Jimmy Carter in Africa

COLD WAR
INTERNATIONAL HISTORY
PROJECT SERIES

James G. Hershberg
series editor

[*continued after index*]

Jimmy Carter in Africa
Race and the Cold War

Nancy Mitchell

Woodrow Wilson Center Press
Washington, D.C.

Stanford University Press
Stanford, California

EDITORIAL OFFICES
Woodrow Wilson Center Press
Woodrow Wilson International Center for Scholars
One Woodrow Wilson Plaza
1300 Pennsylvania Avenue, NW
Washington, DC 20004-3027
www.wilsoncenter.org

ORDER FROM
Stanford University Press
Chicago Distribution Center
11030 South Langley Avenue
Chicago, IL 60628
Telephone: 800-621-2736; 773-568-1550

2 4 6 8 9 7 5 3 1

Library of Congress Cataloging-in-Publication Data

Names: Mitchell, Nancy, 1952– author.
Title: Jimmy Carter in Africa : race and the Cold War / Nancy Mitchell.
Description: Washington, D.C. : Woodrow Wilson Center Press ; Stanford,
    California : Stanford University Press, 2016. | Series: Cold War international
    history project series | Includes bibliographical references and index.
Identifiers: LCCN 2015039576 | ISBN 9780804793858 (hardcover) | ISBN
    9780804799188 (ebook)
Subjects: LCSH: United States—Foreign relations—Africa. | Africa—Foreign
    relations—United States. | United States—Foreign relations—1977–1981. |
    Carter, Jimmy, 1924–
Classification: LCC DT38.7 .M58 2016 | DDC 327.730609/047—dc23
    LC record available at http://lccn.loc.gov/2015039576

Wilson Center

The Wilson Center, chartered by Congress as the official memorial to President Woodrow Wilson, is the nation's key nonpartisan policy forum for tackling global issues through independent research and open dialogue to inform actionable ideas for Congress, the Administration, and the broader policy community.

Conclusions or opinions expressed in Center publications and programs are those of the authors and speakers and do not necessarily reflect the views of the Center staff, fellows, trustees, advisory groups, or any individuals or organizations that provide financial support to the Center.

Please visit us online at www.wilsoncenter.org.

Jane Harman, Director, President, and CEO

To Nancy Roman

Contents

Contents

Maps and Images

Maps

Images and Photographs   *Following page 400*

Acknowledgments

I am lucky. Writing these acknowledgments reminds me of just how fortunate I am to be buoyed by friends, family, and the generosity of strangers. I thank them all.

I dedicate this book to my true friend, Nancy Roman. Nancy is steadfast, smart, and loving. From the walks we took along the towpath when we were in graduate school together until today, we have talked over everything in our lives and minds. Nancy read this entire manuscript when it was an unwieldy draft, and she meticulously helped me refine and shape it. Her family has become my second family. Her husband Steven suited me up in raingear and took me on the back of his Honda 300 scooter to do research in the Communist Party archives in Rome; her son Daniel and her daughter Taylor Beth, as well as her parents, Dave and Ellen, and her brother's family—Scott, Vo, and Mitchell—have listened to endless discussions about "the book." Their extraordinary warmth and support fills me with gratitude.

I benefitted, more than I can express, from the friendship of Donald Easum and his family. Don, who served as US ambassador to Nigeria in the Carter years, shared his love of Africa and of the art of diplomacy with me. His enthusiasm and support for this book gave me courage.

I also thank all the people who agreed to be interviewed for this book. Their insights deepened my understanding of the events about which I was writing.

Lars Schoultz has been unfailingly supportive and has read many chapters in draft form. Michael Hunt very generously read a full draft of the manuscript and offered many helpful suggestions. The enthusiasm of Jim Hershberg, the editor of this series, has been—and continues to be—a source of joy. His astute reading of the manuscript sharpened its argument. It has been a great pleasure and privilege to work with the director of the Woodrow Wilson Center Press, Joe Brinley, and its editor, Shannon Granville.

I also warmly appreciate the friendship of my neighbors: Susan and Walker Casey; Christin, Clement, Nicole, and Joshua Kleinstreuer; and Vicky and Harry McKinney.

Jonathan Ocko, who served as head of the history department at NC State until his untimely death in January 2015, helped fund my travel to archives. I also received a travel grant from the Ford Library. At all the archives I visited—in Africa, Europe, and the United States—I relied on the expertise of the always-overworked archivists. I am indebted to them all, none more so than those at the Carter Library, many of whom—including the great James Yancey—have since retired. In Lusaka, the staff of the US embassy, including Ambassador Donald Booth, kindly facilitated my contacts with President Kenneth Kaunda and Mark Chona.

At North Carolina State University, I marvel at how the interlibrary loan librarians were able to locate every obscure work I sought. And I deeply appreciate the efforts of Darby Orcutt to maintain the excellence of the library's collection in modern US history. It has made my research possible.

I have shared my travails writing this book with many of my graduate students writing their theses: Kelsey Zavelo, Thomas Schultheiss, Ian Lear-Nickum, Drew Wofford, Oliver Ham, Clifford Casper, Brian Trenor, Ian Farrell, Aaron Brown, and Shannon Nix. A special word of thanks to Stephen Harrison, who housed me in London while I did research there. In South Africa, Gcobani Qambela was extraordinarily helpful.

Writing a book must be, at times, a solitary occupation, but I have not been lonely. My family has supported me. I rejoice that my sister Debbie Fitch and her husband Luin have recently moved near to me. I look forward to more adventures and relaxing times with my brother Nick Mitchell and his wife Tricia. And I am enormously grateful for my nephews, Michael Mitchell and Henry Fitch; my niece Sarah Fitch; and their partners Katie, Li, and Daniel.

My intellectual debt to Piero Gleijeses is profound. Thirty years ago, I sat in his class as he lectured about Carter's policy toward the Horn of Africa and Rhodesia. He was the best teacher I have ever known: demanding, precise, humble, and inspiring. He has read and reread every word of this manuscript. We have argued fiercely about some of my interpretations. In an astounding act of generosity, he shared with me hundreds of documents about the Horn of Africa that he had pried from the closed Cuban archives. I thank him for his intellectual rigor, and his friendship.

Jimmy Carter in Africa

Southern Africa, 1977

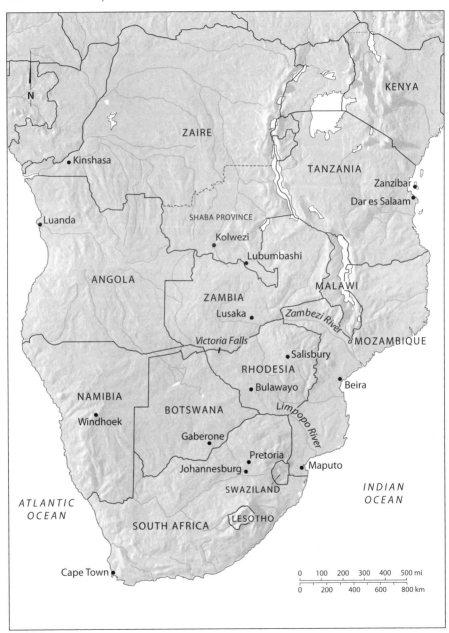

KENYA

ZAIRE

Kinshasa

TANZANIA

Zanzibar
Dar es Salaam

Luanda

SHABA PROVINCE

Kolwezi

Lubumbashi

ANGOLA

MALAWI

ZAMBIA

Lusaka

Zambezi River

MOZAMBIQUE

Victoria Falls

Salisbury

RHODESIA

Bulawayo

Beira

NAMIBIA

BOTSWANA

Limpopo River

Windhoek

Gaberone

Pretoria

Johannesburg

Maputo

SWAZILAND

INDIAN
OCEAN

ATLANTIC
OCEAN

LESOTHO

SOUTH AFRICA

Cape Town

| 0 | 100 | 200 | 300 | 400 | 500 mi |

| 0 | 200 | 400 | 600 | 800 km |

The Horn of Africa, 1977

Legend:
- **– – – –** Boundary of Greater Somalia
- **- - - - -** Boundaries that are disputed or not clearly defined
- ////// Ogaden (Note: the borders of the Ogaden were never clarified)

N

Cairo

Nile River

EGYPT

Riyadh

Jidda • Mecca

SAUDI ARABIA

RED SEA

Khartoum

PROVINCE OF ERITREA

Kagnew (base) • Asmara

NORTH YEMEN

SOUTH YEMEN

Sana

SUDAN

Assab

(Independent, June 1977)

DJIBOUTI

Djibouti

Aden

GULF OF ADEN

Berbera

Arabi

Diredawa

Harar

Jijiga

Hargeisa

Addis Ababa

ETHIOPIA

OGADEN

SOMALIA

UGANDA

KENYA

Mogadiscio

Nairobi

INDIAN OCEAN

TANZANIA

Mombasa

0   100   200   300   400 mi

0   200   400   600 km

Introduction
Race and the Cold War

"**A** lot of times, I think back about mistakes that I made as president, the things I would have done differently." Jimmy Carter was sitting in his modest living room in Atlanta, at the Carter Center, in 2002. He mentioned the first mistake with a wry smile. "Frivolously, I would say—one more helicopter for the Iran rescue mission. Which is where I generally stop."[1]

But this time the president went further. After a pause, he added, "The other thing that I did that doesn't cause me to be proud was letting [Secretary of State] Cy Vance force me in effect to fire [US Ambassador to the United Nations] Andy Young after he had met with the PLO [Palestine Liberation Organization]. . . . I wish I hadn't done it. But Cy Vance threw down his gauntlet and said, in effect, it was Andy or him. . . . I wish I had let Cy resign."[2]

This study of the Carter administration's policies in Africa threw me into the cauldron of still-unresolved, deep, and turbulent emotions. Perhaps if the Carter presidency had been deemed a success, if there had been a second term, nerves would be less exposed.

When I told Anthony Lake—the head of the Policy Planning Staff in Vance's State Department—that Carter wished he had accepted Vance's resignation instead of firing Young, Lake suddenly jumped up. Throughout the interview, he had been reserved. His answers had been careful and measured. Like almost all the State Department officials I interviewed, he unfailingly referred to the late secretary of state as "Mr. Vance." Their respect and affection for Vance were palpable. Respect and protectiveness. When I repeated Carter's comments, Lake muttered fiercely but inaudibly, and began to pace. I asked him what he had said. He paused and looked me straight in the eye: "He didn't even have the decency to come to the funeral."[3]

Cyrus Vance had died after a long struggle with Alzheimer's several months before I spoke with Lake. Carter may have had a good reason to have missed the funeral, but that was not how the people loyal to Vance saw it. Old, unresolved emotions.

The 1970s

Despite the disco music, the garish polyester, the drugs, and the sexual revolution of the 1970s, the global politics of the decade were, for Americans, somber. They grappled with failure in Vietnam and strategic parity with the Soviet Union; they faced the Arab oil embargo and growing economic competition from the European Community and Japan. They suffered through Watergate, the congressional investigations of the Central Intelligence Agency's (CIA) covert activities, and stagflation. They were reminded daily that the United States seemed to be losing power and influence.

The war in Vietnam had sucked the oxygen out of talk of US defense and security, triggered inflation, and constrained the president's ability to use—or threaten to use—force. Given the belief that the Cold War was a zero-sum game, the unfamiliar sense of weakness caused by the US retreat from Vietnam led Americans to assume that the Soviet Union must have grown correspondingly stronger. Moreover, as President Richard Nixon's policy of détente took shape, the Cold War seemed to shift in confusing ways. If the Cold War was an ideological struggle against communism, why was Washington flirting with Mao Zedong's China? And if it was instead a great power struggle against the Soviet Union, how would the United States defend itself and its allies in an era of strategic parity?

This was the world that the Carter administration had to navigate: Americans were trying to draw lessons from their loss in Vietnam, and they were uncertain about the threats they faced. Many of Carter's critics, during his presidency and after, asserted that the hapless president failed to hew a consistent line toward the Kremlin. Carter, however, did not create a contradictory policy toward the Soviet Union: he inherited it.

Détente, bequeathed to Carter by Nixon and his successor Gerald Ford, embodied two contradictory assumptions. On the one hand, it upended one of the fundamental tenets of containment: while the doctrine's author George Kennan had asserted in 1947 that the Kremlin could never envision "a community of aims" with the capitalist West, by the late 1960s President Nixon and his national security adviser Henry Kissinger believed that the Soviet Union had matured into a status quo power.[4] This meant that Washington could—and should—negotiate with Moscow about their "community of aims" to slow the nuclear arms race and ratchet down tensions to create, as Nixon remarked, a "stable structure of peace."[5] This was the side of détente that many Americans, weary of war and anxious about nuclear Armageddon, embraced.

It was, however, less than half the story of Nixon's and Ford's strategic worldview. Even as both presidents pursued arms control negotiations with the Soviet Union, they continued to wage a Cold War against it. US military forces remained on alert, the defense budget remained high, and US nuclear missiles remained trained on Soviet targets. Containment was still US strategy; détente was just "a high falutin' word," as Alabama governor George Wallace said, that tweaked the means—not the goal—of containing the Soviet Union.[6]

This contradiction would not be remarkable, except that the US public expected détente to create a more peaceful and stable world. When war broke out in the Middle East in 1973, the public's confidence in détente was shaken. And when tens of thousands of Cuban troops—considered Moscow's proxies—poured into Angola in 1975 to defend a leftist government, belief in détente was shattered. Americans, the Democratic heavyweight Averell Harriman explained to the Soviets in 1976, were "disillusioned with their own illusions."[7]

In 1976, President Ford and Democratic challenger Jimmy Carter campaigned on these ruins of détente. Ford airbrushed the word from his vocabulary, and Carter sidestepped it. Neither man wanted to discuss grand strategy because neither had an alternative to the discredited détente. Former California governor Ronald Reagan, by contrast, slammed détente as he tried to wrest the Republican nomination from the sitting president. Détente was a "one-way street," Reagan declared. The only thing it had done was "give us the right to sell Pepsi-Cola in Siberia."[8] Both Ford and Carter, however, embraced détente's contradiction: both valued arms control agreements and both remained ardent but quiet Cold Warriors; neither wanted to rattle the sabers.

The American people, by and large, let both Ford and Carter off the hook in the 1976 campaign. Nursing the wounds of Vietnam and of Nixon's abuses of power that had culminated in the Watergate debacle, they had little stomach for high falutin' discussions of US grand strategy in a time of economic and military constraints.

Jimmy Who?

Jimmy Carter's strength as a candidate, beyond his indefatigable ambition, was that he was an outsider—not someone who claimed disingenuously to be an outsider, but a real outsider—more so than any successful presidential candidate in modern American history. "Jimmy who?" became a punch line because it encapsulated a truth: most Americans had never heard of Jimmy Carter until he started to win primaries in early 1976.

Carter did not carry the stench of Washington, a city still reeking of the sordid Nixon tapes and scandals. He came out of nowhere, and he promised to moor America to its moral foundations once more. Flattering his audiences, he promised a government "as good as the people."[9] His resistance to ideology reflected the mood of the 1970s, when Americans were questioning the efficacy of the Great Society and the wisdom of the Cold War. He did not fit any of the usual ideological stereotypes. He was a southern Democrat who seemed relatively liberal on racial issues, but he was a fiscal conservative and a born-again Southern Baptist. His relations with the Democratic Party machine were weak and strained. He had no ties to the Northeast establishment or to the rising Sunbelt. Jimmy Carter was an enigma, and to a very large extent he has remained one.

Carter himself bears some responsibility for this. He seems to have had very little interest in shedding light on his presidency, releasing only a severely edited diary and a memoir that was overwhelmingly concerned with the Camp David Accords, and granting very few interviews to historians. Moreover, he departed the presidency with almost no supporters who took it upon themselves to burnish, defend, or even explain on his record. This absence was particularly damaging, given the sustained and effective assault on Carter's record mounted by the Reagan campaign team in 1980 and maintained almost nonstop since then. Historians have been further hobbled by the dearth of documents from his administration. The National Archives began to release significant numbers of Carter-era State Department documents only in 2014, so scholars had to rely on the sporadic declassification of White House documents at the Carter Library. Finally, assessment of Carter's foreign policy has been befogged by the narrative that has persisted since 1978, when journalists—frustrated by their inability to understand the president—settled on another way to explain his presidency: it was a struggle between Secretary of State Cyrus Vance and National Security Adviser Zbigniew Brzezinski. Jimmy Carter got lost in the shuffle.

Jimmy Carter in Africa returns Carter to center stage. Based on archival materials from the United States, Europe, Africa, and Cuba, plus extensive interviews, it probes this enigmatic president. To find Carter, it was necessary to dig deep into the written record and to immerse myself in his policymaking process. If I skimmed across the surface, I would only repeat the standard narratives. Hence this granular study of two of Carter's foreign policy crises: the search for Rhodesian independence and the handling of the war in the Horn of Africa. Together, these two crises give a more complete picture of Carter's goals and leadership than has been available in previous studies. The long-anticipated dilemma in Rhodesia and the unforeseen war in the Horn were the major African challenges faced by the Carter administration, and they form a fascinating counterpoint.

Why Africa?

The Cold War, which had begun in Europe, had frozen into a nuclear stalemate there. Fourteen years before Carter took office, President John F. Kennedy had declared, "Berlin is secure, and Europe as a whole is well protected. What really matters at this point is the rest of the world."[10] The contest between the superpowers moved to shadowboxing in the periphery, because real war in places that really counted—Berlin, Washington, and Moscow—was unwinnable. By the time Carter took office, the struggle seemed over (however unsatisfactorily) in southeast Asia, quiescent in Latin America, and moving in America's direction tentatively in the Middle East and decisively in China.

In one continent, however, the Cold War was poised to flame into an inferno. The fire had been set almost casually. In 1975, Henry Kissinger had quietly concocted a plot to ensure that the southern African nation of Angola—on the verge of independence after centuries as a Portuguese colony—would fall into the American camp. Kissinger expected this success to provide a sorely needed boost to American morale in the months after the ignominious retreat from Vietnam. As Angolan rebel groups vied for power, Washington sent covert aid to improve the chances of the pro-Western groups, and it encouraged Pretoria to send an army to seal the deal. What neither Washington nor Pretoria anticipated was that, in response, Cuba's Fidel Castro would send 36,000 soldiers to counter the South African attack. Kissinger's plan imploded, the South Africans were driven back, and a leftist government supported by the Cuban troops took power in Luanda. Black African governments—including friends of the United States, such as Ghana—condemned Washington's collusion with Pretoria. US prestige on the continent was at its nadir. Moreover, the complacent assumptions of détente had been jolted: while the Soviet Union might have aged into a status quo power, Castro's Cuba was as revolutionary as ever. Suddenly, American policymakers feared, Moscow had shock troops eager to put muscle behind the Kremlin's expansionist rhetoric.[11]

The continent was also gaining importance in Washington for economic and political reasons. Nigeria shipped the United States one-quarter of all its oil imports; it was America's second-largest supplier, surpassed only by Saudi Arabia. Following the 1973 oil embargo and the resulting energy crisis in the industrialized world, Nigeria had clout. "If you are thinking about these long gas lines," Ambassador Andrew Young—an African American who had been a close aide to Martin Luther King Jr.—noted to a journalist, "one out of every eight gallons of gasoline sold in this nation comes from Nigeria. . . . We are talking about the kind of realities that I think white folk can understand."[12] Moreover, African countries constituted almost a third of the United Nations (UN) General Assembly; the support of the "Africa Group" mattered.[13]

This story, *Jimmy Carter in Africa*, begins at this juncture when the Cold War landed in Africa. In the waning days of the Ford administration and the first three years of the Carter administration, Africa was the heart of the Cold War. Africa was where the superpowers shadowboxed.

"I spent more effort and worry on Rhodesia than I did on the Middle East," Carter told me, reiterating what he had said at a public conference several years earlier.[14] Given the emphasis that the historiography of the Carter years has placed on the Camp David Accords, this statement might seem counter-intuitive or an exaggeration based on the vagaries of memory, but the documentary record supports it. Rhodesia absorbed Carter's sustained attention for three years, it engaged both the struggle with the Soviets and the complexities of race, and it embroiled the president in a prolonged battle with Congress that at times threatened his executive authority. The war in the Horn, by contrast, flared up and led to the landing of 13,000 Cuban troops and 1,000 Soviets in Ethiopia, a country that had long been one of America's closest allies in Africa. Until the Soviet invasion of Afghanistan in December 1979, it was the major Cold War crisis of the Carter years, and in 1978 it was the hottest war in the world.

Counterpoints

The struggles in both Rhodesia and the Horn occurred in the shadow of the Cuban and Soviet intervention in Angola, as anxiety about the expansion of Moscow's influence in Africa spurred Washington's interest in the continent. However, there were also important differences between the crises in Rhodesia and the Horn, and this variance broadens the analysis of Jimmy Carter's foreign policy.

As soon as it came into office in January 1977, the Carter administration mapped out a strategy for Rhodesia, which it pursued with patience and creativity for three years. Its approach to the Horn, on the other hand, was ad hoc and reactive. The contrast between the administration's sure-footed handling of Rhodesia and its fumbling conduct of the crisis in the Horn can be traced to this root. The foreign policy initiatives that the Carter administration anticipated—the Rhodesian settlement, the Panama Canal treaties, the Camp David Accords—were pursued with vigor and harmony, and they achieved their goals.[15] Those that caught the administration off guard—not only the war in the Horn, but also the Iranian Revolution and the Soviet invasion of Afghanistan—produced confusion and heated argument. Carter's lack of a predictable ideology was not a liability when the White House had time to prepare—toward Rhodesia, for example, Carter had made his goals clear—but it was crippling when, as in the Horn, unanticipated decisions had to be made quickly. Carter took time to study the issue before he articulated policy. This delay could be perilous: while Carter contemplated, his administration was rudderless. Uncertain which way the president would lean, frustrated administration officials who hoped to narrow Carter's options would float their proposals (off the record) to the press. The successive leaks helped to generate the image that Carter was overwhelmed and his administration deeply divided.

The Horn and Rhodesia also involved different partners. Whereas policy toward the Horn was discussed in a series of secret quadripartite meetings with British, French, and West German representatives, the Carter administration developed its policy toward Rhodesia in close, sustained cooperation with Great Britain alone. In the first case, the partnership was dysfunctional: Washington's European allies fretted and carped, while offering no constructive aid or ideas. In the latter case, the partnership—though rocky at times—was a rare example of Washington pursuing a genuinely bilateral policy during the Cold War.

Although the independence of Rhodesia was of only marginal interest to the countries of the Middle East, the war in the Horn of Africa was a Middle Eastern crisis, not just geographically but also because Somalia was a member of the Arab League. Carter's diplomacy toward the Horn had to adjust to the influence of Saudi Arabia, awash in petrodollars after the 1973 oil embargo, and of Egypt, a new ally of the United States and a crucial partner in the Arab-Israeli peace process.

Another difference concerned domestic politics. The war in the Horn did not become a political football: Congress displayed little interest in it, and journalists were almost never able to report from the front. Carter's policy toward Rhodesia, however, was the subject of fierce debate in Congress, and the US press covered it extensively. This was an important episode in the battle that Congress waged in the 1970s to wrest power from the executive branch. Rhodesia offered legislators an opportunity to derail presidential plans. From 1977 until late 1979, members of Congress attempted to force the president to lift the UN sanctions on Rhodesia, which had been in place for more than a decade. That the Carter administration defeated these efforts is testament to its willingness to expend vast amounts of sustained political capital on the effort. Carter did not have warm relations with any members of Congress; he disliked deal-making and schmoozing; nevertheless, his administration was more skilled and successful in its dealings with Congress than is generally believed.

Perhaps the most important difference between the two crises concerned race. In the Horn, blacks were fighting blacks; race was not a factor. The conflict in Rhodesia, however, was a struggle of the black majority to wrest power from a white minority regime. The congressional debates about Rhodesia were infused, usually obliquely, with the domestic politics of race. It was much less treacherous for American politicians to discuss the racial politics of a faraway African country than to wade into the explosive domestic topics of busing and affirmative action.

Lifting the Fog

Studying Carter's response to these African crises in the Horn and in Rhodesia clarifies his core values as well as the strengths and weaknesses of his leadership. This study dispels the notion that Carter was an indecisive man torn between two warring aides. In fact, Vance and Brzezinski agreed more often than not, and it was Carter who determined policy, often without sharing his decision-making process with anyone. It highlights how challenging it was for Carter to be an effective leader without an easily pigeonholed ideology, especially when—as in the Horn—he was unprepared.

An analysis of Carter's policy toward the Horn and Rhodesia discredits the narrative that he entered the Oval Office a naive and idealistic crusader for human rights and departed a hardened Cold Warrior. He was a Cold Warrior from day one. This fact is glaring in his handling of US relations with Somalia. Two months into his presidency, Carter ordered Vance and Brzezinski "to move in every possible way to get Somalia to be our friend."[16] Why? To compensate for the fact that Ethiopia, America's erstwhile friend, was moving toward the Soviet camp. This was a classic Cold War, zero-sum swap. It would have been simple, except that the only way to coax Somalia toward the West was to send it weapons that it would use to attack Ethiopia. Carter's Cold War instincts were so ingrained that he overlooked Somalia's war footing. Even after Somalia's invasion of Ethiopia was flagrant, Carter continued to encourage US allies to send weapons to Mogadiscio.

Carter's Cold War motivations in Rhodesia were somewhat obscured by his pursuit of racial justice there, but they were just as real. A clear indication of this is the continuity of goals (if not means) in Rhodesia among Kissinger, British prime minister Margaret Thatcher, and Carter. By repute, the first two were steely-eyed realists while Carter was an inept idealist, but all three agreed that it was essential to resolve the Rhodesian crisis before the Soviets and Cubans moved in and expanded their influence in Africa.

Carter's deep Cold War instincts have eluded most observers' grasp for several reasons. His demeanor encouraged people to think that he was motivated solely by moral concerns. He was a profoundly religious man. He did not flaunt this, but neither did he—or could he—hide it. His Christian faith was at the core of his being. This religiosity coalesced with his interest in human rights and created a powerful, distorting filter: Carter would mention a dozen times in a speech that the United States needed to maintain its strength, and, as an aside, that it should also promote human rights, but what people heard and what the press reported was that Carter had mounted a spirited defense of human rights. Whenever Carter referred to morality, values, or human rights, it was heard at full volume, while his comments about strength and national interest were heard as whispers and forgotten.

The president compounded the confusion by his odd (for a politician) indifference to the impact of his words. Thus, for example, in 1979 when he announced his controversial decision to maintain sanctions on Rhodesia, he duly noted the national security argument—that lifting sanctions would prolong the war and open opportunities for Soviet expansion—but he articulated the moral argument with much more passion: it was "a matter of principle to me personally and to our country," he declared, to do "what's right and what's decent and what's fair and what is principled."[17] This was what the press and members of Congress heard, and it underlined the impression that the president of the United States was driven by morality, not power politics. A more glaring example of Carter's tin ear came in his inaugural address, when he declared that "our commitment to human rights must be absolute," implying that his administration would crusade against human rights abuses, no matter the cost in alliances or dollars. Carter, however, never believed this. What he meant was that his *commitment* to uphold human rights must be unwavering, but his administration's policy would be adjusted to the circumstances of power in the real world.[18]

The problem was that a concern for morality, "idealism," is often construed as incompatible with a concern for the national interest, "realism." For Carter, however, there was no light between them. During the campaign, he argued in almost every speech and press conference that the corruption of Washington's values had weakened America's image, and therefore power, overseas. Carter's promise to restore America's goodness was simultaneously moral and practical.

Timing mattered. Carter governed in the wake of the US defeat in Vietnam, and he and his aides strove with varying success to be sensitive to regional factors that gave rise to conflicts; they wanted to avoid a knee-jerk assumption that every crisis was the result of a malevolent plot hatched in the Kremlin. Carter was determined to pay serious attention to festering problems on the periphery, including seeking a negotiated settlement in Rhodesia. He believed the only way to achieve peace there, and close the door on Soviet expansion, was to forge a settlement that included the guerrillas at war against the white regime. That is, Carter wanted guerrillas armed by Moscow and Beijing—fighters that many Americans considered Marxist terrorists—at the table as equal partners. Thus the logic of Carter's Cold War policy could be counterintuitive: he would fight communism more effectively by not being so obsessed with fighting communism. Instead of turning away from the Cold War, however, Carter was waging a more complex, preemptive, and diffuse Cold War.

Kissinger's Bequest

It is impossible to assess Carter's policy toward the two major African crises without first grasping the situation bequeathed to him by his predecessor. Moreover, Carter's goals and modus operandi become clearer when contrasted with those of Henry Kissinger, who as secretary of state had masterminded Gerald Ford's policy toward Africa. Toward the Horn, Carter inherited a policy of inertia: despite the increasingly leftist turn of the Ethiopian revolutionaries who had overthrown Emperor Haile Selassie in 1974, the Ford administration did not break ties and even increased aid in the hope of moderating the anti-Americanism of the new leaders in Addis Ababa. Toward Rhodesia, however, Carter was heir to Kissinger's activist, even frenetic policy. Throughout 1976, as Carter and Ford campaigned, Kissinger devoted most of his vast energy to his attempt to resolve the Rhodesian problem.

Kissinger's motivation was clear: stop the Cubans, whom he saw as proxies of the Soviet Union. After his covert operation in Angola collapsed, Kissinger feared that the Cuban soldiers might land next in Rhodesia. For the next four years—until its rebirth as Zimbabwe in April 1980—Rhodesia would be at the center of the Cold War. This small, landlocked country, a British self-governing colony since the 1920s, was led by Ian Smith, who in 1965 had declared rebellion from the British Crown to preserve white minority rule. Rhodesia was a domino between Angola and Mozambique—two countries that had established leftist governments after gaining independence from Portugal in 1975—and Kissinger feared it was about to topple into the communist camp.

Although much has been written about Kissinger, little attention has been paid to this strenuous and time-consuming effort in Rhodesia. In his memoirs, Kissinger wrote that "of all the negotiations I conducted, by far the most complex was the one over majority rule in Southern Africa."[19] Kissinger's approach to Rhodesia was similar to his negotiating style in his better-known pursuits: ending the Vietnam War, seeking disengagement in Sinai, and opening the door to China. He relied on his charm and his power to bully and cajole the players, the British as well as the Africans. He demanded secrecy and speed. These tactics kept everyone off balance and allowed Kissinger to narrow the cognoscenti to a very small band of men who were fiercely loyal to him. To get to a deal, Kissinger wove a dazzling web of confusion and half-truths, implying just enough concessions to all participants to keep them in the game. Kissinger described his technique bluntly: "My strategy which is not heroic is to keep the thing sufficiently confused to exhaust them a bit. . . . I am going to keep it confused until somebody's nerves go."[20] He approached Rhodesia as though he were gluing a shattered piece of crockery back together: he hoped his half-truths and exaggerations would hold long enough for the glue to set. He achieved one significant step forward when Ian Smith publicly agreed to the principle of majority rule, but the negotiations collapsed when the participants realized that Kissinger had been leading them on. Carter had to construct his policy toward Rhodesia on these shards.

Race . . .

Rhodesia was not only landlocked; it was also isolated from the world. Its minority white government was condemned by the UN and not recognized by any country. It was engaged in an escalating war against insurgents backed by the Soviet Union and China and given refuge in Zambia, Mozambique, and Angola. As the Rhodesian forces increased the fury of their attacks on their neighbors, it became more likely that Zambia and Mozambique might call on the Cubans for help. If that happened, it would be very difficult for the United States to respond.

Why? Because the essence of American foreign policy during the Cold War—stopping Soviet expansion—slammed up against the most raw and explosive aspect of American domestic politics: racism. The war in Rhodesia was not just a bitter liberation struggle; it was also a conflict that pitted a white minority regime against the oppressed black majority. Opposing the Cubans in Rhodesia would mean supporting the white racist government. Both the Ford and Carter administrations knew that was a nightmare scenario. If Cuban troops intervened in Rhodesia—if men perceived as Soviet proxies marched across Africa and encircled South Africa—Washington would have two choices, both bad. It could look the other way and lose not only southern Africa but also, even more significantly, international credibility and power. Or it could send US troops to fight, risking an imbroglio of racial strife and antiwar protest at home.

For Jimmy Carter, this dilemma hit close to the bone. His childhood in Archery, Georgia, was suffused with the complexities of race in America. Archery, a mere stop along the railroad, was home to two white families (the Carters and the railroad manager) and twenty-five black families, many of them sharecroppers on Carter land. It was dwarfed by the hamlet of Plains, which in turn was dwarfed by the bustling town of Americus. Atlanta was light-years away, and the rest of the world, places like St. Louis and Pittsburgh, existed only because of baseball. Archery, like Walden Pond, was where Jimmy Carter learned about living. It gave him his roots, his bearing, his leaning into life.[21]

Slavery was barely gone on the Carter farm. "Mr. Earl," Jimmy's father, was a fair master and "Miss Lillian," his mother, was enlightened, but the black workers lived in a world of penury, ill health, poor schooling, and severely limited prospects. Mr. Earl accepted the Jim Crow system. When Miss Lillian invited the son of a black bishop into the home to discuss his schooling, Mr. Earl left the house. He talked to African Americans only in the yard. During the 1938 Joe Louis–Max Schmeling match—which pitted the black American heavyweight against the white German who had beaten him two years earlier—Mr. Earl placed the radio by the open kitchen window, so the farmhands could stand in the yard and listen while the Carters sat inside.

This was a world that turned the *Plessy v. Ferguson* decision on its head: it was grossly unequal but not separate. As a young boy, Carter's closest friends were the sons of black tenant farmers; he played, fished, hunted, ate, got in trouble, and worked in the fields with them. He was most comfortable in the home of Rachel Clark, an African American woman who was in many ways a surrogate mother to him because Carter's own mother was often absent attending to her nursing duties. He was aware of the Jim Crow rules—for example, when he took the train to Americus to go to the movies "with" his best friend, A.D., the two separated at the train station and again at the movies to sit in their designated sections—but he did not question them. He never asked why his school was segregated, and he was proud of his purchase (with hard-won savings) of five tenant houses that he rented out for $2 to $5 per month. When he was fourteen, he noticed when his two best friends, both black, stepped back so that he could walk first through a gate. That moment of deference gave the young Jimmy both a thrill and a pang: he had, in a profound sense, lost his friends. Carter was keenly aware of the change, and he accepted it.[22]

Carter went on to observe the civil rights struggle from the wings, and he reaped the benefits. "I would not be here as President," he declared, "had it not been for the Civil Rights Act and for the courage of some leaders—and I don't claim to be one of them—who changed those bad aspects of the South to the present greatness of the South."[23]

It is not surprising that Carter considered the racism of Ian Smith's Rhodesia familiar. In this he was strongly supported by Andrew Young, who frequently drew comparisons between southern Africa and the US South of his—and Carter's—childhood. During the campaign, Young briefed Carter on southern African issues: "I said that basically it boils down to 'one man, one vote.' And . . . he [Carter] said, 'Well, that's not much different from what we had to go through.' I said, 'No—well, it's the same problem, but there are probably lots of differences but it boils down to the same issue.'"[24] Not only was the fundamental issue analogous, but the protagonists were, too: "Some people say that people are not the same, but they are," Young told the Nation of Islam paper, *Bilalian News*. "I know Ian Smith and [South African prime minister] John Vorster. I learned about such men at my mother's knee."[25] Vice President Walter Mondale summed it up: "The analogy with the civil rights movement informed everything we did in southern Africa."[26]

. . . and the Cold War

This conflation of American and African politics was an oversimplification that drew critics from the left and right, from Americans, Britons, and Africans. "The complexities of African politics, the tangle of tribal rivalries, the disparities of a vast continent," the London *Sunday Times* noted, "are hardly comprehended [in the United States]. Issues such as Rhodesia are seen as though they were a question of civil rights in Mississippi."[27]

The critics miss the point. While the analogy with the American South was not apt, it served a purpose: it enabled Carter to envision a clear goal for Rhodesia, and it energized his commitment to pursue it. Carter used the parallel to think about how to promote change in southern Africa. He had seen firsthand how the dogged optimism of the civil rights workers, refusing to succumb to despair and cynicism, had worn down white resistance. Young said of Carter, "He knows very clearly the evils and dangers of racism, and he also knows that racists can change."[28] Based on his own experience, Carter believed that the benefits of change were enormous. In the final presidential debate against Gerald Ford in 1976, he declared, "I think the greatest thing that ever happened to the South was the passage of the Civil Rights Act and the opening up of opportunities to black people. . . . It not only liberated black people, but it also liberated the whites."[29] Donald McHenry, an experienced African American diplomat who was Young's deputy and successor at the UN, explained this mind-set eloquently: "They [Carter and Young] had lived through the unimaginable. And it did not destroy them. And it was good."[30] Carter's belief that there were similarities between Georgia and Rhodesia gave him confidence that resolute optimism and activism could give birth to a more just society in southern Africa, and that everyone—black and white—would benefit. Despite obstacles at every turn and a dearth of public support, Carter doggedly sought a negotiated peace in Rhodesia. He set a goal—peace, justice, and independence—and he pursued it with a determination that rivaled the vigor with which he had sought the presidency.

When I asked Carter to explain the motivations of his policy toward Rhodesia, he cited both strategic and moral concerns. First, he urged me to read the documents about US-Cuban relations during his administration that he had taken to Fidel Castro when he visited Havana in 2002. (These documents emphasize the administration's anxiety that the Cubans would intervene in Rhodesia, checkmating US policy and widening the war in southern Africa.) Then he added: "I would say that reading *An Hour Before Daylight* [his memoir of childhood] pretty well explains where I came from. I felt a sense of responsibility and some degree of guilt that we had spent an entire century after the Civil War still persecuting blacks and to me the situation in Africa was inseparable from the fact of deprivation or persecution or oppression of black people in the South."[31] Viewing the struggle from this perspective enabled Carter to look beyond the communist rhetoric of the black leaders fighting against the racist Rhodesian government and acknowledge that they, like the civil rights activists in the US South, were fighting for basic human rights. Yet achieving peace in southern Africa was not just a moral good for Carter; it was also a strategic necessity. This combination of aims—the national security imperative of stopping a Soviet/Cuban advance and the pursuit of racial justice—meant that Carter's Rhodesia policy had strong support within his administration. Both Vance and Brzezinski backed it. This united support was essential because it helped inspire the administration to stick with Carter's Rhodesia policy, even when it seemed hopeless.

Historians wrestle with memory. We revere it, and we mistrust it. We swaddle it with documents and footnotes in an attempt to square it with facts, hoping that documents—masses of documents—have a special call on truth. Ultimately, however, in human stories, the truth is elusive. When analyzing Jimmy Carter's policy toward Rhodesia, it is impossible to determine whether he was motivated primarily by the Cold War or by the pursuit of racial justice. The dualism of the question distorts reality. Race and the Cold War had always been intertwined.

In the early Cold War, racism in the United States undermined American efforts to "win hearts and minds" in the developing world and provided potent propaganda to the Kremlin. This was one reason President John F. Kennedy grew interested in passing civil rights legislation and President Lyndon B. Johnson was able to persuade a reluctant Congress to pass the Civil Rights Act and the Voting Rights Act in 1964 and 1965. But the fusion of race and the Cold War did not end in 1965. In the early 1970s, the Nixon administration was sympathetic to white minority regimes in southern Africa for two reasons: the whites were considered reliable, and they were anticommunist. Race and the Cold War were inseparable.

During the Ford and Carter administrations, however, the relationship between these two fundamental aspects of the American worldview grew more complicated. The expansion of racial justice at home rendered US support for racist regimes abroad increasingly problematic, yet South Africa and Rhodesia remained anticommunist bulwarks. The equation changed, however, with the 1974 Portuguese revolution that led to the decolonization of Mozambique and Angola. The victories of black leftist governments in both countries shattered the security of the neighboring white regimes. The successful intervention of Cuba and the Soviet Union in the Angolan civil war underlined the vulnerability of white rule in Africa. This was what propelled Henry Kissinger to turn his attention to the continent: complacency was no longer in the US national interest; foreclosing more opportunities for the Soviets was. This required fancy footwork of Kissinger: he had to dance through the complexities of race and national security. This was the challenge the Ford administration tossed to Carter. It was a dilemma that went straight to the heart of the Cold War.

In Rhodesia, Carter succeeded in narrowing the gap between US rhetoric about equal justice for all and its actions abroad. In so doing, he won a Cold War victory. His administration's perseverance in seeking a settlement in Rhodesia, as well as his gutsy decision to defy Congress and refuse to lift sanctions, were essential prerequisites to the Lancaster House Agreement that finally ended Rhodesia's civil war. When the newly renamed country of Zimbabwe was born in April 1980, its sympathies were with the United States and not the Soviet Union. Despite Robert Mugabe's leftist and anti-American rhetoric as a guerrilla leader, when he became the first prime minister of Zimbabwe, he invited the United States to be the first country to open an embassy in Harare—while he made the Soviets cool their heels for ten months.[32]

In the Horn, by contrast, Carter pursued a cynical policy from the beginning, hoping to chalk one up for the Americans despite Somalia's clear irredentist dreams. Cold War reflexes die hard. Carter himself later admitted his error: "Morally or theoretically, we were on the wrong side, and we were defending [Prime Minister] Siad Barre in Somalia, who had invaded Ethiopia."[33] It led to the spectacle of the Carter administration sitting by while the Cubans and Soviets saved Ethiopia from Somali aggression. Carter looked weak. This was a self-inflicted, unnecessary wound. And yet, in real terms the United States lost little, while the Soviet Union lost its prized base in Somalia. The perception of the stakes was very different from the reality.

Complexity and constraint: these are the watchwords that emerge from a close study of Carter's response to the crises in Rhodesia and the Horn. The Cold War in the late 1970s was complicated by doubts inspired by the war in Vietnam, as well as by the rising power of the Saudis and the weakness of the US economy. It was no longer a simple, zero-sum game. And just as the doubts, the diffusion of power, and the sluggish economy complicated US strategy, so too did they constrain the president, who also had to wrestle with the resurgent Congress, a divided public, and his own human failings.

Notes on Sources

Every time I delved into a new repository I was reminded why multiarchival research is essential. I began to piece this story together with US archives, relying largely on the Carter Library, which has declassified material in fits and starts. Its most recently opened documents, the "Remote Archives Capture" material, have proven the most useful. I investigated the Kissinger initiative in Rhodesia at the Ford Library, and the Reagan critique of Carter's policies at the Reagan Library. I supplemented this material with various small collections. The papers of Anthony Lake (the State Department's director of policy planning in the Carter years) at the US National Archives were most useful.

Although it was possible to construct a coherent narrative of Carter's southern African policy from these sources, I could not make sense of his policy toward the Horn. The presidential libraries hold all National Security Council (NSC) documents but only those State Department materials that passed through the White House. The National Archives did not begin to release material from the Carter years until 2014. The result was that until 2014 the vast bulk of available documents about the Horn were from the NSC, and they are written by only one man, a stunningly prolific NSC aide named Paul Henze. For the historian, these papers are both a blessing and a curse: they are voluminous and eminently quotable; but they stubbornly promote a policy (a tilt toward Addis Ababa) that the administration did not follow. They do not begin to tell the whole story. This realization led me, in some desperation, to the Freedom of Information Act (FOIA). Newly declassified documents from the FOIA system finally allowed me to understand the debate within the administration and to trace the development of its policy toward the Horn. My understanding was refined by reading the Carter-era cable traffic released by the National Archives in 2014.

When I first went to the British National Archives, I was hoping to add to my tale of Anglo-American cooperation in Rhodesia. Instead, I transformed it. It was the most exciting experience I have had as a researcher. All the US documents had seemed to tell a story of remarkably smooth cooperation between the two allies, but as I read through the British documents, a much more complicated—and more plausible—narrative emerged. Although the partnership between Britain and the United States was remarkable, it was punctuated by dramatic disagreements about tactics and goals. Once I understood this, I returned to the US documents and grasped the hints that they contained about these arguments. It also spurred me to broaden my FOIA searches to documents about southern Africa.

I was extremely fortunate that my colleague, Piero Gleijeses, shared the hundreds of documents on the Horn of Africa that he had retrieved from the closed Cuban archives. I also consulted the archives of the Italian Communist Party, whose newspaper *l'Unità* carried particularly well-informed articles about the war in the Horn. I supplemented these with East German and Soviet documents.

Realizing that the Americans discussed their Africa policy in secret quadripartite meetings with the British, French, and West Germans led me to archives in France and Germany. To enrich my understanding of the "old Commonwealth" pressures on the British government's formulation of its Rhodesia policy, I consulted the Canadian and Australian archives as well.

It is a challenge to get a comparable African voice. The Ian Smith papers, held in South Africa, were extremely useful. The Zambian and South African archives were helpful. However, I did not venture to Zimbabwe, Somalia has no functioning archive, and the language barrier rendered Ethiopian archives outside my scope. (Gebru Tareke's *The Ethiopian Revolution* helped fill this last void.) I have tried to supplement these archival gaps with a careful reading of the press from many African countries and with African sources available in the United States, such as Aluka and the African News Service.

Interviews with participants have been by far the most helpful additions to these documentary sources. I interviewed many key players—presidents Jimmy Carter and Kenneth Kaunda, Vice President Walter Mondale, National Security Adviser Zbigniew Brzezinski, British foreign secretary David Owen, US Ambassador Andrew Young, Undersecretary David Newsom, and Deputy National Security Adviser David Aaron—as well as many of the men who executed policy. These interviews gave me a sense of the interpersonal dynamics behind the documents; they helped me untangle the contradictions in the documents and fill their gaps; they led me to ask better questions.

As I listened to these men and read reams of documents, I slowly realized that many of my preconceptions about Kissinger, Carter, and the myriad other protagonists in this book had been wrong. This is one of the great pleasures of research. It reminded me of George Orwell's comment that "sooner or later a false belief bumps up against solid reality." Orwell added that this usually occurs "on a battlefield."[34] Happily, scholars can confront reality in the archives instead.

1. Campaigns and Negotiations

The rhythmic whirr of helicopter blades was the sound of the early 1970s. American television reporters in Vietnam positioned themselves near the giant birds as the cameras rolled. The war correspondents ducked, their hair blowing in gusts, and yelled over the din of the ubiquitous Hueys landing or taking off. Until 1973, when the peace treaty ending the war was finally signed, Americans knew that if they turned on their televisions and heard a chopper, it was a report about the war in Vietnam.

It was fitting, therefore, that the final image of President Richard Nixon would be framed by a helicopter. On August 9, 1974, television showed Nixon, tearful after bidding a maudlin farewell to his staff, walking from the East Room of the White House to a Sikorsky helicopter waiting on the South Lawn. The former president climbed the steps of the Sikorsky and turned to the cameras. He raised both arms in an awkward victory sign. Then he turned, and the door closed behind him. The roar of the chopper carrying the disgraced president to seclusion in California marked the end of the long Watergate saga.[1]

Gerald Ford had been president for less than nine months when helicopters again seared themselves onto the American psyche. On April 29, 1975, the North Vietnamese launched their final assault on Saigon. After more than two decades in Vietnam, this—like so much about that country—caught the Americans by surprise.

That Tuesday night, the *NBC Evening News* opened with John Chancellor in the New York studio, a giant picture of three helicopters behind him. In a flat, urgent voice, he told of the collapse of Saigon and the chaotic evacuation of Americans from the city. There was no live video from Vietnam; that technology was still a few years away. Instead, Chancellor stared into the camera and tried to paint word pictures.[2]

"The people leaving were clawed at by desperate South Vietnamese trying to leave with them and fired on by enraged South Vietnamese soldiers who felt that the United States had abandoned them," Chancellor explained. He cut to audio from Brian Barron, a BBC journalist in downtown Saigon. With the screen showing a montage of still photos of helicopters hovering above Saigon, viewers could hear tension in Barron's disembodied voice: "As dusk falls, there are still Americans at the embassy complex. US marines in full combat gear are standing on the embassy walls keeping back crowds of Vietnamese at gunpoint. Some of these desperate individuals are attempting to climb barbed wire barriers into the embassy." Cutting back to the studio, Chancellor repeated Barron's description of the desperate South Vietnamese climbing the ten-foot-tall embassy walls, and added that reporter Jim Laurie had seen them "having their fingers mashed away with rifles and pistol butts wielded by American Marines and embassy civilians." The broadcast turned to Arthur Lord, who had flown out of Saigon that morning, before the evacuation had begun. Lord had carried film to Bangkok, where it could be processed and uploaded to a satellite. The grainy images showed Saigon being pummeled by rockets and explosions and fires; frantic Vietnamese were running through the streets, carrying babies and suitcases and baskets filled to the brim. "In downtown Saigon," Lord said, "the noise of the bombs exploding, and the shooting, started a panic. People ran wildly through the streets without knowing what they were running from. . . . South Vietnamese soldiers shot at each other, and they shot at Americans who were trying to organize them. The South Vietnamese Air Force did not launch one single fixed-wing aircraft to suppress the enemy fire. They seemed leaderless. . . . It's probably only a matter of hours before the North Vietnamese walk into town and take over. Right now, there's nothing to stop them."

After advertisements for Lifebuoy soap and Geritol, the news cut to Henry Kissinger standing behind a podium. "We got out . . . without panic," the man who was serving as both secretary of state and national security adviser declared in his thick German accent. "Objectives were achieved and carried out successfully."

What were the viewers meant to think? That the chaotic flight of Americans from Saigon—leaving their allies on rooftops, scanning the skies for a helicopter to save them—was success? That after almost 60,000 Americans had been killed and more than 300,000 had been wounded, and at least $150 billion in US tax dollars had been spent, US objectives had been achieved? Of course, Kissinger was parsing his words; he did not say *all* objectives. He was deliberately vague and precise at the same time. Americans watching these events unroll on television that dismal night in April 1975 did not react with shock. They felt, instead, the dull, sickening, horrible thud of the familiar.

The Giant Killer

On the evening of March 9, 1976, not quite a year after the fall of Saigon, Jimmy Carter arrived at his hotel room in Orlando, Florida. He had spent the day campaigning in North Carolina while his wife, Rosalynn, held down the fort in Florida. That was a key to their strategy: the campaign was a family affair. Since early 1975, Rosalynn, the Carters' three grown sons and daughters-in-law, and Carter's mother Lillian had fanned out across the country to spread the good news about Jimmy. It kept costs low. After 137 trips to Florida, Rosalynn had shaken off her shyness to become a persuasive campaigner.[3]

Carter had made his decision to run for president in 1972, while he was governor of Georgia. He was barred by state law from running for the governorship again, and he would be only fifty years old when he completed his four-year term in 1975. As much as he loved his hometown of Plains, neither he nor Rosalynn relished the thought of returning to live in that sleepy hamlet. For all his love of fly-fishing and solitude, Carter was no Thoreau. He had propelled himself out of Plains to the US Naval Academy in 1943, served as a career naval officer until 1953 and as a state senator from 1963 to 1966, and launched himself into the governor's office in 1971. Jimmy Carter wanted a big stage.

But what were his options after he stepped down? Business—he had run the family farm and peanut warehouse after his father's death in 1953—or politics. However, his chances of winning the Senate were slim: Georgia's senior senator, the Old South segregationist Herman Talmadge, would be running for his fourth term in 1974, and Carter doubted that he could beat him in a primary.

A number of Carter aides—Peter Bourne and Hamilton Jordan in particular—take credit for planting the idea of running for president in their boss's head, but Carter was already there. He got a taste of national acclaim in May 1971 when *Time* magazine had put the newly elected governor on its cover under the banner "Dixie Whistles a Different Tune." The article described the rise of a vibrant, progressive, and proud South; it led with a sentence from Governor Carter's inaugural address: "I say to you quite frankly that the time for racial discrimination is over." *Time* commented, "A promise so long coming, spoken at last."[4]

In the governor's mansion, the Carters had hosted a number of Democratic hopefuls—senators Ed Muskie of Maine, George McGovern of South Dakota, and Henry "Scoop" Jackson of Washington—as they trooped through Georgia on their way, they hoped, to the 1972 nomination. Before these encounters, Carter said, he had been in awe of presidents (although he "despised" Richard Nixon), who for him were figures in history books. These would-be presidents, however, who relaxed at the mansion and drank too much, under-whelmed Carter. He was, he thought, better.[5]

That 1972 campaign exposed Carter to national politics. In June, he joined other Democratic governors to stop McGovern because, he said, a ticket headed by the liberal South Dakotan would "risk decimating" the ranks of Democrats in Congress and state houses. Then, at the Democratic convention in Miami—the first presidential convention he attended—Carter nominated Scoop Jackson, but behind the scenes he was lobbying the McGovern camp hard for the vice-presidential nod.[6]

From that point on, Carter made a beeline to the White House. Few people noticed it at the time, but with hindsight his trajectory is unmistakable. Following a brilliant strategy laid out in a seventy-two-page memo by Hamilton Jordan, Carter first sought national recognition and then, once he left the governor's office in January 1975, he began to campaign quietly in every state. Jordan had hitched his wagon to Carter early, volunteering as a college kid in 1966 during Carter's first unsuccessful run for governor. Jordan came from a Georgia family with deep political roots, he was smart, and he impressed Carter. Four years later, when Carter again sought the governorship, he hired Jordan as his campaign manager. For the next eleven years, the two men were inseparable. Jordan was "short, ruddy faced, with a Cheshire Cat smile . . . and a thrusting personality," a British official noted.[7] He was a southern boy—he had grown up in Albany, Georgia, not far from Plains—and proud of it. His confidence and youth—thirty-one years old in 1976—exuded the rising New South.

The key to Jordan's strategy was that Carter would contest every primary and establish early, in Iowa and New Hampshire, that he could appeal beyond the South. Then, building on this momentum, in Florida he would try to beat George Wallace, the racist symbol of the Old South who was serving his third term as governor of Alabama. It was audacious. As columnists Rowland Evans and Robert Novak wrote in November 1975, "little Jimmy Carter" intended to be the "giant-killer. . . . No sane Democrat would bet a plugged nickel on Carter's humiliation of Wallace" in the Florida primary.[8] In late January 1976, just six weeks before the Florida primary, Carter was still a very dark horse; Gallup reported that he was the first choice of fewer than 5 percent of Democrats.[9]

The strategy, however, was working. In New Hampshire, on February 24, 1976, Carter won 28 percent of the vote, significantly more than any other candidate on a crowded slate.[10] This landed him on the cover of both *Time* and *Newsweek*. "It's now quite possible," he said, reflecting on his victory, "that I can beat Wallace in Florida."[11]

Sitting on the sofa in their hotel room in Orlando two weeks later, Jimmy and Rosalynn listened as the Florida returns came in. By 8:20 P.M., it was clear: Carter had slain the giant. George Wallace, who had received 42 percent of the vote four years earlier, now culled just 31 percent, as Carter rolled to victory with 35 percent. Wallace was crushed and—more important—from that night forward Carter was the Democrat to beat.

How had he done it?

First, Carter worked harder than any other candidate. He had campaigned in Florida for fifteen months, visiting it thirty-four times. "An ordinary man," wrote a journalist trying to keep up with the candidate, "would die of exhaustion."[12] Carter's aides, young men who had no experience with presidential primaries, and his family also threw themselves into the campaign.

Second, Carter and his team were politically savvy. The fluid politics of race in the New South helped the southern governor. In 1972, Senator Hubert Humphrey (D-MN), Jackson, Muskie, and McGovern had split the anti-Wallace vote. Four years later, the Democratic Party had easily persuaded Carter's rivals for the nomination to bow out of Florida, leaving the bruising and expensive fight to "little Jimmy," whom they underestimated. (Pennsylvania Governor Milton Schapp was the only Democrat other than Carter and Wallace who campaigned actively in the state, and Jackson— after unexpectedly winning the Massachusetts primary—launched a late drive in the Miami area. Mo Udall [D-AZ] was on the ballot but did not campaign.[13]) It was this framing of the contest as anti-Wallace rather than pro-Carter that persuaded the prominent African American leaders Andrew Young and Martin Luther King Sr.—Georgians both—to campaign for Carter in Florida. "They made it clear to me," Carter remembered, "that they just wanted George Wallace defeated."[14]

Young had been one of Martin Luther King Jr.'s closest aides; he had played a key role in the civil rights struggles in Birmingham, St. Augustine, and Selma, and was with King in Memphis on April 4, 1968. He is one of the men on the balcony of the Lorraine Motel in the iconic photograph, pointing to indicate the direction of the bullet, while King lay dying. After King's assassination, Young ran for Congress, and his mostly white district in Atlanta elected him to the House of Representatives three times, with increasingly wide margins. Young was the first African American elected to Congress from the Deep South since 1894.[15]

In the 1976 presidential race, Young planned to support a liberal from Congress—Senator Ted Kennedy of Massachusetts, Representative Mo Udall of Arizona, or Hubert Humphrey—but his first order of business was to crush the bane of the New South, George Wallace. If the old-style segregationist lost one southern state, the idea that he was the true representative of the South might be debunked. Young calculated that the best battlefield would be Florida and the best competitor would be Carter. But he harbored doubts. "It was hard for a black civil rights leader to feel close to a Georgia governor," he admitted.[16]

This was particularly true when the governor hailed from the most racist region of the state, Sumter County. "Martin Luther King used to say that the sheriff there, Fred Chappell, was the meanest man in the world," Young remembered.[17] Young recalled that on his first trip to Plains to see Governor Carter, he had been nervous. "As we passed the courthouse, the sheriff's car pulled out, and I began to tremble a little bit."[18] Upon meeting Carter, Young "told him that the only experience I'd had of Sumter County was Sheriff Chappell, and before I'd finished, Carter interrupted: "'Oh, Fred Chappell's a good friend of mine!'" As Young later remarked, "it took time to reconcile that."[19]

Carter, nevertheless, impressed Young, and he had a chance of defeating Wallace in Florida. "The principles of tolerance and fairness led me into a relationship with Jimmy Carter," Young said in 1976, "but it is hard political reality that keeps me there."[20] He agreed to help Carter through the Florida primary.

Young's support was crucial in several ways. It was Young who first briefed Carter on the problems of southern Africa, which had a lasting impact on how the future president would frame the issues in that region. Not only did Young encourage Carter to draw parallels between the US civil rights struggle and the crisis in southern Africa, but he also led him to view the struggle in Africa through a progressive religious lens. When Carter asked for background information on southern Africa, Young reached for what he had at hand. "I got a lot of the denominational statements, and information from the National Council of Churches, articles from *Christ and Crisis*," he remembered, "and I just packed them up and sent them to him. And he really read them."[21] Thus, Carter's first exposure to southern African politics was through Andy Young's perspective—that of a black civil rights worker who was deeply imbued with the progressive Christian perspective.

To help Carter, Young relied on skills and knowledge he had gathered during the civil rights struggles: he dusted off his piles of index cards with the names of ministers and local black leaders and friendly liberal whites, and he spun an intricate grassroots network of support for Carter. This was new. Previous candidates had encouraged black turnout simply by dispensing largesse to community leaders. Young organized from the grassroots up.[22]

It worked. Carter overwhelmingly won the black vote in Florida. This not only helped him beat Wallace but also—and perhaps more important— encouraged the Democratic Party's liberal wing to give him a second look. Carter did not forget this. In 2013, at the fiftieth anniversary of the March on Washington, he declared: "Every handshake from Daddy King, every hug from Coretta [Scott King] got me a million Yankee votes."[23]

Luck smiled on Carter in the early primaries. The racially charged issue of busing students across school districts to overcome de facto residential segregation was no longer the potent rallying cry for the Wallace forces that it had been in 1972, and Wallace was no longer the same campaigner. Confined to a wheelchair since May 1972, after an attempted assassination paralyzed him from the waist down, Wallace was frail and quite deaf. Moreover, Ted Kennedy, still eviscerated by the Chappaquidick scandal, announced in late 1974 that he would not be a candidate. Finally, the Watergate scandal that consumed the American people in 1973 and 1974, compounded by the retreat from Vietnam and the debacle of the US covert operation in Angola, made the idea of a fresh face, one with no Washington connections, unusually appealing.

Carter astutely capitalized on Americans' disgust with Washington. Many commentators during the campaign and after complained that Carter was "enigmatic,"[24] but his message was clear. He ran on one issue: Jimmy Carter. His campaign can be boiled down to three declarative sentences: "I'm a good man. You are good people. Vote for me." He emphasized his integrity and his competence, and he flattered his audiences. Crisscrossing the country during the primaries, he said again and again and again that his administration would make the federal government more transparent and efficient. Distancing himself from the Washington of Richard Nixon, Carter promised that he "would never lie to the American people."[25]

Back in 1974, as governor, Carter had penned a *New York Times* op-ed that broadcast these themes. After acknowledging the pervasive lack of trust in government, he noted that "the solution may be simple. How can we be considered truthful? Simply by telling the truth!" The op-ed called for governmental reorganization and programs to make the government more accessible to the people.[26] For the next two years, Carter never wavered from these core promises of efficiency, transparency, and honesty. His focus was not on specific issues—although he did address them when asked and in certain speeches—but rather on these mantras of the early twentieth-century progressives. He would reform the federal government, just as he had reformed, he said, the state of Georgia. He mentioned the need for universal health care and environmental reform; for arms control and reductions in arms sales, but these issues were marginal to his message. When he mentioned foreign policy, which was not often, it was to criticize the excessive secrecy of the Nixon and Ford administrations that, he asserted, had led Washington astray. "Unnecessary secrecy surrounds the inner workings of our own government," he said in Chicago in March 1976, "and we have sometimes been deliberately misled by our leaders."[27] Carter made it clear that he was one of these betrayed Americans—one who had grown so disappointed with the nation's leaders, with their venality and their contempt for the common man, that he, Jimmy Carter, a peanut farmer, would go to Washington and throw the crooks out.

The GOP

President Ford had no such luxury. He was a creature of Washington. He had served twenty-five years in the House of Representatives before being appointed vice president following Spiro Agnew's resignation in October 1973, and in 1976 he was living in Washington's cockpit. But the incumbent, elected to neither the vice presidency nor the presidency, had trouble capitalizing on the benefits of incumbency. As the election year opened, Gallup reported that Ford had an approval rating of only 39 percent and a staggering 46 percent disapproval rating.[28] Even though he was considered honest, his decision to pardon Richard Nixon made it difficult for him to run on personal integrity, and the challenge from former California governor Ronald Reagan boxed him in on foreign policy. Ford's achievements in that realm were a continuation of Nixon and Kissinger's détente policy, which promised to reduce tensions with the Soviet Union. But by 1976, prominent conservatives to the right of Ford blasted détente as recklessly naive. The president, therefore, was reluctant to deliver a full-throated defense of his foreign policy, but neither could he renounce its underpinnings. Ford, who had never before run in a national campaign, did not deliver a clear message.

Ronald Reagan, by contrast, was nothing if not clear: the United States was acting weak—and this had to change. In the days before the Florida Republican primary, he stated flatly that the Ford administration's policy of détente had caused the United States to fall behind the Soviet Union militarily. Détente was a "one-way street," Reagan claimed; the only thing it had done was "give us the right to sell Pepsi-Cola in Siberia." He slammed the secretary of state. "Henry Kissinger's recent stewardship of US foreign policy has coincided precisely with the loss of US military supremacy," he asserted. "Mr. Ford . . . has shown neither the vision nor the leadership necessary to halt and reverse the diplomatic and military decline of the United States. . . . All I can see is what other nations the world over see: the collapse of the American will and the retreat of American power."[29]

This was Reagan's resonant rallying cry. In speech after speech, he delivered the same message: Americans, wake up! You are being misled by pessimists who tell you that America is a declining power and must accommodate the world. They are wrong! They are deluded by liberal guilt! In fact, American power—and only American power—can save the world from Armageddon. Americans, be strong! We are strong!

This was the pugnacious message that the emerging neoconservatives had been articulating since the 1960s; it had gained appeal as the US war in Vietnam foundered. Strength of will and strength of arms were key; being strong and feeling strong would counteract the horrors and errors of compromise, negotiation, and self-blame. The choice was straightforward: masculine power or feminine appeasement? Until this campaign, Reagan had been considered an Old Right conservative of the Goldwater variety, advocating small government and strong defense, rather than one of the crusading and intellectual, largely Northeastern neocons who gathered disaffected Democrats to their cause. But in early 1976, Reagan's rhetoric on the campaign trail countered the Vietnam syndrome and stressed all the important neoconservative themes, particularly the need for the growth of US military power to combat the twin evils of communism and Third World radicalism.

Ford tried to cut Reagan off at the pass. On March 2, 1976, the president told a Miami television interviewer that he disliked the word "détente" and did not think it "was applicable any more." However, his administration, he explained, would continue to pursue the policy of "peace through strength."[30] The British ambassador in Washington cautioned London that Ford was merely bowing to his domestic critics; the administration "continues to embrace Kissinger's essential policies." The banishment of the word "détente"," the ambassador assured Whitehall, was a "verbal sleight of hand."[31]

This rhetoric drove Kissinger crazy. "Nonsense to say we are a second-rate power," he groused to former Defense Secretary Melvin Laird. Continuing in the same vein to *New York Times* columnist James Reston, Kissinger remarked on Reagan's characterization of détente as a one-way street: "I could make a strong case that it has been." Then came the punch line: "It has been a one-way street in our direction rather than theirs!" Kissinger wanted the president to hit back hard, defending the administration's (that is, Kissinger's) foreign policy with vigor. But the secretary had lost power, symbolized most dramatically in his loss of the national security adviser hat the previous November to General Brent Scowcroft. For campaign advice, Ford listened not to his secretary of state but to his chief of staff, Dick Cheney, who recommended against attacking Reagan. "Dr Kissinger," a senior US diplomat told the British Foreign Office, "was resigned to the fact that for himself personally 1976 would be a bed of nails. It would be painful and frustrating."[32]

The burden of defending his legacy fell to Kissinger alone. Three days after the Florida primary, he told the Boston World Affairs Council that managing the US-Soviet relationship remained the administration's "most imperative" task, explaining that the threat of nuclear war meant that Moscow had to be handled with firmness, but that it was unwise to "escalate every political dispute into a central crisis." Taking direct aim at Reagan, the secretary of state stated: "No service is done to the nation by those who portray an exaggerated specter of Soviet power and of American weakness." Explaining his policy without using the word détente, he said that in order to "push back the shadow of nuclear catastrophe," Washington sought to find areas of cooperation with the Soviets, especially in curtailing nuclear arms.[33]

Kissinger was suffering. "I was bleeding to death with these guys running around screaming about weak America," he complained to Treasury Secretary William Simon after the speech.[34] Here was the man who less than two years earlier had been portrayed on the cover of *Newsweek* as "Super K"—his smiling face emerging from Superman's body, soaring over the globe[35]—the man who had negotiated the end of the US war in Vietnam and brokered peace agreements in the Middle East. Here was the architect of détente, the man who had endured Nixon's anti-Semitic bullying and maintained US foreign policy throughout the long drawn-out Watergate crisis. Here was Henry Kissinger, who had become a liability to the administration. His policy—summed up in the word détente—was associated with cynicism, secrecy, amorality, weakness, and failure. How had this happened?

The Fall to Earth

In a word, Angola. Of course it was more complicated—a mixture of overexposure, association with Nixon, the fall of South Vietnam, and the stalling of progress in the Middle East—but it all came together in Angola. There, the wax melted.

It was all so unnecessary. Kissinger's *Weltanschauung* had been molded by his youth in Germany, where he had witnessed the rise of Hitler. After immigrating to the United States, serving in the US Army, and completing a PhD at Harvard on nineteenth-century European diplomacy, his worldview was set in stone: for Kissinger, the diplomats of great powers bore onerous and unique responsibilities; they had to focus on relations among the great powers (because the marginal powers were just that, marginal) and they had to establish order before justice. Kissinger put these academic notions into practice, first as national security adviser (1969–75) and then, for an overlapping period, as secretary of state (1973–77). His foreign policy had clear priorities—relations with the Soviet Union were at the core, then China, the Middle East, Europe, and, in the wings, Latin America. Africa was not on his radar.[36]

In a way, this made sense. Kissinger had his hands full, and Africa seemed to have no prospect of affecting the great powers. The continent had briefly flared into America's consciousness in the 1960s with the decolonization struggles, but by 1969 it looked tranquil. The countries that were still ruled by white governments were clustered south of a line that cut across the continent from the southwestern border of Zaire, along the Zambezi River, and up to the southern border of Tanzania. This redoubt was composed of a "tripod of white power"[37]: (1) South Africa and its appendage, Namibia, which Pretoria illegally occupied as South-West Africa; (2) Rhodesia, still technically a British colony but one that had broken from the Crown in 1965, and (3) Angola and Mozambique, still under Portuguese rule.

From its earliest days, the Nixon administration had based its Africa policy on a simple premise, articulated on April 10, 1969, in National Security Study Memorandum 39: "The whites are here to stay."[38] Translated, this meant that there was nothing to worry about: America's friends—the region's Portuguese colonies and the white minority governments of South Africa and Rhodesia—were secure; there was no threat to US business interests and no possibility of Soviet encroachment. Africa, therefore, was not important to Henry Kissinger. A US ambassador put it pungently: in Kissinger's worldview, Africa was "the runt of the international litter."[39]

The continent, and the State Department's Africa Bureau, became the butt of Kissinger's jokes and withering contempt. To Kissinger—who drove his assistant secretaries hard and put them through their paces at weekly meetings of the senior staff—Africa was useful as comic relief. A good joke (even a bad joke) broke the tension; and where better than Africa to find humor? When the assistant secretary for Africa tried to discuss the rebellion in the Portuguese colony of Guinea-Bissau, for example, Kissinger retorted, "That is really what the world needed—a country called Guinea-Bissau."[40] David Newsom, who was Kissinger's first assistant secretary for Africa—and a true gentleman—remembered that the secretary's "jokes were funny, but at the expense of others. He used to embarrass people in ways that were inexcusable." Kissinger's feelings about the Africa Bureau came through in his private telephone conversations: "If you see our position papers written by the African bureau," he told the Israeli ambassador, "you will know why I don't pay any attention to them." Even his memoirs, written a quarter-century after he left office, ridicule the bureau as dealing with "the backwaters of policy."[41]

Kissinger chewed his way through four assistant secretaries for African affairs. Newsom, who stepped down only a few months after Kissinger became secretary of state, warned his successor that "[t]he President [Nixon] tends to favor full relations with South Africa [and] Rhodesia, and . . . [he]

and certain of his advisers have a particular sympathy for the Portuguese. . . . Moral considerations . . . are not usually useful in supporting policy recommendations." He ended his memo with a prescient, "Good Luck!"[42]

Three months later, on April 25, 1974, the bottom fell out of the administration's African policy. A group of Portuguese officers, weary of decades of dictatorship and exhausted by fighting guerrilla wars in Angola, Mozambique, and Guinea-Bissau, staged a bloodless coup in Lisbon. Portugal's colonies plunged toward decolonization.

Soon, Kissinger's prodigious energy and intellect would be riveted on Africa. In Angola, civil war broke out among three liberation movements. To Kissinger, whose eye was always on the great power struggle, the strife in Angola pitted two pro-US groups against the pro-Soviet faction, the Movimento Popular de Libertação de Angola (MPLA). He thought that it would be easy and cheap to tip the scales in favor of the pro-US forces. A small victory, but sweet. It would help expunge the sickening memories of US helicopters whirling off the rooftops of Saigon. Kissinger dismissed the warnings of the CIA station chief in Luanda and the new assistant secretary for Africa, Nathaniel Davis, (who resigned after three months) that his scheme was not in the US national interest. Money and weapons started flowing to the enemies of the MPLA.[43]

Kissinger's goals in Angola dovetailed with South Africa's. Both wanted to prevent the MPLA, which had announced its support for liberation throughout southern Africa, from taking power in Luanda. The earthquake that was the coup in Lisbon had shifted the tectonic plates under southern Africa. Pretoria's buffer zone of friendly white-ruled countries—Mozambique, Rhodesia, Angola—had been fractured. As the National Security Council (NSC) noted, "The Portuguese had been in effect the marcher barons [defenders of the border] of South Africa, holding off the black tide, well away from the white heartlands."[44] For the first time in its history, South Africa would have a hostile black country on its border: Mozambique's liberation movement, the Frente de Libertação de Moçambique (Frelimo), was set to assume control of the country upon independence in June 1975, and its leader, Samora Machel, had declared his passionate opposition to apartheid. This would not only give a psychological boost to black nationalists in South Africa; it would also give them refuge. Moreover, Frelimo promised to help the insurgents fighting for the liberation of neighboring Rhodesia—the next link in South Africa's buffer zone.

A decade earlier, in 1965, the British had been preparing to grant Rhodesia independence. A prosperous colony the size of the state of Montana, Rhodesia had been self-governed by its white population since 1923. The rules of apartheid in Rhodesia were not as stringent as in South Africa, but

Rhodesia's whites—4 percent of the population—dominated the country's six million blacks legally, financially, and socially. "Rhodesia's 275,000 whites had exclusive access to roughly half—the better half—of the country's land," the CIA wrote in 1977, while "Rhodesia's 6.2 million blacks shared roughly the other half."[45] Black income was, on average, 9 percent of white income; the average white farmer owned 6,100 acres, while the average black farmer owned 7 acres; the government spent more than ten times more on white schools than on black schools.[46]

White Rhodesians liked to trace their origins to a band of two hundred pioneers who had trekked north from South Africa in the 1890s in search of gold, but most were in fact much more recent arrivals, having emigrated from Britain in the aftermath of World War II in search of a better life without ration books. Most had been working class in Britain; in Africa, they had houseboys and maids, status and privilege. Yet their roots in Rhodesia were shallow: if they hit hard times or if prospects looked better across the Limpopo River in South Africa or back home in Britain, they picked up and moved. The steady ebb and flow of whites gave Rhodesia what one scholar has called "an illusion of demographic stability [to] . . . one of the most unstable and demographically fragile ruling ethnic castes in any polity anywhere in the world."[47]

Beginning with Ghana in 1957, Britain had recognized that majority rule was coming to its sub-Saharan colonies. Nigeria and British Somaliland (part of present-day Somalia) followed Ghana to independence in 1960; and by the end of 1964 Sierra Leone, Tanzania, Uganda, Kenya, Malawi, and Zambia were also free.[48] In 1964, London set a timetable for the implementation of majority rule in Rhodesia, to be followed by independence.

One year later, Ian Smith burst onto the world stage. Like the Alabama policemen at the Edmund Pettus Bridge who had stopped the civil rights marchers earlier that year in the United States, Smith held back time in Rhodesia. "There will be no African rule in my lifetime," the forty-five-year-old prime minister declared. "The white man is the master of Rhodesia, has built it and intends to keep it." In a desperate attempt to maintain white rule, on November 11, 1965, Smith declared Rhodesia to be independent. This Unilateral Declaration of Independence (UDI) was illegal. British prime minister Harold Wilson immediately condemned it—but his words rang hollow because his Labour government had already announced that it would not use force to reclaim the renegade colony. No nation recognized the new regime. Thirteen months later, Britain camouflaged its inaction by calling on the United Nations (UN) to impose mandatory economic sanctions against Smith's Rhodesia. The UN Security Council obliged, invoking Chapter VII of its charter—the "threat to peace"—for only the second time in its history. (The first was at the onset of the Korean War.) The Smith regime expressed outrage, but the sanctions had no enforcement mechanism and were easily circumvented.[49]

A nationalist movement had been founded in Rhodesia eight years before UDI, but most of its leaders had been jailed. Guerrilla attacks on the white regime had begun in 1972, but these were sporadic and largely ineffective. The 1974 coup in Lisbon, however, presented an existential challenge to Smith's rule because it meant that Rhodesian liberation fighters would have shelter and support across the 800-mile border with Mozambique.[50]

For South Africa, the coup in Portugal also raised the prospect of a black, pro-liberation regime taking over in Angola, a particularly important link in its *cordon sanitaire*. Angola abuts the northern border of Namibia, the barren and beautiful land that South Africa was illegally occupying as its "fifth province." Pretoria therefore welcomed Kissinger's decision to teach the Soviets a lesson there. Both the CIA and South Africa quietly sent money, weapons, and instructors to bolster the foes of the leftist MPLA guerrillas. Nevertheless, by the early fall of 1975 the MPLA was winning the war. South Africa, with US encouragement, upped the ante: in October 1975, its troops invaded Angola and swept toward Luanda, meeting little resistance.[51]

Enter Cuba. Fidel Castro, whose interest in Africa had quickened in the 1960s, decided to challenge South Africa's assault on liberation. He rushed Cuban troops onto Cuban planes and ships to Angola. This changed the equation dramatically for Pretoria. South Africa had expected its march through Angola to be swift and stealthy, not a full-scale war. It also changed the equation for Washington, which had expected tinkering in Angola to be low-risk and easy.

As Cuban troops flowed into Angola, reaching 4,000 by year's end, the South Africans appealed to Washington for open support. Since the Ford administration considered Castro a Soviet proxy (in fact, as historian Piero Gleijeses has shown, he was acting against Moscow's wishes), it saw his intervention in Angola as a flagrant violation of détente and a test of American will.[52] Yet it would be political dynamite for Washington to overtly side with South Africa, and both Congress and the US press were issuing loud warnings against stumbling into another quagmire. In December, the Senate passed the Tunney Amendment, which banned further US aid to the warring factions in Angola; a month later, the Clark Amendment made this ban permanent.[53] In January 1976, while Carter was campaigning in New Hampshire, the South Africans began to withdraw from Angola.

Kissinger's Africa foray had blown up in his face. He had expected to chalk one up for the United States, and instead he had been confounded by thousands of Cubans and befouled by collusion with apartheid. Considered gutless by conservatives and depraved by liberals, "Super K" fell to earth. It enraged him. He blamed Congress for hamstringing the administration with what he considered self-serving, senseless, and sanctimonious opposition to his policy. "The United States is refusing to meet a Soviet challenge in which we would win," he fumed to a sympathetic member of Congress. "It [the Tunney Amendment] is a national disgrace. It is the worst American foreign policy disaster that I can remember."[54]

The 1976 presidential campaign was waged against the backdrop of this debate about US policy in Angola, centered on the morality of covert operations, the proper role of Congress, and the appropriate response to the Soviet threat. In early January, the Senate held hearings on Angola. Kissinger was the first witness, and he did not tell the whole truth. He averred that South Africa had sent "some military personnel" into Angola (it was, in fact, 3,000 troops) "without consultation with the United States." The stakes for the United States, he explained, were high: "If the United States is seen to emasculate itself in the face of massive, unprecedented Soviet and Cuban intervention, what will be the perception of leaders around the world?" Senator Dick Clark (D-IA), sponsor of the Clark Amendment and chair of the Foreign Relations subcommittee on Africa, questioned the essence of the doctrine of containment. Addressing Kissinger, he stated, "We must certainly ask whether it is wise policy to react to Soviet actions anyplace in the world. . . . If we follow this policy, it means that we must react even if the Soviets themselves are making a mistake." Clark lambasted the administration for its failure to fully inform Congress. After listening to Kissinger's testimony, Andrew Young, then a representative from Georgia, observed drily, "What we have heard is a view of Africa through the eyes of a European cold-war man. And I do not think that that is what I see in Africa through my Afro-American eyes."[55]

An Old-fashioned Revival

After winning the Florida primary on March 9, 1976, Jimmy Carter was modest. "I feel good about it, of course," he said, "but we've got a long, hard way to go."[56] Certainly that was true, but after Florida, the field of contenders began to thin. During the long primary season, Carter traveled constantly, packing in as many as sixteen events a day. At his best in small groups, he projected self-confidence and hope. He prided himself on his ability to relate to voters. "I feel at ease with farmers," he told reporter Elizabeth Drew in March. "I feel at ease with blacks; I feel at ease with workers; I feel at ease with businessmen. . . . This is a *very* important political attribute." It was the essence of his campaign. "I honestly believe in the bottom of my soul," he explained, "that

I can accurately represent what our people are and what we want to be and what we can be." This not only helped Carter sway voters, it also recharged his depleted batteries: he enjoyed his success with farmers and businessmen and blacks and housewives. "I believe we've got a bright prospect ahead of us in this country," he would tell them. "I feel good about it. . . . Working together . . . we can accomplish great things. . . . When I'm president," he would conclude, "the country will be ours again."[57]

To the Americans listening, bruised and battered by the sordid revelations of Watergate, Carter was the antidote to Nixon. The other competitive Democratic candidates—Mo Udall, Scoop Jackson, Indiana senator Birch Bayh—had more experience, but in 1976 experience was at best a double-edged sword. Try as they might, not one of these men, sitting members of Congress all, was able to escape the stench of Washington. That Carter couldn't find his way from Union Station to the Capitol was an enormous asset. Carter predicated his campaign on his ability to convince the American people that he would deliver an honorable and open government. He barnstormed the country like a nineteenth-century revivalist. His campaign, he said, was about "whether we can believe again."[58]

The fact that Carter did not discuss issues bothered the press. *New York Times* correspondent James Wooten expressed exasperation with Carter's "uncanny knack of sliding softly over and around the thorniest issues," and many journalists bemoaned the difficulty of deciding if Carter was a liberal or a conservative.[59] It was beside the point. The point was that Carter persuaded one small gathering after another that he was not Richard Nixon.

This odd campaign, which dealt in generalities and failed to grapple with the serious issues facing the country—unemployment over 10 percent, strained relations with the Soviet Union, the debacle in Angola—was defined by small incidents, the first of which was Carter's foray into ethnic purity. Reporters seized on this gaffe (if gaffe it was), and it reverberated in the vast emptiness of the campaign.

On April 2, a reporter from the New York *Daily News* asked Carter what he thought of building low-income housing in the suburbs. Carter and the reporter were on an airplane heading to a campaign stop in upstate New York. The candidate's reply was rambling; he mentioned that inner cities needed the most attention and that his neighbor in Plains, Georgia, was black. Then he added, "I see nothing wrong with ethnic purity being maintained" in a neighborhood. Questioned about these comments four days later, he said, "I have nothing against a community that's made up of people who are Polish, Czechoslovakians, French Canadians, or blacks who are trying to maintain the ethnic purity of their neighborhood. . . . I would never, though, condone

33

any sort of discrimination against, say, a black family . . . moving into that neighborhood. . . . I would not [as governor] have supported a state program to inject black families into a white neighborhood just to create some sort of integration." Asked at the next stop to explain himself again, Carter was visibly annoyed but did not backtrack: "What I say is that the government ought not to take as a major purpose the intrusion of alien groups into a neighborhood simply to establish their intrusion."[60]

Suddenly, Carter's studied vagueness on busing—the most contentious civil rights issue of the day—seemed significant. Carter had projected a multifaceted balance on the issue: he was opposed to busing *and* he was in favor of public funding for students who wanted to be bused *and* he was opposed to a constitutional amendment against busing. By April, Carter enjoyed broad support among African Americans. As historian Jeremy Mayer writes, "Carter's governorship saw the greatest advance for black Georgians since Reconstruction." He had appointed more blacks to high positions than any previous governor—the number of blacks on governing boards and state agencies jumped from three to fifty-three—and he had also made important symbolic gestures such as celebrating the Martin Luther King holiday and hanging pictures of three black Georgians, including the slain civil rights leader, in the state capitol, a venue that had previously been adorned with only white faces.[61] (The former governor, Lester Maddox, vehemently disapproved: "[King] did a disservice to the country, more to advance communism than Americanism. . . . He led this country to anarchy, riots, police deaths."[62]) Moreover, Carter's campaign team was the most integrated in history, and his deputy campaign manager, Ben Brown, was black. Carter clearly felt comfortable with African Americans, and they with him—often because of shared religious roots. Andrew Young recounts that when the Congressional Black Caucus met all the Democratic candidates, Carter stood out. Even though all the other candidates knew many of the members of the caucus personally, "when they came into the room with 15 or 16 black folk, they were all nervous. And it was obvious—they were defensive," Young recalled. "Jimmy . . . immediately was at ease and relaxed. . . . He was more comfortable and relaxed than any of the others, and yet they were supposed to be the liberals."[63]

Carter knew that his record as a Southern progressive on race had, as he said, "political consequences of a benevolent nature."[64] But what exactly had he promised during the campaign? Not full employment (he had not endorsed the Humphrey-Hawkins bill, which mandated government spending to create jobs), or busing, or affirmative action. Against this backdrop, his "ethnic purity" remarks made many, especially hesitant liberals, question whether Carter was the man for them.

Since the only issue was Carter himself, and since Carter was an enigma, these two phrases—"ethnic purity" and "intrusion of alien groups"—became a window on the "real" Jimmy Carter. Were they code language, deliberately voiced two weeks before the Pennsylvania primary to court the state's conservative and ethnic voting blocs? Kissinger, who deemed the remarks "well calculated," suspected so.[65] Or were Carter's comments innocuous words muttered by an exhausted man? If so, what did it say about Carter that he was deaf to the connotations of these words? Who was Jimmy Carter?

The doubts of liberals about this southern governor surfaced with a vengeance. "Jimmy Carter is a wishy-washy, weaseling waffler," Molly Ivins declared in the fiercely independent *Texas Observer*. Carter's most prominent black supporter, Andrew Young, took the heat. "There were a lot of white liberals who were very close to coming around," Young remembered, "and [after Carter's ethnic purity comments] they really jumped on me, especially from the Jewish community." At the time, Young was adamant: "Either he'll [Carter will] repent of it or it will cost him the nomination. . . . I can't defend him on this."[66] Carter and his aides initially failed to grasp how damaging the firestorm was. It was not until six days later, on April 8, that Carter finally apologized, fully and clearly—not for the sentiment but for his "unfortunate" choice of words.

Jesse Hill, a black leader in Atlanta and president of Atlanta Life Insurance Company, whom Carter had known from his days as governor, came to his friend's rescue. He arranged a rally for the embattled candidate on April 13 in Atlanta, with prominent blacks, including Martin Luther King Sr., who, as the *Washington Post* reported, "pulled out all the stops." King's speech roared to a crescendo: "I have a forgiving heart. . . . So, Governor, I'm with you all the way."[67] The Pennsylvania primary was two weeks away.

The brilliance of Hamilton Jordan's strategy to propel Carter to the White House was that it valued every delegate. Jordan did not divide the political landscape into important states and marginal states: a delegate was a delegate, and Jordan wanted them all. Therefore, Carter campaigned in almost every state. This was strikingly different from his competitors, who were hobbled both by their full-time jobs in Washington and by their outdated way of thinking about elections. They planned to contest a few key primaries and then be embraced by the party powerful. The Democratic Party, however, had changed the rules: in 1972 there were only sixteen direct primaries, but in 1976 there were thirty. Jordan grasped that this paved a different path to victory, a bold, lonely, demanding path that would take Carter to almost every state in the union. Hence, Carter felled his opponents sequentially, in battlefront after battlefront.[68] And in Pennsylvania, his competition was Scoop Jackson.

Jackson had served in Congress since 1941, first as a representative and then as a senator. He was the quintessential Cold Warrior, and he thought détente was dangerous. He was adamant that Kissinger, Ford, and Nixon underestimated the gravity of the Soviet threat. That Jackson was a Democrat, and to the right of mainstream Republicans, indicates the complexity of party politics in the mid-1970s. Here is a snapshot of the confusion: speaking at the annual dinner of the Social Democrats, USA (formerly the Socialist Party), Jackson was lionized by prominent Jews, labor leaders from constituencies as varied as longshoremen and teachers, and several eminent African Americans. As Elizabeth Drew noted, "The group here is Old Left . . . bound by fights for social justice . . . but they are fed up now." Alienated by the 1960s, they were convinced that the government had lost its way. And so, these "ex-radicals, ex-Socialists, old liberals, new conservatives . . . have banded together in search of new and common ground."[69] This new coalition—soon to be called "neo-conservatives"—hoped that a crusading conservative Democrat like Jackson would clear that new ground.

Yet Carter won Pennsylvania handily, culling 37 percent of the vote to Jackson's 25 percent, with Udall, Wallace, and the rest of the pack trailing behind. Maybe "ethnic purity" hurt Carter in Pennsylvania—he won only 40 percent of the black vote—or maybe it helped him. Maybe a tactic; maybe a gaffe. But one thing was clear: despite the questions about Carter, he was able to win.

After Pennsylvania, even the doubters assumed that Carter would be the nominee. Liberals' hopes for a brokered convention that would select Hubert Humphrey, who had played "a waiting game" throughout the campaign, dimmed.[70] Democratic leaders who did not want to be left behind threw their support to Carter.

In fact, they jumped the gun: subsequent primaries exposed the fragility of Carter's candidacy. He won nine of the remaining contests, but lost seven to a late ABC (Anyone But Carter) movement spearheaded by Senator Frank Church (D-ID) and Governor Jerry Brown of California. Carter entered the convention in New York City confident, but not certain that he would win on the first ballot.[71]

Support came from an unlikely quarter: a strikingly positive endorsement by none other than Gonzo journalist Hunter S. Thompson, who wrote a glowing encomium in the June 1976 cover article of *Rolling Stone*. Thompson, an influential mouthpiece of the left, had been wowed by a speech Carter had delivered in 1974. "I have never heard a sustained piece of political oratory that impressed me any more than the speech Jimmy Carter made on that Saturday afternoon in May 1974. . . . It was a king hell bastard of a speech, . . . the heaviest and most eloquent thing I have ever heard from the mouth of a politician." Citing Reinhold Niebuhr and Bob Dylan as his lodestars, Carter had excoriated the corrupt legal system. Thompson was confident that this angry, courageous populist was the real Carter, the studied moderation of the campaign notwithstanding: "I still like Jimmy Carter. He is one of the most intelligent politicians I've ever met, and also one of the strangest. . . . Admittedly, a vote for Carter requires a certain leap of faith, but on the evidence I don't mind taking it."[72]

Sanctions and Schisms

The Republican primary focused on an important issue: was US power eroding? Ronald Reagan, whose campaign did not catch fire until he won the North Carolina primary on March 23, 1976, challenged Ford's foreign and defense policies. He mercilessly attacked détente, the Panama Canal negotiations, and Henry Kissinger. Kissinger was the embodiment of the pessimistic foreign policy that Reagan reviled. Kissinger, Reagan asserted, had overseen the decline of the United States. When the Reds launched their final assault on South Vietnam in 1975, Kissinger had wrung his hands and muttered about détente. When the Soviets poured into Angola (in Reagan's mind there was no difference between the Soviets and their Cuban proxies), Kissinger had stood back and muttered about détente. When the communists proposed the Helsinki treaty, which declared the "inviolability of frontiers" of Eastern European countries, Kissinger—incredibly—had put our "stamp of approval on Russia's enslavement of the captive nations."[73] President Ford was a good man, Reagan averred time and again, but his sidekick, Henry Kissinger, was positively dangerous.

The controversial secretary of state became ever more marginalized in the spring of 1976. The previous October, Ford's first campaign chair, Bo Callaway, had advised Ford to dump Kissinger because "what was killing the president was the impression that Kissinger, not Ford, was running foreign policy." In December, Lawrence Eagleburger, one of Kissinger's closest associates, warned him that "things could only get worse" and advised him "to depart with dignity while he could."[74] When Ford, campaigning in Indianapolis, proclaimed that Henry Kissinger "can stay on as secretary of state as long as I am president of the United States," the crowd booed. A *New York Times* columnist pointed out in March 1976 that "Kissinger is not really relevant to the future. Regardless of who wins, he will be finished at the end of the election, if not before." James Baker, then the undersecretary of commerce, announced publicly that Kissinger would not serve in a second Ford administration. (The State Department issued a vehement denial.) One of Kissinger's aides told Elizabeth Drew in March, "The emperor has no clothes. He's down to his underwear in terms of what he has in backing."[75]

What was the proud, ambitious, and driven man to do? He needed one more victory.

Kissinger scanned the globe. "He looked around," an NSC expert who had accompanied him on his travels commented. "He thought about his reputation and asked, 'What am I going to do now?'"[76]

The secretary's favorite place, China, was not available because of its inner turmoil following the death of Mao Zedong in September, and in an election year Ford considered the Taiwan problem too hot to handle. Hawks in the Ford administration, especially Defense Secretary Donald Rumsfeld, had stymied further progress on negotiating the SALT II treaty with Moscow. The Sinai disengagement talks had stalled. In the meantime, Africa had become the main theater of the Cold War, in large part due to Kissinger's misjudgment. Thousands of Cuban troops remained in Angola, and the long-simmering guerrilla war in nearby Rhodesia was beginning to flare up, offering a tempting opportunity for Soviet and Cuban meddling. Perhaps Kissinger would pull the final rabbit out of his hat in Rhodesia.

The irony was thick. Nixon, Ford, and Kissinger had paid scant attention to Rhodesia. After Ian Smith had declared independence (UDI) in 1965, the Johnson administration had voted in favor of selective UN Security Council sanctions against Rhodesia in 1966 and broader UN sanctions in 1968.[77] In so doing, Washington was supporting the UN's first attempt to impose mandatory international sanctions on any regime. Yet many members of Congress were unhappy with the sanctions, which punished a Christian, anticommunist regime (albeit one that was illegal and racist) and hurt some US business interests. Led by Senator Harry Byrd (I-VA), these representatives focused on the fact that the sanctions deprived the United States of its main source of chrome, a mineral essential to the manufacture of stainless steel products, including jet engines. A reliable source of chrome, they asserted, was essential to US national security, and without Rhodesian chrome the United States would be forced to import it from either South Africa or—this was the kicker—the Soviet Union. Surely, they argued, US national security should not be held hostage to a UN resolution.[78]

Opposition to these sanctions came from outside Congress as well. Former Secretary of State Dean Acheson was the most vocal and passionate critic: according to historian Douglas Brinkley, Acheson regarded Smith's regime as "a beacon of European light in a dark continent being overrun by anarchy, Marxism, and demonic black-power propaganda." In a letter responding to a 1966 *Washington Post* editorial about sanctions, Acheson wrote, "You bother me when you write about 'the white minority's transgressions.' Transgressions against what?" In 1968, he told the American Bar Association that Rhodesia "has done us no harm and threatens no one" and described sanctions as "bare-faced aggression, unprovoked and unjustified by a single moral principle." George Kennan, the father of the containment doctrine, agreed. Writing in *Foreign Affairs* in January 1971, he called on the US government to stop "belaboring" its "gestures of goodwill and solidarity" toward black Africans and to reexamine its policy toward southern Africa. Conservative stalwarts such as Barry Goldwater and George Wallace, businesses such as Union Carbide, and Rhodesian lobbyists all joined the assault on sanctions.[79]

These efforts bore fruit in November 1971, when Senator Harry Byrd led a successful drive in Congress to exempt chrome from the sanctions against Rhodesia. His amendment, which prohibited the embargo of strategic material from a noncommunist country if the same material was being imported from a communist country, passed handily in the House, 252 to 100, and overwhelmingly in the Senate, 65 to 19.[80] For the Smith government, the exemption was economically significant: between 1971 and 1975, the Byrd Amendment allowed Rhodesia to export an estimated $80 million of chrome to the United States.[81] It was even more important psychologically: it could be the camel's nose under the tent that would lead to international recognition. The Byrd Amendment also opened a door in US domestic politics to congressional involvement in the formulation of policy toward Rhodesia. For the remainder of the 1970s, the Rhodesian sanctions debate would divide the US Congress. It provided an important locus around which rising neoconservatives in Congress rallied and coalesced. The Nixon administration said that it opposed the Byrd Amendment, but it set a tone that allowed it to pass. President Ford, Kissinger, and the Republican Party failed to convey any interest in repealing it.

To the Byrd Amendment's critics—and they were legion in Africa and in US liberal circles—the idea that American national security depended on Rhodesian chrome was bunk; for them, the amendment screamed of Washington's collusion with white minority regimes. Senator Ted Kennedy damned the Nixon administration's policy of "'benign neglect' for the concerns of disadvantaged people." Parren Mitchell, a Democratic representative from Maryland and founding member of the Congressional Black Caucus, denounced Congress for its "reign of madness" that generated "this racist foreign policy" and rendered the United States an "international outlaw."[82] Liberals in Congress tried to repeal the amendment in 1972, 1973, 1974, and 1975. All these efforts went down to defeat, even in the liberal "Watergate Congress" elected in 1974 when the Democrats had gained forty-three House seats.[83]

Those who opposed the Byrd Amendment based their argument for repeal on principles: justice in southern Africa, respect for the UN, and upholding commitments. Those who argued against repeal based their argument on interests: maintaining access to cheap chrome and reducing trade with the Soviet Union. For many of the latter, race was a factor, although it was not explicit; being in favor of the Byrd Amendment was a way to signal support for Smith's embattled white regime. This combination—race, economics, and anticommunism—proved more potent than the principles of racial equality and international law.

What the press called the "indifferent attitude" of the White House to the fate of the sanctions sealed the fate of repeal.[84] Neither Nixon nor Ford—nor Kissinger—did anything (make phone calls, testify in Congress, give speeches) to help the forces of repeal. This was due to indifference—Rhodesia was very low on the White House priority list—and ambivalence. As Kissinger told the NSC, "I have a basic sympathy with the white Rhodesians."[85]

By 1976, those white Rhodesians were under assault, their privileged way of life threatened by the escalating guerrilla war. The Rhodesian economy appeared fairly robust—inflation was less than 5 percent, its currency had appreciated against the South African rand, and the country was still a food exporter—but the effects of Portuguese decolonization were beginning to be felt. On March 3, 1976, the new black government in Mozambique, declaring that a state of war existed between it and Smith's illegal regime, closed the border and brought much of landlocked Rhodesia's trade to a screeching halt. Rhodesians reacted to this move with "astonishment," according to the local news service in Salisbury.[86] Smith was forced to rely increasingly on South Africa, whose congested railways became the route for 80 percent of Rhodesia's trade. "Rhodesia's main problem," the Rhodesian intelligence service reported in 1976, "is not sanctions but the difficulty over the transport of exports."[87] The country's gross domestic product fell for first time in 1975, and continued its descent in 1976.[88] In the first six months of 1976, manufacturing fell by 9 percent, foreign exchange was "desperately short," and the stock exchange fell to 230 from a high of 490 two years earlier. Most ominously for Smith's regime, more than 1,520 whites a month emigrated, weakening the economy and shrinking the pool of white recruits for the armed forces. Many of the departing whites had been farmers, isolated on large tracts and fearful; others were the urban elite, tired of privation and pessimistic about the future.[89]

The guerrillas fighting the Smith regime were assailed by the Rhodesian army and by their own internal schisms. "The whole history of Rhodesian nationalist movements," a British Africanist observed, "was one of splits and factions."[90] Two liberation movements opposed Smith: the Zimbabwe African People's Union (ZAPU) and the Zimbabwe African National Union (ZANU). ZAPU was led by Joshua Nkomo, who had founded the group in 1961 to advocate for black voting rights and majority rule. Nkomo, an enormous man and imposing presence, had been educated by Methodist missionaries and was a former railway union official and a lay preacher. He considered himself, with much justice, to be the founder of Zimbabwean nationalism. ZAPU was not originally a guerrilla organization, but Smith's regime quickly banned it and imprisoned Nkomo in 1964. Yet Nkomo remained leader of ZAPU during his decade-long incarceration, and resumed active control of the group upon his release in 1974. He was a pragmatist who held open the possibility of achieving his goals—an independent Zimbabwe with himself at the helm—through negotiation, but he advocated armed struggle when necessary.[91]

ZANU emerged in 1963 from a schism within ZAPU that was generated, above all, by conflicts among strong personalities and intensified by disagreements about tactics and ethnic differences. Over time, the differences between the two rebel movements were deepened by geography and regional politics. ZAPU was based in Zambia, separated from Rhodesia by the frequently impassable Zambezi River. It was dependent on President Kenneth Kaunda, a seasoned politician whose landlocked nation relied on the goodwill of its neighbors. Until 1975, ZANU had also been based in Zambia, but Kaunda ejected it—and arrested many of its leaders—after he accused it of carrying out a political assassination. ZANU then moved to newly independent Mozambique, which had a long and porous border with Rhodesia. Mozambican president Samora Machel was a radical leader who could afford to be more bold than Kaunda because his country's long coastline had good ports. By 1976, ZANU was the larger and more active of the two groups. Nkomo's ZAPU, which increasingly became associated with just the Matabele people (only 20 percent of Rhodesia's black population) was estimated by Rhodesian intelligence in 1976 to have 1,400 fighters, of whom 500 had received military training—but almost none of them were operating in the country. ZANU, which drew from the Shona peoples (80 percent of the black population) was estimated to be five times bigger, with 6,000 recruits in Mozambique and 2,000 being trained in Tanzania. In October 1976, Rhodesian intelligence estimated that 1,300 ZANU "terrorists" were operating in the country. The Soviet Union supplied most of ZAPU's weapons and China supplied the bulk of ZANU's weapons, but Beijing's support was more stinting than Moscow's.[92]

Throughout most of 1976, Western observers underestimated the importance of ZANU, despite its size, because it was engulfed in a byzantine leadership struggle. By the end of the year, Robert Mugabe, its secretary general—and, in the words of Colin Legum, "a supremely self-confident and abrasive militant"—would seize the reins.[93]

In spite of their disagreements, the nationalists were united in their demand for immediate majority rule. They were opposed by the Rhodesian government forces—3,669 career professionals in 1976, plus 1,970 conscripts—bolstered by approximately 2,500 South African paramilitary police and pilots, including those who flew the forty Alouette helicopters that Pretoria had loaned to Smith's military. These Rhodesian and South African forces were supplemented by some 2,000 mercenaries, about 400 of whom were American.[94]

The conflict over majority rule in Rhodesia, therefore, had a complicated local aspect: two guerrilla movements—with established arms suppliers and safe havens just outside Rhodesia's borders—were at war with the Smith government. It also had an intricate regional aspect. This can be seen in two intersecting domains: the Frontline States and South Africa. The Frontline States were those bordering Rhodesia—Zambia, Mozambique, Botswana—plus Tanzania and Nigeria. (Angola was occasionally included in Frontline meetings about Rhodesia.) These black African states had a strong interest in the liberation of Rhodesia.[95] South Africa was crucial in two key respects. First, after Mozambique closed its border with Rhodesia in March 1976, all significant roads and rail lines into and out of Rhodesia ran through South Africa. This meant that Pretoria held Salisbury's life in its hands: if it closed its borders with Rhodesia, Smith's economy would suffocate. Second, Portuguese decolonization had shredded South Africa's *cordon sanitaire*. By January 1976, Mozambique and Angola were led by blacks who supported the liberation struggle.

In October 1974, on the heels of the coup in Portugal, South African prime minister Balthazar Johannes ("John") Vorster had changed his tactics. Vorster was a ruthless realist with a clear set of priorities. His government's most important goal was the maintenance of its white supremacist domestic policy. This meant that Vorster needed to identify every possible way to take the heat off his county's internal policies. One option was to use South Africa's enormous economic clout to "make nice" by striking trade deals with the black governments in its neighborhood, hoping that an enlightened foreign policy could distract attention from his country's unenlightened domestic policy. "Africa has been good to us," Vorster announced in the South African Senate on October 23, 1974, "and we are prepared to give back to Africa something of what we have so richly received over the years."[96] With this, Vorster initiated a policy toward black Africa that he called "détente," based, the US State Department noted, on "a mixture of pragmatism and illusion."[97] The premise of Vorster's détente was simple: being a better neighbor would relieve some of the pressure on Pretoria to change its racist policies. To promote détente with black Africa and buy time for apartheid, Pretoria needed to resolve the crisis in Rhodesia, which drew the world's attention to southern Africa and threatened South Africa's own stability. In announcing his détente policy, Vorster had told the South African Senate that his government sought "a durable, just and honorable solution" in Rhodesia and urged "all who have influence to bring it to bear upon all parties concerned."[98]

Would Vorster put the squeeze on Ian Smith?

It would be a domestic political challenge. There was no love lost between Vorster and Smith, and there were tensions between South Africa and Rhodesia—one ruled by Boers and the other by Brits—but their similar racist domestic policies had created a strong bond. Moreover, approximately 40,000 white Rhodesians called themselves Afrikaners; even more—South Africa estimated 50,000—held South African passports and would flood into the country if the war escalated.[99] The last thing that the South African government wanted was a war across its border that could suck in its armed forces.

Beyond its local and regional aspects, the Rhodesian problem had international dimensions. Rhodesia posed a problem for Whitehall—the British government—which retained legal authority for it. Britain had tried several times to resolve the festering issue, which was divisive domestically and strained relations with African members of the Commonwealth. But London's fretting was no match for Smith's determination. Time and again, Whitehall's stabs at negotiation foundered on Smith's intransigence. Having forsaken force, London had no retort.[100]

By 1976, the Cold War was hottest in southern Africa. The sparks from Angola threatened to ignite fires that would smolder in Namibia and South Africa and rage out of control in Rhodesia. Could the "domino theory," one of Kissinger's chief aides asked in February 1976, apply to southern Africa?[101] For the Ford administration, the worst-case scenario in Rhodesia could unfold in a matter of months through a simple, plausible sequence of events. The insurgents fighting against Smith's regime would be strengthened by the support of Samora Machel in newly independent Mozambique, and the liberation war in Rhodesia would escalate. Zambia and Mozambique would be unable to withstand the increasingly violent raids of the Rhodesian army against the guerrilla camps that Presidents Kaunda and Machel allowed in their countries. These two presidents would turn, albeit reluctantly, to Cuban troops for assistance, or the insurgents would establish a beachhead within Rhodesia and call in the Cubans. South Africa would respond to the arrival of Cuban soldiers by rushing in its own troops to help Ian Smith. The United States would be in a double bind: the administration could not allow the Soviet Union (via the Cubans) to get away with another raid on Africa, yet in domestic political terms it was inconceivable to imagine siding with the racist regimes of Salisbury and Pretoria. Compounding Washington's difficulties, given past US support for Africa's white minority regimes there would be no way to persuade world opinion that the United States was not in fact continuing, covertly, to do so. Kissinger put it well: "If we decided to fight such Soviet intervention, we would inevitably be supporting the White regimes. If we didn't fight, we would be seen as caving in to the Cubans." As he told Congress, "It would create impossible issues for us."[102] If a full-scale war, both racial and cold-war-by-proxy, engulfed the region, the United States would be unable to respond. As Winston Lord, the head of the State Department's Policy Planning Staff, declared, this would be "the ultimate nightmare."[103]

Two Headlines in March 1976

As the South Africans completed their humiliating withdrawal from Angola, tensions rose in Rhodesia. On March 10, 1976, the *New York Times* led with two articles. On the right: "Ford Defeats Reagan in Florida; Carter Is Winner over Wallace." On the left: "Rhodesians Face a Wider Conflict with Guerrillas." While the former analyzed why Reagan had lost in Florida and why Carter had won, the latter told of 4,000 to 5,000 insurgents along the full length of Mozambique's border, poised to attack Ian Smith's regime with "Soviet tanks . . . as well as Cuban soldiers." (In fact, there were no Cuban soldiers in Mozambique.)[104]

Pretoria was worried. "There is reason to believe that a limited number of Cuban instructors/advisers/technicians are active there [in Mozambique] now," South African military intelligence reported in April 1976. "There are also signs of a Cuban presence in Tanzania, where they are possibly training Rhodesian terrorists. We must expect that these Cubans would be readily available to act in Rhodesia should the circumstances demand it." Prime Minister Vorster, trying to recover from the fiasco of his Angola adventure, needed to avoid an escalating war in neighboring Rhodesia. He pressed Ian Smith to open talks with ZAPU leader Joshua Nkomo.[105]

In 1976, the war turned nastier. As ZANU infiltrated more guerrillas into Rhodesia, sometimes intimidating black villagers and terrorizing isolated white farmers, Smith's armed forces increasingly retaliated against any blacks they suspected of sympathizing with the "communists" with psychological operations and experimental uses of biological and chemical warfare.[106] Amnesty International reported that the use of torture by the Rhodesian police and army was "routine." Very few prisoners of war were taken. In March alone, the *New York Times* carried six editorials about the "ticking time bomb" in Rhodesia. When Kissinger testified to the House International Relations Committee on March 4 about his recent Latin American tour, he was asked four times about how he would respond if the Cubans intervened in Rhodesia. The secretary ducked the question, saying it was hypothetical. On March 6, President Ford also hedged when asked a similar question. But a week later, when reporters pressed him again, Ford said that the administration had "contingency plans" to deal with the Castro if he dared send troops to Rhodesia. "I can assure you that we will strongly oppose any action by the Soviet Union and Cuba because that is pure international adventurism."[107]

Ford and Kissinger hoped to deter Castro by imposing a blockade that would "clobber" him.[108] "The Fidel Castro regime . . . is acting as an international outlaw!" Ford had exclaimed on February 29, 1976.[109] That the diatribes against Castro escalated in the days before the Florida primary suggests that they were at least in part politically motivated, but there was also serious discussion about how to attack Cuba if it repeated its Angolan adventure. "I think we may have to crack the Cubans on Rhodesia [*sic*]," Kissinger told Ford in early March, "even if it provokes race riots here. . . . we will have to give Cuba a bloody nose." The president told Kissinger to "move forward on our contingency planning."[110]

This worried British prime minister Harold Wilson—who as prime minister in 1965 had failed to respond decisively to Smith's UDI—for two reasons. First, American military action against Cuba would place London in an awkward position; second, pumping up the Cuban threat played right into Smith's hands, rallying his supporters and giving him "material for cheap propaganda." On March 4, 1976, the British ambassador in Washington, Peter Ramsbotham, met with Kissinger to discuss southern Africa. The British are "as apprehensive as the Americans about the possibility of a racial war, with the Cuban weight thrown in," Ramsbotham began, but "there were possibilities of promoting successfully an early transfer of power to black majority rule." Kissinger was not interested. "If the Cubans moved outside Angola," he warned, "the Americans would come after them." He would "blow the roof off" to stop Castro's troops. "The US would not allow the Cubans a second success." Ramsbotham commented to the Foreign Office that Kissinger "is obsessed with the global implications of letting a small communist power loose on a wrecking mission in Africa, with the US powerless to stop it."[111]

The following day, the US ambassador in Zambia, Jean Wilkowski, sent Kissinger an unusually blunt cable urging him to resolve the crisis in Rhodesia before it widened into a regional war. She had been urging this in less blunt terms for six months—ever since President Kaunda had summoned her to the state house to urge that President Ford put America's weight behind the quest for a negotiated settlement in Rhodesia.[112] On March 5, Wilkowski laid out the case urgently. Explaining that the guerrillas had been encouraged by US passivity and "the retreat of the South Africans before the Cuban offensive" in Angola, she advised that the United States "should assert its leadership and play a responsible role by telling Smith how isolated and hopeless his situation has become. . . . Kaunda expects from us some new initiative that will both avert further communist penetration in southern Africa while achieving majority rule without further delay. It is in our own interest to speak out and destroy Smith's false assumptions about where USG [US government] stands. This may be last chance to move Smith toward political settlement." She followed up four days later with a cable suggesting that Kissinger himself travel to southern Africa. "It could mark a dramatic turning point," she wrote, "and take some of the lustre off [the] Soviet star, which has brightened in African eyes following stunning military sweep of Soviet-equipped Cuban troops across Angola."[113] Many years later, President Kaunda explained, "If we did not get this thing sorted out quickly, this problem of East/West competition would arrive here. And what would this mean for us? . . . Britain had a lot of problems in the region. So I always thought the USA had . . . to help Britain do the right thing."[114]

On March 12, Director of Policy Planning Winston Lord sent Kissinger a memo penned by a member of his staff, Tom Thornton. "You may find his approach to the problem a useful alternative optic for dealing with the hard choices concerning Africa," Lord wrote. Thornton had deliberately written his memo in Kissinger's language: he framed southern Africa in Cold War terms, proposed a way out of the morass, and cast the secretary in the leading role.[115] Highlighting the importance of southern Africa, Thornton compared it with the Middle East from 1967 to 1973, where the Soviets had been aligned with "progressive" forces (the Arabs) while the United States was aligned with a nation (Israel) that was becoming an international pariah. Although "the long-term outlook appeared to be very much on their [the Soviets'] side," Kissinger had succeeded in marginalizing Moscow. Likewise in southern Africa, Kissinger must seek to "restructure the political situation in a way that defined the Soviets out of the process." That is, Washington should neither renounce South Africa nor embrace black African liberation, but rather insert itself into the situation in order to lessen tensions. "Defining the Soviets out of the problem would be possible," Thornton concluded, "only if we could present ourselves to both sides as the only party able to bridge between black and white contestants." This would require Kissinger to play America's weak hand boldly.[116]

The Policy Planning Staff developed a detailed strategy along the lines suggested by Thornton. "Convincing the various African partners that the only real solution lies through us . . . will be much more difficult than the Middle East: the Arabs know that only we have the capability to 'deliver' the Israelis; we have nothing like this trump with the white regimes." The United States had to "carve out a role on the side of African aspirations." After a long discussion of the potential pitfalls, the memo suggested, "One possibility would be to . . . enunciate a set of principles concerning African aspirations and problems. . . . Such a statement could be a vehicle for effecting a substantial change, if not in the realities on the ground in Southern Africa, then at least in . . . the strength of our own position."[117]

On March 15, British foreign minister James Callaghan sent Kissinger a long letter about southern Africa, "which is a major preoccupation of ours. . . . There are some very large issues at stake." Callaghan explained that "our main objective must be to deny the communists opportunities for successful intervention in southern Africa." However, he immediately warned Kissinger that the situation was tricky because the communists would try "to pose as the champions of black Africa against white . . . [and], to the extent that we appear to oppose the Russians, we put ourselves on the white side." Therefore, it was essential to attempt to negotiate a settlement. "I am more than ever sure that the right course is to continue to work for an early and peaceful transfer of power to African majority rule in Rhodesia."[118] In the two weeks since he had met with Ambassador Ramsbotham and threatened to "blow the roof off" to punish Cuba, Kissinger had studied the issues and changed his tone. "If I have been a bit hesitant," he replied to Callaghan on March 18, "it is only because . . . we are trying to discipline ourselves to tread the thin line between . . . support for majority rule in Rhodesia and firm public opposition to further Cuban/Soviet interventionism."[119]

The next day, hopes for a prompt settlement in Rhodesia were dashed when talks between Smith and ZAPU leader Nkomo broke down. "I don't believe in majority rule ever in Rhodesia—not in 1,000 years," Smith proclaimed on British television. President Kaunda despaired: Rhodesia's future, he concluded, would have to be decided by "force of arms."[120]

As the Foreign Office noted, "Failure of the Smith/Nkomo talks made it inevitable that responsibility for continuing the search for a settlement would revert to the British Government."[121] On March 22, in what the *New York Times* deemed a "desperate effort," Foreign Secretary Callaghan announced to Parliament new proposals to end the crisis.[122] He envisioned a two-step process. In the first stage, all parties—Smith, the Frontline States, and the insurgents—would agree to the principle of majority rule and the holding of elections in two years. In the second stage, a new constitution would be negotiated.[123]

Ian Smith rejected the British proposals hours after he received them, claiming that they offered "no hope of real progress." Callaghan retorted: "Smith . . .

continues to try to buy time, even though time has almost run out." He told Parliament that his initiative had failed, "like its predecessor . . . because of Mr. Smith's prevarications. . . . I am not hopeful."[124] Nor was the British Parliament, which had no desire for another humiliating imbroglio with the "slippery" (Callaghan's term) Ian Smith. Callaghan's preconditions—agreeing to majority rule and prompt elections—set the bar; until Smith agreed to them, Parliament was loath to engage again. But how could Britain force Smith to agree? A senior British diplomat, Mervyn Brown, admitted, "Essentially what we were trying to do . . . was to solve the problem without getting ourselves involved." British Deputy Undersecretary Antony Duff told the Americans that it was "a hopeless situation." Whitehall had no more cards to play.[125]

On March 24, the North Atlantic Council—the main decision-making body of NATO— met to discuss the crisis in Rhodesia. Bill Schaufele, the US assistant secretary of state for Africa (Kissinger's fourth), was in attendance. The meeting emphasized the "requirement that West must give Soviets no/no pretext for active military involvement" in Rhodesia, the Canadian representative cabled. "The best means to discourage Soviet military adventures would be to remove pretexts for such actions through efforts at peaceful and constructive settlement of problems, in particular our support for concrete and prompt steps toward black majority rule in Rhodesia."[126]

Schaufele wrote Kissinger: "Our essentially passive stance no longer is the most appropriate approach." The CIA agreed. In early April, Kissinger was briefed by the new director of central intelligence, George H. W. Bush. "The essence of his presentation," Kissinger wrote, "was summed up in this pithy sentence: 'It is the intelligence community's prediction that Cuban troops will be involved in Rhodesia before the end of 1976.'" Kissinger got the message. He was going to Africa.[127]

On the eve of Kissinger's departure, President Ford sent a message to the seven African heads of state whom the secretary would meet. "The strengthening of relations between the United States and Africa is a central element of my country's foreign policy. Secretary Kissinger is coming with an open mind and an open heart."[128] Kissinger was not a sudden convert to majority rule. "Basically I am with the whites in Southern Africa," he told an approving President Ford. "But in my comments [in Africa] I will support majority rule in Rhodesia. I will say the same about South Africa, but softer."[129]

The South African government was alarmed. US policy toward southern Africa, Pretoria's ambassador in Washington reported, was "based on the assumption . . . that the fall of Rhodesia can be expected within a matter of months and that South Africa will in turn be under 'majority rule' within a couple of years."[130] Kissinger tried to reassure the ambassador: "I have no sentimental illusion about African countries . . . [but] if we don't get the Cubans out of Africa, we will have a real race war and the Soviets will get in."[131] Before he left Washington, the secretary explained to the NSC, "If the Cubans are involved there [Rhodesia], Namibia is next and after that South Africa, itself. We must make the Soviets pay a heavy price. . . . Otherwise it will be seen as Soviet strength and US weakness."[132] His mission was to cut the Cubans off at the pass.

The Special Relationship

A journalist hurled a question at Kissinger on April 22, 1976, the eve of the secretary's departure for southern Africa. "Mr. Secretary, . . . the administration is on record as opposing the Byrd Amendment but doesn't do anything to get it repealed. . . . How are you going to make credible, now, in view of this past history, this commitment and this desire for change in southern Africa?" Kissinger sighed. "Well," he said, "that will be one of the problems on my African trip."[133]

On his way to Africa, Kissinger stopped in Britain, which was still embroiled in the aftereffects of Prime Minister Harold Wilson's unexpected resignation on March 16. After a hotly contested struggle, Foreign Secretary James Callaghan became prime minister on April 5, and Anthony Crosland, who had been secretary of environment, became the foreign secretary. In his memoirs, Kissinger writes that before his first trip to Africa, "Crosland undertook the undoubtedly painful task of ceding to the United States—at least for an interim period—Britain's traditional role of leadership in Southern Africa."[134] This would have surprised Crosland. There is no indication in the voluminous British files on Kissinger's trip that Whitehall had any intention in April 1976 of ceding anything to the United States. The British officials viewed Kissinger as a pinch hitter at best and a massive pain at worst. A year later, a journalist asked Callaghan if there had been a sense that "the thing had swung too heavily towards America?" Callaghan was jocular. "We all know what Henry was like," he replied.[135]

London acknowledged the importance of American policy in the region. In early 1976, the British, who had been taken by surprise by the Cuban intervention in Angola, were worried that Castro would repeat the feat in Rhodesia. As the Foreign Office's research bureau wrote, "The Rhodesian crisis may be expected to produce just that sort of troubled water in which the Cubans are all too eager to fish."[136] In their postmortem on Angola, Foreign Office officials stressed how US signals would affect Soviet actions: "The Soviet Union will remain on the look-out for similar opportunities elsewhere. . . . Very important among the factors which influence them will be their assessment of the interest or disinterest of the United States and of American resoluteness." The Foreign Office planning staff noted how Washington would also shape the policies of African governments: "If armed confrontation increases in Rhodesia, the Africans may, despite themselves, welcome Cuban intervention. Some African leaders are already saying this. . . . In this context, American reactions are important." The Foreign Office spilled a lot of ink in the spring of 1976 trying to decipher what it considered "confusing signals" from the Ford administration; it worried that an isolationist impulse in Washington would encourage the Soviets, but a militaristic response would be equally dangerous.[137]

"Were Cuba to become militarily involved in Rhodesia there could be serious difficulties for us," the Foreign Office noted drily in May. "Would an invasion of Rhodesia by Cuban regular forces place us, even theoretically, at war with Cuba?" Would Whitehall be obliged to send troops to Rhodesia to protect "kith and kin" which would align Britain with the forces of apartheid and threaten to tear the Commonwealth apart?[138] Approximately 80,000 Rhodesian whites were (or had the right to be) British citizens, and a further 75,000 were eligible to emigrate to Britain. Would they flood into the United Kingdom? "If, say, 20,000–30,000 of these arrived in the United Kingdom as refugees they could present a serious administrative problem."[139] The British, however, were at a dead end in Rhodesia.

Whitehall needed help in two domains. First, convincing Smith that his time was up. "What can we do?" a Foreign Office expert asked. "It is clearly essential," he answered himself, "to bring all possible pressure from Western countries and South Africa to bear on Smith." Second, creating a fund to help Rhodesian whites through the transition to majority rule. This fund, which would be similar to the Land Transfer Programme that London had deployed in Kenya during the latter's transition to independence in 1963, would persuade whites to accede peacefully to majority rule by assuring their pension rights and fair reimbursement for their property. "We must keep the Americans in play," the Foreign Office noted. "Their readiness to find money for this could be decisive."[140]

Against this backdrop, the British welcomed Kissinger's trip. "Given American ignorance of Africa," the Foreign Office seized the opportunity to play "a useful educative role."[141] London did not, however, give it highest priority. Callaghan had been in office for a fortnight, and he was preoccupied with shoring up the Labour Party's fragile governing coalition. Even though as foreign secretary he had forged a good relationship with Kissinger, he decided that campaigning in the north of England was more important than being in London to meet the US secretary. Meanwhile, Foreign Secretary Crosland (who had a reputation for "lofty arrogance") informed Kissinger that because it was "his custom" to spend the weekends with his constituents, it would be inconvenient for him to come to London. "Dr. Kissinger was very welcome to meet him for breakfast," however, at an RAF base in Waddington, near Crosland's Lincolnshire seat. Kissinger, although "unenthusiastic," accepted the invitation.[142]

Moreover, the British were scathing about US policy. "The essential defect of US policy in southern Africa," a Foreign Office expert wrote, is "that it has been reactionary in the true sense of that word. They [the Americans] have not been prepared to do enough of the constructive work, much of it routine and undramatic, needed to prevent disasters from happening. We could not get Dr. K to focus at all on southern Africa until after the Russians had." The North American desk officer at the Foreign Office added that "the Americans . . . had no real African policy; they had an approach. . . . [which] was pretty vague . . . [and] amounted to little more than being in favour of motherhood."[143] The British did not consider this breakfast meeting with the peripatetic secretary to be an occasion at which they "ceded" anything to Washington.

Kissinger sought the benefit of British advice, particularly since he did not trust the bureaucrats he called "retired Protestant missionaries who constitute our African Bureau."[144] He groused to the British ambassador in Washington that "I have no honest account from anyone on anything."[145] This mattered because, as he told Crosland, he "had never been in [sub-Saharan] Africa, . . . had no feel for the situation . . . [and] no knowledge of the psychology of African leaders."[146] The British could not have agreed more. They tried to warn Kissinger of the many pitfalls to avoid, ones they had learned from painful experience during their long history in Africa.

In the meeting with Kissinger at the Waddington airbase, Crosland deferred to Sir Michael Palliser, permanent undersecretary of state, and Sir Antony Duff, a top Foreign Office Africa expert. Crosland was ill prepared for the Foreign Office portfolio; he had hoped instead to be prime minister, or at least chancellor of the exchequer. Even his wife, Susan, noted that he seemed to have been "dropped from the skies into the F[oreign] O[ffice]." Palliser and Duff stressed two things to Kissinger: Africans were deeply suspicious of US policy, and Kissinger should downplay his concern about communist penetration in the continent. Palliser suggested that Kissinger always substitute the word "Soviet" for "communist" and "never forget the extent to which the Africans in south Africa were obsessed with the black/white struggle to the exclusion of wider issues. . . . It was not that they loved the Soviet Union and the Cubans but that they saw them as the supporters of the blacks." Duff recommended that the secretary stress "that there could be no question of a US rescue operation for the whites in Rhodesia."[147]

Kissinger explained that his goals were modest. He wanted the "African situation" to "remain quiescent," and he hoped to "avoid . . . the use in Rhodesia of Cuban troops." The Middle East analogy was on his mind. "The US had found one leader [Anwar Sadat in the Middle East] whom they had convinced that progress depended on Western support for taking concrete measures. He would find the same in Africa." In Lusaka, Zambia, he would give a speech declaring US support for majority rule in Rhodesia.[148]

These goals appeared straightforward, but they were not. Kissinger was going to proclaim his government's strong support for majority rule in Rhodesia, but what exactly did that mean? What was the United States willing to do to support it? A few days before Kissinger's arrival, the US ambassador in London told the Foreign Office, "The Americans did not consider that the liberation movements . . . are, in fact, likely even over a prolonged period of time to bring down the Smith regime on their own. They think this will only be achieved if the liberation movements receive the full support of trained combat forces with sophisticated modern weapons—on the lines of Cuban support for the MPLA in Angola."[149] Was Kissinger implying that he would support majority rule in Rhodesia that came at the point of a Cuban AK-47? Hardly. His goal was to keep the Cubans out of Rhodesia, and this could mean supporting Ian Smith's army. It was not clear how this squared with his newfound support for majority rule in the country.

Senator Clark, chair of the Africa subcommittee, had put the question bluntly to the secretary in March: "Which of these two priorities is greater—majority rule in Rhodesia, or checking Cuban adventurism?" Kissinger had hedged: "We can pursue both of these objectives simultaneously so that the Hobson's choice . . . will not arise." Clark pressed the secretary. Finally, Kissinger had admitted: "We cannot accept the principle that an outside power . . . intervenes militarily all over the world."[150]

Kissinger's declaration that the United States would not come to the aid of the Smith regime was therefore problematic. It was his public message, but in private he would make clear that the United States "would be likely to 'do something'" if the Cubans intervened. This would not only give Ian Smith courage, it might also—as discussed at length in London—encourage the Rhodesians to expand the war in order to provoke a Cuban intervention, thereby triggering US aid.[151] Kissinger would need to do some fancy footwork in Africa.

The very fact that the secretary was traveling to Africa represented change, but his worldview had not budged. Africa, he told the British, "was not a profitable place for a Great Power struggle." Given its "lack of real resources," its importance at that moment "was out of proportion." It had a lot of votes at the UN, but, Kissinger confided, "votes at the UN are not important." Africa mattered for one reason. Kissinger had said it clearly in his congressional testimony in January: "Cuba's unprecedented and massive intervention [in Angola] . . . is a geopolitical event of considerable significance."[152] Henry Kissinger was a bloodhound who followed one scent: Soviets.

It was a long flight from London to southern Africa, and Kissinger had time to worry. His power was ebbing at home, and the warnings of the British about African suspicions were ringing in his ears. The Nigerians, flush with oil and brasher than ever, had refused permission for his jet to land in Lagos, publicly rebuffing the US secretary of state in order to express their outrage over US policy in Angola. The Ghanaians followed Lagos's lead. The *Ghanaian Times* editorialized, "Ghanaians are in no mood to extend their traditional hospitality to a visitor who has been tainted with so much ill-motives." Other African countries had been omitted from Kissinger's itinerary because of concerns for his "personal safety."[153] Not even Prime Minister Callaghan had found time to see him in London, and he had been forced to fly to an airbase one hundred miles north of London to accommodate the new British foreign secretary's schedule. The press covering the trip was jaded. "The simple, unvarnished truth is that Kissinger's interest in African affairs languished on the back-burner until Soviet and Cuban intervention in Angola," Ted Koppel announced on *Good Morning America*. "African leaders will be taking a somewhat jaundiced view of this goodwill tour." Expectations were low. "There will be no miracles, not even for Dr. Kissinger, in southern Africa," the *Washington Star* predicted.[154] Therefore, the US press did not cover this trip with the vigor it had expended on Kissinger's perambulations across the Middle East; it was absorbed in the horse race of the campaign, in which Ford and Reagan were duking it out over détente and the gentleman who was, at that moment, in flight to Africa.

On April 25, 1976, Henry Kissinger landed in Tanzania—whose president, Julius Nyerere, had been a thorn in Washington's side ever since his nation had gained independence in 1961. Just one year before Kissinger deplaned in Dar es Salaam, the outgoing assistant secretary for Africa had written, "One country which has clearly been at the top of the 'enemies' list from the beginning of this Administration is Tanzania. . . . [There is] a long-standing dislike for Nyerere." That had been penned, however, before 36,000 Cubans had landed in Angola. Now Nyerere's status as the unofficial leader of the Frontline States was more important than his questionable politics. "Tanzania is the intellectual leader of Southern Africa," Kissinger told members of Congress, "and as such is the key to the future of the area and whether that future will be violent or not."[155] To keep the Cubans out of Rhodesia, Kissinger would need

Nyerere's help. It would be an uphill climb: only a deputy foreign minister and a crowd of protestors greeted the US secretary of state at the airport in Dar es Salaam. Kissinger took note.[156]

Kissinger opened his conversation with Nyerere with a rare mea culpa: "I am willing to admit the mistakes of the past. We have had Vietnam, the Middle East, Watergate; it was not possible to do everything simultaneously. But I am here now to do something." He then tried to lure the Tanzanian leader. "President Sadat saw that in confrontation with the United States, it was not possible to do anything, and in cooperation with the United States much was possible. Now we're giving $1 billion to Egypt in aid. . . . I like to think we can do the same with Africa . . . and work with you." Nyerere was polite, and evasive. He kept returning to one issue: the liberation of southern Africa. "Our priorities are Rhodesia and Namibia. South Africa is harder." The two men ended with small talk, Kissinger musing about the US presidential contest. "Reagan is a former movie actor," he observed. "He doesn't know what he's saying, but he says it effectively."[157]

Although Nyerere was thoroughly noncommittal as to whether he would be willing to be Kissinger's Sadat in southern Africa, Kissinger told Ford that he found Nyerere "sharp, clever, gregarious and fascinating. . . . He is a man of intellectual range, subtlety, sophistication and wit." However, he added, "I have no illusions: he [Nyerere] will remain ideologically opposed" to the United States.[158]

This was signaled at the state dinner held in the secretary's honor. Delivering the welcoming toast, the Tanzanian foreign minister chose to lecture rather than laud: "Sometimes . . . we feel that you . . . lack the will to help. It is thus our hope that your brief visit . . . will afford you a better perspective so that the United States of America, which at its founding fought hard for independence, shall not turn a blind eye to the situation in southern Africa until it is too late and even then be on the wrong side."[159] As Kissinger flew to Zambia the following morning, he might have been remembering the last such toast he had heard, delivered by Zambia's president, Kenneth Kaunda.

Zambia: "A cheeky little nation"[160]

Of all the Frontline presidents, Kaunda faced the greatest challenges. By exhorting his people from the earliest days of independence about their shared goals—his "one Zambia, one Nation" campaign—he helped forge a Zambian identity. However, as an NSC interdepartmental group noted in 1976, "the one-party state inaugurated by Kaunda . . . has not united the people of Zambia, nor has it improved the administration of the country. Deep divisions along ethnic lines persist." The report stressed that Kaunda's focus was not narrowly on Zambia: "For President Kaunda the attainment of majority rule in Rhodesia and the creation of an independent Namibia have been vital Zambian interests."[161] Southern Africa is liberated today in part because of Kaunda's devotion to the cause, and the sacrifices that he led Zambia to make for it. As Anthony Lake, the State Department's director of policy planning during the Carter administration, would testify to Congress: "No nation has had a greater interest in achieving majority rule in Rhodesia than Zambia, and no nation has made greater sacrifices toward that end."[162]

Zambia has been shaped by copper. The world's fourth largest producer of the metal, Zambia was hit hard when the world price of copper plummeted from a high in May 1974 of $1.40 per pound to $0.53 six months later; copper prices continued to fall until a slight rebound in 1978. Zambia's landlocked position also made it vulnerable. Kaunda could ill afford to antagonize his neighbors: he needed their roads and rails to carry Zambia's copper to a port. In 1973, in retaliation for Kaunda's sheltering of guerrillas fighting in Rhodesia, Ian Smith closed the Rhodesian border with Zambia, and when he offered to reopen it, Kaunda refused. Zambia was obliged, therefore, to cobble together inferior routes to export copper and import necessities such as food and fertilizer. It diverted half its trade to the ramshackle Benguela railway that cut through Angola to the Atlantic, even though this meant paying the Portuguese colonizers for its use. Angola's war of independence, however, brought the railway to a sudden halt in 1975.[163] Kaunda therefore had to look east—to ports in Mozambique, Tanzania, and Kenya. This meant patching together routes that included roads that were often impassable and rickety rail lines that led to undeveloped and congested ports. The Chinese-funded Tazara railway was meant to resolve these bottlenecks. Linking Zambian mines to Tanzanian ports, the Tazara opened in 1976, but it was plagued with problems and carried only 20 percent of the anticipated cargo.[164] In the mid-1970s, when the price of copper collapsed and the war in Rhodesia escalated, Zambia faced almost insurmountable transportation problems that gutted its foreign trade.[165]

The political geography of southern Africa coupled with the ideology of liberation created one circle of problems for Kaunda, but he also had to juggle the superpowers. An ardent member of the Non-Aligned Movement, Kaunda managed to maintain good relations with the United States, the Soviet Union, and China—and at the same time to antagonize all three. The idea of non-alignment defied the Manichaean logic of the Cold War. "Non-alignment," a Zambian diplomat noted, was considered in the West "an aspiration more than a reality."[166] Kaunda was difficult to pigeonhole. On the one hand, he was a devout Christian who wore his religion on his sleeve, and all but 0.6 percent of the investment in Zambia during his presidency was from the capitalist world.[167] On the other hand, he lauded socialist economies, he nationalized industries, and he supported liberation movements.

Washington ignored Zambia, along with all of sub-Saharan Africa, until 1975, when Kissinger began to fathom the repercussions of the Lisbon coup. Then, because Zambia stretched between the hot spots of Angola, Mozambique, and Rhodesia, Kaunda suddenly mattered. He was hastily invited to Washington for a visit in April 1975—ten days before the fall of Saigon—that the *New York Times* aptly called "as important as it is overdue."[168]

At the formal White House dinner in his honor, Kaunda, an emotional man, had shattered decorum. Instead of offering a platitudinous toast, he delivered a courageous rebuke and challenge. After brief pleasantries, he said, "What gives Zambia and Africa great cause for concern is, Mr. President, America's policy towards Africa—or is it the lack of it. . . . American policy . . . has given psychological comfort to the forces of evil. . . . Southern Africa is poised for a dangerous armed conflict. There is not much time. . . . The patience of the oppressed has its limits." The American ambassador to Zambia, who attended the state dinner, said that Kaunda's toast "made Kissinger furious."[169]

The Pivot

As Kissinger's bulletproof Cadillac rolled off his plane after landing on Kaunda's home turf a year later, the *New York Times* editors noted, "the hour is late." Two days before Kissinger's arrival, Kaunda had announced that the time for negotiations about the future of Rhodesia was over. "Henceforth," he said, "Africa and all progressive forces in the world must support armed struggle."[170] Kissinger, however, had come to Lusaka to make precisely the opposite point: that now was the time for negotiations. As the British had predicted, Kaunda was suspicious, and he chose not to give the secretary of state a big stage for his much-touted address in case it turned out to be another in a long string of disappointments from Washington. Kissinger was also wary. "If Kaunda gives a speech in my presence like he did here [in Washington], I would like to talk back," he had told Ford during their last meeting before his departure for Africa. "Go ahead," Ford replied.[171]

After a perfunctory introduction by Kaunda, Kissinger stood at a podium in the dining room of the president's state residence. About fifty people, more than half of them press, were seated at a long table. This was the moment, and Kissinger knew it: he had predicted that his speech would cause "a sensation."[172]

Kissinger began by announcing that he wanted "to usher in a new era in American policy." He then became a new man. "Without peace, racial justice and growing prosperity in Africa, we cannot speak of a just international order," he declared. "I am not here to give American prescriptions for Africa's problems. . . . But we are prepared to help. . . . Of all the challenges before us, of all the purposes we have in common, racial justice is one of the most basic. . . . Our support for this principle in southern Africa is not simply a matter of foreign policy but an imperative of our own moral heritage." Kissinger pledged "support in the strongest terms" for the British proposals that would bring Rhodesia to majority rule and independence in two years. He sent a stern message to Ian Smith: "The United States is totally dedicated to seeing to it that the majority becomes the ruling power in Rhodesia. . . . The Salisbury regime must understand that it cannot expect United States support either in diplomacy or in material help at any stage in its conflict with African states or with African liberation movements." Kissinger promised to work for the repeal of the Byrd Amendment (which breached the UN sanctions on the Smith regime), to provide aid to the Frontline States, and to apply pressure on Pretoria to help resolve the Rhodesian problem. Remarkably, he did not once mention the Soviet Union, the Cubans, or communism. Instead, he called again and again for racial justice. He ended on a soaring note: "So let it be said that black people and white people working together achieved on this continent—which has suffered so much and seen so much injustice—a new era of peace, well-being, and human dignity."[173]

President Kaunda, tears streaming down his cheeks, leapt to his feet and embraced the American secretary of state.[174]

Showdown

Ronald Reagan stood at the doors of the Alamo, the actor Jimmy Stewart at his side. It was April 30, 1976, the day before the Texas primary and three days after Kissinger's Lusaka speech. "I'm afraid that we're going to have a massacre," he told the Texas crowd of about 3,000 people. "I must express my concern over what appears to be a massive shift in US policy in southern Africa. . . . We seem to be embarking on a policy of dictating to the people of southern Africa and running the risk of increased violence and bloodshed in an area already beset with tremendous antagonism and difficulties."[175]

Reagan was echoing a refrain that had emerged as soon as news hit the United States that Kissinger had declared America's support for majority rule in Rhodesia. "Your Lusaka speech is bringing yowls from the conservatives," National Security Adviser Brent Scowcroft had cabled Kissinger, still in Africa, two days earlier.[176] In Texas, Reagan yowled that the secretary of state's call for black majority rule in Rhodesia within two years "undercut the possibility for a just and orderly settlement." It worried him. "It is imperative," he explained, "that we avoid impulsive reactions in a potentially explosive situation. The peoples of Rhodesia [Reagan meant the white people] . . . fought with us in World War II. . . . If they show a creative attitude that can lead to a peaceful settlement, . . . [we] should avoid rhetoric or actions that could trigger chaos or violence." Kissinger's call to repeal the Byrd Amendment was yet another example, Reagan said, of his pandering to the Soviets—it would increase US dependence on communist chrome. Besides, why was the administration focused on Africa and "ignoring the plight of the enslaved millions in the Soviet Union and other Communist countries?" And, Reagan added, looking straight into the eyes of the potential voters, "[We] should not overlook the protection of minority rights."[177]

Seven weeks earlier, on March 10—the morning after the Florida primary—the Reagan campaign had taken note of both of the day's headlines: its candidate's disappointing showing in Florida with his seven-point loss to Ford, and the rising tensions in Africa. Reagan's Plan A—winning New Hampshire and Florida and knocking Ford out early—was in shambles. The campaign shifted to Plan B—it raised the temperature of its attacks on Ford, especially his foreign policy. On the stump in North Carolina, Reagan threw away his notes and spoke freely, hitting hard on his crowd-pleasing lines. About Ford's stewardship: "We have become second to the Soviet Union in military strength in a world where it is perhaps fatal to be second best." About the Panama Canal: "We bought it, we paid for it, it's ours, and we're going to keep it!" And the surest way to get the crowd roaring: "I will appoint a new Secretary of State!"[178]

Reagan's strategy in North Carolina was simple: in foreign policy, attack Ford by vilifying Kissinger as the architect of America's demise; and in domestic policy, wallop him on social issues like abortion, gun control, capital punishment, and God in the classroom. While Reagan's major assault was on détente and Ford's plan to "give away" the Panama Canal, he also railed against the administration's lily-livered response to "Soviet aggression" in Angola. The campaign spread the message by buying a half-hour of airtime in fourteen Tar Heel television markets to show Reagan, seated at a desk, delivering this stump speech.[179]

It worked. This surprised everyone, including Reagan and his "dumbfounded" inner circle.[180] On March 23, Reagan trounced Ford in North Carolina by almost seven percentage points. This was his Inchon—evidence of his almost magical daring. It revived his campaign and infused it with desperately needed cash. It was, however, followed by a perilous lull. The motto of John Sears, Reagan's campaign manager, was "politics is motion,"[181] but it was

Sears's strategy that threatened to throw the campaign into a stall after its jump start in North Carolina. In part to conserve scarce funds and in part because he assessed Reagan's chances poor in the north, Sears pulled Reagan back from vigorous campaigning in the next three primary states—Wisconsin, New York, and Pennsylvania—and Ford therefore chalked up victories in all three. By late April, the Reagan campaign was again short of both funds and motion.

Reagan had to win Texas. Flying on a commercial plane because he could no longer afford a chartered one, Reagan campaigned hard in the Lone Star state. It was make or break. Ford, by contrast, could afford to lose Texas's 100 delegates, but he stumped ferociously anyway, outspending Reagan in the hope of delivering his challenger a knockout blow.[182]

In Texas, the two headlines that followed the Florida primary—the election results and rising tensions in Rhodesia—took on a new importance. In the aftermath of Florida, the Reagan team had focused on the fact that Ford had beaten their candidate. What was much more significant to Reagan's prospects, however, was that Carter had derailed Wallace. Texas was a "crossover" state—Democrats could vote in the Republican primary and vice versa—and it was impossible to know how many Wallace supporters, unhappy with the prospect of a President Carter, might cross over to the Republican side and cast their votes for Reagan. Wallace had won the Texas Democratic Party Caucus in 1972, and his supporters could make the difference again. Reagan appealed openly to the Wallace crowd, inviting former Wallace workers to join him on the platform and handing out fliers with a drawing of a GOP elephant saying, "I'm for Reagan!" and a Democratic donkey adding, significantly, "Me too!"[183] He ran a commercial openly asking for Democratic crossovers because, the narrator explained, "as much as I hate to admit it, George Wallace can't be nominated."[184]

Reagan's criticism of Kissinger's Lusaka speech fit smoothly into his narrative that the secretary of state, Ford's Svengali, was pursuing a reckless and liberal foreign policy that weakened the United States and strengthened the Soviet Union. Kissinger later reflected on Reagan's strategy in Texas: "In the southern states at that time, the issue of voting rights and participation—while mandated by the Civil Rights Act—was still up in the air."[185] Reagan's attack plucked the chords of race in the sweetest way, without striking the discordant alarms of domestic issues like busing and affirmative action. It was, for Reagan, pure gold. Repeating the message he had delivered at the Alamo, the candidate "wowed" crowds in Beaumont, Waco, Dallas, and Texarkana.[186]

"Scowcroft and I are pushing to get a hard response [to Reagan's comments] from the White House," Kissinger aide Lawrence Eagleburger cabled the secretary in Africa. Kissinger cabled back talking points to explain the rationale of his policy, which, he argued, was the only way to save the whites in Rhodesia: "The choice boils down to . . . mounting bloodshed . . . that will remove any real chance for minority rights . . . [or] a negotiated settlement that . . . gives the whites at least a chance. . . . We are trading our diplomatic support for a refusal to let Cubans and Soviets get involved. . . . The approach in the speech, in short, gives us a platform to prevent future Angolas—the only one possible under current conditions."[187]

Ford's internal polling indicated that Reagan's attacks on his foreign policy were hurting the president. In Texas, the day after Kissinger's Lusaka speech, Ford had attacked Reagan frontally. "There are no retakes in the Oval Office," he declared, mocking the erstwhile actor. "Glibness is not good enough; superficiality is not good enough." He continued: "It is irresponsible and a disservice to the American people to lead them to believe that we are inferior when we are not, that our military strength is insufficient when it is not, or that there are pat answers and simple solutions to the complex issues of national security when there are none."[188] But this was no match for Reagan's rousing "we bought it" refrain. Reagan's rhetoric cut through the turgid Kissingerian verbiage about strategic parity, realism, and stable structures of peace. It unleashed rabid American patriotism, pent up by the frustrations of Vietnam, Watergate, Angola, and inflation. Ford's words were, in comparison, pallid and plaintive.

Some of Ford's inner circle advised him to stay above the fray and act presidential—the Reagan phenomenon would pass. Others urged him to go for Reagan's jugular. "We must assert a *strong leadership* stance by the President," the campaign's media expert, Bruce Wagner, wrote. His "recommended message" was that Reagan was "an irresponsible and ambitious man. . . . He would commit our young men to another 'Vietnam war' in Africa or elsewhere. . . . In a nutshell, we must . . . eliminate the credibility of the Reagan candidacy."[189] Wagner's advice gained traction in the days before the vote in Texas: the Ford campaign aired a five-minute television commercial suggesting that Reagan would be "fast on the nuclear trigger."[190]

Perhaps it was the wrong tactic, or perhaps it came too late. In any case, it failed. Reagan took Texas by a landslide, winning every delegate and besting Ford in most districts by at least two to one. The president carried only one congressional district. The press used the verbs "smash," "whip," "crush," and "wallop" to describe what the former governor had done to the incumbent president.[191]

Republican leaders in Congress took note. They marched to the White House. The House minority leader, John Rhodes of Arizona, told Ford that the timing of Kissinger's Africa trip had been "unfortunate." It had been "too politically provocative, especially the stress on ending minority rule in Rhodesia." This would have "a devastating effect" on the southern states, Minority Whip Robert Michel of Illinois explained, and added that it was "a too inflaming type of trip. It aroused people's emotions." Ford had paid in Texas, and they would all pay in November because conservatives—Republicans as well as Wallace Democrats—would stay home. Saying Kissinger had "run out of gas," some suggested that Ford "muzzle" him, and Edward Derwinski of Illinois called for his resignation. In a column on the Texas showdown, William Safire deconstructed Ford's rueful comment that he had drawn from it two lessons: "One is—never underestimate your opponent, and two—always shuck a tamale." (Ford had been photographed in Texas digging into a tamale, husk and all.) Safire opined that the tamale was the least of the president's problems; his real mistake was "his failure . . . to shuck a secretary of state."[192]

On May 7, Brent Scowcroft cabled Kissinger, who was about to return from Africa. "Tempers are short, and the press is looking for blood. . . . Hunker down, grit your teeth and carry on. . . . I do not mean to sound foreboding, but . . . the flak is flying in all directions . . . and you should not lose your cool."[193]

Heat

The next day, Kissinger was back at his desk in the State Department and on the phone with Vice President Nelson Rockefeller. "Do you think my trip hurt him [Ford] in Texas?" he asked his friend, a liberal Republican who had been unceremoniously persuaded to remove himself from the 1976 GOP ticket to make room for a more conservative vice-presidential candidate. Rockefeller deftly avoided answering, but Kissinger persisted, "Do you think I have been hurt in the country by this trip?" Rockefeller ducked again. Kissinger said—on the cusp between playfulness and dead seriousness—"Do you know what they are thinking in the White House? That you fixed up that trip to Africa in order to do Ford in."[194]

Reeling from Texas and anticipating further humiliation in California on June 8, the president was gallant. In his memoirs, he recalled accurately that conservatives "hit the ceiling," but at a special NSC meeting on May 10 about Kissinger's trip, Ford deployed admirable understatement: "We got a little political flak out of the trip," he noted, "but it was totally without merit." Ford then praised the trip, which "halted the radicalization in Africa and opened the door for movement in a positive direction."[195] The following day, Kissinger told a reporter, "If I am the slightest embarrassment for the President, there will be no difficulty about my leaving." The president stood by his man. On May 12, he told members of Congress who complained about the timing of Kissinger's trip, "We couldn't hold foreign policy in limbo every four years. . . . I am willing to . . . take the lumps if necessary." More than twenty years later, speaking about the need to uphold one's principles, Ford cited as his prime example his decision not "to abandon our efforts to promote black majority rule in what was then Rhodesia" despite "facing a stiff challenge from the right-wing of my own party." He remembered: "The polls gave one answer and individual conscience a dramatically different one." Kissinger agreed: in his memoirs, he wrote that it was "one of Ford's noble moments."[196]

But what else could the president have done? Reagan's heavy punches had made him look weak, indecisive, and ineffective. If Ford had fired Kissinger at that moment—or indicated in any way that the secretary had been freewheeling in Africa—he would have confirmed Reagan's imputation that the president was not in charge. Ford had little choice but to stand by his man.

A more interesting question is why he had permitted Kissinger to unroll the new policy in Lusaka three days before the showdown in Texas. Kissinger's explanation at the NSC meeting—that the timing was dictated by Nyerere's travel plans—is not persuasive. Ford writes in his memoirs that his political advisers warned him that the timing was ill advised but that he dismissed these concerns because sending Kissinger to Africa "was the right thing to do." But on March 4, when Kissinger's trip was announced, neither Ford nor his campaign team had grasped the impact of Wallace's eclipse; at that point, Ford had won Iowa, New Hampshire, Massachusetts, and Vermont. Reagan, the White House had believed, could be managed. The day before his Lusaka speech, Kissinger cabled General Scowcroft that he was "totally conscious" of the president's needs, and he was not worried about political fallout because "I suspect that most lovers of the Smith regime are Regan [*sic*] votes already." One White House official succinctly explained the timing of Kissinger's trip: "Politically we're not very ept."[197]

Three months later, the Ford campaign staff was heading to California, Reagan's home turf and a winner-take-all contest with 167 delegates at stake. The polls had once indicated that Ford led Reagan in California by a wide margin, but by June the president had lost his best asset—the invincibility of incumbency—and was trailing Reagan by twenty-four percentage points.[198] The two contenders had split the contests after Texas in a see-saw war of attrition. The *Washington Post* reckoned the race was so close that the winner of California would clinch the nomination.[199]

The Ford campaign staffers were still arguing about how to counter Reagan's challenge when the governor, on June 2—six days before the vote—gave them an opening. At the Sacramento Press Club, a journalist asked Reagan: "On the subject of Rhodesia, you said that we should guarantee that there is no bloodshed. How would we do that? With an occupation force, with military troops, or what?"[200]

Reagan rambled. "Whether it would be enough to have simply a show of strength, the promise that we would [supply troops], or whether you would have to go in with occupation forces or not, I don't know. But I believe in the interests of peace and avoiding bloodshed, . . . I think it would be worth this, for us to do it."

The journalist asked: "You would consider sending US troops if necessary?"

Reagan answered: "You would have to be completely involved with the Rhodesian government, and find out whether that would be necessary. It might simply be that a promise, the treaty or agreement, would prevent it [a bloodbath] from happening."

The next morning, the headline in the *San Francisco Chronicle* read "Reagan Would Send GIs to Avert Rhodesia War." The article continued: "Ronald Reagan said yesterday that if he is elected president he would be willing to send a token force—or even a larger one if necessary—to Rhodesia to prevent a bloody civil war there." The lead editorial warned that Reagan's statement "stands as a classic and ghastly example of why a candidate should not draw up his foreign policy while extemporizing at a microphone. . . . Surely Vietnam is too deep a scar for a scenario of this sort to be countenanced."[201]

At every campaign stop that day—in San Francisco, Monterey, and Santa Barbara—Reagan was grilled about Rhodesia. He tried to dig himself out, saying that "headline hunters" had misrepresented his remarks and that he had not meant that he would send troops. "What I am interested in is peace," he implored. At a hastily called press conference, he declared, "I am not proposing combat."[202] Yet Reagan's remarks about Rhodesia resonated. They slotted neatly into the widespread perception that the governor might be trigger-happy.

The Ford campaign's ad hit twenty-four California television stations and seventy-five radio stations the next day. It had been put together hastily, but the idea had been hatching for months. The production was simple: the camera rested on the face of a woman, perhaps in her late twenties, with minimal makeup, her dirty-blond hair pulled back in a ponytail. She looked like a typical white middle-class mother of young children. She sounded worried. "Last Wednesday," she said, "Ronald Reagan said that he would send American troops to Rhodesia. On Thursday he clarified that. He said they could be observers, or advisors. What does he think happened in Vietnam?" Then the announcer said, deadpan, "When you vote Tuesday, remember: Governor Reagan couldn't start a war. President Reagan could."[203]

The Reagan team cried foul. When asked again about his remarks on Rhodesia, the governor lost his temper in public for the first time during the campaign. The *New York Times* reported that Reagan "reddened and the words poured out of him in angry, snapping tones." Ford, he growled, had taken the "low road." Lyn Nofziger, the manager of Reagan's campaign in California, called the ad "libelous" and said that it was "the kind of dirty tricks that we thought had been thrown out of the White House. It smacks of dishonesty and desperation and unethical conduct. . . . [This is] as low as you can stoop."[204] William F. Buckley leapt to the governor's defense. Explaining that Reagan simply had been trying to assert the need to protect the rights of the white minority in Rhodesia, Buckley reminded his readers of what—in his opinion—was the alternative: "or do we secretly desire that long night of the knives which would visit on the whites of Rhodesia the same fate suffered by black and Asian minorities in other African states?" Barry Goldwater Jr., a Republican representative for California and son of the conservative Arizona senator, expressed his "shock and dismay" at the Ford campaign's attack ad. "This is the same kind of tactic used against my father in 1964 by the Johnson campaign," he charged, referring to the notorious "Daisy" ad that had implicitly linked Barry Goldwater Sr. with the prospect of nuclear war. "In the name of party unity," Reagan asked Ford to withdraw the ad.[205]

Ford refused. He was fed up with Reagan, and he "seemed to relish" the opportunity to "whack" him hard. At campaign rallies in the following days, he doubled down, warning Republicans not to repeat "the tragedy of 1964"— that is, nominate another Goldwater. As he noted philosophically in his memoirs, "Politics is 'hardball' sometimes, and this was one of those times."[206] He said that he had "personally approved" the ad because he wanted the voters to know that "I would not under any circumstances commit US personnel or US troops to Rhodesia." Ford felt good. On June 6, he said, "I think we might win California."[207]

Ford was wrong. Reagan smashed him in California by thirty percentage points, 65.5 percent to Ford's 34.5 percent, and added all California's 167 delegates to his count. At the end of the turbulent and arduous primary season, the *New York Times* calculated that Ford had 957 delegates in the bag, while Reagan had 860.[208] Neither was close to the 1,130 needed to win the nomination. Both would have to engage in frantic haggling for every uncommitted delegate before the GOP met in Kansas City on August 16, 1976.

The president was worried that Kissinger's Rhodesia gambit could cost him crucial support. "One thing to keep in mind," he told William Scranton, the US ambassador to the United Nations, immediately after the California vote. "We will be wooing delegates during this period and some of them are not—to say the least—in sympathy with our African policy." It was, the *New York Times* editorialized, "an amazingly weak position for an incumbent president to be in."[209]

2. Chasing Triumph

"**U**p, up, up, everybody! It's your birthday!" Walter Cronkite, the avuncular news anchor widely considered "the most trusted man in America," had gone off script, startling his producer.[1] At 6 A.M., July 4, 1976, Cronkite was broadcasting from the makeshift CBS television studio in New York City's Madison Square Garden, where the Democrats would convene a week later. His wake-up call set the tone of a day whose exuberance surprised many Americans.

Back in 1964, when planning for the bicentennial began, the dreams had been big. It was, after all, the era when men were heading to the moon. Lyndon Johnson was president, Martin Luther King and Bobby Kennedy were still alive, and no regular US troops had landed in Vietnam. It was before Watts, before Woodstock, before Watergate. It was before conservatives had begun to bend the curve of liberalism. Back in 1964, Americans had imagined a grandiose year-long birthday party that would encompass a World's Fair; the Summer and Winter Olympic Games; a Congress of Liberty; and a federal stimulus program that would pump millions of dollars to uplift blighted cites, renovate public transportation, and protect the environment. The *New York Times* predicted that the city hosting the World's Fair would be transformed "into a glittering cosmopolitan metropolis." The bicentennial would be a party as big and grand as the United States itself.[2]

The subsequent years saw a steady whittling down of this vision. By the early 1970s, the federal government no longer had the funds to underwrite it, and many Americans, including President Nixon, doubted that a huge federal spending program would solve the nation's ills. In 1972, the Bicentennial Committee, which had been established by President Johnson in 1966, declared an international exposition to be of "dubious enduring value."[3] The *New York Times* was dismayed: "The cause of patriotism would be very well served by showing the world how much more there is to the United States than violence, racial tension and the perpetuation of a tragic war."[4]

A year later, on July 4, 1973, Americans contemplated a grim landscape: White House counsel John W. Dean III was testifying to the Senate Select Committee about Nixon's crimes in the Watergate affair; the dollar was plummeting; and Congress, fearing that the president might order US troops back to Vietnam, had just banned any further US intervention in that war-torn country. As columnist Anthony Lewis mused, the problem was not only that the United States had lost the war in Vietnam but also that "some Americans, perhaps most, came to understand something more painful: that our cause was not just." It was difficult to envision a big, bold celebration.[5]

Richard Nixon, in the harrowing months before he resigned in disgrace, tried to put the best face on the dramatic diminution of bicentennial dreams. Since the federal government was no longer willing to bankroll the bash, Nixon announced that he would turn to "the free enterprise system which has made our country . . . the best and strongest nation in history." The inevitable result was that the bicentennial became commercialized, selling everything from star-spangled whoopee cushions to "patriotic moments" on television funded by Exxon and Shell Oil. To its critics, the event became known as the "buycentennial."[6]

When Gerald Ford moved into the White House in August 1974, everything about the bicentennial had become contentious. It was symptomatic of the times: the liberal dreams of the 1960s had shriveled under the pressures of an unpopular war, corruption in the highest places, and doubts about the Great Society. The center had not held. The 1970s were, above all, a fractious decade.

There was, as historian C. Vann Woodward noted, "a certain ambiguity of feelings about what exactly was being celebrated" at the bicentennial. Many Native Americans and African Americans decided that they had no reason to glorify the victory of colonizers and slaveholders. The Peoples [sic] Bicentennial Commission, a small group of 1960s-style radicals, decried the fact that "the White House and Corporate America are planning to sell us a program of plastic Liberty Bells . . . and a 'Love It or Leave It' political program." The Senate held hearings about rumors that the Peoples Bicentennial Commission and Castro-backed "extremists" were planning to disrupt the festivities. Although the logo of the bicentennial, a star surrounded by a red, white, and blue ribbon, symbolized "one nation bound in unity," it seemed that the bicentennial itself would signify the disunity of the nation.[7]

The official Bicentennial Commission deemed more than 64,000 community projects and activities—reenactments, restorations of old buildings and historic objects, and a grab bag of commemorative activities ranging from shuffleboard contests to operas—to be official events. Alistair Cooke, the erudite voice of the BBC's "Letter from America," scoffed, "Anything you can imagine in a nightmare that idiots would do to celebrate the Bicentennial is being thought of."[8]

Many Americans had long ago lost interest. President Ford played golf rather than attend the parade and festivities in Washington.[9] Many tuned in to television, which broadcast sixteen hours of bicentennial celebrations from around the country. If ever there were a patchwork quilt of America, this was it: the video clips jumped from pictures of a man rolling a watermelon to a reenactment of George Washington crossing the Delaware. No one expected it to be riveting.

And yet, for many, the day's events were surprisingly compelling. They defied predictions of irrelevance. As the cameras hopscotched around the modest, idiosyncratic celebrations in hundreds of small towns, the cork popped and long pent-up American patriotism bubbled over. As Elizabeth Drew explained, "We had experienced some terrible things, but we had come through. . . . Vietnam *is* behind us. We *did* survive Watergate." Patriotism—a bruised, sobered patriotism—proved possible even when one had lost confidence in government: the nation was distinct from the government. It felt good. "Some of us," Drew reported, "had emotional reactions today that we did not anticipate." Walter Cronkite agreed: it was "the greatest show I was ever privileged to attend."[10]

The star of the day was not President Ford, the Boston Pops playing on the banks of the Charles River, or the fireworks on the Mall in Washington, DC. It was instead the "tall ships" gliding into New York harbor—more than two hundred large sailing ships, from thirty-five nations, that evoked a romantic, seafaring past. Organized by a private nonprofit group of sailing enthusiasts, the parade of tall ships was never expected to be the centerpiece of the bicentennial or the magic that would transform thousands of disparate events into a national celebration. But the elegant ships captured the American imagination. Woodward, the historian, expressed it well: "Suddenly and mysteriously the 'Tall Ships' became the prime symbol of whatever it was Americans yearned for. . . . What they sought was confirmation of a national myth, the myth of America as the land of youth, always seeking renewal." Renewal, Woodward argued, was sweet succor after the loss of the war in Vietnam, the sordidness of Watergate, and the recent revelations of the transgressions of the CIA and FBI, all of which had struck "a shattering blow to two pillars of the myth, invincibility and innocence."[11]

The bicentennial did not restore either pillar, but for one day it allowed many Americans to feel pride and hope despite the recent past. It revealed the poignant and powerful longing of Americans to feel positive about their country. Even Richard Nixon understood this urge. In a discussion with his chief aide, H. R. Haldeman, during the dark days of Watergate, he said, "From what I've seen they're—you know, they, they [the American people] want to believe; that's the point, isn't it?"[12]

Harmony in New York City

"There is a new mood in America," Jimmy Carter said, accepting the nomination of his party on July 15, 1976. He gazed out at the vast expanse of Madison Square Garden, packed with Democrats waving flags and cheering. "We want to have faith again. We want to be proud again." Carter's delivery was deliberate and steady, masking his high-pitched voice. "I see an America on the move again . . . entering our third century with pride and confidence." Carter ended his speech on a crescendo that recalled the recent bicentennial celebrations: "We will go forward from this convention . . . ready to embark on great national deeds. And once again, . . . our hearts will swell with pride to call ourselves Americans."[13]

Carter had won the nomination on the first ballot. It was an astounding feat. In five months, the one-term Georgia governor had defeated governors George Wallace of Alabama and Jerry Brown of California, Representative Mo Udall of Arizona, and senators Henry "Scoop" Jackson of Washington, Frank Church of Idaho, Robert Byrd of West Virginia, and Birch Bayh of Indiana. He had extinguished the hopes of senators Hubert Humphrey of Minnesota and Ted Kennedy of Massachusetts. He had done it with grit, intelligence, endurance, luck, and vagueness. He had stuck to his message: "You are good people. I am a good man. Vote for me." Carter would bring change and integrity to Washington.

The harmony at Madison Square Garden was a striking contrast to the pitched battles of Chicago in 1968, when the Democratic Party had imploded and exploded in full view of the television cameras, and to the chaos of Miami in 1972, when George McGovern did not receive the nomination of his deeply divided party until 3 A.M., long after most Americans had gone to bed. Four years later, the party orchestrated an elaborate display of unity. It was above all a moment of racial healing, this nomination of a progressive from the Deep South. Seconding Carter's nomination, Andrew Young declared to the assembled delegates, "I'm ready to lay down the burden of race. And Jimmy Carter comes from a part of the country that, whether you know it or not, has done just that." The crowd burst into applause.[14]

The festivities culminated in a love-in on the convention stage—the nominee surrounded by all his defeated rivals, with the crowd cheering and with Martin Luther King Sr., rising to give the final benediction. "Surely the Lord sent Jimmy Carter to come on out and bring America back where she belongs," roared the man who reminded Americans of their profound dreams and profound loss. "Amen!" the conventioneers replied. King began to sing, and all Madison Square Garden joined in, holding hands and swaying. "Deep in my heart, I do believe that we shall overcome someday."[15]

The Democrats were indeed filled with hope: Carter had a twenty-three-point lead in the polls immediately after the nomination, and the Republican convention promised to be a bruising, divisive showdown between Ford and Reagan. Democrats could taste the White House.

There was, however, an undertow of anxiety. The cheers for Carter were genuine, but those for his running mate—Minnesota senator Walter Mondale—were louder and more sustained. Mondale was well known, a champion of liberal causes who had served in the Senate since 1964. Carter, on the other hand, was a newcomer, an outsider, and he was hard to pigeonhole. This was his strength and also his weakness. He had deliberately run a vague campaign, and he was not driven by ideology.

In a way, Carter was transparent: you got what you saw. And what you saw was Jimmy Carter, a driven, intelligent, disciplined, and stubborn man. What did he believe? Above all, he believed that he would be the best president—the most honest, hard-working, and dedicated to the people. But was he a liberal? The power brokers of the Democratic Party were not sure. There were encouraging signs—African Americans supported him, he had selected Mondale, he had not blocked a liberal party platform—but doubts lingered. Carter's rural southern roots, his born-again religion, his comments about "ethnic purity"—all this made Carter's support within the party, especially with its liberal core, tenuous. Disgruntled and disillusioned speechwriter Robert Shrum, who had briefly worked for the campaign and who was well connected to the liberal Democratic insiders, issued a particularly stinging attack in June. "Jimmy Carter was the opposite of what he seemed," Shrum wrote, explaining why he quit the campaign team. "The deceptions, the calculated manipulations of people's yearnings, were routine. . . . The same dichotomy was pervasive . . . public compassion, private callousness."[16]

Carter, especially in the glory days of the convention, papered over the troubling fissures in the Democratic Party, but the divisions that had been exposed so disturbingly in 1968—between Democratic hawks and doves, union workers and hippies, Southern conservatives and blacks—persisted. Carter's support was broad but shallow; the Democrats at Madison Square Garden were filled with hope, not passion.

Promises, Promises

Henry Kissinger was under pressure. After his Lusaka speech in April, American conservatives charged that he had deserted the Rhodesian whites and encouraged "all-out guerrilla warfare and invasion of Rhodesia," as a *Dallas Morning News* columnist wrote: "This is really the message he [Kissinger] carries to black Africa. Have at it, he is saying: the United States is with you." Mail to the State Department and White House was "heavily" opposed to majority rule. The Lusaka speech "provoked 1,800 letters, of which a mere 23 had been in favour," Kissinger told a British official. "I don't think the Americans [Kissinger meant white Americans] like blacks," he commented to President Ford.[17]

By contrast, Washington liberals lauded the secretary's efforts—and demanded more. During hearings in May 1976, senators George McGovern and Chuck Percy (R-IL) praised Kissinger's Africa trip as "superb . . . extraordinary," but agreed with Hubert Humphrey when he said: "We almost missed the boat, and it is very, very late." Humphrey then got to the point: "My concern is," he told Kissinger, "much will depend on our performance, Congress and executive together, over the next few months. I just want to know, if we are all going to charge the barricades: Is the executive branch going to be there too?" Senator Dick Clark (D-IA), chair of the Africa subcommittee, took up the refrain: "If we do not follow through, we will have made a much greater mistake, I think, than if we had not made the speech at all. It will be a great mistake if we once again simply pronounced a number of empty promises. . . . Now, in your judgment, Mr. Secretary, will the administration go all out in implementing the words which you spoke at Lusaka?" Clark placed particular stress on the necessity of repealing the Byrd Amendment, which had legalized US violations of the UN sanctions against the Smith regime: "It will not be possible to repeal that amendment unless the President and others are willing to call people to the White House, and call them on the telephone, to work very closely with them to repeal this amendment. Now, is that going to be the policy of this administration?"[18]

Clark had hit a tender spot. In the days after Kissinger delivered his Lusaka speech, the State Department had geared up for a "major effort in May" to repeal the Byrd Amendment. On May 1, Kissinger had cabled National Security Adviser Brent Scowcroft from Africa: "We should now move ahead and start the procedures to repeal [the] Byrd Amendment. The president should now—immediately—authorize a major effort. Quick repeal would have enormous impact with the Africans, and perhaps a decisive impact on Smith. . . . Failure . . . would literally undermine everything we have achieved here."[19]

But then came Texas, and the brakes went on. "There are . . . grounds for doubt that the White House shares Dr Kissinger's views on the desirability of active lobbying for the repeal of the Byrd Amendment," the South African ambassador in Washington wrote to his foreign minister, "particularly in light of Mr Reagan's convincing victory in the Texas primaries." President Ford could ill afford a battle in Congress in which he would be accused of selling out to the Soviets and deserting white, anticommunist allies of the United States. "We don't want to take the chance of losing on this one," a White House official explained. Ford, he added, "did not want much visibility on the issue." The president voiced support for Kissinger's Rhodesia policy, but it was tepid. He avoided being seen in public with his secretary of state. Ford did not storm the barricades to persuade Congress to repeal the Byrd Amendment. He did not even make a phone call.[20]

Opponents of Kissinger's new policy quickly rallied to obstruct it. One week after Kissinger testified to Congress about his trip, southern Democrats joined Republicans to threaten a filibuster of the State Department's foreign aid bill, which included the $12.5 million that Kissinger had promised to Mozambique. (This was a small fraction of the $165 million that the UN had predicted that Mozambique would lose every year due to its closure of its border with Rhodesia.) These senators asserted that the Frontline States, including Mozambique, were aiding terrorists. They were missing the point, Kissinger argued with exasperation. "Mozambique doesn't need money from us. They can get it from the Russians and China," he explained to Senator Edward Brooke (R-MA). It was the United States that needed Mozambique "to hold down the guerrillas so we can get a moderate black leader in there [Rhodesia]." To stop "Soviets and Cubans," Kissinger told the journalist Phil Geyelin, "12.5 million is chicken feed." He told Geyelin that he was "raising hell" in Congress.[21]

To no avail: the persuasive power of a president was required, and it was absent. Kissinger offered a blunt explanation of the problem to British prime minister Jim Callaghan: "The racists in the United States had made Mozambique a test case in Congress." Liberal senators eventually managed a workaround that promised to free up money for Mozambique, but they understood that the threatened filibuster killed any hope that the Byrd Amendment would be repealed before the election.[22]

Kissinger was not one to let a kerfuffle in Congress slow him down. He had enjoyed his sojourn in Africa, and he smelled opportunity there. "I think we succeeded more than I ever thought possible," he told Ford. "We now have the makings of a platform from which to oppose the Soviets and Cubans. . . . By demonstrating to the Africans that we have similar objectives and by helping them politically, economically, and psychologically, we give them the hope that they can achieve their aims without Soviet or Cuban help. . . . And if we stayed passive . . . we would inevitably face a succession of Angolas."[23] Despite the yowls of conservatives, the mainstream US media reaction to Kissinger's

Africa tour had been positive. Eric Sevareid on the *CBS Evening News*, for example, had gushed that "Kissinger opened up communist China to American diplomacy six years ago. He has now opened up another continent-sized region—sub-Saharan Africa. . . . His speech in Zambia was a blockbuster."[24]

Even Ian Smith's reaction to Kissinger's speech was mildly encouraging. In a radio address to the nation, Smith began with his usual bluster. He bemoaned that the West had "join[ed] in the chorus" against Rhodesia; he warned against "the folly of appeasement" in the face of the Kremlin's attempt to construct "a Marxist-dominated 'saddle' across Africa"; and he swore that "the White Rhodesian has no intention of surrendering his position." But then he announced that he had decided to add four black tribal chiefs to his Cabinet and appoint six black deputy ministers. This did not impress the South Africans: "For . . . [Smith] to accept a multi-racial Government is quite a progressive if not revolutionary step," Pretoria's representative in Salisbury wrote. "But [it] . . . will at this late stage of developments have little if any effect."[25]

Kissinger's trip had been, in the words of an American ambassador, an "eye-opener."[26] The secretary had learned two important things: some African leaders wanted the United States to insert its power into the maelstrom in Rhodesia, and it might be possible to push Smith toward majority rule before the end of the year (while Kissinger was still in office). The first was a direct consequence of the Africans' loss of confidence in the British, who had toyed with the Rhodesia problem since Smith had declared UDI in 1965. The Africans, the British high commissioner in Lusaka admitted, felt "let down by Britain."[27] The second was a consequence of the changing situation on the ground. With the new government in Mozambique supporting the Rhodesian guerrillas, a widening war looked imminent. This made South Africa, as well as Zambian president Kenneth Kaunda and Tanzanian president Julius Nyerere (and, Kissinger hoped, Mozambique's president Samora Machel), eager to hammer out a settlement before the whole region went up in flames.

Meeting with US Ambassador Donald Easum, Kissinger returned to his earlier refrain: "I need to find a Sadat!" he declared. He sought an African leader he could depend on, just as he had relied on Sadat during the recent Middle East negotiations. He explained to the Cabinet, "I realize we don't need more African turmoil in a campaign, but if it doesn't come off now, we are faced with an increasingly brutal war, with the eventual loss of Rhodesia and a race war against South Africa."[28]

The success of Kissinger's April trip surprised—and impressed—the British Foreign Office. After commenting on the ominous portents before the secretary's arrival in Lusaka, the British high commissioner wrote, "That these fears proved groundless was due to a combination of Kissinger's personal charm and skilful diplomacy and to the content of his major statement." Foreign Secretary Anthony Crosland told Kissinger that the speech "hit exactly the right note and was a triumph," and Callaghan congratulated him for giving the Africans "a true realisation of the sense of idealism that underlies American policy."[29]

The British did not yet understand that Kissinger was taking over. In early May, the head of the Foreign Office Rhodesia Department naively recommended that "we should act quickly to involve the Americans as closely as possible in a common programme" and "channel Dr Kissinger's new-found enthusiasm for Africa in a direction which is consistent with our policies." The British were hoisted by their own petard: the settlement proposal that Callaghan had announced to Parliament on March 22, 1976—Smith must accept majority rule and elections—had stymied British diplomacy. Callaghan had put the ball firmly in Smith's court, which had rendered the Labour government's policy "too passive, too immobile," in the verdict of many of his own party leaders. "The British are at a loss for new ideas," the US assistant secretary of state for Africa stated bluntly in a memo to Kissinger on June 5.[30]

As a new prime minister, Callaghan was consumed with pressing domestic matters, especially with shoring up Labour's unsteady hold on power. That Crosland took over as foreign secretary widened the opening for Kissinger: he could ride roughshod over Crosland, with whom he had no relationship and for whom he had little respect. The feelings were mutual, according to the memoirs written by Crosland's wife, Susan: "Dr. Kissinger was a further trial. Backed by White House power, he so dominated international diplomacy that the FO's [Foreign Office's] role in Rhodesia was inevitably hamstrung. What made matters most tiresome was that the FO suspected that Kissinger didn't understand Rhodesian politics."[31]

Kissinger admitted that he was a neophyte when it came to Africa, but he was a master at wielding power. He turned the tables on the bureaucrats at the Foreign Office: in the summer of 1976, they became his support staff, drafting elaborate background papers for the Americans. The British grew uneasy when the State Department put off their requests in May for bilateral discussions on Rhodesia. Their discomfort deepened when they heard rumors that the US secretary of state had met with the South African ambassador to discuss Rhodesia; they began complaining that "Kissinger had played his cards very close to his chest."[32]

The Measure of Vorster

Before staking his reputation on southern Africa, Kissinger wanted to take the measure of the man he considered the central player (after himself, that is): Prime Minister John Vorster of South Africa. This proud Afrikaner led the country that supplied Rhodesia's military, underwrote its currency, controlled its rail and road links to viable ports, and provided much of its oil. An ideologue who had become more pragmatic after taking the reins of power in 1966, Vorster would be the man to convince Smith that it was time to go. He could hold, in the words of British Intelligence, "a pistol to Smith's head."[33]

Kissinger arranged a quiet meeting in Bavaria with Vorster in June. He tried to salve South African fears before the meeting by assuring the apartheid regime's ambassador in Washington: "We are not trying to reform you. We are trying to prevent the radicalization of Black Africa and a race war." Kissinger carefully kept expectations low, telling the West German ambassador: "We cannot afford to look as if great results will happen there [in Germany]." To Congress, he said that it would merely be "an exploratory meeting."[34]

That Kissinger's interest in things African was belated had consequences. The same event that had finally grabbed his attention—the Cuban intervention in Angola—was shaking all southern Africa. It was one of many factors that led to an explosion in Soweto, the vast Johannesburg slum, one week before Kissinger was set to jet to Bavaria. Soweto was a testament to the horrors of apartheid. It was a twenty-eight-square-mile cage trapping a million black South Africans in the racist rules of passbooks, absolute poverty, and hopelessness.[35]

Apartheid looked like America's Jim Crow system—a series of debilitating, humiliating laws that separated the races and ensured that whites were always on top. But apartheid had an important twist, one that increased the pressure in the "townships" ringing South Africa's cities: Vorster's government did not consider the country's eighteen million blacks to be second-class citizens; it did not consider them citizens at all. South Africa's "homelands" policy pulled the rug of citizenship from under the country's majority population. It declared that the four million South African whites, many of them descendants of Dutch settlers who had first arrived in the seventeenth century, were the country's true citizens and therefore had the right to 87 percent of its land. The blacks, Pretoria asserted, were latecomers—"temporary sojourners"[36]—who belonged in nine "tribal homelands" set aside by the apartheid government. The millions of blacks who lived in the townships ringing the cities provided a ready pool of cheap labor, but they did so on sufferance, guests of the whites who could yank their passbooks and ship them off to a desolate "homeland" that had never been home.

This pressure cooker of despair was about to blow. Resentment had been mounting ever since the South African government had announced in 1974 that education would be conducted, in part, in Afrikaans—the language of the oppressors—instead of English. On June 16, 1976, schoolchildren in Soweto, with extraordinary courage, took to the streets. The police opened fire on the unarmed youths, many not yet in their teens. One of the first gunned down was a thirteen-year-old boy, Hector Pieterson, whose murder became a potent symbol of what South African author Nadine Gordimer called "the children's revolt." The rage ignited the slums ringing Johannesburg and jumped 800 miles south to Cape Town. It was the worst rioting in South Africa's history. More than one hundred blacks were killed in the first ten days of raw confrontations.[37]

It shocked the world. Television programs and newspapers showed pictures of wounded and dying black children on the streets of South Africa's slums. The liberal Johannesburg *Rand Daily Mail* ran a front-page photograph of a little black girl dying in a pool of blood, and the lead editorial of the *New York Times* declared, "Southern Africa is drifting toward catastrophic racial war." The UN Security Council unanimously condemned the South African government for "massive violence" against the African people.[38]

On June 23, 1976, in the midst of this uprising, Kissinger met Vorster in an idyllic resort in Bavaria. The press was given very little information about the talks. After the first day, the State Department spokesperson refused to characterize the meetings at all, and at their conclusion no joint press conference was held. Kissinger said merely that the talks had been "businesslike."[39] The transcripts, however, reveal a meeting of minds. The atmosphere was chummy; powerful white men were discussing the future of Africa. Andrew Young, then in the House of Representatives and an adviser to the Carter campaign, noted that none of Kissinger's advisers were black. "It was like dealing with Bull Conors [*sic*, Bull Connor, the notoriously racist official in Birmingham, Alabama, during the civil rights campaign] and not with Martin Luther King." Perhaps Kissinger was trying to put the chain-smoking Vorster at ease, but he did more than jolly him: he colluded with him. In the available transcripts, there is no indication that Kissinger put any pressure on the South African to change apartheid at all, despite the ongoing atrocities in Soweto. In his memoirs, Kissinger spins a different story, saying that he could offer Vorster only the "thin gruel . . . [of] time in which to solve their problems." In fact, according to the available memoranda of the conversation, he did not mention the "problems" at all.[40] Afterward, Vorster told the US ambassador in Pretoria that he was very satisfied with the talks, which he had found "much easier than he had anticipated." *New York Times* correspondent John Burns reported that Vorster and Kissinger had developed "a surprising rapport."[41]

In his talks with Vorster, Kissinger stressed the need to force Ian Smith to negotiate a transfer of power in Rhodesia. He was pushing an open door: as part of his détente policy, Vorster had accepted that it was in South Africa's interest to jettison Smith and nudge Rhodesia toward majority rule. The optimal outcome for Vorster would be to have a moderate black leader in charge in an independent Zimbabwe without an all-out, Angola-style civil war. To this end, Pretoria had quietly reduced its military aid to Rhodesia in March 1976, and the South African ambassador had been clear when he had seen Kissinger in April: "We agree," he had said, speaking for his government, "that Smith is beyond recovery."[42]

Immediately before the meeting in Germany, Vorster had had a tense encounter with Smith in Pretoria. "The Americans have now come into the picture which represents a new dimension," he told the Rhodesian leader. This offered Pretoria a rare opening: "For years South Africa had been ignored [by the United States] and this [the meeting with Kissinger] was the first opportunity of talking. . . . It was unlikely that there would be a second opportunity at this level." Vorster knew that to seize this moment he had to offer the Americans something they wanted, and he knew that what Washington wanted was a date—in the near future—when Smith would hand Rhodesia over to majority rule.[43]

Smith balked. "We are signing our own death warrant and putting a time to it," he insisted. He pleaded with Vorster to urge the Americans to come to Rhodesia so they could see the situation for themselves. He insisted that the insurgency was under control. He was adamant that "we were not engaged in a black and white conflict . . . [but rather] a fight between western ideals and Soviet-orientated Marxists [sic] blacks." Setting a timetable was against the West's interest: "premature majority rule would ensure that Rhodesia would be lost to the free world and would go over to the communists." Vorster had to "wake up" the Americans.[44]

Vorster tried to explain reality to the Rhodesian, who had been isolated from the world for too long. "What is reasonable and logical to us appears quite different to the western powers," he stated patiently but firmly. The Americans wanted to avoid a communist takeover in Rhodesia, but they were convinced that the way to do it was to promote "rapid and significant advancement" of black rights in Rhodesia. "They regard us as expendable and on our own."[45] This was the counsel of bitter experience, as Vorster had been seared by the Ford administration's public condemnation (but private encouragement) of South Africa's invasion of Angola. "The Americans were imbued with the Vietnam complex," he concluded. Neither South Africa nor Rhodesia could expect any help from Washington. "In the event of the Russians and Cubans coming into Rhodesia in full force," Vorster told Smith, "apart from shouting to high heaven nobody in the western world would lift a finger to support us. . . . If South Africa intervened on the Rhodesian side then the West would drop South Africa and that would be the green light for the communists." He repeated: "If the Russians arrived in Table Bay [in Cape Town] tomorrow, the United States would not lift a finger."[46]

The only way to engage the Americans was to give them "something positive." Allowing only "qualified" blacks—those few who owned property and had a high school diploma—to vote would not impress Kissinger. "It must be remembered that we had to deal with western powers who were wedded to one man one vote," Vorster lectured. Moreover, "it was unlikely that we would get them to drop their obsession with a timetable." Time was limited. "Ford would be out by November," Vorster predicted, "and Carter would be the next president." It was in South Africa's and Rhodesia's interest to "make headway with Kissinger before he departed from the scene." Smith was cornered: at the end of the meeting, he snarled at Vorster that Kissinger would surely offer South Africa "glowing rewards" for selling out Rhodesia.[47]

In Bavaria, Vorster was in a good bargaining position. "Talks a Big SA Victory," the Johannesburg *Star* had blared in a banner headline before the meeting had even begun. The talks "would put an end to the country's isolation as the polecat of the world."[48] Given Pretoria's beleaguered diplomatic standing, a high-level meeting between US and South African officials was a victory in itself; Vorster could return home empty-handed. Yet the prime minister was a notoriously tough customer, and he used the encounter in Bavaria to press his advantage.

First, Vorster emphasized the necessity of establishing the fund, initially mooted by the British, to protect the economic interests of Rhodesia's white population. It was "aimed at giving the European [white Rhodesian] certainty as to his future in a multi-racial society." This was not altruism on Vorster's part: the South African government was worried about the destabilizing impact of "a sudden large influx of penniless white refugees" from Rhodesia. "It was, and remains, South Africa's primary concern that there should be no economic collapse in Rhodesia resulting from a mass exodus of whites," the Rhodesian intelligence service explained. Furthermore, helping Rhodesia's whites would protect Vorster from his right flank at home. The South African prime minister's argument was straightforward and, for Kissinger, compelling: without such a fund, whites would flee and Rhodesia would descend into Marxism. Vorster claimed that the country would become "a shambles, and the beautiful cities, Salisbury and Bulawayo, will be in rack and ruin." His minister for foreign affairs chimed in: "It [the fund] could be a great asset to the West, because Communism could be held back."[49]

Moreover, Vorster would be unable to "sell" any deal that got rid of Smith unless it was "reasonable." Kissinger probed: "And your definition of reasonable is something that gives reasonable incentives for the whites to stay and plausible assurance of compensation if they leave?" Vorster replied: "Plausible assurance of life and property." Once Vorster was satisfied with this safety net—which the British estimated would require $110 million to $130 million annually for twenty-five years—he would tell Smith that, in his opinion, it was time to accept a transition to majority rule in Rhodesia. He would not do more.[50]

Beyond getting an American promise to support the fund, Vorster also sought to champion the leader of ZAPU, Joshua Nkomo, as the only acceptable black alternative to Smith. "Nkomo enforced by specific guarantees can save the situation," Vorster stated. "He [Nkomo] won't win prizes with his IQ," Kissinger commented. "No," Vorster agreed, "but he's the best." Exactly how to engineer Nkomo's rise was left murky. Kissinger relied on an anecdote about Kaunda's meeting with President Ford in 1975: "Kaunda . . . said, 'Install Machel in Mozambique.' The President said, 'What about free elections?' Kaunda said, 'Install him and we'll take care of the elections.'" No more was said about how Nkomo would rise to the top.[51]

Vorster seemed to outmaneuver Kissinger, who commented that he was "a newcomer to Africa" and also made a self-deprecating reference to his lame-duck status in the administration: "My weakness is my strength," he noted as the assembled men laughed. "I've got nothing to lose!" Vorster urged the US secretary of state to establish a fund and engineer the rise of Nkomo. "I think we can . . . sell it to the Africans," Kissinger noted optimistically. "And then," Vorster said, "you can look to me." Several months later, Andrew Young offered a stinging critique of Kissinger's performance. "The truth of the matter was that South Africa had bluffed the US," he stated. "Dr. Kissinger got snowed."[52]

The transcripts might omit important items. For example, Kissinger assured Callaghan that Vorster had said he would withdraw South Africa's "helicopters and crews from Rhodesia within the next three weeks"; this appears in neither the US nor South African minutes of the meetings, but the helicopters were indeed withdrawn in August.[53] Kissinger and Vorster, moreover, agreed to be tight-lipped after their encounter. In separate press conferences, Vorster said the talks had been "worthwhile," and Kissinger allowed only that "a process is in motion." Meanwhile, the *Rhodesian Herald* noted that the meeting had "stirred anxiety" in Salisbury. Ian Smith weighed in: "Dr. Kissinger," he told a journalist, "has decided to rush in where angels fear to tread."[54]

Vorster returned home in triumph. He received a loud ovation as he deplaned in Cape Town. He informed the Cabinet that the talks had been held "in a spirit of good will." In discussions with the Rhodesians, however, Vorster was grim. He told them, "They [the Americans] took an amazingly tough and utterly cynical line. . . . They had said again and again the only way to avoid chaos was for us to reach a solution [in Rhodesia]. . . .The American attitude can only worsen if Kissinger goes." The Rhodesians scrambled to figure out exactly what Vorster had given the Americans in Bavaria. They braced for an imminent attempt "to twist arms."[55]

"Unreliable Participants"[56]

Kissinger, meanwhile, stopped in London for talks with Prime Minister Callaghan. If the British and Americans could devise a reasonable settlement plan, he told Callaghan, Vorster would "sell it" to the Rhodesians. They agreed on a three-stage process: first, Vorster would persuade Smith to step down; second, Britain, as the legal authority, would oversee the transition, during which a constitution establishing majority rule would be written and an interim government established; and finally, within two years, Joshua Nkomo would become prime minister of an independent Zimbabwe. Whether elections would be held was left vague in both the US and British schemes. This plan rested on three pillars: inducements to reassure the whites, majority rule, and the establishment of a moderate government.[57]

The Americans and the British disagreed, however, about the mechanics of the crucial middle stage—the transition to majority rule. Kissinger wanted a British governor to assume legal authority of Rhodesia and oversee a brief transition period. Callaghan argued adamantly against this. He was unwilling to spend his scarce political capital on a scheme he suspected was destined for failure like all previous plans to lead Rhodesia to legal independence. "I am totally opposed to putting in a British Governor," he wrote. "We cannot put the clock back like that. Nor can we become responsible for law and order again."[58] He told West German chancellor Helmut Schmidt, "There could be no question of putting British troops back into Rhodesia. This would only lead to another Vietnam." He convinced the Cabinet Special Group to follow his lead, over the objections of his two top foreign policy officials, Foreign Secretary Crosland and Minister of State Ted Rowlands. Callaghan was unwavering: "The United Kingdom must be especially careful to avoid getting exposed politically, or militarily, or administratively, and left with the responsibility for a disaster if and when it occurred."[59] He thought that Kissinger was overestimating Vorster's ability to deliver Smith, and he had no trust whatsoever in the Rhodesian leader. "[He] let Dr Kissinger go ahead, though not without some misgivings," the Foreign Office noted. Callaghan stressed that the Frontline presidents (of Zambia, Tanzania, Mozambique, and Botswana) would have to be brought fully into the process, and he also worried that Nkomo was "losing ground" within Rhodesia and might begin to look like a "stooge." Nkomo might need "covert financial support."[60]

Having declared that his government would never agree to send a governor, Callaghan tasked the Foreign Office with concocting a plan that would return Rhodesia to legality without any direct British participation in the transition. After laborious drafting and a great deal of wishful thinking, the Foreign Office produced a cumbersome two-stage transition plan in which a white interim administration would gradually cede power to a bicameral temporary government that would have a strictly defined balance of races.

This plan was almost unworkable, and Kissinger had cause to be irritated. He vented to President Ford, "I talked Africa with the British. It is obvious they are playing their own game for short-term gains. They want to get Smith out and don't care what happens after. I don't mind that, but if we can't get something for it, I would just as soon let them go to hell on their own."[61]

The British, however, could be useful. "They knew Africa," the assistant secretary of state for African affairs remembered. "They were like oracles for us."[62] Moreover, their presence enabled Kissinger to frame US involvement in Rhodesia as helping an ally resolve its decolonization problems, rather than a Cold War tactic to best the Soviets. London also provided Washington with an escape hatch: if the negotiations failed, the Americans would say that they had done their best to bring peace to Rhodesia, and toss the ball back to White-hall. Throughout, Kissinger was alert to the fact that he needed to keep the British with him—or, more precisely, one step behind him. In the weeks after his meeting with Vorster, Kissinger took over. "Vorster would wish to deal primarily with the US," the Americans explained to Whitehall. "He does not like you British."[63]

Kissinger came to the table with three obvious strengths: he represented the most powerful country in the world; he was the unquestioned architect of US foreign policy (President Ford was almost never mentioned in Kissinger's conversations with the British about Rhodesia); and he still had the dazzle of celebrity. He had heft.

The British welcomed Washington's interest, at first. Callaghan told West German chancellor Schmidt on June 30, "Because of American power, he [Kissinger] could do things which we could not in Southern Africa." Never-theless, Foreign Office officials knew they were playing with fire. "We must get across to him [Kissinger] that we have ideas on a future course of action," Minister of State Ted Rowlands warned, "because he may think that we are planning to do nothing and leave the running to him."[64]

Beyond his gravitas, Kissinger used two levers of power—secrecy and speed—to marginalize the British. He deployed these twin imperatives like a chessmaster methodically moving his rook and knight before his opponent has deduced his strategy. When he briefed Callaghan on June 25, 1976, about his meeting with Vorster, he explained that it was the South African leader who had insisted that leaks or delays would imperil the plan by giving the conservatives in Pretoria time to organize resistance to it. (This does not appear in the transcripts of the Kissinger-Vorster talks.) Kissinger averred that only five Americans (other than himself and, presumably, Ford) were "in the picture." Again and again, he emphasized to Whitehall the need to keep all information about Rhodesia tightly held. The British obliged: it seemed a reasonable request, if a bit excessive. This wove a web of collusion around a privileged few, the chosen ones in Kissinger's inner circle. It would prove to be a perilous privilege.[65] Kissinger's other main tool was speed. He stressed repeatedly that time was running out—that any delay would offer the enemies of a negotiated settlement, on the right and the left, the opportunity to derail the plans. Haste was essential. Callaghan readily agreed, telling Kissinger on June 25, "It was clear that we did not have much time."[66]

A month later, the Foreign Office began to feel the ramifications of Kissinger's insistence on secrecy and speed. On July 20, the *New York Times* printed an article that revealed some details of the Rhodesia negotiations. Rather than fuming and flailing about this leak, Kissinger milked it to his advantage: dispatching his closest aides to express his fury to the British, he tightened his control. The British protested that they were not responsible for the leak, but they obliged Kissinger by creating an entirely new classification for cables about Rhodesia to ensure that they were not seen outside of a tight circle.[67] Nevertheless, there were more leaks, and Kissinger accused the British of being behind all of them.[68] This kept the Foreign Office off balance; it disrupted its normal consultative processes.[69] It also caused the British to worry that the Americans were manufacturing an excuse to fail to keep them fully informed.

The need for speed had even more serious ramifications. In mid-July, the Foreign Office informed Washington that it would be unable to submit its revised Rhodesian settlement proposals by Kissinger's July 23 deadline. This prompted one of President Ford's rare interventions in the Rhodesia saga. "I attach the greatest importance to speed," he wrote to Callaghan on July 20, in a letter that was clearly drafted by Kissinger or one of his close associates. "We must be sure that the Soviets and other outsiders do not have the time to play an unhelpful role."[70] Foreign Secretary Crosland took umbrage. He immediately summoned the American ambassador, Anne Armstrong, and asserted, "There had been no footdragging on the UK side." The delay, Crosland insisted, had been caused by Washington's failure to send him "vital information."[71]

Crosland was on guard. "Kissinger is trying to rush us," he warned at the first meeting of the Cabinet Special Group on Southern Africa. "There is a danger of Kissinger running away with us, and we have to insist on proper consultation and joint control of the whole exercise. I very much welcome the great personal interest he is taking in this subject, but I note that he has not yet told us all that passed between him and African leaders, and possibly not all that passed between him and Vorster."[72]

Thorough consultation is time-consuming. Haste renders it impossible. Kissinger allowed the British inadequate time to reflect, and he railed against their conferring with colleagues. The Cabinet Special Group on Southern Africa meeting on July 28, chaired by Callaghan, tried to resist Kissinger's bullying tactics. Most of the ministers present at the meeting were opposed to supporting Kissinger's plan "because they think success is impossible and because they are concerned that we should get dragged into an impossible situation," Deputy Undersecretary Antony Duff reported. With much effort, Callaghan was able to persuade them to support the plan, but only on the condition that "we really must go inch by inch."[73]

While the British were increasingly apprehensive about hitching their star to Kissinger's wagon, the secretary's patience with the Foreign Office was fraying. Winston Lord, the director of the State Department's Policy Planning Staff, signaled difficulties on July 21, when the Americans were berating the British for leaking and foot-dragging. "Obviously we are running into trouble with the British," he wrote Kissinger. "Crosland . . . is not exactly helpful."[74]

Kissinger later wrote that "of all the negotiations I conducted, by far the most complex was the one over majority rule in Southern Africa." As he told journalist Marvin Kalb, the negotiations had "many of the same characteristics [as the Middle East talks] and even more unreliable participants. If," he added, "that is possible."[75] One reason for this complexity was that the plan was bedeviled—as were most of Kissinger's schemes—by the players he considered marginal. The key actors in Kissinger's scheme were the three white men: Ian Smith, John Vorster, and himself. The next circle of players included Zambia's President Kaunda and Tanzania's President Nyerere, whom he kept informed (but did not truly consult) by letter, cable, and emissary throughout the summer. The British Foreign Office, much to its displeasure, was also in this group. On the outer periphery were Mozambique's President Machel and the guerrilla leaders.

Kissinger had met ZAPU leader Joshua Nkomo for seven minutes on his first trip to Zambia—apparently long enough for him to assess the African's IQ (as he had told Vorster) and for Nkomo to decide that the American was "unpleasant and untrustworthy." Kissinger admitted after he returned from

Africa that he did not even know who Robert Mugabe, the emerging leader of ZANU, was. The insurgents—the "men with guns"—played no role in his gambit. He did not keep them informed; he considered that to be Kaunda's and Nyerere's responsibility. As a leading Africanist and adviser to the Carter campaign noted, Kissinger's diplomacy was "characterized by an absence of contact with the Africans whom the whites have oppressed, deprived, jailed and at times tortured."[76]

Meanwhile, rioting continued in South Africa and the war quickened in Rhodesia. Smith felt increasingly embattled, and he was frustrated because he did not know what the Americans and South Africans had up their sleeves. "If [the] moribund Rhodesian patient is to be disposed of," a top Rhodesian official groused to the South Africans, "he has [the] right to know what is to be done with his remains."[77]

On August 9, 1976, Rhodesian units flattened the Nyadzonia refugee camp that was home to 8,000 people in Mozambique. The operation, Ian Smith bragged, "went like clockwork." Eighty-four Rhodesian Selous Scouts (special forces), many of whom were black, led by a South African officer drove across the border disguised in Mozambican uniforms. (The whites were in blackface.) They arrived at the camp and opened fire at point-blank range. The Rhodesian government claimed that "in a hot pursuit operation . . . more than 300 terrorists were killed," and the *Rhodesian Herald* lauded "the daring raid" as "a legitimate act of self-defense." The British *Guardian* reported that "champagne corks popped in Salisbury bars."[78]

Eyewitnesses and the United Nations High Commissioner for Refugees (UNHCR), however, told a different story: at least 1,000 unarmed refugees, mostly women and children, had been massacred at Nyadzonia. "After gathering together part of the camp population and shouting slogans, they [the Rhodesian soldiers] opened fire indiscriminately with light weapons but also antiaircraft guns," the UNHCR representative in Mozambique reported. "Soldiers pursued fleeing refugees smashing dead bodies with armoured cars. . . .Visit to camp was desolating. Bulldozers were covering ten mass graves . . . dried blood on the ground, stench from graves . . . testified to what must have been a horrifying scene."[79] The Rhodesian government furiously contested this account. "Rhodesia will always be treated . . . as the aggressor, no matter what the evidence adduced to the contrary," the *Rhodesian Herald* grumbled.[80]

This assault represented a dramatic escalation in the ferocity of Rhodesian cross-border attacks and an ominous shift in Salisbury's strategy. The brutality of the attack on a refugee camp—rather than on a ZANU camp—suggested that Smith was deliberately trying to provoke Mozambique to call on Cuban assistance in hopes of bringing in the South Africans, and perhaps even

US aid to Salisbury. Pretoria was alarmed and redoubled its efforts to end the war through negotiation. On August 14, South African foreign minister Hilgard Muller announced that "the South African government welcomes this [Kissinger's Rhodesian] initiative and . . . we are prepared to comply with the request to demonstrate our commitment to Africa by giving our full support for a peaceful outcome" in Rhodesia. "The South African Government has publicly committed itself to the American initiative which rests on the foundation of majority rule within two years," the *Rhodesian Herald* noted, later deeming Muller's announcement "another watershed along the route" to majority rule. Pretoria did more than talk. Fulfilling the promise that Vorster had apparently made to Kissinger in Germany, South Africa withdrew its helicopters and helicopter pilots from Rhodesia. This was a strong signal: during their June meeting, Smith had gone out of his way to thank Vorster for the helicopters, which were playing "a vital role" in the fight against the terrorists.[81]

The attack on Mozambique infuriated Kissinger. "[Is there] no end to what these Rhodesians would do to upset the applecart?" he asked South African ambassador Pik Botha. "Unless Rhodesia could be restrained it would be the end." He explained to the *New York Times*: "Time is running out. . . . If we can't get negotiations started in Rhodesia by the end of the year, it will be a bloody mess." South Africa's Muller was more blunt: "I wish to say unambiguously that I am concerned about the escalation of violence in Rhodesia, for the direction in which the terrorist struggle is developing is exactly what the Russians and Cubans are sitting and waiting for—an excuse." Before the Republican convention, a white South African official noted grimly, "We are very much pinning our hopes on Ronald Reagan."[82]

Ronald Reagan—Off Stage Right

"I have been at the Republican Convention," Kissinger said in late August 1976, "and I wish I hadn't been." President Ford won the nomination, but with no glory. He had scrambled for delegates until the vote was cast on August 18, and he eked out victory by a mere 117 of the 2,258 votes cast. The president had been thoroughly stripped of the glow of incumbency, which made many Republicans fear that they were heading toward a self-inflicted loss in November. Kissinger, moreover, was fuming over the party platform, which Reagan's supporters had managed to pack with criticisms of détente. "The good guys always come out disorganized and the sons of bitches . . . the yahoos . . . [launch] an attack on my foreign policy. . . . I am disgusted," he told Senator Charles "Mac" Mathias (R-MD). "These guys come in every four years and dump ideology all over the place. Then they despair until they can start another crusade."[83]

In fact, Reagan neither despaired nor slowed the crusade. He gave a rousing speech at the convention in which he praised the GOP platform as "a banner of bold, unmistakable colors" and rallied his followers to "go out and communicate to the world that we may be fewer in numbers than we have ever been, but we carry the message they are waiting for." His pungent critique of détente lingered, shaping the debate well beyond the general election. Before leaving Kansas City, he gathered his staff. "The cause, the cause goes on. Don't get cynical," he told them, his voice breaking. "Recognize that there are millions and millions of Americans out there that want what you want . . . that want it to be a shining city on a hill."[84]

Reagan's absence was felt in the general election campaign, which was a lackluster affair. In part, this stemmed from the financial constraints imposed on both Ford and Carter who, for the first time in history, had accepted federal financing of their campaigns.[85] While this certainly lowered the razzmatazz, the problem was more fundamental. In many ways, Reagan and Carter posed a similar challenge to Ford; it was, for the incumbent, a one-two punch. Both challengers ran as outsiders and both criticized the amorality of Kissinger's realism. Both tapped into the frustration many Americans felt with Washington bureaucrats who did not embody—or fight for—America's special mission. And both vied for the Wallace voters, the conservative and mostly southern Democrats who could swing the election for the GOP.

But the fundamental differences between the two governors rendered the general election a much more tepid contest than the Republican primary campaign had been. Reagan, in 1976, was a much less cheery and focused candidate than he would be four years later. In 1976, Reagan led an ideological crusade, while Carter was offering himself alone. Reagan roared that the Ford administration's policy of détente was eviscerating American power; Carter suggested merely that he would be tougher in negotiations with the Soviets. Reagan grabbed his audiences by their gut; Carter tentatively touched their heart. Reagan's city on the hill was exceptionally strong; Carter's city on the hill was exceptionally good. Reagan promised revolution while Carter offered redemption; Ford, in comparison, stood for more of the same.

Ford, therefore, faced a very different opponent after Kansas City. His strategy in the general campaign was straightforward: contrast his experience with Carter's inexperience. Much to Kissinger's dismay, Ford did not trumpet his administration's foreign policy because it was too redolent of Nixon's détente and therefore polarizing in the Republican Party. Ford was determined to minimize dissent from the right wing of his party by putting on hold all talk of renegotiating the Panama Canal Treaties, normalizing relations with China, or pressing Israel toward any land-for-peace deals. The fall of 1976 was a quiescent time in foreign policy; there were no crises in US relations with the countries of Latin America, Eastern and Western Europe, the Soviet Union, the Middle East, or Asia. Even though tens of thousands of Cuban troops remained in Angola, the immediate crisis there was over. Ford did not emphasize foreign policy. Instead, the perils of Jimmy Carter became "*the* issue" of the Ford campaign.[86] The president did not say it out loud, but his bottom line was simple: "better the devil you know."

When the campaign officially opened on Labor Day, Jimmy Carter had a fifteen-point lead. Over the summer months, Carter and dozens of experts who flocked to Plains had developed detailed position papers on seventy-six topics from dairy farming to the B-1 bomber. These papers were handed out at campaign events, and the candidate himself took questions from the press at almost every stop. Carter was a good student, and he gave specific answers to most questions, but he was still perceived as "fuzzy" on the issues. In part this was simply the inertia of image—Carter's reputation for vagueness, acquired during the primaries, was hard to shed, especially when policy details did not make lively copy. Moreover, in an era when television news was crammed into twenty-three minutes each evening, the three networks covered the gaffe of the day and the only way to hear the candidates' stump speeches was to attend their rallies. (C-SPAN began broadcasting in 1979.) The idea that Carter was vague was partly a consequence of his nonideological stance, which made it difficult for him to trot out pat prescriptions to complex problems. And in part it was because his positions rarely posed stark alternatives to President Ford's. He promised to reduce US arms sales worldwide and to pursue nonproliferation vigorously, and he pledged openness and accountability. Unlike Reagan, he did not brutally and frontally attack the Ford administration's competence or worldview.[87]

Both Ford and Carter supported détente, although Ford had expunged that "high falutin' word" (as George Wallace called it) from his vocabulary. Discussion of the Soviet threat left the stage when Reagan did—conservatives continued to raise alarums about Soviet designs, but neither candidate responded. Carter criticized Kissinger's style of doing business, alleging that the secretary of state was conducting "a one-man policy of international adventure" and calling him the "secretive 'Lone Ranger.'"[88] (Kissinger had invited this epithet by describing himself as "the cowboy entering the village . . . alone on his horse" in a controversial 1972 interview with Italian journalist Oriana Fallaci.[89]) Carter's differences with Kissinger were of method, not substance. Kissinger himself acknowledged this. "I can't change my policy because Carter has accepted it," he told newsman Ted Koppel. "Everyone is for more openness and an end to secrecy," he noted, "until they are elected."[90]

Carter did not rewrite his stump speech for the general election, but he did develop variations to suit different audiences and he did hone its emphasis on morality. In the primaries, Carter had promised "a government as good as the people," and he had spoken passionately about the need for the government to return to core US values. America's greatest strengths, Carter argued, were its founding principles. During the primary campaign, Carter rarely expressed this idea in terms of human rights.

The exception is a speech that he delivered on March 15, 1976, to the Chicago Council on Foreign Relations. This was the clearest exposition of his foreign policy goals and vision. For Carter, US competition with the Soviet Union remained a central problem, but it was a mistake to focus too narrowly on it. The increasing complexity and multipolarity of the world required the United States to cooperate with allies and adversaries alike to resolve pressing transnational issues such as pollution, nuclear proliferation, terrorism, and hunger. Carter stressed that to compete—as well as cooperate—effectively on the world stage, it was essential to restore American values to foreign policy. The way to do this was to reestablish the bond between the citizens and the government. In a call that would later morph into the language of human rights, he said that "we should support the humanitarian aspirations of the world's people."[91]

It was after the Democratic convention—after selecting Walter Mondale as his running mate and after extensive exposure to the members of Congress who flocked to Plains to brief the nominee—that Carter began to routinely slip references to "human rights" into his speeches.

Congress had been vigorously debating human rights for two years. This reflected the rethinking of national priorities following the US defeat in Vietnam that some members of Congress believed was necessary, and it signaled the attempt by both houses to reassert control over foreign policy. It was intensified by the disturbing revelations of the Church Committee, which in April 1976 completed its investigation into the unsavory underside of US foreign policy. Congressional interest in human rights drafted in the powerful salience of the idea in Western Europe. The European Community had insisted that the 1975 Helsinki Accords, a set of agreements intended to improve relations between the West and the Communist bloc, include provisions committing all signatories—including the Soviet Union—to uphold basic human rights. In the same year, Congress passed the Harkin Amendment, sponsored by Representative Tom Harkin (D-IA), which banned aid to any country that consistently violated human rights. Congress also created a Bureau of Human Rights and Humanitarian Affairs in the State Department that was charged with submitting an annual human rights report on every country slotted to receive aid. Thus, US legislators were becoming attuned to thinking about US values in the framework of human rights.[92]

By gradually shifting to this language, Carter began to frame his calls for morality and goodness in a relevant and contested terrain. It would be a mistake, however, to claim that Carter campaigned on human rights. He did not. In the extensive compilation of his campaign speeches and in the three major journalistic accounts of the campaign written during and immediately after it, human rights are barely mentioned.[93] Carter campaigned on the restoration of core values and on redemption. He ran on character—his character.

In many ways, Carter was remarkably candid, and the voters should have had a firm grasp of his character: he was smart, organized, demanding, ambitious, and religious. He was, as he wrote of himself, "as stubborn as a South Georgia turtle." He was also, profoundly, a loner. He was incapable of small talk and had contempt for the schmoozing that is the cement of most political deals. After months of campaigning, Jimmy Carter remained an enigma. The Ford campaign capitalized on this: at its core, the president's strategy was to sow doubts about the challenger. Again and again, pundits asked, "Who is Jimmy Carter?"[94]

This was the central dilemma of Carter's campaign: he was running on character, but he was also running as an outsider who had no history in the national political scene and who did not slot easily into the traditional categories of liberal or conservative. The public had trouble putting together the pieces of information about Carter into a picture of a person they could recognize. Jimmy Carter was, as one of his staffers admitted, "a very odd duck."[95]

Moreover, by September, the novelty was wearing thin. Carter had grabbed the public's attention in the spring—the newcomer slaying giants—but his earnestness was beginning to grate and, as he settled into the front-runner position and rubbed shoulders with old pols like mayors Richard Daley of Chicago and Frank Rizzo of Philadelphia, he began to seem more like a traditional politician, albeit in new clothing.

Carter had another problem in the general election. His strength was with small crowds—retail politics—where he could "charm the lard off a hog," as Georgia's secretary of state Ben Fortson put it.[96] But the door-to-door encounters in the snows of New Hampshire were long past. This meant not only that Carter could no longer rely on one of his greatest strengths but also that he lost the important ballast that those interactions had given him during the primary season. For Carter, the loner, this fleeting human interaction—and his almost mystical confidence that he could connect to the people—was his sustenance. As the campaign ground on and the entourage around him grew, the Democratic nominee became more isolated.

In the polls, Carter managed to stay ahead of Ford, who ran an uninspired campaign, but his lead steadily slipped. "I don't think it is impossible for Ford to get reelected," Kissinger told William F. Buckley in late August, but he was worried. "I have an absolute horror of what would come in with Carter." He told his close aide Helmut Sonnenfeldt, "It is going to be a nightmare."[97]

Back to Africa

"Now that we have gotten rid of that son-of-a-bitch Reagan, we can just do what is right," President Ford commented to Kissinger on August 30, 1976.[98]

"You think I should go to Africa?" Kissinger asked. He was contemplating a second meeting with Prime Minister Vorster, followed by shuttle diplomacy between southern African capitals to coax and threaten the parties toward a deal on Rhodesia. There was a catch, however. "What we need to think about is from your political situation. . . . I don't want another Texas situation," the secretary explained, remembering how his Lusaka speech might have cost Ford the Lone Star primary. Ford asked about the chance of success in Africa. "On Rhodesia I'd rate it a little better than 50-50," Kissinger opined. "Go," Ford replied.[99]

Suddenly, "Dr. Kissinger gathered speed," the British Foreign Office noted. On September 6, 1976—one week after his conversation with Ford—the secretary of state was facing the press in Zurich's luxurious Dolder Grand Hotel. He had just concluded three days of talks with Vorster that he deemed "fruitful."[100]

Indeed. Kissinger had explained to Vorster that he was depending on him to deliver Smith before he, himself, would travel to South Africa to meet the outlaw leader of Rhodesia face to face: "You will get Smith to agree 99%, and I will tell him, to explain our moral position—that I, who don't want to do it and who resisted doing it for seven and a half years, now think he has to do it." Vorster's response was all that Kissinger could have desired: "I understand," the gruff South African said. "That is my business."[101]

After this "fruitful" meeting, however, Kissinger could not dispel the unpleasant aura of déja vu that hung over his press conference. Four years earlier, as then–President Richard Nixon had faced an election, Kissinger had famously uttered, in regard to the war in Vietnam, "We believe peace is at hand." Weeks later, however—after Nixon had crushed George McGovern—the war escalated as the United States unleashed the Christmas bombing of Hanoi. In Zurich, Kissinger tried to make light of the parallel. "Should I say 'progress' is at hand?" he bantered.[102]

Almost five thousand miles to the south, Ian Smith was anxiously awaiting word of the talks. "Godspeed and best wishes in your forthcoming talks in Zurich," he had cabled Vorster on the day the South African departed. "I am conscious of the heavy responsibilities you bear at a time when severe pressures are being exerted on the whites of Southern Africa." Smith wanted to be included in the negotiations. "I hope that you will be able to convince Dr. Kissinger that . . . early and direct participation by my government in his discussions is essential if a peaceful solution is to be found."[103]

Vorster informed Smith that Kissinger was open to Smith's "early and direct participation" in the talks. Smith himself might soon be meeting with the American secretary of state: "The time is approaching when it is necessary to have a very frank discussion with Rhodesia," he cabled "Mr. Farmer" (a codename for Ian Smith) after his talks with Kissinger. "He [Kissinger] would like to meet Mr Farmer as soon as possible. . . . Things were moving very fast."[104]

Abruptly, the movement stopped. Kissinger had planned to jet from Zurich to southern Africa to consult quickly with the Frontline leaders before heading to Pretoria where he would meet Smith. But the five Frontline presidents (of Tanzania, Zambia, Mozambique, Botswana, and—on this occasion—Angola) were stuck in an important meeting in Tanzania with Rhodesia's nationalist leaders that was running longer than expected. The Frontline presidents were trying to convince the feuding nationalists to present a united front in preparation for the Kissinger initiative. Unity among the nationalists would strengthen Kissinger's hand in negotiations with Smith, and the secretary accepted the delay graciously. "I appreciate your reasons for saying you need more time," he cabled President Nyerere as he decided to return to Washington to await the outcome of the meeting in Dar es Salaam.[105]

Kissinger stopped in London for consultations with Prime Minister Callaghan. The British were on guard. After meeting with the Americans in Washington three weeks earlier, Deputy Undersecretary Duff had cabled, "Our thinking was markedly diverging. . . . The most disquieting aspect is the US failure to consult us. . . . I fear however we have to accept this and concentrate on damage limitation." He added a strong warning: "We clearly have to keep our eyes wide open." Callaghan agreed: "I feel very strongly about the point Duff has already made, namely that I will not be willing to commit myself to a plan cooked up between Kissinger and Vorster and dumped in our laps." Callaghan knew Kissinger well from his own time as foreign secretary. "Kissinger's method of working will lead him to take initiatives that will not have been agreed by us in advance." Callaghan was resigned to this, but he needed to protect his government. "This being so, Kissinger must understand that we hold ourselves free to disassociate wherever necessary."[106]

The declassified transcripts of the meeting between Kissinger and Callaghan on September 6, 1976, do not mention these doubts and provisos. They focus instead on the details of the next moves, with the British strongly advising Kissinger not to trust Smith or enter into any prolonged negotiations with him. Foreign Secretary Crosland's report to the Cabinet about Kissinger's encounter with Vorster in Zurich was cagey. After wishing "Dr. Kissinger's initiative well," he noted that the British government was "not committed to anything in the plan at this stage." Kissinger had been told that Britain insisted on four points: "that the proposals must be endorsed by the [Frontline] African Presidents; that the United Kingdom could have no responsibility for an interim administration in Rhodesia; that the bulk of finance for a scheme of inducements for white Rhodesians must be found by the United States; and that we could not contemplate negotiations with Mr Smith." It was hardly a ringing endorsement.[107]

Intersection, via Dean Rusk

On September 8, Henry Kissinger was back in Washington, trying to put out another potential fire. That morning, the lead editorial in the *Washington Post* was titled "African Gamble." It warned: "If he [Kissinger] fails [to bring peace to Rhodesia], the United States will have suffered a major blow to its prestige and influence and President Ford will have handed Jimmy Carter a fat campaign issue."[108]

Kissinger phoned Dean Rusk, who had been secretary of state to both John Kennedy and Lyndon Johnson. After leaving Foggy Bottom, Rusk had returned to his native Georgia, where he taught law. He was an informal adviser to the campaign of fellow Georgian Jimmy Carter.

Kissinger needed a favor. Callaghan and Vorster had made clear that the success of his Africa initiative would hinge, to a large extent, on his promise to establish a fund to buy out Rhodesia's whites. However, given the presidential elections in two months, what weight would Kissinger's promise have?

"I needed to talk with you about if I go to Africa next week what commitments I may have to make," Kissinger told Rusk. "I would like to get an understanding with Carter that he would honor those." Rusk asked for clarification: "Is this primarily a financial commitment?" Kissinger said it was and explained that he was turning to Rusk because "there is nobody around Carter that I would trust to talk to." Rusk should come to Washington to discuss it in person. Rusk said he was "pretty sure" he could get through to Carter, but he could not travel to Washington before Kissinger's scheduled departure for Africa. "You can't come up here?" Kissinger asked. Rusk explained that he could not. "Maybe we can send a plane for you," Kissinger replied.[109]

Two days later, Dean Rusk entered the Oval Office. President Ford expressed his appreciation that the former secretary had come to Washington to discuss this "matter of importance." The brief, thirty-minute meeting was not made public. Its purpose was clear: Ford wanted Rusk to persuade Carter to lie low on African policy. He did not want a repeat of Reagan's performance in Texas. Kissinger's upcoming trip could "be damaging . . . in the domestic political context," Ford acknowledged. However, he explained, the United States had a "moral responsibility" to try to negotiate peace in southern Africa. While "there was no certainty of success, . . . possibilities for success would not be enhanced by comments at home which called into question the sincerity of US motives. Were the initiative to be characterized as political grandstanding, it could erode our credibility in negotiations." Ford, for his part, affirmed that he would not "make partisan political capital of our initiative."[110]

Ford had reason to be anxious. That very morning, Carter's advisers, after reading press rumors that Kissinger was organizing a buyout fund for whites in Rhodesia, had urged the candidate to release a statement that strongly condemned the "unnecessary and distasteful secrecy" with which the Ford administration had negotiated a plan "to spend hundreds of millions of American dollars to fund a negotiated settlement of Rhodesia's racial problems." Carter, however, decided to delay until he had checked with "relevant foreign policy people."[111]

This caution was typical of the candidate. Although Carter professed that Africa was "an area of special interest to him,"[112] his neglect of the continent during the campaign was almost complete. The voluminous "Campaign 1976" files at the Carter Library contain a handful of clippings about Africa but fewer than a dozen memos about the candidate's policy toward the continent. Carter mentioned Africa in passing when he criticized the Ford administration for overlooking the Third World, but he always stressed Latin America rather than Africa in this regard. In the early spring of 1976, the campaign had issued a hard-hitting position paper on Kissinger's Angola policy, but instead of amplifying it in a speech, Carter merely mentioned Angola as one item in the litany of Ford's mistakes. The position paper's stinging words therefore received no press coverage.[113]

During the primary campaign, Carter was interviewed by *Africa Report*, the journal of the Africa-America Institute. In the interview, he promised, if elected, to support the work of multilateral international organizations such as the World Bank, as well as bilateral aid programs to promote Africans' "legitimate aspirations for self-determination." But on the campaign trail, the record indicates that he volunteered only two fleeting comments on Rhodesia. Kissinger's Africa trip in April, on which the secretary had pointedly taken the liberal Democratic senator Abraham Ribicoff of Connecticut, had blunted the Democratic critique of the administration's Africa policy: the goals that

Kissinger articulated in his Lusaka speech were from the Democrats' play-book. Carter could not mount a full-throated attack. In late June, answering a question about southern Africa, he said lamely that he agreed with the "long-delayed" Kissinger initiative.[114]

At the Democratic convention in New York in July, Carter approved the Africa plank of the platform. It was a liberal statement that called for "enlight-ened U.S.-African priorities" and "unequivocal and concrete support of major-ity rule in Southern Africa." In the month after the convention, he was briefed on African issues, including Rhodesia, by experts who visited Plains. In response to a question immediately after those meetings, he gave his fullest answer of the campaign on the Rhodesian crisis. He stressed his support for majority rule, and he noted that South Africa could play a useful role in resolving the crisis peacefully. Carter then drew an analogy between the civil rights struggle in the US South and the ongoing struggle in southern Africa, saying that "with that special knowledge in our own country I think we might be a help in Africa. . . . I don't know how to answer your question better than that."[115]

Among the many position papers that the campaign released after the Plains meetings was one on Africa that included a section on Rhodesia. After assert-ing that Rhodesia would be ruled by the majority, the paper noted, "The only question is whether it comes through armed struggle sponsored by the Soviet Union or through an aggressive diplomacy of peace encouraged by the United States." As *Africa Report* noted, it was "a little difficult telling an Elephant from a Donkey so far as policy toward Africa is concerned."[116]

In late August, the campaign toyed with the idea of Carter delivering a major address on policy toward Africa. Anthony Lake, a campaign adviser and Africa expert who would become the State Department's director of policy planning under Carter, drafted a speech that provided a wide-ranging overview of the continent's relevance to the United States. It declared that a Carter administration would treat "African issues on their own merits, instead of largely in terms of East-West competition," and noted that "the gathering war in . . . Rhodesia is the most dramatic manifestation of racial conflict in Southern Africa."[117]

But the speech was never delivered. Andrew Young was one of those who recommended against it. There were several reasons for holding back: people vote on "pocketbook issues," so Carter should focus on domestic policy; Cart-er's comments on Africa after the meeting in Plains would suffice; African issues were "particularly complex" and therefore not suited to a campaign speech; and Kissinger was in the throes of "spelling out the administration policy on Africa" and it would not be "judicious" for Carter to weigh in dur-ing this process. Therefore, a speech on Africa would do more harm than good. "We have a big battle to fight . . . and there is no need to complicate this task."[118] Instead of a major address, Carter simply told the French magazine *L'Express* that the United States "irrevocably supported majority rule," that Rhodesia would "inevitably" be governed by the majority, and that if he became president he would look to Britain to take the lead and coordinate US policy with that of African regional organizations and governments.[119] That was the sum of all his comments on the subject before Rusk was summoned to the Oval Office.

Rusk, therefore, did not have much persuading to do. He contacted Carter immediately and reported back to Kissinger. Rusk asked Kissinger if "representative African leaders" would be "onboard" and if the administration would keep congressional leaders informed about the fund. Kissinger assured Rusk that Carter could "be absolutely sure both of those conditions will be met." Rusk then promised that Carter would not talk even to his staff about the financial agreements Kissinger expected to make in Africa. "Tell him," Kissinger replied, "I think he is behaving very patriotically." On the memo detailing the statement that Carter was set to deliver condemning the administration's secret deals on Rhodesia, there is a scrawled, anonymous comment: "This was killed."[120]

A week later, Kissinger deplaned in Tanzania, where he encountered a pessimistic President Nyerere. Exerting maximum pressure on the fractious nationalists, the Frontline presidents had failed to persuade them to put aside their differences. The internal nationalists (those who lived in Rhodesia and commanded no troops) feuded with the external nationalists (ZANU and ZAPU), who, in turn, argued bitterly with each other. The tumultuous meeting in Dar es Salaam ended in "complete confusion," as one of the Zairean president's informants noted in a detailed account. It had one very important outcome, however: the emergence of Mugabe as the leader of ZANU. Moreover, the Frontline presidents and leaders of ZANU and ZAPU reached unanimity on one point, which Nyerere, who had chaired the meeting, summarized in a one-sentence communiqué: they had agreed "to intensify the liberation war in Zimbabwe."[121]

At a press conference on September 12, 1976, immediately before his departure for Africa, Kissinger had surmised that his chance of success was only a bit better than the twenty-to-one odds that the chair of the Senate's Africa subcommittee, Dick Clark, had given him. Kissinger often referred to the "architecture" of diplomacy, but his construction in Africa was more like an old-fashioned barn raising: it depended on rallying all the parties to work together to build a new Zimbabwe. The Frontline presidents, however, had failed to reconcile the nationalists; Vorster was out on a limb by himself, and Smith was even further out. Meanwhile, the British were anxious, and the election saga in the United States was reaching its climax.[122]

The Rabbit

In Moscow on September 20, 1976, Soviet leader Leonid Brezhnev turned to the Carter campaign's envoy to the Kremlin, Averell Harriman, and blurted, "Why on earth did Kissinger take it into his head [to go] traveling all over Africa?" He told Harriman that he "even thought about it in bed!" Kissinger's perambulations—he had been in Africa for a week—were so confounding, the general secretary explained, that he couldn't think about them "sitting up."[123]

In fact, Henry Kissinger had just pulled a rabbit out of his hat. On September 19, Ian Smith had turned to him and asked, "So you want me to sign my own death note?"[124] Smith had escaped death twice while serving in the Royal Air Force in World War II, and his illegal regime in Rhodesia had lasted more than a decade of international opprobrium and UN sanctions. It appeared, however, that the escape artist had finally been cornered. How had Kissinger achieved this?

In Zurich, in the first week of September, he had convinced Vorster that it was in South Africa's interest to bell the cat—to deliver Smith. This had not been difficult. As Bill Edmondson, the deputy chief of mission in the US embassy in Pretoria, said, "The South Africans wanted a settlement in Rhodesia. It was basically their initiative. They didn't need to be persuaded." On September 14, Vorster had summoned Smith to Pretoria—as he had promised Kissinger he would do—for a "full and frank exchange of views." Smith, Vorster said, had a choice: accept Kissinger's proposals for majority rule, or go it alone without the South African lifeline. At first, Smith tried to slither through the meeting, agreeing in principle to majority rule but refusing to specify how he would qualify the franchise or to give a date certain for the elections. On hearing this, Vorster was, the Rhodesian representative in South Africa reported, "incredulous . . . shattered . . . despondent." And mad. "Even if he [Smith] thought they [the South Africans] were naive," Vorster fumed, "the people they were going to see [Kissinger and his staff] were not. . . . Something must be held out to show Rhodesia was prepared to move towards her goal in a practical way." Vorster had had enough. "He had tried for two years to sell the Farmer's [Smith's] sincerity of purpose . . . but he could not do it . . . now." Nobody—not "the Americans, French, or Germans"—was willing to talk to Smith, he exclaimed, "because they know what to expect." The South African was blunt: "Nobody believes Mr. Farmer [Smith]." The Rhodesians, he complained, "were too sanguine about the possibility of Russians using Cubans or satellites in southern Africa," which, Smith believed, would draw in the South Africans. Concluding the meeting, Vorster emphasized that South Africa "would not come to Rhodesia's aid."[125]

Vorster's words packed a punch: the State Department reported that throughout the summer, "Vorster has removed from Rhodesia South African combat police, helicopter technicians and during September 1976 slowed down ammunition and basic equipment deliveries."[126] Moreover, Rhodesian trade had been slowed by congestion on South African rails and ports.[127] When Mozambique closed its border with Rhodesia in March 1976, Vorster did not pick up the slack. He did not increase the capacity of the rail line that connected Rhodesia to its only remaining path to the sea. Brand Fourie, the director-general of the South African Foreign Ministry, explained that "this meant in effect that the volume of Rhodesian import and export traffic would be reduced by something between 40% and 50%." By October, goods worth $100 million were stuck in Rhodesia awaiting export, and fuel depots held only a twenty-day supply.[128] "Vorster is the bad guy," one of Smith's aides declared. Smith got the message.[129]

On September 14, the day that Vorster gave Smith his marching orders, Henry Kissinger returned to Africa. Vorster immediately informed him of the successful encounter with Smith, and Kissinger made plans to add South Africa to his itinerary. As a South African official explained, had it not been for Vorster's "categorical assurance . . . Henry would not be willing to come to the party."[130]

Kissinger's first stops were Dar es Salaam and Lusaka, where he discussed—in deliberately vague terms—with Nyerere and Kaunda what he would say to Smith. A week earlier, after going over the plan with Vorster in Zurich, he had assured him, "I would not give all this [information] to the blacks." Concerned that the two African presidents would quibble and delay, Kissinger told Callaghan that he was determined "not to give them any details on which to shuffle: we should get them to endorse the approach." Kissinger confidently told the British prime minister that once Smith had accepted majority rule, "Nyerere and Kaunda would come along."[131]

In fact, neither Nyerere nor Kaunda was interested in the details of the scheme because they doubted it would amount to anything. As the British minister of state reported, "They will want to see the colour of Vorster's money before putting their own on the table." Frank Wisner, the director of the State Department's southern Africa desk, who was accompanying Kissinger, noted, "When we arrived in Tanzania for two days of meetings with Julius Nyerere, Kissinger met his match. Nyerere—brilliant, deeply suspicious— . . . told Kissinger to go forth and deliver the Rhodesians." With trepidation, Nyerere and Kaunda watched Kissinger fly into the lion's den: apartheid South Africa.[132]

The rebellion that had begun in Soweto in June had neither died down nor been crushed, despite the South African government's best efforts. By September, "disturbances"—desperate protests quelled by riot police who shot to kill—had spread from Pietersburg in the northeast to Cape Town in the southwest; some 661 people had been killed, almost all of whom were blacks shot by the police, and well-organized strikes had multiplied, depriving the white economy of the black labor on which it depended. Two days before Kissinger arrived in Pretoria, "the biggest strike in South Africa's history"—750,000 blacks and coloreds—effectively closed the Cape Town docks and many other industries.[133]

It outraged many opponents of apartheid that the US secretary of state was visiting South Africa. As Senator Clark explained, "They [the critics] see the Kissinger-Vorster initiative on Rhodesia as a way of giving Vorster more time at home and more prestige abroad." Hours before Kissinger landed at an airbase outside Pretoria, children in Soweto staged a protest. They sang freedom songs and carried placards saying "Dr. Kissinger, Get out of Azania [the nationalists' name for South Africa]!" and "Kissinger – Murderer." Suddenly, the police stormed the protest and, without provocation, opened fire. At least six children were killed, and thirty-five hospitalized.[134]

As Kissinger sped through Pretoria in the armored car that had rolled off his airplane, followed by his entourage of seventy American officials, nearby Johannesburg was rife with rumors, bomb scares, and petrol bomb attacks. That was, however, a world away. In the South African prime minister's residence, perched in the high hills overlooking Pretoria, Vorster assured Kissinger that he had done as promised in Zurich: on September 14, he had called Smith to Pretoria and "read [him] the riot act."[135] Vorster was blunt: "Smith will accept," he told Kissinger. The two men then discussed the problematic details of the plan, and Kissinger mentioned that the British, who refused to take responsibility during the transition, were giving him headaches. "I have been fighting all week with them." Even though he also worried about how Kaunda and Nyerere would respond, he was excited. "This will be a sensation around the world," he told Vorster.[136]

The stage was set for the dramatic climax to Kissinger's Africa gambit. The scene itself was historic—the first visit of an American secretary of state to South Africa and the first meeting of a senior American official with the renegade ruler of Rhodesia—all in full glare of the global media. On September 19, Kissinger met for seven hours with Smith, who had come to Pretoria knowing that he was walking the plank. An aide to Smith who traveled with

him said, "Kissinger was disarming . . . and he kept saying . . . he was only trying to help." Kissinger remembers, "I treated him [Smith] as a fellow statesman rather than as a pariah."[137]

Kissinger had scripted a power play that was both genteel and brutal.
Expressing his personal "regret . . . that we face certain international necessities," he told Smith that no one—not South Africa, not Britain, and not the
United States—would rescue his regime, and he managed to make it seem
more like the counsel of a concerned friend than a threat. "We are caught in a
tragedy," he said. "And we would like as far as possible to find a solution compatible with the dignity of the white population." He dangled the development
fund—the package of financial guarantees for the whites—and the lifting of
sanctions, and he counseled Smith that this was the best deal he would ever
get. He handed Smith the letter from Jimmy Carter pledging to honor the commitments Kissinger was making, but he warned the beleaguered Rhodesian
that if Carter was elected, "you will face active, intense, ideological pressure."
He added ominously, "With Carter in office then, the Lord help us."[138]

Smith said that Kissinger was asking him to "commit suicide."[139] Just six
months earlier, he had announced he would not accept majority rule in a
thousand years, and now he was being asked to accept majority rule in two
years. But even with no cards left to play, this slippery character continued to
place his bets. He still expected to be able to control the situation—that is, he
expected to retain power. He had no intention of committing suicide.

The seven hours of meetings had rhythm. They were like an extended jazz
improvisation, with riffs and caesurae and crescendos. Smith argued vehemently over the composition of the interim government that would rule before
elections could be held. He insisted on a white chairman, and Kissinger
appeared to concede, saying that the United States would "just ram it down
the British throats."[140] Smith also demanded that the key ministries of defense
and law and order would be headed by whites during this interim period. Kissinger agreed, though he cautioned that even though the United States would
support it, "I can't say if the British will."[141]

Smith then asked, "Do we know what majority rule means? . . . If I went
back to Rhodesia and said it meant one man one vote, I would be thrown
out. Could we add one word: 'responsible majority rule'? Can you sell that?"
Kissinger initially demurred, but then said, "You can ask for it." If the blacks
accepted it, "as long as I am in—I would be willing to leave a piece of paper
with my successor saying I've promised this." He hastened to add, "But if you
tell your Parliament that it's qualified voting, all of Africa will accuse you of
tricking me. . . . Just don't be too explicit with your Parliament."[142]

Finally, after what Kissinger called "seven painful hours" on a very long
Sunday, Smith announced, "I accept your proposals." He would take them

to his parliament for approval and, if it agreed, he would announce the plan on Friday. Kissinger cabled the good news to President Ford. He ended on a cautionary note: "But this is Africa, and one can never count on anything until it is completed."[143]

The Master Confusionist

It is understandable that both Vorster and Smith wanted to place dominant power in white hands during the transition, but it is not clear why Kissinger, who appeared to hold all the cards, conceded these critical points. Certainly, he had sympathy for the beleaguered Rhodesian leader. Immediately before meeting Smith, Kissinger had confided to the British high commissioner, David Scott, "I know that what we are doing is right in state terms but I am much less certain about it in purely human terms." In his memoirs, Kissinger wrote that when he saw Smith's party in Pretoria, his "heart went out to the forlorn group." Kissinger's wife, who accompanied him to South Africa, rushed forward to embrace Smith, exclaiming that he was "a great hero of hers." Kissinger told the British that he found the encounter "painful" because "he had liked the Rhodesians. They had not whined. They had behaved like men. . . . They were fine people." Rhodesian intelligence observed that "Kissinger appears more sympathetic to the White position in Rhodesia than does Britain or any of the other Western powers."[144]

Kissinger also misjudged the obduracy of the Frontline presidents on the details of the transitional government. "I am not persuaded that a white majority council of state [one of two governing bodies during the transition] would necessarily prejudice the scheme in the eyes of the black African presidents," he noted immediately before meeting Smith. "I anticipate little objection [from Kaunda] to the proposal for a white chairman," he cabled home immediately after. Kissinger was misled not only by his belief that he could massage all bruised egos, but also by his failure to take the Frontline presidents seriously. "You must understand that what the Black African leaders say to me privately," he told Ford, "is far different from what they say publicly."[145]

Kissinger also might have been thinking of the political consequences at home of pushing Smith so hard that he was ousted or fell from power. Unlike his British counterparts, Kissinger believed that Ian Smith was the best man to lead the Rhodesian whites into negotiations with the nationalists. Whereas the Foreign Office, burned so many times by Smith, feared that no negotiations could succeed as long as he was involved, Kissinger feared that the alternative to Smith—a weaker white leader, or outright chaos—would lead to an ignominious surrender of the whites to the black nationalists. "American public opinion would prefer to see the whites defeated in battle rather than pressured into surrender," he told the British. The negative response to his Africa policy at home indicated "the extent of anti-black feeling in the US."[146]

Kissinger operated with an eye to history. He feared that, in the long term, southern Africa could descend into greater turmoil and his efforts would be judged harshly. "History might not report very kindly on the package which was now being negotiated," he averred to High Commissioner Scott. "For this reason, it would be wrong to push the white Rhodesians beyond the point that was necessary to achieve what we wanted, or to humiliate them gratuitously."[147]

Feeling the urgency of the impending presidential election, Kissinger rushed. Nothing if not confident in his own powers, he believed that he could push the parties closer to consensus before any of them had become fully aware of his assurances to Smith. "What we can do," he explained to the press before his departure on his second African trip, "is bring the parties sufficiently close so they believe in a negotiating effort and establish some of the basic conditions for the negotiations."[148] When Kissinger met resistance, he used ambiguity or outright falsehood to create the appearance of consensus. Thus, he told Smith that he would not balk at a qualified franchise if the Frontline presidents agreed, but there is no indication that he ever even hinted to Nyerere or Kaunda that he had agreed to this enormous loophole. He postponed this bombshell for some time in the future, after—he hoped—all parties had agreed to negotiate. Moreover, he led Smith and Vorster to believe that the Frontline presidents and the British had approved his proposals about whites maintaining control over the interim government—when they had not. "We in fact were not consulted," the Foreign Office fumed. "We do not know exactly what happened at Dr Kissinger's meeting with Mr Smith," the British ambassador in Washington later confided to the Carter administration. What he did know, however, was that Kissinger had unilaterally revised the discussion paper Foreign Secretary Crosland had given him in London, mutating its tone from a discussion paper (the *beginning* of a negotiation) to a list of five points that Smith construed as the *end* of the negotiation.[149]

Kissinger's follow-up meetings in Lusaka and Dar es Salaam were guarded: he was so carefully ambiguous about the deal he had struck with Smith on the composition of the interim government (and he never mentioned qualifying the franchise) that neither Kaunda nor Nyerere understood what had been agreed. Kissinger gave them nothing in writing. He cabled Vorster that the talks with the two African presidents had been "generally encouraging. I anticipate little objection to the proposal for white chairman of the council of state. The designation of white ministers for defence and law and order is a more difficult question. However, the reaction was not unduly hostile." He sent a message to Smith designed to keep him on track: "We understand the anguish that the Rhodesians must be going through at this moment," he wrote, "and we want to be helpful."[150]

The fact was—and Kissinger knew it—that Kaunda and Nyerere were deeply suspicious of what the white men had agreed behind their backs. Nevertheless, they would hold their fire until they heard what Smith had to say. "When it comes to Smith," a Tanzanian official said drily, "Dr. Kissinger is rather innocent." In a press conference after Kissinger's visit, Nyerere noted with wry understatement that "my friend Smith is an imponderable in the equation."[151]

On September 24, 1976, Ian Smith, after conferring with his Cabinet and party caucus, took to the airwaves. In a fifteen-minute televised address to the nation, a bitter, emotional, and resolute Smith told his fellow Rhodesians that "it was made abundantly clear to me . . . that we could expect no help or support of any kind from the free world." Therefore, the Cabinet and the party had reluctantly decided to accept the proposals for majority rule that Kissinger had put forward in Pretoria. He did not mention or even hint that he did not mean one man, one vote. Smith then described the "package deal" in detail. First, the good news: a "cessation of terrorism," the lifting of sanctions, and a generous international program of financial aid. Then, the bad news: "majority rule within two years." Smith described the transition arrangements in detail, stressing that the council of state—one of the key organs during the transition—would be headed by a white man. He concluded, his voice cracking, with "Good night, and may God be with you in these trying times."[152]

Kissinger listened to Smith's speech on a BBC World Service broadcast as he flew home to Washington. He was not jubilant.[153] He knew better than anyone all the truths he had stretched to get Smith to utter his commitment to majority rule, and he was acutely aware of all the work it would require to move forward.

Kissinger earned the sobriquet "number-one confusionist" during his African adventure. In the months after his "Pretoria coup," all his African interlocutors, white and black, struggled to figure out what exactly had been agreed by whom. They tried, and failed, to disentangle the contradictions and ambiguities between the three versions of the Kissinger proposals: the five points the secretary brought to Smith; Smith's own announcement; and the summary that Kaunda gave Nkomo after his meeting with Kissinger. "The differences . . . are far-reaching and fundamental," a team of Nkomo's lawyers concluded.[154] Nigerian foreign minister Joe Garba complained that because Kissinger's talks with Smith were "shrouded in secrecy," he feared "shady deals."[155]

Kissinger himself admitted to his close friend, UN Ambassador Bill Scranton, "My strategy which is not heroic is to keep the thing sufficiently confused to exhaust them a bit. . . . I am going to keep it confused until somebody's nerves go." To French president Valéry Giscard d'Estaing, on the other hand, he wrote, "I do not want to be over optimistic because radical African states encouraged by the Soviet Union could still defeat our efforts." This is "only a beginning," he cautioned.[156]

Kissinger was right: it was only a fragile beginning, and it immediately began to fray. Three days after Smith's speech, Kissinger told Tom Brokaw on the *Today* show, "We should always remember that the biggest steps have been taken and that the differences that remain are relatively small."[157] But the devil, of course, was in those details. Smith's speech contained a critical phrase: by calling the agreement with Kissinger a "package deal," the Rhodesian leader signaled that for him it was nonnegotiable. Smith called it a "firm, binding contract"; the black Africans had a choice—take what the white men had negotiated or leave it.[158] Yet the Frontline presidents, Kissinger, and the British saw the negotiations in Pretoria—especially about the composition of the interim government—as the beginning of a process that would require give and take on all sides. The Frontline presidents immediately denounced Smith's proposals: "If accepted, [they] would be tantamount to legalizing the colonialist and racist structures of power."[159]

Moreover, the idea of a fund to buy out whites offended the Frontline presidents. On ABC's *Issues and Answers*, Nyerere complained that it was based on "an arrogant idea that whites shouldn't have to live in a country where Blacks rule." ZAPU's Nkomo was forthright. There were "very serious flaws" in the plan, he announced. ZANU's Mugabe was contemptuous: "Who will pay blacks for all their years of being exploited by the whites?" he asked when he heard about the financial aid package. And from Mozambican authorities came the ominous word that they "would not support the Rhodesia plan."[160] President Machel, who had been marginalized in Kissinger's machinations, remained deeply suspicious of American policy. The US Congress had weakened Kissinger's hand, voting down all aid for the leftist government of Mozambique. The debacle in Angola, Machel explained, had taught Washington not to "fight against national liberation wars, [but] . . . to subvert them, and instead of trying to protect the rights of privileged minorities individually, . . . to protect the overall rights of capitalism. . . . That was what the Americans were now doing in . . . Rhodesia."[161]

Kissinger made light of this rhetoric. "I think the Black leaders in their public statements," he explained to Ford, "reflected that a Black cannot agree to anything offered by a white like Ian Smith." The South African government was equally dismissive. "Their [black African presidents'] minds work in strange ways," they noted. "The situation is salvageable."[162]

But Smith was preparing to slip the hook. In his speech, he had stated that his acceptance of the plan was contingent on sanctions being lifted and the guerrilla war ending; neither event was likely.[163] Smith's "genius," one of Prime Minister Callaghan's political advisers explained, was "the appearance of movement and momentum he can give to negotiations without conceding anything of substance." A background paper by Smith's deputy summarizes Salisbury's understanding of their agreement. "Kissinger deal: Set up an interim government and would have two years to sort out the constitution, after which majority rule. *Not seen as one man one vote.* America understands the problem better than the United Kingdom."[164]

Kissinger, seeing the house of cards collapsing, tried his level best to keep Smith in line. "I must stress," he wrote the Rhodesian on October 1, "that we reject the proposition that we forced you into making the announcement which you made on September 24. . . . The objective facts in one year would have compelled you to seek a settlement under worse circumstances. Our offer gave you an opportunity—but not a guarantee—for a moderate solution. . . . If you prefer to fight rather than to negotiate, the decision is up to you. Whichever course you choose will have no consequence for the United States. I must remind you, however, that you can expect no help from us." Kissinger was philosophical. He quipped to the British that he had undertaken the Rhodesian negotiations because of "a mixture of extreme naivete combined with extreme arrogance, 'mainly the former.'" He swore he "would never do it again."[165]

In his review of US-British relations in 1976, the British ambassador in Washington, Peter Ramsbotham—one of Kissinger's admirers—identified "three major weaknesses of the Kissinger method" that had been exposed by his foray into southern African affairs.

> First, a tendency to concentrate on one or two issues to the exclusion of others, so that he neglected Africa completely until its problems (i.e. Angola) had reached crisis proportions; second, a predisposition to look at every international problem in terms of the global rivalry between the superpowers . . . ; and third, and for us, I suspect, the most costly, a certain deviousness in negotiation, which resulted in each of his negotiating partners being left with a different impression of what had been agreed—a fault compounded by his passion for secrecy, which left his own Ambassadors in the key posts, and all but his closest collaborators, totally in the dark and unable to resolve any misunderstanding. . . . [Kissinger was] misled by his own exuberance and arrogance.[166]

Nevertheless, no one could undo the fact that Ian Smith had publicly announced that majority rule would be implemented in two years. This was a breakthrough. Henry Kissinger, through trickery, browbeating, hard work, and brilliance, had gotten Smith to concede something of substance. "A tour de force . . . one of the most virtuoso solo performances of Dr Kissinger's career," veteran *Guardian* correspondent Peter Jenkins wrote.[167]

Errors and Omissions

To salvage this tour de force, Kissinger pressed the British to chair a conference in Geneva where Smith and the nationalists would hammer out an agreement on the composition of the transitional government. This was the unwelcome development they had long feared: Callaghan's government had no desire to assume direct charge of the Rhodesian problem and no faith in Kissinger's groundwork. In August, the British had foreseen the problem and had tried to prevent it from being "dumped in our laps."[168] This had always been a delusion: Rhodesia was Whitehall's responsibility, and London could not extract itself from Kissinger's initiative no matter how hard it tried. Frank Wisner, who had accompanied Kissinger in Africa, noted, "For all their protestations of wishing to solve the Rhodesian problem, [the British] didn't want to have to face the awful fact of actually carrying through. . . . Furthermore, I suspect Callaghan never fully explained to his government what he had set Kissinger loose to do. . . . Well, the British began hemming and hawing."[169]

Sir Antony Duff, a leading Foreign Office Africa expert, recalled that "the pressure from Dr. Kissinger, on the Prime Minister and on the Foreign Secretary, by telegram and telephone, to 'get on and call the bloody conference' became so intense that the British Government publicly declared their willingness to do so." As the legally responsible party, the British had little choice. They announced that the conference would begin on October 28. London's timing—five days before the US presidential election—infuriated Kissinger, because he feared that his fragile handiwork would collapse the minute the conference opened. "If this blows up the last week of our election it will be a debacle for us," he told Ambassador Ramsbotham. "I won't understand until my dying day why this thing had to be started this week."[170]

The prospect of a constitutional conference galvanized the Frontline presidents because they knew that as long as the nationalists remained divided, Smith would walk all over them in the negotiations. First, they had to quell the struggles within ZANU: on October 5, they announced that they recognized Mugabe as that guerrilla group's leader. Then, in a series of rapid-fire meetings in Lusaka, Maputo, and Dar es Salaam, they applied intense pressure on Nkomo and Mugabe to put aside their differences and present a united team at the upcoming conference. The rift between the two men was deep. Mugabe was an ascetic, a loner, and an intellectual; he had earned multiple degrees in law and economics. Seven years Nkomo's junior, he had joined the nationalist struggle in 1960, three years after Nkomo had been chosen to lead the movement (then called the African National Congress). He had chafed in Nkomo's shadow, critical of the older man's constant foreign travels, bourgeois proclivities, and willingness to negotiate with the white imperialists. Mugabe was more radical; influenced by his study of Marxism, he opposed compromise on basic principles, he sought not just majority rule but also the transformation of Rhodesia into a socialist state, and he believed in revolutionary struggle.[171]

Mugabe had emerged as the secretary-general of ZANU following its split from Nkomo's ZAPU in 1963. By 1976 he had been challenging Nkomo's leadership of the nationalist movement for more than a decade. Throughout this period, the presidents of the Frontline States had pressed ZAPU and ZANU to bury their grievances and work together. These appeals had gained intensity after the brutal civil war in Angola between rival guerrilla groups. Under the pressure of the impending Geneva Conference and the strong-arm tactics of the Frontline leaders, on October 9, Nkomo and Mugabe announced the union of ZAPU and ZANU in the Patriotic Front. At their press conference, Nkomo and Mugabe emphasized armed struggle, announcing they had decided to intensify the war until "the achievement of victory." Smith's intelligence experts brushed off this latest threat. The Patriotic Front, they declared, was just a "marriage of convenience."[172]

Despite Kissinger's objection to the timing, the Geneva conference opened on October 28. The Callaghan government, bruised by Kissinger's tactics and resentful of being left holding the bag, refused to throw its full weight into it. Crosland, who had conveyed what the *Guardian* called "supercilious distaste" toward the idea of a conference, delegated the role of chair to British UN ambassador Ivor Richard, who did not have the clout to knock heads together. In a meeting with one of Kissinger's aides, British Conservative Party leader Margaret Thatcher said of Richard, "gravitas is what he lacks." The Frontline presidents complained that the negotiations "were too important to entrust to a nation which . . . feared to send its ministers out of the country because its majority was not strong enough in parliament."[173]

Kissinger rebuffed British and African entreaties to attend the conference by explaining that only Britain, the colonial power, could grant independence to Rhodesia; he had gotten the ball rolling, but it was up to Whitehall to finish the job. Kissinger had two further unstated reasons for refusing to attend. With the US presidential election so close, no one in the Ford camp wanted a repeat of the Texas primary fiasco, and Kissinger had no desire to spend what could be his final months in office mired in a futile effort to corral Smith and save the British, who were not willing to save themselves. The Americans, therefore, played no official role in the Geneva talks.

Representatives of the British government, the Smith regime, the Patriotic Front, and the internal nationalists who were not part of the Front gathered in Geneva on October 28. Delegations from the Frontline States, the Commonwealth, and the Organization of African Unity attended as official observers. (A South African delegation was active in the wings, and the US State Department sent a liaison officer who did not attend the meetings.) No longer mediated by Kissinger's power and artifice, the participants succumbed to recriminations and vitriol, and the proceedings soon stalled. Many years later, President Kaunda's close aide Mark Chona remarked: "The British didn't have any leadership to actually take over from where Kissinger left. Ambassador Ivor Richard was too weak, and I think Number 10 wasn't organized for success or failure at that time. So it was clear that they didn't have anyone to handle Kissinger's program in 1976. They were not ready for it."[174]

This was true, but the groundwork of the conference was defective. "You've got to give Kissinger credit for bringing Smith to the Rubicon," the US ambassador in South Africa observed, "but he didn't get him to cross it; Smith just got his feet wet."[175] Kissinger had made several important mistakes. First, and most important, he had ignored Africa for too long, against the well-argued recommendations of a succession of assistant secretaries for African affairs. Second, when he finally did pay attention to the continent, he did it in the worst way—again, against his own experts' advice—by masterminding the US covert operation in Angola that had drawn Washington closer to Pretoria. By the time he finally noticed Rhodesia, Africans thoroughly distrusted him and the Cubans were in Angola. It is a measure of his powers of persuasion and of the potency of US power that in the wake of his Lusaka speech, African leaders—President Kaunda foremost—were able to suspend their anger and fear; they dared hope that this most unlikely of heroes might help them. Their hopes and needs were so great, and the power of the United States so preponderant, that Kissinger was not diminished even when he was unable to make good on his promise to repeal the Byrd Amendment, a failure that many had feared would destroy his fledgling credibility in black Africa.

Kissinger's initiative might have worked despite the residue of mistrust had it not been doomed by a fundamental strategic flaw: he had misjudged the balance of power. His plan did not reflect a clear-eyed sense of reality. Kissinger's concentric circles placed Vorster and Smith in the center, ringed by Kaunda and Nyerere, with Machel and the nationalists relegated to the fringes. If Vorster squeezed Smith, and Smith conceded to majority rule, Kissinger surmised, the search for a solution in Rhodesia would move from the battlefield to the bargaining table.[176] This might have worked two years earlier, but by late 1976, the nationalists (as fractured as they were) believed that time was on their side and that they could get the best deal on the battlefield. Smith was important, but the men with whom Kissinger barely communicated—Machel and the nationalists—could not be ignored. They held the keys to the rising guerrilla war, and it was this war—not Smith's old intransigence—that was the new factor driving the crisis in southern Africa.

This was not an obscure point. In March 1976, a National Security Council expert had advised that "in our efforts to counter Soviet and Cuban influence . . . we should consider responding positively and fast to . . . [Mozambique's] request for assistance." In July, UN ambassador Bill Scranton, one of Kissinger's closest confidants, briefed President Ford about the three-week trip he had just completed through southern Africa. "I have one criticism," Scranton told the president. "We are not making enough effort to get Machel. No American leader has met with Machel." Ford drifted to a discussion of Kissinger's meeting with Vorster, but Scranton returned to the point: "The man with most impact is Machel. . . . He is training troops."[177]

If there was a "Sadat" in southern Africa, Kissinger should have looked in Maputo. That was where ZANU was based, and it was ZANU guerrillas who were doing almost all the fighting in Rhodesia. In Mozambique, Kissinger would have found a leader who might have had the power to deliver the "men with guns." However, Kissinger saw Machel through lenses warped by antipathy to Cuba, and faulty US intelligence fueled his fears. "[The] Cubans had established a base camp in the vicinity of Beira, Mozambique," an intelligence report had stated in March 1976. "Cuban combat troops would be arriving . . . shortly." None of this was true. Until the Angola imbroglio in 1975, Mozambique had been far closer to Moscow's enemies in Beijing than to Moscow's friends in Havana. China and Mozambique, however, had backed opposite sides in the Angolan civil war, and in its wake Machel gradually drew his country closer to Moscow. However, ZANU remained firmly in the Chinese—not Soviet—camp, and, even though the tens of thousands of Cubans in Angola had made Kissinger jumpy, there were no Cuban military instructors in Mozambique in 1976.[178]

Similar fears created domestic constraints: the Republicans had blocked sending Mozambique $12.5 million—"chicken feed," in Kissinger's words—and in an election year, it would have been risky, perhaps foolhardy, to have courted Machel.[179]

Another constraint was Machel himself, who was hardened to any initiatives from Washington. On his first trip to Africa in April 1976, Kissinger had sought an invitation to Maputo, but the proud Mozambican president had been spurned for too long. He summarily rebuffed Kissinger, saying that it was "an inopportune time for the Secretary to visit Mozambique." If Kissinger had acted sooner—in 1974, when Don Easum, the assistant secretary for Africa, had advised a friendly gesture toward Machel—then he might have held better cards in 1976. Back in 1974, Machel had eagerly met with Easum, and afterwards, the assistant secretary had testified to Congress: "I came away . . . convinced . . . that Mozambique wants a mutually beneficial relationship with the United States. . . . [The country's new leaders] are hopeful that the US Government will help them meet the economic and financial challenges their new government faces." Kissinger rejected this advice, and in June 1975, Mozambique did not invite any US representatives to its independence ceremonies. US collusion with South Africa in Angola—compounded by Washington's failure to contribute "meaningfully and significantly," in Machel's words, to an aid program—eviscerated any remaining interest Machel might have had in good relations with the Ford administration. The upshot was that Machel was barely a factor in Kissinger's scheme. "Forget about Mozambique," Kissinger told the South Africans.[180]

By 1976, Henry Kissinger was a lame duck in a hurry. He did not have the power to get Congress to repeal the Byrd Amendment, and the learning curve in Africa was too steep even for him. He made mistakes. He did not coordinate effectively with the British, and his sleight of hand, massaging the truth for his different interlocutors, made magic for a few days but soon was exposed and then seemed tawdry. As a South African observer noted, "Kissinger, Vorster, Smith and the black leaders," he said, "are all dancing on cobwebs."[181]

The Final Stretch

"Recently, Ian Smith, the president [*sic*] of Rhodesia, announced that he had unequivocal commitments from Mr. Kissinger that he could not reveal," Jimmy Carter asserted on October 6, when the fragility of Kissinger's handiwork was evident. "The American people don't know what those commitments are."[182] For a month—the month that Kissinger was shuttling around Africa—Carter had kept his promise, made via Dean Rusk, not to make political hay out of Kissinger's initiative.[183] But by October 6, Kissinger was stateside, Smith had spoken, and President Ford, with whom Carter was sharing the stage, had just lauded his secretary of state's latest diplomatic coup. Carter's gentle criticism of Kissinger's Africa policy echoed the theme he had been hammering ever since he penned his 1974 *New York Times* op-ed: he was opposed to secrecy in government. It was an attack on style, not substance, but it was delivered on a huge stage.

It was the second presidential debate, and the stakes were high. Carter had been slipping in the polls, and as he confronted Ford in San Francisco, the two men—once separated by twenty points—were neck and neck. The race was tightening not because of anything Ford was doing right but because Carter's support was softening. In part, this was due to one of the Carter campaign's few serious missteps. Back in the springtime, Jody Powell, the young Georgian who was one of Carter's closest advisers and who handled the press during the campaign, had thought it would be a good idea to allow Robert Scheer, a self-styled radical journalist known as a probing questioner, to conduct a series of interviews with the candidate that would be shaped into a *Playboy* interview. The popular soft-porn magazine's long interviews with famous people were a standard feature, and in the 1970s had already included talks with Walter Cronkite, Treasury Secretary William Simon, California governor Jerry Brown, and Albert Schweitzer. An interview in *Playboy*, Powell figured, might be just the thing to humanize Jimmy Carter.[184]

Scheer met with Carter several times, for a total of more than five hours. The sessions were unremarkable, until the end. It was after the Democratic convention, and Carter was in Plains. Perhaps he was tired, or exasperated with the line of questioning, or alternatively he simply relaxed with this interviewer who had been trailing him for months. (Carter later claimed that he thought his remarks had been off the record, and Powell complained that Scheer had broken his agreement to allow him to review the article before it appeared in print.) Their last session focused on the relationship between Carter's religious beliefs and his political decisions. The hot-button issues were homosexuality and abortion. Carter tried to explain as carefully as he could that his Southern Baptist religion demanded, above all, humility: he himself was far from perfect and he did not judge others. He decided to be specific: "I've looked on a lot of women with lust. I've committed adultery in my heart many times. This is something that God recognizes I will do—and I have done it—and God forgives me for it. But that doesn't mean that I condemn someone who not only looks on a woman with lust but who leaves his wife and shacks up with somebody out of wedlock. Christ says, Don't consider yourself better than someone else because one guy screws a whole bunch of women while the other guy is loyal to his wife."[185]

Decades later, it is tame stuff, and even in 1976 it was not shocking—except that Jimmy Carter had said it, and said it to *Playboy*. To read about Carter "lusting in his heart" and discussing "screwing" in prose that was sandwiched between airbrushed photos of seminaked women simultaneously amused and alarmed the public. It seemed at best inauthentic and at worst desperate. It created a wave of cognitive dissonance: whatever Jimmy Carter was, he was not one of the boys. Or was he? Who was he? Hamilton Jordan summed up the reaction to the *Playboy* interview ruefully: "It increased the weirdo factor."[186]

It accentuated a fundamental weakness of the Carter candidacy: as the voters got to "know" him better, doubts grew. Poll after poll identified an unprecedented number of "undecided" voters, and as Election Day neared Americans found it hard to decide whether to stick with the uninspiring president they knew or take a risk on the weird Georgian. For most Americans, the stakes seemed low. Once Reagan was ousted and Carter's novelty had grown old, what remained was a campaign with no passion.[187]

The debates, however, did generate a spark of interest. It was only the second time in US history that the campaign included televised debates. (The first were the famous Kennedy-Nixon debates of 1960.) More than ninety million Americans tuned in to the first debate, held on September 23 in Philadelphia. Henry Kissinger rendered a succinct verdict: "It was boring," he told his friend Bill Scranton. Indeed, the high point was an audio failure that occurred immediately before Carter began his closing statement. The television cameras cut away to their anchors who engaged in instant analysis, while the audience in the hall, including 200 members of the press, could observe how these two men handled unexpected adversity. It was not reassuring. Ford remained standing, staring ahead blankly, while Carter eventually sat, smiling wanly from time to time. Neither man acknowledged the other or bantered with the audience; they simply fell silent. For a full twenty-seven minutes. When the audio problem was finally rectified, Carter stood up and resumed his closing speech without missing a beat.[188]

Neither candidate delivered a knockout punch, but most television observers (who, unlike the audience in the hall, had been spared the twenty-seven minutes of awkward silence because the networks had cut to punditry) thought that Ford had appeared more relaxed and in charge than Carter, and had won the first debate. After the debate, Carter's lead shrank to eight points. He commented that he had been "awed" by the experience, an explanation that only deepened questions about this man who until then had seemed to be nothing if not self-confident.[189]

Ford, however, was unable to capitalize on any momentum. Instead, he had his own *Playboy* moment. His secretary of agriculture, Earl Butz, when asked why the GOP could not attract more African Americans, was reported to have said, "I'll tell you why you can't attract coloreds. . . . Because colored [*sic*] only want three things. You know what they want? . . . : First, a tight pussy; second, loose shoes; and third, a warm place to shit."[190] Ford, who liked Butz, thought this was just typical Butzian "rough humor," and he did not expect or understand the political firestorm it ignited. (In a comment that makes 1976 seem a long, long time ago, Butz explained, "You know, I don't know how many times I told that joke, and everywhere—political groups, church groups—nobody took offense, and nobody should."[191]) Nor did Ford want to antagonize the farm states, where Butz was popular. The president dallied for four days, while the press hyperventilated, before accepting Butz's resignation on October 4. Ford thought that his reluctance to fire Butz displayed loyalty to a friend,[192] but with only a month to go before the election, many voters saw instead a president who was out of touch with the times and insensitive to racism.

Four days after Butz left the Oval Office with "tears in his eyes," the president and his challenger stood awkwardly side by side in San Francisco. The second debate focused on foreign policy, and the consensus was that it was Ford's to lose. He was, after all, the sitting president, and he ought to best the one-time Georgia governor on this terrain. "Foreign policy and national defense," Ford wrote in his memoirs, "were my forte."[193]

However, the divisiveness of détente within the Republican Party had led the president to shy away from foreign policy during the campaign. Even after Kissinger's coup in Pretoria, delivering Smith's "head on a platter," Ford had continued to keep his secretary of state at arm's length.[194] Although it was customary for the secretary of state to avoid overtly partisan politicking during an election year, Kissinger wanted to give speeches and appear on television talk shows to discuss his initiatives and his view of the world. Instead, Ford's campaign managers—Dick Cheney and Secretary of Defense Donald Rumsfeld—shut Kissinger down. Throughout the year, Kissinger was uncomfortably and uncharacteristically low-profile, and Africa—the administration's foreign policy focus that year and the site of its major, if fragile, success—did not figure in the general election campaign. With the exception of the brief nods to it in the second debate, both candidates ignored the continent.

It drove Kissinger to distraction. He unburdened himself in a series of conversations with National Security Adviser Scowcroft in the waning days of the campaign. "He [Ford] would be so far ahead of him [Carter]," Kissinger commented wistfully, "if he had done things right." By "right," he meant that Ford should have played his strong card: his secretary of state's triumphs. "If he [Ford] wins, it will be due to me. . . . Everybody believes that I am one of the big assets now." Kissinger groused that he had been left out of the campaign: "The number of people who said to me, why weren't you out campaigning?" He was filled with despair and bile. "The election was blown if we lose it. It was eminently winnable. . . . It never occurred to me that he wouldn't use foreign policy in the campaign."[195]

Under the hot lights in San Francisco, with an estimated 100 million viewers, Ford finally tried to explain his administration's foreign policy. Carter, however, came out swinging, and in his opening salvo he articulated his three themes: "leadership, the character of our country, and a vision of the future. In every one of these instances," Carter explained, "the Ford administration has failed." Carter stuck to these three themes no matter what question he was asked. He would be a better leader, he asserted, because he would listen to the American people, he would not keep secrets from them, and he would not be overshadowed by his secretary of state. "As far as foreign policy goes, Mr. Kissinger has been the President of this country," the Democratic candidate alleged, channeling Reagan. Moreover, "Mr. Ford has shown . . . an absence of a grasp of what this country is and what it ought to be." He, Jimmy Carter, would restore the values that had preceded Vietnam and Watergate. Hearkening back to a "precious" golden age that had been "lost," he said, "I want to see our nation return to a posture and an image and a standard to make us proud once again. I remember the world of NATO and the world of Point Four and the world of the Marshall Plan and a world of the Peace Corps. Why can't we have that once again?" Carter also talked tough, calling for "a defense capability second to none," tougher negotiations with the Soviets, a robust defense of Israel, a greater emphasis on nonproliferation, and an end to the United States being "the arms merchant of the whole world." As Leslie Gelb wrote in the *New York Times* the next day, Carter offered "something for everybody."[196]

Ford was wrong-footed from the beginning. He tried to heap scorn on Carter, saying that the challenger was talking in "generalities" and did not know the facts. But Carter showed time and again that he did know the facts. Ford tried to argue that his administration was pursuing a moral foreign policy, emphasizing Kissinger's recent successes in southern Africa. "The United States of America took the initiative in southern Africa," the president declared, stiffly gripping his lectern. "We wanted to end the bloodshed in southern Africa. We wanted to have the right of self-determination in southern Africa. We wanted to have majority rule with the full protection of the rights of the minority. We wanted to preserve human dignity in southern Africa. We have taken initiative [*sic*], and in southern Africa today the United States is trusted by the black Frontline nations and black Africa."[197]

Carter did not cede ground: "We went into South Africa late," he noted. "We didn't go in until right before the election." In case the audience missed it, he reminded them of the ignominious parallel. "[This is] similar to what was taking place in 1972, when Mr. Kissinger announced peace is at hand just before the election at that time."[198]

Then Ford fell into the sinkhole. Anxious to counteract the widespread impression that he and Kissinger had betrayed Eastern Europe by signing the Helsinki Accords (which not only guaranteed human rights but also recognized the borders of Europe established in the wake of World War II), the president declared, "There is no Soviet domination of Eastern Europe, and there never will be under a Ford administration." Asked to clarify, he dug the hole deeper: "I don't believe . . . that the Yugoslavians consider themselves dominated by the Soviet Union." Ford was on a roll. "I don't believe that the Romanians consider themselves dominated by the Soviet Union. I don't believe that the Poles consider themselves dominated by the Soviet Union."[199]

Carter's response was dry: "I would like to see Mr. Ford convince the Polish Americans and the Czech Americans and the Hungarian Americans in this county that those countries don't live under the domination and supervision of the Soviet Union behind the Iron Curtain."[200]

Henry Kissinger watched the debate, he told his friend Ambassador Anne Armstrong, "with mounting horror." Kissinger was dismayed not just at seeing Ford—and his own future—self-destruct, but also by hearing about Carter's foreign policy. The Democrat's "version of human rights . . . gets us involved everywhere without resources," he told Senator Paul Laxalt (R-NV). "I think it will be a national nightmare."[201]

Kissinger's comment about Carter's human rights policy points to an odd fact about Carter's message. From Kissinger's casual comment to the headline in the *New York Times*—"Human Rights and Morality Issue Runs Through Ford-Carter Debate"—people heard Carter stress human rights.[202] But Carter said "human rights" only once during the debate. Two days after the debate, Carter delivered his first and only speech that dealt specifically with human rights. Delivered at the University of Notre Dame, it was a detailed meditation on both the importance and the manifold difficulties of championing human rights.[203] But these ideas were not on display during the debate three days earlier. Instead, in front of the widest possible audience, Carter stressed the themes he had been highlighting for twenty-two months: character, redemption, and strength. He said "strong" or "strength" thirty-nine times. He underlined repeatedly that America's strength was both military and moral. During the debate and in his stump speeches he was careful to stress both military and moral strength, but the press reported the moral part of the equation and ignored the military.

In part this was due to Carter's persona as America's Sunday School teacher; one theme of his campaign was the need for a spiritual cleansing of the American government. Moreover, for the journalists who needed to sell their story, Carter's call during the debate for "a foreign policy to make us proud instead of ashamed" was certainly more marketable than his explanation of the defense budget.[204] Journalists also had to distinguish the positions of the two candidates in order to make sense of the lackluster campaign.

All of these factors reinforced stereotypes or narratives about Carter that had emerged during the campaign and had come to define him.

What was very difficult to distinguish was the two candidates' views of the Cold War, the central foreign policy issue of the day. One of the questions posed at the second debate was: "What is your concept of the national interest? What should the role of the United States in the world be?"[205] Carter answered, predictably, by talking about the restoration of values, the evils of secrecy, and the importance of strength. Ford rebutted Carter's accusations about his administration's reliance on secrecy. Neither candidate addressed the question. Perhaps this showed good political judgment, but it highlighted a fundamental emptiness at the center of the campaign.

Americans faced a very confusing world in 1976. The loss of the war in Vietnam—burned into the nation's psyche just a few months earlier, in April 1975, when US helicopters clambered off the roofs of Saigon leaving loyal Vietnamese allies behind—had repercussions that were only vaguely understood. The president had lost power—because Congress was demanding more oversight and had constrained covert operations, because the US economy was weak, and because there was widespread popular reluctance to send US troops into another war. Furthermore, according to the CIA's own calculation, by 1970 the Soviet Union had attained "strategic parity" with the United States. There were many theories about the impact of parity on deterrence, but no one knew whether deterrence would work in this new world of strategic parity. Nixon and Kissinger finessed the issue, brilliantly, with détente, with their grand talk of a "stable structure of peace." Détente, however, papered over a deeply contradictory stance toward the Soviet Union: while Nixon and Kissinger talked about cooperation with Moscow, the United States maintained almost all its nuclear warheads trained on the Soviet Union. That is, after all the high falutin' talk, containment remained US strategy.

But containment of what? If US strategy was to contain the spread of communism, how could one explain Nixon's opening to China? If US strategy was to contain the expansion of the rival superpower, the Soviet Union, then how could one explain the fundamental premise of détente, that the Soviet Union had become a *status quo* power? Kissinger's rhetoric had managed to divert attention from these fundamental contradictions—until Angola. If détente could not prevent Moscow from intervening in Angola, of all places, could it do anything? Ford responded by banishing the word, hardly a substantive response, whereas Carter said that he accepted the word but focused on his own competence and honesty. The journalist had asked during the second debate, What was the US role in the world? In the waning days of the long, frequently petty, and increasingly acrimonious campaign, neither candidate wanted to answer this fundamental question.

In the third debate, which was "open" as to subject, the two weary candidates rattled through social and economic issues, without drama. It didn't gain us any votes," Kissinger commented in a testy postdebate exchange with Scowcroft. "I didn't want him [Ford] to be strident but I wanted him to be sharp." Scowcroft explained that the president's caution was campaign manager Cheney's doing. "Cheney is afraid that the President will over-speak," Scowcroft said. Kissinger exploded. "Look, I don't give a good god damn—I think this campaign is lost."[206]

"Trust me"

On November 2, 1976, Jimmy Carter sat in another hotel room with his wife Rosalynn, watching another television. After delivering more than 1,500 speeches and racking up half a million miles, the campaign was finally out of his hands.[207] The race had narrowed to a virtual tie in its waning days, and all the polls showed the contest too close to call. "It's a little like trying to measure wind speed in a hurricane," one pollster said. There were more undecided voters than ever before—one in ten voters—and there were nine toss-up states on the eve of the election.[208]

At 3:30 A.M., the returns from Mississippi came in, and Carter knew he had won. He managed to eke out 50.1 percent of the popular vote, edging out Ford by less than 2 percent. (Carter's margin in the Electoral College was a much more comfortable 55.2 percent to Ford's 44.6 percent.) In the end, the undecided voters had tilted toward Carter by a margin of two to one. "They responded," a Georgian journalist wrote, "to no flash of insight into the candidate, but to their own viscera . . . perhaps above all to some empathy, some mysterious communication with the Georgia peanut farmer which said, 'trust me.' . . . Still, Carter goes to Washington a stranger—at least to most Americans. Trust him? They'd *like* to. . . . They *want* to. . . . They *need* to."[209]

At 4:00 A.M., the victor stepped onto the stage at the enormous conference center in Atlanta where the exhausted stalwarts had been waiting for good news. After thanking them for staying so late and praising President Ford as "a good, a decent man," Carter roared, "Are you proud of our nation?" The crowd yelled, "Yes!"[210]

Hours later, Henry Kissinger was on the phone with National Security Adviser Scowcroft, agonizing about the closeness of the election. Kissinger was particularly focused on Ford's narrow loss of Texas by fewer than 130,000 votes. "Do you think they are going to say I lost Texas?" he asked. "Some s.o.b. [might say] . . . without me he [Ford] could have carried Texas."[211] It is possible that Reagan's attacks on Kissinger's Lusaka speech were still ringing in the ears of Republican voters, causing them to stay home or vote for the conservative third-party candidate. What is certain, however, is that the Ford administration's outspoken support for majority rule in Africa during the election year had not helped them with Texas's black voters. Ford polled less than 3 percent of their vote.[212]

Carter got the remaining 97 percent of the black vote in Texas—259,200 votes, almost double his 3 percent margin of victory in the state. As *Time* magazine explained, "Without the overwhelming support for Carter among blacks . . . Gerald Ford would have been elected." Black turnout was higher than white, and blacks throughout the country gave Carter 90 percent of their votes. In thirteen states, the black vote for Carter exceeded his margin of victory. This was not only a win for Carter, but also an exhilarating culmination of decades of struggle for voting rights. As Andrew Young, the civil rights leader and rising black politician who had worked tirelessly for the Carter campaign, said, "Jimmy Carter would not be President today had it not been for some 11,000 voters in the state of Mississippi. People who produced the margin of victory in that state, who were essentially black, poor and share-croppers . . . turned the tide and gave him victory, so that we shouted that the hands that used to pick the cotton had now picked a president." Historian Thomas Borstelmann pointed out a bit more soberly, "The election of a white president from south Georgia with overwhelming black support symbolized the political reintegration of the South with the rest of the nation."[213]

There were multiple explanations of Carter's victory. Carter himself attributed it to the efforts of his family, others pointed to the critical role played by Mayor Rizzo of Philadelphia in tipping Pennsylvania's twenty-seven electoral votes into Carter's hat, others pointed to the get-out-the-vote campaign of organized labor, and many pointed to Ford's errors. There was a consensus, however, that Carter's strong support among African Americans was critical to his success. While Kissinger had been traipsing around Africa, Carter had performed some magic at home. The lead editorial in the *New York Times* declared, simply, that Carter's victory was "one of the most remarkable personal triumphs in the history of American Presidential campaigns."[214] This white southern governor from one of the most racist districts in the country had persuaded African Americans to vote for him while retaining the confidence of white southerners and northern white liberals. It was a most unlikely and fragile coalition.

"Do you think we can help to unify . . . [the nation] and bring it back together again?" Carter asked the crowd at the Atlanta conference center at 4:00 A.M. "Yes!" the people roared. Jimmy Carter responded with deliberation. "I pray that I can live up to your confidence and never disappoint you," he told his cheering supporters, smiling broadly.[215]

3. Southern Africa Matters

Lifting his newborn son up to the starry night, the father uttered his boy's name for the first time: "Kunta Kinte," he announced, "Behold the only thing greater than yourself!" The camera zoomed out until the father and son were enveloped by the wondrous night skies of Africa.[1]

Two hours later, seventy-five million Americans turned off their television sets and started to talk. *Roots* had begun. After a marathon eight days from January 23 through 30, 1977, airing in one- or two-hour segments each night, *Roots* was seen by approximately 130 million Americans—more than half the population of the United States. The final installment broke records: it was, in 1977, the most-watched show of all time. During "*Roots* Week," restaurants and movie theaters reported a drop in business; sports bars switched the channel from football to melodrama; and all America—black and white—was talking about slavery.[2]

No one had expected this twelve-hour saga in which all the heroes were black and all the villains were white to become a cultural phenomenon. ABC broadcast it on consecutive nights to get it over with quickly in case it bombed and before sweeps week began. Never had American prime time television aired a comparable show.[3]

Based on Alex Haley's 1976 novel of his family history, *Roots* tells the story of Kunta Kinte from his youth in Gambia in the mid-eighteenth century through his capture and passage on a slave ship to America, where he is sold to a planter in Virginia. It is the story of slavery from the victims' point of view. *Roots* traces Kunta Kinte's family through four generations, ending with the US Civil War and, finally, freedom. It is easy to criticize the miniseries: it is hackneyed, sugarcoated, and, as its producer admitted, decidedly "middlebrow."[4] Moreover, while Alex Haley labeled it "faction," it turned out to be significantly more fiction than fact.[5] Nevertheless, *Roots* hit a nerve.

The timing was right. Three days before the first episode of *Roots* aired, Jimmy Carter had delivered his inaugural address on the Capitol steps. "This inauguration ceremony marks a new beginning, . . . and a new spirit among us all," President Carter declared. "The world itself is now dominated by a new spirit. . . . The passion for freedom is on the rise. Tapping this new spirit, there can be no nobler nor more ambitious task for America to undertake . . . than to help shape a just and peaceful world that is truly humane." Carter spoke these words earnestly, in his halting, high-pitched Southern drawl. As he and Rosalynn left the safety of their armor-plated limousine to stroll arm in arm down Pennsylvania Avenue toward the White House, there was a palpable, if fragile, sense of hope. Maybe the years of turmoil—assassinations, riots, war, and corruption in the highest places—were finally over. There were multiple levels of healing: Carter began his inaugural address by thanking Gerald Ford for "all he has done to heal our land"; southerners rejoiced that the country had finally elected a president from the Deep South; African Americans were proud that they had tipped the scales toward Jimmy Carter. "While some aspects of the inaugural ritual," the British ambassador in Washington, Peter Ramsbotham, noted, "may have irritated European observers (many of my colleagues were puzzled by the homeliness, moralising and 'neighbourhood' atmosphere of the whole affair), its mystical qualities are not unimportant."[6]

Roots encouraged Americans, white and black, to rethink their history. For twelve hours, slavery was not an abstraction: it was the institutionalized brutalizing of human beings—human beings like Kunta Kinte, whom the audience, of all races, grew to care about and admire. The white audience identified with this black family that triumphed over evil: in the final episode, Kunta Kinte's grandson intones, "Hear me, Kunta. . . . Hear me, old African. . . . You is free at last!"[7] For all its schmaltz and inaccuracies, *Roots* did something remarkable: it constructed a continuous narrative in popular culture out of three previously separate locales: Africa, slave ships, and America. For *Roots*, the middle passage—the horrific Atlantic journey in slave ships—was not a rupture, but the missing link that tied Africa to America. By putting together the pieces of this narrative, Alex Haley was able to find his own roots and inspire many Americans, of all races, to seek theirs. Africa, for Haley, was not an unknowable void. In *Roots*, it became an Eden: for African Americans, it was a Plymouth Rock.[8]

The series earned immediate acclaim and went on to win nine Emmy awards. Africanist Ali Mazrui asserted that its impact was "comparable in scale" to that of *Uncle Tom's Cabin* and the Harlem Renaissance. Vernon Jordan, former president of the National Urban League, called it "the single most spectacular educational experience in race relations in America." The head of the Congressional Black Caucus, Democratic representative Parren Mitchell of Maryland, admitted that he could not bear to watch all of it because it made him "too angry," but he was glad it had been shown. The story "is as much a part of our legacy," he added, "as Andrew Young being sworn in as US Ambassador to the United Nations by [Supreme Court justice] Thurgood Marshall at the White House."[9]

Three Advisers

Andrew Young hesitated when Carter offered him the UN ambassadorship in December 1976. Young's friends in the civil rights movement advised him not to take the job, thinking that he would have more influence staying in the House of Representatives than in corridors of the global talk shop in New York. "Don't do it, Andy," Georgia state senator and civil rights leader Julian Bond cabled.[10] Young himself tried to dissuade Carter: "I told Carter I didn't want to go to the UN because I thought he needed someone in Congress. Because I knew how Congress worked: it works through the gym and the cloakroom, and if you're not a member you can't get in. And there was nobody close to Carter who could get into the gym and the cloakroom."[11]

Raised in a predominantly white area of New Orleans by middle-class parents (his father was a dentist, his mother a teacher), Young had attended Howard University and Hartford Theological Seminary before serving as a pastor for the United Church of Christ in several Georgia and Alabama churches where, in the mid-1950s, he became increasingly involved in helping his parishioners register to vote. He then worked as one of three black executives of the National Council of Churches from 1957 to 1961, the moment of African decolonization. This introduced him to many future leaders not only of the major African American organizations but also of African liberation movements. "I learned to transcend my Southern roots and prejudices and see religion as a global force," Young recalled of his years with the National Council. "This would get me into trouble later, because my view of the world was from the perspective of the Christian mission, putting me into conflict with the Cold War analysis being advocated by our government."[12] In these years, he became familiar with the "international Black Network . . . [the] 'drum,' as Blacks call it" and he grew highly skilled at working within it.[13]

In 1961, Young turned these skills toward the civil rights movement, moving to Atlanta and joining Martin Luther King Jr.'s organization, the Southern Christian Leadership Conference (SCLC). His friendship with King and his organizational skills, particularly in building bridges to the white community, led to his being appointed SCLC executive director in 1964. Young was passionately committed to the civil rights struggle in the United States, but he thought globally. In 1965, he declared at an SCLC meeting, "We must see that our work extends beyond the South and into the North, and when we have completed our work there we must go from New York to London and Paris and from there to Brazzaville and Johannesburg until the rights of man are secure the world over."[14]

Young's life has revealed three core beliefs: in Christianity, in the importance of voting rights, and in promoting change by listening to all points of view. These beliefs enabled him to straddle many worlds and made him an effective member of the House of Representatives. In 1972, when Jimmy Carter was in his second year as governor of Georgia, Young became the first black person elected to Congress from the Deep South since Reconstruction and perhaps the first ever elected from a mostly white district. "He is the outstanding example of the new breed of southern black politicians opting to work within the system rather than against it," the British embassy noted.[15] In Congress, Young went to prayer breakfasts attended largely by conservative Republicans, he was a member of the liberal Congressional Black Caucus, and he served on the banking committee. He advocated the unorthodox—for liberals—view, forged in his days working with King, that business was an important partner in effecting social change.[16] When Young wanted support for a vote, he paid "pastoral calls" on his colleagues. "I used to think of the Congress of 435 members as my church," he explained.[17]

In November 1976, Young won his third term in the House with a 67 percent majority, a significant feat for anyone and particularly for a black man in a white district in the Deep South.[18] There was buzz about his becoming the first black president.[19] He was a superstar. Moreover, the incoming president was in his debt. In early December, Young went to Plains, Georgia, to talk to Carter about a recent trip he had taken to Lesotho, an impoverished kingdom enveloped by apartheid South Africa. The trip had reminded Young of the continent's yawning needs. He had been struck by black Africans' pervasive optimism that the incoming Carter administration would usher in "great changes," and he was aware of the widespread assumption that he spoke for Jimmy Carter.[20]

Carter talked with Young about his plans for US policy toward southern Africa. "I've decided really that the place where your talents could best be used," the president-elect told the young congressman, "would be trying to restore the United Nations to the kind of place that it had in the eyes of the nation when Adlai Stevenson was there."[21] Carter explained that Young's connection with Martin Luther King would "help people take human rights seriously."[22] He said that he was going to carve out a special place for Young as "point man" for southern Africa, and, more generally, for the whole developing world. "I intend to make . . . [you] a member of the Cabinet, a part of the National Security debate, and you'll have my whole-hearted support."[23]

Young was tempted. He had grown to respect Jimmy Carter. "He's one of the best disciplined, most serious, dedicated and intelligent people I've ever met," Young told a journalist after the campaign. Accepting the UN position "was really a religious decision," he told *CBS News*. It was a job that melded Young's interest in civil rights with his global concerns, and it would give him a platform to steer US power toward the resolution of the turmoil in southern Africa. "His [Carter's] goals and objectives were so noble and so lofty," he later explained, "that I couldn't say no."[24]

It was the *Rand Daily Mail*, a moderate white South African newspaper, that explained most succinctly why Young had accepted the position. Its analysis was ethnocentric, but not wide of the mark:

> Andrew Young is America's Ambassador to the United Nations for one reason above all others: he believes the job gives him scope to bring about firmer US action on South Africa. Young starts from the view, intensely held, that America needs moral regeneration in the aftermath of Vietnam and Watergate. He believes, as deeply, that the cornerstone of his nation's regeneration lies on what it does or does not do about apartheid. . . . Through a new approach on this issue stemming from morality, the US can once more find itself and also regain its world image.[25]

A British diplomat who had observed Young's rise in Atlanta explained: "Andrew Young is an embodiment of the Good American. . . . He is an idealist for whom ethical criteria are paramount. On racial issues, he is a symbol of reconciliation and as much as any other living Southerner has been its instrument. . . . He believes in the greatness of . . . the American political system with the same earnest conviction he brings to his belief in racial tolerance, charity and the other Christian virtues. . . . His blackness will clearly be an enormous asset. . . . When he first stands up to speak he will have made the most eloquent speech on America made in the UN before he opens his mouth."[26]

Young came to his new post with no obligations, with enormous optimism, and with the conviction that to be successful—at the UN, in Africa, everywhere—he had to talk with everyone. He was good at it. "He was like a whale feeding: you've got to strain through a lot of stuff hoping you'll come up with something useful," Assistant Secretary of State for African Affairs Richard Moose explained. "He would talk to anybody. They all mattered. . . . Andy reached in and opened up lines of communication." Young was deft at forging coalitions. During his time in the House, he had earned praise from across the political spectrum. "He's the best bridge between various factions," Representative Charlie Wilson, a conservative Democrat from Texas, said. "He's a man of sweet reason."[27]

Young was also a restless activist and a risk taker. Mark Chona, Zambian president Kenneth Kaunda's closest adviser, got to know Young well, and he drew a surprising parallel: "Young in many ways replaced Henry Kissinger in terms of action. Cyrus Vance was a diplomat, very careful, very cautious, whereas Andy Young would be an action man, and I think Carter used . . . them to an extent that was complementary."[28]

In a ceremony held in the East Room of the White House on January 30, 1977—just a few hours before another episode of *Roots* would glue half the American population to their television sets—Andrew Young was sworn in by Supreme Court justice Thurgood Marshall, the man who had led the NAACP's long fight to overturn *Plessy v. Ferguson* and who had helped draft the constitutions of Ghana, Tanzania, and Kenya.[29] Young was forty-four years old. Jimmy Carter said at the ceremony, "His [Young's] status will be equal to that of the Secretary of State. . . . Of all the people I've known in public service, Andy Young is the best."[30]

Cyrus Vance, who would be the secretary of state, was standing at the president's side. Perhaps he sensed trouble already. Before accepting the job, Young had warned both Carter and Vance that he intended to be outspoken: "I'm going to be like a lightning rod. And they said, 'That's what the country needs.'" Young had a clear vision of his role: "I told him [Vance] that, if he did not mind, I would raise controversial points and talk about them. I said to Cy, 'You can refute and modify what I say, but I'd like to be your point man.'" At his confirmation hearings before the Senate Foreign Relations Committee, Young acknowledged that he would probably be at odds with the administration at times. "I fully expect to stub my toe, make mistakes, and, maybe, even be betrayed by the confusion of a tense moment," he predicted.[31]

It was clear that Young's privileged bureaucratic position could pose problems. He was an ambassador and therefore worked for the secretary of state, but unlike every other ambassador in Vance's State Department he held Cabinet rank. Carter explained, "Andy didn't ever feel that he had to go through Cy Vance to get to me, and I didn't either, and I elevated Andy to be a full member of the Cabinet, and he sat there as an equal member to the secretary of state."[32] The assistant secretary for international organizations, Charles Maynes, who in theory was the conduit through whom the UN ambassador should have reported to the secretary of state, recalled with good humor the impossibility of regimenting Young. "It's kind of like trying to rope in an elephant. Yes, you throw the line over his ear and he'll march the way you want, but if he decides he's going another way, you just can't stop him," he explained.[33]

Unlike every previous UN ambassador, Young would have offices and staff not only in New York but also in the State Department building in Washington, on the prestigious seventh floor around the corner from Vance's office. On the directory of the State Department building, Young's name was listed immediately under Vance, above every undersecretary.[34] Young attended not only Cabinet meetings but also National Security Council meetings. He sent his weekly reports not to Vance but directly to Carter. He was not beholden to the State Department: he was not a career foreign service officer, and he looked forward to returning to politics. His protector was not the secretary of state but the president himself. As Carter said, "Andy . . . had unimpeded access to me at any time, which aggravated the hell out of the State Department."[35] Young agreed, "More than I ever knew."[36]

Cyrus Vance was an old-style diplomat: discreet, gracious, careful. He stood in the shadow while the president lauded the incoming UN ambassador. "He was as liberal and as caring as Young, but from a different tradition," Ambassador Donald McHenry noted.[37] Vance had been born to privilege, growing up in Switzerland and the New York suburbs, attending an elite prep school and then Yale University. After serving in the navy during World War II, he became a lawyer and, in the late 1950s, he served as special counsel to the Senate committee that helped establish the National Aeronautics and Space Administration (NASA). For the rest of his life, Vance would alternate work in a New York law firm with periods of government service. In the 1960s, when Young was marching with Martin Luther King, Vance was working in the Pentagon. He was secretary of the army, and when President Lyndon Johnson decided to send US troops to South Vietnam, Vance was deputy secretary of defense. An initial supporter of the war, his doubts grew, but he kept them to himself.[38] He resigned in 1967 and returned to New York to practice law.

It is true that Vance kept a low profile during the Kissinger years, but then Vance always kept a low profile. "Vance was a gentle soul who was perfectly straight," British diplomat Johnny Graham remembered. "He was a stickler for the truth," Donald McHenry, Young's deputy at the UN, recalled. Bill Edmondson, the US ambassador to South Africa, found him "warm and deep thinking." Vance was "a man of modesty, of precision, a man of the deepest honesty, a man of high principle, high liberal principle. . . . He had an instinctive mistrust of the use of force in world affairs," another US diplomat, Frank Wisner, asserted.[39]

It would be difficult to find a foreign policy maven more different in temperament from Henry Kissinger. The German immigrant craved drama and the limelight; the WASP insider shunned both. As Carter had charged during the campaign, Kissinger was a "Lone Ranger"; he amassed power; bravado and bullying were his essential tools. Vance, on the other hand, was a team captain; he delegated power; discretion and dependability were his essential tools.

Despite these differences in style, Vance and Kissinger agreed that the central challenge of US foreign policy in the 1970s was the reduction of tensions with the Soviet Union; for both, arms control agreements were the crux of that endeavor. But while both men agreed about the central issue, they disagreed about the periphery. The lessons that Vance had learned from the quagmire in Vietnam had deepened his depth of field; for him, peripheral countries mattered—and not just when they affected US-Soviet relations. The debacle of Kissinger's foray into Angola confirmed this central lesson that Vance took from Vietnam: viewing Third World countries simply as Cold War pawns was asking for trouble.

At first glance, Cyrus Vance and Jimmy Carter did not seem to have much in common, the former a northeastern urbane lawyer, the latter a southern populist governor. During the 1976 campaign, Vance threw his support to his friend Sargent Shriver, and after Shriver withdrew in March, Vance kept his powder dry. Approached by friends who were supporting Carter, he occasionally sent advice to the campaign, but he kept his distance until the general election was in full swing. In late October, he wrote an exceptionally comprehensive memo—twenty-five single-spaced pages—outlining what he thought Carter's foreign policy priorities and goals should be.[40] In so doing, Vance was serving his country, and he was also applying for a job. It would be a mistake to underestimate Cyrus Vance's ambition.

After the election, Vance was invited to Plains to meet with the president-elect. "He's not who I wanted to be my secretary of state," Carter said uncharitably in 2002, soon after Vance's death, backing up his recollection with reference to his diary entries from 1976. Carter had wanted to choose George Ball, who had been undersecretary of state in the Johnson years and whose dissent to the war in Vietnam was well known. Ball, however, had criticized Israel, and Carter was concerned that his "outspokenness on the Middle East would have made it difficult for him to pass confirmation hearings. So," Carter explained, "I chose Cyrus Vance."[41]

In his presidential memoir, published in 1982, Carter is less harsh. Describing Vance as "cool under pressure, . . . very knowledgeable" and "a natural selection for secretary of state," Carter writes that "among all the members of my official Cabinet, Cy Vance and his wife, Gay, became the closest personal friends to Rosalynn and me."[42] Of course, the qualifiers are significant, but the more important point is that time had not been kind to Carter's feelings about Vance: the wound caused by Vance's resignation in April 1980 had festered rather than healed. In fact, although Carter barely knew Vance when he selected him to be secretary of state, he soon grew to respect him.[43] From very different starting points—Carter from born-again, populist instincts and Vance from long experience and liberal roots—both arrived at a similar conclusion: pursuing a more humane and humble foreign policy would be in the US national interest. Both wanted to avoid deception and ruthlessness in the formulation of foreign policy.

What led Carter to choose Zbigniew Brzezinski as his national security adviser? The Polish-American professor was an excellent teacher and a skilled courtier. He stimulated and flattered Carter. In 1973, Brzezinski had invited Governor Carter, whom he had not yet met, to join the Trilateral Commission, an elite network of "movers and shakers" from the United States, Western Europe, and Japan that promoted greater cooperation between these three centers of capitalist power. Brzezinski, the founding director of the commission, expected that Carter could represent the rising, progressive US South on the commission. Brzezinski did not know that the governor was already eying the White House.[44] However, when Carter announced his bid for the presidency in December 1974, Brzezinski reacted quickly. He made himself useful: he sent the candidate background material, and he drafted speeches. By the time the first primaries were held, in early 1976, Zbigniew Brzezinski was known to be Carter's top foreign policy adviser.[45]

"My career is in part the product of very deliberate determination," Brzezinski has said, but his path to the White House was unusual. Brzezinski's roots, and in many ways his heart, were in Poland. The son of a diplomat who was a fervent Polish nationalist, Brzezinski remembers, "I was a very patriotic child . . . I was enormously proud of the Polish Army, I enjoyed watching it parade down the streets of Warsaw."[46] He was also imbued with a sense of European history; he had witnessed the rise of Hitler in the early 1930s in Leipzig, and had returned to Warsaw when his father was posted to Kharkov in Soviet Ukraine. Joseph Stalin's purges had made Ukraine too dangerous a place for the family to live, and Zbigniew heard about the terror at his father's knee. "My father told me stories . . . about the mass disappearances. . . . This had an enormous impression on me at a very young age."[47]

In 1938, the Brzezinskis set sail for Canada, where Zbigniew's father would be consul general. In an old photograph, the family looks happy—the elegant parents, the four boys, the governess, the housekeeper, and the German shepherd on the deck of the luxury liner.[48] Zbigniew was ten years old, and he spoke no English. Within months of settling in Montreal, the Brzezinskis' world began to crumble: in the opening salvos of World War II, first the

Nazis and then the Soviets invaded Poland. At war's end, the seventeen-year-old Brzezinski could not celebrate: "I remember above all feeling sad in the midst of all this euphoria. I knew that Poland was loosing [*sic*] her freedom."[49] Brzezinski blamed not only the Soviets, who had perpetrated atrocities and installed a communist government, but also the Western powers that had allowed it to happen.[50]

Chance took Brzezinski to Harvard at age twenty-three: he had hoped to study in England before joining the Canadian foreign service, but because he was still a Polish citizen he was ineligible for a British fellowship. Therefore, he headed south to study, unsurprisingly, the Soviet Union. In three years he earned his PhD, and in five more he became a US citizen. When he moved from Harvard to Columbia University, Brzezinski developed ties with the New York–based Council on Foreign Relations. He began to move in and out of government, advising the Kennedy campaign in 1960 and the Johnson campaign in 1964. During the Johnson years, when Vance was deputy secretary of defense, Brzezinski served on the State Department's Policy Planning Staff, and in 1968 he advised Hubert Humphrey's campaign.[51] By 1970, he focused more on policymaking than on academia.

Brzezinski was attracted to American politics for two reasons: he enjoyed what he called "the game"[52] and he wanted to help the West defeat the Soviet Union. "I felt that America had the greater capacity for influencing world affairs for the good, and thus helping to fashion a more just international system that would therefore also help Poland," he explained.[53]

Brzezinski's analysis of global politics evolved over several decades, and it continued to change over the course of the Carter years, but it revolved around two themes.[54] First, he never shed his contempt for the Soviet Union. A fundamental difference between Washington and Moscow was that the former, with its pluralistic system, could adapt to change, whereas the latter would never change; the Kremlin was irredeemably totalitarian. (Like most academics, Brzezinski stopped using the word "totalitarian" in the 1970s, but the concept remained central to his view of the Soviet Union.[55]) Unlike many Sovietologists in the era of détente, Brzezinski did not believe that a more accommodating US policy would induce liberalization in Moscow, because from his perspective liberalization was impossible. Second, Brzezinski had a strong sense of the fragility of international order; he was acutely aware of the ever-present perils of chaos. This led him to stress the need for the United States to forge networks of cooperation, particularly among developed states. These two principles led Brzezinski to have a complex worldview: the US-Soviet contest was central, but Washington faced other important challenges, particularly adjusting to change and warding off chaos.[56]

Brzezinski was less skeptical about the usefulness of military power than Carter or Vance was. He had been a strong adherent of Johnson's escalation of the war in Vietnam, and despite his assertion in 2012 that his enthusiasm for the war had waned in 1968, his articles published during the Nixon years expressed only the mildest criticism of the war effort. In regretful tones, he noted that the war had fractured the foreign policy consensus at home, distracted the administration, and "weakened the US international position." As a result, "the initiative . . . passed to the Soviet side."[57] He praised Nixon's highly controversial invasion of Cambodia, and in articles written in 1971 and 1974 he gave the Nixon administration a "B" for its Vietnam War policy.[58]

Brzezinski's keynote was that it was dangerous to allow the Kremlin to sense any lack of resolve in Washington. More than any other principal in the Carter foreign policy establishment, Brzezinski argued that it was important to show the Soviets that they could not "get away" with anything. This meant that Brzezinski frequently was the combative voice within the administration.

It would be a mistake, however, to depict Brzezinski one-dimensionally. Although the struggle against the Soviet Union was visceral for him, it was not—in his worldview—the only challenge facing the United States. In this, he differed markedly from his predecessor, Henry Kissinger, who traced all significant threats back to the Kremlin. Brzezinski thought there were problems, such as the gap between the rich and poor nations, that were extremely important and not directly related to the core Cold War struggle. In 1975, in the early days of the presidential campaign, Brzezinski wrote:

> The central question which confronts the United States—and which calls for a new foreign policy—is this: in what way can we cooperate effectively with other countries in a world that is now composed of some 150 sovereign states and that is experiencing in many areas a continuing social and political revolution? . . . The conflict today . . . is increasingly between the First World (notably the United States) and . . . the Third World of the *nouveaux riches* and the Fourth World of the international basket cases. . . . [We must pursue] a policy of "cooperative activism" as an alternative to a posture of confrontation with two-thirds of mankind.[59]

Brzezinski, therefore, combined intensely conservative with progressive tendencies. Toward the Soviet Union, he was a hard-liner, as he believed it to be ossified, degenerate, incapable of change—and a formidable enemy. In this, he resembled the emerging neoconservatives and was more conservative than Kissinger.[60] However, Brzezinski's view of the Kremlin was tempered by his sensitivity to the fact that the Soviet Union was a patchwork of more or less disgruntled nationalities; this led him to believe that an overly aggressive approach to Moscow would be counterproductive because it might unite these disparate parts against a common enemy, the United States. On global politics, by contrast, Brzezinski was a liberal, arguing that the United States had to come to terms with the "social and political revolution" bubbling up from the poor and the powerless and believing, with buoyant optimism, that it could.[61] This was a dramatic change from Kissinger's dour fatalism.

On one issue, however, Brzezinski and Kissinger were in agreement: the US political system complicated their task. The influence of ill-informed public opinion and the attempts of Congress to tie the president's hands made it difficult to maintain an astute foreign policy. Long after Brzezinski had left the White House, he vented his frustration. "Most Americans are close to total ignorance about the world. They are ignorant," he exclaimed to a reporter from the German weekly *Der Spiegel*. "That is an unhealthy condition in a country in which foreign policy has to be endorsed by the people if it is to be pursued. And it makes it much more difficult for any president to pursue an intelligent policy that does justice to the complexity of the world."[62] Both Brzezinski and Kissinger were profoundly annoyed by the influence of public opinion on the execution of foreign policy, but they handled it in different ways. Kissinger went underground, relying to an ever-greater extent on secrecy to implement his plans; Brzezinski did not shun secrecy, but by late 1977 he began to urge and prod Carter to appease the public appetite for shows of strength. Although both Kissinger and Brzezinski assiduously burnished the egos of the presidents they served, they otherwise amassed power in different ways: Kissinger relied on the strength of his personality: he dazzled and bullied; he was like a fighter who throws heavy punches. Brzezinski relied on his quickness: he listened attentively and was fast to shift gears; he was like a fighter who dances while he jabs.

Zbigniew Brzezinski was ambitious, charming, and curious. The people who worked on his NSC staff speak of his exacting standards, courtesy, and fairness. "I had a lot of differences with Zbig," his deputy, David Aaron, recollected, "but he was a terrific boss to work with. He was open to discussion. Totally different from Kissinger. He was not manipulative." Ambassador Steve Low, one of the chief negotiators on Rhodesia who later was head of the Foreign Service Institute, said that "Zbig is the most articulate man I've ever known." Robert Pastor, the NSC Latin America expert, stressed Brzezinski's skills as a manager, his collegiality, and his openness to new ideas.[63] Brzezinski considered himself a "conceptualizer" and was proud of it: he focused on patterns and trends. It would be difficult to find a starker contrast to Vance's lawyerly attention to detail.

Carter wanted what Brzezinski gave him: ideas. He wanted to be bombarded with choices, with alternative explanations and solutions to problems. He trusted his ability to sort through them. He wanted to be presented with the full gamut of possibilities—in a succinct style. "There would be no waste of time," Brzezinski explained. "I'd get in the car and say, 'Look, four things you need to know, the things you need to do, the things you need to say,'—like that, bang, bang, bang." Carter wanted to be intellectually challenged. Thus he was perennially disappointed with the recommendations of the State Department, conveyed in nuanced and balanced memos that had been hammered out by committee. Jimmy Carter preferred a scattershot of ideas, even if some were harebrained. Remembering how valuable Brzezinski had been, Carter explained, "His mind was always functioning in the most brilliant fashion. You know, maybe he'd have ten ideas. Maybe two. . . . I could see some of Zbig's prejudices . . . but he always kept me thinking. Brzezinski," the president paused and leaned forward, "was my treasure."[64]

Plans

The president would be the decider: his advisers would offer their opinions, the more diverse the better. In the Carter White House, there would be no more "Lone Ranger" diplomacy—policy would be set by the president. Nor would there be a filter between Carter and these advisers. Watergate had shown how dangerous it was for the president to be cut off from the world by an "imperial guard," so Carter would not appoint a chief of staff: his door would be open. After receiving advice from diverse viewpoints, Jimmy Carter—former naval lieutenant—would set the course of the ship of state. This would be a welcome change from Nixon's self-imposed isolation and Kissinger's upstaging of Ford, and it suited the new president's temperament: Jimmy Carter liked to be in charge. "I really prefer to be the spokesman for the nation in the area of foreign affairs," Carter told the *New York Times* during the campaign. One of the men who had worked with him in Georgia explained: "[Carter] is a glutton for work. . . . Carter hates meetings: he regards them as a waste of time. . . . But he seeks advice, however conflicting, from all quarters. . . . He then frequently disregards [it]." Richard Holbrooke, the newly appointed assistant secretary of state for East Asia, said: "He's his own Secretary of State. . . . He's at home with it, he loves it."[65]

During the campaign, Carter's right-hand man Hamilton Jordan had told *Playboy*, in a piece accompanying the infamous interview with Carter, "If, after the inauguration, you find a Cy Vance as secretary of state and Zbigniew Brzezinski as head of national security, then I would say we failed. And I'd quit. But that's not going to happen. You're going to see new faces, new ideas. The government is going to be run by people you have never heard of."[66] After Carter won the election, however, reality set in quickly: the fact that an outsider had been elected was novelty enough; now was the time for reassurance. The British Foreign Office noted during the transition, "We know less about President-elect Carter and his future intentions than has been the case with any other recent incoming President."[67] Vance and Brzezinski were well-known establishment figures; appointing them sent a signal that Carter's foreign policy would not veer far from the mainstream, but it did not answer all the questions. Carter's appointments lacked "any clear philosophical complexion," a British diplomat cabled London. "Question marks remain, therefore, over the political flavour of the Carter administration."[68]

In those busy November and December days during the transition, when the country's power base shifted to Plains, Georgia, harmony and anticipation prevailed. "There was an unmistakable atmosphere of excitement," a British diplomat wrote after calling on the transition team, "with no outward hint yet of the frustrations which must inevitably lie ahead."[69] The ideas that the victors talked about, in those heady days when everything was possible, were not new, but they did represent a shift from the Kissinger years. While the core US strategy remained détente with the Soviet Union and the attendant pursuit of a comprehensive arms control treaty with it (SALT II), the incoming administration paid more attention than had previous Cold War presidents to other important regional and transnational concerns. Brzezinski called the strategy "constructive global engagement" and envisioned using US power to bring order to the chaotic world.[70] Vance was a bit more modest. Hoping to bring a new realism and decency to the management of East-West and North-South relations, he identified six areas where he thought progress could be made: the Middle East, SALT, China, Panama, East Asia, and southern Africa.[71]

Both men advised the incoming president to fire on all cylinders: pursue SALT *and* peace in the Middle East *and* the completion of the Panama Canal treaties *and* much, much more.[72] This ambition reflected the pent-up energy of a party that had been out of power for eight years (and waylaid by Vietnam before that), as well as the self-confidence of victors, but it was also an inevitable consequence of broadening US strategy beyond a myopic preoccupation with Soviet relations. Once the depth of field deepened, a plethora of regional concerns vied for Washington's attention. The incoming administration would have to prioritize these clamoring demands.

Yet determining these priorities would not be straightforward. Carter's campaign statements gave little guidance. Beyond continuing SALT and reducing arms sales, the new president's foreign priorities were not clear. He had talked repeatedly about pursuing a foreign policy consistent with American values, and he had indicated a number of goals—peace in the Middle East; pulling US troops from South Korea; normalizing relations with Angola, China, Cuba, and Vietnam; and seeking justice in southern Africa—but he had not revealed how or with what speed he would pursue them.

Moreover, in January 1977, there was no consensus among Americans about the country's most pressing foreign concerns. The confusions of détente had not been resolved: the rising neoconservatives argued with increasing ardor that Washington was underestimating the Soviet threat, while liberals countered that overestimating the Soviet threat had led policymakers to pursue counterproductive policies in Vietnam and Angola. This divide was expressed on January 17, when a coalition of congressional Republicans and southern Democrats torpedoed president-elect Carter's attempt to nominate Ted Sorensen, a liberal who had advised John Kennedy, as head of the CIA. (Members of Congress objected to Sorensen for various reasons, such as his registering for the draft as a conscientious objector; admitting to using classified documents when writing his book, *Kennedy*; and writing an affidavit in defense of the leaking of the Pentagon Papers.)[73] In the weeks before the inauguration, the Sorensen nomination and commentary on Carter's early appointments crowded the front pages. There was a dearth of foreign stories. In the first three weeks of January, page one of the *New York Times*, for example, carried one or two articles each on Israel, Puerto Rico, terrorism in West Europe, Panama, and Soviet dissidents; Rhodesia had the most coverage with three stories. When Carter took office, it was not obvious what challenge he would tackle first.

The new administration began the task of setting priorities at a January 5 meeting of the group that would become the shapers of foreign policy. The president-elect was in the chair, and Brzezinski, Vance, and Young attended. The men who were about to assume the reins of power identified fifteen concerns that demanded immediate attention and required comprehensive interagency reviews called Presidential Review Memoranda (PRMs). Of these fifteen, six addressed core defense concerns (SALT, conventional forces in Europe, defense posture, intelligence, nuclear proliferation, and Europe), whereas nine dealt largely with the periphery (Panama, Middle East, southern Africa, Cyprus, global economy, North/South, arms sales, Korea, Philippines). This list suggests a real broadening of interests—US-Soviet relations remained the heart, but the periphery had come into sharper focus. The PRM on southern Africa was deemed urgent and would be due eleven days after the inauguration.[74]

Henry Kissinger had devoted much of his final year to seeking peace in Rhodesia, but as the Carter team assembled it was unclear whether his efforts had borne fruit. In September 1976, Kissinger had almost cornered Ian Smith, who publicly accepted the principle of majority rule. Then, with the US presidential elections looming, he had tossed Rhodesia back to the British. In late October, London—distrustful of Smith and resentful of Kissinger—had convened the Geneva conference with little enthusiasm. At Geneva, the British hoped that Ian Smith, the Rhodesian nationalists—both internal (without armies) and external (the new alliance of ZAPU and ZANU known as the Patriotic Front)—and the Frontline States would negotiate the details of the transfer of power to an independent, majority-ruled Zimbabwe. However, the talks quickly descended into acrimonious and futile bickering. No progress was made, and on December 14, 1976, Ivor Richard, the British ambassador in charge, decided that all parties needed time to cool off. He adjourned the conference, but expected it to resume in the new year.

On January 18, two days before Carter became president, Vance had a long meeting with Mark Chona, Zambian president Kaunda's top aide. Chona spoke bluntly and urgently about the crisis in Rhodesia. "We are facing a real war situation. Not a local war, but a war with growing international dimensions of an increasingly serious nature." He urged Vance to put the full weight of the United States into the struggle. "The British have not been clear. . . . The nationalists are suspicious of British tactics. . . . Smith needs to be told that the game is up. . . . My President [Kaunda] relies on your commitment." Chona stressed that more than the future of Rhodesia was at stake. "If Zimbabwe and Namibia were independent, change would have to take place in South Africa without a shot ever having been fired." This was why it was so important that Washington voice early, firm commitment to resolving the Rhodesia crisis. "We have pitched our expectations very high, and we believe that the conditions for a settlement have never been better. . . . Under US management and under a new Administration committed to the protection of human rights, there has never been a coincidence of events more favorable than the present."[75]

On the following day, Henry Kissinger gave a valedictory interview to the *New York Times*, summing up the accomplishments of the past eight years and predicting the challenges ahead. Reminiscing about the high points, he mentioned the opening to China and the signing of the first SALT accord in 1972, and his recent experiences in Africa. "I was terribly moved when President Kaunda got up at the end of my Lusaka speech and embraced me." Among his regrets were not completing the SALT II negotiations, failing to answer the challenge posed by the Organization of Petroleum Exporting Countries (OPEC), and not moving faster on southern Africa. He emphasized that the end of the war in Vietnam meant that the United States could focus its attention on other pressing issues, especially those in the Third World. Hazarding a guess about the future, he opined that progress could be made on SALT, the

Middle East peace negotiations, the Panama Canal treaties, and Rhodesia. "It [Rhodesia] will be a murderously difficult, complicated effort," he added. "All I am saying is that conditions exist for a heroic effort." When the interviewer asked why his Rhodesian initiative had "fizzled," Kissinger objected that it had merely "stalled" while the Africans sized up the new administration in Washington. "I don't see any overwhelming crises in 1977," he mused, "unless things in Africa get totally out of control."[76]

Africa Rising

For the incoming administration, southern African was important for several reasons. First, the Cold War: some 30,000 Cuban troops still remained in Angola, where they bolstered a pro-Soviet government that advocated liberation throughout southern Africa. The Cuban troops might enter Rhodesia unless the Smith regime and the nationalists could reach a settlement quickly. Ever since the Cubans had landed in Luanda, Africa had been the hottest theater of the Cold War. The CIA noted, as Carter took office, "Southern Africa has emerged as a world issue. . . . The struggle in southern Africa is not just to determine that region's destiny; it has also become an important element in the overall relationship between East and West."[77] Second, oil: Carter's first domestic priority as president was to develop an energy policy; maintaining the flow of Nigerian crude—a quarter of all US oil imports—was crucial.[78] Most Africa watchers in 1977 believed that the continent was on the upswing: its economic power, based on oil revenues and minerals, was increasing. Third, the UN, where the "Africa Group" comprised almost a third of the General Assembly and formed a powerful voting bloc. Fourth, human rights: Carter's campaign rhetoric had led many to believe he would take a tougher stand against the racist white regimes in South Africa and Rhodesia. During the transition, Carter had told the South African weekly, *The Financial Mail*, that he intended to pursue "an aggressive policy for peace" in southern Africa. American grassroots organizations and black Africans were optimistic; Pretoria and Salisbury were apprehensive. Finally, politics: Carter owed his election to the African American vote.[79]

For the Carter team, there was also a strong emotional reason to focus on southern Africa: to many members of the new administration, it appeared to be a place where the United States could do something *good*, where America could pursue a policy that corresponded to its best ideals. In southern Africa, the Carter administration—led by the first president from the Deep South— could spread the lessons learned in the searing civil rights struggles of the 1950s and 1960s. The new team leaped on the issue with gusto because it offered an opportunity to seize the torch that John F. Kennedy had passed to a new generation, to *their* generation, in his inaugural address sixteen years earlier. "To those peoples in the huts and villages of half the globe struggling to break the bonds of mass misery," Kennedy had said with his voice rising, "we pledge our best efforts to help them help themselves . . . not because we seek their votes, but because it is right."[80] Kennedy's promise to "bear any burden," however, had led not to the spread of liberty worldwide, but instead to the deaths of almost 60,000 Americans and more than four million Vietnamese, Cambodians, and Laotians. For many members of the Carter administration, trying to spread racial justice in southern Africa offered an opportunity to put Kennedy's mission back on track, to return to a more pure, more idealistic—more American—time.[81] Moreover, Carter himself had his eye on Africa. It was indicative of this that on the day after Young was sworn into office as ambassador to the UN, Carter dispatched him to the continent.

No one in the new administration underestimated the difficulties they would face. The fact that they had to construct their policy on the wreckage of Kissinger's heightened the challenge. An adviser to the Carter campaign explained that Kissinger had sharply reduced the next administration's options "through secret dealings and actions. . . . No new administration will be able to directly disavow the moves Kissinger makes. . . . It will rather have to pick up from there."[82] In October 1976, just before the British convened the Geneva conference, Vance sent Carter a memo noting that the "Kissinger proposal [for Rhodesia] is fraught with pitfalls."[83] In November, Carter's key advisers during the transition warned him that "while Kissinger's strategy is couched in terms of support for majority rule, there is considerable suspicion that his main objective is to buy time for South Africa."[84] In December, as the Geneva conference stalled, the South Africans had urged Kissinger himself to go to Switzerland in a last-ditch effort to reinvigorate the talks, but the lame-duck secretary had demurred. Instead, he cynically advised the South Africans to encourage Smith to remain at the conference "at least for a few weeks" after Carter assumed the presidency. "If the talks then fail," the South Africans reported, "Kissinger will at that stage be willing to state in public that there had been a reasonable chance of success but that the Carter administration had caused the peace effort to miscarry."[85]

Three days before the president entered the White House, the State Department reported that the process Kissinger had set in motion had ground to "a virtual impasse." Kissinger's wheeling and dealing had bruised black African sensibilities and steeled Smith's determination to not concede one inch more. The war in Rhodesia had escalated in late 1976, with Smith's troops launching a series of devastating raids on seven suspected guerrilla camps in

Mozambique; reports were that 1,000 people, many of them women and children, had been killed.[86] Pretoria, despairing of a positive outcome at Geneva, had resumed its support of the Rhodesian military. "The odds are heavily against a negotiated settlement," Kissinger's State Department noted.[87] One week later—four days after the Carter administration took over—the Geneva conference came crashing down.

The Southern Africa Policy Review

On January 24, 1977, Ian Smith stared steadily into the television camera. A lanky man with a jutting chin, Smith sighed as though he bore the weight of the world on his shoulders. In a way, he did: the survival of his world—the world of white minority rule and colonial privilege in a sea of black Africans—depended on his own ability to outwit the historical forces closing in on Rhodesia. He had stopped time for over a decade. Could he halt it for a while longer?

Four months earlier, he had stared at the same cameras and announced that because Kissinger had made it "abundantly clear" that the white government in Salisbury "could expect no help or support of any kind from the free world," his Cabinet had reluctantly decided to accept the Anglo-American proposals for majority rule in two years.[88] Therefore, Smith had agreed to go to Geneva.

The conference in Geneva had moved Rhodesia no closer to independence, but it had provided a forum where the nationalists of the Patriotic Front (the makeshift alliance of Nkomo's ZAPU and Mugabe's ZANU) had been able to find a collective voice. The presidents of the Frontline States, worried in the short term about mustering leverage against Smith and in the long term about avoiding an Angola-like civil war in Rhodesia, were eager to reward the Patriotic Front for maintaining unity through the difficult sessions at Geneva. On January 9, 1977, they had met in Lusaka and announced that they saw the Front as the only legitimate voice of the Zimbabwe people, and gave it their unreserved backing.[89]

The Rhodesian armed forces, meanwhile, had been sobered by Kissinger's blunt statement that the United States would never come to the rescue of the white Rhodesians. Ken Flower, the head of Rhodesia's Central Intelligence Organisation, has asserted that from that point forward he knew that the war could not be won militarily. On January 12, he gave Smith's Cabinet "the bleakest picture they've ever had," and two days later he informed the War Council that "the security forces would be unable to hold this position indefinitely."[90]

This was the backdrop to Smith's speech to his nation on January 24. The Rhodesian leader had decided to end what he called "the whole sordid affair" of the negotiations with the Patriotic Front, Frontline States, British, and

Americans about the future of Rhodesia.[91] He spied a better opportunity, one he could more easily control. The formation of the Patriotic Front had elevated ZAPU's Joshua Nkomo and ZANU's Robert Mugabe and left the other blacks who were vying with them for leadership of the nationalist movement—those residing in Rhodesia and not commanding any troops—out in the cold. This is why Ambassador Ivor Richard considered the Frontline leaders' decision to recognize the Patriotic Front as the legitimate representative of the Zimbabwean people "extremely foolish" and a sign of their "growing unreasonableness."[92] Smith, by contrast, welcomed the decision: he hoped to strike a deal with the marginalized would-be black leaders, bringing them into the white government, thereby appeasing his critics while maintaining white privilege.

The Rhodesian leader stared into the blinding television lights and tried once again to reassure his people—Rhodesian whites—about their future, despite the broadening war and their country's deepening isolation. Smith struck his familiar belligerent, dour tone. "After all our efforts and sacrifices which have been made, there can be no question of surrender. If we were to give way now, it would not be to majority rule; it would be to a Marxist-indoctrinated minority." Rather than prolong this humiliating exercise with the British and Americans, Smith would seek an internal settlement. "Instead of looking over our shoulders for outside assistance . . . I have issued invitations to the black leader [*sic*] to join me." Smith hastened to add that he meant those internal leaders who commanded no troops and who had been excluded from the Patriotic Front. "Let me make it clear that I exclude from this exercise anyone who supports terrorism."[93]

When Smith made his announcement, it was early afternoon in Washington, DC, and it was Cyrus Vance's first official day in his office on the elegant seventh floor of the State Department. That night, as the second installment of *Roots* aired, Vance sent the president the first of what would grow to be almost one thousand "Evening Reports." The day's events in Rhodesia figured prominently. "We have urged the British," Vance informed the president, "to move prudently and not change course until we have had a chance to consult."[94] In the margin, Carter wrote, "What to do?"[95]

The next morning, January 25, the news about Rhodesia was plastered all over the front page of the *New York Times*, which quoted British foreign secretary Anthony Crosland warning of the "calamitous consequences" of Smith's decision.[96] A cable to Vance from the US ambassador in London, Anne Armstrong, noted, "Not surprisingly, Britain's major newspapers January 25 carried extensive comment on the apparent collapse of the Richard mission to southern Africa." In England, the *Guardian* observed that the future of Rhodesia "looks, once again, disastrous," while the *Times* was more dramatic: "Smith . . . must know that a mighty cry will now go up in the African world and in the United Nations for an all-out jihad to destroy white Rhodesia. . . . It is difficult to avoid the conclusion that . . . [Smith] has once again come out the victor."[97]

Indeed, Smith, like Harry Houdini, seemed to have eluded inescapable bonds. He had been an affront to Whitehall for twelve years; with Kissinger's insertion of US prestige into the equation, Smith was now also taunting the United States. "Suddenly," the *Washington Post* wrote that morning, "the makings of a major crisis have been dumped into the new administration's lap." The *New York Times* editorialized that Smith's announcement meant that the United States was "the last hope . . . to avoid a vicious racial conflict whose poison would quickly spread to our own multiracial society. . . . It was a devilishly difficult game." Smith's "somersault," as one British diplomat deemed it, shattered the fragile hope of a negotiated settlement to the Rhodesian crisis. With Smith out of the negotiations, a widening war seemed unavoidable.[98]

Cyrus Vance wasted no time. His first official meeting as secretary of state was with the department's Africa specialists, and at 5:00 P.M. on his second day, he ushered the South African ambassador to the United States, Pik Botha, into his office. The two men got right down to business. "The news yesterday [of Smith's rejection of the British proposals] took us by complete surprise," Botha asserted. He blamed the breakdown of the Geneva conference squarely on African "back-sliding" and on Kissinger's lack of clarity. The memorandum of the conversation indicates that Vance listened, without interrupting, to a five-page single-spaced harangue. The South Africans, Botha insisted, had acted "in good faith" throughout the negotiations, but the "Prime Minister [John Vorster] feels that the rug has been pulled out from under him. . . . I must say we feel left in the lurch by the United States." When Vance finally got a word in, he was uncompromising: an "internal solution" in Rhodesia was "not realistic . . . and the United States will give it no support." Washington supported negotiations, and if Smith were not more flexible "he will face nothing short of stiff American opposition." Until Smith moved toward majority rule, "Rhodesia cannot count on American interest or sympathy." The Carter administration would move immediately to repeal the Byrd Amendment and tighten sanctions on Rhodesia.[99]

"Could I ask a question?" Botha inquired. "Yes," Vance replied curtly. Botha asked if the Carter administration would repeal the Byrd Amendment even if Smith showed flexibility. "Yes," was the reply. All Botha could say was "I appreciate the time you have given me," and the meeting was over.[100]

Three days later, the South African ambassador was at the White House, in the office of National Security Adviser Brzezinski. Botha stuck to his script: Pretoria had acted in good faith and had been let down by the British and

Americans. The contrasts, and the similarities, between Vance's and Brzezinski's responses to Botha's spiel are revealing. Fundamentally, the two men were on the same page—both told Botha that the Carter administration considered the aspirations of southern African blacks "legitimate," and both emphasized that Ian Smith could not expect the United States to rescue his regime even if it were threatened by communists. The two meetings differed, however, in tone. Brzezinski jollied and mollified Botha. He began by recalling how, as a boy in Poland, he had reenacted the Boer War many times with his toy soldiers and he had always sided with the Boers. Throughout the encounter, Brzezinski framed the conflict in southern Africa in the broadest possible terms: the problem was that change had been resisted too long. The choice was between—this was Brzezinski's favorite leitmotif—chaos or cooperation.[101]

Botha reported the bad news to Smith. "The poison of the unresolved Rhodesian problem," he explained, was affecting South Africa's relations with the United States. Secretary Vance, Botha said, was "cold and calculating. . . . Ford and Kissinger would be seen as angels compared to Carter."[102]

Vance had a problem. He and, more significantly, the president did not want to let the Rhodesia problem fester, but Smith's announcement meant that the Anglo-American policy in Rhodesia was suddenly in shambles, and it was not obvious what policy could replace it.

"I think this [Rhodesia] is going to be one of the early problems on your table, Mr. President," British prime minister James Callaghan had warned Carter during their first, brief telephone call. "I am not a 'reds under the bed' man," he continued. "In other words I don't look for Soviet influence everywhere, but there is no doubt that in Southern Africa, if we can't ensure a peaceful transition to power, then those people will eventually come to power by force, who will look to the Soviet Union in the future. And this I think is the stake for which we are playing quite apart from the merits, the morality of the issue." Carter replied that he understood and wanted to work "in harmony" with Britain.[103]

Smith's announcement accelerated this search for harmony. Vance urgently consulted the British. Bilateral talks about southern Africa were immediately undertaken at a variety of levels—Carter met with the British ambassador; Vice President Walter Mondale met with leaders in London, Bonn, Brussels, Paris, and Tokyo, and at all stops he discussed the new administration's goals in southern Africa; Vance conferred with Crosland; State Department officials spoke with their counterparts in London; and Foreign Office Africa specialists flew to Washington for intensive meetings. All agreed that, as Mondale told West German chancellor Helmut Schmidt, the Rhodesia negotiations had "run into very heavy water." Crosland was pessimistic. Since he did not have "the foggiest idea as to the next step," he opined that it might be best to "let Smith stew." Prime Minister Callaghan, on the other hand, saw a path forward, and he laid it on the line when meeting Mondale: "[In] southern Africa . . . the United States had 'muscle' and could do things which we could not."[104]

London asked Washington to disabuse Smith immediately of any hope the Carter administration might come to his aid. Vance therefore announced publicly that if Smith opted for an "internal solution," he would "not have the support of the United States."[105] Devising an alternative to Smith's internal solution, however, was not going to be easy, especially given Whitehall's stasis. "Britain's brutally self-deprecating view of its own power has characterized its Rhodesian negotiating attempts for the better part of a decade," the State Department noted in March. "Their sense of impotence results in a stronger desire for greater American support and activity." Vance was "gloomy" and determined: "We would just have to soldier on." To create momentum while they developed a policy, Carter sent letters to ten African chiefs of state "asking them to give diplomacy a chance." Meanwhile, the State and Defense departments, the CIA, and the NSC were busy writing the PRM on southern Africa policy to meet the January 31 deadline.[106]

The PRM was submitted on time, and it was divided into sections on Rhodesia, Namibia, and South Africa. It was discussed at a Policy Review Committee (PRC) meeting on February 8 and an NSC meeting on March 3.[107] (The members of the PRC varied according to the topic being discussed; it was usually chaired by Vance. The NSC was the highest committee, consisting of all principals and usually chaired by Carter.[108]) The PRM presented a snapshot of the administration's aspirations in its earliest days. It began modestly, reminding its readers that "the United States cannot by itself shape the destiny of the people of southern Africa," but it then proceeded to argue in favor of the Carter administration's trying precisely to shape the destiny of the people of southern Africa. Majority rule in Rhodesia, independence in Namibia, and the elimination of apartheid in South Africa were "major US concern[s]" because of the administration's desire to support humanitarian principles, attain regional stability, prevent "increased Communist influence . . . [and a] major power confrontation" in the region, improve US standing at the United Nations, and avoid racial conflict at home.[109]

Although the problems of South Africa, Rhodesia, and Namibia were interrelated, the Rhodesian problem was the "highest priority" because, even though "the prospects for a negotiated settlement are not good . . . this situation contains the seeds of another Angola. . . . If the breakdown of talks means intensified warfare, Soviet/Cuban influence is bound to increase." The PRM presented three policy options for Rhodesia: (1) "press actively and immediately" for new negotiations; (2) back off for a "cooling period" of no more than six months; or (3) "abandon" the effort. The collapse of the Geneva talks had underlined the difficulty of bringing peace to Rhodesia. Smith's declaration of support for the principle of majority rule (whatever he meant by the term) was simply the first step of what promised to be a most delicate process to determine how, exactly, to transfer power to the majority.

The PRM next outlined US policy options toward Namibia, and it ended with a detailed analysis of what was perhaps the trickiest issue, South Africa. Washington wanted three contradictory things from Pretoria. First, because Pretoria was the Smith regime's military and economic lifeline, the PRM stated baldly that "the South African Government holds the key to the white side of the problem" of Rhodesia. Second, because South Africa was illegally occupying Namibia, the PRM noted that Pretoria also held the key to that country's independence. These two facts pulled Washington in the direction of enlisting Pretoria's cooperation. However, the third item—ending apartheid, "one of the major ethical issues of our time"—pushed the administration toward confrontation. The paper presented two "major alternatives" for US policy toward South Africa: either give priority to soliciting Pretoria's help with Rhodesia and Namibia and backpedal US concerns about apartheid, or tell Pretoria that its relations with Washington depended equally on its cooperation in seeking settlements in Rhodesia and Namibia and on its steps toward dismantling apartheid.

When Vance brought the PRC meeting to order on February 8, he opened with this thorniest issue: how should the administration balance its three goals for South Africa? Consensus was never in doubt: all participants agreed that the administration should pursue the second option—tell Pretoria that "the future of our relations would be determined not only by what they do regarding Rhodesia and Namibia *but also by how they handle racism in their country.*"[110] This was both moral (Vance asserted that downplaying US abhorrence of apartheid was "dishonest and wrong") and strategic (Brzezinski warned that if the administration did nothing about apartheid "the possibilities are there to transform this from a black-white conflict into a red-white conflict").[111]

The discussion about the best path in Rhodesia was also harmonious: all thought the United States should pursue the first option, active involvement in renewed negotiations. Anxiety that the British, who had run out of options, were contemplating backing off underlay the committee's activist stance. As the State Department asserted, "A standstill position conformed with neither the ideology or the image of the new administration nor its perception of the continuing threat of escalating violence in the region."[112] Brzezinski expressed "uncertainties" about relying on the British: "The Black African leadership does not really trust them." His deputy, David Aaron, added that the British had done a "lousy job."[113]

There was an air of innocent vigor to this discussion among these men who were just getting to know each other. The Carter administration would move forward on all fronts simultaneously; the contradictions—the "hard choices" that Vance referred to in the title of his memoirs—would appear later.

"More than a social call"[114]

Andrew Young was not at the PRC meeting: he was in Africa. The day after his confirmation as UN ambassador, he was on his way to Tanzania. President Julius Nyerere had invited him to a political celebration that would be attended by many African heads of state. When he had told Carter about it, the president-elect had said, "That's perfect! Go!" Young explained to Brzezinski, "It will give me a good opportunity to speak to the Administration's respect for Africa, and to listen to the views of others."[115] From Tanzania, Young would go to Nigeria, the continent's powerhouse. "I am a firm believer that there can't be any solution to the problems of Africa," Young stated, "unless there is direct involvement of the Government of Nigeria."[116]

A few days before his departure, Young conferred with Carter, Vance, and Brzezinski. The president reminded him that because he would be traveling before the administration had completed its review of its policy toward southern Africa, "you will have the very difficult task of not committing us to anything, but at the same time convincing the Africans that the US won't give up, that we are determined to . . . do whatever needs to be done, and can be done, to reach a settlement [in Rhodesia]. But everything you say is going to be repeated all over Africa, so you are going to have to be very, very careful."[117]

Young got into hot water, however, even before he left the United States. In an interview with Dan Rather on the CBS television show *Who's Who*, on January 31, Young said: "There's a sense in which the Cubans bring a certain stability and order—to Angola, for instance." He went on to explain that, for him, communism was not the worst enemy. Young had been at Martin Luther King Jr.'s side when the FBI had tried to discredit him as a communist. Young told Rather, "Most colored peoples of the world are not afraid of communism. Maybe that's wrong but communism has never been a threat to me. I have no love for communism. I could never be a communist. I could never support that system of government. But—it's never been a threat. Racism has always been a threat—and that has been the enemy of all of my life."[118]

The sound bites that the Cubans had brought "stability" to Angola and that the communist threat was overblown received wide coverage in the US media and produced outrage in Congress. "I caught hell at home," Young remembered, adding with a smile, "but it was the truth, and I gained credibility abroad." John Ashbrook (R-OH) called Young's comments "astounding" and questioned if he was capable of representing the "average American," while Larry McDonald (D-GA) was horrified that "President Carter would send this lamb to the fleshpits of the United Nations where Communist nations . . . run the show," and Robert Bauman (R-MD) called for Young's resignation. In the Senate, minority leader Howard Baker (R-TN), a moderate, criticized Young's propensity for public "self-flagellation."[119]

The State Department tried to defuse the tempest, stating that "[n]either Ambassador Young nor the Secretary condones the presence of Cuban troops in Angola."[120] As the *Washington Post* noted, this statement was "somewhere between a clarification and a reversal," and Baker damned it as "disturbingly mild, under the circumstances."[121] In fact, however, Young's remarks were not very different from comments that Carter had made during the campaign, which had generated absolutely no publicity. "The Russian and Cuban presence in Angola," Carter had told *Africa Report* in May 1976, "need not constitute a threat to United States interests; nor does that presence mean the existence of a communist satellite on the continent." Young's comments, however, roiled the press for weeks. At an April 15 meeting with journalists and broadcasters—ten weeks after Young uttered the remarks—Carter was asked: "Do you agree with Andy Young that the Cuban expeditionary force is a stabilizing influence?" The president began by stating: "I have called publicly for the Cuban expeditionary force to be withdrawn from Africa," and then addressed the question: "I read the whole text . . . of Andy's statement, and . . . I do agree with it. It [the Cuban intervention] obviously stabilized the situation." (Nevertheless, Carter would demand that Castro remove his troops from Angola before there could be any possibility of normalizing relations with the United States.)[122]

Young's rhetoric was implicit in the "decentering" of US foreign policy away from a singular and narrow focus on the bipolar Cold War. Carter, Vance, and Brzezinski—as well as Nixon, Kissinger, and Ford—had all, in less flamboyant ways than Young, modulated their language about the danger of communism. This had led to Ronald Reagan's vehement accusations during the primary campaign that Ford and Kissinger did not understand the "present danger" that communism and the Soviet Union posed to the United States. The debate about the seriousness of the Soviet threat had rumbled throughout the Nixon and Ford years, but when Andrew Young uttered his remarks, many heard them as new, radical, and dangerous. Young was under the microscope for several reasons: he was candid, he was considered a window on what made

Carter—still an enigma to many Americans—tick, and he was the first black American to be one of the principal faces of US foreign policy.

Young, an unflappable sort, was "unperturbed" by the reaction to his comments. Asked about Vance's clarification, Young said cheerfully, "It was my fault. I should have elaborated. I meant to say that the doctors and the electricians [in Angola] are all Cubans and helping to keep things going."[123] He poked fun at himself: the president had given him a very wide remit and, he conceded, "more than enough rope to hang myself."[124] Young had never envisioned his role as UN ambassador as that of a typical diplomat: instead, he was a "point man" who would speak bluntly and take the consequences. He expected to shake things up. He was confident that Carter, also a risk-taker, would support him and that Vance would fall in line; if they did not, Young would move on.

Young sandwiched his trip to Africa between brief stopovers in London. The British were eager to talk with Young; they did not know him, and he made them nervous. Young "may prove a rather awkward colleague and prone to offering hostages to fortune," the Foreign Office briefing notes warned. "It is obviously in our interest that he should be educated to the facts of UN life as soon as possible."[125] In four meetings with the key British experts on Rhodesia, including Foreign Secretary Crosland, Young sought to reassure his interlocutors of his reasonableness. He—more than any of the British, all of whom were white men—stressed the need to protect the rights of Rhodesian whites.[126] The Foreign Office officials, by contrast, stressed that they had "carried the ball about as far as they can." Not one of them was sanguine about resolving the Rhodesia crisis. "We have no idea what to do next," Crosland told Young. "It's as simple as that." Young departed from London for Tanzania pessimistic about the prospect of a quick settlement. "Nobody expects any easy answers," he told the press. "Negotiations (on Rhodesia) are going to be a long and tedious process."[127]

Tanzanian president Julius Nyerere had a deep interest in the Rhodesia negotiations. He was the informal leader of the Frontline States, and he carried moral authority at home and abroad. "His honesty, dedication and intellect, combined with his considerable political skills, have . . . given him and Tanzania a role in Africa and the Third World which Tanzania's circumstances do not otherwise warrant," the State Department briefing notes for Young's trip concluded. Nyerere projected an air of composure, intelligence, and incorruptibility; he listened well, and he impressed people of all political stripes. Nevertheless, the State Department warned, "Throughout the course of our [Kissinger's Rhodesia] initiative Nyerere . . . has proved to be a demanding, tough and elusive partner." The US ambassador to Tanzania recalled that "[Nyerere] was a superb politician. He had an acute brain, the memory of an elephant, intellectual horsepower that was second to none. He was cunning. He could be warmhearted one moment and cut you off at the legs at the next."[128]

A schoolteacher by training, Nyerere had helped lead his country to independence in 1961 in a bloodless transfer of power from the British; he had steered Tanzania toward what he called "African socialism," a merger of socialist economic principles and traditional rural African values. He announced this policy of self-reliance in 1967, in the Arusha Declaration; Young and the assembled dignitaries were celebrating the declaration's tenth anniversary on the island of Zanzibar. Enforcing the Arusha Declaration had meant essentially collectivizing Tanzania's farms and moving its widely scattered fifteen million people to new, more centralized villages. After a decade of dislocation, Tanzania in 1977 remained one of the world's poorest countries. Yet Nyerere had forged a nation, and he commanded respect. "At age 55 Nyerere is at the height of his powers," the US ambassador to Tanzania, Jim Spain, cabled Young on the eve of his arrival in Zanzibar.[129]

The size of France plus Italy, Tanzania has a long coastline on the Indian Ocean and shares borders with eight nations, including Kenya, Uganda, Zaire, Zambia, and Mozambique. Although it does not border Rhodesia, Namibia, or South Africa, it was considered a Frontline State because of Nyerere's passionate commitment to the liberation of southern Africa. This commitment, plus his socialist philosophy and good relations with Moscow (which was Tanzania's arms supplier), put Nyerere at odds with the US government until 1976 when, as Angola exploded in Kissinger's face, the Ford administration decided that it needed to improve US relations with black African states in order to stem the communist tide.[130]

Young's presence at the anniversary celebration of the Arusha Declaration made a strong statement that Carter wanted to strengthen relations with Tanzania. Young, however, had to win over a skeptical audience. The leading Tanzanian newspaper, for example, called his appointment "merely another attempt to appease the Black population with a symbolic gesture of 'good will.' . . . He will be forced to represent the interests of imperialist America; interests which are inimical to those of the people of Africa, and the people of African descent." Young recalls that in Zanzibar, "I met with all of the East African leaders. I met with them together, and I met with them one on one. And they all said the same thing: 'We need help with Zimbabwe. We need the United States . . . to make the British do the right thing.'"[131]

Young was also confronted with the fragility of African politics and alliances. During his brief sojourn, the continent was reeling from the collapse of the Geneva talks on Rhodesia (Smith announced his withdrawal from the talks on January 24); the brutal consolidation of power in revolutionary Ethiopia; and the disintegration of the East African Community, an economic alliance of Kenya, Tanzania, and Uganda.[132] It was hard for Young to ignore this last fact; it led to the collapse of East African Airways, which stranded him and the other hundred VIPs celebrating in Zanzibar.[133] Beyond the inconvenience, it was a potent reminder of the frictions between African states.

This was brought home to Young in his talks in Tanzania with presidents Nyerere and Kaunda of Zambia. The Frontline States tried to present a united face, but their leaders were divided about the best way to proceed in Rhodesia. The State Department had cabled Young to warn him that Kaunda recently had "launched into a bitter tirade against Britain."[134] (Kaunda's fury at Britain was due to rumors—later substantiated—that for years Whitehall had been turning a blind eye to British oil companies' breaking the sanctions on Rhodesia.[135]) Washington feared that Young might come under similar fire. In fact, however, Kaunda received Young with warmth and enthusiasm; and Young left convinced that Kaunda was "by far the strongest and the most intelligent of the moderate African leadership." In an interview in Lusaka in 2009, Kaunda emphasized this encounter, and he explained why he had embraced Young. "The way to get it [Rhodesia] sorted out was to get the United States involved because . . . Britain had problems here, in this area. We had to get the Americans in, to get . . . this thing resolved, and resolved peacefully, as quickly as possible, without getting ourselves enveloped in that confrontation, east/west." Mark Chona, Kaunda's closest aide, agreed: "Britain was unable to do anything."[136]

In Zanzibar, Kaunda told Young, "Britain has not got the will or ability . . . to solve the problem" of Rhodesia. Kaunda had enormous hopes that the Carter administration would pursue a new, enlightened policy toward Africa. Two days before his meeting with Young, he had written the US ambassador in Lusaka, "I have felt a deep compulsion to write to you and let you know . . . the hope I feel that the next four years of his [Carter's] leadership of his people will be a blessing to the entire human race."[137] He then wrote a long, heartfelt letter to President Carter, imploring him to take the lead in Rhodesia. "Following in Britain's reluctant footsteps has led to disaster in the past. America must assume leadership in this area. . . . The consequences of not reaching agreement at the negotiation table are . . . ghastly and will have international repercussions far beyond the borders of our region. Under your leadership, America must do everything to avoid such a catastrophe." Kaunda repeated this message to Young, saying flatly, "The British people and the British government have let us down." Young understood that beneath Kaunda's praise of the United States was a "barely concealed threat" that if Washington did not deliver, Kaunda would look elsewhere—that is, to Moscow and Havana.[138]

Nyerere expressed a different viewpoint. "The US cannot replace Britain" in the negotiations over Rhodesia, he declared in a news conference after the talks with Young. "Britain is the colonial power."[139] Nevertheless, Nyerere agreed with Kaunda that Washington had an important role to play: "We need the United States . . . to make sure the British did right in Zimbabwe [Rhodesia]."[140] He was scathing about Smith's and Vorster's use of the alleged communist threat. "If you want to fight communism in Africa," he told Young, "don't pick South Africa as your ally."[141]

Before leaving Tanzania, Young told reporters that his conversations with the African leaders—he had met with seventeen of them—had been "far more substantive and even moderate" than he had expected. He also said that he did not think that Marxist governments in southern Africa posed a threat to the United States. "What is a Marxist government?" Young asked. "If Angola is a Marxist state and its major trading partner is the United States, that does not worry me. . . . One of the most wholesome things about our administration is that . . . it won't be paranoid about communism."[142] An African politician commented that Young's attitude was "so refreshing it almost makes you suspicious."[143]

From the leisurely streets of Dar es Salaam, Young jetted into the chaos and congestion of Lagos. The city was even more crowded than usual because it was in the midst of hosting Festac, the Second World Black and African Festival of Arts and Culture, a month-long "grand jamboree" that brought together 15,000 black artists and intellectuals from sixty countries and attracted hundreds of thousands of spectators. It had been a long time coming: "Marred by multiple postponements, a civil war, a coup and an attempted coup, mismanagement, extravagant contracts, bribes and inter-African squabbles," the *Washington Post* explained, "the mere fact that the festival is taking place is viewed as an accomplishment."[144] This "Black World's Fair," for which Nigeria had built a network of highways, an enormous National Theater, and numerous exhibition halls, celebrated traditional culture as well as the "fast capitalism" and global aspirations of Nigeria.[145]

Although comparable to Tanzania in size, Nigeria had five times the population. Lagos was bursting at the seams, with exuberance, bravado, and people—perhaps two million of them. Flush with oil wealth (it was the only sub-Saharan African member of OPEC) and boasting one-sixth of Africa's total population, Nigeria in 1977 was the regional superpower. "Nigeria's population (75 million) and wealth make it the most important country in black Africa," the State Department observed in its briefing notes for Young's trip. "Nigerians are justifiably confident (some say arrogant) about Nigeria's manifest destiny." Its 250,000-man army was by far the largest in black Africa, and its economy was equally dominant. The country anticipated earnings of $10 billion in 1977 from its oil exports, nearly half of which (1.1 million barrels a day) were destined for the United States. Because of this, the volume of US trade with Nigeria ($5.5 billion per year) was almost double that of US trade with the former powerhouse, South Africa ($2.9 billion per year). "Some time late this year, or in early 1978, Nigeria's gross national product is expected to overtake South Africa's as the largest in sub-Saharan Africa." the *Washington Post* explained on the eve of Young's departure for Africa.[146] In 1976, American investment in Nigeria was a whopping $340 million and growing. The US trade deficit with Nigeria—almost $5 billion—was second only to that with Japan. In his eighth weekly report to Carter, Brzezinski advised the president to "do more to develop relations with the new emerging powers: . . . In Africa, Nigeria should be our primary target, given its enormous potential." In a marginal note, the president wrote succinctly: "Agree."[147]

Nigeria, however, had big problems, which were exacerbated by the oil revenues that flooded the country's coffers after the 1973 oil embargo. The wealth was diverted by corruption, and it heightened tensions among the Muslim north, the Christian south, and the oil-rich delta. A military coup in 1975, followed by the assassination of the country's leader a year later, led to the rise of Lieutenant-General Olusegun Obasanjo as head of state. "Obasanjo was everything Nyerere wasn't," the American ambassador to Nigeria, Donald Easum, recollected. "He was a big, tough, bright, rude soldier. He was utterly pragmatic."[148] He was just thirty-nine years old in 1977, and he ruled his turbulent country with an iron fist. Force, not philosophy, was what mattered in Nigeria.

Relations between Nigeria and the United States were not good. Kissinger had three times tried to visit Lagos, and three times the Nigerian government had refused his plane permission to land.[149] This was due in part to atmospherics—Lagos thought Washington had not paid it due deference—but it was rooted in serious disagreements with US policy toward southern Africa, especially Kissinger's covert operation in Angola. "Speaking of Marines, we have one in our house all weekend . . . and 25 camped around the corner," Ambassador Easum wrote his parents in January 1976, "because our Angola policy has so angered the Nigerian government, [it] . . . has prompted demonstrations at our consulates . . . resulting in three destroyed flagpoles, some broken windows, two burned flags, burned pictures of Nixon, Ford and Kissinger. . . . Problem is that our policy [in Angola] is in fact highly flawed. . . . I've continued to point out the flaws in the policy from here [Lagos], where my views have been fortified and lent another dimension and complexion from the fact that the Nigerian government has felt much the same way—and when Nigeria speaks, even the Secretary [Kissinger] listens—at least a little."[150]

Obasanjo applauded Kissinger's "change of heart" expressed in his Lusaka speech in April 1976 and welcomed the application of US power in southern Africa later that year—especially in squeezing Smith—because he had no confidence in Britain's ability to influence events in the region. By late 1976, Obasanjo had decided that "the USSR is not as useful diplomatically as the West in dealing with the southern African problems."[151] Nevertheless, Obasanjo still mistrusted Washington deeply because he believed US sympathies remained with the racist white minority governments of Salisbury and Pretoria. Nigeria had funneled more than $50 million to the liberation movements in southern Africa. "Nigeria provides the 'cash,' for much of the armed struggle," Young wrote Carter, Mondale, Brzezinski, and Vance. "[Obasanjo has] the clout to bring Nkomo [and] Mugabe . . . in line."[152]

Andrew Young arrived in Lagos on February 6, 1977, bearing tidings from President Carter that Washington had changed. "I come as a friend and an equal," he told the Nigerian press.[153] The Nigerian government "accorded him exceptional treatment, honoring him as it would a head of state," Easum cabled.[154] Young met with Obasanjo in his military barracks for four hours and delivered a letter from Carter that reiterated "the President's concern regarding events in southern Africa."[155] Young asked Obasanjo to use his power and influence to persuade the Patriotic Front to negotiate. "Nyerere and Kaunda are sound philosophers to whom we listen and from whom we learn," Young told Obasanjo, "but someone has to kick ass."[156] Obasanjo readily agreed to oblige. "If the Americans and British support free and fair elections in Rhodesia," he said, "and if Nkomo and Mugabe refuse to participate in those elections, then we'll . . . get them to the table." When Young asked him how, Obasanjo's reply was curt: "We'll cut off their arms supply, and we'll lock them up."[157] For Obasanjo, the essential factor was that the United States play "a vital role" in the search for peace in Rhodesia. "To achieve any success," Obasanjo said during a news conference following his conversation with Young, "America has to be heavily involved." On national television, Obasanjo announced that "'strained' US-Nigerian relations were a thing of the past."[158]

For Nigerians, Young's position as a senior American official trumped his race—if anything, his being black put them more on guard at first. On the day of Carter's inauguration, the Lagos *Daily Times* had announced: "There is nothing cheerful about Andrew Young's appointment."[159] Young remembers that the headline of a local paper on the day he arrived was "Send a Nigger to Catch a Nigger."[160] But he swiftly began to win the Nigerians over with a long interview on a local television program, in which he was relaxed, charming, and impressive. Watching Young field the questions, Ambassador Easum remembered thinking, "I hope the Soviet ambassador is watching. He doesn't have anyone who could do this."[161] Young used cultural sensitivity to good effect: the Lagos *Daily Times* reported that he "knelt reverently to greet a traditional ruler, the Sultan of Sokoto. . . . Not only that, he shook the Sultan with his two hands instead of the hand to hand fashion of Western culture. Mr Young . . . was also seen regularly sharing kola nuts with Brigadier Joe Garba [the foreign minister] in the true fashion of Nigeria." Young's race gave an added dimension to his attendance of performances at Festac, where he mixed with the crowds and danced spontaneously in the streets. At the closing ceremony, a traditional equestrian spectacular called the Grand Durbar attended by 200,000 people, "the star VIP was none other than Andrew Young," the leading scholar of Festac explains, "whose very body combined the 'blackness' of Africa with American superpower."[162]

It was not just Young's charm or his race that made the difference. As Obasanjo explained after observing how past American administrations had left Africans embittered, "The taste of disappointment needs time to disappear under the sweet taste of actions. . . . You should understand this residue of distrust."[163] In his report on the visit, Ambassador Easum made it clear that it was the Carter administration's promised changes in US policy toward southern Africa that were decisive: the Nigerian government, he cabled, "reflecting important expectations of the Carter administration . . . appears prepared [to] change both tone and substance of its bilateral relationship with the US. The reception tendered Ambassador Young was intended to convey that message."[164]

Passing through London to meet with Foreign Office officials on his way back to Washington, Young first had to smooth feathers he had ruffled with a comment on Nigerian television that Britain was "reluctant to assume" responsibility for Rhodesia.[165] He was asked by the BBC about what Africans thought of him. "A trace of skepticism and a lot of hope," he replied. "Skeptical, wondering if I really was Carter's representative. Full of hope because, if I was, things are really going to change. Well, I tell you, things are really going to change."[166]

Ambassador Easum remained in Lagos with a similar mixture of skepticism and hope. "Big question," he wrote his parents after Young left, "is degree to which his [Young's] approach is accepted by Vance—which really means where does the President stand."[167]

Carter in the Chair

"This could be one of the most important NSC meetings of the year," Carter announced before turning to Vance for an update on Rhodesia. The NSC had gathered on March 3, 1977, to discuss and finalize decisions about southern

Africa. There were several differences between this meeting and that of the PRC on February 8: the president was in the chair; Andrew Young had returned from Africa; and almost a month—a busy month—had elapsed.[168]

The administration's first weeks had sent one clear signal: this would be an activist presidency. Carter had pardoned Vietnam War draft evaders and voiced support for Soviet dissidents; Vance had traveled to Jerusalem, Cairo, Beirut, Amman, Riyadh, and Damascus, and was about to head to Moscow to restart the SALT II negotiations; Mondale had been to Europe and Japan; special negotiators had been appointed for the Panama Canal treaties; and talks with Cuba about improving relations had begun. Carter had mentioned during the campaign that he thought it was time to normalize relations with Havana, which had been severed in 1961, two years after Fidel Castro had rolled into the island's capital city. The main obstacle blocking better relations, from Washington's point of view, was the presence of thousands of Cuban soldiers in Angola. The Carter administration hoped that the carrot of normalization would encourage Castro to withdraw them.[169]

The administration also planned to take an active role in the settlement of the Rhodesian crisis. "I saw at an early stage that in many ways what happened in Zimbabwe, or Rhodesia then, . . . would be a precursor to what happened in South Africa," Carter explained. "They were tied intimately together . . . and it just happened that Rhodesia came along first."[170] The challenge was to find a way toward a negotiated settlement, avoiding the Scylla of all-out war by a continuation of the status quo and the Charybdis of all-out war pursuant to Smith's proposed internal settlement.

Washington needed to identify its levers of influence. The president ordered the CIA to prepare a paper analyzing the effectiveness of sanctions on the Smith government.[171] Young stressed that "the crucial thing in Kissinger's plan was the idea of a development fund," and Vance reassured the group, "We have $100 million in our budget for such a fund." Vance, Young, and Carter attempted to clarify the roles of Britain and the United States in the process. "Great Britain should maintain leadership while recognizing that we are the force behind the British," Carter stated. Together, the two allies would "restate a set of general principles" that would form the basis of negotiations and allow all parties to return to Geneva. "It may fail," Vance admitted, "but it is the best of the alternatives open to us."[172]

The decision to work hand-in-hand with the British had been taken during the preceding month. "The British must be kept in the driver's seat on Rhodesia," Young wrote Carter after his discussions at the Foreign Office, "but they need a lot of help."[173] The path to US-British cooperation was facilitated by a death in London. On February 13, while taking notes on briefing papers about Rhodesia, Foreign Secretary Anthony Crosland had suffered a fatal stroke. His last written words referred to Kaunda's comments to Young: "US must take over."[174] One week later, Prime Minister James Callaghan appointed the young, dynamic, but untested David Owen in his stead. "The American desire for activity [in southern Africa]," the State Department noted, "found a responsive ear in . . . David Owen."[175]

The thirty-eight-year-old Owen was a medical doctor and a Labour MP; he had served in the ministries of defense, health, and foreign affairs. Politically moderate, a strong supporter of the European Community and of human rights, Owen brimmed with energy and its two frequent shadows, impatience and arrogance. He was determined to tackle Rhodesia head-on. "The time of pussyfooting around over Rhodesia's independence was past," he explained.[176]

The problem was that Whitehall had no chips left. "Britain is looking down the dark Rhodesian tunnel," the US embassy in London had reported. "Like a headache, Rhodesia has throbbed in the background of successive British governments for more than a decade."[177] Owen knew that he would need to enlist the help of the United States. With neither credibility nor leverage in its renegade colony, England needed Jimmy Carter. The Labour government had a razor-thin majority and faced vitriolic criticism from the Conservatives: Owen would rely on Washington to give him cover. Moreover, Washington had more sway over Pretoria and the Frontline States than did London. White and black Africa had lost confidence in the British.[178] "The UK doesn't count in Africa," the Nigerian commissioner for foreign affairs told Vance. "We don't talk to the UK any more. We do it instead through you."[179] On the eve of Owen's first trip to Zambia, the government-controlled Lusaka *Daily Mail* called him "a shameless spokesman of the racist den of iniquity in South Africa."[180] The beleaguered foreign secretary knew that London was a "paper tiger over Rhodesia," but he had "no intention of contributing to Mr. Smith's already formidable number of political scalps." Owen was a pragmatist. He faced the fact squarely that "to attempt to settle Rhodesia on our own would be to risk another abject failure. With American strength and power I had a renewed opportunity."[181]

Other US presidents might have pushed the British aside and tackled the problem unilaterally. Whitehall had struck out in Rhodesia for over a decade, and with Cubans in Angola, the problem had grown from a colonial crisis into a Cold War flashpoint. Carter, however, welcomed working with the British to forge a solution. Vance wrote, "David Owen asked that we stand shoulder to shoulder with them. . . . The president agreed." This would give the United States, Vance added, "needed strength in dealing with our own Congress and greater combined leverage with the African parties." Moreover, partnering with London would shield Washington from the accusation that it was injecting East-West tensions into Africa. "We also wanted to limit our involvement so as not to give the Soviets cause to act directly in the matter," the assistant secretary for Africa explained.[182]

On Namibia, the March 3 NSC meeting sketched out a negotiating strategy wherein the five Western Security Council members (United States, United Kingdom, France, West Germany, and Canada) formed a "Contact Group" that would apply pressure on South Africa to demand an end to its illegal occupation of Namibia. If Pretoria failed to comply, the United States "might well vote in favor" of a UN Chapter 7 finding against South Africa—declaring the country a "threat to peace" and triggering the imposition of a mandatory arms embargo—even though this could divide the Atlantic alliance: the NSC was well aware that Britain and France might refuse to support the United States in this vote.[183]

The common denominator to a peaceful settlement of both Rhodesia and Namibia was South Africa: how much leverage did the United States have and how should it use it? When Brzezinski stated, "We have limited leverage with South Africa," Young retorted, "We have a lot of leverage with South Africa." Young did not explain what this leverage was, and no one asked him to clarify his statement. Brzezinski urged the NSC to prioritize US goals: was soliciting South African cooperation in Rhodesia or Namibia most important, or was changing apartheid? The discussion, however, got sidetracked when Carter recollected Young telling him that "we should not be too abusive to South Africa." Young picked up on the idea and explained that US companies in South Africa could apply pressure on the government in Pretoria. He likened this idea to the constructive role that businesses had played in the US civil rights movement. The president agreed: "It does compare with what occurred in Atlanta 15 years ago." Turning to Young, he said, "None of us around this table but you can understand the consciousness of the Black African."[184]

The minutes of the meeting reveal a vague and wandering discussion about US policy toward South Africa, but Carter's impatience was clear. "We are going to have to be forceful soon," he had scrawled ten days earlier in the margins of a memo about the administration's view of apartheid. This impatience emerges forcefully in Director of Policy Planning Anthony Lake's summary of the NSC meeting: the participants, he explained, had decided to inform Vorster, in private, "that our relationship is reaching a watershed and that unless South Africa clearly turns away from apartheid we will be forced to reconsider aspects of our relationship." This might "cause us a problem regarding essential South African cooperation on the Rhodesian and Namibian issues, but this is a risk we feel we must take." It was, they believed, a calculated risk:

the South African government was not putting pressure on Ian Smith to oblige the United States. "Vorster is not doing us any particular favor by working on Rhodesia," Brzezinski asserted. "He is acting in his own self-interest."[185] Therefore, the participants at the NSC meeting agreed that it would be possible to "devise approaches to the South Africans that can be straightforward on apartheid and yet successfully press them on Rhodesia and Namibia."[186]

The NSC meeting concluded with Carter asking for an escalating list of "approaches to South Africa." He wanted to press Pretoria to move from apartheid, but he did not want to destabilize the strategically important country; he sought gradual change. He turned to Young: "I want to have you work with me and the others to evolve a position on South Africa which is correct but as easy on them as possible. We must sell the American people and the South African leadership that we are acting in good faith but at the same time we don't want to turn over South Africa to the Reds." Carter assumed that it would be possible to seek justice in Rhodesia, Namibia, and South Africa while maintaining this Cold War bottom line. Young understood that the president was asking him to proceed with great caution. "If this were leaked," he replied, "I'd be ruined."[187]

Preparing the Ground

One week after the March 3, 1977, NSC meeting about southern Africa, British Prime Minister Callaghan and his newly appointed foreign secretary David Owen were aboard the Concorde heading to Washington. The British "are our closest allies and friends," President Carter effused at the welcoming ceremony on the South Lawn of the White House. It was a warm and sunny winter's day, but there was less pomp and circumstance than usual, not just because of Carter's deliberately homespun style but also because the police had asked that the traditional nineteen-gun salute be canceled. The British had arrived in the midst of a tense standoff in Washington, DC: the previous day, twelve Hanafi Muslims—a splinter sect of the Black Muslims—wielding machetes and rifles, had taken 132 people hostage at three locations around the city, including the District Building two blocks from the White House. Delicate negotiations to free the hostages were underway, and the police feared that the sound of gunfire could "trigger a slaughter."[188]

Inside the White House, the mood was more calm. Callaghan had been foreign minister in the mid-1970s and had worked well with Kissinger; now, he held the slimmest of majorities in Parliament and faced a vote of confidence later in the month. "That he has survived," the State Department noted on January 18, "is evidence of his tactical skills." Callaghan needed to establish a good rapport with Carter. He was a strong believer in the importance of the "special relationship," which, as Foreign Secretary Owen noted, "is the most crucial one for the prosperity and security of our country." On his brief visit, Callaghan wanted to discuss two topics: the global economy and Rhodesia.[189]

The two leaders were already in agreement on Rhodesia: they would work together to try to resolve the crisis through negotiations. "Owen made it clear," Vance wrote, "that any future moves in Rhodesia . . . cannot be sustained by the British unless we work side by side."[190] Owen wanted the initiative "to carry all the clout of American diplomacy." His reasons were both diplomatic and political. The Americans—he believed—had the muscle to persuade South Africa's Vorster to strong-arm Ian Smith to the negotiating table. Moreover, Smith and the South Africans had become expert at using British domestic political divisions to their advantage. If the Americans were fully onboard, the Tories would be less likely to take potshots at Labour's Rhodesia policy. "With American support," Owen explained, "we could have a principled policy and be able to sustain it against the Tory onslaught."[191] The details of the Anglo-American strategy toward Rhodesia would wait until after Owen returned from a tour of southern Africa that he planned to begin in a week. "New moves in Rhodesia," the State Department summarized at the end of the talks, "will be taken in closest consultations with us, and the British will ask us to carry an equal burden of responsibility."[192]

Callaghan, however, was uneasy. The British did not know Jimmy Carter, and they found some omens unsettling. The energy and idealism of the new team were worrisome. A Foreign Office briefing memo for Callaghan's trip explained the anxiety: "President Carter . . . has a strong, almost evangelical, sense of international morality and has assembled an active team which brings together men with previous experience . . . and some bright younger people who share the President's aspirations but on the whole lack experience. There are already some indications that the new team may confront America's friends with problems, arising from the desire to implement policies quickly but without adequate consultation and preparation. . . . The Prime Minister . . . [should] bring home to them the practical realities and difficulties of the situation not only in Rhodesia itself but also in Namibia and South Africa before they launch off—as they may feel tempted to do—on radical new policies without full consideration of all the implications."[193] The Foreign Office noted that "the President . . . is prepared to take risks," and it was uncertain how susceptible he would be to the "impulsive views of Ambassador Young."[194] They had warned Young not to be too tough on the South Africans. "We cannot kick Vorster around in public and still expect him to work with us in private." Even Vance, the most seasoned member of the new team, worried the British.

"I was struck by his [Vance's] insistence on pressing for more rapid and visible progress on all three fronts—Rhodesia, Namibia and relations with South Africa—despite the sober and considered report by officials on all the difficulties," Peter Ramsbotham, the British ambassador in Washington, reported. "We must expect this pressure to continue, although it is not easy at present to see where it will lead."[195]

For the British, this was not an abstract concern. The Africa group at the UN was crafting a resolution on apartheid that was expected to include a call for mandatory economic sanctions on South Africa. The Foreign Office was very worried—panicked would not be too strong a word—that the Carter administration would support the resolution. "They [the Carter administration] take a more radical view of Southern African matters than their predecessors and are reluctant to seem to be resisting black African proposals for increasing pressure on South Africa," Owen told the Cabinet.[196] If trade sanctions were imposed on South Africa, the British economy, which was staggering through a recession, would be profoundly shaken. Sixty-one percent of all foreign investment in South Africa was British. South Africa was Britain's ninth largest export market (£654 million in 1976) and it attracted 10 percent (£3,000 million) of all British overseas investments.[197] Britain could not afford economic sanctions on South Africa, but neither could it afford to be the solitary veto on a UN Security Council resolution calling for them. "A decision to veto a resolution supported by the Americans would be a very serious step having enormous implications," the Foreign Office observed. It would confront Britain with "appalling dilemmas." Owen concluded, "The only way to call a halt on this slippery slope is not to step on it in the first place." The Americans had to be stopped.[198]

The Foreign Office drafted blunt, strong language for the prime minister to use in Washington about the perils of imposing economic sanctions on South Africa. It advised Callaghan to tell Carter that supporting sanctions "would be a major step with far reaching consequences and I would urge you not to take it. . . . This is something which we cannot accept. . . . The consequence is likely to be the complete disarray of the Security Council. I do not need to underline the gravity of this for Western interests in general."[199]

But between the briefing memos and the meetings, something happened. Because when Callaghan was actually in the room with President Carter, his approach was low-key, acknowledging the complexity of the situation and the need for Washington to follow its own interests.[200] It was Owen who pulled out the heavy artillery. At the end of an amiable lunch with Vance and ten other American and British officials, the discussion turned to the possibility of levying UN sanctions on South Africa. Owen did not announce that Britain could not accept them. Instead, he simply stated that "once one had crossed that threshold [that is, once the United States had broken ranks with its European allies to vote in favor of UN sanctions on South Africa] other parts of the world could be affected, eg, Israel, where the Americans would not be able to rely on the French and possibly on the United Kingdom."[201] The threat was stark: if Washington voted in favor of sanctions on South Africa, all bets were off as to whether London (and Paris) would continue to back US policy toward Israel at the UN.

This was the first time that Vance and Owen met. Vance, the suave statesman, was impressed by his young British counterpart. "Brilliant . . . a supple and penetrating mind was matched by courage and vision," the normally reserved Vance wrote in his memoirs. Owen "was to become one of my close friends. . . . I found it both delightful and stimulating to work with him," he added. The sentiments were fully shared. Owen wrote, "We soon developed as close a working partnership and friendship as I suspect ever existed between a US secretary of state and a British foreign secretary." Senior Foreign Office diplomat Robin Renwick described the relationship between the two men in colorful terms: "Vance found himself with this Young Turk in the form of David Owen; he was like an Obi-Wan Kenobi to him." Vance and Owen continued to work together after both had left office, forging the "Vance-Owen plan" for Bosnia in 1993. Twenty-five years after their first meeting, Owen's abiding respect and affection for Vance was palpable. "He was an amazing man," Owen recalled. "I was absolutely devoted to him."[202]

Nevertheless, Owen could be brash and headstrong, and he frequently antagonized the Americans as well as many of his Foreign Office subordinates. A senior British diplomat explained: "[Owen thought] the Foreign Office people were fuddyduddy, old fashioned, out of date sort of people." Renwick added, "Owen was very unpopular in the Foreign Office . . . partly because he wanted to do everything instantly." One senior American official noted that although Owen "had later become something of a friend," in the Carter years he had considered him "an arrogant asshole."[203]

US and British goals overlapped in Rhodesia—both countries wanted a free Zimbabwe governed by majority rule—but differences were evident even in this early meeting. For the British, Rhodesia was a colonial problem that had festered for too long, and as one diplomat with extensive Rhodesia experience explained, "The prime object was to be shut of it."[204] For the Americans, it was a problem of the Cold War and of global justice. This had repercussions that, a year later, would threaten to derail the Anglo-American plans.

Long-term peace in Zimbabwe was both London's and Washington's goal, but the British could achieve their fundamental aim (wash their hands of the problem) with a short-term solution, whereas the Americans could attain their goal (close the door to a Soviet opportunity) only with a lasting peace. This meant that, given the difficulty of negotiating a comprehensive peace, the British were tempted to engineer a solution that would at least create sufficient stability to allow power to be legally transferred from London to a majority government in Salisbury. This could be achieved, they hoped, by arranging, somehow, for ZAPU leader Joshua Nkomo to take over from Smith. Nkomo, they believed, would be acceptable to all sides: he was a nationalist leader and, as the State Department noted, he was "the least unacceptable nationalist to Rhodesian whites and South Africa because he is ostensibly the most moderate of the African leaders, even though ZAPU has been backed by the Soviet Union since its inception."[205] The British had developed good relations with Nkomo over the years, whereas their contact with ZANU leader Robert Mugabe was minimal. Owen was blunt: "Britain would frankly prefer to see Nkomo come out on top in Rhodesia," he told Vance, "and any strategy we follow should be designed to help reach this objective."[206] An agreement that left Nkomo on top would give the British a decent interval to extract themselves from the mess.

It was an appealing idea because the alternative—knocking together the heads of Ian Smith, the Frontline leaders, and the Patriotic Front, not to mention the other black leaders and the South Africans—was a daunting challenge with no guarantee of success. In a carefully argued cable written just twelve days after Carter was inaugurated, the well-respected chargé at the US embassy in London, Ron Spiers, laid out the argument in favor of supporting the British desire to install Nkomo. "Chances for a settlement in Rhodesia have deteriorated considerably over the last several weeks," he began, and "another perhaps more brutal Angola is shaping up." Time was short. Therefore, "we should work for an agreement between reasonable whites . . . and moderate blacks [because] . . . the ends of the Rhodesia political spectrum are irreconcilable. . . . It is essential to bring Nkomo independently to the negotiating table."[207]

The Carter administration resisted the idea for two reasons. First, as Young warned Carter, "doing a deal with Nkomo and not bothering with the others [Mugabe's ZANU]" would not end the war.[208] The US ambassador in Maputo, Willard DePree, echoed Young's point and fleshed it out. "Many of the Zimbabwean guerrillas will continue to fight if Mugabe or ZIPA [the Zimbabwe People's Army, the ZAPU military wing] are excluded. . . . [and they would receive] the encouragement and military and political support of President Machel, as well as that of at least some of the radical African and Third World governments and Communist countries. . . . US interests would be better served if we continue our current 'hands off' policy with respect to the nationalist leadership even though continuation of our present policy is likely to entail further fighting and eventually victory by the guerrillas." DePree argued that

157

no matter who became the next leader of Rhodesia, its "important resources" would continue to be available to the United States. The US ambassador in Dar es Salaam agreed: backing Nkomo would be "dangerous [because] . . . 'the boys' [the guerrillas of the Patriotic Front], as Nyerere calls them, have become a fundamental political (as well as military) force." The paramount US interest was ending the war, and a separate deal with Nkomo would only motivate Mugabe's forces—the bulk of the guerrilla army—to fight on.[209]

There was another reason the Americans were wary of the Nkomo solution: it defied one of the principles that Carter wanted to define his foreign policy. "Africans themselves can best find peaceful answers to African disputes," the president declared. "We stand by you in your work."[210] Young explained the administration's philosophy to Kaunda: "One legacy that [the] new administration wished to eliminate is [the] idea that [the] US should become involved in deciding who other people should have as their leaders."[211] To Obasanjo, he commented, "Every time the US had tried during the past 20 years to influence the selection of the leaders of other countries, we had the wrong results. The Carter administration came to office on a pledge not to intervene in other people's affairs."[212] As Ambassador Jim Spain in Dar es Salaam cabled, "The situation [in Rhodesia] will have to shake itself down. If anyone can help it do so, it is other Africans, not us."[213] This echoed President Kennedy's comment in 1961, "Africa for the Africans."[214] It was an aspiration that would be violated (especially in Angola, where the Carter administration would support a rebel leader[215]), but it shaped the thinking of many of the key formulators of the administration's Africa policy, including the president himself.

For the next two months, the United States and Great Britain struggled to bridge their differences and formulate a joint policy toward Rhodesia. President Carter was actively engaged in this process, making suggestions and asking questions. The State Department informed the Foreign Office that "the president's interest in southern Africa is very strong and he receives a short daily brief on developments in the area."[216] In March 1977, Vance's "evening reports" to Carter, which were generally three pages summarizing approximately five items of interest, almost always included updates on Rhodesia, often as the first item.[217] Also, mid-level American and British officials met regularly and went on several tours of the region to begin rebuilding the peace process.

Repealing Byrd

To make its muscle credible in southern Africa, the White House had to convince Congress to repeal the Byrd Amendment. This legislation, passed in

1971, had declared that the United States could legally import chrome from Rhodesia, thereby breaking the UN Security Council sanctions on all trade with the renegade colony. The United States was the only country in the world to have passed a law that made sanctions-busting legal. Kissinger had promised in his April 1976 Lusaka speech to repeal the amendment, but after President Ford's shellacking in the Texas primary, the administration had abandoned the effort. The Carter team knew that repealing the amendment was the essential first step toward establishing its *bona fides* in Africa—"the acid test of American intentions," as the British ambassador in South Africa noted.[218] If Carter failed to get the Byrd Amendment overturned, then all his rhetoric about a new approach to Africa would ring hollow.

No one argued that the economic impact of closing the chrome loophole would be significant to the Rhodesian economy: Smith had proven his ability to work around sanctions. His government had encouraged measures to improve food security, and with the collusion of many foreign governments it had figured out ways to evade sanctions.[219] As the CIA noted, "Despite a decade of UN sanctions, Rhodesia's economy still ranks about fifth in sub-Saharan Africa, and its manufacturing sector is probably second only to South Africa." In 1977, however, the independence of Mozambique, plus the spike in the global price of oil, had narrowed Rhodesia's economic options, and if the United States suddenly enforced sanctions by suspending its purchase of Rhodesian chrome, the symbolic impact could be significant in Rhodesia as well as throughout Africa. Andrew Young, while still a sitting member of Congress, got the ball rolling on January 11, 1977, by introducing HR 1746—the fifth attempt to repeal the amendment.[220]

One month later, as the legislation moved through Congress and the new administration settled into office, Young was the first witness to testify in favor of the bill. "There is a sense in which the repeal of the Byrd Amendment is a kind of referendum on American racism," he told his former colleagues in the House.[221] "Repeal would show the Smith regime that it could not count on assistance from the US government in its obstinate refusal to accede to majority rule. It would impress on the Africans that the US is serious in its support for majority rule in an independent Zimbabwe. . . . Repeal will have a very positive effect at the United Nations and will enable me to carry out my mission with greater effectiveness. I am convinced that repeal is in the best interests of the United States."[222] Secretary Vance testified before the Senate that the Carter administration was determined to repeal the amendment: "Let no one be in doubt about the strength of our commitment."[223] White House officials called thirty-one legislators who had signaled that they would vote against repeal. Crucially, Carter himself weighed in, personally calling nine members of Congress who had been identified as swing voters.[224] "It was a problem for me," Carter remembered, "because the . . . Byrd amendment obstructed any change, and I had to deal with . . . a whole array of people who were still retaining the commitment—to be generous—that white folks' rights in Africa had to be protected."[225]

The time was ripe for repeal: the administration was fully behind it, scientific advances had reduced US dependence on Rhodesia's high-grade chrome, and the United States had amassed a four-year stockpile of the mineral. For all these reasons, and since most observers believed that the Smith regime's days were numbered (although there was wide disagreement about how long it could hold out), it was sensible to get, in the expression of the day, "on the right side of change."[226] As the chair of the Senate subcommittee on Africa and as sponsor of the bill, Dick Clark (D-IA), explained when he opened the debate on repeal, "If the United States insists on short-run support for the minority racist regimes . . . it runs the risk of permanently alienating the black majorities who are bound to prevail in these countries eventually."[227]

The congressional debate on repeal, however, was heated and long. Two aspects of it stand out. First, a surprisingly large number of representatives in both houses displayed not only a good grasp of the arcane issues concerning the processing of chrome and the politics of Rhodesia, but also passion about both. This was a subject with deep roots in Congress; it had been debated many times, and many members and their staffs had developed considerable expertise on the issues. Second, this was not a partisan issue. The Democrats controlled both houses, with 62 seats in the Senate and a whopping 292 seats (compared with the Republicans' 143) in the House.[228] The Democrats had a veto-proof majority, if they voted as a block, but they did not have a strong whip and their very strength made party discipline difficult to maintain. This was particularly true because by 1977, the Democratic Party was a very uneasy coalition of southern conservatives and northern liberals. Liberal Democrats led the drive for repeal of the Byrd Amendment, but conservative Democrats broke ranks. Repealing the amendment, like any progressive legislation—especially that with a racial dimension—could expect the support of at most two-thirds of the Democrats; it therefore required the backing of Republicans who, like the Democrats, were not united. The GOP moderates were beginning to be challenged by a small group of conservatives. Rhodesia provided a theater for these insurgents.

In February 1977, Congress held hearings on the legislation. By early March, it was sent to the floor for a vote.[229] The White House was eager that President Carter, who was scheduled to address the UN General Assembly on March 17, go to New York with this victory in his pocket. Moreover, Young was president of the UN Security Council (a position that rotated monthly) in March, and repeal of the Byrd Amendment would strengthen his hand. Carter also hoped to inject some momentum into the derailed peace process in Rhodesia.

There was no suspense about the outcome in the Senate, which had passed repeal legislation overwhelmingly in 1975 and was expected to do so even more emphatically two years later. The House, however, was harder to predict. Young was frank about the difficulties that repeal would face: "30% of Congress was still 'white racist,'" he had told Anthony Crosland in February.[230] Tip O'Neill (D-MA), who had been elected Speaker of the House in January, predicted that the vote would be close.[231] O'Neill epitomized the kind of Washington politician that Carter had denigrated during the campaign; the speaker was a back-slapping, hard-drinking Irish-American who loved the deal-making and compromises of the game of politics. "Of all the people I have known," Carter commented, "Tip O'Neill knew best how to enjoy politics." Temperament alone would have separated the two men, but politics widened the gulf. O'Neill was an old-guard New England liberal, a Kennedy man, whereas Carter was something new and hard to categorize—a fiscally conservative, socially progressive, populist Democrat. In early 1977, O'Neill and Carter tried to forge a relationship, but it was rocky from the start. They clashed early over the Byrd Amendment. O'Neill supported repeal, but he bristled at what he considered White House poaching on his prerogative to set the legislative calendar. O'Neill resented the way that the administration dictated the timing of the vote, and he fought back, refusing to exert his considerable muscle in favor of repeal.[232] The White House countered by deploying Andy Young to Capitol Hill to twist arms on the day of the House vote, March 14, 1977.[233]

The debate in the House took all day. More than fifty members rose to express their opinion of the legislation, often with great vehemence. The opponents of repeal argued that the legislation was "steeped in hypocrisy"[234] because it punished Rhodesia while increasing US reliance on Soviet chrome; they bemoaned that it would derail the political progress—Smith's talk of an internal settlement—that was underway in Salisbury. The proponents countered by reminding the House that the Smith government was illegal, and they predicted that the so-called political progress in Rhodesia would lead to intensified civil war.

Toward the end of the debate, the heat that simmered beneath the surface erupted. Robert Sikes, a conservative Democrat from the Florida Panhandle who had entered the House in 1941, became incensed. "This bill must be considered as great a farce as the House has had perpetrated upon it in recent history. The arguments for the bill have defied the imagination. . . . How blind can we be? Talk about international hypocrisy—this is it," he exclaimed. "Historians some day may say that the House is on a lost weekend binge, that we are drunk on morality. . . . We show our allegiance to the UN, but at what cost to the United States?" Parren Mitchell (D-MD), a founding member of the Congressional Black Caucus and, like all seventeen African Americans in Congress, a strong supporter of repeal, disagreed. "Military might alone does not project a nation into world leadership. . . . Economic power alone does not project a nation into world leadership. . . . A nation assumes world leadership . . . because it . . . has the capacity and the will and . . . the deepseated decency to . . . do the right thing. That is all we are asking for today . . . that America live out its role of moral leadership in the world."[235]

This argument was about much more than US policy toward Rhodesia: it was a battle between two dramatically opposed worldviews. Throughout the 95th Congress, both the Republican and Democratic parties were rent by disagreements about how to reassert US power in a post-Vietnam world; these differences were buffeted and fanned by the rising salience of human rights throughout the western world. Conservatives of both parties urged Congress to focus on what they saw as the most serious threat facing the United States—Soviet communism—and stressed that military might was the only way to successfully protect the nation. Their argument against the repeal of the Byrd Amendment was well summed up by John Ashbrook (R-OH): "Chrome is essential to our national security and our economy. It would be foolhardy to deprive ourselves" of ready access to it.[236]

Moderates and liberals urged Congress not to ignore the Cold War, but to think beyond it. They stressed that regional concerns mattered and that US security depended not only on wielding military power but also on commanding the respect of the international community. "This bill is receiving some resistance because it is symbolic," Millicent Fenwick (R-NJ) explained. "It is far more important perhaps than it may seem to be on the surface. What we really are doing in the repeal of the Byrd Amendment . . . is sustaining the position of the United States before the world." The majority whip, John Brademas (D-IN), concurred: "At stake is the integrity of our international legal obligations."[237]

To the conservatives, this smacked of appeasement. "Does the United Nations govern the United States of America?" Robert Badham (R-CA) inquired. "Not yet, by golly." Other Republicans deemed the administration's kowtowing to the UN "laughable," and referred scornfully to the "halo of the UN" that hung over the debate. Robert Sikes took up the charge: "This is a new age when we are told to be kind to our enemies. . . . Russia is the principal beneficiary of the bill, the United States is the loser."[238]

At the end of the day, the conservatives lost the vote by an unexpectedly wide margin, 250 to 146. But in the course of the debate, this loose conservative coalition of ninety-four Republicans and fifty-two Democrats (20 percent of all Democratic representatives) had honed arguments that would gain strength in the remaining years of the Carter presidency.[239] The day after the House vote, the Senate substituted the lower chamber's bill for its own, thereby speeding up the legislative process, and voted in favor of repeal, sixty-six to twenty-six.[240]

Two days later, on March 16, President Carter traveled to the old New England mill town of Clinton, Massachusetts, on the first stop of his "Meet the People" tour, fulfilling his campaign pledge to stay in touch with Americans who never traveled to Washington. Two thousand cheering residents braved the blustery, cold weather to greet the president as he deplaned at Hanscom Field, and in town more awaited his arrival in what the *Washington Post* called a "near frenzy."[241] At the town hall, 850 Clinton residents, who had won their tickets by lottery, peppered the president with questions. For ninety minutes, on live national television, Carter displayed his remarkable grasp of issues, from deregulation of the trucking industry to the closure of a local military base, but he was asked only one question about foreign policy, and it concerned the Middle East. It made the event's only news—and ruffled Israeli feathers—because the president used the politically loaded term "homeland" in relation to the rights of Palestinians.[242] Africa was not on most Americans' minds.

After the town meeting, Carter strolled down Chestnut Street to the home of an "ordinary family," where he spent the night, before flying the next morning to West Virginia to talk to a small group of interested citizens about energy policy.[243] From there, he traveled to New York City, where at the UN he gave the first formal foreign policy speech of his presidency. In a wide-ranging address, he sorted through the myriad initiatives of his first eight weeks to highlight his four overriding goals: peace, arms control, economic justice, and human rights. His speech was ambitious in breadth but modest in tone: "We can only improve this world if we are realistic about its complexities," Carter admitted to the two thousand diplomats in the hall, as well as the millions watching on live television. "The disagreements that we face are deeply rooted. . . . They will not be solved easily. They will not be solved quickly."[244] Although he spoke at greatest length and with most passion about his administration's commitment to human rights—while the Soviet delegates "sat stone-faced"[245]—he gave special attention to southern Africa. "In southern Africa, we will work to help attain majority rule through peaceful means. . . . Anything less than that may bring a protracted racial war, with devastating consequences to all. This week the Government of the United States took action to bring our country into full compliance with

163

United Nations sanctions against the illegal regime in Rhodesia." Looking up from the teleprompter, Carter added with a smile, "And I will sign that bill Friday in Washington." The assembled UN diplomats burst into applause.[246] The speech was well received in the hall—where Carter received a standing ovation—and in the American press.

Less than twenty-four hours later, Jimmy Carter was in the White House surrounded by a bipartisan group of twenty legislators and the world's press to sign the legislation that repealed the Byrd Amendment. The president referred to the repeal's enormous "symbolic importance" and went on to say, "I think it puts us on the side of what's right and proper."[247] His formal statement accompanying the bill explained his administration's Rhodesia policy:

> This measure is a central element in our African policy. Members of my administration have supported it with one voice. . . . Our country is committed to the concept of rapid transition to majority rule in Rhodesia under nonviolent conditions. . . . We have consistently stated our belief that a peaceful solution in Rhodesia depends upon negotiations that involve a full spectrum of opinion among its leaders, both black and white. With the enactment of this measure, there can be no mistake about our support for that principle. I hope that the present Rhodesian authorities, as well as the black African nationalist leaders, will accurately assess the vote of the Congress and this administration's stand on Rhodesia. The solution rests in their hands, not ours. Further delay in negotiations will invite more violence and increase the prospect of outside intervention—an outcome which every person of good will wishes to avoid.[248]

Carter here laid out the structure of his policy: his administration sought rapid transition to majority rule; negotiations must include all parties; the ultimate arbiters were the Rhodesians, black and white; prolonged violence would open the door to outside (Soviet) intervention.

As he signed the bill, Carter had reason to be happy. Everything was working according to the plans he and his principal advisers had drawn up during the transition. They would fire on all cylinders, tackling human rights, SALT II, the Middle East, the Panama Canal, and southern Africa (to mention only the foreign policy initiatives) with vigor. The bill before him represented a significant legislative victory, he had communed with the people in Clinton, and he had been a success at the UN. The polls in March were encouraging: Gallup reported that 70 percent of Americans approved of the way that Carter was doing his job.[249]

The world, however, was about to become more turbulent, and Carter would have to improvise. When Carter, Vance, Young, and the Africa Bureau of the State Department had planned the new administration's policy toward Africa, all had been riveted on the southern cone, where they believed that enlightened US policy could defuse the explosive brew of racism and the Cold War that rocked the region. But the administration soon would be wrenched from its preoccupation with southern Africa and thrust into much more morally ambiguous realms, where its priorities would be harder to determine. In devising policies toward Zaire and the Horn of Africa, the administration would struggle to find the unanimity and enthusiasm with which it tackled the problems of southern Africa. It would be forced to grapple with unanticipated crises where both the national interest and the high moral ground would prove elusive.

4. Unwelcome Surprises

Shaba 1

While President Carter was addressing the United Nations and signing the bill repealing the Byrd Amendment, a crisis—later dubbed Shaba 1—was brewing in central Africa. On March 8, 1977, a group of about 1,500 rebels left Angola to invade Shaba, Zaire's southernmost province, with the intent of toppling the regime of President Mobutu Sese Seko, a dictator who had come to power with the help of the CIA. Not only did this invasion imperil the pro-American leader of one of Africa's largest and most strategically located countries, but the rebels—Zaireans who had fled their country in the turbulent 1960s and taken up residence in neighboring Angola—were presumed to have the support of the Angolan government which, in turn, was supported by more than 20,000 Cuban troops. For Americans, this was a front-page story.[1]

If one were to summarize the pitfalls of Carter's declaration in his inaugural address that his administration's commitment to human rights was "absolute," one need say only one word: Mobutu. The flamboyant dictator had ruled Zaire, an enormous, mineral-rich, and deeply troubled country in the center of Africa, since 1965. Zaire was Mobutu's fiefdom; he robbed its coffers and brutalized its citizens. Journalist David Rieff once observed pungently that "Zaire was not so much a country as a crime scene." Carter's team considered Mobutu "the worst of the worst," as the assistant secretary of state for African affairs recalled, and Washington's cozy relationship with Mobutu epitomized the amoral foreign policy that Carter had promised to change.[2]

America's alliance with Zaire, however, was too big to fail. The former Belgian colony was the geographical linchpin of Africa; it produced vast amounts of cobalt, industrial diamonds, and copper; and US banks held approximately $500 million of its crushing $3 billion debt.[3] There was no alternative to Mobutu: with stone-cold acumen, he had eliminated all viable successors. The bottom line, as the deputy chief of mission in Zaire during the Carter years remembered, was: "We were afraid of the consequences if he [Mobutu] fell: the disorder, the chaos that could occur there in this great big, awkward giant of a country. It was just almost too awful for our policymakers to even contemplate."[4]

The Zairean rebels faced little resistance. Secretary Vance was blunt: "The [Zairean] army is useless," he told West German chancellor Helmut Schmidt in the early days of the invasion. "They flee from the rebels." As commander in chief, Mobutu was equally inept. He spent the war "skulking . . . in the safety of his funk-hole in Kinshasa," the British ambassador in Zaire wrote. "It was a lamentable performance." The rebels advanced ten miles a day; within two weeks, they had occupied a third of Shaba province, and by March 29 they were eighteen miles from its mining center, Kolwezi.[5]

Mobutu knew he could not rely on his army to save him. So he played his trump card: the Cold War. In an interview in *Elima*, the major government-controlled Zairean newspaper, he said that Angola—from whence the rebels had come—"is just a pawn being manipulated by foreign powers." He contacted his friends in Washington, Paris, Brussels, and Rabat. He cried, "Cubans! Russians! Communists!" Meanwhile, his bureaucrats briefed the corralled journalists in Kinshasa, telling them that the rebels were "under the command of specialists . . . from Cuba." The invasion of Shaba, Mobutu's subordinates declared, was the next domino in the Soviet and Cuban takeover of Africa.[6]

Fidel Castro, who was in Tanzania, called a press conference. "I assure you that there is not a single Cuban involved [in Shaba]," he announced. "We have nothing at all to do with it. We have neither equipped nor trained the forces that are fighting the ruling clique in Zaire. The fighting in Shaba," Castro asserted, was an "internal problem" of Zaire. "We have stayed out [of Shaba]," he added, "because we don't want to give the United States any excuse to intervene."[7]

This made sense. By March 1977, Cuba had withdrawn 12,000 soldiers from Angola. For Jimmy Carter, this was a welcome and important development. If the withdrawals continued, it would clear the path toward US normalization with both Cuba and Angola.[8] For Cuba to have fomented the invasion of Zaire would have directly undermined this process. But Castro was not considered credible by many Western observers, and his denials complicated what appeared to be a simple story, one as old as containment: the attack on Zaire was *au fond* a Soviet challenge of the United States, and the Cubans—"the Gurkhas of the Russian empire," according to *Time*—were doing Moscow's bidding. First Angola, then Zaire. Mobutu had transformed an internal threat into a Cold War crisis. The strategy was potent and effective.[9]

It was a cruel and unwanted twist for the Carter team. It threatened to explode the administration's careful and unusual attempt *not* to frame all problems in Africa in terms of the Cold War. In its first six weeks, the Carter White House had gotten a fast start in Africa with Andrew Young's whirlwind tour to Tanzania and Nigeria; this trip had announced with verve and clarity that Carter intended to pursue a new policy toward the continent. The war in Zaire seemed custom-made to derail these plans. First, it had taken Washington by surprise. Moreover, US intelligence about the rebels was spotty: who, exactly, were they? Who had trained and backed them? Second, the Shaba war forced the Carter team, which had hoped to brush the "Mobutu problem" under the carpet, to publicly face the contradiction between its rhetoric about human rights and its continuing support of the African dictator. Third, any efforts to provide emergency military assistance to Mobutu would fly in the face of Carter's campaign pledge to reduce arms transfers abroad. It presented, as Walter Cutler, the US ambassador in Kinshasa said, "a terrible headache for this new Administration."[10]

The threat was potentially grave. The Zambian ambassador in Zaire warned: "if not resolved soon [the war] might end up in Russia and Cuba on the one hand and America and other western countries . . . on the other hand fighting in Zaire." Ambassador Cutler explained, "The whole question for us was how serious a threat was this, and was this, in fact, Soviet-inspired, supported. Were there Cubans, surrogates and so forth? . . . We just didn't know what was going on."[11] Some major US newspapers cast the threat in ominous Cold War terms. The lead editorial in the *Christian Science Monitor*, one week into the war, declared that the Soviets' "ultimate objective seems clear: to deprive the West of Africa's crucial mineral wealth and hamper the sea route around the Cape through which these strategic minerals are carried." The *Chicago Tribune* echoed these sentiments, declaring, "Moscow might well be encouraged to move on toward the control of all of southern Africa and the vital sea lanes which swing around it."[12]

The Carter administration, however, played it cool. On March 15—the day after the House vote on the Byrd Amendment—the White House agreed, as Press Secretary Jody Powell said, "to help an old friend in an emergency."[13] It accelerated the delivery of $2 million in "nonlethal" supplies such as tents, medicine, and food—but no arms or ammunition—that were owed Zaire from its 1976 aid package. To keep these nonlethal supplies at arm's length from the US government, they were flown to Zaire aboard chartered commercial aircraft rather than US military planes.[14] This "gave the impression," the Zambian ambassador noted, that the United States "would rather not go the whole hog for the sake of one man [Mobutu]." Fidel Castro agreed. "The Yankees," he said, "are wavering."[15]

All the same, even a little aid to Mobutu alarmed some in the press and Congress. "The stability of Zaire: is that what the Carter administration's brave new African policy means?" the *Washington Post* inquired, incredulously, in a March 18 editorial that heaped contempt on the new occupant of the White House. "Shades of John Foster Dulles, Dean Rusk, Henry Kissinger and the whole balance-of-power gang. . . . This *is* the Carter administration, isn't it?"[16] When Vance testified to the House Committee on International Relations on March 16, Don Bonker (D-WA), who had led the floor fight against Kissinger's covert operation in Angola, pressed him on the administration's proposed aid for Zaire. What was the rationale? Bonker warned that the explanation would be significant: "This is the first time that the administration will be presented with a situation where its human rights doctrine will come in conflict with its pragmatism." Vance did not reply. Two weeks later, on March 30, Stephen Solarz (D-NY), an intense and occasionally abrasive legislator who had entered the House in 1975, asked the question again: "What is our interest in maintaining Mobutu in power?" Deputy Assistant Secretary of State for African Affairs Talcott Seelye answered succinctly: "We are interested in Zaire essentially to try to preserve the unity and territorial integrity of the country."[17]

During the second week of the war, the State Department, while resisting all attempts to blame the Soviets and the Cubans, did assert that the Angolan government—fed up with the Mobutu-sponsored raids on its country—had supported the invasion. The British agreed, as did the West Germans and the Portuguese, and the Nigerian foreign minister confirmed it, telling Vance that Angola was providing the Katangans "logistic support."[18] This was true, and it had repercussions. First, it transformed the Shaba crisis from an internal affair to an international incident, a violation of the UN Charter. Second, it paved the way for the White House to call on Nigeria, eager to prove its goodwill after Young's visit, to mediate between Angolan president Agostinho Neto and Zaire's Mobutu—seeking an African solution for an African problem.[19] Third, it spurred the administration to put on hold the possibility of normalizing relations with Luanda. Carter had mentioned this goal during the campaign, and Vance had mooted during his Senate confirmation hearing, but on March 21, Vance said that "in view of what was now going on . . . it would be difficult to explain the initiation of such negotiations to the US public."[20]

The Carter administration hoped to dodge a Cold War framework for the turmoil in Zaire. It believed it was a regional crisis that the Organization of African Unity (OAU) should mediate. It urged Mobutu (unsuccessfully) not to stir up anxieties about another Soviet and Cuban grab in Africa.[21] At the same time, it sought ways to quietly help the brutal Zairean regime. At a news conference on March 24, Carter said: "We have no hard evidence or any evidence, as far as that goes, that the Cubans or Angolan troops have crossed the border into Zaire." He added, "But we have been cooperating in exchanging information with the Belgian Government, the French Government, and others, just to try to stabilize the situation and to lessen the chance of expanding the conflict."[22]

On April 1, Secretary Vance stopped in Paris on his return home from discussing the SALT II negotiations in Moscow to confer with President Valéry Giscard d'Estaing. Zaire was the first topic of conversation. Giscard and Vance bemoaned the incompetence of the Zairean army: "How is it possible to help a country that cannot help itself?" Vance exclaimed. He noted that, under the circumstances, it would be very hard for the administration to get congressional approval of lethal aid for Mobutu. Giscard countered that the Shaba crisis "was a test for both the US and France," and the French were prepared to stabilize the situation "ourselves. . . . Even 200 willing and competent fighting men could change the military situation overnight." Giscard added that Morocco would supply "a few 'volunteers.'" Belgian policy was "controlled by business interests," he scoffed.[23] Brussels "will supply ammunition, but they will not send any men.[24]

Thompson Buchanan, the director of the State Department's Office of Central African Affairs, was dispatched to talk with the French about rescuing Mobutu.[25] "It had all come down to just a few practical questions," Buchanan remembered. "How much money? How many guns? How are we going to transport them? Who is going to pay for the transportation?" His conversations with the French went well. The French were "receptive."[26]

Indeed they were. French policy toward Africa under Giscard d'Estaing was increasingly activist. The Soviet and Cuban intervention in Angola had jolted Giscard; he sought to bolster the French position in Africa with increased economic and military assistance. In early 1977, more than 13,000 French troops were stationed in more than fifteen African countries; only Cuba had a larger military presence on the continent. For Giscard, the possibility of strengthening French influence in Zaire was attractive. He was under fire for pursuing a weak foreign policy, and sought an opportunity to look tough. He saw an opening or, as he put it, an obligation, to step up to the plate at a time when Washington's hands were tied by what he considered its squeamishness consequent to its defeat in Vietnam. The French were not happy with "the way things were being allowed to slide in Africa," the British ambassador in Paris reported, and had "little sympathy for what they regard as the excessively easy-going and muddled attitude of the Carter administration and particularly the utterances of Andy Young." Moscow, the French told the British, "is the direct cause of most of the current tensions in Africa."[27]

Giscard urged Carter to stand up to the Soviets. "The situation in Africa is worse than you think," he said when they met in early May. "Last year the moderate [African] leaders—not a particularly brave lot . . . —were ready to throw in the towel. The easiest, and safest, way for them to deal with the pressure from the opposition and with the Soviet blandishments is to choose the Soviet camp. If we don't give them any help, that's what they'll do." Giscard lectured the American president: "We have made it very clear to the Soviets that any attempt to destabilize Africa is contrary to détente. It might be useful for you to do the same. It is important to understand that détente applies to the whole planet; it is not just a game of cards played on the European stage. You should insist on this point with the Soviets."[28]

France had significant investments in Africa, which supplied 75 percent of its energy resources. Zaire provided uranium for France's burgeoning nuclear program. Moreover, it was the largest francophone country in Africa, and loosening it from Belgium's grip pleased many of the conservatives who backed Giscard. By the mid-1970s, France had become Mobutu's main arms supplier. The Belgian foreign minister noted testily, "France has always preferred to help the mineral-rich countries, not the poor ones. . . . It's obvious that France is interested in Zaire's immense mineral wealth."[29]

On April 6, Paris rushed advanced weapons and a team of twenty military advisors to Shaba. As the French foreign minister later noted, "Africa for Africans does not mean Africa for others."[30]

Jimmy Carter welcomed the French intervention: "I think when the European countries . . . because of close political and historical ties with Mobutu and his government, are inclined to be more active in their help for him, we, you know, would certainly approve of that," he told European journalists. He wrote to Giscard to express his "appreciation and approval of your initiative in Zaire."[31]

Much of black Africa decried the internationalization of the war in Shaba; the *Zambia Times*, for example, condemned "the almost obscene haste with which the West has rushed to pour arms into Zaire."[32] But a few African leaders continued to support Mobutu, and it was to them that Carter and Giscard turned. King Hassan II of Morocco was in debt to Paris for its backing of his government's war against the Polisario guerrillas fighting for the independence of Western Sahara (which Morocco had occupied), and he wanted to curry favor with Washington. Vance reported after his April 1 talks with Giscard about Shaba that "King Hassan . . . has agreed to send volunteers."[33] On April 9, 1,500 Moroccan soldiers arrived in Kolwezi aboard twelve French planes. The Saudis bankrolled the operation, and the Americans denied any foreknowledge of it.[34]

Mobutu was saved not by the prowess of the foreign troops, but by what they symbolized: the dictator had powerful friends. The rebels retreated to Angola without fighting. On May 9, Carter told Giscard, "Your actions in

Zaire appear to have been very successful." By late May, the crisis was over. "The whole 'war,'" the British ambassador commented in a retrospective report, "seems to have been pretty mickey-mouse."[35]

Thus, with the Americans discreetly cheering them on, France, Morocco, and Saudi money rescued Mobutu. Rarely "has the world witnessed such a confusion of ideology, adventurism and self-interest," the *New York Times* noted.[36] In fact, the operation was one of the first acts of an informal alliance called the Safari Club. This elusive group of Saudis, French, Moroccans, Iranians, and Egyptians was the brainchild of the fiercely anticommunist director of French intelligence, Alexandre de Marenches, who oozed contempt for "that baby-faced Boy Scout" Jimmy Carter.[37] In the mid-1970s, responding to what they saw as the failures of the CIA, the members of the Safari Club pooled resources to combat the spread of communism, mainly in Africa. The Saudi ambassador to the United States, Prince Turki bin Faisal Al Saud, explained: "Our American friends were in trouble, their intelligence collection and capability has been diminished to say the least and literally they didn't have any more money left to do anything. So we, as friends of the United States, we should get together and try to do something to face the Communist threat on our doorstep in Africa . . . [where] there was a belt of countries that were turning Communist or sympathizing with the Soviet Union." The Safari Club intended to stop the Soviets "whether by money, by human resources, by intelligence work—all kinds of skullduggery."[38] US intelligence noted, "This organization [the Safari Club] provided support to the Zairean government in the Shaba region." Prince Turki confirmed: "The Safari Club provided the military wherewithal, the money and the intelligence to successfully counter that effort [in Shaba]."[39]

The Carter administration's response to the Shaba crisis was measured. It coughed up an additional $13 million in economic aid for Zaire, and it disbursed some of the $38 million military aid that was already in the pipeline. It played it cool about any possible Cuban role in the crisis. "We have no direct evidence at all that there are Cubans within Zaire," Carter said at a news conference on April 22. Two weeks later, he explained to Giscard, "We can't put any public pressure on Castro because it would hurt the movement toward normalization [with Cuba]. . . . Castro has said kind things about me," Carter added, "and I'm reluctant to criticize him in public."[40]

In fact, no one ever provided proof that even one Cuban was in Zaire or had helped the rebels. Mobutu paraded two wounded and terrified Shaban rebels who claimed to have been trained by Cubans, but their testimony, delivered under extreme duress, was more pathetic than credible, leading the British ambassador to comment drily that it "smells strongly of a put-up job."[41]

Mobutu, wearing his leopard-skin cap and leaning on his carved ebony mace, wildly waved allegations and never provided evidence. When the crisis was over, US intelligence concluded that Castro had been telling the truth: "Mobutu's charges of direct Cuban involvement were probably designed to elicit sympathy and assistance from Western countries and to excuse the poor performance of Zairean troops. . . . We have found no reliable evidence of direct Cuban involvement." The Americans were right: Cuba was not involved.[42]

After the war ended, the US press expressed cautious support for the president's levelheaded handling of the crisis: Washington had not plunged into another quagmire. "One of the most remarkable acts of Jimmy Carter's first hundred days as President was a decision *not* to do something: not to plunge into the situation in Zaire," columnist Anthony Lewis wrote. "If Henry Kissinger had still been making United States foreign policy, he . . . would surely have proclaimed the Zaire affair a confrontation with the Soviet Union and demanded strong American action. . . . Carter must have been under great pressure to . . . show his 'toughness' . . . but Mr Carter chose the path of restraint. . . . [There is] hope for wise change in American foreign policy." Brzezinski agreed. "We could all congratulate ourselves on the handling of the affair," he told the head of the British diplomatic service.[43]

Mobutu could not have disagreed more vehemently. "We are bitterly disappointed by America's attitude," he told *Newsweek*. "If you have decided to surrender piecemeal to the Soviet-Cuban grand design in Africa, I think you owe it to us and to your other friends to have the frankness to admit it. Andrew Young says it does not matter if African states go Marxist because they want to go on trading with America. Is that the position of the Carter Administration?"[44]

In fact, Mobutu should have been relieved. Carter's support of his regime was tepid, but it was nonetheless support. As Carter explained to Giscard in early May, "Our freedom of maneuver is constrained, as you know, by the ghost of Vietnam, which precludes all military actions. We therefore have to be very cautious. That said, however, we are determined to support Mobutu." That the Carter administration in its first hundred days—exuberant days trumpeting the new administration's moral foreign policy and support for human rights—would buttress Mobutu was not a foregone conclusion. As British ambassador Peter Ramsbotham noted, it "gives the lie to those of his critics who reproach him for naivete and excessive moralism in foreign policy."[45]

The State Department's Zaire desk officer at the time, Edward Marks, summed up the importance of the episode: the Carter administration was "faced with a very interesting and practical foreign policy problem. A pro-Western, African government with excellent ties to the conservative community and the US intelligence community was under serious attack. So the question clearly posed was whether we would support him even though we now found him personally distasteful." If ever there was a clear case of a government that abused human rights and was pervasively corrupt, it was Mobutu's Zaire. "The Carter Administration was being given an opportunity to get rid of him, without having to do anything nasty with our own hands," Marks mused, many years later. "Merely backing away, not providing help and not encouraging others to help him, might have been sufficient to bring him down, especially if we made no effort to keep our decision secret." (This counterfactual is plausible only if one assumes that the symbolism of US support was crucial; materially, French, Belgian, and Moroccan support could have sustained Mobutu.) "In the African Bureau . . . we wondered what the Carter people would do," Marks remembered. It soon became clear that Carter, despite his ardent desire to implement a policy that "reflected American values," was hamstrung by one fundamental fact: the fall of Mobutu frightened official Washington and America's European allies. It would have invited the balkanization of Zaire, with consequent opportunities for the Soviets and ramifications for American businesses. Therefore, despite his distaste for Mobutu, Carter "ended up fudging the policy question," limiting the aid that Washington sent to Zaire while quietly urging others to swoop in to save the corrupt regime. Carter decided not to "bite the bullet on Mobutu," and the dictator benefited. "Mobutu is now cock-a-hoop," the British ambassador reported. The end of the war "led to a peculiarly nauseating intensification of the cult of Mobutu's personality. He is now not only 'father', 'shepherd' and 'guide' but the 'great strategist.'"[46]

By providing an early, clear clash between human rights and Cold War *realpolitik*, the Shaba crisis opened a window on Jimmy Carter's decision-making. It showed the limits of the desire of Carter and his top advisers to move beyond the knee-jerk assumption that a crisis in the Third World was at bottom a Soviet challenge to the United States. Shaba was a reminder that while the frame might change—while US officials might emphasize the regional roots of a crisis—the canvas remained the same, and it was the Cold War. Had Carter been the radical that some of his critics and supporters expected him to be—and that some of his rhetoric indicated he would be—he would not have sent aid and encouraged others to rescue Mobutu. A State Department postmortem made this clear: "We must . . . play a restrained game lest we justify Soviet involvement [in Africa]. . . . By holding back [in Shaba], we prevented a direct US-Soviet confrontation and thereby did much more to foreclose the Soviets than a confrontationist policy would have."[47] Carter resisted pressure from his right, at home and abroad, to blame Cuba for the invasion of Zaire. Nevertheless, when push came to shove—when the rebels approached Kolwezi—Jimmy Carter was a cold warrior.

Anwar Sadat

As Egyptian president Anwar Sadat flew to Washington on April 4, 1977, he was leaving a troubled country. Egypt was desperately poor, and Cairo had burst its seams; every day for the past decade, at least four hundred impoverished rural Egyptians had poured into the capital city, swelling its overcrowded streets with 1.5 million internal migrants. Sadat's dictatorship cracked down on dissent. The government's modest attempts to liberalize the economy had not borne fruit—or bread. On January 18, 1977, the Egyptian government had reduced subsidies on basic foodstuffs. While festivities for Carter's inauguration were underway in Washington, the Egyptians were rioting; after more than seventy people had been killed, the government rescinded the price changes, but not before the "bread riots" had exposed the cracks in Egypt's economic and political stability. Having renounced his country's friendship treaty with the Soviet Union in March 1976, Sadat's need for US aid was urgent. He had gained legitimacy in Egypt as a result of the 1973 October War and his security apparatus maintained order, but by 1977 he needed to deliver his people economic relief.

Sadat also had to buttress the loyalty of his army by supplying them with modern weapons. He had to avoid a costly war—against Israel or anyone else. Sadat feared encirclement. To the east, the Sinai, still almost entirely occupied by Israel, was very tense. To the west, the border with Muammar Qaddafi's Libya was an armed camp, with frequent cross-border skirmishes. To the south, geography rendered a friendly Sudan critical: a hostile government in Khartoum could control the Nile and choke the country dry. Vance summed up what these fears meant for Sadat's goals in Washington: "In his exposed position, Sadat is highly sensitive to the measure of how much he can rely on us."[48]

Carter prepared assiduously for Sadat's visit. The meeting mattered because peace in the Middle East mattered, and Sadat would be front and center in the peace process. "He has been the pacesetter on the Arab side in the negotiating process," Vance explained. Another Arab-Israeli war would be catastrophic for the United States, threatening another oil embargo at best and a superpower confrontation at worst. Carter threw his energy and intellect into trying to prevent such a cataclysm. This is what both State and Defense emphasized in their briefing memoranda to the president.[49]

Sadat surprised Carter in two ways. First, he broke through Carter's reserve. Despite his broad smile and informal first name, "Jimmy" was hard to know and even harder to befriend. However, he established a rapport with Anwar Sadat almost immediately. After the meeting, Sadat declared Carter "a man of principle" and "a new type of American leader." Carter was even more taken by Sadat, a gracious and gutsy man. "He just charmed the pants off of virtually everybody who came to see him," the deputy chief of mission at the US embassy in Cairo recalled. "Of almost a hundred heads of state with whom I met while president," Carter explained, "he [Sadat] was my favorite and my closest personal friend." There is no evidence that Carter ever addressed the brutal side of Sadat's regime.[50]

The second surprise was what Sadat wanted to discuss. In the days before the Egyptian leader's arrival, the White House, State Department, Defense Department, and the US press focused on his role in brokering the Arab-Israeli conflict. Sadat, however, wanted to talk about Africa. He was concerned about Zaire, where the Shaba crisis was reaching its climax, but his most pressing concern was the growth of Soviet influence in Ethiopia and Somalia. This got Carter's attention.[51]

The tensions between Ethiopia and Somalia would flare into a Cold War crisis by the end of 1977, when 12,000 Cuban troops would begin to arrive in Ethiopia to repel a Somali invasion. This conflict would test Carter's commitment to reducing US arms sales abroad and his respect for international law. It would force him to make hard choices in a morally ambiguous environment that was charged with Cold War tensions. It would reveal the complexity of accommodating Saudi Arabia, flush with cash—and power—after the 1973 oil shock. The Carter administration was prepared for the challenges it faced in southern Africa. When dealing with the racially charged politics of that region, the Carter team stood united on the moral high ground. It was unprepared, however, for the crisis in the Horn. There, Carter and his advisers never found firm footing, and fissures opened.

The Backstory: Ethiopia before Carter

Washington's ties to Addis Ababa had been thrown into confusion on September 12, 1974, the day the aged emperor, Haile Selassie, had been overthrown after failing to subdue a revolution that had been raging since February. Gerald Ford had been in office for less than a month, and his administration was baffled by the group of about 120 midlevel Ethiopian military officers called the Derg (Amharic for "committee") that had seized the reins of power from the emperor.[52]

The Derg was a black hole. Eight months after Haile Selassie had been deposed, all the CIA could say was that it was "an unstable coalition of disparate military figures." What was clear, however, was that it was implementing a violent social, political, and economic revolution. "Ever since the radicals seized control," the State Department's Bureau of Intelligence and Research (INR) wrote in 1976, "their objectives have remained constant—the dismantling of the old feudal society and its replacement with a new egalitarian order." Ethiopia was being turned upside down.[53]

Washington's interest in Ethiopia had quickened in the early Cold War years. The third most populous country in Africa, Ethiopia stretched from the Red Sea toward the center of the continent; its mountains rose 8,000 feet and provided a perfect platform from which to eavesdrop on the Soviet Union and Middle East. The United States, therefore, built a huge land radar system at Kagnew in Eritrea, the country's coastal province. From 1953 to 1974, Ethiopia received more than half of all US military assistance to Africa. In return, the United States gained "almost unlimited rights" to Ethiopia's airfields and ports.[54]

By 1974, however, when the emperor was overthrown, the radar station at Kagnew was growing obsolete and the US public was weary of military involvement in faraway countries. Haile Selassie's friends in Washington did not rush to rescue him. Instead, the Ford administration sought to establish good relations with the Derg "in the belief," the US embassy in Addis explained, "that this would help to strengthen the position of those who will struggle for a continuation of close and friendly relations with the US." After all, as the *Economist* noted, "The young officers who overthrew Haile Selassie . . . were American-trained and American-supplied down to their bootlaces."[55]

The Derg, however, lurched leftward. Within a year, it had nationalized the property of US companies, established diplomatic relations with Cuba, and asked the Kremlin for military assistance.[56] In August 1975, Haile Selassie, who a year earlier had been bundled away from the presidential palace in a Volkswagen and incarcerated, was assassinated. He joined a growing group of people, including many from within the Derg itself, eliminated by the Derg.

Ethiopia was in danger of balkanization. There were rebellions in all fourteen provinces. The Derg "controls, even in a loose sense, less than two-thirds of the country," US intelligence observed. The most serious challenge was in Eritrea, the region along the Red Sea that had long chafed under Addis's rule and was home to the US base at Kagnew.[57]

In 1976, the Derg sent half its army to put down the revolt in the coastal province. "US-supplied arms are being used in the often brutal repression of the insurgency," the State Department reported. Professor Tom Farer told the US Congress that the Ethiopian soldiers "perpetrate[d] My Lais and Guernicas in a random and obscene procession." Despite this onslaught, the Eritrean guerrillas succeeded in wresting control of almost the entire province from the inept, poorly equipped, and demoralized Ethiopian army. As the security situation deteriorated, the Ford administration downsized the staff at Kagnew from a peak of 4,000 in 1969 to just 35 in 1976, but did not close it.[58]

The Peace Corps—which, with 1,000 volunteers, was the second-largest African contingent—packed up in October 1976. Yet Washington did not break relations with the revolutionary regime—"primarily because," as the State Department explained, "we wish to retain both our facility at Kagnew and the access to port and airfields."[59]

The Ford administration was also interested in perceptions: "US disengagement [from Ethiopia] would . . . lend itself to a global perception of a US 'loss' and corresponding Soviet 'gain' in Africa, confirming a trend of diminishing US influence in the world," an interdepartmental analysis concluded in December 1976. Moreover, in the wake of the retreat from Vietnam, it was important to appear "steady and dependable," so as not to "dishearten" America's allies. It was also useful to show the world that the United States was not allergic to revolution. Severing ties with Addis Ababa "might be seen by other nations as motivated by an unwillingness to hew to a difficult course and as demonstrative of US inability to conduct a cooperative relationship with a 'socialist' state."[60]

The Ford administration's decision to maintain relations with Ethiopia came at a high price. US military assistance to Addis had been stable for two decades, but it began an upward climb in July 1974 when Ethiopia's hostile neighbor, Somalia, signed a treaty of friendship with the Soviet Union. Both Haile Selassie and the Derg had told Washington that Ethiopia needed more military aid to counter "an imminent Somali attack."[61]

From late 1974 until the end of Ford's term, US policy toward Ethiopia was pulled in two directions: the increasing anti-Americanism of the Derg alienated Washington, but the increasing Soviet presence in Somalia pushed Washington toward it. The "pull" of the Cold War won: more than half of all US military aid given to Ethiopia from 1953 to 1977 was sent *after* September 1974, that is, after the fall of Haile Selassie. Between 1974 and 1975, US military assistance to Ethiopia "dramatically increased," Kissinger wrote Ford. The CIA and INR estimated that US grant military assistance, Foreign Military Sales credits, and cash sales to Ethiopia totaled $27 million in 1974, $44 million in 1975, and $126 million in 1976. This escalation aroused concern in Congress, which was aware of the Derg's abuses of human rights. It did not, however, satisfy the Derg, which protested vehemently that it needed more arms to counter the Somali threat.[62]

The Ford administration's policy toward Ethiopia was driven by doubt, inertia, and the Cold War. "We . . . have tried to maintain some of our influence," the State Department explained, "by continuing the programs of most interest to . . . [the Ethiopian] government, particularly security assistance, and have tried to use our diminishing influence to slow down or limit . . .

Ethiopia's movement away from the West and toward the Communist world." Washington waited, hoping—with ebbing optimism—that Ethiopia, America's erstwhile friend, would return to "normal," but its assistance failed to sway the Derg from its leftist ideology. The CIA noted in a retrospective study that "what seemed in Washington to be proper caution, and even a degree of humility, in dealing with a fluid situation and a changing cast of characters, was interpreted in Addis Ababa as indifference bordering on outright hostility." One of Henry Kissinger's key aides, while discussing Ethiopia, was more succinct. "Gratitude," he noted, "is not a principle of international relations."[63]

In the days before Ford left the White House, the Derg inked an arms agreement with the Soviet Union. The terms were secret; most US sources believed it to be worth $385 million, but the Soviet defense ministry put it at $100 million. Whatever the amount, the symbolism was potent: the State Department noted drily that this "represents a major departure."[64]

The Backstory: Somalia before Carter

Somalis were watching events in Addis with a mixture of alarm and hope. One fact controlled Somali-Ethiopian relations: Somalis believed that roughly one-third of Ethiopian territory—the Ogaden—was rightfully theirs. The Ogaden region is a 200,000-square-mile triangle of barren land (the size of Mississippi, Alabama, Georgia, and South Carolina combined) that is embraced by the comma-shaped Somalia. It was sparsely inhabited by about one million nomads, the majority of whom were ethnically Somali.

When Somalia gained its independence in 1960, it was an anomaly in Africa: it had only one ethnic group, one language, one religion, and one culture. However, Somalis considered their new state to be a partial birth because it did not include three regions that were—at least in part—ethnically Somali: Djibouti, northwest Kenya, and the Ogaden. The dream of a Greater Somalia that would incorporate all these territories runs deep in Somali lore and politics. The pain of the partial birth is reminiscent of the Republic of Ireland's desire to reunite its "five green fields." Like Ireland, Somalia was a deeply irredentist nation.

It was also desperately poor and undeveloped. Sixty percent of the three million Somalis were nomadic, following their scrawny cattle and camels across the barren scrub brush of their country. Somalia needed foreign aid.[65]

Upon independence, Somalia had turned toward the West. Washington, wary of Mogadiscio's aggressive intentions against Ethiopia, had extended only a modest sum. In 1964, Somalia attacked Ethiopia in an attempt to conquer the Ogaden, but the Ethiopians repelled the invading Somali forces in one week and Somalia's stock in Washington slid lower. The Kremlin stepped up. Over the next decade, it contributed an estimated $35 million in military assistance, and it built a port at Berbera, a seaside town on the Gulf of Aden in northern Somalia. Access to Berbera would give the Kremlin something it coveted: a port on the Indian Ocean.[66]

Somali relations with the United States were further strained when, in 1969, General Mohamed Siad Barre seized power in Mogadiscio. Although he toned down the irredentist rhetoric, Siad Barre promised to implement "scientific socialism," a hybrid philosophy that melded communist rhetoric with Islamic tradition. He introduced the first alphabet for a written Somali language and instituted a massive literacy campaign. He championed the rights of women; indeed, in one of the regime's very rare death penalty cases, ten religious leaders were executed for opposing equal rights for women.[67]

In 1971, Washington discontinued the trickle of aid it had been sending Somalia, and Siad pressed Moscow for more. Three years later, the Soviet Union and Somalia signed their treaty of friendship and cooperation, the Kremlin's first in sub-Saharan Africa. The Soviets, whose access to the growing base at Berbera and the newly opened airport at Harghessa was formalized in the treaty, began pouring aid into Somalia. In 1975, they gave Siad Barre approximately $63 million in economic credits and grants out of $75 million they sent to all of Africa. At roughly the same time, Cuba began training the Somali militia, while the German Democratic Republic trained the intelligence services. "Somalia, though claiming to be non-aligned, is as close to a client state as the USSR has in Africa," the State Department observed in early 1977.[68]

The Soviets transformed the Somali army into "one of the largest and best equipped forces in Africa." According to the CIA, between 1973 and 1976 the Soviet Union tripled its presence in the country. By October 1977, it had extended approximately $280 million in military aid and placed approximately 6,000 Soviet personnel there to train the army, maintain equipment, and manage development projects. Although Somalia had one-tenth the population of Ethiopia, its 35,000 trained soldiers were almost three-quarters the size of the estimated 47,000-man Ethiopian army, and much better equipped. The Somalis had at least 250 tanks (three times more than Ethiopia), 300 armored personnel carriers (twice as many as Ethiopia), 200 coastal batteries, fifty-three MiG fighter bombers, a squadron of bombers, and a ground-to-air missile complex. By contrast, the Ethiopian Air Force had no more than forty fighter bombers. Moreover, most Ethiopian armaments were of World War II vintage, but the Somali weapons were modern and well suited to the Ogaden terrain.[69]

Moscow's growing investment in Somalia worried the Ford administration. The Somali government faced no internal subversion, and it was not threatened by any external enemies. "Siad . . . has permitted the Soviets to establish themselves in Somalia on a scale far beyond that necessary for Somalia's own needs," the CIA noted in 1975. The US embassy in Mogadiscio speculated that Moscow wanted to beef up Somali facilities to support "Soviet naval and aircraft needs in [the] Indian Ocean."[70] In June 1975, Secretary of Defense James Schlesinger showed the Senate Armed Services Committee aerial photographs of purported cruise missile storage units at Berbera. "It is evident," Schlesinger testified, "that the USSR is in the process of establishing a significant new facility, capable of supporting their naval and air activities in the northwest Indian Ocean."[71] This prompted Washington to make a "more positive gesture" toward Siad in the hope that it might lead him, as the US ambassador in Mogadiscio suggested, "to limit military advantages seized by the USSR."[72]

The Ford administration turned to Saudi Arabia. "The Saudi Arabian Government is interested in joint action with us to extract the Soviets from Somalia," the State Department advised Henry Kissinger. "There would be considerable advantage in cooperating with the Saudis." Kissinger agreed, and coordination began with Jidda to lure Siad Barre from the Soviets. In November 1975, the Somali ambassador to the United States, Abdullahi Addou, told the US deputy secretary of state that his country was seeking not just economic aid from the United States but also military aid. The American brushed him off. "Our relations," he said, are "not yet at a point even to discuss such a question."[73]

The crisis in Angola in late 1975 halted any progress toward improving US relations with Somalia. As Cuban troops poured into Luanda, the nuances of US foreign policy—the "big tent" notion that the United States could have good relations with a Soviet ally—fell by the wayside. A meeting in October 1976 between Kissinger and Somalia's acting foreign minister, Hussein Abdulkadir Kassim, symbolized the stasis. In an edgy atmosphere, they discussed Somali claims to the Ogaden. When Kissinger asked about the Soviet base at Berbera, Kassim retorted, "We will never permit a foreign base. . . . We checked your allegation and found what you called a missile was in fact a minaret of a Mosque." Kissinger scoffed. "Perhaps you hide missiles in minarets," he said. Exasperated, he added, "If I became [*sic*] involved in any more African problems I will lose my sanity."[74]

Carter and Mengistu Take Charge

Ethiopia was one of the few countries where it was clear, when the Carter team took office, that US policy would have to change. Once the Derg signed its first arms deal with the Soviet Union in December 1976, the holding pattern that the Ford administration had maintained since the 1974 revolution was unsustainable. Adding to the turbulence in the region, Djibouti—one of the lost fields of Greater Somalia—was slated to become independent in June 1977 after more than a century of French rule. Without France's protection, that destitute city-state would be ripe for the picking of Somali irredentists.

In the last months of the Ford administration, the State Department and CIA focused exclusively on Djibouti, not the Ogaden, as a flashpoint in the Horn.[75] In December 1976, as Kissinger was making his final European tour, he met with French president Giscard d'Estaing. They discussed Djibouti. "What worries me most is what the Somalis might do," Kissinger stated. The two men agreed that it was essential to convince the Soviets to restrain Somalia. "They should be told that any irresponsible action in the Horn of Africa would be considered by us as a serious breach of détente; it would incur serious consequences." Kissinger stressed that Giscard should confer closely with the new American administration. And on January 3, the CIA released an analysis of future threats that included the observation that "there is a serious danger of hostilities between Somalia . . . and Ethiopia."[76] However, the Carter team, embroiled in the chaotic months of the transition, did not pay close attention to the Horn of Africa. There is no indication that the newly appointed leaders of Carter's foreign policy team considered the Horn at all before January 20, 1977—not even as a minor item at the bottom of the elaborately prepared lists of priorities. This is surprising.

Exactly two weeks after Carter entered the White House, Mengistu Haile Mariam, a forty-year-old Ethiopian army officer who had been vying for control of the Derg since 1974, consolidated power with breathtaking brutality Accounts vary: some assert that, having gathered the military council of the Derg for a meeting, Mengistu pulled out his pistol and shot seven of his rivals dead. Others say that he left the room and his guards did the dirty work for him. In either case, seven bodies—all top military officers—littered the room from which Mengistu emerged as strongman. "It was a brawl," an American official declared.[77]

Mengistu was ruthless, suave, and persuasive. The State Department's intelligence bureau observed: "He is a tough ex-NCO. . . . His own political views have been difficult to pin down, other than his single-minded resolve, as the son of a serf, to restructure Ethiopian society." Two US congressmen who visited Addis described him as "thoughtful and determined," while a State Department official deemed him "Robespierre-like."[78]

The new strongman of Ethiopia faced staggering challenges. As a nationalist, he was determined to keep his country united. As a Marxist, he was determined to implement the revolutionary agenda that the Derg had espoused upon seizing power: broad-based land reform, expanded access to primary education, and improved rural health care. The Derg disestablished the Ethiopian Orthodox Church, claimed its land, and seized large estates without compensation. Mengistu relied on desperate measures—murder on a mass scale—to implement these reforms. In Addis Ababa, the revolutionaries fractured in bitter and violent disagreements about their country's future. The capital city was racked by urban guerrilla warfare, exacerbated by skyrocketing inflation. Bands of progovernment vigilantes roamed the streets, killing hundreds—perhaps thousands—of purported enemies of the regime. "The fighting in Addis," the *New York Times* observed, "is devouring its own children." By March 1977, the *Washington Post* noted, Addis Ababa had become "a city of terror."[79]

Mengistu required a strong and loyal military, but the Ethiopian army—the remnants of Haile Selassie's army, trained and armed by the United States—was demoralized. The Derg was, as the State Department's intelligence analysts wrote, "caught in a foreign policy dilemma": its sympathies were with Moscow, but its arms supplier was the United States. The Derg courted Moscow, but the Kremlin's response was cautious because it did not want to endanger its investment in Somalia.[80]

While the arms that Moscow promised Addis in December 1976 did not satisfy Mengistu, they "outraged" Siad Barre.[81] They convinced him that Somalia had a limited window of opportunity to take advantage of Ethiopia's weakness: Somalia had to seize the Ogaden before Soviet arms started to flow to the Derg. The age-old longing for Greater Somalia resurfaced with ferocity. This was Moscow's nightmare: that its oldest ally in Africa would wage war on its newest.

Andrew Young's Recommendation

The Carter administration inherited the assumption that had guided Ford's policy toward the Horn for more than two years: there was time to wait for Ethiopia to "come to its senses" because the Soviet Union would stick with its massive investment in Somalia. This was based on two intelligence assessments, both wrong. The first overestimated the depth of the Ethiopian peoples' pro-Western leanings. The second underestimated the Kremlin's desire to embrace the Ethiopian revolutionaries. "Soviet policy toward Addis Ababa remains cautious," the State Department asserted in January 1977. "The USSR clearly is attracted by the possibilities it perceives in Ethiopia. . . . [but its] relationship with Somalia remains paramount."[82]

Moscow's December 1976 decision to send arms to the Derg, however, did worry the incoming administration. The CIA set up an interagency working group on the Horn and included a brief analysis of the region in its February 1977 "World Trends and Developments," a sixty-nine-page *tour d'horizon*. "Long an area of smoldering tension and turmoil," it noted, "developments in the Horn of Africa during the past year point toward increasing problems." The Kremlin could succeed in maintaining its alliance with Somalia while simultaneously nurturing its budding friendship with Ethiopia. If so, "the reverberations . . . would be felt throughout Africa," the CIA noted. "To many it would reinforce the view that we set in train in Indochina and Angola that the Soviets are a more reliable source of support than the West." An interagency review of the situation in sub-Saharan Africa written in the same month dealt briefly with the Horn: "In southeastern Ethiopia [i.e., the Ogaden], insurgents trained and supplied by the Somali government pose a serious challenge to understrength Ethiopian security units. . . . [Siad Barre] believes that Ethiopia is vulnerable to a Somali challenge. . . . Consequently, there is a greater danger of a Somali move." The analysts predicted, incorrectly, that the Soviets would "*undoubtedly* continue to give the bulk of their aid to the country they currently value the most—Somalia," while at the same time they would "also try to exploit the possibilities" in Ethiopia.[83]

Carter's top foreign policy officials were aware of this danger, but still believed that the Kremlin's focus in Africa paralleled their own: southern Africa was where the action was, and the Horn was a sideshow. "The USSR still sees its best opportunity for gains in Africa . . . in the black-white confrontation in southern Africa," the State Department wrote in a February 1977 review of Africa policy. Furthermore, Washington's preoccupation with the dangers attendant to the independence of Djibouti blinded it to the more imminent threat in the Ogaden.[84] Carter did not even return the Ethiopian government's message of congratulations upon his inauguration, because the Derg leader who had written it had been whacked by Mengistu in the February shootout. There was no US ambassador in Addis Ababa and no plan to send one. The agenda for the spring 1977 chiefs of mission conference in Ivory Coast listed the main item as southern Africa; the Horn was relegated to a side panel for "regional issues."[85]

It was Andrew Young who challenged this assessment. While attending the celebrations in Zanzibar, he met Somalia's Siad Barre. In its briefing notes for the meeting, the State Department had suggested to Young that it was "worth considering . . . efforts . . . to exploit newly aroused Somali displeasure with the Soviets." It added, "We do not expect any abrupt change, however, and do not plan any major gestures, such as a resumed AID program, until we have convincing evidence of a Somali change of heart."[86]

In Zanzibar, Siad Barre regaled Young with his desire to draw closer to the United States. The American responded that the Carter administration's "new approach" was characterized by "readiness to cooperate with all African countries."[87] Young also talked with other African and Middle Eastern leaders about their impressions of the situation in the Horn, and when he returned to Washington, he expressed his concerns with characteristic directness. "Critical situation in Horn of Africa requires strengthening US ties with Somalia," he wrote Carter on February 13, his first day back in the States. "Somalia is strongly expansionist," he warned flatly. He recommended extending economic, not military, aid to Somalia: "[Siad Barre] complained of food shortages. . . . He can't eat Russian weapons and needs other kinds of development assistance."[88]

The following night, at a White House dinner honoring the president of Mexico, Young spoke with the press: The United States should "seek more influence in Somalia . . . and 'monitor very closely' what is happening in Ethiopia," the *Economist* reported him saying. "Mr Young went on to say bluntly that the Russians were 'playing games' in the Horn of Africa, and that the tensions in that area were potentially more explosive than those in southern Africa."[89]

Young discussed his ideas with Carter and Vance and then wrote in a cable circulated to key African and European posts. "As Washington is aware, among the clearest impressions which I brought back from my trip to Africa was the critical need . . . to focus on the problems of the Horn of Africa." Young noted that "Soviet wooing of Ethiopia may lead Somalia to take a new look at the possibility of improving relations with the US," but there was cause for caution. Siad Barre "told me when we met" that he "dreams of a 'Greater Somalia.'" Young predicted that Siad would launch "a concerted effort . . . to reclaim Somalia irridenta."[90]

Young asserted that it was in the US interest to maintain influence in the area. "The Soviets . . . are undoubtedly tempted by the prospect of playing a greater role in the Red Sea, the Gulf of Aden, the Horn, and, thereby, the Indian Ocean." His recommendation was clear. "We are for the moment tagged as being on the side of Ethiopia. . . . This would seem . . . to be a useless, if not dangerous, posture." Young recommended that the United States "reduce its activities in Ethiopia . . . to the absolute minimum necessary to keep our foot in the door." At the same time, Washington should make a serious effort to draw closer to Sudan—for Young, this was the key—and, "while chances seem slight," to Somalia.[91]

Cyrus Vance's Bombshell

Members of Congress, liberal and conservative, had been talking about human rights since the early 1970s. In 1975, Congress had passed the Harkin

Amendment, which required the State Department's new Office of Human Rights and Humanitarian Affairs to submit an annual "Country Report on Human Rights Practices" for every nation slated to receive US aid. The International Security Assistance and Arms Export Control Act of 1976 required the administration to refrain from sending weapons to nations that "engaged in a consistent pattern of gross violations of internationally recognized human rights" unless there were powerful extenuating circumstances.[92]

It was not until the election of Jimmy Carter that the human rights activists in Congress had a president who talked about the need to tie US foreign policy to human rights, and it was not until 1977 that the State Department began submitting country reports about human rights in countries designated for aid. This was the eye of the storm: if human rights were to inform US foreign policy anywhere, it would be in the allocation of security assistance. Carter's vigorous support for human rights in his first weeks in office heightened interest in the State Department's list of countries slated to receive US aid. It would be the first test of the administration's commitment—beyond rhetoric—to human rights.

Cyrus Vance, testifying to Congress about the administration's proposed foreign aid budget, explained: "We must recognize the fact that our foreign policy objectives reflect a range of concerns and sometimes force us to make difficult choices among those concerns. . . . It is our job to make those choices pragmatically, while holding true to our stated principles and purposes. . . . Our concern for human rights must be considered together with other economic and security goals."[93] On February 24, 1977, Vance stressed to the Senate appropriations subcommittee on foreign operations that including human rights considerations in the determination of foreign aid inevitably led to a series of "difficult choices." He also admitted that it was hard to enforce a consistent approach on human rights—the appearance of hypocrisy was an ever-present danger.[94]

Senator Daniel Inouye (D-HI), chair of the subcommittee, then asked Vance if he was prepared, based on human rights concerns, "to reduce aid to some of our friends." Vance's reply was almost offhand. "Yes," he said. "Argentina, Uruguay, and Ethiopia are three that come to mind."[95]

This was a bombshell. "Have they been informed?" Inouye inquired. Vance said, "If they haven't, they will be notified." Inouye stated the obvious: "They are notified now."[96]

In percentage terms, the proposed reductions in aid to these three brutal military dictatorships were a drop in the bucket. For Ethiopia, it amounted to $1 million out of a scheduled $62 million military aid package. Nevertheless, the cuts sent a strong signal. The *New York Times* declared that they were "a first step toward indicating the Americans care deeply about egregious deprivations of human rights." The *Washington Post* agreed: "Their echo is sure to be heard around the world. . . . It is something to applaud."[97]

While the editorial writers hit their keyboards, State Department officers drafted cables to Addis Ababa, Montevideo, and Buenos Aires to inform their embassies of what Vance had just announced to the world. The governments of Argentina and Uruguay loudly and immediately protested. For the latter, it was "unacceptable interference in the internal affairs of Uruguay" based on "total ignorance. . . . The Uruguayan government vigorously rejects it." The Argentine government repudiated Washington's allegations with equal vehemence. "No state—no matter its ideology or power—can arrogate to itself the role of an international tribunal, interfering in the domestic affairs of other countries. . . . This is a lamentable anomaly in the customary conduct of international affairs."[98]

In Addis Ababa, however, the Derg's response was muted. It had already taken compensatory action. The results of its December treaty with the Soviet Union were on their way: Soviet tanks and 76mm guns would begin to arrive in Ethiopia in March.[99] Mengistu, however, was unsure how reliable an arms supplier Moscow—which was still arming Somalia—would be. He had also turned to Cuba.

In late October 1976, Havana had sent a delegation to Ethiopia; it had returned with glowing reports of the revolution.[100] On February 8, 1977—two weeks before Vance's bombshell—Mengistu had summoned the Cuban ambassador in Ethiopia. After explaining that he was modeling revolutionary Ethiopia on "Cuba's example," Mengistu lauded Havana's "help for other revolutionary regimes defending their independence." Referring to the shootout of February 3—five days earlier—he predicted that "we expect the Americans to cut off all aid." The Ethiopian revolution, therefore, had an "immense need of help. . . . Could Comrade Fidel send us small arms?"[101]

Two weeks later, on February 20, a Cuban delegation led by General Arnaldo Ochoa, a close aide of Fidel Castro, arrived in Addis Ababa. During a four-hour meeting with Mengistu, which the Cubans characterized as "friendly and open," the Ethiopian leader explained that "he was not expecting Cuba to provide everything, but that his country needed doctors and medicine and he also hoped that Cuban officers would agree to train the militia that was being organized throughout the country."[102]

The dilemma for Havana as well as for Moscow was their ties with Siad Barre, who was rattling sabers at the new regime in Addis Ababa. The Kremlin strongly wanted to draw closer to Addis without alienating Mogadiscio. Moscow's goal—to straddle both ends of the Horn—was ambitious, though not without precedent: Washington was straddling both ends of the Arab-Israeli dispute. The Soviets launched a frenetic round of diplomacy to defuse the conflict they believed was looming in the Ogaden. General Secretary Leonid Brezhnev himself sent messages to Siad Barre urging him to "reconsider the Somali position with regard to Ethiopia and . . . avoid any exacerbation of the conflict." In reply, Siad oozed reassurance: Somalia, he declared, "was not going to start a war with Ethiopia." He dangled plans for a new naval base near Mogadiscio and a military airfield near Berbera—and then asked the Soviets for more weapons.[103]

Fidel Castro Tries to Mediate

Fidel Castro received "a 'hero's' welcoming ceremony at [the] airport," the US chargé in Addis Ababa cabled, "including full military honors for [a] 'great international revolutionary.'" Deplaning from an Aeroflot jet on March 14, 1977—the day that the US House of Representatives was debating repeal of the Byrd Amendment that would restore sanctions on Rhodesia—Castro was greeted by the Ethiopians with an "orgy of delight." That night, state-controlled television broadcast a one-hour special on the Cuban revolution. The local press speculated that Ethiopia would accrue "all sorts of benefits from the new relationship with 'Freedom Island.'" The American embassy in Addis cabled that the visit "must be seen as a feather in Mengistu's cap."[104]

The State Department followed Castro's African journey, which had begun on March 1, with great interest. It considered its purpose to be, above all, an opportunity for Castro to visit his troops in Angola and cement Cuba's relations with southern African states—Castro would proceed to Tanzania and Mozambique, and he would end his journey in Angola. Castro's decision to spend the first two weeks in North Africa and the Horn was puzzling, but not alarming. US intelligence knew that in late 1976 Castro had attempted to mediate Somali-Ethiopian tensions, and it knew about General Ochoa's February mission.[105] The CIA had concluded that "[Cuban] military assistance [to Ethiopia] was almost certainly discussed [by Ochoa]," a supposition that was confirmed when the US embassy reported on March 5 that a Cuban military mission had arrived in Addis.[106]

"Castro has his own goals and interests to pursue, but they are clearly in harmony with those of the USSR," Vance cabled. "Castro's visit to Addis suggests that the Cubans have decided to provide or are considering sending military advisers to Ethiopia, but Castro would want to avoid undermining Cuba's relationship with Somalia, if possible." Brzezinski wrote Carter that Castro's trip to Addis signaled "an expanded Cuban role in the Horn. . . . The opportunity to gain influence in Ethiopia is too attractive to let pass." By the end of March 1977, the CIA was reasonably sure it had penetrated the mystery: "Castro's decision to visit Ethiopia strongly implies that the Cubans have already decided to provide some military assistance."[107]

This conclusion did not set off alarm bells in Washington. There were at least four explanations for American equanimity. First, Cuba, like the Soviet Union, had close ties with Ethiopia's sworn enemy, Somalia, where forty-two Cuban military personnel were stationed.[108] Second, Cuba had been supporting one of the Eritrean rebel groups in its war against the government in Addis Ababa for many years, both during and after Haile Selassie's reign.[109] Third, the State Department knew that Havana's commitment to Angola was stretching Cuban resources, and it seemed unlikely that Castro would soon launch another "Angola-scale military operation."[110] Fourth, Washington could not shake its conviction that the Horn was a distraction from southern Africa, the real danger zone.

In fact, Havana was mesmerized by the Derg's revolutionary determination to wrench Ethiopia from its feudal past. Castro established diplomatic relations with Ethiopia in July 1975, and he sent an ambassador there in August 1976. In late 1976 and early 1977, this ambassador, as well as the other top Cuban officials in Ethiopia, enthusiastically agreed with Castro's assessment that Mengistu was leading a true revolution. In March 1977, Cuban intelligence paid the Derg the highest compliment: "The social and economic measures undertaken by the leaders of Ethiopia are the most progressive taken by any country since the Cuban Revolution."[111] Associating Cuba with the Ethiopian revolution, however, threatened Cuba's relationship with Somalia, which was making increasingly aggressive claims to the Ogaden. Fidel Castro decided to assess the situation in person, going first to Addis Ababa and then to Mogadiscio.

The goal of Castro's trip to the Horn, the US embassy in Mogadiscio cabled in its "Castro Visit Round-up," was "to mediate [the] subterranean dispute between" Somalia, Ethiopia, and the Soviet Union. "Public aspects of Castro visit [to Somalia] demonstrated conclusively the close ideological and psychological affinity between GSDR [Government of the Somali Democratic Republic] and Castro's Cuba. . . . Siad set tone of visit in his March 12 remarks at airport when he welcomed Castro to his 'second home.'"[112]

Although the US embassy was right about Castro's goals, it misread the atmospherics: Castro did not feel at home in Somalia. "I have figured out Siad Barre," he told East German leader Erich Honecker. "He is, above all, a chauvinist. . . . His socialism is a facade . . . [and] he uses Party simply to enhance his personal power."[113] The new leader of Ethiopia, by contrast, greatly impressed Castro. "Mengistu strikes me as a quiet, honest, and convinced revolutionary leader," he told Honecker. "He is an intellectual who revealed his wisdom on February 3rd." That was the day Mengistu killed, or ordered killed, seven top members of the Derg's military council. Castro explained: "Before [February 3], we could support the leftist forces only indirectly; now we can do so without constraint. . . . A real revolution is occurring in Ethiopia," Castro said. "In this former feudal empire, land is being distributed to the peasants."[114]

Given the brutality of Mengistu's rule, Castro's assessment seems callous, but in many ways the US State Department agreed with him. Mengistu was charismatic, and the yawning needs of Ethiopia called for dramatic change. "Government [the Derg's] policy places primary emphasis on . . . improving living standards for all. . . . Provisions have been made for free education . . . health services . . . a more equal distribution of social benefits. . . . These actions clearly indicate a sincere and meaningful commitment to economic and social reforms related to the improvement in the lives of the rural poor," the State Department explained. This report was not aberrant. Another stated: "After virtually centuries of feudalism, . . . Ethiopia is seeking to create a sectarian, egalitarian, socialist society. Given the problems of a country with a per capita income of under $100 and with 30 million people, it is not surprising that the revolution has been marked by tension, violence. . . . But much has been accomplished."[115]

On March 16, Castro tried to knock Mengistu's and Siad Barre's heads together at an extraordinary summit in Aden. The Cuban leader's goal was to defuse tensions in the Horn by creating a federation of Ethiopia, Somalia, South Yemen, and Djibouti (as soon as it became independent). Mengistu himself had endorsed the idea in an interview with Cuba's *Prensa Latina* on March 2.[116] The negotiations continued into the night. Sometime after 3:00 A.M., Castro decided to give Siad Barre a piece of his mind. The Somali leader's criticism of Mengistu, Castro proclaimed, was wrong: the Ethiopian was a true revolutionary leader—"the events of February 3 proved it." The problem was not Mengistu; it was Siad Barre. It was his irredentism that "threatened the region. It endangered both the Somali and the Ethiopian revolutions and would drive his country into the arms of Saudi Arabia and the imperialists."[117]

Castro's assessment of these talks was blunt. "The meeting was fruitless," he informed Honecker. The socialist countries faced "a great danger" in the Horn. "If we help Ethiopia, we will lose Siad Barre's friendship. If we don't, the Ethiopian Revolution will founder."[118]

Castro had made up his mind. "We must do something for Mengistu," he told Honecker. "We are collecting small arms from our stocks—mostly of

French, Belgian or Czech origin—to send to Ethiopia. About 45,000 men need to be armed. . . . Mengistu asked us to send 100 instructors for the militia, and now he has also asked for military advisers to form regular units." Castro explained his rationale: "The revolution in Ethiopia is an event of momentous importance. . . . We have an opportunity in Africa to inflict a severe defeat on the entire reactionary imperialist enterprise."[119]

In 1977, Fidel Castro wielded enormous clout in the Third World. Fresh off the heels of Cuba's defeat of South Africa's forces—and US policy—in Angola and a leading light in the nonaligned movement, Castro was a very confident fifty-year-old. It is testament to his star power that his tour of Africa utterly eclipsed that of Nikolai Podgorny, the chairman of the Presidium of the Supreme Soviet, who followed in his footsteps. On March 23, when Castro was still in Africa, the Soviet head of state was flying on a Soviet supersonic jet to Tanzania. Podgorny embodied the decay and drift of the Kremlin. An out-of-shape seventy-four-year-old, he and his "retinue of 120 pasty-faced officials," as *Newsweek* noted, seemed awkward and ill-prepared for this African safari.[120]

The State Department viewed Podgorny's trip "a political propaganda exercise" to shore up Soviet influence in the turbulent south of the continent. Vance cabled that the "centerpiece" of the trip was Mozambique, where the Soviet leader was "warmly received" and signed a Treaty of Friendship and Cooperation with the newly independent country.[121] "The Soviets undoubtedly value the treaty as a formal pledge to bring the USSR in on any future Mozambican strategy on Rhodesia," Vance wrote Carter on April 5. Maputo, however, resisted Soviet entreaties for access to naval facilities along its long Indian Ocean coast.[122]

Washington was only vaguely aware that a main topic of conversation in all the capitals that Podgorny visited was the deterioration of relations between Somalia and Ethiopia. The Soviet president added a last-minute stopover in Mogadiscio to personally apply pressure on the Somali leader. Siad maintained his uncompromising line toward Ethiopian "imperialism," despite Podgorny's best efforts to persuade him to embrace Moscow's new friend. And the Somali foreign minister told the Cuban ambassador in Mogadiscio that, for Somalia, gaining the Ogaden was "a matter of life or death."[123]

The House of Saud

Ethiopia, Somalia, the United States, the Soviet Union, and Cuba were not the only players at the table. Saudi Arabia had joined the game, and it had deep pockets. During the Carter years, the House of Saud vied for influence in the Horn. The Carter administration's dilemmas and difficulties in the Horn of

Africa were caused not only by Cold War concerns, but also by the need to adjust to the rise of Saudi Arabia.

The 1973 Arab-Israeli War—and the concomitant Arab oil embargo—had caused a revolution in the global economy that was only beginning to be understood in 1977. Money flowed in ever-increasing torrents from the West to the Middle East and Iran. In the late 1970s, Saudi Arabia—a country with a population of merely eight million, a third of whom were foreign laborers—wielded enormous and increasing power, with oil income that exceeded $40 billion in 1977 dollars.[124] Jimmy Carter's presidency was buffeted by the consequent storms in international relations: the oil shocks of 1973 had changed the global balance of power.

Awash in petrodollars, the Saudi royal family was cautiously exploring ways to exert its newfound political clout. Leading this pursuit after 1975 was Crown Prince Fahd, who, being more energetic and worldly than his half-brother, King Khalid Ibn Abdulaziz, was the de facto architect of Saudi Arabia's foreign policy. As Vance explained succinctly to Carter, "Khalid reigns and Fahd governs."[125] Fahd and his family had to guide Saudi Arabia through a period of extraordinarily rapid and radical change. Their challenge was to modernize the country without unleashing popular pressure to modernize its politics. This would require a deft hand.

Fahd's overriding goal was to use the power of petro-Islam to enhance Saudi security at home and abroad. This meant, above all, defusing the threat to the kingdom posed by radical governments—those supported by the Soviet Union—in the region. "The almost obsessive Saudi concern with communism," to quote Vance, was indigenous and sincere; it was not a sop to Washington. "The Kingdom always looked upon the principles and ideas of communism as being anathema to human thought and well being," the Saudi ambassador to the United States explained.[126] Jidda sought to arrest communism by modernizing the Saudi armed forces and by extending foreign aid to conservative regimes. The Saudi military budget increased almost sevenfold in the early 1970s, from $213 million in 1970 to $1.5 billion in 1974. Its foreign aid budget increased a staggering twenty-five-fold, from $221 million in 1971 to $5.7 billion four years later; by 1977, it was $9 billion. In comparative terms, in 1977 Saudi Arabia's foreign aid was approximately 10 percent of its gross national product, while US foreign aid was 0.27 of 1 percent.[127]

Saudi largesse was doled out carefully, in three concentric circles. In its own peninsula, the House of Saud had been seared by its struggles with the Soviet Union for influence in both Yemens (the communist South Yemen and the military-led North Yemen) and in Oman, neighbors that collectively had a greater population than did Saudi Arabia. The next circle of Saudi concern was the African littoral of the Red Sea. As a French diplomat reported, "The major determinant in Saudi policy toward the Horn . . . [is] the desire for stability in a region which Saudis consider of great (and increasing) importance to their own strategic interests." The key there was Egypt. After Anwar Sadat abrogated Egypt's treaty of friendship with the Soviet Union and expelled the Soviet military and civilian advisers, Saudi Arabia gave Cairo $1 billion a year to purchase arms and extended more than $2 billion of economic aid annually to the destitute nation. Likewise, Saudi Arabia lubricated Sudan's turn toward the West, increasing aid to that troubled country.[128] Saudi ambitions also extended deeper into Africa: at the inaugural Arab-African summit, held in Cairo in March 1977, Jidda pledged $1 billion in low-interest loans to black Africa. "The most spectacular role was played by the Saudis," the *New York Times* reported from the summit. "For the first time on a major scale, Saudi Arabia extended to black Africa the role of political and financial leadership that it has been playing in the Arab world."[129]

The United States watched the evolution of Saudi Arabia's role in the region with great interest. Washington and Jidda, despite their obvious differences, were conservative and capitalist. Their interests were like a set of Venn diagrams: intersecting, complex, and fluid. Yet even the places of overlap—anticommunism and global capitalism—could shift apart, and there was one large area of difference: Israel.

The economic ties between the two nations grew precipitously after the oil shocks. By the time Carter became president, the United States exported more than $3.5 billion of goods (excluding arms) to the kingdom. US weapons sales had jumped from $305 million in 1972 to more than $5 billion in 1975. More than 30,000 Americans were working in Saudi Arabia, most in the oil business, which Americans managed. The Saudis supplied the United States with more than 25 percent of its imported oil. (In contrast, Iran supplied 6 percent and Nigeria 18 percent.) Moreover, Jidda's support of the dollar was critical to the US economy. Carter praised the Saudis for the "responsible and unselfish" way they invested their petrodollars and "saved the entire economic structure of the world from disruption." They had invested approximately $60 billion in the United States, and they bought $1 billion of Treasury notes every three months during 1977. An American diplomat told the *Washington Post*, "We are reaching the point where we are more dependent on them than they are on us."[130]

The security ties were based on the shared US and Saudi interest in containing Soviet influence. The kingdom offered the United States an alluring mix of capabilities and assets, especially after Vietnam when there were constraints on presidential power. First, the kingdom had money—cold cash to fund anti-Soviet ventures. As William Quandt, an NSC official during the Carter administration, told the *New York Times*, "It takes [Saudi] King Fahd about 10 seconds to sign a check. . . . It takes Congress weeks to debate the smallest issue of this sort. If you can get somebody else to pay for it, it's nice and convenient." Second, the kingdom had unequaled prestige in the region. Third, it sat in a strategic location straddling the Red Sea and the Persian Gulf. In return, the United States provided the Saudi royal family with an enormous benefit: a discreet security umbrella. As the British Ministry of Defence explained, "Most Saudis would recognise that the United States represents the best guarantor of the security of a nation which, for all its size and wealth, has a tiny indigenous population."[131]

The security relationship grew more subtle and shadowy in the details: what, exactly, was the nature of the deal between Washington and Jidda? "It's [the understanding between the United States and Saudi Arabia] not written down anywhere," Roy Atherton, US ambassador to Egypt in the Carter years, told the *New York Times*. "It's implicit, but it's unambiguous. The Saudis see this as a special relationship and we do, too." Henry Kissinger confessed in his memoirs, "Often I found through other channels a helpful Saudi footprint placed so unobtrusively that one gust of wind could erase its traces."[132]

The Ethiopian revolution occurred at the same time that Saudi Arabia was spreading its hegemony—and largesse—across the region. By late 1976, the Saudis believed that one repercussion of that revolution might be that Siad Barre of Somalia could be persuaded to turn toward the West. Jidda had rebuffed Siad when he had been joined at the hip to the Soviets. In March 1975, for example, US intelligence reported that "at the burial of [Saudi] King Faisal, the Saudis completely ignored the Somali party." At the time, when Siad had asked for drought aid, the Saudis had "acted angrily and refused to discuss it. . . . President Siad was said to be extremely angry at the cool reception he received from the Saudis."[133] Until Ethiopia signed its arms agreement with the Soviet Union in December 1976, Washington and Jidda were convinced that no amount of money could pry Somalia from the Soviet embrace. "Siad's . . . belief in [the] inexorable march of world socialism and capitalism's inevitable collapse is too conclusive to be abandoned," the US embassy in Mogadiscio reported in 1975. "It is unrealistic for us or Arabs to believe that they could oust Soviet Union by offering to replace Soviet military or economic assistance with their own."[134]

Flip-Flop?

Andrew Young's report after meeting with Somalia's Mohamed Siad Barre and other African leaders in Zanzibar in mid-February 1977 had shone a spotlight on the choices facing the Carter administration in the Horn. A few weeks later, Cyrus Vance's announcement of the reduction in security assistance to Ethiopia hinted at the direction Washington would take.

In Mogadiscio a fortnight after Vance's testimony, Deputy Assistant Secretary of State for African Affairs Talcott Seelye had a three-hour meeting with Siad Barre, who expressed his torment about the arms deal that Moscow had signed with Addis the previous December. The Somali president was frank about the "central role" that Ethiopia played in his strategic thinking. He stated bluntly that the warmth of Somalia's relations with Washington and Moscow would be determined "in good part" by how helpful each superpower was to Somalia in its "long-term contest with Ethiopian 'imperialism.'"[135] The US ambassador in Mogadiscio, John Loughran, thought Siad was serious in his desire for improved relations with the United States. "Embassy strongly believes . . . [the Carter administration] must make tangible gesture in near future," he cabled on March 7.[136]

Thus, in March 1977, while Castro and Podgorny were in Africa and the US Congress was debating the Byrd Amendment, the Carter administration began to develop its policy toward the Horn. On March 17, one day after Castro's failed attempt to mediate the dispute between Somalia and Ethiopia, an interagency group in Washington—State, Defense, CIA, and NSC—was formed to write a Presidential Review Memorandum (PRM 21) on the Horn of Africa. This comprehensive blueprint of US policy toward the Horn was due on April 5.[137]

In the meantime, the Somali ambassador in Washington, Abdullahi Addou, was pressing Siad's case in Foggy Bottom. "I had one mission when I was sent to America," he explained: "to improve Somali relations with the United States." Ambassador Addou was indefatigable. "He was a piece of work," one American official remembered. "Addou was a gifted diplomat and a superb liar," another recalled. "Double-check everything he says," a third recollected, laughing. "Incredible," a fourth said, succinctly.[138] Addou understood the importance of talking to people in Congress (staffers, junior members, committee chairs), as well as in the executive branch (desk officers, NSC staffers, assistant secretaries). His message, which he conveyed to every US official he could buttonhole, was important: Somalia was eager to befriend the United States, if only Washington would replace Moscow as his country's arms supplier.

On March 24, Addou met with Bill Schaufele, the assistant secretary for African affairs. Referring to the collapse of Castro's mediation efforts one week earlier, Addou explained that Siad Barre had rejected the Soviet and Cuban federation of regional states because it would have foiled Somalia's aspiration to claim the Ogaden. Siad was now convinced, Addou said, that the

Soviets had opted for Ethiopia and were willing to sacrifice Somalia "in part because they doubted Siad's commitment to Marxism, given his Islamic faith and the nature of the Somali mentality." But before Somalia could break loose from the Soviets, it had to locate another reliable military supplier. Addou said that he had been instructed to ask if his country could rely on the United States for economic aid and assured access to military supplies.[139]

Vance's Evening Report to Carter on March 24 led with the news that Addou "has approached us to determine whether we would provide them [the Somalis] economic and military aid if they readjusted their close relations with the Soviets. The ambassador [Addou] said that the United States was the only nation with the resources to substitute for the USSR as Somalia's arms supplier." Vance explained that Schaufele had responded that Washington welcomed better relations and might be able to extend economic aid, but military aid "would be more difficult" because the administration had not yet completed its review of arms transfer policy. In this snippet to Carter, Vance did not mention the problem of Somalia's irredentism.[140]

Vice President Walter Mondale, who was always sent a copy of Vance's Evening Reports, circled the part about Somalia wanting improved relations and scrawled a large "Let's move!!" across the top of the memo. He immediately wrote Vance, "I think it is important not to risk the appearance of disinterest at a time when we might have a good chance to lessen Somalia's ties with the USSR. Is there some early action we can take on economic aid? My feeling is that we should follow up quickly on this approach by Somalia." Over lunch the next day, Mondale urged Carter, "This . . . might be what is needed to oust . . . the Soviets from Berbera."[141]

The Saudi royal family agreed. "The Saudis believe the new Ethiopian regime has tilted sharply toward the Soviets, and plan to exploit the opportunity this presents to woo its Somali rival," a senior State Department official had cabled Vance in February. By late March, the White House knew that the Saudis had offered Somalia "up to $300,000,000 to break with the Soviets."[142] A State Department intelligence analyst confirmed that "the Saudi factor was a very important one for the Administration in its policy towards the Horn."[143]

The US embassy in Mogadiscio weighed in. The deputy chief of mission cabled that "atmosphere within Mogadiscio diplomatic corps is changing. . . . Some Arab diplomats . . . are privately urging me to tell Washington that time is right for us to 'move' in Somalia. I agree. . . . Although I recognize difficulties, believe situation warrants serious consideration of modest military assistance."[144]

Thus did US policy morph. Hope—that the new administration could "chalk one up" for the Americans—replaced caution. The Carter administration knew that Siad Barre was itching to invade Ethiopia and seize the Ogaden; both Siad Barre and Ambassador Addou were straightforward about why they sought US arms. In January, the State Department had been unwilling to extend any aid—economic or military—until Siad had provided "convincing evidence of a . . . change of heart." In February, Young recommended modest economic aid. But by late March, Mondale was urging action and the US embassy in Mogadiscio was pushing "modest military assistance." The *Washington Post* opined that a "superpower flip-flop" might be in the offing in the Horn.[145]

Some members of the Carter administration were wary. Brzezinski sent a note to the vice president emphasizing the need to "exercise some caution" because "Somali irredentism is very deep-seated." and Vance told Mondale that the State Department was contemplating only economic aid. Young, who in some ways had set the ball rolling, was growing anxious. He told NSC staffer Paul Henze that "he had come to consider the Horn area much more volatile than South Africa because it was so much less amenable to responsible influences."[146]

Back to Sadat

On April 1, 1977, when Vance was in London talking with Foreign Secretary David Owen about Rhodesia, the conversation turned to the Horn, where Mengistu was veering ever leftward. Asked whether the Carter administration had decided to extend aid to Somalia, Vance replied that the United States "could provide 40 to 50 million dollars in [economic] aid but that no decision had yet been taken about whether to sell arms. The Saudis would finance the purchase of arms." Vance repeated this on April 3 in Paris in talks with French President Giscard d'Estaing in which African issues—especially how to rescue Mobutu—took precedence over discussions about Vance's recent unsuccessful trip to Moscow to jump-start the SALT II talks. Giscard replied that even though Siad Barre was "very unstable," he thought it was "important that we respond favorably to the Somalis."[147] On that same day, Castro was in East Berlin fulminating against Siad Barre, and Podgorny was in Mogadiscio trying to keep Somalia in the Kremlin's corral.

This was the context of Anwar Sadat's first meeting with Jimmy Carter: Podgorny was landing in Tanzania, Castro was in Angola, Moroccan troops were about to land in Shaba, and tensions were increasing in the Horn. On the eve of his arrival in Washington, Sadat told *Le Monde* that he was "worried—very, very worried—about the Soviets' ominous schemes in Africa."[148]

Neither Carter nor Sadat mentioned Africa at the welcoming ceremony, held during a cold, driving rain in Washington on April 4, 1977. During his first conversation with Carter, the Egyptian raised the alarm about Soviet designs on Africa. "The Soviets . . . seized Angola. Now they are using it as a jumping off point," Sadat explained. "They are attacking the richest part of Zaire . . . and they are preparing a second base in Ethiopia. . . . The Soviets support Mengistu. . . . He is a madman. . . . It is about what the Soviets want to do in Africa. All of us feel threatened." Sadat underlined the point: "I am very worried. Saudi Arabia is also worried. The Soviets must be checked."[149] Over lunch, Sadat elaborated on his fears about instability in the Horn, where Ethiopia was convulsed in revolution and Djibouti would soon be independent. Then he got to the heart of the matter: Somalia had turned to Egypt, a fellow Red Sea and Muslim nation, for help. Siad Barre "has asked Egypt for arms." Egypt could be particularly helpful to Somalia because its military was switching from Soviet-supplied arms to US weapons; therefore, it had the Soviet arms with which the Somalis were familiar. Cairo agreed to send small arms to Somalia if Siad Barre distanced his country from the Soviets.[150]

When Vance returned to his office after lunch, a cable from the US embassy in Jidda awaited him. The Saudis had decided "to give up on the Ethiopian regime as hopeless," Ambassador William Porter wrote, "[and to try] to pry the Somalis away from the Soviets." Porter predicted that the Saudis would soon be offering Siad Barre "some firm proposals for economic assistance, including the promise to displace the Soviets as the source of Somalia's petroleum. . . . The SAG [Saudi Arabian government] very much wants our help, but seems determined to move now."[151]

At a working dinner at the White House that night, Carter toasted Sadat: "I've learned a lot from him during this morning's conversation and this evening. . . . His knowledge of the background of developments in the Middle East and south of him, in Africa, are a very valuable reservoir of knowledge and experience and insight that will help to guide me in making the right decisions that apply to our own country's influence."[152] The following day, Carter told Sadat, "We tend to think of Egypt only in relation to Israel, but you helped to explain the problems that you also face in Africa. . . . It was helpful."[153]

Unlike the press coverage before Sadat's visit, which had focused exclusively on his role in the Arab-Israeli peace process, the reports afterward noted that "little attention" had been paid to the peace process because of Sadat's "growing concern over Soviet penetration into African countries. . . . The Egyptian leader repeatedly and dramatically depicted a pattern of Soviet and Cuban involvement in Africa. . . . He said that he needed American arms to help keep all of Africa from becoming Communist." Sadat stressed that because of the deepening Soviet influence in Ethiopia and in the Shaba crisis, Egypt needed "defensive" weapons, including F-5 jet fighters and TOW missiles.[154]

By emphasizing his country's need to defend itself against the Soviet threat in Africa—not the Israeli threat in the Middle East—Sadat changed the context of his request for American arms. Some Israelis, and their friends, were alarmed. "Israel should recognize Egypt's move in the Horn of Africa for what it essentially is—the latest step in an overall design to replace Israel as America's ally in the global competition with the Soviet Union," conservative Israeli scholar Shlomo Slonim warned. "It represents a skilled attempt to neutralize Washington in the Arab-Israeli dispute. . . . American acquiescence . . . to an Arab 'regime' for the Red Sea . . . would seem to be the height of folly."[155]

The Order Is Given

On April 6, 1977, the day after Sadat departed, Carter allowed a *Time* magazine reporter to shadow him for a day. The White House staff hoped that the resulting article would humanize the president. Africa, the *Time* article stressed, was "a continent very much on Carter's mind." One of the president's first actions on April 6 was to call Vice President Mondale at 8:45 A.M. "With an edge of irritation in his voice," *Time* reported, "Carter says, 'I want you to tell Cy [Vance] and Zbig [Brzezinski] that I want them to move in every possible way to get Somalia to be our friend.'" Later that day, Carter wrote a brief memo to Vance: "Find ways to improve relations with . . . Somalia."[156] This changed US policy.

By the end of the day, Vance had sent a memo to Carter entitled "Better Relations with Somalia." The secretary of state explained that the "the Somalis have indicated to us that for them to undertake a major foreign policy shift away from Moscow, they would need an assured alternative source of military as well as economic aid." Vance's memo did not include any explanation or warning about why Somalia—one of the most heavily armed countries in sub-Saharan Africa—would be so adamant about needing more military aid. He merely indicated that the State Department would draw up an economic aid program and "encourage the Saudis—who appear willing—to provide substantial aid to Somalia . . . [including] military assistance."[157]

The following day, Vance cabled the US ambassador in Jidda, William Porter, to "initiate consultations with the SAG [Saudi Arabian government] with the aim of coordinating our respective policies with regard to Somalia." He should inform the Saudis that Somalia had asked Washington for arms and that "we want to be as responsive as possible" in the hope of turning Somalia to the West. "We understand that the SAG is considering the application of substantial resources in an effort to pry Somalia away from the Soviet embrace. For our part, we are actively considering how we might . . . provide Somalia with some economic assistance this fiscal year. It will be far short of Somali desires, but it will, we hope, be a concrete indication of our interest in the GSDR [Somalia] and support for the moderate Arab effort." Vance hedged on the possibility of extending military aid. "In the military field, we recognize Somalia's need to provide for its legitimate defense needs," he wrote, underlining the sentence. "Until we complete our overall review of US arms transfer policy we cannot address this need. We are looking into what non-US sources of arms might be available to Somalia." It was therefore necessary to coordinate with the Saudis. "Given the likelihood that the bulk of the financial resources which might be made available to the Somalis would come from the Saudis, we would welcome their views concerning the most effective application which might be made of the limited US resources." It had taken Vance less than twenty-four hours to act on the president's orders. On his memo informing Carter about the cable to Jidda, the president wrote, "Good."[158] The rest of the bureaucracy also got in gear quickly. On April 6, an NSC staffer wrote Brzezinski that the "President's interest in this area [the Horn] has sparked movement."[159]

The next day, the Presidential Review Memorandum on the Horn of Africa was completed and circulated. It represented a consensus of the opinions of the State and Defense departments, the CIA, and the NSC, but on a fundamental issue—the strategic importance of the Horn—there was, as NSC expert Paul Henze called it, "flak" among the various agencies. "Militarily the Horn is not of great strategic importance to the US," the text of the memorandum asserted boldly. The interdiction of sea routes in the Red Sea was not likely. "The Indian Ocean *per se* occupies a low priority in terms of the global strategic balance." But a telltale asterisk led the reader to the caveat: "DOD [the Department of Defense] disagrees on this point. It holds that US interests in the Horn are primarily strategic, reflecting the area's proximity to Middle East oil fields, the sea oil routes, and the Red Sea passage to the Mediterranean." This profound disagreement complicated the Carter administration's development of a coherent policy toward the Horn.[160]

The PRM conveyed no sense of urgency. It was implausible that Moscow would risk losing Somalia. Ethiopia, it noted, "offers no military-strategic advantages" over Somalia for the Kremlin, other than the "politico-strategic advantage of replacing US" and, possibly, the prospect of gaining more influence over Sudan, Kenya, and countries reliant on the Red Sea oil route. But the committee considered it very unlikely that the Kremlin would imperil its enormous investment in the base at Berbera for these hypothetical gains. The PRM stressed the provincial revolts challenging the Derg and warned that Mengistu might call for Cuban support despite the "adverse reaction in some African and Arab states and in the US."[161] It downplayed, however, the dangers of Siad's irredentism: "The survival of the Somali leadership does not require it to work actively, let alone take risks, for the achievement of that dream [of a Greater Somalia]."[162]

On April 11, the Policy Review Committee, chaired by Cyrus Vance, met in the White House situation room to discuss the Horn. The vice president, the secretary of defense, the director of central intelligence, the national security adviser, the head of the Joint Chiefs of Staff, and the ambassador to the UN were present. Based on the recommendations of the PRM and the stated wishes of the president, the assembled policymakers decided to investigate a warming toward Somalia, but they cautioned that "rushing into too close a relationship with the Somalis too soon . . . [risked] encouraging Somali territorial ambitions toward Ethiopia and Djibouti." Therefore, they agreed to "let the Saudis take the lead in offering money for military aid."[163] The State Department would "actively explore means by which Somalia's legitimate arms requests can be met from non-USSR sources," but with very little hope that Siad Barre would actually switch sides in the Cold War.[164]

Washington had only one decision to make quickly: whether to continue its military supply relationship with Ethiopia. The Department of Defense, reflecting its view of the strategic importance of the region for the United States, argued for "trying to keep . . . a US military relationship with Ethiopia."[165] The PRC tempered this. "It was agreed that we should not pull out of Ethiopia entirely," but neither should the US government extend "further significant support" to the Derg. Nonlethal military aid in the pipeline would be delivered, and military training would continue. "All other military aid . . . will be subject to delaying action. . . . We will simply wait and see."[166]

Jimmy Carter disagreed: the PRC's recommendation was "too easy on Ethiopia. Why just 'wait and see'?" he asked Brzezinski. Then, in another marginal comment, he added: "Need thorough discussion with [Saudi Prince] Fahd re Horn."[167]

At this moment, Mengistu stepped up the terror in Ethiopia. On April 14, he addressed a rally of 200,000 in Addis's Revolution Square. He held up five vials of blood (or a similar red liquid) and smashed them on the podium, declaring: "All the enemies of my administration [including] . . . 'hired fascists, and their running dogs' will see their blood flow!" The "Red Terror" had begun. Hundreds of people who were suspected of being enemies of the state disappeared daily, their corpses later appearing on the streets of Addis with tags around their necks warning onlookers of the price of dissent. "Vultures now roost in center city," the *New York Times* reported.[168]

President Carter overruled his advisers. On April 19, he instructed Brzezinski to inform Ethiopia forthwith that the United States was closing the Kagnew communications center, withdrawing all military advisers, and suspending all military aid.[169] Defense Secretary Harold Brown disagreed: given the strategic importance of the region, he believed Washington should maintain the status quo. This delayed the implementation of Carter's decision.[170]

In the meantime, Mengistu acted: on April 23, he ordered the US government to close all its cultural, medical, consular, and military operations—including the installation at Kagnew. At 5:40 P.M. on April 24, Ethiopian Army personnel "gave the [US] Navy personnel at Kagnew ten minutes warning to get out," Deputy Undersecretary of State Dick Moose reported, adding that in those ten minutes, the Americans had managed to "destroy . . . and to disperse" the guts of the top-secret spying equipment housed at the base.[171] The State Department sent Addis a "strong written protest," but it retained a rump staff at the US embassy in Addis and did not sever diplomatic relations. "Now is a good time to play it cool," the chargé at the US embassy in Addis advised.[172] Because of the delay in Washington, the relationship ended on Ethiopia's terms.

Carter was the driving force pushing the bureaucracy to open doors with Somalia. His reasons were clear: to compensate for the almost certain "loss" of Ethiopia to the Soviet camp, and to please the Saudis and Sadat. On April 15, Carter had written that he wanted to explore ways to improve relations with Somalia. Four days later, the US ambassador in Jidda reported that he had met with Prince Saud, who had said that "his government accepts wholeheartedly the Department's suggestion that we coordinate as much as possible our policies and actions concerning Somalia."[173] What is remarkable, however, is that Carter seemed oblivious to the potential costs of embracing Siad Barre. The Somali leader was refreshingly frank: all he wanted from Washington were weapons, and all he wanted them for was to invade Ethiopia and annex the Ogaden. This was what he told the American ambassador in Mogadiscio, and it was what the Somali ambassador in Washington told every US official with whom he spoke. Moreover, by late April, US intelligence was reporting that the Somali army was preparing to cross the border into Ethiopia.[174] Selling weapons to Somalia would arm an aggressor, and it would contravene Carter's oft-repeated campaign promise to limit US arms sales abroad. This would contradict Carter's stated high moral principles and undermine his administration's attempt to improve US relations with African leaders, for whom the inviolability of borders is the bedrock of peace on their continent. There is no record of anyone bringing these costs to the president's attention.[175] Of course, the Carter administration had not yet agreed to anything; it had merely opened the door. The rewards for doing so—especially in terms of the Saudis—were clear. However, opening that door would entangle the United States in the Horn. Neither Vance nor Brzezinski challenged the wisdom of Carter's decision to improve relations with Somalia. The policy, therefore, drifted forward.

5. Words and Weapons

Energy Week

"At first the price of gasoline climbed—way up. Finally only the well-to-do drove, and that was too clear an indication that they were filthy rich, so any automobile that dared show itself on a city street was overturned and burned. . . . Legs are king in the cities of 1997."

So wrote Isaac Asimov in the April 25, 1977, issue of *Time* magazine. The editors had asked Asimov, a biochemistry professor and prolific writer of science fiction, to imagine the United States at the end of the twentieth century, when fuel had run out. In Asimov's vision of 1997, America's cities are being demolished for scrap, and the rest of the world is in worse straits, especially babies, "the first and most helpless victims of starvation . . . after their mothers have gone dry." In 1997, because no one had done anything in the 1970s to reverse the dependence on oil, the world was roaring back to the preindustrial era. "It must end in subsistence farming and in a world population reduced by starvation, disease and violence," Asimov concluded.[1]

A lot of Americans didn't buy it. An April 1977 Gallup poll showed that 51 percent considered the energy crisis only "fairly" or "not at all" serious. Skeptics suspected that this "energy crisis" was a ploy of big oil to jack up the price of gasoline. "There is not an energy supply crisis," political activist Ralph Nader asserted on *Meet the Press* on April 17. "There is an energy monopoly crisis."[2] No one questioned that there had been a gas shortage after the 1973 Arab-Israeli war, when the price of oil had quadrupled, but President Nixon—fending off his own personal destruction in the Watergate scandal—had had neither the time nor the political capital to fight a battle that would pit the president against the family car and, by extension, the American way of life. Gerald Ford had also punted the problem.

Developing a national energy policy was one of Jimmy Carter's top priorities. Carter was convinced that oil was running out—a CIA analysis that the

White House leaked to the press in early April 1977 confirmed this in apocalyptic terms.[3] The Arab OPEC oil embargo had exposed the soft underbelly of
US defenses: Americans possessed hardened nuclear silos and slippery sub-
marines bristling with nuclear weapons, but the economic and military might
of the United States depended on oil, and the oil producers had proven—
defying all American expectations—that they had the willpower to turn off
the spigot.

On April 18, 1977, the eighty-eighth day of his presidency, Carter addressed
the American people in a prime-time television and radio address. The international context was troubling—the Soviets had rejected the latest SALT
proposals; Moroccan troops were on the ground in Shaba; Fidel Castro and
Nikolai Podgorny had just completed their African tours—but the president's
focus was elsewhere. "Tonight I want to have an unpleasant talk with you,"
a stern Jimmy Carter began. "The energy crisis has not yet overwhelmed us,
but it will if we do not act quickly." The president was in the Oval Office, and
he was not wearing the cardigan sweater he had donned for his first "fireside
chat." This speech was deadly serious, and Carter's pinstriped suit underlined
that fact. "With the exception of preventing war, this is the greatest challenge
that our country will face during our lifetime," he said with earnest emphasis.
It was the "moral equivalent of war." Carter stared unblinking into the camera, in an increasingly close shot that captured only his head and shoulders.
His campaign smile had vanished. "We simply must balance our demand for
energy with our rapidly shrinking resources. . . . The alternative may be a
national catastrophe."[4]

This jeremiad, dubbed "the sky-is-falling" speech by White House aides,
was the opening salvo of what became known as "Energy Week," when Carter
unrolled his policy in a well-planned one-two-three punch: on Monday, the
speech to the American people; on Wednesday, an address to a joint session
of Congress; on Friday, a press conference. Peppered between and after these
presidential moments, all staffers, plus Carter's wife Rosalynn and his mother
Miss Lillian, were deployed to every television show, town meeting, and press
event that would receive them. It was an astounding barrage. "This week
Jimmy Carter will make the most extensive use of the television medium
of any president in our history," columnist William Safire noted. "He will
become the first one-man mini-series."[5]

There was method to the blitz: Carter understood that once the energy
program hit the Congress it would face a withering assault from powerful
special interests. He believed that the only way to steel Congress for the
fight was to create a groundswell of popular support for the energy program. Carter therefore used television to appeal directly to the people. As

Hedrick Smith wrote in the *New York Times*, "President Carter signaled to the nation . . . that he had chosen energy as the issue on which to test and build his presidential leadership."[6]

It was risky, and Carter relished the fight: he believed in the importance of the cause and in his ability to convince the American people of it. He was confident that with his leadership, the enlightened public could persuade Congress to resist the inducements of the powerful oil, coal, and automobile lobbies and enact the painful legislation. Carter had reason to be cocky. After winning the presidency by the slimmest of margins, his popularity had been steady at a sky-high 72 percent approval rating. Carter's consistently high poll results, the *Washington Post* noted on April 17, were nothing short of "astounding."[7]

It seemed paradoxical that the president should be so popular at a time when Americans were deeply disenchanted with government. That April week when the Gallup poll was taken, the movie *Network* swept the Academy Awards; it encapsulated the rage of the day with its chant: "I'm mad as hell, and I'm not going to take this anymore!" Americans' frustration was not—yet—directed at Jimmy Carter, but he knew that in selling his energy proposal he faced an enormous, threefold challenge. He had to convince Americans that the energy crisis was real, persuade them that it was necessary to pay more for energy; and, in a profound way, redefine the American dream. As the *New York Times* banner headline declared on the day after Carter's speech to the American people, "The Message Is Curtailment of the Dream of Plenty."

Despite the speech's grim message—use less, pay more—the initial reaction to it was positive. Immediately before "Energy Week," Carter, trying to control the spin, had predicted that the "thankless" task of addressing the crisis could cause his poll numbers to drop fifteen points. "I'm willing to give up some of my own personal popularity among the people of this nation," he told West Virginians at a meeting about energy policy, "to require them to face the brutal facts." In fact, his numbers rose after his Monday night speech. The press response was generally positive. "The President is right, as well as brave," the lead *New York Times* editorial concluded.[8]

Two nights later, Carter took to the airwaves again, this time to explain the details of the program in a televised address to a joint session of Congress. This was a policy wonk's address, an engineer's speech. It explained a litany of graduated taxes (on gas-guzzling cars, as well as on gas, natural gas, and oil), subsidies (for weatherizing homes), and rebates to cajole and prod Americans toward conserving energy. This program of finely calibrated sticks and carrots was as impressive in its detail as it was mind-numbing. Even the president's mother had trouble with it. "I didn't exactly understand," Miss Lillian, known for her candor, admitted, "but I thought he looked good."[9] The plan's goals, however, were clear: reduce gas consumption by 10 percent by 1985, halve the annual rate of growth of US energy consumption, and begin to shift from imported oil to cleaner coal and solar energy.

The members of Congress applauded politely, but with no gusto. Although Carter's relations with Congress, where the Democrats controlled both houses, were not hostile in those early months of his presidency, neither were they warm; with hindsight, there were reasons to worry. "Congress and the Administration are like alley dogs sniffing each other before deciding whether to have a go," a British congressional expert explained.[10] Carter fully understood the centrality of Congress to his agenda. His White House had more congressional liaisons than his predecessors, he met frequently with members on both sides of the aisle, and contrary to some reports he made many, many phone calls to them to drum up support for bills he cared about. Carter did not neglect Congress, but his relationship with it became increasingly brittle, primarily because of four cooling undercurrents.

First, any president in the late 1970s would have struggled with the legislature, whose members were determined to wrest power from the executive branch. Second, running as an outsider had helped Carter win, but it had repercussions that were exacerbated by the narrowness of his victory: Jimmy Carter had no coattails. No members of Congress felt that they owed their election to him.[11] Third, Carter hated horse-trading. Mutual back-scratching was the engine of Congress, the fuel of politics, but not for Jimmy Carter. When absolutely necessary, as when he was gathering votes for the Panama Canal treaties, Carter would dole out pork, but always with disdain and never as part of a continuing process. Likewise, he shunned currying the favor of the special interest lobbies that were gaining influence on Congress.

Finally, Carter meant what he had told Elizabeth Drew during the campaign: "I honestly believe in the bottom of my soul that I can accurately represent what our people are and what we want to be and what we can be." That belief had helped him exude confidence then, but in the White House it posed a problem: where did Congress fit into Carter's political worldview? Carter *knew* that Congress was important, but given his communion with the American people he *felt* that it was an obstruction. He tried to keep his impatience with Congress in check, but he could not hide it. By April, Senate majority leader Robert Byrd was exasperated, doubting that Carter "really recognized that a President cannot deal with the Congress in the same fashion that a governor deals with a state legislature." In the House, Speaker Tip O'Neill was more blunt. If the president tried to go over the heads of Congress and appeal directly to the public, it would be "the biggest mistake that Mr. Carter could ever make."[12]

The members of Congress listening to the president's speech that April night worried that the voters might make them pay for supporting the president's stringent energy program. "Congress wants to wait for a bit to see which will win—Mr. Carter, with his engineer's mind and his sophisticated planners," the *Washington Post* noted, "or the great human inclination to wait until it starts raining again before deciding whether the roof still needs patching."[13]

Some—perhaps most—members of Congress were also uneasy about Jimmy Carter. "He still baffles the capital," *New York Times* columnist James Reston noted. "He talks like a populist but acts like a conservative. . . . Nobody quite knows where he is going, but it is clear after the last couple of weeks that he is leading the parade." Meg Greenfield of the *Washington Post* agreed. "There is a curiously apolitical and genuinely radical aspect to his method of policymaking," she wrote during Energy Week. "If there is one thing Carter can't abide, it is being told that for some . . . nonsubstantive reason he can't do something he thinks he should. . . . His approach is . . . —in Washington cultural terms—absolutely revolutionary. . . . Conflict is clearly on the way."[14]

Congressional Turbulence

"We are afraid of Congress," a Defense Department official admitted in April 1977. The administration had run into a buzz saw getting its 1978 security assistance budget through the legislature. This mammoth bill—the International Security Assistance Act of 1977—funded everything from jets for Israel to food for Bangladesh. The economic assistance section of the budget was uncontroversial, but the security assistance proposals for Africa drew fire. All of sub-Saharan Africa received only 5 percent of the total security aid package of $4.4 billion; the sums involved were relatively paltry, but they raised many legislators' hackles. When the bill was considered by the House in a long and fiery debate, fully half of the time was spent on African issues; four of the six amendments were about Africa. The Senate debate was less contentious but still disproportionately concerned with Africa: of nine amendments, four dealt with Africa.[15]

The most controversial item, by far, was the $100 million for the Zimbabwe Development Fund—almost half of the entire allotment of $222.8 million for sub-Saharan Africa. This was the fund that Kissinger had promoted in 1976 after his first meeting with South African prime minister John Vorster, but under Carter its purpose had been fundamentally altered. Kissinger's fund had been, as Representative Don Bonker (D-WA) declared, "a thinly disguised bribe" for Rhodesian whites to accept majority rule and to remain in the country. This did not sit well with the Carter administration. By the time Vance presented the proposal to Congress, its rationale had become "to prevent a collapse of the Zimbabwean economy."[16]

Vance might have expected the House subcommittee on Africa to rubber-stamp the budget that proposed increased aid for the continent. The subcommittee's seven members, chaired by Charlie Diggs (D-MI, the first chair of the Congressional Black Caucus), leaned liberal and were pleased with the administration's emphasis on Africa. (The South African ambassador in Washington reported that the subcommittee members "were implacable opponents of the South African government."[17]) But on March 30, tempers flared on Capitol Hill as the subcommittee was holding hearings on the foreign aid bill.

"Mr. Secretary," Steve Solarz (D-NY) began, addressing Deputy Assistant Secretary of State for Africa Talcott Seelye, "I would like to pursue further the question of the Zimbabwe slush fund." Like a prosecutor, Solarz filleted Seelye. He was angry, and he was incredulous. "Mr. Secretary, . . . never have I ever heard a more half-baked, ludicrous scheme than the one I am hearing put before us today." Solarz skewered Seelye with the inconsistencies of the administration's justification for the Zimbabwe Development Fund. "On the one hand," Solarz said caustically, "you are saying the purpose of the fund is to provide an incentive for Smith to agree to majority rule. . . . On the other hand, you said the purpose of the fund is to provide training and other advantages to the blacks. . . . What is it about this fund that creates an incentive for him to come to agreement?" Why did the administration want to throw so much money into a hypothetical country while providing no aid for Zambia, Tanzania, or Mozambique? "Mr. Kaunda [the president of Zambia] is acknowledged as one of the statesmen of the continent, a man of apparently great moral conviction and passion," Solarz declared. "Obviously he has a key role to play in any transition to majority rule. Why aren't we doing anything there?"[18] The questions Solarz posed were valid: in the immediate wake of Kissinger's skullduggery in Angola, the State Department was asking Congress to allocate the bulk of aid for sub-Saharan Africa to a fund that had no clear purpose in a country that did not yet exist.

In the Senate, liberal Republican Clifford Case of New Jersey pilloried the assistant secretary for African affairs, William Schaufele, for presenting Congress with such a poorly prepared proposal. "We do not believe that it is either important or right that we should hand over an authorization with no . . . strings attached," Case said at the end of a long and contentious hearing on April 28. "You keep saying the fund, the fund, the fund," he hurled at Schaufele. "But it hasn't any substance yet. It is just something up there." (Senator Case must have motioned to the ceiling and waved his arms.) "Look, you tribes; look, you guerrilla leaders; look, you whites—look, this is a fund—come." The venerable Republican Jacob Javits of New York ended the discussion: "I am very liberal and I am hot for Rhodesian independence . . . but I will tell you, it will not fly. We will give the State Department no blank check on Rhodesia."[19]

Indeed, neither chamber gave the executive branch what it wanted. The 95th Congress was in no mood to write a blank check, not even to a Democratic president during his honeymoon and not even for a cause—peace in Rhodesia—it supported. Both houses deleted the Zimbabwe Development Fund, the administration's highest priority in Africa, in its entirety. The White House and State Department had miscalculated how much these legislators, still nursing bruises left by Kissinger, were willing to trust Jimmy Carter.

Nevertheless, it was a minor—and in some ways useful—setback. The ruckus in Congress gave administration officials a handy excuse to use with the British that gave them leverage to redefine the fund. Moreover, many members did want to promote peace in southern Africa, and they inserted language back into the bill that it was "the sense of Congress" that the United States should support a development fund "when [there is] progress toward . . . an internationally recognized settlement" in Rhodesia. They also proposed an $80 million "Southern African Special Requirements Fund" for the countries of southern Africa "to address the problems caused by the economic dislocation resulting from conflict in that region." This kicked up another firestorm because it was a transparent sleight of hand—a backdoor to aid for the Frontline States of Zambia, Mozambique, and Tanzania.[20]

Republican senator Jesse Helms of North Carolina, a first-term conservative who was staking out a leadership role on Cold War issues, objected strenuously to aid to the Frontline States. "The issue is communism. . . . There is no question . . . that the Soviets are most anxious to control the sea lanes around the Cape, which carry 70 percent of the strategic materials required by NATO countries." Conservatives in the House agreed. Kika de la Garza (R-TX) waxed poetic: "The Communists and Marxists are . . . lurking like vultures in every African country that assumes independence." Robert Bauman (R-MD) called the aid proposal "blood money from American taxpayers' pockets to finance the communist control of southern Africa." Bill Frenzel (R-MN) and John Ashbrook (R-OH) used more violent comparisons; the former said that extending the aid would be like "pouring gasoline on a fire," while the latter added that it was "pulling the trigger . . . lighting the fuse." Phil Crane (R-IL) summed up the conservative viewpoint: "The Soviets obviously have their foot well in the door in southern Africa; giving the guerrillas encouragement and their backers aid only helps the Soviets reach their objective."[21]

Maybe some legislators were grandstanding, but they were also reflecting the San Andreas fault of US politics in the later 1970s: how serious was the

Soviet threat? The divide between conservatives and liberals (which almost obliterated party lines) was characterized above all by differing interpretations of the seriousness of the Soviet threat to the United States. All politicians agreed that the Soviet Union was America's most formidable military opponent, but they disagreed about the gravity and the immediacy of the threat. Liberals saw an increasingly ossified Kremlin that pursued expansion opportunistically; conservatives looked at the same evidence and saw a Kremlin that was relentlessly unrolling a master plan to crush the United States and take over the world. Therefore, liberals thought conservatives were dangerously paranoid, while conservatives thought liberals were dangerously naive. In the House, Robert Bauman summed up the divide during the floor debate about aid to southern Africa: "I know that our president says that we are not supposed to be paranoid about communism, but we ought to be at least realistic."[22] But what was paranoia? And what was realism?

The fault line fell across Africa more than anywhere in the world. There was agreement across the board that the Soviets would like more influence on that continent; who could deny this, a year after the Cubans had landed in Angola? But liberals and conservatives parted company in assessing how concerted was the Soviet effort to expand in Africa, and therefore they disagreed about what the United States should do about it.

This was where the lessons of Vietnam mattered. Liberals, who drew the lesson that it was dangerous to misperceive regional conflicts through the prism of the Cold War, emphasized the local reasons for instability: revolution in Ethiopia, oppression in Zaire, and racism in southern Africa. They advised Washington to "get on the right side of change" and focus on remedying these regional problems. They thought this was the most effective way to fight the Cold War. Conservatives, by contrast, had learned from the US defeat in southeast Asia that many Americans had lost their will to win, and needed to be awakened to the threat that loomed over them—to "the present danger," as a leading lobby of the era put it. When conservatives looked at Zaire, Ethiopia, and southern Africa, they saw a pattern of Soviet aggression. They could not believe that liberals failed to see it; it seemed so obvious to them. "Just as the Balkans prior to World War I and Southeast Asia in the last decade were tinder boxes of potential world conflict," Bauman declared on the House floor, "Africa has that potential now."[23]

These conservatives, whether paranoid or realistic, wielded power during the debates about security aid to Africa. Congress banned all aid to the Frontline States, albeit with a large loophole that allowed the president to waive the prohibition.[24] And it was only by the narrowest of margins (208 to 204) that the House defeated a motion to strike the Southern African Special Requirements

Fund in its entirety.[25] Even though the administration had stressed the importance of aid for southern Africa, and even though the Democrats in the House outnumbered the Republicans, 292 to 143, the Special Requirements Fund barely survived. This presaged trouble.

It is not surprising that Africa consumed so much of the time of the legislators debating the aid bill. In financial terms, aid to the continent was trivial, but in ideological terms, Africa was central. It was a key theater where the most important foreign policy wars of the late 1970s—about human rights and the Soviet threat—were waged. Members of Congress used this relatively safe terrain to wrestle with the complex issues of the day, honing their own views, listening to their colleagues, and forming coalitions. Africa was ideal terrain for these ideological debates: more distant than Latin America, less explosive than the Middle East, more fluid than Europe, and not as redolent of failure as Asia.

Two Trips

Vice President Mondale and Ambassador Young sat on a balcony of the Ritz looking out at the red roofs of Lisbon. It was an appropriate setting: it had been in Lisbon, in April 1974, that left-leaning military officers had staged the coup that had turned southern Africa—3,500 miles away—upside down. Three years later, on May 15, 1977, two of America's highest officials were discussing how to cope with the continuing aftershocks of the independence of the Portuguese colonies. The two men were both relaxed and serious. They genuinely liked and respected each other, one a liberal champion of the civil rights movement and the other one of its chief activists.[26]

Both faced tough assignments in the following days: Mondale was heading to Vienna where he would meet South Africa's Prime Minister Vorster, while Young would be in Maputo addressing a UN conference promoting the independence of Rhodesia and Namibia. Both were implementing decisions reached at the March 3 NSC meeting on southern Africa, when the administration had decided to "devise approaches to the South Africans that can be straightforward on apartheid and yet successfully press them on Rhodesia and Namibia."[27] In the two months since then, the Shaba crisis, turmoil in the Horn, and Fidel Castro's high-profile tour had raised the stakes. Peace in southern Africa was more important than ever.

In Vienna, Mondale would take the administration's message about apartheid straight to the source: in firm but nonconfrontational terms, he planned to, as he said, "put the burner" on Vorster. US relations with South Africa, he would tell Vorster, had reached "a watershed."[28] Young, meanwhile, would be in Maputo to deliver a speech explaining the administration's new policy to the leaders of African countries and independence movements—most of whom were intensely skeptical of just how new Jimmy Carter's Washington was.

Both Mondale's and Young's journeys were critical to the success of the plan that Washington and London had devised in the two months that had passed since British prime minister Jim Callaghan's visit to Washington the previous March. Foreign Secretary David Owen's April trip to southern Africa—eight days during which he met with the nationalist leaders, the Frontline presidents, Ian Smith, and Prime Minister Vorster—had been a sobering reminder of the damage done by Kissinger's tactics.

Owen had traveled to Africa not just to listen but also to inform the African leaders, black and white, about the most important change in Britain's negotiating strategy for Rhodesia: its full partnership with the United States. Prime Minister Vorster did not object to the Americans' greater role in the Rhodesia talks, but he did allow as how "US involvement would have been more welcome before the appointment of Andy Young." Vorster groused to Owen that he "did not welcome his [Young's] interference." Ian Smith was pleased that the Carter administration was engaged; he assumed that it would continue Kissinger's policies. "American muscle was needed," he told Owen. He was less diplomatic when he reported to his Cabinet about his encounter with the British foreign secretary: "It was obvious that he [Owen] lacked fundamental knowledge about Rhodesia. . . . Britain was in no position to carry out the type of exercise involved on her own and would have to have American assistance."[29]

Zambian president Kenneth Kaunda was in rare agreement with Smith. In 2009, when asked about Owen, he paused before saying, carefully, "It was good that he was interested in moving with Cyrus Vance . . . [because] Britain could not do anything." Nevertheless, American participation made Kaunda and the ZAPU leaders who met with Owen uneasy. "Would they [the Americans] not create another Vietnam?" an aide to Nkomo asked.[30]

Tanzanian president Julius Nyerere was not just uneasy: he was adamantly opposed to an American role. What the negotiations needed was not the heft of a superpower. While "it might be true that the British had not the power," he told Owen, "it might be more true that they had not the will." Mozambique's Samora Machel agreed with Nyerere. He was reserved with Owen, but a few weeks later, he elaborated his thinking to Young: "The British did not use force [against Smith in the 1960s] . . . because of race, not because they were weak. Had it been a black rebellion, they would not have hesitated to use force even today. No one can convince me that the UK doesn't have enough force." ZANU leader Robert Mugabe also considered American participation unnecessary and risky. "It was not yet clear that the situation under Carter had changed significantly," he explained to Owen. Mugabe "did not want the big powers involved or the problem internationalised."[31]

Owen defended his strategy vigorously to the black Africans. Rebutting an editorial in the *Times* of Zambia that labeled him "a toothless bulldog," Owen exclaimed to Nyerere, "It was not fair . . . to call us a toothless bulldog and then criticise us when we looked for someone else's teeth!" Owen tried to convince Nkomo, Mugabe, Kaunda, and Nyerere—their skepticism about American sympathies heightened by the whiff of Kissinger's deals with the white rulers of Rhodesia and South Africa—that there had been a significant change in Washington. Owen asserted that "he had rarely seen a politician so tough as President Carter. . . . That encouraged him to be a bolder Foreign Secretary."[32]

In his memoirs, Owen put a positive spin on his trip, writing that the press reports were "almost universally favorable." He must have been referring to a very select group of newspapers, because the African press was at best mistrustful. The Lagos *Daily Times* announced that "Africa has had enough of masquerades and sweet-lipped antics over Zimbabwe." The Tanzanian *Daily News* concluded bitterly that the "new ideas" Owen promised were "unfortunately . . . not new at all." In Zambia, the *Times* deemed the visit worthy of "a big and loud yawn," while the *Daily Mail* led with a headline quoting ZAPU leader Joshua Nkomo: "Dr. Owen's Tour a Waste of Time." In what the US ambassador to Zambia, Stephen Low, deemed an "authoritative" column, the *Daily Mail* dismissed the 1976 Geneva talks as "chicanery of the imperialists," and explained "Africans have had no alternative but to look to Russia for weapons to . . . win their independence from the white racists in Rhodesia and South Africa who are the open allies of the British and the Americans." Ambassador Low commented that "the atmosphere toward negotiations is becoming more negative and difficult to reverse."[33]

Fulfilling Low's prediction, a week after Owen returned to London, Nkomo and Mugabe held a press conference in which they rejected American participation. "'We . . . cannot have new masters imposed on our situation,'" Mugabe asserted.[34] Owen explained to Vance that "the nationalist leaders had not yet absorbed the importance of the change in administration in the United States. . . . They still keep talking about the CIA and Allende [referring to the CIA-backed coup that had overthrown Chilean president Salvador Allende in September 1973]. . . . I keep telling them that you're more radical than we are." Mondale commented to Carter that the results of Owen's trip "show that progress . . . is . . . not promising."[35]

Against this backdrop, London and Washington developed a strategy to bring Rhodesia peacefully to majority rule. Their plan contained several constants that were fine-tuned in reaction to events in Africa and political imperatives at home. The British and American negotiating team would undertake bilateral negotiations to narrow the differences between all the parties that had been at Geneva—Smith, the black nationalists, and the Frontline States. All would then attend a conference to develop a new constitution that would include a bill of rights and offer protection for minorities. After the conferees had finalized the constitution and the interim arrangements, Smith would resign and Britain would administer Rhodesia for a brief transition period, during which a British Resident Commissioner would organize the new Zimbabwean army and hold elections based on universal suffrage. The Zimbabwe Development Fund would underwrite the transition to majority rule. Zimbabwean independence, which would be finalized in 1978, would be based on "four fundamental principles: democratic elections, universal adult suffrage, a bill of rights which is justiciable and entrenched, and an independent judiciary."[36]

The collapse of the Geneva talks in January 1977 had several important repercussions. The Patriotic Front, the fruit of ZANU's and ZAPU's shotgun marriage in October 1976, had gained strength diplomatically and militarily. The Frontline presidents had recognized it as the sole legitimate voice of the Zimbabwean liberation movement, and it was confident that it would win the war. For the Patriotic Front, the war was the means to undermine white morale; the rising numbers of whites fleeing the country and the swelling Rhodesian defense budget persuaded the guerrillas that they were winning, even though they were engaging the enemy only sporadically and, on average, at least ten of them were killed for every Rhodesian soldier. The Patriotic Front did not focus on the kill ratio: it looked instead at the trend line, and that gave it courage. Therefore, it demanded a stronger role at any future conference, and the Frontline presidents concurred. However, Smith and Vorster dug in their heels, saying they had done what Kissinger had demanded and would do no more.[37]

To break this deadlock, David Owen had to prod his own government out of what he derided as its "masterly inactivity," and he sought US leverage to do so. Carter wanted to help, but—as Owen's Africa tour had shown—the black African leaders did not want American participation because they mistrusted Washington. They had been willing to give Kissinger a chance, but the experience had deepened their doubts about Washington's involvement. They feared being manipulated again, and they worried that the United States would bring Cold War tensions into the region and escalate the war, as had happened in Angola. Mugabe told UN Secretary-General Kurt Waldheim, "If another party with no legal basis [i.e., the Americans] was brought in, the Russians would also intervene and the result would be a big power confrontation." Nkomo expressed similar fears to an American journalist: "Our memories of Vietnam are still fresh. We know how the US moved into Vietnam as the French were withdrawing. We don't want to internationalize the situation in Zimbabwe." Mugabe, Nkomo, and the Frontline presidents feared that adding Washington to the mix would mean one more—very powerful—voice in support of the status quo, and they worried that they would be able to exert less influence on the United States than on Britain.[38]

The other problem with Owen's scheme to bring in the Americans was that it was not clear how much leverage the United States had in the region. The Africa specialists in the Carter administration grappled with this question in the weeks following the March 3 NSC meeting. It was obvious that Washington's past support for the colonizers and the white regimes of southern Africa, as well as the bruises left by Kissinger's failed efforts the year before, harmed its standing with the nationalists. Moreover, the US government did not—and would not—provide the nationalists with weapons, training, or economic aid. In theory, it could dangle a promise of economic and military aid in front of the Frontline States, but Congress had proven that it would bar aid to countries it considered communist, such as Zambia and Mozambique; moreover, Carter had promised to curtail arms sales. Thus, with the Frontline presidents, Washington would have to rely largely on moral suasion, and this would hinge on its ability to convince the black Africans that the Carter administration had broken from past US policies.

As for leverage on Rhodesia, an interagency group composed of representatives from the State, Commerce, Justice, and Treasury departments investigated ways to tighten the screws. It came up with several possible actions, all of marginal merit. The group suggested shuttering the Rhodesian Information Office (a pro-Smith lobby in Washington that functioned as a de facto Rhodesian embassy) and promoting a UN resolution discouraging member states from allowing the recruitment of mercenaries. "There are unsubstantiated reports that as many as several hundred US citizens are fighting for the Smith regime," the memo noted. "Whatever the number, they are an embarrassment to the US government." Nonetheless, it concluded, US law was clear: "There is little that can currently be done to prevent their service." The report also considered ways to tighten the UN sanctions on Rhodesia. It determined realistically that the past decade of sanctions had been "totally ineffective," but it held out hope that Machel's decision to close Mozambique's border with Rhodesia might change this. Smith henceforth would be utterly dependent on the South Africans' continued willingness to break the sanctions. Therefore, the report recommended that the United States tighten its existing sanctions and also support a UN resolution stipulating that countries trading with South Africa ensure that trade was not, in fact, to or from Rhodesia.[39]

The CIA investigated whether tightening sanctions on Rhodesia—or threatening to do so—would give Washington leverage over Smith. On March 31, 1977, Director of Central Intelligence Stansfield Turner delivered a chastening report to the president. "The analysis," he wrote in his cover letter, "concludes that sanctions will not be effective so long as South Africa continues to act as a conduit for Rhodesian trade."[40]

Carter approved the closure of the Rhodesian Information Office, but the State Department worried that doing so would invite a court challenge on First Amendment grounds. Indeed, conservatives in Congress complained bitterly about the planned closure of the Information Office, and the administration put the idea on ice. Carter also approved urging US allies to tighten their enforcement of the sanctions on Rhodesia as well as seeking UN action to expand sanctions to curb South African transhipment of goods to Rhodesia.[41]

Given its dearth of leverage on the Patriotic Front, the Frontline States, and the Smith government, the Carter administration believed that exerting pressure on South Africa would be key to forcing a negotiated settlement in Rhodesia. The president had ended the March 3 NSC meeting with orders to Young to develop "a sequence of events designed to promote the progressive transformation of South African society." Three weeks later, Young's report hit the president's desk. It was cautious, recommending tough rhetoric and weak actions. Administration officials—from the president to ambassadors in the field—should forthrightly and publicly "signal to the world . . . that we strongly oppose apartheid" and this message should be carried directly to Prime Minister Vorster. He should be told that "his government must take steps—very soon—to demonstrate that it is moving away from institutionalized racism and towards full political participation for all the people of South Africa. . . . [If it fails to do so] relations between our countries will inevitably change."[42]

The muscle behind these words, however, was flaccid: limiting cultural exchange programs, tightening loopholes in trade regulations, and examining the nuclear exchange policy. Throughout, the memo dampened expectations: "Our current influence is limited. . . . Our approach . . . may fail." It could even backfire: "There is a risk that in taking a more forthright stand against apartheid we will lose our limited influence and possibly drive the South African government to invoke even more oppressive measures. . . . This is a risk the NSC has decided to take, but it does point up the need to proceed with care." Vice President Mondale summed up the dilemma: "Our economic leverage [with Pretoria] is not as significant as many believe. . . . US private investment accounts for only 16 percent of total foreign investment in South Africa. Further, South Africa's military is the strongest on the continent. Additionally, South Africa knows that its lengthy coastline would make the enforcement of any economic embargo difficult." Therefore, with Pretoria—as with the nationalists, the Frontline States, and Rhodesia—"the real leverage we have is political and psychological." Mondale stressed the perils of the new policy. "Too forceful an application of pressure could drive the already beleaguered and suspicious South African leadership into a self-destructive position of rigid and defensive isolation." He was, he admitted, "not overly optimistic" about the chance of success of persuading Pretoria to support US policy, but he was "hopeful."[43]

On March 23, Vorster wrote Carter that he would like to meet with a representative of the new administration, ideally the president. Carter did not want to reward the apartheid government with a presidential meeting before Vorster had indicated that he was willing to work toward US goals. However, he did not want to offend Vorster. Therefore, he could not delegate the task to anyone of a lower rank than secretary of state, since the Ford administration had twice dispatched Secretary of State Kissinger to meet with the South African prime minister. Vance, however, was in Geneva negotiating the SALT II treaty with the Soviets. It made sense, therefore, that Carter chose Vice President Mondale to sugarcoat the bitter message the administration was planning to deliver.[44]

Moreover, Carter was determined that Mondale play a substantive, policymaking role in his administration. With an office in the West Wing of the White House (rather than in customary vice-presidential exile in the Old Executive Office Building), Mondale had ready access to the president; the two men consulted several times a day. Like other members of Congress who had been hoping that one of their own—Mo Udall or Ted Kennedy or Hubert Humphrey—would be the Democratic standard-bearer in 1976, Mondale had been a late convert to the Carter campaign. However, when he had made the trek to Plains in July 1976 in the parade of vice-presidential wannabes, he and Carter had immediately felt a bond. Both had roots in small towns, eschewed pomposity, and wanted to cleanse America of its recent missteps.[45]

Mondale spent the weeks before he flew to Europe being briefed by State Department specialists (led by the head of policy planning, Anthony Lake) and reading voraciously about Vorster and the complicated issues at stake in southern Africa.[46] In a letter to Carter on April 8, he summarized the purpose of the meeting with Vorster: to confirm, authoritatively, that US policy had changed. Previous administrations, Mondale wrote, "[had] led the South Africans . . . to believe that we cared little about apartheid. And that any solution that kept the Russians at bay would be acceptable." This was not President Carter's policy. "With your election," Mondale noted, "Vorster certainly has become concerned that his fallback assumption which has the West bailing him out in order to 'defend him against communism' (or whatever he may define as 'communism') may be fallacious." The vice president would inform Vorster that the apartheid regime could not rely on the United States to save it—no matter what the threat. The Carter administration's objectives were clear: "We seek a progressive transformation of South African society as well as a constructive South African role on Rhodesia and Namibia." David Aaron, who had worked for Mondale on the Hill and continued to advise him after joining the NSC, wrote succinctly: "The main message we have . . . for Vorster . . . is that the game is up."[47]

The vice president was not expecting it to be an easy assignment. "In dealing with Vorster you will face an intelligent, tough, shrewd negotiator," the State Department warned. "A man who shows his moods, he can be cold, dour and antagonistic or, if things are going well for him, good-humored and pleasant. . . . Your encounter with Vorster will probably be difficult."[48]

The Carter administration's goals might appear quixotic. They were not. Although US officials *hoped* that Mondale's straight talk to Vorster would ease apartheid in South Africa, this was not the purpose of the meeting. "We are under no illusions as to Vorster's likely reaction," Carter wrote Prime Minister Callaghan.[49] "We must be extremely modest," Mondale warned.[50] The State Department agreed, writing Mondale: "There is an outside chance that your statement, in combination with other pressure may lead him to ask for time to reconsider his present course, but this is unlikely."[51]

The administration faced squarely the likelihood that the meeting could have a negative impact: Vorster's response might be "to lead his country into even further isolation from the rest of the world" and to withdraw from the search for majority rule in Rhodesia and independence in Namibia.[52] Washington calculated that this was a risk worth taking, because it was likely that Vorster, even if furious with Washington, would continue to press Smith to accept majority rule because it was in South Africa's national interest. The State Department briefed Mondale about Vorster's reasons to support the Rhodesia negotiations: "By promoting a Rhodesian settlement South Africa hopes to buy time for itself to implement its domestic policy of separate development, win the friendship of the West to counter Soviet influence and activity in the region, and establish neutral, if not friendly, relations with black Africa."[53] Nevertheless, there was still a danger that Mondale would push Vorster too far, backfiring not only in South Africa itself, but also in Namibia and Rhodesia.

What, then, was the administration doing? Mondale's audience was not just Vorster—it was black Africa, the Third World, and liberals at home. "Our meeting will make clear to South Africa—*and equally important to the rest of Africa*—exactly where we stand," Mondale wrote.[54]

This was the crux of the initiative. The Carter administration wanted to persuade South Africa to abolish apartheid, but it knew that this was improbable. The March 3 NSC meeting had implied that ending apartheid, achieving majority rule in Rhodesia, and attaining independence for Namibia were three equal objectives. However, by May 1977, the administration had set implicit priorities: it hoped to resolve Namibia and Rhodesia in the near term; ending apartheid would take longer. What it hoped to achieve in the meeting with Vorster was not ending apartheid but reorienting the image of the United States in the Third World, which was an essential step toward achieving majority rule in Rhodesia. Restoring America's image abroad—as a symbol of freedom, justice, and democracy— was also a national security imperative. This was particularly true in Africa, where Washington's collusion with Pretoria in Angola in 1975 had deepened black African antipathies to the United States and, at the same time, sparked the intervention of the Cubans, seen by many Africans as liberators. Even Henry Kissinger realized the peril: it had impelled him to go to Lusaka in 1976 and declare—for the first time—that the United States sought majority rule in Rhodesia. Kissinger's speech was an important beginning, but it had not applied to the scourge of Africa—apartheid. The Carter administration needed to persuade black Africans that Washington had changed: this administration, unlike its predecessors, would not bail out the apartheid regime no matter the threat it faced. This was an essential step toward gaining the confidence of black Africans—confidence that David Owen's recent swing through Africa had revealed was sorely lacking. "Owen believes that neither the nationalists, nor Vorster or Smith appreciate the fundamental change in policy we have made," the agenda for a late April meeting between Mondale and Carter noted. "Putting them straight on our policy could be a major accomplishment of a meeting with Vorster."[55]

Likewise, at home, Carter wanted to stake out the moral high ground in the debate about southern Africa. The civil rights movement had changed the United States, especially on Carter's home turf, and Carter believed that it was necessary to bring the country's foreign policy in line with this new and much improved domestic reality. While this tapped into the president's idealism, it was rooted in real fears of the potential consequence of a conflagration in southern Africa in which the Soviets sided with the black majority and the Americans sided with the white minority regimes. For the Carter administration (as for Kissinger in 1976), it was imperative to avoid this calamity. Distancing the United States from the South African regime was a way to fight the Cold War. Mondale would make clear to Vorster "our conviction that there must be full and equal political participation," he told Carter, because "the best way to beat communism is to move toward social justice."[56]

As the State Department asserted, Mondale's message risked driving Vorster deeper into the laager; "however, the dangers to us of a standpat policy on South Africa are even greater. They include adverse political and social consequences here at home, and a serious deterioration of our relations with black African countries."[57] Explaining the rationale for his meeting with Vorster, Mondale wrote that *not* meeting could be profoundly damaging: "We are concerned at the growing possibility of a transcontinental race war in Southern Africa that would radicalize black Africans, open the door to Soviet and Cuban penetration, and bring untold suffering."[58]

The British Foreign Office and some American reporters interpreted Carter's tapping of Mondale for the mission to Vorster as a sign of the president's dissatisfaction with Young.[59] Nothing could have been further from the truth. In going to Vienna, the vice president was not assuming the Africa portfolio; his rank was a signal to Vorster that the Carter administration, while delivering a tough message, treated him with respect. It was, David Aaron wrote to Mondale, "a single visit in which you beat up Vorster and Smith," not the beginning of a new—and, in Aaron's opinion, thankless—role. "Africa is a combination minefield and swamp," he commented to the vice president.[60]

Carter's marginalia on Mondale's memo detailing the strategy for Vienna made clear the continuing centrality of Young's guidance: "Get from Andy degree of flexibility and minimum acceptable progress," the president scrawled, and, at another point, "Measure this against Andy's expectations."[61] Mondale was in Portugal not only to recover from jet lag before the important encounter in Austria, but also to receive his final briefing from Young, who flew to Lisbon from an African chiefs-of-mission conference.

The Lightning Rod

Mondale outranked Young, but Young got all the attention. He made, as *Newsweek* acknowledged, "good copy."[62] Young had followed up on his January 31, 1977, comment that the Cubans were "a stabilizing force in Angola" with a torrent of headline grabbers that sold newspapers, led to hasty clarifications, and gave fodder to his critics in Congress. His indiscretions appeared haphazard, but in fact they returned again and again to two interrelated themes: the centrality of racism in world affairs and the dangers of interpreting all events through an anticommunist lens. By talking openly about the continuing salience of racism in the United States and abroad and by downplaying the communist threat, Young challenged the underlying principles of US Cold War strategy. He drew fire.

On race, Young mused that if the United States ever backed the South African government militarily, "You'd have civil war at home. Maybe I ought not to say that but I really believe it. An armed forces that is 30 percent black isn't going to fight on the side of the South Africans." When asked if the South African government was illegitimate, Young replied, "Yeah." He told an audience at Howard University that US blacks could never be free until blacks in South Africa were. In an interview on BBC television, he said that the British "had been a little chicken" about racial questions at home as well as in Rhodesia and South Africa, and that he sometimes thought they "had invented racism." On communism, he declared—in the midst of the Shaba crisis—"Don't get paranoid about a few communists—even a few thousand communists. Americans shouldn't be afraid of communists." He explained his reasoning: "We do almost everything so much better than they [the communists] do that the sooner the fighting stops and the trading starts, the quicker we win." He added, "I think we pandered to a certain paranoia, and it offends me, really. . . . One of the things that I'm concerned about is that we get past the Cold War. I want us to assess the situation and act on that and not with some knee-jerk reaction." As for the war in Shaba, Young opined, "I say, let the Africans settle it. Our policy is to encourage the Africans themselves to settle it." Young told the Chicago press, "It's in the US interest to sit back [in Shaba] and play a supporting role. . . . That's not national weakness, that's national intelligence."[63]

Once again, the State Department hurriedly "clarified" Young's comments, noting, for example that it was "incorrect" to call the government in Pretoria illegitimate, and, after Young mentioned that US troops might be part of a UN peacekeeping force in Rhodesia, commenting that this was not "a serious policy option." Young apologized to the British for calling them racists and chickens, and the Foreign Office decided that "there was no advantage in our getting into a slanging match with Young." At a brief session with the press, Carter was twice asked about Young's comments on British racism. The president noted that the British had accepted Young's apology, and then elaborated: "I certainly wouldn't think the British are any more guilty than we are. I think we've all overcome that facet of our society in a very constructive way, and I don't believe that Great Britain deserves any special criticism."[64]

Members of Congress and the press were less restrained. From the swirling dust of their outrage, three themes emerged: incoherence, hypocrisy, and appeasement. Friends and foes of the administration bemoaned the spate of official "clarifications" that littered Young's wake. The *Washington Post* damned his "indiscreet and careless pronouncements," while the *New York Times* wrote that his "continuing clarifications, amendments and apologies . . . are becoming harmful as well as tedious." *Time* magazine took to calling Young "motor mouth." The House minority whip, Robert Michel (R-IL), asked, "Who is speaking for the Administration—Andy or Vance or who?

When Andy talks, is this administration policy or is he just blowing smoke or raising trial balloons or what?" On the floor of the House, Michel exclaimed, "Not within the memory of anyone in this Congress has there been such a disgraceful lack of coordination and internal discipline among high-level foreign policy makers. . . . This is the kind of blundering that can lead to war."[65]

Many were disturbed that Young criticized America's traditional allies—the British and the South African government—while he embraced black African leaders such as Julius Nyerere and Kenneth Kaunda whom many Americans regarded with suspicion. This inevitably had racial overtones. Some critics questioned Young's choice of friends: "Is it US policy to refuse to trade with tyrants who are white, but to trade openly with tyrants who are black?" one columnist asked. Others questioned the repercussions of Young's own blackness: "Presumably he [Carter] understood that when you start admitting blacks as blacks to the councils of foreign policy," *Washington Post* columnist Stephen Rosenfeld wrote, "you introduce a set of foreign policy priorities that have not been in the white mainstream, even the liberal white mainstream. . . . There is an evident gap between the priorities of many American blacks and Africanists on the one hand, and the premises of many American whites and foreign policy planners on the other." In the House, John Ashbrook (R-OH) stated baldly: "Clearly [Andrew Young] does not speak for a majority of Americans." James Martin (R-NC) summed up the sentiment of many in April when he told a rally in his home district: "[Young] has terrified our allies and insulted the British. . . . [He] misunderstood the rebellion in Zaire, incited revolution in South Africa and Rhodesia, and accused the minority government in South Africa of being illegitimate while endorsing the minority Cuban government in Angola. . . . Enough's enough. I think he needs to resign and go look for another line of work."[66]

Simmering beneath the surface was a more serious complaint: Young and the president for whom he was "point man" were appeasing the enemy. Only William Safire used the word, but it was implicit in the most serious criticism leveled against the UN ambassador. After denouncing "Mr. Young's Cuban appeasement statements," Safire took direct aim at the White House. "Up to now," the *New York Times* columnist wrote on April 14, "most of us have assumed that President Carter, in a mild display of racism, was letting a black United States Ambassador be a hero at the United Nations by publicly opposing US policy. But this week, with non-Communist Zaire under attack from Soviet-Cuban-backed forces from Angola, we see how Mr. Young's 'personal views' are prevailing. . . . Suddenly, Andy Young's aberration has become the Carter Doctrine. . . . The heart of a great continent is being written off to armed Communist aggression. When Americans one day ask 'Who lost Africa?' the finger will point at a leader who underestimated his countrymen's will." This was not necessarily due to perfidy, critics argued, but rather to a fundamental misunderstanding of the world situation. "The thread perceptible in Ambassador Andrew Young's running comments on American policy toward Africa . . . is quite simply that the danger to which the United States ought to respond is less communism than racism," the *Washington Post*'s Rosenfeld wrote.[67]

Many Americans believed Young to be profoundly mistaken. Edward Beard (D-RI), a conservative Democrat, wrote the president: "I cannot understand how a person . . . is able to view everything in this world in the light of racial conflict." The *Wall Street Journal* editors agreed: "The East-West struggle by no means seems to be receding in importance." Conservative columnist Michael Novak declared, "It is imperceptive to hold, despite the evidence, that race is the No. 1 international problem. The spread of tyranny . . . is independent of race." Carl Rowan, the most prominent black journalist at the time, agreed. "The Soviets are moving vigorously all over Africa to exploit every possible conflict while the US is mesmerized by fears of 'another Vietnam,'" he wrote in the *Washington Star*. "The US just licks the scars of Vietnam and watches in virtual impotence as the Soviets operate."[68]

Young saw the world differently. The Carter administration, he thought, was not paralyzed by Vietnam; it was motivated by it. "It seems to me that because our credibility has been so destroyed by Vietnam, the one way of restoring that credibility is to move where we have an administration consensus, and one area where we have that consensus is southern Africa," he told the *New York Times*. One reason he had accepted the job as UN ambassador, he told *Newsweek*, was "to make the American people think about the world in creative terms." This had been the understanding from the beginning. "I believe the foreign policy of the nation is better if you have a free discussion," he explained. "I'm not saying my point has to prevail, but my point has to be made. . . . The President, you understand, can't afford to take any chances, to take any risks. . . . As UN ambassador, it is my responsibility to try to probe and find new avenues of agreement. I can take risks at the United Nations." Therefore, he took the flak with equanimity. "I don't mind being the lightning rod," he concluded.[69]

It was a novel position for Andrew Young. He had dedicated much of his life to controversial causes, but he himself had never been considered a rabble-rouser. Far from it: Young was the "man of sweet reason."[70] He was not a radical in any usual sense of the word—he worked within the system, he believed in gradual change, he advocated nonviolence, and he downplayed the communist threat in part because he was absolutely convinced that capitalism was superior. "I don't think the Marxists can compete," he explained. "There's no Marxist economy that's been able to deliver goods and services to the people like we have. . . . Our most useful relationship to the Marxist world is not to take them on militarily, where everybody loses, but to go ahead and take them on economically, where I am sure we're better prepared to win." Young was prescient about the demise of the Soviet system: "My feeling is that as the Russians begin to evolve, they're going to have more problems rather than less. . . . A massive generation of dissent . . . is probably not ten years off in the Soviet Union," he said in March 1977. "As the Soviet Union becomes more prosperous, . . . they're [the Soviet people] going to rise up *en masse*."[71] He linked those fighting against apartheid with the dissidents in the Soviet Union. "Freedom burns in the hearts of people, whether they are in Soweto or in the Soviet Union," he declared in May 1977. After testifying on the Hill for increased aid to the African Development Bank, he explained to reporters that his goal for South Africa was so "moderate" that militants at home and abroad had complained to him about it. It was, simply, "a peaceful solution that would leave a permanent role for American business and investment."[72]

Why, then, did Young provoke such controversy? In part, it was deliberate. He flaunted protocol to provoke an open debate on delicate and important issues. This was not a role he had assumed as a member of Congress or an aide to King. Young saw the role of UN ambassador as a platform to stir Americans to engage in open debate about their foreign policy. Both he and Carter considered this an essential ingredient of democracy that had been suppressed during the Kissinger years. "Yes, there is a definite risk [to speaking out]," Young admitted, "but the risk is not nearly as great as forming foreign policy in secret." Young drew attention because he spoke for a president who was still an enigma to many. "Andy's never been in a position," civil rights leader Julian Bond explained, "where people were hanging on every word he said." And he was black: he was the first black man to be considered an authoritative voice on the nation's foreign policy. Assistant Secretary Charles Maynes, who worked closely with Young, observed, "Andy's . . . an unbelievably gifted, wonderful man, . . . a 'blithe spirit.' . . . I think he did a great deal of good for the United States . . . and the response of this country to him is very disturbing. It says a lot not very good about the United States."[73]

Young's message kept him in the spotlight. More than anyone in the administration, he articulated a new vision of the Cold War in the mid-1970s. For Young, the Cold War was not over, but it had lost much of its gravitational pull. The Soviet threat had not disappeared, but the United States needed to grapple seriously with other threats as well, particularly those emanating from disorder and injustice in the developing world. Dealing with these issues was the best way to contain the Soviet Union. "In terms of the containment of

Communist expansion in Africa," Young explained to the Senate, "the best thing the Communists have going for them is the presence of racist minority regimes in southern Africa."[74] This vision put Young at loggerheads with the emerging neoconservatives who were convinced that Washington had long underestimated the Soviet threat.

Carter admitted that "Andy would make statements that caused me a lot of concern."[75] But the president stood by his man. Cruising in the limousine to the UN to deliver his address in March 1977, Carter turned to Young, who was sitting beside him. "I hope you're going to stick with me. It gets kind of rough out there. People aren't used to discussing American foreign policy in advance. I don't intend to shut up and I hope you wouldn't let them intimidate you either." On April 13, at the height of the Shaba crisis, the deputy White House press secretary, answering a question, said "His [Young's] basic overview of the African situation is not in disagreement with that of the President." Two days later, Carter confirmed this: "I've never complained about what Andy does," he told reporters. At the dedication of the Africa Room at the Kennedy Center in Washington, DC, Carter was fulsome: "I have had a lot of good teachers in the last 3 months since I have been President, in learning about Africa. I am always interested in what Andy Young is going to say . . . to me, one of his best students." And at the London Economic Summit in early May, Carter told Prime Minister Callaghan, West German chancellor Schmidt and French president Giscard d'Estaing that "he was not going to part company with Andrew Young."[76]

Showdown in Vienna

John Vorster—the dour Afrikaner who had been a member of a pro-Nazi organization during World War II and who had led South Africa since 1966—and Walter Mondale, the crusading American liberal, met at the Hofburg Palace in Vienna, the winter residence of the Habsburgs. Vorster, a large man in his sixties with a square jaw and thinning hair, stared expressionlessly across the blue table at the youthful, earnest, and animated Mondale. Vorster had welcomed the meeting because it was a significant crack in the deepening isolation of his government, but he was not optimistic about it. The South Africans, one of their senior diplomats confessed, wished they "could tell them [the Americans] to go to hell but they can't."[77]

Vorster and Mondale word-wrestled for eight hours over two days in Vienna. Afterward, they described the talks as "cordial," but the transcripts reveal hour upon hour of unrelenting sparring.[78] Mondale struck a combative, bossy tone from the first encounter on May 19 and maintained it through the final hour on May 20. He also set the agenda: first Rhodesia, then Namibia, and then South Africa itself. He was in Vienna not to negotiate but to convey the administration's hardline message to the South African leader "in unambiguous and authoritative terms."[79]

Vorster must have suffered whiplash, so different was this encounter from his chummy, conspiratorial powwows with Henry Kissinger and, more recently, with David Owen. When Owen had met Vorster three weeks earlier, he had not said a word about apartheid, and later admitted to the US deputy national security advisor David Aaron, "[I] ducked."[80] Vorster, Mondale predicted, expected their encounter to be "another Kissinger-type meeting at which he would explain to us that we don't really understand the situation . . . and that South Africa is defending the West against Communism."[81] Mondale immediately set him straight. When Vorster wanted to begin with a private, off-the-record meeting, as was Kissinger's custom, Mondale's response was adamant: "Well, you've got to understand. This is not business as usual. We're not going to talk one way in public and another way in private." Aaron, who accompanied Mondale, noted, "The South Africans expected us to do the same old thing—to say in private 'Don't worry about human rights.' But we weren't going to play footsie any more. And they were shocked."[82]

At one point Vorster said, almost plaintively, "It's a pity that Rogers and Schaufele aren't here," referring to two of Kissinger's aides. In their stead, Mondale was accompanied by a team that included Tony Lake, the head of policy planning and an expert on southern Africa who, the Rhodesians warned the South Africans, had an "anti-Rhodesian background." (They were referring to Lake's 1976 book, *The "Tar Baby" Option: American Policy toward Southern Rhodesia*, which was scathing about the Nixon and Ford administrations' failure to uphold the UN sanctions on Rhodesia.) Also with Mondale was Ambassador Donald McHenry—Young's deputy at the UN—a black foreign service officer with a sophisticated grasp of southern African issues. South African foreign minister Pik Botha told Ian Smith that "he had found McHenery [*sic*], who was a negro, much better than Young" and that he "had clearly been the 'boss'" in the discussions on Namibia. This was a changed world.[83]

In the first session, Mondale sought Vorster's commitment to "press" Ian Smith to agree to get negotiations on Rhodesian independence back on track. Vorster balked: "I have never pressed Smith. . . . I talk sense to him." He agreed, however, to the essential American demand. "If you can guarantee [Patriotic Front leaders] Mugabe and Nkomo will fall in line," Vorster told Mondale, "I will guarantee Smith does."[84] After lunch, which the two parties ate separately, the conversation turned to Namibia, and the two men locked horns. Vorster insisted that Namibia was not a country but rather a collection of tribal areas that should each elect representatives within a loosely federal system. Mondale rejected this as a thinly veiled way for Pretoria to maintain control over the country. Vorster was unyielding.[85]

The following day, Mondale tackled the most "difficult and emotional question." Bluntly, he told Vorster, "We don't believe apartheid or separateness is workable or just." Laced throughout the vice president's speech—which the South Africans deemed a "lengthy homily"—were references to the American civil rights movement. "We have undergone a profound transformation over the past ten years," he explained to Vorster. "We made a long and tortuous march to justice. The result is more peace and good will and strength in the United States. . . . President Carter wanted me to describe this to you." If South Africa did not begin the process of ending apartheid, Mondale concluded, "Our policies will go their separate ways. The choice is yours."[86]

"You mustn't equate the American black with the South African black, and I can argue this until the cows come home," Vorster retorted, time and time again. "Your black man—Mr. McHenry, for instance—I regard not as a black man but as an American. . . . I just read *Roots* recently."

Mondale interjected: "It is required reading for us now."

Vorster seized the opening: "You have divested your blacks of their background."

Mondale: "And it is shameful."

Vorster regrouped. "It is better to understand the situation by comparing our blacks with your Indians. . . . We never took their [blacks'] land. . . . We brought peace. . . . We don't comment on your Indians."

Mondale again: "Our record on that is shameful."

Vorster was undeterred. "The Africans don't regard themselves as members of my nation. South Africa is multinational and not multi-racial." The Afrikaner proceeded to explain the logic behind the homelands policy: South Africa was really several nations, Vorster asserted. "If you think we should scrap governments [in the homelands] and introduce one-man and one-vote in a central parliament, I tell you it can't be done." Foreign Minister Botha interjected: "Let's get down to the bone of the matter. . . . How can we accept a solution that means our own destruction?"[87]

It was an impasse. This did not surprise the Americans. Vorster "countered with standard fare," Mondale reported to Washington.[88] To Yugoslav president Josip Broz Tito, whom he met on the day after he left Vienna, Mondale said sardonically, "Vorster gave us the line about how the Africans are happy, the coloreds are happy, the Indians are happy. They all played football together."[89] Vorster, on the other hand, was stunned. He had expected the tough talk in public, but he had assumed that once they were in private, Mondale would wink, bowing, as had all previous American officials, to the need for anticommunist powers to support each other. Mondale's attack, however, had been relentless, and Vorster was furious. He ended the encounter saying, "There is nothing better I would like than improved relations with US, but it cannot all come from one side. . . . I can take kicks in the pants but don't kick me in the teeth." Leaving the room, Mondale reiterated that if there was no sign of progress in South Africa, "consequences would follow." Vorster acknowledged the threat without comment.[90]

A joint appearance afterward was impossible; the two men faced the press separately. The *New York Times* correspondent, who attended both press conferences, observed that Vorster and Mondale "not only . . . differed fundamentally . . . but also seemed to be living in different political eras." Vorster stressed: "There is a vital difference in outlook between the United States and South Africa. It stems from the fact . . . that the United States wants to equate the position of the American Negro with the African black man."[91]

Mondale's comments to the press made headlines. He removed his gloves. He began carefully, reading prepared comments. "I cannot rule out the possibility that the South African government will not change," he said. "In that event we would take steps true to our beliefs and values." This was widely interpreted as meaning that the United States would support UN sanctions on South Africa. After numerous queries about the details of the talks, a journalist asked what, exactly, the vice president meant by saying that South Africa should move toward "full participation." How did that differ from "one man/one vote?"[92] Mondale knew how freighted the phrase "one man/one vote" was: it destroyed apartheid. "Full participation" was the phrase the State Department had recommended he use; it was vague enough to mean simply that blacks would play a role governing their isolated and artificial homelands, but "one man/one vote" signaled the Carter administration's demand that blacks and whites have equal votes in a unitary state of South Africa. Mondale had avoided the phrase throughout the hours of talks with Vorster.[93] But now he had been asked a direct question, and he was a blunt man.

Mondale had consulted closely with Carter when preparing for the talks, and he called him twice during them. It was Carter who had urged him to emphasize that his administration hoped for an awakening in South Africa comparable to that which had transformed the US South. As Mondale said, "He wanted to explain how good the civil rights movement was for our country." But, more important, it was Carter who gave Mondale permission to go all the way. "I authorized, when Fritz Mondale first met with the South African leader, I authorized Fritz to call publicly for one man one vote," Carter declared.[94]

What was the difference between "full participation" and "one man one vote?" the journalist had asked. Mondale responded softly: "It's the same thing. Every citizen should have the right to vote and every vote should be equally weighted." Everyone present knew what had just happened. "A painful, almost embarrassed silence fell over the room," the *New York Times* noted, "and the press conference came to an end." The State Department reported without comment, "The Vice President put American policy towards South Africa clearly and incisively on the public record in his press conference following the meeting with Vorster."[95]

The South Africans were "really very upset," Bill Edmondson, the US deputy chief of mission in Pretoria, remembered. To Cyrus Vance, Foreign Minister Pik Botha "made an impassioned speech charging that the American endorsement of 'one man one vote' was a 'knife in the back' of the South African Government." The South African notes on the talks reveal their bitterness at the changes in Washington since the Kissinger era. "The first impression of the United States delegation was that of the youth of its members. . . . Mondale was always polite but could not divest himself from giving the impression of a starry eyed liberal out to reform the world. . . . It is most doubtful in view of his background and outlook that he could be anything but condemnatory of our policies." After describing the liberal and youthful American delegation, the South Africans acknowledged, "They are probably the type of Americans we will be compelled to deal with at least during the Carter administration. . . . But," the memo added, "forewarned is forearmed."[96]

This would be the high point of the Carter administration's—or any US president's—opposition to apartheid. The vice president, implementing the president's policy, had declared that US relations with South Africa would deteriorate unless Pretoria began to implement one man one vote. His justification was straightforward: "You can't have democracy with any other principle." The implications for South Africa were profound: it was a call for nothing less than the transformation of its society. The Carter administration seized the moral high ground.[97]

After Vienna, as Washington had feared and expected, the South African government hunkered down. In domestic policy, it refused to budge on apartheid and cracked down harder on dissent. In foreign policy, it dug in on Namibia and increased its economic and military support of Ian Smith in Rhodesia. By the end of 1977, it would be clear that it had given up hope of forging a useful relationship with the Carter administration. The White House, in response, never backtracked, but neither did it maintain the pressure it had threatened at Vienna. By the end of the year, it had established its regional priorities. Changing apartheid would have to wait; Washington focused instead on trying to persuade South Africa to help resolve the crises in Rhodesia and Namibia.

Given the hardening of Pretoria's stance after Vienna, it is easy to criticize the Carter administration for being naive and overzealous. This assumes, however, that a more accommodating—a more Kissingerian—approach at Vienna would have resulted in a more positive outcome. This is unlikely.

First, the intransigence of the Vorster government had many causes, most of them domestic. It would be a mistake to exaggerate Washington's influence. The State Department noted sagely that while "South African Government actions relating to race relations since Vienna have apparently been shaped by immediate internal concerns rather than a response to the American initiative, . . . South African leaders have diverted attention from the real issues . . . by charging that the US has issued a demand for an immediate move to one-man, one-vote which they charge would mean destruction of the white population."[98]

Second, the Carter administration's eye was not so much on Vorster as it was on black Africa. Mondale's forthright statement in Vienna—"every citizen should have the right to vote and every vote should be equally weighted"— was an essential step toward gaining the trust of the black African leaders who would be crucial to the success of the Anglo-American initiative in Rhodesia. "The improved credibility of our southern African policies among leaders of Black Africa," the State Department noted a month after Mondale's meeting in Vienna, "probably stems in large measure from our willingness to confront South Africa."[99]

To Go or Not to Go

On May 19, at almost the precise moment that Mondale walked into the Hofburg Palace for his first encounter with Vorster, Andrew Young was striding to the podium in the crowded hall of what had once been the Portuguese Officers Club in Maputo, Mozambique. The anticipation among the assembled representatives of ninety-two countries and dozen liberation groups was palpable. Even in distant Mozambique, which had just signed a friendship treaty with the Soviet Union, and even in this crowd of delegates from nonaligned and developing nations that were highly skeptical of US policy, Andy Young was a celebrity. "People are coming precisely to hear from Andy Young," an Ethiopian delegate explained.[100]

The meeting, known as the Maputo Conference, had originated in a December 1976 UN General Assembly decision to host a conference "in support of the peoples of Zimbabwe and Namibia." The outgoing Ford administration had not commented on the upcoming gathering, but the other Western members of the Security Council—Canada, France, the United Kingdom, and West Germany—had been sharply critical, predicting that it would provide another platform for Third World rants against Western imperialism, racism, and assorted other crimes. None of these countries planned to attend the conference, and none was going to contribute to funding it, either. The French government expressed "strong disapproval of attendance . . . by any of the Nine [members of the European Community]." British minister of state Ted Rowlands, who ranked just below the foreign secretary, wrote categorically on April 5, 1977, "I am sure we should not attend."[101]

In mid-April, however, the British and French received word that Andrew Young wanted to go to the conference.[102] This was a stunner. The United States had never sent a delegate to a UN conference on decolonization. British Foreign Secretary Owen stalled. He tried to persuade the Americans that attending Maputo "was not a sound idea." A draft of the resolution to be signed at the conference had been circulated, and it was "extreme." Being associated with it would complicate bridge-building with Smith and Vorster, and refusing to sign it would undermine any goodwill generated by attending the conference. Moreover, the draft resolution laid the groundwork for UN sanctions against South Africa, something the British had made clear they could not accept. "The British," Assistant Secretary Richard Moose recalled, "were scared to death of Andy Young going to Maputo."[103]

The White House backed Young, and the British Foreign Office reversed course: "The American decision created a new situation," it noted drily. "I would far have preferred if no major Western country had gone at all," Ivor Richard, the British UN ambassador wrote, "but once Young has decided to go, it will I fear look distinctly odd if we . . . don't turn up as well." Not only did the British want to maintain Anglo-American unity; they also wanted to keep tabs on Young. "There is a danger that Mr Young might be prepared to go further than we would wish in making concessions to radical African opinion. . . . We need a representative [at Maputo] who can . . . deal on all fours with Mr Young." On April 29, Owen announced his decision: "I have no doubt [Minister of State] Mr Rowlands should go. . . . Warn all our EEC colleagues."[104]

All the Western Security Council members, plus Belgium, Finland, Italy, the Netherlands, Sweden, and UN Secretary-General Kurt Waldheim, followed suit, none with any more enthusiasm than that mustered by the British. (Of the nine European Community members, only Denmark had planned to go to Maputo.) "The decision to attend the Conference was taken with great reluctance," the British Foreign Office explained. At a meeting of the foreign ministers of France, Britain, West Germany, and the United States, Owen warned Vance that "the [draft] document was beyond repair"; his West German and French counterparts agreed.[105]

President Samora Machel's greeting to the assembled delegates was not encouraging. "We welcome you to Maputo, a trench in the battle between freedom and colonial oppression," he said in his opening speech. Tensions were heightened when, during the first day of the conference, May 14, the Rhodesian army threatened Zambia and launched its most punishing raid yet into Botswana, claiming to be clearing out Patriotic Front camps. Young's response was immediate. He not only condemned Salisbury's actions but added a comment that played well in Maputo: "Smith is trying to get the liberation movements to bring in Cuban troops."[106]

The next day, President Kaunda sent a long letter to Carter deploring the threats to his country which he blamed not only on Smith but also on Vorster. "We now know that South Africa is involved in the current military plans against Zambia." Kaunda added, flatly: "If Zambia is attacked, it will be war, and Zambia will feel free to call on anyone for assistance in defeating the enemy." Carter replied without delay and in strongly sympathetic terms. "I have issued instructions for representations to be made in Capetown in order that both the South Africans and Rhodesians might know the seriousness with which we regard any Rhodesian incursions into Zambia."[107]

On May 17, during a televised interview, President Carter answered a question about South Africa that ramped up expectations in Maputo that the United States was on the verge of announcing a tough new policy. Asked if he would continue to support South Africa at the UN, Carter strongly criticized apartheid and said, "We've gone to Vorster now and given him a request—a little bit stronger than a request, saying that if you don't do something about Namibia, then we're going to take strong action against you in the United Nations."[108] This could be a signal that the United States would support mandatory UN economic sanctions.

News of Carter's statement spread through the conference rapidly: US action against South Africa at the UN—supporting sanctions—was exactly what the Third World delegates wanted. The new administration's policy began to make sense to them. It would be a one-two punch: at the very moment Mondale was delivering the bad news to Vorster in Vienna, Andy Young would deliver the good news in Maputo.[109] Yet this was precisely what Britain, which adamantly opposed sanctions on South Africa, had been dreading. Ted Rowlands, who was leading the British delegation to Maputo, met with Young on the third day of the conference and tried to persuade him that endorsing the Maputo Declaration, which was bound to be radical, would hurt the Anglo-American effort to negotiate with Smith and Vorster. "We fear the Americans were not convinced," Rowlands cabled Whitehall. "There are problems ahead."[110]

The Old South in Maputo

"I have a speech," Young began, looking out at the eager crowd. It was May 19, 1977, the third day of the Maputo conference—and the very day that

Mondale began sparring with Vorster. "I think essentially it is a good speech," Young noted. "And yet the thinking that I have heard here is not a desire for more statements of policy. . . . The question is not what are the policies that we discuss. The question we face is how believable are those policies. What right have you, as Africans, to believe that anything is any different than it was 5 years ago?"[111]

With that, Young thrust aside the speech that the State Department had cleared and launched into a heartfelt sermon. "I would like to use the time allotted to me to discuss with you the credibility of our policy and why I think these policies represent something of a revolution in the consciousness of the American people." Young had a ringing cadence, and he knew how to orate. He told his listeners about his first meetings with African nationalists in 1951; he waxed lyrical about his work with Martin Luther King; he expounded on the philosophy of nonviolence. He emphasized how US civil rights activists had changed the United States without recourse to violence. "It was in fact an organizing of economic and political forces . . . that brought about the first changes on behalf of black Americans," he explained. "So I would say to you, do not neglect the weapons of economic arsenal that are at your disposal."

Young explained how Jimmy Carter became president of the United States: "People . . . who were essentially black, poor and sharecroppers . . . turned the tide and gave him victory, so that we shouted that the hands that used to pick the cotton had now picked a President. And . . . less than 12 years ago, most of them could not vote at all." He referred to the Africans at the conference as "brothers." He could relate to their struggle. "I say that we are not immune to the struggles which Africa faces for we have known those struggles ourselves." He described Carter's boyhood in Plains, Georgia, where all his playmates were black. "And so the problem of southern Africa and the knowledge of southern Africa is something that goes all the way back to our President's childhood. . . . While I respect your skepticism and even your cynicism, there is in fact a change in America."

Young's speech was optimistic, emotional, and personal. "If we do an analysis of the racism that we find pervasive in southern Africa, we find a phenomena with which I am very familiar and which does not frighten me at all. It has been a part of my whole life, come to me with my mother's milk."

As Young drew to a close, the applause was perfunctory. "What Mr. Young said was totally irrelevant to Zimbabwe," ZANU's Robert Mugabe announced at a press conference after the speech. "Theirs [the Americans'] was an internal situation with rights guaranteed in the constitution. Ours is a colonial situation. There is no comparison. . . . We've tried passive resistance. Our people have been locked up. Our people have been shot. We have now moved a stage up in the struggle. . . . No, I don't see any change in US policy. I don't see any at all." The Nigerian ambassador to the UN, Leslie Harriman, who was a moderate and a close friend of Young, told the press that he was "very disappointed. One could have hoped that Andy Young would contribute to the conference and not lecture us on civil rights. I would have listened ten years ago with some patience. But instead I listened today with considerable irritation."[112]

Mozambican president Machel had greeted Young warmly before the speech. "The dapper Mozambican leader clasped Young on meeting, [and] walked with him hand-in-hand," the *Los Angeles Times* observed. "The two appeared to get along famously." Behind closed doors, Machel was—in the words of Ambassador DePree, who was present at the meeting with Young— "single-minded and tough." Machel charged that "the US has a great responsibility for what is happening in Rhodesia. US purchases of chrome helped put a stamp of legality on the Smith regime" and Henry Kissinger "had deceived the Africans" with his promise before Geneva "that Smith would soon be removed." He then "posed quite forcefully a pair of questions . . . : 'Do you consider the liberation struggle in Zimbabwe and Namibia to be just?' and 'Would the US give help to the liberation movements?'" The Americans explained that they could not offer military aid but could help in other ways. "This line of argument did not seem to impress Machel," DePree cabled. The Mozambican ended the conversation by stressing that "the war against colonialism is not a racial war. It is a liberation war. There are black as well as white colonialists against whom we are fighting. A racial war . . . does not deserve our support." In commenting on the encounter, Ambassador DePree noted that "while he [Machel] came down hard on Ambassador Young . . . [he] was warm in his personal manner."[113]

It was a different story, however, after Young's speech, which Machel believed had been not only misguided but offensive. "Machel . . . patiently explained [to Young] that progressive Africans did not see the current conflicts in southern Africa as race wars—but instead as struggles against colonialism and economic exploitation and domination." Machel then asked Young "to refrain from delivering any more 'racist speeches' while in the country."[114]

Reflecting on this episode, Donald McHenry, Young's deputy at the UN, who also was African American, noted, "Being black . . . does give you an entrée, but that's all. It gets the door opened. . . . Once you're there, you're the American."[115]

Andrew Young "got into trouble here when he started speaking 'as a fellow black man' and tried to tell Africans how to go about winning their freedom," the *Washington Star* reported in a long dispatch from Maputo. With the exception of the *Star*'s report, however, US press coverage was spare and included no editorial comment, despite the intense interest in Young and the bevy of journalists surrounding him. The US press corps tended to like Young, who was refreshing and charming and generated headlines, but it was more interested in him as a personality than in the content of his speeches. The *New York Times* buried a pallid story about the conference on page five. Young "miscalculated," the *Los Angeles Times* wrote, in a story relegated to the "B" section. The *Washington Post* played it on page one, but did not include details: Young "left many of his black African listeners unconvinced, disappointed and even angry," it wrote, omitting analysis or explanation.[116]

The *Washington Star*, whose report was hard-hitting, noted that the negative reaction to the speech "must have come as something of a surprise to Young." Perhaps. But Young was a deliberate provocateur. "Protocol has never been part of my style," he explained. "If ever we believe things are impossible then we've got nothing to live for at all. . . . These impossible dreams make life worthwhile and I wouldn't trade them for any amount of realism, caution and protocol in the world."[117]

Young's style was naivete and innocence, but Andrew Young was neither naive nor innocent. He had learned tactics in the streets and by King's side. He had a purpose at Maputo. It was a gamble, and the stakes were high: he aimed to convince—almost single-handedly—ZANU's Mugabe and Mozambique's Machel to drop their objections to US participation in the Rhodesia negotiations. To succeed, he had to prove that the Carter administration was different from its predecessors and worthy of a chance—but at the same time he had to be careful not to slam the door on Smith or Vorster. Despite the negative reviews of his speech, Young achieved his goals at the conference. He opened minds—just a fraction, and tentatively, but that was an essential beginning to the arduous process of changing perceptions of the United States in Africa.

Young's first tool was to show up. For the US ambassador to the United Nations to go to Maputo—and to tow all the Western representatives in his wake—was a powerful gesture of respect to President Machel and, by extension, to the Frontline presidents, all of whom supported the conference.

Second, Young used rhetoric. By tossing aside the printed speech, which already had been circulated, he was able to give two speeches. His extemporaneous speech was roundly criticized, but in its very unpredictability it broke the mold and helped lay the foundation for real—not bureaucratic—relationships with his interlocutors. It was also moderate: although Young accepted the right of the guerrillas to adopt armed struggle, he argued that his own personal experience had shown him that there was a more effective and peaceful alternative to violence.[118]

Third, Young listened. He walked the halls of the conference, being, as Julian Bond explained, "a skillful, persuasive corridor negotiator." An American observer at Maputo noted, "Andy Young was everywhere and the press people were everywhere following him, so Andy talked all the time." He met Robert Mugabe—the ZANU leader's first encounter with a senior American official. It was an important meeting. "Mugabe was just as ornery as he could possibly be," Moose remembered. "He was his Marxist debating self." Young, however, was persuasive, and he began, slowly, to build fragile bonds of trust with the increasingly powerful guerrilla leader.[119]

David Owen, who had not wanted Britain to attend the conference, acknowledged Young's skill. "At Maputo," he told Vice President Mondale, "just the right balance had been struck and Mr Andrew Young deserved great credit for it." Lord Caradon, a former British UN ambassador who attended the conference, called it "one of the most important and one of the most successful conferences of recent times."[120]

Contrary to all British, French, and West German fears, the fiery rhetoric of the conference's final declaration was tempered. Unlike the circulated draft, the actual resolution signed at the end of the conference did not condemn the Anglo-American negotiating initiative in Rhodesia, did not designate the Patriotic Front the sole representative of the Zimbabwean people, and did not call for sanctions on South Africa. The Carter administration was pleased: this "justified a US decision (much against the UK's better judgement) to go to the conference." The Americans twisted British arms to persuade them not to completely dissociate their country from the declaration, and the other Western powers fell in line. The British Foreign Office noted, "[While it went] beyond anything with which we have hitherto been associated, . . . [it] could have been worse." The final declaration was approved by general consensus.[121]

The West German representative reported that "the mood of the conference was marked by a spirit of mutual understanding and cooperation. It could be called 'a festival of solidarity between the countries of Africa and the West.' Indeed, people are talking about 'the spirit of Maputo.' . . . The results prove that it was the correct decision to participate in the conference." A British UN ambassador, James Murray, conceded, "This was in a sense Andrew Young's conference. His decision to attend turned what might have been . . . 'a minor West-smiting exercise' into a much more important international occasion. . . . [T]he moderate Africans must surely have concluded that they have in Young an impressively powerful supporter and a genuine if unpredictable friend." Owen agreed: "We have gained some time and some goodwill."[122]

Acting Secretary of State Warren Christopher wrote a glowing report of the conference to the president. "The Maputo Conference came out more positively than we expected. The presence of our delegation . . . contributed to a tone of relative moderation." Young wrote to Carter, "The Africans continued to endorse armed struggle but agreed to support our efforts for peaceful settlement as a second legitimate form of struggle." To the Senate, Young explained more fully that the conference had been an encounter between people who believed in armed struggle—the vast majority of those present—and those, mostly Westerners, who believed in negotiations. He had not expected to convince the former to put down their arms, but he was pleased that they had not tried to derail the negotiations. "To get a standoff on that is, to me, a tremendous victory. It means we have a few more months to show that our negotiations can be as effective, if not more so, than their armed struggle. Now, all we have to do is deliver."[123]

Drumming Up Business

As the delegates at Maputo drafted their final declaration, Andrew Young was on a plane to Pretoria, and he was drafting another speech, one intended for a very different audience: 200 South African businesspeople, almost all of whom were white.[124]

The South African government initially had objected to Young's visit, citing safety concerns in public, while in private they had complained to the State Department about Young's "continued torrent of insults." Under strong US pressure, they relented but set limits on who Young could see. Young stayed in South Africa for only thirty-one hours.[125]

Even before Young emerged from his plane in Johannesburg, the South African government expressed its displeasure with his presence. Richard Moose, then the deputy undersecretary for management, was accompanying Young and recalled their arrival: "The South Africans made our plane land way out in a remote corner of the field, near the military part of the airport, far from where any public demonstration could have taken place. [Before we deplaned,] they ringed the plane with soldiers, which was an insulting thing to do—deliberately, egregiously insulting." Young was unfazed. "Outside the ring of soldiers there was a little group of airport employees," Moose continued. "Black, in coveralls. One was sitting on a tractor to pull baggage carts. Andy comes down the steps, delivers a perfunctory acknowledgment of the official party and goes right through the soldiers to the baggage handlers and says hello. That says the whole thing—'You're not going to encircle me.' It was perfect, and I still get goosebumps thinking about it."[126]

The South African government's alleged fear that Young's visit would create disturbances was unfounded. Rather than being inspired to launch a new wave of protests, the more radical black groups, such as the Black People's Convention and the South African Students' Organization, boycotted Young, charging that he was a spokesman for the status quo who wanted to meet with "boardroom blacks" rather than the "true leaders."[127] And while some hardline Afrikaners continued to grumble that Young was "interfering . . . and . . . anti-white," only the gentlest of protests greeted him: bits of paper with the slogans "Young insults us" or "Kick him out" or "Hated Young is our enemy" fluttered from high-rise office blocks near the luxury Carlton Hotel where the ambassador's party was staying.[128]

Young traveled to South Africa to soothe white fears, fanned by the relentlessly negative coverage of him in the government-controlled South African press. Fear, Young believed firmly, retarded progress. He wanted to encourage South Africans "that it is possible to have reasonable change." His message was clear and consistent, whether he was addressing whites or blacks: change is possible, change would benefit everyone, change could occur nonviolently, and change might happen sooner than anyone expected. He called for optimism. "There will not necessarily be a gradual evolution. When things start to happen they will take place very fast."[129]

Young's experience in the US civil rights movement had convinced him that the most effective way to end apartheid would be to convince South African business leaders that reducing racism would benefit their bottom line. "I'm interested in finding a way for South Africans to live together as brothers and live with the rest of the world as brothers," he told the assembled businesspeople. "I've come to think of the business community as in many respects being the key to that hope." He explained: "I hear a lot of talk about revolution around the world, . . . yet as I travel around this world the places where I see the hungry being fed, the places where I see the naked being clothed, the places where I see the sick being healed are places where there happens to be a free market system."[130]

The moderate *Rand Daily Mail* noted, "'The system minus apartheid' was Mr Young's recipe for salvation." It astutely observed that this "persuasive argument" formed "the core of the new American policy towards South Africa. The Mondale stick and the Young carrot go together." In an editorial entitled "Mr Young shows his true colours," it gushed: "When he arrived here this weekend, Mr. Young was an ogre in white South African eyes. But in the flesh he became something very different, as the businessmen at Saturday night's banquet will testify. They went there to hear a man who had been billed as a wild radical and found instead a moderate who took their breath away."[131]

The US ambassador to South Africa, Bill Bowdler, agreed. While acknowledging that white South African opinion of Young remained "divided," he reported that the majority of white South Africans were pleasantly surprised by Young: "His ability to relate to audiences and convey his sincerity, conviction and rational approach disarmed many." Bowdler quoted the director of the South African Chamber of Commerce who, in a note accompanying a videotape of Young's speech sent to all Chamber members, wrote: "Mr. Young showed by this address that he has a keen intellect . . . and is well informed on South Africa. . . . He earned for himself a great deal more respect than many may earlier have been prepared to grant him.'"[132]

At the US embassy the following day, Young gave a speech and fielded questions from a large group of invited guests, including Gatsha Buthelezi, leader of South Africa's 5.8 million Zulus. Buthelezi went up to the dais, embraced Young, and then gave the power salute, shouting "Amandla!" ("Power is ours!" in Zulu). And, in what Africanist Robert Rotberg called Young's "most dramatic act," the American ambassador joined in "the singing of the black anthem of defiance ["Nkosi Sikelel' iAfrika,"] with . . . Buthelezi."[133]

Young's presence in South Africa inspired no violence. The only danger he faced was being mobbed by adoring crowds of South Africans, including some whites, who pushed forward to be near him as he walked to the US embassy: "'Oh, he's so wonderful,' said one middle-aged woman, almost trampled in the crush." The mass-circulation black newspaper *The World* closed its editorial about the visit with "Andy . . . we love you." Conservative white opinion was more mixed. One Afrikaner told Ambassador Bowdler that "it looked as though Young did reflect serious and determined thinking by the Carter administration." This was, the hardline Afrikaner added ruefully, "too bad."[134]

"Our essential character as a nation"
Opinion in the US press of Mondale's and Young's missions was divided. The *Los Angeles Times* and *Christian Science Monitor* gave the president's policy a cautious thumbs-up. Mondale and Young "have produced no solutions," the *Los Angeles Times* admitted. "But the results have been encouraging enough to have justified the effort. . . . No one expected Vorster to be talked out of apartheid. What mattered was the openness of the American Vice President in expressing Washington's disapproval." The *New York Times* emphasized that the jury was still out. "The success of the policy will still depend on . . . the unmistakable threat that we mean to use our diplomatic and military leverage." The *Washington Post* was critical; before Mondale's meeting with Vorster, it had expressed "grave misgivings" about pressuring Pretoria on apartheid. "Is it better to regard the government of South Africa as a partner . . . or as an adversary? Can we have it both ways?" it asked. After the meeting, a tough *Post* editorial titled "A Mixed-Up Africa Policy" took issue with the administration's belief "that apartheid is expendable in South Africa, as segregation

was in the American South. . . . [This is,] in our opinion, [based] on a mistaken view of the nature of the problem in South Africa and of the role open to the United States there. . . . It is at least as likely that American pressure will simply intensify the building racial struggle."[135]

Southern Africa was just one of the issues that preoccupied Jimmy Carter in late May 1977. In the May 18 Israeli elections, the right-wing Likud Party achieved a stunning victory over the Labor Party, throwing all the White House plans for the Mideast peace process into disarray. On May 19, the day Mondale met Vorster and Young addressed the Maputo conference, Carter issued his new policy limiting foreign arms sales. On the 21st, after three days of talks about SALT, Secretary of State Vance and Soviet Foreign Minister Andrei Gromyko announced that no breakthroughs had been achieved. Also on the 21st, Carter "reassigned" (effectively firing) two-star General John Singlaub for publicly criticizing the administration's plan to withdraw US troops from South Korea. It was on the 21st that Young addressed the South African businessmen, and this made the front page of the *New York Times*. On the domestic front, the energy plan was hitting roadblocks in Congress; Carter had proposed a new environmental package; the administration was being pressed by liberal Democrats to implement health care reform; and the White House sold the presidential yacht as an austerity move, netting $266,000. Memories of Watergate and the war in Vietnam were stirred throughout the month as British journalist David Frost's interviews of Richard Nixon were aired.

In the midst of this busy period, Carter traveled to South Bend, Indiana. On May 22, when Young was embracing Chief Buthelezi in Johannesburg and Mondale was in London for debriefings after his meeting with Vorster, Jimmy Carter was sitting on a stage in full academic regalia, replete with the purple-and-gold cowl signifying the honorary degree he had just been awarded.[136] It was a festive occasion: the students threw peanuts, rather than confetti, in the air.

Carter's commencement address at Notre Dame would be the most optimistic and soaring speech of his presidency. "I want to speak to you today," he began, "about the strands that connect our actions overseas with our essential character as a nation. I believe we can have a foreign policy that is democratic, that is based on fundamental values, and that uses power and influence, which we have, for humane purposes."[137]

Twelve times Carter repeated that America was confident—in its democracy, its strength, and its "good sense." Recovering from the sobering experience of Vietnam, "we have now found our way back to our own principles and values, and we have regained our lost confidence." Then, in a much-quoted statement, he announced: "Being confident of our own future, we are now free of that inordinate fear of communism which once led us to embrace any dictator who joined us in that fear." Carter did not say that Americans were free of the fear of communism; he said that because they were confident in the strength and superiority of democratic capitalism, they were free of the "inordinate" fear of communism. For Carter, in May 1977, the Cold War was important, and so, too, was "the new reality of a politically awakening world."

The president then explained the pillars of his foreign policy. Four were easily understood, if difficult to achieve: strengthening alliances among democracies; negotiating nuclear arms control with the Soviet Union; reducing conventional arms sales; and achieving a Middle East peace agreement. Carter dealt at greater length with the fifth pillar, his "commitment to human rights." He was quick to explain that this was a realm of inescapable nuance. "This does not mean that we can conduct our foreign policy by rigid moral maxims." Paraphrasing his favorite theologian, Reinhold Niebuhr, he added, "We live in a world that is imperfect and which will always be imperfect—a world that is complex and confused and which will always be complex and confused."

Carter concluded: "Finally, let me say that we are committed to a peaceful resolution of the crisis in southern Africa. The time has come for the principle of majority rule to be the basis for political order, recognizing that in a democratic system the rights of the minority must also be protected. To be peaceful, change must come promptly. The United States is determined to work together with our European allies and with the concerned African States to shape a congenial international framework for the rapid and progressive transformation of southern African society and to help protect it from unwarranted outside interference."

The Conservative Majority

On that same Sunday, May 22, Ronald Reagan was also on a stage. After the Great Swamp Dixieland Band performed, the former governor strode to the lectern of the Three Saints Cultural Center in Garfield, New Jersey. The audience members—the conservative faithful—were eating Polish sausage, chicken, and pasta. In a wide-ranging speech that extolled the virtues of conservatism, Reagan rallied his base, raised money for conservative candidates, and positioned himself to run in 1980.[138]

After his narrow defeat at the 1976 Republican convention, Reagan had returned to California and been coy about his intentions. But he had kept his campaign structure intact, changing its name from Citizens for Reagan to Citizens for the Republic (CFR) and moving the mailing lists of 190,000 names and the $800,000 of leftover campaign funds (which had arrived too late to be used) over to this political action committee. In September 1976, Reagan's close confidante Lyn Nofziger had declared, "If Ford loses [the general election] . . . we'll take over the party."[139] To this end, Reagan had developed an array of effective mouthpieces: daily broadcasts on 250 radio stations, weekly columns in 100 newspapers, the CFR newsletter, and a busy schedule as a speaker, earning $5,000 a pop. With his easy smile and honed message, Reagan patiently waged a four-year, two-front war: against moderates in his own party and against the Democrats.

In early 1977, the former governor reiterated time and time again his clear message: a majority of Americans considered themselves conservatives. Citing a Gallup poll that he said showed that 51 percent of Americans identified themselves as conservative or right-of-center, whereas only 37 percent considered themselves liberal or left-of-center, Reagan argued that the conservative movement was not a fringe phenomenon. "We are not a cult," he insisted. "We are members of a majority. Let's act and talk like it." (In fact, the poll showed that only 41 percent of Americans considered themselves politically right of center; Reagan must have added the 10 percent who described themselves as "middle of the road" to make them a majority.) The challenge for conservatives was to unite their social and economic wings, and then broaden that base. Well aware of how Carter had eked out his victory, Reagan told conservatives: "We are going to have to come to grips with what I consider to be a major failing of the [Republican] party: its failure to attract black voters."[140]

For three months after Carter became president, Reagan held his fire. He focused instead on winning the fight within the Republican Party, and he waited. Carter, Reagan admitted, remained "kind of a mystery."[141] But Carter's address at Notre Dame was the foil that Reagan wanted. At a meeting of the Foreign Policy Association in New York City, Reagan lambasted the speech and outlined the themes of what would become his sustained attack on the Carter administration. He focused almost entirely on human rights. He began gently, saying that he agreed with the president that "human rights are basic, [and] applicable to all." But, he argued, there were two problems with Carter's human rights policy: hypocrisy and naivete. The White House, he asserted, "has aimed most of its human-rights criticism at . . . our friends." His example: "We insist on applying our own political standards to South Africa. We do not insist on these standards for the rest of the continent." This was dangerous, Reagan explained, because Pretoria was an ally in the fight against the Soviets. "We need our friends in meeting the Soviet challenge." Reagan's vision of Soviet intentions was clear: "The Soviets . . . want . . . the gradual encirclement of the West." Again, his example was from Africa: "In Africa, the Soviets . . . have hit on a winning formula: Use Cuban troops as proxy mercenaries."[142]

Stepping on Headlines

On May 22, as Carter spoke at Notre Dame, Andrew Young flew from Johannesburg to Lusaka, where he had brief talks about the Rhodesian negotiations, and then to Khartoum, where he met with President Gaafar Nimeiry and discussed the Sudanese government's desire to pry Somalia from the Soviets.[143] (Sudan had just ousted seventy Soviet military advisers and asked Moscow to reduce its embassy staff in Khartoum.) From Sudan, Young flew to London. On that last leg of the journey, the exhausted ambassador relaxed with the traveling press corps. The atmosphere on his plane was casual; his staff helped serve meals to the press. Young began to talk expansively about the pervasiveness of racism in the world. "It's impossible not to be a racist if you talk of racism as ethnocentricity. . . . Nobody is immune," he mused. "It's no moral judgment. . . . The worst racists in the world are the Russians." So far so good. But then he uttered a headline: "The Swedes are terrible racists. . . . They have an ideology which makes them very humanitarian and liberal, but when the crunch comes, the black in Sweden is treated just like the black in Queens." And another: talking about his upcoming first meeting with Foreign Secretary David Owen in London, Young said, "I hope he is not trapped by that old colonial mentality. I think it is very strong throughout the island [Britain]."[144]

These comments led British Ambassador Johnny Graham to remark that "Young reminded me of one of the pre-war Schuco toy tin cars—they couldn't go in reverse." The head of the Foreign Office's Rhodesia Department, Robin Renwick, said, "Actually, I liked the guy. He was extremely intelligent, but he was kind of erratic. Very talented. But he'd say things that would drive us screaming up the walls."[145]

At a press conference on the steps outside Owen's official residence, Young delivered a third headline. When asked his opinion of Cuba's decision to send fifty military technicians to Ethiopia immediately and possibly two hundred more later—which the State Department had deemed "a serious development," Young replied, "Well, the State Department expressed grave concern about that. I guess that is what I should do, too." The press corps responded with laughter, and the journalist followed up: "Does that come from the heart?" Young replied: "No, it really doesn't. . . . If Cuban advisers can stop the killing it might be a very good thing."[146]

The evening news on all three US television networks and all the major US newspapers prominently reported Young's comments. An enterprising CBS reporter located the president of the borough of Queens for a response. Young was frustrated that after all his important work in Africa, the headlines were— once again—about his inflammatory asides. "I stepped on my own headlines," he admitted, "and it made me sick."[147]

Young knew that in a few days, the July issue of *Playboy* would hit the stands with a long interview he had given in March, after his first trip to Africa (to Tanzania and Nigeria) and during the early days of the Shaba crisis. Read as a whole, it was—like all Young's interviews—temperate and ardently pro-capitalist, but it had two problems, especially after the brouhaha caused by his remarks about the Swedes, the residents of Queens, and the Cubans. First, he attempted to clarify—but not retract—his early controversial remarks about the Cubans bringing stability to Angola, the British inventing racism, and the South African government being illegitimate, thereby reminding the readers of those controversies. Second, he let drop a few gems that eager journalists mined for headlines. The most inflammatory occurred during a discussion on the pervasiveness of racism, which Young defined—as he had on the airplane—as "ethnocentrism" or having "no understanding of the problems of colored peoples anywhere." In this context, Young said baldly, "Nixon and Ford . . . were, in fact, racists."[148]

This crossed a line, and members of Congress reacted with vehemence. William Broomfield (R-MI) called it "an insult to a great man [Ford]," while Jim Martin (R-NC) deemed it "outrageous" and Robert Bauman (R-MD) called on Carter to "remove Mr. Young immediately." John Anderson (R-IL), normally not a critic, said that he agreed with a recent Harris poll that indicated that most Americans thought Young "should learn to keep some of his thoughts to himself."[149]

Young, however, still had fans, the most important of whom was in the White House. Upon his return to Washington he met with Carter to discuss his trip to Africa. Afterward, they held an impromptu news conference on the White House lawn. Carter stood by Young, literally and figuratively. Asked if the president had encouraged him to speak out, Young replied, "I don't think he had encouraged it, but he didn't tell me to shut up either." Carter said that "his longtime friend" still had his support. In the following days, Carter admitted during a press conference that "the statements that Andy Young has made are different from what I would have said," but he explained that this was due to Young's choice of words, not his meaning. "Andy Young . . . speaks with my full authority and my complete support. . . . We are completely compatible in our hopes. . . . There is actually no disparity of opinion or responsibility among myself, Cyrus Vance, the Vice President, or Andy Young." The president gave Young credit for improving the image of the United States. "Third World nations . . . now look on the United States as having at least one representative—I hope more—but at least one who understands their problems, who speaks their language, who will listen to them when they put forward their woes and their hopes for the future." Carter expressed concern that the press was not communicating this. "I'm disturbed that after he spent 17 days in Africa, . . . that a remark about Sweden was a major headline that derived from that entire, very fruitful visit on his part to that continent. Andy is concerned also."[150]

The Team

It was a natural time to regroup. The administration's goals in southern Africa had been determined, and Young's and Mondale's trips had set its policy in motion. Mondale had thrown down the gauntlet to Vorster, the State Department had begun to work as one of "the Five" (the Western members of the Security Council) to bring about free elections in Namibia, and the administration had devised a plan with the British to bring Rhodesia to majority rule.

This plan had been constructed haltingly on the rubble left by the Kissinger initiative. Throughout, Carter pushed the British forward. "The president wants me to emphasize the necessity for early progress," Vance wrote Foreign Secretary Owen in a typical exchange on April 8, 1977.[151] Through intensive bilateral negotiations on the ground in southern Africa, the Anglo-American team would attempt to steer all the parties that had been represented at Geneva—the Patriotic Front, the Frontline States, Ian Smith, and the black nationalists in Rhodesia—toward an internationally negotiated settlement, rather than toward a solution on the battlefield or in Smith's back rooms. The American press was paying attention: African affairs were regularly on the front pages of the major newspapers and frequently in their editorials; they were featured on all three networks' evening news almost every night in May.[152]

The administration's African policy had been complicated by the war in Shaba and by the intensifying revolution in Ethiopia, but it had not been derailed: southern Africa remained its focus. Moreover, the policymakers in the White House and State Department had not lost their initial confidence and exuberance. They had identified three problems that they were determined to correct. First, the glare of the press had been useful while they had been setting forth their policy, but for the delicate negotiations over Rhodesia and Namibia in the coming months, a lower profile was advisable. Many, including the president, believed that Young's "open diplomacy" had played a constructive role, but it had become a distraction. Young therefore backpedaled. He learned to say—sometimes, at least—"no comment."

Second, some of the "Kissinger holdovers" in the Africa Bureau of the State Department were not comfortable with the direction of the new team. Therefore, in June there were changes. The State Department denied that it was a "purge," calling it instead a "normal rotation," but it was almost a clean sweep at the top: Assistant Secretary of State for African Affairs William Schaufele and two of the three deputy assistant secretaries were replaced.[153]

Schaufele, who had assumed the post in late 1975, had objected to the Carter administration's decision to send Zaire's President Mobutu only a small package of nonlethal supplies during the Shaba crisis, considered the decision to pressure South Africa about apartheid unwise, and disapproved of Young's trip to Maputo. On all three counts, he was overruled. As Schaufele grew increasingly frustrated with "the missionaries" in charge of Carter's Africa policy, Carter's new team grew increasingly concerned that the assistant secretary's close association with Kissinger's policy was undermining its ability to convince black Africans that there had been a sea change in Washington. Overshadowed by Young and overruled on policy, Schaufele did not take the lead in explaining and justifying Carter's policy toward the continent. The result was a growing sense of confusion about who, exactly, was in charge—Young was clearly the man for southern Africa, but who spoke for the administration's policy toward the rest of the continent? This was not a question asked just by conservative columnists; even US ambassadors in the field complained that they were "unclear as to the locus of the administration's Africa policy."[154]

The decision was made in May to replace Schaufele (who was appointed ambassador to Poland) with Wayne Fredericks, who had been deputy assistant secretary in the Africa Bureau from 1961 to 1967. Fredericks was offered the job on May 16. However, before he could begin the confirmation process, he was seriously injured in a traffic accident in London. Deciding that the position was too important to put on hold until Fredericks recovered, on June 4 Vance offered the job to Richard Moose, who was serving as deputy undersecretary for management, a post that ranked fifth in seniority in the department. Heading the Africa Bureau attracted Moose: the continent was a high priority for the Carter administration, and the assistant secretary would have a creative, policy-making position. Dick Moose had been a foreign service officer in Cameroon in the early 1960s, had served on the NSC staff in the Johnson years, and in 1969 had joined the staff of the Senate Foreign Relations Committee. His fascination with Africa had been rekindled in 1975 and 1976, when he had accompanied Senator Dick Clark, chair of the Africa subcommittee, on several wide-ranging tours of the continent. In May 1977—when he was deputy undersecretary for management and Fredericks was still expected to become assistant secretary for Africa—Moose had accompanied Young to Maputo, and he had then flown home with Mondale after the meeting with Vorster. He strongly supported the new administration's call for majority rule in southern Africa, and from his contacts on the Hill he was aware that the Carter administration had not effectively explained its goals to the members of Congress; Moose relished the challenge of rectifying this.[155]

The appointment of Moose as assistant secretary (he assumed office on June 13, 1977) was an important turning point: it helped the Africa team coalesce. Assistant Secretary for International Organizations Charles Maynes observed, "He [Moose] was an important figure in the [State Department] building. . . . He was a major figure." Moose's acceptance of the Africa job signaled the importance that the new administration attached to the continent. Moreover, he was on the same page as the men who were already conceptualizing the policy—Young at the UN and Tony Lake on the Policy Planning Staff. They had known each other for years. Moose was in the "inner circle . . . an inside group that had basically bonded in Vietnam."[156] This group of State Department officials—Moose, Lake, Richard Holbrooke (assistant secretary for Asia), Peter Tarnoff (executive secretary), and Les Gelb (assistant secretary for politico-military affairs)—shared a similar worldview, seared by Vietnam and in some cases by working under Kissinger. (In 1969, Nixon had authorized FBI wiretaps of both Lake and Moose.[157]) Moose was smart and energetic. He succeeded in smoothing many of the rough edges between the new, young members of the team who believed that the time had come to exert stronger pressure on Pretoria and some older career diplomats who advocated caution. The tension between these two camps had been "awkward," in the words of Frank Wisner, an official in the Secretariat of the State Department.[158] Moreover, Moose's experience on the Hill was invaluable to the White House; he understood the nuances of how Congress worked, and he had excellent relations with the key liberals who would guide the Carter administration's Africa initiatives through the legislature. "No one gives enough credit to Dick Moose," the key US negotiator, Steve Low, commented. "He's highly intelligent, and he got along very well with Vance." Moose threw himself into the southern African conundrum—especially Rhodesia—with extraordinary passion. Even decades later, his enthusiasm bubbled over as he answered question after question about the Carter administration's policy toward the region. "It was one of the most interesting and important things I've ever been engaged in," he recalled. "It was the most fun I've ever had."[159]

There was one other significant appointment: Stephen Low, a career foreign service officer who was ambassador to Zambia, was tapped to lead the US side of the Anglo-American team that would undertake the complex bilateral talks to prepare for a negotiated settlement. Ambassador Donald McHenry, who worked closely with Low, said simply that he was "superb." Low's British counterpart was Deputy Undersecretary of State Johnny Graham, who had served as British ambassador in Baghdad as well as head of the chancery in Washington. "Johnny . . . was bright and sound, and a delightful companion," Low recollected. "[He] and I had a wonderful relationship. We kept nothing from each other." Graham concurred: "Steve and I worked together very closely. We didn't always agree with our respective governments, and we got along with each other very well."[160]

Creating the Graham-Low partnership was an essential step in the development of the Anglo-American plan. Low proved to be a creative and diligent coxswain. He and Graham traveled around Africa, logging a half-million miles, Low calculated, to nudge all parties toward agreement. "We went around in circles for three years talking to all the parties," Low recalled. "We talked to every [Rhodesian] Black African Nationalist group, we talked to the South Africans, we talked to all the Frontline heads of state." Vance and Owen sometimes followed, adding their muscle to the negotiations.[161]

The team that oversaw US policy on southern Africa for the remainder of Carter's presidency had several layers. In Washington, White House, CIA, and State Department officials were members of the team, and at the UN in New York, there was Young. In Africa, there were the ambassadors and their staffs. "We had good ambassadors there [in Africa]," Carter remembered, "professionals who knew their stuff."[162] Given the prominence and complexity of southern African issues, these officials were stretched thin. In the coming months, they sustained an impressive juggling act: convincing the leaders of the Patriotic Front and the Frontline States that the Carter administration could be trusted, while simultaneously trying to keep Smith and the moderate blacks in Rhodesia open to talks and persuading South Africa to keep the pressure on Smith.

Each aspect of this performance required diplomatic skill. The Patriotic Front was a fragile alliance between Nkomo and Mugabe, two ambitious men who did not see eye to eye; the Americans wanted to put sufficient pressure on the Front to convince it to come to the table, but they did not want to fracture it. Washington believed that to negotiate effectively with Ian Smith, the Patriotic Front needed to stay united. The Frontline States—represented above all by Zambia's Kaunda and Tanzania's Nyerere—were not united, and the Americans needed to navigate deftly through their differences of opinion. Mondale's tough talk to Vorster complicated the administration's attempt to persuade South Africa to press Smith to make concessions. Another difficulty was that Smith, ever the survivor, had made some concessions to international opinion that had weakened his position at home. In March 1977, he had liberalized the law governing black ownership of businesses, factories, and farms. Although this "symbolic act" contained, in the opinion of the CIA, "little of real value," it was enough to cause Smith's right wing to bolt from the Rhodesian Front party and form a new ultraconservative splinter group.[163] The Carter administration worried that if Smith were forced from office, it could create a dangerous power vacuum in Salisbury. Therefore, while the Americans pushed Smith to agree to all-party talks, they had to be careful not to push so hard that he was hounded from office.

Throughout 1977, Smith dangled the possibility of the "internal solution" that he had first mentioned in the speech he gave in January scuttling the Geneva talks. His idea was that he would convince black leaders within Rhodesia who were not leading guerrilla armies to participate in a government that would be nominally headed by blacks but would guarantee the protection of white interests. Because the Americans wanted, above all, to stop the war and they did not believe that any internal solution would mollify the Patriotic Front, they doggedly and artfully tried to keep open the possibility of a negotiated settlement.

A final and important complication for the Americans was that their partner in this delicate dance in southern Africa was the discredited British. To succeed, the Americans and British needed to speak with one voice. This meant that the ambassadors in the southern Africa and Nigeria, plus the State Department and NSC officials, plus Young and President Carter needed to pull together with the British ambassadors and Foreign Office officials and Prime Minister Callaghan. They all had "to play," as David Aaron told Foreign Secretary Owen, "from the same sheet of music."[164]

The Americans formed a true team: reversing Kissinger's policy of compartmentalization and centralization, Vance encouraged them to circulate all their cables to each other so that they were all always in the loop. It was like an early listserv. "When Carter became president, the tone changed," the deputy assistant secretary for Africa remembered. "It was dramatic." The US ambassador in South Africa told his British counterpart that his position "had changed out of all recognition since the advent of the new administration; he was for the first time receiving copies of all the policy telegrams relating to southern Africa. This meant that he was now in a position to give meaningful advice instead of acting merely as a Post Office."[165] Time and again, American diplomats interviewed about those days used the phrase "we were on the same wavelength," and this is borne out by reading their cables. Moose summed it up: "It was a great team. There was a real sense of excitement."[166]

The infamous wars between Vance and Brzezinski did not occur over Rhodesia. When Carter asked the secretary of state in March 1977 how his recommendations on Rhodesia differed from the national security adviser's, Vance's response was clear: "They are the same."

Brzezinski chose his battles carefully. In 1977, he was gradually earning the president's confidence, and Carter clearly considered southern Africa important and close to his heart. Moreover, Brzezinski believed in majority rule on both moral and pragmatic grounds, as it would provide the only stable structure of peace in southern Africa.[167] Through 1977, he agreed with all the key policymakers that the Anglo-American proposals—negotiation and a constitutional conference—were the surest means to end the war, and ending the war meant closing an opportunity for the Soviets. He met with African leaders in Washington, he chaired numerous meetings on the administration's Africa policy, and his deputy David Aaron met frequently with the team directing it in the State Department. Although Brzezinski understood the importance of Africa—in terms of the Cold War, global capitalism, and US relations with the Third World—the continent was not one of his areas of expertise. He was most comfortable discussing the Soviet Union; Eastern and Western Europe; Asia; and, to a lesser degree, the Middle East. Therefore, on most African matters—especially in his first year—Brzezinski deferred to the State Department. (A significant exception is Angola, which he saw strictly through the prism of US-Cuban relations and about which he was assertive and hardline.[168]) "Zbig didn't know jack about Africa," Henry Richardson, the NSC Africa expert, declared. "Brzezinski had these erratic interventions in the Rhodesia negotiations," Robin Renwick of the Foreign Office recalled. "He was a gadfly. But he didn't really get involved. He didn't have an African policy." As Moose remembered, "Zbig somehow understood he shouldn't get involved in southern Africa. It was a sideshow for him."[169]

In 1977, Brzezinski bridled only at what he saw as US kowtowing to Whitehall. "The British, in particular David Owen, have been conducting our foreign policy for us. . . . Do we wish this to continue?" he asked the president in June. But he did not push this point.[170]

It is a caricature to limn Brzezinski as the realpolitik hawk and Vance as the moralistic dove. For both men, in Rhodesia there was no light between a self-interested policy and a moral one. As Brzezinski told Kaunda's top aide, "In the longer perspective, we must choose between global cooperation and chaos. This is why . . . the Carter Administration attaches such importance to good relations with black African nations."[171] To distinguish between regional and global approaches to crises is misleading. Often, as in Rhodesia, handling a crisis as a regional issue was the smartest way to deal with it in Cold War terms, and Brzezinski understood this.

Carter himself recalled about the team, "We didn't have any arguments in my administration about what we should do about Rhodesia. . . . We had arguments about other things, which I welcomed. But Dr. Brzezinski and [Secretary of Defense] Harold Brown and Cy Vance all understood where I felt very deeply about the African question." The administration's critics agreed: Chester Crocker, who would become Reagan's assistant secretary of state for Africa, wrote, "The administration's key actors on Southern Africa policy at the United Nations, the National Security Council and in State's Africa Bureau and Policy Planning staff operate on a common wave length."[172]

Another striking aspect of the Rhodesia team was that its recommendations were taken seriously: the White House was listening. Diplomatic historians are familiar with the experience of unearthing wise, prescient, and creative memos written by desk officers and ambassadors that appear never to have been read by the higher-ups, let alone acted upon. Yet in reading the full array of documents about Rhodesia there is a striking unity of purpose and an organic flow of ideas from bottom to top.

The reason is straightforward: the principals took a keen interest in the resolution of the crisis in Rhodesia, and all agreed on the broad outlines of the path forward. It is not clear how much time Carter himself spent on Rhodesia in 1977, but he was certainly well briefed: Rhodesia was mentioned at almost every Cabinet meeting, and in that first year Cabinet meetings were held almost weekly. In April, the president admitted, "I have spent an awful lot of time on the African question." Charles Maynes, the assistant secretary for international organizations, who worked closely with Young at the UN, said, "We felt, not a directive hand but a supportive hand. . . . He [Carter] certainly was supportive." Mondale also remained actively involved in southern Africa policy in 1977: "The Vice President's personal attention to the problems of southern Africa," the executive secretary of the State Department wrote in July, "is well known." Secretary Vance also cared deeply about ending the war in Rhodesia, and he set the tone. His key aides on Africa—particularly Moose and Lake—were equally committed to resolving the war and just as convinced that the solution lay in even-handed diplomacy.[173]

Moreover, there was a unique channel from the field to the Oval Office in the person of Andrew Young. He was the roving ambassador for southern Africa and liaison with the British, and most important, he was widely considered a direct route to Carter's ear. "We couldn't have done it without him," one ambassador said. "Andy was crucial," another noted. "He provided the backbone and the spine." The Africa specialist at the NSC called Young "indispensable." Foreign Secretary David Owen extolled Young's "enormous capacity for empathy" and asserted that "he delivered the Patriotic Front. He kept the Patriotic Front on board for us." Young's UN deputy, Donald McHenry, agreed: "[Andy] gave us *time* to try to move away from the previous policy. . . . It gave us entrée with people who were quite negative toward the United States."[174]

When asked if he could imagine developing his Rhodesia policy without Young, President Carter answered, "No. . . . [We had a] superb group of ambassadors in the southern part of Africa, but Andy was the key to it because the African leaders . . . they all came to Andy because . . . people knew the way to get to me with their ideas or hopes or fears was through Andy Young." Carter noted that his communication with Young had been almost always oral: "I didn't order him, 'Don't write to me; talk to me,' but that was just an understanding we had. . . . I think if you search the record," Carter said, "you would find very few [memos] to me in writing, and he would not have submitted his recommendations to me through the State Department in writing."[175]

Young was important because he was an unusually effective US representative in Africa. "He brought the Carter administration credibility with the Africans," Ambassador McHenry explained. Leaders—of all stripes—talked to Young not just because he was a gifted listener, but because he was considered a direct conduit to Carter. The *Bilalian News*, the weekly newspaper of the Nation of Islam, articulated the impression held widely in the United States and abroad: it is "evident that . . . [Young] is indeed an intimate confidant of the President whose public statements are most nearly a true barometer of the chief executive's thinking." Young was forthright about the fact that he did not have a long-standing friendship with Carter. He told *Jet* in early 1977, "I have a really interesting relationship with Jimmy Carter. I don't push him and he doesn't push me. Almost anything I've even hinted to him, he's jumped at and agreed to, I mean in terms of policy things. . . . Anytime I've wanted to call him about anything, I've been able to, and yet, that kind of power is like money in the bank—the less you use it the more you have. . . . When I call him I want it to be a serious policy consideration."[176]

McHenry added, "Andy's belief was that he had a special relationship with the president, and the relationship was regional, southern, spiritual, Christian—that he was chosen [as ambassador] because of those things, that he was articulating what he thought was the president's belief and direction. . . . And if the president wanted to do anything else he would tell him, . . . but the president's a busy person so I don't have to sit there and get instructions from him—I don't want to wear out my welcome." Young attributed his influence with Carter to their shared religious roots. "He and I always related to each other as Christians. . . . Undergirding and wrapping all these things up was the one thing that Jimmy Carter and I shared: we are both religiously motivated." Or, as Moose put it, "With Young and Carter it was a visceral thing."[177]

Carter and Young did not challenge this impression because in broad terms it was true—they respected each other and had similar viewpoints—and also because it was useful: it helped Young gain access and it streamlined US diplomacy. Young was the quarterback; he relied on the full support of the president and the secretary of state, and he led an enthusiastic and competent team in the field. Not even Brzezinski voiced dissent. Young's only problem—and it was a big one—was convincing Smith and the Patriotic Front to play ball.

6. Hopeful in the Horn

Given their druthers, the Africa specialists in the Carter administration would have devoted their full attention to resolving the problems of Rhodesia, Namibia, and South Africa. Unfortunately, they could not stop crises from erupting elsewhere on the continent. This complicated the administration's Africa policy but did not fundamentally change it: the core team maintained its focus on southern Africa. Most other crises—for example, the human rights abuses of Uganda's Idi Amin, and the war in the Western Sahara where rebels were fighting for independence from Morocco—were handled at the State Department regional director level. The main exception was the continuing turbulence in the Horn. Because of its strong Soviet dimension, and because of Saudi Arabia's and Egypt's interest in it, the Horn grabbed the attention of all the principals, including President Carter.

Understanding the fitful evolution of the Carter administration's policy toward the Horn sheds light on the centrality of the Cold War in Carter's thinking. It also shows how hope—wishful thinking—was the engine of incrementalism. The policy developed in three stages. The implementation of the president's April 1977 directive "to get Somalia to be our friend,"[1] proceeded smoothly until mid-summer, when it became impossible to pretend that Somali troops had not launched a war of aggression in the Ogaden. This initiated the second phase, in which the Somali and Ethiopian armies waged war in the Ogaden, while the Carter administration drew back from its promise to send arms to the Somalis (though it continued to help them behind the scenes) and waited optimistically for the Kremlin's dreams of hegemony in the Horn to shatter. The Carter team remained full of hope until late November 1977, when the third and final phase began, in which the administration scrambled to respond to the massive Soviet and Cuban intervention in the war.

Befriending Somalia

The implementation of Carter's policy in the first phase was straightforward. Throughout May 1977, when the spotlight was on southern Africa, Abdullahi Addou, the tireless Somali ambassador, had methodically worked his way up the ladder of American officialdom to deliver the good news about President Mohamed Siad Barre's change of heart: he wanted to ditch his Soviet friends and "go all the way" with the Americans.[2] In April, Addou had seen the assistant secretary of state for Africa, and he kept pounding the corridors and the pavements. In May, he asked to see the secretary of state, the national security adviser, the vice president, and the president.

Granting Addou this access, particularly to Mondale and Carter, would signal Washington's interest in displacing the Soviet Union as Somalia's arms supplier. The argument in favor was clear: Carter, an avid fly fisherman, had Siad Barre on the line, and he wanted to keep him there to compensate for America's loss of influence in Ethiopia to the Kremlin. The possibility of "turning" a Soviet ally strongly tempted Washington. "A most delicate and potentially rewarding opportunity awaits us in Somalia," Vance declared on June 1.[3]

Nevertheless, the argument for caution was also clear. Siad Barre wanted weapons so that his country could attack Ethiopia and annex the Ogaden, and US intelligence reported that war was brewing in the region. A May 1977 assessment estimated that "5,000 to 10,000 Somali-backed insurgents . . . well-armed and trained by Somalia" were operating in the Ogaden, and "very heavy fighting has been occurring around El Kere [a town in the Ogaden]." On June 3, the CIA noted that Somali-backed insurgents, "accompanied by some regular Somali military personnel, are steadily eroding government control of the countryside." Siad Barre denied that any Somali troops were in the Ogaden; all the insurgents, he claimed, were Ogadenis—ethnic Somalis who lived in the Ogaden—who had joined the principal guerrilla group in the region, the Western Somali Liberation Front (WSLF). Based on the WSLF's skills and weaponry, it was obvious that regular Somali forces were helping the guerrillas, but the extent of this aid was murky. This was not an academic question: the answer to it determined whether the war in the Ogaden was a local uprising against Ethiopian oppression—as Siad Barre insisted—or a Somali invasion of Ethiopia, as that country's strongman, Mengistu Haile Mariam, asserted. In June, the White House chose to lean toward Siad Barre's interpretation, despite its own intelligence reports to the contrary. The CIA noted: "The continued dispute over the Ogaden is increasingly likely to lead to conflict between Somalia and Ethiopia. . . . The fear that Ethiopia's success in acquiring foreign [i.e., Soviet] arms may tilt the balance in the Ogaden could lead Somali President Siad to move quickly while Ethiopian capabilities are weak."[4] Any weapons that the United States provided to Somalia, whether directly or through third parties, would be used to wage a war of aggression against Ethiopia.

This fact not only raised a fundamental moral question; it also risked alienating African countries. Somalia's attempt to annex the Ogaden contravened the Organization of African Unity's stricture that the borders in Africa, however arbitrarily drawn, were set in stone. (Otherwise, the OAU explained, the continent would descend into perpetual war.) Moreover, sending arms to Somalia would breach Carter's campaign promise to curb conventional arms transfers. It would also raise questions about the administration's human rights policy, because Siad Barre's record on that score would not bear congressional scrutiny. In May, for example, the State Department included Somalia on a list of nations that supported international terrorism. (When Zbigniew Brzezinski forwarded the report to the president, Carter wrote in the margin, "How the h— does that happen?"[5])

US involvement in the Ogaden would also contradict the administration's promise to see African issues on their own merits rather than as chips in the Cold War. NSC staffer Tom Thornton penned a stiff warning to Brzezinski: "This Administration must not fall into the great power competition trap in the Third World that blighted so much of Kissinger's efforts." Thornton belittled the administration's tilt toward Siad Barre as a "zero-sum, cold war . . . cheap shot [designed to] 'soak the Soviets.'"[6]

Furthermore, it was not at all certain that Washington—if it sent weapons to Somalia—would be backing a reliable horse. Siad Barre was sending what Cyrus Vance rightly called "ambiguous signals." Ambassador Addou was adamant that the Somali leader wanted to sever ties with the Soviet Union. Siad, however, had for weeks rebuffed the US ambassador, whom he knew was carrying a message from President Carter.[7] He had refused to accept a US military attaché, a possible first step toward a military relationship with Washington. He had sent his vice president to Moscow. And in June 1977, he told *Newsweek*, "I can assure you there will be no conflict between Somalia and the Soviets." When asked if he was interested in US military aid, Siad declared: "What we now receive from the Soviet Union is sufficient."[8] Paul Henze, the NSC expert on the Horn, warned that Siad was a "wily nomad" who was merely toying with Washington's fear of expanding Soviet influence and desire to curry the favor of the moderate Arab states.[9]

Carter's desires overrode these misgivings, and on May 3, Addou was granted a meeting with Secretary Vance. The Somali ambassador used the opportunity to confide the "closely held secret" that Siad Barre was determined to move away from the Soviet Union and forge better relations with the

United States. Addou asked for US military aid, explaining that his country was not seeking a huge quantity but rather an "agreement in principle" that Washington would step up. He indicated that the weapons could be channeled through third countries. Could he report to Siad Barre that the United States was "willing in principle" to extend military assistance? Vance did not tell Addou that backing an aggressor would be impossible. In fact, he did not mention the Ogaden. Instead, he dodged the question by saying that he could not answer while the administration's arms transfer policy was still in process (it would be concluded in two weeks) and suggesting that Somalia seek alternative sources. Vance was cautious, but he did not say "no." More significantly, he promised Addou that he would arrange a meeting with Vice President Walter Mondale.[10]

On May 11, Mondale received the Somali ambassador. (A week later, Mondale would face the administration's other Africa crisis during his encounter with South Africa's John Vorster.) The meeting with Addou was remarkable for several reasons. That it occurred was unusual: the vice president had a broad portfolio covering domestic and foreign issues, and he rarely met with ambassadors, especially of destitute countries. The State Department, however, urged Mondale to meet with the Somali ambassador because "we are at a delicate stage in the process of weaning the Somalis away from their heavy dependence upon the Soviets."[11] During the meeting Addou was exceptionally frank about why Somalia was seeking arms from the United States: Siad was unhappy with Moscow's insistence that Somalia renounce its irredentist dreams. Stressing the Somali claim to the Ogaden, Addou told Mondale: "Somalia seeks the self-determination of Somali people throughout the Horn." This was why Siad Barre was turning to Washington for military assistance. Addou then said—with considerable chutzpah—that he required a reply within a month. Mondale repeated Vance's evasive replies, adding that Somalia should try to buy military equipment elsewhere and "we would be supportive of that effort." Like Vance, he did not say "no." In a memo to Carter reporting on this meeting, Mondale wrote that the key question was: Should the United States provide the Somalis military aid? He recommended "testing the Somalis with a modest amount of token assistance," and he thought it was important to act quickly. "By doing nothing in this crucial area, we have failed to explore the possibility that they are sincere in their statements."[12]

The immediate question was whether Carter should agree to see Addou. For a US vice president to meet with the ambassador from Somalia was unusual, but for the president of the United States to do so would be extraordinary. During his four years in the White House, Carter met privately with no other

African ambassadors except those from South Africa and, during the Camp David process, Egypt.[13]

NSC expert Paul Henze, who had been CIA station chief in Addis during the Nixon years, clung to the hope that Ethiopia would return to a pro-American stance. He wrote Brzezinski, "The Somalis are putting themselves up for sale, but they want to be bought on their own terms," and he suggested that instead of extending direct military aid the United States should organize Saudi-funded economic aid. He cautioned against rushing and also noted that the White House must not encourage Somali adventurism. The State Department seemed to agree, at least fleetingly. On May 23, it sent a message to Egyptian president Anwar Sadat that included a rare explanation of the fundamental dilemma: "We do not wish to encourage Somali irredentist ambitions and would not wish to be associated with any military program which would provide a level of arms in excess of Somalia's legitimate defensive needs." The problem was that Siad Barre himself had made it very clear that he was not interested in weapons for his "legitimate defensive needs."[14]

The Saudi Angle

On May 24, two days after Carter's Notre Dame speech, Crown Prince Fahd of Saudi Arabia arrived at the White House for a state visit. The administration had still not realized how important the potential realignment in the Horn was to the House of Saud. In their briefing papers for the president, both Vance and Brzezinski relegated the Horn to an afterthought, just as they had before Sadat's visit the previous month. Vance wrote seventeen pages about all aspects of the Arab-Israeli peace process and the price of oil. Only on the final pages did he discuss the Horn. After observing that "the Saudi Government seems particularly interested in our replacing the Soviet Union as arms supplier to Somalia," Vance advised Carter to say (if asked) that "[w]e share the Saudi desire that Somalia have an alternative to the Soviet Union as a source of military supplies for legitimate defensive needs (as opposed to weapons to further Somali claims on neighboring territory)." Vance failed to alert the president to the imminent danger of an explosive war in the Ogaden; nor did he convey the priority that the Saudi leaders gave to the region.[15]

Somalia was very important to Prince Fahd. His country had already extended $55 million in economic and military assistance to Siad's government.[16] Immediately before his departure for Washington, Fahd had received an urgent telegram from Siad Barre urging him to press President Carter to improve US relations with Somalia. "What alternative do I have if I cannot get Saudi Arabian and American help?" Siad had implored.[17]

Over lunch with Vance, Fahd continued to stress the problems of the Horn. "Somaliland was the chief subject," US ambassador John West, who attended the lunch, noted.[18] Fahd explained that the Saudi government had discerned "new thinking" among Somalis about their alliance with the Soviet Union. The prince stressed that this provided "an opportunity for Saudi Arabia and the West to rush to Somalia's aid, closing out the possibilities for Soviet intervention in Somalia and the Red Sea area." He added that these "efforts will be useful only if the United States and other Western countries join in." Vance responded that US views on Somalia were similar, and he assured the crown prince that the administration "had given much attention and thought to the situation in the Horn of Africa" and was considering economic and military assistance. "In our view," Vance told Fahd, "the United States and Saudi Arabia have an opportunity in the Horn of Africa and should work together." He asked for the prince's advice about "the desirability of forming a consortium of Western countries to provide military assistance to Somalia." Fahd approved of the idea—if the United States was an active participant—and he explained the kingdom's viewpoint: it might be possible to decouple the Somalis from the Soviets, but "the key to this is the question of military supply. Unless Siad is assured in this regard he won't be able to move. It is very important that the US be willing to help."[19]

There is no record of a serious discussion among the principals in the Carter administration about the dilemma that these comments posed. The White House and State Department appear to have been guided by hope: hope that they could devise a way to keep the Saudis happy, win Somali friendship, and yet not be seen to back a war of aggression in which Somalia would annex a third of Ethiopia.

In his remarks to reporters on May 25, after his talks with Crown Prince Fahd, Carter said that they had discussed oil prices and then, "We discussed the Horn of Africa and how to keep the Red Sea region peaceful." The briefing papers had treated the Horn as an afterthought, but when he described the talks to the press, Carter stressed the Horn first and Israel second.[20]

Dousing Rumors about Castro

On that very morning, the *Washington Post* carried a story that raised the stakes. On page one, David Ottaway reported from Somalia that fifty Cuban "military experts" had arrived in Addis two weeks earlier and that 350 to 450 more were expected "in the next few weeks." Ottaway explained that this "appears to indicate that Fidel Castro is prepared to involve his country in yet another major internal African conflict in direct conjunction with Soviet aims and designs on the continent." Ottaway pinpointed the significance of the development: "Cuba is becoming, for the first time, directly involved in the mainstream of Arab as well as African politics."[21]

The Ethiopians immediately denied the report, saying that the only Cubans in their country were doctors and technicians, but the State Department spokesman, Hodding Carter, confirmed that there were indeed fifty Cuban military technicians in Ethiopia. He then sought to lower the temperature. The Carter administration was well aware that Cuba was interested in the Horn—Castro's travels had broadcast it—but it did not believe that this presaged a major Cuban commitment to the region along the lines of Angola. "We don't have any information of his [Castro's] intentions to send more troops," Hodding Carter assured the journalists. When pressed, however, he admitted that if the *Post*'s report that 450 more Cubans could be on their way to Ethiopia were true, it would be "a very serious development." The *New York Times* noted that this was "one of the administration's strongest statements yet about Cubans in Africa."[22]

The State Department's assessment was accurate: scores of Cuban documents show that Castro was impressed by the Ethiopian Revolution and wanted to help Mengistu. He did send a small military mission to scout out the situation, and he sent a team of doctors and nurses, but the scale of his commitment in the summer of 1977 was extremely modest, because he had concluded reluctantly that his country—with tens of thousands of troops remaining in Angola—could not support another major mission abroad. He explained this to US journalist Barbara Walters in an interview on May 20 (broadcast on June 9). In the wide-ranging conversation, Castro insisted that all his "personnel" in Ethiopia were diplomats or doctors. "There are no military advisers there," he said. "I've told you the truth."[23]

It was at this point that Andrew Young—in London after his trip to Mozambique and South Africa—declared that Cubans in Ethiopia "might not be a bad thing" if they could stop the killing. On the *Today* show the following morning, Vice President Mondale corrected Young: the United States would regard the introduction of Cuban troops to Ethiopia as a "very serious" development and "a destabilizing factor." (The following week's *Newsweek* noted that there seemed to be "some disagreement within the Carter Administration over the seriousness of the Cuban threat on the Horn.")[24]

On May 30, the first question reporters fired at Carter as he stood on the tarmac after bidding farewell to his wife, Rosalynn, who was departing for a goodwill tour to Latin America, was about the Cubans in Ethiopia. "Does that bother you at all?" the reporter asked. Carter responded: "We would like very much for Cuba to refrain from this intrusion into African affairs in a military way." This was certainly true, but the key point is that the administration had accurate intelligence that led it to discount the rumors flying in the US news media.[25]

In the following days, therefore, the White House announced movement toward the normalization of relations with Cuba. It was building on the work of the previous four months, when direct talks with Cuba had achieved several small, symbolic breakthroughs: a fishing agreement, the easing of US restrictions on travel to Cuba, and the visits to Havana of a US college basketball team and group of Minnesota businessmen. Carter wanted to encourage Castro to resume withdrawing his troops from Angola, a process that had proceeded smoothly—with 12,000 Cuban soldiers leaving the country—until the Shaba crisis had brought it to a halt. On June 3, 1977, the State Department announced an important step: the United States and Cuba had agreed to exchange diplomats—the United States would set up an Interests Section with ten American staff, just short of an embassy, in Havana, and the Cubans would open a similar bureau in Washington. The next day, it was announced that Castro would free ten of the thirty US prisoners held in Cuban jails. Congressman Ron Dellums (D-CA), who was in Havana at the time, predicted that the establishment of full relations was "near."[26]

The timing was bound to raise questions. "They [the Cubans] sent people to Ethiopia, apparently plan to send more to Ethiopia, and yet the administration goes ahead improving relations," a reporter noted at the State Department press briefing, "which tends to leave the expressions of concern with a rather hollow sound." An editorial in the *Washington Post* called it "puzzling" that the administration would make overtures to the Cubans at precisely the moment that "in Ethiopia, they [Cubans] are lending themselves to a Soviet power play, pure and simple." While this statement was based on rumors and falsehoods, the editors' warning about the domestic consequences of Carter's policy was astute: "The administration is provoking more conservative reaction across the board than its diplomacy may be able to sustain. . . . The Carter administration has stirred the American right."[27]

Carter had "stirred" not only the American right: he had also stirred his own right-hand man. A hint of the difference of emphasis between Carter's and Brzezinski's views can be detected in a conversation they had with French president Valéry Giscard d'Estaing in early May. Carter explained that he hoped to normalize relations with Cuba, "but there are three big problems: (1) the very large number of political prisoners, including several Americans, who have been incarcerated for decades in Cuban jails; (2) the large number of Cuban troops in Africa; (3) the attempts by Cuba to make trouble in Puerto Rico, Latin America, and the Caribbean." Later in the conversation,

Brzezinski reduced this list to one item: "The big problem is that the Cubans are in Africa."[28]

Much Ado about Addou

On June 3, 1977, Brzezinski sent Carter his fifteenth weekly report. "We are at a point when some stock-taking is needed," he began, "and some basic decisions must be made regarding four key areas of our foreign policy." Africa was one of the four. (The others were the Soviet Union, the Middle East, and North/South relations.) "In all four areas . . . our purposes and objectives are clear, and they command respect. However, in all four cases, our immediate tactics and even intermediate strategies need to be reviewed. . . . Before too long, we could begin to look quite bad. . . . With regard to Ethiopia and Somalia," he wrote, "do we simply watch the developments continue or do we make some basic decisions. . . . The Somalians [sic] should either be told that we wish not to support them or, alternatively, . . . that some indirect backing for them should now be more forthcoming." Brzezinski's meaning was clear: it was time to fish or cut bait. Did the United States want to encourage the Somalis' irredentist dream of seizing the Ogaden? Did it want to precipitate the breakup of Ethiopia?[29]

Vance was already several steps ahead of Brzezinski. That was why he had ushered Addou up the chain of command to Mondale. By mid-May, Vance had decided it was in the US interest to help Somalia procure weapons.[30] He knew that these weapons would be used in the Ogaden. What was he thinking?

Vance served the president of the United States, and Carter had made it clear that he wanted to strengthen US ties with Somalia. Carter was fully engaged in this issue. On April 5, he had written Vance: "Find ways to improve relations with . . . Somalia," and he had underlined this the next day with his order to Mondale to "tell Cy and Zbig that I want them to move in every possible way to get Somalia to be our friend." Three days later, the State Department recommended that the United States "actively explore means by which Somalia's legitimate arms requests can be met from non-USSR sources." To determine what "legitimate arms requests" Somalia—a country that confronted no threatening enemies and was already one of the best armed countries in sub-Saharan Africa—might have, Carter suggested sending a military attaché to Mogadiscio. Carter also led policy toward Ethiopia. When, on April 11, the Policy Review Committee—chaired by Vance—had recommended gradually reducing military aid to the Ethiopian Derg, Carter had complained that this was "too easy on Ethiopia" and called for the abrupt cessation of military aid and the withdrawal of all personnel except a rump embassy staff. Carter was the driving force behind the tilt to Somalia, and Vance was obeying orders.[31]

There is every indication, however, that the secretary of state encouraged the direction of the president's policy. The simplest explanation is the best: Cyrus Vance was a US secretary of state during the Cold War. Jimmy Carter had declared at Notre Dame, "We are now free of that inordinate fear of communism," but he had not said that the Cold War was over. The foreign policy leaders of the Carter administration—Carter, Vance, Brzezinski, Defense Secretary Brown, and CIA Director Turner—wanted to stay ahead of the Soviet Union. "My own inclination," Carter explained to the press in mid-June, "is to aggressively challenge, in a peaceful way, of course, the Soviet Union and others for influence in areas of the world that we feel are crucial to us now or potentially crucial 15 or 20 years from now. And this includes places like Vietnam and places like Iraq *and Somalia* and Algeria and places like the People's Republic of China and even Cuba. I don't have any hesitancy about these matters."[32]

Nor did Cyrus Vance. In June 1977, Somalia seemed to offer an opportunity to challenge the Soviet Union, and a cheap one at that. Whereas earlier in the year, it had appeared that Moscow would be able to sustain alliances with both Somalia and Ethiopia, the situation had changed by late May. Washington knew that Moscow's support of the Derg was deepening. Indeed, the conclusions of US intelligence are confirmed by Cuban documents: when Mengistu returned to Addis from Moscow in May 1977, he summoned the Cuban ambassador and the head of the Cuban military mission. Mengistu was "in rare form, happy and cracking jokes," the Cubans reported. "He looked really satisfied, and he seemed to be bursting with optimism." The Soviets had promised him—according to Defense Minister Raúl Castro, Fidel's brother—40 MiG 21s, 8 anti-aircraft missiles, 160 T-55 tanks, and enough weapons to arm one hundred battalions. The Somali government, when it learned of this promise to its enemy, was, Raúl Castro reported, "disgusted."[33]

By June 1977, the Ethiopians, Soviets, and Cubans were facing reality: Siad Barre was waging war in the Ogaden. On June 7, Mengistu warned Arnaldo Ochoa, the general who had led Cuba's February 1977 mission to Addis and was then appointed head of the Cuban military mission in Ethiopia: "The Somalis have moved from word to deed. . . . A full scale invasion is imminent." Several days later, the Ethiopian leader was despondent. "The efforts of the socialist countries have failed," he told Ochoa. "The stance of the Somalis—who said they would not start a war—has changed. . . . We are completely surrounded by the imperialists." In a letter to Mengistu, Castro bemoaned the "betrayal" of Siad Barre.[34]

At the same moment, the Americans arrived at a "rather cheery" assessment of the situation in the Horn. They were buoyed by the recent CIA assessment that Moscow would lose Somalia, its most important asset in sub-Saharan Africa. (Although the Soviets had poured money into Angola in late 1975 and 1976, they had failed to gain access to any Angolan facilities comparable to those they controlled in Somalia.) Moreover, Ethiopia—"ruled by a seemingly insane committee of terrorists" that could not subdue rebellions in eight of the country's fourteen provinces—looked less and less like adequate compensation if the Soviets lost access to their facilities at the port city of Berbera. "Western statesmen view the situation with public neutrality but private pleasure," columnist C. L. Sulzberger wrote in the *New York Times.* "There is considerable confidence that . . . both of them [Somalia and Ethiopia] will be on our side before too long a time has passed."[35]

A Somali invasion of Ethiopia, the Kremlin's new best friend, would ensure a break between Mogadiscio and Moscow. And few events would be more destabilizing to the Mengistu regime than losing a third of his country to the Somalis. All Washington had to do was help Siad acquire weapons and it could reap two sweet victories: prying Somalia from the Soviets and precipitating the fall of Mengistu. It was a reasonable bet in June, when the Derg was besieged by rebellions on all sides, that the Somalis would be able to seize the Ogaden and the Eritrean rebels would succeed in defeating the rag-tag Ethiopian army. "We think likely that Eritrea will have de facto independence within the next 12 months," the US intelligence community predicted in May 1977, "[and] some territory in the Ogaden will be lost."[36] Even if Mengistu managed to survive, the Soviets would be left holding a landlocked and humiliated rump state, and the United States would have allies and bases all along the Red Sea and Horn. The prospect of arming Siad Barre so that he could invade a neighboring country and annex its land seemed to faze no one in the administration, including Jimmy Carter.

The Floodgates

Carter and Vance were also motivated by their desire to forge a peace settlement in the Middle East. This was a matter of paramount national interest. The 1973 Arab-Israeli war had underlined how quickly war in the Middle East could escalate into a superpower confrontation, and the consequent oil embargo had destabilized the global economy. The United States could afford a repetition of neither. Carter was determined to achieve a comprehensive peace settlement between the Arabs and the Israelis. This was one of his major preoccupations in the first months of his presidency when he was also formulating his stance toward the tumult in the Horn.

Anwar Sadat was clearly an important influence. During his first visit to Washington in April, Sadat had convinced Carter of two things: he believed that a pro-Soviet Ethiopia threatened Egypt, and he considered Carter's response to this threat an important indicator of Washington's commitment to him. He did not just talk about Somalia's need for support; on April 26, he informed Carter that because of the perils of "Soviet grand strategy in the Middle East, Persian Gulf and Africa . . . which is directed at weakening the position of the West in general and the United States in particular," his government had sent Siad Barre's government a shipment of weapons.[37]

Saudi Arabia's Crown Prince Fahd was another key player. He did not establish the same rapport with Carter as Sadat had, but he had money. Like Sadat, Fahd stressed the threat to the region posed by a pro-Soviet Ethiopia, and he also discussed the anxieties of the moderate Arab states about Israel's military aid to Ethiopia.[38]

The power struggle in the Horn was in some ways an extension of the Arab-Israeli struggle. Somalia was a member of the Arab League, while Ethiopia—first under Emperor Haile Selassie and then under the Derg—was Israel's closest friend in black Africa. Not only did Ethiopia provide a friendly harbor on the Red Sea for Israeli shipping, but it also was a crucial transit hub for the Israeli flagship airline El Al. "How do we fly to Africa without Ethiopia?" Israeli defense minister Ezer Weizman asked. The April 1977 Policy Review Memorandum on the Horn had therefore predicted correctly that Israel "will probably continue to urge the US to maintain its ties and assistance to the Mengistu regime." Washington's Arab friends, however, pushed in the opposite direction, and in this instance they had more clout.[39]

Carter tilted toward Somalia in part to buy the goodwill of Sadat and Fahd, whose help he required to reconvene the Middle East peace talks at Geneva. It seemed to be a relatively cheap and easy way to signal that the United States took their concerns seriously. That this was part of a new trend—Washington's need to adjust to Saudi power—was masked because Sadat and Fahd cast the crisis in Cold War terms as part of the global war against Soviet imperialism. The Arab dimension lurked beneath the surface.

Gathering Arms

In May, Somalia and its Arab friends—Egypt, Sudan, and Saudi Arabia—approached London, Paris, and Bonn with a pitch similar to the one that Ambassador Addou had used in Washington: Somalia wanted the friendship of the West—if it could be assured an alternate arms supplier.[40]

The American and European responses were coordinated at "quadripartite talks" attended by the foreign ministers of the United States, Britain, France, and West Germany. The existence of these talks, which had been initiated by

Henry Kissinger and James Callaghan (then British foreign secretary), was a closely held secret to avoid antagonizing the allies who were excluded. In 1977 and 1978, the encounters occurred roughly monthly, usually after larger, public meetings that the four foreign ministers had attended. Policy toward the Horn was a frequent topic at these high-level meetings.[41]

On May 9, Vance asked his European colleagues if they "thought that the Soviets would be able to ride both Ethiopian and Somali tigers simultaneously." French foreign minister Louis de Guiringaud thought that the Soviets could succeed for no more than a year, while British foreign secretary David Owen stressed that the West "had a strong interest" in encouraging the Somalis to move away from the Soviets. West Germany's Hans-Dietrich Genscher agreed, opining that "the West has an opportunity to regain its lost position in Somalia."[42]

Three weeks later, at the June 1 quadripartite meeting, the Horn was the second item on the agenda. (Berlin was the first.) Vance hoped "to demonstrate our intention to play a constructive role in an area of potential explosiveness . . . [and] to sound out the three European governments about their willingness to work with us—and the Saudis—in a possible Western arms consortium for Somalia, which avoids encouraging Somali irredentism."[43]

This was the contradiction: the US government wanted to befriend Somalia, it wanted to "play a constructive role," and it did not want to encourage Somali irredentism, but Siad Barre had made it clear that the only way to buy his friendship was to send him arms, and he had all but specified that he wanted the arms to invade the Ogaden. "The Saudis and Somali Ambassador Addou have drummed away at the theme that US involvement in the provision of arms to Somalia . . . is the key to shifting Somalia away from the Soviets," Vance's briefing notes for the June 1 meeting explained. "Without a US commitment to some sort of an arms supply relationship, it is doubtful that we can achieve our objective of reorienting Somalia. . . . While a Western consortium . . . may not . . . be acceptable to the Somalis, it would sufficiently defuse the direct US-USSR rivalry/confrontation to make it politically easier for Siad to disengage from the USSR."[44] As Vance explained to de Guiringaud, working together would give all four donor countries "more control and flexibility." In a separate conversation, President Carter was more direct: "It [a consortium] would be more acceptable to the American people."[45]

Thus did the US government try to square the circle: it would not send arms directly to Siad, but it would encourage its friends and allies to form a consortium to funnel arms to him. The Carter administration's desire to play a constructive role and to avoid encouraging Siad Barre's irredentism remained aspirations—that were contradicted and undermined by the policy.

Forming a consortium of allies to quietly supply Somalia with weapons was difficult. Each of Washington's NATO key partners—the British, French, and West Germans—had their own interests and played their cards close to their chests. Bonn declared that it would not send arms to Somalia because of its policy not to send weapons to "an area of conflict." However, it left the door ajar by promising "firmly but cautiously" to support all attempts to pry Somalia from the Soviets. London and Paris were also drawn to the possibility of luring Somalia from the Soviets, but they too had reservations about sending weapons. The British were reluctant to give Somalia weapons if there was any chance that the arms would be used against their former colony and close ally, Kenya, while the French were hesitant because of the possibility that the weapons would be used against their soon-to-be-independent colony of Djibouti. If Washington wanted to form a consortium, it was essential that it allay these anxieties.[46]

The Kenyans and Djiboutians were worried about the US tilt toward Somalia because they feared that Siad Barre, invigorated by success in the Ogaden, would turn his sights on them. Djibouti and northeastern Kenya, both inhabited by many ethnic Somalis, were coveted by the irredentist Somali government. "They [Kenyan officials] asked me repeatedly whether you and the President really understood the Horn," NSC staffer Paul Henze wrote Brzezinski. "They feel neglected and fear they are getting no credit for having been solidly pro-Western and anti-Communist for 15 years, while everybody fusses about Somalia, which only discovered that it was anti-Communist last summer." The Kenyans had told Henze emphatically, "It is not the Russians but the Somalis who threaten us." Moreover, Kenya was on a precipice because of the impending death of its leader, Jomo Kenyatta. "Kenyatta is failing," the State Department noted in April 1977. "Looks as if we may be nearing X-Day in Kenya."[47]

In June, Dr. Kevin Cahill, a New York physician who knew both Vance and Siad Barre, called the counselor of the State Department, Matthew Nimetz (with whom he was also acquainted), to ask if Vance would like him to carry a private message to Siad Barre, whom he would see in Somalia the following week. Nimetz conferred with Vance and then asked Cahill to tell Siad that "we want to have good relations with Somalia and they have to be very careful. . . . We are very sensitive about Kenya." Three months later, *Newsweek* would report that this was the smoking gun proving that the Carter administration gave Siad Barre a green light to invade the Ogaden. Nimetz speculates that "because we said we wanted better relations and were looking forward to working with him without giving a negative warning about the Ogaden specifically, he might have gotten the impression that he had a *carte blanche* or a wink." Cahill, in any case, was merely repeating the message that Vance himself had already conveyed to Ambassador Addou.[48]

The Pivotal Meeting

Both Andrew Young and Zbigniew Brzezinski had taken a backseat in the development of policy toward the Horn. After setting the ball rolling with his comments upon his return from Africa in February, Young had moved on to other concerns. Although Carter had tilted more strongly toward Somalia than Young had recommended, the UN ambassador remained sanguine. He predicted that the Soviets' embrace of Ethiopia would bring them their "biggest flop," and he told the House International Relations Committee that the Russians "had bitten off more than they could chew" in Ethiopia.[49]

On June 2, 1977—almost a month after Somali Ambassador Addou had seen Vice President Mondale and one day after the quadripartite meeting at which a consortium was first discussed—Vance declared that "a meeting [of Addou] with the President would clearly demonstrate our interest in improving relations and should strengthen the hands of the officials in the Somali government who are arguing for a reorientation of Somalia's policies. . . . [It] would also be warmly welcomed by Egypt, the Sudan, and especially Saudi Arabia. For these reasons the Department recommends that the President receive Addou but give the meeting minimum publicity." This was the pivotal decision. A meeting with the president was scheduled for June 16. Vance was gambling that Somalia could swiftly and easily seize the Ogaden, thereby severing Mogadiscio's alliance with Moscow, weakening the Derg, and pleasing the Saudis and Egyptians.[50]

On June 15, Brzezinski wrote Carter talking points for his upcoming meeting with Addou, scheduled for the following day. "I suggest you emphasize the fact that we are studying the problem [providing arms to Somalia] actively and want to draw in the Saudis and some of our European allies." Brzezinski did not include any warning about the need to restrain Somali irredentism. Nor did the talking points that Vance sent Carter before the encounter with Addou emphasize the need for caution. Vance merely reminded the president that the objectives were to demonstrate US interest in improving relations with Somalia, to tell Addou that US Agency for International Development representatives would arrive soon in Mogadiscio, and to remind him that any arms the United States might supply would be for defensive purposes only, as part of a wider Western effort. The clear warning that the US embassy in Mogadiscio had sent to Washington in March—"We should avoid unintentional signals that US has downgraded its traditional support for territorial integrity of states and for peaceful resolution of disputes"—had been jettisoned.[51]

At 2:02 pm on Thursday, June 16, Abdullahi Addou was ushered into the Oval Office. Addou, who spoke fluent English, was alone. He preferred to attend important meetings unencumbered by staff; that way, no one could contradict him when he reported to Siad Barre. Brzezinski, Deputy Assistant

Secretary for African Affairs Talcott Seelye, and NSC staffer Henze joined
Carter. (Vance was at an Organization of American States meeting in Grenada, and Richard Moose was still settling in as assistant secretary for African
affairs.) Addou repeated much the same pitch he had given Mondale, explaining
that Mogadiscio's relations with Moscow were at the breaking point because
of their differing interpretations of Somalia's borders. "Calling under instructions from Siad," a State Department cable about the encounter explained,
Addou "told the president that the USSR was placing immense pressure on
Somalia to subordinate its national interests to the interests of international
socialism." Addou cast his country's problem as a question of the basic human
rights of the Ogadeni people: the right to self-determination. Therefore, Addou
explained, Somalia sought US economic and military assistance.[52]

Carter's response was disingenuous. "We did not wish to compete with the
USSR," he assured Addou. "We wanted Somalia to be non-aligned and not
dominated by anyone." He then dealt with the request for military assistance,
stressing that he would like to send a military attaché to Mogadiscio and that
his administration was "trying to work with the Saudis and our European
allies to see that Somalia had adequate defense capabilities without relying on
the Soviet Union." Emphasizing this, he added, "In meetings with our European friends we have discussed Somalia and how important it is to have it
associated with us. . . . The trends are all in the right direction." Carter's only
possible reference to Somali irredentism was so oblique that it barely existed:
"We hope your problems with Ethiopia can be peacefully worked out." In
closing, Carter added, "We want the Somalis to recognize their own destiny."[53]

The encounter was "unpublicized," and no reports of it leaked to the press
until much later.[54]

The White House was pleased with the meeting, and Addou was thrilled. It
was, he told a State Department official, "a milestone, especially given Carter's forthcoming attitude to military support." Addou said that Carter "had
indicated his willingness to supply arms to Somalia." When the State Department official insisted that the president had meant defensive arms only, Addou
replied, "That's all Siad wants."[55]

What Siad Barre wanted, of course, was an American commitment. The
fine print did not matter: defensive, offensive, multilateral consortium—it
was irrelevant. What mattered was that the president of the United States had
said that Somalia no longer needed to rely on Moscow as its arms dealer; the
United States would take care of it.

Brzezinski wrote Carter that "the symbolism of this meeting is at least as
important as the substance."[56] But Brzezinski missed the point: the symbolism
was the substance.

Two Conventions

At the end of June 1977, four thousand delegates and visitors converged on the brand-new convention center in St. Louis, Missouri, to attend the sixty-eighth annual meeting of the National Association for the Advancement of Colored People (NAACP), the nation's oldest and largest civil rights organization. Assailed by younger, more militant groups, this venerable body was struggling to retain its power and relevance in the 1970s. *Roots* author Alex Haley got the convention off to a lively start, but the delegates were gripped by a "mood of crisis" brought on by anxiety that the American people were moving to the right and becoming complacent about "covert racism"—deep and persistent economic inequities that caused unemployment and poverty to hit the black community hardest.[57]

The convention's keynote address, however, would tackle a different topic: foreign policy. On the final day of the meeting, July 1, the secretary of state would deliver the first full-length exposition of the Carter administration's policy toward Africa. Cyrus Vance's visit signaled the administration's concern for black American opinion. This was appreciated by the delegates in the hall. African Americans had entertained high hopes when Carter had been elected—they had expected significant acknowledgment of their role in his victory—but by June 1977, they were beginning to grumble. Carter had not appointed as many blacks to high positions as they had expected, Andy Young was under fire, the administration's energy plan seemed designed to hit the poor hardest, and the president's support for social programs and full employment appeared tepid. Benjamin Hooks, the NAACP's incoming executive director, declared to the conventioneers, "Although blacks overwhelmingly voted for . . . Carter, . . . our support is not permanent. . . . We cannot and will not be taken for granted." Vance's presence, therefore, was a welcome sign that the Carter administration did not take the half-million members of the NAACP for granted.[58]

The secretary's speech focused on southern Africa, and its main point was that Africa was a high priority for the administration not because it was "a testing ground of East-West competition," but because of the continent's political, economic, and cultural importance to the United States. Vance explained that Carter had decided to deal simultaneously with the "intertwined" problems of Rhodesia, Namibia, and South Africa. The secretary was modest, yet optimistic. "We cannot impose solutions in southern Africa," he asserted. "Our leverage is limited. But we are among the few governments in the world that can talk to both white and black Africans frankly and yet with a measure of trust." Tagged onto the end of the speech, Vance mentioned the "complex diplomatic challenges" in the Horn. "We will consider sympathetically," he announced cryptically, "appeals for assistance from states which are threatened by a buildup of foreign military equipment and advisers on their borders." (The *New York Times* opined that he was referring to Sudan; the *Washington Post* guessed Somalia.) Vance then drew the long speech to a close. "The future of Africa will be built with African hands. . . . It will require the understanding and approval of this audience, and of Americans everywhere."[59]

The floor was then opened for questions. "That's fine about Africa," the first questioner said, "but . . . what are you going to do for us? . . . What about us?" The conventioneers burst into noisy applause to signal their approval of the inquiry. The second question was about Andrew Young: were the rumors true that he had been muzzled? Vance was categorical: "That is not correct. Andy has not been moved from any committee." The audience began to applaud as Vance added, "Andy is playing a full part." This brought the assembled thousands to their feet, cheering for twelve minutes in the most energetic display of the evening. "Right on!" several exclaimed. Although Vance was asked a few questions about Africa, more were about unemployment, and there was a second about Young, which again brought the crowd to its feet.[60]

Editorial comment in the black press about Vance's speech was positive, but the audience's questions suggested that US policy toward Africa was not at the center of African American concerns. The White House was acutely aware of this. Even on the campaign trail, Carter had bemoaned the lack of a strong Africa lobby. "It would be a great help to this nation," he proclaimed in 1976, "if people in public life were made aware of Africa through a significant Black interest in Africa."[61]

In some ways, Vance's speech was dated by the time he delivered it. The night before, African foreign ministers had gathered to prepare for the fourteenth annual summit of the OAU, which would open in Libreville, the muggy seaside capital of Gabon, the following day. "At the very hour we are assembled here," the Kenyan foreign minister announced to his peers, "we have reliable and authenticated reports that Somalia has sent thousands of troops to our territory, the purpose of which can only be to aggress our territory and realize the dream of a Greater Somalia." The Kenyan asserted that armed Somalis— as many as 6,500—had been crossing into his country for the past week, and he urged the delegates to restrain Somalia "from further acts of interference with Kenyan sovereignty." US intelligence reports agreed that Somalis were entering Kenya, but concluded they were merely traversing the country on their way to the Ogaden.[62]

The OAU summit was a festive affair that celebrated African unity. The small city of Libreville retained much of its French colonial past (more than 1,000 French military and civilian advisers remained in the country), and

Gabon was enjoying an offshore oil boom. Silver Cloud Cadillacs ferried the representatives of forty-eight African countries (including twenty-three heads of state) along the capital's new six-lane highway, built for the occasion and lined with dancing women, to the lavish new conference hall.[63]

Inside, schisms were exposed. "The OAU is really very strong on questions of liberation movements, as far as South Africa is concerned," Andrew Young explained to the Senate subcommittee on Africa, "but when you go beyond that consensus, it is really very hard to keep them together. There is not much that everybody agrees on."[64] This was particularly true in the summer of 1977, when several African states were at war, or on the verge of war, with each other. The hottest fronts were in the Horn of Africa, and there had been ominous clashes between Libya and Chad; between Morocco, Mauritania, and the Algerian-backed Polisario Front over the Western Sahara; between Zaire and the Katangan rebels based in Angola; and between South Africa and the Namibian rebels. Rhodesian raids into Mozambique, Zambia, and even Botswana were increasing, and the guerrilla war for Zimbabwe was intensifying.

The Cold War fanned all these flames. The OAU secretary-general stated, "The rabid rivalry between blocs, big powers and foreign interests has brought to Africa division which seems to have reached a critical point today." Egypt's President Sadat, who was in attendance, added, "The center of international conflict has moved to our continent in the past months."[65]

One bone of contention was the Horn. "Wherever a Somali cow grazes," Mengistu declared sarcastically, "has to be part and parcel of the Somali Republic." In a thinly veiled threat, he warned, "Trying to snatch what belongs to others, one may lose what one already possesses." The Somali delegate accused the Derg of engaging in "black colonialism . . . murder . . . and massacres," and then he stormed out of the proceedings. The delegates established a committee chaired by Nigeria to mediate the dispute in the Horn, but few—at the convention and abroad—held out hope that it would succeed. The French predicted that mediation would fail because "the Somalis will continue to lie."[66]

On Rhodesia, the Africans at the summit agreed that it was essential to end white rule and the only way to do so was through armed struggle. Zambia's Kenneth Kaunda, speaking as the representative of all the Frontline presidents, proposed a resolution to recognize the Patriotic Front as the sole representative of the Zimbabwean liberation movement. "A new Zimbabwe," he declared, "can only be born out of the barrel of a gun!" This was more than rhetoric: OAU recognition would mean that economic and military aid would be directed solely to the Patriotic Front, cutting off the possibility of aid to any of the nationalists who were not in the Front.[67] The British and Americans, forewarned that this resolution would be proposed, had lobbied hard to derail it. By privileging the Patriotic Front, it excluded the black leaders in Rhodesia whom Ian Smith hoped to lure into an internal settlement, and in so doing the State Department feared it "would complicate diplomatic efforts to reach a negotiated settlement." Nevertheless, in the most important accomplishment of the meeting, the delegates unanimously passed Kaunda's resolution, urging all those engaged in the "liberation struggle to fight within the ranks of the Patriotic Front." As the Americans and British had anticipated, the excluded black leaders were outraged and announced that the resolution "makes it impossible for Zimbabwe to unite."[68] Yet the Patriotic Front and the Frontline States celebrated the vote in an "atmosphere of exultation." A spokesman for the Patriotic Front expressed satisfaction: "The British no longer have the excuse," he said, "that there's no single group they can hand over power to."[69]

Omar Bongo, the president of Gabon and the host of the convention, regretted that the delegates had washed "their dirty linen in public" and drew the "summit of reconciliation" to a close—having spent an estimated $800 million, or three-quarters of his country's annual budget, on the proceedings.[70]

Somalia's Friends

In the heat of summer, Carter saddled himself and his staff with an extraordinarily crowded agenda: the energy bill, SALT II, the Panama Canal treaties, southern Africa, the Geneva conference on Mideast peace. An indication of the activity of the Carter team is that by June 1, Vance—who had entered office pledging not to travel as much as Kissinger—had visited Israel, Egypt, Lebanon, Jordan, Saudi Arabia, Syria, Belgium, the Soviet Union, West Germany, Britain (twice), France (twice), Switzerland (twice), Spain, and Iran.

The Horn was not a top priority, but neither could it be forgotten. Washington's efforts to "turn" Siad Barre by funneling him weapons were proceeding. The Saudis were not only bankrolling the enterprise but also spurring their allies to join in. As early as June 30, US intelligence reported that "certain Arab states have delivered or financed large amounts of arms to Somalia recently." President Sadat was eager to help Somalia and to undermine Mengistu, who had become the "super-devil" for the Egyptian government. By early July, the Saudis had supplied Mogadiscio small arms worth $8 million, and the Egyptians had sent another $13 million worth, which was Cairo's second shipment (financed, of course, by the Saudis). The first shipment, which had arrived in Mogadiscio in mid-May aboard four C-130s, had equipped 10,000 men, a third of what Siad had requested.[71]

The Saudis and Americans encouraged other states to pitch in. Somali ambassador Addou recalled that a few weeks after his June 16 meeting with

President Carter, he was contacted by a midlevel State Department official. (He could not remember the official's name.) Over lunch, the American informed the ambassador that "the Shah had agreed to help." Under strong US pressure, the Iranian foreign minister had informed the US ambassador in Tehran that his country "would like to do its share." Iran was sending a military mission to Somalia and would transfer US-made materiel. Addou promised that his country, which did not have diplomatic ties with Iran, would quickly establish relations.[72] Vance cabled instructions to the US ambassador in Tehran that tried to draw the fine line that the administration hoped to tread: "US wished to see Somalia capable of defending existing national territory without relying on Soviets but also without being encouraged to pursue Somali irredentist ambitions." The State Department therefore warned Tehran "to proceed with caution in supplying Somalia with arms not clearly defensive." It never explained, however, what those defensive weapons might be.[73]

An Egyptian official reported in late June, "Arab states have delivered or financed large amounts of arms to Somalia recently." Iraq sent Siad Barre economic aid to purchase weapons. Morocco agreed to help. There are also reports that Sudan, Jordan, Pakistan, Mauritania, and North Yemen sent Somalia light weapons.[74]

The participation of America's NATO allies—France, Britain, and West Germany—in the consortium was discussed at the quadripartite talks of the foreign ministers. The Somalis had asked London for "small arms, anti-aircraft weapons, and machine guns" to arm 80,000 men, and they had asked Paris for arms to supply 100,000 more with "sophisticated weapons, including planes and missiles." The British "were taken by surprise with the size and breadth of Somali requirements," but after getting a tentative okay from the Kenyans, they were prepared to supply small arms (rifles, machine guns, mortars, hand grenades), antitank guns, mines, and ammunition. The French, reassured that the imminent independence of Djibouti was proceeding smoothly, agreed to supply 14,000 to 20,000 Somali soldiers with "small arms and other equipment." The Somalis asked Bonn for "medicines, food, tents, and vehicles," and the West Germans were "willing to supply Somalia with non-lethal items." The Saudis financed all these purchases. The Carter administration's consortium to satisfy Somalia was proceeding according to plan.[75]

At the same time, intelligence reports made it clear that the Western Somali Liberation Front (WSLF) and regular Somali troops were seizing control of ever-larger swaths of the Ogaden. Washington was well aware that this was heightening anxiety in Addis and Moscow. On July 9, Vance wrote Carter that the Soviets, trying to defuse tensions in the Horn, were again promoting a federation of Ethiopia, Somalia, the Ogaden, Eritrea, and possibly Djibouti. The president's response, written in the margins, was nonchalant: "If they succeed, we should take some lessons from them!"[76]

Carter's good humor reflected the administration's mood about the Horn in early July 1977. The gloom of the spring months, when it had appeared likely that Moscow would succeed in winning Ethiopia and keeping Somalia, had lifted by mid-summer, when it seemed that the opposite might occur: Washington could win Somalia and open doors to Ethiopia—to the Derg, if it survived, or to a post-Derg government.

America's divorce from Ethiopia, which had seemed absolute in April, had sputtered on in bitter disputes over property. At issue were US arms in the pipeline (valued at approximately $22 million) for which Ethiopia had paid but which Washington had not delivered. In early June, Mengistu met with the US chargé in Addis—their first meeting—and the encounter had been friendly. Washington believed that the Derg's romance with Moscow was losing its luster. In August, Mengistu complained bitterly to the Cubans about the fact that the Soviets were continuing to help Somalia, and in Washington an interagency intelligence report predicted that "Moscow will acquiesce in Somalia's seizure of the Ogaden."[77] Mengistu was desperate. "How can the Soviet Union send weapons to a government that had clearly betrayed socialism?" he asked. "Ethiopia is utterly alone." He bemoaned the "three year delay" in the Kremlin's response to the Derg's urgent pleas. The Soviets were aware of Mengistu's frustration. "There was some anti-Soviet sentiment in Ethiopia because of the Kremlin's long-standing support of Somalia," a Soviet general admitted.[78]

From the Carter administration's point of view, the good news did not end with the tensions between Addis and Moscow. The independence of Djibouti, which Washington had feared would be a flashpoint between Ethiopia and Somalia, occurred without incident. On July 11, 1977, the colony was officially free, after elections that had elevated an ethnic Somali to the presidency. The French retained 4,000 troops and eighteen warships in Djibouti to protect the hapless little country. "It's costing us a lot of money, and we're getting nothing for it," President Giscard groused to Vance, "but if we just leave, someone else—most probably the Soviets—will come in, and we think it's important that they don't get a new base on the Red Sea."[79]

Asking for the Moon

It was against this backdrop that Ambassador Addou, having given his daughter in marriage to Siad Barre's son, returned to Washington and appeared at Assistant Secretary Moose's door bearing a list of arms that the Somali president considered the "minimum" to fill the gaps in his country's defense.[80] (In fact, the list was—as Peter Tarnoff, the executive secretary of the State Department, noted—"an extensive military supply request . . . composed almost entirely of items readily susceptible of use in the growing Somali guerrilla campaign in eastern Ethiopia." Another State Department official described it as "sufficient for twelve standard Soviet divisions. . . . The total cost would exceed half a billion dollars." Asked for his reaction, the US ambassador in Mogadiscio was sardonic: "Somalis always ask for moon.") Playing his hand with aplomb, Addou told Moose that only after the United States had supplied the arms on the list would it be permitted to station a US military attaché, "preferably a General," in Mogadiscio. Siad Barre, the ambassador declared, required a reply in one week. Addou also floated the possibility that Siad would soon visit Washington, and he claimed—incredibly—that the Soviet Politburo had approved Somalia's seeking a "new relationship" with Saudi Arabia, Egypt, and the United States. Moose (who smiled as he remembered Addou) told the persistent ambassador that he was pleased that US relations with Somalia were improving, but when it came to the arms list it might be best for the United States to be part of a consortium.[81]

Moose, who had been assistant secretary for a month, wrote a memo to Vance about the encounter. "It seems clear that they [the Somalis] are preparing to wrest the Ogaden from the Ethiopians before the Ethiopians receive significant amounts of Soviet arms," he warned. "The US does not want to be identified with this Somali effort, but it does not want to upset their move away from the Soviets."[82]

Vance transmitted much of Moose's memo to the president. "It is . . . a canard," Vance noted, "to describe the items listed, as did Addou, as the 'minimum needed' to fill existing gaps in Somalia's defensive structure: for instance, the 70,785 semi-automatic rifles requested would give each one of Somalia's 30,000 soldiers two such rifles apiece, with 10,785 to spare." Vance then softened Moose's clear warning. "The Somali effort to accumulate new arms," he wrote Carter, "might suggest that the Somalis are planning to press their advantage in the Ogaden." His conclusion, however, seemed as emphatic as Moose's: "This is an effort with which we clearly do not wish to be associated." His memo made it clear that what he meant was that the US government should not be *overtly* associated with Somali aggression: he advised Carter to keep Siad Barre interested in an alliance with the West by encouraging its allies—behind the scenes—to arm him.[83] Vance also sent a circular cable summarizing Addou's spiel to the US ambassadors in twelve capitals in the Horn region and on the list of potential arms donors. After noting that "the gap between our and the Somali definition of 'legitimate defensive needs' is considerable," Vance concluded: "Bear in mind that while we are highly skeptical re list, we do not rpt not wish to upset the momentum of Somali moves away from USSR."[84]

Three days after his meeting with Moose, Addou lunched with Deputy Assistant Secretary Talcott Seelye. Addou was well known in the State Department for inviting his interlocutors to Washington's poshest restaurants, places quiet enough to have a good conversation. Over a gourmet meal, in a voice that was almost a whisper, Addou pressed his case. Siad Barre, he explained, could not shift his policy orientation until he received tangible evidence that the United States was willing to "step into the role"—and he required a reply in one week. Seelye, a most sophisticated diplomat, gently told Addou, "If the United States could not supply arms directly immediately, at least we could permit the Iranians and Saudis to do so." He then explained that it would not be possible for the United States to reply within a week, and he inquired as to the reason for the rush. Addou denied, flatly, that it was due to any plan to invade the Ogaden, and the diplomatic arm wrestling continued.[85]

While Addou was in Washington circulating Siad Barre's wish list, tensions escalated in the Ogaden. "We are keeping close track of the fast-moving events on Somalia's frontier with Ethiopia," Vance wrote Carter on July 13, 1977. "Our most recent intelligence indicates that the possibility of armed conflict between the two nations has increased in the past 48 hours." A week later, Vance cabled Young that the fighting in the Ogaden had escalated to "a high level." Vance was under no illusions: "We have reports that the ranks of the irregular forces [the WSLF] have been strengthened by addition of regular Somali soldiers in mufti. President Siad appears determined to seize the Ogaden now while Ethiopia is weak and before Soviet military assistance to the Addis government can have real effect. . . . We believe he would use the Somali National Army if it were necessary."[86]

The Kenyans urgently warned Washington that they would "react negatively" if the United States provided arms to Somalia. Likewise, they told the British Foreign Office that while they had "initially accepted the idea of Britain sending some arms to Somalia, . . . they had changed their minds after the hostilities in the Ogaden began." The French foreign minister, who had stopped in Kenya during a swing through Africa, got an earful from the Kenyans, who warned him that the Somalis' "next target will be Kenya."[87]

Israel

Jimmy Carter prepared for Israeli prime minister Menachem Begin's visit to Washington on July 19, 1977 like a graduate student preparing for comprehensive exams. Likud's victory in the May elections had been a surprise to Washington, and not a pleasant one. What little administration officials knew of Begin led them to believe he was an inflexible zealot. Carter watched him being interviewed on ABC's *Issues and Answers* and pronounced it "frightening." Begin, like many Israelis and American friends of Israel, was wary of Jimmy Carter, with his talk of a Palestinian homeland and his promise to limit the sales of conventional weapons.[88]

The stakes were high for both men. Carter would require Begin's help for his Middle East policy to succeed, and Begin needed continued American aid and goodwill. After the usual pleasantries on the South Lawn, Carter and Begin retired to the Oval Office. Carter was prepared for tricky discussions about the West Bank, UN Resolution 242, and the upcoming Geneva conference, but Begin wanted to discuss Ethiopia first.

Begin had come to the White House bearing a message from Ethiopia's Mengistu. Worried about the insurgencies in Eritrea and the Ogaden, cut off from the US arms pipeline, and waiting for more supplies from Moscow, Mengistu needed military aid. Begin asked Carter to reverse his decision to cut off US aid to Ethiopia. He also asked for approval for Israel to send Mengistu the US fighter planes and transport assistance that the Ethiopians had requested. Carter, unprepared for the discussion, hedged, not answering Begin's questions directly. "I hope we can keep in touch on Ethiopia," the Israeli prime minister told Carter as he departed.[89]

Begin's queries put the Carter administration in an awkward position. Henze wrote Brzezinski, "Quite a paradox—the Israelis in league with the Soviets, the Cubans, and the Libyans in supporting Mengistu's incompetent and brutal regime." Mossad, the Israeli intelligence agency, untangled the paradox: Israel's position, a Mossad agent explained, was "simple and clear cut. . . . Better to collaborate with [the] Soviet Union than knuckle under to Arabs." The State Department, however, disagreed with its ally in Tel Aviv: it advised the administration against "taking any part of Begin's appeal seriously."[90]

The White House informed Begin that it "was not favorably disposed" to allowing Israel to transfer US arms to Ethiopia, but it had no confidence that it had dissuaded him from continuing to support Mengistu. "Israelis will be sorely tempted to do as much as they can to hold on to one of their last and oldest footholds in Africa," the US ambassador in Tel Aviv, Sam Lewis, cabled, "especially in view of its strategic importance for them."[91]

Begin had barely boarded his plane to return to Israel before the US ambassador in Cairo, Hermann Eilts, reported that President Sadat was "disposed" to accede to Siad Barre's request that Egypt supply pilots to fly Somalia's twenty MiG-21s. Sadat told the American ambassador that Ethiopian MiG-21s had attacked Somali villages, and since no Ethiopians were trained to fly MiGs (having just switched from American fighter planes), "foreign elements"— South Yemenis, Cubans, or Israelis—must have been at the controls. (Sadat did not mention the possibility that Soviets were in the cockpits.) "He [Sadat] wanted President Carter to know [this]," Eilts cabled. Sadat considered the situation critical. "The Somalis, Sadat emphasized, must be helped," Eilts wrote. "If Somalia falls, Eritrea and the Sudan will follow soon afterwards."[92]

Eilts informed Sadat of Carter's "decision in principle to participate in a multilateral effort to provide defensive arms [to Somalia]," but stressed that "we do not wish arms to be used in connection with Somali irredentist aspiration in Ogaden." Sadat was "pleased at President's decision," yet he also chided the ambassador and "candidly acknowledged that Siad Barre's principal reason for wanting arms is to use them in Ogaden."[93] Sadat made an excellent point: Washington's idea that it could provide Somalia "defensive" arms flew in the face of all Siad Barre's explanations of what he intended to do with them. The American position was absurd.

Promises, Promises

Meanwhile, the Africa Bureau of the State Department was drafting the US response to Somalia's arms request. It proposed three options. The most negative was to politely refuse to send any military aid but to continue economic aid. The middle path was to offer vague promises, and the most forthcoming option was to promise to supply certain specific items (e.g., fixed air defense), once a US military attaché had been received in Mogadiscio. The department favored the middle path: giving Somalia a "declaration in principle" that the United States would provide military supplies adequate for its "legitimate defense needs" and would send a team to Mogadiscio to assess these needs.[94]

Carter preferred a more positive response. He told Vance to "keep up dialogue, see if we can't find a few things of purely defensive nature to offer to the Somalis, move ahead with economic aid, and go on trying to get talk of more arms centered on the idea of an international consortium—with nobody moving with great speed because we need to see how the current Ethio-Somali struggle in the Ogaden comes out."[95]

In July, as hostilities increased in the Ogaden, US policy was to keep Siad on the Western hook, while trying to avoid overt association with his war of aggression. As Vance described it, the administration "would seek to fend off the Somali request while at the same time undertaking other activities designed to sustain the momentum" of Somalia's break with the Soviet Union.[96] This led policy in two directions: continuing to quietly encourage America's friends to support Siad and stalling on directly supplying US weapons. The Americans must have been banking on Siad's forces seizing the Ogaden quickly, leaving Moscow's relations with Somalia in shambles and its budding alliance with Ethiopia a quagmire.

It fell to Philip Habib, undersecretary of state for political affairs, to communicate the administration's response to Addou. On July 15, 1977, he "conveyed the President's decision that the US agreed in principle to respond favorably to Somalia's request for arms." Habib elaborated, "While we are not at this stage in a position to be specific, we wish to send a message . . . concerning our agreement in principle to help in cooperation with other friendly countries to meet Somalia's defense requirements." Washington would "study the Somali list and decide what items, what amount, and on what terms" it could proceed. The State Department expected to be able to give Addou a more detailed reply in late August. Habib stressed that the United States wanted to be sure that its assistance was for "defensive weapons" only.[97]

Addou responded that he had expected the American president to be more forthcoming. King Khalid and Crown Prince Fahd, in contrast, had given Siad Barre "all his aims" during his recent trip to Saudi Arabia. Timing, Addou told Habib, was "critical" because Soviet arms were due to arrive in Ethiopia within a month, and Addis would then be in a position to threaten Mogadiscio. When Habib noted drily that the fighting was not in Somalia "but in the Ethiopian Ogaden," Addou retorted that the fighters there were WSLF members, not Somali regulars.[98]

The State Department had devised an elaborate receiving line to ensure that Addou understood the president's message. After seeing Habib, Addou was passed to the East Africa director, who reiterated the hope that "developments in the Ogaden" would not "complicate" Washington's establishment of a military supply relationship with Somalia. Addou next saw Assistant Secretary Moose, who added that Carter's decision should remain confidential until more concrete steps were possible. Notably, Addou was not treated to a meeting with Carter, Mondale, or Vance.[99]

A new note of caution had entered the administration's handling of US-Somali relations. By July, the administration's response to Addou was larded with explicit warnings that it did not want to supply arms that would be used in an invasion of Ethiopia. Given the candor with which both Siad Barre and Addou had discussed Somalia's intention to seize the Ogaden, these American warnings were cynical. "Nice generalities," NSC expert Paul Henze wrote about the administration's calls for defensive weapons, "but no one has managed to draw up much of a list of purely defensive military equipment we could give the Somalis."[100]

Addou told Habib that he was disappointed, but to Siad Barre he cabled that his visit to Washington had been "successful."[101] He then flew to Mogadiscio to deliver the news in person. On July 22, he met with the Somali president. Afterward, he went straight to the US ambassador, John Loughran, to inform him of Siad's response. "Siad's reaction was guarded and he expressed concern about the pace of arms deliveries," Loughran wrote Vance. "According to Addou, Siad is now 'sixty to seventy percent persuaded' that he has solution to his Soviet dependency and a replacement for Soviet military assistance. Addou cautions, however, that Siad will only move away from Moscow when proof of US commitment . . . is in hand. In my view this clearly means that we should not expect the clean or immediate break with the Soviet Union." Addou, Loughran informed the State Department, "assured Siad that President Carter's favorable response meant that he could be certain that US military help would follow in time."[102] This was Addou's distillation of all the State Department's nuance and finesse intended to convey that the United States would not be providing arms soon and that it would work through a consortium: he told Siad that Carter had responded favorably and Somalia could bank on US military aid. The fine print was irrelevant.

War!

On July 23, 1977—the day after Addou told Siad Barre about his meetings in Washington—a barrage of Somali troops, planes, and tanks attacked Ethiopian outposts in the Ogaden, marking the beginning of the war between the two countries. It is tempting to conclude that the Carter administration's promise in principle to supply weapons to Somalia gave Siad Barre a green light to launch the invasion. The truth, however, is more subtle.[103]

The chaos in Ethiopia, where the army was unable to douse rebellions across the country and there was open warfare in the capital city, created an opportunity for Siad Barre: while the Derg was assailed on all sides, Somalia could seize the Ogaden. Siad would achieve one of the deepest dreams of the Somali people. He would be a hero—at home. To the Kremlin, however, the invasion of Ethiopia—a fellow socialist country—would render Siad Barre a villain. This had been obvious for months, certainly ever since Fidel Castro's failed attempt at mediation in March 1977, but it had not dampened Siad Barre's ardor for the Ogaden. That temptation proved overwhelming.

The July attack in the Ogaden had been planned months in advance, and its timing was governed above all by Siad's need to strike before Soviet arms began to flow into Addis Ababa. Siad's decision to go to war was based on two convictions. First, Mengistu was vulnerable; as the US assistant secretary of defense wrote, "We can't overestimate Siad's belief in Ethiopia's disintegration under Mengistu." Second, time was limited. On June 26, Mengistu had proudly paraded his new "People's Army"—a militia of some 70,000 peasants—through the streets of Addis Ababa, and Mengistu's army would soon be bolstered by large deliveries of Soviet weapons. Washington was not the center of Siad's universe: in mid-July, he had gone on a state visit to Saudi Arabia, and the Saudis had promised Somalia $300 million for weapons and an alternative oil supply if it broke from the Soviet Union.[104] The Saudi vice-minister of foreign affairs, Abdul Rahman Al-Mansouri, later bluntly admitted that the Saudis had encouraged Siad to invade the Ogaden because they had believed this would bring down Mengistu: "We did not care who had the Ogaden; we only wanted Mengistu defeated."[105]

The decision to attack was not entirely in Siad's hands. Regular Somali units had moved into the Ogaden in the early summer of 1977, and they began to rack up small victories. The war was creeping from guerrilla to conventional tactics before the frontal invasion on July 23. In June, Somali soldiers—who had removed the insignia from their uniforms—had attacked many Ethiopian towns. Cuban reports in the weeks before July 23 detailed the "enormous tension" along the Somali-Ethiopian border. On July 8, General Ochoa, the head of the Cuban military mission in Ethiopia, wrote Castro that the "Somali troops were at their highest state of readiness, poised to attack." Official Ethiopian documents cite July 13, 1977, as the day the war began. On July 14, Mengistu told Ochoa that fighting had broken out between Ethiopian and Somali troops. On July 21, Raúl Castro reported that "an entire battalion of regular Somali troops had entered the Ogaden." All this had happened before Addou reported to Siad Barre about his talks in Washington.[106]

In the Russian defense ministry's history of the war, there is a long list of reasons why Somalia attacked Ethiopia when it did, and the US promise of arms is not mentioned.[107] The American promise might have given Siad solace as he launched his assault on Ethiopian troops in the Ogaden, but it did not trigger his decision to go to war.

Precarious Success

"The Somali operation into Ethiopia is one of the most skillful the world has witnessed in many years," NSC staffer Paul Henze declared. In late July and August, the Somalis and WSLF rebels easily overwhelmed small garrisons of Ethiopian soldiers and police in the vast southern stretches of the Ogaden—the most arid and underpopulated area—where Addis's control had always been shallow and episodic. The Somali forces—regular and WSLF—were highly motivated and well prepared, whereas the Ethiopian army was demoralized and inept. The Derg, assured by the Soviets that they would restrain the Somalis from invading, had moved troops from the Ogaden to Eritrea, where the insurgency was heating up. As the Zambian ambassador in Addis explained, "Therefore, the invasion . . . caught them flat footed." The State Department explained: "The Ethiopian army (half of which is in Eritrea) is outnumbered . . . and weakened by three years of revolutionary turmoil. . . . Many of the best educated officers have fled." An Egyptian specialist on the Horn estimated in early August 1977 that the WSLF controlled 70 to 80 percent of the Ogaden. The Somali gains looked impressive on a map; [108]

This was, however, misleading. The Somalis had not yet conquered the triangle of towns—Diredawa, Harar, and Jijiga—which were the crux of the war. Diredawa, with a population of at least 70,000, was the third-largest city in Ethiopia; it had a developed industrial base, an airfield, and access to the Addis-to-Djibouti railroad. Harar, twenty-five miles to the southeast of Diredawa, was Ethiopia's fourth-largest city with 48,000 inhabitants and home to Ethiopia's premier military academy. Jijiga, sixty miles east with a population of about 10,000, controlled the Marda pass that led to Harar and Diredawa, and was a major tank base of the Ethiopian army. Technically, these multiethnic towns were not part of the Ogaden, but from the beginning of the war Mogadiscio was determined to take them. In part this was strategic necessity: the three towns formed a defensive perimeter that secured control of the Ogaden and would provide an economic boon. The Somalis' interest in these towns was also rooted in their history, which cast Harar as a glorious Somali city as far back as the sixteenth century. If—and only if—the Somalis could seize and hold all three towns would they declare victory. The race was on: could the Somalis take the towns before the Ethiopians could organize a counterattack?[109]

The battle for Diredawa raged through August, with both sides making conflicting claims about who was winning. A Cuban intelligence report described the battle, noting that on August 31, the Ethiopians—"despite their disorganization"—finally succeeded in pushing back the Somalis. In mid-September, the Ethiopians escorted twenty-five foreign journalists (most of whom were from Eastern Europe) to the virtual ghost city, proving their control of it and showing the journalists evidence of fierce fighting and the remains of sixteen Soviet T-55 tanks—perhaps one-third of the Somali army's entire supply.[110]

Jijiga, however, fell to the Somalis on September 12. After enduring a two-week siege, the Ethiopian Third Division and three battalions of the Tenth Mechanized Brigade dropped their weapons and fled. The victorious Somalis soon captured the Marda pass, putting them in position to attack Harar and

Diredawa. "The Somalis have succeeded beyond our, and very likely their own, expectations," the CIA noted.[111]

The battle for the walled city of Harar began soon afterward. The Somalis predicted confidently that Harar would fall in a week. It did not fall, however, and neither did Diredawa. With hindsight, historian Gebru Tareke writes, "the Somali blitzkrieg had ended and the phase of attrition had begun."[112]

The battles wore on, the Somalis attacking with MiGs and the Ethiopians defending with their thirty-two F-5 jet fighters. These details of hardware indicate the complexity of the conflict: the Somalis, backed by a pro-American consortium, were using Soviet arms, while the Soviet-backed Ethiopians were still using the US arms that Washington had provided in the previous decades (as well as, it was rumored, US arms supplied by Israel). At other times, both sides used Soviet weapons. The Soviets had not stopped shipping equipment to the Somalis, although the pace slowed, the quantities dwindled, and the quality plummeted; there were still Soviet military advisers in Mogadiscio, although they were largely idle. An Italian journalist was struck that the weapons taken from the Somalis and those used by the Ethiopians were "one and the same: all were made by the Soviets." During the Cold War, the simplest way to determine a country's allegiance was to see which superpower had manufactured its weapons, but in the Horn, this offhand analysis fell apart.[113]

Added to this confusion was the fact that the war might as well have been taking place on the moon, so poor was the world's knowledge of it. It was the fiercest war occurring at the time, but journalists covered it only from afar or through rare, well-orchestrated tours led by the government of Ethiopia or—even less frequently—of Somalia. Rumors flew. Diredawa had fallen to the Somalis! No—the battle for the city was still being fought. Or perhaps it had not yet begun. There were 15,000 Cubans fighting in the Ogaden! Or, in another report, there only fifty Cubans in Ethiopia, most of them doctors in Addis.[114]

Underlying all this confusion was Somalia's refusal to admit—whether in public or in private meetings with Americans and Soviets—that the Somali army was involved in the fighting. These protestations shredded Siad Barre's credibility. It was widely known that the WSLF guerrillas did not have the training to fly the MiGs or drive the tanks that were attacking the Ethiopians. And on August 15, when journalists reported from Diredawa that they could see the remains of sixteen tanks and a jet that had clearly belonged to the Somali armed forces, Siad's denials were exposed as bald-faced lies. This did not stop Siad Barre. When he met two American envoys in early September, for example, he told them bluntly that no Somali troops were engaged in the fighting. Henze noted, correctly, that these denials were "ludicrous."[115]

Sparring in Beijing

Insight into the Carter administration's policy toward the Horn can be gleaned from Cyrus Vance's discussions with Chinese officials in Beijing in August 1977. Because events in the Horn would affect the Carter administration's policy toward China, it is worth pausing briefly to reflect on Vance's journey in the summer of 1977, one month into the Ogaden War.

Vance set off for Beijing to restart the process of normalizing relations between China and the United States. President Richard Nixon had had all the fun with China, masterminding the breakthrough and dramatically traveling to Beijing. The arduous and politically costly work—finessing the rupture of the US commitment to Taiwan—had been bequeathed to his successors. Ford had ducked the issue. Carter had promised during the campaign to work toward normalization, and, as president, he fully intended to make good on this promise—even though the "Taiwan Lobby" would make it costly in domestic terms—but he was not in a hurry. His instructions to Vance were clear: "We do not go to Peking as supplicants. . . . We can afford to be patient. The goal here should be to engage the Chinese in meaningful discussion on issues where we potentially can be helpful to each other." The president then listed five such issues, two of which were African: "Korea, southern Africa, the Horn, Southeast Asia, and possibly South Asia."[116]

China had a presence in Africa—particularly in Tanzania, where it had financed the ambitious railway link to Zambia—but its footprint shrank after the 1975 Angolan civil war, when it had backed a movement that lost to the Soviet- and Cuban-backed Movimento Popular de Libertação de Angola (MPLA). By 1977, the State Department noted that Beijing had once again "made Africa a prime focus in its campaign to project an image as a Third World leader" and to foil the growth of Soviet (and to a much lesser extent, American) hegemony. This was a challenge because Beijing had relatively little economic, military, or diplomatic muscle in Africa. The State Department observed that "China has found itself technologically and economically unable to match the Soviet bloc in meeting African arms requirements. . . . Nevertheless the PRC [People's Republic of China] continues its long-standing support for armed insurgencies against white minority governments in southern Africa." In the Horn, however, Beijing's interest was more recent and more tentative. "The PRC has adopted a wait-and-see attitude toward the Horn, . . . ready to take advantage of any Soviet miscalculation," the State Department reported in July 1977.[117]

When Vance arrived in Beijing on August 20, it was clear that the Chinese leaders were particularly concerned about the war in the Ogaden. "They were not even so interested in SALT as in the Horn of Africa," one of the US diplomats accompanying Vance commented immediately after the Beijing talks.[118] It is not accurate, however, to claim that the Chinese leaders wanted to engage in a discussion of African issues; all they wanted was for Vance to tell them what Washington was doing, especially in the Horn, and to bend Vance's ear about the Soviet threat to the entire continent. "The polar bear you are confronting," Vice Premier Deng Xiaoping warned Vance, "is one with wild ambitions—wild ambitions to conquer the world."[119]

Vance explained US thinking on the Horn clearly: the Carter administration had formed a consortium to supply military aid to Somalia, and it believed that the war in the Ogaden would embarrass the Soviets. Washington had kept "in close touch with our Arab colleagues, particularly Saudi Arabia," Vance told Chinese foreign minister Huang Hua, "to provide a coordinated program of assistance [to Somalia] . . . . We got in touch with the French, the British, and the [West] Germans. All agreed that we would supply different kinds of equipment to the Somalis. . . . The French have already supplied small arms." The war had not disrupted that policy, although it had "somewhat complicated the situation." Vance then explained why he was not worried about the war: "It appears as though the Somalis have accomplished 95% of what they set out to do, namely to take over the Ogaden." He predicted, moreover, that "the likelihood is high" that the Eritrean separatists would also defeat the Ethiopian armed forces. Therefore, Vance concluded optimistically, "In our view, this program [US policy toward the Horn] is working. We see the Soviets faced with a very difficult situation where they are trying to ride two horses at the same time in Ethiopia and Somalia and they may well fall off both horses."[120]

Huang was tight-lipped about Chinese policy toward the Horn. The Somali vice president had traveled to Beijing in June, but Huang did not mention his visit, much less what may have been discussed, to Vance in August. Nor did he breathe a word about the rumors that China was funneling arms to Somalia through Pakistan. (The CIA later concluded that in the second half on 1977, China had sent "small arms, ammunition, and anti-tank and anti-aircraft weapons" to Somalia.)[121] Instead, Huang harangued Vance about the Soviet grand imperial strategy in Africa.

Vance pushed back. "As we look at the Soviet efforts in Africa," he said, "we see less a grand strategy in Africa but rather an attempt to pick what they believe to be targets of opportunity. . . . The latest two examples of this are Somalia and Ethiopia. I am not suggesting they will lose all influence in the area, but certainly their influence is less in both these countries than it was several months ago." Vance tried to end the discussion on a positive note: "Our objectives in Africa have many common threads with those of the People's Republic of China."[122] There was, in fact, only one common thread: anti-Sovietism.

The tone of Vance's meetings in Beijing was cordial but stiff. This was a predictable result of Carter's instructions: there was no reason to rush normalization or to grovel. Vance and his Chinese interlocutors exchanged information and sparred. They did not establish a rapport or even try to achieve a breakthrough. The US press, hooked by Kissinger and Nixon on banner headlines after every encounter with the Chinese, was disappointed and conveyed the trip as a failure. The State Department took note. "We do have to counter some of the unfair criticisms being levied at Mr. Vance," the deputy executive secretary of the department cabled his boss, Peter Tarnoff, who was traveling with Vance in China. "We should try to make . . . a virtue out of contrasting his [Vance's] no-nonsense, down-to-earth approach with what has gone before. . . . Mr. Vance's credibility and even his standing in the international community will begin to suffer if the carping, critical commentaries continue much longer." More important, Carter was displeased, and his verdict on Vance's trip was harsh: "The visit was a disappointing failure."[123]

In Moscow: "Lines have now been drawn"

Throughout the first half of 1977, as the men in the Kremlin had tilted toward Ethiopia, they had struggled to restrain Siad Barre and had urged the two sides to negotiate. They had hoped to pull off a diplomatic feat in the Horn comparable to the US accomplishment in the Middle East: by making the Soviet Union the principal ally of the two antagonists as well as the honest broker between them, they would squeeze American influence from the region. To this end, in the months after Fidel Castro's and Nikolai Podgorny's attempts to mediate the dispute, the Soviet leaders maintained normal relations with both warring parties, albeit promising significant military aid to Ethiopia while sending only a trickle of spare parts to Somalia.

As the skirmishes in the Ogaden intensified to war, the Kremlin increased its pressure on Siad Barre to withdraw. The fighting threatened to rupture not only the Soviets' long-standing ties with Siad but also their budding friendship with Mengistu, who had become embittered by the Kremlin's failure to restrain the Somalis. The war also imperiled the Ethiopian state. US chargé Art Tienken, the highest-ranking American in Addis Ababa, noted that this would have calamitous repercussions. "The consequences of an Ethiopian breakup—instability, political vacuum, desire to settle old scores—are immeasurable," he cabled in August. "It may in fact turn out that Soviet Union is the only country that has given these longer term consequences any thought."[124]

In mid-August, Siad sent a high-level delegation to Moscow to try once again to persuade the Kremlin of the legitimacy of the Somali claim to the Ogaden. "The goal of the WSLF is social justice and . . . the construction of a socialist society," the Somali delegation insisted. The Soviets were unmoved.

While the Somalis were still in Moscow, *Izvestia* ran an article that described Ethiopia as "the victim of armed invasion." The Somalis were outraged and rejected "absolutely . . . the claim that it [Somalia] invaded Ethiopia." They went home to Mogadiscio empty-handed.[125]

Two weeks later, Siad Barre himself traveled quietly to Moscow. In a meeting with Leonid Brezhnev, Siad asked for weapons and understanding. "The only thing Siad Barre had on his mind . . . was military assistance," the Soviet ambassador in Addis told his American counterpart. "Soviet efforts to discuss a political settlement in Ogaden fell on deaf ears." The Soviet leaders presented Siad with an ultimatum: get out of the Ogaden or forfeit Soviet arms. If Siad forced the Kremlin to choose between him and Mengistu, he would lose. The meeting therefore grew fiery, and as Siad later admitted, "Brezhnev became angry and left the room."[126]

A fortnight after Siad's calamitous visit, the Kremlin finally faced the fact that, in the words of the Soviet ambassador in Somalia, all its efforts had resulted in "total failure." The Soviets informed Siad Barre that they would not send Somalia any more weapons. "Lines have now been drawn," the US embassy in Mogadiscio cabled on September 20. "Moscow intends [to] support Ethiopia even at risk of losing Somalia."[127] Soviet foreign minister Andrei Gromyko admitted that "Brezhnev was 'annoyed with the mess' in the region," and the Kremlin was "considerably embarrassed" by the Somali attack on the Ogaden.[128] But Moscow still hoped to keep Siad Barre in the fold. "[The] Soviets . . . would continue provide economic assistance [to Siad]," Moscow's ambassador in Ethiopia explained, but "military assistance was now 'impossible.'" Approximately 1,800 Soviet military advisers remained, albeit idle, in Mogadiscio. "We need to keep the Somalis under the influence of the socialist countries," top-ranking Soviet general Sergey Akhromeyev told the Cubans on September 27, 1977. "That's why we keep sending them construction materials and other civilian stuff." Akhromeyev urged the Cubans to keep their forty-two military advisers in Somalia, even though "they have nothing to do."[129]

Somalia's future, the Soviet ambassador to Somalia concluded in late September, was "not promising." The Zambian ambassador in Moscow was more blunt: "Somalia is in a mess," he commented.[130]

In Washington: Schadenfreude

The outbreak of war opened the second phase of the Carter administration's handling of the Horn. After several months of leaning toward sending US arms to Somalia, Washington paused, made minor adjustments, and continued to lure Somalia from the Soviet camp.

It was fortunate for the administration that reports in the US press about the escalating hostilities in the Ogaden were infrequent squibs from the wire services buried in the inner pages. When Mengistu declared on July 24, 1977, that Somali troops had invaded his country, no major US paper reported his speech. Both the *New York Times* and the *Washington Post* simply noted in their world news roundups that Ethiopia had reported increased fighting in the Ogaden.[131]

Behind the scenes, NSC staffers Tom Thornton and Henry Richardson were trying to put the brakes on the administration's decision to arm Somalia. On July 20, they sent Zbigniew Brzezinski a strongly worded memo: "Doing something solely or even primarily to stick a finger . . . in the Soviet eye is a bad reason." Moreover, they added: "Somalia's current national objectives are simply not ones that we want to support. Ripping off Ethiopia . . . in the name of Somali nationalism is not high on our list of international desiderata. It is destabilizing in Africa, [and] goes against everything we stand for. . . . [It] would identify us with aggression."[132]

Their argument fell on deaf ears. On July 26, the State Department publicly announced that it had informed Somalia that the United States was prepared in principle to supply arms "in cooperation with other nations" to "fill any gaps" in Somalia's defense structure. The Carter administration, which had worried—unnecessarily—that the policy might create a stir because it contradicted Carter's campaign promise to curtail US arms sales, had hurriedly issued the statement only after realizing that the promise had already been leaked to the press. (The Americans failed to give advance notice of this announcement to their British and French consortium partners, to the considerable annoyance of London and Paris.)[133]

Facing this new reality, Thornton penned another memo to Brzezinski on July 27. "Obviously, we have a policy. The issue now is to manage it in the most beneficial way." He stressed one principle above all: "We should avoid if at all possible the provision of lethal/combat equipment. . . . The French can take care of arms as such." Thornton added that it would be best to "keep the whole undertaking very low key," and concluded with a flourish: "By any reasonable standard of judgment, Somalia is engaged in simple aggression against Ethiopia . . . on the same ethnic grounds that Hitler used in dealing with Czechoslovakia. Aggression in the name of irredentism is still aggression." Across the top of the memo, Deputy National Security Adviser David Aaron scrawled, "Worth reading," and in the margin Brzezinski wrote, "Give me a memo to Vance."[134]

On August 2, Carter decided to "go slow" on arms for Somalia, but the following day he admitted, "I'm not sure what we should do—best to minimize military aid, probably." Two days later, Brzezinski sent Vance a memo that expressed Thornton's viewpoint and suggestions as his own. (This was, for Brzezinski, an anomalous memo; throughout the Horn crisis he supported doing whatever possible to lure Somalia into the Western camp.)[135]

Vance's reply came swiftly. It was categorical; it reflected the president's thinking, and it determined policy for the second phase: the cost of *not* aiding Somalia trumped all qualms and scruples. "The President asked for an assessment of the effect of our not supplying military equipment to the Somalis," the executive secretary of the State Department informed Brzezinski on August 8. "A flat refusal would almost certainly fail in our objective of easing the Soviet Union out of . . . Somalia. In addition, we would be charged with vacillation by the moderate Arab and African states . . . and we would suffer even more in the eyes of the European and Arab states who have decided to offer military support to Somalia in the legitimate belief that we would be willing to participate." The Carter administration would not condemn Siad Barre's war of aggression. Instead, it would "temporize and delay implementation of the arms supply relationship."[136]

For some in the State Department, this position did not go far enough to distance the United States from an aggressor. Anthony Lake, the Policy Planning Staff director, called for the administration to publicly disavow its decision to send arms to Somalia. The president, however, "felt that it was best just let matters ride for the time being."[137]

The Propaganda War

In a strikingly hypocritical move, in the weeks immediately after war broke out, Carter asked Vance to coordinate "as many African leaders as possible to participate in a call to all outside powers to refrain from supplying arms to fuel the Ethiopian-Somali confrontation." In late August and September, the State Department issued a plethora of cables titled "Drawing African Attention to Soviet activity in the Horn" that called on US ambassadors to fire up their host governments to deplore Soviet intervention in the Horn. These efforts bore no fruit.[138]

There were several reasons for the failure of this initiative. The most important was that Washington's allegations were not credible. It was clear that Somalia was the aggressor in the war, and Washington provided no evidence that Moscow was still supplying it with arms. (On the contrary, US and Saudi attempts to supply Somalia were an open secret.) As for the Kremlin supplying arms to Ethiopia, there were no accounts of significant shipments of arms arriving in Addis, and even if there had been, Ethiopia was defending itself against an invading army. Siad Barre and Ambassador Addou kept frothing about the thousands of Cubans in Ethiopia (though their numbers varied wildly with each repetition), but as Vance commented, "[the] line about Cubans and Soviets has become Somali standard as they seek to find some rationale sufficiently acceptable to the West to warrant Western support for Somalia despite their actions in the Ogaden." The US ambassador in Mogadiscio agreed that the Somalis were "peddling a distorted view," and the chargé in Addis added: "We have absolutely no substantiation of wild stories being spread by Somalis . . . of thousands of Cubans here, there, or someplace else in Ethiopia." This was accurate: Castro's respect for the Ethiopian Revolution had not dimmed, but he did not think that Cuba could afford to send more than the medical mission and military instructors who had been there since the spring.[139]

A second reason that the Carter administration's propaganda war fizzled was that it was overbearing, as the US embassy in Nigeria noted in a stinging response to Vance's request. "Any pointed effort to stimulate Nigerian expression of concern over Soviet activity in the Horn would likely be ineffective and . . . counterproductive. . . . What we consider to be a normal statement of USG [US government] views, Nigerian may testily interpret as a lecture."[140] Washington did not have the leverage or the credibility to whip up an anti-Soviet frenzy without evidence.

Murrey Marder, a seasoned investigative reporter at the *Washington Post*, put his finger on Washington's problem. "Hodding," he said, addressing Hodding Carter at the September 19 State Department briefing, "there seems to be a non sequitur in the basic explanation you have given here which is that Somalia activity in the Ogaden came as a result of the Soviet Union's excessive supply of arms to Somalia. If Somalia had excessive supply of arms then why was the United States considering supplying arms?"[141]

Pulling Back

For the last three weeks of August, as the Somali troops seized enormous expanses of territory in the Ogaden, the administration was mum about its position on arms for Somalia. Finally, on September 1, State Department spokesman Hodding Carter announced, "We have decided that providing arms at this time would add fuel to a fire we are more interested in putting out." The next day, London and Paris issued similar statements.[142]

The Saudis were deeply disappointed. Carter's decision to "temporize" about arms to Somalia confirmed the Saudis' abiding fear that Washington was no longer willing or able to protect them from the Soviet danger. The Carter administration had its priorities backwards, the Saudi leaders charged:

Why let a few scruples about territorial integrity or arms sales derail a perfect opportunity to embarrass the Soviets? From Jidda, US Ambassador John West cabled that the Saudis sought the "liberation of Ogaden Muslims from their Christian rulers," which would leave "a truncated 'Amharic' Ethiopia. By freeing Muslims and, at the same time, giving the pro-Soviet Marxist Mengistu his comeuppance, SAG [Saudi Arabian government] would neatly dovetail its two major foreign policy goals of containing communism and expanding the House of Islam. The additional geopolitical goal of turning vital Red Sea arterial into an Arab lake also an important factor in Saudi thinking."[143]

The Carter administration was in too deep to extract itself, even if it had wanted to. On September 13, Assistant Secretary of State for Africa Dick Moose received an unwelcome phone call from a journalist at *Newsweek*: The magazine had gotten wind of Dr. Kevin Cahill's secret June mission to Somalia, and it was going to print that Cahill, on the State Department's instructions, had given the green light to Siad Barre to invade the Ogaden as long as he left Kenya alone.[144] Moose denied the story "categorically" and promptly phoned Cahill, who unfortunately confirmed that he had delivered a message to Siad "that Somalia should not bother Djibouti or Kenya, but that the Ogaden did not matter so much."[145] Nevertheless, the State Department stuck to its story. When the spokesman was asked about the *Newsweek* article, he "categorically" denied that the United States had "encouraged in any way" Somalia's incursion into the Ogaden.[146]

This would have been a minor incident: but it provided a hook that drew the Carter administration deeper into the narrative of the war. Washington was a player in the crisis, and it was seen to be a player. The Cahill story broke after the Carter administration's tilt toward Somalia was clear, and it helped solidify the perception that Washington was implicated in the war. Nevertheless, most of the policymakers, including the president, were not exercised by *Newsweek*'s scoop: the war was going America's way.[147]

Letting the Soviets Stew

During the opening months of the war, the Horn was not a high priority at Foggy Bottom. In August and September, the seventh floor of the State Department was fully occupied by the SALT negotiations, the Panama Canal treaties, the Anglo-American proposals for Rhodesia, and the attempt to reconvene a Geneva conference for the Middle East. Deputy Secretary of State Warren Christopher acknowledged that the Ogaden war was the "most serious armed conflict that Africa has seen since WWII," but there was not much that Washington could do, or wanted to do, about it.[148] Aside from the East Africa director and the ambassador in Mogadiscio, it was no one's top priority and it generated no dramatic arguments about policy within the administration or among allies.

Washington's policy toward the Horn during this second phase—after Somalia invaded Ethiopia and while it was quickly occupying the Ogaden—was characterized by the administration's public calls for negotiations and its private calls encouraging NATO allies and conservative Arab states to quietly send arms to Somalia.

The White House declared at the OAU and the UN that it sought a negotiated settlement to the war. The State Department fretted that this might be seen as a "half-hearted gesture to score propaganda points."[149] Which is exactly what it was—because ending the war would help the Soviet Union maintain influence in both Ethiopia and Somalia. "We are more eager to end the fighting there than you are," the Soviet ambassador to the United States, Anatoly Dobrynin, told Vance.[150] In September, the Defense Department noted that calling for negotiations "would be strengthening the Soviet position in the Horn." The British, Americans, French, and West Germans discussed the Horn at their quadripartite talks in late September and October, and they agreed with Vance that "the present situation in the Horn continues to offer an opportunity to weaken Soviet influence in Somalia." They considered—and rejected—taking the issue to the United Nations. "The Soviets had made a mess of things and [French Foreign Minister] de Guiringaud saw no reason why the Western countries should help them out of it." De Guiringaud relished seeing the Soviets throw in their lot with the Ethiopians and thereby "annoy all the Arab countries—including Saudi Arabia." Let the Soviets "stew in their own juice," he said. A State Department official summarized the discussion: "We would not want to pull the Soviet chestnuts out of the fire."[151]

The prospects for successful negotiations were minimal in any case. Neither Somalia nor Ethiopia was ready to talk. Somalia expected to conquer Harar and Diredawa, and Ethiopia wanted time to rally and rearm. Moreover, both the UN and the OAU were unenthusiastic about sponsoring negotiations in the Horn.[152]

The war should have been a clear case for the OAU: Somalia had invaded Ethiopia, making a mockery of the principle of the inviolability of borders that the organization championed. Nevertheless, it was reluctant to condemn Somalia. Instead, it dodged and sidestepped. It deferred to the negotiating committee it had formed at the Gabon summit, with Nigeria in the lead, but the parties refused even to meet. The OAU was toothless, and its principles were at odds with its interests: Somalia was supported by the same Arab states that had promised the Africans $1 billion at the inaugural Afro-Arab summit, with the promise of more to come, and the OAU did not relish condemning the Saudis' friend, even if it had invaded its neighbor.[153]

The Arms Bazaar

At the same time that Washington was calling for negotiations, it was also shoring up its relations with regional players, especially Egypt, Iran, Saudi Arabia, and Sudan, by sending more arms and aid.[154]

In the same week in late July that the Carter administration announced its decision in principle to send arms to Somalia, it informed Sudan that it was "prepared to contribute to its legitimate defense needs" and it would send a survey team to Khartoum to study the country's military requirements. Six C-130s were already en route to Egypt, and the administration was contemplating adding fourteen more, along with drones, aerial reconnaissance cameras, F-5E warplanes, tanks, and armored personnel carriers.[155]

It was the proposed sale of sixty sophisticated F-15 Eagle warplanes to Saudi Arabia and seven AWACS (airborne warning and control system advanced radar, mounted on Boeing 707s) to Iran that sparked controversy. The White House had first approached Congress in secret about this sale on June 16, 1977. When the proposal was made public on July 6, it caused a firestorm of condemnation, in part because it so dramatically contradicted Carter's pledge that the United States would never be the first country to introduce new levels of advanced technology into a region, and it made a mockery of Carter's promise to reduce arms sales. The American Israel Public Affairs Committee (AIPAC) warned that "F-15s would enable Saudi Arabia to strike deep into Israel," and the *Washington Post* deemed it a "turkey of a deal."[156]

The arms sales that the Carter administration proposed in the summer of 1977 were designed, in part, to reassure the Saudis, who had expressed alarm about Carter's repeated promise to reduce arms sales abroad. The sales not only added to the total value of US arms transfers but also added four new customers (Chad, Egypt, Somalia, and Sudan)—all in the Horn region—to the list of recipient countries. State Department spokesman Hodding Carter tried to put the best possible spin on this reversal of the president's stated policy: each of the proposed deals, he said, reflected "a limited decision" taken in response to "new situations and new requests." Vance weighed in: "This in no way is to be construed as an attempt to enter into an arms race with the Soviet Union."[157]

The Consortium, with One Degree of Separation

The Carter administration was doing more than calling for negotiations and strengthening its ties to countries in the Horn region: it was also secretly encouraging other countries to send arms to Somalia. This was the most important aspect of Washington's policy, and it is the most difficult to trace. The outbreak of war caused the Carter administration to declare that it would not send weapons to Siad Barre, but it did not lessen its desire to decouple Somalia from the Soviet Union—and this meant continuing to urge its friends and allies to supply arms to Somalia. However, after full-scale war broke out in July, the administration wanted to hide its involvement in the enterprise. Therefore, it began to insist that no US-manufactured weapons be sent to Somalia, and its efforts to rally suppliers were discreet.

The basic outlines of the consortium remained the same. The Saudis and (to a much lesser extent) other oil-rich countries paid the bills, and the arms were supplied by a wide group of regional players as well as America's NATO allies. Even after the Somali invasion of Ethiopia became impossible to deny, Deputy Assistant Secretary Talcott Seelye told a visiting Somali delegation, "We were aware of Somalia's growing arms supply relationship with many of our friends and allies. We had encouraged this relationship and we would do nothing to discourage it now."[158] In late October, US Undersecretary Philip Habib told Ambassador Addou, accurately, that the "US failure to supply arms did not leave Somalia defenseless. Mogadiscio was receiving arms from a number of other countries and was certainly holding its own in the battle in the Ogaden."[159]

The specifics of Saudi aid to Somalia are impossible to determine. If there are relevant US documents, they remain classified.[160] The clearest evidence of Saudi-financed weapons is from Egypt. In early September, returning home from his unsuccessful trip to Moscow and his stormy meeting with Leonid Brezhnev, Siad Barre stopped in Cairo, where "President Sadat promised help and assistance to Somalia." Egypt would send Somalia thirty-one Soviet T-34 tanks, some T-55 tanks, and other arms valued at $30 million. "Fact of the matter is that Sadat has been as generous with arms for Somalia as he can be," the US ambassador in Cairo cabled Washington.[161]

There are also indications that, after the war began, weapons or the money to buy them arrived in Somalia from Jordan, Sudan, Pakistan, Iraq, United Arab Emirates, Kuwait, Morocco, South Yemen, and Singapore.[162] In all of these cases, it is impossible to determine not only the exact quantity or quality of the weapons transferred to Somalia, but also the role of the United States in facilitating these transfers.

There is evidence, however, from Iran. In May, the shah had agreed to send weapons to Somalia, and Siad Barre's invasion of Ethiopia did not affect this decision. On October 10, the US ambassador in Tehran, William Sullivan, cabled Washington in a state of extreme agitation: he had just received a State Department telegram instructing him to stop the Iranian government from flying a C-130 full of US-made M-1 carbines to Somalia. Sullivan, a seasoned career diplomat, was outraged, and he let the State Department know it. He fired off a furious reply to the bureaucrats in Foggy Bottom. He reminded them that they had urged the shah to help Somalia; that they had welcomed Tehran's decision to send a military mission to Mogadiscio to assess the Somali needs; and that they were well aware that the Somalis had accepted the military mission only on condition that it arrive with a large shipment of arms "as good faith." The five-man Iranian military mission had just departed for Somalia, and the C-130 was preparing to take off with the weapons. Sullivan did not hide his anger that Washington had changed its mind at the last moment. He informed the State Department that the Iranian director of political affairs had complained bitterly to him that the "Iranians were totally confused by US position and now found themselves in extremely embarrassing position." The military mission would arrive in Mogadiscio without the weapons and "would be accused of bad faith." Sullivan added that immediately after receiving a blistering tongue-lashing from the Iranian political director, he was confronted by "my volatile little Somali colleague, who had just received a telephone call from Mogadiscio, complaining that the military mission had arrived there 'senza roba' [empty handed]." Sullivan demanded that Washington retract its orders. "Since it was the US which got the Iranians involved in this whole exercise, . . . I see no rpt no alternative to immediate release permitting them to send this load of rifles."[163]

Warren Christopher replied immediately, and he did not budge. The United States "could not rpt not at this moment legally authorize transfer of M-1 carbines." The deputy secretary of state then drew the administration's fine, legalistic line: "US not rpt not discouraging transfer of non-US origin arms by third countries to Somalia."[164] Sullivan did not hide his anger: "[This] will come as considerable surprise to government of Iran." He reminded Christopher that on May 13 Vance himself had asked the shah to help and that on July 6 the Iranians had sent Washington a list of the arms they intended to send Somalia. An objection could have been raised at any point in the three intervening months, not when the loaded plane was set to depart.[165] The Iranians, however, capitulated. Three days later, the C-130 took off for Somalia loaded with German-made G-3 rifles, and the "thorny problem" was resolved.[166]

The entire subject of arms transfers to Siad Barre was cloaked in legalistic fig leaves and punctuated by winks. Washington said that it opposed third-country transfers of US weapons, but the Iranian episode indicates that the policy was not communicated clearly, even to a close ally. There are indications that Washington made little if any attempt to enforce the rule where it most mattered—in Saudi Arabia. At a quadripartite meeting in late 1977, when the French representative asked what the Saudis would do to help Somalia, the American representative replied: "They could transfer weapons of

Soviet, French and US origin . . . even though it would be illegal." Moreover, there is one report—based on oral sources—that between August and December 1977, an arms dealer hired by the CIA "hauled 580 tons of weapons on twenty-eight separate flights to Mogadishu." It is not surprising that US-made weapons did end up in the Ogaden.[167]

The role of the NATO members of the consortium—Britain, France, and West Germany—is also murky. The Western partners at the quadripartite talks did not talk openly even among themselves about what they were doing to help Somalia. There are only hints about arms secretly being shipped to Somalia. Not one of the representatives spoke frankly: not one called Somalia the aggressor, and not one confessed that his government was helping Siad Barre. They spoke in circles, hoping to retain plausible deniability even in these rarefied councils of close allies. The United States, Britain, France, and West Germany said that they were sending increased levels of "development aid" to Somalia while the war was being fought. All of them knew that Siad Barre had no interest in development projects during those months; he was a man obsessed with only one mission: procuring weapons. "Development aid" was a euphemism.[168]

Britain rescinded its offer of weapons in August 1977, as the war in the Ogaden heated up and its fears about Kenyan security spiked. The Saudis, however, continued to urge London to help Siad Barre. In September, Prince Sultan told British defense secretary Fred Mulley that the Saudi royal family "attached overriding importance to the defeat of communism in the Middle East and Africa," and pressed Britain to send weapons to Somalia. Mulley was persuaded: "I believe we should make a positive response in some measure to the Saudi request," he wrote Prime Minister Jim Callaghan. "Failure to do so could bring, in my view, quite disproportionate adverse reactions." Foreign Secretary David Owen, however, advised caution. "We must clearly try to retain Saudi understanding of our position," he told Callaghan, suggesting that the prime minister himself explain to the Saudi royal family why London preferred not to send weapons at this time.[169]

It is unlikely that Britain sent weapons to Somalia during the war, but the French and possibly the Italians did—quietly. In September, French prime minister Raymond Barre explained to Carter, "There can't be a reduction of [arms] deliveries from the Western powers while leaving the field to the Soviets." Later that month, the US chargé in Addis reported that the French had agreed to send arms to Somalia in exchange for Siad's promise not to invade Djibouti, and on the eve of a quadripartite meeting the State Department's assistant secretary for Europe warned Vance that the British and Germans, "as far as we know, [are] still unaware of the French shipment of small arms to Somalia." In October, the Americans told Foreign Secretary Owen that the French had said that they "would be prepared to supply arms . . . [and Washington] would not wish to discourage the French if they did indeed go ahead." In November, Vance reported to Carter that the French and Italians were "discussing secret arms supply to Somalia," and the US ambassador in Paris confirmed that "under considerable pressure from the Saudis and . . . rather than antagonize the Arabs . . . France would be providing limited military assistance to Somalia . . . in great secrecy." This secrecy extended to France's close allies. Guy Georgy, the director of African affairs at Quai d'Orsay, insisted to David Owen that there was no truth to the rumor that France was sending arms to Somalia. Owen told Vance that he was left wondering if "the French are playing straight with us." In December, Undersecretary of State for Political Affairs Philip Habib declared in a meeting of Vance, Owen, and eight other American and British diplomats that he was skeptical about French assurances that Paris was not supplying arms to Somalia. "This might be literally true," Habib explained, but in fact, "the French were supplying arms to Saudi Arabia in the full knowledge that they ended up in Somalia."[170]

West Germany was a special case. Bonn provided only "non-lethal military aid" to Siad Barre—until late October. On October 13, members of the Baader Meinhof terrorist group hijacked a Lufthansa airliner with eighty-six passengers onboard and, after a circuitous journey, ordered it to fly to Mogadiscio. The terrorists gave the West German government five days to meet their demands before they would blow up the plane and all its passengers. On October 17, West German chancellor Helmut Schmidt called Siad Barre and told him that "if Somalia cooperated [with West German plans to resolve the crisis] German aid would be sent to Somalia and extended into other areas." Schmidt then spoke with Hans-Jürgen Wischnewski, a senior West German politician whom he had sent to Mogadiscio to serve as his special representative, and gave him a message to deliver orally to Siad. "I'm going to speak a little cryptically," the chancellor warned Wischnewski. "Tell Siad Barre that . . . his help in this difficult situation will deepen our future cooperation in all realms of our bilateral relations." Ninety minutes before the hijackers' deadline expired, West German commandos—with the permission of the Somali government—stormed the plane and released all the hostages unharmed. "We will never forget," Schmidt cabled Siad.[171]

The Germans did not forget, but they were discreet about it. "Your president took risks to help us," Schmidt told the visiting Somali vice president in November 1977, "and we will incur risks to help you . . . [but] we want to underplay our aid." The West German Foreign Ministry warned, "We have to downplay the details of our help to Somalia, as well as the extent of it." Schmidt then told Callaghan that he "had promised Somalia increased aid and a cash grant; but that no undertaking to supply arms to Somalia had been given."[172]

Schmidt delivered on his promise in several ways. Officially, the West Germans sent Somalia only "economic aid," but they bent over backwards to make the aid fungible. Schmidt was explicit in conversation with the Somali ambassador in Bonn: "It will be very difficult," he admitted, "to disguise German financial assistance to Somalia in order to keep secret its goal, which is to use it to buy weapons. We will have to think about how to do it." The ambassador suggested that they could send arms via the Saudis. Schmidt also promised to talk with Sadat about transferring Soviet weapons from Egypt to Somalia. Bonn sent at least one shipment of arms to Somalia using private chartered aircraft. After the war was over, the Somali security chief visited Bonn to thank the chancellor for "the goodwill and assistance his country had received from Germany."[173]

All these hints and whispers suggest that Siad Barre was receiving weapons from, as Zbigniew Brzezinski said, "a tangle of arms suppliers."[174] The United States encouraged this trade, and the Saudis financed it. The arms flowed primarily from Egypt and Iran, and to a much lesser extent from France. Saudi Arabia, Iran, Egypt, and France: this was the Safari Club, the shadowy international league of intelligence operatives who sought to compensate for what they considered the CIA's failure to stem the communist tide. An NSC document from 1978 noted that this "intelligence organization . . . coordinated strategies in support of Somalia."[175]

The important point remains, however, that Siad Barre had not found a reliable pipeline that could replace the Soviet Union. The Saudis could pay, the Safari Club could help, but Siad still had to scrounge for whatever haphazard stockpiles he could find, and the inadequacies of this supply line would become more debilitating the longer the war lasted. Siad Barre's September trip to Moscow had failed. He needed US help, as quickly as possible.

The Spurned Offer

By mid-September 1977, the Somalis had been fighting in the Ogaden for almost three months, but they had managed to capture only one significant town, Jijiga. Siad Barre's "big gamble has already failed," Brzezinski wrote Carter on September 23, 1977. "No available outside aid can enable Somalia, with its limited population, to win against Ethiopia. Siad will eventually fall. . . . Ethiopian forces should be able to turn the Somalis back." A week later, in talks at the State Department with a West German delegation, Undersecretary Phillip Habib repeated, "Ethiopia will be able to push the Somalis back." He then "reminded the Germans that the US had had long experience in arming Ethiopians and knew what their potential was." The CIA agreed, predicting that the Ethiopians would "regain the military advantage" and launch their final counterattack in the late spring and early summer of 1978.[176]

Yet even though the Carter administration's optimism about Siad's chances in August had given way to predictions of certain defeat, the White House was not willing to send arms to Siad Barre—even to save his troops from being crushed by the Derg. Washington's changed assessment of which side would win the war did not lead to a reassessment of US policy. It did not provoke any discussions (in the declassified record) of arming Siad. The winks at third-country transfers continued as they had since August, when the administration had assumed that Siad's army was marching to victory.

Siad was desperate. In mid-October, two weeks after the Kremlin had told him that it would not send any more arms, he presented the Americans with a deal: Somalia would expel all Soviet military advisers, abrogate its friendship treaty with Moscow, and offer Washington "navy port facilities, as the Soviets have enjoyed" if the United States entered "into an immediate arms supply relationship with Somalia." The Carter administration quickly and summarily rejected this offer. On October 20, Undersecretary for Political Affairs Philip Habib once again "gently" turned down Addou's request for arms "as long as the Ogaden fighting continued." He added that Somalia "did not seem to lack for arms suppliers." In the margin of Vance's report informing the president that the State Department had "turned down the Somalis, but gently," President Carter wrote, "Good."[177]

If Washington had been angling all this time to squeeze the Soviets from Somalia and win it for themselves, then why reject Siad's deal? There were three reasons.

First, if it ain't broke, don't fix it. In mid-October, the Carter administration was confident that the trend in the Horn was going its way. That it suspected that Somalia would lose the war in the Ogaden made very little difference to its calculation: Moscow was estranged from its erstwhile ally in Mogadiscio, and its new ally in Addis Ababa was beset with grave problems. The mainstream US press agreed with this happy assessment. On October 19, for example, a *New York Times* editorial entitled "The Horn—and No Dilemma" praised the administration's "wise policy" of not getting "enmeshed in the conflict" and noted, with evident satisfaction, that "the Russians have gambled their entire position in East Africa on a situation that is beyond their control."[178]

Second, could Siad's offer be trusted? The Somali president, who still denied that his troops were fighting in the Ogaden, had no credibility left. The longer foreigners—whether Soviets, Saudis, or Americans—dealt with him, the less they liked or believed him. Caught in a classic acrobat's dilemma—unable to sever ties with the Soviets before he had a firm grasp on a military alliance with the United States—Siad refused to do the three things that Washington asked: accept a US military attaché in Mogadiscio; guarantee that Somalia would not invade Kenya; and eject the Soviets and Cubans. The Americans, therefore, grew increasingly suspicious of their suitor in Mogadiscio. "He [Siad] is maneuvering, as he has always maneuvered, to both have his cake and eat it too," Ambassador John Loughran cabled from Mogadiscio on August 14. "There is an element of blackmail in this strategy." At the same time that Siad Barre was swearing fealty to the Americans, he was assuring a visiting Italian Communist Party official that he was "a true communist . . . [who] wanted to stay close to the Soviet Union . . . and hated the idea of accepting US aid." Sam Hamrick, a CIA specialist on Somalia, offered an astute assessment: "Siad's tilt to US is a function of war—not an indication of any ideological change. . . . He . . . needs an arms supplier."[179]

Third, Washington hoped that if it played its cards right, it could end up with both Somalia and Ethiopia on its side. The relationship between Mengistu and the Soviet leadership was fraying. Mengistu felt betrayed because the Kremlin had not been able to make good on its promise to restrain Siad Barre, because there were still Russian military advisers in Somalia, and because of the sluggish delivery and disappointing quantity of the arms Moscow was shipping to Addis. (The first shipment did not arrive until April, and it was just a collection of second-hand weapons.) The US chargé in Addis, Art Tienken, noted that the "serious straits" of the Ethiopian military in the Ogaden had caused Mengistu to reexamine his country's relationship with the Soviet Union: "It appears that both partners may have expected too much from each other. . . . Mengistu . . . seems to have overestimated Moscow's restraining influence on Somalia's irredentist ambitions."[180] Moreover, the Kremlin was still trying to balance its old commitments to Somalia with its new commitments to Ethiopia, so despite its grand promises to Mengistu of sophisticated heavy weapons (MiG-21s; T-54, and T-55 tanks; helicopters; rocket launchers; SAM-7 and ASAM-7 ground-to-air missiles; communication equipment and early-warning radar systems), its actual shipments were stinting. This disappointing effort jangled Mengistu's frayed nerves. "There was a lot of resentment in Ethiopia," an Italian journalist reported in August, "because the Soviets so far have sent only light weapons of inferior quality."[181]

The Ethiopian leader therefore turned to the Americans, through Israeli intermediaries, saying that he was "unhappy" with the Soviet Union and wanted to renew the military supply relationship with the United States. The Carter administration listened, floating the possibility of extending more economic aid to Ethiopia and increasing staff at its stripped-down embassy, including sending an ambassador. (The United States had withdrawn its ambassador in July 1976.) Mengistu's probes fueled speculation—voiced most vehemently by Henze at the NSC—that Ethiopia might return to the fold. The CIA's Sam Hamrick disagreed. "Any warming toward US," he asserted, "is tactical."[182]

Carter as Cynic

From July to November 1977, Washington's policy toward the Horn was cynical. The Carter administration wanted Somalia to break away from the Soviet Union, but it did not want to openly arm a state that had invaded its neighbor. Until August, it actively and openly encouraged its friends to help Somalia, but once Somalia had clearly invaded Ethiopia, Washington drew back, not discouraging anyone and allowing Saudi Arabia and the Safari Club to take the lead in drumming up support for Siad Barre.

Carter talked about wanting a negotiated settlement, but his administration put no muscle into the effort. It believed that the war was in America's interest, as it would sever Somalia's alliance with Moscow and weaken the Derg in Ethiopia. "We stand to gain while two Soviet client states slug it out," the State Department noted.[183] Moreover, unlike the conflict in southern Africa, war in the Ogaden desert seemed easy to contain. It would not trigger the racial conflagration throughout the continent and at home that war in Rhodesia portended.

While Moscow appeared to lose its wager in the region, Washington hoped to keep open the prospect of improving relations with both Somalia and Ethiopia. The Carter administration tread a fine line: it withdrew its offer to send arms to Somalia but encouraged its friends to send them; it publicly reiterated its support for the OAU principle of territorial integrity but never condemned the Somalis for their "premeditated aggression," a phrase that was uttered only internally by the Carter White House. Even after it became clear that Siad Barre might not be able to win the Ogaden, Washington remained unperturbed. The policymakers were rarely so blunt as to admit it, but the war suited their overriding purpose: it promised to foil Moscow's plan to befriend both Somalia and Ethiopia. As Deputy Secretary of State Warren Christopher wrote Vance in October, "the Soviets [are] impaled on the horns of a dilemma."[184]

As the Americans and their allies savored the difficulties that awaited the Soviets in the Horn, they were oblivious to the danger that loomed over their own policy. They had agreed at the September 29 quadripartite meeting that "the Soviets would commit any necessary force, equipment or training to

Ethiopia in order to ensure that Ethiopia regained its lost territory."[185] They had known since May that Fidel Castro had sent military advisers to Ethiopia. But they could not believe that Moscow would jeopardize its investment in Berbera, and they were certain that southern Africa was the eye of the storm. They did not question these assumptions—and they failed to anticipate the next phase of the war.

7. Complications

South Africa Faces the New Reality

On May 29, 1977—ten days after Vice President Walter Mondale had confronted South African prime minister John Vorster in Vienna—the Rhodesian Army launched its biggest raid yet against a neighboring country. Five hundred soldiers, with cover provided by the Rhodesian Air Force, attacked what the Smith government deemed "a guerrilla camp" sixty miles across Mozambique's border. General Peter Walls, the head of the Rhodesian Army, led the attack. Two days later, the *New York Times* reported—on page one above the fold—that General Walls had declared that his troops had seized the Mozambican town of Mapai and would remain "until all the guerrilla forces in the area are driven out."[1]

The Carter administration was outraged. The State Department fired off a "strong representation" to the Smith government (via the South Africans) asserting that "such actions are not in Rhodesia's ultimate survival interests." The flagrant act of aggression against Mozambique threatened to derail months of the Carter administration's careful diplomacy in Africa and provide an opening for the Soviet Union, which had just signed a treaty of friendship with Samora Machel's government. Moreover, the attack occurred when the US and British diplomatic team of Johnny Graham and Steve Low, on its first tour of the region, was in Maputo meeting with ZANU leader Robert Mugabe. South African foreign minister Pik Botha told Ian Smith that the raid "caused the Americans to see red."[2]

Botha had been stewing for a month, ever since he had sat opposite Mondale and at Vorster's side in Vienna. Immediately after those talks, he had briefed the Rhodesians in apocalyptic terms. "The battle for S.A. [South Africa] . . . was now joined," he had declared. "This was a new American team and a new ball game," he explained. "The screws were on RSA [Republic of South Africa] and the Carter people were thoroughly vindictive towards her." Botha summed up his assessment of what the talks meant: "South Africa was in for 'a hell of a time.' . . . [She] was now on a collision course with the US. She would have to look at her resources and her power very carefully."[3]

Botha made it clear that the screws were not only on South Africa. "With the previous American government they [the South Africans] had felt they had some time left for manouevre," he explained. "But not now. The Carter people wanted to 'get at them,' and this would happen immediately. It was not months ahead. There was a possibility of sanctions against RSA. Both [the US] Congress and the US military/industrial complex would follow the Carter line on RSA, and Rhodesia." Botha warned: "Neither of us [South Africans and Rhodesians] should indulge in any wishful thinking on this score."[4]

Three days later, General Walls had stormed into Mozambique and announced that he was going to stay. Pik Botha was caught in the cross fire: the US ambassador to South Africa immediately phoned and demanded he "urge the Rhodesians to get out of Mozambique." Botha, however, was fed up with the Americans. "The Carter administration were like religious converts whose belief in their own righteousness was unshakeable," he later told Smith. To the US ambassador, he declared that US policy—not Rhodesian actions— was the problem in southern Africa.[5]

At 11:30 P.M. that night, Botha's phone rang again. It was Warren Christopher, acting secretary of state (Cyrus Vance was traveling), and it was urgent. The Americans had "good intelligence" that Mozambique had asked the Soviet Union for assistance. "An emergency meeting of the Security Council had been called," Christopher said, "at which it was intended that sanctions against South Africa would be invoked because she was supplying the arms which made the Rhodesian raid possible." Botha lamely protested that South Africa was not supplying the arms, but he did not press the point. Instead, he tried to turn the tables, complaining that the encounter with Mondale had convinced the South Africans that they could expect "no cooperation . . . from the Americans who wanted power to be handed over to the terrorists." Christopher shot back: "The Security Council would meet and the Americans would not use the veto to safeguard South Africa." Botha retorted: "It would be better to get on with sanctions and have the race war."[6]

Despite Botha's intemperate reply to the Americans, the South African government wanted to avoid a UN Security Council debate, and it immediately pressed the Rhodesians to withdraw. Suddenly, General Walls ordered his troops out of Mozambique. "The behind the scenes US pressure on South Africa, leading to the withdrawal of Rhodesian troops from Mozambique, seems to have been most effective," Mondale commented to Carter in June 1.[7]

Two weeks later, on June 15, Pik Botha was face to face with Smith. They commiserated about the Americans who were "entirely selective in their morality" and had "a naive concept of our part of the world." Nevertheless, Botha asserted, the Carter administration was ruthlessly looking after its long-term interests: it was currying favor with African blacks. "Their [the Americans'] actions were quite cold-blooded. . . . [Their] feeling was 'The Blacks will take over in any case, so we must co-operate with them.'" Washington's objective "was to bring about a position where Southern Africa was governed by blacks who would hopefully be well-disposed to the United States." Therefore, "if a few million [South African and Rhodesian] whites had to be sacrificed . . . then so be it."[8]

Botha's assessment was grim. South Africa, he told Smith, was "well on the way to complete isolation." There was no hope of any rapid change of heart in Washington. "Andrew Young would not be fired. This was a reality and a fact of life."[9] The trump card of the white African governments—that they were holding the line against communism—had been shredded by the crisis in Angola and by the advent of the Carter team. Botha reiterated: "The Carter men . . . were like religious converts who would burn you to save your soul." It was infuriating, because the Americans "had the power to take drastic measures unless their terms were complied with."[10] Botha stated flatly: "US power and technology were awesome. This was a reality we must face." And South Africa was vulnerable because it "was very short of money. . . . If she were cut off from her markets she would be in severe trouble." Botha expected economic sanctions to be levied, and he had heard rumors of Carter officials making "veiled threats against American companies operating in South Africa."[11]

Formulating the Anglo-American Proposals

Throughout the summer and early fall of 1977, Washington's goal in Rhodesia was, as Andrew Young told the Senate on June 6, "to maintain a kind of momentum that the first four months, in my opinion, has produced." This was complicated not only by events like the Rhodesian raid on Mapai, but also by the fact that, as Vance wrote Carter, "the two sides remain far apart."[12]

This was an understatement. There were many more than two sides, each with multiple constituencies, and they were very far apart indeed. Imagine a six-ring circus—Rhodesia, the Patriotic Front, the Frontline States, South Africa, Britain, and the United States—and imagine two circus masters, British and American, trying to persuade the acrobats in all six rings to trust each other and swing together. Now imagine that the circus is located in the earthquake zone that is being jolted by the aftershocks of the Angolan revolution. The Americans and British tried to cope by taking what they called "the salami approach," slicing the movement toward Rhodesian independence into the smallest possible steps and trying to persuade each of the parties to agree to just the next step.[13] Occasionally, they made progress, but it was fleeting and fragile.

The enormity of the challenge can be seen in the transcripts of Johnny Graham's and Steve Low's first meetings with the Rhodesians in Salisbury. That these two senior diplomats, one British and one American, agreed to travel to Salisbury to talk with Ian Smith was a diplomatic coup for the isolated leader of a regime that neither Britain nor the United States recognized. Yet if Graham or Low had expected gratitude, they were sorely disappointed. Their Rhodesian interlocutors were rigid, and every discussion landed in a dead end. The Rhodesians wanted guarantees for the whites, including restricted suffrage, pensions, and control during the transition period. Low and Graham stressed that suffrage had to be universal, that the US Congress would not underwrite pensions for Rhodesians, and that the details of the transition period would have to be negotiated. As Graham and Low departed, a member of Smith's government wrote that they were "nice chaps but [we were] glad to see the last of them."[14]

The talks occurred against the backdrop of the intensifying war. Salisbury, however, was cushioned from the horrors of the struggle roiling the countryside. "No capital city reflects the country as a whole and Salisbury less than most," an American diplomat cabled on a rare official visit to Rhodesia. "Whites in Salisbury know there is a war going on somewhere beyond the green hills that surround the town . . . [but] Salisbury sees little sign of the war." Nevertheless, the city was tense. "Beneath all this gleam and comfort and safety, there is real anxiety . . . among the whites of impending change, of an era coming to a close, of an anachronism about to be jerked up to date, and of decisions long-postponed that must soon be taken, if not today then maybe tomorrow."[15]

Throughout 1977, an increasing number of ZANU guerrillas—based in Mozambique—were establishing informal control over ever-larger areas of the Rhodesian countryside. Rhodesian officials retreated from rural areas, and basic services—schools, hospitals, local governments—collapsed. The government implemented a strategic hamlet policy, rounding up and moving rural Africans to "protected villages." By 1978, half a million black Rhodesians had been displaced. At the same time, the Soviet Union was shipping sophisticated weapons to ZAPU camps in Zambia. Deaths escalated dramatically. From 1973 through 1975, the estimated number of guerrillas killed was 502; in 1976, the toll climbed to 1,244; and in 1977 it rose to 1,774. (This does not include guerrillas killed in the raids on the Frontline States.) Although the "kill ratio" remained strongly in the Smith regime's favor, the trend line was ominous: in 1977, the guerrillas killed almost as many Rhodesian soldiers (195) as they had in the previous five years combined. Moreover, both wings of the Patriotic Front were tapping a seemingly inexhaustible supply of recruits, while the Rhodesian armed forces were stretched to their limit. All white, colored, and Asian Rhodesian men between the ages of eighteen and thirty-eight were drafted for more than half of every year; men up to the age of fifty served shorter periods, and men up to the age of sixty were expected to volunteer. (Until 1978, all blacks in the Rhodesian armed forces were volunteers.)[16]

In February 1977, the CIA had predicted that "the odds [in Rhodesia] favor the insurgents," and in November, the Agency noted succinctly, "The march toward a [Rhodesian] settlement . . . may be at an impasse. Each step in the process has created new complications and the numbers of participants and the differences among them have thwarted efforts to reach any basic understandings. . . . The search for common ground . . . may not only be impossible but impractical."[17] Among the myriad problems that the Carter administration faced while implementing its Rhodesia policy in the second half of 1977, two stand out: corralling the British and dealing with the South Africans.

Strains in the Special Relationship

For Washington and London, cooperating in Rhodesia carried mutual benefits. Britain was legally responsible for its renegade colony, but a decade of failure had gutted its credibility in the region. The power of the United States and the goodwill that the Carter administration had generated among black African leaders gave the British an essential boost in southern Africa. Carter's support also gave Prime Minister James Callaghan leverage at home when arguing with the opponents of his fragile coalition government. Washington, meanwhile, was able to cast its involvement in Rhodesia as aid to its close British ally rather than as superpower interference in southern Africa. In many ways, the cooperation between the two allies was remarkable. "I think that the American position and the British position are really very close . . . we are working together very well," Young reported in June. "But," he added, "there are all kinds of problems." The British were irritated by the Americans. "[It was] quite difficult dealing with the Carter administration on this issue," Robin Renwick, the head of the Foreign Office Rhodesia Department, noted.[18]

The fundamental difficulty was that London and Washington had different goals in Rhodesia. The Callaghan government wanted to wash its hands of a problem that had bedeviled British domestic, Commonwealth, and foreign affairs for more than a decade. Whitehall dreamed of a solution that created peace and prosperity in Zimbabwe, but it would settle for one that rendered the renegade colony independent and gave Britain a credible way to claim that it had discharged its duty honorably. The Carter administration, on the other hand, had two goals: it wanted to create stability in Rhodesia so that the Soviets would have no opening to extend their influence, and it wanted to manifestly do the right thing for both ideological and practical reasons. London confronted the Rhodesia problem as a jaded and exhausted metropole; it had dealt with all the players for years, and it had firm opinions about them all. Washington approached Rhodesia with enthusiasm and optimism; it was learning on the fly. Both countries chafed at having to take the other's views into account, but both knew that it was in their mutual interest to do so.

Many of the resulting tensions were minor and easily managed. Washington was peeved that London sent two of its diplomats to reside in Rhodesia, "despite," the NSC informed Brzezinski, "a last minute appeal from us" not to do so. The White House feared that this quasi-recognition would appear to be a tilt toward Smith, but it did not press the issue. Foreign Secretary David Owen urged Vance to agree to use the Zimbabwe Development Fund to cover the pensions of whites after independence—an issue that was important to the British public—but Vance resisted, and Owen gave up. During the summer of 1977, the Graham/Low group conferred extensively with all parties to develop the Anglo-American proposals for a negotiated settlement. "We would talk to every person who felt he or she had something to contribute," Low remembered. They discussed a new constitution and the mechanics of the transition to independence. In public, the two allies supported these nascent Anglo-American proposals wholeheartedly, but behind the scenes both tried to do end runs around them. This caused significant friction. [19]

Law and Order

Elections could determine the leader of Zimbabwe, but what armed forces would be at his command? The Rhodesian army or the Patriotic Front forces, or a combination of both? The answer to this question cut through the legalistic verbiage of the Anglo-American negotiations and forced the Americans and British to reveal their hand: who would have power in Zimbabwe after independence? This was the question that Ian Smith, Zambian president Kenneth Kaunda, Tanzanian president Julius Nyerere, and the Patriotic Front leaders asked the Americans and British. Who would enforce law and order during the transition period?

Washington and London tried to fudge the issue. In the early months, they talked of a Commonwealth force—three battalions of approximately 650 men each—that would patrol Rhodesia during the transition. The Patriotic Front guerrillas, Owen told Vance, "would remain alongside" the Commonwealth force, and the Rhodesian army would be disbanded, although its soldiers could join the new, combined force. The evolving Anglo-American plan envisioned a British resident commissioner who would govern Rhodesia during the transition to independence, and his major challenge would be forging a new army. Owen admitted that "the new Zimbabwean defense force would have as a major task to integrate the guerrilla elements." He did not explain when Smith's army would disband or what the "new Zimbabwean defense force" would be.[20]

Johnny Graham—the key British diplomat in southern Africa, and US Ambassador Low's counterpart—later explained that the British "had a good deal of experience with this kind of thing, with merging two armies, like in Oman [in the late 1950s]."[21] But Jimmy Carter found Owen's vagueness annoying. He considered it Whitehall's responsibility to figure out how to maintain law and order in what would be, once again, a compliant British colony. He decided in late June that while the United States would help with the logistics of the Commonwealth force, "no American forces" would join it.[22]

The plan suffered a debilitating defeat when, on July 7, 1977, Owen presented his proposal for a Commonwealth force to the British Cabinet. Fearing a quagmire, and loath to send any Britons into harm's way in Rhodesia, the Cabinet nixed the idea. An enormous hole was shot through the Anglo-American scheme. London's dilemma had not changed since the declaration of UDI in 1965: Britain was unwilling to use force to discipline Ian Smith. The British, Andrew Young complained, were "scared of a Vietnam-like situation and worried about money." The State Department concluded, "This means that law and order must either be maintained by the existing Rhodesian armed forces or taken over by the guerrilla fighters."[23]

On July 23, David Owen flew to Washington to meet with an impatient President Carter. Carter expressed his deep disappointment that Owen had failed to deliver on the promise of a Commonwealth force. Three times during the long and contentious meeting Carter vented his frustration, exclaiming, "We cannot allow the situation to drift. . . . We must get off dead center." Owen expressed the hope that "the US Government will agree not to give anything away to the Patriotic Front at this stage." He then returned to the need to provide guarantees for the whites, and Carter countered, "We will never be able to devise a solution that would please Rhodesian whites. An ultimatum from [South African Prime Minister] Vorster is the key to Smith's accepting a settlement proposal."[24]

This sentence—"We will never be able to devise a solution that would please Rhodesian whites"—opens a window on Carter's thinking at the time. He supported the proposals that the US and British diplomats were developing, but he did not expect any settlement to satisfy Ian Smith. Ultimately, Smith would have to be strong-armed to hand over power, just as the whites in the US South—including Carter's father and, to a certain extent, Jimmy Carter himself—had been strong-armed into accepting change. And their lives, Carter was convinced, were better for it. "I think the greatest thing that ever happened to the South was the passage of the civil rights act and the opening up of opportunities to black people," Carter had declared during the final presidential debate in 1976. "It not only liberated black people but it also liberated the whites."[25]

The Carter administration spent a great deal of time in the summer of 1977 developing lists of graduated pressures to put the squeeze on Smith. Most went through South Africa: "I believe we can get Vorster to put extreme pressure on Smith," Carter told Owen in July. This delusion, which informed Washington's policy that summer, would erode by the end of the year when it became clear that Vorster was not susceptible to American suasion and that efforts to impose penalties on Pretoria would incur costs, domestic and international, that the Carter administration was not willing to pay. But in August 1977, Carter was still optimistic that "extreme pressure" could be applied from two directions: Vorster would deliver Smith, and the Frontline presidents would deliver the Patriotic Front [26]

Against this backdrop, two weeks after meeting with Owen, Carter welcomed Tanzanian president Julius Nyerere to Washington on August 4. Even though it was the height of summer and Congress was in recess, the administration was on overdrive: at home, the energy program remained its priority; abroad, brokering Arab-Israeli peace, negotiating the Panama Canal treaties, finalizing the SALT II agreement with the Soviets, and seeking a peaceful settlement in Rhodesia absorbed the attention of the principals. The Somali army had invaded the Ogaden two weeks earlier, but the White House was more absorbed with southern African affairs than with the Horn.

Nyerere was the first head of state from sub-Saharan Africa to visit the Carter White House, and the timing was fortuitous. Carter feared that the Rhodesia negotiations were stalling, and he wanted Nyerere to help reinvigorate them. "Nyerere . . . is an introspective, intellectual Catholic . . . [with] warmth, eloquence [and] humor," Vance wrote Carter. "His honesty, dedication, intellectual leadership and considerable political skill . . . have given him a role in Africa and the Third World which Tanzania's circumstances would not otherwise warrant." The administration's immediate need was to persuade Nyerere to call a meeting of the Frontline presidents with Owen and Young to discuss the draft Anglo-American plan for Rhodesia. Vance stressed that the "difficult subject" of the draft plan was "the maintenance of law and order" during the transitional period. "You decided last weekend to take advantage of his [Nyerere's] presence to gain his support for our initiative on Rhodesia," Vance reminded the president. "He can be extremely helpful."[27]

Zbigniew Brzezinski was on vacation in the days preceding Nyerere's visit, leaving his deputy David Aaron in charge. The NSC Africa expert, Henry Richardson, an African American lawyer, drafted a briefing memo for the president and sent it to Aaron for approval. Richardson's analysis of the crisis in Rhodesia was similar to that of Young and the Africanists in the State Department. His six-page memo conveyed a thorough grasp of arcane issues and stressed that speed was of the essence. Borrowing Carter's phrase, he argued that it was time to "to move off dead center." Aaron summoned Richardson. "Henry, I have only one question for you," he said. "This guy who's coming next week, is he for us or against us?" Richardson replied: "David, he's for us." The briefing memo that the NSC sent to Carter over Brzezinski's signature was blunt. "We want something from Nyerere. . . . We desire an African solution in Rhodesia, and feel one must be negotiated at an early time."[28]

The British were on guard. Hours before Carter met with Nyerere, Prime Minister Callaghan sent him last-minute guidance. Effusive in his praise of Carter's "decisive involvement . . . [and] personal commitment" to resolving the crisis in Rhodesia, Callaghan mentioned the impossibility of determining at this stage "what scope there is for an arrangement between the Rhodesian defense forces and the liberation armies."[29] Carter brushed Callaghan's concerns aside. He was frustrated by Britain's failure to resolve the law-and-order problem. It was time to move.

In the first session with Nyerere, there was no small talk. The Tanzanian got to his point right away, and he never lost sight of it. "I do not believe in a multi-army [sic] system," he insisted. "Now, the problem is that we have two armies. One will have to go, and that is Smith's army. It cannot become the independence army, just as the French army could not become the independence army of Algeria." His question to the Americans—Carter, Mondale, Brzezinski, Young, and Christopher—was direct: "Who is the power during this interim period?" Carter dodged the question. Nyerere did not let it go: "The army is key! Which of the two armies is to be the base army? This is a serious question. . . . The Zimbabwean army must be the base army."[30]

Carter changed the subject. He asked Nyerere if he would call a meeting of the Frontline presidents to rally their support for the draft Anglo-American proposals and then press the Patriotic Front to the bargaining table. This was what Carter sought, and he anticipated a tough negotiation. "No problem," Nyerere responded. Carter had other requests: would Nyerere support elections? "All will accept elections," Nyerere promised, adding, "I will tell them to prove your popularity by helping us to shorten the war." Would he press the Patriotic Front to observe a cease-fire during the transition? "By all means," was the immediate reply. Carter told Nyerere he was "very encouraged" by these responses and that he looked forward to the dinner with Nyerere that night and to continuing the talks the next day.[31]

Nyerere had given the Americans a clear proposition: he would enthusiastically support every aspect of the Anglo-American proposals *if* the Patriotic Front controlled the Zimbabwean army after independence. Although there are only hints of the lively discussions that must have ensued after Nyerere left the room, their result is clear. In a memo written hours after the meeting, Brzezinski noted that "Dick Moose [the assistant secretary of state for Africa, who attended Carter's meeting with Nyerere] and I agree that we should make this concession [basing the army on the Patriotic Front forces] to Nyerere." He added that the promise "probably goes further than the British are prepared to go."[32]

After a working dinner with Nyerere that night, Carter escorted him to the more intimate quarters of the second-floor residence in the White House. There is no declassified record of their talk, which lasted for just over half an hour, but the following morning Carter opened the second formal meeting with Nyerere (with all the same attendees as at the first meeting) by summarizing what he and Nyerere had decided the night before. "I just want to reiterate the points we agreed on. . . . The settlement would be based on the principle of one person, one vote; majority rule, free elections during the interim period, [and] *one army built predominantly on the basis of the Patriotic Front* by the government emerging from the elections." Nyerere repeated, "The army is key." Carter concluded, with trenchant understatement, "The United Kingdom might have some qualms about some of our proposals."[33]

The British were livid. It was "dynamite," Owen declared in his memoirs: "President Carter came very close to destroying the whole initiative."[34] He thrust all the blame on Carter, while turning a blind eye to the significance of the British Cabinet's refusal to send troops or approve a Commonwealth force to keep the peace during the transition period. Owen was sure that neither Smith nor Vorster would ever accept an agreement that dismantled the Rhodesian security forces. Decades later, Owen still fumed about what he continued to see as Carter's inexcusable blunder. "Relations [with the Americans] were fine until this fateful meeting [with Nyerere]. I am convinced that the Anglo-American proposals could have worked without it."[35]

In his own memoirs, Vance implies that President Carter misstepped because he had not been well briefed. Carter, Vance writes, "was not as current on the issues or the nuances of the parties' positions [on Rhodesia in the summer of 1977] as he was with those of the Middle East or the SALT negotiations."[36] Perhaps Carter was bamboozled by the charming and wily president of Tanzania.

Perhaps. But Jimmy Carter was nothing if not deliberate. He had followed southern African issues closely, and it was no surprise that military matters arose in his meeting with Nyerere. As early as February 21, 1977—five months before the encounter with Nyerere—Carter had mentioned to Canadian prime minister Pierre Trudeau that "the major unresolved question [in the Rhodesia negotiations] . . . is who will control defense and the police."[37] This question had been the central focus of Carter's talks with David Owen. Weeks before Nyerere arrived in Washington, Young had explained that the maintenance of law and order would be "an important subject" in the talks with Nyerere. Carter was a military man. It is likely that he understood exactly what he was doing.[38]

Vance writes in his memoirs that Assistant Secretary Dick Moose and the Africa experts present at the meeting (Vance was in Syria) were "dismay[ed]" at Carter's pledge. The documentary evidence indicates otherwise. Owen was convinced that Moose was behind it all, persuading Carter (in Vance's absence) that this was the only way to push "the fuddy-duddy Brits" into action. "I love Dick," Owen said, "but he did it." Six months after Carter's fateful encounter with Nyerere, Owen was still complaining about it to Vance. The Foreign Office reported that Vance "paid very careful attention. He had clearly not understood beforehand the extent of our irritation over the lack of consultation on 'based on the liberation forces' and *appeared quite shocked that we had not known in advance*."[39]

Carter was impatient. He wanted, as he had said three times in the meeting with Owen, "to get off dead center." The British could wrangle forever trying to come up with, as Callaghan had written, "an arrangement between the Rhodesian defense forces and the liberation armies."[40] It had not led to success, and it was unlikely to do so. Therefore, Carter tilted toward the nationalists; they represented the black majority, and the United States needed to gain their trust. What the United States wanted to do was end the war, and the war would not end until the Patriotic Front put down its guns. The nationalists would not put down their guns until they were confident that their forces would be in charge after independence. That was what they were fighting for. For Jimmy Carter, ending the war was a Cold War imperative, not a feel-good exercise. The settlement in Rhodesia could not be a balanced negotiation: the whites would have to accept a negotiated surrender. This was the inevitable result of majority rule. No one could be sure who would win democratic elections in Rhodesia, but it was obvious that the white minority would no longer wield power and the new army would have to reflect this reality. Carter had empathy for the whites: he believed that he not only *could* walk a mile in their shoes, but that he already had, in his own lifetime in the US South. He was not oblivious to the profound differences between the two situations, but in this case he was guided by his gut. He believed that change in Zimbabwe would be painful for the whites, but it would be good: the US South, Carter was convinced, had been reborn and invigorated by the civil rights movement. Everyone had benefited, just as all Rhodesians—black and white—would benefit from a more just and democratic political system.

It is possible that Carter did not understand the significance of the promise he offered Nyerere, but given his attention to detail and his interest in southern African affairs, this is unlikely. If Carter's pledge was deliberate, as the evidence indicates, his vision of the future of Zimbabwe had the Patriotic Front in charge.

London swallowed hard after Carter's unexpected pledge to Nyerere. Carter wrote a three-page, single-spaced letter to Prime Minister Callaghan describing the encounter which had gone, he said, "extremely well." After pleasantries, Carter declared: "Of all the points which he made, Nyerere placed greatest stress on the creation of a new Zimbabwe army. . . . In his view the new army must be based predominantly on the forces of the Patriotic Front." Carter then thanked Callaghan for his government's "unfailing cooperation" in this "formidable" endeavor.[41]

The British got a sense of just how formidable the task would be when Owen met Nyerere on August 13, nine days after Carter had made his promise. Nyerere insisted that by agreeing that the Zimbabwean army would be "based predominantly on the liberation forces," Carter had pledged that the Rhodesian army would be dissolved as soon as the transition period began. "Mr. Smith's army must go," Nyerere asserted. "It could not be the army of independent Zimbabwe. President Carter had told him that this posed no problem. . . . He [Nyerere] had said very clearly both to President Carter and to Mr Vance that the Smith army must be 'out' during the transitional period." If he could not rely on President Carter's statement, the deal was off: Nyerere would not urge the other Frontline presidents and the Patriotic Front to support the Anglo-American proposals.[42]

"My spirits were somewhat dampened by a subsequent discussion with Dr. Owen," Nyerere wrote Carter. "I have since received a message from Mr. Callaghan, the result of which is to confirm my worry about British intentions concerning the Smith Army and the future of forces of the Patriotic Front."[43] Nyerere's concerns were well founded: London was engaged in its own freewheeling diplomacy.

Tilt toward Nkomo

The British and Americans disagreed about more than how to maintain law and order during the transition; they also debated how best to select the new leader of Zimbabwe. From the time that Prime Minister Callaghan and President Carter first met in March 1977, it was clear that the British were open to the idea of moving Rhodesia to independence via negotiations that did not include free elections.[44] The Carter administration, however, feared that anything short of a transparent democratic process would not stop the war. This difference in viewpoints helps to explain the differing British and American attitudes toward the possibility that Smith would develop an "internal" settlement as an alternative to the "external" Anglo-American settlement that, in his view, would be foisted on the Rhodesian people. Ever since January 1977, when Smith had announced he was withdrawing from the Geneva talks and opening discussions with "responsible" blacks, he had been angling to devise a system that would give blacks some power while preserving white privilege.

Smith's talk moved beyond the theoretical on July 18, when he announced in a speech to the Rhodesian people that "last week we were informed [by the British and Americans] that there was no hope of anything other than one man, one vote" in the draft Anglo-American proposals. "It was absolutely clear to us that the Patriotic Front were calling the tune," Smith explained. This "surrender," which would "betray those principles for which so many sacrifices have been made," was "completely unacceptable." Nonetheless, Smith continued, the white Rhodesians who refused to accept any change were "out of touch" and advocating a course that would lead to "disaster." Smith proposed a "road between these two extremes": an internal solution. The details were unclear, but Smith promised a general election (in which very few blacks would be allowed to vote) on August 31, 1977 as the first step toward creating "a broad-based government, incorporating those black Rhodesians who are prepared to work peacefully and constitutionally with Government . . . to draw up our future constitution." He called on white Rhodesians to unite and give him a clear mandate in the upcoming election to proceed with this plan. This was, he assured his war-weary listeners, "the final lap of our settlement marathon."[45]

Earlier in the year, the *Rhodesian Herald* had declared Smith's objectives "laudable" but his methods "vague." After listing all the hurdles that Smith would face, it concluded that the internal settlement was a "tall order—almost an act of desperation." It noted that there were two black leaders with whom Smith "would be happy to negotiate": Abel Muzorewa and Ndabaningi Sithole.[46]

Abel Muzorewa, a dapper Methodist bishop who had studied in Tennessee and Missouri, had been thrust to the forefront of the nationalist struggle in the early 1970s when ZAPU leader Joshua Nkomo was enduring his decade-long imprisonment in Smith's jails. When Nkomo was released in 1974, the two men vied for leadership of the nationalist movement. By late 1976, it was clear that Nkomo had won the struggle, and Muzorewa was marginalized—an erstwhile leader with no troops.[47]

Ndabaningi Sithole was in a similar position. A Methodist minister who had founded ZANU in 1963, Sithole had been another of the nationalists incarcerated from 1964 to 1974. While in detention, he was convicted of plotting the assassination of Ian Smith, but at trial he publicly renounced violence. Many nationalists never forgave him, and, after he was released in 1974 his leadership of ZANU was challenged. The emergence of Robert Mugabe as ZANU's leader in late 1976 meant that Sithole was cast aside. As British Ambassador Graham said, "Sithole had turned his coat too many times." Like Muzorewa, he commanded no troops. Both men were ripe for Smith's picking.[48]

Almost all Carter administration officials wanted to steer clear of any internal settlement. For the principals—Carter, Vance, and Brzezinski—the reason was pragmatic: they did not think that any settlement that excluded the guerrillas would end the war. "Our longer term objective is to create positive relationships with the African countries," Brzezinski wrote Carter on July 22, 1977. "From a practical point of view, an internal solution would probably not endure," and a continuing war would create an opening for the Soviets to support "the extremists." In conclusion, Brzezinski wrote, "we do not wish an internal solution." In the unlikely event that the leaders of the Patriotic Front accepted an internal settlement and laid down their arms, the Carter administration would support it. Therefore, although Carter, Vance, and Brzezinski did not reject an internal settlement in principle, they set the bar so high as to be virtually unattainable.[49]

For the British, the bar was lower. Many Foreign Office officials hoped to shepherd into existence an independent Zimbabwe governed by Joshua Nkomo, the Rhodesian leader they had long preferred. "We did think Nkomo was the best bet," Graham later acknowledged. The British hoped to persuade Nkomo to join in an internal settlement with Smith, Muzorewa, and Sithole. Because this would leave ZANU leader Mugabe (who controlled the vast majority of armed guerrillas) in the cold, it was unlikely to stop the war, but it might create space for Britain to discharge, at long last, its legal responsibilities to Rhodesia.[50]

Joshua Nkomo was an enormous man, a back-slapping *bon vivant*. After his release from prison, he spent much of his time traveling abroad to drum up support for ZAPU, staying in luxury hotels and savoring the good life. David Owen voiced the opinion of many British officials when he told Carter, "You feel you can do a deal with Nkomo."[51]

There were several problems, however, with the idea of doing a deal with Nkomo. First, although he had an illustrious past as a nationalist leader, Nkomo was losing power and authority to Mugabe, whose ZANU troops were leading the war against the Smith regime. The British had been aware of this for at least a year. In June 1976, Prime Minister Callaghan had told Henry Kissinger, "Nkomo had recently been losing ground." In the same month, the head of the Foreign Office's Rhodesia Department reported that Nkomo was "despondent" and in danger of being relegated to "the sidelines as an impotent, embittered observer."[52]

Moreover, Nkomo was a complex man. British ambassador Johnny Graham, who had extensive contact with him, remembered Nkomo as "generally a very pleasant fellow to deal with, but extremely volatile: He was like a pan of milk—all of a sudden he would boil up, and then, just as suddenly, subside." Nkomo relied on the Soviet Union for almost all of his guerrillas' weapons and on the Cubans for military training, and he had good relations with the Soviet and Cuban leaders. His anti-Western rhetoric could be as harsh as his appreciation of things Western was heartfelt. Graham's American counterpart, Steve Low, also knew Nkomo well: "He was not a communist! But he knew what side his bread was buttered on, and he said what he had to say to keep getting Soviet weapons." It is a measure of Nkomo's plasticity that he was both Moscow's protégé and South African Prime Minister Vorster's top choice to lead an independent Zimbabwe. Nkomo's great strength was his ability to move between these worlds, convincing all sides that they were the true objects of his affection and that his truck with the others was purely tactical. As one journalist wrote, "Nkomo could have breakfast at the Kremlin, lunch in the Lonrho boardroom [a British conglomerate that helped finance his travels—and was also close to Ian Smith], and dinner at the White House in the same day."[53]

On July 19, 1977, one day after Smith announced elections to endorse the idea of an internal settlement, the British told the Americans that they were considering a scheme that would grant Rhodesia independence *before* elections. They would hold a referendum on a draft constitution, and if it gained support from a majority of all Rhodesians, they would immediately grant independence to an interim government that would hold elections when the situation was stable. "Nkomo would have to be the leader of such a government," they explained, adding that it would not include Mugabe. The State Department commented that this "would be difficult to achieve," and the Policy Review Committee noted that "British objectives are ambiguous."[54]

The subject came up during Owen's July 23 meeting with Carter. "Nkomo wants an election, but he wants to win it, or you might say, to rig it," Owen explained, and added, "We have some sympathy for his position." Carter's response was categorical: "We cannot agree to install Nkomo by fiat, no matter how much African support he might have." Carter's reasoning was pragmatic—installing Nkomo would not stop the war—though it was reinforced by sentiment. Owen, Carter observed, "thought more of Nkomo than Vance did. . . . Nkomo made a very bad impression on Cy." Deputy National Security Adviser David Aaron summed up why Washington "wasn't too hot on Nkomo: he was massively corrupt." Vance was not reassured by a second encounter with Nkomo in July, when the ZAPU leader ignored the Americans and "obviously saw the meeting as a discussion between himself and the British." Carter mused, "My guess is that Nkomo would lose [elections in Zimbabwe]." Carter pursued this line of thought in the conversation with Owen: "There is some hesitation about Nkomo in the United States."[55]

Four days later, Nkomo was at 10 Downing Street, talking with Prime Minister Callaghan. He was not pliant. Callaghan averred that "the best solution would be if he [Nkomo] and Bishop Muzorewa were to agree to work together for the future of Zimbabwe." Nkomo, who had a long and stormy history with the bishop, said flatly that cooperating with Muzorewa would be impossible because "he could not deal with liars."[56]

In less than a fortnight, however, Owen had brushed aside Nkomo's reservations. "We believe that Nkomo . . . would be prepared, if necessary, to break with Mugabe," Owen told South African foreign minister Pik Botha on August 12. "This is a development we [the British and South Africans] should wish to encourage. We have made it plain to Nkomo that we would like him to reach some form of accommodation with Muzorewa and/or Sithole."[57]

Smith won the Rhodesian elections in a landslide on August 31, and he interpreted the result as a mandate to pursue an internal settlement. In his victory speech, he lambasted the proposals that the British and Americans had been circulating all summer, calling them "a very cunning scheme to insure that the Patriotic Front will be the next government of Rhodesia." Smith found himself in rare agreement with Mugabe, who also heaped scorn on the proposals, albeit for different reasons. They were, in the ZANU leader's opinion, Britain's attempt to create a "neo-colonial state" in Zimbabwe.[58]

It was at this point, on September 1, 1977, that the faltering Anglo-American proposals were published and presented to the British Parliament. The plan was still a work in progress—the negotiations were ongoing—but its three-step outline was set: a new constitution, a transition period of direct British rule, and free elections. The road to independence would begin with—in a phrase that enraged the Rhodesians—"the surrender of power by the illegal regime and a return to legality." A caretaker British commissioner would govern for a three- to six-month transition stage, during which time a cease-fire would be called, UN sanctions would be lifted, a new Zimbabwe Army would be formed, and democratic elections based on universal suffrage would be held. The victor of these elections would become the first leader of an independent Zimbabwe. A development fund of $1 billion to $1.5 billion would be established "for the economic stability and development of an independent Zimbabwe." (The Carter administration was confident the US Congress, once it was convinced that Zimbabwe was going to gain independence, would allocate money to the fund.) The British and Americans hoped that this path to independence would be so "manifestly fair" that any party that refused to accept it would be exposed as unreasonable.[59]

These proposals would be fine-tuned and debated for more than two years, but they endured to form the basis of the eventual independence settlement. They marked a clear shift from the Kissinger plan: the new proposals would be the result of transparent negotiations between all the parties, they would not be hurriedly imposed by any outside party, and all the details were open to debate. This meant that the plan would not be built on sand, but it also invited carping and bitter argument between the parties, which would prolong the process. Although the specifics were still being negotiated, it was clear that the new plan would offer less protection for white privilege than had Kissinger's scheme. Also, in a departure from Kissinger's *modus operandi*, the negotiations undertaken during the Carter administration included the black Africans—the Patriotic Front and the Frontline States—as equal partners.

When Owen submitted the proposals to the Cabinet, American and British diplomats were gathering votes at the UN Security Council to ensure passage of a resolution appointing a UN representative to help implement the Anglo-American proposals. On September 19, Assistant Secretary Richard Moose and Policy Planning Staff director Anthony Lake declared that "the Rhodesian settlement effort is at a critical juncture."[60]

David Owen's Gambit, First Try

On the surface, Anglo-American cooperation in Rhodesia was going swimmingly. In late August, David Owen and Andrew Young went on their first joint tour through southern Africa. Young was "euphoric" about his relationship with Owen, while Owen cabled London that "Andy Young is a delight. . . . Very easy and extremely effective." Owen went on to note that the British members of the team had been a steadying influence on the Americans. "Certainly our people's caution has stopped some of the wilder aspects of US thinking on Africa." His cable then became cryptic. "It was probably always going to be very difficult but the decision is now made." Referring back to

Carter's August meeting with Nyerere, Owen wrote, "In its way, the crunch was 'based on liberation forces'." The final sentence is ominous: "But it goes deeper than that."[61]

Owen was secretly doing an end run around the Anglo-American proposals. He was trying to facilitate a deal between Smith and Nkomo that would bypass the arduous negotiations and declare Nkomo leader of an independent, moderate Zimbabwe. On September 25, Tiny Rowland, a British wheeler-dealer who had amassed a fortune in various businesses throughout Africa, especially in Rhodesia, secretly arranged for Ian Smith to fly to Lusaka. In strict confidence, Smith met with President Kaunda and Joshua Nkomo. The purpose of the encounter was to bring Nkomo back to Rhodesia to lead what Smith called a "government of national unity." For Smith, this could be the best possible outcome.[62]

Kaunda wanted the meeting because he feared that both alternatives—escalating guerrilla war, and the Anglo-American proposals—were likely to lead to civil war between ZANU and ZAPU. He hoped that a direct transfer of power to Nkomo—whom he had known since the 1950s and whose troops he had long protected—could avert "major violence" and lead to a government of "national unity."[63] When asked in 2009 about his role in this meeting that could place Joshua Nkomo in charge, Kaunda stressed, counterintuitively, that he had not been trying to split the Patriotic Front. "For the Rhodesia thing to be settled, you could not afford to think of Nkomo and Mugabe, the two parties, separating," he explained. "It would not work. At all. No way. No way. It would be introducing a civil war." He said he simply believed in talking to one's opponents. "There was no harm in the two [Smith and Nkomo] meeting," he explained. "No harm."[64]

Ambassador Steve Low, the lead US negotiator on the ground in southern Africa, disagreed. The initiative had "real pitfalls," he commented in a cable written in the aftermath of Nkomo's meeting with Smith. "Smith is devious and clever enough to lead us along toward . . . taking steps which would make it appear that we were favoring him." Low had been working closely with the Foreign Office in London all year. "The British have, from the beginning, been tempted by a manipulative approach. Whenever we have run into a road-block they have wanted to turn to the idea of selecting a leader and trying to impose him on the situation. Fortunately or unfortunately, the day has passed when either they or we have the power to do such a thing. An attempt to do so will only backfire." Low wanted to stick with the Anglo-American plan. "We may not like some of the ZANU leaders or their ideas but in our view they are less dangerous included in the process . . . than excluded from it. . . . Trying to split ZAPU and ZANU does not serve our interests; it will increase suspicion of our motives; and it is likely to backfire against us."[65]

The meeting between Smith, Kaunda, and Nkomo bore no fruit—there was no deal—but as Low predicted, it had consequences. It deepened Kaunda's skepticism that Smith would ever step down. "We are back to square one," he reportedly declared.[66] When word of the encounter between Smith and Kaunda (Nkomo's presence was a closely guarded secret) leaked, Mugabe's doubts about Kaunda's trustworthiness intensified. The Zambian government quickly released a statement explaining that Smith had asked Kaunda if he could talk with him, "and President Kaunda, as a humanist who always seeks peace, could not stop Smith from coming to see him in a hope that Smith, in desperation, might have some constructive ideas." Mugabe, however, feared this was far from the full story; he suspected but could not confirm that Nkomo had also been present. Old suspicions resurfaced with a vengeance. As Field Marshal Lord Carver, who was slated to become the resident commissioner in Rhodesia if the Anglo-American proposals were implemented, noted, "the solidarity of the Front Line Presidents was put at risk" by the meeting, "and the already fragile unity of the Patriotic Front was severely tested."[67] Moreover, the secret meeting outraged the Americans, who had not been informed about it. There was a slow burn in Washington as details emerged about the British gambit, which hit the press on October 1.[68]

Three weeks after Smith flew to Lusaka, the Carter administration reacted. Vigorously.

After reading "new reports of secret contacts between Ian Smith and Joshua Nkomo," Vance told Carter that he had told Assistant Secretary Moose to fly forthwith to London. "He [Moose] will tell David Owen that we feel very strongly that we must stick to the Anglo-American proposals . . . as originally envisioned and agreed upon. From the very outset . . . we have all agreed that our objective should be an open election based on universal suffrage with all contenders competing on an equal basis. For us to do anything which would appear to give Nkomo a preeminent role would risk driving Muzorewa and Sithole into a deal with Smith, exacerbate the already existing strains between Nkomo and Mugabe and lead almost certainly to continued civil strife." After clearly stating US policy, Vance turned to his disquiet about the partnership with Britain. "We find it hard to believe that David [Owen] would seriously consider abandoning our agreed plan, but we remain concerned by his apparent attraction to the idea, which we believe is illusory, that a Smith and Nkomo deal offers an easy solution. In any event, it is best to clear the air before the matter goes any further." In the margin, Carter wrote, "Good."[69]

Vance also wrote a personal letter to Owen. Sandwiched between the warm salutations was iron. He brought the full weight of the presidency of the United States to bear. "Both President Carter and I believe that the surest route to a successful transition is with proposals which will be universally recognized as fair and reasonable. . . . We believe that great care must be taken to avoid allowing any individual to be or to appear to be singled out for preferential treatment which would give him an inside track in the election. Moreover, we believe that we must adhere fully to the President's undertaking to President Nyerere, regarding the future Zimbabwe army." In case Owen had not fully understood who was in charge, Vance added the courteously devastating sentence: "I am glad that you want to be closely involved in the coming round of talks."[70]

Three days later, Vance reported to Carter that Moose's conversation with Owen had been "tough and frank." After Moose's "strenuous critique," the British foreign secretary had backtracked fast, stressing "his commitment to cooperate with us, to treating the Nationalists equally and he disclaimed any interest in dealing unilaterally with Joshua Nkomo." Carter was pleased. "All good," he wrote in the margin of Vance's report.[71]

The contretemps between Vance and Owen, which was never reported in the press, revealed an instance when Washington treated London as its junior partner in Rhodesia. The US ambassador in Tanzania summed up the Carter administration's role: "As Nyerere, hand-on-shoulder, enjoined Moose during visit here, [we must] play our essential role in 'keeping [the] British honest.'"[72]

South Africa and the Complexity of Sanctions

Corralling their wayward partner was not the Americans' only concern. As Moose flew to London in mid-October, the Carter administration was at a crossroads in its policy toward South Africa. The future of Pretoria's cooperation with the Anglo-American plan for Rhodesia was at stake.

The October crisis had deep roots. The Africa hands in the administration had been debating ways to apply pressure on South Africa ever since Jimmy Carter had been inaugurated. There was enthusiasm within the administration—at the highest level—for tightening the screws on Pretoria. The broad outlines of the policy were clear: condemn apartheid while at the same time securing South Africa's help in resolving the crises in Rhodesia and Namibia. Vice President Mondale's meeting with Prime Minister Vorster had been the opening salvo, but it was followed by a fierce debate about what steps to take next.

There were four fundamental dilemmas. First, to gain the confidence of black Africa, the administration had to condemn apartheid, and not just with words. The Anglo-American plan for Rhodesia, however, depended on Pretoria's delivering Ian Smith. In President Kaunda's phrase, it was South Africa that would "bell the cat."[73] Washington therefore had to calibrate its pressure against the apartheid state very carefully: enough to satisfy black Africa, but not so much as to alienate Pretoria.

Second, the evolving situation on the ground in southern Africa changed the equation for Pretoria. Whereas Vorster had been eager to help Kissinger put the squeeze on Smith in 1976, he drew back in 1977. The failure of the Geneva conference not only increased South Africa's skepticism about the likelihood of a negotiated solution; it also gave rise to Smith's announcement that he sought an "internal settlement" bringing blacks into his government. From Pretoria's point of view, this proposed internal settlement could be the answer to its Rhodesia problem, paving the way toward a moderate black government with international recognition. Therefore, in 1977, the Carter administration faced a less pliant Pretoria than had Kissinger. Instead of wanted to oust Smith, it wanted, as US ambassador Bill Bowdler cabled, "to shore up Smith in the hope he can work out some kind of internal settlement."[74]

Third, the Cold War. The Angolan crisis had shown that chaos and civil war provided an opening for the Soviet Union (and Cuba). This was why the Carter administration placed such high priority on achieving negotiated settlements in Rhodesia and Namibia. But South Africa itself was where the most dangerous civil war could erupt, in a cataclysmic struggle against apartheid. To avoid this nightmare, the Carter administration was convinced that the government in Pretoria had to reform apartheid and eventually eliminate it. This reform, however, would shake the foundations of the most anticommunist country in the region, which in turn could precipitate the very chaos that the Carter administration sought to deflect. Once again, Washington had to calibrate its pressure against the apartheid state, applying just enough force to induce Vorster to reform but not so much as to tip South Africa into chaos.

Fourth, race and domestic politics. Carter needed to be wary of the rising conservative chorus that pilloried him as a naive, crusading liberal who was more interested in human rights and currying favor in the Third World than in protecting American citizens from Soviet communism. Again, he had to calibrate his administration's pressure against the apartheid state very carefully: enough to bolster his liberal Democratic base, but not so much as to swell the ranks of his domestic critics.

In addition to these dilemmas, there was one major complication: to be effective, the United States could not act alone. Unilateral sanctions packed only a symbolic punch. Therefore, while Washington contemplated a range of unilateral actions, the real pressure would have to come from multilateral action at the United Nations. However, Washington's Western allies with veto power at the UN Security Council—London and Paris—balked at mandatory sanctions, not because they wanted to protect apartheid but because they wanted to protect their own economies. This was because mandatory sanctions of any stripe would open the door to mandatory economic sanctions. According to chapter 7 of the UN Charter, the Security Council could impose mandatory sanctions only if it determined that there was a "threat to peace." Once the Security Council had determined that apartheid was a threat to peace—in order, for example, to impose an arms embargo on South Africa—the foundation would be laid to extend this to sweeping mandatory economic sanctions. For Britain and to a lesser extent France, cutting off trade with South Africa would grievously weaken their economies, which were already mired in deep recession. Thus, mandatory UN sanctions of any type on South Africa were a slippery slope that Whitehall was determined to avoid. Prime Minister Callaghan had been blunt about this when talking with Vice President Mondale in May 1977. "The British are very nervous about our new policy," Mondale reported to Carter. "The Prime Minister emphasized to me that he was not proud of the fact, but he had to look to their [the British people's] interests, rather than their principles."[75]

The Western allies had narrowly ducked the issue in March when Andrew Young had persuaded the African Group at the UN to withdraw its resolutions calling for mandatory sanctions on South Africa.[76] But Whitehall remained worried. David Owen warned the British Cabinet that Washington was "producing . . . 'alarming resolutions' on South Africa including a suggestion that Britain actually be asked to introduce economic sanctions." The impact of losing trade with South Africa would cause the "immediate loss of 75,000 jobs . . . [and] be crippling to British industry," he told the Cabinet in late June.[77]

Nevertheless, in the wake of Mondale's meeting with Vorster, the Carter administration appeared to be leaning toward mandatory sanctions. The State Department asserted boldly that although "we shall have to consider the views of our traditional allies . . . we are prepared to act unilaterally." On July 5, Don Petterson, director of the southern Africa office at the State Department, told the British that the Carter administration had decided that Kissinger's policy toward South Africa—"to hope for evolutionary change"—must be firmly rejected. "It was not acceptable to wait for evolutionary change which was never going to occur. Instead President Carter had taken a decision to embark on a policy of active involvement to bring about a fundamental transformation of society in South Africa. . . . If the South Africans did not show evidence of change 'within a year' there would be consequences." Later that day, the British warned the West Germans about the danger that the United States would push for sanctions against South Africa, and grumbled that "the Americans are inclined to think that their own experience with race relations is relevant to South Africa."[78]

Two weeks later, however, the Carter administration retreated. The preparatory notes for the Policy Review Committee on July 22 began with the sober observation that although Mondale's meeting with Vorster had given the administration "credibility in Black Africa," the response of South Africa's leaders "had been strongly negative." The committee debated a spectrum of measures to express Washington's displeasure with Pretoria. It acknowledged that minor steps, such as closing a missile tracking station, would be meaningless, while the most significant action—mandatory UN economic sanctions—would be vetoed by Britain and France. The conclusion of the discussion was anticlimactic: "it was decided that now was the time to begin taking smaller steps." To start, Washington would tighten "grey area" sales to the South African police. (The grey area included items, such as tear gas, that were not covered by the UN voluntary arms embargo first enacted in 1963.) The administration also decided to encourage US companies doing business in South Africa to uphold the "Sullivan principles," a code of conduct that promoted corporate social responsibility to improve the lot of black workers. Quietly, the administration was talking with Iran, which supplied 90 percent of South Africa's oil, about using this avenue to put pressure on Pretoria. A fortnight later, Policy Planning Staff director Anthony Lake wrote Warren Christopher that the review of US economic ties with South Africa was complete: "We have a clear idea of steps that might be taken. We simply do not wish to begin them now."[79]

The exuberance of the first PRC meeting on southern Africa, held just five months earlier, had been tempered. Then, the administration had vowed to pressure South Africa simultaneously on three fronts: seeking its help with Rhodesia and in Namibia while at the same time condemning apartheid. In May, Mondale had skewered Vorster. But instead of loosening the rules of apartheid, the South Africans had cracked down at home and cranked up their rhetoric abroad. "Increased sanctions," Pik Botha threatened in the course of a contentious conversation with Vance and Owen in August 1977, "would mean war in southern Africa."[80]

Nuclear Anxieties

On August 6, the day after the talks with Nyerere ended, Carter received a note from Soviet general secretary Leonid Brezhnev about a matter "of quite considerable importance . . . to the development of the international situation and furtherance of detente." The Soviets had detected signs that South Africa was preparing to test a nuclear weapon in the Kalahari Desert. A US spy satellite confirmed the Soviet report. This "nuclear problem," as Vance called it, changed the equation. A nuclear South Africa would threaten the entire region.[81]

The discovery, however, was not entirely unexpected in Washington. In May, before Mondale met Vorster, the State Department had observed that "the political and psychological climate in South Africa would support the development of nuclear weapons." The analysis explained Pretoria's possible motivation: "Its sense of isolation and insecurity has been intensified by the shrinking of its buffer areas, concern over Rhodesia, uncertainty about the intentions of the new US administration, and apprehension about relations with the West generally. The convergence of these concerns has heightened Pretoria's fear that it may have to 'go it alone.'"[82]

For Washington, the immediate priorities were to persuade Pretoria to refrain from testing a nuclear device and to sign the Non-Proliferation Treaty, which mandated international inspection of nuclear facilities. The US ambassador in Pretoria met with Foreign Minister Pik Botha to convey a stern message from Carter: "Any further steps to acquire or develop a nuclear explosive capability would have the most serious consequences for all aspects of our relations and would be considered by us as *a serious threat to the peace*." By invoking the language of the UN charter's Chapter 7, Washington signaled that it would vote to support mandatory sanctions. The meeting of the US ambassador and the South African foreign minister was "stormy," according to British accounts.[83]

Vorster's reply to the Americans was "extremely sharp," Vance told Carter. The South African prime minister decried the US message as "unacceptable," and warned that "if you persist in this course, then I see grave consequences in our relations." He flatly rejected the American allegation that South Africa was preparing to test a nuclear weapon, but he then gave Washington what the State Department deemed "some dubious assurances" that it was not developing a bomb, and "basically told us to mind our own business."[84]

The Carter administration wanted to lower the temperature. On August 23, President Carter began a news conference with the announcement that "South Africa has informed us that no nuclear explosive test will be taken in South Africa now or in the future. . . . We will, of course, continue to monitor the situation there very closely." But in a defiant speech the next day, Prime Minister Vorster vented his outrage at the world's unfounded accusations and "discrimination against South Africa." He concluded his address to his party congress in Cape Town with a threat: "If these things continue . . . the time will arrive when South Africa will have no option . . . [but] to say to the world: So far and no further, do your damndest [*sic*] if you so wish." The crowd of National Party supporters burst into thunderous applause.[85]

Vorster was lying about his government's nuclear program. In 1974, South Africa had decided to build a bomb, and it had sped up its plans after the 1976

Soweto riots. The South African government had guarded the secret closely to avoid international opprobrium and its fruit: mandatory economic sanctions. Pretoria might have closed down the Kalahari site after it was exposed, but it did not cease its nuclear weapons program, and the Americans knew it. "Vorster has publicly lied about his assurances to the President," David Aaron wrote Zbigniew Brzezinski on November 11.[86]

The revelation of the test site, however, may have been part of a complicated and calculated diplomatic gamble. A top secret US assessment noted that "the South Africans may well have wanted the [Kalahari] site to be discovered."[87] Vorster, after the meeting with Mondale, had faced the grim fact that Pretoria had lost its most significant leverage in Washington: being the region's anti-communist bastion no longer excused apartheid. The Carter administration had turned the security question on its head: it believed that, rather than containing communism, the South African government invited communist expansion because of its racist policies. The nuclear threat helped Pretoria redress the balance and gain new leverage in Washington.[88]

This, however, was a most dangerous game. Played badly, it could lead to mandatory economic sanctions.[89] South Africa therefore vehemently denied the existence of the program and simultaneously sought to remove another tripwire to UN sanctions, its military support of the illegal Smith regime in Rhodesia. On September 5, General Magnus Malan, chief of the South African Defence Force, met with his Rhodesian counterpart Lt. General Peter Walls to demand that the Rhodesians immediately "eliminate any incriminating documentary evidence of the RSA's [Republic of South Africa's] military involvement in Rhodesia." He also ordered that all future correspondence about military cooperation between South Africa and Rhodesia "be kept to an absolute minimum . . . [and] no further documents are to be held in Rhodesia." Malan's motivation was straightforward: "At present the RSA is under tremendous political pressure and threats of sanctions from the Western nations. . . . Any sanctions . . . on the RSA would naturally also have a direct effect on Rhodesia and it is, therefore, in both our interests that everything must be done to eliminate any written evidence which could be use [sic] as a lever to get sanctions applied against the RSA." Malan barked: "The urgency of the matter cannot be overstressed." It was "imperative" that the documents be destroyed by September 30, 1977. Then, he flashed his weapon: "Unless and until I have satisfied myself that this has in fact been done, it is impossible for me to continue to supply further military support."[90]

Walls was alarmed, and immediately wrote to Smith, drawing the prime minister's attention to Malan's threat. "This sentence, I am sure you will agree, is of great significance to us." The problem was that it would be impossible to destroy all the relevant documents by the requested date. The South Africans had temporarily paused their military aid to Smith during Kissinger's initiative, but since then they had resumed it with a vengeance, sending new French Alouette 3 helicopters, 105mm recoilless rifles, mortars, and 5.5 howitzers, and promising twelve Mirage jets. "There is reference to it [South Africa's military cooperation with Rhodesia] on practically every file in Security Force registries, on many files in Ministries, and in the minutes of various committees, such as War Council, OCC [Operations Coordinating Committee], etc.," Walls explained to Smith. Malan's demand was so outrageous that Walls wondered "if this is an excuse to cut off further supplies."[91]

While the South Africans worried about sanctions, in the wake of the Kalahari incident the Carter administration backed further away from them. The CIA warned that the only immediate effect of sanctions would be to antagonize Pretoria: "It is our judgment . . . that the impact of sanctions, even under the most optimistic assumptions about the universality of application, would not be felt for at least a year." The Defense Intelligence Agency added that they "would escalate an already precarious situation." Riling the South African leaders seemed unwise while Washington was trying to persuade them to sign the NPT. The intelligence community recommended that, rather than wield a feeble stick, the administration dangle a carrot: "South Africa's leaders . . . might be persuaded to delay a scheduled test for a short period if there were indications that a major turnaround in US policy towards South Africa was possible."[92]

As nuclear anxieties swelled in Washington in late August 1977, Owen and Young traveled to South Africa for a long-scheduled meeting with Prime Minister Vorster about the Anglo-American plan for Rhodesia. Vorster was obdurate: it was up to the Americans and the British to sell their scheme to Smith. The South African government "would not use its influence on him."[93]

Less resilient secretaries of state might have despaired, but not Cyrus Vance. On September 12, he sent Carter a "status report" on Rhodesia. "Our success to date lies . . . in the fact that none of the parties has rejected it [the Anglo-American plan]." As for Vorster's refusal to play ball, Vance thought that the plan could survive. "At this point it appears likely that US pressure on South Africa will not be necessary to gain agreement from Smith to participate" in the Anglo-American talks.[94]

"Oh Biko, Biko!"[95]

On September 12, the day that Vance penned his status report, the anti-apartheid activist Steve Biko died in a South African jail. Biko was the brave founder of the South African Black Consciousness Movement, which had played a seminal role inspiring the 1976 Soweto uprising. "The South Africans allege that he died of natural causes following a hunger strike," Vance wrote Carter, "but given the fact that 17 other nationalists have died in South African jails, their explanation is open to question."[96] Indeed. Biko, who had been arrested a month earlier although he had committed no crime, had been tortured and beaten by the South African authorities. The police had refused to give him medical attention, and he died of massive head injuries.

Biko's charisma and courage, coupled with the brazen lies of the South African officials, created a tipping point: international fury at the brutality of the apartheid regime gathered momentum. The Carter administration expressed its condemnation by calling for an international inquiry into Biko's death and by sending both US Ambassador to South Africa Bill Bowdler and Deputy UN Ambassador Don McHenry to the funeral, a massive ritual that was simultaneously a political protest.

In Washington, the administration's horror and exasperation merged with its heated debate over the most effective measures to apply pressure on the regime. Moose warned Vance in preparation for the September 20 PRC meeting that "there are some marked differences of opinion within the Department on how, or even whether, we should proceed to tighten the screws on the SAG [South African government]."[97] The State Department presented an array of possible pressures on the apartheid regime, including voting in favor of a mandatory UN arms embargo, cutting the flow of oil, restricting trade and investment, and curtailing export credit facilities for trade with South Africa. In considering the immediate future, the PRC arrived at a cautious conclusion: "There is no reason at this time to apply any pressures on South Africa." However, it did recommend that Carter give preliminary approval to several significant steps that might be taken in the near future, including supporting a mandatory UN arms embargo. Carter agreed that the United States would support a mandatory arms embargo if the conditions were right. This step, as theoretical as it was in September, was significant because it positioned Washington at loggerheads with its NATO allies. Although a mandatory arms embargo would make little practical difference in terms of US military hardware going to South Africa—the United States had observed the voluntary UN arms embargo imposed in 1963—it would carry potent symbolic weight. It would be the first time that the United Nations had imposed mandatory sanctions on a member nation.[98]

Carter explained why he was not doing anything to punish Pretoria immediately to the Nigerian head of state, Lt. Gen. Olusegun Obasanjo, during talks in Washington in early October. "We have made it clear to South Africa that sanctions will be applied . . . if progress is not made," he told Obasanjo. "But we believe that it is easier for [Ian] Smith and South Africa to cooperate if the pressure applied to them is done in private."[99]

Walter Mondale's frank and open condemnation of apartheid to Prime Minister Vorster in May had been an essential step in the process of building trust in black Africa, which was necessary for progress toward a negotiated settlement in Rhodesia. But it had deepened Pretoria's alarm, which complicated the Rhodesia negotiations that relied on Vorster's ability to deliver Smith to the negotiating table. The Americans still hoped that the South Africans would cooperate with their plans, but relations between the two countries were increasingly strained.

At the United Nations
There was cause for celebration on September 29, 1977, when the UN resolution supporting the Anglo-American proposals for Rhodesia passed thirteen to zero. (The Soviets abstained, and China was absent.) It was "miraculous," UN Secretary-General Kurt Waldheim declared. On October 4, Carter addressed the opening session of the UN General Assembly in high spirits. Waldheim told him of his "astonishment" at how quickly and dramatically the United States had improved its standing at the United Nations, "particularly among the African states which heretofore had been very critical of the American government." Carter built on this goodwill by hosting a luncheon for African heads of state and by meeting one-on-one with several African leaders.[100]

One of these private meetings was with Mozambique's president Samora Machel, the Frontline president with the closest relationship with—and most leverage over—ZANU's Robert Mugabe. Just as Mugabe was the Rhodesian leader who was the least known in the West, Machel was the least-known Frontline president. He had refused to meet with Henry Kissinger, and his reputation in Washington was that of a hardline Marxist-Leninist, a man who had led Mozambique's guerrilla war against the Portuguese and then quickly consolidated power as his country's first head of state. The Carter administration, however, needed Machel. "The success of the United States' initiative to foster a negotiated settlement to the Rhodesian conflict hinges, to an ironic degree, on the actions of a nation which is fiercely suspicious of our motives," the State Department noted.[101]

This would be Machel's first meeting with an American president, and he did not mince words. Forgoing pleasantries, he launched into a remarkably blunt explanation of why he did not trust Washington. "We got . . . only hostility" from the Nixon administration, Machel explained. "It was as if we had become a devil for the United States." Relations with the Ford White House, after Mozambique had become independent, were not appreciably better. Machel told Carter that he had refused to meet with Kissinger because "I didn't trust Secretary Kissinger then and I don't trust him now." Machel was angry that the Carter administration criticized his country's support of the guerrillas fighting in Zimbabwe. "Mr. President, southern Africa is . . . a problem for all of us. We are the flesh surrounding the wound, and it is very painful. We see discrimination, hangings, and massacres every day in Zimbabwe, Namibia and South Africa. . . . We must ask, where lies the responsibility for these conditions? Who has been strengthening Rhodesia for twelve years?"[102]

Machel did not pause. He let Carter have it. "The United States is deeply involved in economic investment in Southern Africa, which . . . leads to killing and humiliation. . . . With the consent of the United States, South Africa has acquired a nuclear capacity. . . . That is a crime, and why we think of North America when we think of imperialism, because North America has always been involved in unjust causes."[103]

Carter interrupted. "You have a very mistaken, distorted viewpoint of our country. . . . I am proud of my country; it is a country dedicated to justice and freedom."

Machel changed tack. He praised Carter's "very positive and solid steps" in Zimbabwe. Carter replied graciously, and the stormy meeting ended, a long hour after it had begun.

The next day, Carter met with Secretary-General Waldheim, and said that "Machel had given him hell. . . . But," he added—undoubtedly flashing his famous smile—"[I] liked him."[104]

Smoke or Fire? The October Crisis

"South Africa," the State Department reported in late September after the death of Steve Biko, "appears bewildered and beleaguered. Its friends are no longer so easily identifiable and their number seems to be shrinking. Its enemies are many, and their hostility seems implacable."[105]

The apartheid government lashed out. On October 13, Vorster wrote Carter a belligerent, aggrieved and, to quote US Ambassador Bill Bowdler, "petulant" letter.[106] "We cannot escape the impression that the United States . . . while expecting our further active co-operation in the search for peace, nevertheless continues to take steps which we cannot interpret as otherwise than hostile and which endanger our future cooperation," Vorster complained, referring to Washington's intense pressure to sign the NPT and to the rumors of sanctions. "This was my clear impression in Vienna during the talks with Vice President

Mondale and it is regularly being confirmed by . . . deliberately discriminatory and even vindictive actions against South Africa." Vorster attacked what he viewed as Carter's distorted worldview. "It would seem, therefore, that the United States officially hold the view that stability in Southern Africa and the future of our country is to be sacrificed in the hope of stopping Soviet expansionism. This is a vain hope. On the contrary, by simplistically insisting on majority rule in South Africa, the United States . . . will pave the way for . . . conflict on a catastrophic scale." He then levied his threat: "Such an approach [is] . . . making it extremely difficult, if not altogether impossible, for my country to continue the constructive role it has accepted."[107] On that same day, October 13, Foreign Minister Pik Botha erupted in an anti-American tirade at an election rally in rural South Africa. "The United States is a greater enemy than is Russia to South Africa," the foreign minister thundered. "The US is a so-called friend which really wants to choke South Africa to death."[108]

Five days later, on October 18, the Vorster government decided to launch a brutal, comprehensive crackdown on all prominent opponents of apartheid, black and white. It banned *The World*, the country's largest circulation black newspaper; two other publications; and eighteen opposition groups. At least seventy activists were arrested; others were banned. The State Department took stock. "The South African Government has crossed a critical line. It has made a fairly clean sweep of the moderate black leaders and organizations that seek evolutionary change through dialogue with the government. The government has made clear to opponents that conversation will not work, that it will not recognize or deal with black political leadership. . . . [The crackdown has] aroused considerable outrage in this country."[109]

The outrage spread well beyond the United States: it was global. At the UN, Andrew Young braced for the inevitable. In his heady early days as UN ambassador, he had managed to persuade the Africa Group to withdraw its resolutions calling for wide-ranging, mandatory sanctions on Pretoria based on designating apartheid a threat to peace. Now the Africa Group threatened to revive the resolutions it had tabled in March, and it would be impossible to hold off a UN Security Council debate on the crisis in South Africa. Young knew that the Carter administration would not be able to go as far as the Africans wanted, but he wanted to minimize the damage to the administration's standing in the Third World and to his own reputation. Suddenly, after months of debating how to calibrate pressure on Pretoria, the Carter administration would have to decide.

Young penned a long, passionate letter to Carter and Vance on October 22. "We are clearly in for a very rough time in the [Security] Council." Young knew well that "our close allies—the British in particular—will be trying to restrict Security Council activity largely to the rhetorical." Carter had to resist this because "in very real terms, the credibility of our Africa policy is at stake." Young carefully explained that the success of the Rhodesia negotiations depended on "a growing African trust in American policy toward Africa. But that trust is indeed fragile." Black Africans, Young wrote, believed that the United States was "sucker[ed] into" a continuing alliance with South Africa due to their shared anticommunism and racism. "And they believe that economic imperatives underlying our relationship cause us to balk at the most crucial truth of all—South Africa and its system survive because we continue to do business with them."[110]

Young then turned to his policy recommendations. "I do not dispute the basic wisdom that US policy toward South Africa should continue to be based on the belief that . . . a series of continuous, progressively appropriate pressures can be effective. . . . But a carrot-and-stick policy needs an occasional stick. And now is the time for a stick." It was imperative that the Carter administration respond to the crackdown. "The latest series of arrests and bannings is widely (and I believe correctly) interpreted as a clear indication that the SAG [South African government] is now betting that US policy, because of our domestic constraints, will be more smoke than fire. . . . Accordingly, the primary question that I urge you to consider is what real actions the United States is prepared to take in response to Vorster's challenge."[111]

Young, despite his reputation as a firebrand, was a pragmatist. He understood that, due in large part to Britain's vigorous dissent, Carter could not support the mandatory economic sanctions that the Africans would demand. "Our ability to resist unacceptable extreme measures may well hinge on what we are willing to do bilaterally." Therefore, he recommended that the administration curtail its economic ties with South Africa (ending Export-Import Bank credit guarantees and discouraging new US investment), stop all intelligence cooperation, and withdraw some US military attachés. That would send a signal, but it would not be sufficient; Carter also needed to support a mandatory UN arms embargo. Young, who was very familiar with the British resistance to sanctions, insisted that voting in favor of a mandatory arms embargo "does not mean a 'slippery slope' to a full range of economic sanctions." He explained—and this was the heart of his letter— that the arms embargo could be justified on narrow grounds that would not lead to the "slippery slope." It should not be based on the "threat to peace" posed by the apartheid system, because once apartheid was declared a threat to peace, economic sanctions would surely follow. Instead, it should be based on the "threat to peace" posed by South Africa's military buildup and continuing aggression toward its neighbors. This finesse, and strong US leadership, was needed to convince

Britain and France to support a mandatory arms embargo. In turn, US, British, and French support for such an embargo might be enough to dampen the Africans' demands for full economic sanctions.[112]

On October 24, the PRC met to discuss the situation. A briefing paper asserted, "Urgent action is necessary to convey to South Africa and other nations the seriousness with which we regard events in that country." Even though taking action against Pretoria could complicate the Rhodesia negotiations, it might not, because South Africa's cooperation to date had been "in accordance with its own interests. . . . In any event . . . we must be prepared to run certain risks. . . . One of our basic objectives is to confirm the credibility of this Administration with African and other Third World states while resisting their pressure to take action based on a Chapter VII finding that the South African situation presents a threat to the peace." After a vigorous discussion, the PRC decided to recommend "that the United States support or initiate a resolution on a mandatory arms embargo."[113]

Washington rejected Young's suggestions to curtail Export-Import Bank credits and intelligence cooperation, but it did take several unilateral measures: the United States recalled its ambassador from Pretoria for "consultations," withdrew one of its five naval attachés, and halted all "grey area" sales. (This last action had been delayed for three months because of concerns that it would complicate the administration's Rhodesia policy.) It also initiated reviews of its economic, intelligence, and nuclear relations with South Africa.[114]

It was too late. Young had not been able to convince his African colleagues to modify their resolutions. Therefore, on the day that the PRC met, debate opened at the UN Security Council on four resolutions calling for comprehensive mandatory sanctions. [115]

The European allies scrambled. Worried about what the Carter administration might do, they made their position clear. "Not one EC [European Community] member is prepared to support sanctions against South Africa," Belgian prime minister Leo Tindemans informed Vance.[116] The French told Washington that they had "an objection 'at this point' to any Chapter 7 reference to South Africa in a SC [Security Council] resolution."[117] Vance paid a call on the British ambassador in Washington to discuss British policy at the United Nations. "Prompt actions, not simply words, are needed," the American secretary of state declared.[118] The Carter administration had some reason to hope that the British might soften their hardline stance against any sanctions on South Africans. Foreign Secretary David Owen had reconsidered after Pretoria supported Smith's brutal May raid of Mapai in Mozambique. Personally, Owen thought that some form of a mandatory arms embargo might be required, but he did not have his colleagues behind him. "Owen will have real trouble with the Cabinet," Assistant Secretary Moose observed after talks in London, "unless the President lays down the law."[119]

On October 27, Jimmy Carter announced the policy the United States would pursue against South Africa at the UN. "The crisis was engendered last week when South Africa took away the rights of the free press and eliminated many of the organizations . . . working toward improved equality for the citizens of South Africa," the president explained. "I think it's important that we express in no uncertain terms our deep and legitimate concern about those actions of South Africa. . . . My decision has been to support strong sanctions against the sale of weapons to South Africa." Carter had just laid down the law: would the allies support a mandatory arms embargo?[120]

Behind the scenes, the Americans were working the French and British. They stressed that the embargo they proposed would be based on a very narrow Chapter 7 finding, as Young had suggested, and would not lead to economic sanctions. They insisted that they had to propose the arms embargo or they would be cast "in the role of defenders of South Africa."[121]

Years later, David Owen recalled the struggle. "We were most reluctant," he explained, "but I said to our Cabinet, 'Look, unless we move a bit, we will lose the Americans. . . . They aren't as economically vulnerable as us, and they're not going to take a hands off position.' Callaghan understood that we had to bend on this issue." On October 31, London and Paris relented. "HMG with reluctance and misgivings has agreed to go along with our South Africa resolution," Kingman Brewster, the US ambassador in London, cabled. But the Callaghan government remained "troubled that a Chapter Seven determination, no matter how narrowly defined, does put in fact put the UK at the top of a slippery slope." Brewster remained worried: "It is not inconceivable that there may be a parting of the ways in the United Nations."[122]

At the Security Council, the hardline African resolutions calling for mandatory economic sanctions were moving to a vote. Young pleaded with the Africans to withdraw their resolutions because they knew that he, and his British and French colleagues, would veto them. This would only broadcast the UN's division, which would help Pretoria. Instead, Young urged his African colleagues, support the mandatory arms resolution that the West could back.

Young, however, failed to work any magic. On October 31, he delivered a pained speech to the UN Security Council. "I think everybody around this Council knows that there has never been an administration in the United States that has struggled more determinedly against these policies of apartheid. Our resolution remains undiminished." Young then explained why he was going to veto the resolutions for economic sanctions, and he repeated Carter's call for a mandatory arms embargo. He ended with the words of Steve Biko that "racial justice will come to South Africa." He then cast three vetoes on the African resolutions. This "deepened an atmosphere among Africans of frustration and disappointment," Young cabled Washington. "Things were rough tonight."[123]

Four days later, on November 4, the Security Council voted on Resolution 418, which imposed a mandatory arms embargo on South Africa based on the "threat to peace" posed by Pretoria's military buildup. If it passed, it would represent a long-fought victory: a mandatory arms embargo had been proposed in 1963, 1975, and 1976, but had fallen to US, British, and French vetoes. This time, the mandatory arms embargo passed unanimously. It was a significant step—the first time that the UN had imposed mandatory sanctions on a member state—but it was enacted with disappointment and bitterness on all sides.[124] "We could have gone further," Mondale explained on *Meet the Press* on November 6. "But . . . you need the cooperation of other nations. Even the step that we took was taken with some difficulty."[125]

Looking back several weeks later, Young was philosophical. Carter administration officials (he included himself) had been "particularly susceptible to over-optimism." They had deluded themselves that the goodwill they had engendered in Africa and at the UN would enable them to persuade the Africa Group to temper their resolutions and accept—indeed celebrate—the narrowly defined mandatory arms embargo that the West could support. They had been so focused on corralling the British and French that they had dismissed the Africans' resolutions in a "high-handed" manner. The Africans resented this. "We knew how delicate the compromises struck among the Five were," Young said, referring to the wrangling among the five Western nations—Canada, France, the United Kingdom, the United States, and West Germany. "It was difficult for Africans to see our inflexibility as the product of a difficult compromise among the Five. . . . In short, we played our initiative as a weighty policy switch and assumed that the Africans would understand and respect both it and our limited flexibility."[126]

The Americans had overlooked the passions that the South African crackdown had aroused, and they forgot how entrenched was the Africans' suspicion that "in a crunch, Western policies, as opposed to Western words, toward South Africa had not changed." They underestimated, Young admitted, the desire of some radical Africans to show "the world the limits of the Carter administration's new policies toward Africa . . . and to undercut Andrew Young."[127]

The Carter administration was assailed from both sides—too conservative for the Africans and too radical for the other Westerners. "The suspicion among the Four . . . that the Carter administration would break ranks," Young observed, "interfered with straight talk among the Five. . . . The British, French and Germans, wary of the concessions the US might be prepared to offer under African pressure, insisted on initially offering the Africans as little as possible." As disturbing and disappointing as the incident had been, however, Young did not despair. Ultimately, he thought that it had not undermined the credibility of the Carter administration, but had shown "how fragile it still is."[128]

Troubles at Home

Despite the war in the Horn and the fragility of the talks in Rhodesia, the administration's handling of African affairs was a bright spot in what was a difficult autumn for the White House. First there was the Bert Lance affair, or, as it was quickly dubbed, "Lancegate." In June, allegations had surfaced that Lance, Carter's close friend and confidant, had employed questionable banking practices in Georgia before being appointed head of the Office of Management and Budget. As the summer wore on, a steady drip of stories about Lance's shady (or at least sloppy) deals spilled across the front pages. The Senate held televised hearings about the scandal; Lance, a large, affable man, performed well, but too much damage had been done, and he tendered his resignation on October 22, 1977.

Lancegate tarnished Carter's squeaky-clean image. Not only was he slow to fire his budget chief, but the press also implicated Carter in some of Lance's questionable deals. More important than its effect on Carter's public approval ratings, however, was its impact on the internal dynamics and mood of the White House. Carter trusted Bert Lance, and he had relied on him as a sounding board for many issues. He believed that his friend had been hounded out by his critics in the press and Congress in what was, in part, a cheap shot against a southerner. From Carter's perspective, it was the end of the honeymoon, and it embittered him.

At the same time, the Senate was gutting the president's energy program—nixing, for example, the tax on gas-guzzling cars. Moreover, economic growth was more sluggish than expected, and worries about inflation were intensifying. The *New York Times* noted in September, "Paradoxically, Mr. Carter's best prospects for political success now lie in foreign policy."[129]

While the Lance story was developing in the middle of the summer, the White House was also deeply involved in the process of negotiating the Panama Canal treaties, which would restore sovereignty of the Canal Zone to the Panamanians in 2000. As with China, Carter was attempting to complete a process that previous presidents had started but had been unwilling to complete because of its domestic political costs. In October 1977, General Omar Torrijos of Panama and Jimmy Carter signed the treaties in a White House ceremony. The real challenge then began as the administration struggled to round up two-thirds of the senators to ratify the treaties. Although the treaties enjoyed widespread bipartisan support—Gerald Ford, Richard Nixon, Henry Kissinger, and many leading conservatives such as William F. Buckley spoke ardently in favor—there was also a potent populist, conservative fervor against them. Ronald Reagan had brought this antipathy to a head during the primary campaign in 1976 with his memorable (if inaccurate) phrase, "We bought it, we paid for it, it's ours!" Opposition to Carter's Panama Canal policy served as an important stimulus to the emerging neoconservative movement: it forged alliances, honed direct-mail politics, and raised money. It also consumed the time of the Senate and many members of the administration for months.

By far the most important issue in the fall, however, was the pursuit of peace in the Middle East. Carter sought a comprehensive peace, and he went back to basics. In the immediate aftermath of the 1973 Arab-Israeli war, Washington and Moscow had co-convened a peace conference in Geneva, but the talks had collapsed in disarray. Carter struggled throughout 1977 to reconvene this conference. On October 1, the United States and the Soviet Union issued a joint declaration articulating the goals of the conference, which was expected to open before year's end. The communiqué mentioned "the legitimate rights of the Palestinian people."

With this phrase, all hell broke loose. The Israeli government, led by Prime Minister Menachem Begin, rejected the communiqué as "unacceptable," and Israelis across the political spectrum denounced it. A poll taken two weeks after the communiqué was issued showed that a staggering 70 percent of American Jews disapproved of Carter's Middle East policy. By the end of October, the *New York Times* commented that "President Carter's Middle East initiatives over the last nine months have opened a breach between the Administration and the organized American Jewish community that poses a potentially serious threat to both his policy and his political future."[130] The uproar surrounding the communiqué also led some Americans to question why the Carter administration had invited Moscow back into the peace process. This fanned concerns that Carter was either naive about the Soviet threat or willing to sacrifice Israeli interests to pry concessions on SALT from the Soviet Union.[131] Both alternatives were devastating for Carter's image.

Carter's approval rating had dropped in the polls from the heady days of spring. In October, he was at 48 percent, which was not in itself cause for alarm. But Lancegate, and the troubles of the energy bill in the Senate, and the dissension over the Panama Canal treaties, and the uproar about the Middle East were causing many Americans to wonder if the Carter White House knew how to govern. In mid-October, liberal columnist Tom Wicker posed the question: "Is Jimmy Carter a one-term President?" The British embassy in Washington noted that "there is scarcely a powerful lobby he has not challenged head on." Carter was disappointing all the core Democratic constituencies—his fiscal conservatism dismayed blacks, his pressure on Israel inflamed Jews, and his refusal to bargain with special interests frustrated labor.[132]

On October 27, Carter held his eighteenth news conference. The first question was a zinger. "[Do] you believe," the reporter asked, "that there's anything to the idea that people still think, as a Georgian, that you don't belong here?"[133]

Carter was good at press conferences. He enjoyed displaying his command of the issues, and he was confident. He replied with a smile. "I remember in this room last May someone asked me if my administration was . . . all style and no substance. Lately the criticisms have been that there's too much substance and not enough style." The president explained that he was trying to address "the most difficult questions that face our Nation"— peace in the Middle East and in Africa, nuclear disarmament, energy, and welfare and social security—and it could take a long time to resolve these festering problems, but it was useful to get them "on the table, [to] have an open debate."[134]

Commenting on the press conference, columnist Meg Greenfield wrote, "Something has gone wrong. . . . His presidency is widely regarded as weightless and formless, lacking in coherence, direction and order. . . . What is odd is that this most disciplined of men is failing to impose a discipline on his government or to . . . convey a sense of . . . mastery . . . to the American public."[135] After almost a year in office, Jimmy Carter remained an enigma. In a way, this was not surprising: most people are hard to understand. He was no more enigmatic a man than, say, Richard Nixon. But in Carter's case, it mattered. His policy decisions reflected his personal judgment, rather than an ideology or a grand strategy. Therefore, because the public could not be sure of his lodestars, they could not predict his policy. Uneasiness spread.

8. War and Settlement

The Cubans Are Coming?

In April 1977, Jimmy Carter had wanted to seize the opportunity to embrace Somalia, coaxing it from the Kremlin's arms. In August, as Mohamed Siad Barre's troops invaded Ethiopia, Washington backed off, unwilling to openly assist a war of aggression. But the Carter administration was unable to resist the lure of wooing Somalia from the Soviets, and it was reluctant to oppose Siad Barre, a friend of Saudi Arabia. It therefore engaged in a balancing act, encouraging friends of Siad to transfer non-US weapons to him even as it refused to open a pipeline of US-supplied arms. By early November, the Carter administration had decided that Ethiopia would rout the Somali forces in a matter of months. Disillusioned with Siad's lies and exaggerations, it looked on the situation with equanimity, knowing that it had little leverage in the region and that Moscow's relations with Mogadiscio would be damaged, probably irreparably.

The Carter administration's focus was elsewhere. It was closely following the congressional debates on the energy plan and the Panama Canal Treaties, it was making progress on the SALT II negotiations, it was determining its response to South Africa's nuclear ambitions and crackdown after Steve Biko's death, and it was dealing with the collapse of progress toward a Geneva conference for the Middle East.

Siad Barre tried to get Carter's attention by waving the red flag of Cuba under his nose. On October 21, 1977, he publicly accused Cuba of intervening in Ethiopia, and on November 2 he repeated the charge, telling the foreign press that there were "about 15,000 Cuban soldiers" in Ethiopia.[1]

Washington had heard it all before. Siad had been hyperventilating about the Cubans since early August, when he had told the Americans that 15,000 Cuban soldiers were about to be transported aboard Soviet planes from Angola to Ethiopia. The CIA had dismissed the charge, and the State Department spokesperson had told the press that there were only "about fifty" Cuban military advisers in Ethiopia. (In fact, according to Cuban sources, there were about 280, a figure that had crept up from the 200-man military mission that Havana established in April 1977 to train Ethiopian troops.) A weary Paul Henze, the Horn expert on the NSC staff, wrote Zbigniew Brzezinski, "The Somalis continue to make wild charges about large numbers of Cubans in Ethiopia, but . . . the Cubans are proving to be quite wary of deepening their involvement in Ethiopia for the time being."[2]

At quadripartite talks on November 10, Vance estimated (accurately) that "there were no more than 200 Cuban technical experts with the Ethiopian forces."[3] The four foreign ministers agreed that the tide of the war was about to change—Siad's forces were stretched thin and had failed to seize the major population centers—and they predicted that "the heavy Soviet arms support for Ethiopia . . . [was] likely to tip the scales against Somalia in the coming months." Nevertheless, Vance reported to Carter that "none of the four powers appeared prepared to respond to Somali appeals for arms . . . [and all] agreed that the time is not ripe for a Western mediation effort or a Security Council resolution." No one, including Vance, considered the possibility that the Cubans might intervene *en masse*, as they had two years earlier in Angola.[4]

Washington's calm was the result of a serious misreading of what motivated Fidel Castro. No one in the Carter administration expected Cuba to become a significant player in Ethiopia. Castro would send some advisers; perhaps there would be some mission creep. But not another Angola. Administration officials were lulled into complacency by their knowledge that Cuba was already straining to meet its commitment to Angola (where it still had more than 20,000 soldiers) and by their confidence in three assumptions—all of which were wrong.

First, the Carter administration believed that since southern Africa, not Ethiopia, was Castro's priority, Cuba would not sacrifice its long-standing commitments to Somalia and to the Eritrean liberation movement to throw all its support to Ethiopia's Derg. (Washington was unaware that Havana had stopped aiding the Eritrean guerrillas, a fact that is clear in the Cuban documents.)

Second, they were confident that the promise of normalization with the United States would prove irresistible to Castro. The tenacity of this assumption is remarkable. Castro had already proven that he could resist the carrot of normalization: he had rebuffed the Ford administration's overtures by sending Cuban troops to Angola, and he had insisted, time and again, that his troops were in Angola at the invitation of President Agostinho Neto, and he would consult with Neto—not Jimmy Carter or any other American president—to determine when they were no longer required. It should have been apparent that Castro would formulate his policy toward Ethiopia based on his perception of Cuba's needs and his conversations with Mengistu, not in accordance with the desires of any American official.[5] The Carter team, however, deluded itself that its proffers of normalization were so sincere that Castro would change his stripes.

Third, the administration believed that the Ethiopians did not need the Cubans—eventually, they would win the war without outside troops. Therefore, even though the top officials in the White House, the State Department, and the CIA were aware that the number of Cubans in Ethiopia had edged upward, they all were confident that Castro would behave sensibly and that Siad Barre was crying wolf.[6]

Washington also misread Soviet policy. It underestimated the importance that the Kremlin attached to supporting the Ethiopian revolution. The high profile of the region for Moscow should have been clear, given Soviet leader Nikolai Podgorny's visit there, but the administration found it difficult to believe that the Soviets would renounce Somalia—their most important client in sub-Saharan Africa and the location of their base at Berbera—for the Derg. Carter administration officials were on guard in southern Africa, not in the Horn.

Siad's Gamble and Carter's Image

Siad Barre was a gambler: he emptied his pockets and placed his last bet. At 8 P.M. on November 13, 1977, Radio Somalia broadcast the announcement: effective immediately, all Somali military ties with the Soviet Union were severed; the Somali-Soviet friendship treaty was abrogated; and relations with Cuba—which had continued to station a forty-two-man military mission in Mogadiscio—were broken.[7]

This was big news: Moscow had lost its most important client in Africa; it had been ejected from its strategically located base at Berbera; its multimillion-dollar investment in Somalia had gone down the drain; and the 6,000 Soviet military and civilian advisers still in Somalia were sent packing. The *New York Times* covered the Soviets' catastrophic loss on page one: "Setback for Moscow Is Worst Since 1972 In Such a Key Area," the headline declared, reminding readers of President Anwar Sadat's eviction of the Soviets from Egypt five years earlier. The US ambassador in Moscow, Malcolm Toon, cabled: "The abrogation of the friendship treaty must be interpreted as a severe blow to Soviet international political prestige [and] . . . a great loss of face for the Soviet Union in the Third World in general and in Arab/Muslim world in particular." This was a sensitive point for the Kremlin in late 1977; in the wake of the uproar over the joint US-Soviet communiqué of October 1, the Carter administration had reneged on its promise to include Moscow in the Middle East peace negotiations.[8]

One day after making his dramatic announcement, Siad explained his new policy to an enthusiastic crowd in Mogadiscio. Although he was critical of the Soviet decision to arm Ethiopia and brand Somalia as the aggressor, Siad spewed particular venom on Havana, swearing that the Cuban "mercenaries . . . would never succeed in their misadventure."[9]

A few hours later, Carter's Cabinet assembled for its regularly scheduled November meeting. Vance reported on Siad's decision to expel the Soviets, calling it a "major step," but it generated absolutely no discussion. Instead, Carter and Vice President Mondale focused on the good news that US corporations in South Africa were adopting the Sullivan principles (which improved conditions for black workers); as in the US South, the president said, "by keeping enlightened business leaders working with us . . . we will prevail."[10]

Brzezinski, true to form, left the discussion about southern Africa to the president and the secretary of state. But uncharacteristically, his remarks at the Cabinet meeting focused on Africa. Inexplicably, he did not celebrate Siad's important decision—he completely ignored it. "The NSC is increasingly concerned," he informed the Cabinet, "about the scale of Cuban involvement in Africa, especially in Somalia and Angola." The fact that Somalia had just severed relations with Cuba did not enter Brzezinski's equation, and Ethiopia was not on his radar. Instead, he zeroed in on Castro's recent decision to pause his phased withdrawal of Cuban troops in Angola. (The Cubans had been slowly withdrawing troops for a year, but in the wake of the Shaba crisis in March 1977 the Angolan government had asked Castro to reconsider the drawdown.) Castro's change of course in Angola deeply disappointed the Carter team, which had hoped for progress in the normalization talks with Havana. For Brzezinski, it was an affront, a challenge to the administration's vigor, one that hurt America's image abroad. He asserted that the Cuban posture in Angola was one more step in Castro's plan to spread revolution in Africa. Foreign leaders, Brzezinski explained—referring to the shah of Iran, the Saudi royal family, French president Giscard d'Estaing, West German chancellor Helmut Schmidt, and the Chinese leadership—"are increasingly critical of US foreign policies." Carter responded without waiting for any discussion. "The United States," he told his Cabinet, "will begin to express its frank criticism of the 'Cuban intrusion' into Africa."[11]

In fact, the verbal barrage had already begun. In prepared remarks to journalists three days earlier, Carter had lambasted Cuban policy in Angola. "The Cubans have, in effect, taken on the colonial aspect that the Portuguese gave up in months gone by. . . . They are now spreading into other countries in

343

Africa, like Mozambique. Recently, they are building up their so-called advisors in Ethiopia. . . . We consider this to be a threat to the permanent peace in Africa." The State Department spokesman stayed on message, announcing that Cuban troop levels in Ethiopia had grown to an estimated 550 in recent weeks.[12] In spite of these remarks, there was some push-back within the administration. NSC aide Henry Richardson wrote Brzezinski, "It is one thing to aim to get Cubans out of Angola. It is another to aim to remove every Cuban from anywhere in Africa. First, we can't do it. Second, American interests in Africa don't demand it. Third, it sounds somewhat hysterical." Richardson's warning, however, was a voice in the wilderness.[13]

Carter kept up the pressure on Cuba. In the margins of Vance's November 15 Evening Report about the shah's anxieties that "the Soviets would pump more arms into Ethiopia," Carter wrote, "We should get Andy to deplore publicly SU-Cuban involvement in Africa. Make it as strong as possible." Two days later, the front page of the *New York Times* was emblazoned with a large map of Africa that showed in bold graphics everywhere the Cubans had a "military or advisory" presence. "The Carter White House is seriously disturbed by the steadily expanding Cuban military presence in Angola, Ethiopia and other African countries and sees no possibility of reestablishing full diplomatic relations with Havana under these circumstances," was the lead. State Department officials were caught off guard by the story and suspected that the map had been prepared by the CIA for the NSC.[14]

The White House should have been capitalizing on the devastating Soviet loss in Somalia, but it had decided to attack Cuban policy in Africa and it was not sufficiently deft to adjust course. Instead of building on the *New York Times'* November 14 headline about the dramatic Soviet loss of influence from Cairo to Mogadiscio, the administration buried the story of its real success in Somalia by raising alarums about Cuban adventurism in Africa. It mounted a concerted campaign on the Voice of America and deployed administration officials to the Sunday television talk shows. On *Face the Nation*, Andrew Young condemned Cuba's "new colonialism" in Africa.[15]

This anti-Cuban barrage not only swamped the more important headline— the Soviet Union's grave loss in Africa—but also marked the tentative beginning of an important shift in the way the Carter administration explained global events. For almost a year, the White House and State Department had emphasized the contingent, regional roots of troubles around the world; while still waging the Cold War, Carter and Vance had doggedly refused to frame all the world's troubles in Cold War terms. Drawing lessons from the war in Vietnam and from the nuance that détente added to the international system, they described the Soviet leaders as opportunistic rather than as megalomaniacal masterminds. They saw the dots, but they resisted drawing Cold War lines between them. With the administration's public assault on Cuban policy in Africa, which began in early November, the White House began connecting some dots.

Brzezinski explained the logic of the anti-Cuban policy in his thirty-seventh weekly report to the president, penned on November 18, 1977. He was worried about Carter's image at home and abroad. "Soon it will be one year since you assumed office," he began. Carter's policies had been "right," but there was a growing problem of the "public perception of the general character of that policy." Brzezinski cast the problem in sweeping terms. "For much of the last thirty years our foreign policy could focus simply on . . . the Soviet threat. [This] permitted Presidents to mobilize public support through an appeal to emotion." The emotion to which Brzezinski referred was fear. "In contrast, we now confront a much more complex world. . . . This necessarily means greater reliance on reason, but the public is not inclined to support foreign policy through reliance on cerebral processes alone." A foreign policy without the organizing principle of fear was, Brzezinski explained, "simply and quite bluntly . . . seen as 'soft.'"[16]

The national security adviser had learned how to get the president's attention. Telling Carter that he was "soft" was sure to galvanize him. "Our critics," Brzezinski continued, "will ask for some examples of 'toughness', and exploit against us such things as . . . the current Cuban activity in Africa." (He was referring to Castro's decision to halt the withdrawal from Angola.) Brzezinski recommended: "You ought to take, before too long, a decision . . . that has a distinctly 'tough' quality to it." He then praised Carter for his announcement four days earlier to the Cabinet that his administration was going to express "frank criticism of the 'Cuban intrusion' into Africa." Brzezinski commented, "The public pressure on Cuba regarding Africa came none-too-soon." In the margin, the chastened president wrote—perhaps ruing his measured response to the Shaba crisis the previous spring—"It took me 6 months to get it done."[17]

The administration's public assault on Cuba's policy in Africa reflected its genuine distress at Castro's decision to stop withdrawing his troops from Angola, but it was also intended to handle the domestic political problem of Carter's perceived lack of toughness. It was an attempt to depict a virile administration on guard against a communist takeover of Africa. There is no evidence that when the public relations blitz was initiated—on November 11—and for the subsequent month, administration officials thought that Cuba would intervene substantially in Ethiopia. There were no contingency plans to determine a US response if it did; not one meeting was held at any level to prepare for such an eventuality. Cuba was barely mentioned at the quadripartite talks on the

Horn held on November 10, and at a NATO meeting a fortnight later the possibility of Cuban aid to Ethiopia was mentioned, but with no sense of anxiety.[18]

The Carter administration was complacent about the situation in the Horn. The Americans had won: the Soviets had lost access to Berbera, and were left only with a weak and unreliable regime in Addis that faced a growing insurgency in Eritrea. That Siad Barre, who had won no friends in Washington with his demands, exaggerations, and lies, would eventually lose the war in the Ogaden was a minor point. For the Carter administration, Somalia's expulsion of the Soviets and Cubans meant that the course it had set was correct.

Washington's failure to trumpet this Cold War victory is difficult to explain. Perhaps the Carter administration did not want to provoke the Saudis, who were still hoping that Siad's irredentism would lead to Mengistu's downfall and the expulsion of the Soviets from Ethiopia. The Saudi leaders stressed to Washington that Siad had not only switched sides in the Cold War, he had also—at long last—said that he would sign a nonaggression pact with Kenya. (He soon reneged on this promise.) In light of these two reversals of past Somali policy, on November 17 the Saudis urged the White House to "review its policy on military assistance to Somalia." Two weeks later, Prince Sultan repeated the plea, adding a note of pathos: he had just come from a three-hour meeting with Siad Barre, and "Siad had cried during most of the session." Siad said that he needed armored personnel carriers, antitank weapons, ammunition, and food. "His troops are forced to fight hungry."[19]

To no avail. Carter sent a message to Siad, reiterating "the US view that, while the conflict in the Ogaden persists, the United States cannot supply arms to either side."[20] On November 24, Cyrus Vance explained the Carter administration's logic in a long cable to the US ambassador in Jidda. "If the US were to supply arms to Somalia . . . the Ogaden conflict would take on the character of a surrogate super-power confrontation," which, Vance asserted, was not only unwise but also unnecessary. If Ethiopia won the war, the victory would be pyrrhic for the Soviet Union because it had lost Somalia and the insurgency in the Ogaden would continue. Vance hastened to add that the United States was taking the Saudi position seriously: it would continue to quietly encourage its friends to send weapons to Siad. Vance instructed the ambassador to remind the Saudis that "Somalia continues to receive arms shipments [because] . . . we have not sought to discourage arms not of US origin from being sent to Somalia."[21]

Washington also refused President Sadat's request to provide arms for an Egyptian contingent that Cairo proposed sending to Berbera, prepositioning its troops in case of an Ethiopian invasion. "It is not just my battle," Sadat told the US ambassador when pitching the idea, "but yours as well."[22] On

November 27, Vance cabled that the Carter administration would not accede to Sadat's request. While "it is logical for Siad to assume that Ethiopia . . . [will] mount a counter-offensive," Vance wrote, he thought it likely the counterattack would be delayed for several reasons. First, it would take time, "probably several months," for the Ethiopian armed forces to become familiar with the advanced weapons that the Soviets had delivered. Although Vance accepted that "if Siad's claim that there are 15,000 to 20,000 Cuban troops in Ethiopia were true," the offensive could occur sooner, he dismissed Siad's estimate. "Our intelligence is only able to confirm the presence of some 400 Cuban military in Ethiopia." Second, the Ethiopian armed forces would not be able to focus on the Ogaden because they had to suppress the revolt in Eritrea. Third, Somali morale was "high," and Siad had "managed to arrange arms deliveries from a number of sources." The Ethiopian troops, on the other hand, were "shaken" and would "clearly face a hostile environment" in the Ogaden.[23] Vance—whose policy in southern Africa was shaped by the fear that Zambia or Mozambique might call for Cuban aid—failed to imagine that Mengistu might choose not to delay but instead to call for help and that Castro might answer the call.

Sadat was not impressed with Vance's logic. "The Americans always go to extremes," he complained to Chancellor Schmidt. "In Vietnam, they lose 50,000 men; in Africa, they do nothing."[24]

Castro Responds

The Castro government was irritated by Washington's sudden barrage of hostile rhetoric. On November 18, Cuban vice president Carlos Rafael Rodríguez met with Lyle Lane, the ranking US diplomat in Havana, to tell him that Havana had not significantly increased its military presence in Africa "even though it has had urgent requests to do so." As for Ethiopia, Rodríguez insisted that "Cuba had no intention of joining the fighting there. . . . Ethiopia does not need foreign military manpower." Carter's attacks on Cuba, he added, either reflected "serious misconceptions and misinformation" or served "internal political requirements in the US." To the Canadians, Rodríguez speculated that Carter was trying to create a "power image" to counter his drop in the polls.[25]

In Washington, the chief of the Cuban Interests Section toed the same line: "Cuba has never denied its assistance to Ethiopia but there are no combat troops there," he told the assistant secretary of state for Latin American affairs on November 21. "Cuba has no intention of repeating the Angolan experience elsewhere."[26]

Castro had been impressed by Mengistu and the Ethiopian revolution when he had toured the Horn in March 1977. He had wanted to help the Derg ever since, and had urged Moscow to do so, but he did not think that Cuba could undertake another major intervention in Africa. On April 12, Mengistu had pressed Castro: "Time is passing. . . . The Ethiopian people are placing their hopes in the arrival of Cuban troops." The Cuban ambassador in Addis, José Pérez Novoa, reported that the Ethiopian revolution was confronting such dire threats that it "desperately needed Cuban troops." When Castro explained that Cuba was unable to send troops, Pérez Novoa cabled that Mengistu understood and accepted the decision.[27]

Instead of troops, Castro had sent instructors to train the Ethiopian militia. This militia would become the "new backbone" of the Ethiopian armed forces, Mengistu explained. "The [old] army is useless. . . . The real problem is that it's not just the senior officers who don't share our worldview, but also the mid-level officers," Mengistu told Cuban general Arnaldo Ochoa, who had arrived in Addis Ababa on April 17, to set up a 200-man military mission there. (Cuba also sent a medical mission, as Mengistu had requested.) Ochoa soon reported to Havana that the Ethiopian army, rent by purges and schisms, was incapable of dealing with the rebellions that roiled almost every province. There was a danger, Mengistu told Ochoa in July, that "Ethiopian soldiers might turn their weapons against the revolutionaries."[28]

On the other hand, from April through July 1977, Defense Minister Raúl Castro sent weekly reports to Fidel indicating that despite the weakness of the Derg's military, the Ethiopian revolution was gaining popular support. In Moscow, the Soviets agreed to send more weapons and prepared to dispatch a 240-man military mission (which included 40 doctors) to Addis Ababa. Mengistu explained that the Cubans and Soviets had a formidable task: "to transform the militia of workers and peasants into a modern army with modern weapons."[29]

Then, in July, Somalia invaded the Ogaden. Mengistu again implored Castro to send troops, but the Cuban leader reluctantly declined. "Despite our sympathy for the Ethiopian revolution and our profound indignation at the cowardly and criminal aggression to which it has fallen victim, it is frankly impossible for Cuba to do more in the present circumstances," Castro wrote Ochoa on August 16. "You cannot imagine how hard it is for us to constantly rebuff these requests."[30]

Beginning in August and continuing through the end of the year, the Somalis launched a sustained offensive to capture Harar. The Cubans feared that the Ethiopians might be unable to hold the city. An official Cuban history of the war notes that this "might have meant the collapse of the entire eastern front [the Ogaden]." In September, Mengistu met with the head of the

Cuban military mission and the Cuban ambassador in Addis. He explained that the situation on the battlefield "was very bad. Our enemies are getting stronger, and we still don't have the skilled personnel to use the weapons that the Soviet Union is sending us." He wanted more instructors and weapons to train and equip 100,000 more men. "This is the decisive moment," Mengistu declared. "Either we rally to save the Revolution, or we allow the imperialists to destroy it."[31]

In late October, Mengistu made a last-ditch effort, hurrying first to Havana and then to Moscow to plead for help. On October 28, he met with Fidel Castro and spoke frankly: "Not long ago, four of our divisions were wiped out by the Somalis. . . . The Somalis, after taking control of the entire south, launched three attacks on Jijiga, and the third attack forced us to withdraw. . . . In Eritrea, we have lost the countryside; we control only two large towns, and if we lose them we might lose the revolution. But we don't have enough troops." Mengistu then praised the work of the Cuban military mission in Ethiopia, which was training the 98,000-man militia. "Without it, the Ethiopian revolution would have been utterly crushed. The fact is that, today, our only hope, our only defense is the militia." Mengistu could do nothing but plead. "Comrade Fidel, the situation is grave."[32]

The atmosphere of the meeting was warm. "I have listened carefully," Castro told Mengistu. He then lambasted Siad Barre, whose "chauvinism and aggression" had caused this situation, despite all Fidel's efforts. Castro wanted to help. "All is not lost," he assured Mengistu. "We can help with some things—we can provide more training," he said, "but we cannot provide weapons." He ended with a promise: "We will think about what else Cuba would be able to do."[33]

Mengistu's trip to Moscow was more encouraging. A secret Cuban report noted that "the determination of the leaders in the Kremlin to do more to help Ethiopia was getting stronger and stronger."[34]

In the first week of November, the Cuban military mission sent Havana another grim report: the Somali military was improving "in every sphere," and the Ethiopian revolution was in peril. "The revolution is not consolidated and there is a grave danger of a coup d'état." It was clear to the Cubans that "the Ethiopian army and militia were not strong enough to turn the tide of the war."[35]

At almost the same time—on November 10—the four Western foreign ministers held quadripartite talks on the Horn. Their assessment of Somalia's prospects was starkly different from the Cubans'. The Somalis were "by no means as strong as a few weeks ago," the Americans asserted. They had lost 40 percent of their tank force and half their airplanes, the French added. The discussion concluded "that there was likely to be a stalemate in the fighting for several months, but that it was thereafter likely that the Ethiopians would begin to gain the upper hand. . . . There was general assent [that] . . . the present situation was moving in favour of the Russians."[36]

The four Western powers were relying on logic—the Somali supply lines were attenuated and not being replenished, while the Ethiopians would soon absorb the Soviet supplies; this would enable Ethiopia to retake Jijiga. Their assessment of Ethiopia's prospects was blinkered: they focused narrowly on the war in the Ogaden, failing to view it as one theater in the Derg's multifront war against insurrections throughout Ethiopia. The most important other front was in Eritrea. If the Derg lost its war there, could it then hold onto the Ogaden? Moreover, based on Mengistu's dire prognostications as well as their own observations on the ground in Ethiopia, the Cubans and the Soviets feared that the leaders of the revolution in Addis would lose control of the undisciplined and poorly led troops in the field. The Western powers savored the fact that Moscow had saddled itself with an embattled ally in Addis, but they had an exaggerated sense of the vigor of the Ethiopian army. The Soviets and Cubans, on the other hand, were acutely aware of the interconnectedness of the insurgencies, and they knew that the morale of the Ethiopian armed forces was collapsing. They believed that the Ethiopian revolution was in danger.

Then, on November 13, Siad ejected the Soviets from Berbera and broke relations with Cuba. Moscow's policy toward the Horn was in shambles. It had lost its entire investment in Somalia, and it had gained only a besieged regime in Addis. First Egypt's Sadat, then Sudan's Gaafar Nimeriy, and now Somalia's Siad Barre had all rejected their Soviet patron: Moscow's relations with Muslim clients in the Horn was checkered indeed. "Moscow has an extremely low opinion of the reliability and trustworthiness of the Muslim Arab states in the Middle East and North Africa," a French analysis posited. "Ethiopia . . . will represent an area of pro-Soviet continuity . . . unaffected by the political vicissitudes that often sway or reverse orientations of governments in the Arab world."[37]

The Kremlin was determined to "save the Ethiopian Revolution," a senior Soviet official asserted.[38] This marked the turning point: for months, the Kremlin had been trying to straddle the fence, strengthening its bonds with Mengistu while not severing ties with Siad Barre. In November 1977, Siad made the choice for the Soviets. From that moment on, Moscow was fully committed to saving the revolutionary regime in Addis Ababa. The Soviets hurriedly airlifted weapons to Addis Ababa and sent more military advisers. "Somalia's treachery was not just an attack on Ethiopia," Soviet defense minister Dmitriy Ustinov announced. "It was a betrayal of the Soviet Union and Cuba." On

November 17, four days after the expulsion from Somalia, "approximately 250 Soviet officers" arrived in Ethiopia, the CIA reported. They were led by General Vasily Ivanovich Petrov, first deputy commander of Soviet ground forces. Soon, there would be more than a thousand Soviet military advisers and technicians in Ethiopia. The State Department noted that the Soviet officers had "begun to participate actively in Ethiopian military planning and to counsel a more ambitious counteroffensive."[39]

One week later, on November 25, Fidel Castro cast aside his doubts about Cuba's ability to sustain another African intervention: he decided to send troops to Ethiopia. Leonid Brezhnev immediately wrote Castro to thank him for his "timely decision."[40]

The response of the Carter administration to this dramatic change in the Horn was anything but timely. At least ten Soviet planes laden with materiel for the Ethiopian army landed in Addis Ababa before Washington had an inkling of what was happening. It was not until December 11 that Deputy Secretary of State Warren Christopher cabled Vance, who was engaging in shuttle diplomacy in the Middle East, that "the Soviets could be on verge of mounting major upgrading of their military materiel and personnel assistance to Ethiopia." Although Carter administration officials had thought for some time that Siad would eventually lose the war, they had imagined that it would be as a result of arduous attrition over many months. The possibility that the Soviets had decided to substantially increase their support for Mengistu's army changed the equation; it introduced momentum. The Ethiopians might be able to rout Siad's forces and storm toward the undefended borders of Somalia. They might not stop. Christopher noted this in his December 11 cable: "Further, we must look ahead to the possibility of a successful Ethiopian strike towards Somalia."[41]

The following day, the American ambassador in Moscow, Malcolm Toon, called on Soviet foreign minister Andrei Gromyko. The White House wanted to voice its "serious concern" to the Kremlin. Gromyko vigorously defended his government's actions in the Horn. Unlike the Americans, in early 1977, "when the winds of war began to blow," the Soviets had openly pleaded with Siad Barre not to invade Ethiopia and for the past five months they had been publicly calling on him to withdraw his troops. Moreover, Gromyko assured Toon, "Soviet arms supply to Ethiopia is insignificant . . . [and the Ethiopians] don't have any plan to invade Somalia."[42]

The State Department was not mollified. It sent cables to leaders in the region—Iran, Pakistan, Turkey—asking them to refuse the Soviets permission to overfly their countries. At the same time, it urged its NATO and Arab allies to loudly and vehemently protest Soviet actions. "We consider Soviet airlift . . . egregious interference by superpower in African dispute which should be left to Africans themselves to resolve," Christopher cabled.[43]

Neither appeal was particularly successful. Turkish aviation had been rerouted over Bulgaria as a consequence of Turkey's war with Greece over Cyprus, and Istanbul feared that Moscow, if told its planes could not fly through Turkish airspace, would retaliate by imposing further limits on Turkish routes. And while Iran and Pakistan were eager to stop the overflights, the American warning had come too late. The Iranian foreign minister was irate at Washington's intelligence failure: Iran had already given overflight permission to at least four Soviet planes headed for Addis Ababa or Aden (a staging area for the airlift) before Christopher's warning had arrived. In Tehran, US Ambassador William Sullivan—not one to mince words—was apoplectic. "By sheer gall and because countermeasures have been neglected, the Soviets have already managed to send a number of flights to Aden. . . . If they [the Soviets] get away with this, they [the Iranians] will have a pretty low estimate of our resolve . . . [and] be contemptuous of the quality of our leadership." Sullivan suggested that the State Department stop "fussing around with mediation proposals" for the Ogaden and pay attention to halting the flow of Soviet weapons to Ethiopia.[44]

David Ransom, the deputy chief of mission at the US embassy in North Yemen, who witnessed the Soviet planes flowing into neighboring Aden, shared Ambassador Sullivan's outrage. "Surely we should not fail to signal our strong opposition to Communist intervention of sort successfully practiced in Angola. . . . Is there not some level of Soviet involvement which would lead us to help Somalia?" Ransom cabled on December 6. "Soviets have a history of pushing until they meet resistance, and they are pushing . . . hard . . . in Horn [ellipses in original]." Ransom did not hide his disgust. "Intervention of Soviets in Ethiopia could be test of our determination. Certainly Yemenis will look at it this way."[45]

The Carter administration turned to diplomacy. "We are seeking [US Ambassador to Nigeria] Don Easum's suggestions as to how we might get the Nigerians to rebuke the Soviets publicly for flagrant interference in an African dispute," Christopher cabled Vance on December 11. Easum's response was frank and courageous: the Department's idea was unwise. The Ethiopians were the victims of Somali aggression, and they had the sympathy of the vast majority of Africans. "We must be wary not to overexploit our improving relations with FMG [the Federal Military Government of Nigeria] by asking for too many favors," Easum cabled from Lagos. "We must husband our chips carefully and spend them deliberately." Vance wrote Carter that the response to the administration's request that African heads of state protest the Soviet airlift was "not as positive as we would have liked."[46]

Ostriches

Rallying the Western allies was also difficult, in large part because they were caught in the same dilemma that hamstrung Washington: drawn to helping Somalia because they wanted to defeat the Soviets and please the Saudis, they were unwilling to openly support Siad Barre's war of aggression. At a meeting of European Community leaders on December 6, several of the nine called for less complacency toward "the Soviet thrust into Africa." West Germany's Helmut Schmidt, grateful for Siad's help during the Lufthansa hijacking in October, "urged that the Governments of the Nine should give their backing to Somalia. . . . [They] should make an approach to the Saudis on Somalia's behalf." Britain's Jim Callaghan countered that this would antagonize the OAU and Kenya, and he cautioned Schmidt not to "overreact." Vance warned that "Somalia is playing with fire."[47]

At a quadripartite meeting the following day, the foreign ministers (with West German state secretary Günther van Well standing in for an ill Hans-Dietrich Genscher) fretted about the situation in the Horn. It was a revealing discussion. For the first half of the five-hour meeting, they talked about the possibilities and perils posed by Sadat's recent trip to Jerusalem and badgered Vance about the SALT negotiations. Then they settled into a discussion of African issues. Foreign Secretary David Owen opened the discussion of Rhodesia expressing his concern about "the grave danger" that the war could explode in Zambia. "The South Africans know that [Zambian president] Kaunda is moving toward accepting Cuban support," Owen said. If that happened, then "Smith would invade Zambia."[48]

But it was the crisis in the Horn that generated the longest conversation, as the assembled men batted around ideas about supplying arms to Somalia. Van Well said that West Germany "was increasing its assistance to Somalia considerably" but was not sending arms, and Vance reported afterward to Carter that "even the French may be backing away from providing arms to Somalia."[49] The men repeated their anxieties about Kenya and Djibouti and worried about an Ethiopian attack on Somalia, but they felt no urgency: they were confident that it would take months for the Ethiopians to learn how to use the new Soviet weapons, and they therefore failed to understand that the war could accelerate quickly. "Siad paints an exaggerated picture of Ethiopian capabilities," the State Department wrote in Vance's briefing book for the meeting, and emphasized that the Ethiopian army, facing multiple insurgencies and "serious morale and unity problems," would need time to regroup. No one's imagination stretched far enough to conceive that the Cubans, rather than marching to Zambia, might well land in Ethiopia.[50]

A week later, the allies again conferred about the latest round of Somali arms requests. "The Somalis seem to want to replace their entire arsenal with western weapons," the French representative declared. But as long as the war in the Ogaden continued, all asserted that they could not send weapons. This was doubletalk, since they all knew that the Americans and the French (at a minimum) were greasing backchannels to get arms to Mogadiscio.[51]

Throughout late November and December, the Carter administration was fundamentally in the dark. Despite hints of the Cuban shift of policy in Ethiopia, it failed to predict or prepare for a major Cuban intervention there. The US Interests Section in Havana cabled the State Department on December 9 that Castro had declared that an Ethiopian defeat would be "intolerable" and that Cuba would "do everything possible" to prevent it. But section head Lyle Lane did not grasp that Castro was signaling a change of policy; instead, he speculated that the speech reflected merely Cuba's disappointment with Somali advances in the war.[52]

Reality began to dawn on Washington the following week, when the CIA reported from Addis that "more than 400" Cubans had been airlifted there, bringing the total number of Cuban military personnel in Ethiopia to "more than 1,000," while there were "slightly more than 500" Soviet military advisers. (Cuban sources indicate that these were accurate estimates.) The CIA predicted that these numbers would double "in the next months"—a gross underestimate of what would actually occur. Moreover, in mid-December the administration received multiple intelligence reports that Cubans were fighting in the Ogaden and in the Eritrean port of Massawa, a key point of entry for Soviet supplies. (The reports were erroneous: Cuban sources are clear that there were never Cuban troops in Massawa—although there was a Cuban medical mission there for a short time—and no Cuban troops fought in the Ogaden before January 22, 1978.) NSC staffer Paul Henze wrote Brzezinski: "What we seem to be faced with," and he began to underline, "is another major escalation of Soviet involvement in the Third World, analogous to the Angola adventure."[53]

Brzezinski's tone was muted when he reported this information to Carter on December 16. "The evidence seems to indicate that they [the Soviets] are involved in a major escalation of their involvement in Ethiopia and that they are using the Cubans in much the same fashion as they used them two years ago in Angola," he wrote. "We are going to have to consider much sharper approaches to the Soviets on the Horn than we have made to date."[54]

Suddenly, the Carter administration's public relations blitz against Cuban policy in Africa—which had begun in early November as a low-cost way for the administration to flex its muscles—looked foolhardy. Why would Havana or Moscow hesitate to help Addis when it appeared that Washington was going to blare about Cuban intervention in Africa no matter the facts? Therefore, although the administration had lambasted Cuban interventionism in the Horn in November (when it was largely theoretical), its response to a real threat in December was subdued. A full-throated public denunciation of Soviet and Cuban escalation in Ethiopia would make it more difficult, the State Department explained, to induce Moscow and Havana "to exercise restraint."[55]

The US press was stirring. At the December 20 noon briefing at the State Department, spokesman Hodding Carter was grilled about the number of Cubans in Ethiopia. "I am obviously not being very precise with you," Hodding Carter admitted. "The reason is that we do not feel capable of being very precise now." Asked what pressure the United States could put on Cuba "other than words," the spokesman confessed that the available options were "limited."[56]

The administration, however, remained calm. It was unhappy about the Soviet airlift of materiel, but it did not consider it a crisis. The Soviets had gotten into a mess in the Horn, and they were trying to salvage what they could by buttressing the Mengistu government. Despite Brzezinski's memo, there is no indication that others in the administration believed that a thousand Cubans in Ethiopia presaged another Angola-scale intervention. Still confident that the Ethiopians would not need Cuban or Soviet troops to repulse the Somalis, the White House played it cool. By late December, it had faced the fact that it had little leverage: its attempts to rally its friends in Africa and the Middle East to denounce Soviet policy had fizzled, its protests to the Kremlin had been rebuffed, and its threat to Havana that sending troops to Ethiopia would halt the normalization process had been ineffective. The administration decided to avoid any more initiatives that would only expose its impotence, and congratulated itself for attaining a position in the Horn "that permits us maximum flexibility with minimum risk."[57]

"They have failed."[58]

In late November and December 1977, the Carter administration officials dealing with Africa were much more worried about the fate of the Anglo-American proposals for the resolution of the Rhodesian crisis than about Soviets and Cubans landing in Ethiopia. Their concerns were shaped by the need to respond to three events: Ian Smith's attempt to construct an internal settlement, blistering Rhodesian attacks deep inside Mozambique, and the continuing South African crackdown at home. Their anxieties were given urgency by a looming rupture in Anglo-American cooperation in Rhodesia.

On November 24, Ian Smith announced that Bishop Abel Muzorewa, Reverend Ndabaningi Sithole, and Chief Jeremiah Chirau—three black leaders without troops—had agreed to begin discussions with him to forge an "internal settlement" based on "one man, one vote." He bluntly explained his rationale to a group of white Rhodesian businessmen: "Even if you believe that all nationalists are devils, you have only one choice: find the better of the devils."[59]

Muzorewa, Sithole, and Chirau fit the bill. The first two had old, albeit compromised, nationalist credentials, but they had been shunted aside by the power struggles that roiled through the nationalist groups and by the creation of the Patriotic Front in late 1976. Chirau, by contrast, was a Shona chief who had always supported the illegal, racist Smith regime; he was, the British Foreign Office noted, "a pleasant individual . . . but lacking in punch." By including all three blacks, Smith not only broadened support for the internal settlement but also created a structure he could manipulate to his advantage, dividing and conquering the three restive black leaders. He had been signaling all year that he was interested in an internal settlement as a way to hijack the Anglo-American initiatives and blunt the momentum of the guerrilla war, but this was the first time he had convinced the nationalists to dance with him. When asked what this development indicated about the Anglo-American proposals, Smith was frank: "They have failed."[60]

Meanwhile, the war in southern Africa escalated. Four days after Smith announced the internal settlement talks, his government disclosed that it had launched two crushing air and ground assaults on "guerrilla bases" in Mozambique. Since the Rhodesian army lacked the manpower to recover the vast rural regions of Rhodesia that the Patriotic Front had taken over, its strategy shifted to punishing the countries that harbored the guerrillas' bases. Smith also had a political reason to launch these raids, Vance believed: "With the internal option now launched, he wants to be seen to be dealing from strength. A successful cross-border operation helps project the kind of image he needs right now—reassuring potential allies, intimidating foes." Dropping napalm and fragmentation bombs from helicopter gunships and Mirage fighters before landing 185 troops to mop up, the Rhodesians flattened camps at Chimoio, 54 miles inside Mozambique, and at Tembue, 134 miles from the border, dealing what Rhodesian military commanders called "a crippling blow" to Mugabe's ZANU forces. A huge banner headline in the Salisbury *Herald* proclaimed "1200 TERRORISTS KILLED." (Later estimates were that two to three thousand people were slain.) "Security forces lost one man in the operations. . . . Rhodesians greeted the news . . . with delight." An editorial lauded the "magnificent feats of arms" and asserted that "no amount of propaganda can disguise the fact that the operations were mounted purely in self-defence."[61]

Reports from the scene cast doubt on the Rhodesians' claims. A UPI reporter wrote that among the wounded were "boys and girls in their early teens," while the London *Guardian* noted that the bodies were "mainly of children." ZANU leader Robert Mugabe passionately denounced the "naked and unprovoked aggression by the rebel forces of Ian Smith and his imperialist masters . . . [that] . . . cold-bloodedly massacred . . . children, mothers, patients, and physically handicapped people. In one case, thirty-five children . . . were burnt in a classroom."[62] The Tanzanian state-owned newspaper, *The Daily News*, published grisly photographs on its front page allegedly showing Rhodesian soldiers torturing their victims at the two camps.[63] *Noticias*, the state-owned paper in Mozambique, printed two full pages of photographs from the scene showing what the US ambassador described as "a gruesome spectacle of death and destruction." The Mozambican government declared that "the attack's fundamental objective was the deliberate massacre of defenseless civilians." Even the Rhodesian pilot charged with going to the scene immediately afterward to analyze the effectiveness of the various types of bombs noted that "the air strike effects were very troubling. . . . Never again did I accept airstrike casualty numbers . . . without remembering the horror of what I saw at Chimoio."[64]

Bishop Muzorewa, who had just entered internal settlement talks with Smith, tried to take a stand. He publicly criticized Smith's government for these "diabolical acts" and called for a week of mourning. "Zimbabweans . . . must be informed that the people massacred in Mozambique were for the most part men, women, and children who fled from the land of their birth to seek asylum. . . . I vehemently condemn these massacres." After this brave protest, however, the bishop—who had nowhere to turn—fell silent and continued to negotiate with Smith. "Muzorewa was an incredibly weak man," Ambassador Steve Low commented.[65]

Three days after the Rhodesian government disclosed its "victory" at Chimoio, South African whites loudly announced their intransigent commitment to apartheid. In elections that excluded all the country's nonwhites, Prime Minister John Vorster's National Party won the biggest majority it had ever enjoyed: 134 of 165 parliamentary seats. "I think the electorate has spoken louder than any man could ever have spoken," Vorster proclaimed after the results were in. It was one month after the UN Security Council had imposed a mandatory arms embargo on South Africa. Vorster continued: "I think people will take note of . . . the determination with which South Africa will resist [outside pressure] if attacked."[66]

The following day, the inquest into the death of Steve Biko, the charismatic black leader who had been beaten to death in South African police custody, was released. It absolved the police of any responsibility. Many jaws dropped. The US State Department spokesperson delivered an unusually harsh comment, stating that the United States was "shocked by the verdict. . . . Mr.

Biko's death clearly resulted from a system that permits gross mistreatment in violation of the most basic human rights." The *New York Times* published a strong editorial calling the inquest a "whitewash [that] . . . shakes any remaining hope that blacks can receive justice from white South African courts."[67]

Thus, during the week after Thanksgiving—when Castro made his decision to send troops to Ethiopia—Washington was faced with multiple crises in southern Africa. Its pressure on Pretoria seemed to have backfired, galvanizing white South Africans to rally around their embattled leader and his party's racist policies. The Anglo-American proposals for Rhodesia had failed to stop the devastating raids on Chimoio and Tembue, and they appeared to have been preempted by Smith's internal settlement talks.

Exhorting Owen

Cyrus Vance knew that he had a problem. The moment he heard Smith's November 24 speech announcing that Muzorewa, Sithole, and Chirau had joined him in talks about an internal settlement, his mind turned to David Owen. The British foreign secretary was under intense pressure from the Tory backbenchers, and he was getting cold feet about the Anglo-American plan; therefore, Smith's internal settlement might lure him from the policy that the British and the Americans had jointly pursued for almost a year. "Owen and the FCO [the British Foreign Office] may be inclined to follow a more passive course," Vance cabled two days after Smith's announcement. Passivity was the opposite of what Vance thought the situation demanded. "We believe . . . that we should develop with the British a scenario for further moves. . . . Our intention is to press for a Frontline meeting before Christmas."[68]

The Carter administration's response to Smith's speech was guarded. State Department officials expressed grave misgivings because they did not see how Smith's plan could stop the war. The reason was simple: since the Patriotic Front guerrillas were excluded from the internal talks, the fighting would intensify. "[An] election from which the Patriotic Front is excluded would signal the start of a new round of violence in Rhodesia," Vance wrote Carter.[69] Nevertheless, the officials understood that it would be unwise to dismiss Smith's plan out of hand for two reasons. First, they were keenly aware that Smith's promise to construct a multiracial government in Rhodesia would appeal to many Americans, especially when the Anglo-American strategy had not borne fruit and the leaders of the Patriotic Front continued to trumpet their anti-American and prosocialist views. Refusing to even consider Smith's proposed solution would invite fierce criticism at home, and would cement the view of many conservatives that Jimmy Carter was in fact a dangerous radical.

The second reason was the opposite of this: Carter thought that there was an outside chance that Smith's talks could result in a just, independent Zimbabwe. Carter had grown increasingly wary of Joshua Nkomo after the latter's secret negotiations with Smith in September 1977. "At some point we should comment on Nkomo's unwillingness to face the electorate in an open campaign," he grumbled. Carter thought that Bishop Muzorewa might be a better leader of Zimbabwe. And Washington received some glimmers of hope that the internal settlement could be viable. After talks with Sithole, for example, the US ambassador in Malawi cabled: "Smith is at last prepared to concede ostensible black rule but clings to hope he can maintain some degree of white control. . . . [Sithole insisted that the] internal settlement talks . . . were an honest effort and therefore merited UK/US support." Thus an internal settlement with two highly unlikely provisos—that Smith was serious about sharing power and that it included the Patriotic Front—might not be without merit. As Carter wrote on the margin of one of Vance's evening reports, "Internal settlements are better than nothing."[70]

Therefore, the Carter administration did not slam the door on the internal settlement, but at the same time it struggled mightily to reinvigorate the Anglo-American negotiations. This was very challenging. "Smith's timing, as so often in the past, is excellent," the State Department admitted on November 30. Due to the fallout from the meeting between Ian Smith and Zambia's Kenneth Kaunda (and, as was widely and correctly suspected, Nkomo) the previous September, the Frontline presidents were scarcely talking to each other and the fissures between Nkomo and Mugabe had deepened. "He [Smith] has grabbed center stage at a time when the other principal actors on the Rhodesian drama are in varying stages of confusion and contradiction," the State Department observed. The real danger was that in this situation, the Frontline presidents would give up on a negotiated solution, Smith would pursue his settlement, and the war would expand, drawing in increasing Soviet aid and Cuban troops.[71]

Moreover, the South African government, already deeply disgruntled with the West, might decide that Smith's internal settlement plan was good enough and stop pressing him to do more. This possibility shook the core of the Anglo-American plan. If Pretoria refused to exert pressure on Salisbury, what leverage did London and Washington have to force Smith's hand? The State Department memo of November 30 dealt with this dilemma. Optimistically, it posited that "the South Africans still appear willing to cooperate with us on Rhodesia—within the same limited parameters as before." Nevertheless, the internal settlement would inevitably create a delay—and doubts. "As long as there is a plausible chance . . . that Smith's gambit could produce a moderate black government and a diminution of the war, it is unlikely that South Africa will take stern action to attempt to dissuade Smith from his present course." This meant that the Frontline presidents and the Patriotic Front would question more vigorously than ever whether the Anglo-American plan could really deliver on its promises.[72]

For the State Department, there was only one way forward. The Americans and British had to convince the South African government, the Frontline presidents, the Patriotic Front, and the world that the Anglo-American proposals were still alive and that they offered the best path to peace and justice. There was even reason for some optimism: the threat of an internal settlement could jolt the Frontline States and the Patriotic Front back to the negotiating table. "It could induce a more reasonable attitude on the part of Nkomo and Mugabe, and even serve to reunite Kaunda with his Frontline colleagues," Vance wrote Carter five days after Smith's announcement. However, there was no time to waste: the proposals were in danger of becoming irrelevant.[73]

The State Department's most immediate problem, however, was not in Salisbury or Pretoria, but in London. "David Owen is most reluctant to pursue an active strategy," a departmental discussion paper observed. "We conclude, as we always have, that it is essential to stick with the British-American Plan. Indeed . . . it is more important than ever to demonstrate that our plan is still alive." On November 27, Vance sent a long, assertive letter to Owen urging him to stand firm: "Pressing forward with our plan is the wisest course. . . . [It is] important for us to demonstrate our determination. . . . If we appear to hesitate at this critical moment, or if we appear too interested in Smith's proposal, we are likely to be placed on the defensive and charged with having abandoned our commitment. We should be faithful to our undertakings." Vance proposed calling a meeting with the Frontline presidents as soon as possible. He implored Owen, in these difficult circumstances, to help him create momentum.[74]

In London, Ambassador Kingman Brewster commented that "the Secretary's letter [to Owen] . . . will crystalize US-UK differences on how to proceed. . . . Owen is firmly against a meeting with Frontline presidents." Instead, Owen wanted to blame Zambia's Kaunda and Tanzania's Nyerere for the lack of progress in the Anglo-American initiative, and let them stew. "Owen is discouraged," Brewster explained, "[and wants to] 'throw the ball into their [the Frontline presidents'] court.'" The Americans suggested to Owen that "this would seem to throw in the towel as well."[75]

The "Oily Tinge" at the UN

It was a UN debate that goaded David Owen from his torpor. In late November, just as Ian Smith announced that Muzorewa, Sithole, and Chirau were joining him in internal settlement talks, the General Assembly, the Apartheid Committee, and the Decolonization Committee (the "Fourth Committee") were all considering action to tighten the screws on Rhodesia. The Smith regime was being kept alive by clandestine oil shipments, thought to be largely from South Africa; these shipments broke the mandatory UN sanctions on Rhodesia, and therefore each of the three groups at the UN was discussing imposing oil sanctions on South Africa to force it to stop the illegal activity. (In 1978, the Bingham Report would reveal that British oil companies had also been routinely violating the mandatory UN sanctions on Rhodesia.[76]) These deliberations, Andrew Young cabled in early December, "would give the UN atmosphere an oily tinge."[77]

In response, the British and the Americans almost parted ways. The Carter administration stressed that the sanctions could be limited to oil and based not on a Chapter 7 finding (that South Africa was "a threat to peace") but on the need to enforce existing sanctions on Rhodesia. Whitehall rejected this argument and threatened to veto any oil sanctions, even if it had to do so unilaterally. The British regarded oil sanctions as a dangerous step, a slippery slide closer to mandatory economic sanctions. They argued that oil sanctions were unnecessary "we had 'done enough' about South Africa." They also would be counterproductive because "the threat was more useful" than the deed. Washington struggled for weeks to persuade the British to reconsider.[78]

At a quadripartite meeting on December 7, when Vance inquired about the response of the other governments to oil sanctions, Owen unleashed a tirade. The only way to enforce such sanctions would be a naval blockade, and that "was virtually a declaration of war." Vance asked about more modest steps, such as requiring South Africa to provide end-user certificates that would certify that the imported oil would not be shipped to another party. Owen responded that any embargo, no matter the fine print, "would be very difficult to get through Parliament." Moreover, it "would be valueless." Acceding to the Africans' demands at the UN would be dangerous. "There would inevitably be demands for further sanctions," Owen asserted. "The South Africans would resist. They were tough," he reminded his three colleagues. "They would really go nuclear and would fight." Only a month had passed since London had reluctantly acceded to US pressure to vote in favor of the UN mandatory arms embargo on South Africa. It was enough. Best to wait and see whether Smith's internal settlement developed and what its impact would be on the Frontline States and the Patriotic Front. Owen was emphatic: "If he regretted anything it was that the Western powers had accepted too much," bending over backwards to satisfy the African Group at the UN. In answer to Vance's query as to how Britain would respond if a vote were called, Owen said flatly: "The UK would unilaterally veto any such UN resolution."[79]

The French and West Germans agreed that there was no need to rush into oil sanctions. West Germany's UN ambassador noted, "Ever since the inauguration of President Carter, the British and French have looked on US policy toward South Africa with nervous suspicion. . . . The French are already working with their major allies to construct a Maginot line against further sanctions." Paris let London take the lead in opposition to oil sanctions. The French government also wanted to avoid sanctions, and it implied that it would support a British veto, but it stayed on the sidelines as Owen battled it out with Vance.[80]

The Americans saw the situation differently from their European allies. Their reputation in black Africa and the Third World had been bruised by the triple vetoes that Young had cast in November against the UN mandatory economic sanctions on South Africa. The viability of the Anglo-American proposals had been put in doubt by the recalcitrance of the Frontline States, the Patriotic Front, and the Smith regime, and the relevance of all-party talks was undermined by Smith's efforts to reach an internal settlement. Therefore, despite its initial uneasiness, the Carter administration decided in December 1977 that vetoing UN oil sanctions, as Britain desired and general Western unity demanded, could deal a death blow to its hopes for a negotiated settlement in Rhodesia and to its overarching attempts to change the developing world's opinion of the US government.

The Americans saw a way to avert disaster: inject enough life into the Anglo-American proposals to relieve the pressure at the UN for immediate sanctions. Young laid out the strategy. On December 2, after explaining that "the Africans will use it [a UN Security Council meeting on Rhodesia] to attempt to force oil sanctions on South Africa . . . in the near future," Young warned that "[h]ow well we survive such sessions depends very much on how well the UK/US effort on Rhodesia is doing at that time. If there is no progress . . . then US and UK calls for patience and restraint will fall on absolutely deaf ears. If we are forced to veto an oil sanctions resolution . . . the credibility of the UK/US promise to take the necessary measures to remove Smith will be severely undercut and with it, our effectiveness to continue negotiating." In other words, "clear progress on the UK/US initiative will buy us more time. Stagnation . . . presents the near certainty of Donneybrook [sic] SC [Security Council] sessions on Rhodesia."[81]

To reinvigorate the Anglo-American proposals, Washington decided to focus on the Patriotic Front, which had been squeezed out of Smith's internal settlement talks. Although the Carter administration still hoped and expected that Pretoria would press Smith to negotiate a transfer of power, by late 1977 it had accepted that its leverage was limited: the South African government would pursue the policy it believed to be in its best interest; therefore it was not useful for Washington to apply further pressure. Instead, the Americans concentrated on rallying the Frontline presidents to push Mugabe and Nkomo to the negotiating table, and then present Smith with a fait accompli—a proposal supported by the Patriotic Front, the Frontline States, the Americans, and the British.

Young also proposed a much more dramatic move to restore America's credibility at the UN and in the developing world: "a pre-emptive UK/US resolution on oil."[82] Young explained the urgency of the situation in a long cable to Vance and Brzezinski on December 17. "We have reached a point in the overall negotiations in Rhodesia where the absence of effective action to back up our promise not to let Smith impede an equitable settlement is becoming a key obstacle." Continued failure to act would doom the peace process. "Nkomo simply does not believe we will act, and appears to be planning his own strategies accordingly," Young asserted. "A similar skepticism adds to the incentives of Muzorewa and Sithole to obtain through internal settlement . . . what they doubt will ever be delivered to them by US/UK pressures on Smith." America's inaction made it more difficult for Kaunda and Nyerere to stay the course. "Centrifugal tendencies among the Frontline presidents feed on the same doubt," Young commented, adding, "and, of course, the intransigence of Smith and Vorster is affected by the degree to which they believe we are bluffing."[83]

Given the stakes, Young called for action. "Contrary to David Owen, . . . I suggest that we seize the opportunity of the upcoming SC debate on Rhodesia to manifest, for the first time, a concrete willingness to remove Smith. While the British appear to be scratching for other options, I believe that the only one that could be effective both in New York and in Africa is UK/US support for Council actions tightening oil sanctions." Young then referred to a recent Harris poll that showed strong US domestic support for applying pressure on South Africa. (The poll, taken before the details of Biko's death were public, showed that 63 percent of respondents thought apartheid was not justified, while only 12 percent disagreed; 45 percent favored applying pressure on South Africa, with only 26 percent disagreeing; and 41 percent supported a ban on new investment, while 33 percent disagreed. The arms embargo was supported by 51 percent of the respondents and opposed by only 24 percent.) This persuaded him that oil sanctions were "within the bounds of measures the American people could be led to accept."[84]

Supporting oil sanctions on South Africa, especially over British objections, would be playing, one NSC expert opined, the "heavy chip."[85] Vance was hesitant, but did not dismiss the idea. He did not want to veto oil sanctions that had strong African support. Therefore, Vance pressed Owen to join the United States in supporting an oil resolution that would be the "least of the evils."[86] Owen would hear none of it.[87]

The Carter administration moved forward. "While we are naturally sympathetic to UK concerns," Christopher cabled, "we feel that Indian resolution [which would impose oil sanctions only if South Africa refused to comply voluntarily with the prohibition on selling oil to Rhodesia] is least painful among various alternatives."[88]

The prospect that the United States might support sanctions and leave Britain to veto them alone lit a fire under Owen. He threw his weight behind "plan A"—getting the Anglo-American negotiations on Rhodesia rolling again so that the African Group at the UN could be persuaded that this was not an opportune time to impose punitive and disruptive sanctions. The British UN representative, Robin Byatt, put it succinctly: "The deader the [Anglo-American] plan looks, the more difficult it will be for us to turn down oil sanctions." After refusing to move for weeks, Owen swung into action: he invited Nkomo and Mugabe to London and agreed to call a meeting of the Frontline presidents. Mugabe and Nkomo refused imperiously to jump to Owen's call, but the important point was that the Anglo-American process was back on the table.[89]

President Carter entered the fray, writing to Nyerere that he agreed that it was imperative to "move forward rapidly." He urged Nyerere to persuade Mugabe and Nkomo to agree to meet with British and American representatives. "For this meeting to succeed, however, we should avoid any precipitate moves in the UN . . . which could complicate or divert attention from our efforts. I hope that you and our other African friends agree and will collaborate with Andy Young to this end."[90]

The crisis was averted. A vote on oil sanctions was delayed indefinitely, the British had climbed back aboard the Anglo-American train, and in January 1978 Nkomo and Mugabe agreed to participate in talks in Malta with the Frontline presidents, the British, and the Americans.[91]

Hoping for the Best in the Horn

Jimmy Carter lifted his glass. He was relaxed, away from Washington, celebrating New Year's Eve in Tehran with America's friend, the shah of Iran. Carter's toast is remembered for its characterization of Iran as "an island of stability" when, unfortunately, the country was on the precipice of revolution. This phrase was embedded in boilerplate praise for Iran and the shah, but Carter's brief toast included a substantive comment on policy. "We also had a chance to discuss," Carter revealed about his talks with the shah, "the Horn of Africa."[92]

In fact, Somalia's Siad Barre had just flown out of Tehran the day before. "The primary purpose" of Siad's trip, the Iranian foreign minister said, "was to persuade Shah to lean on Pres[ident] Carter for greater assistance."[93]

The Horn was very much on the shah's mind. He impressed on Carter his concern that "the radical Arab states, in cooperation with the Soviet Union, might create a 'red crescent'" to satisfy the Soviets' growing energy needs. Soviet influence would expand from Syria and Iraq to Lebanon and Jordan, "and eventually Kuwait and not even Saudi Arabia would be safe." The Soviets were shifting "all their weight to this part of the world, directing their efforts toward the Indian Ocean." The following day, the shah promised Carter that Iran would help Siad if the Ethiopians attacked Somalia. "Not only Iran, but also Egypt, Jordan, Saudi Arabia and other regional states could not stand by if Ethiopia crossed [the] Somali border," the shah pledged.[94]

On January 4, 1978, Carter stopped in Paris, where President Valéry Giscard d'Estaing was adamant that Washington had to respond to Soviet intervention in the Horn. Giscard considered the Americans "a little naive in an involuntary way." He lectured Carter. "What the Russians were doing was incompatible with détente," he asserted. "The only way of stopping them would be a strong warning to Moscow from the American president. . . . You have to make it clear to the Soviets that détente is global, and if they want détente then they cannot pursue a policy of destabilization in the Horn." Giscard, however, offered Carter no help and no ideas, just harsh words.[95]

A week later, Carter faced the press in the Old Executive Office Building. It was his first news conference of the new year, and it was televised live. "It's nice to be back home," Carter began. Perhaps, but it was certainly not restful: Carter returned to an administration on overdrive. Many of the major initiatives that the White House had launched in its first year were reaching critical junctures—the Panama Canal treaties, the energy policy, SALT II, southern Africa, peace in the Middle East—and added to these were unpredicted events, like the strike of the United Mine Workers of America (which had begun in December) and the war in the Horn.[96]

US policy toward the Horn was the subject of the second question hurled at Carter. "Mr. President, everywhere you traveled, except Poland [Carter had also visited Iran, India, Saudi Arabia, Egypt, France, and Belgium], . . . you . . . talked about Soviet and Cuban penetration in the Horn of Africa. . . . Can you enunciate the depth of our concern, and what can we do about it except jawbone?"[97]

Carter had anticipated the question. He began by explaining his administration's African policy: "We've taken a position concerning Africa that we would use our influence to bring about peace without shipping arms to the disputing parties and without our injecting ourselves into disputes that could best be resolved by Africans." He drew a stark contrast with the Kremlin's policy. "The Soviets have done just the opposite," Carter said. "They sold excessive quantities of arms and weapons both to Somalia and to Ethiopia . . . and now they are shipping large quantities of weapons, some men, and they are also dispatching Cubans into Ethiopia, perhaps to become combatants themselves." Carter sketched the two trajectories of the US response: vague threats and calls for negotiations. "We have expressed our concern to the Soviets in very strong terms," he said slowly and deliberately. "I hope that we can induce the Soviets and the Cubans not to send either soldiers or weapons into that area and call for and achieve a rapid initiation of negotiations."[98]

The truth was that Carter administration officials could do little more than hope: the Soviets had legality and African sentiment on their side. TASS, the Soviet news agency, slammed the president's remarks, saying they "distorted the true state of affairs" in the Horn and implied that Cuba was "not a sovereign state." Carter's statement, Ethiopian radio claimed, was "a tasteless joke." Addis hinted that it would break relations with Washington.[99]

The British Foreign Office noted that "warning signals of a general kind have now been hoisted publicly by the Americans." It was disgruntled that Carter had issued this public reprimand to Moscow without consulting London. "We should have welcomed advance notice," Johnny Graham, the head of the British negotiating team in southern Africa, complained to Assistant Secretary Richard Moose. Moose responded with resignation: "[I, too,] would have liked to have been consulted."[100]

As the NSC's Paul Henze wrote on the day of the president's press conference, "The Carter administration inherited a mess [in the Horn]."[101] Washington's rupture with Addis had been unavoidable, given the pro-Soviet ideology of the Derg. From April to August 1977, the White House had hoped to compensate for America's "loss" of Ethiopia with the "gain" of Somalia. By November, Siad Barre's invasion of Ethiopia had changed Washington's calculus. First, it rendered a US alliance with Somalia impossible, at least in the short term. Second, and more important, it caused the rupture between Moscow and Mogadiscio. Thus, by November, the Carter administration had achieved one of its primary aims: the Soviets had failed to straddle both ends of the Horn. Courting Siad Barre, therefore, was less necessary.

The walls were closing in on Siad. On January 2, 1978, he vented his frustration to West German chancellor Helmut Schmidt. "I have received no support from the West," he declared. "From France, nice words but nothing useful. . . . From non-western states, very little. Iran would like to help, but has been told it can't. Egypt 'will see what it can do.'" The Saudis had sent

$100 million to pay for oil and transportation costs, but Somalia had not been able to locate a reliable arms supplier. For all his efforts imploring the West, Iran, and the conservative Arabs, Siad had received only a small, haphazard assortment of heavy weapons; some small arms; and empty promises.[102]

Siad tacked once again. On January 16, he summoned the American, British, French, West German, and Italian ambassadors in Mogadiscio to inform them that "a Russian inspired attack on northwest Somalia was imminent. . . . Soviet ships would land Cuban and other black troops at Berbera." Simultaneously, the Somali ambassadors in each of the five Western countries delivered a formal request to their host governments: "Forces from the Soviet Union, Cuba, Hungary, Czechoslovakia, East Germany and other Warsaw Pact countries are now poised to strike at Somalia," the letter explained. Somalia therefore required "immediate aid."[103]

On January 20, the quadripartite group met in Washington to coordinate its response to Siad's newest request for arms. They agreed that an Ethiopian invasion of Somalia would be a matter of "utmost seriousness." However, American and British intelligence believed that "the threat . . . is not as immediate as President Barre maintains." While the four allies had "no desire to see Somalia crushed," they were all aware that "Somalia has put herself in the wrong." They therefore fell back on calling for negotiations, with little expectation of success. On the following day, the four foreign ministers—who did not want other NATO members to know about their meetings—invited the counselor of the Italian embassy in Washington to join their working group for a special "Five Power Meeting on the Horn." Given Italy's historical ties with the Horn, the allies hoped that the Italian embassy's representative might shed new light on the crisis. The conclusions of this meeting, however, duplicated those of the day before: seek negotiations without much hope they would lead anywhere and with no urgency. The five were confident that they had several months to consider other options. "It is unlikely EPMG [Ethiopia] can launch a successful general counterattack before June."[104]

The Western countries failed to imagine the scale of the Soviet and Cuban intervention in Ethiopia. There were still no reporters on the front lines of the war, and the information from official Ethiopian and Somali sources was almost comically unreliable. The Somalis still denied that any of their troops were in the Ogaden, and Siad Barre had cried wolf for so long about the Cubans that it was impossible to take his claims seriously. The Ethiopians denied that the Cubans and Soviets were arriving. As late as February 7, 1978, for example, when thousands of Cubans were fighting in the Ogaden, the spokesman for the Derg assured the press corps in Addis that "there were no Soviet or Cuban troops in Ethiopia—only technicians and medical personnel. . . . Some Soviets and Cubans are training our soldiers, but they are not participating in the fighting, and they are not even near the front. Moreover, there are only 'about 100' of them." The Soviets likewise lied, denying that they were airlifting weapons to Ethiopia.[105] Throughout January 1978, US intelligence expected that it would be at least four months before the Ethiopians, armed with Soviet weapons and "backed by a Cuban mechanized battalion," would be capable of mounting a counteroffensive against the Somalis.[106]

The View from Havana

The Cubans had come to a different conclusion: the Ethiopian army was broken. The Cuban military mission reported recurring problems with its discipline, command structure, and morale. In November 1977, it noted three episodes of fragging. On December 4, General Ochoa, the head of the Cuban military mission in Addis Ababa, cabled Havana that Ethiopian soldiers on the front lines were engaging in self-mutilation so that they would be evacuated. Part of the problem was that the army was overextended. "The Ethiopian army lacks reserves, particularly of artillery and tank units," the Cuban armed forces reported on December 12. Compounding these problems was the fact that the Ethiopian troops had trained with American weapons, and they did not know how to use the Soviet arms that were flowing into Addis. The conclusion was inescapable: "The Ethiopian army is incapable of mounting offensive operations," the Cuban mission reported in December. "Only the active participation of Cuban troops can change this."[107]

Historian Gebru Tareke arrived at a similar conclusion thirty years later based on research in the Ethiopian archives. By October 1977, the Ethiopians had stalled the Somali advance, but foreign intervention was necessary to achieve victory. "That Cuban-Soviet assistance was instrumental in both their [the Somalis'] defeat and their expulsion is . . . incontrovertible." While this was in part due to the Ethiopians' unfamiliarity with Soviet weapons, the more serious problem was the weakness of command and control. The Derg had purged Emperor Haile Selassie's officer corps, but it had not succeeded in replacing it with well-trained leaders who were reliably loyal to the revolution. This worried the Kremlin. The US chief of mission in Addis, Richard Matheron, reported that in his conversations with Soviet ambassador Anatoly Ratanov "a basic point to which Ratanov returned repeatedly during our discussions was the lack of control of the central government . . . over the military forces."[108]

In early January 1978, Fidel Castro sent his brother Raúl, the minister of defense, to Addis Ababa to assess the military situation. On January 6,

Mengistu delivered the grim news to Raúl: "The Ethiopian Armed Forces," he said flatly, "are nonexistent. There are really only two functioning divisions—the 'Flame' and the 7th division—plus a handful of men from the old army. That's what we now call the army. The militia is a hundred thousand strong, but it's composed of peasants who have no revolutionary consciousness, and all they want to do is go home." Mengistu and Raúl were particularly worried that countries supplying weapons to Mogadiscio might decide to send troops to Somalia. "We have to accept the possibility," Raúl Castro told Mengistu on January 10, 1978, "that Siad will receive additional help—troops from Iran and, after a while, from Egypt."[109]

Raúl Castro made a quick trip to Moscow to consult with his counterpart, Soviet defense minister Dimitriy Ustinov. "How much longer can we continue to help them [the Ethiopians]," Ustinov asked, "when they still haven't been able to create an army—even a small army, but at least one that is organized? No matter how much we help them, we can't take their place. We'll help—but it's up to them to solve their problems!" The Soviets and Cubans decided that a massive effort, larger than they had foreseen in November, was required and that speed was essential: Harar must not fall. On January 19, 1978, from Moscow, Raúl Castro and Ustinov sent a message to the heads of the Soviet and Cuban military missions in Ethiopia. "We understand the complexity of the situation in the Ethiopian army and the difficulties of mounting the offensive. . . . But time is of the essence. Do not delay the counteroffensive. In the last ten days of January, advance toward Harar. Then, in the first ten days of February, launch the major offensive toward Diredawa."[110]

The Americans were well aware that Cuban troops were arriving in Ethiopia, but their imaginations failed them when they tried to analyze what it meant. US intelligence experts kept tabs on the escalating numbers of Cubans in Ethiopia: in early January they predicted the number would crest in April at 2,000; by mid-January they had added 3,500 to the total; by early February the anticipated total had grown to 7,000. This estimate was not made public; the official US estimate of Cubans in Ethiopia in early February was 3,000.[111] The American estimates, public and private, were wrong—by a long shot. The Cubans sent 12,000 troops to Ethiopia, 70 percent more than Washington expected. On February 12, there were already 5,132 Cubans on the ground. This number jumped to 8,224 by February 24, and peaked several weeks later.[112]

American officials were always playing catch-up. Throughout the crisis, US intelligence was groping in the dark, perpetually surprised by the numbers of Cuban troops arriving in Addis. A cable from Lyle Lane, head of the US Interests Section in Havana, summed up the confusion. Titled "Whereabouts of Raúl Castro?," it noted that the Cuban defense minister and brother of the president had skipped an important meeting in Havana. Could he be in Ethiopia? (The answer, the Americans learned a week later, was yes, he was indeed in Addis.) There were glimmers of comprehension, as in Paul Henze's note to Brzezinski on January 10 that the "scope of the Soviet investment [in Ethiopia] is staggering." But they were just glimmers. At no point did the Carter administration understand that the Cubans had made a decision to intervene *en masse* and bring an end to the war.[113]

The dominant viewpoint was expressed by an interagency intelligence report prepared for a late January meeting on the Horn. "For the next three to four months the Somalis have a reasonable chance of defending most of their gains in the Ogaden," the analysts predicted. They asserted that Ethiopia was held back mainly by its "critical deficiency . . . in experienced leadership" and disciplined troops. They failed to realize that men from Havana and Moscow might solve these problems. Instead, the American experts concluded, "There will be no massive foreign intervention on either side. . . . A critical pushback of the Somalis any earlier than May is unlikely." Therefore, the five men—Cyrus Vance, Zbigniew Brzezinski, CIA Director Stansfield Turner, Defense Secretary Harold Brown, and Chairman of the Joint Chiefs General George Brown—who gathered on January 26, 1978, for the year's first high-level meeting on the Horn believed that they had time to sit back and observe the situation. "It was the consensus of the group that the US Government should be cautious about taking actions that would . . . encourage a sense of crisis or confrontation with the Soviets."[114]

Last Chance at Malta

"The Horn is a sideshow," the CIA's national intelligence officer for Africa wrote in late January. Even with US intelligence estimating more than 2,000 Cuban troops and 1,000 Soviet advisers in Ethiopia, the Carter administration's attention remained riveted on southern Africa. (The estimate of the Soviet presence was accurate, but close to 5,000 Cubans were already in Ethiopia.) The State Department and CIA were convinced that southern Africa was where the most dangerous conflagration could occur. That Havana and Moscow would go to such lengths to save the Derg only underlined the possibility of a true nightmare scenario in the southern third of the continent. The State Department redoubled its efforts to prove that the Anglo-American proposals for a Rhodesian settlement were not, as the US ambassador in Tanzania wrote, "dead in the water."[115]

Under strong Frontline pressure (the Nigerians had promised "to talk turkey" to Nkomo and Mugabe), the Patriotic Front had accepted the British and

American invitation to meet them in Malta to discuss the proposals.[116] This would be the first substantive meeting of the Americans and British with the Patriotic Front. During January 1978, State Department officials prepared for this encounter, which they thought could be "the last chance for the Anglo-American settlement proposals." If Washington could not persuade the Patriotic Front to support the proposals—Smith and the nationalists by his side had already rejected them—the American people might ask who *did* support them and "domestic pressures . . . [would] increase dramatically" for the administration to accept an internal settlement instead.[117]

At Malta, the American team decided not to administer "shock therapy"—threatening to walk out if the Patriotic Front proved obdurate—and to rely instead on the people skills that Andrew Young had honed during his days at Martin Luther King's side. Young signaled his approach before he arrived on the island. "Amb. Young believes that it is important for US side to be lodged in same hotel as Patriotic Front in Malta," the State Department cabled the US embassy in Valletta, "in order to permit best opportunity for in depth discussions. (On any other visit, Amb. Young would be pleased to accept Amb. Laingen's invitation to stay at the residence.)" Foreign Secretary David Owen, by contrast, stayed at the British high commissioner's residence and did not fraternize outside the formal meetings.[118]

Persuading the Patriotic Front to consider the Anglo-American proposals was not the Americans' only challenge: they also had to restrain their partner. David Owen was angling once again to persuade Nkomo to join the internal settlement talks. "The British are clearly anxious to explore the possibilities of splitting Nkomo from Mugabe," Vance informed Carter. This was in part a response to domestic pressures on the Callaghan government. The heat of the debate in the British Parliament can be gleaned from a question hurled at Owen while he was explaining the importance of the Malta meeting: "How much longer," a Conservative member of Parliament asked, "does he [Owen] propose to prefer the company of murderers to that of moderates?"[119]

Callaghan expected to have to call a general election within the year, and Owen was on the defensive. This revived the old dream of a quick and slippery deal with Nkomo. The Americans worried that Owen, who had agreed to the Malta meeting only to avoid a UN vote on oil sanctions, might use the occasion to justify jettisoning the Anglo-American proposals. In their preparatory papers for Malta, State Department officials noted that one of their main objectives at the conference was to "counsel Owen not to overreact."[120] A breakdown in the talks might suit Whitehall's purposes by opening a path to a deal with Nkomo.

As the Americans, British, and Africans converged on the rooftop lounge of the Grand Verdala Hotel, all were under pressure. Almost 4,000 miles to the south, Ian Smith, Bishop Muzorewa, Reverend Sithole, and Chief Chi-rau were hammering out the final details of the internal settlement. Smith's proposal of a biracial government was sure to gain popular support in the United States and in Britain, making it harder for Owen and Young to sell their Anglo-American proposals at home. The war was spreading, wreaking havoc on the Rhodesian economy. Fully a quarter of the workforce was unemployed, and the cost of living was skyrocketing. In January, 401 Rhodesians were killed by the guerrillas—the highest death toll since the war began. The Smith regime struck back with devastating attacks on Mozambique, and the "kill ratio" remained 5 to 1. The Frontline presidents felt increasingly vulnerable: that was why they had urged Nkomo and Mugabe to go to Malta. If the Malta talks failed—if the Anglo-American proposals collapsed—the Rhodesian war would intensify and Mozambique's Samora Machel and Zambia's Kenneth Kaunda would need Soviet and Cuban help. "It could lead to the destruction of southern Africa," Young told a reporter.[121]

The Malta talks, which stretched over three days, were "direct, but non-confrontational." Each side made concessions about the transition period: the Patriotic Front would consider allowing UN peacekeepers to play a role; and the Americans finally persuaded the British to give the Patriotic Front more power (but not the "dominant role" that the Front requested) during this period. Ambassador Steve Low commented that "at Malta, Owen finally accepted that the Patriotic Front would play a major role during the transition. This was an important change." Many difficulties, however, remained. As Owen told the BBC, "Negotiating a cease-fire when neither of the two armies [the Patriotic Front and the Rhodesian Army] have won or lost a war is an appallingly difficult problem."[122]

The Americans were more upbeat despite the lack of substantive progress in the negotiations. "Much was achieved," Young told the Baltimore *Afro-American*, "in the realms of trust and understanding." It was, Ambassador Low wrote, "a happening of considerable importance." The Americans had feared that Patriotic Front intransigence and British ambivalence would lead to a breakdown of the talks. Instead, they had managed, as Young reported, to find enough common ground with the Patriotic Front "to maintain British interest." This was crucial to the survival of the Anglo-American initiative.[123]

To the extent that the talks succeeded, it was due in large part to the shoe-leather skills of Young and his staff, almost all of whom were black. Between the formal meetings, they worked the hallways, restaurant, and bar of the hotel. They chatted incessantly, sometimes late into the night, with Mugabe and Nkomo and (perhaps more significantly) with their negotiating staffs. They were well aware, as Young noted, that "there probably were more British/

American PhD's on their side of the table than there were on our side." The *Malawi News* reported that the Americans established "a mately approach . . . with jolly working lunches." Young told an anecdote that conveyed the atmosphere at Malta: "A big, burly guy comes over to me and put his hand on my shoulder and said, 'I need to talk to you.' I didn't know him. As big as he was, I was kind of nervous. He was in his battle fatigues, long-bearded. He was one of their [ZANU's] military commanders from out of the bush. He pulled me off to the side and said, 'What really happened to the Oakland Raiders? . . . They were supposed to be in the Super Bowl this year. What happened?'" At another moment, when Nkomo was annoyed with the British and considering quitting the talks, Young and Ambassador Low appeared at his hotel room door to talk about it. "Nkomo," Low cabled Washington, "clearly felt himself in the presence of a friend in Andy Young, with whom he was sharing his private feelings." The effect of Young's personal diplomacy was most pronounced on Mugabe, who previously had resisted American participation in the Rhodesia crisis. At Malta, he began to believe that Young and the Americans could deflect Owen and the British from the siren of the internal settlement. Mugabe told the press that Young's contribution at Malta had been "tremendous." He never again railed against American involvement in the negotiations; at Malta, Moose noted, "Andy became a brother."[124]

Mugabe's change of heart led to the other shift that occurred at Malta. David Ottaway, who covered the meeting for the *Washington Post*, reported, "The United States appears to be taking over from Britain the main burden of selling their joint peace plan for Rhodesia to the black guerrillas." This reflected Owen's uneasiness about the future of the Anglo-American proposals. On February 12, he complained "very frankly" to Vance about promises Young had made to the Patriotic Front at Malta. "We cannot afford a situation in which we discovered that the US side had made hidden commitments. . . . [I]t could come to an open breach between us." Owen also revisited his irritation about Carter's promise to President Nyerere six months earlier that the Zimbabwean armed forces during the transition would be "based on the liberation forces." Five days after his "frank" talk with Owen, Vance chaired a Policy Review Committee meeting at which it was concluded that the British, "who are under great domestic pressure, . . . would be glad to see us carry the ball [in Rhodesia] by ourselves for a while."[125]

When Owen reported on the Malta talks to Parliament, it was clear why he needed American cover. As he explained that the Labour government would continue to pursue the Anglo-American proposals, Tories yelled "Shame!" and "Resign!" Winston Churchill, the grandson of the former prime minister, closed the debate by asking, "Is the Foreign Secretary aware . . . that the

British people . . . resent his most recent cavortings with the terrorist leaders in the Mediterranean?"[126]

The American team, meanwhile, fanned out to consolidate the fragile gains it had made at Malta. On February 9, 1978, Ambassador Low had a long meeting with President Kaunda, who spoke with "a new note of urgency." The Zambian president feared that "without progress on our proposal, this part of the world faced a real calamity."[127]

In the Ogaden, the Game Changes

On that same February 9, the State Department began to grasp the dimensions of the problem it faced in Ethiopia. What had begun in early January as an expected battalion of Cubans (fewer than 1,000) had swelled to a full division (10,000 to 15,000) "intended to operate in combat." (In fact, Cuban troops were already in combat.) More than a thousand Soviet advisers had arrived in Ethiopia, and Moscow had shipped approximately a billion dollars' worth of materiel to the Derg—including MiG fighter bombers, heavy tanks, giant helicopters, rocket launchers, armored personnel carriers, antitank missiles, heavy mortars, air defense systems, and "the BMP-1, a devastating . . . armored vehicle . . . which the Somalis named the 'moving castle.'"[128]

The impact was immediately reflected on the battlefield. On January 22, the Somalis had launched what would be their final assault on Harar. They surrounded it, fighting their way to within three kilometers of the city walls. Suddenly, they confronted two Ethiopian armored columns with Soviet T-54 tanks and a company of Cuban artillerymen with tanks. Overhead, a squadron of Cuban pilots flew MiG-17s and two MiG-21R reconnaissance jets. The Somalis were used to fighting the Ethiopians, but this was their first encounter with the Cubans. A fierce battle raged for five days until the Somalis were forced to withdraw, "leaving a lot of weapons on the battlefield." The Somalis, who had mounted, in the words of the Cuban commander, "a strong resistance," suffered perhaps 3,000 casualties. (Ethiopian casualties were not reported.) The Cubans lost four men, including a captain. "Congratulations to all of you for your great victory!" Fidel Castro wrote General Ochoa, the head of the Cuban military mission in Ethiopia. "This was the first victory of the Ethiopian/Cuban troops," an official Cuban history of the war notes, adding correctly that "it was the point at which the enemy [the Somalis] lost the initiative."[129]

Washington did not have a clear sense of what had happened at Harar. "It seems that not much has changed," Henze wrote on January 25, three days after the battle for Harar began. "Scrappy SIGINT [signals intelligence] indicates that the Somalis are being pushed back in this area [Harar]," he added a week later. By February 9, however, one thing was clear: Cubans were involved in the fighting. "Airstrikes by at least 40 Cuban pilots have destroyed equipment, depressed morale, and restricted movement, and the Somalis are in retreat in several key areas," intelligence analysts wrote Vance. "The current Ethiopian drive, with Cuban units serving as the cutting edge . . . is proving so successful that . . . we think they will have taken Jijiga and be at the Somali border within three-five weeks. . . .Somali forces throughout the Ogaden will probably be defeated in the next month or two . . . a far more rapid victory than previously seemed likely." On February 10, Cyrus Vance called a press conference. "The Cubans have been flying aircraft and indeed have been involved in other ground activities," he announced. The game had changed.[130]

The problem for Washington was that even though the stakes were suddenly higher, it had no chips to play. Most US officials, including President Carter, believed that calling for negotiations, even if a long shot, was at least harmless. "I have decided we have nothing to lose," Carter wrote several heads of state, "by making a major effort to keep this situation from going from bad to worse."[131]

Grasping at these straws, the State Department convinced itself that the combatants in the Horn might agree to negotiate rather than fight. It pursued this pyrrhic quest with staggering vigor. From January through March—even after the war ended—cables flew to and from Foggy Bottom about negotiating strategies. The basic outline of the proposed settlement remained consistent, no matter what was happening on the battlefield. The State Department proposed a five-step negotiating strategy, which Vance discussed with the British, Canadian, French, and West German foreign ministers: (1) cease-fire; (2) withdrawal of all foreign forces, meaning not only Somali troops from the Ogaden but also Cuban and Soviet withdrawal from Ethiopia; (3) no Ethiopian invasion of Somalia; (4) a semiautonomous Ogaden within an Ethiopian federation; and (5) international observers in the Ogaden to ensure that there were no reprisals against the people.

This scheme was riddled with insurmountable problems. The Somalis dismissed it as "ludicrous" and the Ethiopians charged the Carter administration with "a coordinated plot" to destroy the revolution. The reaction of Egyptian ambassador Ahmad Sidqi was typical, if more candid than most. When informed about the US proposals, "Sidqi's reaction was one of mirth, followed by incredulity. . . . The idea that Soviet/Cuban forces would withdraw from Ethiopia at same time as Somalis left Ogaden," was, Sidqi told the US ambassador, "a chimera."[132]

The fundamental flaw was that the US negotiating points implied that Ethiopia and Somalia were equally at fault, when in fact Somalia had invaded

Ethiopia. To call for withdrawal of all foreign troops equated the invading Somalis with the invited Soviets and Cubans. The Americans condemned the Soviets for supplying weapons to the victims of aggression, while they remained silent about their friends' well-known support of the aggressor. The Carter administration compounded this error by steadfastly refusing to condemn the Somali invasion. US officials talked about Somali aggression only in "a whisper," in the apt words of the Soviet ambassador in Washington, Anatoly Dobrynin. Soviet foreign minister Andrei Gromyko had reproached the American ambassador about it in December: "The main difference in the US and Soviet position on this [Somali withdrawal from Ethiopia] is that Moscow states it both privately and in public, whereas . . . the US . . . has not called for withdrawal of Somali troops." The head of the Cuban Interests Section in Washington raised a similar complaint in January: "Havana is puzzled by the fact that no one [in the Carter administration] expressed concern when Somalia . . . attacked Ethiopia and appeared to be on the way to rolling over half the country. Only when Cuba . . . came to Ethiopia's assistance did the US raise a cry." The Carter administration claimed that it was refraining from condemning Somalia to maintain influence in order to resolve the crisis, but it also wanted to avoid alienating the conservative Arabs. Paul Henze was blunt: the administration "keeps weaseling on the territorial integrity issue," he wrote Brzezinski.[133]

There was no hope that either side would accept a cease-fire. Siad Barre still dreamed of winning on the battlefield. As late as February 20, the Somalis refused to back down; the exasperated British ambassador in Mogadiscio wrote that the Somalis wanted "to have their cake and eat it too." Meanwhile, the Ethiopians were girding with Soviet weapons and Cuban troops. The idea of placing international observers in the Ogaden to guard against reprisals was a nonstarter: "The concept was insulting," an Ethiopian official exclaimed.[134] Mengistu flatly rejected all calls for negotiation. "President Carter has attempted to project the invader as a peace seeker and invaded Ethiopia as an aggressor," he railed in a speech to the nation on January 30. "Do they consider the Ethiopians . . . no better than dead donkeys?"[135]

Playing a Bad Hand

The State Department was keenly aware of America's lack of leverage in the Horn, and it struggled to deal with it in four ways.

First, it tried to dampen media scrutiny. "Our intention," Vance wrote Carter on January 27, "[is] to downplay public affairs attention to the Horn situation."[136] Second, Washington communicated its displeasure to Moscow directly. "There had been more communications with the Soviet leadership over the Horn than any other subject," a State Department Soviet expert stated in February 1978, reflecting back on the previous three months.[137]

Third, it spread the burden by rallying an international coalition to support its call for a negotiated settlement. Enlisting the help of its NATO allies, the United States pressed the friends of Ethiopia (identified as the Soviet Union, Cuba, India, and Yugoslavia) and the friends of Somalia (identified as Saudi Arabia and other conservative Arabs states, as well as Iran) to urge the two warring parties to the table. This was done at the highest level—Carter and world leaders exchanged letters.[138] The Carter administration also turned to the OAU with newfound seriousness. Washington had been rhetorically supporting OAU mediation for months, but its interest became real when the Cubans started to flood into Ethiopia. Going to the OAU conformed with the Carter administration's stated belief that "this is an African problem which requires an African solution," and it also put welcome distance between Washington and the long-shot negotiations.[139] However, the warring parties refused even to meet with the Nigerians, whom the OAU had designated as the mediators. On March 2, after months of wrangling, the Nigerians announced that they had achieved "zero progress." The State Department considered taking the issue to the UN Security Council, but, as Washington's African friends said, the idea of a UN Security Council resolution was "academic since the Soviets will in the end have the power to veto it." In its pursuit of negotiations, Washington had struck out.[140]

The fourth way that the Carter administration grasped for leverage was to think creatively about carrots and sticks. Washington had little direct influence on any of the warring parties, so it sought indirect means of exerting pressure, especially on the Kremlin. That is, the Carter administration considered "linking" Soviet behavior in the Horn with other aspects of the Soviet relationship with the United States.

The State Department, however, was wary of deploying indirect measures of pressure for two reasons: all carried costs and risks, and none was likely to get the Soviets and Cubans out of Ethiopia. Thus, from the beginning, it took many coercive actions off the table. "We almost certainly cannot manipulate grain sales or other elements in our economic relationship [with Moscow] as a form of coercion on Soviet behavior," State Department officials noted in mid-January. "MBFR [Mutual and Balanced Force Reduction, talks to curb conventional weapons in Europe] offers nothing useful: it is too remote, multilateral and stagnant to give us a handle on Soviet policy in Africa. SALT is none of these things, but the situation and prospects in the Horn at present do not warrant jeopardizing our own interest in these negotiations in an attempt to use them as a lever against the Soviets." A week later, the assistant secretary for Africa and others elaborated: "We never do ourselves good by publicly raising the stakes in a game in which we do not hold cards equivalent to the size of your bets," they wrote Vance. "We would recommend that . . . [we] not make threats we cannot back up."[141]

The chief CIA analyst for Africa, Bill Parmenter, agreed. In a seventeen-page analysis of the situation in the Horn, he emphasized that the Soviets had acted with caution, not recklessness, in the region. "I feel very strongly that the Soviet motive here has been primarily to avert disaster . . . and I am strongly skeptical that the airlift was viewed in Moscow as . . . a 'challenge' to the US. These concepts sound more like Washington putting on its white hat and beginning to believe its own propaganda." Parmenter did not think that events in the Horn would result in "traumatic damage" to US national interests. His assessment was clear: "It's really up to us whether we permit that sideshow, on which we are likely to have minimal influence, to affect to our detriment the atmosphere in the main ring."[142]

Those were fighting words for the NSC's Paul Henze, who believed that the Horn was anything but a sideshow. "This judgment is parochial and bespeaks a neo-isolationist approach to foreign policy," Henze wrote Brzezinski. Henze hammered Brzezinski with memos, all arguing with rising frustration that the State Department had lost sight of what he saw as the real prize in the Horn: improved relations with Addis Ababa. Ethiopia was, he reminded Brzezinski, "by far the most important country in the Horn."[143] In the margin of a State Department report asserting that "the time was ripe for . . . negotiation," Henze scrawled: "Total misconception!" The pursuit of negotiations, he asserted, would antagonize the Ethiopians. "How diplomats love to negotiate!" he exclaimed in exasperation.[144] Years later, Brzezinski smiled as he remembered this avalanche of memos. "I didn't have time to read them all," he admitted. (On an average day, Brzezinski received a total of 400 pages of memos.) The problem, however, was not just lack of time: it was that Henze was stubbornly advocating a policy that President Carter had rejected. The administration wanted to keep a door open to improved relations with Ethiopia, but its tilt toward Somalia—even after it invaded the Ogaden—was clear.[145]

Henze enlisted the support of two members of the House International Relations Committee, Don Bonker (D-WA) and Paul Tsongas (D-MA), who had recently returned from a junket to Ethiopia. They met with Carter, urged that he pursue "a more even-handed" policy in the region, and suggested that he send a high-level emissary to Addis Ababa to reassure the Derg that the United States still valued relations with Ethiopia. The White House decided to give it a try: Carter sent a message to Mengistu, who replied that the visit of "a senior emissary . . . is most welcome."[146]

Attention Must Be Paid

While mid-level professionals in the State Department and NSC were pursuing pyrrhic quests in the Horn, the attention of the three principals—Carter, Vance, and Brzezinski—was largely elsewhere. Throughout January, as the war began to escalate in the Ogaden, not one of Brzezinski's weekly reports to the president even mentioned the Horn, nor did the State Department's own *Bulletin*. Carter had taken a personal interest in the Horn after Anwar Sadat's April 1977 visit, but he had backed off four months later when Somali troops invaded Ethiopia. From that point on, Carter intervened only when needed (urging heads of state to support a negotiated settlement, for example) and left the formulation of policy toward the Horn to others.[147]

In January 1978, Carter was focused on the Middle East peace process. Sadat's November 1977 trip to Jerusalem had simultaneously energized and derailed the administration's efforts to resolve the explosive Arab-Israeli problem. Carter's attempt to reconvene the Geneva conference, which had occupied much of 1977, was in shambles, but the White House hoped to use the momentum of Sadat's trip to push the Israelis and Egyptians toward a comprehensive settlement brokered by the United States alone. From Washington's point of view, excluding Moscow from the Mideast peace process was unavoidable, given the uproar that the joint communiqué had caused and the jubilation with which the American public had greeted Sadat's visit to Israel. From the Kremlin's point of view, however, the Carter administration's change of policy was treacherous and humiliating. Moscow had welcomed Carter's request in early 1977 that it use its influence in the Middle East to bring its allies to the negotiating table, and it was shaken when the invitation fell by the wayside. The reversal enraged and shamed the leaders in the Kremlin. As the US ambassador in Moscow noted, "such factors loom large here."[148]

Cyrus Vance was vigorously supporting Carter's Middle East peace initiative; he traveled to Jerusalem and Cairo in January. He was also preparing for April meetings in Moscow to get the SALT II negotiations back on track, and was under considerable time pressure on this front, as the first SALT agreement had expired in October 1977. Both countries had agreed to extend the treaty informally, but they needed a new agreement urgently: delay would put additional roadblocks in their path, and Leonid Brezhnev, the champion of SALT in the Kremlin, was in increasingly poor health. For Vance, successfully negotiating a new SALT agreement was central: it would stabilize the US-Soviet relationship, which was key to global peace. "It's life or death," Vance explained.[149] Vance also focused in January 1978 on southern Africa, where Ian Smith's attempt to forge an internal settlement threatened to bury the Anglo-American accords. The State Department feared that the internal settlement would not stop the war. A widening guerrilla war in southern

379

Africa, Vance believed, would be catastrophic for US interests. The crisis in the Horn, by contrast, was a tragic regional problem about which the United States could do little more than encourage the warring parties to negotiate.

Through January 1978, despite Paul Henze's deluge of memos about the importance of US ties to Ethiopia, there is no documentary evidence that Zbigniew Brzezinski considered the situation in the Horn of prime significance. In his memoirs—written after he left the West Wing—he highlighted his escalating concern about the Soviet challenge in Ethiopia, but the available record indicates that there were thousands of Cubans in Ethiopia before the national security adviser decided that they posed a grave challenge to the United States.[150]

America's European allies were increasingly uneasy about Washington's complacency. The British, who had toed the American line on the Horn, were worried about the assertion of Soviet power there. "We should ask ourselves whether we are prepared to see Somalia crushed," Prime Minister Callaghan noted, while instructing the Foreign Office to do more to help Siad Barre. In Paris, the secretary general of the foreign ministry said that he "was surprised that the US government was not reacting more strongly."[151]

The Saudis concurred that the passivity of Washington's response was alarming. Speaking with the US ambassador, Foreign Minister Saud described "the Soviet airlift to Ethiopia as the biggest and most effective in the history of the world . . . and pictured the combination of Russian and Cuban activities in Africa . . . as being the most threatening situation that could be imagined."[152] The Saudi royal family was appalled by what it saw as Carter's reluctance to stand up to the Soviet threat. It did not share crucial information with the Americans: in early 1978, US documents bristle with questions about what the Saudis and their friends were doing to help Somalia.[153] In late January, Saudi Arabia signaled its displeasure with Carter's Washington in a more pointed way. The House of Saud, which had shunned all relations with the godless Soviet Union, made direct contact with Moscow for the first time. A US intelligence report observed that this represented a "Saudi step toward establishment of international options in light of growing Saudi disenchantment with US policy in the area," and the NSC staff mentioned the possibility of "the Finlandization of Saudi Arabia."[154] Despite the criticism of its friends, throughout January the Carter administration held firm: it called for negotiations, and it hunkered down, waiting for Siad Barre to be defeated.

It was the magnitude of the Soviet commitment to Ethiopia that changed Washington's calculus. In early February 1978, some administration officials began to worry that Moscow was supplying the Derg with more arms than it needed to expel the Somalis from the Ogaden. This revived the threat that Siad

Barre had mentioned weeks earlier: would the advancing Ethiopian and Cuban troops invade Somalia? The Kremlin might instruct the Ethiopians to occupy the northern tip of Somalia, slicing from Harar to Hargeisa and straight to the sea. This was a variation on an old war plan that the Pentagon had developed for Ethiopia, back in the days when it had advised Haile Selassie's army, that had encouraged the Ethiopian army to take advantage of the geography of Somalia, quickly severing its northern tip—from Berbera northward—to gain leverage over the government in Mogadiscio, almost a thousand miles away. If the Soviets encouraged the Ethiopian army to implement this old scheme, it would return the base at Berbera to the Soviets and give Addis Ababa leverage to dictate peace terms to Mogadiscio, perhaps toppling Siad and returning Somalia to the Soviet fold.[155] "An Ethiopia in control of Hargeisa, Berbera and parts of the Ogaden would give the Russians the best of both worlds: influence in Ethiopia and on the Red Sea and an emasculated Somalia," a worried British diplomat explained. Moreover, as the State Department's intelligence experts reported, "The Ethiopian military commanders are smarting for revenge." Ethiopian planes had already attacked Hargeisa, the second-largest city in Somalia.[156]

In January, the Carter administration had felt reasonably comfortable observing the war in the Horn from the sidelines. But if the advancing Ethiopian and Cuban troops invaded Somalia, could Washington afford to be passive? The United States would be perceived as flaccid in the face of the Soviet Union's next step—after Angola—in its grand strategy of expansion in Africa.

President Carter got an earful about the Horn during Anwar Sadat's trip to Washington in early February 1978. On the eve of Sadat's arrival, Carter received a letter from French president Giscard d'Estaing urging him to respond assertively to the "massive reinforcement of the Cuban and Soviet position in Ethiopia." Giscard had three principal recommendations: a "massive action" to shape public opinion in the West; an explicit warning to Moscow that its policy was "not compatible with . . . the pursuit of the SALT negotiations"; and the provision to Somalia of "immediate military support to assure its protection within its national frontiers, [with] Iran . . . to provide aircover." The French president lectured Carter but offered no help. "These are, my dear Jimmy, the broad lines of a possible action," he concluded, adding the suggestion that "perhaps you can take advantage of the presence of President Sadat to examine the practical modalities with him."[157]

Documents detailing Carter's talks with Sadat remain classified, but their tenor can be gleaned from a statement that the latter made during a meeting on Capitol Hill. "For all practical purposes, the Soviet Union has taken over in Ethiopia," Sadat asserted. "It is now a Soviet base. . . . Half the water of the

Nile comes from Ethiopia. Naturally, I am alarmed with the Soviet's [*sic*] controlling half my water. After the Soviets knock out Somalia, they will then turn on Sudan and Egypt. . . . What is happening in Ethiopia is part of the Soviet international game." Sadat told the US press that Egypt was "sending arms to Somalia" and considering sending military personnel as well.[158]

While Sadat was in Washington, Israeli foreign minister Moshe Dayan announced that the Israeli government was still "selling some arms" to Ethiopia. The Israeli newspaper *Ha'aretz* claimed that the supplies were "mainly limited" to small arms and supplies, but Saudi radio broadcast that Israel "had delivered napalm bombs and air-to-ground missiles to the Derg." At the State Department noon briefing, the press grilled Hodding Carter about Israel's support of Ethiopia, and all three networks covered the story in their evening news broadcasts.[159]

"African eyes [are] now on US response," the US ambassador in Cairo cabled. "Africans were wondering . . . why US has not perceived Soviet grand design for Africa, particularly in the Horn. . . . Nightmares [are] coming true."[160]

"Containment has now been fully breached."

On February 9, as Sadat left Washington, Brzezinski finally focused on the Horn. His forty-sixth weekly report to the president opened with a segment titled "Strategic Deterioration," in which he warned that three developments could "adversely affect the overall global position of the United States." The first was the threat posed by Eurocommunism to NATO.[161] The second was the US failure to move more quickly toward normalization of relations with China. This subject was much on Brzezinski's mind. Carter had hoped to visit China in 1978 but had decided it would be impossible due to the pressing demands of the Panama Canal Treaties, the Middle East negotiations, and SALT II. In mid-January, therefore, Han Hsu, the highest-ranking Chinese diplomat in Washington, had again mentioned the possibility of Brzezinski traveling to Beijing. (This idea had first been floated by a member of the NSC staff to the Chinese in late October; on November 3, 1977, Han Hsu's predecessor had informally invited Brzezinski.)[162] On January 23, Carter had approved a proposal that Brzezinski help develop a plan to increase US trade of advanced technology with China; this would not only help the US economy, it would also strengthen China "as a counter to the USSR." On February 1, David Broder in the *Washington Post* had commented in glowing terms on Senator Ted Kennedy's recent trip to China. Describing Kennedy as "the most skilled politician of the left in America," Broder mused that "he can quite conceivably do more than anyone else just now to nudge along the US-China relationship." Later that day, Brzezinski's aides had sent him a memo urging: "The time has come to nail down your trip to East Asia. . . . You are the person to visit the region. . . . Vance cannot go to China unless we're prepared to discuss normalization, which we're not." Not only Brzezinski was intrigued by the prospect of his going to Beijing: so too was Carter. On February 7, the president mentioned the possibility in a meeting attended by Vance.[163]

The third threat that Brzezinski mentioned in his February 9 Weekly Report was "the potential consequences of major Soviet/Cuban success in Ethiopia." In the margin, Carter noted, "agree." Brzezinski elaborated: Soviet "success" in the Horn would have "a very direct psychological and political impact on Egypt, Sudan, Saudi Arabia and Iran. It will simply demonstrate to all concerned that the Soviet Union has the will and the capacity to assert itself." This would have consequences: "This will . . . make more likely increased Cuban involvement in the Rhodesian conflict." Brzezinski pushed further: "First through proxy (as in Angola) and now more directly (as in Ethiopia) the Soviet Union will be demonstrating that containment has now been fully breached."[164]

Brzezinski's analysis did not have broad support, even within the NSC. "I dispute the idea that the Horn is of notable strategic value unless you are going to fight World War II over again," NSC staffer Tom Thornton wrote Brzezinski on February 10. "We have quite a bit to gain internationally by standing above the battle. . . . The worst thing that can happen to this Administration . . . is to be seen as . . . talking big and not being able to follow up. . . . These views . . . find substantial support among those of us [on the NSC staff]."[165]

The CIA, Defense Department, and State Department concluded that it was unlikely the Soviets would instruct the Ethiopian and Cuban troops to cross the Somali border. "Moscow almost certainly does not believe that its interests would be served by a large-scale Ethiopian invasion of Somalia," a CIA memo from February 2 concluded. A longer CIA report about Soviet motivations in the Horn agreed that the Kremlin would counsel caution, because an invasion of Somalia "would greatly raise the political costs to the Soviets in their relations with the US, the Africans and the Muslim states [and] . . . Iran." It also would provoke the Saudis and Americans to increase their aid to Siad. This report emphasized that in Ethiopia, Moscow hoped to enhance its great power status, not engage in a raw power grab. "They [the Soviets] are influenced by . . . their view of their rightful place in the world," the CIA explained. "They are aware that their setback in Somalia was widely regarded as part of a pattern of recent injuries to Soviet prestige, particularly in the Middle East [their expulsion from Egypt and exclusion from the peace talks]. The concern to rescue the credibility of the Soviet claim to a growing place in the sun has been reinforced by Moscow's sense of rivalry with the US and its accumulated resentments over aspects of US policy in the Third World."[166]

Sam Hamrick, a defense intelligence analyst who had served in both Somalia and Ethiopia, disagreed with this assessment of Soviet motivations. For Hamrick, the key was not the Kremlin's view of global competition, its bruised pride, or its pursuit of strategic advantage; it was, instead, ideology. "We should not underestimate the Soviet commitment to its own revolutionary ideology or tradition, even at this late date," Hamrick asserted on February 15. "The Soviet commitment to Ethiopia derives fundamentally from Moscow's support for the Ethiopian revolution." The Kremlin admired the Derg's goals and its willingness to use the necessary tool—"terror"—to achieve these goals. These were "ingredients," Hamrick wrote, "which have been lacking in other Islamic or African societies where the Soviets have supported progressive change, as in Somalia. . . . Ethiopia thus provides the Soviet Union with a unique revolutionary opportunity in Africa which is unlike any of those provided previously, even in Angola." This was why Moscow chose Addis over Mogadiscio.[167]

Hamrick asserted that the Soviets would not encourage the Ethiopians to invade Somalia. "There is little basis—except the assumption of Soviet recklessness, which past performance doesn't sustain—that the Soviet presence in Ethiopia is committed at present to any goal other than the immediate restoration of Ethiopian territorial integrity and Ethiopian nation-building afterwards." The Soviets were seizing opportunities, not unrolling an imperial master plan. "It is not Soviet adventurism that has created these opportunities but rather the dynamics of African politics, beginning with the collapse of the Portuguese Empire in 1974 as well as the beginning of the dissolution of the old Ethiopian kingdom during the same period," Hamrick explained. "In both Angola and Ethiopia the Soviet Union did not act unilaterally or alone, [and it] didn't sponsor aggression." In both cases, its "military support had been sanctioned by diplomatic or legal convention and a majority of African states." That is, "the Soviets seized opportunities because it was safe to do so." Hamrick drove this point home: "The question which must be asked is not why the Soviets acted as they did but whether they had any alternative. . . . The answer must be no . . . since failure to do so [come to the Derg's aid] would have signalled [*sic*] an ideological retreat. . . . The Soviet [Union] . . . could not have made such a retreat without . . . proving to its critics, like the Chinese . . ., that it had surrendered the substance of its ideological conviction. This the Soviet leadership cannot do."[168]

At the State Department, Richard Moose was excited by Hamrick's memo. "This is the first thing I've read that makes sense," he remembered thinking. He brought Hamrick into the Department and listened intently to his advice.

"Everyone read Hamrick's analyses of the Horn," Moose's deputy Don Petterson remembered.[169]

Brzezinski, however, viewed the Horn through a different prism. The fine points of Soviet motivations were secondary: what mattered was that Soviet actions challenged the United States and made it look weak. Carter had to respond. In late January, Brzezinski had received a useful letter about the Horn from a friend and fellow Sovietologist, William Griffith, who taught at the Massachusetts Institute of Technology. Griffith wrestled with ways to force the Soviet Union to curb its adventurism in Ethiopia. He focused on China. "The Soviets clearly fear more extensive US involvement with the Chinese. To prevent this has been one of Moscow's main motives for Soviet-US detente. The US objective, therefore, should be to make the Soviets believe that if they continue in the Horn, we will move farther toward Peking. This should initially involve expanded U.S. consultations with the Chinese on the Horn."[170] Brzezinski saw the Horn in global, strategic terms; it would also be his springboard to Beijing.

The Paralyzed Giant

US policy began to show small signs of change. At a press conference on February 10, 1978, Vance called for the "withdrawal of Somali forces from the Ogaden . . . and *in return* . . . a withdrawal of Soviet and Cuban forces from Ethiopia." This was new: it moved the administration from the call for simultaneous withdrawal—which had encountered derision from all sides—to a call for a phased withdrawal that would begin with the Somalis. It came closer to a condemnation of Somalia than had any other public pronouncement from Washington. That night, both CBS and ABC devoted long segments of their evening news broadcasts to the war in the Horn. The three networks had mentioned the crisis on average three times a week since the beginning of the year, but it was not a war made for television. Only once did US television broadcast video from near the front, a brief clip filmed under the watchful eyes of Ethiopian handlers. The nightly news broadcasts had to settle for brief updates from the studio.[171]

On February 12, the foreign ministers of the five Western members of the Security Council (Britain, Canada, France, the United States, and West Germany) met secretly to discuss the Horn. "There was no way," Vance admitted at the outset, to avoid a Somali defeat, but US policy remained "not to deliver arms to Somalia so long as the Somali army was in the Ogaden." Vance was stating the administration's public policy, knowing that all the participants at the meeting knew that Washington had encouraged third-party transfers of weapons to Somalia. Vance's European counterparts now wanted more, and they criticized Washington's spinelessness. Britain's David Owen said that "he personally thought we should have been tougher [toward the Soviet Union] over the Horn in the past." While Britain "would prefer not to supply arms to Somalia openly . . ., he would have a relaxed attitude to their supply by the Arabs." France's Louis de Guiringaud feared that Moscow's success in the region could lead—if Siad fell—to "Soviet puppets" in Mogadiscio as well as Addis. "The Soviet Union would have won out on both sides. . . . This could have serious consequences for Saudi Arabia." The Europeans carped and scoffed, but they offered Vance not one constructive idea of how to counter the Soviets in the Horn. Instead, they came to a grudging consensus that the least worst option was to press Siad to withdraw from the Ogaden.[172]

On February 16, Carter for the first time publicly called for Somali withdrawal without linking it to the withdrawal of the Cuban and Soviet troops. Vance followed up by asking the US embassy in Mogadiscio to send "your best reading of the willingness in principle of Siad to withdraw his forces from the Ogaden."[173]

At the same time, Owen briefed Prime Minister Callaghan about the meeting of the Western Security Council members. A successful Ethiopian invasion of Somalia would mean "the possible establishment of another Soviet puppet regime in Mogadishu," he explained. "The Soviet Union would thus have scored a double victory with serious implications for Africa as well as . . . Saudi Arabia." Because of the gravity of the threat, "the United States has asked for our permission to pre-position stores and fuel at Diego Garcia for possible high altitude surveillance flights of the Horn by SR71 [Lockheed 'Blackbird'] aircraft." Callaghan agreed to the American request.[174]

When Saudi Crown Prince Fahd was informed of the recommendation of the five Western foreign ministers that Siad be pressed to withdraw his troops, his reaction was, according to the US ambassador in Saudi Arabia, John West, "extremely negative." Fahd refused to recommend to Siad Barre that "he make a unilateral withdrawal of Somali forces from the Ogaden" because doing so would lead, first, to reprisals against the Ogadenis, many of whom would be "massacred"; and, second, to the overthrow of Siad and his replacement with a Soviet "puppet." This would have a profoundly demoralizing effect on the states in the region. "Any future attempts by anticommunist forces to oust Soviet-dominated regimes would probably fail because Somalia could be pointed to as an example of the uselessness and futility of such an attempt." Ambassador West, speaking on instructions, said that the Carter administration did not disagree with the prince's assessment but that "the military situation was of such a critical nature that the only alternatives presented were a voluntary withdrawal or a crushing military defeat." Fahd ended the meeting with a warning: "The United States must shoulder its responsibilities if we are to avert a disaster in Somalia."[175]

Meanwhile, the attempt to improve US relations with Addis Ababa—encouraged by representatives Bonker and Tsongas—was underway. On February 17, Deputy National Security Adviser David Aaron and NSC staffer Paul Henze faced Mengistu in the old imperial palace in Addis Ababa. This was the first meeting of a senior US official with the Ethiopian strongman, whose reputation for brutality preceded him. Aaron admitted, with real emotion, that he had been terrified. "There was fighting in the streets of Addis when I was there. It was the first time I'd seen children armed with AK-47s shooting each other." Throughout the two-and-a-half-hour meeting with Mengistu, Aaron could hear the roars of Haile Selassie's pride of lions, symbols of his imperial rule, that roamed the palace grounds and were sheltered under the throne room. "The whole floor would shake," Aaron remembered vividly. "No one had warned me. I literally looked down to see if there was a trap door that would disappear me. It was so disconcerting that it was hard to keep talking."[176] Aaron told Mengistu that the Carter administration wanted good relations with Ethiopia; Mengistu lambasted the Americans for their silence while his country was invaded. "The people of Ethiopia were dying left and right. . . . Really, isn't it your responsibility as members of the UN . . . to condemn this aggression?" Aaron's reply was succinct: "It is very hard to help someone who is poking you in the eye with a stick." He added that the United States was not supplying weapons to Somalia. Mengistu retorted that he would give Aaron the serial numbers of US-manufactured weapons that his troops had captured from the Somalis. As for Washington's push for a negotiated settlement, Mengistu was sarcastic: "Would you like us to advocate the autonomy of Texas?" He reserved his harshest criticism for the Arab countries that were helping Somalia. "Ethiopia is a Christian country. . . . This is the main cause of the problem we are having in this region." After venting his outrage, Mengistu made an important promise: his troops would not invade Somalia.[177]

Aaron, despite his anxiety about the lions, was impressed by Mengistu. "He was in full grasp of what was going on. He knew what he wanted to do. He had some charisma. I suspect that when he came to the United States in the 1950s [for military training] he'd been treated badly as a black man and he never got over it."[178]

As Mengistu was meeting with Aaron in Addis Ababa, Ethiopian and Cuban troops were zeroing in on Jijiga, the last remaining Somali stronghold in the Ogaden. The "backbone" of the Ethiopian army "was a Cuban armored brigade," Gebru Tareke, who has written the only history of the war based on research in the Ethiopian archives, explains. The State Department, assessing the war several months later, also gave credit to the Cubans: "Three mechanized [Cuban] brigades . . . were largely responsible for overcoming Somali forces in the Ogaden. About 40 Cuban pilots flew combat missions in the Ogaden. There are at least five Cuban generals in Ethiopia, three of them veterans of the Angola campaign." After crushing the Somali offensive against Harar on January 27, Cuban and Ethiopian troops had systematically evicted the Somalis from the small towns west and north of Jijiga. Swooping to the north, they captured Arabi—a town twenty miles north of Jijiga—on February 17, the day Aaron heard the lions roar. This put the Ethiopian army in position to launch its final assault on Jijiga.[179]

Three days earlier, on February 14, Siad Barre had received John Loughran, the US ambassador to Somalia, at the presidential palace in Mogadiscio. "It appears to me we may lose," Siad admitted, drawing deeply on his cigarette. "We cannot fight against modern Soviet weaponry, tanks, and aircraft." The US intelligence community concurred: the "Ethiopians and Cubans . . . [will achieve] a far more rapid victory than previously seemed likely."[180]

The Elephant in the Room

When Brzezinski, Vance, Defense Secretary Harold Brown, General David Jones of the Joint Chiefs of Staff, CIA director Stansfield Turner, Dick Moose, and David Aaron met to discuss the Horn on February 22, the collapse of Somalia's fortunes was not the focus. The key question was what the United States could—and should—do if the Ethiopian and Cuban troops invaded Somalia.

The minutes of the meeting reveal an administration that was floundering. Aaron opened by reporting on his "fairly fruitful" talks in Addis, but then the discussion lapsed into a tragicomic debate on how to promote a negotiated settlement in the Horn (resurrecting the harebrained notion, at this late stage, of a simultaneous Somali and Soviet/Cuban withdrawal).[181] The meeting then wandered into the question of how to respond to an Ethiopian/Cuban invasion of Somalia. The consensus was that an invasion was possible but unlikely. "Our judgement is that Mengistu would prefer not to cross the Somali border," Vance explained. "Nevertheless . . . if there appeared to be no other way . . . to get Somali forces out of all of the Ogaden, . . . he probably would be prepared to cross the border."[182] Brzezinski asserted that if Somalia were threatened, "the Administration would initiate action to provide third country arms transfers." When Brown asked if Washington should encourage transfers even if the Somalis refused to withdraw from the Ogaden, Brzezinski referred to the elephant in the room. "We do not want to oppose the Saudis politically on the Horn," he said curtly. This was the theme of the second half of the meeting. Brzezinski returned again and again to the Saudis, saying that "we must assure the Saudis that the United States is not bugging out or washing our hands of the Horn."[183]

It was this concern about the ramifications of a Saudi loss of confidence in Washington that led Brzezinski to suggest sending a US carrier task force to the region as "a confidence building measure, encouraging countries in the region that the US is present, [and] stands with them." The carrier would also provide cover for the US arms that Brzezinski imagined Washington would encourage friendly countries to transfer to Somalia. He went further: "It is in our interest to get the Saudi Arabians and the Iranians into Somalia if it looks like the Somalis will be defeated [i.e., successfully invaded by the Ethiopians]." He added, "The Saudi Arabians and Iranians will have to match the Cubans."[184]

In his memoirs, Brzezinski recalled that the secretary of state "for the first time . . . [started] to get red in the face and to raise his voice."[185] Vance insisted that the first order of business was to get Siad Barre to withdraw from the Ogaden. To that end, the administration should not dangle any promises of arms to Somalia if it was attacked, and it should discourage the Saudis from sending Siad any more weapons. Brzezinski asked Vance if he was saying that the United States "should do nothing in the event Ethiopia crossed the frontier." Vance replied: "Yes."

That one word pinpointed the gap between the two men. A State Department official summed up their contrasting styles well: "Brzezinski reacts 'Don't just sit there, do something,' while Vance reacts 'Don't just do something, sit there—until you understand the consequences of what you want to do.[186] It would be wrong to exaggerate their differences—both were in the mainstream of the moderate internationalist Democrats of their generation, and usually they had no significant trouble working together. But tensions did slowly accumulate for several reasons: there is unavoidable structural friction between a secretary of state and a national security advisor; Vance's low-key diplomacy contrasted with Brzezinski's theatricality; and they disagreed sharply about the priority of finalizing SALT II—for Brzezinski it was desirable, while for Vance it was essential. Wrestling with the complex problem of the Horn in February 1978 was one of the early instances of these tensions gelling. In the Horn, the two men disagreed about the gravity of the threat, the way to handle it, and the most effective way to rebuild US credibility in the wake of Vietnam. Each man believed that the other's advice imperiled fundamental US interests; therefore, the divide was deep.

Vance wanted to protect the SALT negotiations: as secretary of state, his overriding goal was to shepherd SALT II to a successful conclusion. For him, it would be disproportionate to imperil US-Soviet relations because of a regional crisis in the Horn. Brzezinski, however, considered SALT expendable. "A SALT agreement, though a useful and positive element in the US-Soviet relationship, is not likely to alter profoundly the nature of the US-Soviet relationship," he wrote Carter. He later expressed his disagreement with Vance more pungently: "I don't make a fetish out of SALT. I don't think SALT is the most important thing in the world."[187] For Brzezinski, the priority was to show strength. Vance did not disagree about the need to display strength—but he did not think anyone, including the national security adviser, had proposed any viable way to do it.

Brzezinski argued that in the Horn of Africa, the Soviet Union was posing a direct challenge to the United States. He proposed that to meet this affront the administration should promote direct US arms transfers to Somalia, ask the Saudis and Iranians to intervene militarily if Somalia was invaded, and offer to provide air cover from a US carrier group offshore. Brzezinski was convinced that if Washington failed to respond, it would lose credibility globally, and especially with the Saudis. "To a great extent," he explained in his memoirs, "our credibility was under scrutiny by new, relatively skeptical allies in a region strategically important to us."[188]

Vance disagreed on every count. He did not think that the Soviet Union had set out to challenge the United States: he believed that they were taking advantage of an opportunity. He rejected all three of Brzezinski' responses. Congress had made it almost impossible for the administration to encourage third-country arms transfers. The Saudis and Iranians were no match for the Cubans and would refuse to go. Secretary Brown and General Jones agreed, pointing out drily, "The Cubans . . . would 'kick the shit out of those forces.' [Then] what would we do?" Sending an aircraft carrier to the region would be reckless. "We would be playing a bluff we cannot carry through," Vance asserted.[189]

Brzezinski believed in the utility of bluster, in the theater of hawkishness. For him, the important thing was that the White House do *something*. "The threat of military force carries with it a message," he later explained. "Our presence in the area would . . . be a complicating factor. . . . It would maximize the complexity of the environment that they [the Soviets] were confronting." Moreover, Brzezinski was worried about "the effects of seeming US passivity on Egypt, Israel, and Saudi Arabia . . . about the consequences domestically and abroad of doing nothing."[190] Bluffing, Vance countered, would weaken— not strengthen—US credibility. It was unlikely that the Ethiopians would cross the border, and it was important that the United States not overreact to that remote possibility. Building credibility, for Cyrus Vance, was a painstaking process of proving the trustworthiness of one's word. Issuing empty threats was the opposite.

The meeting on February 22 was brutal: seven men in a room with not one good idea among them. All were trying to figure out how to position the United States vis-à-vis a war about which they knew very little and that was raging in a virtual desert 8,000 miles away. Vance, supported at almost all times by everyone except Brzezinski, saw the situation clearly: the United States had no leverage. It should do nothing. It was unfortunate and even humiliating, but it was a fact. The administration could weather it, particularly if it kept a low profile in the press and if—as Vance thought most likely—the Ethiopians did not invade Somalia.

Brzezinski's dismay was understandable, but his proposed alternatives were nonsensical. Did he believe that the Saudis would be reassured by Carter urging them to confront the well-armed Cubans and Ethiopians and their Soviet advisers? Did he believe the House of Saud was so naive as to be mollified by an American carrier group loitering pointlessly offshore? Did he imagine that the Saudis or Iranians would send their men to confront the Cubans? The British Foreign Office, when informed of the options Brzezinski had proposed, noted drily: "None of these responses (except the first [direct US intervention] which is excluded ex-hypothesi) is likely to meet an invasion situation in the time scale required. . . . The administration have therefore little leverage they can apply to secure their policy aim of a removal of Soviet and Cuban troops from Ethiopia."[191]

Washington Post columnist Meg Greenfield pinpointed the essential problem: "The Horn of Africa provides a model of the current American foreign policy dilemma in the world. And in this situation, people seem to be flailing about foolishly in search of new levers of power."[192]

Carter Stumbles

On February 23, less than twenty-four hours after Vance and Brzezinski had locked horns, the NSC convened with Jimmy Carter in the chair. It was 11:10 A.M., and Carter had already chaired a meeting about the SALT negotiations, talked with House Speaker Tip O'Neill (D-MA) and senators Robert Byrd (D-WV) and Alan Cranston (D-CA), and met with ten members of the White House staff and Cabinet. He entered the White House's Situation Room, turned to the CIA's Stansfield Turner for an intelligence briefing on the Horn, and peppered him with questions. Was an Ethiopian invasion of Somalia likely? Turner said that the Soviets would "counsel restraint . . . but there will be great pressures on the Ethiopian leadership to go into Somalia."

What would the Iranians and Egyptians do? How much information should be released to the press? Then Carter proffered his first opinion: "The more publicity we make available . . . the better off we will be."[193]

One can almost hear the sharp intake of breath: everyone around the table had already agreed that the less publicity, the better. Secretary Brown noted that publicity would "raise the stakes."[194]

Brzezinski then changed the subject, recommending third-party transfers of US weapons to Somalia. Carter cut the discussion off: "We must look to what we want in the area. We want peace there, we want to get the Soviets and Cubans out, and we want the Somalis to withdraw from Ethiopia. . . . The most important of these is to get the Soviets and Cubans out. This is compatible with third country arms transfers if Somalia withdraws or if Cubans cross the border." Vance asked, "Is this the case [that transfers should be approved] even if the Somalis are still in the Ogaden?" The president replied, "That is my inclination." Vance noted that Siad would then refuse to withdraw from Ethiopia, and Carter said cryptically, "Don't rule out direct US aid. . . . We need to be forceful without prolonging the conflict." Vance repeated that this would cause Siad to hang on and his moderate Arab friends to increase their aid.[195]

This point led to a recapitulation of the previous day's debate about the aircraft carrier: was it reassurance for the Arabs (as Brzezinski saw it) or a risky empty threat (as the others saw it)? After several minutes of argument, the president had heard enough. "Congress would react with horror at the prospect of American military help for Somalia," Carter noted, flatly contradicting the call to be "forceful" he had uttered only a few minutes earlier. "We should get our allies and the OAU to understand the situation and collectively deplore it," he declared.[196]

At least this comment clarified the problem: Jimmy Carter was unprepared. He seemed not to know that the State Department had been working for weeks with US allies and the OAU to collectively deplore the situation. Vance said, "We are attempting to do just that." But the president turned immediately to what was on his mind. "Sadat seems eager to send forces to Berbera," he stated. Then, channeling Brzezinski, he added that the Saudis and Iranians would be "fighting in the air against the Cubans." With this, the meeting ended. Confusion reigned.[197]

Carter had articulated three goals and offered no way to achieve any of them. He wanted peace, Somali withdrawal from the Ogaden, and above all Soviet and Cuban withdrawal from Ethiopia. He approved third-party arms transfers if Somalia was invaded, even if Siad's troops were still in the Ogaden. He advocated a "forceful" response but recoiled from "American military help to Somalia." How did he propose to get the Soviets and Cubans out of Ethiopia? Or Siad out of the Ogaden? Or to end the war?

It is not surprising that Carter was not on top of the issue. He was very, very busy. He had developed a highly centralized structure that relied on his making all the key foreign and domestic policy decisions. To some extent, this was a consequence of the US presidential system, but recent American history and Carter's character accentuated it. Carter had railed against the excessive power that Henry Kissinger had amassed; Kissinger, Carter claimed, had not only usurped power that should have rested with the president but also had used this power to implement a secretive, undemocratic foreign policy. Carter was determined to correct this trend. Moreover, centralization suited his character. Carter was intensely curious; he wanted to understand everything before he made any decision about it. He expected his advisers to present him with many points of view. With supreme self-confidence, he would sort through the alternatives and set policy. He seemed to harbor no doubt that he would be able to understand every issue quickly and completely. He misjudged the chasm between the governor's mansion in Atlanta and the White House. Moreover, Carter underestimated the complexities of leadership. He had told his team that he expected collegiality; he considered it self-evident that collegiality was the right way to behave; therefore, he expected his administration to act collegially. He did not see any reason to inspire or frighten them into collegiality, and in any case he did not have the temperament to do either. He believed that because he was president, because what he asked for was right, and because he was Jimmy Carter, his staff would do as he expected.

This approach had worked fairly well for a year, but it depended on luck and on Carter's own ability to be on top of every issue. On February 23, 1978, Carter went to an important meeting badly unprepared. An explanation might be found in his diary. On January 27, a month before the NSC meeting on the Horn, he wrote with relief, "During 1978 I won't have to do the hundreds of hours of detailed study of issues that I had to do last year, since I'm now fairly familiar with most of them."[198] Carter had taken a crash course on the Horn in 1977, and he thought he knew the issues. Given the centralized system of decision-making in his White House and the disagreements among his advisers, Carter's lapse had consequences.

Perhaps more revealing than Carter's failure to lead at the NSC meeting is the pusillanimity of Brzezinski, Turner, Vance, and Brown when confronted with the train wreck of a meeting. They gently posed questions and proffered comments, but not one of these principal advisers challenged the president or directed the meeting to a more constructive discussion. Instead, as the minutes of the meeting discreetly note, "the principals continued to discuss the issues of the NSC meeting after the President left." The disjointed and inconclusive discussion left them unable to answer the key questions, and the president's directive that "the more publicity . . . the better" guaranteed that this confusion would be broadcast.[199]

Fallout

"President Carter has come to one of those forks in the road," James Reston wrote in the *New York Times* on February 24, the morning after the NSC meeting. "The idea is getting around that he's not very effective. . . . They [people] talk, not about the complexity of the problems but about the President's failure to solve them." The *Washington Post*'s lead article that day asserted that twenty-five to fifty Cubans were in Zambia preparing Nkomo's 8,000 ZAPU guerrillas for battle.[200] (This was partly true: since August 1977, some 200 Cubans had trained approximately 4,000 ZAPU guerrillas at a camp in Angola, near the Zambian border. By October 1978, 6,000 ZAPU fighters had passed the course. In Zambia, there were only about twenty Cubans, under cover of a medical mission. Half of them were indeed doctors, but the other ten trained ZAPU troops in Zambia.[201])

At a White House press briefing later that day, Brzezinski stirred the pot. He announced that 10,000 to 11,000 Cubans were in Ethiopia, doubling the estimate that the administration had offered a week earlier. He added that the Cubans were bolstered by 400 Soviet tanks and 50 MiG jet fighters, and that Soviet General Vasily Petrov was directing the campaign from army headquarters in Addis. "This is clearly an external, foreign intrusion into a purely regional conflict," Brzezinski told the press. All three network nightly news programs reported the national security adviser's remarks.[202]

For Brzezinski, the tipping point had been reached. He had not reacted when Washington had believed that the tide of the war was turning against the Somalis. What triggered Brzezinski's response was the scale of the Soviet and Cuban intervention: it was a direct challenge to Carter's leadership. He was worried that Carter did not grasp this. After he addressed the press briefing, Brzezinski wrote his forty-eighth weekly report. It began with a riff titled "On the Psychology of Presidential Power." The national security adviser was playing the role of coach, trying to motivate his quarterback after a lackluster first half. "A president must not only be loved and respected," Brzezinski wrote. "He must also be feared. . . . Occasionally . . . a touch of irrationality can be an asset. Those who wish to take advantage of us ought to fear that . . . the President is prepared, and willing, to hit the opponent squarely on the head." He primed Carter to be on the lookout for an opportunity: "I think the time may be right for you to pick some controversial subject on which you will deliberately choose to act with a degree of anger and even roughness, designed to have a shock effect." Brzezinski then, none too subtly, played on the president's pride: "If we do not do this soon to somebody, we will increasingly find Begin, Brezhnev, Vorster, Schmidt, Castro, Qadhafi, and a host of others thumbing their noses at us."[203]

After every NSC meeting, a Presidential Directive was issued summarizing the decisions that Carter had taken. After the February 24 NSC meeting, penning this directive required clarifying what had transpired at the meeting. It summarized the opinion of the majority, flatly rejecting Brzezinski's proposal to station an aircraft carrier offshore.[204]

Vance had won that round, but he knew that Brzezinski would not give up. Although Carter had rejected the most bellicose of Brzezinski's suggestions, Vance worried that the president might be persuaded to adopt measures to—as Brzezinski had declared at the meeting—"make the Soviets and Cubans bleed." Vance thought that punitive measures would be ineffective and counterproductive: they would not force the Soviets to withdraw from Ethiopia, but they would damage US-Soviet relations. Moreover, they were unnecessary: Ethiopian nationalism would chafe against the Kremlin's embrace, and Mengistu would eventually eject the Soviets, as had Sadat before him. Vance accepted that US relations with the Soviet Union would be a mixture of competition and cooperation; Brzezinski, on the other hand, thought, as he explained in a later interview, "You can't have your cake and eat it too. . . . There is a real choice: either détente across the board, or competition across the board, but not détente in some areas and competition in those areas in which we [the United States] were vulnerable."[205]

As Vance feared, after the NSC meeting, Brzezinski immediately tasked his staff with investigating ways to "raise the costs"—in other words, to study linkage—of the Soviet and Cuban intervention in the Horn. He considered "having the President announce a decision to produce the neutron bomb in reaction to Soviet activities in Ethiopia," but his staff advised that "there is a certain disproportionality to this response."[206] Another staffer suggested persuading "Egypt to close the Suez Canal to Soviet shipping." Mike Armacost, the NSC staffer responsible for East Asia, honed in on the link that Brzezinski was already savoring: "The most effective means of sending this signal" of disapproval, he wrote, "is to worry them [the Soviets] about our future relations with China." Brzezinski then penned a formal memo to the president: "Bearing in mind developments in the Horn and the related need to send a sensitive signal to the Soviets, the time is ripe for your decision" on whether "a visit by me to China would be useful." On January 28, 1978, Carter had asked Vance about the "advisability" of sending Brzezinski to China. Vance was, Carter noted in his diary, "strongly opposed."[207]

On March 1, a week after the NSC meeting, Brzezinski faced the press. "If tensions were to rise because of the unwarranted intrusion of Soviet power [in the Horn]," the national security adviser observed, "that will inevitably complicate . . . not only the negotiation process [of SALT] itself, but [also the] ratification process." Brzezinski added, "We are not imposing linkages, but linkages may be imposed by unwarranted exploitation of local conflict for larger international purposes."[208] Linkage was the only issue that the journalists wanted to discuss at the State Department's noon briefing, where Hodding Carter tried to control the damage. "In fact, we don't have a policy of linkage," he declared; all that Brzezinski had done was to "state the obvious." One skeptical journalist retorted, "Dr. Brzezinski always seems to speak out much more strongly and stridently than the secretary does." That night, all three networks noted the threat to the SALT talks posed by Soviet behavior in the Horn. "President Carter is facing his first war-like crisis," ABC's Howard K. Smith announced. "This could turn into another Vietnam or Angola."[209]

On the next day, the argument came to a head. The *Washington Post* carried news of Brzezinski's press conference on the front page. "The White House for the first time yesterday directly tied the fate of the strategic nuclear arms negotiations . . . to the . . . Horn of Africa." Hours after the *Post* appeared on his doorstep, Senate minority leader Howard Baker (R-TN), turned to Cyrus Vance, who was testifying to the appropriations committee about the budget. "I read with great interest the statement attributed to Dr. Brzezinski in this mornings [*sic*] press," Baker began. "I would be very happy to have your comment."[210]

Vance was direct: "There is no linkage between the strategic arms talks and the situation in Ethiopia. . . . I believe very strongly that it is in our national interest to proceed with the SALT talks." Vance then emphasized that Somalia should withdraw from the Ogaden.[211] Vance left the Hill at 11:00 A.M. to prepare for a meeting about the Horn.

At 12:20 P.M., President Carter held a news conference. Predictably, he was asked about the linkage between the Horn and SALT. The United States did not "initiate" a policy of linkage, he explained. However, the Soviets, having "over-armed to the teeth" both Somalia and Ethiopia, had "caused a threat to peace in the Horn." This would affect the American people's opinion of Moscow, which would in turn affect Congress, which would in turn affect the ratification of SALT. "Therefore, the two are linked because of actions by the Soviets. We don't initiate the linkage."[212]

Minutes later, the principals—absent the president—convened in the Situation Room. When told what Carter had just said, Cyrus Vance, normally a reserved and self-controlled man, blurted, "That is wrong." He continued, "Zbig, you yesterday and the President today said it may create linkage and

I think it is wrong to say that." Brzezinski responded that he and Carter had simply offered "a statement of fact." Harold Brown jumped in: "Not all statements of fact should be made," he noted. Vance explained his reasoning: "We are on the brink of ending up with a real souring of relations between ourselves and the Soviet Union and it may take a helluva long while to change." (Vance uncharacteristically said "hell" three times during the meeting.) "We will end up losing SALT and that will be the worst thing that could happen. If we do not get a SALT treaty . . . that will be a blemish on his [Carter's] record forever."[213]

Brzezinski retorted that the administration's "pattern of behavior of the last few months" had been "noise but no follow-through," and he declared that the Soviets "must understand that there are consequences in their behavior." Vance concluded: "This is where you and I part."[214]

Carter's Manhood

Once again, Vance prevailed. Carter refused to help Siad Barre until he "withdraws his forces immediately and completely from Ethiopian territory," and did not link progress on SALT to Soviet behavior in the Horn. The only measure he approved to express his displeasure at the Kremlin's actions was to "increase in our scientific and technological cooperation with the Chinese."[215]

Brzezinski was filled with contempt. Everyone, other than him, had been "badly bitten by the Vietnam bug," he wrote in his diary.[216] He immediately regrouped, sending Cater a staccato three-page memo titled "The Soviet Union and Ethiopia: Implications for US-Soviet Relations," in which he argued that the president's response did "not go far enough." The first half of the memo laid out energetically and persuasively why the United States should react to the Kremlin's projection of power in Africa. "The Soviets are becoming bolder. . . . What is even more disturbing is that the Soviets apparently have concluded that they can run such risks and get away with them. . . . It is unwise, potentially very dangerous, to reinforce them in this conclusion." Brzezinski then highlighted the devastating repercussions of US passivity. "Soviet success in Ethiopia . . . will also free the Cubans . . . to become engaged in the struggle against Rhodesia. . . . The impact on Saudi Arabia and Iran will be significant." At home, the right wing would accuse the administration of "incompetence as well as weakness."[217]

The memo then fell apart. Brzezinski trotted out his ideas of deploying an aircraft carrier, playing the China card, canceling some cooperative ventures with the Soviets, and telling them that their behavior would derail SALT. He also called for negotiations based on the familiar formula of Somali withdrawal from the Ogaden, Soviet-Cuban withdrawal from Ethiopia, peace-keeping monitors, and no further arms for Somalia. The Americans had been touting this plan for months, and it had gotten nowhere: Washington had no leverage to achieve any of these goals. For the US national security adviser to promote this "good, four-point approach" on March 3—when the Ethiopian and Cuban troops were routing the Somalis—is astounding.[218]

"Top Carter Aides Seen in Discord," led the *New York Times* on the day that Brzezinski wrote his memo. The *Washington Post* blared, "Linkage Rift Exposes a Split at Heart of Détente Strategy" and commented on the "serious fissures within the high councils of the executive branch."[219] A theme had emerged: Jimmy Carter was an incompetent president. The *Los Angeles Times* noted that "the nagging question . . . is whether Carter and his foreign-policy advisers are up to the task." The banner headline in the *Christian Science Monitor* was: "How many challenges can a president handle?" At a March 2 news conference, journalist Judy Woodruff pulled no punches when she asked Carter, "How concerned are you that your administration is perhaps developing a reputation for fumbling and ineptitude?" Carter responded characteristically: first a smile and then a slow, careful answer. "We have . . . decided to deal with some longstanding, very difficult, controversial issues that in some instances had not been adequately addressed by my predecessors." He then explained yet again why energy reform and natural gas deregulation and peace in the Middle East were needed. He discussed the difficulty of dealing with inflation, unemployment, and the coal strike. He reminded the audience that "the polls show that my own personal popularity is very high" (he had a 57 percent approval rating) and pointed out that the resolution of all these matters required cooperation, which took time. "Government doesn't have the unilateral, autocratic control over some of these very difficult issues." He ended on a positive note. "I'm not disappointed at the progress that we have made. I'm certainly not disappointed at our willingness to tackle issues that have historically been difficult to resolve."[220]

Washington Post columnist William Greider explained one reason that Carter was being accused of being weak. "Jimmy Carter, during his first 12 months, did not invade, bomb, or otherwise plant our flag in somebody else's war. Jimmy Carter is the first president since Eisenhower who can make that claim," Greider noted. "Obviously," he added, "it's an awkward thing for the White House to brag about. . . . Nothing makes a president 'presidential' more effectively than a foreign crisis. If Carter had gone to the barricades, committed US power to an overseas war, even spilled some blood, you would not be reading so much about his 'fuzzy' image." Greider echoed Brzezinski's weekly reports to the president, but while Brzezinski was deadly serious,

Greider was sardonic when he observed that the Ogaden war was a place "where Carter can demonstrate his manhood."[221]

At long last, the press had a handle to discuss the Horn crisis: was Jimmy Carter man enough? This was an enormous relief to editors who had struggled for months to make the war in the Horn—which was clearly important—intelligible and interesting to their readers. Both the *New York Times* and the *Washington Post* had dispatched crack journalists to Ethiopia and Somalia to cover the war, but they had been unable to get to the front and had been reduced to filing picturesque travelogues and human interest stories from Mogadiscio and Addis. Often these stories were run side-by-side on the first page—one from Ethiopia and the other from Somalia—and their contradictory and hazy reports of what was happening in the Ogaden only deepened the mystery of the war. When the Cubans intervened, the press had a villain, but the war still did not make good copy because there was no hero and no likelihood that the Americans would rush in to save the day. The humorist Art Buchwald made fun of this complexity in a syndicated column (with a sexist tone that dates it) that imagined a wife asking her husband, "Would you explain to me what's going on in the Horn of Africa?" As the husband launches into a detailed explanation of the war, his wife's eyes "started to glaze" and she begged him to stop.[222] The wife symbolized those Americans who were unable to make any sense out of the war in the Horn.

This was not just because the story was complicated. By 1978, the Cold War itself was not making much sense. The *New York Times* noted in late February that Americans' declining interest in foreign policy was not the result of a new isolationism. "They have turned away from public affairs, not out of callousness or irresponsibility," the editorial asserted, "but out of genuine confusion."[223] The attempt to locate US national interest in the crisis in the Horn revealed cracks in the logic of the Cold War: Ethiopia had been pro-American and now was pro-Soviet; Somalia had been pro-Soviet and now wanted to be pro-American (or at least get American weapons), but what did these words mean? Were Ethiopia or Somalia in any meaningful sense "pro-" either superpower? And what were the stakes for America? As the *Wall Street Journal* asked, "Does this gritty little war have any importance to the United States?"[224] Did it matter that Moscow had flipped to ally itself with Somalia's enemy? Should the United States care? Why? What were Americans meant to think and feel as thousands of Cubans poured into Ethiopia, to be commanded, they were told, by a Soviet general and armed with Soviet tanks and MiGs?

Journalists had tried to report on the war and explain its regional and global significance, but always at the risk of boggling their readers, whose eyes, like those of Buchwald's archetypal wife, would start to glaze over. Finally, in early

March 1978, they were handed an angle that readers could understand: discord at the heart of the administration was a story that would sell newspapers.

It was, ironically, the Cuban and Ethiopian troops that saved the Carter administration from this line of attack by bringing the war to a swift conclusion. Their assault on Jijiga began on March 1.[225] "The Somalis had organized an effective defense of the city," a Cuban history of the war records, "and they mounted a tenacious resistance." But on March 4, some Somalis began to flee from the city, and by March 5 it was a rout. The Somalis, who had fought with great courage and dwindling supplies, lost thousands of men. From Jijiga, the Cubans and Ethiopians headed south—not east to invade Somalia, as the Americans had feared—to expel the Somali forces from the entire Ogaden. An Ethiopian commander bragged, "Our tanks have been moving just like Patton's."[226]

Vance increased the pressure on Siad Barre. On March 7, he sent John Loughran, the US ambassador in Mogadiscio, a blunt message for Siad. First, Vance asserted that the situation was hopeless: "Somali troops cannot survive this offensive." Second, he insisted that Siad withdraw his troops: "The President believes that . . . [you must] announce . . . a withdrawal of Somali forces from the Ogaden." After Somali troops had been withdrawn—and not before—Vance suggested that "the President [would] begin consultations with congress to provide Somalia with some defensive weapons and discuss with other nations the possibility of their also supplying such weapons." At that time, Carter would also ask Congress for "additional economic assistance to Somalia." Vance's message to Siad concluded ominously: "You should be under no illusion that if you do not . . . withdraw your forces from the Ogaden, the United States will come to your assistance if you are invaded."[227]

Siad received this message from Vance in silence. He told Loughran he could not understand "why the United States chose to side with the Soviets and the Cubans against a poor and tiny country."[228]

1. In Lusaka, Zambian president Kenneth Kaunda congratulates Secretary of State Henry Kissinger, who had just announced a dramatic reversal of US policy: the Ford administration would henceforth support the quest for majority rule in Rhodesia "in the strongest possible terms." *Courtesy of the Ford Library*

2. Henry Kissinger told members of Congress in 1976 that Tanzanian president Julius Nyerere "is the intellectual leader of Southern Africa, and as such is the key to the future of the area and whether that future will be violent or not." *Central Press/Getty Images*

3. South African prime minister John Vorster chats with Henry Kissinger in September 1976 about the latter's upcoming encounter with the leader of Rhodesia, Ian Smith. Soon, when dealing with the Carter administration, Vorster would sorely miss Kissinger's chummy camaraderie. *Central Press/Getty Images*

4. During the 1976 campaign, Carter conveyed a smiling, folksy image, but Andy Warhol, who painted this portrait to help raise campaign funds and attract younger voters, depicted a brooding and pensive man. Carter liked it: "It kind of grows on you," he commented. It is a portrait that captures the complexity and contradictions of Jimmy Carter, a man who lived humbly but was not humble; who believed in forgiveness but was unforgiving; who embraced the cause of human rights but exuded little human warmth; who sought the acclaim of the crowd but was, above all, a solitary man. *Andy Warhol / Artists Rights Society (ARS), New York. Photo © Art Resource, NY*

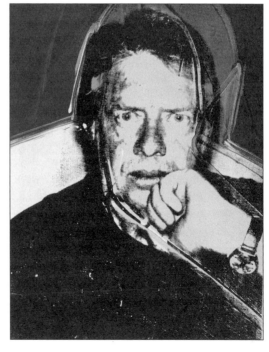

5. The simplest way to make sense of Carter's foreign policy is to assert that it was a battle between the hawkish national security adviser Zbigniew Brzezinski (left) and the dovish secretary of state Cyrus Vance (right). This is inaccurate. *Courtesy of the Carter Library*

6. Andrew Young, the prominent civil rights leader whom Carter appointed ambassador to the United Nations, spoke bluntly and ruffled many feathers. Carter, however, told the press in 1977: "Andy Young . . . speaks with my full authority and complete support. . . . We are completely compatible in our hopes." *Oliphant © universal uclick*

7. In April 1977, Carter and Egyptian president Anwar Sadat met for the first time. The State Department had prepared extensive briefing papers on the Israeli-Palestinian conflict, but Sadat wanted to talk about Soviet penetration of the Horn of Africa. *NBC NewsWire/Getty Images*

8. During an extraordinary meeting in June 1977 with Somali Ambassador Abdullahi Addou, President Carter promised to try to provide arms to Somalia, an irredentist regime that was preparing to attack Ethiopia. Carter's desire to pry Somalia from the Soviet embrace trumped any scruples about supplying weapons to an aggressor. "Morally or theoretically," Carter later rued, "we were on the wrong side." (Zbigniew Brzezinski is in the background.) *Courtesy of the Carter Library*

9. In February 1978, an Ethiopian soldier poses next to a poster showing Ethiopians and Soviets hurling the Somalis out of the Ogaden, the Ethiopian region that the Somalis were attempting to annex. *Keystone-France/Getty Images*

10. Fidel Castro and Ethiopian strongman Mengistu Haile Mariam in Addis Ababa, September 1978. Castro, in close coordination with the Kremlin, had sent thousands of Cuban troops to Ethiopia to defend Mengistu's government against the Somali invasion of the Ogaden. *Photograph by Shemelis Desta, courtesy of Autograph ABP*

11. "There will be no African rule in my lifetime," Rhodesian leader Ian Smith declared in 1964. "The white man is the master of Rhodesia, has built it and intends to keep it." In a desperate attempt to maintain white rule, Smith declared Rhodesia independent on November 11, 1965. *Keystone/ Getty Images*

12. Robert Mugabe (*left*) and Joshua Nkomo (*right*) led the two guerrilla groups fighting Ian Smith's government. Nkomo's strength was his ability to move between worlds: he was both Moscow's protégé and Pretoria's top choice to lead an independent Zimbabwe. Mugabe was an ascetic, a loner, an intellectual, and a radical. He criticized Nkomo's foreign travels, bourgeois proclivities, and negotiations with white imperialists. Despite their deep rift, in October 1976 they joined together in a loose alliance, the Patriotic Front. *Popperfoto/Getty Images*

13. Andrew Young, US ambassador to the United Nations, and David Owen, the British foreign secretary, traveled through southern Africa to sell the Anglo-American proposals to resolve the Rhodesian war. Whereas Kissinger had browbeaten the British, the Carter administration treated them as equal partners. The cooperation between the two allies was remarkable. *Lawrence Harris/AP Photo*

14. In early 1978, US and British negotiators met with the Patriotic Front in Malta to discuss proposals to bring peace and independence to Rhodesia. The stakes were high. Failure of the talks "could lead to the destruction of southern Africa," Ambassador Andrew Young warned. Here, British foreign secretary David Owen, Ambassador Young, and US assistant secretary for Africa Richard Moose (right to left) face representatives of the Patriotic Front across the table. *AFP/Getty Images*

15. In March 1978, Carter visited Nigeria—a country that had thrice refused entry to Henry Kissinger. Yet Carter was greeted on the tarmac by the head of state, and thousands of Nigerians lined the streets waving placards saying "Welcome Carter!" and "Hooray Carter!" UN Secretary-General Kurt Waldheim expressed his "astonishment" at how quickly the United States had improved its standing "among the African states which heretofore had been very critical of the American government." *Dieter Endlicher/ AP Photo*

16. In Guadeloupe in January 1979, the leaders of the United States, Britain, France, and West Germany discussed the state of the world. Giscard d'Estaing said that they had been like four "friends on a holiday." Perhaps, but Giscard and Schmidt harbored grave doubts about Carter's leadership, while Carter admitted that "Jim [Callaghan] is the one person I enjoy being with." Carter and Callaghan stayed in Guadeloupe an extra day to discuss the crisis in Rhodesia. (L to R) Helmut Schmidt, Jimmy Carter, Valéry Giscard d'Estaing, and James Callaghan. *Courtesy of the Carter Library*

17. Bishop Abel Muzorewa, who joined Rhodesia's erstwhile all-white government, was championed by conservative North Carolina senator Jesse Helms. Many white American southerners, annoyed that their own "sacrifices" to accommodate blacks had not been appreciated, resented President Carter's refusal to praise Ian Smith's attempts to accommodate Rhodesia's blacks. *Courtesy of the Jesse Helms Center Archives*

18. In April 1979, Rhodesian leader Ian Smith called elections to select a black prime minister. As this May 1979 *Dayton Daily News* cartoon shows, many Americans, including President Carter, concluded that Smith had no intention of sharing power with the black majority. They believed that Smith, nicknamed "the eel," was simply slithering to retain power. Others, including a large and vocal group in the US Congress, applauded Smith for taking a significant stride toward majority rule. *Courtesy of Mike Peters*

19. At the 1979 Commonwealth Conference in Lusaka, British prime minister Margaret Thatcher (here dancing with Zambian president Kenneth Kaunda) surprised everyone by announcing that her government would maintain sanctions on Rhodesia and call a conference of all participants—including the guerrillas—to resolve the crisis. She was following the lead of Jimmy Carter. "A . . . crucial problem," she explained, "was . . to receive United States support." *MF/AP Photo*

9. Worrying about Cuba

"Genuine, or a fake?": The Internal Settlement[1]

"It's been a victory for moderation," Ian Smith announced with a broad smile on February 15, 1978. Bishop Abel Muzorewa, Chief Jeremiah Chirau, and Reverend Ndabaningi Sithole were at his side. After two months of "sometimes acrimonious bargaining," as the CIA reported, Smith and the three black leaders in Salisbury had finally signed an internal settlement that they claimed would lead Rhodesia to majority rule. The details were still being worked out, but the "Salisbury Four" had agreed to share power until a general election could be held to determine the leader of a new Zimbabwe.[2]

From one angle, it appeared to be a breakthrough: Smith was accepting majority rule and relinquishing some power to blacks. An election would be held in which blacks and whites would vote. Muzorewa, who was normally ebullient, was ecstatic. And yet the weaknesses of the internal settlement were glaring. First, Smith was still very much in the picture, and he had proven his supreme ability to hold onto power. Second, the Patriotc Front was banned in Rhodesia and it would not participate in the elections; how, then, would the internal settlement end the war? Third, although the Salisbury Four planned to spend the coming months hammering out a constitution, the signs were already clear that the government proposed by the internal settlement would entrench white power and privilege. For ten years, whites—3 percent of the total population—would hold a guaranteed 28 seats in the 100-member parliament. Even though the new Rhodesia would have a majority black parliament, would the new constitution withhold effective power from this majority?

Members of the press corps cornered Andy Young on the street outside the UN and asked for his reaction to Smith's announcement. "The problem with an internal settlement is that it is no settlement," the blunt ambassador said, without having cleared his statement with the State Department. "A free election, involving all of the parties in Rhodesia [i.e., including the Patriotic

Front], is the only thing that can stop the killing." Young explained that failing to stop the killing would have ominous repercussions. "We have had evidence that there would be a massive commitment of Soviet weapons." This warning resonated during a week when the headlines focused on the thousands of Cubans in Ethiopia. "So what you have done really is not settle the situation," Young concluded, "but you have created a black on black civil war."[3]

The ambassador's comments hit a nerve. The *Wall Street Journal* castigated him for criticizing the peacemakers rather than those "supplying the arms and doing the shooting." Young's remarks, the *Journal* asserted, revealed that the Carter administration's Africa policy was driven by its desire to prove that it was not racist: "At the end of the day, in order to demonstrate your opposition to the racists you end up supporting the Russians." This meant, according to the *Wall Street Journal*, that the White House had rejected moderation and embraced radicals and terrorists. "They are writing off the National Association for the Advancement of Colored People . . . and . . . throwing their support to the Black Panthers."[4] Young argued that supporting the internal settlement would help the Soviets, whereas the *Journal* argued the opposite: rejecting the settlement would help the Kremlin.

The Policy Review Committee gathered on February 17, 1978, to discuss the Salisbury agreement. The mood was somber: all agreed with Assistant Secretary Dick Moose that the internal settlement placed the administration in a "dreadful situation," made all the more acute by the spiking concerns about the Cuban intervention in Ethiopia.[5] "Greatly increased Soviet and Cuban involvement [in Rhodesia] looks likely," the participants—who included Zbigniew Brzezinski, Cyrus Vance, and Andrew Young—concluded. They decided that the objective of their policy toward Rhodesia—"majority rule emerging from an electoral process"—remained unchanged. All were doubtful that the internal settlement would bring peace to Rhodesia, but thought that it would be premature to condemn it before its details were known; in the meantime, they tried to maintain open minds. The agreement of the Salisbury Four might "be a significant step in the capitulation of Rhodesian whites—the start of an inexorable and accelerating transfer of power." It would all depend on "how rapidly it promises to get Smith out." If it seemed possible that the settlement would remove Smith faster than the Anglo-American accords could, then it would be worthy of support. For this reason, plus the fact that US public opinion seemed to welcome the accord, the committee decided that the administration should describe the internal settlement "as a possible constructive step, provided it leads to a rapid transition to majority rule." It was difficult to predict whether the internal settlement was the first step in a real transfer of power in Rhodesia or just another of Smith's ruses. "Anybody who was at all honest at this point," Ambassador Steve Low, the lead US negotiator in southern Africa, recalled, "had to accept that it could have gone either way."[6]

Soon, however, the skepticism of the Carter administration deepened. The details of the internal settlement agreement were made public on March 3. The accord established an Executive Council composed of Smith, Muzorewa, Sithole, and Chirau that would govern during the transition, but Smith would remain as prime minister and the white-dominated parliament would continue to function. Elections for the 100-member parliament (with its 28 reserved seats) would be held by December 31, 1978. No matter who won the contest, the constitution ensured that whites would exercise effective control over the defense structure for at least ten years, and constitutional amendments would require the support of seventy-eight members of parliament; that is, no amendment could be passed without at least six white votes.[7]

The US State Department cautioned that "Smith and the nationalists still face a protracted negotiating process." Rhodesia—under Smith or under his internal settlement—remained a renegade, illegal regime. The settlement could succeed only if it gained international recognition and the UN lifted sanctions. Bishop Muzorewa, who had taken the lead in the negotiations with Smith, immediately flew to London to begin to garner the international support that would be crucial to the success of the Salisbury accord.[8]

Opinions of the accord—in Britain and in the United States—were divided. The *Washington Post* summed up the quandary: was it "genuine, or a fake?"[9] The answer to this question was in the eye of the beholder. US press comment was generally favorable, but editorial writers at some papers, such as the *New York Times*, expressed skepticism: "The deal is little more than a device for keeping real power in the hands of Rhodesia's small white minority," its editors opined. "Andrew Young . . . characterized them as a recipe for civil war. Now that the details are known, his fears appear justified."[10]

Most Britons seemed relieved, hopeful that an end to their involvement in Rhodesia was finally in sight. They had been wrestling with Smith ever since he had unilaterally declared Rhodesia's independence in 1965, and they were weary. Even the liberal *Guardian* concluded that "Britain has now got what it insisted upon: the full commitment to majority rule." In the Cabinet, Foreign Secretary David Owen supported the internal settlement, saying that it was "a much better deal for the [black] Africans" than any of the previously considered accords: "Smith had moved a long way in comparison with his position a year ago." In Parliament, a Conservative backbencher demanded that Owen explain Young's comment that the internal settlement was "no settlement" and that he "urge the United States Ambassador to the United Nations to be far more cautious." Fellow Tories yelled their agreement. The beleaguered Owen explained, "The Americans carry great influence in Africa at the moment—greater influence than they have ever carried before. . . . One of the people who has made a major contribution to this end has been Ambassador Young."[11]

Despite Owen's spirited defense of the Carter administration, a rupture between Washington and London was in the offing. In public, the allies glossed over their different attitudes toward the internal settlement. "There are always differences of nuance," Owen told a British television reporter, "but I don't think there is any fundamental difference." The CIA disagreed. "The UK-US initiative has reached a critical juncture," the agency warned. "After 12 years of protracted negotiations and guerrilla warfare, Britain is tempted to accept the internal agreement and relieve itself of a last vestige of the colonial empire."[12]

David Owen's Gambit, Part Two

Not only was the British Foreign Office's assessment of the internal settlement more positive than was the US State Department's, its commitment to the Anglo-American proposals was weaker. The Carter administration continued to believe that the painstaking Anglo-American proposals were the best hope to end the war, but the British government harbored grave doubts that they would lead anywhere. British Ambassador Johnny Graham, the lead British negotiator in southern Africa, summed up the sentiment in the Foreign Office: "I see little prospect of their [the Anglo-American proposals] ever being put into effect in anything like the form we envisaged them," he wrote the private secretary on February 22, 1978. Moreover, the Anglo-American proposals had become a Tory cudgel against the Callaghan government. "This had become a domestic battle," Owen explained.[13]

Owen sought an alternative course: one that would result in ZAPU's Joshua Nkomo as the leader of Zimbabwe. He wanted to persuade Nkomo to enter into talks with Smith, Muzorewa, Sithole, and Chirau. That is, Owen wanted to widen Smith's internal settlement so that it could include—and indeed be led by—Nkomo. This could give birth to a government that would gain international acceptance and provide Britain a decent interval in which to grant independence to the new nation of Zimbabwe and wash its hands of the burden. In late February, Owen met with Assistant Secretary Moose to discuss "the involvement of Nkomo" and the desirability of reviving "high level contacts between President Kaunda and Smith," with the clear hope that Nkomo would join these talks.[14]

The State Department's Africanists disagreed sharply: they doubted that Nkomo could be persuaded to join the internal settlement, and they wanted to stick with the Anglo-American proposals. A discreet tug of war between the two allies ensued. "As Dick Moose and company pointed out to Owen," Ambassador Low wrote, "our assessment seems to be very different than his on the ultimate success of the Salisbury talks and Nkomo's willingness to join them. . . . We completely fail to follow Owen's logic. . . . [We must] dissuade Owen from what seems to us to be an ill-advised course."[15]

Owen saw it differently. "I fear I have roughed up the Americans over Rhodesia but I am quite unapologetic about it," he wrote to Peter Jay, the British ambassador in Washington, on February 24. "After spending five hours with Dick Moose where he rambled on, refusing to face facts, I cut the meeting off and showed my exasperation. . . . The fact is that Dick Moose, much as I like him, is hung up on Vietnam. . . . Guilt still predominates and while he is prepared to exert influence, he is not prepared to exert power. It is as if they are operating with one ball. . . . They are looking at Africa somewhat naively . . . and tending to brush off as insignificant the Marxist and revolutionary element that exist in quite large measure in [Mugabe's] ZANU."[16]

Owen then wrote a six-page personal letter to Vance. "I have spent about five hours discussing Rhodesia with Dick Moose over the last days," he began. "For the first time since we started our joint initiative I detect the possibility of a different analysis of the problem. This is potentially serious and is why I write. Let me assure you that I will not take any unilateral decisions. . . . We start, I am sure, from an agreed position. Our long-term objective, besides bringing about a genuine transfer of power and fair and free elections for Zimbabwe, must be to prevent increased Cuban involvement in the Rhodesian situation."[17]

Owen tried to enlist Vance on the side of what he considered pragmatism. He explained that the Anglo-American proposals had been predicated on the assumption that Britain and the United States would be able to "remove Smith," but this task—challenging at the best of times—had been made immeasurably more difficult by the internal settlement. They would now have to get rid of not only Smith but also the internal settlement government. How could they do it? "We could . . . be severely attacked for backing the forces of violence in an attempt to overthrow a genuine democratic settlement." Owen summed up: sticking "rigidly" to the Anglo-American proposals—which he feared some people in the US State Department wanted to do—"will not, in my view, achieve either a ceasefire or a negotiated settlement. . . . It is important to state this brutally and frankly now."

There was an alternative. Owen continued. "Reality dictates that our objective now should be to accept that we will have to somehow widen the area of agreement . . . between the Salisbury talks and the Anglo/US initiative." While Robert Mugabe might refuse to join talks with the Salisbury Four, and therefore make it impossible to fully stop the war, there was still a way to "minimise the fighting." Owen returned to his favored scheme. "Realism dictates that . . . Joshua Nkomo must come into some arrangement involving Smith, Muzorewa, and Sithole. . . . If that meant Joshua separating from Mugabe, he would be able to do it under the respectable umbrella of our proposals." He tried to rope Vance into his plan. "I tend to believe . . . that if it were possible by clandestine means to involve Nkomo before the Salisbury talks firm up . . . this would be better [than sticking to the Anglo-American proposals]." Owen wanted Vance's agreement to initiate secret talks with Nkomo. The potential pitfalls were serious. "I well recognise that to do this without alienating the front-line presidents is extremely difficult. . . . I do not underestimate in any way the difficulty of walking this tightrope." But the risks of doing nothing were greater. Once the internal settlement government got established, "the only way the Patriotic Front will then be able to influence Salisbury is to increase the violence." Owen pulled out the last stop: the Patriotic Front could only increase the violence by bringing in "reinforcements, probably Cuban."

On February 27, Owen received a brief and cryptic reply to his heartfelt missive. "I have studied your letter and I believe that there are really no substantial differences between us as to our objectives," Vance wrote. He stressed that it was important to continue to support the principles of the Anglo-American plan and to keep the Frontline presidents onboard. Owen later paraphrased Vance's message: "Look, I'm not with you on this . . . but I won't stop you. Keep me informed, but I don't want the Americans involved."[18]

Vance's aides sensed trouble immediately. Owen's strategy struck them as a dangerous pursuit of fool's gold: if Nkomo agreed to it (which they considered improbable), the Patriotic Front would be destroyed. Not only would US relations with black Africa nosedive, but an Angola-style civil war would be more likely. Moose could not forget what Tanzanian president Julius Nyerere had whispered in his ear the last time they had met in Dar es Salaam: "Dick, don't trust the British."[19]

All their problems, however, were not across the pond. In the first week of March, when the war in the Horn was cresting, Vance's aides did battle with Brzezinski's aides over the direction of US policy in Rhodesia. On March 4, Deputy National Security Adviser David Aaron wrote Brzezinski a closely argued memo in support of Owen's plan to convince Nkomo to join the internal settlement. "If there is a good internal settlement that really gives the blacks control and a stake in that government, we will [be] . . . in a very strong position to humiliate the Soviets, Cubans and any other diehards." Several days later, Aaron followed up: "The British have to get Nkomo into power politically and not through the force of Soviet and Cuban arms. This makes a lot more sense to me than fooling around with the AAP [Anglo-American proposals]." Aaron underlined the next sentences: "It is important to remember that Rhodesia is a British colony and they could put into office anybody they want. . . . We must not become hung up on the 'free elections' aspects of the AAP." Although there is no declassified record of Brzezinski taking up this line of argument vigorously, he was clearly in sympathy with it. "I am beginning to lean to the notion that we ought to let . . . the moderate Africans take over," he wrote in his diary.[20]

At the State Department, Dick Moose and Anthony Lake strongly disagreed. They worked hard to stiffen Vance's resolve to stick with the Anglo-American proposals. "We could be heading into a dangerous situation on Rhodesia, if David Owen pursues his strategy of encouraging Nkomo into an internal settlement," Lake and other senior State Department officials wrote the secretary. If Owen persisted, "we will lose all credibility with the Frontline States" whose leaders had spent political capital backing the Anglo-American proposals. One official expressed this pithily: it "would kill Andy Young with the Africans." Moreover, it would be for naught, since "it is most unlikely that Nkomo will enter into the internal arrangement." Therefore, the State Department had "to turn off Owen's current efforts."[21] (A quarter-century later, when Owen read this memo, he remarked, "That's true. There is no doubt. I wanted Mugabe to be in a secondary role. I thought Nkomo would make more compromises, while Mugabe was zealous and intransigent."[22])

On March 8, two weeks after the Owen-Vance exchange, a reporter asked Andrew Young whether a rift had developed with the British about the internal settlement. Young responded with a stinging reference to Britain's relinquishing the mandate for Palestine. "What are they [the British] going to do? Chicken out and leave us with 30 years of trouble the way they did in 1948?"[23]

Later that morning, Bishop Muzorewa arrived in Washington, continuing his tour to gain international backing. The bishop, a gracious and unprepossessing man, was riding a fragile wave of power: he had been well received in London, and now he sought to persuade the Americans to take, as he said, "a courageous lead to endorse and accept what we have done." It was rough going for him. For ninety minutes, he faced the withering questioning of Vance, Moose, and Lake. He asserted that the internal settlement's transfer of power was genuine—Smith would be prime minister "in name only . . . real power, including control of army and police, will pass to executive council." The Americans pointed out, however, that the leaders of the Frontline States did not perceive it as a genuine transfer of power. Vance asked what would happen if Smith "changes his mind?" Muzorewa's reply was devastatingly lame. He said it was "very unlikely" that Smith would change his mind. "I can almost rule it out," he added. The Americans then pressed him about how the internal settlement would end the war. "We estimate warfare will escalate," Vance told him, "and there will exist a greater possibility of Soviet, Cuban, and South African intervention." As Muzorewa tried to explain why the Patriotic Front would lay down its arms, "his voice grew fainter . . . and finally trailed off."[24]

A few hours later, David Owen flew to Washington. He met first with President Carter and then, for four-and-a-half hours, he discussed Rhodesia with Vance. No account of these talks has been released, but they must have dealt extensively with Owen's continuing desire to open a secret backchannel to Nkomo. Owen was undeterred by the failure of the meeting he had arranged between Smith, Nkomo, and Zambian president Kenneth Kaunda the previous September, and he had not been chastened by the tensions it had caused in the Anglo-American partnership as well as on the ground in Africa. After sunset that day, the State Department spokesman emerged to deliver a terse, carefully worded statement. "There was full agreement that the two governments will jointly continue their efforts to facilitate a settlement among all the parties, in accordance with the principles the two governments have previously put forward: free and fair elections, a transition to majority rule and independence, and respect for the individual rights of all citizens of an independent Zimbabwe."[25]

For the next five weeks, the people in the State Department most concerned with Africa scrambled to get the Anglo-American proposals on track so that they could deflect Owen's desire to reach a secret deal with Nkomo, one that they believed would fail and in the process destroy America's credibility in Africa. Young used the press to signal his distress. "I frankly think that the British people want to wash their hands of the Rhodesia issue and almost don't care what happens," he told the *Zimbabwe Times*. "They would like a quick solution that would turn it over to Smith and they would look the other way." This prompted former Prime Minister Harold Wilson to remark to the BBC that the British people were "a little tired" of the pronouncements of Andrew Young. "A period of silence on your part would be welcome," he said publicly to Young.[26]

London was only one source of difficulty. Bishop Muzorewa had returned home from his foreign travels to a huge, cheering crowd of some 200,000 Rhodesians in Salisbury. He claimed that 85 percent of the population supported the internal settlement. The Salisbury Four believed that they were on the path to power and they had no interest in returning to the Anglo-American proposals; the Patriotic Front dug in its heels; South African prime minister John Vorster urged Britain and the United States to pursue Owen's gambit.[27] And the Cuban intervention in Ethiopia upped the ante.

Worries

Joshua Nkomo and Robert Mugabe, the leaders of the Patriotic Front, confronted Vance at the State Department on March 12. A week earlier, Nkomo had told the press that he would seek Cuban help to fight Smith's forces if necessary. At the State Department, he and Mugabe accused the Americans and British of "abandoning the Anglo-American proposals" and they flatly rejected participating in any "'appeasement meeting' at which the US and UK would try to 'marry' the Anglo-American proposals and the Salisbury agreement."[28]

The Carter administration was worried. "The failure of efforts to get negotiations [on the Anglo-American proposals] started again," Vance wrote after the distressing meeting with Mugabe and Nkomo, "offers only the prospect of long, destructive warfare with tragic consequences for all concerned." Adding to the Americans' concerns was that the war in Rhodesia was escalating at the same time as the crisis in the Horn. American officials had worried about Soviet and Cuban interference in southern Africa ever since the Cubans had appeared in Angola, but they had not thought that the danger was imminent—until the Soviet airlift to Addis Ababa. The Carter administration had been confident that Moscow would not jeopardize détente by mounting another Angola-style intervention in Africa. It had been sure that Castro would pause long and hard before derailing normalization with the United States. It had been reassured by Castro's promise that he would gradually withdraw troops from Angola. This complacency was summed up in a US intelligence report from May 1977: "We doubt that we will see any special new Soviet 'drive' in southern Africa in the next three to five years. But nine months later, in February 1978, not only had Castro stopped his troop withdrawal from Angola, but thousands of Cubans armed with sophisticated Soviet weapons were entering Ethiopia. "We have had a setback," Vance acknowledged.[29]

Robert Gates, who had moved from the CIA to the NSC staff, wrote to Brzezinski in late February 1978. "The USSR's efforts in the Horn have not diminished its determination to pursue its African involvement on a number of other fronts as well." Gates analyzed Soviet policy in Angola, Guinea (Conakry), Nigeria, Tanzania, and, in particular, Rhodesia. Nkomo had recently returned from the Kremlin, where he had been greeted by Politburo member Boris Ponomarev and reportedly had arranged additional ZAPU training and materiel. Gates wrote that Nkomo and Mugabe had reached a similar agreement with Cuba. (He was mistaken: in 1977, Cuba had agreed to train 6,000 ZAPU fighters, but it had no agreement with ZANU.) On February 24, the CIA concluded: "In the wake of their success in Angola and Ethiopia—the Soviets are psychologically prepared for additional involvement in Africa. . . . Castro has the military personnel to support an expanded effort." It added that it was unlikely that any type of US pressure would "deter policymakers in Moscow and Havana from increasing their support for Nkomo." There was only one effective constraint on Castro: "He is likely to be reluctant to commit major combat units to ZAPU . . . as long as increasing numbers of Cuban forces are needed in Ethiopia."[30]

The War Is Over

Suddenly, in the early hours of March 9, a flash cable arrived at Foggy Bottom from Mogadiscio. "Siad summoned me at 0200 hours local," the US ambassador to Somalia, John Loughran, wrote. "He asked me to inform President Carter that he accepts the proposals." Somali president Mohamed Siad Barre was referring to the blunt cable that Vance had sent two days before: if Siad withdrew his troops, Washington would consider providing Somalia defensive weapons and economic aid; if Siad did not withdraw, he would face the consequences alone. Siad told Loughran that "he was personally shocked and disappointed at the language . . . of the proposals but nevertheless he accepted it." He had given the order for his troops to withdraw.[31]

In fact, Siad Barre had faced reality before receiving Vance's stern demands. On March 5, Jijiga, which the Somalis had held since September, fell to the Ethiopian and Cuban forces. On March 6—one day *before* Siad's stormy meeting with US Ambassador Loughran—a cable from Fidel Castro reveals that Siad Barre had written Moscow "acknowledging Ethiopia's victory, asking for a ceasefire, and offering to withdraw his troops." Siad had also asked the Kremlin if "the ties of friendship between Somalia and the Soviet Union could be renewed," and Moscow had agreed to serve as mediator between Ethiopia and Somalia if Siad Barre promised "to cease all aggression against Ethiopia." Castro summed up the situation: "In a word, Siad Barre wants peace." It was the rout of his troops on the battlefield, not Washington's threats and promises, that had convinced Siad to wave the white flag. To General Arnaldo Ochoa, the head of the Cuban military mission in Addis, Castro cabled, "Congratulations on your brilliant victory!" To General Vasily Petrov and the Soviet military advisers in Ethiopia, Castro sent his "hearty congratulations and thanks for their extraordinary cooperation . . . in the victorious operation."[32]

The following day, March 7, Castro sent Ethiopia's Mengistu a long cable reflecting on the dramatic events of the preceding months. "We have followed day by day every detail of the heroic and victorious actions of the revolutionary Ethiopian soldiers and internationalist fighters on the eastern front [the Ogaden]. The turn-around in the military situation . . . seems truly unbelievable. From January 22, 1978—the day the Somalis launched their final assault on Harar and the Cuban fighters had the honor of participating on the front line for the first time—until March 5, the day Jijiga was captured, was only forty-two days, forty-two days of military victories." Castro then turned to Siad Barre's peace probe. "Our opinion, if it is useful, is that you cannot reject a peace proposal from an enemy who has acknowledged defeat. It is a matter of principle." He then turned to the issue that had consumed Washington. "It is even more sensible and correct to accept the peace proposal because the international political situation dictates that it would not be useful to carry out military operations on Somali territory." Castro concluded with fatherly advice. "Now, Comrade Mengistu, you have the immense boon of a great victory. It is your challenge to use it responsibly."[33]

On March 9, the morning that Washington received the news of Siad's offer, Vance was scheduled to testify before the Senate Appropriations Committee about the foreign aid budget. He and Carter had learned the hard way that it was important to verify Siad's promises, and Vance therefore was determined to be circumspect before the committee. He need not have worried: the members expressed scant interest in the Horn. Congress had not gotten involved in the issue: it concerned almost none of their constituents, it attracted no lobbies, and—until the Cubans appeared—it provided no fodder with which to attack the administration. Only one senator asked a question about it, and Vance replied coyly that "there are indications that a withdrawal may be underway."[34] No senator expressed the slightest curiosity, and the discussion returned to appropriations.

The journalists at the hearing, however, smelled a story. The State Department spokesman was peppered with questions at the noon briefing. Would the United States now be sending Somalia military aid? "Are they [the Somalis] the good guys now?" By three o'clock, Washington had received "independent indication [that Somali troop] withdrawals . . . are . . . in process," and Carter called allied foreign leaders to tell them the news.[35] "This gives us some hope," he told West German chancellor Helmut Schmidt, "that we may be able to get the Cubans and Soviets out of Ethiopia." At a televised news conference in the Old Executive Office Building, Carter made the announcement. "Last night, I was informed by President Siad Barre of Somalia that he was agreeing to withdraw his forces from the Ogaden area. . . . As soon as Somali forces have withdrawn completely, and as soon as Ethiopian forces have reestablished control over their own territory, withdrawal of the Soviet and Cuban combat presence should begin."[36]

The *New York Times* editorial the next day was titled, "Somalia Retreats, Everyone Gains." Certainly, the Carter administration gained: the longer the war had continued, the more vigorously the press would have probed the divisions

411

it exposed among the administration's high officials. Carter was lucky that the media had not gotten a handle on the war until the fateful February 23, 1978, NSC meeting when Brzezinski had linked "the unwarranted intrusion of Soviet power [in the Horn]" to the ratification of the SALT treaty, Vance had rapidly contradicted him, and the president had failed to lead his troops.[37]

Hindsight

Two years later, after the Soviet Union invaded Afghanistan in December 1979, Brzezinski asserted that the moment when "things [would] begin to go genuinely wrong in the US-Soviet relationship" was that day in late February 1978 when Carter had not sent a carrier task force to the Horn. This failure to respond, Brzezinski argued, "emboldened" the Soviets and therefore led less than two years later to their march to Kabul. "SALT," he proclaimed, "lies buried in the sands of the Ogaden."[38]

The Kremlin's successful intervention in Ethiopia did deepen its self-confidence. As Odd Arne Westad, the historian who has had greatest access to the relevant Soviet documents, writes: "To many Soviet leaders of the World War II generation, it was the successful intervention in the Horn of Africa that established the Soviet Union as a real global power—a power that could intervene at will throughout the world with decisive consequences."[39] No one in the Carter administration would have disagreed: Moscow was emboldened by its ability to intervene in the Horn.

At the pivotal meeting of February 23, 1978, all the principals—Vance, Brzezinski, Defense Secretary Harold Brown, CIA director Stansfield Turner, and Joint Chiefs of Staff chair David Jones—had agreed in theory that a US response would have been useful, but they had not agreed with Brzezinski that the Soviets had violated "the rules of détente."[40] Addis had requested help to repel the Somali invasion, and Moscow and Havana had responded. If the Ethiopian and Cuban troops invaded Somalia they would become aggressors, but all signs were that this was very unlikely—which was extremely fortunate, because none of the responses that Brzezinski suggested made any sense. Transferring arms to the Somalis would be a futile gesture that would break US law. Encouraging the Iranians and Saudis to intervene would only embarrass Washington: they would refuse to send their troops because they knew that the Cubans would "kick the shit" out of them. Stationing a US carrier group offshore would be "ineffectual."[41] The Somali army had been defeated. All except Brzezinski had looked at this fact and grimly determined that in practice, the best policy would be to do nothing—to hunker down, hope (as they all expected) that Somalia would not be invaded, and wait for it to blow over. Four of the most powerful men in the United States—Vance, Turner, Brown, and Jones—did not think that there was any way to force the Soviets to change their policy in Ethiopia that would be worth the price to the United States. (They did contemplate measures to punish the Soviets and Cubans for their behavior, but none to counter it in the Horn.) They were pursuing a bitterly realistic policy.

Even though Brzezinski's proposals had received no support at the meeting, they had alarmed Vance for two reasons. First, it was possible that Carter would implement them. No one could be sure what Jimmy Carter would decide. This provided fertile ground for Vance's second worry: the debate would be played out in the press. Brzezinski was agitated and outnumbered; the president had not yet weighed in. Therefore, there would be a temptation for someone who supported Brzezinski's policy to use a press leak to bend the debate. For Vance, it was very important that the administration minimize public interest in the Horn. Denouncing Soviet behavior in the Horn would only underline US passivity and raise the American people's anger at the Soviet Union. This would endanger SALT II—needlessly, in Vance's opinion. That was why, with the exception of Brzezinski, the principals wanted to avoid talking in public about the war.

To a large degree, the administration succeeded in minimizing interest in the war. In the final week of hostilities, there was a flurry of articles about the disarray within the administration, especially about the divide between Vance and Brzezinski, but even then the US press did not focus on the war itself. One of the most striking aspects of the Ogaden war is how little interest it generated in the US press, even though it involved Soviet and Cuban forces and was by far the most lethal conflict occurring at the time. Although the number of Somali dead is unknown, at least 5,000 and possibly more than 6,000 Ethiopian soldiers perished, as well as 163 Cubans and an untold number of Ethiopian civilians.[42] However, from January 1 to March 9, when the war was at its peak, the *New York Times*, *Washington Post*, and *Christian Science Monitor* published only three editorials each about it, and the *Los Angeles Times* none. (In contrast, in the same period the *New York Times*, *Washington Post*, and *Christian Science Monitor* ran at least ten editorials each about the Middle East peace process, while the *Los Angeles Times* published five.) Likewise, there were four times more articles about the Middle East on America's front pages than there were about the Horn of Africa.[43] The war was hard to explain, the stakes for the United States seemed low, and it was even more difficult to help readers see a satisfying US response to it. Less than three years after the fall of Saigon, no Americans wanted to jump into a guerrilla war in east Africa (or anywhere else).

Nevertheless, the war in the Ogaden had a significant impact on the Carter administration. It changed the atmosphere; it sharpened the edges between Vance and Brzezinski; and it weakened Carter, who was seen by those paying attention as unable to respond to the Soviet and Cuban intervention. Brzezinski drove this point home in his missives to Carter. In reacting to the crisis in the Horn, Moscow felt triumphant, while Washington—and Jimmy Carter—felt cornered.

The actual stakes, however, bore no relation to these powerful feelings. The Soviet Union lost: it gambled that it could befriend both Somalia and Ethiopia, and instead it was hurled out of Mogadiscio, its most important sub-Saharan ally, and lost Berbera, its only base in Africa. By hitching its wagon to Ethiopia, Moscow failed to gain a replacement for Berbera and inherited a desperately needy and fractured state in Addis. It had shipped $1.5 billion worth of arms to Ethiopia. (By 1980, Mengistu had given the Soviets access to the Dahlak Islands, "a small naval base" in the Red Sea. The Americans followed this development "very easily through satellite reconnaissance," the deputy chief of mission in Addis remembered. In terms of access, size, and location, this base was inferior to Berbera.) As the Soviet ambassador to the United States, Anatoly Dobrynin, admitted in April 1978, "They [the Soviets] were better off when they had their relations with Somalia instead of taking on the problems of Ethiopia."[44]

In the zero-sum calculations of the Cold War, the United States correspondingly won. As Young said on *Face the Nation* in May 1978, the United States was "in a better position now in the Horn than we were last year" when the Soviets had been welcomed in both Ethiopia and Somalia. As soon as Siad Barre's troops had retreated from the Ogaden, Washington made overtures to strengthen its relations with Somalia. NSC staffer Paul Henze's analysis was correct: "We have not failed in the Horn," he wrote immediately after the war ended, "we have only managed to give the impression that we are much worse off than we really are."[45]

Yet there were other peripheral costs for the United States. For example, its relations with Kenya—threatened by Somali irredentism and alarmed by Washington's tilt toward Siad Barre—were temporarily strained.[46] More significantly, the war in the Horn provided an early learning experience for both Jidda and Washington about the complexities of adjusting to newfound Saudi power. Initially, in early 1977, Carter was swayed by the conservative Arab point of view. Immediately after Egyptian president Anwar Sadat's visit in April, Carter told Vance: "Get Somalia to be our friend." Likewise, in 1977, Jidda had imagined that money—lots of it—would make Siad Barre malleable. By early 1978, however, the White House was separating its policy in the

Horn from that of Saudi Arabia, and the Saudis were holding back information about what weapons they were sending to Siad. Moreover, the Saudis—learning their own lessons in power—had grown disenchanted with Siad, who was happy to take their money but not their advice. The Saudis, Henze wrote on March 6, 1978, were reacting "grumpily . . . to the dishonesty of Somalis who, they maintain, are mis-spending money they give them for military equipment." There is evidence that in the final days of the war, the Saudis joined with the Americans in urging Siad to withdraw his troops. "The Saudi mission took more than it gave," one of Siad's top aides complained ungratefully.[47]

The war in the Horn also deepened the chill in Washington's relations with Moscow, which had been cool ever since March 1977 when Vance had ventured to the Soviet Union, new SALT proposals in hand. However, contrary to Brzezinski's post facto claim that "SALT lies buried in the sands of the Ogaden," the Kremlin's intervention in Ethiopia did not cause a major rupture in superpower relations. The Ogaden war killed neither SALT nor détente.[48]

Vance succeeded in shielding SALT from the administration's rising frustration with the Kremlin's policy toward the Horn, and the arms control talks continued without interruption. Although the war did exacerbate US senators' distrust of Moscow, it is important to remember that Congress all but ignored this crisis; the Senate's failure to ratify the SALT II treaty occurred in the wake of much more inflammatory incidents, such as the Cuban minibrigade crisis a full nineteen months later (see chapter 15). The Carter administration, despite Brzezinski's rhetoric, managed to tamp down the impact of the Horn on US-Soviet relations.

This was due, in part, to luck: the war ended just as the US press was beginning to get a handle on it. The triumphant Ethiopian troops did not invade Somalia. For this, Jimmy Carter had the Cubans—who had imposed discipline on the Ethiopian troops—and the Soviets to thank. (In a conversation with Soviet foreign minister Andrei Gromyko, Vance acknowledged that the Kremlin had persuaded the Ethiopians not to invade Somalia.)[49] The incipient criticism of the Carter administration's inability to exert leverage in the Horn was abruptly cut short. The impact of the Horn crisis was also defused by horizontal escalation. Unable to punish Moscow for its legal intervention in the Horn, the Carter administration found other ways to express its frustration, cooling relations with Havana and warming them with Beijing.

Castro's intervention in the Horn helped sink the Carter administration's talk of normalization of relations with Cuba. On February 27, Vance announced that he did not see normalization in the immediate future. The State Department also launched initiatives, soon to prove ineffective, to undermine Cuba's stature in the Non-Aligned Movement and to press US allies to limit economic credits extended to Havana. At the same time, however, the talks among high officials that the two countries had secretly initiated in 1977 staggered forward.[50] Young explained, "We must avoid allowing the spectre of the 'Cuban threat' to distract us from basic problems in Africa." But Brzezinski wanted to take a harder line against Havana. "Why not make them increase their involvement in Angola? Let them be pinched by it," he declared in the March 2, 1978, meeting on the Horn. Brzezinski argued that the United States should increase US aid—indirect and covert—to Jonas Savimbi, the rebel leader who continued to wage a guerrilla war against Angola's Cuban-backed government. Vance vigorously opposed the idea. The 1976 Clark Amendment prohibited direct US aid to Savimbi, but there are indications that the war in the Horn opened the door wider to indirect aid. Or perhaps the door had never really been closed. As Dick Moose later commented, "Those CIA guys know that presidents come and go. They just hunker down and maintain their contacts. Have you ever had a computer screen go completely black, and you think you've lost everything? Then, ping! You touch one key and it all magically reappears."[51]

Playing the China Card

Although the Carter administration's feelings of impotence and frustration soured its relations with Cuba, their impact was felt most strongly in US relations with the People's Republic of China. It was while the war in the Horn was reaching its apogee that Jimmy Carter decided to send Brzezinski—not Vance—to Beijing. Carter might have tapped Brzezinski even without the Soviet and Cuban intervention in Ethiopia, but the evidence suggests that it was under the pressure of the rising frustration with America's impotence in the Horn that Carter's decision about China crystallized.

Jimmy Carter was not accustomed to being seen as weak. He had been an achiever all his life, an activist prone to bold decisions—applying to the US Naval Academy; running for governor and then president; and, as president, in one year, developing an energy program, seeking peace in the Middle East and southern Africa, and negotiating the Panama Canal treaties. Nevertheless, his approval rate was slipping, and domestic critics as well as foreign leaders were complaining that he was not tough enough, especially in response to the Soviet Union's boldness in the Horn. Carter agreed with Vance and the rest of his top foreign policy advisers—except Brzezinski—that Washington had no cards to play there and it was best to fold. But Carter was uncomfortable, and he felt the need to flex his muscle, and America's muscle, somewhere.

Why not China? As a candidate, Carter had promised to normalize relations with Beijing, and time was wasting; it would not be smart to provoke the

Taiwan lobby during the presidential election cycle, which would be underway in 1979. However, moving too quickly toward normalization could threaten the SALT II negotiations which, Vance argued, had to be the administration's priority. For Vance, diplomacy was a delicate and deliberate construction of fragile bonds of trust, and the US-Soviet bonds that had been woven during the détente years were fraying. Sending Brzezinski to Beijing, Vance believed, would send the wrong signal at the wrong time: the Kremlin would interpret it as a profoundly anti-Soviet move, as Washington playing the "China card." Vance considered it inappropriate and unwise. He did not believe that the Soviets had violated the rules of détente by intervening in Ethiopia; the administration's unease at being unable to counter the Soviets in the Horn did not justify a response that would imperil both détente and SALT. Vance was not "soft" on the Soviets, but he had clear priorities, and the arms control process was at the top of them. Moreover, Vance worried about relying on Brzezinski as the messenger. The national security adviser was widely known to have an impetuous, impulsive side; he was a man of enthusiasms. He might go off script in Beijing. Finally, as Vance wrote, sending Brzezinski to China "would bring into sharp relief the question of who spoke for the administration on foreign policy. . . . There could only be two spokesmen, the president and the secretary of state."[52]

On February 27, 1978, Brzezinski sent Carter a memo urging him to choose the next emissary to China: "Bearing in mind developments on the Horn and the related need to send a sensitive signal to the Soviets, the time is ripe for your decision on this subject." Unsaid but understood was that he would be the emissary. Brzezinski was careful to specify that he would consult with Vance and that his proposed trip to Beijing would be "consultative" only. It would, nevertheless, give "the Soviets some food for thought."[53]

Secretary of Defense Harold Brown weighed in. "Initiating talks with the PRC [People's Republic of China] . . . would surely cause the Soviets to be concerned. It would be a response to their actions in the Horn of a kind appropriate in magnitude and in nature, being political and strategic. . . . That can be carried out as part of a visit by Zbig to Peking, a visit which I strongly support," Brown wrote Carter on March 11, as the Somali troops were beating a hasty retreat. "An advantage, in my view, (others might say a risk) of using Brzezinski visit for this purpose is its stronger impact." Brown's opinion carried weight: Carter respected his intelligence. Moreover, Brown had sided with Vance against Brzezinski in the debates about sending an aircraft carrier and foreign troops to Somalia; his support of Brzezinski for Beijing therefore seemed to be based on his carefully considered analysis of the problem. "I know that Cy believes this could be a dangerous move," Brown added, "[but]

I believe we must be prepared to upset the Soviets as much as they have upset us by their actions in the Horn, in order to discourage them from expanding such activities into even more dangerous places. . . . stirring the waters in Rhodesia and then fishing in them."[54]

Carter agreed with Vance about the centrality of SALT, but he believed that a tilt toward China would light a fire under the Soviets and help bring SALT to its conclusion. He also agreed with Vance that Brzezinski needed watching. That did not worry him: he would control Zbigniew Brzezinski. In 1999, Carter reflected on this. "My national security adviser never departed from the instructions I gave him. . . . I do not believe there was ever any doubt about who was in charge."[55]

On March 14, Carter returned Vance's Evening Report to its author, with his customary marginalia. But at the bottom was a handwritten note. "Cy—Let's move on a visit to PRC [China]. Either Fritz or Zbig & you to SU [Soviet Union]." It was signed simply "J."[56] The following day, Carter made it official in a terse, handwritten note on White House stationery to Vice President Walter Mondale and Vance. "I've decided it would be best for Zbig to go to China—perhaps as early as next month."[57]

National Insecurity

"This morning, I would like to talk to you about our national security—where we now stand, what new circumstances we face, and what we are going to do in the future."[58] President Carter was standing at the pulpit of Wait Chapel at Wake Forest University in Winston-Salem, North Carolina. It was March 17, 1978—one week after Siad Barre had announced that he was withdrawing his troops from the Ogaden and two weeks after Ian Smith had announced the internal settlement in Rhodesia.

March had been a difficult month for American officials focused on relations with Africa. The good news was that the Somali troop withdrawal had proceeded swiftly, there were no reprisals against the Ogadeni people, and the Ethiopian and Cuban troops had not invaded Somalia. The hot war was over. But an estimated 14,000 Cuban troops were in Ethiopia, Havana showed no interest in withdrawing them, and Washington had no way to get them out. Carter looked weak. Moreover, the end of the war in the Ogaden meant that the Cubans would be free to move south, to Rhodesia. As the French magazine *Jeune Afrique* wrote in March 1978, "Yesterday, Angola; today, Ethiopia; tomorrow, Rhodesia." Washington's fears about southern Africa, where its diplomatic efforts were challenged by Ian Smith's internal settlement as well as David Owen's gambits, spiked. In March, the State Department's Bureau of Intelligence and Research analyzed Fidel Castro's goals in Africa and drew ominous conclusions. "Cuba's symbiotic relationship with the Soviet Union in Africa has enabled Castro to play a major role as a supporter of revolutionary movements and 'progressive' governments. . . . Improved relations . . . with the US . . . are clearly secondary in priority." The danger was obvious. "Recent information . . . suggest[s] that Cuban military personnel may begin accompanying guerrilla units into Rhodesia. . . . [This] would incur the risk of bringing South Africa into the conflict on the other side."[59]

US intelligence feared that Zambia and Mozambique might turn to the Cubans to help them repel Smith's raids. Even though Mozambique was hardest hit, the State Department was more worried about Zambia. This was in part because the Soviet bloc's relations with Mugabe (based in Mozambique) were strained. "The Cubans and the Soviets seem to have largely written off Mugabe and ZANU," the State Department asserted. Washington was also pleased that Samora Machel's government "has become warmer and less doctrinaire during recent months." The United States had condemned the Rhodesian raids on Chimoio and Tembue, and it had sent emergency aid to Maputo. The Carter administration had worked around the constraints that Congress had imposed on aid to Mozambique; it was determined to do everything legally possible, Vance wrote, "to reinforce current Mozambican resistance to a major increase in such foreign military involvement." It therefore sent more food aid than Mozambique could absorb, knowing that it would be sold for hard currency, and extended $1.45 million to refugees living in Mozambique and $1 million in other aid projects. President Machel told Andrew Young that he credited the turnaround in his government's attitude to the United States to "the personal relationship he believes he established in his meeting with President Carter." (This was the contentious encounter at the UN in October 1977, when Machel had berated the US government.) Machel added, "After my meeting in New York with President Carter, good relations began. . . . Now we want to have good relations with the US."[60]

Zambia's Kenneth Kaunda, however, was in dire straits, and Nkomo's ZAPU had long-standing ties to the Soviets and Cubans. On March 12, 1978, the Rhodesian armed forces launched "one of their largest attacks to date" on a ZAPU camp in Zambia. Ten Rhodesian jets and two hundred troops in Chinooks pummeled a Zambian village for seventy-two hours, killing at least eighty people. Although cross-border raids had occurred before, this was the first attack on Zambian territory that the Rhodesian armed forces publicly acknowledged. The CIA reported that "[President] Kaunda doubtless would like to make some military response to save face, but he is frustrated by the weakness of his own forces." This was the avenue to disaster: Kaunda told

419

the US ambassador that "he was under great pressure to retaliate . . . [and] he would have no choice but to go to the Eastern countries [Cuba and the Soviet Union] for support."[61]

Five days after the Rhodesian attack on Zambia, Jimmy Carter was delivering his speech at Wake Forest. He had had three weeks to mull over Brzezinski's advice that "the time may be right for you to pick some controversial subject on which you will deliberately choose to act with a degree of anger and even roughness, designed to have a shock effect." The president was about to land the first punch. He began with a fact: "Over the past twenty years, the military forces of the Soviets have grown substantially, both in absolute numbers and relative to our own." And then, his voice insistent and slow-paced, he said: "There also has been an ominous inclination on the part of the Soviet Union to use its military power—to intervene in local conflicts, with advisers, with equipment, and with . . . mercenaries from other Communist countries, as we can observe today in Africa." *Mercenaries.* That was an angry word, straight out of Henry Kissinger's playbook.[62]

Within hours, the Soviet Union's TASS news agency responded. In a column entitled "Distortions," it declared that Carter's speech marked "a shift of emphasis in American foreign policy." The president who had talked about negotiations and peace a year ago was signaling a new "buildup of tension." The West Europeans, on the other hand, were relieved. "Good," West German foreign minister Hans-Dietrich Genscher told the US ambassador in Bonn. "The West has to make it clear to the East that détente is not regional; it is global."[63]

Arm-Twisting in Lagos

It must have been with some relief that Jimmy Carter set off for foreign climes. After brief sojourns in Caracas and Brasília, the president, accompanied by his wife Rosalynn and young daughter Amy, alighted in Lagos on March 31, 1978. Lieutenant-General Olusegun Obasanjo, whom Carter had welcomed to the White House the previous October, was on the tarmac to greet him, and thousands of Nigerians lined the streets waving placards saying: "Welcome Carter!" and "Hooray Carter!" It was the first state visit of a US president to sub-Saharan Africa, and the fact that Carter was welcomed in Nigeria—a country that had refused entry to Henry Kissinger barely two years earlier— was testament to the dramatic improvement in US relations with Africa. The lead article in the Nigerian *Daily Times* stated, "Here is an American President . . . sitting down in the 'heart of darkest Africa' and inviting Nigerians to join him in pursuit of diplomatic goals. . . . Not even the most rabid optimist could have predicted this five years ago."[64]

420

Carter's three-day trip to Lagos symbolized this change, which Brzezinski—who along with Cyrus Vance and Andrew Young had accompanied the president—characterized as "spectacular."[65] It was due above all to Carter's commitment to majority rule in southern Africa. It had been facilitated by the skillful work of the US ambassador, Donald Easum—"the most genuine, lovable, unpretentious and generous guy you could imagine," the economic counsel at the embassy recalled—who had deftly and consistently communicated the Nigerian viewpoint to Washington. Andrew Young's frequent visits to Lagos signaled the Carter administration's identification of Nigeria as the most important country in Africa: the one with the most oil, the largest population, the greatest military and economic potential, and the loudest megaphone to express African concerns. Whereas previous US presidents had tilted toward Zaire as the powerhouse of black Africa, Carter tilted toward Nigeria as the powerhouse of all Africa.[66]

That the Americans had come to this conclusion did not impress the Nigerians. It was, they thought, long overdue. They welcomed Carter warmly, but they were not bowled over by the fact that he had traveled to their country. Their press—a raucous, gritty affair with at least thirty daily papers—covered the visit but tended to give more prominent headlines to the rising price of cars or the latest rugby match. The state-run television channel broadcast a tennis tournament rather than Carter's keynote address. Nigeria in 1978 shouted swaggering self-confidence; it had no inclination to kowtow to an American president. Moreover, suspicions and resentments lingered. Nigerians had not forgotten Washington's sympathy for the separatists in the Biafran war in the late 1960s, or President Gerald Ford's support of the South African invasion of Angola in 1975, or the rumors of CIA complicity in the 1976 attempted coup in which Nigerian leader General Murtala Muhammed had been killed. Jimmy Carter could not rest on his laurels. He had his work cut out for him.[67]

In Lagos, Carter delivered a public address about US relations with Africa that stressed his administration's interest in human rights, majority rule, economic development, and peace on the continent. Cognizant of African desires not to be cast as pawns in the Cold War, Carter mentioned the Soviet Union only once, obliquely, when he decried the "military intervention of outside powers" in Africa. He focused instead on his administration's pursuit of justice in southern Africa. He insisted that he would stand firmly behind the Anglo-American proposals for Rhodesia. "Let there be no question of the commitment of the United States," the president announced, "or our determination to pursue a just settlement [in Rhodesia] which brings a cease-fire and an internationally recognized legal government. . . . That is our Nation's position. We will not depart from it."[68]

Woven through the speech were references to the civil rights struggles in the US South. "I know something about social change," Carter told the Nigerians. "In my own lifetime, I've seen the region of my birth, the southern part of the United States, changed from a place of poverty and despair and racial division to a land of bright promise and opportunity and increasing racial harmony." He added caveats: "I know that our own society is different from any other, and I know that we still have much to do in the United States. But nothing can shake my faith that in every part of the world, peaceful change can come and bless the lives of human beings." He concluded: "We know that this continent will enjoy the liberation that can come to those who put racial division and injustice behind them. . . . And on that day, blacks and whites alike will be able to say, in the words of a great man from my own state, Dr. Martin Luther King, Jr., 'Free at last, free at last, great God Almighty, we are free at last.'"[69]

When Carter and Obasanjo settled into their private sessions, Rhodesia was the most important item on the agenda. "Time is not on our side," Obasanjo warned. "The more that Muzorewa and the other nationalists in Salisbury enjoy the trappings of office, the more they will wish not to give up their office. . . . We must act fast." Both Obasanjo and Carter understood that the situation in southern Africa had become even more precarious due to the Cuban and Soviet success in the Ogaden. Both men wanted to avoid a widening war in southern Africa. "The internal settlement will not bring peace," Obasanjo asserted. "We fear and shudder to think of civil war in Zimbabwe." Carter agreed wholeheartedly: "We share your concern that war could break out with Muzorewa and Vorster on one hand, against Nkomo and Castro on the other. . . . If a war breaks out, it would be a very great challenge between the US and the USSR."[70]

Having agreed on the stakes, the meeting quickly settled into a substantive brainstorming session between Carter and Obasanjo about how best to proceed. This was an extraordinary meeting, presaging the intense negotiations between the Egyptians and Israelis that Carter would undertake at Camp David several months later. There was nothing ceremonial about this conversation: it was a working session, with two national leaders trying to figure out how to energize the Anglo-American proposals. Vance, Young, and Nigerian foreign minister Joe Garba offered rare interjections (Brzezinski said nothing), but they were marginal.

The challenge that Carter and Obasanjo faced was that the linchpin of the Anglo-American proposals—holding all-party talks—seemed unattainable: the Rhodesian "internal settlement" government of Smith, Muzorewa, Sithole, and Chirau had no interest in talks, and the Patriotic Front had been recalcitrant even to voice support for the idea. Obasanjo and Carter agreed that an interim step toward the goal of holding all-party talks was required.

To that end, they both wanted to convene a follow-up to the Malta Conference that the Americans and British had held with the Patriotic Front in late January 1978. At "Malta 2," US, British, Patriotic Front, and Frontline States representatives would continue to discuss the issues (which centered on control of the military during the transition) that had been raised at Malta.

Tanzanian president Julius Nyerere had promoted the idea of a follow-up to Malta in an attempt to distance Washington and London from the internal settlement. He and Kaunda, who also supported the idea, had promised to "deliver" Nkomo and Mugabe to a second Malta meeting. Kaunda had implored Carter to stay the course. "As I have said before, I remain of the firm belief that the resolution of the Rhodesian problem . . . depends entirely on you, Mr. President," he had written Carter immediately before the Lagos meeting. "America must take the front seat in ending the war in Zimbabwe. . . . I have great respect for Britain, but it is increasingly becoming clearer that Britain, if left to her own devices, would accept any solution . . . as long as it absolves her of the problem."[71]

Indeed, the British had already balked. They had complained to the Americans that meeting again with the "terrorists" would inflame British public opinion, and they had refused to contemplate holding a second Malta conference. They took it to the brink. "There seems to be no resolution of this impasse," the State Department concluded on April 1, hours after Carter landed in Lagos. With characteristic understatement, the cable noted "[the] lack of [a] concerted position with [the] UK . . . would seem to limit the president's flexibility in his conversations with Obasanjo." At the last minute, however, the British had relented. "British relax conditions for meeting with Patriotic Front [that is, for a Malta 2 meeting]," the State Department cabled Vance when he was en route to Lagos. "Owen would not wish to tie the secretary's hands in Lagos. . . . Owen . . . is content to rest with the secretary's judgment on this issue."[72]

In Lagos, with the British agreement to holding a follow-up to Malta in hand, Carter strongly pressed Obasanjo to work harder to convince Nkomo and Mugabe to support the Anglo-American initiative. "Your point is well taken," Obasanjo conceded. "You are saying we have not done enough to enable you to do more." Carter then suggested that immediately after Malta 2, the Americans and British should go to Salisbury and talk with Smith and the internal nationalists. This could be a path toward all-party talks. "If Smith won't come to a meeting, then go and see him," Carter commented.[73]

At the end of the conversation, Obasanjo said to Carter, "I like very much what I hear you saying about the Rhodesian situation." In 2002, Carter explained that during these long talks almost a quarter-century earlier, "a real personal friendship [developed] between me and Obasanjo. We hit it off. And we're still friends."[74]

Behind the scenes, Vance, Young, Dick Moose, and Don Easum scrambled to set up the followup conference. Young had arranged for the foreign ministers of the Frontline States to be present in Lagos, and together, these Americans and African foreign ministers hammered out the details of Malta 2, which would be held in Dar es Salaam.[75] Then and only then did the British High Commissioner in Lagos, Sir Sam Falle, pick up the phone and call David Owen in London. It was late, and the call woke Owen up. "David, can you show up in Dar es Salaam three weeks from now to talk to Mugabe and Nkomo?" Falle asked. Owen retorted, "Who's guaranteeing they'll be there?" Falle replied: "General Obasanjo and President Jimmy Carter . . . and . . . all the foreign ministers of the Frontline States."[76] Malta 2 was a done deal—whether Owen liked it or not.

The final communiqué that Carter and Obasanjo issued after their talks indicated the distance that Carter had traveled. Before Lagos, the Carter administration had straddled the fence, calling the internal settlement "inadequate" but potentially useful. The communiqué issued on April 2, however, asserted that the internal settlement was "unacceptable" because it did not "guarantee a genuine transfer of power . . . nor take into consideration the views of all Zimbabwean nationalist groups."[77]

The world noticed this change of tone. "Frankly, we liked the administration's Rhodesia/Zimbabwe policy better before the president dropped in on Nigeria," the *Washington Post* commented on April 4. "Mr Carter seems to have succumbed to Nigeria's uncomplicated fervor for a Popular [*sic*] Front guerrilla victory. . . . His performance is all the more baffling when you consider that the internal settlement looks to be more democratic, moderate and multiracial than any government the guerrillas might construct." In Salisbury, the supporters of the internal settlement agreed with this criticism, damning Carter as "the running boy of Soviet communism."[78] Others had more approving words. The *New York Times* praised the "commendable goals" that Carter had espoused in Nigeria. An African diplomat commented, "I love the rhetoric. Keep it coming." President Kaunda wrote Carter that his statements in Lagos had "brought . . . hope that America, under your leadership, will not retreat in the face of the grave crisis . . . in southern Africa." He urged him to persevere. "No American president in history has been closer to the problems of Africa than you. . . . Having come so far, I urge you not to stop on the threshold, but to go beyond and save the situation."[79]

Rocky Times

As Carter flew back to Washington, a storm of criticism was descending upon him. On April 4, the *New York Times* announced that the president had decided not to approve production of the neutron bomb because the "weapon ran counter to his goals of nuclear disarmament."[80] The neutron bomb had fallen prey to the central conundrum of American weaponry in the 1970s. To strengthen deterrence in the new age of "strategic parity" with the Soviet Union, the Pentagon sought to develop smaller, smarter nuclear weapons that it could credibly threaten to use, but this new generation of weapons—precisely because they posed a credible threat—struck terror in the hearts of the growing legions of antinuclear activists in the United States and Western Europe. It was an impasse with which Carter, who fancied himself something of a nuclear specialist, had wrestled for over a year, initially leaning toward authorizing the neutron bomb's production. The Pentagon, Vance, and Brzezinski all supported this decision. In the meantime, the neutron bomb became a *cause célèbre* because the public believed that it was designed to kill people while leaving most buildings intact. This struck many people as unbearably gruesome. Feelings were especially heated in West Germany, where neutron bombs were most likely to be used in a war between the United States and the Soviet Union. Chancellor Helmut Schmidt, who did not like Carter at the best of times, had stuck his political neck out to support the president's apparent decision to authorize the weapon.

It turned out that the *New York Times* had jumped the gun. The White House denied that the president had decided to nix the bomb, explaining that the issue was still "under review."[81] For the next three days, upon his return from Lagos, Carter cogitated. He studied the issue again and sought outside counsel. Sixty members of the House of Representatives and a slew of conservative senators urged Carter to support the neutron bomb. So, too, did Chancellor Schmidt. But no one, not even Carter's closest aides, could predict what he might decide.

In governing, suspense is corrosive. Carter's style—nonideological and centralized—meant that to a greater extent than usual, the key decisions of the US government hung on his unfathomable inner processes. Previous Cold War presidents, from Truman to Ford, had all seemed more predictable. Jimmy Carter was different. During this three-day period while Carter thought about the neutron bomb, the fact that he had not yet made up his mind was plastered all over the front pages of the nation's newspapers. Into the vacuum rushed anxiety and irritation.

On April 7, Carter announced that he had decided neither to cancel nor to approve the production of the neutron bomb, but to delay it. This mollified no one. Antinuclear activists simply moved to the next fight, while American conservatives pilloried the president for being indecisive and soft on defense. The Germans were scathing. "So far, this Jimmy Carter has been a statesman in name only," *Der Spiegel* wrote. "Never in the existence of NATO has the

425

alliance seen such a serious crisis and has the force of the . . . United States been so greatly doubted."[82]

Many on Carter's staff were worried. The president's inability to respond to Soviet intervention in the Ogaden war was still reverberating. "Was the failure of the Americans to stand up to the Soviets and Cubans in the Horn of Africa a sign that the erstwhile 'world policemen' are now impotent?" *Jeune Afrique* inquired. "America's paralysis in the wake of Vietnam is much more serious than we thought." Joseph Kraft, the respected and widely syndicated American journalist, filed a series of reports from Mogadiscio. "America changed its mind seven times," one of Siad Barre's top aides told Kraft. "First President Carter said he would do 'anything' to help us. Then he said the United States wanted to take Russia's place. . . . Then he offered us arms 'in principle.' Then he insisted the arms could only be defensive. Then he refused us arms. . . . Then he said help would be available. . . . That's too much."[83]

What would happen if the Cuban battalions headed north from the Ogaden to the Ethiopian coastal province of Eritrea, where the rebellion against the Derg was raging? "We may yet see Cuban troops fighting against the fighters [the Eritrean guerrillas] they previously supported," David Owen declared in a hard-hitting speech that cited intelligence reports about Cubans flying to the beleaguered garrison of Asmara. That possibility, which many American and British officials considered likely, would place Cuban troops along the Red Sea, heightening Saudi and Egyptian fears of expanding Soviet power. Many believed that it would make Cuban intervention in southern Africa more likely. It also would make Carter look weak. (In fact, American and British concerns about the Cubans fighting in Eritrea were misplaced. Cuban documents show clearly that Castro consistently insisted that his troops would not fight there; he considered the Eritrean insurgency to be an internal Ethiopian problem, unlike the Somali invasion of the Ogaden. No Cubans fought in Eritrea.)[84]

In mid-April, after accompanying Carter in Lagos, Vance traveled to Moscow on an important mission to get the SALT negotiations back on track after his rocky trip a year earlier. Carter's detailed instructions to Vance concerned, above all, the paramount importance of Soviet restraint in Africa:

> You should explain to the Soviets that their military intervention in Africa is becoming intolerable, and ask when Soviet/Cuban forces will be withdrawn from Ethiopia. You should indicate that . . . Soviet/Cuban military intrusion into Southern Africa will jeopardize détente as a whole and the US will react strongly. This should be stated at the highest levels directly, unambiguously, and forcefully. . . . Efforts to fan the flames of a major racial war in Southern

Africa can only provoke the most profound and adverse reaction on the part of the American people. For this reason you should explain to the Soviets that we believe our relationship is now at a watershed. . . . We cannot accept a selective détente.[85]

Vance's presentation to Soviet leader Leonid Brezhnev followed the president's instructions to the letter. Brezhnev, who was in very poor health and who often drifted through meetings, was on this occasion feisty and alert, frequently interrupting the American secretary of state. Soviet relations with Africa "had no bearing" on relations with the United States, Brezhnev asserted. He could "not understand . . . why all sorts of pernicious plans were ascribed to the Soviet Union" just because it had helped Ethiopia defend itself against aggression. When Vance warned the Soviets not to intervene in Rhodesia, Brezhnev scoffed. "This was totally in the realm of fantasy," he exclaimed.[86] The Carter administration disagreed. If Smith's raids continued, either Kenneth Kaunda or Samora Machel might turn to Brezhnev and Castro for help. Angola and Ethiopia had proven that fantasies could come true.

Malta 2

The State Department officials concerned with policy toward Africa were busy laying the groundwork for an all-parties conference by preparing for the Malta 2 meeting that Carter, Vance, and Young had strong-armed into existence in Lagos. It was a challenging task. Nkomo and Mugabe had agreed to attend, but because they knew that London was drawn to the internal settlement, they were more wary than usual. Meanwhile, the Salisbury Four—Smith, Muzorewa, Sithole, and Chirau—had dismissed the American initiative. In a meeting with Bill Bowdler, the US ambassador in Pretoria, they "turned down flatly any thought of an all-parties meeting." Laying the groundwork for such a meeting was the reason for holding Malta 2. Bowdler commented ruefully, "One could not escape the impression that the two sides are further apart than they have been."[87]

David Owen had agreed to attend the April meeting in Dar es Salaam, but he was not happy about it. Several days after Sir Sam Falle's middle-of-the-night phone call from Lagos, Owen briefed the Cabinet about "the many problems he was having to negotiate not only with the Patriotic Front, Frontline presidents and Salisbury Four but at times also with the United States. American long term interests in South Africa were not necessarily the same as ours." He then flashed concerns about Young: "So far the President and Mr Vance had supported the joint United Kingdom-United States policies against the more idealistic, United Nations oriented, side of the Administration. But," he continued, "we might have to make a difficult judgment." Although Owen did not mention making a deal with Nkomo—he intended to keep it secret—this was the fork in the road to which he referred. Owen then cast the problem in its Cold War context, explaining that if the Rhodesian raids against Zambia and Mozambique grew more punishing, presidents Kaunda and Machel "might be unable to resist" asking Havana for help. This could draw in the South Africans. "It was a fairly somber picture," he noted, drily. Prime Minister Callaghan intervened to say that the Cabinet "attached importance to maintaining the closest possible co-operation with the United States." [88]

Five days later, on April 11, State Department policy planning chief Anthony Lake flew to London to confer with Foreign Office officials. Owen did not waste words: "Why did we [Americans] want the Dar meeting [Malta 2]?" Lake explained that Washington thought it essential to give it a try, since "the risks of a future civil war, etc., are so much greater." Owen, with resignation, told Lake that he was "relying on our [Washington's] judgment."[89]

On April 13, Owen admitted to the Cabinet that "he was not very optimistic" about the upcoming talks.[90] Callaghan tried to strengthen his foreign secretary's resolve to work in tandem with the United States. He praised the Cabinet for not joining in "the current general criticism of President Carter. It was particularly unfortunate that the Germans were making their discontent with him known." He was referring, above all, to the fracas over Carter's neutron bomb decision. "It would be quite wrong to regard President Carter as an indecisive man. He was a man of principle who was the first to admit that he lacked experience. . . . Our role was not to voice criticism but to give the President the fullest possible support."[91]

The Malta 2 meeting was held in Dar es Salaam on April 14 and 15. As with Malta 1, the Americans, British, and Patriotic Front arrived with large negotiating teams. But this time, Vance attended. He and Owen engaged in three lengthy and "heated" meetings with the Patriotic Front. They debated the crucial details that would determine who exerted power during the transition period. From the American and British point of view, Mugabe and Nkomo ceded some minor ground but generally were inflexible. The Patriotic Front saw it differently: they asserted that they had conceded major points about the balance of power during the transition and that they had agreed to attend all-party talks.[92]

Andrew Young, who believed that the Anglo-American proposals were on the line and who wanted to derail the Owen gambit, grew exasperated with the guerrilla leaders. He had hoped and expected that Nkomo and Mugabe would realize that the internal settlement threatened to make the Anglo-American proposals irrelevant, and this meeting was a last-ditch opportunity for the Patriotic Front to reinvigorate them. When Nkomo and Mugabe kept upping their demands about their control during the transition, Young exclaimed that they "had changed the ball game." The Patriotic Front leaders retorted that they were "very sad that the US/UK were being so intransigent." Tony Lake remembered how contentious the meeting became. "There was a horrible evening meeting in Dar when I almost jumped over the table at Edgar Tekere [a key Mugabe aide] who came in roaring drunk and then began yelling and abusing Vance, and I came as close as I ever had to just wanting to hit him." Ambassador Steve Low recalled, "The meeting in Dar was unbelievable. Some of the Africans seemed to be on drugs. They kept shouting at us. It was bedlam." NSC expert Tom Thornton, who had just received the southern Africa portfolio, cabled Brzezinski an edited account: "Conference is going very badly."[93]

At the last minute, Mugabe and Nkomo made a bad situation worse by reneging on their promise to attend all-party talks. And at the press conference after the meeting ended, Mugabe deepened the damage by announcing publicly that he looked forward to establishing a one-party Marxist state in Zimbabwe. Vance wrote Carter that even though his expectations for Malta 2 had been low, he was "disappointed."[94] This was an understatement. Vance had struggled mightily to get the original Anglo-American plan for all-party talks back on track. In Lagos, he had brought in his heaviest equipment—the president himself. He had strong-armed Owen to attend Malta 2. But at the meeting, the leaders of the Patriotic Front had refused to show any willingness to play ball. Vance's plan was in shambles.

Meanwhile, Owen's gambit quietly gathered steam. According to British Field Marshal Michael Carver, who attended the Malta 2 summit, it was there that Owen "thought that Nkomo, beneath the obvious posturing, . . . was ready to negotiate seriously with the Salisbury parties."[95]

Vance and Owen followed through on their original plan—suggested by Carter at Lagos—that they fly from Tanzania to Rhodesia, where they met for the first time with all the Salisbury Four. They had expected to arrive strengthened by having secured the Patriotic Front's agreement to engage in all-party talks, and they had hoped to resuscitate the Anglo-American proposals by persuading Smith and his cohorts that it was in their interest to accept the invitation to the talks.[96] But the contumacy of Mugabe and Nkomo in Dar es Salaam meant that Owen and Vance had no momentum as they headed to Salisbury. Their encounter with Smith was depressing. Smith saw no reason to return to the table. "Past experience had shown," he reminded the Americans and British, "that round-table conferences had had very little success."

His internal settlement plan was progressing, and elections were scheduled. "For the first time in the history of Rhodesia," Smith explained, "an agreement had been formulated by white and black leaders." Smith said that he failed to understand "why the British and United States Governments had not supported it." He declined their invitation to another conference. "The trip was a disaster," Dick Moose recalled. "Smith was so rude, so rude. He treated Owen with contempt, and Owen, of course, had an ego. Smith just walked all over him, and Owen got up on his high horse. It was hopeless. We turned with our tails between our legs and fled to our waiting plane."[97]

Attacks from All Sides

The American initiative had failed. The Patriotic Front was unwilling to negotiate seriously, and the Salisbury Four saw no reason to even entertain the notion of all-party talks. In public, Washington and London continued to stand by the Anglo-American proposals, but many Carter administration officials, dispirited and busy with other crises, thought it made sense to sit back and let the situation develop.[98] It would give everyone time to observe the durability of the internal settlement. Would it collapse or gain strength? Would the war ebb or escalate?

During this lull in overt diplomatic activity, the rhetoric on all sides in southern Africa grew more intemperate. "We will not be a party to any internal agreement," Mugabe told Britain's *News of the World* tabloid in July. "We want genuine independence, not some phoney, neo-colonial stuff. Total power to the people." Smith told the press that the idea of all-party talks was "madness."[99]

Adding to the pressure that Carter administration officials felt was the fact that the president's job approval rating was slipping. Gallup tracked its fall from a high of 75 percent in March 1977 to a low of 47 percent the following February, the final ten points peeling off since December. An AP/NBC poll was even more dire. "Carter's Plus Rating at New Low of 34%," was the headline of a February 25 article in the *Washington Post*: "The downward trend has been uninterrupted since last May."[100]

The decline was not stanched even by the administration's impressive victory when, on March 16, 1978, the Senate ratified the first Panama Canal treaty. (The negotiations divided the return of the canal to Panama into two treaties: the first guaranteed the US right to defend the canal's neutrality, and the second, ratified on April 18, guaranteed the transfer of the canal to Panama on the last day of 1999.) The White House, which had waged trench warfare for every vote, celebrated, while the neoconservatives regrouped. They had mounted a passionate fight against the treaty, which they had cast as a patriotic crusade. Although the neoconservatives lost the treaty vote, they gained from the struggle. They had coalesced around the issue, honed their organizational skills, and swelled their direct-mail lists. They had established themselves as a powerful voice decrying what they deemed the loss of American pride and willpower. Many of these conservatives had voted for Carter in 1976, but fifteen months later they had buyer's remorse. "The American instinct for a bold crusade, for a visible enemy and a fast horse," the British ambassador in Washington commented, "[does not] derive much fulfilment from the . . . alien and strange causes of détente, interdependence, SALT . . . and their ilk."[101]

Ronald Reagan filled the void. He used his daily radio addresses to mount a relentless attack on the administration. His tone was astounded and friendly: he seemed to be asking his audience, "Can you believe this guy?" His subjects appeared spontaneous, but they focused laser-like on one theme: American greatness. In foreign affairs, he heaped special ire on the Panama Canal treaties, SALT II, and Carter's human rights policy. Cuba was also one of his favorite targets. "I'm sure you're all aware of the Cuban and Russian presence in Africa," he began a broadcast in mid-March 1978. "Are we just as aware that they haven't limited their tourism just to Africa?" Reagan proceeded to talk about "Cuban infiltration" of Panama. In early April, he excoriated the State Department for expressing "a hope that Cuba will '*reduce*' the number of troops in Africa. . . . This hardly has the sound of a bold trumpet," he commented, adding that the Cubans had just announced that they had no intention of changing their Africa policy. "The State Department will probably react to this by saying 'pretty please—with sugar on it.'"[102]

At the annual meeting of the Conservative Political Action Conference (CPAC) in March, Reagan let fly. He began softly, with a few jokes needling the Carter administration, but then, suddenly, he grew serious. Looking directly at the crowd, Reagan said: "Few Americans accept the belief of some of those now in positions of importance in guiding our foreign policy that America's purpose in the world is to appease the mighty out of a sense of fear or to appease the weak out of a sense of guilt." Pow! The Carter administration's foreign "policy is rooted in well-meaning intentions, but it shows a woeful uncertainty as to America's purpose in the world," Reagan explained.[103]

In Reagan's opinion, America's purpose was clear: the United States—freedom itself—was locked in a titanic struggle against the Soviets, who were trying to "dominate the world." In the face of this challenge, "the Carter administration seems confused and torn." Reagan then launched into a detailed examination of what he considered the clearest example of the administration's confusion. "Today," he said, "we can see the brunt of the Soviet Union's capabilities at work in the Horn of Africa. . . . From there, it can threaten the sea lanes, . . . destabilize those governments on the Arabian peninsula, [and then] turn its full attention south. . . . It takes no great stretch of the imagination to see that Rhodesia is a tempting target. . . . In a few years we may be faced with the prospect of a Soviet empire of protégés and dependencies stretching from Addis Ababa to Cape Town." In his rousing conclusion, Reagan used one of his favorite images: "We must be willing to carry out our responsibility as the custodian of individual freedom. Then we will achieve our destiny to be as a shining city on a hill for all mankind to see." The crowd roared.[104]

Brzezinski agreed with the thrust of Reagan's speech. He was feeding Carter a steady dose of pep talks about the need to convey strength. "We should . . . tell the Soviets very frankly that their behavior in Africa is intolerable," he wrote on April 7. "You will have to take some decision in the near future that conveys clearly your toughness in dealing with the Russians," he wrote a week later. And the following week: "In some cases what is needed is a demonstration of force, to establish credibility and determination and even to infuse fear."[105]

Shaba 2

Late April 1978 was a busy time at the Carter White House. Cyrus Vance was following up on the SALT talks that he had jump-started during his trip to Moscow, and he was pushing hard for a Middle East peace treaty in the wake of Anwar Sadat's stunning trip to Jerusalem. The Senate narrowly ratified the second Panama Canal treaty and took up consideration of the package of sales of fighter planes to Israel, Saudi Arabia, and Egypt that Carter had proposed in June 1977.[106] Zbigniew Brzezinski was making his final preparations for his trip to China. Then, on April 27, 1978, a coup in Kabul led to the assassination of Afghanistan's prime minister, a swift and bloody purge, and the installation of the head of the radical wing of the Afghan communist party as the country's new leader. The Soviet Union was the first state to recognize the new government, and in Washington it was widely assumed that the Kremlin had been behind the coup. "My own inclination is not to view the Afghanistan development in isolation but possibly to see it in relationship to the Horn," an NSC specialist wrote to Brzezinski. "American passivity [toward the coup in Kabul] . . . is likely to increase the chances of Soviet intervention in southern Africa."[107] In early May, Carter attended an economic summit in London; he was confronted by European leaders who expressed doubts about his ability to lead. The Europeans also worried about domestic terrorism: on May 9, the bullet-riddled body of former Italian prime minister Aldo Moro, who had been kidnapped by a home-grown revolutionary organization known as the Red Brigades, was discovered in the trunk of a car in Rome.

In Africa, the Rhodesian internal settlement was weakened when Byron Hove, the new black co-minister for Justice, Law and Order (all ministries of the internal settlement government were co-led by one black and one white), was fired. Hove had been outspoken, criticizing police brutality and the dearth of job opportunities for blacks in the police. When his white counterpart at the justice ministry told him to retract his statements, Hove refused and was sacked. This was a direct challenge to Muzorewa: Hove had occupied one of the highest positions in the new internal settlement government, and he was a member of the bishop's party. Muzorewa could have resigned in protest, but he had nowhere to turn. He knew that Sithole and Chirau would have happily filled his place in Smith's scheme, and he also knew that he could never hope to be embraced by the Patriotic Front after having colluded with the enemy. And so, the bishop buckled. It was a revealing moment, exposing who was really in charge. "Far from adjusting to majority rule," Hove exclaimed as he left Rhodesia to resume his law practice in London, "Smith and his machinery are trying to cheat us, to take us for a ride, and to cheat the whole world."[108]

This impression was deepened by the fact that, despite its promises, the Salisbury Four government delayed four months before eliminating any of the laws enforcing racial discrimination; on August 8, it took its first timid step, opening public facilities to all races. For many, Ian Smith's idea of "power sharing" was a sham. The Patriotic Front guerrillas did not lay down their arms and the population did not stop supporting them. Thinking back on those months, Ambassador Low mused, "If Smith himself had had one ounce of self-discipline, it could have worked. Instead, he humiliated Muzorewa on a daily basis; he destroyed him. He left Muzorewa out there without so much as a fig leaf for protection."[109]

On May 12, Vance testified before the Africa subcommittee of the Senate Foreign Relations Committee, and despite the turbulence in southern Africa, the atmosphere was celebratory. "I want to congratulate you for the real change in direction that has occurred," Senator Dick Clark said. "If there is one area of American foreign policy that has undergone the greatest change . . . it is that policy which is directed toward that continent [Africa]." After admitting that increasing Soviet and Cuban intervention "raises serious problems," Vance stressed that the United States had formidable economic tools at its disposal and that "our continued support for peaceful resolution of disputes . . . is . . . a barrier to Soviet and Cuban designs." After Vance had explained US policy in all the major conflict zones on the continent, Senator John Sparkman, a conservative Democrat from Alabama who was chair of the Africa subcommittee, told him, "This is about the finest presentation I have ever seen on any subject." Vance was modest. "Major challenges lie ahead," he said.[110]

433

At dawn the next day, May 13, Katangan rebels invaded Zaire for the second time in little over a year. This time, the rebels—approximately 2,500 of them—were better organized than they had been in 1977. They achieved surprise by quietly infiltrating through Zambia and attacking Shaba from the east, rather than from Angola. They headed directly to Kolwezi, the sprawling regional capital of Zaire's mining industry, the economic lifeblood of the country. The rebels had "a strategy and not simply an objective," the British ambassador in Kinshasa wrote. That strategy was to seize Kolwezi, shut the mines, and precipitate the fall of President Mobutu. The rebels captured Kolwezi easily—they were supported by the townspeople, and the demoralized Zairean army did not fight. Mobutu's ability to retain control of his vast country was threatened.[111]

The White House response to the second Shaba crisis unfolded in two steps. First, it acted quickly to bolster Mobutu's hold on power. As in 1977, it let others take the lead, in this case the French and the Belgians. This time, however, instead of doling out paltry amounts of aid as it had in 1977, Washington immediately expedited the $17.5 million in "nonlethal" aid that Congress had earlier earmarked for Zaire. More significantly, it provided eighteen C-141s to airlift 1,300 French and Belgian troops to Kolwezi on a "humanitarian mission" to save the white residents, including approximately ninety US citizens whose lives were believed to be in danger.[112] The American press reported that ghoulish massacres were taking place in Kolwezi. The *Chicago Tribune*, for example, wrote that a sixteen-year-old white girl was beheaded, and a ten-year-old white girl was raped in front of her parents. Although these reports were later discredited, they shaped American attitudes toward the crisis.[113]

The State Department's opinion of Mobutu had not changed—Assistant Secretary Moose referred to him as "the big turkey"—but Washington's explanation of its forceful actions betrayed none of the hesitation at propping up a brutal dictator that it had expressed a year earlier. "Zaire remains one of our important friends in Africa," Vance wrote. "We have shared a commonality of views on many issues." The *New York Times* noted that the White House, "with quiet pride," referred to the airlift as its first "military operation."[114]

The airlift met with rapid success: the first French paratroopers arrived in Kolwezi on May 19, six days after the Katangans had entered Zaire; the Belgians arrived less than twenty-four hours later. They evacuated approximately 2,500 whites. By sunset the next day, the Europeans had retaken the city and routed the invaders. Mobutu was safe once again.[115]

The administration's actions were widely applauded. They garnered "broad support on the Hill," the newly appointed NSC congressional liaison, Madeleine Albright, wrote Brzezinski, who had been her professor at Columbia

University.[116] Senator Robert Byrd (D-WV) praised the administration for its "measured, deliberate and adequate" reaction to the crisis. The US press followed suit. Carter's response "strikes us as on the money," the *Washington Post* wrote, while the *Christian Science Monitor* lauded the president's "prudent . . . [and] measured" policy that exhibited "a degree of boldness."[117]

Carter, however, did not stop at the aid and airlift. He added a rhetorical component that had been absent a year earlier: he blamed Fidel Castro for the crisis.

Perhaps it was inevitable. Carter joined a long line of finger-pointers. Mobutu had immediately blamed the Cubans, just as he had in 1977. The French agreed. "We know from several different sources that Cuban instructors . . . helped train the Katangans," French foreign minister Louis de Guiringaud declared. Headlines in the US press emphasized Cuban complicity; buried deep in the articles was the caveat that there was no proof, "yet," of their allegations. The conservative British papers were even more strident. "The West is behaving like some hapless victim of [boxing champion] Cassius Clay in his prime," the *Daily Telegraph* scoffed, while the *Daily Mail* ordered Washington to "stop shilly-shallying in Africa."[118]

The allegations of Cuban involvement were more plausible in 1978 than they had been in 1977: the attack seemed professionally planned and executed, and the Cuban intervention in Ethiopia had demonstrated Castro's willingness to defy the Carter administration. Moreover, it occurred against a backdrop of Carter's severe criticism of Cuban "mercenaries." As one administration official explained, "Even if the Cubans are not leading the charge, the chances are extremely good that these guys [the Katangans] are getting help and training from the Cubans. . . . This time, the atmosphere is different." A White House aide added, "You really have a different situation from last summer. There has been a doubling of Cuban combat forces [in Africa], mostly in Ethiopia, and more than $1 billion in Soviet military equipment pumped in. There's a more expansive Soviet and Cuban presence."[119]

Indeed, the temperature on the Hill rose during the early days of the Katangan invasion. The controversial Middle East arms package came to a vote on May 16, three days after the rebels descended on Kolwezi. In the critical week before the vote, the Saudis had lobbied the senators hard. With little subtlety, they had roiled Cold War anxieties. King Khalid wrote to senators to emphasize that his country needed the advanced weapons to combat "communist expansion in the area." During the debate, even Senator Mac Mathias (R-MD), who was considered a liberal, warned: "The Soviet noose around the Middle East is tightening. This is no time to make mistakes." The Carter administration mustered a slim majority in support of the controversial arms package by appealing directly to hardline anticommunists such as Barry Goldwater (R-AZ) and Jesse Helms (R-NC). It was a hard-fought victory, and it had consequences. "Not for years has Washington rung with such anticommunist fervor," the *Washington Post* noted the day following the vote.[120]

Nevertheless, for several days after the Katangans' May 13 attack on Kolwezi, Carter had refrained from blaming Cuba, despite pressure to do so from Paris, Jidda, Beijing, Tel Aviv, and Kinshasa; from a broad swath of US conservatives and liberals; and from most of the nation's editorial pages. The administration's caution was based on two facts: the evidence that Cubans had participated in the invasion was circumstantial, and Castro himself emphatically denied that his troops were involved.

On May 17, for the first time since the US Interests Section had opened in Havana, Castro summoned its head, Lyle Lane. "There is not even one Cuban with the Katangan forces in Shaba," the Cuban leader insisted. "Cuba has had . . . no participation either directly or indirectly in the Shaba affair." Cuba had not provided weapons, it had not provided training, and it had not "had any contact . . . with the Katangans . . . for at least two years." The Shaba crisis was contrary to Cuban interests, Castro explained to Lane, because it threatened to draw Western troops into Zaire, which would increase turbulence on Angola's northern border. Moreover, as the CIA pointed out, the Katangan attack on Zaire was an invasion of a sovereign country; it violated international law, something Cuba assiduously had not done in Angola or in Ethiopia. "Havana's credibility as a responsible actor on the African continent would be seriously undermined," a US intelligence memo noted, with emphasis. "Castro's worries were illustrated by his unprecedented conversation [with Lane]," the CIA explained. "We have no evidence that Soviets or Cubans are involved in the present fighting."[121]

Also on May 17, President Kaunda arrived in Washington for a state visit, and he poured cold water on the idea of blaming the Cubans for Shaba. It was the first time the Zambian president had been to the White House since his infamous toast in 1975 that had so irritated Henry Kissinger. "Being in the United States today is not the same . . . as being here a few years ago," Kaunda said as he was welcomed on the White House lawn. "This new atmosphere which has brought America closer to many nations . . . is the product of President Carter." But at a press conference a few hours later, when asked about reports that Cubans were in Zaire, Kaunda defended Havana. "I am not sure there is a single Cuban on the African continent who has not been invited. . . . [Therefore] it is not easy to condemn their presence." Kaunda's message was clear: he hoped that the driving motive of US policy toward southern Africa would remain the desire to implement majority rule rather than the desire to oust the Soviets and Cubans. Please, Kaunda pleaded with Carter, do not view Africa as a Cold War battlefield.[122]

New York Times columnist Tom Wicker also encouraged Carter to show restraint. "There is a strong American tendency—one widely shared abroad—to believe that 'nerve' and 'leadership' are shown by a President only when he sends troops and bombers and cloak-and-dagger men," Wicker wrote on May 23. "But what will really require nerve and leadership by Jimmy Carter, as events unfold in Africa, is that he stay cool and keep his knee from jerking every time someone shouts 'The Cubans are coming!' or accuses him of being weak or indecisive."[123]

Two days later, Carter's knee jerked. "Carter's instinct was of a politician watching his flank," Ambassador Donald McHenry explained. "His instinct was also one of anticommunist, anti-Cuban beliefs." Carter had held this instinct in check during the first Shaba crisis, but now, bruised and frustrated by Castro's intervention in the Horn and continuing presence in Angola, he saw the situation differently. He kicked the dog. On May 25, at a nationally televised press conference in a crowded Chicago hotel, Carter announced: "We believe that Cuba had known of the Katangan plans to invade and obviously did nothing to restrain them from crossing the border. . . . We also know that the Cubans have played a key role in training and equipping the Katangans who attacked." Carter's words consumed just a few minutes of a long press conference, but the headline writers seized on them: "Carter Blasts Cuba's Role in Zaire Invasion," the *Chicago Tribune* blared. "Carter Accuses Cuba on Zaire Raid," the *Washington Post* screamed. "Jimmy Carter," *Time* reported, "was mad as hell."[124]

This tough talk pleased conservatives, but it alarmed some of the administration's stalwart supporters such as Senators George McGovern (D-SD) and Dick Clark (D-IA). McGovern was skeptical about the White House's evidence and about its motives. Clark's confidence in the Carter administration had been shaken in late April 1978, when Brzezinski's deputy David Aaron had asked him, "Couldn't we interpret the [Clark] amendment to mean we could give weapons to the rebels fighting against the Cuban-supported government?" And he became even more alarmed on May 4 after CIA head Stansfield Turner told him that the United States was considering secretly resuming aid to the Angolan rebels in an attempt to raise the cost of Cuba's African adventures.[125]

The Carter-versus-Castro showdown was high drama, and the press loved it. On May 28, Brzezinski went on *Meet the Press*, expecting to opine about his triumphant trip to Beijing where, he believed, he had established a useful rapport with the Chinese leaders and restarted the momentum toward normalization. However, the moderator's first question was about the evidence of Cuban involvement in Shaba. "I can assure you that what the President said was right," Brzezinski asserted. "Cuba shares the political and the moral responsibility for the invasion." The panel of journalists went on to ask him ten questions about Cuban policy in Africa and only two about Beijing. Brzezinski launched into a freewheeling attack on the Soviet Union's "shortsighted . . . effort to . . . stir up racial difficulties in Africa and . . . to seek more direct access to the Indian Ocean." This "pattern of behavior," he asserted, was not "compatible" with détente and could not be "cost free."[126]

Fidel Castro fanned the flames, telling the *New York Times* that the allegation of Cuban involvement in the Shaba invasion was "not a half-lie . . . It is an absolute, total, complete lie." He followed up with an equally emphatic performance in an interview aired on all three US television networks. "Castro has made something of a cult about not lying," the State Department observed, "and that partly explains the heat of his attack when his honesty was questioned."[127]

Carter had ignited a firestorm he could not douse because his evidence of Cuban involvement—which was shown to the Senate Foreign Relations Committee and the House International Relations Committee, but not released to the public—convinced only those who wanted to be convinced. "You'd get a divided jury," Senator McGovern declared after studying the evidence. The CIA reported that "two bearded, long-haired men" might have been spotted in Kolwezi. Other reports were even sketchier, based on information from prisoners (who had been interviewed only by Zairean officials), diplomats, and other intelligence assets.[128] The Americans' prized source is revealed in a Soviet transcript of a conversation between Soviet foreign minister Andrei Gromyko and Vance. Vance asserts, "As for the sources of our information, it was the Commander of Katang armed forces, General Mbumba, and Cuban sources in East Germany." (This line is redacted from the American account of the conversation.) Gromyko reacts with incredulity. "You are simply victims of disinformation. . . . Who on Earth knows what kind of General this is? Who does he serve? Is he really the only one to tell the truth, like Jesus Christ of the Bible legend? . . . Maybe [he] is only saving his skin?"[129]

The Americans' evidence was weak because, as the painstaking research of historian Piero Gleijeses has shown, the Cubans were not involved in the Shaba invasion. Perhaps Carter was convinced by his flimsy, circumstantial evidence. "It is impossible to believe," the CIA asserted, "that the Cubans had no part in the plans or training or foreknowledge of the attack in a country in which they play a major role in civilian administration and a dominant role in internal security."[130] A year earlier, however, when faced with comparable evidence during the first Shaba crisis, Carter had not jumped to such conclusions. The difference was not in the evidence but in the context. It would be an exaggeration to say that Carter was beleaguered in the spring of 1978, but the constraints and the isolation of his job had taken a toll. The buoyant optimism of a year earlier had been battered by criticism at home and abroad and by the logjams that his programs faced in Congress. Jimmy Carter's world had changed.

NATO vs. Cuba

At the end of May, with French and Belgian forces still in Shaba, the leaders of fourteen NATO nations assembled in Washington for their annual meeting. In his opening remarks, Carter set one of the themes of the gathering: "As I speak today, the activities of the Soviet Union and Cuba in Africa are preventing individual nations from determining their own future."[131]

It was an edgy topic. The Belgians were bruised by what they perceived as French high-handedness in Shaba, and the British were wary of French president Valéry Giscard d'Estaing's pursuit of a special French destiny in Africa. The Europeans, who had been badgering Carter to stand up to the Soviets, were now alarmed by his heightened anti-Sovietism. Prime Minister Callaghan tried to dampen the concerns with dry humor that was widely interpreted as a jab at Brzezinski. "There seem to be a number of new Christopher Columbuses setting out from the US to discover Africa for the first time," Callaghan told the press. "Before we rush into instant solutions, we had better be sure we get the analysis of the problem right."[132]

Over lunch with Giscard during the NATO summit, Carter talked for more than an hour about Africa. He thanked the French president for his actions in Zaire and complained that "his own hands had been tied by Congress." He agreed to provide airlift for a pan-African (largely Moroccan) force that Giscard was mounting to replace the French and Belgian troops in Shaba. In a surfacing of the Safari Club, the Saudis agreed to pick up the tab. Carter's orders to the Defense Department were crisp: "Keep the US involvement [in the pan-African force] limited and secondary to that of others." As for Giscard's idea of creating "an international force that would be available to intervene in Africa as needed," Carter's instructions to the State Department were emphatic: "pour cold water" on it. "We will not be instruments of French and Belgian neo-colonialism."[133]

Détente and Containment

The second Shaba crisis stirred anxieties about America's ability to stand up to Moscow. Although the Carter administration's response had been much sharper than it had been during Shaba 1, the perception remained that the Soviets and their Cuban proxies were marauding through Africa and that Washington was impotent or unwilling to counter them. Conservatives placed Carter's actions in a continuum beginning with the retreat from Vietnam, followed by the debacle of Watergate, the curbing of presidential powers by Congress, the fiasco in Angola, and the Carter administration's mild response to the first Shaba crisis and the Soviet/Cuban intervention in Ethiopia.

Three emotions coalesced. Competitiveness: Americans did not want to be bested by the Soviets. Fear: the Saudi royal family, Egypt's Sadat, the shah of Iran, and other leaders of moderate Arab states worried that without an effective American shield, they would be encircled by hostile pro-Soviet states; this anxiety was also expressed by Washington's NATO allies, especially Giscard and Schmidt. And confusion: what was US policy?

Jimmy Carter got blamed for this confusion, but it was not entirely his fault. He had inherited it. Richard Nixon's and Henry Kissinger's rhapsodic descriptions of détente earlier in the decade had obscured the fact that containment in its most raw form was still in force. The war in the Ogaden proved it. The Carter administration's inability to keep the Soviets (and Cubans) out of the Ogaden—a barren land that had no bearing on American security, history, or economic well-being—was felt and seen as a failure. In the zero-sum logic of containment, it was a Soviet gain and a corresponding American loss.

Carter tried to clarify the complex reality of the Cold War in his June 7 commencement address at his alma mater, the US Naval Academy at Annapolis. Although the myth has developed that Carter "stapled" this speech together out of a hawkish draft written by Brzezinski and a dovish draft written by Vance, Carter himself had drafted the speech alone at Camp David over the previous weekend. While the brouhaha over Castro and Shaba swirled around him, Carter wrote the speech on a yellow legal pad, referring at times to more than a hundred pages of suggestions from myriad experts, including Vance and Brzezinski. Returning to Washington, he convened a small group—Vance, Brzezinski, Defense Secretary Harold Brown, top aide Hamilton Jordan, and Andrew Young—on Sunday evening to go over it; all suggested additions, but no one expressed strong disagreement with any part of it. The speech that Carter delivered on June 7 was essentially the speech he himself had drafted on June 3 and 4.[134]

Jimmy Carter stood under gray skies at an open podium at midfield of the football stadium, surrounded by midshipmen in their starched summer whites. It was a remarkable homecoming: thirty-five years earlier, he had entered the Naval Academy, a raw Southern boy who had never ventured out of Georgia. In his campaign biography, *Why Not the Best?*, he wrote that "one of the most fearsome requirements" of the academy was having to give speeches which, he remembered, would cause him to break out in a "cold sweat." Now he was addressing the world about what he deemed "one of the most important aspects" of international politics: America's relationship with the Soviet Union.[135]

It was not a great speech, but it showed Carter wrestling with the meaning of détente. It echoed the instructions Carter had given to Vance for his meeting with Brezhnev in April. "The word 'détente' has a different meaning to different people," Carter hand-wrote in a paragraph that survived intact to the final draft. It was "simplistic," he said, to think of détente as "an easing of tensions." Détente, he explained (albeit not clearly), was an evolving process between two nations that were trying to find grounds for cooperation. To be meaningful, détente had to be "truly reciprocal," Carter asserted, but recently the Kremlin had not adhered to this principle of reciprocity. "To the Soviet Union, détente seems to mean a continuing aggressive struggle for political advantage and increased influence . . . [especially through] military power." In particular, Carter criticized the "increasing military involvement of the Soviet Union and Cuba in Africa." In a sentence that was added to Carter's original draft—and not in Carter's hand—he presented a stark choice: "The Soviet Union can choose either confrontation or cooperation." He added: "The United States is adequately prepared to meet either choice." Carter concluded with a paragraph that was in his handwritten draft: "By a combination of adequate American strength, of quiet self-restraint in the use of it, of a refusal to believe in the inevitability of war, and of a patient and persistent development of all the peaceful alternatives, we hope eventually to lead international society into a more stable, more peaceful, and a more hopeful future."[136]

The journalists covering the speech had a tough assignment. They agreed that they had heard a major speech, and they agreed that the fracas that had erupted during Shaba required the president to clarify US policy toward the Soviet Union. But they did not agree on what Carter had said. Some, like Joseph Kraft and Mary McGrory, dismissed it as "a muddle."[137] Many, like the *New York Times*, deemed it Carter's "toughest speech" and stressed the choice it posed between confrontation or competition.[138] Still others praised Carter for staking out a "middle ground . . . a more realistic view of détente . . . détente without illusions."[139] The *Washington Post* conveyed the most sensitive grasp of Carter's meaning: "The message that Mr. Carter was trying to convey at Annapolis was that while the United States is eager to seek the benefits of détente, it insists on a measure of [Soviet] restraint."[140]

Carter, unfortunately, had not been as clear as the *Post*. And he compounded his troubles by adding the sentence that the Soviets would have to choose either cooperation or confrontation. That statement contradicted the rest of the speech, which was more subtle, using "competition" rather than "confrontation." Vance had stressed competition in an eleven-page letter about the US-Soviet relationship that he sent the president on May 29: "We cannot object to competition," Vance wrote with lawyerly clarity. "It is inherent in our relationship [with Moscow]."[141] Carter's decision to assert that the Kremlin had to choose between confrontation or cooperation also positioned the United States in a passive role—the onus was on Moscow to make the choice—that was not consistent with the rest of the speech. But the speech that Carter delivered was so murky that few people noticed these contradictions. They grabbed onto the one clear, catchy sentence and considered it the key: cooperation or confrontation.

This accelerated the construction of the narrative that Carter was torn between two advisers: Vance whispered "cooperation" in his left ear and Brzezinski whispered "confrontation" in his right, as the indecisive president wobbled between them. This vision of Carter had gained enough traction by the summer of 1978 that it became an *idée fixe* when the Iranian Revolution crescendoed a few months later. This was, however, a serious misunderstanding of Carter's leadership. Carter's vacillation in response to the revolution in Iran was atypical; it was a consequence of the extraordinary complexity of the issue rather than of his work habits. In other areas—Rhodesia, the Horn, Panama, the Middle East, the Soviet Union, China—Carter was his own man, and he stuck to his guns. Jimmy Carter was not in the thrall of his advisers. He ran the ship. He made the decisions. If those decisions appeared inconsistent, it was because Carter had a complex, nonideological worldview, not because he was listening to Vance one day and to Brzezinski the next. "The point is," Carter said in a news conference on June 26, "that I make the ultimate decisions in foreign policy. . . . I do get advice from various sources, both in and out of Government. . . . I make the judgment and neither the Secretary of State nor Dr. Brzezinski makes those judgments. . . . I'm the President, I make the decisions, and I want to be responsible for those decisions once they are made."[142]

The most striking aspect of Jimmy Carter's leadership is that he so rarely listened to anyone. To an extraordinary degree, he made decisions by himself. He immersed himself in the issues. He was an impressively diligent student; during the learning process, he listened attentively and was very curious. But when it came to making policy, Carter looked inside himself. He thought deeply about what was the right thing to do. He prayed about it. It was not a *political* process. It bore none of the consensus building or favor swapping that characterized the policymaking of, for instance, Lyndon Johnson or Bill Clinton.

This is not to say that Carter was incapable of politics. His 1976 campaign had proved that he could be as political as anyone, as did the successful passage of the Panama Canal treaties. He used his political skills when he thought they were required, but these were the exceptions. Carter's conception of the presidency was intensely solitary: he had been elected president, and that meant that the American people had selected him to make the decisions. Wasn't this what the campaign had been about—that the American people trusted his judgment?

Carter was a man of such discipline and energy that this policymaking style often worked. But it had consequences. First, it meant that relationships—the stuff of politics—failed to thrive. In his first year, Carter was the new man on campus. He had critics from the beginning, but it was in almost every politician's interest to get along with the president. Carter could have developed a broad base of support in the capital. But his policymaking style rendered building relationships with other politicians a waste of time, and Carter did not waste time. Networking and back-slapping were beneath him. The West German ambassador in Washington noted that the American president's press conferences were "brilliant intellectual performances but, at the same time, there was something mechanical [*schmächtig*] and impersonal about them. This might be the real mystery and the tragedy of the man: . . . he is what the Americans call 'a loner.'"[143]

Moreover, Carter's lack of an easily understood ideology frustrated and occasionally alarmed even his allies. He seemed to "lurch" from issue to issue, with unpredictable outcomes.[144] From Carter's point of view, he was being absolutely consistent—he was *always* guided by his best judgment of what was true to American values, trimmed to realist sails; the charge that he was inconsistent must have mystified him. He took pride in the fact that he was not easily categorized: how could he be reliably liberal or reliably conservative if he believed that "doing his best" meant to apply his best judgment afresh to every decision? He was consistent to himself, the man the American people had elected president. If others found this inconsistent, well, they were in the grip of an ideology.

There were consequences. During the campaign, people assumed that Jimmy Carter was simply playing his cards close to his chest and he would reveal his true leanings after the election. By the middle of 1978, it was dawning on many politicians and government officials that Carter's "true leanings" were complicated and decisions would be made on a case-by-case basis. Would he approve the neutron bomb? Would he link the SALT negotiations to Soviet behavior in Africa? These would have been difficult decisions for many presidents, but the centralization of power in the Carter administration, plus the fact that Carter had no track record on national or international issues, accentuated the unpredictability of the answers.

One result was a sense that the Carter White House was erratic and overwhelmed, not up to the task. Because journalists and politicians could not divine which way Carter might tilt, the utterances of Vance, Brzezinski, and unnamed "high administration officials" gained unusual significance. This created a vicious circle of leaks and added to the sense of disarray. Carter was so busy making decisions and so convinced that this was his most important job that he failed (ironically, for a former naval officer) to run a tight ship.

Another effect was that it was hard to build trust. In part, this stemmed from the theological nature of Carter's governing style. Many factors entered the calculus of Carter's decision making, but every policy choice was subjected to his moral compass. Once Carter made a decision, he was convinced that it was right. Anyone who disagreed was wrong. (An important exception was with leaders of Third World nations. Although Carter could be arrogant in his dealings with other Americans, West Europeans, and Soviets, he displayed a striking lack of arrogance when dealing with leaders and people from the developing world.) When this rigidity was added to Carter's distaste for building networks, the result was a corrosive absence of ties of loyalty during the Carter years. Carter did not believe that he owed loyalty to members of Congress who supported his policies: they should support his policies because those policies were right, not out of loyalty to him. If a member of Congress objected to his policy but out of loyalty or for political reasons voted for it anyway, Carter was not impressed: the legislator should have understood that the policy was right. Thus, as the months rolled on, members of Congress felt less—rather than more—loyalty to the president.

The second Shaba crisis highlighted the complexity of the Cold War in the late 1970s and the character of the Carter presidency. The invasion of the Katangan rebels threatened Mobutu, but what did it have to do with the Cold War? This question pitted the lessons of World War II against the lessons of Vietnam; that is, it pitted containment against regionalism. Was the invasion another in a series of Soviet affronts and probes, or was it a tribal crisis in central Africa? Did Washington have to raise the costs for Moscow before Cuban troops ventured across the continent to Rhodesia? Would choosing not to respond be appeasement? "There is a lot of soul searching . . . going on," one State Department official said five days after the Katangans invaded Zaire. "It looks as though we 'overlearned' the lessons of Vietnam."[145]

The pressures on Carter to hit the Soviets were intense. Criticizing the Soviets would reassure the administration's domestic critics, which would make it more possible to get key legislation, especially SALT, through Congress. The pressures were not just at home. "Far from Africa are other audiences—the NATO allies, the Soviet Union, China—who have been wondering how long Americans would be traumatized by Vietnam," a *New York Times* editorial noted on May 22. Even though some officials in Washington wanted to move US foreign policy away from a narrow anti-Soviet orientation, US allies in the Middle East, Western Europe, and East Asia made this difficult. At a NATO meeting in May, for example, the West German foreign minister announced, "The struggle between East and West has extended into Africa, and our job is to figure out how to stop it from spreading further." At the July 1978 Economic Summit in Bonn, Giscard d'Estaing urged Carter "to demonstrate the true strength of the United States." America's allies wanted reassurance that Washington would continue to aggressively counter the Soviets in their backyards: blowback from decades of waging the Cold War.[146]

The stakes were high. The evidence that the Katangan invasion was another Soviet/Cuban intervention in Africa was weak (because it was not true), but the administration remained concerned by the possibility. If the invasion it was a sign of increased boldness in Moscow and Havana, and if the Soviets and Cubans got away with it, then they would be more likely to intervene in Rhodesia. This would be the nightmare scenario, with the Soviets backing the blacks and the Americans either doing nothing or backing the white minority. Washington would be checkmated the minute the war for Rhodesia began. Carter understood this.

Jimmy Carter was in a difficult position. The confusions of détente had fueled polarization of opinion about the Soviet threat, and Carter's governing style had given him no cushion of safety on either side. No one was sure where he would head next, and many people were anxious.

10. The War at Home

The boil had been lanced. Pressure had been building on Jimmy Carter—stoked by Brzezinski, conservatives in the United States, and leaders in Europe, the Middle East, and Asia—to stand up to the Cubans and Soviets, to stop being a wimp, to be a man, to *do something*. Carter had succumbed. He had lashed out against the Cuban "mercenaries" and declared Castro a liar. He had stopped the talk of normalization with Cuba. He had launched a "military operation"—his first—in Zaire.

Many at home and abroad applauded the president's display of toughness and wanted more, complaining that the administration should have done more to help Mobutu and halted the SALT talks to punish Moscow. Others, including some of the administration's allies in Congress as well as its newfound friends in Africa, were alarmed and feared that the enigmatic Jimmy Carter was revealing his true colors as a hardline cold warrior.

The African continent had claimed a great deal of attention in the early months of 1978, but by June, the war in the Horn was over (although skirmishes began anew in the Ogaden); Shaba was under control; and the administration was attempting to conduct its southern African diplomacy more quietly. The effect was immediate: Africa fell from the front pages and from the public's consciousness. In the first six months of 1978, Carter was asked seventeen questions about Africa at news conferences; in the following six months, he was asked only one.[1] From January through June 1978, stories about Africa appeared on the front page of the *New York Times* 150 times; from July through December, only 25 times. On the three nightly news broadcasts, Africa was mentioned 221 times from January through June but only 59 times for the rest of the year. After the turmoil of the first half of the year, the Carter administration returned to focus on the issue that had gripped it from its earliest days: southern Africa.

Stasis and War

The reverberations of Ian Smith's internal settlement rumbled through the remainder of 1978. As the Salisbury Four—Smith, Bishop Abel Muzorewa, Reverend Ndabaningi Sithole, and Chief Jeremiah Chirau—worked out the details of the government they planned to create, they had no interest in pursuing the Anglo-American proposals. These proposals, formally announced in September 1977, had three basic provisions: (1) a cease-fire, after which Smith would step down and a British commissioner would take charge for a transitional period; (2) a constitution that would guarantee equal rights for all; and (3) internationally supervised elections to select the leader of an independent Zimbabwe. All three aspects required negotiations among all parties— Smith and his three black associates as well as the Patriotic Front. But the Salisbury Four refused to attend the all-party talks that were the *sine qua non* of the Anglo-American proposals. They told the Anglo-American negotiating team of Ambassadors Graham and Low that merely asking them to attend another conference to discuss the proposals was "an insult."[2]

The internal settlement created almost insuperable barriers to the implementation of the Anglo-American proposals, but at the same time it made those proposals more necessary because the internal settlement did not stop the war. Muzorewa, Sithole, and Chirau had assured Smith that the internal settlement would inspire many Patriotic Front guerrillas to renounce armed struggle, return home, and allow peace to descend on their troubled land. However, the opposite had occurred: the war had grown ever more violent. This threatened the internal settlement itself. The Salisbury Four were "sitting on a volcano," the Rhodesian finance minister admitted to Graham and Low.[3]

Throughout 1978, the number of trained Patriotic Front insurgents swelled. Joshua Nkomo's ZAPU had an estimated 10,000 to 12,000, and the Soviet Union was shipping them ever more sophisticated weapons. The brunt of the fighting, however, continued to be borne by Robert Mugabe's ZANU, whose numbers doubled in 1978. Unlike ZAPU, which had only about 1,000 fighters in Rhodesia, most (approximately 8,000) of the ZANU insurgents were deployed in the country. Their goals were to expand control of the countryside and to launch sporadic assaults on the Smith's regime's economic infrastructure. The overstretched Rhodesian military of approximately 50,000 men, bolstered by South African support, could neither stop the bloodshed nor control large portions of the countryside.[4]

For the Carter administration, stopping the Rhodesian war was even more imperative in 1978 than it had been in 1977 because fears of Cuban adventurism had spiked due to Havana's intervention in Ethiopia, the allegations of its complicity in Shaba, and its decision to increase its troops in Angola in the wake of Shaba 2. In May 1978, the CIA warned that "the USSR in recent weeks has clearly shifted its attention to the Rhodesian crisis in order to . . . maintain the momentum of recent Soviet successes."[5]

Add to this Washington's deteriorating relations with Pretoria, and the dilemma that the Carter administration faced in Rhodesia becomes clear. More than a year earlier, at its first NSC meeting on Africa, the administration had decided to avoid the moral ambiguity of the Ford administration and pursue peace in Rhodesia, the independence of Namibia, and the end of apartheid simultaneously. By the middle of 1978, however, that pristine policy had been battered by reality. Vice President Walter Mondale's bold talk with South African prime minister John Vorster had helped improve US relations with black Africa, but it had not borne fruit with the South African government, which had cracked down even harder on its nonwhite population and steadfastly refused to sign the Nuclear Non-Proliferation Treaty. Washington feared that Pretoria was continuing to develop nuclear weapons. "Some eight months after the discovery last August in the Kalahari Desert," the CIA declared in July 1978, "We are still far from certain what the South Africans are up to. . . . We think it likely they will continue to pursue such a program."[6] Moreover, Smith's internal settlement presented Pretoria with an attractive alternative to the Anglo-American proposals. The bottom line for Carter's Rhodesia policy was that Vorster refused to play the heavy to bring Smith to heel, as Washington had hoped in 1977 that he would. Ending the war in Rhodesia was the only way Washington could foreclose an opportunity for Soviet/Cuban intervention that would lead to a devastating wider war pitting whites against blacks backed by the Soviet bloc. Nevertheless, by June 1978, the administration could see no way forward. The Anglo-American proposals could not get off the ground, and Pretoria refused to help.

The internal settlement not only affected the dynamics in Rhodesia; it also had an impact on US politics. Many Americans believed that Ian Smith had taken a significant step forward toward majority rule, and they thought that his efforts should be acknowledged. A broad swath of senators and representatives—conservatives and liberals alike—were troubled by the Carter administration's refusal to embrace Smith's compromise. "Concerned Democrats are wrestling with the problem," an NSC aide wrote Brzezinski. "Even Dick Clark [the liberal chair of the Senate Africa subcommittee] is unwilling to publicly outright condemn an internal settlement." Madeleine Albright, the NSC expert on congressional affairs, noted, "Only the [Congressional] Black Caucus has taken a public stance opposing the internal settlement." Likewise, in Britain, the Callaghan government faced a growing chorus of criticism of its Rhodesia policy.[7]

On the surface, both Jimmy Carter and Jim Callaghan stood firm in their stalwart support for the Anglo-American proposals. Beneath the surface, reality was more complicated. Both governments were wedded to the proposals only so long as they appeared to be the best means to their chosen ends: for London, to bring Rhodesia to legal independence; for Washington, to end the potentially catastrophic war. Carter was not opposed to the internal settlement per se; if it seemed to be a more sure or swift path to peace than the Anglo-American proposals, he would support it. Carter's willingness to consider approaches other than the Anglo-American process—at the internal settlement as well as British foreign secretary David Owen's attempts to broker a separate deal between Joshua Nkomo and Ian Smith—shows that his fundamental goal was not to lead Zimbabwe to pure democracy but rather to end the war.

Whitehall thought that it could build on the internal settlement to construct a path to Rhodesian independence. Owen continued to believe, ardently, in a deal that would leave Nkomo on top. "Now is the time to apply maximum pressure," Owen urged the other foreign ministers at a quadripartite meeting in late May 1978. "It's in the West's interest that the internal settlement . . . gain enough strength to really join the negotiations. . . . Nkomo is still the key figure, and there are indications that he's ready to deal." One month later, Owen was beating the same drum in a Cabinet meeting: "There was a basic common interest between Mr Nkomo and Mr Smith who both, for different reasons, wanted a settlement, and we should do our best to build on this."[8]

Carter and Vance understood Owen's need to take risks. In Britain, Labour was under brutal pressure from the Conservatives; opposition leader Margaret Thatcher had called for a debate in the House of Commons on the "very urgent" Rhodesia situation.[9] The Callaghan government—the Carter administration's staunchest friend in Europe—was hanging by a thread, and general elections were anticipated in the fall.

Thus, the "Owen gambit" went forward. In public, both allies continued to give their full support to the Anglo-American proposals, while in fact, the Owen gambit was their major diplomatic initiative in Rhodesia in 1978. It was a disaster that sheds light on Anglo-American cooperation under strain; clarifies the leadership style of Cyrus Vance, who bucked the advice of his staff; and complicates the image of Jimmy Carter as a naïf who believed religiously in democracy. In approving this gambit, Carter authorized a path that he hoped would end the war in Rhodesia but not one that would lead to democratic elections: the point of the gambit was that Nkomo end up in charge, even though, as Owen admitted, he "could not win a fair election on his own."[10]

While the Owen gambit was underway, in the summer of 1978, the State Department pursued a two-track policy toward Rhodesia. At the highest level—Vance and his reluctant aides—the focus was on supporting the British attempt to arrange the secret Smith-Nkomo meeting. But at all other levels it was business as usual: the regional directors and ambassadors in the field worked tirelessly to reinvigorate the Anglo-American proposals. They traveled widely and ceaselessly throughout southern Africa; they talked to the Patriotic Front, the Frontline States, and the Salisbury Four; and they drew up draft transition arrangements and draft proposals for all-party talks. These efforts were fruitless in 1978, but they would lay the foundation for the Lancaster House negotiations a year later.

"We are in grave danger."[11]

Congressional critics of the Carter administration had sensed opportunity the minute Ian Smith had emerged from the governor's mansion in Salisbury on March 3, 1978, with the internal settlement in hand. Even though none of the essentials—such as the constitution—had been worked out, Smith had compromised, and many senators and representatives believed that the White House should celebrate it.

Three days later, Representative Richard Ichord, a conservative Democrat from Missouri, called for the Byrd Amendment to be immediately reinstated. He believed that in light of the progress Smith had achieved in Salisbury, the United States should once again break the UN sanctions and import Rhodesian chrome "in the interest of human rights as well as our own economic and national security interests." The next day, Republican senator Robert Dole of Kansas and twelve co-sponsors introduced a concurrent resolution that instructed the president to tell Andrew Young "to lend his dedicated efforts towards gaining international support for the internal agreement," which it deemed "a momentous accomplishment." The House followed suit with a resolution urging the administration to support the internal settlement by lifting sanctions and thereby undercutting "the radical Marxist . . . terrorist guerrillas committed to violence."[12]

In early April 1978, Congressional Liaison Frank Moore wrote Carter that the mood in the Senate was "one of uneasiness and extreme caution. . . . Many on the Hill perceive us as uninspiring, indecisive, disorganized, and undisciplined. . . . Even more disturbing is the growing notion that those who 'walk the plank' for us get little thanks or recognition . . . and run the real risk of being abandoned if we feel it politically expedient to do so. . . . All this erodes confidence in the President." The administration could not afford to be complacent. Although the 292 Democrats in the House had a filibuster-proof supermajority against the 143 Republicans, in the Senate the Democrats' supermajority was razor-thin (61 Democrats, plus one Independent who caucused with them, to 38 Republicans) and unreliable. The Democrats, split between conservatives and liberals, did not vote as a bloc. "In such an environment, a small minority of Senators, adamant in their opposition, can take advantage of Senate rules to prevent action on any issue they choose. . . . The 8 to 10 Republican 'moderates' often hold the balance of power in the Senate." Moore went on to sound a warning: "We are in grave danger. . . . Our political capital will have been exhausted in the Senate and in the country as a result of the divisive fight on Panama in an election year. [The midterm elections would be in November.] . . . We must concentrate our energies, time, and resources on priority issues, committing ourselves only to endeavors in which we have a reasonable chance of prevailing." Across the top of the memo, Carter wrote, "I don't mind the criticism, but is morale this low?"[13]

The White House and State Department worked with the Senate Foreign Relations Committee to draft a report on the internal settlement that would clarify the administration's doubts about it. "On the surface, this option seems highly attractive," the report explained. However, it cautioned, it would be a mistake for the US government to endorse it. The internal settlement left "land tenure, the public service, the judiciary, the police, and defense forces" in the control of whites; it did not grant "majority rule based on one man, one vote." It was suffused with "pervasive ambiguity," and it did not "ensure the 'end of white rule.'" Endorsing the internal settlement would "damage US policy in Africa . . . [and] put the United States on the same side as the white regimes."[14]

Jesse Helms did not agree. On June 28, the Republican senator from North Carolina rose to speak. "The amendment I propose is a simple one," he began. "The transitional government [in Salisbury] is struggling to provide the necessary economic and social stability for free elections to be held in December 1978." The United States should assist this valiant effort. Therefore, Helms proposed that sanctions against Rhodesia be lifted "during the most critical period"—that is, until October 1979, which would allow the new multiracial regime in Salisbury several months to establish itself after the scheduled December 1978 elections. Helms was appalled by the Anglo-American proposals, which he called "a vindictive plan" demanding Smith's "unconditional surrender." The internal settlement, by contrast, was "reasonable, humane . . . [and] based upon traditional Western concepts of equity and justice. . . . It deserves to be given a chance." Helms, a verbal slugger, did not mince his words. Asserting that the Anglo-American proposals kowtowed to the "Marxist" Patriotic Front, he rose to a crescendo: "A Rhodesian settlement that succumbs to the claims of aggressors will be another Munich settlement, touching off a continental war with chaos of epic proportions."[15]

Republican Senator Sam Hayakawa of California concurred. "We at least should give that group which is making groping steps toward interracial harmony and democracy a fighting chance to survive," he argued in a hard-hitting speech. Harry Byrd (I-VA) and Barry Goldwater (R-AZ) rose to support Helms' amendment.[16]

Those senators who supported the administration's Rhodesia policy were caught off-guard. Only George McGovern (D-SD) and Dick Clark (D-IA) rose to counter Helms' argument. Both explained that lifting sanctions would make it more difficult for the administration to persuade all parties to return to the negotiating table. "By what stretch of the imagination is the war going to end simply because we endorse the internal settlement?" Clark inquired. "If we are interested in keeping Soviet and Cuban penetration out of southern Africa, if we are serious about getting a diplomatic and, therefore, a peaceful transition to majority rule in Rhodesia, we will certainly support the Anglo-American plan and not adopt this amendment." McGovern added, "It is the overwhelming conviction of the majority of the Foreign Relations Committee that we ought to stay with our present policy with regard to Rhodesia and not make the change proposed by the Senator from North Carolina." He moved to table the amendment.[17]

Helms had the last word: "If the Senate tables this motion the blood will not be on the hands of the Senator from North Carolina, but it will be on the hands of those Senators who vote to table."[18]

A vote on Helms' amendment was immediately called, and the closeness of the vote was a surprise, even to Helms: forty-two for and forty-eight against. Why did it fare so well? The *Washington Post* boiled the answer down to two reasons: "First, the moderate one-man, one-vote multiracial system promised by the 'internal' government . . . looks better to many senators than the communist-oriented black guerrilla regime they see as a likely alternative. Second . . ., these senators thought that by temporarily lifting sanctions, they might even the odds in a struggle the guerrillas now seem almost sure to win. . . . The State Department treats Salisbury like a leper and courts the Popular [*sic*] Front. The United States funnels economic aid to the Frontline States sponsoring the guerrillas, and enforces no-trade sanctions against Rhodesia."[19]

The allegation that the administration's bias was blinding it to the virtues of the internal settlement was not the preserve of one party. Most Republicans voted with Helms and most Democrats against him, but ten Republicans (the reliable liberals, most of whom were from the Northeast) and seventeen Democrats (more than a third of those voting, and all but one Southerner) crossed the aisle. Carter would need these Democrats to pass important legislation, including SALT II. For the White House, the close vote on the Helms Amendment was an unwelcome wake-up call.[20]

David Owen's Gambit, Part Three

"With misgivings," Vance wrote in his memoirs, "I agreed to secret British attempts beginning in late June [1978] to arrange an exploratory meeting between Smith and Nkomo." On June 23, the first hint that Vance had bowed to Owen's pressure appears in a report from Andrew Young about a conversation he had with Nigerian foreign minister Joe Garba. It was cloak-and-dagger stuff. Garba, who had previously been the Nigerian UN ambassador and was close to Young, alluded to the behind-the-scenes machinations of arranging the Nkomo-Smith meeting, and Young responded "that the US would not discourage such a settlement plan if it included all parties and succeeded in avoiding civil war." A week later, Brzezinski wrote Carter that Vance and Owen had agreed that "a secret British intermediary [Tiny Rowland, the British tycoon who had lived in Rhodesia and befriended Smith] will inform [Zambian president Kenneth] Kaunda, possibly today, of Smith's proposal for a secret meeting with Nkomo." (Although Smith did want the meeting, the evidence points to Owen, not Smith, as the instigator.) Kaunda, who had been burned by Smith many times before, harbored grave doubts about his intentions. "Smith's last fling may be the worst," he told the British high commissioner. "He may feel he has nothing to lose." Nevertheless, on June 30, Kaunda met with Nkomo to discuss the idea. Two days later, on July 2, Assistant Secretary Dick Moose—whose objections to the scheme Vance had overruled—wrote the secretary a handwritten letter. "Nkomo is interested in meeting Smith," he announced.[21]

Brzezinski was uneasy, and he voiced his concerns about the administration's southern Africa policy to Carter. That Brzezinski inserted the topic into one of his weekly reports indicates not only that he felt strongly about it (he had carefully avoided debating Rhodesian or South African policy with the president) but also that he sensed that Carter was open to criticism of it. "We plunged heavily into African problems—which, alas, the British created," Brzezinski wrote on July 7. "But should we be so heavily engaged?" He rejected the State Department's assertion that its policy was balanced; instead, he posed the question that the administration's conservative critics had long asked: why favor the radical Patriotic Front over the moderates in Salisbury? "Should we really lean towards Nkomo . . . —and not Muzorewa?" Brzezinski then dealt with the issue at hand: the secret dealings with Nkomo. "Perhaps the British will succeed in seducing Nkomo," he wrote, "but if they do not, then maybe we should choose to quietly disengage and lower our own direct involvement." The underlining was Carter's and in the margin the president wrote, in his terse style, "A good possibility."[22]

Carter was deeply worried. Over dinner on the first night of the G7 Summit in Bonn on July 16, he "urged all present [the leaders of West Germany, Britain, France, Italy, Japan, and Canada] to consider how they would react to a blood bath in Rhodesia if the search for a settlement failed." He explained that he approved Owen's gambit because the war in Rhodesia was intensifying, the Anglo-American proposals were stalled, and he had no better options.[23]

A few days later, Vance and Owen met quietly in New York with South African foreign minister Pik Botha and his senior aide Brand Fourie (who was the liaison between Pretoria and Salisbury) to ask them to confirm that Smith would be willing to meet with Nkomo. Owen took the lead, but Vance's presence at the meeting was the US imprimatur. "Basically the British Government wanted the Prime Minister [Smith] to meet Mr. Nkomo," Fourie reported to Smith on July 31. If Owen was "convinced that it would lead to something successful," he was prepared to fly with Nkomo to Salisbury to meet with Smith, Fourie said. "Both Dr. Owen and Mr. Vance were of the opinion that, without Nkomo being part and parcel of any settlement exercise, the war would continue." Fourie described Owen's and Vance's plan, which was, he said, "very vague" in some respects. "What they had in mind was to enlarge the present Executive Council by inclusion of the Patriotic Front members." The council would expand from its current four members—Smith and his three black colleagues—to eight: "two from the Nkomo faction and two from the Mugabe faction. . . . The British hoped," Fourie said, "that Nkomo would be the Chairman."[24]

Smith asked whether Owen "had said anything about driving a wedge between Nkomo and Mugabe." Fourie stressed that he and Botha had "gained the very firm impression that, as far as the British were concerned . . . Mugabe was probably of little consequence." From the British point of view, "there were now only two key figures in the Rhodesian settlement exercises, namely, the Prime Minister [Smith] and Joshua Nkomo." An internal Foreign Office history of the negotiations notes that "Mr Nkomo's belief was that Mr Mugabe would accept his [Nkomo's] leadership." Many years later, Owen asserted, "I was definitely not trying to push ZANU out, or to break up the Patriotic Front." It is difficult to accept this claim, however, because there was no reason to believe that Mugabe—whom Owen himself called a "zealot"—would accept playing second fiddle to his rival, Nkomo. Owen might have indicated his true plan in a comment he made to Sithole: "The real question, is how do we bring Nkomo in. . . . Before he breaks with Robert [Mugabe], he must be assured of success."[25]

Within the week, Owen was back in London. Nkomo, Chief Chirau (one of Smith's three black colleagues), and a delegation of traditional chiefs were in town. A subterranean momentum toward a breakthrough, which would propel Nkomo to the top, was growing. The British Foreign Office wanted it; Smith, Nkomo, and the chiefs wanted it; Kaunda wanted it; the South Africans wanted it; and the Nigerians wanted it. As Owen explained: "I couldn't have done it, and I wouldn't have done it, if it had been just a British initiative. It would have been much too damaging." The Nigerians, eager to throw their weight around, helped with the logistics. But Owen expressed the bottom line when he said, "I was masterminding it."[26]

In a conversation with the chiefs, Owen did not mention that he was arranging the secret meeting, but he did assert that the government in Salisbury had to "take in Joshua Nkomo." Nkomo was the natural leader, the "eldest statesman of nationalism in Rhodesia"; he had "high ambitions" and "support all around the world." Owen envisioned cornering Mugabe and giving him the option of accepting Nkomo's dominant role in the Executive Council or being left out in the cold. "If Mugabe proved to be unrealistic, and all could see this, then Nkomo would be forced to leave him out."[27]

Political Prisoners

While Owen masterminded the delicate negotiations between Smith and Nkomo, Vance was focused on the SALT talks in Geneva, and Carter was increasingly preoccupied with preparations for the Camp David summit with Egypt's Anwar Sadat and Israel's Menachem Begin. Also, the administration's human rights policy came to the fore.

In the summer of 1978, Anatoly Shcharansky—a Jewish dissident whose request to emigrate from the Soviet Union had been refused, who had joined a group protesting Soviet violations of human rights, and who had been accused by the Soviet authorities of working for US intelligence—was put on trial in Moscow after a fifteen-month imprisonment. An explosive stew of human rights, antisemitism, and espionage allegations, the case attracted enormous attention in the United States and globally. Carter, Vance, and the US Congress condemned Shcharansky's arrest and trial.[28]

The timing upped the ante: the trial opened on July 10, as Vance was heading to Geneva. Many Americans, led by Senator Henry "Scoop" Jackson (D-WA), called on the administration to cancel the SALT talks in protest. On July 11, Carter denounced the trial as "an attack on every human being who lives in the world who believes in basic human freedom."[29]

At almost the same moment that Carter was condemning the trial in those soaring terms, Ambassador Andrew Young was chatting with a reporter from the French socialist daily *Le Matin*. In the course of a long interview, Young compared the dissidents in the Soviet Union with civil rights workers in the United States, who, like him, had been jailed. "It was only ten years ago that I myself was arrested . . . in Atlanta, Georgia, for organizing garbage workers and ended up spending—fortunately—not too long a time in jail. . . . Down south in the 1950s, they used to accuse us of being communists, and they used to say that everything the civil rights movement did was inspired by the communists." This line of thought led Young to the soundbite that ricocheted around the world: "There are still hundreds of people I'd categorize as political prisoners in our jails. Maybe even thousands."[30]

This remark was the lead in *Le Matin*'s account of the interview, and it was the sentence that was repeated across the US press. The White House and the State Department immediately announced that Young's comment did not "reflect the policies of this administration." Carter declared he was "very unhappy" with Young's statement. On July 13, Young flew to Geneva to meet with Vance. Afterward, Vance said that he was "very displeased" and had let Young know that it had better not happen again. Young was uncharacteristically terse. He read a mimeographed statement explaining that he had never meant to equate the "status of political freedom in the United States with that of the Soviet Union," and he refused to take questions.[31]

The frenzy that had swirled around Young's first months on the job returned. His old comments were recalled, and they became a conservative refrain: Presidents Ford and Nixon were racists; the British were chicken; the Cubans were stabilizing Africa, and so on. These oft-repeated remarks reinforced the image of the Carter administration's policy—especially toward Africa—as beyond the pale.

Senator Harry Byrd, the Independent senator who in 1971 had authored the amendment breaching UN sanctions on Rhodesia, exclaimed that US foreign policy "is being shaped by a few extremists in the State Department and by another extremist, . . . Mr. Andrew Young . . . the same Ambassador Young who yesterday . . . stated that the United States itself 'has hundreds and perhaps thousands of political prisoners.'" It was extremists like Young, Harry Byrd argued, who were "insisting that the internal settlement [in Rhodesia] . . . should not be permitted to go into effect unless Russian-oriented terrorist guerrilla leaders . . . are made a part of the government."[32]

The Senator from North Carolina

Jesse Helms was a bulldog. He had drawn blood in June with the closeness of the vote on his amendment on the internal settlement in Rhodesia. He had superb political instincts, and he had mastered parliamentary procedure. He was a formidable opponent.

Throughout the 1960s and early 1970s, Helms had been part-owner of a local television station in Raleigh, North Carolina, where he made a name for himself with his feisty, folksy commentaries that aired every night on the local evening news. Similar to Ronald Reagan's radio broadcasts a decade later, Helms' "Viewpoints" covered a broad range of subjects but stressed a consistent, conservative theme: freedom was threatened by communism abroad and liberalism at home. The civil rights movement was undermining American strength. Black people had a "right to pursue progress," Helms stated in a 1964 commentary, but not "to misbehave and violate the law demanding what they vaguely call 'freedom.'" Rhodesia was one of his favored topics in his television commentaries. As Helms saw it, Ian Smith, like many white southerners in the United States, was holding the line against communism and chaos. *New York Times* columnist Tom Wicker noted that Jesse Helms was Ian Smith's "kindred soul."[33]

For Helms to move from commentator to politician made sense, but his timing—1972—rendered his choice of party affiliation complicated. Jesse Helms was by temperament a Wallace Democrat, but the Democratic Party had shifted under George Wallace's feet. Helms was one of those southerners who fulfilled President Lyndon Johnson's prediction that the Democrats would lose the South because of the Civil Rights and Voting Rights acts. In 1972, Helms ran for the Senate as a Republican in North Carolina, a state that had not sent a Republican to Washington since 1903. His victory marked a turning point in American political history.

Ambitious, competitive, and hard-working, Helms quickly became an important voice of the emerging conservative movement. As two analysts of the movement noted, "Helms expressed without visible embarrassment many of the racial, social, and economic views of Old South Democrats," and he was skilled at using race as a campaign theme. On that subject, Helms was unreconstructed, never once supporting any civil rights legislation and conducting a one-month filibuster against the Martin Luther King holiday.[34]

Helms was in campaign mode again in 1978, and Rhodesia was an attractive issue. First, the close vote on his June amendment had shown that the president's policy was vulnerable. Second, helping Ian Smith construct a biracial government that was fighting against black "Marxist terrorists" hit the right notes for a conservative Republican politician running in North Carolina in 1978. It captured the resentment of many white southerners, annoyed that their "sacrifices"—like those of Ian Smith—to accommodate blacks had not been appreciated. His support for the internal settlement could also be used to signal that Helms was not a racist: he was in favor of including blacks in the government in Salisbury, as long as they were the "good" blacks and white rights were protected. Rhodesia could help Helms get votes back home, and he would need them to win what his own aides admitted was shaping up to be a "tough race."[35]

"Helms now claims that he has the votes [in the Senate] for a six-month lifting of sanctions," a State Department official wrote Assistant Secretary Moose on July 13. The senator from North Carolina was preparing to strike again. This time, he would try to rope in the handful of votes he needed to ensure passage of his resolution by shortening the period of time that sanctions would be lifted and by stressing that it was a temporary measure, a brief respite to give the Salisbury government time to prove itself. The State Department was worried. By trying to force the US government to lift sanctions, Helms was using the leverage that Congress could muster to compel the White House to openly embrace the internal settlement. This, the Carter administration believed, was dangerous: it would not stop the war and it would preclude further negotiations with the Patriotic Front. It would mean that Washington could no longer play the role of honest broker. "Given the closeness of the last vote," Deputy Secretary of State Warren Christopher wrote, "[the Department is] . . . working closely with key Senate staffers and private lobbying groups (Washington Office on Africa, TransAfrica, etc.) to develop an effective strategy for countering the Helms Amendment." The Carter administration did its homework. It analyzed congressional voting patterns and targeted swing votes. It paid particular attention to the ten members who had been absent for the vote on the first Helms Amendment.[36]

To explain why Helms's amendment was ill-advised, the administration had to rely on a counterintuitive argument: including the leftist guerrillas in talks was the best way to stop the Soviets and Cubans. The State Department tried to clarify its policy in an announcement on July 17. The Helms Amendment "would damage our relations throughout Africa, and reduce our ability to urge a fair settlement on the Patriotic Front. It would remove an incentive for the internal parties to negotiate about an inclusive, balanced agreement. It would undercut African governments which agree that peaceful settlements to these problems are possible without resorting to increased foreign intervention."[37]

That justification of US policy, Helms proclaimed on the floor of the Senate, was "another outburst of Andy Young mentality." Helms and his supporters—who had drawn useful lessons from the Panama Canal debate—had the advantage of simplicity. The discussion, as congressional liaison Frank Moore wrote Brzezinski, "has been narrowed down to a simple question of why are we supporting Marxists—against those who are trying to set up a democratic government."[38]

This stark framing of the debate presented a special challenge for those senators who were facing tight races in November. Supporting "Marxists" in Rhodesia was dicey during an election season. For the White House, this mattered. Senator Dick Clark, who was up for reelection in Iowa, had been the most articulate and effective supporter of the administration's Africa policy in the Senate. Moore noted: "We cannot count on Clark to take as much of a leadership role on Rhodesia as previously because of his re-election."[39]

Helms formed a close, mutually beneficial partnership with lobbyists from the Rhodesian Information Office—the de facto Rhodesian embassy that the Carter administration, bowing to congressional pressure, had failed to close in 1977.[40] "We see them [officials from the Rhodesian Information Office] all the time buttonholing our Congressmen," Young commented. "It reminds us that democracy is a constant struggle."[41] The Information Office not only educated members of Congress about Rhodesia (always, of course, from Smith's point of view), but also fed them a steady stream of newspaper reports, letters, and political statements supporting the internal settlement and painting the guerrillas as bloodthirsty communists. These reports—transcripts of Smith's speeches and lurid articles about the crimes and atrocities of the guerrillas—peppered the *Congressional Record* in 1978 and 1979. Members of Congress who had no prior knowledge of (or interest in) Africa rose to expound on the virtues of the internal settlement, freely citing arcane details of Rhodesian history. The Rhodesian Information Office worked on overdrive after the near success of Helms' amendment in June. It also funded congressional junkets to Rhodesia where officials of the internal settlement government regaled the visiting Americans with professions of their love of democracy and Western civilization.

The Rhodesian Information Office suggested to Helms that he invite Bishop Muzorewa to Washington in order to lobby in person for the internal settlement. Muzorewa, who arrived on July 16, spent two weeks on the Hill talking to every member of Congress who would listen. He met with Henry Kissinger, who afterward urged Carter to give the internal settlement "a fair chance." Muzorewa also delivered speeches. "America must honour her traditional principle[s] of justice, human rights, and national sovereignty," he told an audience at Georgetown University. "Like America, we wish to create a Zimbabwe . . . in which we can say we have a government of the people, by the people, for the people and a society in which we too can say, 'In God We Trust.'" But after a most unproductive meeting with Vance, Muzorewa gave interviews to the press, explaining how he found it "puzzling" and "unfair" that the Carter administration was refusing to help the new democracy in Rhodesia. The bishop, journalists Evans and Novak wrote, "was in a state of distraught perplexity."[42]

The Case-Javits Amendment

While the Rhodesian Information Office was pulling out all the stops to support the Helms Amendment, the Carter administration was working feverishly to defeat it. One hundred Senate staffers were invited to the White House for a two-hour briefing on the issue by top State Department and NSC officials. Vice President Mondale, Brzezinski, and State Department officials lobbied individual senators. On July 20, Vance and David Owen held a joint press conference in London to denounce Helms' attempt to lift sanctions on the Smith regime. "I can think of really nothing that would be more unwise and more dangerous than to take such a step at this time," Vance, who was not given to theatrics, stated. As soon as he returned to Washington, Vance asked Vernon Jordan, president of the National Urban League, "to get his troops working," and he extracted a promise from Henry Kissinger that he would refrain from commenting further on the issue. Vance then appeared on the ABC newsweekly *Issues and Answers* and repeated the message: "It is of vital importance that we not lift these sanctions."[43]

Behind the scenes, State Department and White House officials were working with Senator Clark to devise language for a compromise amendment that would incorporate some of the sentiment of the Helms Amendment but stop short of forcing the White House to lift sanctions. Assistant Secretary Moose, who had traveled through Africa with Clark in 1975 and 1976, played a key role. Two liberal Republican senators agreed to sponsor the compromise amendment: Clifford Case, whose days in the Senate were numbered because New Jersey Republicans had recently opted for his opponent in the primary election, and New York's Jacob Javits, who had been weakened politically by his loyalty to Nixon and who was turning to foreign affairs to refurbish his liberal image prior to his 1980 reelection bid. Both senators sat on the Foreign Relations Committee. Also active in support of compromise language were Henry "Scoop" Jackson (D-WA) and Daniel Patrick Moynihan (D-NY), two anticommunist firebrands who sought to arrest the growing power of Jesse Helms.[44]

The State Department's proposed amendment was simple. It had two parts. First, sanctions would remain in place until the Salisbury regime had fulfilled two conditions: agreed to participate in all-party talks and held an election that was deemed "free and fair" by international observers. Second, President Carter would determine when and if these conditions had been fulfilled.

The White House would have preferred a free hand to develop its southern African policy, without congressional interference. However, the Case-Javits Amendment, the administration said with flat understatement, was "much less damaging" than the Helms alternative. While it gave senators a vehicle to express their anxiety about the administration's Rhodesia policy, it kept sanctions in place and it preserved presidential authority. It was a brilliant defensive maneuver. But it was important that the amendment not be associated with the administration. "Our posture in public and private is to continue to oppose Helms and not be identified with a compromise," Deputy Secretary of State Warren Christopher wrote Carter.[45]

For the White House, the vote was a nail-biter. If it was forced by Congress to lift sanctions on Rhodesia, its Africa policy would be in shambles. It had painstakingly persuaded many black African nations that US policy had changed and that American support for majority rule was sincere, but this trust was fragile. If Congress forced the White House to lift sanctions on Rhodesia, the Anglo-American proposals would be dead in the water. On July 22, Frank Moore wrote Carter that "Helms may have the votes necessary to prevail." It had come down to a handful of swing votes. Moore informed the president that Majority Leader Robert Byrd might vote with Helms. In the margin, Carter wrote, "Let Byrd know how important this is."[46]

A measure of its importance was that all the major US newspapers weighed in. The *Wall Street Journal*, *Chicago Tribune*, and *Washington Post* criticized the administration's Rhodesia policy for tilting toward the guerrillas, but they came down on different sides of the Helms Amendment. The *Tribune* and the *Journal* thought that "lifting the sanctions for a while may help redress the balance," while the *Post* thought that the Helms Amendment promised "no more than messy confusion." The *New York Times* was adamantly opposed to the Helms Amendment, which it called "tragically misguided." If it was adopted, the *Times* warned, "American policy would be left bankrupt."[47]

The showdown began in the early afternoon of July 26. Bishop Muzorewa was a spectator in the Senate gallery, sitting beside Ken Towsey, the head of the Rhodesia Information Office. The administration forces scored an early victory, outmaneuvering Helms so that the Case-Javits Amendment was debated first. Helms, clearly annoyed, tried to turn the tables on the administration. He rose to speak. This maneuver "indicates a certain nervousness on the part of Senators who oppose the lifting of sanctions on Rhodesia," he observed. "It may be that they are worried about whether they have the votes, despite the fact that the administration and State Department have pulled out all the stops." Helms declared that voting for Case-Javits would be "endorsing the State Department policy." It was an astute observation, but Helms could not make it stick: the hand of the administration was hidden, and because Case-Javits called for sanctions to be lifted, it seemed to challenge rather than support White House policy. Even the well-informed *CQ Weekly* reported that the administration "objected to the [Case-Javits] compromise."[48]

Republican John Danforth of Missouri also spoke against Case-Javits. "In a distant corner of the world, a small country is struggling on a pilgrimage from repression to democracy," he said. "It asks our support in this effort. It asks us to stand for democracy—not for conferences, not for a role for guerrillas, not for popularity with the Frontline States—to stand for democracy. . . . That is the issue before us today." While the opponents of Case-Javits described with great passion atrocities attributed to the guerrillas, not one word was said about the violence perpetrated on the black population by the Smith regime.[49]

Danforth and Helms were wrong-footed by the fact that the administration's supporters had managed to get the vote on Case-Javits to precede that on Helms. The eloquent defense of the internal settlement mounted by the supporters of the Helms Amendment might have persuaded their colleagues to vote *for* it, but it did not convince them to vote *against* Case-Javits. The Case-Javits supporters capitalized on this. All of them stressed that Case-Javits was, as Dick Clark said, "a middle course" between Helms and the White House. Javits explained his decision to cosponsor the amendment by asserting that it restored balance to US policy: whereas the Carter administration favored the Patriotic Front, his amendment tilted toward the internal settlement. His amendment, Case concluded, "shares Helms' purpose, but without denying the administration the needed flexibility to make policy."[50]

Senate minority leader Howard Baker, who supported Helms, moved to table Case-Javits. With hindsight, the vote on this procedural maneuver was the key vote of the day. The tally was not even close. Fifty-seven senators—forty-six Democrats and eleven Republicans—opposed tabling the amendment.[51]

Case called for a vote on his amendment and the result was decisive: fifty-nine in favor; thirty-six opposed. (Forty-five Democrats and fourteen Republicans voted for Case-Javits; twenty-four Republicans and twelve Democrats—ten of whom were from the South—voted against it; five were absent, all Democrats.) Moore, the congressional liaison, sent an urgent note to President Carter. "Now pending is the Helms . . . amendment. The vote should come between 5:00 and 5:30. Both Senator [Robert] Byrd [the majority leader] and Senator [Howard] Baker [the minority leader] support the Helms Amendment. The vote will be close."[52]

In fact, it was anticlimactic. Helms proposed his amendment that forced the president to lift sanctions immediately for six months. He reminisced about his recent travels with Bishop Muzorewa. "I was deeply touched by a visit that he paid to an 83 year old former missionary, a delightful lady, who now lives in a Methodist home in Asheville NC. I do not think I will ever forget the scene of the bishop embracing and being embraced by this gracious lady who not only taught him to speak English but converted him to Christianity." He laid it on the line: "[I am] pleading with the Senate not to dismiss the dreams, the hopes, and wishes of 80 percent of the Rhodesian people."[53]

But Helms knew parliamentary procedure. He had been beaten. Danforth tried to salvage the situation, proposing a substitute amendment that watered down Helms' own by suspending sanctions for only three months. Helms withdrew his amendment, and the vote proceeded on the Danforth substitute. It was defeated soundly, fifty-four to forty-two. The State Department immediately issued a statement: "We are encouraged by the Senate rejection of the extreme approach advocated by Senator Helms." It added that "the thrust of the Case/Javits amendment is consistent with the goals of our Rhodesia policy."[54]

Lobbies

The fight was not over. Congressman Richard Ichord, one of the most conservative members of the House, was planning to introduce an amendment similar to that of Helms. The State Department was on guard. Two days after the Senate vote, Christopher wrote that Department officials "are working closely with . . . NGO's [nongovernmental organizations] to defeat any House attempts to modify our policy on sanctions." By "working closely," Christopher meant that the State Department was trying to galvanize a small group of overworked NGOs and then take cover behind them. Many black pressure groups such as the NAACP, the Southern Christian Leadership Conference, the National Committee of Black Lawyers, and the Urban League had a long commitment to the principle of global solidarity, but by the time Carter became president they were focused on the crushing problems that American blacks faced at home. The NAACP was typical: it established a Task Force on Africa in 1976, and the committee duly reported on the continent at every national convention during the Carter years.[55] Leaders of the NAACP occasionally were briefed on Africa policy by State Department officials, testified on African affairs before Congress, and wrote op-eds on the subject.[56] And yet, understandably, Africa always seemed to be an afterthought; as Vance learned when he had addressed the group in June 1977, their passion was reserved for the plight of blacks at home.

In the 1970s, several grassroots organizations such as the Washington Office on Africa were lobbying against US policy toward the white-ruled governments of southern Africa. Although these groups—some minuscule, fleeting, and passionate—were rarely specifically African American, they recognized that rallying African Americans was their best path to influence. They could expound in the wilderness about the immorality of US support for apartheid, but until they had significant numbers—that is, voters—on their side, they would be marginal to the policymaking process. After wrestling with the apathy and resistance of the Nixon and Ford administrations, the grassroots organizers had high hopes for Carter, with his emphasis on human rights. Their shoestring budgets and small staffs meant that they had to choose their battles, and particularly after Soweto they had an almost single-minded focus on South Africa: apartheid was the abomination, and US policy toward Pretoria had to change. Now was the time.[57]

This affected the pressure that these groups brought to bear on the administration's Rhodesia policy. Rhodesia was a distraction: it was less dependent than South Africa on US support, and racism in Smith's Rhodesia was less obscene than was apartheid in South Africa. Moreover, the Carter administration appeared to be heading generally in the right direction in Rhodesia. Therefore, these lobbies did not focus on Rhodesia. The exception was Trans-Africa, whose goal was to influence US policy toward Africa. TransAfrica, which would become powerful in the 1980s during the South African sanctions debates, cut its teeth on the Rhodesia issue. Inaugurated in late 1977 by Randall Robinson, an African American lawyer who had been administrative assistant to influential black Congressman Charles Diggs, it remained closely allied to the Congressional Black Caucus. It was nurtured by State Department and NSC officials who believed that it could be a useful voice. "I needed all the heat that Randall could generate," the NSC expert for Africa remembered.[58]

The State Department did more than encourage NGOs like TransAfrica to speak out. It also worked directly with friendly members of Congress and their staffs, shadowboxing the Rhodesian Information Office.

Where one might expect to find a locus of pressure on the White House about Rhodesia was the Congressional Black Caucus. Formed in 1970 by thirteen African American representatives "to promote the public welfare through legislation designed to meet the needs of millions of neglected citizens," the caucus had a direct tie to the Carter White House: Andrew Young had been its treasurer from 1972 through 1976. In September 1976, five weeks before Carter was elected president, Young had signed the caucus's "African-American Manifesto on Southern Africa," which had announced: "We, the descendants of Africa, . . . proclaim our unswerving commitment to immediate self-determination and majority rule in Southern Africa. We do this because we are African-Americans, and because we know that the destiny of Blacks in America and Blacks in Africa is inextricably intertwined, since racism and other forms of oppression respect no territories or boundaries."[59]

Nevertheless, the sixteen Black Caucus members did not focus on Africa. They were too busy trying to improve the lives of African Americans at home. (Young, had he stayed in Congress, might have encouraged more interest in Africa, and Charlie Diggs, chair of the Africa subcommittee and "a one man band in respect to Africa policy," would have focused more on Rhodesia, had he not been embroiled in a tawdry scandal involving payroll kickbacks.[60]) Moreover, Carter was slow to meet with the group, apparently ducking its requests for a meeting in May and June 1977 and not having a formal encounter until September 1977, after news broke that the black jobless rate had climbed to 14.5 percent, and amid turmoil over the president's reluctance to wholeheartedly support the Humphrey-Hawkins full employment bill (sponsored by caucus member Augustus Hawkins of California) and his lack of a clear stance against the challenge to affirmative action posed by the *Bakke* case being argued before the Supreme Court. In the summer of 1978, the Congressional Black Caucus members were almost silent during the debate on lifting the Rhodesian sanctions.

A Sharp Rebuke

On August 2, 1978, Robert Bauman (R-MD) opened the House debate on Ichord's version of the Helms Amendment in grandiose style. "There comes a time in the history of each nation that fundamental decisions must be made, a point which is commonly referred to . . . as a crossroads. There is no question," he asserted, that US policy toward Rhodesia would be seen "as indicative of the fundamental purpose and direction we as a nation will take in the future." Bauman framed the decision in the most redolent of terms: "Even those with but a cursory knowledge of history remember . . . Munich. Ever after Neville Chamberlain's name will be associated with . . . appeasement. We today have to make a decision about whether or not we are going to continue a policy in Africa which . . . has failed miserably."[61]

Bauman had put his finger on one aspect of the debate that was about to rock the House. The discussion was, in part, about appeasement's inverse: containment. It was about how to assess and counter the communist threat. Bauman and his supporters argued that the White House, in the thrall of Andrew Young, was cavorting with communist terrorists and refusing to acknowledge the enormous strides that the internal settlement represented. The Salisbury accord, Bauman asserted, reflected "more significant peaceful progress toward change than has occurred in any African state."[62]

Be it sinister or naive, Carter's policy was dangerous, in the opinion of Bauman and his supporters. John Ashbrook (R-OH), who slammed the administration's Africa policy as "absolutely disgusting" and "ridiculous," introduced a complaint that would stick: the Carter administration, he exclaimed, was pursuing "détente with our enemies but a cold shoulder for those who would be our friends."[63] The debate in the House was cast in stark terms: communism versus freedom.

Democrats Clement Zablocki of Wisconsin, chair of the International Relations Committee, and Steven Solarz of New York, who had strategized with State Department officials prior to the debate, argued that Bauman and his supporters had framed the discussion incorrectly. Everyone was opposed to communism; the question was how best to deny the communists opportunity in southern Africa. Zablocki and Solarz asserted that the administration's policy was the most effective way to minimize communist influence. Moreover, the internal settlement was not "freedom": it did not represent fundamental change, as Rhodesia's black majority still faced "the same army, the same police, the same civil servants, and even the same Smith parading around." Therefore, lifting sanctions would be "premature," a word used by almost every member in this camp.[64]

Differing ideas about how to combat the communist threat and about what constituted adequate racial progress stirred deep passions: there were so many interruptions from the gallery that the chair had to call for order, and one member was forced to retract offensive comments. Late in the day, the voting began. First, a strongly anti-administration amendment stipulating that sanctions be lifted immediately was defeated. This seemed to clear the path for Zablocki's substitute amendment, which was almost identical to the Senate's Case-Javits, but Ichord maneuvered to have his amendment considered first. Ichord's proposal called for sanctions to be lifted on December 31, 1978—immediately after the scheduled elections in Rhodesia. It added that the president could choose to reimpose sanctions, but only if elections had not been held. That is, unlike Case-Javits, Ichord did not leave the decision to lift sanctions in the president's hands, he did not mention the need for Salisbury to participate in all-party talks, and he did not require international observers at the elections.

In what the *Washington Post* called "a sharp rebuke to the Carter administration," the Ichord Amendment passed decisively, 229 to 180. The Carter administration lost more than a third of the 292 Democrats in the House. Half of the 102 Democrats who voted for Ichord were from the South, but the remainder represented almost every other state in the union. Only a dozen Republicans, almost all of whom were well-established liberals from mid-Atlantic states, crossed the aisle to vote against Ichord. The House, the *Washington Post* declared in a blistering editorial on August 3, had gone "off half-cocked."[65]

In Conference

It was, however, a one-week wonder. Immediately after the vote on Ichord, Vance assured Carter that the State Department was working with senators Clark, Javits, and Case as well as Congressman Solarz, all of whom would serve on the conference committee, "to preserve as much as possible of the flexibility allowed us in the Senate version." In the margin of Vance's report, Carter wrote: "Important. Fritz [Mondale] & I will help." From the State Department, Dick Moose and Tony Lake then offered Solarz "suggested language" and worked with him to draft a compromise resolution. This resolution, Warren Christopher wrote Carter on August 8, "would preserve the substance of the Senate version but give something to the House."[66]

The conference committee, which met on August 10, was tilted in favor of Case-Javits. Chaired by Zablocki, its nineteen members skewed liberal.[67] Clark took the lead arguing fervently for preserving the language of Case-Javits, and Zablocki agreed. "I would hope that . . . we would hold very close, as close as we can, to that language," Zablocki said. "It seems to me that if we go very far from it, I don't think it is too much to say for all intents and purposes it is the destruction of this Administration's policy in southern Africa." Nonetheless, Zablocki knew that the committee had to acknowledge that "the Ichord amendment was accepted by a very substantial margin [in the House]. So we must come back with something that the proponents for lifting the embargo support." Zablocki faced a challenge: US policy toward the internal settlement in Rhodesia was "a very political, emotionally charged issue."[68]

Solarz whipped out the compromise language. His amendment stipulated that sanctions against Rhodesia would be lifted when the president determined that the government of Rhodesia had fulfilled two conditions (1) "demonstrated its willingness to negotiate at an all parties conference" and (2) installed "a government which is chosen by free elections under international auspices." His draft added language to mollify the opponents, but it maintained the crux of Case-Javits: the president would decide when to lift sanctions. Case congratulated Solarz on "an extraordinarily fine effort," and the compromise language was accepted. Vance was pleased: "I think we have managed to construct a compromise version which embodies the essence of all of these essential provisions of the Case-Javits amendment . . . and it would also fly on the floor of the House," he wrote Carter. "We are satisfied with the conference action."[69]

On September 11, 1978, the Senate adopted the bill in a voice vote with no debate. The House debated the Foreign Assistance Act, with all its amendments, the following day. Toward the end of a long debate, the Rhodesia amendment came up. It was dispatched with quickly. A handful of representatives protested, but the vote to accept it was decisive: 225 to 126. The critics of Carter's policy had drawn some blood, they had waved a caution flag at the White House, but they did not want to expend political capital in a pyrrhic attempt to force the conference committee to change its decision.[70]

At the end of the year, Brzezinski opined that Congress had cast four key foreign policy votes in 1978, and Case-Javits was one of them. (The others were the Panama Canal treaties, arms sales to the Middle East, and the lifting of the arms embargo on Turkey that had been imposed following Turkey's 1974 intervention in Cyprus.) The passage of the Case-Javits amendment was significant in several ways. First, as the *Economist* noted, it was evidence that US policy toward Rhodesia had become "snared in domestic politics." The British weekly added: "Ask the average American to find Zimbabwe (or even Rhodesia) on the map, and he is almost sure to be baffled. . . . Yet letters-to-the-editor columns of American newspapers have, in recent weeks, been packed with pleadings of the Rhodesian issue, generally taking the position that the Carter administration should . . . put its prestige behind the internal settlement." This marked a significant change. "For nearly two years, Africa had been that part of the world where the new administration seemed to have the greatest foreign policy flexibility."[71] That had changed. By late summer, southern Africa had become terrain where liberals and conservatives would spar, define themselves, and build coalitions.

Second, the passage of Case-Javits shed light on the complexity of the Carter administration's relations with Congress. Even though not one member of either chamber had warm relations with the president, the administration won most—70 percent—of its battles with Congress. This was in part because there were Democratic majorities in both chambers, and many members supported the president's policies. But it was also because many Carter administration officials, in the White House and in the State Department, compensated for the president's lacunae. Unlike Carter, these men and women were intimately familiar with the subtleties of the congressional process and they enjoyed maneuvering through them. This was evident in the behind-the-scenes crafting of the language of Case-Javits, both in its original Senate form and in conference. The solid teamwork among administration officials, Senator Clark, and Representative Solarz belies the common complaint that the Carter administration had bad relations with Congress. Reality was more complicated: Carter himself was not beloved by members of Congress, but his policies had strong adherents, and his administration included officials who knew how to work the system.[72]

Third, by kicking the ball down the road—by putting off the day when sanctions would be lifted—the passage of Case-Javits set the stage for the drama of 1979. For the administration, it was a defensive victory. It had avoided an outcome—mandatory lifting of sanctions—that would have derailed its entire African policy. It had been saved from disaster by skillful behind-the-scenes maneuvers, but it had exposed its vulnerability. Frank Moore warned:

"We are going to face some very difficult decisions on Rhodesia over the next six months."[73]

The passage of Case-Javits sent a chill through the regime in Salisbury. The Rhodesian Ministry of Foreign Affairs noted: "Perhaps the aspect of the motion which should give rise to most concern is that it gives the final power of determination that the conditions have been met to the President of the United States." This was ominous because "President Carter has demonstrated that his African policy is guided by a belief that the views of radical African states are of prime importance, and by a State Department which is implacably opposed to the Salisbury Agreement." This was particularly unwelcome news, given the deteriorating situation on the ground in Rhodesia. "The scene is more than sombre," Rhodesian intelligence chief Ken Flower announced at a high-level meeting in Salisbury on August 3. "It's pretty desperate and needs desperate remedies. . . . The Patriotic Front . . . is gaining support. . . . The security situation has never been so desperate."[74]

David Owen's Gambit, the End

Cyrus Vance did not mince words: the meeting between Ian Smith and Joshua Nkomo was a "fiasco." After weeks of elaborate and closely guarded preparations, the two men met in secret on August 14 at the State Lodge on the outskirts of Lusaka, Zambia. President Kaunda and Nigerian foreign minister Joseph Garba also attended. (General Garba brought Nigerian clout to the table.) The initial reports were encouraging: "The atmosphere was good but the meeting was brief," an NSC staffer informed Brzezinski.[75]

During the clandestine meeting, Smith and Nkomo focused on how to proceed to a second encounter at which more comprehensive matters would be discussed. "The meeting was exploratory," Jack Gaylard, the Rhodesian cabinet secretary who accompanied Smith, wrote. "PM [Prime Minister Smith] probed Nkomo regarding basis on which he would return [to Rhodesia]." Although details of a government that included Nkomo were not discussed, two points were clear. "After much sparring Garba eventually said Nkomo must have preferential place as permanent chairman of ExCo [Executive Council] during interim period. Nkomo confirmed this and said he would not come in without Mugabe. PM [Smith] . . . asked whether Mugabe would accept second fiddle to Nkomo. Nkomo said several times that he would have no problem with Mugabe." Gaylard explained: "[The] plan was for Garba to take Mugabe to Lagos to be 'persuaded' by [Nigerian head of state Olusegun] Obesanjo [sic]." After Mugabe had been "persuaded," he and Nkomo would meet with Smith, and the details would be hashed out.[76]

The gathering seemed promising—to the participants. But it left Smith's black partners out in the cold. Muzorewa and Sithole knew that their shaky hold on power would evaporate if Smith brought Nkomo into the internal settlement. Not only were relations between the bishop and Nkomo frosty— "Muzorewa should go back to the church," Nkomo had quipped to West German chancellor Helmut Schmidt in June—but the overture to Nkomo was proof of Smith's disillusionment with his black partners, who had failed to deliver on their promise to end the war. This broken promise "shows how slippery and inconsistent they are," an exasperated Smith fumed. (Chirau wielded little weight and might have stayed in an Nkomo-led government.)[77]

On August 31, Muzorewa and Sithole counterattacked. "In an obvious effort to head off another meeting [between Smith and Nkomo]," Vance wrote Carter, "representatives of Muzorewa and Sithole revealed publicly yesterday that Smith and Nkomo met."[78]

This was a bombshell. No one had informed the other Frontline presidents or Robert Mugabe about the meeting before it occurred. David Owen blamed the Nigerians, Nkomo, and Kaunda for this "big mistake." He explained that none of them had wanted to tell Mugabe or Mozambique's Samora Machel, and that Garba had promised to inform Tanzania's Julius Nyerere. "I was apprehensive," Owen remembered, but when he had suggested sending a British diplomat to speak with Nyerere, Garba had gotten "very upset. . . . There were limits to what we [the British] could do."[79]

When Mugabe found out about the meeting, he was "incensed," Ambassador Low reported to Washington from Mozambique. "He blamed the U.K. and did not exonerate the U.S. or Nkomo." The whole affair had an air of déjà vu for Mugabe: he had been arguing with Nkomo since 1963 about the advisability of negotiating with Smith, and his mistrust of Kaunda had deep roots. "Zambia needs South African goods," Mugabe had written in 1974. "So we did not trust Kaunda, especially not since he is a friend of Nkomo and trying to raise him to be our equal." A year later, Mugabe's seething contempt for Kaunda had deepened; following the assassination of Herbert Chitepo, a ZANU leader, in 1975, the Zambian president had banned ZANU and arrested 1,660 of its members, including most of its top leaders. On BBC radio in January 1976, Mugabe had said, "I think President Kaunda has been the principal factor in slowing down our revolution." That Nkomo, Kaunda, and Smith were up to their old tricks infuriated Mugabe, but it did not surprise him.[80]

Samora Machel summoned the US ambassador in Maputo, Willard DePree. "He chewed me out," DePree remembered. "He felt he'd been double-crossed." Machel delivered what the US ambassador deemed an eighty-minute "harangue that was the most hard-hitting public attack on US/UK diplomatic efforts since beginning the Anglo-American initiative." The speech was much more than an attack on American and British policy. It was an analysis of imperialism in southern Africa that recalled Machel's criticism of Andrew Young's speech in Maputo in 1977. It explained why the Smith/Nkomo meeting had confirmed Machel's darkest suspicions about Western imperialism. The West had never supported the liberation struggle, Machel asserted, and it had used two strategies to destroy it. First, "Western propaganda tries to reduce the conflict to a racial struggle. This masks the true struggle for national liberation, for structural economic transformation." This fundamental misreading of the war allowed the West to position itself as "the enemy of white minority racist regimes, but the protector of white settler lives and property." Second, with the Smith/Nkomo talks, the West had tried to breathe new life into the internal settlement and thereby maintain the status quo. "The main objective of imperialist action is not to overthrow Smith," Machel declared. "The main objective of imperialism is to destroy the liberation movement."[81]

Nyerere was also irate. At a meeting of the Frontline presidents on September 2, the fragile edifice of Anglo-American diplomacy in southern Africa seemed to crumble as the Frontline imploded. "Nyerere as usual dominated [the] proceedings," Steve Low commented. The Tanzanian president delivered a jeremiad: Nkomo and Kaunda had "sold out to the imperialists." They had played into Smith's attempt to divide the Patriotic Front. "Smith had come out to get Nkomo," he charged. "There is nothing of value to be had from any more secret meetings with Smith."[82]

Nyerere was acting like a "prima donna," a Nigerian who attended the meeting fumed. The Tanzanian's accusations had made Nkomo "livid." Nkomo, Kaunda, and Garba asserted that "Smith had been serious," and that by objecting to any further meetings with Smith, "Nyerere and Machel had wrecked a golden opportunity." It meant that "the best opportunity for a peaceful transfer of power had been lost." Kaunda, according to Low, "was speechless with anger."[83]

Dick Moose's report about the Frontline meeting to Vance, who was at Camp David participating in the Egyptian-Israeli peace talks, pulled no punches. "All the major actors are now in disarray. . . . The prospects for achieving an early peace in Rhodesia [have been set back.] . . . The fear of a civil war [ZANU vs. ZAPU] is real and justified." For the remainder of the year, Moose predicted, the war would escalate and the internal settlement would weaken.[84]

On September 6, 1978, the day Moose wrote Vance, the situation worsened. Air Rhodesia Flight 825, a Viscount turboprop flying from Victoria Falls to Salisbury, was shot down by a Soviet SAM-7 missile. There were eighteen survivors, but thirty-eight passengers, almost all of whom were vacationing white Rhodesians, were killed instantly. Nkomo, humiliated by the rhetorical blows of Nyerere and Machel, immediately claimed responsibility on behalf of ZAPU for the downing of the Viscount.

But then the situation took a ghoulish turn, as reports surfaced that the eighteen survivors of the crash had been beset by "guerrillas" who massacred ten of them, including seven women and two children. Nkomo denied that ZAPU fighters had been involved in these atrocities, but since he had claimed responsibility for shooting down the plane, the Western press did not believe his denial. Deepening the damage to his image, during an interview with BBC radio about the murder of the survivors, Nkomo made a noise that sounded like laughter. He was belligerent in the face of the ensuing outrage: "You forget that the regime kills 30 of our people a day," he told a journalist. "So the life of a black person is different from a white person. A European child is supposed to be worth a million blacks."[85]

Ian Smith publicly called Nkomo a "monster" and hurriedly cabled South African Prime Minister Vorster, seizing the opportunity to ask for "stronger support in the security field." Smith assured Vorster that "this would certainly have the full support of black Exco [Executive Committee] members [Muzorewa, Sithole, and Chirau]." Smith was forthright about his desperate straits: his black "partners" were feckless, and Nkomo was beyond the pale. "Situation here which had already become serious because of continued failure of black . . . colleagues to live up to their optimistic promises to achieve ceasefire has taken a dramatic turn for the worse. . . . Viscount atrocity . . . has raised serious doubts about majority rule and handing over to such people."[86]

Vorster had a more pressing matter on his mind. On September 20, he announced that he was resigning for "health reasons," while in fact he was dodging the simmering information scandal that was about to scorch him. "Muldergate," named for South African minister for information Connie Mulder, would boil over in November, exposing the South African government's illegal funding of a covert propaganda war since 1973 that had involved attempts to bribe domestic and foreign journalists (some at the *Washington Post*), surreptitiously buy media outlets (including a failed bid for the *Washington Star*), fund travel of "opinion makers" to South Africa (including Congressman Richard Ichord), and siphon money to US political campaigns.[87]

The British government, meanwhile, was reeling from its own "-gate," a scandal that the press dubbed "Rhodesiagate." A year earlier, Parliament had established a commission, led by lawyer Thomas Bingham, to investigate whether British oil companies had violated the UN sanctions against Rhodesia. In September 1978, the "shabby story," as the London *Times* called it, was made public: from 1966 to 1977, oil giants BP and Shell (which were owned in part by the British government) had illegally supplied Ian Smith's regime with more than half its total oil. Even worse, the highest levels of the British government had known about it and done nothing to stop it. "We were doing everything possible to avoid a confrontation with South Africa," Michael Stewart, who had been foreign secretary in 1968, explained a decade later. The credibility of Prime Minister Callaghan, who had served as foreign secretary from 1974 to 1976, took a beating.[88]

Given the preoccupation of the British and South African governments, the flaring tempers among the Frontline States and Patriotic Front, and the heightened sensitivities toward Rhodesia in the US Congress, the State Department decided on September 16, 1978, to wait to launch any new initiative "until the dust of the current upheaval settles." Neither side was desperate enough, yet, to negotiate. The Patriotic Front, especially Mugabe's ZANU, seemed willing to wage a long war of attrition, and the Salisbury Four were buttressed by increasing South African support. The Americans and British, therefore, decided that all-party talks would remain their "ultimate goal" but would not be their "immediate objective." Instead, Washington and London would simply try to narrow the yawning gap between the parties.[89]

Pushed Back into the Fray

The Carter administration could not afford to disengage from events in Rhodesia. In Zambia, President Kaunda was increasingly vulnerable, and the Cubans were waiting in the wings.

An emotional man at all times, President Kaunda was under intense pressure. Not only had Frontline unity fractured because of the Nkomo/Smith meeting he had hosted, but his country was in a financial and security crisis; he was facing his first serious electoral challenge on December 12, 1978; and his opponent's main line of attack was that Zambia was sacrificing too much for the liberation struggle in Rhodesia. In the summer of 1978, the NSC had noted that "Rhodesian forces have been operating inside Zambia's southern border with near impunity. . . . Kaunda . . . is outraged, frustrated, and probably a bit desperate." The Zambian government had imposed a curfew and blackout on Zambia's cities. Kaunda wrote British Prime Minister Callaghan on September 19 to request an urgent meeting. "Kaunda was in a very emotional state. . . . It was imperative to prevent him [Kaunda] taking some drastic action [that is, turning to the Soviet bloc]," Callaghan explained to his Cabinet before flying to Nigeria to meet with Kaunda. (Kaunda asked if Cyrus Vance or Andrew Young would join, but Carter demurred. "We should stay out of this meeting," he wrote Vance. The United States did send an extra $500,000 in aid to Zambia, and it convinced the International Committee of the Red Cross to send $1 million.)[90]

Three days later, Kaunda implored Callaghan for additional economic and military aid. He feared that the Rhodesian attacks deep into Zambia were going to increase, which "could eventually force Zambia to seek Cuban and Soviet military support." Callaghan offered economic aid, but he was able to extend only limited military assistance without the consent of the Cabinet. Upon his return to London, the Cabinet offered its "full support for the offers of help" to Kaunda but cautioned that "we should need to take great care not to . . . become militarily involved in Rhodesia."[91] Kaunda had worried that the British government would balk at providing heavy equipment because of his reliance on Soviet and Cuban aid to support Nkomo's ZAPU guerrillas in Zambia. Upon his return to Lusaka after meeting with Callaghan, Kaunda asked Nkomo to get the Cubans to downplay their assistance to ZAPU in Zambia. He agreed to a "sleight of hand" which would label the Cuban instructors at ZAPU camps in Zambia as members of a medical mission rather than military officers.[92]

The Americans' anxieties were exacerbated by a series of high-level US secret conversations with the Cubans in which Havana had insisted that its policy in Africa was none of Washington's business. It was "a complete impasse," David Aaron reported after one meeting.[93] The Carter administration knew that Cubans were training ZAPU guerrillas in Zambia, Angola, and Cuba. In May 1978, it reported at a NATO meeting that "due largely to Soviet/Cuban efforts, Nkomo's ZAPU forces have been rapidly enlarged." The CIA reported—erroneously—that the Cubans had begun training ZANU insurgents in Ethiopia, as well as delivering arms to them in Mozambique.[94] In September, Fidel Castro appeared again in Africa, attending the Afro-Arab Solidarity Conference in Addis Ababa, where he delivered a speech that "condemned the US-UK plan [for Rhodesia] in unprecedentedly harsh terms," according to US intelligence, and declared that Cuba's "resolute cooperation" with the Patriotic Front would continue.[95] The *New York Times* drew a foreboding conclusion: "In the same way that Premier Fidel Castro's trip to Africa last year led to Cuban intervention in the Horn of Africa, his recent journey . . . seems to portend a deepening Cuban involvement in the Rhodesian conflict."[96]

Under these pressures, the CIA posited that it might be worthwhile to reinvigorate the Anglo-American negotiations. "Although the short term outlook for further Rhodesian settlement negotiations is not good," it noted drily on September 20, the leaders of the government in Salisbury and of the Patriotic Front remained "interested in talks because of the shortcomings of their military positions." The Rhodesian army was unable to stop the guerrillas from infiltrating into Rhodesia and operating virtually freely within it because the size of the guerrilla armies was growing: the CIA estimated that the Patriotic Front could call on 59,000 troops.[97] Mugabe, Nkomo, and the Frontline presidents, on the other hand, were open to negotiations because they thought it would take two or three more years for the guerrillas to win the war. Fighting for several more years would not only imperil Kaunda and strain Machel; it would also destroy the infrastructure of Rhodesia and risk the internationalization of the war.

There was another reason for the Carter administration to reenter the fray. On September 14, twenty-seven senators, led by Jesse Helms, had invited Ian Smith to Washington "to put his case directly to the American people." Helms hoped that Smith's presence would boost support for the internal settlement, and he knew that the invitation would put the Carter administration in an awkward situation: granting Smith a visa would violate UN sanctions on Rhodesia, which required member states to bar entry to anyone traveling on a Rhodesian passport who had "furthered or encouraged the unlawful actions of the illegal [Rhodesian] regime." If Ian Smith did not fit that description, no one did. (Muzorewa, Sithole, and Chirau were exempt from this ban because they had never supported the illegal UDI regime.) Smith had not left his country since the UDI, except to attend meetings in South Africa or the 1976 Geneva Conference. The Callaghan government had denied him a visa. If Washington decided to let Smith in, it would break international law as well as upset black Africans, the British government, and American liberals, including African Americans. It was, as the Baltimore *Afro-American* asserted, "a major diplomatic hot potato."[98]

The State Department opposed granting a visa to Smith. An NSC staffer wrote Brzezinski that Andrew Young's deputy, Don McHenry, predicted "more or less, the end of the world if we give a visa to Smith." The staffer then advised Brzezinski, "You should take a hand; there are important domestic political aspects that may outweigh the foreign policy concerns." Helms would have a heyday if the administration appeared to be unwilling to let Americans hear what Ian Smith wanted to say; it would be a violation of free speech. Since the administration had issued a visa to Nkomo—"the Soviet-backed guerrilla who has brazenly claimed responsibility for shooting down a commercial jetliner," as Senator Orrin Hatch (R-UT) put it—denying Smith entry would strengthen the perception that Carter preferred terrorists to moderates. Muzorewa had also received a visa. A journalist asked the State Department spokesman why the black bishop had received better treatment than Smith. "Is it the fact that he [Smith] has the wrong skin color?"[99]

Dwindling Black Support

The November midterm election season was in full swing while the administration was debating whether to grant Ian Smith a visa. This muffled the voices of the liberals in Congress who might otherwise have loudly opposed letting Smith visit the United States. Senator Clark and Representative Solarz, for example, did not want to be tarred as lovers of communist terrorists a mere month before the midterms. The NAACP, TransAfrica, and the National Conference of Black Lawyers wrote the White House to urge it not to give Smith a visa, but it was not the most important issue on their agendas.[100]

Carter had four problems maintaining the support of African Americans. First, hopes among many blacks had been so high after the 1976 election that Carter was bound to be a disappointment. Second, the US economy was in recession and unemployment was high, especially among young blacks. Third, Carter was a fiscal conservative, loath to expand social programs. And finally, Carter believed that the civil rights struggle had achieved its fundamental goals—some tinkering might be necessary, but the playing field was essentially level.

Black leaders and many liberals disagreed passionately with the president. They "are coming to view him as a kind of skinflint, a warmed-over Gerald Ford on domestic issues," columnist Meg Greenfield wrote in the *Washington Post*. Fellow *Post* columnist William Raspberry added: "He certainly campaigned 'blacker' than he is administering." As Young told a Cabinet meeting, "Many Americans view the term 'balanced budget' as a code word. . . . To them it means anti-poor and anti-black." In 1978, Carter met more frequently with minority leaders than he had in his first year, but the fundamental problems remained and festered.[101]

Carter's fiscal conservatism clashed with his commitment to the civil rights struggle. African Americans, who had greeted Carter's election with high hopes, were deeply disappointed by his failure to effectively address the domestic issues—unemployment and poverty—that mattered most to them. Carter countered that he appointed more black federal judges than any previous president, that he had stood firm on the principle of affirmative action, that he sent his daughter to a desegregated public school, that he had used the bully pulpit to support civil rights, and that he had pursued a progressive policy in Africa. But he stubbornly refused to expand the Great Society programs created by the Johnson administration a decade earlier. Andrew Young's explanation of why Carter was more progressive in his foreign than his domestic policy was succinct: "It's simple. Because at home it costs money, and Carter inherited a country in debt. He did everything he could do—that didn't cost money."[102]

By September 1978, when the administration was debating the Smith visa issue, tensions between Carter and the Congressional Black Caucus erupted on national television. The caucus felt that Carter should capitalize on his momentum from the successfully concluded Camp David negotiations to put his full weight behind the Humphrey-Hawkins Full Employment Act in the congressional session scheduled to end on October 14. Carter feared that the bill—which committed the government to reducing unemployment to 4 percent within four years—would be inflationary, and he hesitated. On September 20, Congressional Liaison Frank Moore told him that caucus chair Parren Mitchell (D-MD) felt "intense anger" toward Carter. "[He] has indicated that he can no longer support the President. . . . He feels the President has not been a full partner with the Black Caucus." Moore explained why this mattered: "Parren's support is important to the administration. . . . The Caucus considers him their leader and takes his lead. Currently, however, he feels let down and left out. . . .You need to reinstate the faith he had in you."[103]

Five days later, on September 25, Carter met with the caucus members at the White House. The president intended to talk first about Africa, but Moore explained that employment and job creation were "the two most important issues, and the two with which the Caucus will spend the majority of their time." Indeed they were. The ensuing discussion between the fiscally conservative president and the disappointed caucus members grew so heated that Michigan representative John Conyers stormed out in anger—under the glare of the television lights. All three networks' evening news programs described the tumultuous meeting, which had included, ABC reported, "a shouting match."[104]

In the wake of this meeting, the Congressional Black Caucus issued a six-page review of the Carter administration's "achievements and shortcomings." Of twelve categories, only one concerned foreign affairs. It gave Carter credit for lifting the Byrd Amendment, opposing the internal settlement in Rhodesia, and appointing Andrew Young, but it criticized his failure to harden the US stance toward South Africa and to provide sufficient foreign aid to black Africa. The overwhelming focus of the document was the unemployment crisis. (The unemployment rate dipped in 1978, but the gap between black and white unemployment rates widened: in July 1978, 13 percent of blacks were unemployed versus 5 percent of whites.)[105]

When Carter met again with the caucus on September 29 in an attempt to mend fences, he had mellowed. He promised to press for the passage of Humphrey-Hawkins. The following night, he spoke at the caucus's annual convention. Conyers boycotted the event, and although the audience applauded the president's speech, the *Washington Post* noted that "later they grumbled . . . [that] the administration has shortchanged the pivotal black vote of 1976." Late in the night, Stevie Wonder stole the show, singing a ballad with the refrain "For a country that's the richest country in the world—four percent [the target unemployment rate of Humphrey-Hawkins] . . . that's the thing that I call bullsh--." The crowd roared.[106]

It was against this backdrop that the Smith visa debate occurred, and the Congressional Black Caucus members paid it little heed. They made it clear that they opposed issuing the visa, but they had more pressing matters, including the midterm elections, on their minds.

On October 2, Minority Leader Howard Baker stood in the well of the Senate and called the administration's delay in granting Smith a visa "unconscionable." Senator Hayakawa added, "What we are witnessing is an incredible display of spinelessness and pusillanimity." The two Washington newspapers, the *Post* and the *Star*, agreed that the State Department was continuing to "dawdle disgracefully."[107]

Assistant Secretary Moose came up with an elegant way to sidestep the Smith visa problem. It was a long shot, but worth trying: if Smith entered the United States to attend all-party talks, granting him a visa would not violate the UN sanctions. Smith had, after all, traveled to Geneva to attend the talks in 1976. Why not New York in 1978? Cabling the ambassadors in the Frontline States on October 2, the State Department admitted that the attempt to hold talks might fail, but the slower, step-by-step process of narrowing the differences between the parties "would take more time than the urgency of the situation now permits."[108]

It took less than twenty-four hours for Machel and Nyerere to nix the idea. All-party talks "would be fruitless," Nyerere explained. Worse, they would be "a ready made forum to show the reasonableness of Smith . . . and . . . the inflexibility of the Patriotic Front." Before talks could be held, Nyerere wanted to be more sure of Smith's intentions. "Smith is the stumbling block. He is the millstone around all our necks."[109]

Welcome, Mr. Smith

The White House regrouped. Further delay in deciding whether or not to give Smith a visa would only invite more criticism. Vance feared that a refusal would prompt "an emotional response" in Congress and could add fuel to the effort to lift sanctions. Jesse Helms had already threatened to hold up the confirmations of three ambassadors. Granting a visa to Smith was, Vance said, "an agonizing decision for the President . . . a decision he wished he could have avoided making."[110]

On October 4, the State Department announced that it would issue a visa for Ian Smith "because we believe the visit can contribute to the process of achieving a settlement of the Rhodesian conflict."[111] (A standard business visa, not a diplomatic one, was issued.)

Smith was ebullient. This was "the biggest diplomatic coup since UDI," an official exclaimed in Salisbury. The mainstream US press was more subdued, but it supported the administration's decision. "Welcome, Mr. Smith," the *Washington Post* declared.[112]

Landing in Washington on October 7, Smith was accompanied by Ndabaningi Sithole. The lean, dour white man and the rotund, jolly black man made a potent symbolic statement, and Sithole softened Smith's sharp, abrasive edges. The duo was immediately whisked to an estate owned by the American Security Council, a conservative group that had helped organize and fund their two-week visit, where Smith addressed a select crowd: "It seems the leaders of the Free World are siding with the Marxist terrorists," he declared. Smith met with Henry Kissinger, who said afterward that the internal settlement should be "given a chance." On October 8, Smith and Sithole appeared on *Meet the Press*. Asserting that the internal settlement fulfilled all the demands that Kissinger had made in 1976 and that it implemented the principle of "one man, one vote," Smith asked plaintively, "What more do the Americans want us to do?"[113]

On October 9, Vance answered that question. In a tense meeting at the State Department, he informed Smith and Sithole that the Carter administration wanted them to agree to attend all-party talks. Smith said only that "he would think about it." Smith repeated again and again that the United States should support the internal settlement. When the Americans pointed out that violence in Rhodesia had intensified after the internal settlement had been declared, Smith responded that "the reason for this was that the Patriotic Front had Russian support whereas the transitional government had no support."[114] Summing up the two-hour encounter, a State Department spokesman said it had been a "meeting with all the bark off. Both sides expressed their points of view very clearly and very forcefully. There was no progress made." The *New York Times* reported that Smith appeared "crestfallen" after the meeting. Asked if he was disappointed, Smith replied, "Yes, whenever I don't get my way, I am disappointed."[115]

Other disappointments awaited Smith. President Carter refused to see him. Twenty-seven senators had signed the letter inviting him to Washington, but for most of them—winding up a frenetically busy session—Ian Smith was not a priority; only ten senators showed up at the meeting on Capitol Hill to welcome him. And the mainstream US press, which had supported giving Smith a visa, was underwhelmed by the man himself, who seemed to be a vestige of a bygone era. This led some editorial writers to express sober criticism of the internal settlement.[116]

Meanwhile, Smith and Sithole were ushered around the country—to California (where they met with Ronald Reagan) and Texas—by the American Conservative Union and the American Security Council, the organizations backing them. They encountered scattered demonstrators, who yelled "Hitler rose! Hitler fell! Ian Smith, go to hell!," but most of the time security was so tight that not even the press knew where they were going to speak next.[117]

Upon his return to Washington, Smith met with the Senate Foreign Relations Committee. Aptly dubbed "the eel," Smith had changed his tune: of course he would attend all-party talks; he had always been open to them; Carter administration officials had misunderstood him. A surprised State Department decided to give it one more try. The timing was inconvenient because Cyrus Vance, Undersecretary David Newsom, and Assistant Secretary Dick Moose were in Pretoria for talks about Namibia, following which Vance was due to depart for Geneva and Moscow for SALT talks. Newsom and Moose abruptly flew back to Washington to meet, again, with Smith and Sithole. Chirau and Muzorewa had just arrived in Washington, and they too were invited to the State Department on October 20.

On the eve of the meeting, the Rhodesian armed forces launched raids deep into Mozambique and Zambia. It was the second major assault on Mozambique in a month, and even more ominously, it was the most brazen attack yet on Kaunda's vulnerable regime. The shooting down of the Air Rhodesia Viscount flight on September 6 and Nkomo's subsequent chuckle had changed the Rhodesians' strategy. Previously, they had focused their wrath on ZANU targets in Mozambique, launching more than 200 raids across that border, but they had left the ZAPU strongholds in Zambia relatively unmolested in order to keep open the possibility of some accommodation with Kaunda and Nkomo. But after the Viscount incident, the floodgates to Zambia were opened. For almost an hour, six Rhodesian jets accompanied by helicopters (and allegedly by South African Mirages) strafed, bombed, and dropped napalm on a camp twelve miles from Lusaka. Residents of the Zambian capital could hear the bombs falling. Approximately three hundred people were killed, and many more were wounded.[118]

The Rhodesians claimed that the target was Nkomo's headquarters and that Cubans had been killed there. Nkomo, however, asserted that the Rhodesians had attacked a camp for refugees and the sick, and the United Nations supported his claim. A UN spokesperson in Geneva said that the organization had visited the camp less than a month earlier, and it was indeed a haven for refugees.[119]

The raids continued: in four days of pitiless attacks on Zambia, whose army could mount no effective defense, the Rhodesians leveled three major camps and nine smaller ones. It was the deadliest series yet of cross-border incursions of the war. The Rhodesians killed an estimated 1,500 people, including several hundred young women training to be police and customs officers. Only one Rhodesian soldier was killed. The Salisbury Four expressed no regret. Smith said, with bravado, that he was "very happy" with the raids and that they would become "bigger and better" as long as the guerrilla war continued. They provided a "salutary lesson" to the terrorists in Zambia "for their continuing cowardly attacks on innocent Rhodesian civilians," Smith wrote. They were "even more successful than we anticipated."[120]

It was while Rhodesian planes were strafing Zambia and Mozambique that Smith extended an olive branch to the Americans. It was an old and familiar gambit, one that Richard Nixon had used as he juggled war and peace in Vietnam. Newsom and Moose, jet-lagged and jaded, could not be hopeful about the outcome of their meeting with Smith.[121]

The encounter at the State Department was chilly and businesslike. Newsom, third in seniority and serving as acting secretary of state in Cyrus Vance's and Warren Christopher's absence, began by saying that the Carter administration was "very disturbed" by the raids on Zambia and Mozambique and expressed its "strong objection" to them. Beyond the loss of life, the Americans were concerned that the raids would spur Machel to seek Cuban assistance. Newsom then asked Smith to confirm that he was willing to attend all-party talks. Smith did so, but the remainder of the two-hour meeting degenerated into acrimonious and fruitless arguments over issues large and small, past and present. Smith was "cold," Newsom remembered. "He made his *pro forma* statements, he trotted out the communist card, and I reiterated why it would be difficult for the United States to accept the internal settlement."[122]

From one perspective, Smith had gotten the better of the Americans: by agreeing to attend talks he had positioned himself to look like the reasonable party, and by authorizing the cross-border raids he had ensured that no talks would happen. As Smith knew they would, the raids drove the Patriotic Front and Frontline States from the table. "Forget about the whole damn thing," Nkomo told a reporter who asked about all-party talks. "How do you talk with these criminals who use napalm against us?"[123]

Smith squandered the goodwill he had hoped to gain in the United States: the brazen raids, launched while he was a guest on American soil, left a bitter aftertaste. Before Smith's arrival, Vance had expressed the hope that Smith's sojourn would expose the leader of Rhodesia "as a devious and deceitful man."[124] For many Americans, Vance's wish had come true.

11. Discerning Intentions

PRM 36: The Soviet/Cuban Presence in Africa

"State keeps me on the periphery," the NSC southern Africa expert Tom Thornton had complained to Zbigniew Brzezinski in the summer, when Joshua Nkomo was secretly meeting Ian Smith. The NSC was largely sidelined during the tumultuous events in Rhodesia in the summer and fall of 1978—Smith's meeting with Nkomo and his visit to the United States—and the State Department was in charge. Brzezinski admitted that he had been "out-manoeuvred by the State Department." It was the State Department that urged President Carter to order four agencies—State, Defense, NSC, and CIA—to develop a Presidential Review Memorandum about the "Soviet/Cuban Presence in Africa" that would provide a forum to air the disagreements about the subject and, Cyrus Vance bargained, allow the State Department's viewpoint to emerge as official policy.[1]

The draft memorandum, labeled PRM 36, was completed in August 1978 and debated throughout the fall. It laid out the dimensions of Soviet and Cuban penetration of Africa: it estimated that there were 15,000 Soviet and 45,000 Cuban military and civilian officials in Africa. The PRM noted that there were 20,000 Cuban soldiers in Angola; 17,000 in Ethiopia (this was inaccurate; there were about 12,000); and 500 military advisers in Mozambique. (The PRM overlooked the thousand Cuban soldiers in Congo-Brazzaville.) The Kremlin had inked military assistance agreements with twenty countries in sub-Saharan Africa totaling $2.3 billion, and it had negotiated friendship treaties with Ethiopia and Mozambique.[2]

That much was agreed, but determining Soviet intentions was "a subject of vigorous debate." The fundamental divide was between those who believed that the Kremlin was implementing "a grand design" and those who believed it was engaged in "a purely opportunistic exploitation of instability." The PRM managed to bridge this divide by establishing a consensus that "sub-Saharan

Africa . . . remains the most attractive region for expanding Soviet third world interests and influence." Whether Moscow was implementing a master plan or merely seizing opportunities, its "objectives in Africa have been relatively coherent and consistent over the years." The Kremlin sought to "diminish Western and Chinese influence while expanding its own," it sought access to military bases, and it hoped to expand trade.[3]

The PRM's analysis of Cuban motivations exposed more stark differences of opinion within the administration. "Some see Cuba as little more than a Soviet puppet. Others hold that Cuba is a self-directed nonaligned state dedicated to the defeat of imperialism." The latter view, centered in the State Department, dominated the PRM. "Soviet and Cuban objectives in Africa are harmonious but not necessarily synonymous. The Soviets and the Cubans have developed a symbiotic relationship. . . . Cuba is not involved in Africa solely or even primarily because of its relationship with the USSR. Rather, Havana's African policy reflects its activist revolutionary ethos and its determination to expand its own political influence in the Third World." The Defense Department lodged the lone dissent, but its argument that it was "misleading" to characterize Cuba as acting independently of the Soviet Union was relegated to a footnote.[4]

Having grappled with the extent of the problem, the PRM turned to what the United States should do about it. The White House had the means—military, covert, and economic—to punish the Soviets and the Cubans but chose not to deploy them because they would hurt US interests, appear to be disproportionate, or run counter to "current legislation and sentiment on the Hill."[5] Therefore, the administration stressed rhetoric and, in Cuba's case, halting progress toward normalization. All the agencies involved in the study were resigned to the fact that these tools had countered neither the Kremlin's ambitions nor Fidel Castro's messianic zeal. (There is no mention in the declassified record of the PRM about US covert aid to Jonas Savimbi, the Angolan guerrilla leader waging war against the Cuban-backed government in Luanda.)

The administration's admonitions to Soviet leaders and its muttering about the fate of the SALT talks had fallen on deaf ears. Anatoly Dobrynin, the seasoned Soviet ambassador in Washington, was unfazed by the president's occasional threats. In July 1978, he brushed off Carter's combative speech at the Naval Academy: "Carter frequently resorts to anti-Soviet rhetoric in order to, as they say, win cheap applause," he explained to Soviet foreign secretary Andrei Gromyko.[6]

The Cubans, likewise, had ignored Washington's attempts to influence their behavior in Africa. In the series of secret talks with high US officials, the Cubans had not budged: they categorically refused to negotiate their policy in Africa, even though the Americans repeatedly insisted that it was the main stumbling block toward improved relations. Moreover, Castro had emerged unscathed by the State Department's campaign to discredit his nonaligned credentials. At the Belgrade conference of nonaligned foreign ministers, held in late July 1978, "solidarity" had prevailed. "The attacks on Cuba's . . . non-aligned credentials have not impaired Cuba's leadership role in the movement," the State Department concluded. Castro mocked his critics at the conference, joking that they were "speaking with a Yankee accent." The drafters of the PRM were pessimistic about the administration's ability to effect change in Cuba. "Cuba is not likely to abandon its objectives in Africa easily or soon. . . . Our warnings to Havana . . . had no appreciable effect. . . . While the Cubans attach some value to improved relations with us, they attach even more to their political goals in Africa."[7]

The PRM was more optimistic about the long-term outlook in sub-Saharan Africa, where American influence, ideals, and business interests would ultimately triumph. "African nationalism," the memorandum declared, "would not allow a permanent Soviet domination."[8] The question, then, which was debated for months, was what to do in the short term. The basic issues had not changed: South Africa still had an apartheid system, Namibia was not independent, there were still Cubans in Angola, and Rhodesia was still governed by the white minority. On apartheid, there was a reluctant consensus that Washington needed to proceed slowly, but on the other three issues there was sharp disagreement.

In the autumn of 1978, the laborious negotiations that the State Department had been pursuing to dislodge South Africa from Namibia had reached a crisis point. In September, the South African government, after months of giving the Carter administration hope that it would agree to withdraw from Namibia, flatly refused to cooperate further with the negotiations. In Angola, Carter's move to normalize relations had hit a wall—a wall of Cuban soldiers. Carter was unwilling to recognize Angola while the Cuban troops remained, and Castro was unwilling to withdraw them until the Angolan president determined they were no longer needed to protect his country from the South Africans, whose army had never fully left southern Angola. It was an impasse. And in Rhodesia, the Anglo-American proposals were stalled, while the internal settlement had not dampened the war.[9]

The State Department espoused dealing with the Rhodesia, Namibia, and Angola problems discretely. To deal with the stasis in the Rhodesian negotiations, the State Department was united in advocating a vigorous and sustained effort to breathe new life into the Anglo-American proposals. To force South Africa to comply with the UN Security Council and International Court of Justice rulings that it cease its occupation of Namibia, Vance suggested imposing limited sanctions on Pretoria that would curb, for example, air travel and food imports. As for Angola, the State Department itself was divided. Some officials, led by Andrew Young, urged Carter to proceed with normalization despite the presence of the Cuban troops. These officials stressed that even the CIA admitted that the Cuban troops were "necessary to preserve Angolan independence" against the continuing threat posed by South Africa, and they predicted that US recognition would help Luanda lessen its reliance on Moscow and Havana. Others spoke against normalization and expressed the hope that the continuing talks with the Cubans would eventually persuade them to withdraw their troops.[10]

Brzezinski disagreed on all counts, not just on the specifics but also on the diagnosis. He believed it was a fundamental error to see the problems of southern Africa as separate. For Brzezinski, they were three manifestations of the same problem: Soviet adventurism. The real enemy was in Moscow (and its sidekick, Havana), not in Pretoria or Salisbury. Therefore, the key was to address the real culprits—the Soviet Union and Cuba—and not get bogged down in the details in Africa. Regarding Rhodesia, Brzezinski believed that since the administration's influence was limited, it should curtail its involvement there. He had scant interest in the Namibian negotiations, and he was vehemently opposed to any thaw in relations with Luanda, advocating instead raising the cost for the Cubans in Angola by covertly helping Jonas Savimbi's guerrilla movement.[11]

Brzezinski argued that the State Department's failure to correctly identify the root cause of the turmoil in southern Africa doomed all its proposed solutions. He would devote most energy to influencing the administration's policy toward Angola, but while the PRM was being hammered out, he also weighed in on Rhodesia. "An activist policy on behalf of a moderate solution"—a high-profile attempt to achieve a negotiated solution in Rhodesia—would fail, he asserted, unless the administration dealt with the "militant alternatives." That is, American policy in Rhodesia could not succeed until the Patriotic Front was convinced that it could never win on the battlefield. "That is why tolerating the Sov[iet]/Cuban presence has had such pernicious effects," Brzezinski explained. Furthermore, berating Pretoria and threatening to impose sanctions on it played into the hands of the Soviets—something "we don't want" to do.[12]

Brzezinski was caught in a dilemma. The paradox of embracing Soviet-armed Marxist guerrillas in order to counter the Kremlin's expansionist policies in Africa was, simply, a bridge too far for him. He did not believe it would work. Nor was he impressed with the internal settlement. He informed the British ambassador in Washington that "he was even more opposed to supporting the internal settlement than Andy Young." Brzezinski could not come up with a policy for Rhodesia that he considered viable; therefore, he wanted the administration to back off. He summed it up best himself in the subtitle of an analysis of the issue he sent the president: "If You Can't, Don't."[13]

The final draft of the PRM tackled Brzezinski's argument head-on: "To lower our profile . . . would be the surest way to open the doors to wider Soviet/ Cuban involvement." The PRM embraced the State Department's viewpoint emphatically. "Africa deserves a *higher* priority in our policy deliberations and in our assistance allocation," it asserted before reaffirming the administration's focus on southern Africa. "Our best tactic in this regard is to pursue our efforts toward achieving majority rule in southern Africa."[14]

Brzezinski remained unconvinced. On October 6, he tried to relitigate the issue at an NSC meeting on southern Africa chaired by Carter and attended by all the principals. If the administration was determined to give Africa such a high priority, then it must not maintain a narrow regional focus: it had to explicitly link US relations with the Soviets to their behavior in Africa. Otherwise, the policy was flaccid and would fail. "The President's prestige is involved," Brzezinski explained. He presented a stark choice: the administration could make Soviet policy in Africa "a major issue in our relations with them . . . [or] we should slowly and subtly lower our level of involvement [in Africa]."[15]

Vance told Brzezinski he was wrong. "There is a third way," he said, "and that is bringing about peaceful solutions. We should continue along that route."[16]

Vance prevailed because this was also the president's opinion. Carter had given Africa high priority from the beginning of his presidency, and despite setbacks his conviction that southern Africa merited high-level attention had not wavered. Carter knew full well that it was not a popular decision, but he was convinced that it was necessary: war in southern Africa would threaten the fabric of the United States. Just a week before the NSC meeting, he had told Soviet foreign minister Andrei Gromyko, "The most serious threat to good relations between us and the Soviet Union . . . resulted from Soviet activities in Africa . . . even more threatening was the dispute concerning Rhodesia. . . . If there were any Soviet military involvement in the area, that could have very serious consequences," Carter warned.[17] This helps explain his decision not to lower the US profile in southern Africa, despite Brzezinski's argument. Carter still believed what he had told Nigeria's General Olusegun Obasanjo several months earlier: "I concluded that it was in our interest to become more involved with Africa than perhaps the American people would currently wish to be."[18]

At the conclusion of the October 6 NSC meeting, Carter ordered the State Department to try once again to persuade all parties in Rhodesia to agree to the Anglo-American plan. Although he advised Vance to reassure the South

Africans that "our intentions towards South Africa are not hostile," he also talked vaguely of getting "a process started on apartheid."[19]

In contrast to the NSC meeting on southern Africa of March 1977, this gathering had a sober and contentious tone. Brzezinski believed that US policy in Rhodesia was likely to fail because the Soviet-backed guerrillas would never surrender, and it was therefore foolish to squander the president's prestige on it. It would be better to behave as though Rhodesia were a marginal theater and focus instead on countering the Soviets and Cubans in Angola and Namibia. Carter and Vance, by contrast, believed that US policy in Rhodesia could succeed and that it was essential to keep trying because Rhodesia was a pivotal Cold War theater. Carter's conclusions were strikingly similar to those he had reached fifteen months earlier: southern Africa mattered and the United States should stay engaged on all fronts. Having failed to convince the president to disengage from Rhodesia, Brzezinski took his own advice: while he continued to voice his misgivings on the subject he lowered his profile in discussions about implementing the Anglo-American accords.

A Sense of Impending Crisis in Rhodesia

The NSC meeting was the easy part; figuring out how, exactly, to breathe new life into the Anglo-American accords was the hard part. "The Rhodesian situation remains muddy," Vance had confessed to Carter before the meeting.[20] Everything about it was muddy. The British, propelled by Foreign Secretary David Owen, were still trying to find a way to do a deal with Nkomo even after the debacle of the ZAPU leader's meeting with Smith. The new South African prime minister P.W. Botha, who took office in October 1978, was more hardline than his predecessor John Vorster and was even less likely to put his government's weight behind the Anglo-American proposals. US intelligence analysts reported that P.W. Botha was "a mercurial personality, prone to hasty, ill-considered decisions," and he would prove even more obdurate than Vorster. When Bill Edmondson, the US ambassador in South Africa, paid a courtesy call on the new prime minister he was subjected to a philippic: "He [Botha] was very, very, very bitter about the United States and about our policy," Edmondson reported. Moreover, the Frontline presidents and the Patriotic Front were still fuming after Nkomo's meeting with Smith, they were outraged by the Rhodesian raids on Zambia and Mozambique, and they had lost confidence in any plan concocted in London and Washington. "The all-party conference," Nkomo announced, "is on the battlefield."[21]

In 1978, the war exacted a heavy toll inside Rhodesia. It was costing $1.2 million every day, a whopping 40 percent of government revenue. The country's gross domestic product had fallen by 15 percent, and per capita incomes had plummeted by almost 30 percent. It was not surprising that the country suffered an acute shortage of foreign exchange. Compounding the regime's fiscal worries was the fact that the tax base was shrinking: every month in 1978, Rhodesia suffered a loss of more than 1,500 whites on the "chicken run"—the derisive term used by Rhodesian whites to describe the flight of their white compatriots. In December 1978 alone, there were 2,937 net departures. There had always been considerable fluidity in the Rhodesian white population, but until the war there had been a net inflow of whites. By 1978, however, there was a net decline of 13,709. The impact on the farms— vast, fertile tracts in white hands—was devastating as white farmers, feeling isolated and vulnerable, joined the chicken run. Food shortages became endemic. The armed forces lost potential conscripts. As South African military intelligence had predicted in 1976, the only way Smith's forces could keep up with the guerrilla threat was to conscript more and more men. Virtually every white male between the ages of eighteen and fifty had been called up, potentially serving half of every year, and even the "Dad's Army" of men aged fifty to fifty-nine had to serve forty-two days a year. This level of conscription had, as Pretoria had predicted, "a grave impact on the country's economy." In August 1978, Rhodesian intelligence chief Ken Flower admitted that despite the draconian draft, the army was diminishing "in numbers and effectiveness." In October 1978, the Smith government announced that it would begin to con- script black Rhodesians—many of whom had already volunteered to serve in the regular army—in 1979.[22]

The Rhodesian army was losing control of the countryside, even though 90 percent of it had been placed under martial law. In November 1978, ZANU insurgents brought the war to the outskirts of Salisbury for the first time. In December, ZAPU guerrillas launched rockets at Salisbury's main oil storage depot and blew it up; 17 million gallons of fuel went up in acrid smoke that hung over the capital for days. Firefighters from South Africa were called in to help douse the fire, which raged for six days.

Smith's regime simply did not have enough men to control the ever- increasing waves of recruits joining the Patriotic Front. In desperation, the internal settlement government imposed martial law over 85 percent of the country, and Smith allowed Bishop Abel Muzorewa and Reverend Ndabaningi Sithole to build their own private armies of "auxiliaries," which officially were composed of guerrillas who had deserted the Patriotic Front but in reality were conscripted prisoners and thugs. With the internal settle- ment unable to quell the fighting, Ian Smith faced increasing pressure from his right flank, which had been appalled by his decision to bring Muzorewa,

Sithole, and Chief Jeremiah Chirau into the government. When Smith addressed a crowd of whites in Salisbury and defended his decision to share some power with blacks, members of the audience roared "Rubbish!" By late October, Smith and his black colleagues faced the reality that the internal situation was so chaotic that it would be impossible to keep the promise they had made the previous March that elections for the new majority-rule government would be held in December 1978. They declared that those elections—in which both blacks and whites would vote—would not be held until April 1979.[23]

At almost the same time, William Parmenter, the national intelligence officer for Africa, sent a "Warning Report" to Stansfield Turner, the head of the CIA. "Intelligence Community specialists are particularly concerned . . . that the situation in Rhodesia . . . is moving downhill. . . . They have a sense of impending crisis that is accompanied by a general feeling that the Soviets/Cubans place increasing emphasis on supporting the creation of conventional forces. . . . We have a sense that the Rhodesian situation is now tilting more steeply both toward intensified military operations on all sides and toward the possibility of a sudden break in white morale. . . . At the same time . . . Frontline unity . . . [could] collapse. If this happens, civil war among the black nationalists in Zimbabwe appears an even surer bet. . . . [President Kenneth] Kaunda's position in Zambia will become desperate. . . . In sum, the Rhodesian situation has reached a point where a dramatic turn is in the offing."[24]

Portents

From the Carter administration's point of view, the US midterm elections on November 7, 1978, were well timed. Flush with victory from the Camp David accords, Carter managed to hold onto Democratic majorities—albeit a bit slimmer—in both houses. Republicans gained three Senate seats and fifteen House seats, but Democrats retained 59 Senate seats and had a 119-seat lead in the House. Pundit David Broder declared it "a nothing election."[25]

Embedded in the results, however, were several red flags for the White House. The strength of the Democratic Party masked the underlying trend in US politics, which was that the country and its representatives were becoming more conservative. Just as the 95th Congress, which entered with Carter, had been more conservative than its predecessor, so too was the 96th Congress, which would take office in January 1979. This reflected the rightward turn of the US electorate, which was growing increasingly concerned the United States was being bested by the Soviet Union. Zbigniew Brzezinski warned the president before the election, "Recent polls indicate that a majority of

Americans are now dissatisfied with how US military power compares to that of the Soviet Union."[26]

This posed particular concerns for the passage of the SALT II treaty, which would have to be approved by two-thirds of the Senate. Even before the midterms, this was a high bar for the White House because it could count on the votes of only fifty-one senators, while it was writing off twenty-five. After the midterm election, the odds were worse: forty-seven were in favor and twenty-nine were opposed.[27]

One race above all sent shockwaves through Congress. Dick Clark, the liberal senator from Iowa who had won in a landslide in 1972, went down to an unexpected defeat. On the eve of the election, every poll had shown him leading his Republican challenger, Roger Jepsen, by at least ten percentage points. As a first-term senator, Clark had made a name for himself as chair of the Africa subcommittee. In 1975, he had sponsored the amendment that stymied the Ford administration's covert operation in Angola, and he had championed majority rule in southern Africa. He had carved a national profile.[28] Jepsen, a conservative former lieutenant governor, was not given much of a chance even by his supporters. The *Washington Post* observed that "Jepsen's bumbling has been a harsh blow to Republican leaders." He had suggested, for example, that Social Security should be privatized and that he supported South African apartheid. Political scientist Richard Fenno, who accompanied Senator Clark on the campaign trail immediately before the election, noted that there was "no sense whatever that Dick Clark was, or could be, in trouble." Clark himself exuded confidence. "It's gone a lot easier than we expected," he said. "Their [Jepsen's] campaign hasn't seemed to make any headway."[29]

But then the returns came in. Clark lost decisively, 48 percent to Jepsen's 52 percent. Every election produces upsets, Al Hunt mused in the *Wall Street Journal*, but Clark's defeat was "at the head of the shocker list."[30]

The Monday morning quarterbacking began immediately. People hazarded a plethora of explanations. Clark was too liberal for Iowa. His vote for the Panama Canal treaties did him in. Some voters thought that Clark was "more interested in Africa than Iowa." As Ronald Reagan said in one of Jepsen's ads, "As a former Iowan myself," alluding to the years he had spent in the state as a radio announcer, "it's about time Iowa had a senator who votes for Iowans." Some argued that Clark's liberal stance toward the African continent, which Jepsen had characterized as "advancing the Soviet cause" and "helping Russia and Cuba with an appeasement policy," had killed his chances. Others said that his campaign against Jepsen had been too low-key and polite. Many, including Clark himself, thought that he had failed to comprehend the potency of the abortion issue; in the campaign's final weeks, antiabortion groups—using direct mail tools honed by conservative political action committees during the Panama Canal treaty fight—suddenly mounted an expensive, all-out attack on Clark's support of a woman's right to choose. And some asserted that Clark was too tied to President Carter, whose popularity had "nosedived an astonishing 35 percentage points—from 80 to 45" in 1978 in Iowa.[31] No one could be sure, however, why the voters had turned against Senator Clark. This uncertainty sent shudders through the Congress: if Dick Clark—popular, prominent, and ahead by ten points—could lose, then they all were vulnerable.

Clark's loss had several effects on the 96th Congress that spelled trouble for the future of Carter's foreign policy. At the practical level, it meant that the administration's most reliable advocate would no longer chair the Senate's Africa subcommittee. As columnist Anthony Lewis wrote in the *New York Times*, "Clark's defeat . . . will increase the already considerable domestic difficulties for the Administration on African questions. It may well encourage the white regimes of southern Africa in their resistance to western policy." The significance of Clark's loss to the Africa subcommittee deepened when it became clear who was going to be the new ranking minority member: Jesse Helms. The administration braced for the worst: "It is clear," Lake wrote, that the conservatives "are feeling their oats after last Tuesday [the midterm election], and we should not underestimate their ability to cause trouble in the next Congress."[32]

More broadly, Clark's defeat intensified the feeling on the Hill that, as White House aide Frank Moore had warned Carter in April, "those who 'walk the plank' for us get little thanks or recognition."[33] Not only Clark, but also Democratic senators Thomas McIntyre of New Hampshire and Floyd Haskell of Colorado—both of whom had stuck their necks out supporting the administration and voting for the Panama Canal treaties—had gone down to defeat. These losses reverberated through the ranks of the Democrats and seemed to confirm that walking the plank for Carter was a fool's errand.

Finally, the members of the 96th Congress would not only be ideologically more conservative, but they also would learn from Clark's loss and be less willing to take risks. In 1978, members of Congress were beginning to grasp the impact of powerful single-issue lobbies. "Less and less, it seems, are Iowans defining themselves in broad and traditional categories: as Republicans or Democrats; liberals or conservatives; internationalists or isolationists," the *Wall Street Journal* noted. "More and more they're defining themselves in narrow categories."[34] Clark had dismissed the importance of these narrow categories such as the opponents of a woman's right to choose, the Panama Canal treaties, or gun control—and he had suffered the consequences. He and all the pollsters had failed to understand how these issues would energize small but

significant groups of voters that could turn elections. Clark had been a courageous senator, a crusading liberal. He had believed that this big picture would
carry the day with enough like-minded Iowans to propel him to victory again.
His defeat had a sobering effect in Congress. It meant that courage would be
harder to find.

A footnote to the Clark-Jepsen battle emerged five months after the election. Jepsen was estimated to have spent at least $600,000 on the campaign,
most of it in the direct-mail assault launched in the final three weeks. "Where
is that money coming from?" the *Wall Street Journal* inquired in the days
before the election. The British knew the answer. Commenting on Clark's
surprising defeat, the British Foreign Office noted on November 10, 1978,
"the considerable effort, including money, which the South African Government was putting into lobbying." The answer did not emerge publicly until
March 1979 when Eschel Rhoodie, a former senior official in the South African Information Department, told the BBC that "$250,000 of South African
money was passed through . . . various 'front organizations' . . . into the campaign of . . . Jepsen." Jepsen denied it, but the *New York Times* reported that
Jepsen's campaign records "disclosed a pattern of involvement by South Africans or people strongly supportive of South Africa." Rhoodie later wrote that
Clark had been "a real thorn in our side."[35]

The impact of the midterms—the rightward tilt, the increasing caution, the
reluctance to "walk the plank" for Carter—made the path forward in Rhodesia
even more "muddy," to use Vance's term. The State Department, strengthened
by the PRM, set forth in late 1978 to revive the Anglo-American proposals
virtually single-handedly. It was beset with obstacles not only in London and
southern Africa but also in Washington itself.

Brzezinski nursed his doubts about the wisdom of spending energy on the
fight. As the British ambassador reported after a talk with him, "The White
House staff . . . do not like seeing the President actively committed to a policy
which is not succeeding. They do not like conflict with either the public or
the Congress where it can be avoided and at a time when the President will
be having to use all his political capital to secure the ratification of SALT."[36]

The next three to six months would be critical, NSC expert Tom Thornton
warned in a prescient analysis. If the conservatives in Congress, fired up by
the Case-Javits debates, succeeded in forcing the White House to lift sanctions, Smith would be able to stagger on for "several years." If, however,
sanctions survived for several more months, Smith "will have failed and be
more ready to negotiate." Thornton understood that the priority for the Carter
administration was not to convince the parties in Africa to attend talks but
rather to convince Congress not to lift sanctions. "The key to strategy, then, is

to see that there is no breaking of sanctions. This is the battle to be fought out with the Congress." Thornton was emphatic. "Following this strategy should be one of the Administration's major foreign policy initiatives over the next several months."[37]

David Owen's Gambit: The Repercussions

By late 1978, a war that embroiled southern Africa—and beyond—seemed more likely than it had a year earlier, not only because of escalation on the battlefield but also because of the damage caused by Nkomo's August 1978 meeting with Smith. That was a corrosive encounter. In the ensuing months, the loss of trust it had caused—between Mugabe and Nkomo, among the Frontline States, and toward the British and Americans—deepened rather than healed.[38]

The Patriotic Front, cobbled together in late 1976 under the duress of the Frontline States, had never been more than a bureaucratic fiction. Robert Mugabe's ZANU and Joshua Nkomo's ZAPU had continued to field entirely separate guerrilla armies, under different leaders, with different arms suppliers, and different strategies. Nkomo's meeting with Smith exploded the paper-thin facade of unity. "The Frontline presidents must realize that Patriotic Front unity is a lost cause," the CIA reported in the months after the meeting with Smith.[39]

The meeting did more than fracture the Front: it changed the balance of power within it. The damage to Nkomo's reputation was deeper than the Americans and British had realized immediately after the ill-fated encounter. Joshua Nkomo had bargained with the enemy one time too many. He was discredited, while Mugabe gained stature and support. Ambassador Steve Low cabled from Lusaka: "Mugabe's . . . political position has clearly been strengthened. . . . Mugabe, for the first time, may see himself emerging as the preeminent nationalist leader." By the end of 1978, Americans who spoke with Mugabe were struck by his confidence. "They [ZANU] are winning the war," Ambassador Willard DePree cabled from Maputo. "They view [the] Nkomo-Smith meeting as [a] major setback for Nkomo, as a result of which they claim Zimbabweans inside Rhodesia are shifting their support from Nkomo . . . to ZANU." Nkomo fell back on his support within the Ndebele people, only 20 percent of the total population of Rhodesia. "Nkomo has become the leader of a minority tribal bloc," Australian intelligence (which had a particular interest in southern Africa) noted, while Rhodesian intelligence chief Ken Flower concluded that "Nkomo's position had deteriorated so seriously that he really had little chance of playing a major role in the future. . . . He has no chance . . . [to] win an election."[40]

Nevertheless, the idea of a united Patriotic Front remained useful. If ZAPU and ZANU publicly split, civil war in a newly independent Zimbabwe would appear inevitable. The Frontline presidents, as well as the British and American governments, clung to the increasingly desperate hope that Patriotic Front unity, however fictitious, could be sustained until a peaceful solution had evolved. The CIA, for example, reported that Tanzanian president Julius Nyerere was convinced that it was "essential that at least the semblance of unity, as symbolized by the Nkomo-Mugabe relationship, be maintained."[41]

The Kremlin continued to back Nkomo, despite his dwindling chances. Nyerere pleaded with the Soviet leaders that they also extend aid to Mugabe— treating the two leaders of the Patriotic Front "on an equal basis"—but the Soviets demurred. (The Americans, however, continued to worry that Moscow would begin to back Mugabe, the rising star.) The Kremlin considered the ZANU leader pro-Chinese, and it wanted to avoid backing both sides in what could develop into a brutal civil war. The Soviets urged Mugabe to accept the primacy of Nkomo. Mugabe would not forget this.[42]

In early 1979, Cuba, on the other hand, began to extend some technical assistance to Mugabe's ZANU because, as Castro noted, "ZANU has been fighting much harder [than ZAPU]." Nevertheless, Cuba sent no military aid to ZANU.[43]

The Smith-Nkomo meeting also deepened the simmering mistrust among the Frontline States and affected African attitudes toward London and Washington. Black Africa's newfound hope in the Carter administration had been shaken by Carter's tough rhetoric during the second Shaba crisis, and it sustained a direct hit with the Smith-Nkomo meeting. The State Department explained that the meeting had given "rise to [the] suspicion that we were abandoning [a] comprehensive settlement based on AAP [Anglo-American proposals] in favor of [a] deal that would leave both PF [Patriotic Front] and Frontline divided." Doubts about the Carter administration's sincerity, never far below the surface, were accentuated by the decision in October 1978 to grant Ian Smith a visa to visit the United States and by the raids on Zambia that Smith launched during his American tour.[44]

The loss of confidence in the British went even deeper. Mugabe told Senator George McGovern (D-SD), who toured southern Africa in December 1978, "that he had no confidence in future British initiatives because [the] events of July and August [the Smith-Nkomo meeting] demonstrated that they clearly wanted a government which excluded ZANU and himself." Mozambique's President Samora Machel was succinct: "The British," he told Dick Moose and Andrew Young in December, "are not serious." Kenneth Kaunda was grim, warning Moose and Young that "if the US followed the British lead, they would fail."[45]

The Nkomo-Smith meeting also had ramifications for Anglo-American cooperation in Rhodesia. David Owen, who had pushed indefatigably for the encounter, was weakened. The NSC advised Carter to talk directly with Prime Minister James Callaghan about the next moves in Rhodesia "in order to circumvent Owen." Within the Foreign Office, irritation with Owen's allegedly imperious ways grew. "He was a very difficult man to work with," Ambassador Johnny Graham admitted. By November 1978, Owen finally stopped actively promoting an Nkomo solution. Senior Foreign Office officials were convinced that "it is in our interests . . . that the Patriotic Front should come to power united." Yet what could the British or the Americans do to ensure that this happened peacefully?[46]

By late 1978, pundits were declaring the Anglo-American proposals for Rhodesia dead, and it was difficult to argue with them. One of the NSC Africa experts concluded, "What we are searching for here is the least bad approach to a set of problems that just may be insoluble." The State Department agreed that there was not much to be done to bring about a settlement "except keep our channels open and appear virtuous." On November 17, Brzezinski wrote Carter: "We are at a hiatus in our Rhodesia policy. . . . Fruitful negotiations [are] unlikely. . . . In Ambassador Low's words, 'We may be going through all the motions of support for a policy (The All-Parties Conference) that is no longer viable.'" In the margin of Brzezinski's memo, Carter wrote: "Callaghan called me. He wants to move on his own—with some US involvement. I told him o.k."[47]

Prime Minister Callaghan was fantasizing about a master stroke. He was dreaming that he could follow in Carter's footsteps and pull off his own "Camp David" to resolve the Rhodesian crisis. He proposed sending a special emissary, Labour MP Cledwyn Hughes, to southern Africa to determine if the conditions were opportune for an all-parties conference that he, Callaghan, would host in London. Carter, the British Foreign Office reported, "thought this a good idea because we had almost reached the end of the present path."[48]

It was a desperate scheme—neither the first nor the last in the saga of Anglo-American diplomacy toward Rhodesia. Hughes diligently traipsed around southern Africa for weeks, accompanied by US Ambassador Steve Low. The two men talked to everyone, and by the middle of December 1978 they had come to a flat and predictable conclusion: "Such a conference would have no prospect of success in the present circumstances."[49]

This was, Owen remembered, "a tricky period" for the Callaghan government. The prime minister was "deeply disappointed" by the stasis in Rhodesia, but Owen was "absolutely convinced" that the time was not yet right to hold a conference. Coming to this conclusion was, in Owen's words, "the most important decision I've made in my political career."[50]

Callaghan decided to reach out to Carter. Would the president be willing to stay "an extra day" after the summit meeting in Guadeloupe, planned for early January 1979, "with a view to having a long private talk . . . about the whole situation [in Rhodesia] and what should be the next steps"?[51]

The Widening War

Callaghan was anxious to confer with Carter because the war in southern Africa was widening. In late 1978 and early 1979, the Rhodesian armed forces escalated their attacks on their neighbors. The CIA noted that Rhodesian officers had figured out how to inflict "heavy personnel and equipment losses on the insurgents." The Rhodesians would wait until the camps they planned to destroy were filled with people. Then, before striking, they paradropped troops to block all escape routes. "When the firing begins, the guerrillas normally break ranks and flee from the camp into ambushes set by the blocking forces."[52]

In addition to cross-border raids to clear out ZANU camps, the Rhodesians' targets in Mozambique—but not yet in Zambia—included civilians and infrastructure: they bombed bridges and gasoline depots and trains and buses. On December 30, 1978, they launched their deepest raid yet into Mozambique, all the way to the coast, battering the Mozambican air force base in Beira, the country's second largest city. President Machel's paltry military could not mount a response. The Soviets stepped up their arms deliveries to Machel's beleaguered defense forces, but never went full throttle; they feared that Machel, like Mugabe, could lean toward China.[53]

Zambia, too, was hammered. This heightened dissension within the Zambian military, which was unable to defend the country. The Rhodesian attacks also shook Zambia's fragile racial harmony. Blacks suspected that their white fellow citizens must have been feeding intelligence to the Smith regime. Angry scuffles broke out in the streets of Lusaka. Kaunda was humiliated and desperate. "Up to now, the West hasn't really given us anything real," he told the New York Times. The weapons the British had sent were "Roy Rogers stuff, inadequate even to defend Lusaka airport," he complained to Ambassador Young and Moose, and hinted darkly that "I know that the East . . . is ready to help us."[54] In September, the State Department noted that Kaunda "may be obliged to trim his sails." Indeed, on October 6, Kaunda—seeing no other way to salvage Zambia's economy—announced that the financial crisis had forced him to reopen the rail line through Rhodesia, which had been closed since 1973 in protest against Smith's regime. The loss of this vital transportation link had cost Zambia $744 million, but reopening it while Smith was still ruling Rhodesia was difficult for Kaunda and enraged Nyerere and Machel.[55]

Even Botswana was sucked into the maelstrom. Tens of thousands of black Rhodesians—many simply fleeing the war, others seeking to join ZAPU—flooded into makeshift camps in Botswana as they crossed the Zambezi River by ferry or plane to reach refugee or training camps in Zambia. Salisbury responded by kidnaping suspected guerrillas from the refugee camps in Botswana, infiltrating spies into their camps, and engaging in acts of intimidation. The Botswana government was powerless to respond: it did not even have an army until 1977, when it began to build a token defense force. The Botswanans tried to draw a line in the sand, declaring that refugees could not bear arms, but their resources were stretched thin and they could not or would not stop the armed ZAPU guerrillas based in Zambia from passing through their country on their way to Rhodesia. This drew the ire of the Rhodesian military, which launched cross-border raids. The attacks were infrequent, and not as ferocious as the assaults on Zambia and Mozambique, but they were enough to convince Botswana's president, Sir Seretse Khama, that he had to beef up his fledgling army. On December 3, 1978, Khama poured out his worries in a frank conversation with Young and Moose. "Botswana's inability to control its borders makes it a 'playground.' And there is nothing we can do about it," he told the Americans. Khama begged for US military aid, adding that he had declined the Soviets' "open invitation to provide arms." The Americans explained that sending military aid to Botswana would be "counterproductive in Congress, which sees Botswana as peaceful." Khama despaired: "Our democracy has become an albatross around our neck. . . . The sad fact is that Botswana cannot defend itself. We will wake up one morning and find out we don't exist."[56]

The Abyss between Washington and Havana

In December, at the invitation of the Cuban government, Peter Tarnoff, the executive secretary of the State Department, and Robert Pastor, the Latin American expert at the NSC, met with Fidel Castro in Havana. It was an extraordinary encounter. Fifteen years earlier, Americans had been trying to assassinate Castro; now two emissaries from the president of the United States were on a secret mission to create an opening. The transcript of the five-hour talks clarifies the gulf between the two countries.[57]

Tarnoff's opening remarks were straightforward: "Africa is central to our concerns. . . . As I look over the transcripts of our talks [with Cuban first vice president Carlos Rafael Rodríguez], I see that we have spent 70 percent of our time on Africa." The United States was asking only that Cuba curtail its adventurism in Africa and, most important, that Castro promise not to intervene in Rhodesia. In return, Tarnoff implied that relations could be normalized and the embargo lifted.

From the US point of view it was a sweet and generous deal, but from Castro's point of view it was an insult. The deal was built on the assumption that the United States had the right to determine Cuba's foreign policy. It assumed inequality between the two nations; the assumption was so thorough that it was invisible to the Americans. But not to Castro. He bristled. "We never have discussed with you the activities of the US throughout the entire world," he asserted. "Perhaps because the US is a great power it feels it can do what it wants and what is good for it. It seems to be saying that there are two laws, two sets of rules and two kinds of logic, one for the US and one for the other countries."

This gulf between these two different conceptions of how states should relate to each other permeated the talks. Castro repeated the main lines of Cuba's approach to the Rhodesia conflict. He preferred peace but doubted it could be achieved through diplomacy; he would prefer not to intervene but would make no promises; if invited by the Africans—a possibility that Castro considered unlikely—then Cuba would intervene in any way that the Africans deemed useful. Because Castro had said that he was not opposed to a diplomatic solution in Rhodesia, Tarnoff and Pastor asked him to voice his support for the Anglo-American proposals. "An indication of Cuban support . . . could make a difference," Tarnoff explained. "For the Anglo-American plan . . . such an indication could be very important." Castro, however, suspected that the Anglo-American plan was a ploy to preserve white privilege in Rhodesia and impose a pro-Western government in Salisbury. If he announced that Cuba would not intervene, it would give Smith courage. "Why is the US so concerned about the presence of Cuban soldiers in Africa?" he asked at the beginning of the talks. "We have no troops in areas with common borders with Zimbabwe." He concluded: "It seems to be a psychosis." Pastor commented: "As we go marching further into the woods, it is becoming clear that we each see the trees differently."

Upon their return to Washington, Tarnoff and Pastor wrote an unusually frank debriefing memo to Carter. "It seemed to us that we were viewing a man who has bottled up 20 years of rage and was releasing it in a controlled but extremely impassioned manner. . . . His principal message was that Cuba wants to be treated with respect, as an equal, by the same rules. . . . The major point the Cubans made was that Cuba's African policy was not negotiable. . . . On Rhodesia, Castro said that under present circumstances, he did not see a need to become involved, but that would change if South Africa got involved. He stressed his preference was to see independence achieved by local forces." Pastor wrote more informally to Brzezinski and his deputy David Aaron. "The transcripts are a little flat and completely fail to convey what it was like to be there on the receiving end. . . . I was struck by how different our goals are. . . . They think their military presence [in southern Africa] is helpful in preventing mass killings by the whites; we believe that their presence undermines the possibility of negotiating a peaceful solution. There really is no way to bridge the gap in our positions. However, I do believe that they will give us the room to seize the initiative (if we can do it). I believe Castro when he says that Cuba will not be an obstacle to peace. They won't be helpful . . . but they won't be an obstacle, at least in their terms, at this time." He underlined the next sentence: "You can be sure, however, that if we trip, they will strike like vultures."[58]

The focus of the Carter administration's concern was Rhodesia. Pastor's debriefing memo to Brzezinski dealt with no other topic (except for a brief appendix on Puerto Rico). Tarnoff and Pastor took their historic trip to Havana because the White House was worried about what was happening in Rhodesia, where the internal settlement had failed to staunch the intensifying war, Anglo-American diplomacy had faltered, and the specter of Cuban intervention loomed.

Memories

Motivations are complicated. Although it is incontrovertible that the attention of the US government at the highest level—Carter, Brzezinski, and Vance—was directed to Rhodesia because of the need to contain Soviet and Cuban inroads, it is also clear that this was not every US official's primary interest. When, many years later, I asked officials charged primarily with African affairs—US ambassadors posted to southern Africa, members of the Africa team at the State Department and NSC staffers—why they focused on Rhodesia, not one mentioned the Cubans. When I showed them the documents that clearly indicated the importance that the White House attached to the possibility of the Cubans entering Rhodesia, they were—to a man—surprised.[59]

Ambassador Steve Low, the point man in southern Africa, explained: "First of all, the Russians were so ham-handed they shot themselves in the foot every day. . . . No one who knew anything about Africa took it [the communist threat to Africa] very seriously. . . . The Cubans trained some ZAPU fighters—fine. . . . Racism was more of a factor." Ambassador Donald McHenry, Young's UN aide, remembered, "In Rhodesia you didn't have this strong Cuban dimension." Dick Moose said, "We didn't see the Soviet Union or the Cubans as a factor. . . . Carter never bought Mugabe and Nkomo as tools of the Russians. . . . Carter was right on that. I think that he really believed that the Soviets were not the menace—that the South Africans were the threat to democracy in southern Africa, not the Soviets." When I showed him the documents about the conversations with the Cubans, Moose was startled at the content of the talks—and at the fact that he had not been informed. "Very interesting," he said. "If I had been asked, 'What does Castro have to do with it?,' I would have seen their role as tangential. Curious."[60]

The British agreed. "I don't think the Cuban threat was taken seriously by us," David Owen said. "Most of us thought it was rather farfetched that they would come into Rhodesia." When I showed him the US documents, he said, "It's not what I remember. . . . It surprises me." Robin Renwick, head of the Foreign Office's Rhodesia Department, concurred: "I was never very impressed by the Soviet threat to Africa. . . . I didn't worry that the Cubans would intervene." Ambassador Johnny Graham, Low's counterpart, agreed: "I don't think the Cuban thing figured in our thinking much."[61]

Of course, memory plays tricks. If the struggle against racism was the primary concern of these Africanists in the State Department and NSC, why did they focus on Rhodesia rather than South Africa, where the institutionalized racism was more noxious? In the complicated, shifting tangle of motivations that explain a diplomatic effort that spanned years, it is only human to remember one's most noble impulses and to minimize (to the point of forgetting) one's more worldly Cold War concerns about a Cuban threat that never materialized. In their memos and cables penned during the Carter years, these men referred frequently to a possible Cuban threat to Rhodesia. Were these comments just a tactic to grab the attention of their superiors? Moose recalled, "We would manufacture anticommunism. Tony [Lake] and I would concoct it in order to defend the policies of the administration." Tom Thornton, an NSC aide, remembered, "It was always politic in writing—and to no small extent we were writing for Brzezinski—to throw in the Cubans." Anything to do with Cuba was bound to get attention. NSC aide Henry Richardson observed that "Cuba has been literally a sore tooth in American foreign policy. . . . It turns otherwise reasonable policy makers crazy. . . . Bring up Cuba and meetings go crazy. I've seen them dissolve. Spit coming out of their mouths." David Aaron, Brzezinski's right-hand man, noted that "Zbig used to refer to Cuba as 'the erogenous zone of foreign policy'—everyone got overheated talking about it." It made sense, Aaron added, that administration officials would emphasize the communist threat: "Nobody wants to look like they aren't hairy chested."[62]

Moreover, there are indications that the Africanists' fears about a Cuban intervention were muted. In an off-the-record speech about Rhodesia in 1979, for example, Ambassador Low declared: "As far as Cuba's coming into the fight, I think it is much over-rated as a threat or probability. . . . It is unlikely that they will want to invite further attacks on them although they have enough trained forces to do it. . . . I think they have their platter full. They're not going to want to intervene."[63]

Perspective matters. These men—senior officials, but not the principals—did not have to worry about the worst-case scenario. Their job was to focus on Africa. Carter, Vance, and Brzezinski agreed with Low that it was unlikely that Cuba would intervene—but it was possible. And that possibility fueled their worries and drove their policy. The Africanists had the luxury of tunnel vision; the principals had to worry about the possibility of a "nightmare scenario." Their recollections are useful reminders of the complexity of motivations within the layers of the US government, but they do not reflect the perceptions of Carter, Vance, or Brzezinski.

When asked about the impetus for his Rhodesia policy, the first thing that Carter said was to read the transcripts of Pastor's and Tarnoff's talks with Castro. These talks stress Washington's fears of Cuban intervention in Rhodesia. Pastor and Tarnoff were following Carter's instructions. Undersecretary for Political Affairs David Newsom noted: "Especially in matters concerning Cuba, we were carrying a presidential mandate: it was the president who made the decisions."[64]

The Sunshine Summit

Both Jimmy Carter and Valéry Giscard d'Estaing claim credit for the idea of a "sunshine summit" in the French Caribbean island of Guadeloupe. Carter writes that he thought that an informal meeting with the British, French, and West German leaders would be more useful than the scripted encounters at the routine NATO and G7 meetings. Giscard, however, notes in his memoirs that a meeting was needed to heal the growing rifts between the Carter administration and its European allies. Although the initial focus of the meeting was SALT II, the agenda quickly broadened. The purpose of the gathering, Giscard announced on his departure from Paris, was "to evaluate the situation in the world."[65]

Meeting in a thatched cabana on January 5 and 6, 1979, with no aides or interpreters, the four leaders discussed the SALT II agreement, relations with China, the energy crisis, inflation, and five flash points: Iran, Turkey, Pakistan, southeast Asia, and southern Africa. Carter opened the conversation about Africa by explaining America's "new interest" in the continent and by saying "how much Andy Young had helped—which," Carter added in his notes of the meeting, "drew a frown from Valery [Giscard]." Callaghan remembered that during the "long discussion [about southern Africa] . . . Carter and I ran in double harness for most of the time."[66]

After the two-day summit, all four leaders stressed its usefulness as well as the camaraderie that had developed among them. "We spent forty-eight hours together, living cheek by jowl in adjacent simple holiday accommodation," Callaghan noted. At their final dinner together, Giscard wrote, they were like four "friends on a holiday." Helmut Schmidt deemed the encounter "harmonious and pleasant," and Carter told *Time*, "I have never attended a conference that was more beneficial to me nor more substantive in nature."[67]

This image "of four utterly congenial and satisfied men" was, *Le Monde* observed, what the heads of government wanted to convey, "but, in fact, some were more happy than others." There were deep political and personal tensions among these four leaders. Schmidt was pleased to have been included in a meeting of the elite "nuclear club" of Western allies, but he was nursing a long list of grievances that ranged from the specific—the Carter administration's positions on SALT, human rights, the Middle East, the neutron bomb, energy, and economics—to the general. Schmidt had not hidden his frustration with what he viewed as the ineptitude of the Carter administration. As a British official later told Vance, "Herr Schmidt appears to regard President Carter as at best woolly-minded and unpredictable and at worst downright incompetent. . . . The Chancellor has not helped matters by repeatedly telling journalists and others what he thinks of Mr Carter." Giscard had been more discreet, but his contempt would burst forth at a press conference soon after his return from Guadeloupe in which he bemoaned "the void left in the world by the Americans' handling of foreign policy." Nor did he hold back in his memoirs: "When Carter talked," Giscard wrote, "we could sense in our bones that he had arrived in Washington straight out of Georgia, without a stop or a detour." In his informal notes of the encounter, Carter wrote, "Schmidt['s] . . . whole attitude was very negative. . . . Jim [Callaghan] is the one person I enjoy being with." Callaghan noted that "Schmidt was at his most illogical . . . [and] Giscard was detached." Nevertheless, he concluded, the talks were "immensely worthwhile."[68]

One reason that Callaghan was pleased was that he achieved one of his key goals at the summit: to get Carter's promise that Washington would remain actively involved in the Rhodesia negotiations. He and Carter held two long bilateral meetings about Rhodesia after Giscard and Schmidt had departed. The first was during a long drive across the island to a dinner at the prefect's house. In the privacy of the limousine, Callaghan handed Carter a copy of Cledwyn Hughes' yet-unpublished report and observed that its conclusions required "some radical re-thinking of the options open to us." The second meeting was onboard the HMS *Scylla*, docked in the harbor, where the two men "spent a happy couple of hours sitting in the captain's cabin." At the end of these bilateral talks, Callaghan was delighted to report that Carter had given him "his complete assurance that the United States would stand firmly with us over Rhodesia and had no intention whatever of trying to disengage."[69]

Carter stayed in the game for three reasons: the Anglo-American alliance, the Cold War, and domestic politics. The most straightforward explanation is the first: Callaghan wanted him to. The British prime minister, who was Carter's personal favorite among the European leaders, was on the brink of a tough general election; moreover, Britain was America's stalwart ally.

But it was not just loyalty or the "special relationship" that determined the Carter administration's decision to stay engaged in Rhodesia. It was also the need to implement containment. Zambia's President Kaunda summarized this realpolitik argument during a discussion with Andrew Young and Dick Moose in December 1978. "It was becoming increasingly clear that the Cubans would become involved whatever anyone wanted," Kaunda asserted. "For the West to sit on the fence was to invite disaster."[70]

Seeking Leverage in Congress

Carter did not want to cede Rhodesia policy to the US Congress. This was the third reason he told Callaghan at Guadeloupe that he "had no intention whatever of trying to disengage" from Rhodesia. "The Rhodesian problem," the newly hired NSC Africa expert Jerry Funk wrote Brzezinski in January 1979, had become "a very serious domestic political problem."[71]

This had not been the case in the administration's first year: then, the Carter team had been able to pursue its southern Africa policy largely free from interference. But in June 1978, Jesse Helms had fired a shot across the administration's bow when his amendment to lift sanctions on Rhodesia had almost passed in the Senate. One month later, Helms had been determined to make his amendment stick, but the White House, working feverishly behind the scenes, had outmaneuvered him and overseen the passage of the Case-Javits Amendment. Although Case-Javits had opened the door to lifting sanctions, it had left the prerogative with the president to decide whether the Rhodesians had fulfilled the two conditions: agreeing to all-party talks and holding "free and fair" elections. Thus it was a victory for the White House, but a narrow and temporary one.

Since most members of the administration thought that Smith had agreed to all-party talks during his visit to Washington in October 1978 (others dismissed Smith's promise as a cynical tactic because it had been accompanied by the brutal assault on Zambia), the crux of Case-Javits would be Carter's assessment of the elections, scheduled to be held in April 1979. If Carter decided they had been "free and fair," the United States would lift sanctions; if not, sanctions would remain in place.

With Case-Javits, Carter had won round one, but he had riled his opponents and exposed his vulnerability. Rhodesia had become a political football in the United States. "The Achilles heel" of Anglo-American policy toward Rhodesia, Moose and Lake observed in late 1978, "was the US Congress." The White House warned Whitehall that "next to SALT, the Administration's biggest foreign policy battles in the Congress [in 1979] will be over Rhodesia."[72]

In November 1978, the British ambassador in Washington had written David Owen a long letter. "We face a potential shift in United States policy on Rhodesia," he began. "We need to be prepared for it. . . . US policy towards Rhodesia could become an issue with mass opinion if, as Dr Brzezinski put it to me, white nuns were daily being raped on national TV by black soldiers with red stars on their caps. . . . From the New Year onwards the attitude of the Congress, especially the Senate, is going to be increasingly important. In my judgement, unless we have a conspicuous diplomatic success in the next 3 or 4 months, Congressional pressure on the White House to forget the Anglo-American proposals and to lend a friendlier countenance to the Salisbury parties will grow." The Foreign Office drew the logical conclusion. "Much will depend, therefore, on how determined President Carter shows himself to be to resist a change of course which would put the United States in breach of its international obligations and cause the most serious damage to the US position throughout Africa."[73]

The need to achieve "a conspicuous diplomatic success" that could dampen the congressional revolt propelled Carter's policy toward Rhodesia in early 1979. In January, NSC aide Jerry Funk explained the State Department's thinking to Brzezinski: "The gut emotional potential of this issue cannot be overstated. In order to position the President politically, we have to be doing something other than 'awaiting events' as April approaches [when the elections would be held in Rhodesia]. Therefore, we must develop a new initiative, now."[74]

For all these reasons—maintaining the special relationship with Great Britain, containing the Soviet/Cuban advance, and girding for the looming battle with Congress—at Guadeloupe, Carter agreed with Callaghan. Although it was impossible to be sanguine about their chances, they would continue to actively pursue a peaceful solution in Rhodesia. The stakes were too high for them to give up now.

Gathering Clouds

The Cold War dimension of the Rhodesian problem was underlined in late January 1979 when UN Secretary-General Kurt Waldheim informed Carter that Mozambican President Machel had asked Castro for military assistance. Waldheim, who had been in Cuba on official business, had gone fishing with Castro. While they were cruising near Havana harbor, the Cuban had reached into his pocket and pulled out "a scruffy piece of paper." It was Machel's letter: "The Rhodesians were trying to destroy Mozambique's economy," Machel had written Castro. "It was essential . . . [for Mozambique to] receive military help." Castro turned to Waldheim. "Why [was it that] people thought Cuban troops were the answer to all African problems!" he exclaimed. "Cuba was not a bottomless pit!"[75] Revealing his hand, Castro asked Waldheim to get "the United Nations to do something to stop Rhodesia's systematic aggression against Mozambique" and to urge the Americans "to use their influence with South Africa to stop the Rhodesian raids."[76] Castro was using Waldheim as a conduit to Carter who, he hoped, would understand the implicit warning and therefore restrain Smith's armed forces from attacking Mozambique.

What made the threat of Cuban intervention to help Mozambique all the more plausible was that in Rhodesia the internal settlement was facing a deepening crisis. The essential task of the Smith, Muzorewa, Sithole and Chirau government—announced with such fanfare in March 1978—was to write a new constitution. This document, released after a long delay in early January 1979, made a mockery of the notion that Smith was sharing power with his black "partners." Martin Meredith, an authority on Rhodesia, summed it up: "The constitution was so devised that every instrument of power except Parliament remained under white control. . . . The civil service, the defence forces, the police and the judiciary" would continue to be controlled by the 3 percent of the population that was white. Political power would remain in white hands: twenty-eight seats in parliament, five cabinet posts, and effective control of the Senate.[77] On January 30, the government held a referendum on the new constitution, and it was approved overwhelmingly—by 85 percent. Underlining the continuing privileged position of whites, only they were allowed to vote.

The war was devastating Rhodesia. The International Committee of the Red Cross estimated that in January 1979, half a million Rhodesians were in need of "immediate assistance" and another half-million were "not receiving adequate food and medical aid." Hundreds of thousands of blacks had fled the country and were filling refugee camps in Mozambique and Zambia. More than 25,000 people had been killed since hostilities had begun in earnest in 1972.[78] All the while, Mugabe's ZANU and Nkomo's ZAPU were gaining recruits. In February 1979, the State Department estimated there were 10,000 Patriotic Front troops in Rhodesia, and "more are on the way." ZANU, which continued to send many more guerrillas into Rhodesia than did ZAPU, controlled ever-larger areas of the Rhodesian countryside. (The State Department estimated that there were eight thousand ZANU and two thousand ZAPU guerrillas in the field.) On February 12, ZAPU guerrillas used one of their sophisticated Soviet heat-seeking missiles to shoot down a commercial Air Rhodesia jet, their second such attack since September. All fifty-nine people aboard Air Rhodesia Flight 827, white Rhodesian vacationers, were killed. Ian Smith lashed out at Carter and Callaghan, who, he declared, "have it in their power as no one else does to bring an end to all this inhuman terror."[79]

Five days later, Smith's forces unleashed their fury. Nkomo's camps in Zambia near Victoria Falls were hit first. Then ZANU camps and arms depots in Mozambique were flattened. Then came a devastating attack on an enormous camp in Zambia, home to an estimated 14,000 people, many elderly refugees and children.[80]

In this wave of assaults, on February 26 the Rhodesian armed forces attacked Angola for the first time. It was their widest ranging attack of the war. Four Canberra bombers took off from Wankie air base in western Rhodesia and flew 650 miles, traversing either Zambia or Botswana to travel 180 miles deep into Angola. The Cuban military mission in Angola reported that the Canberras were accompanied by three Mirage fighters, presumably South African. Pretoria denied the report, but a Rhodesian pilot later confirmed that it was a combined operation because the base was "too large to be covered by the formation of only four [Rhodesian] Canberras." (He asserted that the South Africans flew three Canberra B9s, not Mirages.) The well-planned attack targeted the camp at Boma, Angola, which was home to 1,552 ZAPU insurgents, 125 Cuban military instructors, and six Soviet experts. According to Cuban sources, six Cubans, one Soviet, and 191 trainees were killed instantly; 532 people were wounded.[81]

The Salisbury government celebrated. "The countries that lend themselves to these activities [sheltering guerrillas] must accept the fact that they will suffer in the same way that innocent civilians were killed in their tens of thousands by Anglo-American bombing raids on Germany in the last war," the Rhodesian foreign minister explained. The comparison with World War II was ominous. "This far-reaching air attack not only escalates the Rhodesian conflict," the *Washington Post* observed, "but raises the possibility of direct retaliation by the estimated 20,000 Cuban troops and 2,000 East German and Soviet military advisers stationed in Angola." The British *Guardian* agreed: "It brings closer the inevitable day when the undoubted airpower of South Africa will confront

Russian fighters flown by an assortment of East European or Cuban pilots over Central and Southern Africa. That day may not be far off."[82]

The Mother of Invention

In Washington, the battle to lift sanctions on Smith's internal settlement government was gaining momentum on Capitol Hill. It was led by a small group of conservatives who had seized on it as a winning issue, one that allowed them to slam the Carter administration as radical and inept; they railed against a White House that embraced Marxist terrorists and rebuffed moderate pro-Western leaders who, they believed, had taken huge strides toward creating a more just regime in Rhodesia. This was a potent attack, especially in early 1979, after the shah of Iran, a staunch US ally, had fled his country in the throes of revolution; the Taiwanese were complaining loudly that the United States had abandoned them when Carter had normalized relations with the People's Republic of China; the pro-Cuban leftist Maurice Bishop had seized power in Grenada; and the Sandinista rebellion against Nicaraguan strongman Anastasio Somoza, another US ally, was gaining strength.

It was important for the White House to counter the criticism. First, Carter did not want this narrative to gain traction, especially when he was looking toward the 1980 election and when SALT II was expected to come before the Senate. Second, if the United States lifted sanctions on Rhodesia, then the Patriotic Front and Frontline States would see no alternative to war and be more likely to call in the Cubans and Soviets. Third, lifting sanctions would turn black Africa against the United States by confirming the simmering suspicion that, despite all of the Carter administration's rhetoric, Washington still supported white minority rule.

Therefore, the White House had to blunt the congressional move to lift sanctions, but how? If the administration stated that the Anglo-American proposals were still on the table, it would simply fuel Helms' argument that Carter had no policy except to stubbornly back the terrorists. If the administration proposed pausing the pursuit of the Anglo-American proposals until the parties were ready to negotiate, it would leave its allies with no ammunition. Most members of Congress had not yet made up their minds about US policy toward Rhodesia. They were, as NSC aide Jerry Funk wrote, "looking to the President for leadership and alternatives." Therefore, to take "the steam out of the Rhodesian lobby" the administration sought to develop a policy beyond the Anglo-American proposals.[83]

It is a cliché, but it is apt: necessity is the mother of invention. The State Department and the White House needed to develop a Rhodesia strategy that they could take to Congress, even though they knew that neither Smith nor the Patriotic Front was ready to negotiate. The British, fully cognizant that the battle was now to persuade the US Congress not to lift sanctions, joined in the Carter administration's efforts. They all, therefore, invented a world in which negotiations would be possible. The key was the wild hope that the South African government would help.

It was Cledwyn Hughes, Callaghan's special envoy, who planted the seed. During his tour in late 1978, Hughes met with South African foreign minister Pik Botha. In his report, which Callaghan showed Carter in Guadeloupe, Hughes suggested that Prime Minister P.W. Botha "could press Smith and, as a carrot, meet with Carter." The State Department and the Foreign Office seized on the idea. On January 29, 1979, Vance wrote Carter, "Owen seems to share our view that we should now seek South Africa's cooperation in pressing Salisbury to accept a framework for an internationally acceptable settlement." At long last, Pretoria might be willing to oblige. "We know that Prime Minister Botha has become increasingly concerned about the deteriorating situation in Rhodesia and the consequent threat of increased instability and expanded Soviet influence in the area." Owen himself echoed these thoughts in a letter to Callaghan, adding another reason to hope: "The Iranian oil situation [the revolutionary Iranian government had suspended oil deliveries to South Africa in January] gives them [the South Africans] an added reason to be working with us for a negotiated settlement in Rhodesia."[84]

On February 2, Owen flew to Washington for talks about Rhodesia with Vance. That night, Vance opened his evening report to Carter with an update on Rhodesia. "South Africa is the most likely key to the situation," he wrote, explaining that he and Owen would meet with Foreign Minister Pik Botha to persuade Pretoria to "endorse UN-supervised elections in Rhodesia." That is, the Americans and British hoped that South Africa would convince Smith to scuttle the elections planned for April, and instead allow the UN to hold its own internationally supervised election.[85]

Vance did not tell Carter that South Africa appeared to be pursuing the opposite tack. He did not mention the "disturbing information about increased South African military help to Rhodesia" that he and Young had discussed with Owen. Nor did he relay to Carter the question that Young had asked: "How could we induce them [the South Africans] to make a commitment of this kind?" Vance merely added the caveat that "this will be a difficult undertaking."[86]

That was an understatement. As prime minister, P.W. Botha had consistently refused to side with the American or British governments. He had blocked progress on a settlement in Namibia; he had not halted South Africa's nuclear weapons program, promises to the Americans notwithstanding; he had refused to sign the Non-Proliferation Treaty; and he had increased military aid to Rhodesia. P.W. Botha was, David Owen observed, "a really tough character." William Edmondson, the US ambassador in Pretoria, sent a blunt cable: "It is unthinkable that the SAG [South African Government] would agree to compel the Rhodesians to abandon the April elections."[87]

Washington and London ignored the evidence and pursued their plan. On February 14, Assistant Secretary Dick Moose and his British counterpart Antony Duff went on "a quiet mission" to Cape Town to talk with Brand Fourie, the South African director-general of foreign affairs. Moose and Duff stressed their "grave concern over continuing deterioration [in Rhodesia] leading to further heavy Cuban or Soviet involvement." They asserted that South Africa was "the only force who can directly influence Smith." They pitched their idea of holding UN-sponsored elections as "the only way to keep the Cubans and Soviets away from the Limpopo [the river separating Rhodesia and South Africa]." They also asked South Africa to urge Smith to stop the raids on the Frontline States. Fourie was pessimistic, saying that little could be done before the April elections, but he promised to "refer the question higher up."[88]

That thin reed was enough for the Americans and the British. Stressing that lifting sanctions would give a "tremendous boost to Soviet propaganda and policies throughout Africa," British and American officials hawked their plan to the members of Congress. On March 17, Vance and Owen released a joint statement on Rhodesia. In emotional terms, they described the suffering of the Rhodesian people and emphasized the "growing opportunity for Soviet and Cuban involvement." They stated flatly that lifting sanctions prematurely would "encourage Salisbury's insistence on its own plan for the future of Rhodesia, a plan we do not believe can succeed." They then called for UN-supervised elections before April 20, 1979.[89]

This was a policy that the administration could take to Congress and to the press. Never mind that the UN-sponsored elections would not actually happen. As Jerry Funk admitted, "It will put the President in a better situation politically, for having tried."[90]

12. Adjustments and Showdowns

President Carter grabbed the phone. "What's going on?" he asked Secretary Vance.

It was at 3:19 in the morning of February 14, 1979. Vance had disturbing news. In Afghanistan, the American ambassador, Adolph Dubs, had been kidnapped and was being held hostage in a hotel room in Kabul. In Iran, a heavily armed mob had stormed the US embassy, trapping more than one hundred Americans.[1]

The first cable from Kabul had arrived at the State Department's Operations Center just after midnight Washington time (and just after 9:30 A.M. Kabul time). "Ambassador Dubs was apprehended at gunpoint by unknown terrorists this morning and is being held at the Hotel Kabul," Bruce Amstutz, the deputy chief of mission, cabled. "The hotel is swarming with [Afghan] police," he added twenty minutes later. "When the police said their plan was to break in and teargas the room, our response was not to do so yet. The important thing was to be patient, take no precipitous action and try to talk to the terrorists." Seventeen minutes later, Amstutz cabled that "Afghan police are now being advised . . . by a Soviet police adviser." The Americans at the scene urged the Russian to be patient. Just after 1:00 A.M. Washington time, Amstutz asked the State Department to notify Dubs' wife that "we are doing all we can to get him released unharmed." By 1:30 A.M., Amstutz had learned that the kidnappers sought "the release of three political prisoners [who] . . . may be Shiias [*sic*]." At 2:04 A.M., Vance, who had been called the moment the crisis broke and had gone immediately to the Operations Center, sent a cable to Kabul: "Precipitous action should be avoided at all cost." Less than ten minutes later, a reassuring cable arrived: the Afghan police commissioner had assured Amstutz that he had "no intention to break into the room by force."[2]

Kabul, long an exotic backwater for US diplomats, had been gaining the attention of Washington since July 1973, when King Mohammed Zahir Shah had been overthrown and a republican government had been established. A second coup in April 1978 installed a communist government in Kabul. The Carter administration did not consider Afghanistan a high priority, but it was concerned about the growing Soviet influence there. It was less interested in the shadowy Islamic rebels—mujahideen—who were mounting an insurgency against the communist government. The kidnapping of Adolph Dubs was one of Washington's first encounters with the mujahideen.

In February 1979, when Dubs was kidnapped, Americans were struggling to make sense of what was happening in neighboring Iran, once their stalwart ally in the region. The revolution there, which had jolted Washington in late 1978, crescendoed in early 1979 when the shah fled. On February 1, 1979, Ayatollah Ruhollah Khomeini had returned to a tumultuous welcome in Tehran. Within days, the Iranian army, bristling with American weapons, collapsed; arms caches were raided and chaos spread through the country. The transitional government, with Khomeini as its de facto head, labored to assert control. On February 13, the Carter administration, hoping to calm the volatile situation, expressed its desire to have a "stable relationship" with the new government and offered its cooperation. That night, Khomeini delivered a televised address to his nation. "Our inheritance [after the victory of the revolution] is a country lying in ruins, a country wallowing in confusion. . . . All of us, no matter where we work, should join hands to achieve the Islamic and humanitarian goals of the revolution."[3]

Iran was the linchpin of America's regional containment of the Soviet Union, and it sat on 10 percent of the world's proven oil reserves. In January 1979, the State Department had ordered all dependents of embassy personnel in Tehran to evacuate, and it had set up an open telephone line to the embassy in the Operations Center.[4]

At 2:25 A.M. on February 14, in one corner of the Operations Center, diplomats huddled to read the incoming traffic from Kabul and devise a strategy to obtain the release of Ambassador Dubs. In another corner of the room, the open line from Tehran suddenly cackled with the sound of machine-gun fire. It was 10:55 A.M. in Iran, and a Marine guard at the US embassy—one of nineteen stationed there—reported that a mob had begun to scale the walls. Communication became erratic, but the outlines of a carefully executed attack emerged: snipers stationed on rooftops shelled the embassy and invaders scaled the twelve-foot walls on three sides of the embassy compound. (To this day, it is not clear who the invaders were. Some identified themselves as members of the fringe Marxist group Fedayeen-i-Khalq; most accounts label them "Marxists" to distinguish them from Khomeini loyalists.) US Ambassador William Sullivan, communicating with the Marine guards by walkie-talkie, ordered them not to fire unless essential for self-defense. He called

Khomeini's government and urgently asked for help. The sound of gunfire, broadcast by speakerphone, filled the Operations Center until 3:00 A.M.— when the phone line went dead.[5]

It was then that Vance awoke the president. Vance's first concern was Iran, where many Americans were at risk; in Kabul, by contrast, the hostage stand-off appeared to be settling in for a prolonged period of negotiations.[6]

Communication with the Americans besieged in Tehran was sporadic, and was maintained for a while by a telex machine in the US embassy's chancery and later by a ham radio operator in Florida. As the invaders shelled and gutted the ambassador's residence, the approximately 100 Americans retreated to the communications vault on the second floor of the chancery. A journalist noted that it was "the worst attack on a US diplomatic mission since the Vietcong assault on the American Embassy in Saigon during the 1968 Tet offensive." Suddenly, at about 11:30 A.M. (3:00 A.M. in Washington), a Marine guard yelled, "They're in the building!" Ambassador Sullivan barked: "Destroy all equipment! Destroy everything!" The diplomats frantically shredded documents and destroyed code machines with sledgehammers while the Marines flooded the first floor with tear gas and locked the metal door leading to the second floor. As the invaders stormed in, they killed an Iranian cook who worked in the embassy and wounded a Marine. They plowed through the tear gas and blew open the metal door. The Americans emerged from the vault and surrendered to the mob. They were herded at gunpoint, hands over their heads, to the ambassador's office. "The next half hour was a nightmare," a *Los Angeles Times* reporter who happened to be among the hostages remembered. "I thought we were going to be killed," the army attaché recalled. "There wasn't any other thought in my mind."[7]

All of a sudden, a bullet "came flying in the window" of the ambassador's office "and hit the picture of Secretary Vance that was on the wall," the press attaché remembered. "The picture fell to the floor. It just dropped straight down. That was how the counterattack started."[8] Indeed, at 11:49 A.M. (3:19 A.M. in Washington), word came through on the ambassador's walkie-talkie that Khomeini's forces had arrived. The Americans in the ambassador's office could hear the frenzied eruptions of the automatic rifles, submachine guns, and 30-caliber heavy machine guns as a fierce battle between the attackers and Khomeini's counterattackers was waged in the courtyard.

One minute later, a cable from Kabul peeled off the machine in the Operations Center. Amstutz had been sending rapid-fire cables all night, expressing his cresting frustration at the Afghan authorities who were stonewalling his attempts to get information about Ambassador Dubs. One US embassy officer was cooling his heels in the Afghan Interior Ministry waiting to talk with the chief of police. Three US diplomats were at the Hotel Kabul, trying unsuccessfully to talk with the Afghan policemen and the four Soviets who were clearly directing the response to the kidnapping. "Situation at 12:45 hours [Kabul time; 3:15 A.M. in Washington] is as follows," Amstutz cabled in his ninth "sitrep" of the night. "[Afghan foreign minister Hafizullah] Amin will not talk to me on the phone. . . . I have talked again to [Afghan deputy foreign minister Shah Mohammad] Dost stressing the importance of no forced action. . . . Our contingent at hotel . . . are doing same."[9]

Suddenly, Amstutz interrupted his own cable. "FLASH," he wrote. "Hotel group reports that break in is scheduled in omi [*sic*; one] minute." He added, "Apparently government has decided to reject the terrorists [*sic*] demands and respond by forced action." Then, "FLASH: They went in and firing is over."[10]

Secretary Vance waited with the other officials in the Operations Center for five minutes, until 3:25 A.M., before word arrived from Kabul. Amstutz was terse. "Amb[assador] is dead," he cabled.[11]

In Tehran, the tension escalated. The Americans cheered the news that Khomeini's forces had arrived to rescue them, but the fighting outside the chancery escalated as the "Marxists" battled Khomeini's "soldiers of Islam," who had arrived by the truckload, brandishing automatic weapons. Provisional Foreign Minister Ibrahim Yazdi, armed with a bullhorn, stood atop a pickup truck and implored the "Marxists" to lay down their arms. "The Americans were rescued by Yazdi," Johnny Graham—erstwhile partner of Steve Low in southern Africa who had become the British ambassador to Iran in January 1979—declared. By 12:30 P.M. (4:00 A.M. in Washington), the "Marxist" attackers had surrendered and the tension in the chancery eased. "You are our brothers," Khomeini's loyalists assured the Americans. "Don't worry." Yazdi apologized to the Americans: "In times of revolution, mistakes occur."[12]

Less than four hours later, Carter and Vance were aboard Air Force One, en route to Mexico. US-Mexican relations were rocky. Mexican president José López Portillo deeply resented that Washington had reneged on a deal to import Mexican natural gas. The Carter administration, determined to keep a lid on energy costs, countered that the Mexican government's price had been too high. Carter's trip was an important step toward healing relations with America's southern neighbor, and the president decided that despite the crises in Afghanistan and Iran, he should not cancel it. From Air Force One, he telephoned Adolph Dubs' widow to express his sympathy for the murder of her husband. He and Vance were exhausted. A State Department official accompanying them noted that "Mr. Vance was so hurt by that incident [the assassination of Dubs] and felt so strongly that he had lost a friend and one of his people, that you could see it etched on his face. . . . His face was somewhat grey. . . . He was so tired it looked as if he was about to fall on his face."[13]

The arrival ceremony at the Mexico City airport was cool, but nothing prepared Carter for López Portillo's toast at the state luncheon. After four hours of meetings and treks to tourist sites, Carter sat at the banquet table in the Mexican Foreign Ministry. Mexican television broadcast the event live. López Portillo rose to toast his guest of honor but delivered instead a stinging rebuke. "Among . . . neighbors, surprise moves and sudden deceit or abuse are poisonous fruits," he warned. Referring to his country's recent discovery of vast oil reserves, López Portillo observed that Mexico's newfound power inspired "fear" in Americans "much like the recurring vague fears you yourselves inspire in certain areas of our national subconscious."[14]

Jimmy Carter stared intently at López Portillo. He did not smile, but his face conveyed "surprise and some anguish," according to one journalist. Another noted that the president was "looking weary." He rose to toast his host. He began by trying to lighten the atmosphere, bantering about how much he and López Portillo had in common—their fascination with archaeology, their "beautiful and interesting wives," and their love of running. "As a matter of fact," Carter continued, going off-script, "I told President López Portillo that I first acquired my habit of running here in Mexico City. My first running course was from the Palace of Fine Arts to the Majestic Hotel. . . . In the midst of the Folklorico performance, I discovered that I was afflicted with Montezuma's revenge."[15]

Rosalynn Carter "covered her face in embarrassment." The Mexicans deemed it "a typical Yankee slur" that was "unworthy of a world leader." The headline in the *Los Angeles Times* the following day was "Carter humor falls flatter than a tortilla."[16] Other US headlines were equally harsh: "Carter Greeted by Record Chill;" "Blunt Warning from Mexico"; "Mexico Lectures the US"; "Little Enthusiasm for Carter in Mexico."[17]

These eighteen hours on Valentine's Day—from the seizure of Adolph Dubs to the gaffe in Mexico—encapsulate Jimmy Carter's challenges and problems in early 1979. He appeared to be swamped, and he was assailed from all sides.

This aura of weakness invited attacks from afar. On February 15, while Carter was still in Mexico, French president Valéry Giscard d'Estaing launched an unusually sharp attack on his leadership. At a press conference in Paris, when asked what France intended to do about "the void left in the world by the Americans' handling of foreign policy," Giscard responded: "The speed of change and . . . the profound tensions in various parts of the world require clear vision and bold, firm execution of international policy. This is what France is doing." Giscard proceeded to stake out independent ground for France in key domains: relations with the Soviet Union, nuclear arms, and international finance. Pointedly dissociating France from US policy toward Iran, he promised that his administration would "take advantage" of its good relations with the Saudis and Iranians to persuade them to sell more oil to Europe. This upended a long-standing US-led effort to avoid competition among Western countries for oil.[18]

On the same day, European bankers and officials at a trade conference in Frankfurt expressed their "deep-seated lack of faith in the Carter Administration and its economic policies." Moreover, Abu Dhabi and Qatar announced an increase in the price of oil, which would trigger another round of price increases. "The dominoes are starting to fall," one pricing expert observed. Inflation, already at 10 percent in the United States, would rise.[19]

Americans were experiencing an unaccustomed sense of weakness. The *Christian Science Monitor* observed that "to Americans there was the sobering spectacle of vulnerability [during the Valentine's Day takeover of the embassy in Iran] in a land where they had been top dog." The *New York Times* tried to explain what had happened. "Americans have become the obvious targets of angry movements in many places. To the weak, we represent power; to the poor, we stand for exploitation." The *Wall Street Journal* was unsentimental: "In the world of geopolitics, if you lose in one place you will be tested in another." The *Los Angeles Times* intoned ominously: "Other bad days may lie ahead."[20]

This sense of impotence and foreboding mattered. While inchoate, it gravitated toward one symbol, and that was Jimmy Carter. From early 1979 onward, Carter was shadowboxing with this image that he was weak and indecisive. It had become, to use a current cliché, "the narrative" about Jimmy Carter. His politically gutsy decision in December 1978 to normalize relations with China, defying the conservative Taiwan lobby, was forgotten; it did not fit the narrative. Richard Nixon and Henry Kissinger, who had done the glitzy easy work earlier in the decade, got all the credit for the opening to China. Carter's resolute pressure on Israel and Egypt to follow through on the September 1978 Camp David Accords and sign the peace treaty was also cast as weakness. His 1979 State of the Union address, in which he declared inflation to be "the persistent, historic enemy of a free society," was belittled by his conservative critics and bemoaned by liberals as a betrayal of Lyndon Johnson's Great Society.[21] By early 1979, Jimmy Carter, who had been narrowly elected by a fragile and unlikely coalition, had no cheering section. He had no political base. He and his team had to construct a new coalition to support every issue. And, in the distance, they stared at the next election.

Rhodesia: The Most Fertile Field

On April 16, 1979, the CIA scanned the globe to determine where the Kremlin might strike next. "The Soviets still see Africa as the most fertile field for asserting themselves," the agency concluded. The shah had fled Iran, and Afghanistan was in turmoil, but US intelligence believed that Africa was the Soviets' most probable target. The Soviets "are driven to this by (1) ideology . . . [and] (2) geopolitical/strategic reasons," the CIA explained. "Cubans see Africa as fertile too. . . . The record shows increasing Cuban penetrations. . . . [The] most dramatic cases, of course, are Angola & Ethiopia. Rhodesia," the report added, was the most likely place for "possible future Cuban involvement."[22]

This preoccupation with the vulnerability of Africa was evident at meetings with allies. At a December 1978 NATO meeting, "next to human rights, the subject which drew most attention was . . . Africa," the State Department informed Carter.[23] At the Guadeloupe summit of the American, British, French, and West German leaders in January 1979, Africa was not only discussed as one of the key "flashpoints," but Carter and British prime minister James Callaghan stayed behind for a day specifically to talk about Rhodesia.

Hindsight might be 20/20, but it can also be very distorting. The overwhelming complications of the final Carter years obscure the fact that in early 1979, the simmering crisis in southern Africa loomed large in the anxieties of policymakers in Washington. By then, the disaster that had haunted Washington since the Cubans had landed in Angola in 1975 seemed imminent and unstoppable. The longer the Rhodesian war continued, the more likely it was to explode into a conflagration involving Cubans, South Africans, white and black Rhodesians, and the Frontline States. Unless the United States publicly and materially backed the rebels, world opinion would assume that it was backing its long-time ally, white South Africa. Both options—backing the rebels or backing South Africa—would have explosive domestic and foreign consequences. Backing the rebels would signify a profound change in policy, one that would be unacceptable to all but the most radical Americans. Yet backing South Africa, implicitly or explicitly, could cause all black Africa to turn against the West, stopping oil shipments, blocking access to strategic minerals, and closing key ports. Moreover, it would galvanize the Cubans and Soviets.

The 96th Congress

Senator Harry Byrd (I-VA) was not a quitter. He was, as the *Rhodesian Herald* had noted, "one of our [the Rhodesian government's] staunchest friends in Congress." His amendment exempting chrome from the sanctions on Rhodesia had been overturned in early 1977, but as the 96th Congress convened in January 1979, Byrd believed that the time was right to lift sanctions once again. "The Department of State is pursuing an outdated and unrealistic policy toward Southern Africa," he declared in the Senate on January 29. "This policy, I believe, is based at least in part on a misplaced nostalgia for the politics of the civil rights movement of the 1960s and an almost 19th century missionary attitude toward the solution of African problems." Byrd called on the United States to lift sanctions "immediately."[24]

Both the White House and Whitehall were expecting Byrd's move. The Case-Javits resolution had been only a makeshift dam, hastily constructed the previous summer to divert support from the much tougher Helms Amendment. It was designed to hold off the congressional pressure to lift sanctions until Rhodesia held elections, which at the time Case-Javits was passed had been scheduled for December 1978. Smith's decision to delay the elections until April 1979 meant that those who had hoped that sanctions would be lifted by the new year were disappointed, and restive.

"The first skirmish in what has become an annual congressional battle over US policy toward Rhodesia" began on February 9, *CQ Weekly* noted. Two centrist senators, Republican Richard Schweiker of Pennsylvania and Democrat Dennis DeConcini of Arizona, introduced a concurrent resolution that "it is the sense of the Congress" that the Salisbury Four had already fulfilled the first stipulation of Case-Javits—agreeing to all-party talks—and that holding the April elections would fulfill the second stipulation; therefore, within ten days of those elections, President Carter should lift sanctions. This was a warning to the administration to be on guard. As a "sense of the Senate" resolution, it would not compel the White House to obey, but it would cast a broad net, putting many members of Congress on record supporting the internal settlement.[25]

The Schweiker-DeConcini resolution stalled (it would be revived later) because a more immediate opportunity to affect the president's policy toward Rhodesia arose. It addressed the conundrum at the core of the Case-Javits Amendment: how should the president determine whether or not the Rhodesian election had been "free and fair"?

The answer might seem simple: the administration should accept the Salisbury Four's invitation to send a team of official observers to Rhodesia to report on the election. The Salisbury government, however, was illegal and not recognized by any country. The administration worried that sending official US observers would imply recognition.[26] At the first hint that the United States might send observers, the UN's Africa Group issued a statement expressing its "dismay and indignation" that the Carter administration would do something "tantamount to legitimising and giving credibility to the 'internal settlement.'"[27] The Patriotic Front and Frontline States also strongly objected.[28]

Domestic groups weighed in, voicing opposition to sending observers. The White House received letters from TransAfrica, the Black Economic Research Center, leaders of the major civil rights organizations, and black mayors of major cities. All seventeen members of the Congressional Black Caucus wrote the White House and issued a press release explaining their opposition to official observers.[29]

Yet refusing to send observers was sure to rile many other members of Congress. It would reinforce the widespread belief that the Carter administration was irrationally opposed to the Salisbury Four and in the thrall of the Patriotic Front. It would convince some members that Carter was not taking their point of view—expressed in Case-Javits—seriously. As the US ambassador in Tanzania noted, the administration was "on the horns of a classic dilemma: if we send observers, we damage our credibility in Africa; if we don't, we damage it with Congress. How to balance the horns?"[30]

While the White House struggled to answer that question and delayed responding to Salisbury's invitation, members of Congress contemplated sending their own team of observers to the elections. The arguments in favor and against were similar to those being debated by the White House, except that a congressional team was less likely to be seen as signaling an official US tilt toward the internal settlement government.

Senator George McGovern (D-SD), who had assumed the chair of the Africa subcommittee of the Senate Foreign Relations Committee after the defeat of Iowa's Dick Clark, supported the administration's southern Africa policy but considered it doomed on the Hill. He told British foreign secretary David Owen that he "could see little possibility of heading off another Byrd type amendment. There was a growing current of feeling on the Hill and elsewhere," he explained, "that the US administration should not be backing communist terrorists." McGovern doubted that the administration was capable of mounting a persuasive defense of its own policy. Given this pessimism, McGovern adopted a defensive strategy in an attempt "to prevent," he explained, "the initiative being seized by Senate conservatives led by Helms." To this end, he decided that he should introduce a resolution proposing that Congress send a team of observers to the Rhodesian elections. He thought this would be doubly useful: it would release some congressional steam and dull the push for sanctions to be lifted immediately; and, since McGovern was confident that the observers would find that the elections were not free and fair, their report would give Carter important backing for a negative determination on Case-Javits.[31]

The liberal senator from South Dakota managed to persuade an unlikely ally: Sam "S. I." Hayakawa (R-CA), the ranking Republican on the Africa subcommittee. Hayakawa hailed from the conservative end of the GOP, and he had much more in common with Jesse Helms than with George McGovern. He was one of the leaders of the fight to lift sanctions. Unlike McGovern, he was convinced that observers would declare the elections "free and fair" and that this would force Carter to lift sanctions. Thus, although their expectations of what the resolution would accomplish were diametrically opposed, the two senators agreed that Congress should send observers to the elections. They consulted Vance, who advised them that the administration would not oppose the resolution if it included the proviso that sending observers did not imply recognition of the internal settlement government.[32] On March 1, McGovern and Hayakawa cosponsored a concurrent resolution in the Senate that the Congress should send a team of twenty-five to fifty observers to the Rhodesian elections. The observers would not be members of Congress; instead, they would be "recruited from private life" and their presence would not imply US recognition. "The objective of the resolution," the Senate report noted, "is to provide a mechanism for obtaining accurate, impartial, and first-hand information which would be available to the US Government in making a determination" on the election.[33]

That night, Vance wrote Carter a long memo about the observers issue. Vance was sensitive to the need to protect the president's time; he chose his topics with care and did not overload Carter with peripheral issues. On March 1, when he penned the memo on Rhodesia, Vance was preparing to accompany Carter on a state visit to Egypt and Israel the following week to finalize the Egyptian-Israeli peace treaty, which seemed to be unraveling; both men were dealing with the fall of the shah and the revolutionary chaos in Iran; they were preparing for a summit with Soviet leader Leonid Brezhnev to sign the SALT II accord, scheduled for June; and they were overseeing Congress's final passage of the Panama Canal treaties. Sending observers to the Rhodesian elections received top-level attention in the midst of such a crowded agenda.

In his memo, Vance explained that the president would need a factual basis to make his decision on Case-Javits but that sending official observers "would violate our international legal obligations by awarding a degree of legitimacy to the Smith regime." It would be "interpreted negatively" by Africans and "seriously erode our negotiating capability." Therefore, he recommended that Carter decline the Salisbury Four's invitation to send official observers. Vance then dealt with the congressional debate about election observers, and he recommended that the executive branch take "a neutral position." Vance knew that the opponents of the administration's Rhodesia policy were waiting for an opportunity to pounce—forcing the president to lift sanctions—and he believed that the opponents could command a majority in both houses. Vance wanted to avoid doing anything to raise the temperature on the Hill about Rhodesia. "To oppose Congress's sending observers would only increase the chances for an undesirable Congressional resolution calling on the Administration to designate observers."[34]

Andrew Young—who had stirred more controversy when he announced that "only neo-fascists in this country would be willing to support the neo-fascism of the Smith regime in Rhodesia"—disagreed. His soundings on the Hill led him to believe that the administration could rally a majority, however slim, in support of its Rhodesia policy. "Without making this a major test of will," Young asserted, "the administration should oppose Congress sending any officially appointed observers."[35] He was overruled. The president followed Vance's advice.

On March 5 and 7, the Foreign Relations Committee held hearings on the McGovern-Hayakawa resolution to send observers. Assistant Secretary Dick Moose deftly dodged questions about the administration's stance toward the resolution. "We certainly respect the reasoning that has led you . . . to introduce this resolution," he said. "We certainly recognize the right of the Congress to inform itself in whatever way it sees fit." The congressional expert from the British embassy attended the hearings and noted their "relaxed" and "non-confrontational" tone. "I suspect," he added, "the hardliners like Helms . . . are . . . keeping their powder dry for a later stage—perhaps after the April 20 elections. In the meantime, the McGovern/Hayakawa Resolution strikes me as . . . the best available means of holding the line (at least for the time being) against strong Senate pressures to lift sanctions after 20 April."[36]

On March 14, the resolution to send observers passed in the Foreign Relations Committee with only one dissenting vote. Two weeks later, on March 28, it was debated by the full Senate. McGovern and Hayakawa struck a cordial, bipartisan tone when their resolution came to the floor. The debate, however, was dominated by critics of the administration's Rhodesia policy. Helms and Schweiker orated at length about the "odd . . . stupid . . . inexcusable" policy of the Carter administration. Liberals who opposed sending observers, deserted by McGovern and the "neutral" administration, had nowhere to turn. Massachusetts Democrat Paul Tsongas, who had moved from the House to the Senate in the last election, mounted a hopeless battle against the resolution. "This resolution . . . is unnecessary; it is impractical; and it would involve great foreign policy risks," he exclaimed. He was almost alone. The final vote was as lopsided as had been expected: sixty-six to twenty-seven.[37]

Moose and Solarz to the Rescue

A similar story seemed likely to unfold in the House. The day after the McGovern-Hayakawa resolution passed in the Senate Foreign Relations

Committee, William Carney, a New York freshman representative who belonged to the state's Conservative Party, introduced an identical measure in the House to send observers to the Rhodesian elections. Carney's measure, however, followed a different trajectory. This can be explained by two names: Dick Moose and Stephen Solarz.[38]

Before his appointment as assistant secretary of state for African affairs, Moose had served on the staff of the Senate Foreign Relations Committee from 1969 to 1976. He not only had an intimate knowledge of how Congress worked; he also had good relations with key senators and their staffs. He was smart, passionately committed to the administration's policy in southern Africa, and willing to work discreetly behind the scenes. He understood that it was imperative to keep the hand of the White House hidden.[39] Solarz, a liberal New York City Democrat in his third term, was ambitious, energetic, and intensely curious. "I came to Congress feeling very strongly that I wanted to make a difference," he explained. "I quickly concluded that the way to make a difference was within the framework of my committee assignments. . . . And it quickly became clear to me that in order to make a difference, one had to master . . . the intricacies of the issues with which the [foreign affairs] committee was dealing. I quickly concluded that the best way to achieve that mastery was to go to the various areas of the world where there were important issues at stake." In July 1976, two months after Henry Kissinger's speech in Lusaka, Solarz traveled to South Africa, Rhodesia, and Mozambique; he returned to Washington determined that the US government promote change and justice there. "[It was] where one could most meaningfully try to reaffirm some of the fundamental principles and values upon which our own country had been founded two centuries earlier."[40]

Other than raising his profile, championing African issues did not help Solarz politically. He did not have a close relationship with Carter, who appears never to have seen him on his own, despite the State Department's strong suggestion that it would be smart to do so. Nor did it curry the favor of his Brooklyn constituents—overwhelmingly Democratic and Jewish—who expressed no particular interest in the continent. Only 8 percent of his district was African American. "What I did in southern Africa was not in any way whatsoever a response to concerns or pressure on the part of my constituency," Solarz asserted, "but emanated entirely from my own view of America's interest and values as they apply to that part of the world." He explained to Vance, "The lifting of sanctions by the United States would be a disaster for us with the Africans and present a golden opportunity for the Soviet Union and Cuba."[41]

By early 1979, Solarz feared that the administration's improved relations with black Africa would go up in flames if Congress lifted sanctions on

Rhodesia prematurely. He was convinced that sending congressional observers to the April elections would be perilous: by signaling a US tilt toward the Salisbury Four, it would remove incentives for them to negotiate. Many years later, he explained, "My sense was that if the delegation went, they would look at the voting and probably on election day it would be reasonably honest. . . . They would give the elections a good government seal of approval and then we would be in a position where we had, in effect, legitimized the process which was inherently unfair." Therefore, Solarz decided to fight— hard—against sending observers to the Rhodesian elections. He and Moose joined forces.[42]

Solarz was in a good position to lead the battle. He had just assumed the chairmanship of the House Africa subcommittee after Charlie Diggs had stepped down. In the House, the resolution on observers to the Rhodesian elections would be debated first in the Africa subcommittee and referred to the full committee only if the subcommittee failed to achieve unanimity. (This differed from the Senate, where the resolution had been debated by the full Foreign Relations Committee without being considered in subcommittee. Frank Church [D-ID], chair of the Foreign Relations Committee, wanted to centralize power, while Clement Zablocki [D-WI], chair of the House International Relations Committee, gave the subcommittees more autonomy.) Moreover, the House Africa subcommittee members leaned liberal. The six Democrats included Solarz; three members of the Congressional Black Caucus (Charlie Diggs, Cardiss Collins, and Bill Grey); and Howard Wolpe, a Michigan freshman who had a deep interest in Africa. The sixth Democrat, Nebraskan Floyd Fithian, was a middle-of-the-road conservative. None of the three Republicans on the subcommittee was a firebrand like Helms or Hayakawa: Alabama's John Buchanan was a pastor who cared about human rights; New Jersey's Millicent Fenwick was a moderate Republican who championed civil rights; and Pennsylvania's Bill Goulding was a small-government conservative who focused on domestic affairs.

Working together, Moose and Solarz took no chances. With Moose advising from the wings, Solarz obtained Senator McGovern's agreement that observers should go to Rhodesia only if both houses of Congress voted to send them. Then he pulled out all the stops to persuade his colleagues on the committee that they should vote against the Carney resolution. Solarz realized that the argument in favor of supporting the internal settlement government had merit, but he tried to convince his colleagues that it would be "counterproductive." He did this by holding extensive hearings over four days that educated the committee about the background to the elections. With Moose's discreet help, Solarz moved the debate from a simple up/down vote on Carter's policy to a broader consideration of the impact that US support for the internal settlement government would have in southern Africa and on US interests in the region. To this end, he invited the African ambassadors in Washington to meet with the committee members. The ambassadors, who represented widely varying political points of view, were unanimous and adamant that the internal settlement government would not bring peace and Congress should not send observers to the election.[43]

By late March, when Moose testified to the House Africa subcommittee, the administration was "confident" that the Carney resolution would be voted down in committee. Vance wrote the House International Relations Committee that "the Administration strongly opposes any legislative initiative that could be interpreted as US support for one side or the other in the Rhodesian conflict." Moose toed this fine line in his testimony.

> Mr. Solarz: Clearly you believe that a group of *executive* observers would [damage the prestige of the country], that is your testimony?
>
> Mr. Moose: I do believe that.
>
> Mr. Solarz: Do you believe that a group of *congressional* observers could seriously damage the prestige of the country . . .?
>
> Mr. Moose: In the absence of a keen understanding on the part of others of the American constitutional process, that effect could occur.
>
> Mr. Solarz: Do you think that keen understanding exists?
>
> Mr. Moose: I have some doubts. [Laughter]
>
> Mr. Solarz: We ought to take this show on the road. [Laughter][44]

On April 2, the subcommittee voted on the Carney resolution. By then, it was clear that Moose and Solarz had five votes of support, but had they persuaded the three Republicans and one conservative Democrat? Decisively, yes: the Carney resolution was defeated unanimously—which meant that it would not be referred to the full committee. "It was an enormously significant moment in history," Ambassador Steve Low, not a man given to overstatement, remarked. Solarz agreed: "It was a rather extraordinary legislative achievement." Immediately after the vote, he announced confidently, "The matter has now come to an end."[45]

Not quite. The critics of Carter's Rhodesia policy hoped to tack an amendment calling for observers onto pending legislation on the House floor.

However, they had two big problems: time was running out (the Rhodesian elections would begin on April 10) and House rules require that an amendment be "germane" to the bill to which it was attached. Days passed with no appropriate legislation coming to the floor. Finally, on April 9, the foreign assistance bill was debated. This bill could serve as a vehicle for amendments about Rhodesia. "The President, being unable to veto the Aid Bill, will find it very difficult to resist such a move," Moose explained to the British Foreign Office. "We must take very seriously the likelihood of Congressional action."[46]

Pennsylvania Republican Robert Bauman led the charge, proposing an amendment that would send congressional observers to Rhodesia and also (to make it germane to foreign assistance) extend $20 million in aid to the newly elected government. The amendment had one purpose: to signal congressional support for the internal settlement. Bauman himself admitted that it was "too late" to actually send observers. Moreover, the $20 million in aid was a transparent bow to the germaneness rule. The long and heated debate that followed was not about observers or aid; it was about the future of US policy toward Rhodesia in particular and the world in general.[47]

Solarz went on the attack. "This amendment would alienate literally every country in Africa," he declared. "This amendment would be a passport to the Russians and the Cubans to become infinitely more involved in the Rhodesian conflict than they are today." Solarz brought out the heavy weapons: "We will be stuck with another Vietnam-like situation . . . supporting a government which has the support of only one other country on the globe, the Government of South Africa." He reached a crescendo: "Forget about our relations with the rest of Africa. Forget about the possibility of a peaceful transition to majority rule in Rhodesia. . . . If this amendment is adopted it will constitute an unmitigated disaster." There was scattered applause as the representative from New York sat down.[48]

Ed Derwinski, an arch-conservative Republican from Illinois, spoke next. "I join in the applause," he began, "because I consider it to be one of the most masterful overstatements of a case I have ever heard." Derwinski elaborated on the reasons the United States should support the Salisbury Four, and he concluded with the suggestion that "those who are concerned with the use of Cubans as a foreign legion by the Soviets in Africa, [must] not be lulled by the wonderful, glowing oratory of my friend, the gentleman from New York."[49]

After many representatives had weighed in—displaying an impressive command of the intricacies of the Rhodesian crisis—the two camps engaged in a rapid-fire series of complex parliamentary moves. Moose and Solarz worked furiously behind the scenes. They pleaded. They twisted arms. They had very little time. After a brief debate, Bauman's amendment was put to a vote. Moose and Solarz had performed magic: the amendment went down to defeat, 190 to 180.[50]

Reading the Tea Leaves in Pretoria and London

"While we are somewhat encouraged by this result," Vance wrote Carter about the House vote on observers, "we do not consider it a reliable indication of how the House may vote on sanctions after a black government is installed." Would Congress vote to lift sanctions if Carter delivered a negative determination on Case-Javits? The Senate had voted overwhelmingly to send observers, but some, like McGovern, had done so hoping to help Carter maintain sanctions whereas others, like Hayakawa, had done so hoping the opposite. In the House, it was much clearer that those who voted in favor of observers (the Bauman resolution) would be likely also to support lifting sanctions, but the extraordinary closeness of the vote made it a poor predictor. Moreover, between fifty-five and sixty-four representatives had been absent. It all came down to interpretation or, in other words, guesswork.[51] Moreover, as the Carter administration strove to read the tea leaves in Congress, the situation on the ground—particularly in South Africa and Britain—was changing.

The desperate hope that Pretoria would rescue the Anglo-American proposals by tightening the screws on Smith collapsed in the weeks following Brand Fourie's lame promise to Dick Moose and Antony Duff that he would "refer the question higher up." One month later, on March 24, Ambassador Steve Low met with Ken Flower, the head of Rhodesian intelligence. "The South African government has taken a new look at the Rhodesian situation," Flower announced bluntly, "and decided to support the internal settlement." Flower pointed out that Pretoria was giving "significant financial support" to Bishop Abel Muzorewa and Reverend Ndabaningi Sithole. The Americans had relied on South African foreign minister Pik Botha for insight on Pretoria's policies, but the new prime minister, P.W. Botha, "was turning away from the Foreign Office for advice and towards [Chief of the Armed Forces] General Magnus Malan. Malan's view had always been more supportive of Smith and his efforts than the Foreign Office." Pretoria had hoped to engineer a diplomatic solution that would put ZAPU leader Joshua Nkomo on top, but after the failed meeting with Smith and the downing of the Viscount in September 1978, Nkomo's star had fallen. Therefore, Flower concluded, Pretoria "felt that neither the British nor the Americans had anything to contribute to resolving the situation." The South Africans had given up on diplomacy. The internal settlement government was their best bet, and they were committed to helping it survive.[52]

Flower had a vested interest in this interpretation of Pretoria's policy, but he was supported by the evidence. The Botha regime was cracking down internally and externally, and any hope that P.W. Botha would be flexible on granting independence to Namibia had been dashed. "It now looks as if a minor miracle will be required to get the Namibian settlement plan back on track," congressional liaison Madeleine Albright wrote on March 10. Two weeks later, Botha delivered a scathing indictment of the Carter administration. "America," he told the London *Sunday Times*, "is in the grips of a sickly humanism trying to appease Africa and at the same time feed the hungry crocodile from Moscow." On April 12, relations soured further when Pretoria expelled three American embassy officials, including the defense attaché and the assistant air attaché, for spying; Washington responded by expelling the South African defense and air attachés. A well-informed *Sunday Times* correspondent with close ties to Foreign Minister Pik Botha wrote that the South African government was fed up with Washington's "'reproving nanny' attitude" and doubted that it could still consider the United States "a friendly country." P.W. Botha told the South African Parliament that South Africa would not be the "doormat of any superpower."[53]

The Carter administration had a number of sticks to use against South Africa. It could have repeated the firm anti-apartheid message that Vice President Walter Mondale had delivered in Vienna in 1977; it could have recalled its remaining military attachés and its ambassador; it could have stalled or stopped cooperation on nuclear energy and research; or it could have supported mandatory UN economic sanctions. Anti-apartheid activists called on Washington to take all these measures. The Carter administration, however, demurred. All the sticks were boomerangs. Mondale's words had not alleviated apartheid at all. By late 1978, even Mondale rued his call for one man/one vote in South Africa. "I think I did speak inartfully in that one," he admitted to the *Washington Post*. US officials had concluded that cutting ties—anywhere along the spectrum from pulling out a military attaché to breaking relations—might give short-term satisfaction to Pretoria's critics in the United States but would inflame Carter's conservative critics and reduce Washington's influence and information. Economic sanctions were anathema not only to London but also to the galvanized conservatives in the US Congress. Senate Foreign Relations Committee chair Frank Church predicted that "Congress would vote to roll back sanctions against South Africa within 6–9 months of the US voting for them in the Security Council." The Carter administration decided, therefore, to absorb P.W. Botha's rebuff in silence.[54]

Instead of using a stick, it dangled a limp carrot. Soon after Prime Minister Botha had told James Callaghan's envoy Cledwyn Hughes that he sorely wanted to meet with the American president, Carter had embraced the idea, telling Callaghan, Helmut Schmidt, and Valéry Giscard d'Estaing at Guadeloupe that he planned to extend the invitation "fairly soon." On April 6, at the bottom of a formal letter to P.W. Botha, Carter added a postscript in his own handwriting: "If there is agreement on the UN proposals [for Namibia], I believe it would be useful for us to get together at an early date." By the time he penned the letter, it was an empty formality: no one expected an agreement on the UN proposals. A month later, Carter expressed resignation about the situation. On a memo about South African obduracy, he wrote, "I guess our only option is to continue dreaming." Then he crossed out dreaming and wrote "hoping." Finally, he crossed out hoping and wrote "trying."[55]

The Callaghan government, meanwhile, was battling labor strikes at home sparked by its anti-inflation measures. As 1979 began, it was clear that a British general election was a matter of months away, and by February the omens for Labour were grim: public opinion polls gave the Conservatives a nineteen-point lead, signaling "a Tory landslide of epic proportions."[56] On March 28, the Labour government lost a vote of confidence, and a general election was called for May 3, 1979. For the Carter administration, this meant that the years of careful cooperation with Whitehall might be screeching to a halt.

The British Conservative Party hid neither its respect for the tenacious white Rhodesians nor its disdain for the sanctions that Labour Prime Minister Harold Wilson had asked the UN to impose in the late 1960s. Nevertheless, when Parliament had to renew the sanctions every November, almost all Tories had bitten their tongues and either voted for their renewal or abstained. They groused, but they did not mount a campaign to lift the sanctions because they accepted the government's demand that Rhodesia had to move toward majority rule. Their mood changed, however, in March 1978 when Smith announced his internal settlement. Like their counterparts across the Atlantic, British conservatives applauded the internal settlement and pilloried the Anglo-American proposals for their failure to recognize the fledgling biracial government in Salisbury.[57] By October 1978, these conservatives, who packed the Tory backbenches, were raring for a fight.

On October 4, 1978, the top officials of the Conservative Party met to prepare for the annual party conference that would open a week later in the seaside resort of Brighton. One topic dominated the meeting, which was chaired by party leader Margaret Thatcher. "Rhodesia," one of the participants warned, "was by far the likeliest subject of a revolt at the Conference."[58] Thatcher and her shadow cabinet had a problem: the backbenchers were restless; they wanted the party to call for the immediate lifting of sanctions on Rhodesia's internal settlement government.

Lord Carrington, the leader of the Tories in the House of Lords, opened the discussion by explaining why lifting sanctions was "a road that we could not sensibly take unilaterally." He explained his reasoning pungently in his memoirs: "I was already, sadly, convinced that the 'internal settlement' was probably a fudge. . . . Above all . . . it could not possibly be sold to the international community."[59] It would be dangerous, diplomatically and economically, for Britain to lift sanctions before the rest of the world recognized the Rhodesian government. "Once we were in office, a commitment to remove sanctions . . . would put us in an extremely weak position to act as any kind of bridge between the various parties," Carrington noted. "It was also vital to bear in mind that enormous economic and diplomatic interests would be at stake if we pursued this course." Patrick Jenkin, the shadow secretary of health and social services, added that he had received "a very firm warning . . . from a contact in Nigeria" that if London lifted sanctions, Lagos would nationalize British companies operating in Nigeria. Lord Thorneycroft, who had been chancellor of the exchequer in the 1950s, inquired: "Why on earth should the next Tory Government be landed in still more trouble by an impractical motion about sanctions which would create nothing but complications?" Not one of the assembled leaders, including Thatcher, spoke in defense of the backbenchers' desire to lift sanctions. They agreed unanimously: "Our best line to take, therefore, would be to concentrate on attacking the Labour Party in general and Dr. Owen in particular, indicate some of the difficulties of removing sanctions, and state that we understood and sympathized with the powerful emotions of the Conference but could not accept any motion or amendment to end sanctions unilaterally."[60]

It fell to John Davies, shadow foreign secretary, to break the news to the delegates crowded into the hall. In what a *Guardian* editorial deemed "a speech of truly memorable inadequacy," Davies conveyed what the leadership had decided—that it would be unwise for the Party to box itself in by promising to lift sanctions. "He said nice things about Mr Ian Smith . . . and nasty things about Dr David Owen," the *Guardian* noted. "But that is the Tory way of disguising that what it would actually do in office is not so very different from what Dr Owen is now doing." The disguise fooled no one. While Davies was speaking, the "rank and file howled . . . with a fury." The hapless Davies was "heckled and jeered." Catcalls and cries of "Sack him!" echoed through the hall.[61] (Days after this debacle, Davies was diagnosed with inoperable brain cancer; he stepped down from his post as shadow foreign secretary and died soon thereafter.)

Two days later, Margaret Thatcher addressed the crowd. Hammering hard on her promise to shrink government, cut inflation and curb the unions, she was greeted with rapturous applause by the assembled Tories, who could taste victory. "I hope after this afternoon . . . that it will not be possible for anyone to say: 'There's really not much difference between the parties.' There's all the difference in the world," she roared.[62] She did not mention Rhodesia.

When Parliament debated the sanctions bill in November 1978, the Tory leadership issued a "blanket condemnation of the Government's handling of the Rhodesia situation," but it also announced that official Conservative policy was to abstain on the vote, although it would not punish backbenchers who refused to obey. The opponents of sanctions were outraged by the idea of abstention. They believed passionately that the internal settlement had brought majority rule to Rhodesia, and therefore sanctions must be lifted. "This debate is about ourselves," the fiery Ulster Unionist Enoch Powell declared in the House of Commons. "It is about our honour and about, if such a word may still be used without laughter, our greatness." In 1976, only twenty Tories had bucked their leaders' advice to abstain, and in 1977 only seven more had joined them, but this time fully half of the backbenchers rebelled. The motion to renew carried in the lower house, but with 121 dissenting votes. This was, Thatcher's authorized biographer Charles Moore writes, "the largest Tory rebellion since the Second World War."[63]

The next day, the *Guardian* headline blared: "Tory Right Score Psychological Victory on Sanctions Vote." (The *Times* was on strike.) The Conservative leadership was challenged not only by the backbenchers but also by two of their own: both Winston Churchill, the grandson of the former prime minister, and John Biggs-Davison voted to lift sanctions. Biggs-Davison promptly resigned his post as a shadow spokesman for Northern Ireland, and Thatcher summarily fired Churchill from his post as shadow spokesman for defense. "You felt strongly about this matter—and voted accordingly, . . . but the front bench has to act on the principle of collective responsibility," she wrote Churchill, adding in her own hand at the end of the letter, "I too feel strongly about events in Rhodesia—we all do."[64]

The debate then moved to the House of Lords, where the sanctions on Rhodesia had been controversial ever since they were first imposed.[65] Lord Carrington bore the responsibility of persuading his Tory colleagues to abide by the leaders' recommendations and abstain on the vote. "The test . . . is solely this," Carrington explained, "whether or not sanctions removal will be more or less likely to make a peaceful settlement attainable. . . . Let us make no mistake about it. A repeal of sanctions by this country would bring great hostility upon us and . . . would lead not only to an intensification of the dispute but would remove Britain's ability to play a useful role."[66] The debate was long and heated. Finally, at 2:30 A.M. the motion was put to a vote. Carrington had succeeded beyond expectations: only 65 of the 231 Lords balked, and sanctions remained in place.

Although the Tory leaders, including Thatcher, were sympathetic to the internal settlement, they believed that for the time being, practical considerations overrode sentiment and necessitated the maintenance of sanctions. The backbenchers, by contrast, were mounting an increasingly strong revolt in favor of Smith and Muzorewa.

In the spring of 1979, the Tory leaders had to deal with two new factors: the Rhodesian elections and the imminent British general election. The former increased the backbenchers' pressure to lift sanctions, and the latter meant that Tory policy was no longer the chatter of the opposition: it was probable that it would soon be British policy. The leaders wanted to acknowledge the importance of the Rhodesian elections, dampen a full-fledged rebellion in their ranks, and also avoid limiting their options once in power. They accomplished this by doing what politicians do best: they parsed their words.

In early March 1979, the Tories announced that they were sending a team of observers to the Rhodesian elections. A month later, in a major policy statement, the new shadow foreign secretary Francis Pym seemed to promise that a Tory administration would recognize the new government in Rhodesia and do "everything possible to make sure that the new independent state receives international recognition . . . if the election takes place in reasonably free and fair conditions." On April 11, Margaret Thatcher unveiled her party's "fresh approach" to southern Africa in the Conservative Manifesto: Thatcher, who routinely labeled Nkomo and Mugabe "terrorists," repeated Pym's pledge to recognize the new government in Rhodesia. If the elections were free and fair, "the next [British] Government will have the duty to return Rhodesia to a state of legality, move to lift sanctions and do its utmost to insure that the new independent state gains international recognition." She and Pym stressed the seriousness of the communist threat to Africa, which, they asserted, has "never loomed larger."[67]

While it was clear that the Tories were much more sympathetic to the internal settlement than were the Labour government or the Carter administration, Washington had reason to doubt that they would act precipitously once in office. Tory rhetoric was strident, but its leaders quietly assured Washington that their actions would be more measured. After a meeting with Lord Carrington in February 1979, Vance informed Carter: "I was pleased to see that he takes a more moderate approach on southern Africa . . . than many of his Conservative colleagues." In early March, Carrington assured American officials "that a Conservative Government would more or less follow the Government's present line on Rhodesia," and the US ambassador in London,

Kingman Brewster, cabled that the "Tory leadership . . . recognize the dangers of a hasty embrace of the Salisbury government should the Conservatives come to power."[68]

The State Department and the CIA believed that two dates in 1979 would affect the timing of British decision-making on Rhodesia. In August, the biennial Commonwealth conference would be held in Zambia, and in November, Parliament would have to vote to renew the sanctions on Rhodesia. "If Congress voted to lift US sanctions," the CIA observed on April 6, 1979, "a Tory government might be emboldened to act sooner."[69]

Thus, the messages from London were mixed. Everyone expected a change of government as a result of the May election, and the Carter administration accepted that this would spell the end of its close cooperation with Whitehall on Rhodesian policy. Nevertheless, it was not yet clear how widely or quickly the two allies' paths would diverge. As Ambassador Brewster cabled in early April, immediately before the Rhodesian elections: "There is little Conservative sympathy for the Anglo-American proposals and considerable support for the internal settlement. Nonetheless, there is in Conservative ranks a growing appreciation of and caution about the Rhodesia problem. We have been told repeatedly that Mrs Thatcher . . . wishes to keep her options open."[70]

Washington Wobbles

The combined pressures on the Carter officials who were formulating Rhodesia policy—Congress threatening to lift sanctions, South Africa refusing to play ball, the imminent demise of the Callaghan government, the unwavering intransigence of all parties in Rhodesia, and the escalating war—took their toll. The friendship between Dick Moose and Tony Lake, a key partnership in support of the State Department's Africa policy, frayed. Moose and Lake were a powerful duo. As assistant secretary, Moose influenced the Africa Bureau and the ambassadors in the field, while as head of the Policy Planning Staff, Lake—who had a close relationship with Vance—held sway through the department's upper echelons.[71]

By the end of March 1979, Moose and Lake disagreed about how to handle the prospect that Congress might lift sanctions. Moose thought that the Carter administration should pull out all the stops to persuade swing voters in Congress to maintain the sanctions. In this, he had the key support of Solarz, who had told Carter that he believed that "at the end of the day the House would be prepared to sustain his determination if he concluded the elections were not free and fair."[72] Lake, however, was pessimistic about the administration's chances in Congress and thought that the White House had to reshape its policy to face the new reality: Congress was going to lift sanctions, South Africa was not going to cooperate, and the Callaghan government was going to fall.

The matter came to a head in the wake of Carter's routine intelligence briefing on March 28, 1979. The president, who had been preoccupied with the Iranian Revolution and the Egyptian-Israeli peace treaty, had not been focusing on Rhodesia. But as the April elections approached, he knew that he would have to decide whether they had been "free and fair." Therefore, he showed "keen interest" when Deputy Director of Central Intelligence Frank Carlucci briefed him on the situation in Rhodesia. Carlucci noted that "the South African attitude was hardening and . . . the possibility of Thatcher coming into power [in Britain] was giving heart to Rhodesian whites." He added "that Congress could preempt our options." Carter was open to a shift in policy. He mused to Carlucci that "one possibility would be to cut a deal with the South Africans where they support us on [UN supervised elections in] Namibia and we would agree to recognize the internal settlement [in Rhodesia]." He ordered Brzezinski to hold an immediate Policy Review Committee (PRC) meeting on the issue.[73]

The PRC was called for April 5. This gave the officials concerned with Rhodesia one week to hone and pitch their ideas. They had the president's attention. Yet even though there was quiet confidence that Carter would maintain the policy they had been pursuing for two-and-a-half years and keep sanctions in place, there were two reasons why no one could be sure.

First, Carter was unpredictable. His April 1978 decision to delay the development of the controversial neutron bomb was only the most glaring example. Carter absorbed information and advice from many sources, but he delegated no important decisions. Everyone who worked with him knew that he would diligently study the reports of the Rhodesian elections and the memos about it and he would look within himself and come to his own decision. Second, it was a tough call. Although Moose had been fairly confident on February 16, telling the British Foreign Office that he expected Carter to make a negative determination on Case-Javits (that is, that the elections were not "free and fair"), much had changed in the intervening seven weeks in the US Congress, South Africa, and Britain.[74] Would it be wise for the president to refuse to lift sanctions on Rhodesia and thereby antagonize a sizable group in Congress at a time when he needed their support on SALT? The answer to this question involved two judgments: how important was Rhodesia and, even if it was important, would maintaining sanctions make any difference? Would a widespread war break out in any case? If he refused to lift sanctions, would Carter be wasting precious political capital on a hopeless cause?

Tony Lake was worried about the president's political capital. He thought the administration was going to lose the fight on the Hill. "Congress would certainly lift sanctions," he wrote Vance on April 4. One reason was that the administration's strategy was backfiring: "The nub of our problem with both the Congress and the Salisbury parties is that the harder we fight against lifting sanctions, the more we are perceived as favoring the Patriotic Front." Therefore, he argued, the State Department had to face reality, however painful. It had to change tactics. Lake's new proposal was to offer the new Rhodesian government elected in April (and presumably led by Muzorewa) a deal: if it agreed to "internationally supervised elections and a new or significantly amended constitution," President Carter would lift sanctions. The key change here was that the choice was given to the new Muzorewa government alone. Even if the Patriotic Front refused to participate in the process, the United States would lift sanctions if the Muzorewa government agreed to rewrite the constitution and hold internationally supervised elections.[75]

Lake knew that this plan, with its apparent tilt toward the new government elected in Salisbury and away from the Patriotic Front, would be costly. He admitted that it "would be unpopular with the Africans." Moose let him know in no uncertain terms that he thought that Lake was "compromising on a matter of principle." Lake remembered the argument ruefully. "Ah yes, I had a case of moral turpitude." He smiled. "Moose said, in front of Vance: 'Tony, of all the issues you've been wrong on, you're more wrong on this one than on any other.'"[76]

Lake vehemently disagreed. "I take severe exception to any implication that I was leaning toward the internal settlement; I was just more anxious to try to find a compromise with our critics in Congress. Because I thought we'd be dead in the water if we didn't." This desperate situation called for a desperate measure—but it was a shift in tactics, not an abandonment of principle. Lake figured that the majority of the US Congress would welcome, and consider reasonable, the deal he proposed that Carter offer to the newly elected Muzorewa government. His plan, he wrote Vance, would be seen "as more fair than our current position," and it would give Carter political cover if he decided to declare that the April elections were not free and fair. Moose understood this clearly: "Tony said we have to make sure that the president—if he makes a negative decision [on Case-Javits]—has a defensive rationale for it."[77]

But Lake's plan was not just a way to protect the president; it was also an attempt to protect the policy. Lake knew that it was highly unlikely that the new government, flush with victory after the April elections, would agree to the two conditions he proposed (a new constitution and new elections). This refusal, Lake figured, would weaken support on the Hill for Muzorewa. Then—if the bishop rejected the deal, as Lake expected—the administration would have a chance of defeating any congressional attempt to lift sanctions. Lake knew that Vance was open to the idea, but he suggested that Vance "first explore it with Andy Young. His support and efforts would be very important."[78]

Moose was aware that Vance was tempted by the idea of taking some of the congressional heat off the president and smoothing the path for the ratification of SALT II; he suspected that Carter might also be so inclined. But he considered the Lake gambit not only a sacrifice of principle but also unacceptably risky for two reasons. First, it gave Muzorewa alone the prerogative: if he accepted new elections and a new constitution, Washington would lift sanctions no matter what the Patriotic Front did. Whatever Lake's intention, this would be seen as a tilt toward Muzorewa and damage Carter's image in Africa and the Third World. Second, Muzorewa just might accept the deal, and then the administration would have to lift sanctions even though the war would not end.

Moose immediately fired off a memo to Vance, strongly urging him not to scuttle the administration's established policy and instead to "make the strongest effort possible to prevent a Congressional lifting of sanctions." Moose was not unrealistic about the administration's chances of success, but he believed that this policy would serve US interests better than the Lake plan. "If, as now seems likely, we lose the battle [with Congress to maintain sanctions], we would have done so in a way that would still permit us to play a role [negotiating a settlement in Rhodesia] in the future."[79]

The PRC met in the midst of this exchange, on April 5, with Vance in the chair and top people from the CIA, the Joint Chiefs, the Departments of Defense and Treasury, as well as Brzezinski in attendance. They discussed Namibia and debated the normalization of relations with Angola, but the bulk of the meeting concerned Rhodesia. There was almost unanimous pessimism about the ability of the administration to head off a congressional move to lift sanctions. Lake outlined his "Sanctions-Leverage Strategy," and although some participants raised "serious questions" there was "a great deal of interest" in it. They could not reach a consensus and decided to hold another meeting on April 12 to decide the future direction of US policy toward Rhodesia. Time was running out. The Rhodesian elections were set to begin on April 10.[80]

Jerry Funk, who had been recruited to the NSC staff as an African expert in November 1978, attended the meeting, and as soon as he left it he penned a lengthy analysis of the Lake strategy to Brzezinski. Funk, formerly with the CIA, had quickly gained Brzezinski's confidence in his time on the NSC. His inclinations were to be tough on the Soviets and pragmatic on US policy toward Africa. He was not ideologically liberal, but he had a sensitive grasp of the nuances of African perceptions, and—a personal detail that might have colored his views—he was married to an Ethiopian. Funk spoke Brzezinski's language, but his conclusions tended to be consonant with those of the State Department's Africa Bureau. When working for the AFL-CIO in early 1978, he had gone to Rhodesia to assess the internal settlement, and his judgment had been critical. "While Bishop Muzorewa was a very nice man, he basically represented a commitment to maintain the status quo of racial inequality, with Ian Smith pulling the strings and the South Africans yanking his chains. . . . Any new [internal] election was very very unlikely to be open or fair." The British assessment of Funk was apt: "He is short, square, has a ginger beard and his views are down to earth." In the development of Africa policy in 1979, Funk played an important role guiding Brzezinski toward the State Department's point of view. Moose recalled that "Jerry very quickly became a member of the team. We were all on the same wavelength."[81]

Funk's memo to Brzezinski about the PRC meeting helps explain why Brzezinski did not ultimately join the fray in support of Lake's proposal. "The pitfalls" of Lake's scheme "are many and obvious," Funk noted. Liberals and blacks would see it as "a sell out to racism . . . [but the] real problem—it is unlikely to end war (or bring parties to table) and it could damage our credibility." Funk was blunt: Lake's scheme was "not . . . a very good idea. . . . I think there is more long-term political gain in sticking to our present 'high ground' position." The Case-Javits Amendment had put President Carter in a tough position: "He is going to make some people mad" no matter what he did. The Lake gambit might mollify his domestic critics but it would infuriate everyone else, and so the president "must choose . . . who he wants to make mad."[82]

On April 11, on Carter's instructions, his close aide Hamilton Jordan called an informal meeting to discuss Lake's plan. Moose and Lake had fleshed out a detailed scenario of the steps needed to implement it, which included consultations with all parties (Muzorewa, Smith, the US Congress, the Frontline presidents, and the Patriotic Front). To succeed, the plan required that not one of these parties leak one word of these discussions. "The chances of success are 17 to 1 on a dry track," Funk wrote Brzezinski. After a spirited debate, the participants, who included Lake, Moose, and Funk, agreed that it was important for Andrew Young to weigh in. Reporting on the meeting, Moose wrote Vance: "[Hamilton] Jordan stressed the need to get Andy Young's views as the President attached great importance to them."[83]

Later that day, Young wrote Carter a long memo exhorting him to show courage, optimism, and leadership. Lake's "proposal involves serious risks," Young declared, and it would not appease the administration's foes. "This administration cannot afford to ignore the Baumans, Helms, Hayakawas,

Symms, Rousselots [its critics in Congress], but we also cannot expect rational support from them either." Young then attacked the pessimism that underlay Lake's scheme. He encouraged the president to have the optimism and
the courage to counter Congress's move to lift sanctions "head-on." Young
zeroed in on an argument that resonated with Carter: "We have assumed that
fiscal conservatism [of our opponents in Congress] is also anti-black and racist. I contend that the American people are neither and will respond to leadership." In other words, it was *not* inevitable that Congress would lift sanctions;
Jimmy Carter could lead his critics to a more enlightened position. As Young
said, "I insist that this administration has won all foreign policy issues that it
has fought to win." This was true in April 1979: Carter had won congressional
support for the Panama Canal treaties, the Middle East arms package, and the
normalization with China. Young exhorted Carter to stick to his principles
and fight for them. "Our objectives [in Africa] have been: stable conditions to
facilitate trade and development; political and economic approaches toward
majority rule and democratic conditions; to minimize Soviet influence, violence and chaos." Young then cast Lake's scheme for "*de facto* recognition
of the internal settlement" in terms designed to make Carter recoil: "I'm not
interested in . . . cutting deals with Smith or South Africa." He ended his
missive on a note of powerful optimism: "Soon, someone is going to need
an impartial party with credibility to mediate a cessation of hostilities; internationally recognized elections, a negotiated settlement in Rhodesia. At that
point, I want the US to be credible."[84]

The Lake plan reveals how difficult were the decisions about Rhodesia.
The internal settlement—a biracial government that would soon be confirmed
by elections—had changed the equation. The rebellion in Congress, at a time
when the administration needed to rally support for other policies, including
SALT II, was a major headache for the White House. The failure of the Anglo-
American proposals to gain support and the expected change of government
in London indicated that a new policy might be needed. The administration's
policy toward Rhodesia was not set in stone; Vance and more significantly
Carter were drawn, however briefly and tentatively, to the idea of "cutting a
deal" (as Young put it) to mollify their foes in Congress. Yet Andrew Young
knew how to talk to Carter. His argument—carefully constructed and from
the heart—rallied Carter's pride, optimism, ego, and faith. Lake's argument,
on the other hand, was pragmatic and political. It was clear which way Carter
would lean.

Lake's proposal was dead. On April 12, 1979, the PRC concluded that the
administration would "maintain our present policy" and "launch a major Hill
effort to sustain sanctions."[85]

536

13. Jimmy Carter's Determination

The Rhodesian Elections

"The elections in Rhodesia have been a public relations coup for the internal government," NSC expert Jerry Funk wrote Zbigniew Brzezinski on April 23, 1979. Bishop Abel Muzorewa's party won an overwhelming majority of the black seats, taking fifty-one of seventy-two set aside for blacks. (The twenty-eight seats reserved for whites had been determined by an all-white poll on April 10.) The Patriotic Front did not mount the massive disruptions at the polling places it had promised, and the Rhodesian government declared that 64 percent of registered voters had cast their ballots. Against all expectations, the election period was remarkably quiet in Rhodesia.[1]

This was due, in part, to what the White House Situation Room called "dramatically escalating attacks" of the Rhodesian military on the Frontline States. In a particularly audacious operation, on April 13 Rhodesian forces targeted Joshua Nkomo's headquarters in Lusaka—"less than two blocks from the residence of President [Kenneth] Kaunda"—in an attempt to assassinate the ZAPU leader. In an ominous escalation of the war, the Rhodesians also sank a Zambian commercial ferry, an attack on infrastructure "with no pretense of [being a] ZAPU target," the US ambassador in Pretoria, William Edmondson, noted. Ian Smith crowed about this "success which exceeded our expectations," and added: "Poor old Kaunda: I felt a certain sympathy for him, having to put up with all these humiliations."[2]

The Patriotic Front lay low during the elections because the Rhodesian government deployed a massive security force of approximately 100,000 police and troops at the polls. This followed an unprecedented call-up of reserves, including men up to age sixty, who were supplemented by Muzorewa's and Reverend Ndabaningi Sithole's "auxiliary forces." The election was held in two stages. The white poll was held first, on April 10, and then from April 17 the polls opened on a rolling basis throughout the country for five days until all Rhodesians, white and black, had been able to cast their ballots for the remaining seventy-two seats. This five-day sequential voting process enabled the Rhodesian government to blanket the polling places with security forces. This convinced the Patriotic Front not to squander its resources. As Ambassador Edmondson reported after the polls closed, "The much vaunted guerrilla offensive never materialized."[3]

What did the massive turnout signify? This was the hotly contested question. To Rhodesian officials, the answer was obvious: their new government enjoyed overwhelming approval. They were "jubilant," Edmondson, whose embassy had sent unofficial observers to Rhodesia, noted. The more than two hundred members of the international press (including fifty Americans) who were deployed to report on the elections received "kid glove treatment," as they were ferried to selected polling places and exhaustively briefed by government officials. Cyrus Vance wrote President Carter that "[US television] network coverage has been generally favorable, showing long lines of happy voters." The Defense Intelligence Agency summed up the reporting: "Even the most hostile of the press corps could raise not more than piffling criticisms."[4]

With a handful of exceptions, the seventy election observers—sent by nongovernmental organizations from around the world and also by Britain's Conservative Party—came to similar conclusions. This was true even of traditionally liberal organizations like Freedom House, which announced that the Rhodesian elections were "a useful and creditable step toward the establishment of a free society."[5]

Nevertheless, buried beneath the headlines and in some observers' reports, there were other interpretations. NSC Africa expert Jerry Funk explained: "Smith has been able to focus press attention almost exclusively on the numbers of people voting. . . . You have to go to the small print to read negative comments and questions of fairness."[6]

The most important complaint about the turnout was that it was the result, in part, of intimidation. There were few reports of overt intimidation at the polling places, but there were widespread allegations that government officials and white employers had subjected Rhodesia's blacks to "both overt and implicit" intimidation to go to the polls. The CIA had predicted that "government pressure and intimidation by the black parties [of the internal settlement government] and their auxiliary forces should result in a fairly high turnout." Congressman Stephen Solarz (D-NY), who traveled widely through Rhodesia on the eve of the election, noted how vulnerable blacks were to intimidation. "At least 50 percent of the black population either lives or works on white farms, is in the employ of white businessmen, or lives in government-controlled protected villages." Many might have voted without intimidation, but "it is also possible that many of them would have expressed their opposition to the internal settlement by not voting if their welfare was not so clearly at stake," Solarz observed.[7]

Also, while the claim that 64 percent of the population voted sounded like a hard statistic, it was based on soft science. No one knew how many potential voters were in Rhodesia: there had not been a census, and there was no registration list. The government came up with the figure of 2.9 million possible voters, but most observers considered this a deliberately low estimate intended to inflate the percentage of people going to the polls. Vance wrote Carter that it was more realistic to assume a voting population of 3.6 million.[8]

Nevertheless, almost everyone was impressed by the fact that, even allowing for intimidation and fuzzy statistics, a significant number of black Rhodesians had gone to the polls. Bayard Rustin, an African American who had been a leader in the civil rights movement and who served as co-chair of the Rhodesian election observer team sent by Freedom House, commented that since "turnouts in American elections were often less than fifty percent" it would be "inappropriate" for Carter—who had won the presidency in an election with only a 59 percent turnout—to take a "high and mighty" view of the elections in Rhodesia.[9]

But what did it mean? What did the people who voted think they were voting for? They had a choice of candidates from four parties: one led by each of the three black leaders of the internal settlement government (Abel Muzorewa, Ndabaningi Sithole, and Chief Jeremiah Chirau) plus one led by a conservative chief, Kayisa Ndiweni. Muzorewa took the lion's share with his fifty-one seats; Sithole's party won twelve seats; Ndiweni won nine; Chirau won none. The Patriotic Front, which clearly commanded significant support in Rhodesia, had not been allowed to field candidates. (At the last minute, the government had invited the guerrillas to return to Rhodesia and vote, but only if they laid down their arms, accepted the constitution and the internal settlement, and voted for the registered candidates—none of whom represented the Patriotic Front. This was not a serious offer.) No one had been allowed to organize opposition to the elections.

At the opposite extreme to the Rhodesian government's claim that the election legitimized the internal settlement was the report of Lord Chitnis, a delegate from the British Parliamentary Human Rights Group. "The recent election in Rhodesia was nothing more than a gigantic confidence trick designed to foist on a cowed and indoctrinated black electorate a settlement and a constitution which were formulated without its consent and which are being implemented without its approval," Chitnis concluded. The election was a "brilliantly stage-managed performance. . . . It was not a valid test of opinion and its results are meaningless." Stephen Low, who had been based in Zambia since Henry Kissinger's dramatic 1976 visit, was more diplomatic. In a sober cable analyzing the election, he wrote: "Rhodesian authorities scored an impressive success in the 64 percent turnout for the April elections. While the figure is undoubtedly exaggerated . . . nevertheless it seems likely that over half the voting age population did participate, the principal significance of which is to demonstrate how susceptible the people of Rhodesia are to pressure."[10]

The meaning of the election was unclear, but its effect on US politics was obvious: it greatly increased pressure on the Carter administration to support the new Muzorewa government. Many members of Congress declared that it was time for Carter to accept that Ian Smith and his three colleagues had done everything the president had asked of them—agree to all-party talks and hold a "free and fair" election—and therefore they had satisfied the demands of the Case-Javits resolution that Congress had passed the previous September, which meant that Carter was obliged to lift the sanctions. Removing the sanctions would have a positive impact on the struggling Rhodesian economy, but much more important was that it would signal US support for the fledgling Muzorewa government. In so doing, the proponents of lifting sanctions argued, it would give the new regime a fighting chance to survive.

The Pressure Mounts

On April 23, 1979, the day before the results of the Rhodesian elections were officially declared, Senator Richard Schweiker (R-PA) reintroduced the resolution that he and Senator Dennis DeConcini (D-AZ) had co-sponsored in February, calling for the president to lift sanctions ten days after the new Rhodesian government was installed. It was anticipated that it would take Muzorewa four weeks to form the government of the "new" country of Zimbabwe-Rhodesia; therefore, Schweiker and DeConcini asked for sanctions to be lifted in early June. On April 24, Senator Jesse Helms (R-NC) introduced a bill that would lift sanctions immediately. He congratulated the Rhodesians on holding "the most free and open election in the history of the continent of Africa," and added, "Surely all fair-minded Americans will now acknowledge that Rhodesia has become a model for other African nations." He cast the decision that the Senate faced in stark terms. "On the one hand," he declared, "we have a Marxist terrorist supported by Communist guns and money who calls for one party rule. On the other hand, we have a Methodist bishop elected by the majority of the country's voters." In the House, Robert Bauman (R-MD) put forward a similar resolution, and Richard Ichord (R-MO) railed against the Carter administration's policy. "When, oh when, President Carter, when, oh when, Secretary Vance, when, oh when, Andy Young, will you change your minds and admit you are wrong?"[11]

Vance was not optimistic that the administration would be able to convince Congress to sustain sanctions. On April 24, he wrote that the "public image of Smith and the internal coalition has improved considerably in the past few weeks. . . . Among the major [US] newspapers . . . only the *New York Times* continues to support the administration's position." The media reports of the election would "provide new ammunition to proponents of lifting sanctions." The Senate's strongest supporter of the administration's Rhodesia policy, Paul Tsongas (D-MA), lost heart: "I can't imagine that, given the limited ammunition supplies the White House has, they will spend it on Rhodesia."[12]

President Carter immediately called a meeting to map out Rhodesia strategy with Walter Mondale, Vance, Brzezinski, and Young, plus Hamilton Jordan and White House congressional liaison Frank Moore. No minutes of this April 24 pivotal meeting have been declassified (and perhaps none were taken), but the brief and cryptic notes Carter wrote during it are available, as is a memo from Brzezinski to Funk about it and a comment by British ambassador Peter Jay. "The President raised three basic questions," Brzezinski noted in his memo. "1. How can we move the Muzorewa government in the right direction?" This hints that, contrary to the allegations of his critics, Carter accepted that the elections had created a new reality and contemplated figuring out a way to work with it rather than reject it out of hand. "2. How can we better compete with the Soviets/Cubans for Machel, Nyerere, etc.?"[13] In his notes, Carter indicates that the men at the meeting answered that it was advisable to maintain the policy they had pursued for two and a half years: "US policy kept SU [Soviet Union] out of Zambia, Mozam[bique], etc. . . . No worry re SU in Africa—unless we alienate F[ront]line States."[14] The challenge was to steer a course that would "move Muzorewa in the right direction" while not at the same time alienating the leaders of the Frontline States. Brzezinski listed the president's final question: "3. Can we, and if so how, take an open stance on the recent elections without having to wait six weeks [until Muzorewa forms a government], given Congressional pressures?"[15] This went to the heart of the administration's immediate dilemma. Case-Javits stipulated that the president carefully analyze the evidence before determining if the elections had been "free and fair." Therefore, a precipitous determination—particularly if it were negative—would trigger outrage in Congress. But delay was deadly. The longer the president said nothing, the more time his opponents would have to grandstand and organize. Nevertheless, as Carter's notes make clear, the consensus of the meeting was that it was best for the president to "delay decision until early June," which would allow the administration to "consult $\bar{c}$ [with]

Great Britain." In the meantime, Carter, Mondale, Vance, or Brzezinski should deliver an "early statement"[16] explaining the administration's Africa policy and, Ambassador Jay reported, "lobby Congress to forestall action in advance of his [Carter's] determination."[17]

Carter's notes are very clear on one point: "All - No on Case/Javits." That is, Carter's entire foreign policy team and his closest domestic aides advised him to decide that the Rhodesian elections were not free and fair. They had two reasons: "what is right [and] US interests." Carter's notes end philosophically: "Admin & Congress may go separate ways."[18] This was perilous because the administration needed Congress—not only to ratify SALT II and pass other important legislation, but also to enable it to pursue a coherent policy in southern Africa. Only the executive branch could recognize the new regime in Rhodesia, but Congress could strip it of its most potent instrument of influence: sanctions. The British Foreign Office, which was following events in Washington closely, understood the danger. It noted on April 25: "All sources (black/white, liberal/conservative, government/non-government) believe that conservatives in the Congress are likely to make an early move to lift sanctions . . . and . . . may well succeed."[19]

Jesse Helms' chief foreign policy aide, John Carbaugh, was at that moment in London meeting with the Foreign Office and with leaders of the Conservative Party—who expected to win the general election on May 3. The hard-driving, rabidly anticommunist Carbaugh had been trying for months to determine if the Tories were going to lift sanctions, and he had made the Foreign Office nervous. This aggressive intervention of a US congressional staffer in British foreign policy was unusual and unwelcome. One British diplomat noted that Carbaugh "comes from the south of the United States, and is unashamedly right-wing in his views." Another wrote that "Mr Carbaugh sounded like the sort of lunatic who had talked the United States into 20 years of ultimately disastrous involvement in Vietnam. . . . [But] we have to take the Helms/Carbaugh line seriously, since it has such a strong appeal on the Hill."[20] On April 26, at a meeting in the Foreign Office, Carbaugh exuded confidence and spoke in what a British diplomat described as "his usual pungent way." Carbaugh declared, for example, "'that black son of a bitch' Muzorewa had better move fast." He predicted that the Senate would wait two to three weeks before introducing an amendment to lift sanctions. "He was totally confident that both in the Senate and in the House the votes would be available to lift sanctions . . . [and it] would damage the President."[21]

Days later, Carter received a telegram from Senator Helms. "Mr. President, I have this information and I do not wish to use it to your disadvantage," Helms wrote. (The implied threat was left vague: it is not clear what "information," if any, Helms may have had.) "Therefore, I solicit in the most sincere way possible your consideration of an immediate lifting of sanctions." The NSC congressional affairs liaison, Madeleine Albright, noted that the threat could have substance: "It may be only bravado, but his [Helms'] staff man, John Carbough [*sic*], claims he is in close touch with Thatcher's people and they are 'trying to work together.'"[22]

These were awkward weeks for Anglo-American cooperation. American policy toward Rhodesia was on hold until the president made his determination on Case-Javits, expected in early June. The British thought that Carter would resist the congressional drive to lift sanctions, but they were not sure. "President Carter is a fair-minded man; given the heavy turnout [in the Rhodesian elections], he is likely to acknowledge that the voting was fair even if the circumstances of the election were not (martial law, censorship, restrictions in political parties and campaigning)," a senior British diplomat reported. "[This] argues for a qualified negative [determination on Case-Javits] until the black government has shown whether they are indeed Uncle Toms or not."[23]

Madeleine Albright was pessimistic. "The outlook on the Hill looks pretty bad at the moment," she wrote Brzezinski on May 2. "We stand a good chance of losing on a probable Helms amendment to lift sanctions." She estimated that only thirty-four senators would support the administration's policy versus sixty-six who would oppose it. Losing the vote would mean more than having to lift sanctions on Rhodesia. "The vote on the Helms amendment," she explained, "will be a referendum on our African policy."[24]

Thatcher Leans to One Side

American policy was in limbo, but British policy was even more so. The British election campaign was in its final days, and the race had tightened. The Tories attacked Labour's economic policy; both parties shied away from debates about foreign policy in general and Rhodesia in particular. Labour wanted to avoid the Rhodesia question because its policy—the Anglo-American proposals—had failed to show results, and the Tory leaders were happy to oblige because, as their October 1978 annual conference had demonstrated, discussing Rhodesia would divide the leadership from the rank and file.[25]

Thus, on May 3, when the Tories won with a comfortable margin, their only specific policy toward Rhodesia was a short statement in their manifesto that if the elections were free and fair, then "the next Government will have the duty to return Rhodesia to a state of legality, move to lift sanctions and do its utmost to insure that the new independent state gains international recognition." This formulation had satisfied the Tory backbenchers, who were confident that Thatcher—the "Iron Lady"—would lift sanctions. It also encouraged American opponents of sanctions, and gave hope to Rhodesian whites. "All Rhodesians thank God for your magnificent victory," Smith immediately wrote Thatcher. The *Rhodesian Herald* announced, "It is the best possible result. . . . There is little doubt that her [Thatcher's] approach to our problems will be far more sympathetic than that of her predecessors." The editor then tackled the real problem. "The complicating factor here, of course, is the attitude of the Carter administration. . . . Should an early move in Congress to remove sanctions be successful it would surely encourage the Tories also to remove sanctions. . . . Let us hope that the Iron Lady will be able to put some steel into the souls of Western politicians in general and President Carter in particular."[26]

On the afternoon of May 4, the queen bade farewell to Prime Minister Callaghan and asked Margaret Thatcher to form a government. Jimmy Carter, who was en route to Des Moines, Iowa, called the new prime minister from Air Force One. After conveying his congratulations, he said that "there were important issues to discuss, including that of Rhodesia. . . . The United States wished to act in harmony with the UK to the greatest possible extent." He followed this up with a letter stating that "the stakes [in southern Africa] for both of us—and for the West in general—are high."[27]

By evening of the next day, Thatcher had chosen her cabinet. Filled with predictable choices, it contained only one appointment that surprised many. "The most striking event," the *Guardian* noted, "is Lord Carrington's elevation to Foreign Secretary."[28] Francis Pym, the shadow foreign secretary, had been the obvious choice, and former Conservative prime minister Edward Heath had also made it clear that he wanted the post. But Thatcher passed over Pym and Heath to tap the hereditary peer Lord Carrington. Carrington had fought in World War II and had since then had alternated careers in business and politics. He had served as high commissioner in Australia, secretary of defense and of energy in the Heath government, chair of the Conservative Party, and leader of the Tories in the House of Lords. But he was considered a "Heath man," that is, loyal to the former prime minister, with whom Thatcher had a frosty relationship. And, like Heath, Carrington did not share Thatcher's passion to shrink government.

Why did Thatcher select Carrington? He was widely respected, hardworking, and experienced. He was suave but not pompous. As one of his biographers notes, "On the international stage Carrington acted as a foil to Mrs Thatcher: the pragmatist to her idealism, the Tory Grandee to the grocer's daughter from Grantham; the gentleman to the lady ready to give a good hand-bagging."[29] All this is true, but Margaret Thatcher was not interested in atmospherics: she wanted results. Britain's most pressing foreign policy problem was Rhodesia, and Carrington's position on it was clear. It was Carrington who had persuaded the Lords, against the odds, to uphold sanctions the previous November. It was Carrington who had stressed repeatedly the high cost for Britain of lifting sanctions prematurely. It was Carrington who had said in a radio interview on April 25, 1979, immediately after the Rhodesian elections, "If you are going to bring Rhodesia back to legality it will be necessary to get the support and agreement of the international community."[30] Thatcher knew what she was getting: by giving the nod to Peter Carrington, Thatcher gave the nod to the result she wanted in Rhodesia.

Had Thatcher wanted to lift sanctions quickly, she would have chosen Pym. Instead, she chose Carrington and, in so doing, she maintained the stance she had adopted at the party conference in Bristol. She leaned to one side— the side of her fellow Tory leaders, the previous Labour government, and the Carter administration—all of whom were wary of lifting sanctions quickly.

Many pundits and scholars assert that in the days immediately after he was appointed, Lord Carrington took the fiery Iron Lady in hand and persuaded her to refrain from lifting sanctions immediately. Charles Moore, Thatcher's authorized biographer, asserts that Carrington "succeeded in deflecting Mrs Thatcher from acceding to the internal settlement."[31] To depict Thatcher as meekly accepting the older man's firm hand is to ignore her mastery of the theater of leadership. Thatcher corralled the sexism of the era to her benefit. When it suited her, she became the pliant lady listening to the big men. This allowed her to maintain her unwavering conservative credentials while not pursuing unwaveringly conservative policies. With her rhetoric, Thatcher continued to appease her rank and file, but with her actions she signaled that she had decided to pursue a moderate policy toward Rhodesia. Thatcher was canny: Carrington would get the blame if—as was likely—another attempt to resolve the Rhodesian crisis failed. Meanwhile, she would keep her hardline credentials burnished. Thatcher could have it both ways: her heart was with Smith, but her policy was not.

Senator Helms Attacks

Jesse Helms, who feared what the appointment of Carrington as foreign secretary might signify, sprang into action. He timed his amendment to exert maximum pressure on the new Thatcher administration before it declared its Rhodesia policy.[32] On May 14, he introduced an amendment, co-sponsored by Harry Byrd (I-VA), to the Foreign Relations Authorization Act that would lift sanctions on Rhodesia as soon as the Muzorewa government was installed.

The long, heated debate about it the following day was punctuated by arcane parliamentary maneuvers.[33]

Those arguing in favor of the Helms Amendment—led by Helms, Harry Byrd, Sam Hayakawa (R-CA), and Orrin Hatch (R-UT)—stressed the significance of the high turnout at the recent Rhodesian election and the positive observers' reports. They also argued that President Carter was needlessly delaying making his determination. "The administration has been deliberately dragging its feet," Helms declared. "What kind of game are they playing? . . . It is time for a decision."[34] Those opposing Helms stressed that his amendment would subvert what the Senate itself had decided in the Case-Javits resolution: the Senate had voted to give the president time to assess the elections before making his determination. Carter had promised to abide by this and deliver his ruling two weeks after the installation of a new government in Rhodesia.

The debate raged for most of May 15. Its length as well as its vehemence stemmed from many factors unrelated to Rhodesia. It was useful for the conservatives to lean on the politics of Rhodesia to add nuance to their stance on race relations. In discussing Rhodesia, they were able to flaunt their open-mindedness: they liked Bishop Muzorewa, whom they regarded as a responsible, sensible black man. They contrasted Muzorewa not with Joshua Nkomo or Robert Mugabe but with someone closer to home: Andrew Young, the irresponsible, irrational black man. Helms, for example, first praised Muzorewa by retelling how he had escorted the bishop to North Carolina to visit the "beautiful little white-haired lady who . . . converted him to Christianity. . . . I heard him discuss with this dear lady his hopes and dreams for his people. . . . This is the man who is now pleading with the president of the United States, 'Don't delay further . . . set us free.'" Then Helms unloaded on Young: "If ever there were a man afflicted with foot-in-mouth disease, it is our Ambassador Young. . . . Mr Andrew Young is running the show, not Secretary Vance. Not President Carter but Andrew Young. . . . I have some resentment at the fact that he is taking over as Secretary of State in this matter."[35] By embracing Muzorewa (literally), Jesse Helms blazed the trail for southern Republicans who wanted to broaden their base to include centrist whites without alienating their core, far-right supporters.

The debate about US policy toward the internal settlement government of Rhodesia was a safe forum—compared, for example, to the explosive domestic topics of busing and affirmative action—to discuss how much change in race relations was desirable and at what speed it should occur. These senators were still adjusting to the world that emerged after the 1954 *Brown v. Board of Education* decision and the 1965 Voting Rights Act. Many of them had roots deep in Jim Crow. When Harry Byrd asked, "What more does President Carter want [of the white Rhodesians]?,"[36] the echo for conservatives was clear: what more will liberals and radicals demand of *them*?

This debate about Rhodesian sanctions also formed an episode in the ferocious tug of war between the executive and the legislature. Since 1973, with the passage of the War Powers Resolution, Congress had hacked away at the power of the executive branch in repeated attempts to restore the balance that members of Congress believed had existed before the rise of the "imperial presidency." Jesse Helms and his supporters heaped scorn on the White House. Orrin Hatch bemoaned its "total incompetency" and called on the Senate to show courage. Richard Schweiker reminded his colleagues that Congress was "a coequal partner." Helms and Sam Hayakawa complained bitterly about the administration's refusal to consult seriously with them. "They totally ignore us," Hayakawa groused. "We might just as well be dropped in a deep, deep, deep canyon. . . . Therefore we are compelled to force the issue."[37]

By 1979, however, senators on both sides of the aisle were wondering if the process had gone too far. George McGovern (D-SD) noted that Helms' amendment "invades the president's territory." Ed Muskie (D-ME) explained, "As lawmakers we can help chart the President's direction as he carries out this country's foreign policy. But when we attempt to unilaterally take charge of the helm of the ship, Congress becomes irresponsible." John Glenn (D-OH) announced that he would vote against the Helms amendment because the tasks of examining and assessing the Rhodesian elections "are careful decisions best left for Executive determination."[38]

Helms' reasons for introducing his amendment were also tactical. He was not sure he would win the vote, but lifting the Rhodesian sanctions was not his only goal: he wanted to force his colleagues to go on the record. Helms was a street fighter. On issue after issue—the Panama Canal treaties, UN funding, aid for Egypt, to name just three of dozens—he engineered votes that impelled all the senators to reveal their gang colors. And he put those votes in his back pocket; they could come in handy. Helms was a prime mover in the increasing polarization of the Senate.[39]

This strategy not only intensified the partisan divide. It also erased nuance. In 1977, the shapers of the Carter administration's African policy—Vance, Brzezinski, Young, Lake, Moose, and the president himself—had hoped to introduce some of the lessons of Vietnam into their actions. They were still waging the Cold War, but they wanted to be less "knee-jerk" in their response to threats. They wanted to assess each threat carefully before assuming that it emanated from Moscow. Richard Nixon's détente policy had led the way, and many of the same people who lambasted Nixon and Kissinger for their dangerous naivete were in the forefront of the attack on Carter. The right wings of both the Republican and Democratic parties believed, when it came to fighting communism, that nuance was just a polite word for appeasement. Their assault on détente was unrelenting.

In Congress during the Carter years, Rhodesia was favored terrain to pursue the battle against nuance in the Cold War. For the conservative critics of détente and all it represented, there was no downside to challenging the president on his Rhodesia policy, because at a gut level it was an easy fight to win. Helms' case was compelling: the president, in the thrall of Andrew Young, was mollycoddling black Marxist terrorists and turning his back on the pro-American, moderate black bishop. This was a boon to Moscow. "If . . . sanctions against Zimbabwe-Rhodesia are not lifted," Harry Byrd predicted, "then it will be merely a matter of time before a pro-Soviet police state will be established [there] . . . , and a great experiment in African democracy will end." The administration's policy was also, they argued, immoral. Conservative firebrand Roger Jepsen (R-IA), turned the tables on Carter by seizing the moral high ground: "The sad fact is that President Carter, Andy Young, and Moose already have their minds made up: strangle the last breath out of a young new nation that wants to live." Jepsen then exhorted his colleagues to support the Helms Amendment: "Let us vote for something that is morally, economically, and basically right, good and fair."[40]

In the Senate debate on the Helms Amendment, the administration's supporters scarcely tried to counter these attacks; they focused instead on the procedural argument that the amendment was unnecessary because Case-Javits was yet to be decided. "The Carter administration seems embarrassed," Utah Republican and Helms supporter Jake Garn announced, "by the stark simplicity of the situation."[41]

Garn was right: the administration's supporters knew that their reply lacked the punch of Helms' Manichaeism. The White House had argued repeatedly that lifting sanctions prematurely would widen the war and provide an opportunity for Cuban and Soviet intervention, but this argument was very hard to sell. It was much easier to pillory the Patriotic Front as Soviet-backed, anti-American guerrillas and extol Muzorewa and Smith as peace-loving democrats than to argue—as did the Carter administration—that both sides should be treated as equal parties in the negotiations. No matter how astute tactically, Carter's policy struck many as a tilt toward the Patriotic Front. The idea of giving equal treatment to "Marxist terrorists" was so new, so alien to past American practice, that to a great many Americans it seemed as though the Carter administration had gone, at best, berserk.

Carter's close cooperation with the British, his multilateralism, also came under fire. When Senator Ted Kennedy (D-MA) observed that it would be "unseemly" for the United States to lift sanctions "before the new British Government can decide what its policy . . . is to be," Hayakawa exclaimed, "Is the United States a world leader? The United States must act unilaterally when everybody else is too timid to do so."[42] McGovern noted that Vance was going to London on May 20 to discuss policy toward Rhodesia with Carrington; he argued that the Senate should delay voting on sanctions until after this meeting.[43] Helms wanted precisely the opposite: he hoped that a Senate vote to lift sanctions would affect the Vance-Carrington talks, weakening Vance's hand and spurring Thatcher to heed the Conservative Manifesto's call to lift sanctions.

The White House had anticipated Helms' move and prepared for it. The key was Senate Majority Leader Robert Byrd. Byrd had pulled himself up from a hardscrabble life in West Virginia. By dint of ambition, hard work, and a daunting command of Senate rules, he had risen in 1977 to majority leader. But his past continued to hound him. In the early 1940s, Byrd had been an enthusiastic leader and recruiter for the Ku Klux Klan. In 1945, he opposed the integration of the armed forces, writing a senator that he would rather "die a thousand times, and see Old Glory trampled in the dirt never to rise again, than to see this beloved land of ours become degraded by race mongrels." In 1946, he wrote the Klan's Imperial Wizard that "the Klan is needed today as never before and I am anxious to see its rebirth here in West Virginia." He backtracked in 1952, during his first run for the House of Representatives (he would serve three terms before going to the Senate), averring falsely that he had been a member of the Klan for little more than a year and had severed his ties in 1943. During the 1960 presidential campaign, in which he was a leader of the "Stop Kennedy" forces, Byrd's membership in the Klan—a virulently anti-Catholic as well as racist organization—briefly became a national issue, but he doggedly refused to apologize for his past actions. In 1964, Byrd was the only Democrat to join his southern colleagues in opposing the Civil Rights Act, personally filibustering it for more than fourteen hours. A year later, he again joined his southern colleagues to vote against the Voting Rights Act, and in 1967 he opposed the nomination of Thurgood Marshall to the Supreme Court.[44]

Robert Byrd had not hidden his respect and sympathy for the white Rhodesians; he had voted for the Byrd Amendment (sponsored by Virginia's Harry Byrd) in 1971 and voted against overturning it in 1977. He had told the White House after the April 1979 Rhodesian elections that he supported lifting sanctions. The administration had sprung into action: on May 3, Carter placed a personal call to Robert Byrd, and on May 4, he wrote Byrd a personal letter asking for more time to make his determination, as Case-Javits had specified.[45] It had an impact. Robert Byrd held a press conference, circulated the president's letter, and announced that he supported giving Carter more time.[46] Moose worked with Byrd's staff behind the scenes. On May 14, Vance wrote Carter, "In response to your May 3 call, Bob Byrd has taken the lead in putting together a substitute which he will offer tomorrow when Jesse Helms offers his sanctions lifting amendment." Robert Byrd's alternate amendment would require the president to announce his determination within fifteen days of the installation of the new government in Salisbury, which, Vance noted, was "something you have already said you will do." Vance was cautiously optimistic: "My staff think we have a fair chance of beating Helms."[47]

The debate proceeded as the administration had planned: Helms offered his amendment, and Robert Byrd, with Senator Frank Church (D-ID) as cosponsor, countered with the substitute that would give Carter more time to make his determination. The purpose of the substitute, Church explained, "will simply be that of giving the President an opportunity to do what Congress told the President to do."[48]

Then Helms struck. In what two experts who served as congressional staffers in the 1970s called a "deft parliamentary maneuver," the senator from North Carolina outsmarted the administration. He proposed an amendment that would suspend sanctions for one year—until June 1980—at which time the president would determine whether to lift sanctions permanently or to reimpose them. This would give "us time to see how the Muzorewa government works out," it would preserve the presidential prerogative, and it would maintain the leverage of threatening to reimpose sanctions. By proposing an amendment to his amendment, Helms prevented an early vote on the Byrd-Church substitute.[49]

Church, the floor manager, was irate that Helms had "hijacked" his substitute. Objections flew. Accusations were hurled. Parliamentary inquiries accumulated. The (Robert) Byrd-Church team hurriedly conferred with Dick Moose in the cloakroom. Robert Byrd feared that the revised Helms Amendment would pass. "Dick," he told Moose, "you're going to have to find another way out of this. You're going to get rolled over." Moose hurriedly called Vance, who was in a meeting with Carter. Vance briefed Carter and returned to Moose with explicit instructions: "Dick, don't give ground on this."[50]

Moose consulted with Jeff Davidow, a bright young foreign service officer. Together, they came up with language that resurrected the Schweiker-DeConcini "sense of the Congress" resolution originally proposed in February, which had called on the president to lift sanctions on Rhodesia but had not required him to do so. "Helms bought it," Moose recalled. "It was language that appeared to open the way for Helms to get what he wanted." It offered Helms a surefire way to get a majority of senators on record in favor of lifting sanctions against the Muzorewa government. But Helms committed a fundamental error: he miscalculated the willingness of the House to go along with the Senate. Moose explained: "I was counting on Solarz to control the House."

Robert Byrd, who had always been lukewarm about the president's policy, was happy to throw his support to the Schweiker-DeConcini resolution that Moose and Davidow proposed. Paul Tsongas protested that voting for Schweiker-DeConcini would have a devastating impact because it would signal that the US Senate supported the Muzorewa government, but he did not carry the argument.[51]

"There have been huddles in the cloakroom," Helms said wryly when the Senate returned from the brief and frantic recess. "They were afraid they might lose." After the long debate, the resurrected Schweiker-DeConcini resolution came to a vote first. With Robert Byrd and Church announcing that they would vote for it, it was sure to pass. "Finally we have arrived at the moment of truth," Helms intoned. "The Senate is finally going to say, 'Lift the sanctions, lift the sanctions against Rhodesia.'" The measure was carried by an overwhelming majority, seventy-five to nineteen.[52]

"I cannot tell the Chair how delighted I am with the sequence of events here today," Helms crowed. "All that the senator from North Carolina has wanted is for this Senate to send a message to the President of the United States that enough is enough. . . . I think he is going to get the message." Helms promptly declared that he would withdraw his own amendment.[53]

Schweiker-DeConcini, which put seventy-five senators on record opposing the Carter administration's policy, satisfied Helms. It did not lift sanctions on Rhodesia, but it was another step in the senator's escalation of pressure on the president. Helms assured the *Rhodesian Herald* that he would take "more forceful steps to lift sanctions" if Carter ignored the Senate's wishes. Schweiker agreed with Helms that, as he told the *Herald*, "the vote was a signal. . . . But it was also a threat because, frankly, if sanctions are not lifted by the end of June we are going to vote again and mandate it." Ken Towsey, the head of the Rhodesian Information Office in Washington and de facto Rhodesian ambassador, emerged from the Senate chamber "broadly smiling. . . . 'You can say that I am satisfied with events,'" he announced.[54]

Ian Smith was overjoyed: "This was a major victory," he wrote, "giving us a great boost." Salisbury's *Sunday Mail* declared, in a headline, that Carter's "Rhodesian policy lies in ruins." It rejoiced, "Unless the world has gone completely crazy, the lifting of sanctions must be around the corner." Helms also celebrated. "One thing is clear," he exclaimed: "This message will not only get to Salisbury, Rhodesia, it is going to get to London, and the new government there will hear it."[55]

Before the London Talks

"Well, I wouldn't call it a ringing affirmation," Hodding Carter admitted at the State Department press briefing when asked about the previous day's Senate vote. "I don't think our Senate has the slightest idea what is going on in Africa," a frustrated Andrew Young told the BBC. While the Senate had not voted to trump the president's authority and lift sanctions forthwith, its "lopsided" decision, as the *Washington Star* wrote, was "an unexpectedly severe, almost stunning, vote of no confidence." The significance of the vote was not in what it did (which was, in fact, nothing), but what it portended. As British Ambassador Peter Jay cabled, "The Senate action demonstrates there are sufficient votes in Congress to overturn a presidential determination . . . and to lift sanctions." When Hodding Carter was asked what the administration was going to do about it, he replied that the State Department was "relying heavily" on Vance and Carrington to "devise a new joint strategy."[56]

Vance had a very difficult task: he had to hold Congress at bay. This would have been difficult at any time, but it was particularly so in May 1979. Vance was busy. He was preparing for the Vienna summit with Leonid Brezhnev to finalize the SALT II agreement, dealing with the Iranian Revolution, navigating the aftereffects of normalization with China, assessing the rising tide against Nicaraguan leader Anastasio Somoza, addressing the ongoing difficulties implementing the Camp David Accords between Israel and Egypt, and handling countless minor crises. And yet, everyone in the administration agreed that to have any chance of persuading Congress not to lift sanctions, Vance would have to take the lead. Carter's participation would be crucial, but Vance would have to do the testifying, lobbying, and schmoozing to make it happen. Solarz thought that he might be able to hold the line in the House, but he would need help from a senior official.[57] Vance would be the face of the administration's Rhodesia policy in Congress. The timing could not have been worse. SALT II was within Vance's grasp. More than anything, Vance wanted the treaty to be signed and ratified. This meant that he could not afford to antagonize the Senate.

As he headed to London to confer with Carrington, Vance was worried not only about the Senate vote on Rhodesia but also about the Thatcher administration's plans. If the British lifted sanctions, the pressure in the US Congress to follow suit would be irresistible and the Carter administration would be helpless to stop it. The repercussions, Vance feared, would be dire. As Moose and Lake wrote Vance on the day of the Senate vote, "Continued violence [in Rhodesia] will provide the Soviets and Cubans with fresh opportunities to expand their influence, and domestic reaction to further Soviet advances will be sharply critical of our inability to impede these advances."[58] That would make the ratification of SALT less likely. Vance had been reassured by Thatcher's selection of Carrington, but there was still reason to worry. Throughout her campaign, Thatcher had said that her policy toward Rhodesia would be guided by the findings of the team of observers that the Tories had sent to the Rhodesian elections. Vance had just read their report, and it stated that the Rhodesian elections had been "free and fair."[59] What would Thatcher do?

It was crucial, Vance told Ambassador Peter Jay, that he and Carrington "reach common ground on Rhodesia." Carter agreed. "He [Carter] set a good deal of store," Jay reported, "on keeping the policies of our two governments in step, . . . 'nudging our boat alongside yours.'"[60]

The signals from London were mixed. Brzezinski warned that "[w]hile US-UK objectives in southern Africa should remain broadly congruent under the new Prime Minister, the issues there offer the greatest potential for differences with us, . . . especially in connection with Rhodesia." In a *Time* magazine interview with Thatcher, conducted while she was still campaigning but not published until May 14, the first question was about Rhodesia. Thatcher's reply delighted American and British conservatives and gave the White House pause. "There . . . was an election, one person-one vote," Thatcher declared. "Where else would you get that in Africa? . . . There's . . . no reason to have the sanctions at all."[61] Yet the selection of Carrington and the private comments of British officials to their American counterparts indicated that Thatcher, despite what Brzezinski called her "hard-driving nature and her tendency to hector," intended to proceed cautiously. The State Department observed that "a Tory government probably would not lift sanctions immediately, lest it foul lines of communication with the US and harm relations with the Commonwealth and the UN. If the US Congress lifts sanctions first, a Tory government might then follow suit."[62]

On May 15, the same day that the Senate debated the Helms Amendment, Thatcher made her first public comments as prime minister about her government's policy toward Rhodesia. Addressing the House of Commons, she gave solace to the Tory backbenchers in her opening remarks. The government welcomed "the major change" that the Rhodesian elections had wrought, she announced. "It is our objective to build on that change to achieve a return to legality," she said, but added, "in conditions that secure wide international recognition." That was the trapdoor out of the promise of the Conservative manifesto: Thatcher's objective was to lift sanctions—she *wanted* to lift them—but it would take time. Carrington wrote years later in his memoirs that the stipulation that the new state had to gain "international recognition . . . was the crux—and the problem" because it could only be achieved through "some sort of universal suffrage" that included the Patriotic Front. As Brzezinski's aide Jerry Funk observed, "The Tory pledges on sanctions have contained loopholes all along."[63]

Thatcher hedged: "We shall need to consult many people in the coming days and weeks, including our own partners in the Nine and in the Commonwealth. . . . The United States Government should be one of the first to be consulted in view of their involvement in the Rhodesian question. Therefore, I am particularly glad that Mr. Vance will be here next week for talks with my noble friend the Foreign and Commonwealth Secretary."[64]

The backbenchers were irate, but Thatcher had reason to back away from the certainty of the manifesto. As Carrington explained in his memoirs, "To have recognized the 'internal settlement' at that time would have led to embargoes on British goods around the world . . . and within Rhodesia Nkomo and Mugabe would have done all in their considerable power to step up the insurrection—with Soviet and Chinese assistance respectively." The prospect that Britain might lift sanctions had already stirred opposition in the Commonwealth. On the morning that Thatcher took office, the *Times* of Zambia had warned in an editorial that if Britain lifted sanctions, the queen would face a frosty reception at the Commonwealth Heads of Government Meeting that would open in Lusaka on August 1, 1979. Queen Elizabeth II might "address empty seats with only Australia, New Zealand, and Canada listening to her."[65]

It was possible that even Australia would refuse to attend. Prime Minister Malcolm Fraser, a conservative with close ties to the British Tories, had carved out an unlikely role as champion of majority rule in southern Africa. In part, Fraser was trying to save the Commonwealth—which was a useful forum for Australia—from fracturing along racial lines. "I thought the Commonwealth was an organisation well worth preserving," he explained. "Apart from the intrinsic justice of majority rule, that's why I did what I could to make sure it survived." Moreover, he was eager to play an influential role on the world stage, and helping end the war in Rhodesia could appeal to Australian liberals, who supported majority rule, as well as to conservatives, many of whom sympathized with Rhodesian whites. "[The] kith and kin issue was [an] important one for Fraser's own party," a Canadian diplomat observed.[66]

At the previous Commonwealth Heads of Government Meeting, held in 1977 in London, Fraser had joined with an improbable ally, Jamaica's leftist Prime Minister Michael Manley, in stressing the need for a quick settlement in Rhodesia. Two years later, on May 5, 1979, Fraser called his chief of staff, who was in London wrapping up his duties as an adviser to the Tory election campaign. Thatcher had declared victory the previous day. "Look," Fraser said, "I am very worried about Margaret's attitude on Africa."[67]

So were his fellow Australians. On the very day that Fraser expressed his concerns about Thatcher's plans for Africa, Andrew Young began a six-day tour of Australia, where he was bombarded with questions about American and British policy toward the Muzorewa government in Rhodesia. The British high commissioner in Canberra reported, "Given the firebrand image that the Ambassador has often presented in public, Ambassador Young impressed generally in his private and public meetings." At every venue, Young explained why sanctions should remain in place. He called on Thatcher to delay her decision on sanctions. Everywhere, his message was warmly received. This bode ill for Thatcher if she lifted sanctions.[68]

The Commonwealth was spurred to action by the overwhelming US Senate vote on May 15 calling on Carter to lift sanctions. Three days later, on May 18, thirty-four high commissioners from Commonwealth countries, anxious to make their muscle felt before Vance and Carrington decided on a joint policy, assembled in emergency session in London. During a three-hour meeting, they "agreed unanimously to send a delegation to warn Carrington of the dangers of recognizing the Muzorewa government" and to present Carrington with a declaration damning the Rhodesian election as "an exercise in mass deception." Vance immediately informed Carter of this meeting. Stressing Australian fears that the Commonwealth could split over the issue, Vance noted that the assembled high commissioners included representatives of all but five of the thirty-nine Commonwealth countries; and Canada, Australia, India, Nigeria, and Zambia—that is, the most powerful Commonwealth countries as well as the host of the upcoming summit—had endorsed the declaration condemning the Rhodesian elections.[69]

The following day, Australian foreign minister Andrew Peacock wrote Vance: "With Rhodesia occupying our minds so much at the moment, I thought I would outline some of our views on what is going to be a very difficult question over the next few months." With an eye to Vance's imminent talks with Carrington, Peacock noted that "Rhodesia clearly is an issue which is going to put Western credentials in Africa to a severe test. . . . A matter of immediate concern is the danger of a serious rift within the Commonwealth . . . with damaging consequences for Western interests in Africa and elsewhere." Peacock stressed the importance of withholding recognition from the Muzorewa government. "Can Muzorewa be persuaded that it would be to his advantage . . . to offer . . . real negotiations with the Patriotic Front?"[70]

Just as Vance was "nudging" his boat close to Britain's, so too did Carrington want to align his policy with Washington's. The two men were facing strikingly similar situations. Both needed each other's support to stave off domestic pressures to lift sanctions immediately. The Foreign Office explained British desires: "We want to achieve a realignment of US policy with our own. . . . We are much more vulnerable to African retaliation than they are. We need to carry them with us." If the United States lifted sanctions, Carrington's options would evaporate.[71]

Peter Carrington and Cyrus Vance had known each other since the 1960s, when the former had been First Lord of the Admiralty and the latter, Secretary of the Army. They respected each other. Both wanted to settle the Rhodesia problem once and for all. Just as Vance longed to focus on other issues, Carrington wanted to clear the decks so he could concentrate on British relations with Europe. "Far too much of a Foreign Secretary's time was being spent on Rhodesia," he wrote in his memoirs.[72]

That much was certain. So, too, were three deadlines. First, Carter would announce his decision on Case-Javits in early June. This complicated Vance's task in London: he had to negotiate with the British without being able to guarantee what the president would decide. The next deadline was the Commonwealth Summit, which would open on August 1 in Lusaka. Immediately prior to Vance's arrival, Thatcher had announced that Britain would not lift sanctions before the Commonwealth conference, giving her government two months to determine the best way forward. The third deadline, the real crunch, was the British Parliament's annual vote in November to renew sanctions on Rhodesia. The trend line of the annual renewal votes had been unmistakable: in 1976 there had been 20 votes against renewal; in 1977 the number had risen to 27; and in 1978, despite the official Tory policy to abstain, 121 members had voted against continued sanctions. The April 1979 Rhodesian elections as well as the May British elections, which had swept a Conservative majority into office, further eroded parliamentary support for sanctions. Were Thatcher to try to buck the trend and renew sanctions in November, she would spark a ferocious fight within her party. Therefore sanctions almost certainly would not be renewed. Whatever Carrington and Vance planned to do to bring peace to Rhodesia, it would have to be completed by then. "Time is running out," Vance noted.[73]

In May, immediately before Vance and Carrington met, a curious event occurred in southern Africa. It began in a routine way: Fidel Castro sent a top aide, Raúl Valdés Vivó, to talk with Mugabe, Nkomo, and the Frontline presidents. "I was tasked," Valdés Vivó explained to a Soviet diplomat in Havana, "to convey to J. Nkomo and R. Mugabe that Cuba is unable to satisfy their request to send pilots." But Valdés Vivó went much further: he promoted what he called a "Cuban plan for the creation of a provisional government in Zimbabwe." If the Patriotic Front declared "a government in exile" in a region in Rhodesia that it controlled, with Nkomo as president and Mugabe as prime minister, Havana would recognize it. When Valdés Vivó returned to Havana,

Castro summarily dismissed him, saying that he had raised issues "he did not have the authority to discuss. And this resulted in damage to our activities, and raised a host of doubts and false rumors."[74]

A May 19, 1979, US intelligence report accurately described Valdés Vivó's scheme. Two intelligence reports written later in the summer refer to it in passing. However, no declassified document indicates that anyone in the Carter administration took it seriously.[75] Moreover, not one of the administration officials interviewed for this book said that they remembered it. Perhaps the written and oral record has been carefully redacted, but it seems more likely that the Carter administration was quickly convinced by one (or several) of the Frontline presidents that they would not approve the scheme, or perhaps Castro himself had swiftly and decisively persuaded Carter that Valdés Vivó had exceeded orders. The incident died without a trace.

Vance and Carrington Nudge Their Boats Together
On May 21, the first day of Vance's talks with Carrington, Vance spent the morning session ensuring that he had London's support for the SALT II treaty. In the afternoon, they tackled Rhodesia.

Vance explained that the dangers of lifting sanctions were twofold: it would be seen as "aligning the US with South Africa against black Africa . . . [and] it would increase the opportunities for Soviet and Cuban penetration." Therefore, he expected Carter to announce that he would not lift sanctions, but would keep the situation under review and lift them as soon as the Muzorewa government took three specific steps that hinged on the successful convening of all-party talks: Muzorewa would have to (1) attend these all-party talks where (2) the constitution would be revised and (3) arrangements would be made to hold new, internationally supervised elections. The crucial difference between this plan and the plan that Anthony Lake had suggested was that the Patriotic Front also would have to be at the table. However, Vance hastened to add, the president was still evaluating the Rhodesian election results, and he might surprise everyone, as he had with his neutron bomb decision.[76]

Carrington, who wanted to be able to work his way through the Rhodesian morass without constraints, did not find these specific benchmarks "attractive." The idea of all-party talks "is so well worn that it would likely be greeted with a horse laugh." He wanted President Carter to say simply that he would keep the situation under review. This worried Vance, who knew that specifying the steps Muzorewa had to take to satisfy the Carter administration would strengthen the president's hand in the looming battle with Congress. After extensive negotiations, however, Vance agreed to suggest a more general framework to Carter.[77]

Carrington would later navigate the Rhodesian shoals brilliantly, but during these talks he was naive. His plan was vague and unworkable. "Bishop Muzorewa wants to cooperate with us," he told Vance. "He will be open to influence." Britain would send a senior official to Salisbury to open lines of communication and press Muzorewa to amend the constitution. This assumed that Muzorewa wielded real power. Vance did not object to the British taking the lead. It was important to be able to tell Congress that the administration was not slavishly following the Anglo-American proposals; it was useful to shove Britain out front. His position was that "it might be better in most cases to act separately, rather than hand in hand." This was a departure. The public cooperation between the two allies that had been begun in March 1977, when Jim Callaghan and David Owen first met with Jimmy Carter in Washington, had ended.[78]

But the odd thing is that the talks reveal that Britain and the United States needed each other more than ever. Thatcher's policy hung on Carter's decision, just as the looming battle in the US Congress hung on Thatcher's decision. It was absolutely critical that they were "nudging" their boats together. This is indicated by the fact that Vance, at a particularly busy time, traveled to London to talk primarily about Rhodesia. When the first session ended inconclusively, he extended his visit by two days. He met three times with Carrington and once with Thatcher, and in all instances Rhodesia was the prime topic. The policy of the two allies was, in fact, more interdependent than ever.

Carrington drew a bright line between the policy of Thatcher and that of the Callaghan government. "Our predecessors, with respect, sought to make the facts fit their policies; we shall ensure that our policies fit the facts," he declared in the House of Lords the day after his first talks with Vance. In fact, however, the Thatcher administration was moving closer to Carter's and Callaghan's views. In April 1979, the Tories had all but promised to lift sanctions forthwith; by May, Carrington assured Vance that nothing would happen before August. During the talks, Robin Renwick, the head of the Foreign Office's Rhodesia Department, noted that "Vance speculated about the possibility of some revisions of the constitution; an attempt to move the Salisbury government towards an all-party conference; and elections under some form of international supervision." The structure of the Anglo-American proposals was intact.[79]

Options

Jimmy Carter faced a mountain of memos: backgrounders on Rhodesian history, sanctions, and the legal requirements of the Case-Javits Amendment; reports from the observers of the Rhodesian elections; exhaustive lists written by the State Department and the NSC of the pros and cons of various verdicts Carter might deliver on the Rhodesian elections; letters and telegrams from leaders of African American organizations, conservative groups, liberal groups, members of Congress, and concerned citizens pleading with him to reject the elections—or, with equal passion, to accept them.

The Case-Javits Amendment required the president to determine if the Salisbury regime had fulfilled two conditions: agree to participate in all-party talks, and hold a "free and fair" election. If he agreed that both conditions had been met, then he should lift sanctions on Rhodesia. The Case-Javits Amendment had bought the administration time, preventing Senator Helms from pushing through his sanctions-lifting motion in July 1978. Nevertheless, just shy of a year later, it was an unwelcome distraction. Carter was preparing to travel to Vienna for his summit with Leonid Brezhnev, during which the two leaders would sign the SALT II treaty; he was trying to steady US relations with Iran, in the throes of revolution; he was worried about growing Soviet influence in Afghanistan; he was beginning to face the fact that Nicaragua's Anastasio Somoza was not going to be able to hold onto power; and he was pressing Israeli prime minister Menachem Begin to uphold the US interpretation of the Camp David Accords. In addition to these foreign policy concerns, he was moving forward with his ambitious domestic agendas on energy and healthcare; he was grappling with an inflation rate of 11 percent (double what it had been when he took office) and an unemployment rate of almost 6 percent; he was still calming the public's nerves after the near-meltdown of Pennsylvania's Three Mile Island nuclear plant on March 28; he was trying to manage an increasingly partisan and obstreperous Congress; and he was beginning to prepare for the 1980 election.

The Carter administration would have preferred to have waited to see what happened in Rhodesia and in London before making a pronouncement on the Muzorewa government, but Case-Javits made that impossible. On June 1, 1979, Bishop Muzorewa would take office and form a government, and Carter had promised to announce his determination no later than two weeks after Muzorewa became prime minister. As Vance concluded his talks in London on May 23, the pressure on the US president was mounting.

Vance brought back a clear message: the British wanted Carter not to lift sanctions and to give them maximum flexibility to develop their own policy by offering only a very general description of the changes that Muzorewa would have to make before the United States would lift sanctions. "What we wanted," the Foreign Office expert on Rhodesia, Antony Duff, told US ambassador Kingman Brewster, "was for the US to take the same line as we were taking: i.e. that a new situation existed [after the elections in Rhodesia] on which we ought to try to build in order to put Rhodesia on the road to independence."[80]

Dick Moose and Tony Lake met with Brzezinski's aide Jerry Funk to develop a series of options for the president. They identified three possibilities: a positive assessment of the elections, which would mean that the United States would lift sanctions immediately, or two variations of a negative determination, one specifying exactly what Muzorewa had to do before Carter would lift sanctions (which Carter preferred) and the other offering Muzorewa only general guidelines (which Carrington had requested).[81]

Over the following two weeks, as Carter contemplated his decision, the State Department, NSC, and CIA weighed in, all agreeing that the president had to choose among these three options. However, the first option—a positive determination—was included merely as a theoretical possibility: Carter *could* choose it. It is striking that not one official even hinted that he should. All agreed that the elections had been superficially free but fundamentally flawed. Their unanimous advice, therefore, was that Carter make a negative declaration on Case-Javits.[82]

There were good reasons to urge Carter to come to the opposite decision: lift sanctions and then try to persuade Muzorewa to broaden his system. First, the elections were widely considered a step forward. Ian Smith had stepped aside (although he would remain a minister without portfolio) and a black man would be prime minister of Rhodesia. Although there were serious questions about how much real power blacks had under the new constitution, there was no doubt that they had more than at any time since colonial rule had been established. Second, the past two years of painstaking Anglo-American negotiations seemed to have reached a dead end. Third, lifting sanctions would have pleased Carter's opponents in the Senate, who were precisely the people whose votes he would need to ratify SALT II. Rhodesia's white population clung to this argument: "Will he [Carter] let a secondary issue such as sanctions jeopardise his chances," the *Rhodesian Herald* asked, "to win congressional approval of the new strategic arms limitation agreement with Russia?"[83]

This is what makes the unanimity of Carter's advisers noteworthy. At an extraordinarily hectic time, both Vance and Brzezinski considered that upholding sanctions on Rhodesia was worth risking a major confrontation with Congress that would demand a significant commitment of the president's (and their own) time and political capital. This was because the arguments against lifting sanctions trumped political expediency: US security was in play. Lifting sanctions would tie the US government to the Muzorewa regime, which had shown no indication of being able to stop the war, and it would enrage the Frontline presidents, who might, in desperation, call on the Cubans and

Soviets for help. Moreover, on ethical grounds, Vance believed strongly that the Rhodesian constitution was flawed and that the April elections were consequently invalid. Brzezinski did not disagree. "He agreed with Vance, Carter, and Young about the need for majority rule," NSC expert Bob Pastor asserts. "There was no doubt about that."[84]

The only disagreement among the advisers concerned the merits of specific versus vague benchmarks. The State Department, opting to stay in step with Britain, recommended that Carter announce the vague benchmarks that Carrington had requested, coupled with a promise that the administration would review the situation in six months—"immediately after the [British] vote on sanctions in Parliament in November." This would signal that the ball was in London's court and give "us a good argument for urging Congress not to take actions that would undercut the British." However, citing only vague benchmarks would infuriate the administration's critics, who thought that Carter was constantly moving the goalposts for judging Muzorewa.[85]

When he was briefing Brzezinski, Funk addressed this problem head on. "The major advantage" of offering specific benchmarks, Funk explained, "is that it . . . answers the conservatives' inevitable question: 'What in the hell do you want'?" Brzezinski liked specific benchmarks because they would flush the British out of "their present strategy of waffling until we go first." If Carter announced that the United States would not lift sanctions until Muzorewa had implemented "a more equitable constitution" and held UN-sponsored elections, then the Conservative government in London would be put on the defensive. If Thatcher decided to lift sanctions, she would be forced to explain why she found the constitution and elections acceptable while the Americans did not. This, Brzezinski wrote Carter, would "force the UK to 'get out front' on the sanctions issue and . . . put some distance between ourselves and the UK without an open break."[86]

British desires were, however, only one of the many factors Carter weighed when making his decision. Determining whether the Rhodesian elections had been free and fair was a challenging conundrum. What is a free and fair election? There were few reports of blatant fraud in the Rhodesian elections; turnout was high and the polling places orderly. And yet the Rhodesians were not offered a free choice: blacks had not been allowed to vote on the constitution that preserved white control in many important domains, and they could not vote for Nkomo or Mugabe or anyone associated with them in the Patriotic Front.

The problem with Case-Javits was that, although the question it raised was intriguing, it was the wrong question. It distracted attention from the fundamental question that drove US policy: would the Muzorewa government gain, or lose, legitimacy? The answer to this question would determine if Muzorewa could end the war. If Muzorewa demonstrated that he wielded real power, if he was able to improve the lot of black Rhodesians, if the civil war ebbed, and if he gained the support of other African leaders, then Carter would lift sanctions. The ball was in Muzorewa's court.

The Bishop's Challenges

Black trumpeters in elaborate costumes sounded a fanfare on May 29, 1979, as Bishop Abel Muzorewa ascended the steps of Government House in Salisbury to be sworn into office as the first black prime minister of the country that at midnight would be reborn as Zimbabwe-Rhodesia.* In a short speech, Muzorewa called on "all true Rhodesians" to cooperate with the new government. "Good Luck, Mr. Prime Minister," the African American *Atlanta Daily World* newspaper declared.[87]

Muzorewa would need it. He faced a country ravaged by a brutal war that had raged for six years and claimed approximately 20,000 lives. At least one Rhodesian was killed every hour. "War fatalities," Brzezinski wrote Carter, "reached their highest levels in April." In May, after the elections, a record 891 people were killed in Rhodesia.[88] Martial law had been declared in all but 10 percent of the land; that meant curfews, censorship, detentions, and summary justice. The rural population was caught up in what the International Committee of the Red Cross described as "a rapidly deteriorating humanitarian situation." Rural Rhodesians were fleeing to the country's few cities or to camps in Botswana, Mozambique, and Zambia, which provided shelter for more than 200,000 war refugees. The Rhodesian economy had been decimated by the cost of the war. Defense spending rose by 610 percent from 1971 to 1978, and tourism revenue, an economic mainstay, plummeted. White flight doubled in the first four months of 1979 compared with the previous year. The draft of black Rhodesians, a desperate measure to bolster the armed forces, was instituted in early 1979, but the vast majority of conscripted blacks failed to show up. Likewise, an increasing number of whites dodged the draft.[89]

Prime Minister Muzorewa had two imperative, intertwined, and extraordinarily challenging tasks: he had to end the war and he had to convince the international community to recognize his fledgling regime. Soon after he won the election, and before he formed a government, he addressed both imperatives

---

*I do not use the name "Zimbabwe-Rhodesia" in the text because it was not recognized by any country. The Carter administration continued to refer to the country as "Rhodesia" but also used the new name on occasion.

in "an urgent appeal" he sent to President Carter and also released in full to the *Rhodesian Herald.* "During the month of April, 837 people lost their lives in fighting in my country. No fewer than 811 . . . were blacks," he wrote Carter. "I have no doubt that if you, as the acknowledged Leader of the Free World, were to give and [*sic*] immediate and positive indication of your intention to . . . lift sanctions, it would have a dramatic effect on the situation . . . [and] go a long way towards alleviating the suffering of my people. . . . All I am asking is that you should remove the fetters which you imposed on the previous white minority government."[90]

Muzorewa promised to form a government of national unity that would not only gather together Rhodesia's white and black citizens but would also heal the fissures dividing the fractious political and tribal groups that had loosely joined together to form the transitional internal settlement government. Yet even before Muzorewa formed his cabinet, the old antagonisms resurfaced. In a cable titled "Cracks in the Foundation," Bill Edmondson, the US ambassador in Pretoria (who reported on Rhodesia because the United States had no official representation there), noted that Reverend Ndabaningi Sithole, Muzorewa's partner in the internal settlement government, challenged the results of the elections and announced on May 1 that his party (which had the second-largest bloc of black-held parliamentary seats) would boycott the new government, refusing to accept any cabinet posts in it. Chief Kayisa Ndiweni, the leader of the only other black party that had won any seats, also announced that his party would go into opposition rather than partner with Muzorewa. (He later reversed this decision.) Chief Jeremiah Chirau, whose party won no seats, bitterly questioned the integrity of the elections. James Chikerema, a leader in Muzorewa's own party, was outraged when the new prime minister selected cabinet members only from his own ethnic subgroup, and he publicly accused Muzorewa of "tribalism, nepotism, and dictatorship." Edmondson cabled on May 30, "As the new government seems to be moving toward realization, the facade of national unity is crumbling away." Within days, the ambassador's pessimism had deepened. "On a more ominous note," he cabled on June 2, Muzorewa's police had arrested fourteen officials of Sithole's party and charged them with plotting to assassinate the prime minister. This was "a very unsubtle threat to Sithole to discontinue his boycott." It did not, he added, "augur well."[91]

In his first televised address as prime minister, Muzorewa was frank. "Nowhere, throughout history, has any new government come into power beset with more problems than those I see facing my Government." He announced that it was his government's "first priority to stop the conflict."[92] His election, however, did nothing to quell the war. Fighting had ebbed during the elections only because the government had deployed almost 100,000 men—every ounce of manpower it could muster. This was unsustainable. "The public must not think that any of the problems have been solved," the white co-minister of defense, Hilary Squires, warned.[93]

Muzorewa responded to the war in three ways. First, he offered amnesty, "the hand of fellowship," to any Patriotic Front fighter willing to lay down arms and accept the new government as legitimate.[94] This was a repetition of the offer that had been on the books for over a year, ever since the internal settlement government had been in office. It had not attracted the guerrillas before Muzorewa became prime minister, and it did not attract them now. Second, Muzorewa—who was also serving as his own co-minister of defense alongside Squires—promised to wage the war vigorously. On June 4, immediately after extending the hand of friendship to the guerrillas, his troops launched an aerial and ground assault on ZANU bases in Mozambique. Third, quietly, Muzorewa reached out to Pretoria.

This epitomized Muzorewa's problem. He had to achieve peace in order to achieve legitimacy, but he did not have the manpower, money, or materiel to quell the guerrillas. Having won a landslide election, he was loath to open the Pandora's box of negotiations with the guerrillas. Instead, he wanted to achieve enough peace to convince Washington and London to lift sanctions and recognize his regime. But to achieve this prospect of peace, he turned to the only government that would offer military assistance—apartheid South Africa. This undermined his legitimacy as the leader of the black majority.

South African prime minister P.W. Botha was happy to help. While still toying with the Western governments who sought negotiated solutions in Namibia and Rhodesia, Botha was circling the wagons. "Those of us who believed in the same ideals of democracy and civilisation," he told two Rhodesian officials in April 1979, "had to stand together." Botha sought to protect South Africa by forming what he called a "constellation of states" that would be economically and militarily dependent on Pretoria. South Africa would shore up its defensive line—breached by Samora Machel's black nationalist government in Mozambique—with a nominally independent Namibia, hapless Botswana, and—the plum—Rhodesia led by Abel Muzorewa. Prime Minister Botha proceeded discreetly. In April, he and Ian Smith had agreed on "a treaty of cooperation and mutual support in the security field" that would be implemented after the election. Pretoria increased its military and economic aid to the Rhodesian regime. In his memoirs, Smith cast a cold eye on Botha's motivations: "The South Africans were . . . trying to bring our new government under their wing in order that they might control and direct our future policy . . . by using security and financial assistance as a lever."[95]

Immediately after the elections, P.W. Botha noted at a press conference that Muzorewa "had told him on several occasions . . . that he was willing 'to cooperate with South Africa in the interests of Rhodesia,'" and at a news conference Muzorewa had announced, "We will take help from anyone who can help us." Pretoria increased its shipments to Salisbury of ammunition and sophisticated materiel, including helicopters; its advisers were attached to the Rhodesian military; its border patrol police spilled over into Rhodesian territory; and its soldiers were given generous terms if they chose to be seconded to the Rhodesian army.[96] Prime Minister Botha carefully avoided saying if he would formally send troops to help Muzorewa but, in a BBC interview on May 29, he said that his government would extend "*de facto* recognition*" to the new government in Rhodesia. He added, somewhat cryptically, "If there is an attempt on the part of foreign interests, foreign powers, to create chaos in Rhodesia by foreign interference, then the South African parliament will have to take cognizance of such a state of affairs. . . . We cannot afford chaos on our borders." Washington understood what this signified. Jerry Funk wrote Brzezinski that South Africa would give "strong support" to the new Rhodesian government. "This means we can expect an expansion and intensification of the war, and the Soviets/Cubans will become more deeply involved."[97]

Africa's Opprobrium and Obasanjo's Muscle

"I was delighted that the United States Senate voted so overwhelmingly to remove sanctions," Prime Minister Muzorewa wrote Walter Mondale—in the latter's capacity as president of the Senate—on May 24, 1979. "I am confident that President Carter, himself a true Christian and champion of human rights, will have the honesty and courage to lift economic sanctions."[98]

All the other African leaders, including the heads of pro-Western governments such as Liberia, Botswana, and Kenya, wrote to Carter asking that he do the precise opposite—that is, not lift sanctions. The Organization of African Unity released an uncompromising statement: "No true African can accept a government based on such a constitution [as the Rhodesian one]. . . . The war will not stop until the black majority achieves real power in Zimbabwe."[99]

General Olusegun Obasanjo, the leader of Nigeria, agreed with the OAU, and he had clout—not only in Africa but also in Washington. In October 1978, when Iranian oil exports were disrupted by the revolution, Lagos had increased its shipments to the United States by 10 percent. The United States was importing one million barrels of Nigerian crude every day—at a cost of $5 billion annually—which equaled 15 percent of US oil imports.[100]

Moreover, in 1979, Nigeria was expected to displace South Africa as the largest market in Africa for US exports—worth more than $1 billion—and US firms had invested approximately $1.2 billion in the large, populous country. Obasanjo's stock in Washington was not based solely on oil and greenbacks. He had forged a personal relationship with Carter, and US-Nigerian relations had never been stronger, due in large measure to Obasanjo's respect for Carter's policy in southern Africa. For his part, by 1979 Carter's admiration for Obasanjo had deepened as he observed the Nigerian strongman fulfilling his promise to return Nigeria to democratic rule. The Obasanjo administration had drafted a presidential constitution, and free elections were scheduled for October 1979. US officials listened, therefore, on May 4, when the Nigerian government announced that if the United States lifted sanctions on Rhodesia, it could expect an "appropriate response" from Lagos.[101]

Fears of Nigerian retaliation had been swirling for months. In March 1979, in the wake of the US Congress's moves to send observers to the Rhodesian elections and to lift sanctions, the American ambassador in Lagos, Donald Easum, warned that "Nigerians are studying actions they might take against sanctions lifters." This could include using economic levers such as "a trade cut-off or the nationalization of companies . . . and the denial of some new contracts." This worried Washington and alarmed London. Nigeria was Britain's tenth largest market, with investments totaling £375 million and exports worth more than £1 billion annually. Britain, like the United States, depended on Nigerian oil. Moreover, Nigeria was a powerful member of the Commonwealth, and a threat by Obasanjo to withdraw from that body would have profound consequences. The *Guardian* reported that "confidential warnings came up the line from Nigeria to the FO [Foreign Office] during the general election campaign [in late April]."[102]

In the United States, the fears crystalized in the weeks before Carter's highly anticipated announcement required by Case-Javits. Obasanjo, who called the Rhodesian elections "a mockery of democracy," was concerned that Carter would cave to congressional pressure and declare the Rhodesian elections free and fair. In late May, Ambassador Easum cabled that "a substantial amount of media attention in Nigeria has been devoted to discussion of measures which might be taken against countries . . . which . . . lift sanctions." Easum speculated that economic retaliation against the United States "could range from an oil embargo . . . to a variety of lesser measures . . . [such as] the withdrawal of ambassadors, the cancellation of visits or meetings, and the denial of some new contracts." If the United States did lift sanctions, Easum was convinced of two things: Nigeria would "take some such action to demonstrate its commitment to the cause of Zimbabwe" and the "new era of improved Nigerian-American relations which began with the Carter administration [would] . . . come to an end." Lifting sanctions would signal to black Africa that Washington had never truly supported majority rule. "Nigerians would feel hoodwinked and believe they had been duped by a big power which was now once again showing its true colors."[103]

In February, the CIA had dismissed the prospect that cash-starved Nigeria would invoke the oil weapon if the United States lifted sanctions on Rhodesia, but the idea gained credence in the subsequent months. "While we continue to consider such action unlikely," the oil expert at the US embassy in Lagos wrote on May 18, "the arguments against it from the FMG's [Federal Military Government of Nigeria] standpoint are not as overwhelming as first appear." Nigerian officials warned the US embassy that their response would be "far stronger than Washington now anticipates." On May 29, the Nigerian ambassador in Washington announced that if the Carter administration recognized the Muzorewa government, "we will, of necessity, then review our bilateral relations, both political and economic, with the United States."[104]

An article about Nigeria's threat to retaliate where it hurt—at the pumps—if Carter lifted sanctions was splashed across the front page of the *Washington Post* on May 31. The journalists attending the State Department's daily press briefing pummeled the spokesman with questions about the story, which he said was "accurate." The Nigerian threat was carried that night on the television evening news and picked up by other major newspapers. "US officials . . . are taking the Nigerian warning extremely seriously," the *Baltimore Sun* reported. "The Nigerians mean it."[105] The words were given teeth when Lagos announced that British companies would not be allowed to bid on a $235 million port construction contract, which London had fully expected to land. Even more ominously, a Nigerian official declared that his government would not "entertain any new proposals from British companies" until London clarified its attitude toward the regime in Rhodesia. "The Nigerians have made their point," the *Washington Post* noted. "Nigeria is experimenting to see how much leverage a million barrels a day can exert. It is invoking the oil weapon."[106]

The Black Vote

"There's no constituency for an intelligent Africa policy in this country," Andrew Young said to a crowded room of civil rights leaders in Atlanta in January 1979. "Where is the constituency for an intelligent, long range policy?" he asked. "We know where the constituency is for Cyprus. When I was a congressman in this district we had less than two percent Greek population but I got almost a thousand letters when the Turks invaded Cyprus [in 1974]. I must confess that I didn't get ten letters when Soweto [the South African slum outside Johannesburg] was overrun [in 1976] and thousands of black children were killed."[107]

Young was talking about a problem that had bothered liberals for years: there was no effective domestic constituency that pressured Washington about Africa policy. Many liberals who cared about Africa looked to African Americans to express a particular interest in the continent. They wanted black Americans to form an engaged constituency that could press the US government in the same way that Jewish Americans lobbied for Israel or Irish Americans lobbied for Ireland. This line of thinking, of course, overlooked the fact that few African Americans knew from which part of the vast continent their ancestors had been wrenched, and also glossed over the more pressing problems of poverty and unemployment confronting African Americans in the late 1970s. Nevertheless, it was a persistent theme. Senator Dick Clark, for example, later rued, "When I was chair of the Africa subcommittee [from 1975 to 1979], I can't remember any black members of Congress coming to talk with me about Africa. There was no pressure at all." Although the leaders of civil rights organizations such as the NAACP and the Urban League said that they supported Carter's Rhodesia policy, they did not rally their followers to help the president counter his critics. "There is not much grass-roots interest [in Rhodesia]," a top State Department official told the *New York Times* in 1979. "While black leaders had voiced concern . . . , it was not a matter of high attention for blacks."[108]

Carter's policy toward Africa helped politically active African Americans justify their continuing support for the president. "The president was still rather conservative on fiscal policy, and black people didn't want to hear that," Young explained. "And he didn't agree with quotas, so when they asked him how many blacks he'd appoint, he wouldn't make any commitments. But saying he was in favor of one man, one vote in southern Africa was politically helpful. Lots of liberal Democrats weren't ready yet to come out in favor of one man, one vote. They were still kind of caught up in the Cold War view of Africa. So Carter's policy gave him the political credential that made it possible for blacks to support him when he was against many other things that they were for."[109] Nevertheless, Carter's policy toward Africa, however praiseworthy, was simply not as important to African Americans as was his policy on jobs and the economy.

By the late 1970s, in large part due to appointments in the Carter years, there were for the first time many career black professionals in the executive branch. They formed the Tuesday Afternoon Club, where they occasionally discussed African issues; their focus, however, was closer to home. "There wasn't any consistent strain of organizing," Henry Richardson, a member of the group during his time at the NSC, recalled. "But there was a gradual rising of consciousness."[110]

In 1979, the administration instituted a series of regular meetings with the minority community in an effort to rally broader and more active support for its Africa policy. In January, Vance held a reception for one hundred African American leaders to discuss foreign policy—the gala launch of the ongoing series of smaller, lower-profile meetings. He wrote Carter that he had been "concerned that this would be a very difficult and non productive meeting but I was wrong. . . . The dialogue was serious, frank and informative on both sides." In the margin of the memo, Carter wrote, "These meetings are very helpful to me." The gathering, as Vance implied, had not been a lovefest. Predictably, it was the representatives from TransAfrica, the group that had been established in 1977 as a foreign policy lobby, who expressed the most passionate concern about the direction of US policy toward Africa. Richard Gordon Hatcher, the chair of TransAfrica, complained bitterly that the Carter administration had "failed to deliver" on its promises to promote change in southern Africa. "We find it incredible," Hatcher told Vance, "that the mightiest power in the world cannot put enough pressure on two hundred and some odd thousand whites in Rhodesia, or even South Africa, to end their illegal and repugnant domination of Rhodesia and Namibia." This complaint exemplifies the challenge that the administration faced: its policy toward Africa was marginal to the vast majority of African Americans and disappointing to the small minority that focused on it.[111]

As the recession deepened, interest in Africa grew more attenuated. For example, when the Congressional Black Caucus met with the president in February 1979, while the Rhodesia debate was in full swing, the caucus wanted to discuss the budget; it was Carter who wanted to focus on Rhodesia.[112] The president's relations with the caucus were not easy. Although the public argument that had erupted between Carter and Representative John Conyers (D-MI) the previous September had been papered over, feelings of disappointment and grievance had deepened on both sides.

Through the spring of 1979, as Salisbury held its elections and Muzorewa took office, it was difficult to gauge how important Carter's decision on Case-Javits would be for African Americans. It clearly mattered to a handful of leaders. Randall Robinson, the founder of TransAfrica, was blunt: "What we're dealing with here is racism. . . . A response to Rhodesia is a response to us." In March, Andrew Young wrote Carter, "While there is little in the way of an organized African policy among Black voters, any collapse of our African policy will be used to confirm the growing cynicism and racial distortion of Administration policies." A few weeks later, Jerry Funk was emphatic in a memo to Brzezinski: backing away from the Anglo-American proposals, he warned, would be seen by blacks as "a sell out to racism." On April 25, the Congressional Black Caucus wrote Carter that "the Black community has come to perceive the lifting of sanctions against Rhodesia as a major issue of commitment for which the Administration is held responsible, an issue which goes to the basic attitudes of fairness towards all persons of African descent." Maynard Jackson, the first African American mayor of Atlanta, was more direct. He told Carter: "Do not to underestimate the issue. Africa is our Israel."[113]

Was it? The Congressional Black Caucus, for example, went through the motions—writing to the White House and testifying before at least one hearing—but not one member of the caucus played a leadership role in the congressional debates about Rhodesia before Carter's decision on Case-Javits. They left that to white liberals such as New York's Stephen Solarz. Clearly, this reflected the caucus constituents' focus on domestic concerns, but it also was the result of its rocky relationship with the president. NSC Africa specialist Tom Thornton recalled that the "CBC [Congressional Black Caucus] was not a factor. There was no Black pressure group on Rhodesia that I can remember." Dick Moose explained: "They [the members of the caucus] were preoccupied with the economy. At the end, it was me trying to get [caucus member Charles] Diggs to move. . . . But [John] Conyers, [Charlie] Rangel—not a word."[114] Even TransAfrica, which was focused on foreign policy, had trouble exercising any leverage. At a fundraiser in Baltimore in early June 1979, Randall Robinson declared, "Black Americans provide the margin of Democratic presidential electability. . . . A wrong decision on Rhodesia could cost the president that margin." Talking to a small group of black officials in the White House, Robinson was more sober. The real problem was not lack of funds (although TransAfrica did lack funds), Robinson admitted; it was that, "We are a leadership without a following."[115]

This left it to the White House to create the appearance of a groundswell of support for its Rhodesia policy. Andrew Young quietly got out the Rolodex that had helped him rally votes for Carter in 1976. He used his connections in the black churches and civil rights organizations. "We literally mobilized an opposition to that election [in Rhodesia]," Young explained. "We had two thousand Africanists and ministers from key congressional districts that we wrote to and urged them to visit their congressmen, and we sort of set up a model which was the old civil rights movement model that eight or ten preachers and ministers would get together and visit the congressman." As

Tom Thornton recalled, "Liberals in the White House pleaded with the black organizations, 'Here's our arm. Please twist it!'"[116]

In May, letters from black organizations—mayors, community organizers, women's groups, lawyers, churchmen, Republicans and Democrats—flooded into the White House and Congress, expressing passionate opposition to the lifting of sanctions. The *Rhodesian Herald* was all over the story, which confirmed its conviction that Carter was motivated by his desire to maintain black support. The US press attributed the sudden interest to the efforts of Trans-Africa and the Washington Office on Africa. No one identified the hand of Andy Young.[117]

The apparent outpouring of black support gave the president cover, particularly with his British partners. For example, in his first meeting with Carrington, Vance said that "the [Carter] Administration faced a very divisive political battle, with the black community feeling particularly strongly." As Robin Renwick of the Foreign Office's Rhodesia Department remembered: "They [the Americans] would say, 'We have to carry the Black Caucus with us.' That was a kind of Carter refrain."[118] It was, for the White House, more a wish than a reality.

Congress Pauses

If Carter decided to maintain sanctions, would Congress overrule him? If it did, would Carter veto legislation that lifted sanctions? Could he sustain the veto? Was Rhodesia worth a fight with Congress, when its support was needed to pass SALT II and when the 1980 elections were approaching?

The Senate had made its stance toward the Rhodesian elections clear with its lopsided (75 to 19) vote on May 15, which declared that it was "the sense of the Congress" that the provisions of Case-Javits had been "substantially complied with" and that the president should lift sanctions forthwith. On May 25, the indefatigable Senator Harry Byrd attached an amendment lifting Rhodesian sanctions to the Defense Authorization bill. This was a smart move for two reasons: the $40 billion bill, which funded all major military procurement, was considered veto-proof; and it would be debated in the notoriously conservative Armed Services Committee. As expected, on May 31 the committee voted to accept Byrd's amendment. The bill was not expected to reach the Senate floor before June 11, when Helms would spearhead the battle.[119]

The administration did not give up on the Senate, but it placed its hopes on the House. There, Solarz continued to lead the fight and, as Funk noted, "carry our water on the Hill." As part of his continuing drive to persuade swing votes in Congress, Solarz had led a group of members of Congress to southern Africa over the Easter recess. Upon his return, he wrote a concise and well-informed report explaining why it would be "both precipitous and premature" to lift sanctions immediately. This report sheds light on the arguments that Solarz employed to change the minds of his colleagues in the House. Although he stipulated that the Rhodesian elections had been "a watershed," Solarz argued that lifting sanctions would increase the likelihood of "major" Soviet and Cuban involvement in the conflict. It would give the United States "a stake" in the survival of the Muzorewa regime, which meant that Washington might be faced with the choice of either sitting by as Muzorewa tottered or going to the "aid of a hated regime." Either way, "we will have maximized rather than minimized Soviet influence through this minerally rich and politically important part of the world." There was an alternative, Solarz asserted. "Used creatively, sanctions and recognition could be an effective lever to get the Salisbury group and the Patriotic Front to accept a new Anglo-American proposal." What Solarz had in mind was a "streamlined" version of the proposals, one that did not get bogged down in the details of the transition period or the constitution.[120] On May 23, Solarz wrote Carter that the administration could win the battle to retain sanctions "if, and only if, you are willing to actively undertake an effort to persuade the Congress that it would not be in the best interest of our country to lift sanctions at this time." He summed up his argument in three words: "Members," he reminded Carter, "are educable."[121]

One week later, Solarz hosted a lunch for six African ambassadors, seventeen members of the House, and a diplomat from the British embassy. The ambassadors explained why lifting sanctions was a bad idea. The Nigerian said that "Nigeria would be bound to react." The British diplomat reported that "things began to get interesting when Millicent Fenwick (R-NJ) started to stoke her pipe—usually a sign that sparks will begin to fly. . . . Fenwick said she hadn't received a single letter from her district in favour of keeping sanctions. If she was going to work to keep them in place she would have to have arguments that she could use with her constituents."[122]

These arguments began to materialize in the days before Carter made his determination. They were, essentially, a one-two punch. The threat of a Nigerian oil embargo grabbed the public's, and Congress's, attention. It was a splash of cold water that made people ready to listen to the argument that it would be rash for the United States to lift sanctions before Great Britain—the legal authority—did. Why not let the British take the heat?

Andrew Young emphasized this on the weekly television news program *Meet the Press* on June 3. Young had recently compared the executions in revolutionary Iran with a contested death penalty case in Florida, a comment that had revived the furor over all his past incendiary statements. The interviewer asked him about his "controversial statements . . . with kind of an anti-American—" Young interrupted. "Let's call them editorial statements to make people think," he said, closing that line of questioning. The interviewer then asked if he would resign if Carter lifted sanctions on Rhodesia. Young smiled. "I didn't get into this job thinking I was going to win every battle," he answered. In discussing Case-Javits and the sanctions issue, Young mentioned Nigerian oil and added, "I think the British . . . are basically stalling to see what happens. I think that is pretty wise. I don't know that we ought to plunge in and take this problem off their hands. This has not been an American problem; we did not create it." Young also sent a letter to every senator "warning them that an immediate lifting of sanctions might provoke reprisals from black African nations, including Nigeria."[123]

Two letters signaled that this argument was gaining traction. The first letter was to Carter from ten representatives—five Democrats and five Republicans, all moderates and all swing voters. On May 31, they wrote the president that, after hearing the "persuasive testimony" of numerous witnesses who cautioned against a precipitate lifting of sanctions during the hearings Solarz had organized on the Rhodesian elections, they thought that "a reasonable delay is justified" and urged the president to "defer" any decision to lift sanctions at least until the Commonwealth met in Lusaka in August.[124] The second letter was from Republican John Erlenborn of Illinois and Democrat Don Pease of Ohio, to all their House colleagues, on June 4. There was nothing polemical about this letter. It was plain-spoken and nonpartisan. "The key point is this," Erlenborn and Pease wrote. "Now is not the time for Congress to take actions on the sanctions question." They mentioned the importance of Nigerian oil, and they asserted that "by hastily lifting sanctions, Congress would play right into the hands of the Soviets and Cubans." Finally, they wrote, "Let's remember that Rhodesia is primarily a British problem." This letter packed a particular punch because Erlenborn had switched camps: he had been one of the conservatives who voted to send congressional observers to the Rhodesian elections. Senator Henry Bellmon, a Republican from Oklahoma, was succinct. Africa "has us over a barrel," he announced on the Senate floor. "An oil barrel to be exact." On June 5, Vance told Carrington that there was "growing caution" on the Hill about lifting sanctions on Rhodesia.[125]

The Case-Javits Announcement

Carter did not like the draft speech that the State Department sent him to announce his decision on Case-Javits. It focused exclusively on the tragedy of the war in Rhodesia, emphasizing the suffering of the Rhodesians who lived "in daily terror . . . their lives a walking nightmare."[126] It did not embrace the full complexity of the decision the president was about to announce.

Nothing about Carter's Case-Javits determination was simple. The domestic costs of a negative determination—that the Rhodesian elections were not "free and fair" and therefore the United States would not lift sanctions—seemed straightforward at first: it would antagonize many members of Congress whose votes Carter needed to pass important legislation, particularly SALT II. Declaring the elections "free and fair," however, would antagonize his more liberal base in Congress and would undermine his support among African American leaders. But how much would this matter? Would Carter's congressional critics oppose his policies no matter what he did about Rhodesia? Would any foreign policy issue sway the attitudes of African American leaders?

The impact in black Africa of accepting the Muzorewa government and lifting sanctions was clear: it would set back the progress that the Carter administration had made improving the US image in the eyes of black Africa. And yet, would this matter in material terms? Would Nigeria really stop shipping its oil?

Carter's determination would have the most immediate dramatic impact in Rhodesia itself. Lifting sanctions would give the Muzorewa government a significant boost, and it would almost certainly lead to Britain's lifting sanctions as well. The question with which Carter had to wrestle was: would that boost be enough to allow the new government to take root, begin to stabilize, and stop the war? If Muzorewa could not stop the war—and the early signs were that he could not—then the war would escalate.

This brought in the next circle of complexity: the Cold War. Here, Carter could not escape the counterintuitive logic of his policy. If, on one hand, he supported the pro-American and pro-capitalist Muzorewa, it was reasonable to expect that the Patriotic Front or the Frontline presidents would call for Soviet and Cuban assistance; this would bring the Cold War to southern Africa in full force. If, on the other hand, he rejected Muzorewa and kept lines of communication open to the Patriotic Front, he might be able to avoid the polarization of the Cold War and continue to pursue a negotiated settlement.

Finally, beyond the political considerations, there was a moral argument. Had the elections been free and fair? Was the Muzorewa government based on true majority rule? It is foolhardy to try to read Carter's mind and determine the precise weight of all these considerations. Carter himself, years later, stressed both the Cold War and moral dimensions.[127] Indeed, in June 1979, this was what he wanted his speech announcing his decision to emphasize. Thus, he tore the State Department draft apart, crossing out whole paragraphs and adding new ones in his own hand. The speech Carter delivered late in the afternoon of June 7 bears almost no relation to the draft the State Department suggested. It was his own speech.[128]

At 5:15 P.M., the president walked from the Cabinet room to the White House Press Briefing room with Vance at his side. Carter then announced his decision: he was not lifting sanctions on Rhodesia. He stressed that he had made his determination only after intensive consultations with the British, "who retain both legal and historic interests and responsibilities for that country." He asserted that retaining sanctions on Rhodesia was in America's interest. First, it would "limit the opportunity of outside powers"—the Soviet Union and Cuba—"to take advantage of the situation in southern Africa at the expense of the United States." Moreover, it "should preserve our diplomatic and ties of trade with friendly African Governments . . . in a region of the world of increasing importance to us."[129]

The thrust of the speech, however, was an impassioned explanation of the inequalities that remained in Rhodesia. Carter explained that only whites had voted to approve the constitution and that "opposing political parties" (he avoided using the term Patriotic Front) had not been allowed to participate in the election. Therefore, although the election "appears to have been administered in a reasonably fair way . . . I cannot conclude that the elections were either fair or free." Retaining sanctions on Rhodesia would encourage Muzorewa, Carter said, "to achieve genuine majority rule, [and] an end to apartheid and racism." If Muzorewa made these reforms, if he moved toward "a wider political process and more legitimate and genuine majority rule"— the vague benchmarks that the British desired—then Carter would lift sanctions. His administration would keep the situation under constant review and inform Congress of its findings every month.

Carter was forthright about the fact that his decision would not be popular in Congress. "I recognize, to be perfectly frank with you, that I do not have a majority of support in the United States Senate. My guess is that at the present time in the House we would have difficulty in this position prevailing." And he threw down the gauntlet: "But because it is a matter of principle to me personally and to our country, because I see the prospect of our Nation being seriously damaged in its relationship with other countries, in southern Africa, and elsewhere, because to lift sanctions at this time would directly violate international law, . . . I intend to do everything I can within my power to prevail on this decision. . . . [Retaining sanctions is] what's right and what's decent and what's fair and what is principled."

14. Surprises

"Good Heavens!" Edward Gierek, the first secretary of Poland's ruling communist party, exclaimed. He turned to his wife. "A Pole has become the Pope."[1] It was October 16, 1978, and the white smoke was still wafting over St. Peter's Square in Vatican City. Karol Wojtyła, born fifty-eight years earlier in a small city in southern Poland and for twenty years the archbishop of Cracow, had just been become Pope John Paul II.

Wojtyła was not only the first Polish pope; he was the first non-Italian pope in 455 years. His selection stunned the world. The KGB saw Zbigniew Brzezinski's hand behind it, informing the Kremlin that Brzezinski had been one of the three Poles "masterminding the election of the Archbishop of Cracow." (The others were Cardinal John Krol of Philadelphia and Cardinal Stefan Wyszyński of Poland.) It rendered the leaders of Poland speechless. They offered no official comment for twenty-four hours while they argued about how to react to the news.[2]

Poland in 1978 was a study in survival. Its economy was in free fall, caught between the inefficiencies of Soviet central planning and the inexorability of the $13 billion in Western loans that would come due in 1979. Gierek tried cutting subsidies—and the people rioted. So he backtracked. Over the course of the 1970s, he had worked out a delicate balancing act: he avoided provoking the Kremlin, but he liberalized just enough to secure Western loans and he struck a deal with the Polish Catholic Church. The church, despite the state's earlier attempts to crush it, claimed more parishioners than ever: 90 percent of the thirty-five million Poles. Under Gierek's leadership, the church received a circumscribed zone of freedom so long as it refrained from attacking the state. At the same time, the church gave quiet and conditional support to the rising dissident movement in Poland.[3] It was a paradoxical and deft balance, a sophisticated and uniquely Polish arrangement, but it worked fairly well— until a Pole was named pope.

It became clear within weeks that this Pole wanted to visit his homeland. No pope had ever been allowed to travel to a communist country. (The Polish authorities had refused permission to Pope Paul VI to visit in 1966.) After difficult negotiations with the Catholic hierarchy, Gierek approved the visit of John Paul II for June 1979, despite the strong opposition of the Soviet Union. Soviet leader Leonid Brezhnev phoned Gierek twice to demand the cancellation of the visit, "which would endanger the entire socialist community."[4]

On May 29, 1979, Cyrus Vance had an audience with the pope at the Vatican. They discussed arms control, China, and Carter's imminent decision on the Case-Javits Amendment. "The pope was very sensitive to the intense attention that non-aligned countries in general and the Africans in particular are paying to the Rhodesian situation," Vance cabled Carter. The pope was also anticipating his own trip home. "I found the pope exhilarated at the prospect of his nine-day trip to Poland, starting at the end of this week." Vance departed feeling hopeful. "I came away from my audience with him convinced that his common sense, vitality and humanity will be extremely powerful forces for good in the year to come."[5]

Pope John Paul II landed in Warsaw four days later. For the following nine days he crisscrossed Poland, delivering thirty-three sermons and speeches to an estimated thirteen million people. It was a week that overwhelmed. It overwhelmed language and it overwhelmed emotions.[6]

Western journalists tried to convey it, but, as the *New York Times* West German bureau chief admitted, "the situation was totally new and difficult to grasp."[7] Newspapers carried reports of the enormous crowds, of John Paul's ability to create a sense of intimacy with a throng of thousands, of the pride, the fervor, and the joy. Journalists highlighted anything the pope said that could be interpreted as coded political language. But this missed the key point. The point was not the pope's subtle language. It was his presence, his galvanizing presence.

The pope—the *Polish* pope—symbolized and embodied the past ten centuries of Polish history. He hearkened back to it constantly. Totally overlooking the Soviet present, he reminded his audience again and again of their shared Catholic and Polish past. He burst exuberantly into traditional Polish folk songs, and the crowds sang with him and begged for more. And, again utterly ignoring the Iron Curtain, John Paul II looked to the future, a future that would unite Christian Europe—if his fellow Poles called on their faith and displayed their courage. "Is it not the intention of the Holy Spirit that this Polish Pope—this Slav Pope—should at this precise moment manifest the spiritual unity of Christian Europe?" he asked in the midst of a sermon in Gniezno. By ignoring the Soviet Union, John Paul II not only deftly avoided transgressions that would invite a crackdown, he also, more importantly, pulled back the curtain on the circumscribed power of the state. Suddenly, the weight of the Soviet state was merely a transient episode in the long, glorious struggle of the Polish people.

The pope's visit did more. It gave the Poles—those who attended the events and those who watched the snippets shown on the state-controlled television—a "movement high," a rush of power, purpose, and community.[8] Perhaps even more important, it showed the Polish people that they could dare to organize and to defy the authorities—parishes and communities decorated their towns with yellow and white bunting; they developed transportation networks to ferry each other to the papal events; they defied the state's orders not to skip work or school; they released balloons stamped with the insignia of the World War II anticommunist resistance movement—and the result was not chaos. It was, instead, happy, friendly, and well-behaved crowds. The nationalism that for decades had been implied behind church doors was suddenly voiced openly and joyfully in public squares. The Poles' small steps toward organization, their individual acts of minor defiance did not unleash forces that they could not control. Instead, they allowed the people to feel the power of the mature, dignified, patriotic Polish people—their power. They were stirred, inspired, and reborn. As a Russian historian noted, "The nine-day visit transformed the Pope, a spiritual leader, into also being the political leader of the Poles."[9]

The coverage in the mainstream US media was, on the one hand, exuberant. The papal visit was a glorious miniseries that distracted Americans from the steady diet of depressing articles about lengthening lines at the gas pumps. On May 31, 1979, a man had been shot dead in Brooklyn after he cut into a queue of irate, frustrated motorists waiting to fill up.[10] Journalists turned to the "remarkable" . . . "fantastic" . . . and "astounding" story of the papal visit with relief.[11]

On the other hand, the US press was flummoxed. "What will happen now?" the cover story in *Time* asked. "Will this visit . . . eventually weaken the hold of the Soviet Union?" Many editorials noted that the pope's visit was, as the *Christian Science Monitor* wrote, "making the Kremlin squirm." The *New York Times* deemed John Paul II "the most formidable opponent Polish Communism has ever faced." The *Washington Post* noted that "the Communist authorities are being revealed as bereft of . . . legitimacy." It then observed that "the fragility of the Communist order in Poland, elsewhere in Eastern Europe and even . . . in the Soviet Union itself, is a political fact."[12]

And then they all drew back. After that bold beginning, the *Post* editorial ended with the timid prediction that the papal visit might "strike a new religious-secular balance" in Poland. *Time* concluded that "the Pope's visit is unlikely to produce any dramatic result." The *Christian Science Monitor* asserted that the impact would not be "an overthrow of the Marxist system, certainly." The *New York Times* agreed. "As much as the visit of John Paul II to Poland must reinvigorate and reinspire the Roman Catholic Church in Poland, it does not threaten the political order of the nation or of Eastern Europe."[13]

Cardinal Wyszyński, the head of the Catholic Church in Poland, offered a more astute verdict. "The visit of the Holy Father," he observed, "spells the end of communism in Poland."[14]

The Case-Javits Decision: Black America Reacts

On June 7, as the pope returned to Cracow after praying at Auschwitz and Birkenau, President Carter returned to the Oval Office from the White House briefing room, where he had announced his decision on the Case-Javits resolution. Two hours later, he and Rosalynn strolled onto the South Lawn of the White House where Chuck Berry, Barry White, Patti La Belle, and Curtis Mayfield were milling among the crowd of 800 people—"a who's who in the black music industry"—celebrating the Black Music Association. As soon as Carter appeared, he was surrounded by people congratulating him on his courageous stance toward Rhodesia. Randall Robinson, the head of TransAfrica, vowed that "Black America will be four score behind you on this issue." It was "the first time in months," *Time* magazine noted snidely, that Carter had been "surrounded by applauding blacks."[15]

The evening, which the White House had been planning since February, was a success, but other than the last song—gospel singer Andrae Crouch belting out "Jesus Is the Answer," which brought everyone to their feet—it was a subdued affair. The White House had invited 1,000 people, but only 800 showed up, and many big young stars such as Stevie Wonder and Diana Ross had declined President Carter's invitation. "A lot didn't want to come to the White House," a founder of the Black Music Association said. "They are unhappy over government priorities, and I can understand that."[16]

This unhappiness was reflected in the way the black press covered the president's determination on Case-Javits. Studying the coverage of nine black newspapers—*Afro-American* (Baltimore), *Amsterdam News* (New York), *Atlanta Daily World*, *Los Angeles Sentinel*, *Philadelphia Tribune*, *Pittsburgh Courier*, *Sun-Reporter* (San Francisco), *Tri-State Defender* (Memphis), and *Washington Informer*—for the month following Carter's announcement, the absence of interest in Rhodesia is striking. Three of the newspapers did not mention Rhodesia in their reporting or commentary, and three others ran only one editorial each, with at most one news story. The *Philadelphia Tribune* identified Rhodesia as "that northwestern African nation."[17] Only the conservative *Atlanta Daily World* displayed interest in Carter's decision to maintain sanctions—and that was because its editor wanted to express his strong disagreement with the president.

In many ways, the black press's lack of interest in Rhodesia is not surprising. Most of the black papers were weeklies: their focus was overwhelmingly local and their interest in politics was domestic. The jobs crisis—black men were suffering from almost 40 percent unemployment in some cities—sucked all the energy out of talk about any other political topic. Carter's conservative budgets hurt African Americans disproportionately. "Carter doesn't care what black folks think," the *Washington Informer* noted on June 7, 1979, the day Carter delivered his Rhodesia speech.[18] The anger of blacks at the president's failure to address the jobs crisis pushed foreign affairs to a footnote. In June 1979, for example, of the approximately seventy-five editorials run in the nine papers sampled, only fifteen dealt with foreign affairs, and half of these were from the *Atlanta Daily World*, which was unusual among black papers because it appeared four times a week.

While the dearth of articles about Rhodesia reflected the low priority of foreign stories, it is also clear evidence that the editors did not agree with Atlanta's Mayor Maynard Jackson that Africa was black Americans' Israel. For some black leaders—perhaps most—Carter's policy toward Rhodesia was, as the State Department's Dick Moose asserted, "a litmus test" of his attitude toward matters close to home.[19] They welcomed Carter's determination, but their congratulations were not effusive. Vernon Jordan, president of the National Urban League, offered the warmest response when he noted that "Carter acted boldly and decisively."[20] For the readers of the black press, however, the racial injustice of southern Africa merited only slightly more attention than any other foreign story.

More unexpected is the tone of the few editorials that did comment on Carter's decision not to lift sanctions. The *Amsterdam News* was the only paper to express fulsome praise. On June 16, it ran an editorial that applauded the president's "highly principled action" and called on black Americans to tell Congress to maintain sanctions. The *Afro-American*, the *Washington Informer*, and the *Sun-Reporter* were stinting in their praise, while the *Tri-State Defender*, which was drawn to Muzorewa, expressed ambivalence toward Carter's decision.[21] The *Atlanta Daily World*, which alone among the black press was keenly interested in Rhodesia, expressed no ambivalence at all about Carter's decision. The paper had long hewed a cautious editorial line—for instance, it had demurred from supporting the sit-ins of the 1950s and 1960s—and it assailed Carter's refusal to accept the Muzorewa government. On June 12, it announced, "It is with deep regret that we read that the President is not going to lift sanctions against Zimbabwe-Rhodesia, which recently elected a black

Prime Minister. . . . The new government should be supported and given a chance to succeed." Two days later, the *Daily World* returned to the topic, saying boldly that it agreed with the white Rhodesian commander of the armed forces, General Peter Walls, that Carter's decision would "prolong the killings." The paper called on Atlantans to start a fund to support the Muzorewa government. On June 19, declaring that Rhodesia was "the second strongest anti-Communist country in Africa," it called on the US government to "promptly act to strengthen the newly elected government headed by Abel Muzorewa."[22]

What the Mainstream Press Heard

On June 8, the major US daily newspapers gave prominence to Carter's decision, running stories about the Case-Javits Amendment on page one on a busy news day: Carter's announcement competed with stories about the pope praying at Auschwitz, Carter's approval of $30 billion for the advanced nuclear intercontinental MX ballistic missile system, Sandinista rebels closing in on Nicaragua's Anastasio Somoza, and the downturn in leading economic indicators. And yet, the huge banner headline in the *Los Angeles Times* was "Carter Won't Lift Trade Ban"; the Baltimore *Sun* also featured it in a banner headline, and in both the *New York Times* and *Washington Post* the story earned the coveted top right-hand column on page one.[23]

All the major papers commented editorially. The response ranged from the *Christian Science Monitor*'s praise of Carter's "wise" and "politically courageous decision" to the *Chicago Tribune*'s bitter attack on the president's "astonishing lack of imagination, leadership, and political realism." Yet not one of the papers, no matter how scathing its comments about Carter's speech, roundly condemned the decision he made. Not one argued that the president should have lifted sanctions immediately.[24] They bowed to the logic of letting Britain take the lead, and they noted the Nigerian threat to cut oil supplies. The *Chicago Tribune* wished that Carter had "initiated a carefully calibrated policy" to gradually lift sanctions, and the *Los Angeles Times* regretted that he did not explain "just what he expects" the Muzorewa government to do.[25]

Only the *Christian Science Monitor* and the *New York Times* focused on the content of Carter's policy. It was his speech that drew the attention and fury of most editorial boards. The *Washington Post*, which had been consistently critical of Carter's Rhodesia policy, explained why it was exasperated. "Is it not possible for Jimmy Carter to say, just once, that the elections in Zimbabwe-Rhodesia were an impressive feat?" It went on to describe Carter's "blunder" and his lack of "political tact" and his "clumsiness" and "arrogance." It was the tone, rather than the substance, of Carter's speech that so riled the *Post*. The *Wall Street Journal* agreed: Carter's "little piece of tawdriness . . . did more of the thing that's been getting everyone so mad at his Africa policy in the first place, which is to yell at the Rhodesians in the voice of outraged morality." Even the *New York Times*, which called Carter's policy "shrewd and prudent," admitted that "he has not explained it well."

The *Times* was right: Carter had not explained his policy effectively. Most editors did not notice the nuances in his speech. Four days after Carter's announcement, the *Christian Science Monitor* noted correctly that "too little attention has been given to the conciliatory challenge to the Muzorewa regime" that Carter had included in his speech. In fact, by saying that he would keep the situation under review, Carter did initiate the "carefully calibrated program" that the *Chicago Tribune* said it wanted, and he was not specific about his benchmarks only because the British had asked him not to be. Carter also explained the national interest arguments for his decision—foreclosing an opportunity for Soviet and Cuban expansion, maintaining good relations with black Africa, and letting Britain take the lead—that the *Washington Post* and *Wall Street Journal* alleged were absent from the speech.

What these editors heard was the preachiness of the speech, its holier-than-thou tone. This drowned out everything else Carter said. He had a politically tin ear. He cast aside the speeches others had drafted because he wanted to speak, as one of his advisers told the *New York Times*, "from the heart"—his heart: "It's the President's policy and always has been." Carter labored over the speech so that he could carefully, even meticulously, explain his thinking. But he failed to remember what had been obvious three years earlier, during the campaign: when Jimmy Carter spoke, almost no matter what he said, people *heard* moralizing. During the second presidential debate in 1976, he had stressed American strength, but the newspapers had not reported that: they had reported his few comments about human rights. And with his Rhodesia speech three years later, even though the editors agreed with the thrust of the policy, the *Washington Post* titled its editorial "The President's Rhodesia Blunder" and the *Chicago Tribune*'s headline was "An Africa Policy Disaster." It was the conclusion of Carter's speech—"It means a lot to our country to do what's right and what's decent and what's fair and what is principled. And in my opinion, the action that I've described fulfills these requirements"—that rang in the editors' ears, and it drove most of them crazy.[26]

Reverberations in Britain and Africa

The Thatcher administration agreed. Even though Carter had bowed to London's wishes (and made his own task in Congress more difficult) by being deliberately vague about what benchmarks Muzorewa had to reach to get sanctions removed, the Foreign Office was disgruntled. "We had hoped that the President would be much more positive about what has been achieved in Rhodesia," Robin Renwick, the head of the Foreign Office's Rhodesia Department, wrote Antony Duff, the head of the Africa Department. Another senior British official told Warren Christopher that "the President had used some unhelpful expressions," and then gave vent to his frustration: "If the Americans could get off principle and on to detail, this would be helpful." Carter was unmoved. "The monkey belongs on Britain's back," he commented to Vance. None of this mutual irritation emerged in public. "There are no policy differences" with Washington, the Foreign Office assured the *Guardian*.[27]

Behind the scenes, however, Whitehall scrambled to deal with the ramifications of Carter's speech. "The presidential 'determination' has revealed a difference of emphasis between the American approach and our own," a Foreign Office official noted drily. Carter's criticism of the Muzorewa regime put unwelcome pressure on the Thatcher government. The tone of Carter's message made it more difficult for Whitehall to pursue the policy it preferred—shun the Patriotic Front and persuade Muzorewa to make changes so that his government could gain international acceptance. The British hoped to convince the Frontline presidents—Zambia's Kenneth Kaunda, Tanzania's Julius Nyerere, and Mozambique's Samora Machel—to accept this improved Muzorewa government and to persuade the Patriotic Front to lay down its arms. Carter's speech, however, did the opposite: it gave courage to the Frontline leaders and strengthened their resistance to Muzorewa. "The clear UK preference at this time is to seek improvements in Salisbury's arrangements," Dick Moose and Tony Lake told Vance, "grant independence and lift sanctions on that basis, and hope Front Line support for the PF [Patriotic Front] eventually will diminish."[28]

The Carter administration believed that only a political settlement—all-party talks—would end the war. Even though the previous two years had proven that arranging the talks would be difficult, in June 1979 Washington saw reason to be hopeful. The Frontline States, increasingly weary of war, were interested in a negotiated solution. "Botswana, Tanzania, Zambia . . . have urged an early all-parties meeting," Lake and Moose noted. The State Department believed that Muzorewa would agree to talks if he failed to achieve international recognition, but "progress . . . in negotiations . . . could be impossible if Salisbury has reason to hope that sanctions will be lifted soon."[29]

Whitehall, however, thought that Washington was dreaming. "We do not ourselves believe that it is likely to be possible to achieve wider agreement," Renwick wrote Duff, and Carter's speech announcing his Case-Javits determination added to their pessimism. It had offered Muzorewa little reason to hope for recognition in the near future, the British grumbled, and it had encouraged the Commonwealth and black African states to oppose the internal settlement.

Therefore, it forced London to reconsider its strategy. The Zambia *Times* understood the impact of the speech: "The American decision is a setback for the Bishop, for Ian Smith, and for the British." Moreover, the tone of Carter's Case-Javits speech caused the Thatcher administration to keep Washington at arm's length as it worked out its next steps in Rhodesia. "We had previously thought that, once the President's determination was out of the way, we would ask the Americans to support our approaches to African governments," Duff wrote. "However, if they do so now they will be acting against the background of the unhelpful language used by the President and are likely to foul up . . . [our] cultivation of the Front Line ground."[30]

London, however, wanted to maintain as united a front as possible in public. On June 15, Thatcher wrote Carter, "We wish to keep in the closest touch with you over this problem [Rhodesia]." The Foreign Office was realistic: "There could be a parting of the ways in the future." On this point, the Americans were in full agreement. "We should recognize that their [the British] criteria for lifting sanctions and recognition in the end may differ from ours and that we may have to seek independently progress beyond what the UK wishes to achieve," Moose and Lake observed. Vance noted: "This is correct, but we should try to keep as much in step as possible."[31]

Throughout black Africa, the reaction to Carter's decision was ecstatic. Kaunda was emphatic when, many years later, he reflected on it. "It was extremely important. Extremely important. . . . I knew that he had many people . . . who were pushing him to go ahead and recognize Muzorewa. . . . He was under great pressure. . . . It was, for us, a godsend. A godsend."[32] After months of anxiety about the possible erosion of US influence in black Africa, the US ambassadors stationed in Africa sent cables to the State Department suffused with relief and even joy. Willard DePree wrote from Mozambique, "News of Carter's decision has electrified the diplomatic community. . . . It is indeed a proud day to be US Ambassador in Mozambique." The ambassadors reported African press reaction: from Zambia—"President Carter has shown rare courage"; from Mozambique—"It's been a long time since the press here has reported that the US has done something 'positive' about southern Africa"; from Nigeria—"God Bless Jimmy Carter." Ambassador DePree remembered seeing President Samora Machel at a crowded diplomatic reception soon after Carter's decision was announced. "Machel walked diagonally across the open space, lined with foreign dignitaries and diplomats—and this was at a time when Mozambique's relations with the United States were not considered good—and took me by the hand and walked me across the square and asked me to send a cable to President Carter congratulating him for his courageous decision not to lift the embargo."[33]

In Washington immediately after the speech, Dick Moose briefed a gathering of the African ambassadors. They were, to a man, "thrilled."[34] The Tanzanian ambassador extolled Carter's "wise and timely" decision. As Moose concluded his remarks, the ambassadors gave him a standing ovation.[35]

The South African government did not comment, but its press did. The official television station, SABC, ran "a scathing attack on President Carter," and the Afrikaans newspapers stressed that the United States had caved in to Nigerian threats. The Rhodesian papers likewise expressed outrage. "The role of Pontius Pilate is ill-suited to such an avowed Christian and champion of human rights as President Carter. Yet there can be little doubt that this is the part he has elected to play by refusing to lift sanctions against this country," the *Rhodesian Herald* fumed on the day after Carter's determination. The editors then hearkened back to their familiar theme that Carter was motivated by his craven search for black support. "He knows that the maintenance of sanctions will be popular with the black despots his Government is so assiduously courting. He also knows that it will be equally popular with his black voters." Salisbury's *Sunday Mail* agreed: "The mindless prejudice against Zimbabwe-Rhodesia reached a new low last week," it announced. "Although the President made the announcement, it seemed much more like Andy Young opening his mouth and Carter putting his foot in it."[36]

Prime Minister Muzorewa called Carter's determination "a blatant example of political expediency and double standards. . . . This is an insult." The American president, Muzorewa claimed, was "appeasing Black Africa . . . and pandering to votes of Black Americans." Chester Crocker, an American academic touring Rhodesia after the elections—and who would become Reagan's assistant secretary of state for Africa—encouraged Muzorewa to hope that the US Congress would "surmount this temporary hurdle."[37]

The Senate Responds

This time, the White House was prepared for the battle with Congress. It would not again be caught flatfooted, as it had been a year earlier when Jesse Helms had first proposed his sanctions-lifting amendment. The administration knew that the ardor in the Senate to force the president to lift sanctions had been dampened by the desire of some senators to give him time to act on Case-Javits. Now that Carter had determined not to lift sanctions, the White House girded for battle.

On the table was the Defense Authorization bill, the Senate version of which had emerged from the Armed Services Committee with Senator Harry Byrd's amendment calling for sanctions to be lifted immediately. The Carter administration expected this amendment to pass when the full Senate debated it on June 12, but it was important that it pass with the smallest possible margin. This would weaken the Senate's hand in the conference committee. Meanwhile, the administration hoped to persuade the House not to vote to lift sanctions. The White House strategy focused on the conference committee. If the Senate vote to lift sanctions was not overwhelming and the House had voted against it, then the language that emerged from conference might be acceptable to the Carter team. This would require high-level, sustained, and creative lobbying. The White House did its homework. In the words of *CQ Weekly*, it "lobbied heavily" for more leeway on the sanctions issue. The president and all the principals telephoned members of Congress, the State Department hosted breakfasts, and "nearly a dozen administration aides pressed Carter's case on Capitol Hill."[38]

The administration had a particularly daunting task in the Senate, which less than a month earlier, on May 15, had voted seventy-five to nineteen in favor of a nonbinding resolution to lift sanctions. Although the White House remained "gloomy" about its chances of winning the next round, it made an all-out effort to narrow its opponents' margin of victory.[39] This was not only to blunt the Senate's weight in the conference committee but also to set the stage for Carter's threatened veto of the bill. If the nineteen senators who had voted against Helms on May 15 held firm and the administration managed to persuade fifteen senators to change their votes, then Carter's veto would be sustained. Therefore, even though the administration expected to lose in the Senate, the stakes were high.

Vance, who was about to depart for the Vienna summit where Carter and Brezhnev would sign SALT II, spent the entire morning of June 12 testifying about Rhodesia before the House and Senate foreign affairs committees. Vance considered Carter's decision to defy Congress "courageous" and he backed it fully, even though it meant that the administration had a fight on its hands. In the course of a two-hour grilling by the senators, Vance sought to make the president's announcement more palatable by repeatedly acknowledging that the elections in Rhodesia represented "encouraging progress" and created a "new reality." Nevertheless, he argued, it would not be in the US national interest to lift the sanctions immediately.[40]

Vance offered a multipronged explanation. The fundamental US interest was peace, and, Vance explained, unless the Muzorewa government made "further progress and accommodation, there will not be peace." Lifting sanctions prematurely would give the Soviets and Cubans "new opportunities to expand their influence in Africa at our expense" and "undercut" Great Britain. Moreover, it would be seen as the United States siding with Salisbury, which would make it impossible for the Carter administration to continue working for peace in the region and would "undermine the significant progress we have made in improving our relations throughout Africa." Summing up, Vance declared, "We would tarnish our image abroad and divide ourselves at home." If, therefore, Senator Harry Byrd's amendment lifting sanctions were attached to the Defense Authorization bill, it was "quite likely" that the president would veto it.[41]

In the questions after Vance's statement, the conservative senators assumed their well-rehearsed positions. Jesse Helms (R-NC) once again reminisced about escorting Muzorewa through the North Carolina mountains, and Sam Hayakawa (R-CA) complained that the White House was embracing the Patriotic Front.[42]

Yet Vance's efforts and the administration's lobbying had made an impression on the members of the Foreign Relations Committee, most of whom had grown leery of forcing a confrontation with the administration over Rhodesia at a time when the situation in both Salisbury and London was so fluid. Vance's clear presentation, particularly his acknowledgment that progress had been made in Rhodesia, had smoothed feathers ruffled by Carter's Case-Javits speech. After Vance's departure, the committee hammered out a substitute to Harry Byrd's sanctions-lifting language that preserved the president's authority. The new amendment stated that the United States would lift sanctions on Rhodesia by December 1, 1979, unless the president determined it would be in the national interest to lift them sooner. This was approved in an eight-to-one vote; even Hayakawa agreed to support it. (He would later renege and vote against it on the floor.) Jacob Javits (R-NY), the ranking Republican on the committee, agreed to propose the substitute amendment—perhaps because he had received a warning from the Egyptians (Javits's main foreign policy interest was the Middle East) that if the United States lifted sanctions on Rhodesia, it would "hamper Egyptian efforts to secure moderate black African support for the Israel/Egypt peace treaty."[43]

The committee members rushed to the Senate chamber, where the debate on the Defense Authorization bill was underway. As Javits introduced his amendment, Frank Church (D-ID) explained, "What this amendment obtains for us is time—time to be certain we are doing the right thing; time to give the United Kingdom . . . an opportunity to act. . . . Nothing is to be gained for the United States by rushing to judgment on the Rhodesian question, and a great deal could be lost."[44] The debate would last four hours, and it would be the full Senate's final extended debate on the issue. This was a much more challenging forum for the administration than had been the Foreign Relations Committee; it was more partisan and less well informed.

Those senators who opposed the immediate lifting of sanctions, led by Church, Javits, and Paul Tsongas (D-MA), stressed one question: "Why must we rush to judgment?" Helms, Harry Byrd (I-VA), and Richard Schweiker (R-PA) countered by reminding the senators that just three weeks earlier a "stunning majority" of them had determined that the Rhodesian elections had been free and fair and that the United States should lift sanctions forthwith. "What has happened that in any way has changed the situation?"[45]

Helms' opponents were ready. Three things, they asserted, had changed. First, it had become clear that Prime Minister Thatcher was not going to act precipitously. As Tsongas asked, "Why should we rush in where Maggie Thatcher fears to tread?" Second, Nigeria had intimated that it would cut oil supplies if the United States lifted sanctions. "Why lengthen service station gas lines in the name of haste and poor judgment on the sanctions issue?" Tsongas asked. McGovern piped in: "Why take the risk?" Finally, the president had made his determination, and overturning it would provoke a major confrontation with the executive branch. Larry Pressler, a freshman Republican from South Dakota who had been a foreign service officer, expressed his discomfort with this "very difficult" vote. "Under our system of formulation of foreign policy," he explained, the Senate should "assist" and the president should "lead." Pressler pointed out that if the Senate, when it voted on May 15, had wanted to require the president to lift sanctions, it should have passed a law rather than a "sense of the Congress" resolution.[46]

Helms and his supporters summoned their colleagues' patriotism. When the Nigerian threat was mentioned, Helms scoffed at the administration's "scare tactics,"[47] and Roger Jepsen (R-IA) declared, "We are the United States. . . . [We need not] fear the retribution of smaller states." They also called on their fellow senators' pride. Carter, in his "supreme arrogance," had given "a slap in the face" to all of them, and had not even had the honesty to acknowledge that the elections had changed Rhodesia. What the White House had done was "bury its head in the sand and pour cement around it." It was wrong to let "Bishop Muzorewa dangle in the breeze." Gordon Humphrey (R-NH), one of Helms' strongest supporters, turned Carter's words on their head. "What is right, Mr. President, with a decision that undermines the honest attempt of Rhodesia's blacks and whites to live in harmony? What is decent, Mr. President, with a decision that encourages Communist-backed . . . guerrillas . . . ? And, finally, what is fair, Mr. President, with a decision that summarily invalidates the results of an election?"[48]

No one, not even the administration's most ardent supporters, revisited the argument Carter had stressed in his speech about how US foreign policy should reflect American ideals. "The so-called 'moral' arguments . . .

persuaded no one," the State Department's congressional liaison wrote. The president's speech announcing his Case-Javits determination was "a political liability."[49] The debate on June 12, 1979, was not about American idealism. Nor was it about democracy in Rhodesia. Toward the end of the session, Church reminded Helms that the sanctions had never been effective and lifting them would not "save the government in Salisbury. . . . This is not a question of substance," he added. "It is a question of symbolism." That symbolism, after Carter's determination, was about the balance of power in Washington, not in Rhodesia. Helms said disingenuously, "It is time to stop playing domestic politics with the future of Zimbabwe Rhodesia." But Gordon Humphrey admitted, "Let us face it . . . what is occurring here in the Senate Chamber is a contest between the President and this body."[50]

The real news about the vote at the end of the debate was not that Helms' forces carried the day. After all, less than a month earlier, seventy-five senators had voted to lift sanctions. The real news was that twenty-three senators jumped Helms' ship. The tally on June 12—fifty-two to forty-one—was dramatically closer than it had been on May 15. The administration lost the vote, but forty-one senators voted to delay the decision on sanctions until December 1. This was more than enough to sustain a veto. Therefore, wrapped in the technical victory for the Helms' forces was a stinging defeat that would stall their momentum.[51]

It had been a bad week for Jimmy Carter. On June 10, the *New York Times* headline declared, "Carter's Standing Drops to New Low in Times-CBS Poll." The president's overall approval rating had crashed twelve points since March, from 42 percent to 30 percent. Only Richard Nixon and Harry Truman had ever polled worse. In the same poll, Senator Ted Kennedy, whom many expected to challenge Carter for the Democratic nomination in 1980, garnered high approval ratings even from southerners, conservatives, and Republicans. Carter responded fiercely. At a White House dinner for seventy-five members of the House, the president declared: "If Kennedy runs, I'll whip his ass." The polls, however, revealed an American public not only upset about inflation and unemployment but also worried about Carter's lack of "strong and uncompromising positions on the issues." The *Christian Science Monitor* noted, "The dominant element in the public view of the President today is that he should be more assertive—that somehow he should take command." At the annual US Conference of Mayors on June 11, the Democratic mayor of Chicago, Jane Byrne, expressed the sentiments of many: "President Carter is in trouble."[52]

When the Senate voted to lift sanctions the following day, it was predictable that the *Rhodesian Herald* would exult: "By voting to end sanctions," it declared on page one, "the Senate has put a half-nelson on the remains of President Carter's African policy." The US press agreed, reporting the vote prominently, on page one, as another "blow" to the White House, and as "a major foreign policy setback" and "a political thorn" for the administration. All three US television networks covered the story in their evening news programs; all depicted it as a loss for the administration. On NBC, which led with the story, David Brinkley announced that "President Carter is already irritated with Congress and now has cause to be more so." Rather than citing the relatively close vote on the sanctions-lifting amendment, Brinkley mentioned the final vote on the defense bill, which had passed eighty-nine to seven, thereby giving the impression that the president had been overwhelmingly defeated.[53] NBC then cut to a White House official who claimed to be "extremely satisfied" with the vote. Given the preceding story, he sounded like a fool.[54]

The Battle Moves to the House

"We're halfway there," Prime Minister Muzorewa exclaimed after the Senate vote. "Let us hope the House will not be taken in by the bluster of President Carter or the blandishments of Mr Vance," the *Rhodesian Herald* proclaimed. "If democracy and justice are to be preserved in this country [Rhodesia], Congress must convince the quixotic occupant of the White House and his Sancho Panza at the United Nations that there really is no future in tilting at windmills."[55]

Speaker Tip O'Neill (D-MA) predicted that the House would indeed follow the Senate, thereby forcing Carter to lift sanctions or to veto the defense bill. Steven Solarz (D-NY), however, disagreed. There was "more than a fighting chance," he asserted, that the House would part ways with the Senate.[56]

The White House lobbying machine revved into top gear. "Following yesterday's more encouraging Senate vote on Rhodesia," Vance wrote Carter on June 13, "we are focusing attention on the House." The administration, which was busy preparing for the Vienna summit, spent a great deal of time and energy on Rhodesia, courting labor, black leaders, churches, foreign policy organizations, businesses, and the Democratic National Committee. It convened a White House working group to brainstorm the best ways to persuade swing voters. Carter, Vice President Walter Mondale, and Vance hosted breakfasts, lunches, dinners, and other gatherings for members of the House.[57] Now that the president had made his Case-Javits determination, the administration could shift its emphasis away from the gnarly issue of passing judgment on the Rhodesian elections and focus instead on the nuts-and-bolts ramifications for the United States of lifting sanctions on Rhodesia. Solarz stated this clearly:

"Our decision on this issue ought to be based not so much on the conduct and character of the [Rhodesian] elections but on the interests of the United States itself." The *New York Times* noted that the administration was playing "a losing hand shrewdly."[58]

Vance played the Nigeria card in, as the *Guardian* noted, "a stage whisper." In response to a State Department request for more information about the possibility of an oil embargo if the United States did lift sanctions, US Ambassador Donald Easum sent a series of cables from Lagos to help the administration's lobbying effort. The Nigerian government would view the lifting of sanctions, Easum reported, as "a deliberate challenge to the black race." After traveling widely in eastern and central Nigeria, he cabled that he had been "deeply impressed by the strong feelings" he had encountered everywhere "regarding the possible lifting of US sanctions against Rhodesia." He was "convinced that a lifting of those sanctions would lead to a number of damaging retaliatory measures by the Nigerian government [and] . . . the consequences for the U.S.-Nigerian bilateral relationship . . . would be serious." Easum listed a range of retaliatory measures the Nigerian government might take, including putting diplomatic relations on hold and excluding US companies from lucrative contracts. "There might well be demonstrations directed against the American embassy in Lagos." He concluded this cable with a clear indication of his intended audience. "The [State] Department is requested to consider," he wrote, "the appropriate method for passing the above message to the Hill."[59]

The most important weapon the White House had, however, was not Nigerian oil but Steven Solarz. Once again, the representative from New York, working closely with Assistant Secretary Moose, came to the rescue. To build the bipartisan consensus he required, Solarz was indefatigable. In early June, he traveled with two Republican members of the Africa subcommittee of the House Foreign Affairs Committee, Millicent Fenwick and Bill Goodling, to London to consult with Foreign Secretary Carrington about Rhodesia. And in Washington, he painstakingly educated, arm-twisted, and cajoled his colleagues.[60]

On June 13, in close cooperation with the State Department, Solarz introduced a bill in the House that gave a little to all sides. Its preamble stated unequivocally that the Rhodesian elections had been "a significant step" forward. It stressed that Britain remained the legal authority. And it directed the president to keep the situation under review, and to lift sanctions by October 15, 1979—unless he reported to Congress that it was not in the US national interest to do so. The House Foreign Affairs Committee planned to consider the bill immediately. The acting assistant secretary of state for congressional relations, Brian Atwood, described the bill accurately: "an artfully crafted compromise bill which said nice things about the elections and new government in Salisbury, but whose bottom line was keeping sanctions on."[61] The Solarz bill was, essentially, another Case-Javits amendment. No one was thrilled with it, but its careful phrasing succeeded in drawing together a coalition that included the Congressional Black Caucus as well as some conservatives. It was a model of compromise. The White House was mightily pleased. Vance assured Carter, "We are working with the [House] leadership, and will be actively supporting the Solarz effort. . . . I am hopeful that with our help this House effort will succeed."[62]

Vance then departed with the president to meet the Soviets in Vienna. Carter's meeting with Leonid Brezhnev—the first between an American and Soviet leader since Gerald Ford had met Brezhnev in 1975—was the culmination of seven years of painstaking work hammering out the SALT II agreement. The accord set limits on the number and type of nuclear weapons and delivery vehicles both superpowers could build and test. Vance in particular had worked tirelessly for the moment when Carter and Brezhnev would sign the treaty.

Yet the summit was a dull thud. Brezhnev was a hulk. He had been ailing for years. In happier times, Americans might have stressed the symbolism of the moment, the shell of decrepit Soviet authority encountering the energetic American president. They might have noted the crushing economic problems that Brezhnev faced at home and the profound challenge to the Kremlin's legitimacy that Pope John Paul II had so recently posed in Poland. They might have reflected on the impact in Moscow of the US normalization of relations with China and its growing closeness to Egypt. But the US press did not emphasize Soviet travails. Instead, it cast a cold light on Jimmy Carter. The SALT agreement had been knocked around for too long. It excited no one, and it had something to irritate everyone, especially the multiplying neoconservatives who considered its acknowledgment of Soviet nuclear parity with the United States as—in Democratic senator Scoop Jackson's pungent word—appeasement. The specter of Munich hung over Vienna. At the opening ceremonies, Jimmy Carter stood bareheaded in the rain. "'I'd rather drown than carry an umbrella,' the President declared firmly," referring to the iconic photographs of Neville Chamberlain with his bumbershoot in 1938. "President Carter came a cropper on the umbrella problem," the *Wall Street Journal* commented.[63]

The neoconservatives were so transfixed by RAND reports about Soviet military strength and corresponding American weakness that they neglected to notice the Pope or the failure of the Soviet economy or the encirclement of the Soviet Union. In *Newsweek*, columnist George Will explained their fears: "In the last year alone, the USSR has added 1,000 warheads to its strategic arsenal. . . . The Soviet buildup will produce military superiority in the mid-1980s. . . . Brezhnev almost surely came to Vienna believing the US is in decline." In this context, Will saw the president's Rhodesia policy as worse than inept—it was dangerous. "On the eve of Carter's Vienna summit, . . . Carter risked Senate defiance on Rhodesia and got it. Defiance gets easier each time. The debate about SALT is, at bottom, about what the US can do, militarily and diplomatically, to pull itself from the hole it is in. . . . [Carter's] desire to continue sanctions against southern Africa's most democratic government, sanctions that benefit Communist guerrillas, does not help him."[64]

It was heat like this that made Solarz's attempt to strike a compromise on Rhodesian sanctions so important. The opening salvo of his fight was encouraging. While Carter and Brezhnev were meeting at Vienna's Hofburg Palace, the House Foreign Affairs Committee considered the Solarz bill. The committee members were aware that much hung on their meeting. "The question of whether the United States should lift or maintain the UN-imposed sanctions against the Government of Zimbabwe-Rhodesia is one of the most complex, critical, and controversial issues currently before the Congress," the official report noted. This is striking language, considering that Congress was also studying the SALT treaty, the energy bill, the Panama Canal implementation legislation, and the defense budget. Given the significance of US policy toward Rhodesia, the committee "felt that it was in the interest of the Nation to reach a constructive compromise." Once again, Solarz, aided behind the scenes by the State Department, performed magic. "In a spirit of conciliation and cooperation and despite deeply held and widely divergent views," the report explained, the committee passed the bill unanimously, thirty-three to zero. "These guys are a bunch of statesmen," Douglas Bennet, State Department congressional liaison, exclaimed when he heard the vote count.[65]

Vance, who was in Vienna, received an urgent request from Bennet. Could the secretary make time in his schedule on the day after he returned to Washington to meet with a group of House members? "If we can get a really substantial vote on the House floor, we may be able to block sanctions lifting efforts by the Senate," Bennet wrote. "As a result of your testimony [to the Senate Foreign Relations Committee], we have made steady gains. I recommend that it is worth a little more of your time to see if we can clinch our position on the House."[66]

On June 20, Vance penned his regular evening report to the president. This was a frenetic time—he and Carter would be in Washington for only five days after returning from Vienna and prior to departing for the Tokyo Economic Summit, and they were juggling the SALT II treaty, the aftereffects of the meeting with Brezhnev, the energy bill, the continuing Iranian Revolution, and the Sandinistas' impending victory in Nicaragua. Nevertheless, the first two items of Vance's memo concerned Rhodesia. "The House floor vote [on the Solarz bill on Rhodesian sanctions] . . . promises to be close. . . . To bolster support for your position, Fritz [Mondale] invited some 100 undecided Congressmen to breakfast on Thursday [June 21] and we are putting together a bipartisan leadership team that is prepared to fight for the Administration position on the House floor."[67]

Carter himself was on the case. In the five days he was in Washington, he spent a great deal of time cajoling members of Congress to support his Rhodesia policy. He hosted a breakfast, he made many phone calls, he held a meeting with representatives, and he was in almost constant communication with his congressional liaison.[68] As Carter, Vance, and Brzezinski flew to Tokyo for the G7 Economic Summit—and Carter's first encounter with Margaret Thatcher as prime minister—Moose, Lake, and many other administration officials continued to pound the halls of Congress.

Events in Rhodesia strengthened their argument. Muzorewa's position was crumbling faster than anyone had expected. He was assailed politically, militarily, and internationally. Politically, his "government of national unity" was weakened not only by Reverend Ndabaningi Sithole's walkout on May 1, which had resulted in twelve representatives refusing to take their seats in Parliament, but also by the June 20 defection of James Chikerema, a senior official in Muzorewa's own party, who set up an opposition party with seven other representatives. Senator Helms claimed that this proved "that democracy is at work" in Rhodesia, but the New York Times noted that it would make Muzorewa "more beholden than ever" to the twenty-eight white representatives who were loyal to Smith. Vance wrote Carter that "Chikerema's defection reduces Muzorewa's flexibility in making needed internal reforms." Indeed, when the new Rhodesian government presented its domestic program on June 28, there was nothing to alleviate unemployment or to institute land reform. Columnist Anthony Lewis summed up the situation: "Muzorewa is not master in his own house."[69]

The war, contrary to Muzorewa's promises, escalated. Disillusionment pervaded the countryside. "We voted for peace," a Rhodesian said, "but the situation has only gotten worse."[70] On June 20, word leaked that for four days the previous week, Muzorewa had been on a secret mission to South Africa, meeting with Prime Minister P.W. Botha to ink a mutual defense treaty that Smith had approved in April. South Africa had been footing half the cost of the war since 1976; it was providing Salisbury financial support to the tune of $25 million to $30 million a month. When questioned, Muzorewa stoutly defended his reliance on South Africa. "If I get in trouble and the Devil comes to help and says, 'I am going to save you,' I will let him save me," he averred. An official close to the prime minister, however, fretted about the impending vote in the US House of Representatives. "The timing [of Muzorewa's trip] is all wrong," he muttered to a *Washington Post* reporter. "It'll make [the U.S.] Congress as uneasy as hell."[71]

One week later, Muzorewa's actions spread even more alarm. At dawn on June 26, residents of Lusaka awoke to the sound of bombs being dropped from jet fighters and gunships. Five helicopters targeted houses in a heavily populated section of the city, raking them with machine-gun fire and grenades and then dropping troops on what they alleged to be ZAPU leader Joshua Nkomo's intelligence headquarters. A fierce thirty-minute gunfight ensued, killing twenty-two alleged guerrillas and injuring a score more. US Ambassador Stephen Low cabled that "detonations of bombs [were] clearly heard by members of embassy staff." He commented, "We begin to wonder if in fact these raids are not designed to show that security conditions in Zambia make it impossible to carry out the Commonwealth conference in Lusaka." Indeed, London noticed. "The sounds of battle could be heard clearly at the conference center where the Queen, Mrs Thatcher, and more than 30 other Prime Ministers and Presidents are due to assemble [for the Commonwealth conference] at the end of next month," the *Guardian* reported in a page-one article titled "Air-Raid renews fears for Queen." The Rhodesian soldiers withdrew, having sustained no injuries, and moved on to attack an alleged ZAPU camp twelve miles north of the capital.[72]

As these raids were occurring, a grand ceremony was underway in Salisbury. Sporting a top hat and tails, the new president (a largely ceremonial post) opened Parliament. He demanded international recognition, and he promised that the new government "desires only to live in peace and harmony with neighboring states." In fact, however, all Africa was showing what the *Washington Post* deemed "an unexpected degree of solidarity" in its rejection of the Muzorewa government. Not only were pro-Western countries such as Kenya, Liberia, Senegal, Zaire, and Gabon keeping their distance, but Malawi shuttered its diplomatic office in Salisbury. (Alone among African countries, Malawi had maintained this office throughout the Smith regime.) "Things are crumbling," a white Rhodesian told a journalist from the *Christian Science Monitor*. "We gave them [black Africans] the power, and now things are falling apart."[73]

This was the backdrop on June 28, as the House considered the Solarz bill. The debate was long, occasionally acerbic, and substantive. The choice was between the Solarz bill, which left the decision about sanctions in the president's hands, and an amendment offered by Michigan Republican Bill

Broomfield, which mandated that sanctions be lifted on December 1, 1979, unless Congress—not the president—decided otherwise.[74]

The debate differed from the Senate debate as well as from past House debates about Rhodesia in several key respects. First, Solarz had meant what he said when he had written Carter that "members are educable." He had educated them: the House had held eight hearings on Rhodesia, and the debate on the Solarz bill was well informed, which cut down on the grandstanding.[75] Second, the Congressional Black Caucus, which had been peripheral in past debates on Rhodesia, sprang to life. It played an active role, with seven of its members making substantive contributions and its chair, Cardiss Collins (D-IL), assuming a leading role. The caucus members stressed that this was an issue that was important to African Americans. "It is a matter of high principle," Ron Dellums (D-CA) asserted. Collins stripped the veneer from the coded language about race that had permeated past debates about Rhodesia. "Some people have openly regretted that the question of prematurely lifting sanctions has become 'political' and treated as a 'civil rights' issue in the black community. It could not be otherwise. The deceptions and games of racial injustice in southern Africa are quite familiar to us." This, plus the physical presence of eighteen black representatives, shifted the tone of the House from the more chummy and less well-informed Senate, which had not one black member.[76] Third, time had elapsed since the April elections in Rhodesia. The glow of those elections had faded, and reality had seeped in. It was evident that Muzorewa was not a savior and Thatcher was not going to act swiftly. Carter would veto a sanctions-lifting bill, and his opponents did not have the two-thirds majority needed to overturn it.

The terrain of the debate had shifted. The discussion was no longer a megaphone to spout about American values or engage in a coded discussion of race; it now focused on the calculation of US national interests. "What am I going to say to my constituents who are already waiting in three-block long gasoline lines . . . [if] we needlessly took precipitous action we did not have to take" that could lead Nigeria to cut oil supplies, asked John Buchanan, a conservative Republican from Alabama who had always supported lifting sanctions immediately. "Let Great Britain take the first action," he concluded. "We need not serve as moral judges here," the pipe-smoking Millicent Fenwick added. The question was not whether the Rhodesian elections had been fair, but why the US House should risk any important national interests for this issue, especially when it seemed highly probable that the British Parliament would lift sanctions in November. Why not wait?[77]

Broomfield and all who supported his amendment were hard pressed to provide a convincing answer to that question. Jonathan Bingham, a liberal

Democrat from New York, commented astutely on the weakness of the speeches in favor of the Broomfield amendment. "Very little discussion of the national interest occurs in support of the argument that we should lift sanctions now," he noted. "The arguments there have to do with a kind of feeling of emotionalism perhaps, some references to morality, but very little reference to the national interest." Indeed, those who supported Broomfield implored their colleagues to remember that the United States was "a leader" that should "cease kowtowing to . . . African nations" and "show some guts." After the Nigerian threat had been repeatedly mentioned, Robert Bauman exploded: "Do you suggest that we vote not on the basis of what is right or wrong or moral or immoral but rather in response to economic blackmail? Have we come to that?"[78]

The answer arrived late in the evening, when the House voted. The Broomfield amendment came up first. It went down to decisive defeat: 147 to 242. It was clear, then, that the Solarz bill would pass, but the margin of victory came as a surprise: 350 to 37. It was an overwhelming victory for the administration.[79]

Three weeks earlier, all the major papers had carried prominent, page-one stories accompanied by editorials about the "blow" that the Senate vote on sanctions had dealt the White House. It had been a lead story of all three networks' evening news programs. How did the US media cover the House vote on June 28, which dealt a stunning blow to the opponents of Carter's Rhodesia policy? ABC and CBS did not mention it, and NBC gave it one sentence in its "News in Brief" segment, sandwiched between stories about a tornado in Iowa and a big fish caught off Long Island. In the print media, the administration's success fared little better. Only in the *Washington Post* did it merit a front-page story with a byline, and even there, in the paper that prided itself on its congressional coverage, it was below the fold. The *New York Times*, *Los Angeles Times*, Baltimore *Sun*, and *Chicago Times* buried brief wire service reports about the vote in their inner pages. The *Christian Science Monitor* and *Wall Street Journal* did not mention it. In fact, the *Journal* wiped the House vote out of history, writing in an editorial about SALT on July 9 that "the Congress cannot get the president to follow its clear wishes and the spirit of the laws it has passed in lifting the trade sanctions against Rhodesia." Not one paper ran an editorial, column, or opinion piece about the House vote. It was as though it had never happened.[80]

One reason that the House vote received so little attention was that everyone anticipated that it would be followed by many more fights on Rhodesian sanctions. "Last week in the House, we won a major battle, but not the war," the acting assistant secretary of state for legislative affairs, Brian Atwood, noted. "More battles loom ahead." Two engagements—conference committees reconciling Senate and House versions of bills containing sanctions-lifting language—were foreordained. The Senate had passed two sanctions-lifting pieces of legislation. On May 15, it had tacked the "sense of Congress" amendment onto the State Department Authorization Act, and on June 12, it had tacked a tougher amendment, requiring sanctions to be lifted, onto the Defense Authorization Act. The House versions of these two bills had not mentioned Rhodesia, but the Solarz bill on June 28 expressed that body's decision that sanctions should remain until October 15, when they should be lifted only if the president determined that it was in the national interest to do so. It was up to the conference committees to reconcile all these charges. "We face an incredibly messy legislative situation," Atwood wrote Vance on June 30. Beyond these two unavoidable clashes, the administration, Congress, and the press fully expected a barrage of "torpedoes"—sanctions-lifting amendments that Helms might add to any bill passing through the Senate.[81]

The White House was not sanguine. The NSC and State Department congressional liaisons threw cold water on any glimmer of complacency the success of the Solarz bill might have inspired. "We should not misinterpret the size of the vote as an endorsement of our policy," Madeleine Albright wrote Brzezinski on June 30. "Most importantly," Brian Atwood warned Vance, "we must conclude that this 'victory' does not represent an endorsement of the Administration's Rhodesia policy." The Solarz bill had passed because of "the weight of the national interest argument . . . hard work . . . and, for once, poor organization and tactical blunders by our opponents," Atwood explained. "The vote bought time." Nothing more.[82]

Malaise and Muzorewa

On June 28, as the House was debating the Solarz bill, Jimmy Carter was in Tokyo at the G7 Economic Summit. In his diary that night, he wrote, "This first day of the economic summit was one of the worst days of my diplomatic life." The European leaders, including Thatcher, had ganged up against his energy proposals. "Thatcher is a tough lady," Carter noted, "highly opinionated, strong-willed, cannot admit that she doesn't know anything." The mood at lunch was "bitter and unpleasant," and West German chancellor Helmut Schmidt "got personally abusive." While the summit was underway, OPEC announced an oil price rise that, Carter wrote dourly, "amounted to a 60 percent increase in prices since last December."[83]

Then he read a memo from Stu Eizenstat, his top domestic policy adviser. After describing the lengthening gas lines, Eizenstat wrote: "Nothing which has occurred in the Administration to date . . . [has] added so much water to our ship. Nothing else has so angered, frustrated, confused, angered the American people—or so targeted their distress at you personally. . . . All this is occurring at a most inopportune time. Inflation is higher than ever. A recession is clearly facing us. . . . OPEC is raising prices once again. The [presidential approval rating] polls are lower than they have ever been . . . [Ted] Kennedy's popularity appears at a peak. And the Congress seems completely beyond anyone's control."[84]

Carter returned from the G7 summit to a country of angry motorists waiting in long lines to fill up for the Fourth of July weekend. He had planned to deliver another nationally televised speech to rally support for his energy program, which Congress had alternately shredded and stalled. It would be another explanation—the fifth in a series of speeches about energy—of the nuts and bolts, an "engineer's speech," as befitted his professional roots. But as Carter contemplated drafts his advisers had given him, he began to think that a different approach was needed, one that would address the question, as he put it, "Why have we not been able to get together as a nation to resolve our serious energy problem?"[85]

Carter abruptly canceled the speech and retreated to Camp David. He holed up there for eleven long days, wiping his official calendar clean, backing out of a planned trip to Louisville, and proffering no explanation. Inevitably, this fueled increasingly wild speculation about his health, mental and physical. The federal government, enveloped in an uneasy aura of mystery, ground to a halt. Many presidential aides, rattled and insecure, leaked their disagreements about the administration's policies to the press. Hedrick Smith, writing in the *New York Times*, declared that the "president stands on the precipice. His political peril matches the policy paralysis of the nation."[86]

There was something poignant about this lost week of the American president. Jimmy Carter was trying—with some desperation—to reestablish, however fleetingly, the connection with the American people that had buoyed him during the campaign. It had been his ballast, his wellspring, and after two-and-a-half years in the splendid isolation of the presidency he needed to feel it again. He traveled, with as little fanfare as possible, to the homes of "average Americans" in nearby West Virginia, and he invited writers, pundits, "prominent citizens," politicians, religious leaders, journalists, and labor organizers to eclectic meetings at Camp David to talk about where America was heading and what he should do about it. In its almost freakish abnormality, it was as close to normal human interchange as the president could get.[87]

Carter kept one official engagement while "on the mountaintop," as the press called his vigil. On the afternoon of July 12, Prime Minister Muzorewa emerged from a helicopter and strolled with Cyrus Vance toward Holly Lodge, where the president was staying. Muzorewa had been invited to Washington by his most ardent US booster, Senator Helms. On the day after the Case-Javits determination, Carter had acceded to Helms' request to meet the embattled Rhodesian prime minister, but as the appointed time approached, many voices advised him to cancel the encounter. Brzezinski warned the president that the conclave would be interpreted as "an endorsement of the Muzorewa administration by you." In what the *Rhodesian Herald* termed "an almost hysterical appeal from black American radicals," TransAfrica head Randall Robinson declared that the meeting "approaches a recognition of a regime that is unthinkably undemocratic." The Nigerian ambassador in Washington added, "[It is] recognition without the name."[88]

Carter was undeterred. He and Muzorewa met alone for twenty-five minutes. The substance of the encounter (they prayed together, and Carter urged Muzorewa to work closely with the British) was less important than the fact that Carter—who had refused to meet Ian Smith—had received the new Rhodesian prime minister at Camp David, an honor accorded to few legitimate heads of government, let alone one the administration regarded as illegitimate. The *Rhodesian Herald* appreciated the symbolism of the encounter: "Perhaps the greatest success was the enhanced prestige and stature which talks with President Carter and the Secretary of State gave to the fledgling Prime Minister." Salisbury's *Sunday Mail* was less restrained: "It is one of those moments of history. The deliberations will . . . go a long way towards deciding . . . whether good or evil will triumph."[89]

Carter disregarded Brzezinski's advice and met with Muzorewa for two reasons. The first revolved around Jesse Helms; the second around Margaret Thatcher.

When Helms first proposed the meeting, "political prudence alone" suggested that Carter agree to it, as the *Christian Science Monitor* noted.[90] The administration needed to buy time, and Helms was the man selling it. If meeting with Muzorewa would appease Helms and hold him off from pushing another sanctions-lifting resolution, it was worthwhile. Therefore, Carter gave his word to the pugnacious senator. Helms then turned to London. He wrote 10 Downing Street to request "a private and confidential discussion" with Margaret Thatcher about Rhodesia, and on July 4 his wish was granted. Thatcher's first words to Helms were to insist that the meeting receive "no publicity." He acquiesced, the British minutes note, "but with evident reluctance." Helms got to the point: Britain should recognize Muzorewa before the August Commonwealth meeting in Lusaka. Thatcher politely disagreed. It was not a good idea, she stated, to present "the CW [Commonwealth] Heads of Government Meeting with a *fait accompli*." In closing, Thatcher repeated that she wanted "knowledge of her meeting with Senator Helms to be confined to the smallest possible circle."[91]

Conservative journalists Rowland Evans and Robert Novak could not disguise their glee when they wrote about the encounter in their widely syndicated column. They predicted that Thatcher, dubbed "Attila the Hen," would refuse to "be pushed around by Carter's liberal activists in the State Department. . . . [This] could spell trouble between the United States and its closest ally." Evans and Novak noted that Rhodesia was the "likeliest source of trouble." Thatcher was moving fast to lift sanctions, they claimed. "She spent 50 minutes with Helms in an unpublicized July 4 meeting in London," and through him she conveyed "to Carter her refusal to extend sanctions beyond their November expiration date." (When leaking the story, Helms—or one of his aides—doubled the length of time the senator spent with the prime minister.)[92]

Thatcher was indeed moving fast, but in the opposite direction. In July, the Foreign Office was in the throes of a major shift in its Rhodesia policy. Its goal remained to grant Rhodesia independence with the greatest possible international acceptance, but was beginning to accept that this would require more than tweaking the flawed Rhodesian constitution. It was contemplating inviting Muzorewa and the Patriotic Front—whom Thatcher had dismissed as "terrorists"—to a conference. This was a closely held secret, and it was still in its formative stage. Evans and Novak were right that "Attila the Hen" would never bow to the liberals in Cyrus Vance's State Department, but Thatcher was following a circuitous route back to the Anglo-American proposals. The fundamental problem, as Carrington admitted to UN Secretary-General Kurt Waldheim, was that "[r]ecognition by the UK alone would not be much help to Rhodesia." Whatever Britain did, it needed to get the United States on board. Carter's obduracy over lifting sanctions meant that Britain would have to devise a settlement that gained at least some African acceptance. This was the only way to satisfy Washington, and it led the British back to all-party talks. One of Carrington's chief aides explained this forthrightly: "It will be important in carrying the Americans with us to place some emphasis on the need to offer the Patriotic Front an opportunity to participate."[93]

It was the US House of Representatives that gave Thatcher the running room she needed. As Ambassador Stephen Low wrote, "It seems very likely that if the House had supported the Senate and required the president to lift sanctions, the Conservative Party in Britain might have forced Prime Minister Thatcher to do likewise. She would then have been deprived of the flexibility to make a new attempt at an agreed settlement when she went to the Commonwealth Conference in Lusaka." This "new attempt at an agreed settlement" was a plan hatched by senior Foreign Office officials, particularly Antony

Duff and Robin Renwick, who had long chafed under the imperious leadership of David Owen. They suggested that Thatcher dispatch Lord Harlech, a distinguished Conservative politician, to Africa to determine what might persuade the African presidents there to recognize Muzorewa. After his trip, Harlech's conclusions were as categorical as they were unwelcome to Thatcher.[94]

On July 4, shortly after meeting with Jesse Helms, Margaret Thatcher received a call from Jimmy Carter, who was at Camp David. Carter warned: "We're on an open line, so I'll be—" Thatcher interrupted him: "You'll be circumspect." Carter then asked Thatcher to "expedite getting me your advice after the visit to Rhodesia"—Carter was referring to Harlech's report—"because Muzorewa's coming over here shortly and I need to have your—" Thatcher interrupted again: "Yes, indeed. I will see to that immediately."[95]

On July 7, Thatcher cabled Carter a summary of Harlech's findings. (1) "An internationally acceptable solution will have to stem from Britain as the legal authority." (2) The constitution will have to be rewritten. (3) "There should be a final attempt to achieve a wider agreement which could bring an end to the war." Harlech had also recommended that Britain convene an all-party conference, a point made clear in the proviso that Thatcher added: "If the Patriotic Front fail to respond to a genuine attempt to involve them that would create a new situation." Thatcher explained that she wanted to recognize Muzorewa and lift sanctions, "but it would be essential to carry our friends and partners with us." The path forward was becoming clear. "The Bishop's real need was for international acceptance," Thatcher concluded. "This was the way to bring an end to the war." The *Rhodesian Herald* was more blunt. When it got wind of Harlech's conclusions, its summary was succinct: "Muzorewa will be 'squeezed.'"[96]

In a second cable to Carter on July 7, Thatcher asked for the president's help. Referring to his upcoming meeting with Muzorewa, Thatcher wrote, "It would help us if you would impress upon him the need to work closely with us to enable us to fulfil our constitutional responsibility." The "tactics for the Muzorewa visit," Dick Moose confided to an official at the Australian Foreign Office, "had, in fact, been closely coordinated" with Downing Street.[97]

This was the second reason Carter did not cancel the meeting with Muzorewa: Thatcher was moving toward the solution he had long advocated. The Conservative government was, as the Australian high commissioner in London wrote, "nerving itself to make one more real try, quite soon, to solve a problem that has dogged successive British (and other) governments for nearly fifteen years." Not only was Thatcher contemplating all-party talks, but she wanted Britain to take the lead. This, more than anything else, would help Carter hold his congressional opponents at bay. "The most persuasive argument on the Hill," State Department congressional liaison Brian Atwood had noted in an analysis of the House vote on the Solarz bill, was that "it was sensible to let Britain go first. . . . Our chances of continuing our winning streak [in Congress] depend on . . . our ability to keep the British out in front on Rhodesian policy."[98]

The White House press release after Carter's encounter with Muzorewa was clear: the president "had restated his commitment to work closely with the government of the UK" to reach a settlement based on "full political participation." Moose reiterated the centrality of the administration's cooperation with Britain when he presented to Congress the first monthly update on Rhodesia that Carter had promised in his Case-Javits determination. "I want to emphasize," Moose began his prepared remarks, "that we are continuing to consult closely with the British Government." Indicating that London had moved beyond tweaking the constitution, Moose said, "The British have embarked on a serious effort to resolve this problem in a way that satisfies the legitimate aspirations of the people of Zimbabwe-Rhodesia for self-determination." When asked to elaborate, he ducked, referring the committee to Carrington's announcement in the House of Lords that "after the Lusaka [Commonwealth] conference we [Britain] intend to make firm proposals of our own."[99]

Thatcher was pushed further along the path to all-party talks by the bull-headedness of Muzorewa, who flew to London from Washington. In both capitals, in every meeting, Muzorewa was described as "[displaying] almost no flexibility" . . . "essentially non-responsive" . . . "did not . . . make any significant concessions."[100] Vance described him as "depressed and disappointed." Muzorewa was, as US and British intelligence reported, "fading fast as a viable leader." Perhaps to shore up white support back home, he brushed off all appeals to change the constitution. And at Heathrow airport, after his meeting with Thatcher, Muzorewa boldly announced to the press that he expected Britain and the United States to recognize his government. His "man to man" talk with the American president had been, he asserted, "a great day for Zimbabwe."[101]

In the immediate afterglow of the visit, the *Rhodesian Herald*, which considered it "a make or break" event for the new government's pursuit of Western acceptance, dared agree: Muzorewa's trip might mean that sanctions, "this fearful drag on our economic progress, may soon be lifted." Three days later, however, the *Herald* plummeted back to earth. "There may not be much reason for optimism," it admitted on July 17. The bishop, who had been put up in a Stouffer's Hotel in Arlington, Virginia, had not received "the red carpet treatment accorded to heads of government," noted the *Herald*'s reporter who covered the trip. "Sadly," Ian Smith concluded, "Muzorewa's faith and trust were misplaced. . . . He was out of his depth."[102]

The Jeremiad

On July 15, three days after his encounter with Muzorewa, President Carter descended from Camp David. He went to the Oval Office and delivered what became known as the "malaise speech." He did not use the word *malaise*, but he did tell his sixty million viewers that the nation faced "a fundamental threat to American democracy." The country was suffering from "a crisis of confidence . . . a crisis that strikes at the very heart and soul and spirit of our national will. We can see this crisis in the growing doubt about the meaning of our own lives and in the loss of a unity of purpose for our nation." The public responded favorably to the "malaise speech"; Carter's popularity ratings jumped from 26 percent before the speech to 37 percent immediately after it.[103]

In the speech, Carter mentioned that during his retreat he had asked "men and women like you" to tell him their impressions of his administration. One of their "typical comments" was: "Some of your Cabinet members don't seem loyal. There is not enough discipline among your disciples." Two days later, to emphasize what Vice President Mondale explained was the "new direction" that the president was determined to pursue, Carter asked for the mass resignation of all members of the cabinet, three cabinet-level officials, and eighteen senior members of the White House staff. He explained to his startled aides that he wanted a free hand to reshape his administration and to change "my lifestyle and my way of working." He then proceeded to publicly criticize individual members of the cabinet and staff. He was particularly scathing about the State Department. Andrew Young was not excluded: Carter rebuked him for his sometimes careless rhetoric, but added that he had played a very constructive role at the UN, improving US relations with "perhaps fifty countries."[104]

"Armageddon happened yesterday," a cabinet member told the *New York Times*. "He [Carter] really did it. You don't know what he's going to do. Lots of people talk out their decisions with their staff, almost get them to ratify it. But not Jimmy Carter. With him, you never know."[105] Carter's dramatic cabinet shake-up fed fears that he was coming unglued. The malaise speech boomeranged: perhaps the country was in a "crisis of confidence" because its leader did not know what he was doing. Anxiety crackled through Washington; the dollar fell; critics took to the op-ed pages.

After all the *Sturm und Drang*, on July 19, Carter announced that he had accepted the resignations of only five cabinet members, none from the top ranks of the foreign policy team. "It looks as though we will have to put up with the ineffectual Mr Vance and the insufferable Mr Young for a bit longer," the *Rhodesian Herald* noted.[106]

Happy Compromise

The fact that the Thatcher government was actively engaged in seeking a solution to the crisis in Rhodesia, however vague the outline, sucked the urgency from the calls in the US Congress to force Carter to lift sanctions immediately. When the conference committee reconciled the State Department Authorization Act on July 30, a compromise was struck between the widely disparate Senate and House recommendations about Rhodesian sanctions, the former taking the initiative away from the president and the latter leaving the decision to him. Steven Solarz, once again, carried the administration's water. Stressing that the Congress ought not to "pull the rug out from under the British" who were on the verge of announcing a new initiative, Solarz introduced a substitute amendment like the one he had succeeded in persuading the House to pass. It praised the Rhodesian elections and stated that sanctions should be lifted by October 15, 1979—unless the president determined that it would not be in the national interest to do so. That is, it expressed the desire of Congress that sanctions be lifted but preserved Carter's prerogative to do whatever he thought best.[107]

"You will probably fall over in a dead faint, but I look with favor on almost all of this substitute," Jesse Helms replied. He mentioned that he had met with Carter, and he announced, "We ought to help the president." Carter's meeting with Muzorewa had indeed bought the administration time. Helms then referred to his July 4 meeting with the "Iron Lady" and said to Solarz, "You can change October 15 to whatever date you want. The point is that sanctions are going to be lifted by Britain." After some fine-tuning, the committee approved the essence of Solarz's resolution but changed the deadline to November 15, 1979—after the British Parliament would have voted on renewing its sanctions on Rhodesia. "All I want to do is send a signal," Helms explained, "that we are not just sitting around here with our thumbs in our mouths." On August 2, without debate, both houses passed what Jacob Javits called this "extremely happy compromise." The *Rhodesian Herald* expressed a different opinion. The vote was "disappointing." It noted, accurately, "The next move is up to Mrs Thatcher."[108]

Storm Clouds over Lusaka

Prime Minister Thatcher was playing her hand very close to her chest. Lord Harlech's tour of Africa had convinced her that the Rhodesian constitution, which entrenched white power, would have to be changed. She continued to talk, however, a very hard line, implying that she would recognize Muzorewa as soon as he tweaked the constitution. This led to widespread fears of fierce fights at the upcoming Lusaka Commonwealth Heads of Government Meeting.

In late June 1979, in anticipation of the discussion about Rhodesia at Lusaka, the Commonwealth Committee on Southern Africa released a report on Muzorewa's election. This committee included representatives from all but the smallest Commonwealth countries. That is, it contained members of both the "old Commonwealth" (the majority-white countries of Britain, Canada, Australia, and New Zealand) and the "new Commonwealth" (the nations of the former British empire). After welcoming Carter's "principled decision . . . not . . . to accept the Senate's recommendation on the lifting of sanctions," the committee delivered its verdict on the Rhodesian elections. "The elections could not, and indeed were not intended to, produce majority rule. . . . The elections were in effect a choice between the internal settlement groups for an essentially subordinate role in the administration of the country. That they took place is a fact. That they did not usher in majority rule is also a fact." The report added, "The British Government Representative did not concur with all aspects of the preceding paragraphs."[109]

It is not surprising that London distanced itself from this hard-hitting report, whose conclusions did not represent Whitehall's policy. It is striking, however, that the British representative was not joined in dissent by his old Commonwealth colleagues from Australia, Canada, and New Zealand. Britain stood alone.

Canada, long a conciliator between Britain and the African members of the Commonwealth, was not in a position to step in. Canadians were still reeling from a turbulent election campaign and a dramatic change of government: on May 22, 1979, the Liberals were ousted for the first time in sixteen years as the young Conservative leader Joe Clark cobbled together a shaky coalition. As journalist David Martin noted in the London *Observer*, while Canada was embroiled in this turmoil, Australian prime minister Malcolm Fraser "inherited [Pierre] Trudeau's mantle as the peacemaker of the old Commonwealth."[110]

The mantle, however, did not fall to Fraser: he grabbed it. It would be an essential tool to fix the problem that was worrying him deeply: Thatcher's intransigence on Rhodesia could lead to a breakup of the Commonwealth, an organization that was central to Australia's global reach. "The Commonwealth link constitutes an important check to the spread of Soviet power in developing countries, especially in Africa," the Australian government explained. "The continued viability of the Commonwealth is thus of basic importance to Australia's longterm strategic interests."[111] This is why it mattered that, as Fraser jotted in his notes for the Lusaka meeting, "Commonwealth in jeopardy if no settlement."[112] This was not an idle fear: Rhodesia had figured prominently and divisively at Commonwealth gatherings since 1966, and at the 1971 meeting in Singapore, London's resumption of arms sales to South Africa had so outraged some members that they had called for the expulsion of Britain from the Commonwealth.[113]

Moreover, Fraser did not want to have to make a choice between his country's old ties of kith, kin, and history with Britain and its burgeoning relations with Africa. He had cultivated ties with African leaders, particularly those in the Commonwealth, and although he was a Conservative he had steered a progressive stance on matters of importance to Africans. Australia's policy toward Rhodesia was clear. As the Canadian high commissioner in Canberra cabled: "Fraser . . . has no intention of granting any form of 'recognition' to the Zimbabwe-Rhodesia regime. Fraser is convinced that no solution that does not have the backing of frontline gov[ernmen]ts will succeed."[114]

Although the Australian Conservative backbenchers grumbled, the Department of Foreign Affairs in Canberra fully concurred with the prime minister. Part of its concern was practical, as the war in Rhodesia could lead to an unmanageable influx of refugees in Australia: "It is likely that an increasing number of those leaving Zimbabwe permanently will seek to enter Australia." The Australian government's underlying interest, however, was more profound. A report jointly written by the Prime Minister's Office and the Department of Foreign Affairs cast the repercussions of failure to bring peace to the region in ominous terms: "The future stability of world order depends very greatly on the achievement of peaceful and lasting solutions to Southern African political and racial problems." A deepening war in southern Africa would create opportunities for the Soviets. "If the Africans become disaffected with the Western approach to the Rhodesian question, Western interests and influence in southern Africa would be put at risk and the opportunity for further Soviet advances would arise," the department asserted. "Australia would be most concerned to prevent this happening." Fraser's challenge, therefore, was to convince Thatcher to move closer to the African point of view on Rhodesia. He tackled this in two ways: by directly talking with British officials and by rallying other Commonwealth members to join with him in pressing Thatcher to moderate her stance.[115]

Fraser gave Thatcher only a fortnight to settle into 10 Downing Street before beginning his offensive. "I am especially concerned that the Rhodesian issue . . . could split the Commonwealth," he wrote her on May 19. "It is important I think for all of us to put stress on some form of all party talks. . . . We must all do what we can to avoid an explosive confrontation there [in Lusaka] between the old and new commonwealth over African issues." Thatcher's reply was polite but noncommittal. Fraser therefore welcomed the opportunity to talk with her about Rhodesia "behind closed doors" in late June, one month before the Commonwealth meeting, when she visited Canberra on her way home from the Tokyo G7 Summit.[116]

Many observers expected sparks to fly at this meeting. The Canadian high commissioner in Canberra wrote, with diplomatic understatement, that "differences of view might develop between PM Fraser and Mrs Thatcher on legitimacy of Zimbabwe-Rhodesia Govt." The talks, however, were calm and "particularly useful," Fraser told Canada's new prime minster, Joe Clark. "Our discussions were lengthy and frank." Fraser stressed the deficiencies of the Rhodesian constitution and the necessity of garnering African support for whatever plan Britain pursued, and he believed that Thatcher agreed with him. He told Clark that he was "heartened by some aspects of Mrs Thatcher's response," and an Australian Department of Foreign Affairs memo noted that in "useful private discussions on Saturday . . . Lusaka had been discussed, and they thought they could see a way through the problem."[117]

The British were less sanguine. They summarily refused to accept the Australians' summary of the talks, and they bristled at what they saw as Fraser's "seeking a role for himself as an intermediary between Britain and the black African states." Moreover, when the Iron Lady addressed the Australian National Press Club the following day, July 1, she reverted to form, calling the Patriotic Front "terrorists" and announcing that she doubted "that a renewal of sanctions would go through the British Parliament" when it was debated in November.[118]

This got a response. The US State Department said that it was "embarrassed" by Thatcher's remarks. UN Secretary-General Waldheim met with Thatcher to warn her of the negative reaction in the UN and to implore her to hold new, internationally supervised elections in Rhodesia.[119] Thatcher's comments also fueled African suspicions that London was stalling until after the Commonwealth meeting to announce that it would recognize Muzorewa and lift sanctions. Tanzania's Julius Nyerere sent her an impassioned letter. "I cannot believe that Britain wishes to defy Africa and the world in the interests only of supporting a constitution in Rhodesia which entrenches racialist privilege behind a camouflage of a superficially democratic veneer." In the British Foreign Office, Antony Duff groused that "[Nigerian leader Olusegun] Obasanjo evidently thinks [we are] being deceitful." This raised fears, as the British high commissioner in Lagos cabled, that Nigeria "might decide to take drastic measures against British interests if [the] British government moves towards recognition of Muzorewa or is even suspected of stalling." It also raised the possibility, the Australian high commissioner in Lagos cabled, that Nigeria would leave the Commonwealth. That is, it could precipitate the breakup of the Commonwealth.[120]

The Organization of African Unity, which gathered in Liberia for its annual summit on July 16, sent a clear warning to Thatcher and to the US Senate that recognizing Muzorewa would be considered "an act of war against the Front-line States" because it would enable Rhodesia to buy legally more weapons with which to pummel its neighbors. Muzorewa, who had intended to attend the OAU meeting, had been banned from it. Obasanjo was particularly fiery about Muzorewa, denouncing Rhodesia's "sham elections . . . [and] phantom black government." He added, "In many ways, the desire of the British government [to recognize Muzorewa], if carried out, is more reprehensible than the position of the United States Senate, where, clearly, there is an astonishing degree of ignorance." In the summit's final hours, the members passed a resolution recognizing the Patriotic Front as the "sole, legitimate and authentic representative" of the people of Zimbabwe.[121]

This was more radical than both the 1978 OAU summit, which had deemed lifting sanctions "an unfriendly act," and the 1977 summit, which had called the Patriotic Front "the sole liberation movement." It surprised the British, who had expected a more moderate tone to prevail, and it worried them, as it augured that the Africans at the Commonwealth meeting would toe a radical line. Thatcher called the outcome "discouraging."[122] The tone of the summit reflected the Africans' fear of what Thatcher might announce at the Commonwealth meeting. "Many members of the OAU believed that the United Kingdom had already made up its mind [to lift sanctions and recognize Muzorewa]," the Kenyan foreign minister explained. "The toughness of the OAU declaration . . . [was] in great part tactical." The heads of state at the summit wanted their voices to be heard, but they did not mean to scotch a diplomatic settlement. However, in what turned out to be a meaningful threat, the organization called on member states to "apply effective cultural, political, commercial, and economic sanctions against any state which accords recognition to the illegal, racist minority regime in Zimbabwe, or lifts the mandatory sanctions against it."[123]

Ten days later, Nigeria made good on the threat. "Effective August 1, 1979," the US ambassador in Lagos, Donald Easum, cabled, "the FMG [Federal Military Government of Nigeria] will take over British Petroleum [BP]." The entire staff of BP was ordered to leave Nigeria by August 31. The Nigerian government explained that it was nationalizing BP to protest Britain's decision to ship North Sea oil to South Africa. "Nigeria sees this as a screen," the official Nigerian communiqué explained, "permitting BP's Nigerian oil to be sold to South Africa and ultimately Zimbabwe-Rhodesia." Easum commented, "The motivation behind the move is clear: to demonstrate that a strong African country is not necessarily powerless in the face of what Nigeria sees as continuing perfidy on the part of multinational companies and their supporting governments." The Nigerian government, which was still smarting from Nyerere's wrath after the aborted Smith-Nkomo meeting a year earlier, was flexing its muscles.[124]

The rambunctious Nigerian press exulted. "Attila the Hen could only cackle in sheer trepidation," the *Nigerian Standard* crowed, while the more staid *Daily Times* deemed the nationalization "an immense contribution to the liberation struggle of southern Africa." The *Rhodesian Herald* understood the magnitude of the threat and lashed out. "Nigeria's military bullyboys have shown a crudeness and arrogance that even by their standards is breathtaking," it announced. "[It shows] the frightful dilemma in which Mrs Thatcher has been placed. Will she . . . have the resolution and honesty to challenge these apostles of hate and violence?"[125]

Iron Bends

Under very tight security, Queen Elizabeth II flew on July 27, 1979, to Lusaka, a city that was still clearing the debris of the recent Rhodesian raid. On August 1, she would open the biennial Commonwealth Summit, attended by twenty-seven heads of government and twelve representatives from other Commonwealth countries; no member was absent. Tensions about the precarious security situation in Lusaka and the potential explosions in the meeting ran high. US intelligence sources noted on the eve of the summit that "the British will need immense skill and patience if they are to avoid an irrevocable split with the Frontline States and Nigeria."[126]

Whites in Salisbury looked anxiously toward the gathering 250 miles to their northwest. "There is no end to the number of people ready and willing to interfere in the affairs of this country, to regard everything that happens here as evil," the *Rhodesian Herald* noted in a bitter editorial. "The Lusaka summit conference is, in fact, being used as a pistol to our heads." The newspaper excoriated Australian Prime Minister Fraser, whom it called "selfish, power-hungry, ruthless and insufferably arrogant." The Rhodesians sensed that the axe was going to fall. The Commonwealth was going to demand changes to their constitution. "It is the extent of these changes that forms the crux of the problem," the *Herald* noted grimly on the eve of the summit.[127]

On the opening day of the meeting, Fraser announced, "time is running out."[128] He had been working on overdrive to build a coalition of Commonwealth members to convince Thatcher to modify her stance toward Rhodesia. Working closely with Commonwealth Secretary-General Shridath Ramphal, he and his foreign minister, Andrew Peacock, maintained close contact with the heads of government of key new Commonwealth countries—Tanzania, Zambia, Nigeria, and Jamaica—and lobbied the leaders of the old Commonwealth nations of New Zealand and Canada.[129]

New Zealand was less than amenable to Fraser's overtures. Prime Minister Robert Muldoon was preoccupied with his country's economic woes, caused in part by the Arab OPEC oil embargo. His political instincts were deeply anticommunist, and he had a combative personality that clashed with Fraser's. Furthermore, the State Department had noted in 1978 that "there is considerable sympathy in New Zealand for the whites in Rhodesia." Alone among the Commonwealth leaders, Muldoon had refused to sever sporting ties with South Africa in protest against the apartheid regime, arguing that it was not the role of government to interfere in sporting events. He told Thatcher that Fraser's approach to the Rhodesian problem "contained an excessive element of appeasement."[130]

Therefore, Canada, due to its size and heft in the Commonwealth, would be a particularly important ally for Fraser, and his courting of Prime Minister Clark was persistent. "You will of course have a great many urgent matters to occupy your attention during your early days in office," Fraser wrote Clark on June 4, the day that Clark took office. "I would, however, like to mention to you at this stage my concern about the difficulties that are likely to be facing us at the Lusaka meeting on Southern African issues and, in particular, Rhodesia. . . . I believe the Rhodesian issue has the potential to split the Commonwealth and—in its wider implications—could have a crucial impact on the prospects for long term stability in Southern Africa and on the future of western interests in Africa as a whole." Fraser got straight to the point: "Canada . . . could, I believe, play a particularly constructive role." Fraser followed up by sending a high-level Australian delegation of Africa experts to Canada, while Peacock met with his Canadian counterpart, Flora MacDonald. Several weeks later, Clark was on board: "Canada is prepared to do what it can to assist the building of a consensus at the Lusaka meeting," he wrote Fraser.[131] Thus Fraser, Clark, and all the Africans were prepared for battle as they convened in Lusaka.

On the evening before the formal opening of the meeting, President Kaunda, his aide Mark Chona, Secretary-General Ramphal, Thatcher, and Carrington dined together. Thatcher tipped her hand and enlarged the group of people who believed that their intercession had been decisive. "Mrs. Thatcher and Lord Carrington . . . came [to Lusaka] determined really to say, 'Well, we recognize Bishop Muzorewa,'" Chona recalled, "but . . . it was a very good meeting, and I think she abandoned the idea of the internal settlement."[132]

Indeed, Margaret Thatcher astounded everyone. On Friday, August 3, she delivered a speech that, as Vance wrote Carter, showed "movement" on British thinking about Rhodesia. Thatcher was emphatic that the Rhodesian constitution had to be changed, and she opened the door to an all-party conference. Salisbury's *Sunday Mail* was appalled at this "cold douche of political depression" and by Thatcher's "talk (shudder the thought) of an all-party con-ference."[133] Vance, on the other hand, was delighted. "The only thing missing from her speech," he noted, was "a clear call for new elections."[134]

This absence worried Malcolm Fraser. He had heard a clear message from Nyerere, Kaunda, and Obasanjo. They would support another diplomatic ini-tiative, but two items were nonnegotiable: the constitution must be changed and new elections must be held. "These were," Nyerere said, "the essential minimal requirements." He explained the importance of elections eloquently: "It is necessary for us to remember that those who are fighting now for the liberation of their country are doing so not because they prefer the bullet, but because they were denied the ballot."[135] Carrington, however, had assured Australia's Andrew Peacock that Nyerere would be satisfied with Thatcher's call for changes in the constitution and all-party talks. The British wanted to avoid pinning themselves down to holding elections. Carrington told Peacock that he had convinced Nyerere that Thatcher sincerely wanted to return Rho-desia to legality and majority rule by "giving him a wink."[136]

Fraser had reason to believe the wink had not worked. When he met with Thatcher immediately after the meeting opened, the need for Britain to orga-nize fresh elections in Rhodesia was uppermost in his mind. "Not only was there a need for constitutional changes but the elections would need supervi-sion"—that is, Britain must call for and oversee new elections. Fraser stressed that the Frontline presidents would be unable to persuade the Patriotic Front to participate in a conference unless Thatcher called for new elections. Thatcher, however, resisted, saying that supervised elections had not been necessary when other British colonies had gained their independence. She feared offending Muzorewa so gravely that he would refuse to negotiate, and she feared that the Patriotic Front would stall by nitpicking and quibbling about all aspects of the British plan. Therefore, she would call for a new constitution and all-party talks, but otherwise would be as brief and vague as possible. "The communique should not describe future elections as free and fair, since many people already felt that the April elections deserved that description," she informed Fraser.[137]

It was then that the negotiations began in earnest. Commonwealth summits followed a traditional pattern: the formal meetings sandwiched a weekend, which was when the real work was done; during the weekends, the heads of government gathered in small groups to thrash out the contentious issues. The Canadian Department of External Affairs, briefing Prime Minister Clark on the eve of his first summit, explained it well: Commonwealth heads of govern-ment meetings "are unique. Their main 'business' is to discuss, consult and, where possible, to achieve some convergence of views on important and often controversial political, economic, and other questions of mutual interest. The intent is to encourage informal and frank discussion, with no formal agenda or set speeches, in an atmosphere conducive to friendly and better understanding of differing points of view. Any decisions are by consensus."[138]

In August 1979, all eyes were on Margaret Thatcher, who would be corralled during this working weekend with the "group of six"—Fraser, Kaunda, Nyerere, Secretary-General Ramphal, Jamaican prime minister Michael Manley, and Nigerian foreign minister Henry Adefope—to discuss one topic: Rhodesia. Their goal was to draft a communiqué to present in formal session on Monday, August 6.[139]

On Saturday morning, before this group convened, Malcolm Fraser and Andrew Peacock met with Thatcher and Carrington privately. Thatcher was on guard from the first moment. Her opening comment was that "it was important that she not be asked for too much in the communique." She cited the "domestic rumblings" of her backbenchers and the importance of not "creating unmanageable suspicions in Salisbury." Fraser knew it was important to "jolly along Mrs. Thatcher," who had a "short fuse."[140] He was, however, undeterred. "We must not lose sight of the requirements of the Front Line Presidents . . . [who] needed and wanted the maximum arguments and the best case in order to persuade the Patriotic Front to participate in negotiations," he observed. He mentioned the need to set a date for the new elections. Peacock stressed that "genuine elections" had to be mentioned in the communiqué. Thatcher dug into her handbag—"the most secure place in Whitehall," she quipped, "my armory"—for her notes about Tanzania. Nyerere had waited four years before holding elections, she announced with a flourish. "Supervised elections" in Rhodesia, Thatcher implied, "would be unacceptable." Carrington jumped in. It was impossible, he insisted, to get into these details. "If they [the Patriotic Front] were given new proposals outside the constitution about which to argue, they would find pretexts for aborting negotiations . . . [and] Muzorewa would go wild." He was unyielding: "The United Kingdom could not accept any reference [to elections] at all." The communiqué would be "a paraphrase" of the speech Thatcher had delivered the previous day.[141]

Thatcher explained the logic of her policy. "There was a strong moral case," she said, for recognizing Muzorewa immediately. However, "even if she were to . . . go down that road, she could not carry other countries with her. The Government had therefore embarked on its present course and it was not an easy one." As for Fraser's worries that the Frontline presidents needed arguments to persuade the Patriotic Front to come to the table, that was not her concern. If the Patriotic Front balked, so be it. "*A much more crucial problem*," Thatcher declared, "*was . . . to receive United States support.*"[142]

Thatcher then entered into the discussions with the "group of six"—all of whom, not coincidentally, had been on Fraser's shortlist of contacts before the meeting. Approximately twenty-four hours later, the Iron Lady emerged. She had abandoned her opposition to elections.

At 8:00 P.M., the breakthrough was made public. The communiqué specified that Britain was responsible for establishing peace in its renegade colony; that the current Rhodesian constitution was defective; that all parties had to be involved in the solution and should be invited to a conference; and, most significantly, that new elections must be held under British supervision. "The new and crucial element at Lusaka," Robin Renwick wrote, "was the commitment to new elections, under British supervision. . . . In taking that step the Conservative government had been persuaded to go back to the principle underlying the Anglo-American proposals—that of impartially supervised elections, which alone afforded the prospect of avoiding a fight to the finish in Rhodesia."[143]

The Commonwealth and black Africa celebrated. The Lagos *Daily Times* boasted that "the African heat in the conference room [was] much more than she [Thatcher] could bear." Ian Smith, by contrast, was outraged. "There was no question of another election in Zimbabwe-Rhodesia," he vowed. The *Rhodesian Herald* asked, "Is Mrs Thatcher really a Labour Prime Minister in drag?" Her purportedly new scheme "sounded like an old record being replayed. . . . [It is] a rehash of previous . . . proposals. . . . [We have been] let down."[144]

Carter immediately wrote Thatcher to congratulate her for this "significant step forward."[145] In some ways, however, as the *Rhodesian Herald* lamented, Thatcher had taken a step back—to the Anglo-American proposals.

614

15. Lancaster House

"It's him or me"

The challenge, Jimmy Carter noted in his diary on August 3, 1979, was to "move toward peace without committing political suicide." How could he push Israel to begin to implement the promise of the Camp David Accords for Palestinian autonomy without losing the Jewish vote?[1]

The issue had come to a head a few weeks earlier, when the UN committee on Palestinian rights had quietly circulated a draft resolution authored by Yasser Arafat, the head of the Palestine Liberation Organization (PLO). The resolution gave the Carter administration hope that the impasse might be broken: its wording suggested that the PLO was prepared to accept Israel's right to exist—the essential breakthrough—but it also mentioned a Palestinian "state," a word that would render the resolution unacceptable to Israel. Cyrus Vance and Carter sought a delay at the UN to give Ambassador Andrew Young time to change the resolution's call for a Palestinian "state" to the more acceptable call for Palestinian "self-determination."[2]

On July 26, 1979, Young invited the Syrian and Kuwaiti UN ambassadors to lunch at his apartment to seek the support of the Arab bloc for a postponement. When they told him that it would be necessary for him to speak directly with the PLO permanent observer, Zehdi Labib Terzi, Young agreed to do so.[3] Several hours later, Young walked four blocks from his suite at the Waldorf Towers to Kuwaiti Ambassador Abdallah Yaccoub Bishara's townhouse. He was aware that Henry Kissinger had promised the Israeli government in 1975 that no US official would meet with a PLO representative until that organization had recognized Israel's right to exist; he therefore tried to make the meeting look like a chance encounter. As he strolled down Park Avenue, he was holding the hand of his six-year-old son, who was a playmate of Bishara's son. As the two little boys played on the floor of Bishara's living room, Terzi arrived; he and Young spoke for less than thirty minutes.[4] Four days later, the Security Council postponed consideration of the PLO resolution for one month.

Young sent the State Department a report about the lunch which mentioned that the Arab representatives had suggested he meet with Terzi, but he did not send a report about the meeting itself. Young later explained that he had wanted to create a firewall to protect the department, and that he considered his meeting with Terzi procedural—to discuss a postponement of the vote—rather than a substantive discussion of issues.[5] In fact, Young was working in the grey area that ambassadors frequently navigate, where the administration's goal was clear but the means to achieve it were deliberately vague.

That the Camp David Accords between Egypt and Israel were at a critical juncture led Young to break the rule about not meeting with PLO representatives, and it also caused the Saudis to apply pressure on the Carter administration. On August 2, one week after Young met Terzi (and before the meeting became public knowledge), the *New York Times* reported that the Saudis had threatened to reduce oil supplies to the West unless there was "noticeable progress in negotiations on Palestinian autonomy." This threat alarmed the Israelis: would the Carter administration cave in to the Palestinians in exchange for cheaper gas? "The US does not stand in the exact mathematical middle between the two sides," the Israeli interior minister declared on July 27. "They differentiate between the holy places [i.e., Jerusalem] and the oily places." Israeli foreign minister Moshe Dayan did not mince words: "There has been a shift in US policy," he announced on August 9. "The US wants to arrive at an understanding with Saudi Arabia, and that country is making this understanding contingent on the Palestinian issue."[6] On August 11, Carter, seeking to reassure Israel, publicly reaffirmed Kissinger's 1975 pledge. "I will not deal with the PLO," he told reporters. "This is a commitment we've made. We've never deviated from it. We're not going to deviate from it."[7]

Unbeknownst to Young, Israel's intelligence agency, Mossad, routinely tailed Terzi and, it was reported, had bugged his apartment.[8] On the day that Carter reaffirmed Kissinger's pledge, a *Newsweek* correspondent called the State Department to follow up on a tip (from an Israeli source, presumably Foreign Minister Dayan) that Ambassador Young had met with Terzi. Assistant Secretary of State for International Organizations Charles Maynes called Young, who was in New Orleans, to ask what had happened. Young later said that he prefaced his response with the phrase "the official version is" to signal—on an open phone line—that it was not the full truth, before answering that the meeting had been accidental: he had happened to run into Terzi while his son was playing at Bishara's house.[9]

By the time this information was conveyed to Vance, who was en route to Washington from Uruguay, the nuance had been wiped clear: Vance was told that Young had said that the encounter with Terzi had been accidental and social. Young had not bothered to call the State Department back on a secure line to clarify what had happened, and so at the noon press briefing on Monday, August 13, the department's spokesperson announced that Young's meeting with Terzi had been "accidental."[10]

Young believes that the State Department understood his coded language. Therefore, this public announcement made him suspect foul play. (He does not suspect Maynes, a close friend, of distorting his message.) Young was a free-wheeling ambassador with special status who had irritated many people. "A cabal at the State Department," *Washington Star* columnist Mary McGrory reported, "resentful of his [Young's] direct line to the president and his direct style of operation, was waiting in the weeds to pick him off." The *New York Times* noted that "long knives were out in the State Department for Andy Young."[11]

The Israeli ambassador to the UN, Yehuda Blum, had gotten wind of the encounter and asked Young if they could discuss it. Young thought that he had a good relationship with Blum, and they met for ninety minutes on August 13—the day that the State Department had declared Young's meeting with the PLO representative "accidental." Blum pressed Young for details, saying, ominously, that he could "prove" that the meeting had been substantive. Blum knew, he told Young, that "what they [Young and Terzi] discussed wasn't the weather."[12] Young decided to tell Blum the whole story—that it had not been a chance encounter—in the hope that this would mollify him. "I thought that my relationship with Israel was good enough," Young rued years later. He had wanted to stop Blum from going public with the story, not because it would create an awkward situation for him in the State Department—he had weathered many awkward situations—but because he feared that if it appeared that Israel was trying to bring him down, it would escalate tensions between blacks and Jews in New York City.[13]

This was not an idle fear. The previous summer, simmering resentments had burst into the open in the Crown Heights section of Brooklyn, sparked by blacks' anger over what they considered police bias in favor of the area's large Hasidic population and fueled by a widening schism between the two communities—erstwhile allies—over issues such as affirmative action.[14] Young himself had been on the receiving end of these tensions. Despite his impeccable record of support for Israel while a member of Congress and his affiliation with Jewish leaders while working with Martin Luther King, Young had encountered swift and fierce opposition from American Jews when he had accepted the UN post. Assistant Secretary Charles Maynes recalled, "The theory was that he was going to adopt the Third World agenda . . . that there was no way that a black American could serve in that job and then not become pro-Third World, pro-Palestinian." That Young received "hate mail . . . the minute he got the job—and much of it from Jewish sources—reflected this black-Jewish rift that had developed." Maynes then corrected himself: "Hate mail's too strong: fear . . . from below."[15]

Young had tried to remedy this by his characteristic outreach, speaking in synagogues and to Jewish organizations. He realized the peril of the schism. In 1977, he had told *Playboy*, "When you divide blacks and Jews, you're not helping anybody, . . . you're not helping black Americans, you're not helping forward-moving politics."[16] Two years later, on August 13, 1979, Young told Blum that "a big uproar over this issue only creates a constituency [African Americans] on the Palestinian issue that does not exist." When the two men departed, Young believed he had Blum's word that he would not go public.[17]

The Israeli government, however, wanted to stop what it feared was momentum toward a Palestinian state. At 4:30 A.M. on August 14, Young received a phone call from the US mission in Tel Aviv informing him that the Israelis were going to lodge a formal protest about his meeting with Terzi. Just a few hours later, Vance arrived at the State Department to find the letter of protest from the Israeli embassy. Vance called the Israeli ambassador in Washington to apologize, and then he called Young to deliver what in official parlance is called a reprimand. Young conceded to journalists that his initial account of the encounter with Terzi had not been forthright: "That was not a lie—it was just not the whole truth."[18]

For Cyrus Vance, it was the last straw. "If he [Young] had picked up the phone and told me that he had the meeting—that night, the next day," he told a friend over lunch a year later, "there would have been no problem at all. Unfortunately, that phone call did not come."[19] Perhaps. But Vance had seen his authority chipped away: Zbigniew Brzezinski had taken charge of relations with China, and Carter had appointed a special envoy to handle the Middle East. Vance had spent the summer in bruising battles with the Senate trying to round up the necessary sixty-seven votes to ratify SALT II, and he had failed. Vance remembered Young's remarks about political prisoners in the United States; about the Cubans stabilizing Angola; about the racism of the British, the Swedes, and former American presidents. The State Department had "corrected" all these statements, while the president had defended his unconventional UN ambassador. Young had caused the department—Vance's department—to backtrack one time too many.

Cyrus Vance went to see the president, bearing a document with all his grievances against Young. He told Carter that Young had lied to the department and, therefore, to him. "It's him or me," he announced.[20]

Jimmy Carter told Vance that he needed to think about it. He was in a terrible bind. He could ill afford to antagonize Israel, but he was furious that the

Israelis had "very unwisely" (as he wrote in his diary) gone public with their accusation against Young. "It is hard to remember when a friendly Government has put an American President in a worse political spot," a journalist noted.[21]

The political costs of not firing Young would have been enormous. On the night before Vance delivered his ultimatum, all three networks led with the Young story. "Good evening," David Brinkley intoned on NBC. "UN Ambassador Andrew Young is in trouble again." After explaining the sequence of events, Brinkley said, "The Israelis erupted in anger. They said that if the US talks with the PLO, Israel will withdraw from all peace negotiations." The segment, which ate up four minutes of the broadcast—an eternity in the abbreviated world of network news—included an interview with Young and a report from the State Department, where Vance's "dressing down" of the ambassador was emphasized. "But the big questions now," Brinkley concluded, "are how displeased is Carter and can Ambassador Young survive through another diplomatic flap?"[22] The following morning, the story was emblazoned across the front pages of all the nation's newspapers. There were calls from both sides of the aisle to oust Young, including from Senate Majority Leader Robert Byrd and Republican presidential candidates Bob Dole and George H. W. Bush.[23] In the *New York Times*, a "high official" commented, "This is very damaging to the President, very damaging."[24] The damage was particularly acute in the Jewish community. "All day Wednesday [August 15], government officials and party leaders discussed whether his [Young's] departure would cost more heavily with American blacks than his retention would cost with American Jews," the *New York Times* reported.[25]

Carter thought that "a mountain was made of a molehill," but it was, in a way, a mountain of his own making: he abhorred dishonesty, and Vance had flatly accused Young of lying. Moreover, just one month earlier, Carter had made a flamboyant show of exerting control over his cabinet. Defending Young's alleged insubordination and losing Vance would be very awkward.[26]

Carter sought the advice of his friend, Jesse Hill, a man who *Jet* magazine had called "perhaps the closest black to Jimmy Carter" and "braintruster number one." Hill was a prominent Atlanta businessman; he had campaigned for Carter in 1976 and traveled with him to Lagos in 1978. He had also been Young's campaign manager during his runs for Congress. On August 14, after receiving Vance's ultimatum, Carter and Hill spoke on the phone three times before 11:40 P.M., when the president called the switchboard to say he was going to bed. But shortly after midnight, Carter was on the phone again with Hill, and an hour later, at 1:00 A.M., Hill was talking with Young.[27]

The next morning, August 15, Jesse Hill flew to Washington from Atlanta and Young flew in from New York. They met at the airport and rode downtown together. Young handed Hill his letter of resignation to give to the president. He then went to see Vance, while Hill headed to the White House.[28]

"Jesse Hill was kind of a daddy to Andy," Carter explained, "as far as financing Andy's campaign for Congress and so forth. Jesse Hill came up to see me, and we sat on the Truman balcony and discussed it. He thought it was time for Andy to step down." Carter read Young's letter. "I am afraid," Young had written, "that my conduct has created serious difficulties for the administration."[29]

A few hours later, Young left Foggy Bottom, where Vance had welcomed his decision. Young joined Hill and the president on the Truman Balcony. The three men talked for ninety minutes. Young thought it was important to resign quickly because he was worried about what might happen if the story dragged on: "If I don't go now, we'll have a race riot in front of the UN," he told Carter, "and I don't want that, and you don't need it."[30]

While they were talking, Carter's aides were on the phone to Tel Aviv, trying to persuade the Israeli government to publicly oppose the ouster of Young. However, their attempts, complicated by the sudden illness of Prime Minister Menachem Begin, foundered. Young later said, "If they had gotten the approval from Begin, I probably would have stayed on."[31]

The decision to fire Young was painful to Carter personally and politically. In a 2002 interview, he said: "[The] thing that I did that doesn't cause me to be proud was letting Cy Vance force me in effect to fire Andy Young after he had met with the PLO. . . . I wish I hadn't done it. . . . I wish I had let Cy resign."[32] Firing Young was "one of the most heart-wrenching decisions I had to make as president," Carter wrote. "He was a close and intimate friend, and the prohibition against meeting the PLO was preposterous."[33] Carter and Young had not known each other long, and they did not often see each other. They never socialized, but they shared roots from the two sides of the Jim Crow South as well as a deep Christian faith. Jimmy Carter respected Andrew Young, and he valued what Young brought to his administration. Moreover, his decision to fire Young would further erode his dwindling support in the black community and accelerate the rush of liberals to Ted Kennedy.[34]

On the Truman Balcony, sitting with Hill and Young, Carter agreed with "deep regret" that Young had to resign. Later that afternoon, White House Press Secretary Jody Powell broke the news. His voice choking with emotion, he read aloud the three-page handwritten letter that Carter had written to Young, accepting his resignation. "You have helped to prove," Carter had written, "that we are sensitive to the demands for world peace and racial justice, and have earned for us the friendship, trust and respect of many nations which had previously considered the United States to be suspect and unworthy of such a relationship."[35] The press corps was so stunned that no one asked a question.[36]

When Young faced the media hours after his meeting with Carter, he was unbowed. To the packed press room at the State Department, he said, "I come before you not at all bloody. . . . I really don't feel a bit sorry for what I've done." He added ominously that "there are sharks smelling blood in the water." He explained his predicament succinctly: "I found myself caught between two groups of people, both quite desperate in their own way. . . . Palestinians, desperate for recognition and Israelis, desperate for security."[37]

As Young had predicted, tensions between blacks and Jews spiked. "Out on the streets, the perception, the feeling, is that the Israeli government went out of its way to embarrass and humiliate a black man," Representative Parren Mitchell, the former chair of the Congressional Black Caucus, explained. "The feeling is that somebody did Andy Young in. And when you ask who did him in, the people say the Israelis." African American groups threatened to march in front of the UN; Jewish groups threatened counterprotests. Historian Leonard Dinnerstein noted, "It is impossible to exaggerate the impact of Young's resignation. . . . Young's ouster shattered any possible reconciliation between Jewish and Black leaders."[38]

That night, civil rights leader Jesse Jackson spoke at the annual convention of the Southern Christian Leadership Conference in Norfolk, Virginia. "The Klan didn't move in on Andy," he roared: the "real pressure" had come from "our former allies, the American Jewish community." Author James Baldwin weighed in. Writing in the *Nation*, he proclaimed Young "a hero, betrayed by cowards." He added that "the Jew, in America, is a white man. . . . [H]e is still doing the Christian's dirty work, and black men know it."[39]

On August 22, more than two hundred leaders of black organizations—the largest gathering of African American leaders since the 1963 March on Washington—met at NAACP headquarters in New York City and issued a statement condemning the State Department's "history of racism" and calling its treatment of Young "abhorrent . . . callous . . . ruthless." Young was a "sacrificial lamb." He had been "nailed to the cross." The statement, prominent black psychologist Kenneth Clark declared, "was our declaration of independence."[40]

Leonard Fine, editor of *Moment*, the leading US magazine of Jewish affairs, expressed his dismay at the alarming rise in black anti-Semitism: "It's not the vandals, the unwashed, the slum-dwelling hordes. Not this time. It's the middle class blacks, the best and the brightest of Black America, the ones who are supposed to know better. . . . You frighten us just now, with your loose accusations and your superficial analyses. You frighten us and you offend us." The leader of the Jewish Defense League was blunt: Jews, he warned, "must be ready with guns."[41]

Jimmy Carter, meanwhile, was steaming down the Mississippi on the *Delta Queen*, merging his summer holiday with stump stops to promote his energy program, which was being gutted and delayed by Congress. While tensions between blacks and Jews rose to the boiling point, the president cruised from St. Paul to St. Louis. Representative Parren Mitchell despaired. "I can't think of anyone who's better off because Andy has left public service," he told *Washington Star* columnist Mary McGrory, "unless it's Ian Smith."[42]

Carrington's Stage

In London, Foreign Secretary Carrington had acted quickly to implement the plan that had been agreed at the Lusaka Commonwealth Heads of Government meeting. On August 14, the day Vance delivered his ultimatum about Young to Carter, Britain extended invitations to the Muzorewa government and the Patriotic Front to attend a conference that would open on September 10 at Lancaster House, an imposing building in central London. "We didn't think there was a chance of getting a successful conclusion, but it was the only conceivable thing to do," Carrington told a journalist in 1983. "Recognition of the Bishop's regime would have led to the most appalling problems—not least the isolation of Britain by the rest of the world, including the United States. And it would have intensified the war in Rhodesia." Lord Harlech, who had led the mission to Rhodesia in June, quipped, "Better to end with a disaster than to have disaster without end."[43]

The Thatcher administration had two enormous advantages over the diplomats who had struggled for years to enact the Anglo-American proposals. First, unlike her predecessor James Callaghan, Margaret Thatcher did not have to contend with the Tories in opposition. The Callaghan government's Rhodesia policy had been crippled by its inability to battle the Tories; given the weakness of Labour's hold on power, Callaghan had not dared to put the full weight of the British government behind negotiations in Rhodesia. Thatcher operated under no such constraints. For the first time, Britain was willing to commit its troops to bring Rhodesia to legal independence. This willingness—not changes to the Anglo-American proposals—made the critical difference. Andrew Young noted this when he testified to Congress in October 1979. "I think Margaret Thatcher and Lord Carrington have done an excellent job up until now," he said. "I would like to point out, though, that they are only doing what we tried to get them to do three years ago, and which they said was not right."[44]

Second, Whitehall had a credible and imminent deadline. It had been clear since May 1979 that in November the British Parliament would almost certainly remove sanctions on Rhodesia. This meant that the British government, which did not want to defy the United Nations, would inform the UN Security

Council that Rhodesia, having established majority rule with the election of Bishop Abel Muzorewa, was no longer in rebellion against the Crown and the sanctions were therefore no longer relevant.

This deadline was Carrington's leverage, and he used it masterfully. At every stage in the process, he wielded the threat that if the Patriotic Front dragged its feet, Britain would recognize Muzorewa.[45] It was a fully credible threat, because it was clear that the Thatcher government preferred the bishop to the "terrorists" in the Patriotic Front. The deadline also gave Carrington leverage over Muzorewa. It was worth the risk for Muzorewa to enter negotiations—which would annul the landslide elections he had won the previous April—for three reasons. First, the internal settlement had neither slowed the war nor been recognized by any government; the Lancaster House conference offered a way to push the reset button. Muzorewa needed the international recognition, particularly from Washington, that could flow from participating in the negotiations. Second, it was widely expected that the Lancaster House talks would collapse because the Patriotic Front would walk out. In this case, Muzorewa would get the prize of international recognition without having to sacrifice anything. It was a high-stakes game of chicken: if the Patriotic Front swerved first (which seemed likely), Muzorewa would win; but if Muzorewa swerved first, he would lose; therefore, it made sense for him to stay in the game. Finally, in the unlikely event that the Patriotic Front did not walk out and new elections were held, Muzorewa believed that he would win. Carrington encouraged his confidence. "Everyone knows you are going to be the incoming prime minister," he assured the bishop, "so you may leave your slippers behind in your office to await your return."[46] The looming deadline generated momentum for both sides, a key factor that had been absent from all previous settlement talks.

Carrington sustained this momentum in three ways. First, he was dictatorial. He set the rules, and he set the schedule. He was an impatient conductor of a fast-moving train yelling repeatedly, "All aboard! This train is leaving the station!" Second, he sliced the negotiations into three rapid, successive agreements on a new constitution, the transition process, and the cease-fire. By the time the parties got to the cease-fire arrangements—the most contested issue—they would have so much skin in the game that it would be hard to back out. Third, he simplified the negotiations. As he explained in his memoirs, "the previous proposals had been overelaborate." The Lancaster House talks were a stripped-down version of the Anglo-American proposals: only the British, the Patriotic Front, and the Muzorewa government were at the table.[47]

Something else had changed during the long months of war and Anglo-American diplomacy: Ian Smith no longer wielded the power that had enabled him to block progress at Geneva in 1976. When Smith arrived in London—a member of Muzorewa's twenty-two-man team—he was feted at conservative gatherings as though nothing had changed. Yet behind the closed doors of Lancaster House, Smith failed to sway the votes of the querulous Salisbury group, which included seven whites. These whites were led by Smith; they represented his Rhodesian Front party and included his closest aides. But Smith could not persuade his white cohorts to follow him down the path of rejectionism. He had been fighting a rearguard action to shore up white supremacy ever since 1976, when he had declared that he was handing his head on a platter to Henry Kissinger. He had hoped to retain white power by handing the title of prime minister to a black man, but his gamble had failed because the war had continued to escalate: white supremacy, even if masked, could not survive. Smith went to London the defender of a lost cause.[48]

No Americans negotiated at Lancaster House, but the Carter administration wielded great influence nevertheless. Britain convened the conference to bring Rhodesia to legality "in conditions that secure wide international recognition"—the goal Thatcher had articulated in her first speech as prime minister. Although the British hoped that the conferees would negotiate a lasting peace, their bottom line was that they would hand over power to a government that had "wide, international recognition"—even if that government was unable to stop the war. At Lancaster House, the British had to be seen to offer both sides a transparently fair solution. This was the safeguard against the eventuality that was widely expected—ZANU's Robert Mugabe and perhaps ZAPU's Joshua Nkomo would walk out. If Carrington manifestly treated all sides equally, the conference could survive such a walkout and the participants who remained (presumably Muzorewa) would be able to form a government that could have legitimacy.[49]

The legitimacy of the new regime would hinge on Washington. If the Carter administration was satisfied that Britain had offered all sides a fair deal, then it might recognize the new government even if it did not represent all parties, and "wide international recognition" would follow. If not, Britain would be in a worse position than before Lancaster House: the Rhodesian government would still not have wide international recognition; the war would continue; and all black Africa, the Commonwealth, and the Third World would be inflamed. Therefore, although there were no American representatives around the conference table, their presence was palpable. Behind the scenes, throughout the conference, the British scrambled to attain American agreement to the process. When Carrington yelled "All aboard!" he was addressing not only Muzorewa and the Patriotic Front; he was also pleading with the Americans to jump on the train.

Carter wanted to help. In August, before the Lancaster House talks opened, the British had told the Americans that "it was essential that the US should back us up in public and in private when the difficult issues came to the fore." Carter had agreed. He was happy that Britain was taking charge: this would help him persuade Congress to delay lifting sanctions, and it enabled him to focus on other pressing issues. In 1977 and 1978, there had been wide agreement that the region of the world most vulnerable to the Soviet threat—and that posed the greatest peril to US domestic harmony—was southern Africa, but by 1979 the locus of the Cold War had shifted to Iran and Central America. And while in 1977 Carter had agreed with Prime Minister Callaghan's assessment that Britain required American help to resolve the Rhodesia problem, by late 1979 he thought that the time for Britain to take the reins was nigh. This would be, Carter believed, "best for the success of the negotiations." The frustrating years of trying to enforce the Anglo-American proposals had demonstrated how skilled the Rhodesian government and the Patriotic Front were at exploiting differences between the British and the Americans. Having one country in charge would streamline the process. Carrington's plan, the White House thought, "offered the best chance of a way forward, though the odds remained long."[50]

One problem, however, continued to dog the negotiations. "The major difficulty," a ZAPU official told US Ambassador Donald McHenry (Young's replacement at the UN), "[was] one of trust—the Patriotic Front did not trust the British." The Patriotic Front had been skeptical of the US government in early 1977, the ZAPU official explained, but in the ensuing negotiations Washington "had always been more 'realistic' than . . . London."[51] The Patriotic Front's and Frontline States' lack of faith in the British was accentuated by the omnipresent threat that if the talks failed, London would recognize Muzorewa. This tactic created momentum, but it corroded trust.

As the conference moved through the three stages Carrington had prescribed—agreement first on a new constitution, then on arrangements for the transition, and finally on the terms of the cease-fire—a pattern emerged. At each juncture, Muzorewa was the first to agree to the British terms, while the Patriotic Front held out for more changes. And at each juncture, the British turned to the Americans to press the Patriotic Front to sign on the dotted line, while the Patriotic Front and Frontline presidents turned to the Americans to press the British to make concessions. It was a process, the *Economist* noted, of "huff, puff and fudge."[52]

In mid-October, after a month of hard bargaining, the first phase—writing the new constitution—was drawing to a close. The draft constitution was almost identical to that envisioned by the Anglo-American negotiations. It prescribed universal suffrage and a Bill of Rights. A bicameral legislature would consist of a 100-member lower house with 20 seats selected (for seven years) by a whites-only poll, and a 40-seat upper house that would elect a president as head of state and commander in chief. The key new aspect of this constitution was its regulation that for ten years the new government of Zimbabwe could not seize land from whites. Land could be redistributed only if whites freely decided to sell and the government could pay the market price. This would cost billions of dollars; hence, the idea of a development fund was resurrected. Tanzania's Julius Nyerere had revived the concept in his opening speech at the Lusaka Commonwealth conference, and Carrington gave it flesh in early October.[53]

Muzorewa was relatively satisfied with the draft constitution, and he asked his delegation to vote it up or down. Ian Smith protested loudly. He told South African foreign minister Pik Botha that "he could not accept the constitutional proposals of the British . . . [and] the armed struggle must continue." He then cast the sole, bitter vote against compromise, astounded that his closest aides had deserted him.[54] The Patriotic Front, on the other hand, was united in its opposition to the proposed constitution because of the way it dealt with the critical question of land. The Foreign Office asked the Americans to "use their influence with ZAPU/ZANU in order to help secure agreement." Vance instructed the US ambassadors in Lusaka, Maputo, and Dar es Salaam to meet with the heads of government and convey the stern message: "We believe that the constitutional proposals which the British have advanced will be perceived as fair and democratic by the world community and by our Congress." The ambassadors were told to add the threat: "If the conference were to break down due to PF [Patriotic Front] refusal to accept these proposals, the [US] Congress would undoubtedly move to lift sanctions."[55]

The Carter administration put money behind its words. Zambian president Kenneth Kaunda's aide, Mark Chona, who was attending the Lancaster House conference, recalled one night when "Mugabe called me to his flat and told me that the negotiations were going to collapse over land. 'Could you please call your American friends and ask them if the Kissinger pledge [for a development fund] . . . was still on the table?' So I picked up the phone that was sitting next to me and I called [US diplomat] Gib Lanpher, who was . . . an observer there [at Lancaster House]. And I asked him a straight question, if that offer was still available, and Gib said, 'Well, Mark, I can't say that it's still viable, but we'd be prepared to consider the possibility of funding that kind of program.'"[56] Kaunda immediately wrote Carter: "If we do not provide for this contingency [a fund for land reform] now," he pleaded, "the sufferers will be the whites of Zimbabwe."[57] London followed up on October 12, asking if the Carter administration would agree to participate in a fund that would help buy out white farmers and provide "general economic development assistance."[58] On October 15, the State Department announced: "We believe a multidonor effort would be appropriate to assist in the agricultural and economic development of an independent Zimbabwe . . . and we would be prepared to cooperate in such an effort." This reassured Nkomo and Mugabe. "It gave them enough of a hook and a sense of commitment that about two days later they agreed to the British constitutional proposal. It broke the logjam," Gib Lanpher, the American diplomat who conveyed the news to the Patriotic Front leaders, remembered. "If the US had not stepped in," Nkomo told *Time* magazine, "it would have been very difficult to move on this question. The war is about land."[59]

When Carter thought that the leaders of the Patriotic Front were being unreasonable, he did not hesitate to tell them so. At one point, when Nkomo implored Carter to weigh in on a contested point, he received a gruff response from Vance: "There is no possibility whatsoever of President Carter's intervention. . . . It is essential to get on with the Lancaster [House] negotiations without delay or interruption." However, in late October, when the Patriotic Front explained to the Americans why it could not agree to Carrington's transition arrangements—the second stage of the Lancaster House process—because they did not include a voter registration system, an international supervisory force, and adequate time for the Front to repatriate its forces, Carter decided that "there is some justice in these concerns" and urged the British to make concessions.[60] The British acceded in part, but Carrington called in the American ambassador, Kingman Brewster, "to comment candidly" on the situation. Carrington's "impression was that the Americans thought that he had only one customer to satisfy: the Patriotic Front. In fact," he reminded Brewster, "he had two customers: one already in possession with an election and a 64% turnout . . . and the Patriotic Front." Brewster protested, "The important thing was that neutral countries should not say that the arrangements were unfair. This was the only motive behind American recommendations. . . . The main concern of the Americans was that the arrangements should not appear to have been rigged up for the Bishop."[61]

The appearance of fairness mattered: on it hung the possibility that Carter would lift sanctions. Therefore, London courted Washington, however grumpily. "The Carter Administration will want them [the Patriotic Front] to be seen to have been given the fairest possible chance to participate," the Foreign Office noted. "The Americans will want to get the fullest information they can on our thinking . . . but it would be wise to avoid going very far at this stage." From the State Department, Dick Moose and Anthony Lake traveled frequently to London during the conference to be briefed by the British and to "offer our thoughts."[62] During an October visit, they pledged Whitehall "our continuing support . . . while maintaining our distance from day-to-day activities at the conference table." They assured Vance, "We shall emphasize your view that Lancaster House is their show."[63]

Nevertheless, the British worried. They were unsure how fully they could count on Jimmy Carter. In September, the British embassy in Washington tried to reassure the Foreign Office. Asked by Carrington to speculate about what Carter would do if Muzorewa accepted "what we regard as a reasonable settlement" but the Patriotic Front rejected it, the embassy noted that US domestic politics would come into play.[64] By the fall of 1979, Carter could ill afford another fight with Congress. His administration was under fire. Its failure to counter the fall of the shah of Iran in January 1979, the leftist revolution in Grenada in March, and the Sandinista victory in Nicaragua in July—plus its inability to reduce inflation and unemployment—fueled frustrations and fears.

This was the context of the British attempts to predict how Carter might react to a failed conference at Lancaster House—one in which the Patriotic Front walked out but Muzorewa stayed on. The counselor at the British embassy in Washington, William Squire, thought there was reason to believe that Carter would recognize a Muzorewa government that emerged from Lancaster House, even if the Patriotic Front had balked, because failing to do so would "hurt the President domestically." Dealing with Rhodesia held no political benefit for Carter—it won him neither friends nor respect among the broad electorate. If Carter maintained sanctions on Rhodesia after a Lancaster House agreement, however incomplete, it would "increase domestic criticism of his dealings with the USSR. . . . The voters expect the US to 'stand up to the Russians' and their proxies [such as the Patriotic Front]." Squire concluded, "The logic of this analysis is that the US will normalise relations when Britain . . . does so." He ended with the important proviso, however, that "the less credible the constitution or subsequent test of opinion, the more difficult it will be to achieve full Administration backing."[65]

If Carter proved recalcitrant, the British had another trick up their sleeves: they would convince a veto-proof majority of the US Congress that it was time to lift sanctions. Lord Harlech, one of Thatcher's most trusted advisers, traveled to Washington, talked to a wide array of officials and politicians—including Ted Kennedy, George McGovern, Sam Hayakawa, Stephen Solarz, and Warren Christopher—about Rhodesia. Harlech reported: "He [Carter] is not well placed to have a head-on collision with them [Congress] with his campaign for re-election . . . underway. Therefore, the stronger and more widespread those forces in the Congress which favour lifting sanctions can be made, the more likely the President and his Administration will be to support our actions." Harlech recommended that the Foreign Office get busy. "I have been disagreeably surprised by the attitude of the Administration and their disinclination to face unpalatable facts," he reported. "It is of the greatest importance that our Embassies in Washington and New York [at the UN] use all available means to gain support for our position and our actions not only within the Administration where it will be more difficult than I had expected, but in both Houses of Congress and among influential columnists and leader [editorial] writers in the 'New York Times' and 'Washington Post.'"[66]

Senator Jesse Helms was eager to help the British. On September 12, he wrote Margaret Thatcher. He congratulated her on the Lancaster House conference, which had just opened, but he added that he remained "deeply concerned" about "the pressures on the Muzorewa government." He then reminded her of the status of the US Congress's attempts to lift sanctions. There were two relevant pieces of legislation. The State Department Authorization Act, passed by both houses on August 2, stated that the sanctions should be lifted by November 15, 1979—unless the president determined that it would not be in the national interest to do so. Helms claimed credit for the November deadline, explaining to Thatcher that he had chosen that date "in order to give the British Government time to secure a consensus for the lifting of sanctions." The Defense Authorization Act was about to go to conference committee; the Senate version required the president to lift sanctions immediately; the House version did not mention Rhodesia, but the Solarz bill (passed on June 28) had repeated the language of the State Department Authorization Act—the House thought that Carter should lift sanctions in the fall, but left the decision to him. Helms assured Thatcher that the final Defense Authorization Act would force Carter to lift sanctions. "At the very minimum, the conference [reconciling the House and Senate drafts] is sure to provide for the lifting of sanctions on strategic minerals. Once the finger is pulled out of the dyke even to that extent, the whole edifice of sanctions will come falling down." Helms, however, was beginning to worry about Thatcher's resolve. "If the lifting of sanctions is delayed [by the British] . . . for any reason," he lectured the prime minister, "the consequences will be disastrous not only for Rhodesia, but for all of southern Africa." He concluded: "It is therefore urgent that the Constitutional [Lancaster House] conference extend some hope to the Muzorewa government immediately." Helms signed off with a personal note, written in pen: "I remain very proud of you!"[67]

Helms also sent a message of encouragement to the Muzorewa government. "Moderates, both black and white, throughout Zimbabwe should clearly understand that they no longer stand alone."[68] He despatched two of his legislative aides, John Carbaugh and James Lucier, to London. There, they urged

Smith to hang tough, and Carbaugh—extraordinarily—was granted a meeting with Thatcher. According to Carbaugh's account, he brashly told Thatcher, "Peter Carrington is not serving you well," a comment that she brushed off with "That is not for you to decide."[69] In the Foreign Office, the American duo provided comic relief. "Tweedledum & Tweedledee (C[arbaugh] & Jim Lucier). We spoke!" one diplomat wrote, using the nicknames the Foreign Office had dubbed Helms' aides. "Tweedledee has given me copies of memoranda he has sent to Jesse Helms following his visit with Tweedledum to southern Africa." In a cover note forwarding these memos, a Foreign Office official opined that his colleagues might be "amused by the stuff being fed to Senator Helms by his staff." Another diplomat cautioned, "Carbaugh is well capable of shooting a line [exaggerating]." Lord Harlech was not amused. "The one thing calculated to reduce any vote [in the US Congress] in favour [of lifting sanctions] will be the activities of Senator Helmes [*sic*], whose reactionary and racist views repel most Senators."[70]

Gib Lanpher, the American diplomat stationed in London who followed the Lancaster House negotiations closely, cabled Washington about the activities of Jesse Helms' two aides. "When your cable on Carbaugh and Lucier hit Mr. Vance's desk," Moose told Lanpher, "he had to be scraped off the ceiling." Lanpher remembered, "Vance just went ballistic."[71] Vance feared that Helms' meddling would derail the delicate Lancaster House talks by convincing Muzorewa that he need not make concessions since the US Congress was going to lift sanctions.

Lake and Moose were dispatched to London to discuss the problem with Robin Renwick, the head of the Rhodesia Department. Renwick later noted, "I do think Jesse Helms was a bad influence throughout this. I really do." With the help of Moose and Lake, he drafted a statement objecting to Carbaugh's and Lucier's presence because, as he wrote Carrington's private secretary, "Mr Vance would be relieved that we had found a way to help him."[72]

Lanpher recalls that Vance, as soon as he had Carrington's oral approval of the statement, "told his staff to clear his schedule, get his car, he was going to the Hill. He went up to the Hill and grabbed Senator [Jacob] Javits (R-NY) and maybe a couple of others and briefed them on what was going on and got the Senate to get to Jesse Helms and order his aides out of London." Lucier and Carbaugh were back in Washington the following day. "I was very glad to hear this morning that the problem which blew up . . . about Senator Helms' aides seems now to have subsided," Carrington cabled Vance. "But if there is anything more we can do to help, do let me know."[73]

Vance was on edge. The conference committee on the Defense Department Authorization Act was about to meet, and at stake was the possibility that it would adopt the Senate version that lifted sanctions on Rhodesia immediately. The administration was concerned for two reasons. First, the armed service committees, from whom the conferees were chosen, were (unlike the foreign affairs committees) very conservative. "This task is complicated," the State Department explained, "as the majority of conferees are not sympathetic to Administration's African policies."[74] Second, it was the autumn of 1979, and SALT II was in dire straits in Congress. No one had expected it to be easy to round up two-thirds of the senators to ratify the treaty, but in August, when Congress went on summer recess, Vance had been sanguine about its prospects. By October, that had changed.

The hearings about SALT, which had begun in the Senate Foreign Relations committee on September 6, had added fuel to the debate about détente that had raged for a decade. The most passionate participants in that debate were neoconservatives, an eclectic group of Republicans and Democrats united in their certainty that the Soviets were gaining strength while naive American bureaucrats wallowed in liberal regrets about Vietnam. The neoconservative message was clear, and it hearkened back to George Kennan's diagnosis of the world situation thirty years earlier: the Kremlin was a mortal enemy and could not be trusted, negotiations with the Soviets were a fool's errand, and the only appropriate response to the Kremlin's desire to dominate the world was to confront it with greater strength. In the turbulent world of 1979, when Americans waited in lines for gas, watched friendly dictators in Iran and Nicaragua fall, and nursed the wounds of Vietnam and Watergate, the neoconservatives' call to revive American power was seductive. This was particularly so for many senators who faced reelection in November. SALT, for the neoconservatives, was the apogee of liberal naivete and appeasement.

The heightened anti-Soviet sensitivities of the day were exemplified in the tempest that blew up over the discovery—or rather, the rediscovery—of a combat unit of about 2,600 Soviet soldiers stationed in Cuba. In the wake of the Cuban Missile Crisis, the Kennedy administration had tolerated Moscow's keeping this one unit in Cuba. Over time, however, US intelligence had forgotten about it. The CIA was therefore alarmed when, in August 1979, it "discovered" a Soviet unit in Cuba. In the overheated atmosphere of Washington, this "discovery" confirmed alarmist fears of brazen Soviet expansion perilously close to home. Carter, misled by his intelligence community and desperate to look strong, drew a line in the sand, stating publicly on September 7 that the presence of this combat unit was "a very serious matter and . . . not acceptable." He demanded that Moscow remove the brigade forthwith. Leonid Brezhnev was unimpressed. A painful month ensued, with Carter continuing to fume about the brigade in public, while in private the CIA informed him that the brigade had been in Cuba since the Missile Crisis. On October 1, Carter stepped back, announcing that although the unit remained a "serious concern" that his administration would continue to monitor closely, the White House had been assured by "the highest level of the Soviet Government" that the brigade was not a combat unit but merely a training center. Carter's fumbling of the issue was a costly, self-inflicted error. The SALT treaty was not its only wreckage. It also annealed the impression that the Carter administration was inept and weak.[75]

It was in the midst of this crisis that the Defense Authorization Act resurfaced, and the administration had to rally its demoralized forces in Congress to defeat another move to lift sanctions on Rhodesia. Lifting sanctions at this point would derail the Lancaster House talks because it would remove the main incentive for Muzorewa to be flexible and it would alienate the Patriotic Front; therefore, lifting sanctions would widen the war. In September, Vance assured his French, British, and German colleagues at a quadripartite meeting that Carter would veto the Defense Act if it contained language lifting sanctions, but the administration was loath to be put in this position.[76] At a time when the administration needed to affirm its toughness, Carter did not want to veto a bill funding the Department of Defense.

The White House, State Department, and Defense Department deployed their top people in a sustained effort to maintain sanctions on Rhodesia. Carter, Vance, Vice President Mondale, Secretary of Defense Harold Brown, undersecretaries and assistant secretaries, the American ambassador in London, and other members of the administration telephoned, wrote letters to, and breakfasted, lunched, and dined with the conference committee members in a dramatic attempt to persuade them to strike the language lifting sanctions from the Defense Authorization bill.[77] In September and October, when the struggle was raging, Rhodesia was often the first topic on Vance's (or Christopher's, when Vance was away) evening reports to the president. When Christopher warned that the vote count looked grim, Carter wrote, "Go all out on this." One member of the conference committee stated that it was "the hardest press [lobbying] I've ever seen."[78]

These efforts paid dividends, and the administration also benefited from movement at Lancaster House, where Carrington had clinched agreement on the new constitution and was moving forward on the terms of the transition period. On October 24, at the end of a grueling battle in the conference committee, Senator John Tower (R-TX), who previously had supported lifting sanctions, "made a statesmanlike presentation recommending caution," the State Department congressional liaison wrote, "in light of the ongoing negotiations" at Lancaster House. The conference committee then voted unanimously to back a flaccid "sense of Congress" resolution that the United States should lift sanctions.[79]

On October 27, the day after the House passed the Defense Authorization Bill, State Department officials were drafting memos to prepare the president for the determination on Rhodesian sanctions that the State Department Authorization bill mandated he make by November 15. (When it had been passed on June 25, 1979, this compromise provision had seemed to apply to the distant future.) Carter's decision was inextricably tied to two events in London: British sanctions would lapse on November 15 unless the British Parliament renewed them, and the Lancaster House conference was progressing rapidly. Washington and London, therefore, needed to synchronize their policies toward sanctions. This would not prove easy.

Carter Decides, Again

On November 4, 1979, Iranians stormed the US embassy in Tehran, taking sixty-six Americans hostage.[80] The Carter administration, although alarmed, believed that this siege, like that of February 14, would end quickly.

On November 5, Vance sent an urgent cable to Ambassador Brewster in London. "[We need] a clear view of where the British are going [with their Rhodesia policy] . . . The sanctions question poses a particular problem for us." Carter would have to make his determination in ten days. "If HMG [Her Majesty's Government] were to allow the Order in Council [sanctions] to lapse . . . it could be extremely difficult for President Carter to maintain sanctions."[81] Two days later, Brewster met with Carrington. The British Foreign Office was going to finesse the issue. Carrington would soon announce that Thatcher would not ask Parliament to renew sanctions. However, the Foreign Office had figured out that approximately 80 percent of the sanctions were "double-banked," that is, they were maintained not only by the Order in Council that Parliament renewed annually but also by other legislation.[82] Therefore, Britain would maintain the great bulk of sanctions, creating "a rather gray, undefined area of trading activities," until the Lancaster House talks were concluded.[83]

On November 10, Vance met with the new British ambassador in Washington, Nicholas Henderson, who informed him that Carrington was going to "play a forcing hand" at Lancaster House. Even though agreement had not been reached on the transition and talks had not begun on the cease-fire, Whitehall was planning to send a British governor to Rhodesia to assume control of the colony and rule during the transition. "Henderson said it would be crucial," Vance wrote Carter, "when you make the decision on sanctions next week to state that the United States would lift sanctions when the British

Governor arrives in Salisbury. I said I understood the problem fully and that we were studying the question. I said we wanted to be as helpful as possible."[84]

The Foreign Office was apprehensive. It had been irritated by the statement that Carter had made in June announcing his decision on Case-Javits, which it had considered unjustly critical of Muzorewa. It was therefore worried about what Carter might say when announcing his imminent decision about sanctions. Lord Harlech expressed this anxiety: "We must insist that as regards any statement to be made by the President," he wrote, "we are fully consulted beforehand on the text. A repetition of the serious inaccuracies and confused thinking contained in his June statement would on this occasion be extremely dangerous."[85]

There was never any doubt that Carter would refuse to lift sanctions on November 15, when the talks at Lancaster House were at a critical juncture, but there were questions about exactly how he would justify maintaining them. His reasoning mattered because it would affect the response in Congress. "A decision to retain them [sanctions], depending on its justification, would probably be overturned in the Senate, but might be sustained in the House," Vance wrote Carter. The State Department developed three options for the president: simply announce that he was maintaining sanctions; announce that he was maintaining sanctions but would lift them when a British governor arrived in Salisbury; or announce that he was maintaining sanctions but would lift them when a British governor arrived in Salisbury and "a process leading to impartial elections begins."[86]

Carter and Vance were leery that the British might renege at the last moment on their promise to hold new elections in Rhodesia. Vance, therefore, recommended the third option. It would allow the administration to "maintain flexibility until we see what the final UK proposals look like, retain some influence over UK decisions, and maintain credibility with the Africans and in the UN." Brzezinski agreed. The second option, he wrote Carter on November 13, "would tie ourselves too closely to the British, and would be seen by many as a total capitulation to the will of the UK," whereas the third "will avoid giving a complete 'blank check' to the UK."[87]

On November 14, the tenth day of the Iranian hostage crisis, Carter issued his decision on Rhodesian sanctions—his second in six months. "Encouraging progress has been made," his announcement began. "However, . . . a termination of sanctions at this stage could lead all the parties to harden their positions and would jeopardize the chances for a successful settlement for Zimbabwe-Rhodesia. . . . We would, however, be prepared to lift sanctions when a British Governor assumes authority in Salisbury and a process leading to impartial elections has begun."[88]

The following day, there was a breakthrough at Lancaster House. After weeks of haggling, "a grim-faced Mugabe," in the words of the US embassy in London, agreed to the transition arrangements. This was where the Lancaster House agreement differed dramatically from the Anglo-American proposals: the Tories gave Britain full responsibility for governing Rhodesia during the brief transition, with a British governor who would maintain law and order and create conditions in which free elections could be held.[89]

All that remained was accord on the terms of the cease-fire. This, and the hostage crisis, overshadowed the press coverage of Carter's decision to maintain sanctions: most Americans' attention was elsewhere, and those who focused on Rhodesia were optimistic that the crisis there would soon be settled.[90]

Reaction in the Frontline States to Carter's announcement was "very positive," Vance wrote the president. "Our ambassador in Lusaka reports the Zambians were extremely pleased at the good news from London [the agreement on the transition] and attributed your decision on sanctions as being a significant influence on the breakthrough at Lancaster House."[91] Mozambique's President Samora Machel agreed. "Had [the] US lifted sanctions . . . [the] chances of settlement [would have been] jeopardized." The response from Rhodesia, on the other hand, was chilly; the *Rhodesian Herald* once again attributed the decision to Carter's need to court the black vote. The American president, it explained, was "concerned about his popularity after the departure of Ambassador Young."[92]

London's reaction was subdued. Vance began his evening report on November 15 with the comment that "though they would have preferred an unconditional statement that you would lift sanctions when the British Governor arrives in Salisbury, the British have expressed their appreciation for your decision."[93]

In the Senate, Sam Hayakawa (R-CA) immediately moved to overturn Carter's decision, and Ed Derwinski (R-IL) did likewise in the House. The administration was not worried about the House, where the rules would slow down the progress of Derwinski's bill. "The entire House Democratic leadership . . . have promised to help us bottle up sanctions-lifting resolutions," Vance assured Carter on November 15. However, he warned, "the situation is slightly less useful in the Senate."[94] Hayakawa's bill was referred to the Senate Foreign Relations Committee, and Jesse Helms intended to force it to the floor after ten days' debate in committee. Assistant Secretary Moose appeared before the committee three times, engaging in testy exchanges with Helms, who was at his most combative. "Helms . . . knows what he wants, and he sticks to it like glue," Jacob Javits observed. "Helms argued tenaciously," Moose wrote Vance. Helms wanted to give Congress the power to decide when the sanctions should be lifted. Moose countered that the administration would never accept this encroachment on its authority.[95]

There was a purity and simplicity to this debate. The senators barely mentioned race or Rhodesia or American values. As Javits declared, "The only nuance, which is the nuance I am interested in, is that the Congress remains a partner in the deal."[96] This was a brute struggle of the legislature to assert control over foreign policy.

By November 30, when the committee was in its third day of hearings on the subject, Moose reported encouraging news from Lancaster House. The negotiations on the cease-fire—the final stage of the agreement—were proceeding well. The mood in London was "upbeat. . . . We are very close," Moose told the committee. It was important that the Senate do nothing to upset this "delicate balance."[97]

Frank Church (D-ID) and Javits broadened the discussion in the Senate Foreign Relations Committee. The world was in turmoil in Iran, Nicaragua, and Afghanistan. The Grand Mosque in Mecca was under siege by Islamic militants, and that morning, the Mexican government had rejected the US request to allow the exiled shah of Iran to return to Mexico after having had medical treatment in New York. "Mobs have formed in front of the American embassy in Kuwait and . . . the Mexicans have clearly cast their lot with the third world," Church said. Javits noted, "This [Rhodesian sanctions] is a more serious matter I think than perhaps meets the eye. We are a nation under assault today in a very serious way in the third world. We need successes in the third world very urgently. . . .This is a big test for us. . . . Can the western world contrive anything that is successful? This [Lancaster House] looks like it is on the verge of success." Struggling to restore a modicum of "national unity," Javits reminded his colleagues of the need to respect the office of the presidency. Referring to Carter, he added, "We may not like the guy but that is the institution."[98] He then asked if Vance would assure Helms that "when the British Governor arrives in Salisbury to implement an agreed Lancaster House settlement, we will immediately lift sanctions."[99]

Moose sent Javits' request—repeating the senator's precise wording—to Vance, who sent it to Carter, who edited it. In his own hand, the president inserted a phrase and added a second sentence. The revised statement, with Carter's insertions here rendered in italics, was: "When the British Governor arrives in Salisbury to implement an agreed Lancaster House settlement, *and the electoral process begins,* we will immediately lift sanctions. *This will be done no later than one month after his arrival.*" In a marginal note, Carter explained, "Cy, I cannot violate my commitment to black leaders given as you proposed. J." Vance dutifully sent Helms a letter including the two sentences written by the president.[100]

This letter, and the speed of events at Lancaster House, mollified Helms, who was confident that Muzorewa would win another election. "I think we have reached the point where good faith needs to take over, and I think it has," he announced on December 3, when the committee reconvened. Helms and his colleagues then unanimously approved a resolution calling for sanctions to be lifted by January 31, 1980, unless—the familiar presidential prerogative loophole—"the president determines it is not in the national interest."[101]

Vance's letter to Helms, which the British Foreign Office obtained, had the opposite effect in London.[102] The Lancaster House negotiations were at a critical juncture: the constitution and transition arrangements had been agreed; on November 26, Muzorewa had accepted the rules for the cease-fire. These declared that all hostilities of the Patriotic Front and the Rhodesian army would cease by December 28; a 1,200-man Commonwealth force led by the British would monitor compliance; the Rhodesian armed forces would stand down; and the disarmed Patriotic Front guerrillas would congregate in "assembly points" prior to the elections.[103]

All that remained was for the Patriotic Front to agree to these protocols. Whitehall had put the squeeze on the Front by preparing to send the governor to Salisbury and by announcing that as soon as he arrived, the British sanctions would be ended. It was crucial, the Thatcher administration believed, that Washington make a similar statement. If Washington announced that it would lift sanctions, the Patriotic Front would sign the Lancaster House agreement, because otherwise Muzorewa would take charge of an internationally recognized, independent Zimbabwe. However, if Washington refused to make the announcement, the Patriotic Front could hang tough and walk out. Then the British would be faced with the worst possible outcome: it would be fully committed to a Muzorewa government that had failed to gain international recognition and faced an intensifying war. Thus Carrington uttered the final call of the Lancaster House train: "All aboard!" The British wanted— needed—the Americans on board.

From the British point of view, Jimmy Carter's insistence on waiting until "the electoral process begins" was infuriating and potentially catastrophic. The Foreign Office noted that it was "highly unsatisfactory . . . [and] would cause us serious concern." It was, moreover, embarrassing. Margaret Thatcher was flying to Washington on December 17 for her first state visit. In preparation for the trip she had met with the US ambassador on December 5. Rhodesia was the first topic. "It would be very awkward," Thatcher observed caustically, "if the United States was still applying sanctions against Rhodesia at the time of her arrival [in Washington]."[104] On the same day, a British diplomat, Ray Seitz, who had been closely involved with the Rhodesia negotiations for years, called on Vance. The Thatcher administration, he said, appreciated Washington's assistance—Carter had approved the use of US aircraft to lift helicopters and heavy equipment to Rhodesia that would be needed during the transition (which, as Rhodesia Department head Robin Renwick said, was a "crucial contribution to the success of the negotiations"[105])—but it was troubled by its reluctance to lift sanctions. The Foreign Office had a copy of Vance's letter to Helms. Why did Carter insist on waiting until the electoral process had begun?

Vance confided that the phrase about the electoral process "had been argued intensely within the administration. It had been pointed out," he said, that "it would look crazy" if the Americans maintained sanctions while its military aircraft were lifting equipment into Rhodesia. Moreover, Vance admitted that "it would imply doubt" about British dependability and "strain bilateral relations on other fronts just when the Americans needed friends." (Washington was seeking support for UN sanctions on Iran to force it to release the hostages.) Vance found these arguments convincing, but "the President believed that he had committed himself to this wording to a significant political group (our guess is that this is the Black Caucus in Congress)." Seitz explained to Vance that "what mattered to us was that the Americans should not under any circumstances maintain sanctions for more than a day or two after the arrival of the governor." Vance could not give him that assurance. This caused, he admitted in his memoirs, "a serious irritant" in US-British relations.[106]

On December 7, Carrington cabled the British ambassador in Washington. "Unless and until the Patriotic Front are aware that the . . . [US] lifting of sanctions [is] . . . imminent, they will have no incentive to reach final agreement on our proposals." He instructed the ambassador to tell the Americans: "We hope, therefore, that . . . the lifting of sanctions by Britain will be accompanied by . . . a clear indication that the Americans will follow suit: this will greatly increase the pressure on the Patriotic Front to accept our proposals." In case he had not been clear, he repeated, "Any suggestion that the lifting of sanctions . . . will be delayed will encourage the Patriotic Front to hold out . . . and this would be extremely dangerous."[107]

Carter did not budge. On the same day, Moose and Lake met with a diplomat from the British embassy "to convey the hope that the British could set a date for the elections, and come up with other concrete indications that the 'process leading to impartial elections' had actually begun when the Governor General arrived in Salisbury." Several hours later, the British diplomat called Lake to say that the government had announced "ordinances which [mean] the electoral process will have begun" when the governor arrived in Salisbury. "This was very helpful," Lake responded.[108]

It was not, however, sufficient. At the Foreign Office, Robin Renwick was losing patience. "Our recent exchanges with the Americans have revealed hesitations in Washington about the timing of the lifting of sanctions," he wrote Antony Duff, the head of the Africa Department, on December 8. "The Americans asked if we could say 'something more concrete on the question of the electoral process.'" Renwick pointed out that "the ordinance establishing the Electoral Commissioner, an Election Council and assuming control of the Rhodesian election machinery will come into effect immediately on the Governor's arrival in Rhodesia. . . . [This] really ought to satisfy the Americans." It did not. "Mr Lake is now asking if we could announce the date for elections simultaneously with the date of the Governor's arrival." Renwick was beaten: "If this is really necessary to secure immediate US action in lifting sanctions . . . we should consider this." The Americans had the Foreign Office over a barrel. Thatcher was departing for Washington, the governor was departing for Salisbury—and Britain wanted Carter to lift the sanctions.[109]

Two days later, Renwick returned to the subject. "The Americans have got themselves into some difficulty over the precise timing of the lifting of sanctions," he wrote Duff. "The difficulty lies in President Carter's commitment to his liberal and black supporters in Congress."[110]

The US officials were playing for time. Carter had given his word to the leaders of the Congressional Black Caucus that he would not lift sanctions until he was sure that the election process was underway.[111] He did not promise anything lightly. Therefore, the question must be asked, why would Carter have committed himself to this proviso that so irritated the British? And why would he have made the promise to the Black Caucus in particular?

Lifting sanctions was Carter's trump, and before he played it he wanted to be as sure as possible that Britain would follow through on its promise to implement a fair electoral process in Rhodesia. His administration had harbored doubts about Thatcher's commitment to holding elections from the day the idea of a conference had been mooted at the Commonwealth meeting in Lusaka. At Lancaster House, the British had been coy about elections, leading General Peter Walls, the head of the Rhodesian military and a powerful member of the Muzorewa negotiating team, to believe that Carrington had signaled "with winks and nods" that Mugabe would be excluded from the final deal, one way or another.[112] At the end of the negotiations, the British were still refusing to change key aspects of the cease-fire arrangements that the Patriotic Front claimed would bias the election process in favor of Muzorewa. This might have been a way to keep the Rhodesian whites on board, as London claimed, or it might have been a way out of holding a fair election, as the Patriotic Front and members of the Carter administration feared.

The British were playing a complicated game; to keep the conference going, they were winking at everyone. Who could trust that the wink the British gave them was the sincere, the meaningful one? Mugabe feared that the whole conference was "a British maneuver . . . in favour of Muzorewa and Smith." Suspicion was endemic to the process, not just within the walls of Lancaster House, but also in Washington and every other interested capital. In Canberra, for example, diplomats struggled to make sense of what Robin Renwick told them about his conversations with South African prime minister P.W. Botha. "Botha had begun with a long tirade about how the whole thing [Lancaster House] was a disaster and a grave mistake," Renwick recounted. "At the end of the discussion, Prime Minister Botha had said that he now understood what Britain was trying to do. He thought it very risky." Had Renwick confided a secret plan to the South Africans, or had he just winked again?[113]

These doubts about British intentions help explain Carter's promise to the Congressional Black Caucus. In these subtle negotiations, Carter's insistence that London commit to elections before he would lift sanctions bought him credibility with Mugabe, who was more skeptical about the process than Nkomo; this could help the Americans persuade Mugabe to sign the final accord. Carter was using US leverage to ensure that the British would follow through on their promise to hold free elections. Washington did want to help London, and it was delighted with the imminent success of the Lancaster House conference, but it worried about Thatcher. It feared that at the last minute—after the United States had lifted sanctions and lost its leverage—Britain might backtrack and seal a deal with Muzorewa. It wanted to lock Britain into holding elections.

The promise to the caucus, therefore, gave Carter and his staff an excuse to twist Britain's arm. When explaining the administration's policy abroad, US officials often stressed that they had to take African American opinion into account. "The Carter administration was very much subject to the Congressional Black Caucus," Robin Renwick asserted, many years later. "They talked about it a lot; it was a kind of refrain." This impression—encouraged by the Americans—did not reflect reality, but it was useful. It was a conversation ender: there was nothing the British, Rhodesians, or South Africans could say to counter it. It meant, however, that foreigners had a highly exaggerated impression of the importance of African Americans in the creation of Carter's policy toward Rhodesia.[114]

The Foreign Office prepared hard-hitting briefs for Thatcher's upcoming conversations with Carter in Washington. The first objective of the talks was to signal the importance that Britain attached to its relationship "with our most powerful ally," and the second objective was "to ensure that the United

States continues to adopt a helpful attitude" toward British policy in Rhodesia. Although the prime minister should thank the president for his support "in earlier phases of the negotiations" at Lancaster House, she should emphasize that "this is the decisive phase." Thatcher should lodge a clear protest at Carter's recalcitrance. The British governor, Lord Soames, had arrived in Rhodesia on December 12 and formally reestablished British rule over the colony. Smith's UDI was thereby defunct. "The sending of Lord Soames," Carrington explained, was "the final ultimatum: the Patriotic Front knew that they risked getting left behind." And yet Carter continued to drag his feet. "Despite strong requests by us, the Americans have not yet begun any action to lift sanctions," the briefs for Thatcher's trip noted. "This could cause the Patriotic Front to procrastinate; will cause additional difficulties for us in the Security Council; and will also cause some of our other allies to hesitate before lifting sanctions."[115]

Hoping to clear this obstacle before she arrived in Washington, Thatcher sent Carter an urgent letter on December 14. "I am sorry to have to raise Rhodesia with you when the very worrying situation in Iran is taking up so much of your time," she began, "but there is one important point on Rhodesia on which I hope we can make progress before then [her arrival on December 17]." She praised Carter for his support, which had "been a major factor in helping us to get this far," and tried to impress on him the critical status of the negotiations: "Carrington has . . . called a final session of the [Lancaster House] Conference for tomorrow. There is a fair chance that the Patriotic Front will initial the agreement then, if it is made absolutely clear to them that they will get no support for staying out." Thatcher implored the president directly: "I hope that now you can help us to bring home to the Patriotic Front the need to agree to a cease-fire and participate in the elections." She was specific: "This might be done by a statement that the United States will not continue sanctions against Rhodesia under a British governor." She reiterated: "Action on these lines could help us to clinch the final agreement." In closing, she added the velvet: "I hate troubling you at a time when you have such appalling troubles of your own. But I believe that action by you on the lines I have suggested would greatly increase the chances of a successful outcome."[116]

The pressure on Carter mounted. Vance was frustrated with him, and Vance's close friend, US ambassador to Britain Kingman Brewster, threatened to resign if Carter did not accede to Thatcher's request.[117] At Lancaster House, Carrington played his last card, closing the conference without succeeding in persuading the Patriotic Front to sign the cease-fire agreement. The Salisbury group—which had signed—packed its bags, while Carrington continued to press Nkomo and Mugabe to sign this final document. A British governor had been in charge in charge in Salisbury for two days.

Late on December 14, Carter cabled Thatcher, satisfied that she would ensure that fair elections were held in Rhodesia. He thanked Thatcher for her letter and assured her that he would announce the following day that he would lift sanctions. "I am communicating this to the Frontline leaders along with a strong plea for support to conclude the negotiations tomorrow. . . . I have also instructed our embassy to make the same point to Nkomo and Mugabe."[118] The US ambassador in Mozambique, Willard DePree, received an urgent cable from Washington telling him to "request President Machel to use his influence with Mugabe." DePree met with Machel and, he recalled,

> delivered President Carter's request . . . emphasizing that the US would work with the British to ensure free and fair elections. This is what the Zimbabweans and front line states had been fighting for. They had won. I told him [Machel] that we believed he was the one person who could persuade Mugabe to agree. Would he do it? He looked me in the eye and said, "Yes, I will do it. Tell President Carter that I will try my best." . . . The British, who were monitoring telephone calls, later told us that Machel called Robert Mugabe. Machel told him that he had this appeal from President Carter, that we had assured him that there would be free and fair elections. . . . He urged Mugabe to sign.

Vance explained, "Because we had good relations with Machel, we were able to enlist Samora Machel's support in the final hours . . . to bring Robert Mugabe to initial the ceasefire."[119]

On Sunday, December 15, Lord Carrington agreed to make the changes to the cease-fire arrangements that the Patriotic Front had been demanding. The major concession was the establishment of more places within Rhodesia where the guerrillas could gather before the vote was held. All three phases of the negotiations were thus completed: the constitution, the transition, and the cease-fire. Almost simultaneously, Jimmy Carter announced publicly that he had decided to lift US sanctions on Rhodesia, effective at midnight December 16. "At the end of the day," Robin Renwick remembered, "the administration came through, and it did lift sanctions. That was crucial to the success of the negotiations." Dick Moose announced that the administration had determined that the Lancaster House agreements were "fair, and make possible an impartial election leading to a just settlement of the Rhodesian conflict."[120]

At 10 a.m. the following day, Jimmy Carter greeted Margaret Thatcher on the White House's South Lawn. No one had high expectations for the encounter: Thatcher and Carter had little in common, and their previous meetings had been testy. Ambassador Nicholas Henderson noted, "Gloomy had been the foreboding in London and Washington on how the two heads of government would get along together. . . . [We] watched eagerly as the two came out of their corners." After pleasantries, Carter said that the American people were "deeply grateful and filled with admiration at the successful efforts that you have brought to resolving the longstanding problems in Zimbabwe-Rhodesia." Thatcher acknowledged "the grievous events in Iran" and alluded to the recent tensions between the allies by thanking Carter for his "understanding and support throughout the negotiations, and not least in the last few days."[121] This tone continued in their formal meeting. Carter told Thatcher that he was "full of admiration" for her handling of the Rhodesian problem, despite "the slight hiccough" about when Washington would lift sanctions, and Thatcher responded that she was "extremely grateful for everything that the American government had done to help over Rhodesia."[122]

At a luncheon in the British embassy, Thatcher delivered good news: there had been a final breakthrough at Lancaster House. Nkomo and Mugabe had agreed to sign the cease-fire accords. The conference had succeeded.[123]

Thatcher then met with members of the US Congress. "Rhodesia had been at the top of the agenda following the General Election," she told them. She explained her government's policy: "Some in Britain had advised the Government to recognise the outcome of those elections [the April Rhodesian elections] straightaway. Had Britain done so, however, the war would not have stopped and other nations would not have followed suit. Moreover, there were defects in the Rhodesian Constitution." She added that she appreciated "all the help" offered by the United States.[124]

At the state dinner that night, Carter warmly congratulated Thatcher "for the tremendous achievement that was announced today when the Patriotic Front initialed the agreement on which you've worked so successfully." He praised Thatcher as "a distinguished and strong and courageous leader," and he called the success of Lancaster House "a triumph." Thatcher graciously thanked the Americans for the "stalwart support they've given us unfailingly over Rhodesia. And you, Mr. President, and you, Mr. Vance, we would like to give our warmest and most heartfelt thanks, because without your support the whole process would have been incomparably more difficult, and we may never have reached success."[125]

The US Role

Hindsight might make the success of Lancaster House appear inevitable because the Rhodesian conundrum was finally "ripe" for resolution. In fact, there was nothing inevitable about it. It was touch-and-go until the last moment, and it depended on bullying, arm-twisting, and hazardous leaps of trust. And although Lord Carrington deserves the high praise he has received for his management of the conference, the success of Lancaster House rested on many factors. It would not have occurred without the war on the ground. The guerrilla struggle, begun in 1972 and strengthened every year thereafter, made it imperative to try to resolve the Rhodesian crisis through diplomacy. The diplomatic effort involved many players beside the British: Abel Muzorewa and his team, who agreed to give up power (believing they would regain it); the Patriotic Front, which conceded important points on the constitution, transition, and cease-fire; the Frontline presidents, especially Samora Machel and Kenneth Kaunda, who kept Robert Mugabe and Joseph Nkomo at the table, and Olusegun Obasanjo, who deployed Nigeria's economic clout; the Commonwealth leaders who backstopped Margaret Thatcher's commitment to new negotiations; and the Carter administration, which played a decisive role.

Thatcher was right: Jimmy Carter had been critical to the success of the Lancaster House conference. Had Carter lifted sanctions in June 1979, when the Senate had pressed him, Muzorewa's government would have staggered forward, anticipating that Thatcher would follow suit and recognition would result. There would have been no Lancaster House, because Muzorewa would have had no reason to take the huge gamble of agreeing to new elections. Representative Stephen Solarz understood this. "If Congress had lifted sanctions," he surmised on December 5, 1979, "there wouldn't have been a Lancaster House conference at all." Turning to Dick Moose, he added, "I think you [the Carter administration] saved this country from what otherwise would have been an enormous diplomatic disaster. You have helped pave the way . . . for a resolution of this conflict which has caused so much suffering. I think all of us can be proud as Americans for having helped set the stage for this agreement."[126]

Moreover, had Carter capitulated to Congress, the fragile trust that his administration had established with the Frontline States and the Patriotic Front would have been shattered. The war would have settled into the expected pattern: the United States supporting the white-dominated government (albeit led by a black prime minister) and the guerrillas relying more and more on the Soviet bloc and China for support. The war would have escalated. Carter's June 1979 decision on Case-Javits was a turning point.

It was a decision that was politically costly for Carter. William Squire, who noted that Rhodesia "can only hurt the President domestically," was right.[127] Rhodesia was a thankless issue: maintaining sanctions gave fodder to Carter's conservative critics and risked irritating moderate members of Congress, while it gained few kudos from liberals and African Americans who were much more concerned with myriad other issues. Rhodesia was low on their list of priorities.

The damage was magnified because the Carter administration failed to explain its policy persuasively. This is not surprising: it was the first time in the Cold War that the US government treated leftist guerrillas as freedom fighters with legitimate grievances. Carter and his team explained that taking the Patriotic Front seriously was the best way—the only way—to preclude Soviet and Cuban advances in the region. They asserted it again and again, but it did not stick. It went against the grain of Cold War thinking. The administration never overcame this hurdle; the charge that they were coddling terrorists and stabbing America's friends in the back trumped their more subtle message.

Perhaps some of Carter's critics in Congress understood his policy. But they were politicians: they smelled blood. Carter's counterintuitive Rhodesia policy was a soft target. It gave the Congress a toehold to challenge his foreign policy, his leadership, and his worldview. It was not a naive policy, but it could easily be made to look naive.

It could also be made to look irrelevant. Lord Carrington stole the show. His handling of the conference was a tour de force. Jeffrey Davidow, the first US diplomat stationed in Zimbabwe, spoke for most when he concluded that peace came because of—above all—the "dexterity of Carrington . . . [his] clarity of goals . . . [and his] British diplomatic heritage." Ted Kennedy, locked in a brutal fight with Carter for the Democratic nomination, announced on the floor of the Senate that the question that arose from Carrington's triumph at Lancaster House was "why it did not happen sooner. President Carter set this as one of his highest foreign policy goals. . . . [But the] 'Anglo-American Plan' . . . succeeded only in alienating everyone and influencing no one. . . . Britain has fulfilled our ambitions for us."[128]

Carrington has overshadowed analyses of the peace process not only because of his bravura performance at Lancaster House but also because the myth of Margaret Thatcher—the Iron Lady who broke the mold—has masked the continuity of the Anglo-American diplomatic effort in Rhodesia from 1976 through the signing of the Lancaster House agreement in 1979. That agreement built on the plan that Prime Minister Jim Callaghan had announced to Parliament on March 22, 1976: majority rule; free elections; no delaying tactics. It was almost identical to the Anglo-American proposals: a constitution, a transition period of direct British rule, and elections. Yet well-informed analysts routinely miss this point. As Robin Renwick noted in his explanation of Lancaster House: "It was apparent that there was no possibility of agreement on the Anglo-American proposals, and that a new basis for a settlement would have to be worked out."[129]

Renwick—together with all British diplomats who have written about the Rhodesian peace settlement—asserts that Carter's August 1977 promise to Julius Nyerere that the Zimbabwean army would be "based on the liberation army" doomed the Anglo-American proposals. "That was the fatal flaw," he declared. "It was Carter who had rendered the AAP [Anglo-American proposals] non-negotiable by accepting Nyerere's demand that the future army should be 'based on the liberation forces.'" This sets up the conclusion that Thatcher and Carrington swept in with new ideas. "The attitude of the Conservative government to the [Rhodesia] problem was very different from that of the Carter administration."[130]

As plausible and pervasive as is this interpretation, it is not accurate. First, Carter's pledge to Nyerere did not torpedo the negotiations; talks about the Anglo-American proposals were pursued with vigor for a year after that promise, and the promise itself was essential to keep the Patriotic Front on board. If anything threatened to render the proposals "non-negotiable," it was Foreign Secretary David Owen's pursuit of a separate deal with Nkomo and Callaghan's inability to persuade the British government to assume control of Rhodesia during the transition. Second, in 1979, the Anglo-American proposals were not dead; they were in abeyance until after the Rhodesian and British elections. Third, although Renwick is correct that the "attitudes" of the Carter and Thatcher governments differed, their policies were fundamentally identical. Neither recognized the Muzorewa government, and both believed it was essential to include the Patriotic Front in the settlement talks (although Thatcher came reluctantly and slowly to this conclusion). Finally, although Lancaster House did resolve the dilemmas of the transition by putting a British governor in charge and introducing a Commonwealth force, it did not offer a "new basis" for a settlement: it continued the efforts of James Callaghan, Henry Kissinger, and Jimmy Carter. It built on the success—not the failure—of the Anglo-American accords.

In her memoirs, Thatcher gave the Anglo-American proposals the back of her hand: they "had got nowhere." This is not true. They not only set the structure of the eventual settlement, but as Davidow writes, they "kept a negotiated settlement on the table." The lesson for diplomats was: "It pays to keep plugging away."[131] Carter's and Callaghan's dogged pursuit of negotiations kept an alternative to a military solution in the mix; it created an international forum that compelled the two guerrilla armies to present a united front. The Patriotic Front was created because of the demands of the 1976 Geneva Conference, and it persisted due to the pressure of the Anglo-American process. Without the Front, negotiations would have been immeasurably more complicated and probably impossible.

The pursuit of negotiations also enabled all sides to learn about each other. Carrington was able to crack the whip at Lancaster House and maintain a fast clip because his team was already familiar with their interlocutors' passions and peccadillos. Moreover, the arduous Anglo-American process had built fragile bonds of trust. When the process began in early 1977, Britain had failed too many times in Rhodesia: it had lost credibility on all sides. As David Owen admitted frankly, London needed Washington. In June 1979, after the election of Margaret Thatcher, the Foreign Office noted that "in our most important overseas venture, the formulation and negotiation of an Anglo-American Plan for Rhodesia, we needed US muscle to supplement and strengthen British experience. . . . The present position looks different." That was because, in the intervening years, the Carter administration had established some credibility with the Patriotic Front and the Frontline presidents, and this was essential to the success of Lancaster House. "One of our most important contributions throughout the LH [Lancaster House] Conference," Cyrus Vance noted in his memoirs, "was to vouch for British sincerity and impartiality with the suspicious Africans."[132]

Carter's relationship with Samora Machel—the fruit, in part, of their stormy encounter in October 1977 when the US president had listened to the Mozambican's grievances—was especially important. "Machel had a great respect for President Carter," the US ambassador in Mozambique, Willard DePree, remembered. Carter's decision on Case-Javits "persuaded Machel and Mugabe that President Carter and the US could be trusted." This was critical to the final breakthrough: the knowledge that Carter was twisting Thatcher's arm to ensure that elections would be held in Rhodesia convinced Machel to urge Mugabe to sign the accord. Mugabe was confident that he would win a fair election; he could compromise on all other issues as long as he believed that Britain would oversee a fair election. "We had got the main concession on the creation of democracy," Mugabe noted when explaining why he made concessions at Lancaster House. "There would be democratic elections in the country, and [the democratically elected government] . . . would, in due course, bring about the necessary changes." Carter's insistence on fair elections and the brittle trust Mugabe had developed in him were essential.[133]

Also essential were the changed external circumstances of Lancaster House. The war had settled into a "hurting stalemate."[134] Time was on the side of the guerrillas, but no one expected a rapid victory. In the meantime, Zambia, Mozambique, and the entire region suffered. More than 27,000 Rhodesians had been killed and an estimated 300,000 had been wounded. White flight from Rhodesia continued unabated, averaging a loss of 1,000 people per month in the final two years of war. Presidents Kaunda and Machel were straining under the human, economic, and political costs of the war: harboring guerrilla armies threatened to destabilize their own regimes. Observing sanctions on Rhodesia had cost Zambia $750 million by 1977 and was costing Mozambique $100 million every year.[135] Machel acknowledged that 1,338 Mozambicans, half of them civilians, had been killed in the Rhodesian attacks on his country.[136]

Rhodesia's ruling elite had diminishing options. In January 1979, as Ian Smith prepared the country for the April elections, he was confronted by an angry and fearful white Rhodesian woman at a town hall meeting. "Does the Prime Minister think God wants us to be ruled by thugs, murderers and terrorists?" she demanded as the audience of 700 whites applauded. An exasperated Smith retorted, "To think we can mount an operation and defeat terrorism is moonshine. . . . We simply haven't got enough men. . . . Airy-fairy talk about 'go on and win the war' . . . is absolute pie in the sky." He continued: "If I thought time was on our side, I wouldn't be doing this, but time is not on our side."[137] Smith, therefore, bet the farm: in April 1979, he handed his office to a black man.

Smith's gamble was not crazy. It was almost good enough: a majority of Tory backbenchers supported it, and so did much of the US Congress. This right-wing pressure on Thatcher and on Carter gave substance to the threat that Britain would recognize Muzorewa if the Patriotic Front walked out of Lancaster House, and this threat generated the momentum. And yet Smith lost his bet: Carter refused to lift sanctions on Rhodesia, even though Congress had all but ordered him to. The war and the hemorrhaging of whites on the "chicken run" continued. The mood of Rhodesia's whites was conveyed by a Salisbury dentist who told a journalist: "When I tell a patient to come back in six months, we look at each other and we know what we are thinking: where will we be in six months' time?"[138] Margaret Thatcher dashed the hopes of Rhodesia's beleaguered whites. She wielded her party's strong majority in Parliament and conservative credentials not to rescue Smith's internal settlement but instead to do what had been impossible for her predecessor—in December 1979, Britain, at long last, assumed direct control of Rhodesia, sending a British governor and British troops.

By December 1979, when the Lancaster House accords were signed, the question that Kaunda had posed to Vance in February 1978—"Who would bell the cat?"—finally had been answered.[139] Who had forced Smith to cede power? The answer was not flashy: Smith was not "belled" in one fell swoop by Carrington's brilliance. He was belled by the war, by the years of unrelenting Anglo-American pressure, and by Carter's refusal to lift sanctions. He was "belled" before the negotiations at Lancaster House began—that is why they could begin.

"I did not disdain the attempt to keep America with us," Carrington has written, "but to involve too many people . . . would be a mistake." He added, "We excluded all the Front Line States and the Americans, and it became an entirely British responsibility."[140] Rhodesia was indeed a British responsibility, but the American role at Lancaster House was not, as is often asserted, peripheral. Carter forced Thatcher to make concessions to the guerrillas, and he helped persuade the Patriotic Front that the process was aboveboard. As one British diplomat noted, "The job could simply not have been done without them [the Americans], and it was worth almost any irritation to secure their help." Another added, "When really serious issues arose . . . the Americans came up trumps. These were difficult political decisions for the President to take, and it is encouraging that when it really mattered he came down on our side. He deserves credit for this."[141]

Thatcher's comment to Australian prime minister Malcolm Fraser at the Lusaka Commonwealth meeting in August 1979 cut through Carrington's bluster. If the Patriotic Front balked, she said, so be it. "A much more crucial problem for her was that she was able to receive United States support."[142] Lancaster House was about achieving a settlement that the Carter administration would consider fair. This, of course, overlapped with a settlement that the negotiating parties would consider fair—but US acquiescence was the key for the British. If Carrington came up with an agreement that Carter refused to accept as fair, Britain would be in a desperate situation. It would be duty-bound to pursue the agreement and lift sanctions on Rhodesia, but it would do so alone and in support of an agreement that its most powerful patron had rejected. UN sanctions would remain in place and the war in Rhodesia would continue, with British credibility in Africa, the Commonwealth, and the UN at its nadir.

Dénouement

At midnight on December 16, 1979, when the United States finally lifted sanctions on Rhodesia, its prominent role in the saga ended. Lord Soames, who assumed control in Salisbury as the governor, had one of the most challenging tasks of all those Westerners who had plied their diplomatic skills in Rhodesia: in the midst of war, he had to hold elections. To keep the peace, he relied on a Commonwealth force of 1,319 "ceasefire monitors," largely British, but also including troops from Australia, New Zealand, Fiji, and Kenya.[143] London knew that this lightly armed force would be quickly overwhelmed if fighting broke out either during the transition or after the elections. Therefore, Britain unofficially depended on some 6,000 South African troops secretly stationed in Rhodesia—some in Rhodesian army uniforms and others flying South African helicopters—as well as 250 South African soldiers who served openly to protect the critical road and rail link at the Beit Bridge over the Limpopo River.[144] Above all, Soames relied on his formidable diplomatic skill to keep the Lancaster House process moving forward.

There were violations of the cease-fire, and there were arguments among the parties, especially about the presence of the South African soldiers and about alleged British bias against Mugabe. The Carter administration tried to soothe these waters, but in this phase its role was marginal.[145] At the time, twin crises gripped Washington: Iran continued to hold the American hostages and, on Christmas Eve, the Soviet Union invaded Afghanistan. In an interview in 2002, Carter drew attention to "the massive effort I made in Afghanistan. All this was secret. We worked primarily through the Egyptians and the Saudis, and we . . . filled . . . Afghanistan with weapons. . . . These were all weapons that the Soviets had sold to the Saudis or to Egypt. . . . It was tens of millions of dollars."[146] The Carter administration also slapped economic sanctions on the Soviet Union, withdrew SALT II from the Senate, and increased US defense spending.

When the elections were held in Rhodesia, they were overshadowed in America by the hostage crisis, the war in Afghanistan, and the presidential election campaign. Nevertheless, on March 4, 1980, after five days of voting, Zimbabwe garnered page-one attention.

The elections surprised almost everyone. First, they had not been marred by violence but had occurred in a "calm, purposeful atmosphere," as Jeffrey Davidow reported from Salisbury. Although there were sporadic reports of intimidation, virtually all observers agreed with him.[147] Second, the outcome stunned almost everyone—except the victorious Robert Mugabe, who called the result "right on the nose," the US ambassador in Mozambique noted.[148] The leader of ZANU won in a landslide. He garnered fifty-seven of the eighty black parliamentary seats and 63 percent of the popular vote. Nkomo trailed with a mere twenty seats—the same number reserved for whites, all of which went to Smith's party. Muzorewa, who had celebrated victory a mere ten months earlier, suffered a catastrophic reversal, winning only three seats.

The scale of Mugabe's victory suddenly and dramatically simplified the situation in Rhodesia: there would be no need to form a wobbly coalition government. It was, the *Guardian* noted in its leader following the election, "the clearest and the best outcome. Anything else would have been not a decision but a lack of a decision, leading to long and damaging in-fighting or worse."[149] Many had expected the war to resume after the election, but Mugabe's triumph stopped it cold.

Nonetheless, peril remained. There were fears that disgruntled white officers, backed by South Africa, would launch a coup. "The road ahead is going to be rough," an NSC aide wrote Brzezinski on March 4, 1980. Mugabe, however, had another surprise up his sleeve: in the days immediately after the election, this elusive man, who had shunned publicity while his enemies painted him as a radical Marxist and ruthless terrorist, assumed power with grace. He appointed Nkomo minister of home affairs, selected two prominent white politicians for cabinet posts, and retained General Walls as head of the armed forces. Moreover, his rhetoric soothed the rattled nerves of white Rhodesians and Westerners. He spoke of reconciliation and peace, and he vowed to pursue a nonaligned foreign policy. A white Rhodesian journalist wrote in early March, "We were all wrong about him [Mugabe]. Everyone's got egg on his face."[150]

On April 18, 40,000 invited guests—representing 104 countries—jammed into a soccer stadium in Salisbury to witness Britain's Prince Charles hand the official independence documents to the new leaders of Zimbabwe. As Mugabe arrived in a white Mercedes, the crowd cheered and danced joyfully to Bob Marley and the Wailers singing their hit song, "Zimbabwe." At midnight, the Union Jack was lowered as a solo bugler played "The Last Post," and the flag of Zimbabwe—green, yellow, black, and red—was hoisted. The crowd burst into "God Bless Africa," the anthem of the nationalists. White officers in the uniforms of Smith's army sang beside guerrillas recently emerged from the bush. The crowd fell silent as Mugabe lit an eternal flame to commemorate the 27,000 Rhodesians, black and white, who had been killed in the war. "If yesterday I fought you as an enemy, today you have become a friend," the prime minister said. "If yesterday you hated me, today you cannot avoid the love that binds you to me and me to you. . . . Is it not folly, therefore, that in these circumstances anybody should seek to revive the wounds and grievances of the past? The wrongs of the past must now stand forgiven and forgotten."[151]

Mugabe's rhetoric pleased American officials, but it was the tilt of his policies that delighted them. Elder statesman Averell Harriman, who was a member of the US delegation attending the ceremonies, sent a glowing report to President Carter. "I feel that Mugabe's strongly anti-Russian position . . . bids fair to stop the Russian advance in Southern Africa." Mugabe invited the United States to be the first country to establish diplomatic relations with his country. "We opened our embassy twelve hours after independence!" Dick Moose exclaimed. The Soviets, by contrast, were forced to wait ten months before Mugabe extended the same courtesy to them.[152]

"The successful settlement of the Rhodesian problem was important not only because it satisfied the legitimate aspirations of the Zimbabwean people," Brzezinski wrote, "but also because it foreclosed a major avenue for

Soviet and Cuban meddling in southern Africa." Mugabe's hostility toward Moscow surprised and gladdened the Carter administration. "Significantly, Mugabe has been cool toward the Soviets, who gave him little support during the guerrilla conflict," the CIA noted in April 1980. "He has stated that he looks upon the US as an 'ally rather than an opponent' because of our support for the negotiated Lancaster House settlement."[153] The journalist Xan Smiley, writing about the election of Mugabe in *Foreign Affairs* in 1980, noted that "American policy toward Africa under Carter has . . . been widely appreciated in many African and Zimbabwean circles." The Soviet Union, which had staked its bets on Nkomo and steadfastly refused to back Mugabe, found itself in the opposite position. "We are not cold toward the Soviet bloc," Mugabe explained. "They have been cold to us."[154]

Mugabe's guest list for his inauguration expressed this frisson. The high-level six-person US delegation, led by Andrew Young and Dick Moose, was treated royally. The Soviets were snubbed. They were allowed to send only a three-man delegation led by a deputy foreign minister, whom Mugabe refused to meet. No East Germans, Poles, Hungarians, or Czechs were invited, while delegations from China and Albania—the Soviet Union's archenemies—were received warmly.[155]

Mugabe's message was not lost on America's editorial writers. Mugabe "seems more favorably disposed to the United States than to the Soviet Union," the *New York Times* noted. "Mr Mugabe has gone out of his way to praise the United States for playing an 'honorable role' in the independence talks." The *Christian Science Monitor* observed that his election was "a solid setback for the Soviet Union," and even the *Atlanta Daily World*, which had excoriated Carter's failure to support Muzorewa, crowed: "The United States and Britain won over Russia. . . . We won."[156]

Conclusion
Jimmy Carter

> I think what has chiefly struck me in human beings is their lack of consistency. . . . It has amazed me that the most incongruous traits should exist in the same person and for all that yield a plausible harmony. I have often asked myself how characteristics, seemingly irreconcilable, can exist in the same person.
> —W. Somerset Maugham, *The Summing Up*

Jimmy Carter was a complex man who led the United States in a complex era. He lived humbly but was not humble. He exercised patience but was impatient. He believed in forgiveness but was unforgiving. He promised that his administration would be transparent, but he personally was the least transparent of men. He embraced the cause of human rights but exuded little human warmth. He questioned, in the wake of Vietnam, the need to contain the Soviet Union everywhere, but he did not want it to expand anywhere on his watch. He sought the acclaim of the crowd but was above all a solitary man.

These contradictions were perfectly attuned to the United States in the late 1970s, years of discord and disappointment when many Americans were grappling with the meaning of the US failure in Vietnam, the Watergate scandal, and the future of liberalism. The consensus with which Americans had fought the early Cold War had been shattered. Jimmy Carter governed in—and reflected—this era of fracture.

Carter was, as a campaign staffer noted in 1976, "a very odd duck."[1] Four years in the most public of spotlights—five years, including the campaign— did not change this assessment. "Carter was impossible to understand. I know that Mr. Vance felt that very strongly," David Newsom, who as the undersecretary for political affairs had worked closely with Cyrus Vance, declared.

Zbigniew Brzezinski described Carter as "a deeply private man." When Andrew Young was asked if he felt he really knew Carter, he admitted, "I do, and I don't."[2]

This flummoxed journalists, who sought clarity and snappy leads. At first blush, during the primary campaign, attempting to understand Jimmy Carter posed an interesting challenge, but as his campaign and then his presidency wore on, Carter's opacity became a source of frustration. How many stories could a journalist write about what made Jimmy tick?

To understand the Carter years, it is necessary to clear away several myths: that Jimmy Carter was a weak, indecisive, and irresolute man torn between the advice of Vance the dove and Brzezinski the hawk; that he was a naive idealist who belatedly "saw the light" and became a hard-nosed realist; and that he left the country in worse shape than he found it. Not one of these narratives is true.

Carter did articulate a vision: in the campaign and throughout his presidency, he promised repeatedly to align the US government's actions with its stated ideals of peace and justice. This is as clear a vision as other twentieth-century American presidents articulated, including those most often associated with one: Franklin Delano Roosevelt's determination to pull America out of the Great Depression, Lyndon Johnson's call for the Great Society, and Ronald Reagan's promise to make Americans feel strong again. Carter promised moral restoration. In the wake of Vietnam, Watergate, and the revelations about the CIA's illegal activities, this was an alluring vision.

Carter had a vision, but he lacked a clear ideology. Was he a liberal or a conservative? A realist or an idealist? Jimmy Carter was an anomaly: he had no track record in foreign affairs, he was not a typical Democrat, and he never developed strong ties to the Democratic Party. He was a fiscally conservative southern Democrat who was liberal on race, unwilling to expand Great Society programs, and ready to use calls for human rights as a cudgel to bash the Soviet Union. He did not fit easily into any category; he was not a man of the right, left, or center; he was not an internationalist or an isolationist; he was not a typical southern Democrat or northern Democrat or western Democrat.

When Carter took the time to plan his strategy toward an issue, such as the Panama Canal and the independence of Rhodesia, he conveyed his priorities and goals. But when crises arose unexpectedly, such as the war in the Horn and the Iranian Revolution, doubts about his ideology meant that there was no roadmap to help people—the American public, foreign leaders, and even the president's closest advisers—predict what choices he would make. Every decision seemed to begin with a *tabula rasa*. Therefore no one could sit back, confident of the outcome. Anxiety crept into the public's perception of his presidency like rising damp.[3]

This created corrosive suspense. For instance, would he stop the SALT negotiations with the Soviet Union if the Ethiopians and Cubans invaded Somalia? Jimmy Carter got advice from many quarters, but ultimately he would sit at his desk, read a mountain of memos, and come to his decision alone, guided by his personal belief system. The upshot was that almost every key decision was preceded by a period of suspension—like a spacecraft's reentry blackout—when Carter was cogitating.

That pause was dangerous. It created a void that inevitably was filled with information, misinformation, and speculation—not just in the media, but also at dinner tables and in the upper echelons of the US government. While the president cogitated, his aides worried. Excluded from the process, unsure of the outcome, and hounded by the hungry press, some aides leaked. There was nothing new about this. But given the opacity of Carter's decision-making process—given his lack of identifiable political ideology—the leaks became the story, the only story. And in early 1978, during the war in the Horn of Africa, a narrative emerged from this confusion: the story of the Carter administration became the story of Cy Vance versus Zbig Brzezinski.

When the National Security Council met on February 23, 1978, to determine the US response to the Cuban intervention in the Ogaden, Carter was ill-prepared to lead the discussion. Had the meeting occurred in the Ford or Nixon administrations, Henry Kissinger would have seamlessly taken control of the conversation. Nixon's and Ford's intentions were predictable because their ideology was clear; both were center-of-the-road, internationalist Republicans. Carter's aides, however, could not be confident that they knew Carter's wishes. When the president dropped the ball, no one was able to pick it up. Vance gently posed a few questions, but he did not take over. The meeting ended in disarray, with none of the attendees sure what had been decided.

The following day, Brzezinski held a press conference in which he implied that the future of SALT would depend on Soviet restraint in the Horn. Vance immediately "clarified" this statement, saying that the SALT negotiations would proceed as scheduled. Journalists seized on the contradiction. At long last, they could make sense of the Carter administration: the president was an indecisive pawn torn between the dovish advice of Vance and the hawkish counsel of Brzezinski. The battle was on, in the press, between Brzezinski and Vance. Jimmy Carter got lost in the shuffle. This undermined the public's perception of his presidency. "Carter should have fired Vance," Brzezinski opined thirty years later. "Or he should have fired me. Or I should have shut up. I didn't know how much it was hurting the presidency."[4]

The damage was galling because the narrative was false. Vance and Brzezinski did disagree at times, but their differences were typical of presidential advisers and they were rarely critical to the formulation of policy. Carter did

655

vacillate at several key moments, especially in response to the Iranian Revolution, but overall he was a decisive president. Hamilton Jordan, one of his closest aides, put it succinctly: "Anybody who . . . has watched him [Carter] operate knows that he's a mean son of a bitch. The one thing he is not is indecisive." Kissinger agreed: "One would have to go back to FDR," he told the British ambassador in Washington, "to find a President who took on himself so much of the decision-making." Carter made hard choices and stuck with them even when they were politically costly—in Panama, in China, and in Africa. Did any other modern US president so consistently and doggedly stake out such controversial terrain? His predecessors had dodged making the tough calls on Panama, Taiwan, and South Africa; they had been unwilling to risk their personal prestige on the Arab-Israeli crisis. "I can't think of anything we did that was popular," Carter noted, thinking back on his presidency. "We were skating on thin political ice, and there were people who were at my political throat." When Carter did waver, as on Iran, it was because these decisions were very difficult. He wavered because he could not determine the best course to follow in a radically new and poorly understood situation; it was not because he listened one day to Vance and the next to Brzezinski.[5]

One of the striking aspects of Carter as president is how rarely he relied on anyone's counsel. The British ambassador in Washington, Peter Jay, captured this in the annual review he sent London in January 1979: the president "walks alone. He does the unexpected. . . . He is politically insensitive. He can be diplomatically inept. But he is unmistakenly in charge. He is tough and decisive."[6] Carter studied the issues carefully, and then he relied on his judgment. That the idea of Carter being torn between Vance and Brzezinski gained currency is testament to the president's utter failure to convey to the public a sense of who he was. He was tarred with the image of hesitancy and self-doubt; in a word, he was increasingly (and to this day) seen as a "wimp." In fact, it would be more accurate to stress Carter's supreme self-confidence and even arrogance.

Carter's conception of leadership accentuated the remote and inscrutable parts of his character. He believed that if the goals he set were correct (and he always believed that they were), then all he needed to do was demand that everyone follow his example and do their best, as his mentor Admiral Hyman Rickover had demanded of him in the US Navy. "He is so righteous he makes everyone else feel guilty," Andy Young pointed out when trying to explain Carter's character. "He's not self-righteous. That's not his problem. And it's not a matter of any piety on his part . . . . He'll have a scotch and soda. . . . It's just that he is so disciplined about everything, and he is so organized, you just feel guilty when you're around him."[7] Carter was so earnest that he made everyone around him feel frivolous. The British Foreign Office agreed with Young. In November 1976, Ambassador Peter Ramsbotham sent a character study of the president-elect to London: "What I find most interesting is the unanimity of view about certain aspects of Carter's character and personality from his admirers and detractors alike—the intelligence, capacity for hard work, methodical approach to decision taking . . . . There is a toughness and a single-mindedness about him which, though perhaps necessary to achieve power, are not always endearing qualities."[8] The head of Prime Minister James Callaghan's political office summarized the reports coming into Number 10 Downing Street: Carter was "someone admired and respected rather than loved. He is a rather distant, calculating man."[9] The West German ambassador noted that the American president's press conferences were "brilliant intellectual performances but, at the same time, there was something remote and impersonal about them. This might be the real mystery and the tragedy of the man: . . . he is what the Americans call 'a loner.'" The *Guardian* may have put it best: "He performs many feats; but he never, ever catches the imagination."[10]

There was indeed a bloodlessness to Carter's leadership. His was a "passionless presidency," as James Fallows, one of Carter's speechwriters, noted in an influential article published while Carter was still in office. Carter believed passionately in many causes, but he stubbornly refused to grasp the importance of the human element in governing: an effective leader must persuade people to follow. "Jimmy Carter was a difficult man to work for," Hamilton Jordan, one of his longest-serving lieutenants, observed. "He was very demanding." Fallows noted: "Carter seemed to believe that organizations would run in practice as they did on paper; people would perform their assigned functions and seek no others; orders, once given, would be carried out."[11]

Carter not only recoiled from massaging egos, he also shunned the theater of leadership. Carter did not think he should have to engage in subterfuge to convince anyone to follow his lead.

The contrast with Margaret Thatcher is stark. Between her election as prime minister in May 1979 and the Commonwealth conference in Lusaka three months later, Thatcher let everyone believe she was leaning toward recognizing the Muzorewa government. She met with Americans, Africans, Australians, and members of her own government who tried to persuade her to pursue a different path. She played her cards close to her chest. When she finally announced her decision to engage in another round of negotiations, Zambia's Kenneth Kaunda, Tanzania's Julius Nyerere, Nigeria's Olusegun Obasanjo, Australia's Malcolm Fraser, Jimmy Carter, and a host of others swelled with pride because they all believed that they had provided the decisive argument that had persuaded the "Iron Lady" to change her mind. Thatcher had played, masterfully, this theater of politics. This was something Carter could not bring himself to do. Although the record shows that he met frequently with members of Congress and that he consulted often with the leaders of allied countries, none of them ever got the delicious—and important—sense of ownership of any of Carter's decisions. He was polite; he listened; but his decisions were his alone.

Beyond making it more difficult to lead people toward his goals, Carter's bloodless style of governing also failed to build bonds of loyalty. Like any human being, Carter valued loyalty. It was one of Brzezinski's traits he praised most highly: "Brzezinski was always intensely loyal, and I could tell Zbig how I felt and what my doubts were with as much confidence as with Rosalynn."[12] Loyalty, in Carter's book, was a characteristic of an honorable person. It was never, however, a good reason to support a policy. Unlike most politicians, Carter was almost constitutionally incapable of asking anyone to support his policies as an expression of personal loyalty to him. He believed his policies should be supported because they were right, not because they were his.

Carter, a stunningly ambitious, driven, and successful man, shunned all aspects of a cult of personality. Not only did he forgo the pomp of the office (and require his aides to do likewise), but he also abjured putting his character in the center of policy debates. This was unusual. Politicians tend to have egos that leave a mark; Carter had a very healthy ego, but he believed that what mattered were his actions, not himself. Thus, consistently, he set a policy—and he withdrew to study the next pressing issue.

This not only intensified the doubts and questions about what made Carter tick, it also meant that he squandered his power to weave the webs of loyalty—the cheering sections—that can buoy a president in hard times and burnish his reputation after he departs. Carter did not build an effective team—not because he micromanaged but because he did not see how necessary it was to bring his top aides into his decision-making process. Even when he articulated his goals clearly—to draw closer to Somalia or to bring peace to Rhodesia—he rarely explained how he would resolve the inevitable conflicts that arose among goals. Thus, he said that he would curb US arms sales abroad, but he nevertheless decided it was in the national interest to sell enormous and unprecedented packages of weapons to Israel, Iran, and Saudi Arabia—and to begin selling US arms to countries, including Somalia, that had not previously received them. There is no evidence that he ever explained this contradiction between his goals and his policies in internal discussions or to the American public. He brushed it under the carpet. The same disconnect between goals and praxis occurred in the administration's attitude toward the human rights records of the shah of Iran, Zaire's Mobutu Sese Seko, and the Chinese leadership, and toward Somalia's warmongering president, Mohamed Siad Barre. There was nothing unusual about these contradictions. They are rife in the annals of US foreign policy: goals conflict, and the calculation of national interest trumps all else. Nevertheless, during the 1976 campaign, Carter had stressed that he would "never lie," and he had been given the mantle—fairly or unfairly—of the nation's Sunday School teacher. Therefore, these contradictions struck at the core of the public's inchoate understanding of the man, and it was an error not to explain them explicitly.

Carter even eschewed planting the seeds of loyalty: unlike other presidents, he expected all his top aides to hire their staffs free from White House pressures. Thus he began his presidency with few built-in loyalists.[13] This had a double impact: not only was there a dearth of people beholden to Carter in the upper echelons of the administration, but there was also a plethora of people beholden to Vance or Brzezinski. This encouraged leaks, as members of the State Department and National Security Council increasingly went to the media to lobby for the agenda of their boss, whom they saw as Vance or Brzezinski, not the president.

Carter left a record of achievements and failures, but he did not leave a personal footprint. Every group in the fragile and improbable coalition that had carried him into the White House—African Americans, organized labor, evangelicals, liberal Democrats, Wallace Democrats, Jews, and the poor—felt neglected and disappointed four years later. When Ronald Reagan entered the office in January 1981 and claimed Carter's successes as his own, almost no one, including Carter's closest aides, tried to protect Carter's reputation.

Furthermore, Carter's vision increasingly fell from favor. Although he benefited from the complications and the doubts of the era—he would not have been elected at another time—he was also hurt by them. Electing an outsider—"Jimmy who?"—lanced the wounds of Vietnam and Watergate. Having made a powerful statement rejecting the Nixonian status quo, many Americans began to long for something more familiar as the Carter years unfolded. Vice President Walter Mondale understood the shift in the public's mood. In January 1979, the midpoint of Carter's presidency, Mondale warned: "Vietnam tugs in opposite directions—against foreign military involvements and for not being 'pushed around.' . . . We need to . . . emphasize our strengths."[14] A growing number of Americans were weary of their own doubts, and they pined for full-throated strength. They had rejected Ronald Reagan's bravado in 1976; they embraced it four years later. Carter, therefore, was to some extent a victim of his own success. The voters, having vented their frustration in 1976, were free to embrace the "feel good" politics of Reagan in 1980. Many Americans had grown to feel that Carter's vision—honesty, caution toward the use of force, modesty abroad—was inadequate. It failed to galvanize, unite, and motivate them. They wanted swagger.

Despite Carter's presence in the public eye for forty years, he has given historians surprisingly little with which to work. Most fall back on the Brzezinski-Vance story and leave Carter a shadowy figure in the background. Carter's famous saying that he "lusted in his heart" is emblematic: his lusts and passions were hidden in his heart; his memos and marginalia were almost always dry and unrevealing. This contrasts dramatically with Henry Kissinger, for example, whose passions, peeves, and foibles were obvious for all to see.

It is often asserted that part of Carter's difficulties stemmed from his mind-set as an engineer—that he saw each problem as a discrete puzzle awaiting the correct solution.[15] Jimmy Carter's five years working in engineering-related fields while he was in the US Navy were, however, anomalous. In his many memoirs and reflections on his life, he has rarely discussed this interlude. He has, however, written extensively about the profession and mindset that permeated his bones. Jimmy Carter was a farmer. Farming shaped his outlook on life. As a young boy, tilling the fields alone, he learned the rhythms and rigors of nature; as he matured, he learned when to bow to nature and when to try to tame it. This respect for the natural forces of life and death, deepened by his faith, affected his view of the international system. He assumed that there were laws and rhythms and an underlying order, and he saw his job as tilling those fields with the diligence he had applied to the red clay of south Georgia. What he failed to understand, however, was that his job—his ability to lead—would have been greatly enhanced had he also tilled the human fields, sowing bonds of trust, and commitment, and loyalty.

The Mercury of Détente

Was it possible to implement containment with less fear? Jimmy Carter tried. He was following in Nixon's and Kissinger's footsteps. Nixon's ebullient embrace of Mao Zedong and his pursuit of arms control with the Kremlin signaled that, as Carter would later say, "we are now free of that inordinate fear of communism."[16] That was détente.

All three US presidents of the 1970s were Cold Warriors: their foreign policy priority was to improve the position of the United States vis-à-vis its foremost competitor, the Soviet Union. However, unlike the presidents of the early Cold War, Nixon, Ford, and Carter did not expect the Cold War to end in the foreseeable future; they settled in for a prolonged contest. Moreover, they governed in the shadow of Vietnam (the war cast a shadow even as it continued to rage in the early 1970s) and of the Soviet Union's achievement of "strategic parity"—approximate equivalence of nuclear weapons—with the United States. These three presidents, therefore, believed that it would be smarter to fight the Soviets with a bit more cooperation and a bit less confrontation. Their ultimate goal remained the defeat of the Soviet Union, but their immediate and medium-term goal was peaceful coexistence—with a twist: the United States must remain on top. The three presidents of the 1970s sought one-upmanship for the long haul without nuclear Armageddon. That, too, was détente.

Détente clouds the 1970s like a thick fog. It dazzles scholars. And yet it is as elusive as mercury: just when it seems to adhere and make sense, poof! it shatters into tiny globules and defies definition. Détente is not all it is cracked up to be.

The "era of détente"—the 1970s—was an organic continuation of the previous decades of Cold War and containment. As early as the Eisenhower years, American officials had attempted to talk with the Soviets about areas of mutual concern; these efforts accelerated in the wake of the 1962 Cuban Missile Crisis and persisted even during the US war in Vietnam. Nixon and Kissinger were not radicals. They tweaked containment, and they called it détente. Building on the work of previous administrations, they made overtures toward China, pursued arms control talks and tried (with little success) to deploy economic incentives to contain the Soviet Union. They sought to adjust containment to changing circumstances, particularly strategic parity. They wanted to cut the US defense budget and reduce the risk of nuclear holocaust. This required a slight ratcheting-down of the fears that decades of Cold War propaganda and policy had engendered in the American people.

This evolution of the doctrine of containment alarmed some people—Republican and Democrat, American and foreign—who remained convinced that the only way to deal with the Soviet Union was to threaten it with preponderant power. Nuance and negotiations were anathema to these hardliners; profound fear, they believed, was the appropriate response to the existential Soviet threat. This conservative backlash to détente (which would coalesce into the neoconservative movement) reified Nixon's modest idea, swelling and stiffening détente into what these conservatives declared was a radical and dangerous departure in American foreign policy. But détente was no departure. Containment remained the core of US foreign policy throughout the 1970s. Nixon, Ford, and Carter were not "post–Cold War," but the opposite: they sought to fight the Cold War more effectively.

Nixon's reputation as a crusading anticommunist helped shield him from the full fury of the hardliners, but Ford did not have that luxury. During the 1976 campaign, the Republican right-wingers, led by Ford's nemesis, Ronald

Reagan, were inflamed by Kissinger's pursuit of peace in Rhodesia, which they claimed epitomized the perilous naivete of détente. Ford was under so much pressure that he purged the word "détente" from the Republican lexicon. Jimmy Carter—a political outsider and a Democrat with no foreign policy credentials—was exposed to the unmitigated outrage of the rising neoconservatives, many of whom hailed from the Northern intellectual elite, who feared the unseasoned Southerner would catapult the United States toward disaster.

Carter did bring a new perspective to the White House. He was the first post-Vietnam president, and he was determined to avoid the mistakes that had led the United States into that war. He was wary of deploying combat forces abroad. He sought to see regional crises not just as Soviet challenges to US power but also as complex phenomena with local roots and, perhaps, local solutions. He hoped to resist the urge to automatically attribute all US travails abroad to the machinations of the Kremlin; he wanted to think before he connected the dots into the long-accepted pattern of Soviet malevolence. Yet in strategic terms—détente—there was continuity between Carter's worldview and that of his predecessors. This was obscured not only by the change of party in power but also by the excitement—positive and negative—about Carter's embrace of human rights. Carter, like Nixon and Ford, often spoke of the need for US strength, but the press focused almost exclusively on his less frequent calls to respect human rights. Carter seemed oblivious that his comments about human rights were drowning out his other, often more important points. One result was that he acquired the image of being an idealist, whereas he was in fact also a hardline realist.

The notion that Jimmy Carter, peanut farmer, arrived in Washington wet behind the ears has confused the analysis of his presidency. It is satisfying to impose a narrative arc on the Carter years: in 1977, a starry-eyed Georgian arrives in Washington, pursuing naive foreign policy goals; in 1978, when the Soviets and their Cuban "proxies" intervene in Ethiopia, the president begins to discern the clear and present danger of Soviet communism; in 1979, as Soviet troops roll into Afghanistan, the scales fall from his eyes, and Jimmy Carter becomes a Cold Warrior. This story plays into well-worn assumptions about the parochialness of southerners, and it superimposes an easily understood plot line on the turbulence of the Carter years.

The problem is that it is untrue. Jimmy Carter did have a steep learning curve when he became president, but it was not from idealism to realism. He was a Cold Warrior before he came to Washington. How could it have been otherwise? He was a white southern Democrat who came of age during World War II; he was a graduate of the Naval Academy and a naval officer for six years. He saw the world through Cold War glasses.

The Resistance to Change

Carter's approach to the Cold War mobilized fierce and broad-based opposition. In part, this reaction was predictable: Americans disagreed, more sharply in the 1970s than in the previous two decades, about the immediacy of the Soviet threat. Carter (and Nixon and Ford before him) believed that the Soviet leadership had gained a stake in the status quo and therefore the threat that they posed to the United States was less immediate than it had been in the early Cold War. The Kremlin, they argued, was seizing opportunities to expand rather than methodically pursuing a master plan. A rising chorus of conservatives from both parties called this analysis of Soviet strategy dangerous naivete.

Naivete is a corrosive accusation; a president will be forgiven for being wrong or for overreacting, but not for being naive. The conservatives' bill of indictment lengthened with Carter's every move. They were apoplectic when he "gave away" the Panama Canal Zone; they were anxious when he opened talks with Havana to improve relations; they were horrified by his tepid support of Zaire's Mobutu during the first Shaba crisis; they were incredulous when he issued a joint statement with the Soviets about the Arab-Israeli struggle that mentioned the rights of the Palestinians—all during Carter's first year in office. Carter's critics were galvanized.

It was difficult for Carter and his aides to counter the charge of naivete. The president failed to persuade his growing legion of critics that his path was sensible, and the ranks of his detractors grew. His opponents organized, raised funds, and gained strength.

The assault on Carter's foreign policy was compounded by the revolt of the US Congress in the 1970s to curtail the excesses of "the imperial presidency."[17] Members of Congress, ruing their quiescence while the White House had conducted the war in Vietnam, were bent on asserting their powers and reclaiming those that they believed the executive branch had poached. In their battles with the other end of Pennsylvania Avenue, the 95th and 96th Congresses stalled Carter's nominations and gutted his energy program. They used their control of the purse to maul the executive's foreign aid proposals and scrutinize its recommendations for arms sales abroad. And when, in June 1978, Senator Jesse Helms' amendment demanding that the president lift sanctions on Rhodesia almost passed in the Senate, the battle was joined: Carter's critics in Congress seized on the issue, and for the next eighteen months they debated the wisdom of the president's policy toward Rhodesia.

In the contest between the legislature and the executive, Congress nipped incessantly at Carter's heels. The antagonism transcended party: even in 1977 and 1978, when the Democrats enjoyed a veto-proof majority in both houses,

Carter could not be confident that his proposals would pass. The composition of both the Republican and the Democratic parties, still reeling from the realignment of southern Democrats after the 1965 Voting Rights Act, was changing. Moreover, Jimmy Carter was a reluctant and lackluster persuader. The upshot of all of this was that Carter's modest attempts to rethink containment encountered ferocious criticism in both the House and the Senate.

Foreign leaders also joined in the attacks on Carter. In Paris, Bonn, Jidda, and Tokyo, the heads of government reacted swiftly and negatively to suggestions that Washington was flirting with any softening of containment. All had grown used to and dependent on America's Manichaean reflexes in the Cold War, and none relished change or complexity in the White House. Even Britain's James Callaghan, the leader of the Labour Party, and West Germany's Helmut Schmidt, a Social Democrat, pushed Carter to the right. At the secret quadripartite meetings, the British, French, and West German representatives urged the Americans to take a tougher line against the Soviet airlift of men and materiel to Ethiopia, while they surreptitiously slipped military aid to the Somalis. At summit meetings, Schmidt and France's President Valéry Giscard d'Estaing criticized Carter to his face. At the July 1978 G7 economic summit, for example, Giscard urged Carter "to demonstrate the true strength of the United States." At a NATO meeting in May 1978, West German foreign minister Hans-Dietrich Genscher announced that the "struggle between East and West has extended into Africa, and our job is to figure out how to stop it from spreading further." The allies derided the American president behind his back. "When Carter talked," Giscard wrote, "we could sense in our bones that he had arrived in Washington straight out of Georgia, without a stop or a detour." Britain's *Daily Telegraph* summed up Schmidt's assessment: "the White House is in the hands of holy idiots."[18]

The Cold War had come full circle: blowback had arrived in Washington. These foreign leaders worried about the Soviet threat that Washington had emphasized for so many decades. They rued the possible loss of the knee-jerk response. They feared nuance in the White House.

Beyond the resistance of the neoconservatives and foreign leaders, the subtle shifts in containment—especially the attempt to ease the fear of communism—made it harder for the president to rally the mass of the American people. In 1978, British ambassador Peter Jay presciently noted why Ronald Reagan's candidacy in the 1980 elections would be appealing: "The American instinct for a bold crusade, for a visible enemy and a fast horse . . . [does not] derive much fulfilment from the . . . alien and strange causes of détente, interdependence, [and] SALT."[19] In one of his early weekly reports, Brzezinski tried to warn Carter why supporting détente could hurt his image and effectiveness: "For much of the last thirty years, our foreign policy could focus simply on . . . the Soviet threat. [This] permitted Presidents to mobilize public support through an appeal to emotion." That emotion was fear. "In contrast, we now confront a much more complex world. . . . This necessarily means greater reliance on reason, but the public is not inclined to support foreign policy through reliance on cerebral processes alone." A foreign policy that was not based on fear was, Brzezinski explained, "simply and quite bluntly . . . seen as 'soft.'"[20] This was particularly true when a policy that dialed back on fear was combined with caution about the use of force. These two aspects of Carter's foreign policy made some of his critics, especially neoconservatives, fear that the inscrutable Georgian was pursuing a radical and dangerous agenda.

The Target

Those who alleged that Carter was implementing a radical foreign policy were given fodder by Andrew Young. Young's vision of the Cold War overlapped with that of Carter, Vance, and Brzezinski: all believed that the best way to fight the Cold War was to avoid a tunnel focus on the Soviet threat; all believed that it was critical for world peace and prosperity that the capitalist, democratic system triumph over the communist system. Where Young differed was that he did not consider Soviet communism to be America's greatest threat. Young did not fear communism; he had contempt for it. He was an ardent capitalist, believing that business had been an engine of change in the US South and that it could be a potent engine of global change. As a civil rights worker, he had learned to be skeptical of people wielding the anticommunist cudgel. "Down south in the 1950s, they used to accuse us of being communists," Young told a French journalist, "and they used to say that everything the civil rights movement did was inspired by the communists."[21]

Young's life, his theological training, and his work with the civil rights movement and the World Council of Churches had led him to view the fundamental problem of the world not as the communist threat but as racism. "Most colored peoples of the world are not afraid of communism," he told journalist Dan Rather. "I have no love for communism," he continued. "I could never be a communist. I could never support that system of government. But—it's never been a threat." Young framed the world differently: "Racism has always been a threat—and that has been the enemy of all of my life."[22]

This was not an idle comment. In the midst of the first Shaba crisis, when exiles based in Angola threatened the pro-American dictator of Zaire, Young counseled, "Don't get paranoid about a few communists—even a few thousand communists. Americans shouldn't be afraid of communists." He explained his reasoning: "We do almost everything so much better than they [the communists] do that the sooner the fighting stops and the trading starts, the quicker we win." He threw cold water on Washington's "panic" about the war in the Horn of Africa. He observed drily that most Americans had never heard of the Ogaden until the Soviets and Cubans had gone there. "Then all of a sudden . . . we . . . decide there is this enormous strategic significance in a thousand miles of sand. . . . That's ridiculous."[23] He put his finger on a great divide: "If one tends to see all this as a great Soviet design, and lapses back into the domino theory, then there may be some cause for concern. But we should have learned the weakness of the domino theory in Southeast Asia." Summing up, he declared: "We ought to have a rational, analytical response to the Russians and the Cubans in Africa, and not respond emotionally."[24]

Carter admitted that "Andy would make statements that caused me a lot of concern,"[25] but for two-and-a-half years—until Young met with the PLO's representative at the UN—the president stood by his man. "Andy Young . . . speaks with my full authority and my complete support," Carter told the press. "We are completely compatible in our hopes."[26] This complicated the public's understanding of Carter's worldview. Carter never publicly distinguished between his and Young's visions of the world. This mattered, because Young's views were pithy and memorable, while Carter's were stubbornly opaque. In fact, Carter did not see racism as the central threat confronting the United States; for Carter, the Soviet system remained the greatest threat. Yet he never distanced himself from Young, because he had, politically speaking, a tin ear; Jimmy Carter lacked the typical politician's instinct for creating and grooming his public persona. Moreover, Young embodied the president's commitment to human rights, and he was a strikingly effective ambassador to the developing world and at the UN. As Young noted, "I caught hell at home, but I gained credibility abroad."[27]

Young and Carter also had a fundamental bond: their shared Christian faith. They leaned into life in the same way. Faith was the bridge across their different worlds; it was the glue that tied them to each other. "He and I always related to each other as Christians," Young explained. "Undergirding and wrapping all these things up was the one thing that Jimmy Carter and I shared: we are both religiously motivated."[28]

Young brought the sensibility and the reputation of Martin Luther King Jr. and of the civil rights struggle into the Cabinet room. Carter told Young that appointing him would "help people take human rights seriously."[29] For Carter, the campaign for human rights was the US civil rights struggle writ large (albeit applied inconsistently in practice). He had lived through the transformation of his world: the "New South" was built on the courage, sacrifice, and vision of the civil rights workers. Although Carter had not aggressively sought change, the revolution in his own neighborhood had liberated, humbled, and inspired him. He expounded on this in an off-the-cuff response to a question from a housewife in Yazoo City, Mississippi, about how his southern roots had informed his interest in human rights. "In the South," the president said, "we were guilty for many years of the deprivation of human rights to a large portion of our citizens. . . . [That] is an indictment on us. I think it was with a great deal of courage that the South was able to face up to that change. I personally believe it was the best thing that ever happened to the South in my lifetime. . . . It's strengthened the South. I would not be here as President had it not been for the Civil Rights Act and for the courage of some leaders—and I don't claim to be one of them—who changed those bad aspects of the South to the present greatness of the South."[30] Carter's decision to bring one of Martin Luther King's closest aides into the heart of his administration—into the cabinet, with a direct line to the president—was his way of signaling his commitment to carry forward the transformative power of the civil rights movement.

It is tempting to see Carter's firing of Young in August 1979 as the turning point, the moment when the president lost his liberal bearings—his innocence—and turned to the right. In fact, however, Carter began as a Cold Warrior, and circumstances—the Iranian hostage crisis that began in November 1979, the Soviet invasion of Afghanistan the following month, as well as the rightward turn in the United States—caused Carter to implement harsher policies toward the Soviet Union.

Carter regretted firing Young for a more personal reason: with hindsight, he wondered if he had made a mistake. In 1979, he had accepted Cyrus Vance's allegation that Young had lied to the State Department about his meeting with the PLO representative; as time passed, he grew less sure. Young did not tell the State Department the whole truth right away, but Carter himself had encouraged him to operate in the "grey area" of diplomacy—bypassing the circuitous reporting procedures of the State Department. In 2002, reflecting on Young's report of his meeting with the PLO representative, Carter mused, "I don't know that Andy lied."[31] Moreover, nine months after Carter fired Young, Vance resigned to protest Carter's decision to launch a mission to rescue the American hostages in Iran; there is no indication that he and Carter ever spoke afterwards. Had Carter chosen to side with Young in August 1979 when Vance had delivered his ultimatum—"it's him or me"—Carter would have been spared the pain of his secretary of state resigning at the nadir of his presidency.

Carter also regretted firing Young because it narrowed his world. Carter and Young were not friends in any conventional meaning of the word, but they understood each other at a deep religious and cultural level, and they respected each other. Young stretched Carter. He represented an aspect of the president—his rebellious side—that Carter rarely allowed to emerge. "The President, you understand, can't afford to take any chances, to take any risks," Young explained. "I can."[32]

Rhodesia

Africa was where the Cold War was hottest when Jimmy Carter became president. It had been the focus of Washington's attention ever since thousands of Cubans had landed in Angola in late 1975. Throughout 1976, as Carter felled his Democratic contenders and then battled Gerald Ford, Henry Kissinger shuttled around Africa.

Kissinger's purpose was clear: to close the door to further expansion of Soviet influence in southern Africa. This was pure Cold War, pure containment. Angola had changed the equation; suddenly, the Kremlin had a ready force of "Ghurkas," as *Time* magazine pungently deemed the Cubans.[33] That the Cubans were not Moscow's proxies was irrelevant: in Washington in 1976, the Cubans were seen as tools of the Soviet Union, and that perception changed the calculus of power. All of a sudden, Moscow had a means to project force swiftly and decisively thousands of miles from home.

Rhodesia could be next. And if Rhodesia slid into the Soviet orbit, South Africa and Zaire might not be far behind. Kissinger therefore threw his immense energy into resolving the civil war in Rhodesia. This was his top priority throughout 1976. He rode roughshod over the British. He soaked up information about Africa, a continent that had previously been only the butt of his jokes. He alternately charmed and browbeat the Africans, white and black, to goad them toward a settlement. By the end of 1976, he had racked up a signal achievement along the long road to failure: he had forced the illegal white leader of Rhodesia, Ian Smith, to publicly agree to majority rule in two years.

The civil war in Rhodesia, however, was hotter than ever as Kissinger bowed out of power, and all the participants—in London, Salisbury, Pretoria, and the Frontline States—felt bruised by his manipulative tactics. Kissinger had stretched the truth to paper over differences between the parties; his handiwork began to crumble before he boarded his jet in Africa in September 1976 to return to the United States. He had focused on the whites, the men who, in his book, wielded the power: Ian Smith and South African prime minister John Vorster. He had cajoled Kenneth Kaunda of Zambia and Julius Nyerere of Tanzania, while leaving them outside any substantive negotiations; he had been snubbed by Mozambique's Samora Machel; and he had ignored "the men with the guns"—the guerrillas who were waging the war.

In his climactic meeting with Kissinger in September 1976, Ian Smith declared, as he promised to pursue majority rule in Rhodesia, that he was handing the American "his head on a platter." In fact, it was a head with many, many strings attached, as Kissinger well knew. Smith would spend the next three years tugging at those strings in one desperate attempt after another to hold onto power. This was the legacy of all Kissinger's efforts: Smith's slippery pledge, and mistrust all around. "Of all the negotiations I conducted," Kissinger admitted in his memoirs, "by far the most complex was the one over majority rule in Southern Africa."[34]

As the Carter administration took charge in Washington in January 1977, the Cold War was being fought in southern Africa above all, and US officials considered Rhodesia the most vulnerable prize for the Soviets and their Cuban surrogates. This contrasted with the rest of the world in early 1977: in Latin America, there was no expectation of an imminent communist advance; nor was there a fear of rapid communist gains in southeast Asia; the Soviets had lost influence in the Middle East; the West European communists were nettlesome but had been kept out of power. Africa was the hotbed.

Any American president in 1977 would have paid attention to Rhodesia for the same reason that Kissinger had devoted his time to it: in the calculus of the Cold War, it was the soft underbelly of Africa. There was a seamless continuity of goals in the Rhodesia policy of the Ford and Carter administrations: both wanted to end the war, thereby diminishing opportunities for the Kremlin to gain more influence in Africa.

When I asked Carter to explain the motivations of his policy toward Rhodesia, he first urged me to read the documents he had taken to Fidel Castro when he visited Havana in 2002. These transcripts of conversations between high-ranking US and Cuban officials during the Carter administration highlight one fact: Washington was very concerned that Cuba might intervene in Rhodesia. This was apparent in the conversation that Peter Tarnoff, the State Department's executive secretary, had with Fidel Castro in December 1978. Tarnoff's opening was: "Africa is central to our concerns." Brzezinski summarized the encounter for Carter. "As in the past, much of the conversation was devoted to Africa. . . . The Cubans . . . hinted that their support of liberation movements might draw them in before too long. We should have no illusions about their intentions in Africa."[35]

This had been Kissinger's nightmare, and Carter inherited it. As president elect, he told the Johannesburg *Financial Mail*. "As long as the Soviet Union is willing to sponsor aggression and unrest there [in southern Africa], the threat to the US is a serious one."[36] At the same time, during the transition, Senator Dick Clark, chair of the Africa subcommittee, sent Carter a report of the trip he had just completed in southern Africa. "Should the Cubans come in [to Rhodesia], with sophisticated Russian arms, the South Africans would have great difficulty in staying out and the consequence would be a massive and tragic racial war, the outcome of which is uncertain," Clark wrote. "American-Soviet détente would be put in jeopardy. . . . Furthermore . . . racial tension would be strained at home. It is clear that we must do whatever we can to prevent these eventualities."[37] This anxiety was repeated in reams of documents during the Carter years. Predictably, it was Brzezinski who expressed the problem in its most graphic and dramatic terms: the crisis for Carter's Rhodesia policy would come "when white nuns being raped by black guerrillas wearing red stars on their armbands start appearing on nightly television news."[38]

The particular challenge in Rhodesia was that if the Cubans did intervene on the side of the guerrillas, the United States would have two choices. It could do nothing, sitting on the sidelines while the Soviets and Cubans grabbed another territory in Africa. This option was clearly unacceptable from a strategic and political perspective. Alternately, Washington could counter the Soviets by aiding Smith's white minority government. This option was almost unthinkable for Jimmy Carter. Throughout his quest for the presidency, Carter had reiterated his goal to strengthen America by restoring the moral foundations of the United States after the decade of Vietnam and Watergate. This was the driving force behind his human rights campaign and a key component of his Cold War strategy. Fighting on behalf of white minority rule would negate everything that Carter was trying to accomplish.

Therefore, in Rhodesia, Carter faced a delicate challenge: he had to figure out how to claim the moral high ground but not end up on the same side as the Soviet Union. He was saddled with untying the knot that had been created by decades of American hypocrisy, when Washington had claimed to be the great supporter of democracy while it had in fact buttressed white minority governments in Africa. Those lies, those prevarications, those convenient compromises came home to roost during the Carter years.

What Was New?

The Cold War underlay Carter's focus on Rhodesia, but he had other reasons to take note. He was indebted to African Americans, who had overwhelmingly supported his election. As Andrew Young declared, "The hands that used to pick the cotton had now picked a president."[39] Although most black Americans, like their compatriots, were more concerned with domestic affairs than with foreign policy, black leaders tended to regard Carter's policy toward the white racist regimes in Africa as a barometer of his commitment to racial equality. This was particularly important, given Carter's roots in racist southern Georgia and his fiscal conservatism. The leaders of African American organizations would have roared had Carter followed a different policy in Rhodesia, but they gave him little credit for what he did. No one in the administration argued that Carter's Africa policy would be a crowd-pleaser or a vote-getter.

Africa was not only the main Cold War theater in 1977; it was also important in its own right. Carter and his top foreign policy aides were determined to apply lessons learned in Vietnam. They sought to look beyond narrow East/West frameworks. This was true even of Brzezinski. The difference between the Ford and Carter years, observed Willard DePree, who served as US ambassador to Mozambique during both administrations, was that for Carter, "Africa was an issue in and of itself, as opposed to a means to send signals to the Soviet Union."[40] The refrain of the Carter administration's policy toward the continent—"Africa for the Africans"—paid homage to the significance of this regional viewpoint.[41] The administration zeroed in on Nigeria, the only African member of OPEC, as the regional powerhouse. US relations with Lagos had taken a nosedive in late 1975 because of the Ford administration's collusion with South Africa in Angola. Three times, the Nigerian government had refused Kissinger permission to land in Lagos. It welcomed Young to Lagos, however, a week after he had been confirmed as the UN ambassador. Young's visit was the first step in the Carter administration's careful courtship of the country; Young had opened the door, but it was the clear shift in Washington's policy toward southern Africa that mended relations. It was not just Young's charm or his race that made the difference. As the US ambassador in Lagos wrote after Young's departure, "Big question is . . . where does the President stand."[42]

Jimmy Carter answered that question quickly. In May 1977, he authorized Vice President Mondale to call publicly for one man, one vote—that is, the end of apartheid—in South Africa.[43] Carter was already pursuing a new tack in Rhodesia that represented a sharp break with Kissinger's tactics. In the Ford administration, the Rhodesia negotiations had been a one-man show run by Henry Kissinger. He had wielded power through his driving personality, his charisma, his insistence on speed and secrecy, and his adroitness at spinning webs of almost-truths. In the Carter administration, many people—from the president to ambassadors in the field—contributed substantively to the development and implementation of policy toward Rhodesia. They relied on inclusion and transparency as they sought to build consensus. Moreover, Carter truly cooperated with the British, who were still recovering from Kissinger's whirlwind diplomacy. In contrast to the prickly relationship between Kissinger and British foreign secretary Anthony Crosland, a deep bond based on mutual respect developed between Cyrus Vance and the new foreign secretary, David Owen.

During the three years that the administration developed and executed policy toward Rhodesia, there was not one significant clash between Vance and Brzezinski. Brzezinski muttered about the administration kowtowing to the British, but he never questioned Carter's fundamental commitment to majority rule there. Nor did the NSC staff. The president made it clear that this was an issue about which he felt deeply, and he set the policy.

The White House deliberately slowed the pace in the Rhodesia negotiations. Correcting errors caused by Kissinger's frenzy to achieve results before the 1976 US presidential election, the Carter team laboriously prepared the ground in southern Africa. This meant that Carter's Rhodesia policy was no longer a secret shared only among the secretary of state's inner circle: reversing Kissinger's procedures, Vance opened up channels of communication, circulating relevant memos to all the US embassies in Africa. The Americans and British established multiple layers of diplomacy that included their ambassadors in Africa; their bureaucrats in London and Washington; the negotiating team of US ambassador Stephen Low and British diplomat Johnny Graham; Young, who sometimes worked with Graham and Low and sometimes flew solo; the higher-level team of Vance and Owen; and, finally, Carter and Prime Minister Callaghan. All of these groups worked toward the same end: stopping the war in Rhodesia.

Carter opened up the process in another, even more crucial way: he looked beyond the white leaders in Africa—Ian Smith and John Vorster—who had been Kissinger's focus. Carter included the Frontline leaders—Kaunda, Nyerere, Machel, and Obasanjo—as full partners in the negotiations, and he shoved Smith to the sidelines. This was not surprising: it was obvious that Kissinger's failure to consult fully with the black presidents had torpedoed his efforts; and at almost the moment Carter took office, Smith removed himself from the Anglo-American talks.

What was remarkable was that Carter opened up the process to the guerrillas—to the men whom many called terrorists and communists. Kissinger had met only with the leader of ZAPU, Joshua Nkomo, and had given him short shrift, never consulting or negotiating with him. Kissinger did not meet with any other guerrilla leader. He and his aides would inform Kaunda and Nyerere what had been decided and leave it to them to inform the guerrillas. When Carter was president, the guerrillas were full participants in the negotiations to resolve the war.

Race

In the late 1970s, the contradictions between US racism and Washington's claim to be the city on the hill—a claim that was central to its fight against communism—had come into stark and perilous relief in Africa. At home, the United States had made strides against institutional racism, but when Carter took office, US foreign policy was still mired in its old racial preferences in southern Africa. Kissinger had belatedly scrambled to change this with his Lusaka speech in 1976, but it was up to Carter to follow through with a sustained policy toward Africa that was no longer based on Washington's cozy relationship with white minority governments.

This shift in policy exposed the extraordinary complexity of the Cold War in the late 1970s. To preclude the Cubans and Soviets, the war in Rhodesia needed to end; to end the war, the guerrillas had to be included in the settlement; therefore, to end the war, Carter needed to talk with men deemed Marxist-Leninist terrorists. This, however, was a bridge too far for many Americans, who could not stomach the idea of top US officials seeking meetings with black Soviet-backed rebels accused of massacring innocent white civilians.

Carter's policy—treating communist-backed rebels as equal partners with moderate, pro-American politicians—was exceptional in the annals of US foreign relations and in the history of the Carter years. In all other cases, the Carter administration followed the customary US practice of refusing to talk with opposition groups that were deemed radical leftists or anti-American: it shunned the Iranian opposition until the shah was in exile; it opened no channels to the Sandinistas in Nicaragua until Anastasio Somoza was teetering; it banned contact with the PLO. Why were the Rhodesian guerrilla fighters different?

Carter himself answered the question. When I told him I wanted to understand his policy toward Rhodesia, he first suggested I read the documents that he took to Cuba—but then he added, "I felt a sense of responsibility and some degree of guilt that we had spent an entire century after the Civil War still persecuting blacks, and to me the situation in Africa was inseparable from the fact of deprivation or persecution or oppression of Black people in the South."[44] Carter drew a parallel between the civil rights struggle in the US South and the liberation war in Rhodesia. His first exposure to southern African politics was through Andrew Young's perspective, that of a black civil rights worker who was deeply imbued with the progressive Christian viewpoint. After reading the background material about Rhodesia that Young had sent him during the 1976 campaign, Carter commented, "Well, that's not much different from what we had to go through."[45] Carter retained this conceptualization of Rhodesian politics throughout his presidency. He saw the crisis in Rhodesia through the prism of the US civil rights struggle.

This mattered. It helped Carter believe that he understood the problem and could envision a solution. It convinced him that the result—majority rule—would benefit everyone. As Young noted in a 1976 interview, "He [Carter] knows very clearly the evils and dangers of racism, and he also knows that racists can change."[46] This parallel between Rhodesia and the US South, however flawed from a historian's point of view, was critical to the development of Carter's policy. In southern Africa, because of race, Carter was able, with difficulty, to step outside the conventional Cold War framework; the resonance of racism in America enabled him to see the war in Rhodesia not just as a forum of East-West conflict but also as a struggle for justice, as a nationalist struggle. It helped him remain optimistic that a solution could be found, even when the pursuit appeared futile. It enabled him to see Nkomo and Mugabe—men whom he otherwise would have labeled "terrorists"—as freedom fighters. The trope of racial justice added nuance to the trope of the Cold War. Race helped Carter frame the crisis in southern Africa outside the strict confines of the US-Soviet conflict. In two key ways—motivation and method—race mattered.

Realpolitik and race, the two aspects of Carter's commitment to resolve the Rhodesia crisis, strengthened each other. Realpolitik explained the time and high-level attention devoted to Rhodesia. "I spent more effort and worry on Rhodesia than I did on the Middle East," Carter declared in a personal interview.[47] The racial component—the search for racial justice—not only broadened the appeal of the policy through all layers of the US bureaucracy, it also personalized the issue for Carter. He believed that he understood the problem and that he knew the solution. This gave him the courage to stay the course.

The Internal Settlement

Negotiating with the guerrillas was facilitated by one unintended consequence of Kissinger's efforts: the creation of the Patriotic Front. In late 1976, as the Geneva conference was about to open, the Frontline presidents were finally able to persuade the feuding guerrillas to unite so that their delegation to the talks would be as strong as possible. This had several results. First, ZANU was forced to resolve its protracted leadership struggle, clearing the path for Mugabe to emerge. Second, the merger of ZANU and ZAPU into the Patriotic Front—however strained the union—marginalized other nationalists, foremost Bishop Abel Muzorewa and Reverend Ndabaningi Sithole.

The significance of this last development became clear a year later, on February 15, 1978, when the bishop and the reverend flanked Ian Smith as he announced that they, together with the conservative Chief Jeremiah Chirau, had hammered out an internal settlement for Rhodesia. Smith and his black colleagues were attempting to preempt an Anglo-American settlement by ushering in a government in which blacks and whites, Smith claimed, would share power. Most members of the Carter administration responded to the internal settlement with deep skepticism because it left real power in the hands of the white minority. But the British government, bone weary of Rhodesia, found Smith's solution alluring.

On the surface, Anglo-American cooperation continued unabated. The protracted Anglo-American cooperation in Rhodesia is an unusual instance of the United States pursuing an almost truly bilateral policy; the Carter administration treated the British as almost equal partners. "In the past, we had always been the junior partner," David Owen later explained, "but this time, because of our knowledge of Africa, it was as near as could be to a fifty-fifty partnership. It was a serious partnership, helped by my and Cy Vance's remarkable relationship."48 Brzezinski's complaint that Washington had ceded too much control to London fell on deaf ears. The alliance worked well and was strong. Nevertheless, Smith's internal settlement exposed a fissure in the two countries' goals in Rhodesia. A tug-of-war ensued, with Owen attempting to expand the internal settlement by persuading Smith to include Nkomo in it, while Cyrus Vance and his aides, worried that Owen's gambit would not end the war, warned the British not to exclude Mugabe. The Carter administration could have imposed its view—throughout the negotiations, it pushed London to the left—but in the summer of 1978 Vance gave Owen latitude to pursue his plan.

Owen's gambit, however, came to naught, as the Americans had predicted. By the time Owen's scheme collapsed in the disastrous encounter between Smith and Nkomo in August 1978, Carter's policy toward Rhodesia had become a political football in the United States. Smith's announcement of his internal settlement had set the stage by offering an alternative to negotiating with the "terrorists" in the Patriotic Front. Senator Jesse Helms led the charge, proposing on June 28, 1978, that Congress lift sanctions on Rhodesia to give the internal settlement a chance. Smith's proposal, Helms argued, was "reasonable, humane, . . . just to all parties . . . [and] based upon traditional Western concepts of equity and justice."49 His amendment was defeated by a mere six votes. Carter's opponents smelled blood. Congress and the president were locked in a struggle that was ostensibly for the soul of US policy toward Rhodesia but was also about domestic politics.

Rhodesia was ideal terrain for Carter's critics for several reasons. First, the Cold War. They could tap into the widespread unease about the administration's negotiations with the Patriotic Front. Jimmy Carter, they alleged, was in the thrall of Andrew Young. Surely, they argued, it made more sense—and was more American—to bolster Smith's internal settlement than to chat with terrorists. Smith's internal settlement, pro-Western and anticommunist, was the side that the United States should be supporting.

Second, the battle against the imperial presidency. If Congress could muster the votes—and the tally on the Helms Amendment indicated that it could—then it could force the administration to lift the sanctions on Smith's regime. This would pack a significant symbolic wallop, not only in Africa, by putting the weight of the United States behind the internal settlement government, but also at home, by demonstrating that Congress had the power to hijack the president's foreign policy.

Third, race. The debates gave conservative politicians an opportunity to signal their stance toward race on terrain—far away in Africa—that was much less explosive and divisive than the domestic policy debates about affirmative action, busing, and unemployment. Smith's internal settlement, they argued, was a significant step forward and should be rewarded. Rising white conservatives, riding the early swells of the Reagan tsunami, glommed onto Bishop Muzorewa like a long-lost relative. Jesse Helms' grand tour through North Carolina with Bishop Muzorewa drew a not-so-subtle distinction: Helms had no problem with reasonable blacks like Muzorewa; he objected only to unreasonable blacks like Andrew Young and terrorists. Even if the debate appeared to be about an overseas crisis, it was often about politics and values at home. Members of Congress knew this. Dennis DeConcini's staff, for example, eager to preserve the senator's centrist reputation, strongly advised him not to testify in favor of lifting the Rhodesian sanctions to the Foreign Relations Committee because "the issue . . . has been perceived . . . in racial terms, . . . [especially given] the general stripe of the persons" voting for it. Charles Maynes, assistant secretary of state for international organizations during the Carter years, understood this: "I've always thought the American interest in the racial issue in southern Africa is directly related to our own racial problem here," he mused. "I never heard it expressed by anybody, but I think that's the reality, that there is a special intensity, a special sensitivity on this questions [sic], and we're fools if we don't recognize it."[50] The domestic politics of race were an undercurrent throughout the congressional debates on Carter's policy toward Rhodesia.

Bucking Trends

Jimmy Carter understood the power of the argument that the internal settlement was a step forward and should be encouraged. In early 1978, when Smith announced his solution, Carter instructed his administration to refrain from condemning it. He gave it a chance, even though he was deeply skeptical that it would lead to true power-sharing or end the civil war. On at least one occasion, it was a close call. In April 1979, when Vance wobbled toward the internal settlement, Young put his hand on the scale. He reminded Carter, in a preacher-like tone, of the power of optimism over caution. "I contend that the American people . . . will respond to leadership," he wrote Carter. "I insist that this administration has won all foreign policy issues that it has fought to win." He cast the notion of accepting Rhodesia's internal settlement in terms that would make it abhorrent to Carter: "I'm not interested in cutting deals with Smith or South Africa," Young wrote to the president who loathed both horse-trading and apartheid.[51] On June 7, 1979, Carter announced that he had decided to reject the internal settlement. Bucking the will of the Congress and rejecting the reports of almost all the election observers that Muzorewa's victory had been free and fair, Carter declared the election invalid and refused to lift sanctions on Rhodesia.

With this decision, Jimmy Carter ventured into new territory for an American president. He rejected what appeared to be a moderate, pro-American solution in favor of a comprehensive settlement that required negotiating with "Marxist-Leninist terrorists." This was radical. Up to this point, Carter's Rhodesia policy had borne strong continuities with that pursued by Henry Kissinger in 1976. Their methods were different, but both sought majority rule, peace, and the foreclosure of opportunity for the Soviets. With his Case-Javits decision, however, Carter parted ways with the previous administration. Although it is impossible to be certain, all indications are that Gerald Ford would have recognized the election of Abel Muzorewa. Kissinger made this point clear in an interview with the *Washington Post* in the days after Carter's announcement. "The administration . . . should not develop a public position which undermines the one elected official in Rhodesia and encourages guerrilla war rather than negotiations," he declared. "That course will lead to war between the races."[52]

Carter's critics claimed that he was blinded by ideological fervor, by his naive tendency to see the war in Rhodesia through the prism of the US civil rights struggles, and by his predilection to side with the Third World underdogs. This was not, they asserted, a realistic policy. Carter himself opened the door to this attack in his speech announcing his decision not to recognize the Muzorewa government. He did not explain his motivations well. He noted the pragmatic, realpolitik logic behind his decision—to "limit the opportunity of outside powers to take advantage of the situation in southern Africa at the expense of the United States"—but this was not what his critics heard. They remembered instead the more impassioned conclusion to his announcement, when Carter declared, "It means a lot to our country to do what's right and what's decent and what's fair and what is principled." This call to principle was what commentators of the speech derided, claiming as did Senator Gordon Humphrey that there was nothing right, decent, or fair in encouraging communist-backed guerrillas, undermining the efforts of Rhodesians blacks and whites to live in harmony, and invalidating the results of a free election. Carter, his critics charged, was pursuing a perilous policy warped by idealism.[53]

The irony is that it was Carter who was the realist. It was Carter who transcended his anticommunist blinkers to see clearly that the Muzorewa government was incapable of ending the war. As Muzorewa, following in Smith's footsteps, deepened the Rhodesian army's attacks on Mozambique and Zambia, it would become more likely that Machel or Kaunda—and possibly both—would call for Cuban assistance. This, in turn, could draw in the South Africans to support Muzorewa, and the imbroglio would be underway, with the United States siding with South Africa or sitting on the sidelines. This, Carter reasoned, could be avoided only if the Patriotic Front was included as a full partner in a settlement.

Kissinger predicted that Carter's refusal to recognize the election of Muzorewa would "lead to war between the races" in southern Africa, but in fact Carter's diplomacy had the opposite effect. It created conditions that allowed the Lancaster House conference to occur, the essential precondition that brought peace to Zimbabwe. On the day the new government in Salisbury declared independence, it rushed to establish diplomatic relations with the United States, while it ignored Moscow's pleas to open an embassy for ten months.[54] In retrospect, it is clear that Robert Mugabe turned out to be, as Carter has declared, "a disaster" for Zimbabwe,[55] but his election in 1980 was a solid and remarkable Cold War victory for the United States: a potential avenue for the expansion of Soviet influence in southern Africa, one that could have inflamed race relations at home and humiliated the United States, had been blocked.

Jimmy Carter deserves credit for this. He focused sustained presidential attention on Rhodesia; had he chosen the politically easier path and lifted sanctions in June 1979, Prime Minister Margaret Thatcher would not have been able to buck the pressure from her own backbenchers to do likewise, and the Lancaster House conference would never have happened. Thirty years later, Zambia's Kenneth Kaunda and his close aide Mark Chona vividly remembered Carter's fortitude. "If President Carter had recognized the internal settlement, then Thatcher would have gone ahead . . . . So President Carter's decision was *hugely* important," Chona remarked. "If President Carter had recognized the internal settlement, it would have been a disaster because the war wouldn't have ended. It would have actually intensified, and history would have taken a very different course. . . . South Africa would have been sucked in." President Kaunda, who had been nodding in affirmation as Chona spoke, interjected, "Totally. Totally." Chona continued: "So the region as a whole would have been a real mess." Kaunda interjected again, "Totally."[56]

Carter, however, has received little credit for this achievement for three reasons. First, the resolution of the Rhodesian war was a defensive victory. Failure—allowing the Soviets and Cubans to expand their influence to Rhodesia—would have grabbed the attention of most Americans. Success—precluding Soviet expansion—was, by contrast, of no interest to the vast majority of Americans. Members of Congress debated US policy toward Rhodesia not because their constituents cared about it, but because it exposed a vulnerability in the president.

Second, the Thatcher government claimed full credit for the Lancaster House settlement. This was ungracious and inaccurate. It is a claim that has been given credence by historians and political scientists who have proclaimed that the situation in Rhodesia was not "ripe" for settlement until Thatcher appeared.[57] This discounts the contingency of negotiations and the importance of keeping the talks alive, even when they seemed pointless. Carter's team kept slugging away at the Rhodesia talks, although Smith denounced them, the Patriotic Front refused to meet, the Frontline States despaired, the British pursued their own wrongheaded policy, and the US Congress virtually ordered the president to change course. The Carter administration deepened its understanding of the participants. It built trust with the British, who had been bullied by Kissinger. It built trust with the Frontline presidents—including Mozambique's Samora Machel—who understandably were skeptical that the US government, with its habitual support of white minority rule, had had a change of heart. It even built some trust with the leaders of the Patriotic Front, who turned to Carter for reassurance during the Lancaster House negotiations. It enabled Thatcher to resist the relentless pressure of her backbenchers. These were remarkable achievements, and they made the success of Lancaster House possible.

Third, as Robert Mugabe descended into murderous thuggery, it became awkward to say anything positive about his rise to power. Nevertheless, it is only fair to judge Carter's policy on its own terms: his policy was a Cold War victory for the United States that helped give Zimbabwe a chance to establish majority rule and a democratic system. That Mugabe squandered this opportunity ought not be blamed on Carter.

The Horn

A more complete picture of Jimmy Carter emerges in the contrast between his handling of the crisis in Rhodesia and the war in the Ogaden, the only other African crisis that demanded sustained presidential attention. Unlike the insurgency in Rhodesia, the conflict between Ethiopia and Somalia caught the administration off guard. It carefully planned its moves in Rhodesia, but its response to the crisis in the Horn was ad hoc. The crisis in the Horn also involved different subsidiary players: the US Congress was barely engaged; the United States had no close partner comparable to the British in Rhodesia; and, given its location at the nexus of Africa and the Middle East, the Horn was of great interest to the Saudis, the Egyptians, and the Iranians. Moreover, race did not play a role in the US response to the crisis in the Horn.

Carter himself got the ball rolling. In April 1977, lured by the prospect of extracting Somali president Siad Barre from the Soviet orbit, he instructed Vance and Brzezinski "to move in every possible way to get Somalia to be our friend."[58] Carter had been in office for little more than two months, and he was prone to dashing off brief memos about ideas that flickered into his mind. It took him some time to appreciate that no presidential statement was received as exploratory or casual: it was, instead, policy.

Thus did Carter set the direction of US policy toward Somalia as he, Vance, and Brzezinski turned to more pressing concerns. The Somali ambassador in Washington, Abdullahi Addou, moved into the void, plying his message that Somalia was weary of the Soviets, who had pumped more than $400 million in military hardware into the country, bloating its army and constructing a naval base at Berbera, on the Gulf of Aden. Somalia, Addou insisted, wanted to be America's friend. At the same time, Ethiopia, in the throes of revolution, moved decisively into the Soviet camp. Therefore, it was tempting for Washington to imagine a square dance in the Horn of Africa: "Switch your partner, do si do!" Ethiopia would join the Soviets, while Somalia would join the Americans. In a classic zero-sum Cold War swap, the Soviets' loss would be the Americans' gain and vice versa. Wresting Somalia from the Soviet embrace would have the added benefit of pleasing Egypt's Anwar Sadat as well as the leaders of Saudi Arabia, who wielded newfound clout after the 1973 oil embargo and who were partners in the Middle East peace process.

The problem was that Siad Barre wanted arms for one reason and one reason only: to attack Ethiopia. Giving weapons to Somalia would mean arming an aggressor and also contradicting Carter's fervent campaign promise to reduce US arms sales abroad. And yet, when Carter initiated the tilt toward Somalia, neither Vance not Brzezinski—busy with other priorities and just getting to know the president—challenged him, despite clear signs that it was an unwise policy. On June 16, 1977, Carter met with Ambassador Addou. After the encounter, the Somali ambassador was overjoyed. The president of the United States, he declared, "had indicated his willingness to supply arms to Somalia."[59]

The Cold War shaped Carter's decisions in the Horn. This was logical: the Cold War permeated the region. Berbera—the large and well-equipped naval base in a strategic location near the oil routes and the Indian Ocean—was the Soviets' jewel in Africa; and America's alliance with Ethiopia had been one of its most enduring on the continent. Moreover, both regional actors—Mengistu in Ethiopia and Siad Barre in Somalia—were expertly playing the Cold War game, using the competition between the superpowers to eke out leverage for their destitute countries.

As more and more Somali troops crossed into the Ogaden in the weeks after Carter met with Addou, the attention of the principals was elsewhere. Those weeks in the summer of 1977 were characterized by a striking lack of curiosity in Washington about what the Somali troops were doing in Ethiopia and by the fog of wishful thinking. It was not until the Somali invasion of its neighbor was flagrant that Washington drew back, suspending its promise to deliver arms to Mogadiscio.

Yet the White House did not forgo its dream of befriending Somalia, even as regular Somali troops stormed through the Ogaden. The year had begun with the Soviets securely in Somalia and on the verge of pocketing Ethiopia. By late summer, the Carter administration thought it likely that the Somalis would successfully seize the Ogaden, which would mean an almost certain rupture in Somalia's relations with Moscow and—even sweeter—Mengistu's likely ouster.

America's allies in Europe and in the Middle East pressed Carter not to give up, and the administration turned to them in order to carve out indirect ways to siphon arms to Siad Barre, still hoping to buy his allegiance. At secret quadripartite meetings, Vance tried to coordinate US policy toward the Horn with his French, British, and West German counterparts. These talks did not reflect well on the alliance. The Europeans, especially the French and West Germans, sniped at the Americans' policy after the Cubans intervened, but offered no useful suggestions. Like spoiled children, they belittled what they deemed the spinelessness of the Carter administration in the face of a Soviet power grab, but they did not lift a finger to help. Unnerved by the combination of détente, the Vietnam syndrome, and Jimmy Carter, they pined for the certitude of the pre-détente days.

Washington's messy gamble paid off on November 13, 1977, when the Somalis cut all military ties with the Soviet Union, abrogated their friendship treaty with Moscow, and broke relations with Cuba.[60] A fortnight later, however, the Cubans responded: Fidel Castro, strongly supported by the Kremlin, decided to send troops to help the Ethiopians repel the Somalis. By the middle of December, there were 1,000 Cuban soldiers in Ethiopia. By late January, there were 5,000; by the end of March 1978, 12,000. In addition, approximately 1,000 Soviet military advisers landed in Addis Ababa. As the Cuban and Ethiopian troops, aided by Soviet planes, turned the tide of the war, the United States was in a box. It would look passive if it did not vehemently protest the Cuban presence, but if it complained loudly it would raise expectations that it should stop the Cubans and Soviets, or at least make them pay.

But how? The Carter administration had made the possibility of normalizing relations with Cuba contingent on its restraint in Africa, but Castro's soldiers kept pouring into Ethiopia. As Carter explained, many years later, "Castro had to make a decision between normal relations with the United States of America, which was an attractive prize, and his heartfelt obligations to struggling people in Africa."[61] Castro chose the latter. The Carter administration exerted public and private pressure on the Soviets to withdraw from Ethiopia, but the uncomfortable facts were that the Soviet actions were legal and the United States had little useful leverage. Carter fussed and fumed and called for a (far-fetched) negotiated settlement.

The situation came to a head in Washington in mid-February 1978, when the defeated Somalis were racing home with the Ethiopians and Cubans in pursuit. The question that gripped the Carter administration was: Would the Ethiopians invade Somalia? An Ethiopian/Cuban invasion of Somalia would have three unfortunate repercussions in Washington. It would alarm the Saudi royal family, who would expect a vigorous US response. It would mean that in the Cold War game, the score in the Horn would be: USSR, 2 (Ethiopia and Somalia); US, 0. And finally, unless Washington could come up with a reply, it would look weak before the entire world.

This is when Brzezinski broke ranks, urging his fellow top officials on February 23 to approve the deployment of a carrier group to the region and to encourage the Saudis and the Iranians to send troops to defend Somalia. No one agreed with him—not the secretaries of state or defense, the director of the CIA, the head of the Joint Chiefs of Staff or, most important, the president of the United States. In his memoirs, Brzezinski penned a compelling first draft of this episode. All his peers, and by implication the president, had been "badly bitten by the Vietnam bug," he fumed.[62] Carter's failure to heed his advice and respond assertively to Soviet aggression in the Horn was, he explained, the president's critical error. Brzezinski drew a straight line from the Soviets' success in Ethiopia to their invasion of Afghanistan in December 1979 and, from there, to the collapse of the SALT II negotiations. "SALT," Brzezinski proclaimed, "lies buried in the sands of the Ogaden."[63]

It has a lovely ring to it, that sentence. It is, however, wrong.

First, the principals rejected Brzezinski's suggestions not because they were suffering from the "Vietnam bug" but because Brzezinski's proposals were, in Donald McHenry's words, "really silly." Brzezinski could not seriously imagine that Saudi and Iranian troops could counter crack Cubans troops backed by the Soviets; Jidda and Tehran would not send their troops to this battle. Defense Secretary Harold Brown dismissed the idea so categorically that not even Brzezinski mentioned it again, omitting it entirely from his memoirs. And what would the naval group be doing, loitering offshore? What did Brzezinski propose the US troops on the aircraft carrier do if the Ethiopians and Cubans called the Americans' bluff and stormed across the Somali border? All of Carter's top officials, and Carter himself, wanted to respond to the Soviets in Ethiopia—but no one, including Brzezinski, proposed a viable response. That is why, when Brzezinski asked Vance if he honestly meant to say that the United States "should do nothing in the event Ethiopia crossed the frontier [into Somalia]," Vance replied, "Yes."[64] Vance was the realist.

Second, the war in the Horn was a pivotal moment for the Carter administration in only one respect: although Vance and Brzezinski continued to cooperate well on most matters—as evidenced by their harmony on policy toward Rhodesia—after the crisis in the Horn, the battle of the two advisers for the ear of Jimmy Carter became the dominant narrative of journalists' explanations of the Carter administration. Carter, whose defiance of categorization had frustrated the media for two years, was shunted to the background while journalists had a field day documenting the bureaucratic wars churning around him.

In the two ways that Brzezinski asserts that the Horn was a critical moment—the education of Carter and the deterioration of détente—the record does not support him. The first, which places Brzezinski in the role of professor to the prince, falls back on the idea that Jimmy Carter needed to be trained in the cruel ways of the world. In fact, Carter's policy toward the Horn indicates the opposite: it was cynical from the start. There was nothing starry-eyed or moral about it. Siad Barre wanted arms to invade Ethiopia, and Carter wanted to supply them in order to stick it to the Soviets and to curry the favor of the moderate Arabs. This was Carter's policy, and he initiated it just ten weeks into his presidency. It led to a self-inflicted and avoidable wound. Carter admitted his mistake in 2002: "Morally or theoretically, we were on the wrong side, and we were defending Siad Barre in Somalia who had invaded Ethiopia."[65]

Likewise, Brzezinski's claim that the war in the Ogaden killed SALT is inaccurate. The Senate was not exercised about Soviet behavior in the Horn. There were stray comments about it on the floor, but the war was over before the Senate weighed in. The second Shaba crisis, which followed on the heels of the Horn, got the dander up of many more senators. The debates over the Panama Canal treaties and Rhodesian sanctions prepped the rising neoconservatives for the fierce debate over SALT II. Yet, on June 18, 1979, when Carter and Brezhnev signed the agreement, the administration was still hopeful that it would be ratified by the Senate. That autumn, however, ratification was dealt an "almost fatal" blow, as Brzezinski himself wrote in his memoirs, by the furor over the pseudo-crisis caused by the Soviet combat brigade in Cuba.[66] It is inaccurate to attribute the Senate's failure to ratify SALT II to the events in the Horn.

Where Brzezinski makes some sense is in his assertion that the lack of a US response to the Horn emboldened the Soviets. But the key point is that the alternatives he proposed—the aircraft carrier, plus Saudi and Iranian troops— were not viable. The United States had no effective response to Soviet actions in the Horn, not because of Carter's ineptitude or inexperience but because of reality. The Soviets had achieved strategic parity, the Americans had hurt themselves in Vietnam and in Angola, and the Cubans were challenging the Kremlin to be bolder and were providing the troops to make it possible.

The Soviet Union—the purported victor in the Cold War stakes in the Horn—ended up losing more than the United States. The Soviets had hoped to add Ethiopia to their stable while continuing to maintain their alliance with Somalia, but Siad Barre tossed them out and evicted them from Berbera, their preeminent base in Africa. They got no comparable base from Mengistu and they were saddled with Ethiopia, a country that had ten times more desperately needy people than Somalia and was wracked by revolution and revolt. By 1980, the Americans, considered the losers in the crisis, were moving their own troops and materiel into Berbera.

The debacle in the Horn exposed the inadequacy of the simple bipolar worldview that underpinned the conception of détente. It presaged the cracks in the zero-sum calculus of the Cold War that would widen a year later with the Iranian Revolution, which was a loss for both Washington and Moscow. It exemplified the watchwords of the late 1970s: complexity and constraint.

Together, the study of Carter's handling of the two major African crises— Rhodesia and the Horn—elucidates his priorities, strengths, and weaknesses. Both crises reveal the centrality of the Cold War in Carter's worldview, and counter the assumption that he assumed office as an unsophisticated if well-intentioned dreamer and departed an unsentimental realist. The Horn underlines this. It was a stripped-down crisis, not befogged by issues of race, human rights, and congressional wrangling. Carter's policy toward it was a conventional Cold War power play, tempered by the constraints of the post-Vietnam environment, until the last moment, in February 1978, when he refrained from escalating. (It is true that there was no effective way to escalate, but that fact might not have stayed all presidents' hands.) Likewise, Carter's interest in

Rhodesia stemmed from the same realpolitik roots that had driven Kissinger to devote so much time to it.

Carter's Rhodesia policy was bolstered by his belief that the struggle in southern Africa bore parallels to the civil rights movement in his native South. He anticipated the crisis in Rhodesia, and he developed a clear viewpoint toward it. His rhetoric and his goals aligned, and this gave him the fortitude to pursue a controversial policy until it bore fruit. The war in the Horn, by contrast, caught the administration off guard. Carter never explained how his immediate goals in the Horn—besting the Kremlin and pleasing the conservative Arabs—aligned with his overarching promise to restore American honor and reduce arms sales. This muddied the message he sought to convey to the American people, as well as to his inner circle, about his values and priorities. This helps to explain why he remained an obscure figure, relegated to the shadows of the alleged war between the flamboyant Brzezinski and taciturn Vance. However, the reality is that Jimmy Carter ran his ship; he was in charge; he set the policy.

Not in the Stars

It is easy to criticize Jimmy Carter. He was a true outsider, and in many ways he was not prepared for the job. He made mistakes. He tried to do too much too fast. He did not convey a clear sense of his priorities. He and his top aides were overwhelmed implementing the ambitious policies they planned—the SALT II negotiations and Panama Canal treaties, normalization of relations with the People's Republic of China, and peace efforts in the Middle East and in southern Africa—which meant that unexpected crises such as the war in the Horn, the Iranian Revolution, and the turmoil in Afghanistan were ignored for too long. Moreover, with so much legislation crowding Congress's agenda, it was inevitable that some of the president's initiatives would fail. This gave his critics fodder. Carter himself reflected on this in an interview during Reagan's first term. Almost wistfully, he contrasted his cluttered agenda in 1977 with what "Reagan did, I think wisely, in 1981 with a major premise and deliberately excluding other conflicting or confusing issues. It . . . gave the image . . . of strong leadership and an ultimate achievement. We didn't do that."[67]

By temperament, Carter was aloof, and he failed to build the personal relationships that grease effective leadership. He was an earnest but uninspiring speaker, and he often did not predict how his words would be interpreted. Thus, for example, he was unprepared for the derision that greeted his 1977 commencement address at Notre Dame, in which he announced that "we are now free of that inordinate fear of communism which once led us to embrace

685

any dictator who joined us in that fear."[68] He was not saying anything new; presidents had tried to ratchet down Americans' "inordinate fear of communism" ever since the 1962 Cuban Missile Crisis. Nevertheless, this phrase became emblematic of Carter's alleged weakness, naivete, and ineptitude. "When we talk about defense," Ronald Reagan told his audience in 1983, "I think we should remind people what things were like back in 1980. . . . One weapons program after another was being eliminated or delayed. America was falling behind. . . . But what we heard from our leadership was lectures on our inordinate fear of communism."[69] Three years later, during the run-up to the 1986 midterm elections, Reagan was still hammering Carter: "What they [the voters] do this November will decide whether the days of . . . national malaise and international humiliation, the days of 'Blame America First' and 'inordinate fear of communism,' will all come roaring back at us once again."[70]

Carter was unlucky. The late 1970s would have been challenging years for any US president: the economy was reeling from the 1973 oil shocks; the nation was fractured by Vietnam and exhausted by Watergate; and several foreign crises erupted—such as the Iranian Revolution—that, to the extent the United States was the cause, were more attributable to Carter's predecessors than to Carter himself. This was not, however, how Carter's critics saw it. "Look at what has happened since 1975," Kissinger told the *Economist* in February 1979. "In the space of a little more than four years: we have had Cuban troops in Angola, Cuban troops in Ethiopia, two invasions of Zaire, a communist coup in Afghanistan, a Communist coup in South Yemen, and the occupation of Cambodia by Vietnam, all achieved by Soviet arms . . . so that Cuban pilots and aircraft are operating all around Africa—also presumably against us. . . . To my mind, [this signifies] . . . American geopolitical decline."[71]

Memories of the Carter presidency have been shaped by factors that militate against a positive assessment. First, Carter's failure to win reelection colors the judgment of his presidency. Second, the spin of the Reagan team, in full force in 1980, was sustained for the subsequent eight years and beyond. In 2006—almost thirty years after Carter's Notre Dame speech—President George W. Bush proclaimed, "At the height of the Cold War, a Democrat President told the country that America had gotten over, quote, 'inordinate fear of communism.' . . . Fortunately, in the 1980s, America had a Republican President who saw things differently."[72] The image of an inept Carter serves as a necessary foil to the dominant narrative of Ronald Reagan as the nation's rescuer. "Reagan sucked all Carter's successes up," Andrew Young commented.[73] Third, memories of feelings trump recollections of facts. Americans who lived through the Carter years tend to remember their feelings of impotence in gas lines and rage at the Iranian hostage crisis much more vividly than they can recollect what Carter actually did.

Confronting Reality

The striking feature of this widespread perception of American weakness at the end of the Carter years is how wrong it was. The United States was winning the Cold War. At the end of the Carter presidency, the United States was in a stronger position vis-à-vis the Soviet Union than it had been when Carter entered the White House.

There had been glaring defeats, especially in Iran, but there were huge gains in Africa, China, the Middle East, and Eastern Europe. And even in the areas normally considered Cold War losses for the United States during the Carter presidency, such as the Horn, the impact was not as damaging to the United States or as beneficial to the Soviet Union as most Americans believed.

In Iran, the Carter administration was slow to grasp the gravity of the shah's plight and it fumbled its response. On January 16, 1979, the shah fled into exile—the most significant loss of an ally in US history. The shock was later compounded by the humiliation of the hostage crisis. The Iranian Revolution, however, was also a loss for the Soviet Union: the rise of an Islamist state on its border threatened its security in much more immediate ways than it imperiled the United States. A world that had heretofore been defined in Manichaean terms suddenly and unexpectedly had a third way, an Islamist way. Washington, however, reeling from its own losses, failed to understand this.

Likewise, the Soviet invasion of Afghanistan, which many Americans considered proof of their president's incompetence, was an act of desperate overreach for the Kremlin. The Politburo meetings show that the Soviets sent troops to Afghanistan in a frantic attempt to shore up a shaky ally on their border. They were propelled by weakness, not adventurism. With hindsight, the invasion was a catastrophic mistake for the Soviets, but at the time it outraged Jimmy Carter. In a cold frenzy, he pulled out all the stops. He dramatically increased aid to the mujahideen and to Pakistan. "All this was secret," Carter later noted with pride. "We . . . filled Afghanistan with . . . weapons that the Soviets had sold. . . . It was tens of millions of dollars."[74] This was not evidence of a sudden awakening on Carter's part: his view of the Soviets had always been hardline. His courting of Soviet dissidents had signaled this early in his presidency; his desire to befriend Somalia and to settle the Rhodesian war continued the trend, as did his policy toward China. What had changed were the circumstances. By December 1979, with the American hostages languishing in Iran and Ted Kennedy harassing him for the Democratic nomination, Carter had had enough. As Mondale explained, "Carter had been worn down by all these constant challenges and political bruises. He needed to show strength."[75]

Nevertheless, the US gains in the Carter years struck at the heart of the Soviet empire. Regarding China, Nixon got all the kudos, but it was Carter—not

Nixon or Ford—who had the moxie to take the politically costly step of abrogating the Taiwan Relations Act, without which US normalization of relations with Beijing could not have been achieved. This not only opened economic opportunities for the United States; it also threatened the Soviet Union with the prospect of a two-front war. Carter gloated about this many years later: "Normalizing relations with China drove the Soviets up the wall," he said with a grin.[76] In the Middle East, Carter staked his personal prestige, and that of the United States, on his ability to hammer out a peace accord between Egypt's Anwar Sadat and Israel's Menachem Begin. Carter did not achieve the comprehensive peace he sought, and he received unending venom from friends of Israel for his purportedly strong-arm tactics, but the Camp David Accords served US (and Israeli) interests by precluding a major Arab-Israeli war, by anchoring Egypt as a US client, and by marginalizing Soviet power in the region. Throughout the developing world, America's standing was improved by Carter's negotiation of the Panama Canal treaties, his ardent support of majority rule in Rhodesia, and his championing of Andrew Young. And in Eastern Europe, the heart of the Soviet empire, the Carter administration quietly encouraged dissent by espousing human rights, bolstering Radio Free Europe, and lauding prominent Soviet and Eastern European dissidents.[77] The peril to Soviet authority was most acute in Poland, where the message of Pope John Paul II had strengthened the opposition. For the Kremlin, the unrest in Poland was a disaster, a slow and inexorable sinkhole. On August 14, 1980, Lech Wałęsa, a man who took seriously the idea that he and his fellow workers had human rights, began to lead a strike that cascaded into a wave of unrest that paralyzed the country. The strikers succeeded in forcing the government to recognize independent unions with the right to strike—a first for a state in the Soviet orbit—and to promise to allow freedom of expression. This challenged the very foundation of Soviet authority.

Thus, while the Carter administration was consumed in those waning months with the hostages in Iran and the battle against Reagan, the Kremlin leadership was facing an impending catastrophe: losing control of Poland, the linchpin of the Warsaw Pact. Washington failed to appreciate the formidable power of the doctrine—human rights—that Carter himself had proclaimed with such passion a mere three years earlier, and it failed to grasp the impotence of the Kremlin. It was the Soviets, not the Americans, who could not defend themselves.

In the balance sheet of the Cold War, Carter's policies—and Soviet incompetence—led the United States to the winning side of the ledger. Washington won the significant battles in Rhodesia, China, the Middle East, and Eastern Europe, while Moscow won in Ethiopia and Nicaragua. Both superpowers lost in Iran. Even 1980, that *annus horribilis* when the Carter administration seemed unable to do anything right, was a good year for the United States in Cold War terms. The Soviets faced two of their worst nightmares: in Afghanistan, their army was bogged down by mujahideen supported by the United States and China working together; and in Eastern Europe, the Polish government had capitulated to Solidarity. But Americans, humiliated by Iranian "students" and alarmed by the Soviet troops marching into Afghanistan, were not able to penetrate the fog of war: they felt that their hapless government was being outmaneuvered, time and time again.

Although Carter wanted US foreign policy to be more sensitive to regional issues than it had been in the past, and he wanted to wring some of the fear out of the conduct of foreign policy, he was, from the beginning of his presidency to its end, a Cold Warrior. But he governed in the shadows of the war in Vietnam. It was obvious that the US defeat in that war made Americans wary of projecting their military power; what was less apparent was that it also caused Americans to exaggerate their weakness. The attempt of the Carter administration to craft a foreign policy that added nuance to the Cold War foundered because Soviet advances anywhere, no matter how pyrrhic (as in Ethiopia), could not be dismissed: they stung like another humiliation of America. That sense of vulnerability, compounded by stagflation; setbacks in the Horn of Africa, Iran, Afghanistan, and Nicaragua; and day after day of news coverage of "America held hostage," created an ineluctable narrative of American impotence. Given the belief that the Cold War was a zero-sum game, this intensely painful and unfamiliar sense of weakness similarly led Americans to exaggerate Soviet strength: if the United States was weak, then the Soviet Union must be strong. This conviction, plus the bewildering complexity of international affairs in the late 1970s, caused even well-informed and wise commentators to underestimate the perils the Soviet Union faced.

It also led Americans to overlook Carter's accomplishments. Jimmy Carter's foreign policy record is impressive: the Camp David Accords, the Panama Canal treaties, normalization with China, and majority rule in Zimbabwe, plus the institutionalization of human rights as a pillar of US foreign policy, and caution in the use of force. David Newsom, who was a seasoned diplomat as well as an academic, chose his words carefully. In 2001, he looked back on the Carter years: "If you put Jimmy Carter up against any recent administration in terms, first, of specific accomplishments that changed the course of events, it stands very high. Panama and China and Zimbabwe were major accomplishments in executive and legislative terms. . . . I don't think there's another president with comparable successes."[78]

Abbreviations in Notes

AAA	African Activist Archive
AAPD	*Akten zur auswärtigen Politik der Bundesrepublik Deutschland*
ACR	*Africa Contemporary Record*
ADR	Accredited Diplomatic Representative (Rhodesia and South Africa, which did not have formal diplomatic relations, exchanged ADRs in lieu of ambassadors.)
Aluka	Digital library of scholarly resources from and about Africa; summary at http://www.aluka.org; full content available by subscription
ANS	Leroy T. Walker Africa News Service Archive, Special Collections Library, Duke University, Durham, North Carolina, USA
APP	American Presidency Project, edited by John T. Woolley and Gerhard Peters, University of California, Santa Barbara, California, USA, http://www.presidency.ucsb.edu
BDOHP	British Diplomatic Oral History Programme, Churchill Archives Centre, Cambridge University
Berlin	Politisches Archiv des Auswärtigen Amts, Berlin
CAB	Cabinet Office (National Archives, UK)
Canada	Library and Archives Canada, Ottawa, Canada
CBC	Congressional Black Caucus
CD	Congressional Document (see list in bibliography)
CHOGM	Commonwealth Heads of Government Meeting
Christopher/	followed by box number. Records of Deputy Secretary Warren Christopher, RG 59, National Archives, College Park, Maryland, USA
Church Papers	Papers of Frank Church, Albertsons Library, Boise State University, Boise, Idaho, USA
CIA	Central Intelligence Agency (USA)

CIA-rr	CIA Freedom of Information Act Electronic Reading Room, http://www.foia.cia.gov/
CIO	Central Intelligence Organisation (Rhodesia)
CL	Jimmy Carter Presidential Library, Atlanta, Georgia, USA
CPP	Carter Presidential Project, Miller Center, University of Virginia
CR	*Congressional Record*
CREST	CIA Records Search Tool, National Archives, College Park, Maryland, USA
CSM	*Christian Science Monitor*
CT	*Chicago Tribune*
CWIHP	Cold War International History Project
DCI	Director of Central Intelligence
DDRS	Declassified Documents Retrieval System, by subscription
DFA, SA	Archives of the Department of Foreign Affairs, Pretoria, South Africa
DGFL	Digital Gerald R. Ford Presidential Library, http://www.fordlibrarymuseum.gov
DMN	*Dallas Morning News*
DNSA	Digital National Security Archive, by subscription
DOS	Department of State, United States
Easum Papers	Donald Easum generously gave me papers he had preserved
edit	editorial
ER	Evening Report (During the Carter years, Vance or the acting secretary of state wrote Evening Reports, but did not always label them as such; therefore, I do not use this label for their reports.)
FBIS	CIA, Foreign Broadcast Information Service *Daily Reports*
FCO	Foreign and Commonwealth Office, United Kingdom
FD	Frontline Diplomacy, The Foreign Affairs Oral History Collection of the Association for Diplomatic Studies and Training, Library of Congress, Washington, D.C., http://memory.loc.gov/ammem/collections/diplomacy/
FOIA	Freedom of Information Act (declassified for this study)
FOIA-mf	Freedom of Information Act document collection (microfiche). (Until 1980, the Carrollton Press Retrospective Collection; from 1981 to 1996, produced by

	Primary Source Media. Some but not all of these documents are available on DDRS.)
FRUS	*Foreign Relations of the United States*
GFL	Gerald R. Ford Presidential Library, Ann Arbor, Michigan, USA
Gleijeses Papers	Piero Gleijeses shared documents he gathered from the closed Cuban archives.
GPO	US Government Printing Office
HAKto	Message from Kissinger to . . .
Hamrick Papers	Sam Hamrick generously gave me papers he had preserved.
Harriman Papers	Averell Harriman Papers, Library of Congress, Washington, D.C., USA
HC	High Commissioner
HK	Henry Kissinger
INR	Bureau of Intelligence and Research, US State Department
Koblenz	Bundesarchiv, Koblenz
KTT	Kissinger Telephone Transcripts, available by subscription to Digital National Security Archive; and at the State Department Electronic Reading Room, http://www.state.gov/
Lake/	followed by box number. Records of Anthony Lake, RG 59, National Archives, College Park, Maryland, USA
LAT	*Los Angeles Times*
LNA	Lexis Nexis Academic (database)
LOC	Library of Congress, Washington, D.C., USA
Lord/	followed by box number. Director's Files of Winston Lord, RG 59, National Archives, College Park, Maryland, USA
Memcon	Memorandum of conversation
MINFAR	Ministerio de las Fuerzas Armadas Revolucionarias, Cuba
MisNY	United Kingdom Mission to the United Nations, New York
Mog	Mogadiscio, Somalia
NA	National Archives (US), College Park, Maryland, USA
NA-AAD	National Archives, Access to Archival Databases, Central Foreign Policy Files, RG 59, 1976 Electronic Telegrams and 1977 Electronic Telegrams

NAACP	Papers of the National Association for the Advancement of Colored People, Library of Congress, Washington, D.C., USA
NA-AUS	National Archives of Australia, www.naa.gov.au
NA-UK	National Archives of the United Kingdom, Kew, UK (formerly the Public Records Office)
n.d.	not dated. Estimated dates given in hard brackets where possible.
NIE	National Intelligence Estimate, CIA
NLC-	followed by a string of numbers. Remote Archive Capture documents at the Jimmy Carter Library, Atlanta, Georgia, USA
NPT	Nuclear Non-Proliferation Treaty
NSA	National Security Archive, George Washington University, Washington, D.C., USA
NSA-online	National Security Archive online, www.gwu.edu/~nsarchiv
NSC	National Security Council
NYT	*New York Times*
PMAC	Provisional Military Administrative Council, Ethiopia
PRC	Policy Review Committee, USA
PREM	Prime Minister's Office (National Archives, UK)
PRM	Presidential Review Memorandum
PS	Private Secretary (UK)
PUS	Permanent Under Secretary
RAC	Remote Archives Capture
RG	Record Group
RL	Ronald Reagan Presidential Library, Simi Valley, California, USA
RSA	Republic of South Africa
SAPMO	Stiftung Archiv der Parteien und Massenorganisationen der DDR im Bundesarchiv, Berlin, Germany
SCC	Special Coordinating Committee, USA
SCPC	Papers of John C. West, South Carolina Political Collections
SecTo	Message from Secretary of State to . . .
SH Chron	"Sam Hamrick Chronology." Included in Hamrick Papers was a detailed chronology that Hamrick compiled about the Horn, with quotations from key documents. I was able to verify more than 60 percent of

	these quotations and therefore was comfortable relying on this document for sources that have not yet been declassified.
Smith Papers	Ian Smith Papers, Rhodes University, Grahamstown, South Africa
Telcon	Telephone Conversation
Thatcher Papers	Margaret Thatcher Foundation Archive, http://www.margaretthatcher.org/
toHAK	Message from . . . to Kissinger
ToSec	Message from . . . to Secretary of State
UNIP	United National Independence Party, Zambia
UNSC	United Nations Security Council
USUN	United States Mission to the United Nations
VNA	Vanderbilt Television News Archive, summary available at http://tvnews.vanderbilt.edu/; full archive available by subscription
WHCF	White House Central File
Wits	University of Witwatersrand, William Cullen Library, South African History Archive, Johannesburg, South Africa
WP	*Washington Post*
WOA	Washington Office on Africa Papers, Yale University, New Haven, Connecticut, USA
WR	Weekly Report
WS	*Washington Star*
WSJ	*Wall Street Journal*
ZB	Zbigniew Brzezinski
ZUPO	Zimbabwe United People's Organization

Notes

Introduction

1. Author's interview with Carter.

2. Ibid.

3. Author's interview with Lake.

4. Kennan, "Sources of Soviet Conduct," 572.

5. Nixon, Third Annual Report to the Congress, 9 Feb 1972, APP.

6. Wallace, quoted in *Times* (London), 14 Oct 1975, 1.

7. Memcon (Harriman, Arbatov), 17 Sep 1976, 596/6, Harriman Papers.

8. Drew, *American Journal*, 48.

9. Carter used this phrase in an early campaign ad (*LAT*, 16 Feb 1976, B1) and repeated it often on the stump.

10. Schlesinger, *Thousand Days*, 872.

11. See Gleijeses, *Conflicting Missions*.

12. Bill Drummond, "Young Pushes for Black Lobby on Africa: Black America's Stake in Rhodesia," *Pacific News Service*, 19 Jun 1979, US Foreign Relations: Rhodesia/253, ANS.

13. In 1977, 49 of the 147 UN member countries were African. Djibouti, which joined in September 1977, brought the total to fifty. This was the largest geographical voting bloc in the UN. It did not, however, always vote as one. See, for example, Herzog, "UN at Work."

14. Author's interview with Carter. Carter also said this at a news conference during "The Carter Presidency: Policy Choices in the Post New Deal Era," 20 Feb 1997, The Jimmy Carter Presidential Library and Museum, Atlanta, GA.

15. The negotiation of the SALT II accord was pursued with vigor and a great deal of harmony within the administration, but it ran aground in Congress; the normalization of relations with China was pursued with vigor and apparent harmony, but behind the scenes it deepened the animus between Vance and Brzezinski.

16. *Time*, 18 Apr 1977, 18.

17. Trade Sanctions against Rhodesia, 7 Jun 1979, APP.

18. Inaugural Address, 20 Jan 1977, APP. For a more nuanced description by Carter of his human rights policy, see Address at Notre Dame, 22 May 1977, APP. See also Clymer, "Cambodia"; Stuckey, *Jimmy Carter*; Soares, "Strategy"; Dumbrell, *Carter*, 150–78; Strong, *Working*, 71–97; and Kaufman, "Bureau."

19. Kissinger, *Renewal*, 972.

20. Telcon (HK, Scranton), 14 Oct 1976, KTT.

21. For Carter's childhood, see Carter, *Hour Before Daylight*; and Carter, *Remarkable Mother*. For Carter's views on race, see Borstelmann, *Cold War*, 242–59; and Dumbrell, *Carter Presidency*, 86–109.

22. See "The Pasture Gate," in Carter, *Reckoning*, 33–34; and Carter, *Hour*, 229–30.

23. Dumbrell, *Carter Presidency*, 86.

24. Author's interview with Young.

25. *Bilalian News*, 21 Oct 1977, 19.

26. Author's interview with Mondale.

27. *Sunday Times* (London), 8 Oct 1978, 9.

28. *WS*, 10 Sep 1976, 21.

29. Presidential Campaign Debate, 22 Oct 1976, APP.

30. Author's interview with McHenry.

31. Author's interview with Carter.

32. See Solodovnikov, "K istorii," 137–38.

33. Author's interview with Carter.

34. Orwell, *In Front of Your Nose*, 124.

Chapter 1

1. *NBC Evening News*, 9 Aug 1974, VNA.

2. This account is based on *NBC Evening News*, 29 Apr 1975, VNA. ABC and CBS carried almost identical reports.

3. In this chapter, unless otherwise specified, when discussing the events of the campaign I have relied largely on two classic books about it: Drew's *American Journal* is a diary of the campaign that first appeared in the *New Yorker*; Witcover's *Marathon* is based on his reporting in the *Washington Post*. Also useful are Carter and Ford, *Campaign*; Wooten, *Dasher*; and Anderson, *Electing*.

4. *Time*, 31 May 1971, 24.

5. See Wooten, *Dasher*, 314–16; Carter, *Why Not the Best?*, 137; and "Interview with Hamilton Jordan," 6 Nov 1981, CPP.

6. *NYT*, 4 Jun 1972, 60. See also *NYT*, 12 Jul 1972, 1.

7. Ramsbotham, Washington 862, 28 Feb 1977, FCO 82/755, NA-UK. Also Davidson to Hughes, 7 Feb 1978, FCO 82/876, NA-UK.

8. *St. Petersburg Times* (FL), 20 Nov 1975, 24.

9. See Gallup Organization, "Gallup Poll #944," 23–27 Jan. 1976. Ahead of Carter were Kennedy (21%), Wallace (18%), Humphrey (16%), Muskie (7%), and Jackson (6%).

10. The final tally was Carter (28.4%), Udall (22.7%), Bayh (15.2%), Harris (10.8%), and Shriver (8.2%). The following were write-in candidates: Humphrey (5.6%), Jackson (2.3%), and Wallace (1.3%). Congressional Quarterly, *Guide to 1976*, 26.

11. *NYT*, 25 Feb 1976, 1.

12. *Guardian*, 17 Apr 1976, 3.

13. In the Florida primary, Jackson won 23 percent, and Schapp and Udall won 2 percent each.

14. Author's interview with Carter.

15. Young won with margins of 53 percent (1972), 72 percent (1974), and 80 percent (1976) in a district that was 60 percent white. In 1972, Barbara Jordan, a black Democrat from Texas, was also elected to the House.

16. Author's interview with Young.

17. Ibid.

18. "Statement of the Honorable Andrew Young," in Democratic National Convention, *Official Proceedings 1976*, 302.

19. Author's interview with Young.

20. Young, "Why I Support Jimmy Carter," 397.

21. Author's interview with Young.

22. Ibid.; and Mayer, *Running on Race*, 131.

23. Carter, speech at anniversary of March on Washington, Washington, DC, 27 Aug 2013.

24. See, e.g., Rovere, "Letter," 120; and James Wooten, "The Well-Planned Enigma of Jimmy Carter," *NYT Magazine*, 6 Jun 1976, 16, 76–89.

25. Carter made this promise at the launch of his campaign and repeated it throughout. Carter and Ford, *Campaign*, 11.

26. *NYT*, 12 Aug 1974, 23.

27. "Our Foreign Relations," 15 Mar 1976, in Carter and Ford, *Campaign*, 110.

28. *LAT*, 11 Jan 1976, 6.

29. Drew, *American Journal*, 48 (10 Feb 1976); Cannon, *Governor Reagan*, 420; and *NYT*, 5 Mar 1976, 1. On the Republican primary, in addition to the sources in note 3 above, see Shirley, *Reagan's Revolution*; and Cannon, *Governor Reagan*, 393–436.

30. *Boca Raton News* (FL), 3 Mar 1976, 2.

31. Ramsbotham, [10] Mar 1976, FCO 45/1876, NA-UK.

32. Telcon (HK, Laird), 10 Mar 1976, KTT; Telcon (HK, Reston), 9 Apr 1976, KTT; and Russell to Greenstock, 8 Jan 1976, FCO 82/641, NA-UK. See Ford, *Time to Heal*, 374–75.

33. *NYT*, 12 Mar 1976, 4.

34. Telcon (HK, Simon), 12 Mar 1976, KTT.

35. *Newsweek*, 10 Jun 1974, cover.

36. On Kissinger, see especially Isaacson, *Kissinger* and Hanhimäki, *Flawed Architect*. However, neither analyzes Kissinger's policy toward Africa, the continent that absorbed most of his energy in his final year.

37. Colin Legum, "The End of Cloud-Cuckoo-Land," *NYT Magazine*, 28 Mar 1976, 52.

38. El-Khawas and Cohen, *Kissinger Study*.

39. Author's interview with DePree.

40. Minutes of the Secretary of State's Staff Meeting, 10 Jul 1974, *FRUS 1973–1976, vol. E-6: Africa*, doc. 73.

41. Author's interview with Newsom; Telcon (Dinitz, HK), 22 Apr 1976, KTT; and Kissinger, *Renewal*, 799.

42. Newsom to Easum, 15 Jan 1974, Easum Papers.

43. For the covert operation in Angola, see Gleijeses, *Conflicting Missions*, 246–372; Gleijeses, "Interview with Hultslander"; and Westad, *Global Cold War*, 218–45.

44. [Thornton], [17 Mar 1977], "Southern Africa," NLC-24-114-12-5-0.

45. CIA, "Rhodesia: A Political Challenge to Prime Minister Smith," 13 Apr 1977, NLC-4-32-7-1-4, CL.

46. The literature on Rhodesia under Ian Smith is extensive. See especially Meredith, *Past Is Another Country*; Martin and Johnson, *Struggle*; Smith, *Betrayal*; Caute, *Under the Skin*; Godwin and Hancock, *Rhodesians Never Die*; Verrier, *Road to Zimbabwe*; and Flower, *Serving Secretly*.

47. Brownell, "Hole," 592. See also Brownell, *Collapse*; and Mlambo, *White Immigration*.

48. Tanganyika became independent in 1961 and merged three years later with Zanzibar, which had gained its independence in 1963; Botswana, Lesotho, and Gambia became independent in 1966; Mauritius and Swaziland followed in 1968.

49. *Time*, 6 Nov 1964, 49 (interview with Smith). See also Murphy, "intricate and distasteful"; Palmer to Lord, dissent channel, 3 Jul 1975, Lord/355, NA; and Cohen, "Lonrho."

50. On the guerrilla war, Martin and Johnson, *Struggle*, is authoritative. See also Sibanda, *Zimbabwe African People's Union*; Callinicos, *After Zimbabwe*, 24–51; and Moorcraft and McLaughlin, *Rhodesian War*.

51. Gleijeses, *Conflicting Missions*, 230–395 is the definitive source on the Angola debacle. On South African policy, see Spies, *Operasie Savannah*; also Miller, "Things Fall Apart"; Miller, "Yes, Minister"; and du Preez, *Avontuur in Angola*.

52. See Gleijeses, *Conflicting Missions*, 365–72.

53. See Johnson, "Unintended Consequences," and Johnson, *Congress and the Cold War*, 222–24.

54. Telcon (Mahon, HK), 14 Jan 1976, KTT.

55. US Senate, "Angola," CD38, 10, 7, 2, 55. For the number of South African troops, see Spies, *Operasie Savannah*, 215.

56. *NYT*, 10 Mar 1976, 18.

57. Drew, *American Journal*, 105 (emphasis in original), 101, 94.

58. Ibid., 94.

59. Wooten, *NYT*, 15 Mar 1976, 1.

60. For the best account, see Witcover, *Marathon*, 302–9.

61. Mayer, *Running on Race*, 129, 127. See also Henderson and Roberts, *Georgia Governors*, 242–43. In 1973, Georgia became the first southern state to declare Martin Luther King Day a holiday.

62. *NYT*, 5 Jan 1974, 25.

63. Shartar, "Carter Promise," 39–40.

64. Author's interview with Carter.

65. Telcon (Lord, HK), 14 Apr 1976, KTT.

66. *The Texas Observer* (Austin), 23 Apr 1976, 22; Joseph Lelyveld, "Our New Voice at the UN," *NYT Magazine*, 6 Feb 1977, 56; and Witcover, *Marathon*, 305.

67. Witcover, *Marathon*, 307.

68. See Kamarck, *Primary Politics*, 27–28. Carter did not campaign in West Virginia, where favorite son Senator Robert Byrd was running.

69. Drew, *American Journal*, 132–33. See also Fitzgerald, "Warrior Intellectuals."

70. *NYT*, 14 Mar 1976, edit E14.

71. Congressional Quarterly, *Guide to 1976*, 26–30. After winning Pennsylvania, Carter also won Georgia, Indiana, Michigan, Arkansas, Kentucky, Tennessee, South

Dakota, New Jersey, and Ohio. He lost four to Church (Nebraska, Idaho, Oregon, Montana), three to Brown (Maryland, Nevada, California), and one (Rhode Island) to "unpledged delegates."

72. Thompson, "Jimmy Carter."

73. *WP*, 1 Apr 1976, 1.

74. Naughton, "Campaign," 62; and Eagleburger quoted in Sykes to Thomas, 31 Dec 1975, FCO 82/641, NA-UK.

75. Rowland Evans and Robert Novak, *Free Lance-Star* (Fredericksburg, VA), 30 Apr 1976, 4; *NYT*, 10 Mar 1976, 35; *Pittsburgh Post-Gazette*, 6 Apr 1976, 2; Kissinger, *Renewal*, 956; and Drew, *American Journal*, 83. See John Osborne, "Kissinger's Future," *New Republic*, 1 May 1976, 5–7.

76. Author's interview with Low.

77. UN Security Council resolution 232, *Southern Rhodesia*, S/RES/232 (16 Dec 1966), http://undocs.org/S/RES/232(1966); and UN Security Council resolution 253, *Question concerning the situation in Southern Rhodesia*, S/RES/253 (29 May 1968), http://undocs.org/S/RES/252(1968).

78. For a scholarly presentation, see Randolph, "Byrd Amendment."

79. Brinkley, *Acheson*, 316; *WP*, 11 Dec 1966, 106; *LAT*, 25 May 1968, 20; and Kennan, "Hazardous Courses," 236.

80. See Lake, *Tar Baby*, ch. 6; DeRoche, *Black, White, and Chrome*, 170–77; and Horne, *Barrel*, 145–53.

81. Democratic Study Group, "Fact Sheet no. 94-12: Rhodesian Chrome," 19 Sep 1975, Campaign 1976/132, CL.

82. *CR-House*, 20 Mar 1972, 9069; and *CR-House*, 10 Aug 1972, 27672.

83. Repeal passed in the Senate (54–37) on December 18, 1973, but failed in the House. On September 25, 1975, a coalition of Republicans and southern Democrats in the House again defeated repeal (209–187); only twenty-two Republicans voted for repeal. See Randolph, "Byrd Amendment," 58.

84. *NYT*, 14 Nov 1971, E4. See Lake, *Tar Baby*, 270–75; and Strack, *Sanctions*, 146–51.

85. HK to Ford, [1975,] "The Byrd Amendment," Country/5, GFL; and NSC Meeting, 11 May 1976, NSC Meetings/2, GFL. For avowals of support: US Senate, "Nomination of Henry A. Kissinger," CD35, 48; *NYT*, 21 Aug 1974, 8.

86. Milne (Rhodesian Broadcast Company), "World Survey," 7 Mar 1976, 1/156/1, v82, DFA, SA.

87. CIO, "The Settlement Proposals," 8 Oct 1976, Background, Smith Papers.

88. Astrow, *Zimbabwe*, 60.

89. *Guardian*, 30 Sep 1976, 16. See "Rhodesia: Economic Aspects of White Resettlement," 22 Jul 1976, DDRS; INR, "Namibia: Assessment of Current Situation," 17 Jan 1977, Lord/363, NA; and Meredith, *Past Is Another Country*, 291.

90. Memcon (Richard, Duff, Young), 2 Feb 1977, FCO 36/2006, NA-UK.

91. On Nkomo, see D. Mitchell, *African Nationalist Leaders*, 41–52. For his relations with the Soviet Union, see Kempton, *Soviet Strategy*, 95–99; Nkomo, *Story*, 173–77; Schleicher, "Befreiungskampf"; Shubin, *Hot "Cold War,"* 151–75; Somerville, "Soviet Union"; and Vorotnikov, *Gavana—Moskva*, 49–50, 147–48.

92. See Mtisi, Nyakudya, and Barnes, "War in Rhodesia"; Astrow, *Zimbabwe*, 30–56, 76–94; and Ndlovu-Gatsheni, *Reconstructing*.

93. *Observer*, 27 Sep 1976, 9. On Mugabe's rise, see Martin and Johnson, *Struggle*, 202–14.

94. Figures based on South African Military Intelligence, "Rhodesië: Militêre Bedreiging en Veiligheidsmagte," 23 Apr 1976, 1/156/1, v82, DFA, SA. On mercenaries, see Voss, *Washingtons Söldner,* 197–246 and 296–382; and Horne, *Barrel*, 25–32 and 233–38, and *passim*.

95. See Jaster, *Regional Security*, 2–19.

96. Vorster, 23 Oct 1974, RSA Senate, *Debates*, 1974, c. 3340.

97. "Annex: Outline of the Rhodesian and Namibian Negotiations," attached to [DOS], "Southern Africa: Policy Options," [filed under "Jan. 7"], Lord/363, NA.

98. Vorster, 23 Oct 1974, RSA Senate, *Debates*, 1974, c. 3340. See Giliomee, *Last Afrikaner*, 116–19.

99. Sole, "Verwikkelinge in Rhodesië," 2 Apr 1976, 1/156/1, v82, DFA, SA.

100. For background on Britain's policy toward Rhodesia, see Martin and Johnson, *Struggle*; Meredith, *Past Is Another Country*; and Charlton, *Last Colony*.

101. Undersecretary of State for Political Affairs Joseph Sisco in Memcon (Sisco, Sonnenfeldt, Duff), 13 Feb 1976, FCO 7/3128, NA-UK.

102. Memcon (Ford, HK, members of Congress), 12 May 1976, Memcons/19, GFL; and US House, "Report of Secretary of State Kissinger," CD9, 28.

103. Lord, "Strategy for Southern Africa," 12 Apr 1976, in Lord to HK, 12 Apr 1976, Lord/357, NA.

104. *NYT*, 10 Mar 1976, 1. See Gleijeses, *Visions*, 86–87.

105. South African Military Intelligence,"Rhodesië: Militêre Bedreiging en Veiligheidsmagte," 23 Apr 1976, 1/156/1, v82, DFA, SA. On the talks: "Index to Scope of the Contents of the Attached Memorandum" in [unsigned] to Smith, 13 Apr 1976, ibid.

106. For the Smith regime's use of anthrax and cholera, see Flower, *Serving Secretly*, 137–38; Parker, *Assignment Selous Scouts*, 157–68; Martinez, "Bacteriological and Chemical Agents"; Mangold and Goldberg, *Plague Wars*, 214–23; and Brickhill, "Zimbabwe's Poisoned Legacy."

107. *NYT*, 4 Mar 1976, edit 29; and Remarks at Wheaton College, 12 Mar 1976, APP. See *NYT* editorials of March 3, 9, 21, 23, and 29, 1976; US House, "Report of Secretary of State Kissinger," CD8, 16, 19, 23, 34; and Exchange With Reporters on Arrival at Champaign, Illinois, 6 Mar 1976, APP.

108. Memcon (Ford, HK), 15 Mar 1976, Memcons/18, GFL. See Memcon (Ford, HK), 26 Feb 1976, DDRS.

109. *NYT*, 29 Feb 1976, 1.

110. Memcon (Ford, HK), 4 Mar 1976, Memcons/18, GFL. See LeoGrande and Kornbluh, *Back Channel*, 145–50.

111. Rhodesia Department, "Visit to Washington by Mr Aspin," 16 Mar 1976, FCO 36/1823, NA-UK; and Ramsbotham, Washington 794, 4 Mar 1976, ibid.

112. See Wilkowski, Lusaka 1685, 4 Sep 1975, NSA—Presidential Correspondence with Foreign Leaders/5, GFL; Kaunda to Ford, 28 Jan 1976, ibid.; and Kaunda to Ford in Sisco, State 30929, ibid.

113. Wilkowski, Lusaka 556, 5 Mar 1976, DNSA; and Wilkowski, Lusaka 584, 9 Mar 1976, Country/8, GFL.

114. Author's interview with Kaunda.

115. Thornton, "Southern Africa: The Soviet Role," in Lord to HK, 12 Mar 1976, Lord/358, NA. Also, author's interview with Thornton.

116. Thornton, "Southern Africa: The Soviet Role," in Lord to HK, 12 Mar 1976, Lord/358, NA.

117. Lord, "Strategy for Southern Africa," in Lord to HK, 12 Apr 1976, Lord/357, NA.

118. Callaghan to HK, in Callaghan, FCO 537, 15 Mar 1976, FCO 82/662, NA-UK.

119. Ramsbotham, Washington 794, 4 Mar 1976, FCO 36/1823, NA-UK; and HK to Callaghan, 18 Mar 1976, in HK, State 68649, 21 Mar 1976, Country/16, GFL.

120. Schaufele and Lord to HK, "Statement on Rhodesian Crisis," 19 Mar 1976, Lord/358, NA; UNGA Special Committee, "Southern Rhodesia," 23 Apr 1976, in Steward to Müller, 28 Apr 1976, 1/156/1, v82, DFA, SA; and *NYT*, 13 Mar 1976, 2.

121. "Rhodesia: Recent History," in Wall to Renwick, 2 May 1979, FCO 36/2493, NA-UK.

122. *NYT*, 23 Mar 1976, edit 26. See Callaghan, *Time and Chance*, 378–82.

123. Callaghan, "Rhodesia," 22 Mar 1976, *Parliamentary Debates*, Commons, 5th ser., vol. 908, cols. 30–31.

124. UNGA Special Committee, "Southern Rhodesia," 23 Apr 1976, in Steward to Müller, 28 Apr 1976, 1/156/1, v82, DFA, SA; Callaghan, FCO 69, 23 Mar 1976, FCO 36/1849, NA-UK; and Callaghan, "Rhodesia," 22 Mar 1976, *Parliamentary Debates*, Commons, 5th ser., vol. 908, cols. 29, 33 (for full debate, cols. 29–45).

125. Brown, 24 Oct 1996, BDOHP; and Memcon (Mulcahy, Duff), 13 Feb 1976, FCO 36/1823, NA-UK.

126. Menzies, CanDelNATO 255, 26 Mar 1976, box 11493, pt. 2, block 21, RG25-A-3-C, Canada.

127. Schaufele to SecState, 1 Apr 1976, DNSA; and Kissinger, *Renewal*, 921. Also, NSC Meeting, 11 May 1976, NSC Meetings/2, GFL.

128. HK, State 97581, 22 Apr 1976, Lord/363, NA.

129. Memcon (Ford, HK), 21 Apr 1976, Memcons/19, GFL.

130. Shearar (for Pik Botha) to Müller, 5 Apr 1976, 1/156/1, v82, DFA, SA.

131. Memcon (HK, Pik Botha), 15 Apr 1976, Memcons/19, GFL.

132. NSC Meeting, 7 Apr 1976, NSC Meetings/2, GFL.

133. "Transcript of a Press Conference," 22 Apr 1976, FCO 45/1876, NA-UK.

134. Kissinger, *Renewal*, 927.

135. "On the Record: Blair House/British Press," 10 Mar 1977, PREM 16/1486, NA-UK.

136. Joint FCO Research Department, "Cuba and the Afro-Asian Worlds," 3 May 1976, FCO 7/3130, NA-UK. See: Joint Intelligence Committee, "Soviet-Cuban Involvement in Rhodesia," 12 Mar 1976, PREM 16/1091, NA-UK; and these files: FCO 7/3125, FCO 7/3129, FCO 7/3333, FCO 51/425.

137. Duncan, "Post Mortem on Angola," 3 May 1976, FCO 51/425, NA-UK; Smith to Newton, 25 Mar 1976, ibid.; and Collins to Jackson, 24 Feb 1977, FCO 7/3333, NA-UK.

138. Cable, "Anglo-Cuban Political Relations," 17 May 1976, FCO 7/3125, NA-UK; and Reid to Duff, 19 Feb 1976, FCO 7/3129, ibid.

139. UK Cabinet Meeting: Conclusions, 4 Mar 1976, CAB 128/58/8, NA-UK. Also Palliser to Prime Minister, 1 Mar 1976, PREM 16/1091, ibid.

140. Reid to Duff, 19 Feb 1976, FCO 7/3129, NA-UK; and Marginalia on Barlow to Laver, 30 Apr 1976, FCO 36/1824, ibid. For British desire for Vorster's help with Smith: Memcon (Sisco, Sonnenfeldt, Duff), 13 Feb 1976, FCO 7/3128, ibid. For the

fund: "International Economic Support for Rhodesian Settlement," in ADR to Gaylard, C204, 15 Sept 1976, Rhodesia-RSA, Smith Papers.

141. Thomas to Duncan, 29 Mar 1976, FCO 7/3131, NA-UK; and Samuel to Aspin, 23 Mar 1976, FCO 36/1823, ibid. Also Foreign Secretary to HK (draft), in Reid, "Central and Southern Africa," 10 Mar 1976, FCO 7/3130, ibid.; and Telcon (HK, Callaghan), 22 Mar 1976, KTT.

142. Daddow, "Anthony Crosland," in Theakston, *British Foreign Secretaries*, 69; Crosland, *Crosland*, 325; and Ramsbotham, Washington 1340, 14 Apr 1976, FCO 45/1876, NA-UK. On Callaghan's refusal: Callaghan to HK, 28 Apr 1976, in Armstrong, London 6581, 29 Apr 1976, Country/16, GFL.

143. Reith, on Thomas to Cartledge, 9 Apr 1976, FCO 45/1876, NA-UK; and Thomas to Duncan, 29 Mar 1976, FCO 7/3131, ibid. Also Campbell, "Minutes of the 80th Meeting of the Planning Committee," 4 Feb 1976, FCO 51/425, ibid.

144. Memcon (Mobutu, HK), 30 Apr 1976, *FRUS 1973–1976, vol. E-6: Africa*, doc. 295.

145. Telcon (Ramsbotham, HK), 13 Apr 1976, KTT. Also Telcon (Schaufele, HK), 21 Apr 1976, KTT, in which Kissinger hangs up on the assistant secretary.

146. Memcon (Crosland, HK) on 24 Apr 1976, 1 May 1976, FCO 45/1876, NA-UK.

147. Crosland, *Crosland*, 324; and Memcon (Crosland, HK), 24 Apr 1976, FCO 36/1824, NA-UK. Also UK Cabinet Meeting: Conclusions, 29 Apr 1976, CAB 128/59/2, NA-UK. On the appointment of Crosland: Jefferys, *Anthony Crosland*, 196–99.

148. Memcon (Crosland, HK), 24 Apr 1976, FCO 36/1824, NA-UK.

149. Reid to Aspin, 31 Mar 1976, FCO 45/1876, NA-UK. See "Transcript of a Press Conference," 22 Apr 1976, FCO 45/1876, NA-UK.

150. US Senate, "International Security Assistance," CD41, 17.

151. Memcon (Crosland, HK on 24 Apr 1976), 1 May 1976, FCO 45/1876, NA-UK. Also Wilkowski, Lusaka 559, 5 Mar 1976, FOIA.

152. Memcon (Crosland, HK on 24 Apr 1976), 1 May 1976, FCO 45/1876, NA-UK.

153. *Ghanaian Times* (Accra), 28 Apr 1976, edit 6; 22 Apr 1976, *NYT*, edit 31. Also author's interview with Easum. On Ghana: Scowcroft, toHAK 25, 27 Apr 1976, Africa Trip/32, GFL; Black, toHAK 22, 27 Apr 1976, ibid.; and Black, Accra 277, 2 May 1976, Africa Trip/34, GFL.

154. Koppel transcript in Sisco, ToSec 11003, 23 Apr 1976, Africa Trip/33, GFL; and *WS*, 27 Apr 1976, edit. 10.

155. Newsom to Easum, 15 Jan 1974, Easum Papers; and Memcon (Ford, HK, members of Congress) 12 May 1976, Memcons/19, GFL.

156. Kissinger, *Renewal*, 931.

157. Memcon (Nyerere, HK), 25 Apr 1976, DNSA.

158. HK to Ford (via Scowcroft), HAKto 6, 26 Apr 1976, Africa Trip/32, GFL; and HK to Ford (via Scowcroft), HAKto 7, 26 Apr 1976, ibid. Also HK to Schmidt in HK to Scowcroft, HAKto 17, 29 Apr 1976, ibid.

159. *NYT*, 26 Apr 1976, 1.

160. Zambian HC in London, "Commonwealth Conference Brief: 1979," 152 UNIP 7/23/70, Zambia.

161. NSC Interdepartmental Group for Africa, "Zambia: African Policy Analysis and Resource Allocation Paper," Nov 1976, NLC-21-37-4-19-4.

162. Lake, 22 Mar 1979, in US House, "United States Policy Toward Rhodesia," CD26, 5. See also Kaunda and Morris, *Humanist*; and Mwaipaya, *African Humanism*.

163. CIA, "Rhodesia: Economic Situation and Outlook," [4 Apr 1979,] CREST. Stretches of the line reopened in subsequent years, but Zambia remained cut off.

164. Contingency Planning Secretariat, *Why Zambia Re-Opened the Southern Railway Route*, Lusaka: GPO, [1978,] 67 UNIP 6/5/33, Zambia. See also Monson, *Africa's Freedom Railway*, 101; Gleave, "Transport Corridor," 259–65; and Mwase, "Tanzania-Zambia Railway."

165. In 1977, the US Congress estimated the four-year cost to Zambia of the border closure to be between $750 million and $800 million. (*CR*, 24 May 1977, 16184)

166. Zambian HC in London, "Commonwealth Conference Brief: 1979," 152 UNIP 7/23/70, Zambia.

167. See Southall, "Comment," 118.

168. *NYT*, 18 Apr 1975, 31.

169. Toast of President Kenneth D. Kaunda of Zambia, 19 Apr 1975, APP; and Jean Wilkowski, FD, 23 Aug 1989.

170. *NYT*, 22 Apr 1976, edit 31, and 14. For Kissinger's arrival: Miles, 11 Nov 1996, BDOHP.

171. Memcon (Ford, HK), 21 Apr 1976, Memcons/19, GFL. See Kissinger, *Renewal*, 939.

172. Memcon (Ford, HK), 21 Apr 1976, Memcons/19, GFL. For wrangling over the draft speech: Scowcroft to HK, 24 Apr 1976, Africa Trip/32, GFL; and HK to Scowcroft, 25 Apr 1976, ibid.

173. "Address by The Honorable Henry A. Kissinger at a luncheon in his honor: 'United States Policy on Southern Africa,'" 27 Apr 1976, Raoul-DuVal/16, GFL.

174. See McQuiggan, Lusaka 1025, 27 Apr 1976, FCO 45/1876, NA-UK; HK to Ford (via Scowcroft), HAKto 11, 28 Apr 1976, Africa Trip/32, GFL; WOA, "Washington Notes on Africa," 27 May 1976, 7; Lord to Schaufele, 11 Jun 1976, Lord/362, NA; and Colin Legum, "Southern Africa: The Year of the Whirlwind," in Legum, *Africa Contemporary Record: 1976–77*, A4.

175. Eagleburger to HK in Sisco, ToSec 110304, 29 [*sic*] Apr 1976, Africa Trip/34, GFL; and *NYT*, 1 May 1976, 10.

176. Scowcroft to HK, toHAK 42, 28 Apr 1976, Africa Trip/32, GFL. George Kennan was one of the critics: Kennan, "Black Rule in Rhodesia: Some Implications," *NYT*, 2 May 1976, E15.

177. *NYT*, 1 May 1976, 10; and *LAT*, 1 May 1976, 26.

178. Cannon, *Governor Reagan*, 423, 422; and *NYT*, 26 Mar 1976, 16.

179. See Shirley, *Reagan's Revolution*, 158–76.

180. Ibid., 174.

181. Drew, *American Journal*, 353.

182. *LAT*, 1 May 1976, 1. On Ford's campaign in Texas: Pilas to Wagner, 29 Mar 1976, Committee/E5, GFL.

183. *LAT*, 1 May 1976, 1; Shirley, *Reagan's Revolution*, 192; and Witcover, *Marathon*, 419.

184. Ford, *Time to Heal*, 381.

185. Interview of Kissinger, 29 Apr 2008, African Oral History Archive, www.africanoralhistory.com.

186. *DMN*, 1 May 1976, 24.

187. Eagleburger to HK in Sisco, ToSec 110304, 29 Apr 1976, Africa Trip/34, GFL; and HK to Scowcroft, HAKto 18, 29 Apr 1976, Africa Trip/32, GFL.

188. Remarks at Tyler Junior College, 28 Apr 1976, APP. See Remarks in Fort Worth, 28 Apr 1976, APP.

189. Wagner to Morton, 7 Apr 1976, Committee/B4, GFL (emphasis in original).

190. *LAT*, 1 May 1976, 1.

191. *DMN*, 2 May 1976, 1 ("smash" and "whip"); *LAT*, 2 May 1976, 1 ("crush"); and Naughton, "Campaign," 61 ("wallop"). For analysis of the vote: Eagleburger to HK in Sisco, ToSec 110562, 2 May 1976, Africa Trip/34, GFL; Eagleburger to HK in Sisco, ToSec 110636, 3 May 1976, ibid.; and Scowcroft to HK, toHAK 80, 3 May 1976, ibid.

192. *NYT*, 7 May 1976, 30; and *NYT*, 3 May 1976, 31. For "muzzle," Naughton, "Campaign," 64.

193. Scowcroft to HK, toHAK 106, 7 May 1976, Africa Trip/33, GFL.

194. Telcon (Rockefeller, HK), 8 May 1976, KTT. Also Telcon (Scowcroft, HK), 29 May 1976, KTT; and Kissinger, *Renewal*, 955–57.

195. Ford, *Time to Heal*, 380; and NSC Meeting, 11 May 1976, NSC Meetings/2, GFL.

196. *NYT*, 10 Jul 1976, 2, citing interview conducted on 11 May 1976; Memcon (Ford, HK, members of Congress), 12 May 1976, Memcons/19, GFL; "Gerald R. Ford's Remarks at the Harry Middleton Lecture," Lyndon Baines Johnson Library, Austin, 7 Feb 1997, DGFL; and Kissinger, *Renewal*, 956.

197. Ford, *Time to Heal*, 380; HK to Scowcroft, 25 Apr 1976, Africa Trip/32, GFL; Naughton, "Campaign," 15. See NSC Meeting, 11 May 1976, NSC Meetings/2, GFL; and Ford, *Time to Heal*, 373–75.

198. See *LAT*, June 5, 1976, 8.

199. See *WP*, May 26, 1976, 19.

200. This account is based on *San Francisco Chronicle*, 3 Jun 1976, 1, and Witcover, *Marathon*, 430. See also *LAT*, 4 Jun 1976, B12, and *NYT*, 11 Jun 1976, 22.

201. *San Francisco Chronicle*, 3 Jun 1976, 1; and *San Francisco Chronicle*, 4 Jun 1976, edit 44.

202. *NYT*, 4 Jun 1976, 12; *LAT*, 4 Jun 1976, B12; and *San Francisco Chronicle*, 4 Jun 1976, 1.

203. Ford Campaign ad, "Rhodesia," XXPF 3836, GFL; *NYT*, 6 Jun 1976, 1. Lou Cannon writes that immediately before the ad's tag line, a hand was shown reaching for a red phone (*Governor Reagan*, 427). This was not in the version of the ad I viewed at the Ford Library.

204. *NYT*, 6 Jun 1976, 1. See John Coyne, "Eating Crow in California," *National Review* 28, 9 Jul 1976, 726.

205. Buckley, *DMN*, 19 Jun 1976, 3; and *LAT*, 8 Jun 1976, 14.

206. John Coyne, "Eating Crow in California," *National Review* 28, 9 Jul 1976, 726; *WP*, 8 Jun 1976, 1; *LAT*, 5 Jun 1976, 8; and Ford, *Time to Heal*, 388. See also Cannon, *Time and Chance*, 406.

207. *LAT*, 7 Jun 1976, 5. See also *St. Petersburg Times* (FL), 9 Jun 1976, 15; and *DMN*, 10 Jun 1976, 38.

208. *NYT*, 9 Jun 1976, 1.

209. Memcon (Ford, Scranton), 4 Jun 1976, Memcons/19, GFL; and *NYT*, 10 Jun 1976, 35.

Chapter 2

1. Cronkite, *Reporter's Life*, 320.
2. *NYT*, 22 Jun 1969, 10:14. See *WP*, 16 May 1964, 1; and American Revolution Bicentennial Administration, *Bicentennial*, 1:58.
3. *NYT*, 17 May 1972, 1.
4. *NYT*, 21 May 1972, edit E14.
5. Anthony Lewis, "The System," *NYT Magazine*, 4 Jul 1976, 7.
6. Radio Address About the American Revolution Bicentennial, 10 Mar 1974, APP; Capazzola, "It Makes You Want to Believe," 33; and *NYT*, 11 Mar 1974, 17. See also Randel, "The Fife and Drum."
7. Woodward, "The Aging of America," 583; Peoples [sic] Bicentennial Commission, *America's Birthday*, 9; and *NYT*, 9 May 1971, 59. See US Senate, "The Attempt to Steal the Bicentennial" CD40; and US Senate, "Threats to the Peaceful Observance of the Bicentennial," CD42.
8. Cooke, quoted in McWilliams, "Thoughts on the Bicentennial," 420. See Lowenthal, "Bicentennial Landscape"; and Gordon, *Spirit of 1976*.
9. *NYT*, 4 Jul 1976, 1.
10. Drew, *American Journal*, 282 (emphasis in original); and Cronkite, *Reporter's Life*, 319. For dissenting views: Bernstein, *Founding Fathers*, 137; Unger, *Recent America*, 193; Steinberg, "Philadelphia," 124; and and Rehnquist, "A Tribute," 984.
11. C. Vann Woodward, "The Graying of America," *NYT*, 29 Dec 1976, 25.
12. Telcon (Nixon, Haldeman), 25 Apr 1973, Watergate Trial Conversation 38-150, Nixon Presidential Library online.
13. "Address of Jimmy Carter," 15 Jul 1976, in DNC, *Official Proceedings 1976*, 401–6. On the Democratic Convention: Reeves, *Convention*; Stroud, *How Jimmy Won*, 312–32; Drew, *American Journal*, 284–317; Witcover, *Marathon*, 355–70; and Schram, *Running for President*, 200–17.
14. "Statement of the Honorable Andrew Young," 14 Jul 1976, in DNC, *Official Proceedings 1976*, 302.
15. "Benediction by The Reverend Martin Luther King, Sr.," 15 Jul 1976, ibid., 408.
16. Shrum, "No Private Smiles," 24.
17. Robert Baskin, *DMN*, 30 Apr 1976, D3; *NYT*, 9 Sep 1976, 3; Memcon (Crosland, HK), 4 Sep 1976, PREM 16/1094, NA-UK; and Memcon (Ford, HK), 30 Aug 1976, Memcons/20, GFL. For letters from irate citizens: Subject/CO124, GFL; Committee/80, GFL; and Gergen/1, GFL.
18. US Senate, "US Policy toward Africa," CD39, 181, 182, 205–6, 212.
19. Seelye to Schaufele in Sisco, ToSec 110386, 30 Apr 1976, Africa Trip/34, GFL; and HK to Scowcroft, HAKto 25, 1 May 1976, Africa Trip/32, GFL. See "Talking Points on Byrd Amendment," 30 Apr 1976, Press & Congress/8, GFL; Ramsbotham, Washington 1531, 30 Apr 1976, FCO 45/1876, NA-UK; and HK to Ford, "Repeal of the Byrd Amendment," [Spring 1976,] DDRS.
20. Shearar (for Pik Botha) to Müller, 6 May 1976, 1/156/1, v82, DFA, SA; and *NYT*, 21 Jun 1976, 1. For the brakes: Scowcroft to HK, toHAK 67, 2 May 1976, Africa Trip/32, GFL; DOS Press Briefing, in Scowcroft to HK, toHAK 107, 7 May 1976, Africa Trip/33, GFL; and Janka and Horan to Scowcroft, 18 May 1976, Subject CO124/43, GFL.
21. Telcon (HK, Brooke), 1 Jul 1976, KTT; and Telcon (HK, Geyelin), 28 May 1976, KTT. The UN estimated that closing the border with Rhodesia had cost Mozambique $550 million by 1980. (Gregory, "Zimbabwe Election," 20)

22. Memcon (Callaghan, HK), 25 Jun 1976, PREM 16/1092, NA-UK. See *CQ Weekly*, 19 Jun 1976, 1569; and Telcon (HK, Mansfield), 9 Sep 1976, KTT. The work-around was not finalized until September; the funds were drawn from the $25 million economic aid appropriated for southern Africa.

23. Memcon (Ford, HK), 9 May 1976, Memcons/19, GFL; and HK to Ford (via Scowcroft), HAKto 11, 28 Apr 1976, Africa Trip/32, GFL.

24. *CBS Evening News*, 28 Apr 1976, VNA.

25. "Prime Minister's Address to the Nation," 27 Apr 1976, Détente-RSA, Smith Papers; and ADR to Müller, 29 Apr 1976, 1/156/1, v82, DFA, SA. Pretoria did not rec-ognize Smith's regime; therefore, the two countries exchanged Accredited Diplomatic Representatives (ADRs) instead of ambassadors.

26. US Ambassador to Botswana David Bolen, quoted in Emery to Reid, 13 May 1976, FCO 45/1876, NA-UK.

27. McQuiggan, Lusaka 708, 18 Mar 1976, PREM 16/1091, NA-UK.

28. Author's interview with Easum; and Cabinet Meeting, 30 Aug 1976, Mem-cons/20, GFL.

29. McQuiggan to Reid, 28 Apr 1976, FCO 45/1876, NA-UK; Crosland to HK, 5 May 1976, Africa Trip/32, GFL; and Callaghan to HK, 28 Apr 1976, in Armstrong, London 6581, 29 Apr 1976, Country/16, GFL.

30. Laver to Aspin, with marginalia, 6 May 1976, FCO 36/1824, NA-UK; Laver to Aspin, 23 Jun 1976, PREM 16/1157, NA-UK; and Schaufele to HK, 5 Jun 1976, DNSA. See "Note for the Record: Rhodesia," 6 May 1976, PREM 16/1092, NA-UK.

31. Crosland, *Crosland*, 336. See: Callaghan, *Time and Chance*, 358–60; and Mor-gan, *Callaghan*, 439–42.

32. Muir to Samuel, 18 May 1976, FCO 36/1824, NA-UK. See Crosland, FCO to Washington 970, 10 May 1976, PREM 16/1092, NA-UK.

33. Joint Intelligence Committee, "Soviet-Cuban Involvement in Rhodesia," 12 Mar 1976, PREM 16/1091, NA-UK. See ADR (Hawkins) to Gaylard, c217, 22 Sep 1976, Rhodesia-RSA, Smith Papers. Harold Hawkins was Rhodesia's de facto ambas-sador to South Africa.

34. Memcon (HK, Pik Botha), 14 May 1976, Memcons/19, GFL; Telcon (von Staden, HK), 15 Jun 1976, KTT; and US House, "Report of Kissinger on Visits," CD9, 18.

35. Estimates of the population of Soweto in 1976 vary from 700,000 to 1.5 mil-lion, the latter figure taking account of the estimated half-million people who lived there illegally (Transnational Institute, *Black South Africa Explodes*, 44); estimates of its size ranged as well, with the *NYT* and Transnational Institute calling it approxi-mately thirty-five square miles.

36. Lord to HK, 27 Feb 1976, Lord/358, NA.

37. Nadine Gordimer, "Apartheid, the 'Agitator,'" *NYT*, 27 Jun 1976, 4. The final death toll after two months of unrest was more than 400. On the Soweto uprising, see the primary sources and detailed account in Kane-Berman, *South Africa*.

38. *NYT*, 13 Jun 1976, edit 18; and UN Security Council resolution 392, *South Africa*, S/RES/392 (19 Jun 1976), http://undocs.org/S/RES/392(1976). Also *Rand Daily Mail*, 19 Jun 1976, 1. The UN resolution was a consensus motion, without a vote. Western support was contingent on its containing no call for punitive action against Pretoria.

39. *NYT*, 24 Jun, 1976, 3. See HK, State 122047, 18 May 1976, DNSA.

40. Young quoted in Morgenthau, "Southern Africa in Crisis," 15 Sep 1976, in Morgenthau to Eizenstat, 15 Sep 1976, Campaign 1976/1, CL; and Kissinger, *Renewal*, 959. See also Memcon (Vorster, HK), 23 Jun 1976, Memcons/20, GFL. Vorster and Kissinger had two private meetings, with no other participants present (ADR to Brice, c98, 1 Jul 1976, Détente-RSA, Smith Papers). I have located no record of these meetings.

41. Bowdler, 29 Jun 1976, Pretoria 2867, DNSA; and *NYT*, 20 Sep 1976, 6.

42. Memcon (HK, Pik Botha), 15 Apr 1976, Memcons/19, GFL. See Gleijeses, *Conflicting Missions*, 327.

43. Memcon (Smith, Vorster), Pretoria, 13 Jun 1976, Gaylard Meetings, Smith Papers. Also Onslow, "We Must Gain Time."

44. "Notes on a Meeting," 13 Jun 1976 in Hawkins to Gaylard, 15 Jun 1976, Gaylard Meetings, Smith Papers; and Memcon (Smith, Vorster), 13 Jun 1976, ibid.

45. "Notes on a Meeting," 13 Jun 1976 in Hawkins to Gaylard, 15 Jun 1976, ibid.

46. Ibid.; and Memcon (Smith, Vorster), 13 Jun 1976, ibid.

47. Memcon (Smith, Vorster), 13 Jun 1976, ibid. The CIA later received an accurate, but not full, account of this meeting. Bush (DCI) to HK, 19 Aug 1976, *FRUS, 1969–1976, v. 28: Southern Africa*, doc. 201.

48. *Star* (Johannesburg), 4 Jun 1976, 1.

49. Untitled, 21 Sep 1976, Background, Smith Papers; CIO, "The Settlement Proposals," 8 Oct 1976, ibid.; and Memcon (Vorster, HK), 23 Jun 1976, Memcons/20, GFL.

50. Memcon (Vorster, HK), 23 Jun 1976, Memcons/20, GFL. Also Lord to HK, 8 Jul 1976, Lord/368, NA.

51. Memcon (Vorster, HK), 23 Jun 1976, Memcons/20, GFL.

52. Ibid.; and Memcon (Richard, Duff, Young), 2 Feb 1977, FCO 36/2006, NA-UK.

53. Memcon (Vorster, HK), 23 Jun 1976, Memcons/20, GFL; and Memcon (Callaghan, Kissinger), 25 June 1976, PREM 16/1092, NA-UK.

54. *NYT*, 25 Jun 1976, 1; *Rhodesian Herald* (Salisbury), 30 June 1976, 1; and *NYT*, 29 Jun 1976, 13.

55. South African Cabinet Meeting, 3 Aug 1976, in Onslow and van Wyk, eds. *Southern Africa*, 239; ADR to Gaylard, C93, 29 Jun 1976, Détente-RSA, Smith Papers; and Brice to Gaylard, 2 Jul 1976, ibid.

56. Telcon (HK, Kalb), 26 Jul 1976, KTT.

57. Memcon (Callaghan, HK), 25 June 1976, PREM 16/1092, NA-UK. See "Extract from a note by Sir A. Duff," 22 Mar 1977, FCO 36/2135, NA-UK; and "Speaking note for Sir P Ramsbotham," in Harrison to Duff, 31 Jan 1977, FCO 36/2005, NA-UK.

58. Callaghan's marginalia on Wright to Callaghan, 10 Jul 1976, PREM 16/1092, NA-UK. On the studied vagueness about elections, see, e.g., the joint British/US paper given to the South Africans, in Moreton, Washington 2762, 16 Aug 1976, FCO 36/1829, NA-UK.

59. Memcon (Callaghan, Schmidt), 30 Jun 1976, PREM 16/1092, NA-UK; and Memcon (Callaghan, Rowlands), 4 Aug 1976, ibid. On Crosland's and Rowland's objections: FCO, "Rhodesia: Meeting of GEN 12 on Wednesday, 28 July," FCO 36/1827, NA-UK; and Rowlands to Callaghan, 4 Aug 1976, PREM 16/1092, NA-UK.

60. "Speaking note for Sir P Ramsbotham," in Harrison to Duff, 31 Jan 1977, FCO 36/2005, NA-UK; Memcon (Callaghan, HK), 25 June 1976, PREM 16/1092, NA-UK; and Lord to HK, 8 Jul 1976, Lord/368, NA.

61. Memcon (Ford, HK), 13 Aug 1976, Memcons/20, GFL.

62. Author's interview with Easum.

63. Duff to Laver, 1 Jul 1976, FCO 36/1826, NA-UK.

64. Memcon (Callaghan, Schmidt), 30 Jun 1976, PREM 16/1092, NA-UK; and Rowlands to Crosland, 24 Jun 1976, FCO 36/1826, NA-UK.

65. Memcon (Crosland, HK), 8 Jul 1976, PREM 16/1092, NA-UK. The inner circle was initially National Security Adviser Brent Scowcroft, Undersecretary for Political Affairs Philip Habib, Director of Policy Planning Winston Lord, NSC staffer Peter Rodman, and Assistant Secretary of State for African Affairs William Schaufele; this was later broadened to occasionally include Undersecretary for Economic Affairs William D. Rogers, Executive Assistant Lawrence Eagleburger, Chargé Ronald Spiers (US embassy, London), and ambassadors Anne Armstrong (UK) and Bill Bowdler (RSA). On Kissinger's insistence on secrecy, see Duff to Laver, 1 Jul 1976, FCO 36/1826, NA-UK; Duff to Wright, 9 Jul 1976, ibid.; Aspin to Scott, 9 Jul 1976, ibid.; Ramsbotham, Washington 2409, 13 Jul 1976, ibid.; Ramsbotham, Washington 2427, 14 Jul 1976, ibid.; Ramsbotham, Washington 2464, 17 Jul 1976, ibid.; and Aspin to Duff, 19 Jul 1976, FCO 36/1827, NA-UK.

66. Memcon (Callaghan, HK), 25 June 1976, PREM 16/1092, NA-UK.

67. For the leak, see *NYT*, 20 Jul 1976, 1; and Ramsbotham, Washington 2503, 20 Jul 1976, FCO 36/1827, NA-UK. The new classification was "Rhodesia Joint Planning": see Crosland, FCO 1653 to Washington, 20 Jul 1976, FCO 36/1827, NA-UK.

68. For other US accusations of British leaking: Fergusson to Duff, 21 Jul 1976, FCO 36/1827, NA-UK; Crosland, FCO to UKMisNewYork 564, 26 Jul 1976, ibid.; Moreton, Washington 2740, 12 Aug 1976, FCO 36/1829, NA-UK; Crosland, FCO 1749 to Washington, 13 Aug 1976, ibid.; and Ramsbotham, Washington 3016 and 3023, 9 Sep 1976, PREM 16/1094, NA-UK.

69. The British Treasury Department complained bitterly to the FCO about its failure to consult it. See Duff to PS, 27 Jul 1976, FCO 36/1827, NA-UK; and Duff to Wass, 6 Aug 1976, FCO 36/1828, NA-UK. So did Britain's European allies (Aspin to Samuel, 12 Aug 1976, FCO 36/1829, NA-UK) and the Canadians (Duff to Laver, 7 Sep 1976, FCO 36/1832, NA-UK).

70. Ford to Callaghan, 20 Jul 1976, PREM 16/1092, NA-UK. Callaghan responded by phone (Wright (PS) to Fergusson, 22 Jul 1976, FCO 36/1827, NA-UK).

71. Fergusson to Duff, 21 Jul 1976, FCO 36/1827, NA-UK.

72. "Rhodesia: Meeting of GEN 12 on Thursday, 22 July," 22 Jul 1976, ibid.

73. Duff to Laver, 30 July 1976, FCO 36/1828, NA-UK. See "Rhodesian Settlement: Financial Arrangements," 21 Sep 1976, CAB/129/192/6, NA-UK.

74. Lord to HK, 21 Jul 1976, Lord Papers/368, NA.

75. Kissinger, *Renewal*, 972; and Telcon (HK, Kalb), 26 Jul 1976, KTT.

76. Nkomo, *Story*, 170–71; and Morgenthau, "Southern Africa in Crisis," 15 Sep 1976 in Morgenthau to Eizenstat, 15 Sep 1976, Campaign 1976/1, CL. On Kissinger's meeting with Nkomo: Spain, Dar 1371, 16 Apr 1976, HK Trip/33, GFL; McQuiggan, Lusaka 1052, 29 Apr 1976, FCO 36/1787, NA-UK; and Memcon (Callaghan, Nkomo), 18 May 1976, ibid.

77. Brand Fourie quoted in Bowdler, Pretoria 3062, 10 Jul 1976, DNSA. See Lord to HK, 21 Jul 1976, Lord/368, NA.

78. Smith, *Betrayal*, 195; Official Communiqué, in *Rhodesian Herald*, 11 Aug 1976, 1; *Rhodesian Herald*, 11 Aug 1976, edit 10; and *Guardian*, 12 Aug 1976, 10. For

the raid, see Moorcraft and McLaughlin, *Rhodesian War*, 43–44; and Petter-Bowyer, *Winds of Destruction*, 390–93.

79. UNCR, "Report on Massacre," in Burns, UKMisGeneva 263, 1 Sep 1976, PREM 16/1094, NA-UK. See *NYT*, 21 Aug 1976, 11; and Martin and Johnson, *Struggle*, 240–41.

80. *Rhodesian Herald*, 13 Aug 1976, edit 10. South African author Peter Stiff also strongly contested the reliability of the UN account. See Stiff, *Silent War*, 241–42. The British Foreign Office concluded that there was "no reason to question the UNHCR's account." (FCO Rhodesia Department, "Monthly Summary No. 8," Aug 1976, FCO 36/1814, NA-UK)

81. Muller in *Rhodesian Herald*, 14 Aug 1976, 1; *Rhodesian Herald*, 14 Aug 1976, edit 4; *Rhodesian Herald*, 17 Aug 1976, edit 6; and Memcon (Smith, Vorster), 13 Jun 1976, Gaylard Meetings, Smith Papers. See also Moorcraft and McLaughlin, *Rhodesian War*, 44. The number of South African helicopters in Rhodesia is difficult to determine; forty is the most widely cited figure.

82. HK, quoted in ADR to Gaylard, c162, 13 Aug 1976, Rhodesia-RSA, Smith Papers; *NYT*, 8 Sep 1976, 4; Muller, speech to National Party Congress, 13 Aug 1976, excerpted in *NYT*, 14 Aug 1976, 8; and *Newsweek*, 31 May 1976, 35.

83. Telcon (Pastore, HK), 27 Aug 1976, KTT; and Telcon (Mathias, HK), 20 Aug 1976, KTT. The delegate tally was Ford, 1,187; Reagan, 1,070; and Elliot Richardson, 1.

84. Reagan, "Remarks at the 31st Republican National Convention," 19 Aug 1976, Reagan 2020, http://reagan2020.us/speeches/rnc_1976.asp; and "Reagan's Impromptu Speech at 1976 GOP Convention," YouTube video, 3:04, posted by "krb3141," February 6, 2008, http://www.youtube.com/watch?v=n-p-Nuu8hYQ.

85. In 1974, the Federal Election Campaign Act set a $25 million cap on campaign spending. The Nixon campaign had spent $61.4 million four years earlier.

86. Ford, *Time to Heal*, 412 (emphasis in original).

87. For the position papers: Carter and Ford, *Campaign*, 586–698. See Anderson, *Electing*, 80 and *passim*.

88. Wallace quoted in *Times* (London), 14 Oct 1975, 1; and Carter, "Relations between World's Democracies," 23 Jun 1976, in Carter and Ford, *Campaign*, 266. Carter himself added the phrase "secretive, Lone Ranger" to the speech draft. (Anderson, *Electing*, 42)

89. Fallaci, "Kissinger," 22. See also Kissinger, *White House Years*, 1409–10.

90. Telcon (HK, Koppel), 9 Jul 1976, KTT; and *NYT*, 27 Jun 1976, 4.

91. Carter, "Our Foreign Relations," 15 Mar 1976, in Carter and Ford, *Campaign*, 112. This became the foreign policy component of his presentation to the platform committee. See "A New Beginning: Jimmy Carter's Platform Program," 16 Jun 1976, ibid., 245–49. Other than this, Carter mentioned human rights in passing three times during the primary campaign: "Formal Announcement," 12 Dec 1974, ibid., 3; "Relations between World's Democracies," 3 Jun 1976, ibid., 270; and "Meet the Press," 11 Jul 1976, ibid., 298.

92. See Moyn, *Last Utopia*, 120–55; and Thomas, *Helsinki Effect*, 27–88.

93. During the general election, Carter addressed human rights at four campaign events in September and four in October: "Addressing B'nai B'rith," 8 Sep 1976, Carter and Ford, *Campaign*, 709–14; "For a Strong Sunset Law," 9 Sep 1976, ibid., 714–16; "At Oregon Rally," 27 Sep 1976, ibid., 829–35; "Opposes Arab Boycott," 30 Sep 1976, ibid., 835–38; "At Notre Dame University," 10 Oct 1976, ibid., 993–98;

"Competent, Compassionate Government," 10 Oct 1976, ibid., 998–1001; "Polish-American Dinner," 10 Oct 1976, ibid., 1001–6; and "Our Country is Drifting," 16 Oct 1976, ibid., 1037–45. He answered questions about human rights in three interviews: "Views Self as 'Populist,'" 13 Sep 1976, ibid., 734–45; "*Playboy* Magazine," November 1976 (interviews conducted, Aug–Oct), ibid., 939–64; and "Religion and the Presidency," 9 Oct 1976, 965–74. Not one of the classic books on the campaign, all of which were published in 1977 or 1978—Drew's *American Journal*, Witcover's *Marathon*, and Wooten's *Dasher*—mentions human rights once.

94. Carter, *Why Not the Best?* 139; and Reston, *NYT*, 7 Jul 1976, 25. On Ford's strategy: Greene, *Presidency of Ford*, 177; Schram, *Running*, 252–68; and Witcover, *Marathon*, 530–35.

95. Unnamed staffer quoted in Shrum,"No Private Smiles," 42.

96. Ben Fortson quoted in Wooten, "The Well-Planned Enigma of Jimmy Carter," *NYT Magazine*, 6 Jun 1976, 78.

97. Telcon (HK, Buckley), 26 Aug 1976, KTT; and Telcon (HK, Sonnenfeldt), 16 Aug 1976, KTT. Ford, of course, had not previously been elected president.

98. Memcon (Ford, HK), 30 Aug 1976, Memcons/20, GFL.

99. Ibid.

100. "Extract from a note by Sir A. Duff," 22 Mar 1977, FCO 36/2135, NA-UK; and and *NYT*, 7 Sep 1976, 1.

101. *NYT*, 27 Oct 1972, 18; and Memcon (Vorster, Kissinger), 6 Sep 1976, *FRUS, 1969–1976, Vol. 28: Southern Africa*, doc. 203.

102. *NYT*, 7 Sep 1976, 1.

103. Smith to Vorster in Gaylard to ADR, c204, 3 Sep 1976, Rhodesia-RSA, Smith Papers.

104. Vorster to Farmer (Smith) in ADR to Gaylard, c192, 8 Sep 1976, ibid.

105. HK, State 218974, 3 Sep 1976, DNSA. See HK, State 218978, 3 Sep 1976, DNSA; and HK, SecTo 26015, 4 Sep 1976, DNSA. On the Dar meeting: Martin and Johnson, *Struggle*, 242–46.

106. Moreton (from Duff), Washington 2789, 19 Aug 1976, PREM 16/1093, NA-UK; and Callaghan to Meadway, "Rhodesia," 22 Aug 1976, ibid.

107. Crosland, "Rhodesia: Memo for Cabinet," 21 Sep 1976, CAB 129/192/5, NA-UK; and Annex, UK Cabinet Conclusions, 9 Sep 1976, CAB 128/60/1, ibid. See Memcon (Callaghan, HK), 6 Sep 1976, PREM 16/1484, ibid.; and "Speaking note for Sir P Ramsbotham," in Harrison to Duff, 31 Jan 1977, FCO 36/2005, ibid.

108. *WP*, 8 Sep 1976, edit 14.

109. Telcon (HK, Rusk), 8 Sep 1976, KTT.

110. Scowcroft, "Meeting with Rusk," 10 Sep 1976, DGFL.

111. Zeidman, "Statement on Rhodesia, draft," 9 Sep 1976, Campaign 1976/1, CL; and Gwirtzman to Eizenstat, 10 Sep 1976, DGFL.

112. *NYT*, 1 Jul 1976, 43.

113. Jimmy Carter Presidential Campaign, "The U.S. and Angola," [early 1976,] Campaign 1976/132, CL.

114. "Election '76: Jimmy Carter on Africa," 18; and *NYT*, 24 Jun 1976, 22. For Carter's brief references to Africa: "Our Foreign Relations," 15 Mar 1976, and "Discusses Childhood, Religion," 6 May 1976, in Carter and Ford, *Campaign*, 109–19, 163–82.

115. Democratic Party Platform of 1976, 12 Jul 1976, APP; and "Foreign Policy," 29 Jul 1976, in Carter and Ford, *Campaign*, 371–77, quotation 375.

116. "Policy on Africa," n.d., in Carter and Ford, *Campaign*, 684–88, quotation 686; and Kornegay, "Africa and Presidential Politics," 20.

117. Lake, "Africa Statement, 2nd Draft," 21 Aug 1976, in Holbrooke to Aaron, 21 Aug 1976, Campaign 1976/132, CL.

118. Butcher to Lake, "Timing of an Africa Speech," 4 Aug 1976, Campaign 1976/1, CL. For similar advice: Clark, "Background Information on Southern Africa," in Clark to Eizenstat, 27 Apr 1975, ibid.; and Morgenthau, "Southern Africa in Crisis," in Morgenthau to Eizenstat, 15 Sep 1976, ibid.

119. "Jimmy Carter à *L'Express*: 'Voici ma politique étrangère,'" (interview with Pierre Salinger), *L'Express*, 23 Aug 1976, 40–44, quotations 42.

120. Telcon (HK, Rusk), 11 Sep 1976, KTT; and marginalia on Gwirtzman to Eizenstat, 10 Sep 1976, Campaign 1976/1, CL.

121. Zairean intelligence report in Cutler, Kinshasa 7761, 16 Sep 1976, NA-AAD; and Nyerere quoted in *Guardian*, 8 Sep 1976, 2. For Nyerere's astute assessment of the state of play: Nyerere to Callaghan, 12 Aug 1976, PREM 16/1093, NA-UK; and Nyerere "Memorandum on Southern Africa," in Brown, Dar 288, 29 Aug 1976, ibid. For a full account of the meeting based on Zairean intelligence sources: Cutler, Kinshasa 7761, 16 Sep 1976, NA-AAD.

122. For the odds: *NYT*, 12 Sep 1976, 1. For the British, see the tense exchange with Crosland as Kissinger was en route to Tanzania: Telcon (Crosland, HK), 14 Sep 1976, KTT.

123. Memcon (Brezhnev, Harriman), 20 Sep 1976, 596/6, Harriman Papers.

124. Memcon (ZB, Pik Botha), 28 Jan 1977, NSA-subject/33, CL.

125. Author's interview with Edmondson; Bowdler, Pretoria 4171, 16 Sep 1976, NA-AAD; and ADR to Gaylard, 14 Sep 1976, Geneva Conference, Smith Papers.

126. DOS, "South African Negotiations: Perspective of the Participants," [Apr 1977,] NLC-133-15-3-1-3.

127. See DOS, "An Approach to Prime Minister Vorster on Rhodesia," May 1977, NLC-133-13-26-16-4.

128. Fourie quoted in Scott, Cape Town 114, 24 Mar 1976, FCO 36/1849, NA-UK. See Sisco, ToSec 110389, 30 Apr 1976, Africa Trip/34, GFL; FCO, "Rhodesia: Meeting of GEN 12 on Wednesday, 28 July," FCO 36/1827, NA-UK; Smith to Vorster in Gaylard to ADR, C258, 7 Oct 1976, Rhodesia-RSA, Smith Papers; and Callinicos, *Southern Africa*, 15.

129. Nöthling, *Geskiedenis*, 24. See Smith, *Betrayal*, 198–99. On South Africa's relations with Rhodesia: Fourie, *Brandpunte*, 107–47.

130. Short, quoted in ADR to Gaylard, C209, 17 Sep 1976, Rhodesia-RSA, Smith Papers.

131. Memcon (Vorster, Kissinger), 6 Sep 1976, *FRUS, 1969–1976, Vol. 28: Southern Africa*, doc. 203; and Memcon (Callaghan, HK), 5 Aug 1976, PREM 16/1157, NA-UK. See Memcon (ZB, Pik Botha), 28 Jan 1977, NSA-subject/33, CL; and "Annex: Outline of the Rhodesian and Namibian Negotiations," attached to [DOS,] "Southern Africa: Policy Options," n.d., [filed in "Jan 77",] Lord/363, NA.

132. "Rhodesia: US/UK consultations with presidents," in Aspin to Dales, 3 Sep 1976, FCO 36/1832, NA-UK; and Frank Wisner, FD, 22 Mar 1998. See HK to

Scowcroft (for Ford), HAKto 9, 15 Sep 1976, HK Trip/42, FL; Memcon (Kaunda, HK), 17 Sep 1976, DNSA; Memcon (Nkomo, HK), 17 Sep 1976, DNSA; and HK to Scowcroft (for Ford), HAKto 11, 17 Sep 1976, HK Trip/42, FL.

133. Transnational Institute, *Black South Africa Explodes*, 39–40. See Kane-Berman, *South Africa*, 27–28.

134. Clark, "Memorandum for the Record: Africa Trip Impressions," 27 Nov 1976, DNSA; and Transnational Institute, *Black South Africa Explodes*, 41. See Kane-Berman, *South Africa*, 32. For protests: American Committee on Africa, "News," 24 Aug 1976, Aluka; HK, State 218272, 2 Sep 1976, FOIA; and *NYT*, 3 Sep 1976, 4.

135. *Observer*, 26 Sep 1976, 8. The *Observer*'s account of the Kissinger-Vorster meeting is by the well-informed journalists David Martin and Colin Legum. The declassified notes of the formal meeting do not include Vorster's description of his meeting with Smith. Vorster and Kissinger also met privately, and records of those meetings, if they exist, have not been declassified.

136. Memcon (Vorster, HK), 17 Sep 1976, DNSA. The following day they went over more details. See Memcon (Vorster, HK), 18 Sep 1976, DNSA.

137. Rhodesian delegate to talks quoted in Martin and Johnson, *Struggle*, 250; and Kissinger, *Renewal*, 998. See Kissinger, *Renewal*, 998–1001; and Smith, *Betrayal*, 201–6.

138. Memcon (Smith, HK), 19 Sep 1976, 10:00 am, DNSA; and Smith, *Betrayal*, 202. See Kissinger, *Renewal*, 1001.

139. Memcon (Smith, HK), 19 Sep 1976, 10:00 am, DNSA.

140. Ibid.

141. Memcon (Smith, HK), 19 Sep 1976, 5:55 pm, DNSA.

142. Memcon (Smith, HK), 19 Sep 1976, 10:00 am, DNSA.

143. HK to Scowcroft (for Ford), HAKto 22, 20 Sep 1976, HK Trip/42, GFL; Memcon (Smith, HK), 19 Sep 1976, 5:55 P.M., DNSA; and HK to Scowcroft (for Ford), HAKto 22, 20 Sep 1976, HK Trip/42, GFL.

144. Scott to Duff, 19 Sep 1976, FCO 36/1837, NA-UK; Kissinger, *Renewal*, 1000; Martin and Johnson, *Struggle*, 252; Memcon (Richard, HK), 30 Sep 1976, FCO 36/1840, NA-UK; and CIO, "The Settlement Proposals," 8 Oct 1976, Background, Smith Papers.

145. HK, SecTo 27022, 14 Sep 1976, DNSA; HK, SecTo 27225, 20 Sep 1976, DNSA; and Cabinet Meeting, 28 Sep 1976, DGFL. See Telcon (HK, Marder), 26 Oct 1976, KTT.

146. Memcon (Crosland, HK), 4 Sep 1976, PREM 16/1094, NA-UK.

147. Scott to Duff, 19 Sep 1976, FCO 36/1837, NA-UK.

148. *NYT*, 12 Sep 1976, 1. See HK, SecTo 27225, 20 Sep 1976, DNSA; HK, SecTo 27248, 21 Sep 1976, in Mokoena, *Zimbabwe*; and *NYT*, 16 Nov 1976, 16.

149. "Speaking note for Sir P Ramsbotham" in Duff to Ramsbotham, 2 Feb 1977, FCO 36/2006, NA-UK. For the five points: HK to Smith, in ADR to Gaylard, c217, 22 Sep 1976, Rhodesia-RSA, Smith Papers. For the disagreement with London: HK, SecTo 27022, 14 Sep 1976, DNSA; Crosland to HK, 21 Sep 1976, Crosland Papers 5/14, London School of Economics; Cabinet Minutes, 23 Sep 1976, FCO 36/1839, NA-UK; Memcon (Crosland, HK), 6 Oct 1976, FCO 36/1840, NA-UK; Telcon (HK, Ramsbotham), 13 Oct 1976, KTT; Telcon (HK, Richard), 24 Dec 1976, KTT; HK to Crosland, in Duff to Rowlands, 17 Jan 1977, FCO 36/2006; Kissinger, *Renewal*,

1006–12; and Crosland, *Crosland*, 361–65. For Smith's insistence on the five points: Smith to HK in Bowdler, Pretoria 4249, 21 Sep 1976, DNSA; and HK to Wisner, State 264172, 26 Oct 1976, in Mokoena and Gaymon, *Zimbabwe*.

150. HK to Vorster in ADR to Gaylard, c215, 21 Sep 1976, Rhodesia-RSA, Smith Papers; and HK to Smith, via Bowdler, in ADR to Gaylard, c217, 22 Sep 1976, ibid. See Memcon (Kaunda, Kissinger), 20 Sep 1976, 1:45 pm, DNSA; Memcon (Kaunda, Nkomo, Kissinger), 20 Sep 1976, DNSA; HK to Scowcroft (for Ford), HAKto 27, 21 Sep 1976, HK Trip/42, GFL; and HK to Scowcroft (for Ford), HAKto 32, 21 Sep 1976, HK Trip/42, GFL.

151. *Observer*, 19 Sep 1976, 1; and Nyerere quoted in Brown, Dar 350, 22 Sep 1976, FCO 45/1876, NA-UK. For Kaunda's summary of Kissinger's proposals and Nkomo's objections: Appendices A and B, 21 Sep 1976, Background, Smith Papers. See Kissinger, *Renewal*, 1003–5.

152. "Prime Minister's Address to the Nation," 24 Sep 1976, Background, Smith Papers. For "cracking": *NYT*, 25 Sep 1976, 1.

153. *LAT*, 25 Sep 1976, 1.

154. *Ghanaian Times* (Accra), quoted in Burns, Lusaka 2476, 18 Sep 1976, DNSA; and Legal Team of ANC Zimbabwe, "On the Proposed Transitional Government," 27 Oct 1976, Appendix D, Background, Smith Papers.

155. Garba, Press Briefing (transcript), 7 Oct 1976, 1/156/1, v84, DFA, SA.

156. Telcon (HK, Scranton), 14 Oct 1976, KTT; HK to Poncet (for Giscard), 23 Sep 1976, Présidence/5AG3-983, Paris; and *NYT*, 25 Sep 1976, 1.

157. "Secretary Discusses Southern Africa in Interview for NBC 'Today' Show," 28 Sep 1976, DOS *Bulletin* (25 Oct 1976): 529.

158. Smith to van der Byl, 29 Nov 1976, Telex Messages, Smith Papers.

159. *NYT*, 27 Sep 1976, 1.

160. *Issues and Answers*, 26 Sep 1976, quoted in *MACSA News* 59 (Oct 1976), 9, Aluka; *NYT*, 23 Sep 1976, 3; *NYT*, 17 Sep 1976, 8; and *NYT*, 23 Sep 1976, 3.

161. Martin and Johnson, *Struggle*, 236, citing authors' interview with Machel.

162. Cabinet Meeting, Sep 28, 1976, DGFL; and ADR to Gaylard, c228, 27 Sep 1976, Rhodesia-RSA, Smith Papers.

163. For Smith's slipping the hook and endless quibbling: "Statement Released by Ian Smith's Office," in Gaylard to Laver, 28 Sep 1976, Rhodesia-RSA, Smith Papers; Smith to Crosland, HK and Vorster in Gaylard to ADR, c242, 30 Sep 1976, Rhodesia-RSA, Smith Papers; and ADR to Gaylard, c282, 19 Oct 1976, Rhodesia-RSA, Smith Papers.

164. Martin and Johnson, *Struggle*, 239, citing authors' interview with Tom McNally, 28 Jun 1977; and "Rhodesian Strategy memorandum," in Baumhogger, 202 (emphasis added).

165. HK to Smith in ADR to Gaylard, c243, 1 Oct 1976, Rhodesia-RSA, Smith Papers; and Scott to Duff, 19 Sep 1976, FCO 36/1837, NA-UK.

166. Ramsbotham to Crosland, 3 Jan 1977, FCO 82/725, NA-UK.

167. *Guardian*, 22 Sep 1976, 12.

168. Callaghan to Meadway, "Rhodesia," 22 Aug 1976, PREM 16/1093, NA-UK.

169. Frank Wisner, FD, 22 Mar 1998.

170. "Extract from a note by Sir A. Duff," 22 Mar 1977, FCO 36/2135, NA-UK; Telcon (HK, Ramsbotham), 27 Oct 1976, KTT; and Telcon (HK, Ramsbotham), 13

Oct 1976, KTT. See Crosland's statements and debates in Parliament, 12 Oct 1976 and 20 Oct 1976, *Parliamentary Debates*, Commons, 5th ser., vol. 917, cols. 240–53, 1474–619.

171. On Mugabe: Meredith, *Mugabe*; Meredith, *Past Is Another Country*; and Blair, *Degrees in Violence*, 17–27.

172. *Observer*, 10 Oct 1976, 1; and CIO, "Formation of the Patriotic Front," 14 Oct 1976, Background, Smith Papers. On the creation of the Patriotic Front, see Dumiso Dabengwa, "ZIPRA in the Zimbabwe War of National Liberation," in Bhebe and Ranger, *Soldiers*, 24–35.

173. *Guardian*, 11 Oct 1976, 10; Rogers to HK in Katz, US Mission OECD Paris 30261, 13 Oct 1976, DDRS; and Low, Lusaka 335 in Vance, State 26132, 4 Feb 1977, FOIA.

174. Author's interview with Chona.

175. Author's interview with Edmondson.

176. See Undersecretary for Economic Affairs William D. Rogers, statement to Senate Africa Subcommittee, 30 Sep 1976, DOS *Bulletin* (25 Oct 1976): 533.

177. Horan to Scowcroft, 8 Mar 1976, Country/5, GFL; and Memcon (Ford, Scranton, Scowcroft), 8 Jul 1976, Memcons/20, GFL. Also Hartman to Scowcroft, 8 Mar 1976, Country/5, GFL.

178. INR, "Cuba-Southern Africa," 8 Mar 1976, Country/5, GFL. See "Intelligence Materials for President Nixon," [late May 1976,] Nixon/2, GFL; Gleijeses, *Visions*, 86–87; and Taylor, *China and Africa*, 96–99, 106–14.

179. Telcon (HK, Geyelin), 28 May 1976, KTT.

180. Machel quoted in Willard DePree, FD, 16 Feb 1994; Easum, in US House, "State Department Trip," CD5, 4; Carson, Maputo 218, 5 Mar 1976, NA-AAD; and HK quoted in ADR to Gaylard, c298, 8 Nov1976, Rhodesia-RSA, Smith Papers. See Easum, "Hard Times"; and Scowcroft to Ford, 26 Apr 1976, Africa Trip/32, GFL. Also author's interview with DePree.

181. *NYT*, 5 Sep 1976, D1.

182. Presidential Campaign Debate, 6 Oct 1976, APP.

183. Carter did twice mention Rhodesia. On September 13, he brushed off a direct question ("Views Self as 'Populist,'" 13 Sep 1976, in Carter and Ford, *Campaign*, 734–45), and on September 27—four days after Smith's historic speech—when asked by reporters, he said that he supported majority rule but ruled out US military intervention "unless our security is directly threatened." He added, "There was [sic] seven years of ignoring African policy on the part of Nixon-Ford administrations. . . . It took the election of 1976 to get them involved." (*The Bulletin* [Bend, OR], 27 Sep 1976, 1; and *NYT*, 28 Sep 1976, 31)

184. For the backstory: Witcover, *Marathon*, 561–70; and Anderson, *Electing*, 110–16.

185. Scheer, "Playboy," 86. The story broke when Scheer was interviewed on the *Today* show, September 20, 1976.

186. Witcover, *Marathon*, 570.

187. A Harris poll on election eve indicated that fewer than half of the voters felt strongly about their choice. (*NYT*, 2 Nov 1976, 1)

188. Telcon (HK, Scranton), 25 Sep 1976, KTT. See Drew, *American Journal*, 437–40.

189. See Presidential Campaign Debate, 23 Sep 1976, APP. On the polls: Ford, *Time to Heal*, 416; and Gallup, *The Gallup Poll: Public Opinion, 1972–1977* (online database), 1:906.

190. Dean, "Rituals," 57. John Dean, who overheard the remark while traveling with Butz after the GOP convention, included it in an article he wrote for *Rolling Stone*, demurely attributing it to "a distinguished member of Ford's Cabinet." *New Times* investigated and soon reported that Butz was the distinguished member. (Tony Schwartz, "The Insider," *New Times*, 13 Oct 1976, 27) The vulgarity of the comment led most editors to redact it. (See Alexander Cockburn, "Butz is an . . . [anatomical term]," *Village Voice*, 11 Oct 1976, 34.) Of the daily newspapers, only the *Toledo Blade* and the *Madison Capital Times* printed the comment in full.

191. *Time*, 18 Oct 1976, 25.

192. Ford, *Time to Heal*, 420.

193. Ibid.

194. *Observer*, 26 Sep 1976, 8.

195. Telcon (HK, Scowcroft), 26 Oct 1976, KTT; Telcon (HK, Scowcroft), 2 Nov 1976, KTT; Telcon (HK, Scowcroft), 1 Nov 1976, KTT; and Telcon (Scowcroft, HK), 27 Oct 1976, KTT.

196. Presidential Campaign Debate, 6 Oct 1976, APP; and Leslie Gelb, *NYT*, 8 Oct 1976, 19.

197. Presidential Campaign Debate, 6 Oct 1976, APP.

198. Ibid.

199. Ibid. For explanations: Greene, *Presidency of Ford*, 184–85; and Witcover, *Marathon*, 597–99.

200. Presidential Campaign Debate, 6 Oct 1976, APP.

201. Telcon (Armstrong, HK), 13 Oct 1976, KTT; and Telcon (Laxalt, HK), 13 Oct 1976, KTT. Polls indicated that Carter had won the second debate by a wide margin. (*WP*, 7 Oct 1976, 7)

202. *NYT*, 8 Oct 1976, 19.

203. "At Notre Dame University," 10 Oct 1976, in Carter and Ford, *Campaign*, 993–98.

204. Presidential Campaign Debate, 6 Oct 1976, APP.

205. Ibid.

206. Telcon (HK, Scowcroft), 25 Oct 1976, KTT. See Presidential Campaign Debate, 22 Oct 1976, APP.

207. See *NYT*, 3 Nov 1976, 18.

208. *NYT*, 1 Nov 1976, 1. Turnout was about 53.8 percent, only slightly down from 1972.

209. Bruce Galphin, "Jimmy Who Goes to Washington," 82 (emphasis in original).

210. "Atlanta Campaign Headquarters," 3 Nov 1976, Carter and Ford, *Campaign*, 1122.

211. Telcon (HK, Scowcroft), 3 Nov 1976, KTT.

212. See CQ, *Guide to 1976*, 23; and Joint Center for Political Studies, *The Black Vote*, 52. Thomas Anderson ran on the "American Party" ticket in Texas, winning 11,442 votes.

213. *Time*, 15 Nov 1976, 18; "Statement by Ambassador Andrew Young, May 19, 1977," United States Mission to the United Nations *Press Release*, USUN-27 (77),

May 24, 1977, WOA 58-210, Yale; and Borstelmann, *Cold War*, 247. See Joint Center for Political Studies, *The Black Vote*, 11 and 44; and Lawson, *Running*, 194. The thirteen states were Alabama, Florida, Louisiana, Maryland, Mississippi, Missouri, New York, North Carolina, Ohio, Pennsylvania, South Carolina, Texas, and Wisconsin.

214. *NYT*, 4 Nov 1976, 38.

215. "Atlanta Campaign Headquarters," 3 Nov 1976, Carter and Ford, *Campaign*, 1122; and Drew, *American Journal*, 533.

Chapter 3

1. Wolper Productions, "Roots."

2. For Nielsen ratings, *WP*, 26 Jan 1977, B7; and *WP*, 2 Feb 1977, 1.

3. Wolper, *Inside Story*, 137–38, 151.

4. Ibid., 142.

5. *Sunday Times* (London), 10 Apr 1977, 17.

6. Inaugural Address, 20 Jan 1977, APP; and Ramsbotham, Washington 274, 24 Jan 1977, FCO 82/726, NA-UK.

7. Wolper Productions, "Roots."

8. Fishbein, "*Roots*," 65.

9. Mazrui, "End of America's Amnesia?" 6; and *Time*, 14 Feb 1977, 69.

10. Range, "*Playboy*: Young," 62. See *Newsweek*, 28 Mar 1977, 25; and Haskins, *Andrew Young*, 141–43.

11. Author's interview with Young.

12. National Council of Churches, "Andrew Young." See Young, *Easy Burden*, 57–59, 116–21.

13. *WP*, 8 Aug 1979, E1. See Young, *Way Out of No Way*, 71–72; and Young, *Easy Burden*, 117–23. See also DeRoche, *Andrew Young*.

14. Young, "An Experiment in Power," 11 Aug 1965, quoted in DeRoche, "Andrew Young and Africa."

15. Bridges, Washington 4248, 15 Dec 1976, PREM 16/1909, NA-UK.

16. Documenting the American South, "Interview with Andrew Young," 16–17.

17. Young, "Interview of Mayor Andrew Young."

18. CQ, *Guide to 1976*, 50.

19. See Andrew Greeley, *CT*, 17 Feb 1977, B4; Shartar, "Carter Promise"; *Newsweek*, 28 Mar 1977, 30; and *Guardian & Observer* (London), 23 Apr 1978, 13.

20. *NYT*, 25 Dec 1976, 11. See *Daily Mail* (Lusaka), 23 Nov 1976, 4, Diggs Papers/192, Howard University; and Bowdler, "South African Press Comment on Congressmen Young, Diggs, and Clark," 14 Dec 1976, DNSA.

21. Johnson, "Helping Blacks" (interview with Young), 13.

22. DeRoche, *Andrew Young*, 75, quoting Young.

23. Johnson, "Helping Blacks," 13.

24. Shartar, "Carter Promise," 40; *WP*, 1 Feb 1977, 17; and Young, "Interview of Mayor Andrew Young."

25. *Rand Daily Mail* (Johannesburg), 9 Feb 1977, 11.

26. Kennedy to Russell, 17 Dec 1976, FCO 36/2005, NA-UK.

27. Author's interview with Moose (2001); and *NYT*, 14 Jul 1976, 19.

28. Author's interview with Chona.

29. See Dudziak, *Exporting American Dreams*.

30. Remarks at the Swearing In of Andrew J. Young, 30 Jan 1977, APP.

31. Author's interview with Young; *WP*, 13 Mar 1977, 1; and US Senate, "Nomination of Young," CD45, 12.

32. Author's interview with Carter.

33. Charles Maynes, FD, 4 Aug 1998.

34. See Haskins, *Andrew Young*, 152.

35. Author's interview with Carter.

36. Author's interview with Young.

37. Author's interview with McHenry.

38. Walker, "Yesterday's Answers," 4–5, based on an unpublished chapter of Vance, *Hard Choices*. Also MacLellan, *Cyrus Vance*, 1–9. These are the two best secondary sources on Vance.

39. Author's interviews with Graham, McHenry, and Edmondson; and Frank Wisner, FD, 22 Mar 1998.

40. Vance, "Overview of Foreign Policy Issues and Positions," 24 Oct 1976, Vance Papers/8, Yale.

41. Douglas Brinkley, "The Lives They Lived: Out of the Loop," *NYT Magazine*, 29 Dec 2002, 43. See Ball's account in Galsworthy to Palliser, 11 Nov 1976, FCO 82/650, NA-UK.

42. Carter, *Keeping Faith*, 50–51.

43. Vance and Carter had met twice, briefly, in Atlanta in 1971 and at the Trilateral Commission, of which both were members. Vance, *Hard Choices*, 29.

44. Shoup, "Jimmy Carter and the Trilateralists" and Chomsky and Otero, *Radical Priorities*, 136–42. Nearly a dozen members of the commission (which had fewer than 200 US members) joined the Carter administration: Brzezinski, Mondale, Vance, Harold Brown, Warren Christopher, Paul Warnke, Anthony Lake, Richard Holbrooke, Leslie Gelb, Samuel Huntington, and Henry Owen. Carter was not a particularly active member. See "The Trilateral Commission," *Trialogue* 12 (1976):10; and Carter, *Why Not the Best?*, 141.

45. *NYT Magazine*, 23 May 1976, 13. The best secondary sources on Brzezinski are Gati, *Zbig*; Lubowski, *Zbig*; Bonafede,"Zbigniew Brzezinski"; and Vaughan, "Zbigniew Brzezinski."

46. Ziołkowska, *Dreams*, 147, 141–42.

47. Vaughan, "Brzezinski and Afghanistan," 111. Brzezinski's dissertation, published in 1956 by Harvard University Press as *The Permanent Purge: Politics in Soviet Totalitarianism*, was a study of the purges. See the chapter on Tadeusz Brzezinski in Ziołkowska, *Dreams*, 111–40.

48. M. Brzezinski, *Casino Moscow*, 44–45.

49. Ziołkowska, *Roots Are Polish*, 33–34.

50. Ziołkowska, *Dreams*, 120. After the war, Zbigniew's father—who no longer had a government to represent—lost his job; he became a Canadian citizen in 1951.

51. For Brzezinski's service during the Johnson administration: Brzezinski, FD, 12 Nov 1971.

52. Brzezinski, quoted in Bowden, *Guests*, 123.

53. Ziołkowska, *Dreams*, 144.

54. See especially Brzezinski, *Africa and the Communist World*; Brzezinski, *Between Two Ages*; and Brzezinski and Huntington, *Political Power*.

55. Engerman, *Know Your Enemy*, 208–9, 221–22; and Mark Kramer, "Anticipating the Grand Failure," in Gati, *Zbig*, 42–59.

56. See especially Brzezinski, "U.S.-Soviet Relations."

57. Brzezinski, "How the Cold War Was Played," 196–97. For ZB's 2012 interview, see Gati, *Zbig*, 232.

58. For Cambodia: Brzezinski, "Half Past Nixon," 17. For grades: "Half Past Nixon," 19; and Brzezinski, "The Deceptive Structure of Peace," 50. See also Brzezinski, "US Foreign Policy: the Search for Focus"; and Brzezinski, "America and Europe."

59. Brzezinski, in Auspitz, "America Now," 26, 27.

60. See Engerman, *Know Your Enemy*, 282; and Pipes, "Team B."

61. See ZB, Richard Gardner, and Henry Owen, "Foreign Policy Priorities: A Memorandum to the President-Elect," 3 Nov 1976, Vance Papers/8, Yale.

62. "Spokespersons of US Right 'In Most Cases Stunningly Ignorant,'" *Der Spiegel* online, 6 Dec 2010, www.spiegel.de/international (interview with ZB).

63. Author's interviews with Aaron and Low; and Robert Pastor, "The Caricature and the Man," in Gati, *Zbig*, 105. See interview with Brzezinski, Albright, Denend, Odom, 18 Feb 1982, CPP.

64. Interview with Brzezinski, Albright, Denend, Odom, 18 Feb 1982, 61, CPP; and author's interview with Carter.

65. *NYT*, 7 Jul 1976, 12 (interview with Carter); Bourne quoted in Palliser to Duff, 8 Nov 1976, FCO 82/650, NA-UK; and *Newsweek*, 28 Feb 1977, 16.

66. Scheer, "Jimmy, We Hardly Know Y'all," 192.

67. Melhuish, "Future US Foreign Policy," [Dec 1976,] FCO 82/650, NA-UK.

68. Bridges, Washington 4356, 23 Dec 1976, PREM 16/1909, NA-UK.

69. Davidson to Melhuish, 22 Nov 1976, FCO 82/650, NA-UK.

70. Brzezinski, *Power*, 53.

71. Vance, *Hard Choices*, 31.

72. See Vance, "Overview of Foreign Policy Issues and Positions," 24 Oct 1976, and ZB, Richard Gardner, and Henry Owen, "Foreign Policy Priorities: A Memorandum to the President-Elect," 3 Nov 1976, Vance Papers/8, Yale.

73. See US Senate, "Nomination of Theodore C. Sorensen," 17 Jan 1977, CD44.

74. See Brzezinski, *Power*, 51; and ZB to Mondale et al., 21 Jan 1977, PRM/NSC 4, NCLC-12-37-8-4-8.

75. Memcon (Vance, Chona), 18 Jan 1977, FOIA.

76. *NYT*, 20 Jan 1977, 16. Also *NYT*, 20 Jan 1977, 1.

77. CIA, "World Trends and Developments," n.d., Feb 1977, CIA-rr. See Gleijeses, *Conflicting Missions*, 246-372.

78. See Inderfurth to ZB and Aaron, 5 Apr 1977, Brzezinski/14, CL.

79. *Financial Mail* (Johannesburg), 5 Nov 1976, 1. See Memcon (Chona, Kamana, ZB), "Southern Africa," 19 Jan 1977, NSA-staff/118, CL; and Lewis to Huntington, "Task Force Report—Africa," 29 Apr 1977, "Podgorny's 1977 Africa Tour/11," Program Files on Soviet Foreign Policy, RG 59, NA.

80. Inaugural Address, 20 Jan 1961, APP.

81. Author's interviews with Carter, Young, Moose (2001, 2002), Lake, Easum, DePree, and Petterson.

82. Morgenthau, "Southern Africa in Crisis," 15 Sep 1976, in Morgenthau to Eizenstat, 15 Sep 1976, Campaign 1976/1, CL.

83. Vance, "Overview of Foreign Policy Issues and Positions," 24 Oct 1976, Vance Papers/8, Yale.

84. Watson, Aaron, and Lake to Carter, "Your Meeting with Secretary Kissinger," 16 Nov 1976, NLC-133-212-1-1-6.

85. Kissinger quoted in ADR to Gaylard, C343, 6 Dec 1976, Rhodesia-RSA, Smith Papers.

86. *NYT*, 10 Nov 1976, 3. See Moorcraft and McLaughlin, *Rhodesian War*, 45–46.

87. INR, "Rhodesia: Assessment of Current Situation," 17 Jan 1977, Lord Papers/363, NA.

88. "Text of Address by Rhodesian Prime Minister," *NYT*, 25 Sep 1976, 4.

89. DOS, "Rhodesia: Negotiating Options and Elections," [30 Mar 1977,] NLC-133-14-13-25-7.

90. Flower, *Serving Secretly*, 177.

91. Smith, *Betrayal*, 221.

92. Halsted, Zanzibar 43, 4 Feb 1977, NLC-6-88-2-1-6.

93. Full text of speech in Scott, Cape Town 34 to FCO, 24 Jan 1977, PREM 16/1426, NA-UK.

94. Vance to Carter, ER, 24 Jan 1977, NLC-7-17-7-7-2, CL. See Ramsbotham, Washington 298, 24 Jan 1977, FCO 36/2005, NA-UK; and Crosland, FCO 171, 25 Jan 1977, FCO 36/2005, NA-UK. Vance was confirmed on January 20 and sworn in on January 23; his first day in the office was January 24.

95. Carter, marginalia, on Vance to Carter, 24 Jan 1977, NLC-126-6-3-2-0.

96. *NYT*, 25 Jan 1977, 1.

97. Armstrong, London 1449, 26 Jan 1977, FOIA; *Guardian* (London), 25 Jan 1977, edit 10; and *Times* (London), 25 Jan 1977, edit 15.

98. *WP*, 26 Jan 1977, edit 18; *NYT*, 27 Jan 1977, edit 34; and Richard in Memcon (Rowlands, Richard, Duff, Young), 2 Feb 1977, FCO 36/2006, NA-UK.

99. Memcon (Vance, Pik Botha), 25 Jan 1977, FOIA. See "Talking Points for Secretary Vance's Meeting with the South African Ambassador," in Vance to Carter, 25 Jan 1977, NLC-128-12-5-2-9.

100. Ibid.

101. Memcon (ZB, Pik Botha), 28 Jan 1977, NSA-subject/33, CL. Later Brzezinski told Botha, "We have great . . . empathy with you." Memcon (Carter, Pik Botha, Mondale, Vance, ZB), 23 Mar 1977, NLC-133-123-6-12-8.

102. Memcon (Smith, Pik Botha on 31 Mar 1977), 1 Apr 1977, Gaylard Meetings, Smith Papers.

103. TelCon (Callaghan, Carter), 13 Jan 1977, in Wright to Fergusson, 13 Jan 1977, PREM 16/1485, NA-UK.

104. "Mondale's Visit to Bonn: Talking Points," NLC-133-10-2-27-1; Gammon (from Mondale), Paris 102, 29 Jan 1977, "Vice President's Meeting with Prime Minister Callaghan," NLC-133-10-18-12-0; and Memcon (Callaghan, Mondale), 27 Jan 1977, FCO 82/762, NA-UK. See "Vice President's Trip to Europe and Japan, Jan 23–Feb. 1, 1977: Southern African Negotiations," NLC-133-12-1-6-3; "Mondale's Visit to Belgium, Jan. 24, 1977: Talking Points," NLC-133-119-5-1-6; "Meeting with EC Commission President Jenkins, Jan. 24, 1977," NLC-133-119-6-1-5; "Meeting

with President Valery Giscard d'Estaing, Jan. 29, 1977," NLC-133-10-23-2-5; "Visit of Vice-President Mondale: 27 January; and Steering Brief," FCO 36/2005, NA-UK.

105. Vance to Carter, 26 Jan 1977, NLC-126-6-6-1-8. Also *NYT*, 27 Jan 1977, 2.

106. Schaufele to Vance, 2 Feb 1977, NLC-133-14-13-26-6; Vance to Carter, 7 Feb 1977, NLC-7-17-7-11-7; and Ramsbotham, 26 Jan 1977, Washington 338, PREM 16/1909, NA-UK.

107. PRM [4]: Rhodesia, Namibia and South Africa, [Jan 1977,] DDRS; Special Coordination Committee Meeting (SCC), 8 Feb 1977, Vertical/Classified, CL. These minutes refer to it as an SCC meeting, but it was a PRC meeting. (The SCC dealt with intelligence matters that cross-cut across departments; it was generally chaired by Brzezinski.) See ZB to Carter, "PRC Meeting on Southern Africa—PRM 4," 9 Feb 1977, Vertical/Classified, CL; Schaufele and Lake to Vance, "NSC Meeting on South Africa, Rhodesia, and Namibia," 1 Mar 1977, Lake Papers/2, LC; NSC Meeting (minutes), 3 Mar 1977, DDRS; and NSC Meeting (summary), 3 Mar 1977, FOIA.

108. Carter, "Presidential Directive/NSC 2," 20 Jan 1977, CL online; and Inderfurth and Johnson, *Fateful Decisions*, 71.

109. PRM [4]: Rhodesia, Namibia and South Africa, [Jan 1977,] DDRS. Covers next two paragraphs.

110. ZB to Carter, 9 Feb 1977, Brzezinski/24, CL (emphasis in original). See Tuchman to ZB, 7 Feb 1977, Brzezinski/24, CL.

111. Minutes of PRC meeting, in ZB to Carter, 9 Feb 1977, Brzezinski/24, CL.

112. Backgrounder in Maynes to Vance, 28 May 77, FOIA.

113. Minutes of PRC meeting, in ZB to Carter, 9 Feb 1977, Brzezinski/24, CL.

114. US Information Agency (Lagos), "Andrew Young in Nigeria: More than a Social Call," Easum Papers. This glossy brochure about Young's trip was produced by the US embassy in Lagos.

115. Author's interview with Young; and Young to ZB, 24 Jan 1977, NSA-Agency (8)/22, CL.

116. US Information Agency (Lagos), "Andrew Young in Nigeria: More than a Social Call," Easum Papers. This glossy brochure about Young's trip was produced by the US embassy in Lagos.

117. [Vance,] "Talking Points for President Carter" (meeting with Young), [late January 1977,] NSA-Country/2, CL. Also Vance and Young to Carter, 27 Jan 1977, NLC-128-12-5-4-7; Carter, handwritten note to ZB, 28 Jan 1977, WHCF 11-10, CL; and *NYT*, 30 Jan 1977, 3.

118. *WP*, 1 Feb 1977, 17.

119. Author's interview with Young; *CR-House*, 2 Feb 1977, 3385 (Ashbrook); *CR-House*, 2 Feb 1977, 3385 (McDonald); *CR-House*, 3 Feb 1977, 3473 (Bauman); *CR-Senate*, 7 Feb 1977, 3753 (Baker). Also: Dewey Bartlett (R-OK), *CR-Senate*, 4 Feb 1977, 3719; Jesse Helms (R-NC), *CR-Senate*, 7 Feb 1977, 3754; Jim Martin (R-NC), *CR-House*, 8 Feb 1977, 3886. See, e.g., *NYT*, 1 Feb 1977, 2; *CBS Evening News*, 4 Feb 1977, VNA; *LAT*, 3 Feb 1977, B1; *CT*, 16 Feb 1977, edit B2; and *CSM*, 16 Feb 1977, 27.

120. *LAT*, 3 Feb 1977, B1.

121. *WP*, 3 Feb 1977, 1; and *CR-Senate*, 7 Feb 1977, 3753.

122. "Jimmy Carter on Africa," *Africa Report* 21:3 (May/June 1976):18–21, quotation 19; and Question-and-Answer Session with a Group of Publishers, Editors, and Broadcasters, 15 Apr 1977, APP. See Gleijeses, *Visions*, 98–103, 119–26; 158–63.

123. Mary McGrory, *CT*, 18 Feb 1977, B4.

124. Brighty to Tait, 18 Feb 1977, FCO 36/2006, NA-UK.

125. "Meeting with Young: Line to Take," in Harrison to Laver and Duff, 1 Feb 1977, FCO 36/2005, NA-UK. See Schaufele to Young, 28 Jan 1977, NLC-133-175-9-6-5.

126. See Memcon (Rowlands, Richard, Duff, Young), 2 Feb 1977 at 11:25 am; Memcon (Crosland, Duff, Young), 2 Feb 1977 at 12:00 pm; Memcon (Luard, Palliser, Young), 2 Feb 1977 at 12:30 pm; Memcon (Richard, Duff, Young), 2 Feb 1977 at 4:25 pm; and all FCO 36/2006, NA-UK.

127. Halsted, Zanzibar 43, 4 Feb 1977, NLC-6-88-2-1-6; Top Secret, 3 Feb 1977, NLC-1-1-8-19-1; *LAT*, 3 Feb 1977, B7. See *WP*, 3 Feb 1977, 16; and Vance to Carter, 4 Feb 1977, NLC-128-12-5-13-7.

128. DOS, "Your Visit to Tanzania," [Jan 1977,] NLC-133-175-9-28-1; and Richard Viets, FD, 6 Apr 1990.

129. Spain, Dar 314, 26 Jan 1977, NLC-133-175-9-38-0. See DOS, "Zanzibar," July 1977, NLC-133-159-2-10-5.

130. The Soviet Union and Tanzania signed arms agreements in 1974 for $83 million, in 1976 for $34 million, and in 1977 for $58 million. The terms were very liberal (2 percent interest; repayment in ten to fifteen years). Soviet economic aid was limited, approximately $600,000 in 1977; US economic aid was $22.3 million in 1978. State/NSC Paper #3, "Improving US Relations with African Countries," in Spiegel to Thornton, [16 Aug 1978,] Lake Papers/2, NA.

131. *Daily News* (Dar), 30 Jan 1977, 4; and author's interview with Young.

132. See: Vance, State 26383, 5 Feb 1977, NA-AAD; Mayondi (Zambian embassy, Dar) to Mwale, 25 Feb 1977, 150 UNIP 7/23/64; Mayondi to Mwale, 24 Mar 1977, 150 UNIP 7/23/64; Mayondi to Mwale, 22 Mar [must be Apr] 1977, 150 UNIP 7/23/64; and Makasa (Zambian High Commissioner, Nairobi) to Mwale, "Political Report No. 1 for January–April, 1977," n.d., 147 UNIP 7/23/55. On the East Africa community: Nabudere, "Role of Tanzania"; and Green, "East African Community."

133. Makasa to Mwale, "Political Report No. 1 for January–April, 1977," n.d., 147 UNIP 7/23/55.

134. Vance to Carter, 1 Feb 1977, NLC-128-12-5-9-2. See Spiers, London 1992, 3 Feb 1977, NA-AAD.

135. See Miles, BDOHP, 11 Nov 1996; and "Secretary's Visit to Iran and Saudi Arabia, 13–15 May 1977: Current African Issues," FCO 31/2117, NA-UK.

136. Young, "Reflections on an African Policy," in Katzen to Mondale, 3 May 1977, NLC-133-107-3-10-1; and author's interview with Kaunda and Chona.

137. *NYT*, 6 Feb 1977, 5; and Low, Lusaka 500, 3 Feb 1977, NSA-country/88, CL.

138. Kaunda to Carter in Low, Lusaka 338, 4 Feb 1977, NA-AAD; Halsted, Zanzibar 57, 5 Feb 1977, NA-AAD; and Ramsbotham, Washington 562, 9 Feb 1977, FCO 36/2006, NA-UK. See Vance to Carter, 10 Feb 1977, NLC-6-88-4-8-7.

139. *NYT*, 7 Feb 1977, 8.

140. "Nyerere appeals to US: topple Smith," *Rand Daily Mail* (Johannesburg), 7 Feb 1977, 5. See "Young outlines Africa policy," *Daily Nation* (Nairobi), 8 Feb 1977, 1, 16. See Spain, Dar 672, 14 Feb 1977, NA-AAD.

141. Halsted, Zanzibar 49, 5 Feb 1977, NA-AAD. See Ramsbotham, Washington 561, 9 Feb 1977, FCO 36/2006, NA-UK; and Easum, Lagos 1584, 10 Feb 1977, NA-AAD.

142. *WP*, 6 Feb 1977, 14.
143. *WP*, 8 Feb 1977, 10.
144. *WP*, 15 Jan 1977, C1.
145. Apter, "Pan-African," 441, 442; and *Newsweek*, 14 Feb 1977, 40.
146. DOS, "Your Visit to Nigeria," NLC-133-176-1-1-7; and *WP*, 20 Jan 1977, 35. Nigerian population statistics are inexact; because the results of the 1973 census were canceled, there are no census figures from 1963 to 1991. For trade, see Young's address to South African business leaders in Bowdler, Cape Town 838, 24 May 1977, NA-AAD.
147. ZB to Carter, WR, 9 Apr 1977, Brzezinski/41, CL. See "Background Information for Senator Percy," in C. to Rick [Inderfurth], 16 Nov 1978, NLC-20-19-4-1-4.
148. Author's interview with Easum. See Christopher to Carter, 6 Oct 1977, NLC-133-160-5-2-9.
149. See [no author,] State 192690, 4 Aug 1976, FOIA.
150. Easum to family, 10 Jan 1976, Easum Papers. See Easum, Lagos 798, 21 Jan 1976, Country/5, GFL.
151. DOS/NSC Paper #3, "Improving US Relations with African Countries," in Spiegel to Thornton, [16 Aug 1978,] Lake Papers/2, NA.
152. Young to Carter, Mondale, Vance, ZB, "Recommendations for Discussion Resulting from African Tour," 13 Feb 1977, NLC-7-17-8-12-5.
153. US Information Agency (Lagos), "Andrew Young in Nigeria: More than a Social Call," Easum Papers.
154. Easum, Lagos 1681, 12 Feb 1977, FOIA.
155. Vance, State 22058, 1 Feb 1977, NA-AAD. See *Newsweek*, 21 Feb 1977, 24.
156. Easum, Lagos 1683, 13 Feb 1977, NA-AAD.
157. Author's interview with Young.
158. Easum, Lagos 1681, 12 Feb 1977, FOIA.
159. Haroun Adamu, "Carter's Limitations," *The Daily Times* (Lagos), 20 Jan 1977, 3.
160. Author's interview with Young. In a May 18, 1979 speech in Houston, Young also mentioned this headline. See Young, USUN 2413, 6 Jun 1979, FOIA. Nigeria had a rowdy and chaotic press, much of which has not been preserved on microfilm or in the Library of Congress. I was unable to find this headline that Young remembered vividly.
161. Author's interview with Easum.
162. Apter, "Pan-African," 457.
163. Memcon (Carter, Obasanjo), 11 Oct 1977, NLC-20-7-7-2-3.
164. Easum, Lagos 1681, 12 Feb 1977, FOIA.
165. BBC, "Britain Reluctant to take Responsibility," 11 Feb 1977, FCO 36/2006, NA-UK. See Memcon (Richard, Young), 11 Feb 1977, FCO 36/2006, NA-UK.
166. *International Herald Tribune* (Paris), 14 Feb 1977, 6. See Young to Carter, "Recommendations for Discussion Resulting from African Tour," n.d., NLC-128-12-5-23-6.
167. Easum to Mr. and Mrs. Chester Easum, 23 Feb 1977, Easum Papers.
168. NSC Meeting (minutes), 3 Mar 1977, NLC-17-1-5-9-8.
169. Presidential Directive/NSC-4: "Cuba," 15 Mar 1977, DNSA.
170. Author's interview with Carter.

171. Presidential Directive/NSC-5, 9 Mar 1977, DNSA.

172. NSC Meeting, 3 Mar 1977, NLC-17-1-5-9-8. See Vance to Carter, 10 Feb 1977, Brzezinski/24, CL; and Hartman, State 35287, 16 Feb 1977, FOIA.

173. Young to Carter, Mondale, Vance, ZB, "Recommendations for Discussion Resulting from African Tour," 13 Feb 1977, NLC-128-12-5-23-6.

174. "Mr. Crosland's notes written on Sunday 13 February," FCO 73/244, NA-UK. See Crosland, *Crosland*, 394.

175. [DOS,] "Southern Africa—Policy Review," in Dodson to Mondale, 19 Jul 1977, Vertical/Cuba-Defense, CL. That this is the State Department's draft is clear in Richardson to ZB, 19 Jul 1977, Brzezinski/24, CL.

176. Owen, *Time to Declare*, 291.

177. Spiers, London 3315, 2 Mar 1976, FOIA.

178. See "PRM: Rhodesia, Namibia and South Africa," [late January 1977,] DDRS; and "Rhodesia: Recent History," in Wall to Renwick, 2 May 1979, FCO 36/2493, NA-UK. For South Africa's attitude toward the Anglo-American diplomatic offensive: Onslow, "South Africa" and Smith, *Betrayal*, 228–48.

179. Memcon (Vance, ZB, Garba), 21 Mar 1977, FOIA.

180. Burns (Lusaka) to US Information Agency, 20 May 1977, FOIA.

181. Owen, *Time to Declare*, 271, 284. Also author's interview with Owen.

182. Vance, *Hard Choices*, 264; and Schaufele to Young, 28 Jan 1977, NLC-133-175-9-6-5.

183. NSC Meeting, 3 Mar 1977, NLC-17-1-5-9-8. See INR, "Namibia: Assessment of Current Situation," 17 Jan 1977, Lord Papers/363, NA; Gleijeses, *Visions*, 92–96; and Gleijeses, "Test of Wills."

184. NSC Meeting, 3 Mar 1977, NLC-17-1-5-9-8.

185. Carter's marginalia on Vance to Carter, 22 Feb 1977, NLC-7-17-8-13-4; Lake and Petterson to Spiegel, 10 Mar 1977, Lake Papers/2, NA; and SCC Meeting, 8 Feb 1977, Vertical/Classified, CL.

186. Lake and Petterson to Spiegel, 10 Mar 1977, Lake Papers/2, NA.

187. NSC Meeting, 3 Mar 1977, NLC-17-1-5-9-8.

188. *Time*, 21 Mar 1977, 18. The hostage takers killed two people but released the remaining hostages unharmed thirty-eight hours later.

189. INR, "Constraints on the Callaghan Government,"18 Jan 1977, NLC-133-12-3-4-3; and Owen, *Time to Declare*, 283. See Callaghan to Carter, [1 Mar 1977,] FCO 36/2006, NA-UK.

190. Vance to Carter, 11 Mar 1977, NLC-128-12-6-11-8.

191. Owen, *Time to Declare*, 284; and author's interview with Owen.

192. Memcon (Vance, Owen), 11 Mar 1977, FOIA. See Vance to President, "Rhodesia: Reactions to Owen Trip to Africa," 20 Mar 1977, FOIA; AmEmb London to SecState, 31 Mar 1977, NLC-133-14-13-11-2; and "The Owen Brief: An Analysis and Recommended Response," [Apr 1977,] NLC-133-14-13-4-0.

193. "Prime Minister's visit to Washington," in Vile to Private Secretary, 22 Feb 1977, FCO 66/870, NA-UK.

194. "Brief for the Secretary of State," in Melhuish to Private Secretary, 25 Feb 1977, FCO 66/871, NA-UK; and Russell to Greenstock, 9 Mar 1977, FCO 82/726, NA-UK.

195. Halsted, Zanzibar 43, 4 Feb 1977, NLC-6-88-2-1-6; and Ramsbotham, Washington 810, 24 Feb 1977, FCO 36/2010, NA-UK.

196. Owen, "Cabinet: South Africa at the United Nations," [1 Mar 1977,] FCO 36/2034, NA-UK.

197. See DOS, "Southern Africa," [Jan 1977], NLC-133-10-18-5-8; "Background: Rhodesia," attached to "Visit by the Vice-President of the United States: Southern Africa Brief," 26 Jan 1977, FCO 36/2005, NA-UK; and "Secretary's Visit to Iran and Saudi Arabia, 13–15 May 1977: Current African Issues," FCO 31/2117, NA-UK.

198. Reid to Mansfield, 4 Mar 1977, FCO 36/2011, NA-UK; "Speaking Notes: UN-Chapter VII," in Reid to Dales, 8 Mar 1977, FCO 36/2010, NA-UK; Owen, "Cabinet: South Africa at the United Nations," [1 Mar 1977,] FCO 36/2034, NA-UK. See Memcon (Richard, Vance), 8 Feb 1977, NLC-133-42-3-2-2; and Memcon (Vance, Owen), 11 Mar 1977, NLC-133-42-3-4-0.

199. "Speaking Notes: UN-Chapter VII," in Reid to Dales, 8 Mar 1977, FCO 36/2010, NA-UK.

200. See Memcon (Owen, Mondale), 10 Mar 1977, FCO 36/2011, NA-UK; Memcon (Callaghan, Carter), 10 Mar 1977, PREM 16/1486, NA-UK; Memcon (Callaghan, Senate Foreign Relations Committee), 10 Mar 1977, PREM 16/1486, NA-UK; and Memcon (Callaghan, ZB), 10 Mar 1977, PREM 16/1486, NA-UK.

201. Memcon (Owen, Vance), 10 Mar 1977, PREM 16/1486, NA-UK. Giscard said something similar to Vance. See Gammon, Paris 09751, 3 Apr 1977, FOIA.

202. Vance, *Hard Choices*, 262; Owen, *Time to Declare*, 283; and author's interviews with Renwick and Owen.

203. Henderson, BDOHP, 24 Sep 1998; Renwick, BDOHP, 6 Aug 1998; and author's interview with Aaron.

204. Author's interview with Graham.

205. DOS, "Briefing Paper: Rhodesia," 6 Dec 1976, NLC-133-213-5-6-6.

206. Memcon (Vance, Owen), 11 Mar 1977, NLC-133-42-3-4-0.

207. Spiers, London 1792, 1 Feb 1977, NA-AAD.

208. Author's interview with Young.

209. DePree, Maputo 118, 7 Feb 1977, NA-AAD; and Spain, Dar 701, 15 Feb 1977, NA-AAD. See Low, Lusaka 406, 1 Feb 1977, NA-AAD.

210. Remarks at the National Arts Theater, Lagos, Nigeria, 1 Apr 1978, APP.

211. Halsted, Zanzibar 57, 5 Feb 1977, NA-AAD.

212. Easum, Lagos 1683, 13 Feb 1977, NA-AAD.

213. Spain, Dar 701, 15 Feb 1977, NA-AAD.

214. Kennedy, News Conference, 1 Mar 1961, APP. Kennedy was defending his assistant secretary of state for African affairs, "Soapy" (G. Mennen) Williams, who first used the phrase.

215. See Gleijeses, *Visions*, 51–53.

216. Ramsbotham, Washington 735, 21 Feb 1977, FCO 36/2006, NA-UK.

217. See, e.g., Vance to Carter, 4 Mar 1977, NLC-128-12-6-4-6; Vance to Carter, 9 Mar 1977, NLC-128-12-6-9-1; Vance to Carter, 11 Mar 1977, NLC-128-12-6-11-8; Vance to Carter, 18 Mar 1977, NLC-128-12-6-1-0; Vance to Carter, 19 Mar 1977, NLC-128-12-6-16-3; Vance to Carter, 20 Mar 1977, NLC-128-12-6-16-3; and Vance to Carter, 30 Mar 1977, NLC-128-12-6-28-0. Also Carter to ZB, in ZB to Aaron and Thornton, 29 Mar 1977, NSA-staff/119, CL.

218. Scott, Cape Town 170, 3 May 1976, FCO 45/1876, NA-UK.

219. Mtisi, Nyakudya, and Barnes, "Social and Economic Developments," 128–37.

220. *CR-House*, 11 Jan 1977, 957. Clark simultaneously introduced a similar bill (S. 174) in the Senate: *CR-Senate*, 11 Jan 1977, 789.

221. Young, 24 Feb 1977, US House, "Rhodesian Sanctions Bill," CD8.

222. Young, 7 Mar 1977, US House, "Amending the UN Participation Act," CD5.

223. Vance, 10 Feb 1977, US Senate, "Rhodesian Sanctions," CD58. See *CQ Weekly*, 19 Feb 1977, 308–10. The new head of policy planning at the State Department, Anthony Lake, was an expert on the amendment, and he had a sophisticated grasp of the machinations of Congress. A foreign service officer who resigned in 1970 to protest the invasion of Cambodia, Lake had written a study of US policy toward Rhodesia from 1965 to 1976 that is a well-informed and well-argued call for change, beginning with the repeal of the Byrd Amendment. See Lake, *"Tar Baby" Option*.

224. Moore to Carter, 5 Mar 1977, Plains/19, CL. Carter urged action on repeal during his first week in office. Marginalia on Vance to Carter, 25 Jan 1977, NLC-128-12-5-2-9. Vance also made calls. Vance to Carter, 11 Mar 1977, NLC-128-12-6-11-8.

225. Author's interview with Carter.

226. See Julius Katz in US Senate, "Rhodesian Sanctions," CD46, 67–81.

227. Clark in US Senate, "Rhodesian Sanctions," CD46, 3–4. Technically, the bill did not repeal the Byrd Amendment; it simply declared that it no longer applied to Rhodesia.

228. Harry Byrd (I-VA) caucused with the Democrats.

229. The Senate Committee on Foreign Relations voted it out, 15–1; the House Committee on International Relations followed suit, 27–5. See US Senate, "Rhodesian Sanctions" CD45 and US House, "Rhodesian Sanctions Bill." CD11.

230. Memcon (Crosland, Young), 2 Feb 1977, FCO 36/2006, NA-UK.

231. *LAT*, 15 Mar 1977, 1.

232. *NYT*, 6 Jan 1994, 1. See O'Neill, *Man of the House*, 297–329; Carter, *Keeping Faith*, 71–73; Farrell, *Tip O'Neill*, 440–62; and *CQ Weekly*, 26 Feb 1977, 361–63.

233. *NYT*, 15 Mar 1977, 1.

234. Dick Ichord (D-MO), *CR-House*, 14 Mar 1977, 7412. For the debate, *CR-House*, 7410–48, and 7454–56. The Byrd Amendment had not reduced US reliance on Soviet chrome; in 1976, 41 percent of US chrome imports were from the Soviet Union, while only 5 percent were from Rhodesia.

235. *CR-House*, 14 Mar 1977, 7445–46 (Sikes), 7421 (Mitchell). In the 95th Congress, there were sixteen African Americans in the House, all of whom were Democrats, and one in the Senate, who was a Republican.

236. Ibid., 7427 (Ashbrook).

237. Ibid., 7414 (Fenwick), 7426 (Brademas).

238. Ibid., 7434 (Badham), 7413 (Robert Bauman, R-MD), 7439 (Edward Derwinski, R-IL), 7446 (Sikes).

239. Thirty-nine Republicans (30% of all GOP representatives) joined 211 Democrats in support of repeal.

240. For the Senate debate, *CR-Senate*, 14 Mar 1977, 7385–404; and *CR-Senate*, 15 Mar 1977, 7526–606. It was not a party-line vote: eighteen moderate Republicans joined forty-eight Democrats in favor, whereas eight conservative, southern Democrats and one Independent joined seventeen Republicans in opposition. Four Democrats and three Republicans abstained.

241. *WP*, 17 Mar 1977, 1.

242. Remarks and a Question-and-Answer Session at the Clinton Town Meeting, 16 Mar 1977, APP. See *NYT*, 17 Mar 1977, 1. For the reaction to "homeland," see *NYT*, 18 Mar 1977, 11; and *LAT*, 18 Mar 1977, 1.

243. *LAT*, 17 Mar 1977, 1.

244. Address Before the General Assembly, 17 Mar 1977, APP.

245. Richard, UN 322, 17 Mar 1977, FCO 82/748, NA-UK.

246. *LAT*, 18 Mar 1977, 5.

247. Remarks on Signing H.R. 1746 into Law, 18 Mar 1977, APP. Also, "Bill Signing—HR 1746," 18 Mar 1977, Name/Dick Clark, CL.

248. Statement on Signing the Bill into Law, 18 Mar 1977, APP.

249. *NYT*, 27 Mar 1977, 2. The poll was taken from March 4–7, 1977.

Chapter 4

1. Zaire has had several name changes: before independence in 1960, it was the Belgian Congo; from 1960–64, Congo (Léopoldville); from 1964–71, Democratic Republic of the Congo; from 1971–97, Zaire; in 1997, it reverted to Democratic Republic of the Congo. I refer to it as Zaire, the name it had throughout the Carter years. For Shaba 1, see especially Gleijeses, "Truth." See also Ogunbadejo, "Conflict"; and Hull, "Internationalizing."

2. Inaugural Address, 20 Jan 1977, APP; Rieff, "Realpolitik," 20; and William Schaufele, FD, 19 Nov 1998.

3. Vance to Carter, 18 Mar 1977, NLC-128-12-6-16-3.

4. Allen Davis, FD, 26 Jun 1998.

5. Memcon (Schmidt, Vance), 31 Mar 1977, doc. 82, *AAPD 1977*, 420; and Stratton to Owen, 9 Jun 1977, FCO 31/2117, NA-UK. See Walker, Kinshasa 2089, 10 Mar 1977, NA-AAD; and Glickson, "Shaba," 186.

6. *Elima* (Kinshasa), 12 Mar 1977, 1; and Munkanta to Mwale, "Political Report for March 1977," n.d., 150 UNIP 7/23/63. See Walker, Kinshasa 2096, 10 Mar 1977, FOIA; and Cutler, Kinshasa 2362, 16 Mar 1977, NA-AAD.

7. *WP*, 22 Mar 1977, 12; Memcon (Honecker, Fidel Castro), 3 Apr 1977, DY30 JIV 2/201/1292, SAPMO. Also: FBIS Trends, "Analysis of Communist Media Treatment of African Developments," 30 Mar 1977, CREST; and Malley, "20 heures."

8. See Department of Agriculture Remarks, 16 Feb 1977, APP; Memcon (Vance, ZB, Garba), 21 Mar 1977, FOIA; Schoultz, *That Infernal*, 296–308; Gleijeses, *Visions*, 43–45; and LeoGrande and Kornbluh, *Back Channel*, 155–68.

9. *Time*, 28 Mar 1977, 43. See Cutler, Kinshasa 2321, 22 Mar 1977, NA-AAD.

10. Walter Cutler, FD, 15 Sep 1989. See Edward Marks, consul general at Lubumbashi, FD, 12 Aug 1996.

11. Munkanta to Mwale, "Political Report for March 1977," n.d., 150 UNIP 7/23/63; and Cutler, FD, 15 Sep 1989. See Cutler, Kinshasa 2321, 16 Mar 1977, FOIA.

12. *CSM*, 17 Mar 1977, edit 32; and *CT*, 19 Mar 1977, edit N8.

13. *LAT*, 20 Mar 1977, E1.

14. See William Schaufele, FD, 19 Nov 1994; Vance, State 80399, 9 Apr 1977, NA-AAD; and Minutes of Cabinet Meeting, 11 Apr 1977, Plains/18, CL.

15. Munkanta to Mwale, "Political Report for March 1977," n.d., 150 UNIP 7/23/63; and Memcon (Honecker, Fidel Castro), 3 Apr 1977, DY30 JIV 2/201/1292, SAPMO.

16. *WP*, 18 Mar 1977, edit 26 (emphasis in original).

17. Bonker, 16 Mar 1977, US House, CD15, 33–34; and Solarz, Seelye, 29 Mar 1977, US House, "Foreign Assistance 1978, Part 3," CD16, 223, 227, 218, 220, 229, 230.

18. Gammon, Paris 09751, 3 Apr 1977, FOIA. For US: Vance to Carter, 9 Mar 1977, NLC-128-12-6-9-1; March 18 State Department Press Briefing in Vance, State 62587, 21 Mar 1977, NA-AAD; Vance, State 64045, 23 Mar 1977, NA-AAD; and Vance, State 64155, 8 Apr 1977, NA-AAD. For UK: Memcon (Owen, Sadat), 26 Apr 1977, FCO 31/2116, NA-UK. For FRG: Bonn, Federal Cabinet, "Assessment of the Situation in Zaire" 14 Apr 1977, in Young to Rosling, 18 Apr 1977, FCO 31/2115, NA-UK. For Portugal: Young to Ibbott and Reid, "Call by Counselor, Portuguese Embassy," 22 Apr 1977, FCO 31/2116, NA-UK. See also Gleijeses, *Visions*, 37–43.

19. See Vance in US Senate, "Foreign Assistance Authorization," CD49, 22; Benson in US House, "Foreign Assistance Appropriations for 1978, Part 1," CD10, 771; and Seelye in US House, "Foreign Assistance 1978, Part 3," CD16, 208, 228.

20. Memcon (Vance, ZB, Garba), 21 Mar 1977, FOIA. See Intelligence Review, 23 Mar 1977, NLC-1-1-3-42-0; and Vance to Carter, 6 Apr 1977, NLC-128-12-7-5-4.

21. See Cutler, Kinshasa 2644, 23 Mar 1977, NA-AAD; and Cutler, Kinshasa 2742, 25 Mar 1977, NA-AAD.

22. News Conference of March 24, 1977, APP. See Vance, State 67025, 25 Mar 1977, NA-AAD; Strausz-Hupé, USNATO 1740, 26 Mar 1977, NA-AAD; Cutler, Kinshasa 2760, 26 Mar 1977, NA-AAD; and Christopher, State 69120, 29 Mar 1977, NA-AAD.

23. Gammon, Paris 09751, 3 Apr 1977, FOIA. See Vance, SecTo 3108, 2 Apr 1977, NA-AAD; and Vance, State 78877, 8 Apr 1977, NA-AAD.

24. Memcon (Carter, Sadat, Mondale, Vance, ZB), 5 Apr 1977, NLC-25-109-8-3-2. On March 26, 1977, while attending a NATO meeting in Brussels, Vance conferred with the Belgians about Shaba. See ibid.

25. See Gammon, Paris 09751, 3 Apr 1977, FOIA; and Thompson Buchanan, FD, 15 Mar 1996.

26. Thompson Buchanan, FD, 15 Mar 1996.

27. James to Owen, 24 Apr 1977, FCO 31/2115, NA-UK; Mansfield to James, 10 May 1977, FCO 31/2117, NA-UK. See Christopher, State 240039, 21 Sep 1978, FOIA; Goldsborough, "Dateline," 174–78; and Lellouche and Moisi, "French Policy."

28. Memcon (Giscard, Carter), 9 May 1977, 5AG3-984, Archives de la Présidence, Paris.

29. Belgian Foreign Minister Renaat Van Elslande, quoted in *Knack* (Brussels), 20 Apr 1977, 217–18.

30. Jean François-Poncet, quoted in *Le Monde* (Paris), 21 Dec 1979, 1.

31. European Newspaper Journalists: Question and Answer Session, 25 Apr 1977, APP; and Memcon (Soutou, Aaron), 15 Apr 1977, 5AG3/984, Archives de la Présidence, Paris.

32. *Times of Zambia* (Lusaka), 21 Mar 1977, edit 1.

33. Memcon (Carter, Sadat, Mondale, Vance, ZB), 5 Apr 1977, NLC-25-109-8-3-2.

34. For Saudi funding: Vance, State 79669, 8 Apr 1977, FOIA; Cutler, Kinshasa 3668, 19 Apr 1977, NA-AAD; and *NYT*, 21 Jun 1987, 1. For US denial: *NYT*, 9 Apr 1977, 5. For US foreknowledge: Porter, Jidda 2297, 26 Mar 1977, NA-AAD; Memcon (Carter, Sadat, Mondale, Vance, ZB), 5 Apr 1977, NLC-25-109-8-3-2; Easum, Lagos 3962, 10 Apr 1977, FOIA; and Haskell, *CR-Senate*, 15 Jun 1977, 19285.

35. Memcon (Giscard, Carter), 9 May 1977, 5AG3-984, Archives de la Présidence, Paris; and Stratton to Owen, 9 Jun 1977, FCO 31/2117, NA-UK.

36. *NYT*, 13 Apr 1977, edit 23.

37. Marenches with Ockrent, *Dans le secret*, 248.

38. SURSIS, "A Conversation with Saudi Arabia's New Ambassador." On the Safari Club: Haykal, *Iran*, 113–16; Haykal, *Illusions*, 56, 82–83; Mamdani, *Good Muslim, Bad Muslim*, 84–87; Trento, *Prelude to Terror*, 99–106; and Bronson, *Thicker Than Oil*, 132–36.

39. [CIA,] "Considerations on Regional Conflicts" (follow-up to 10 May 1978 NSC meeting on Defense Department Consolidated Guidance), [10 May 1978,] Serial Xs, Brzezinski/36, CL; and SURSIS, "A Conversation with Saudi Arabia's New Ambassador."

40. News Conference of April 22, 1977, APP; and Memcon (Giscard, Carter), 9 May 1977, 5AG3-984, Archives de la Présidence, Paris.

41. Stratton, Kinshasa 122, 25 Apr 1977, FCO 31/2115, NA-UK. See Cutler, Kinshasa 2761, 26 Mar 1977, NA-AAD; Harlan, Paris 11651, 21 Apr 1977, NA-AAD; and Anderson, Rabat 2186, 21 Apr 1977, NA-AAD.

42. Situation Room to ZB, 7 May 1977, NLC-1-2-2-47-5. On the lack of Cuban involvement in Shaba 1: Gleijeses, *Visions*, 41–42.

43. *NYT*, 28 Apr 1977, 29 (emphasis in original); and Memcon (Palliser, ZB), 26 May 1977, FCO 82/749, NA-UK. For two exceptions to the praise: "Triple Play," *National Review,* 15 Apr 1977, edit 425; and *CT*, 8 Apr 1977, edit B2.

44. *Newsweek*, 18 Apr 1977, 49. See Cutler, Kinshasa 2670, 24 Mar 1977, NA-AAD.

45. Memcon (Giscard, Carter), 9 May 1977, box 5AG3-984, Archives de la Présidence, Paris; and Ramsbotham to Palliser, 25 Mar 1977, FCO 36/2011, NA-UK.

46. Edward Marks, FD, 12 Aug 1996; Stratton to Owen, 9 June 1977, FCO 31/2117, NA-UK; and Stratton to Osborn, 14 May 1977, FCO 31/2117, NA-UK.

47. "President's Briefing Book [for London Summit]," 4 May 1977, NLC-24-97-7-3-8.

48. Vance to Carter, 25 Mar 1977, NLC-128-11-19-2-5.

49. Ibid. See Holcomb (DOD) to Cabinet Secretary, 30 Mar 1977, NSA(5)-VIP visits/3, CL; and Vance to Carter, "Official Working Visit by Egyptian President Anwar Sadat," n.d., NLC-133-157-3-3-4.

50. *CSM*, 8 Apr 1977, 3; Memcon (Owen, Sadat), 26 Apr 1977, FCO 31/2116, NA-UK; H. Freeman Matthews, FD, 20 Apr 1993; and Carter, *Palestine*, 89.

51. The short shrift the State Department gave to the Horn in its briefing memos for Carter is puzzling. The declassified record contains at least fifteen cables from January through March about "Egyptian concern about Soviet activities in Ethiopia." See, e.g., from January alone: Cairo 1197, Cairo 1262, Cairo 1299, Khartoum 278, Addis 498, Addis 534, Khartoum 317, and Khartoum 328; all NA-AAD.

52. See, e.g., Washington Special Actions Group Meeting, "Ethiopia," 24 Apr 1974, Kissinger Papers, Box TS 81, NSC Committees and Panels, Washington Special Actions Group, LOC; and Secretary's Staff Meeting, 3 Jan 1975, Kissinger Transcripts, DNSA.

53. DCI/NIO, "East Africa: Outside Influence and Potential Conflict," 7 May 1975, *FRUS 1969–1976, E-6*, doc 142; and INR, "Ethiopia: Radicals Stave Off New Challenges," 26 Aug 1976, ibid. On the Ethiopian revolution: Tareke, *Ethiopian Revolution*;

Westad, *Global*, 250–61; Haile-Selassie, *Ethiopian Revolution*; Keller, *Revolutionary Ethiopia*; Ottaway and Ottaway, *Ethiopia*; Lefort, Éthiopie; Tubiana, ed., *La révolution*; Tiruneh, *Ethiopian Revolution*; and Marcus, *History*, 181–96. For an overview of US policy: Woodroofe, *Buried*, 14–28.

54. See Lefebvre, *Arms for the Horn*, 278–80; "Issue Paper on Ethiopia," attached to Springsteen to Scowcroft, 10 Jan 1975, Ethiopia: DOS memos, box 1, NSA; and DOS/NSC Paper #3: Improving US Relations with African Countries, in Spiegel to Thornton, 18 Aug 1978, Lake/4, NA.

55. Wyman, Addis 14026, 25 Nov 1974, *FRUS 1969–1976, E-6*, doc 118; and *Economist*, 19 Feb 1977, 61. See "Economic Assistance to Ethiopia," n.d., NSA-country/21, CL; and DOS, "Review of Foreign Assistance Policies toward Ethiopia," in Shurtle to Oxman, 4 May 1978, Christopher Papers/16, NA.

56. See Hummel, Addis 8717, 22 Jul 1975, NA-AAD; Soviet Foreign Ministry and CPSU CC International Department, "About the Soviet-Ethiopia Conflict," 3 Apr 1978, in Hershberg, "Anatomy," 92–94; Brind (British ambassador to Somalia, 1977–80), "Soviet Policy in the Horn," 93; and Westad, *Global*, 261–72.

57. "The Ethiopian Revolution and its Implications," 28 May 1977, NLC-23-13-5-3-4.

58. DOS, "The Horn of Africa: US and Soviet Involvement," 27 Jan 1977, NLC-133-175-9-23-6; and Thomas Farer in US House, "Foreign Assistance 1978, Part 3," CD16, 153. On security at the base: Lt. Gen. Howard Fish in US House, "Foreign Assistance 1978, Part 3," CD16, 193–94.

59. Interdepartmental Group for Africa, "US Policy toward Ethiopia," 10 Dec 1976, *FRUS 1969–1976, E-6*, doc 170. On the Peace Corps: Agency for Volunteer Service, *Action: Fiscal 1976 Budget and Transition Estimate, International Programs (Peace Corps)*, February 1975, 70, appendix D; and Henze to ZB, 8 Feb 1978, Horn/2, CL.

60. Interdepartmental Group for Africa, "US Policy toward Ethiopia," 10 Dec 1976, *FRUS 1969–1976, E-6*, doc 170.

61. DOS to Scowcroft, 10 Jan 1975, Ethiopia: DOS Memos, box 1, NSA.

62. HK to Ford, 10 Jun 1975, DDRS. Figures from Habib, State 14991, 22 Jan 1977, FOIA, citing a joint CIA/INR study. Also HK to Ford, 24 Jun 1975, DDRS; Henze, "Arming the Horn"; and Lefebvre, *Arms for the Horn*, 280. US intelligence in 1977 estimated total US post–World War II military aid to Ethiopia at $286 million, and total economic aid at $352 million. "The Ethiopian Revolution and its Implications," 28 May 1977, NLC-23-13-5-3-4.

63. Habib, State 14991, 22 Jan 1977, FOIA; [Parmenter (NIO Africa),] "An Alternative View of the Situation in the Horn of Africa," [20 Jan 1978,] NLC-15-17-2-3-2 (for author and date of this document: Henze to ZB, 1 Feb 1978, "Comments on CIA Paper," Horn/2, CL); and "Ethiopia," attached to Lord to Sisco, 24 Jan 1975, *FRUS 1969–1976, E-6*, doc 129. For an astute analysis from the US ambassador in Somalia, 1978–82, see Petterson, "Ethiopia Abandoned?"

64. Hartman, State 35287, 16 Feb 1977, FOIA. See Habib, State 14991, 22 Jan 1977, FOIA; Russian Republic, *Rossiya*, 107; David, "Realignment in the Horn of Africa," 4; and Ofcansky, "National Security." For Soviet policy toward Ethiopia, see Westad, *Global*, esp. 261–72.

65. For Somalia in the first fifteen years of independence: Lewis, *Understanding Somalia*; Samatar, *Socialist Somalia*; Laitin, "Political Economy"; and Mehmet, "Effectiveness of Foreign Aid."

66. Brind, "Soviet Policy in the Horn," 80. See also Mehmet, "Effectiveness of Foreign Aid."

67. See Hamrick, Mog 506, 7 Apr 1975, Hamrick Papers; and "Human Rights Country Evaluation Plan: Somalia," in Derian to Christopher, 8 Dec 1977, Christopher Papers/24, NA.

68. DOS, "Somalia," [Jan 1977,] NLC-133-176-1-49-5. See CIA, "Communist Aid to LDCs," 6 Jan 1977, CIA-rr; and Henze to ZB, 8 Apr 1977, Ethiopia/2, NSA.

69. Brind, "Soviet Policy in the Horn," 83. See CIA, "NIE: Soviet Military Policy in the Third World," NIE 11-10-76, 21 Oct 1976, CIA-rr; CIA, "Communist Aid to LDCs," 6 Jan 1977, CIA-rr; "The Ethiopian Revolution and its Implications," 28 May 1977, NLC-23-13-5-3-4; Memcon (Ochoa, Ratanov), 17 Jul 1977, CWIHP-va; Tareke, *Ethiopian Revolution*, 183; Laitin, "War in the Ogaden," 99; Robbs, "Africa and the Indian Ocean"; Ghebhardt, "Indian Ocean," 677; and Marcus, *History*, 197.

70. CIA, "Intelligence Information Cable: Somalia/USSR," 29 Mar. 1975, Hamrick Papers; and Loughran, Mog 1169, 8 Aug 1975, NA-AAD.

71. US Senate, "Construction Projects on the Island of Diego Garcia," CD36. For the photographs: attachments to HK, State 142400, 17 Jun 1975, Hamrick Papers; and sheaf of photos in NSA Country/5, GFL. See also *Newsweek*, 17 Mar 1975, 46; *NYT*, 7 Apr 1975, 2; and *US News & World Report*, 26 May 1975, 24. Cruise missiles required refueling every sixty to ninety days; therefore, the ability to refuel in theater was a boon.

72. Loughran, Mog 1169, 8 Aug 1975, Hamrick Papers; and Mulcahy to HK, 19 Aug 1975, ibid. Also Loughran, Mog 1287, 3 Sep 1975, *FRUS 1969–1976, E-6*, doc 145; and HK to Ford, 24 Sep 1975, NSA-Country/5, GFL.

73. Mulcahy to HK, 19 Aug 1975, Hamrick Papers; and HK, State 277323, 22 Nov 1975, *FRUS 1969–1976, E-6*, doc 152. See HK to Ford, c. 16 Sep 1975, NSA-Country/5, GFL.

74. See Memcon (Kassim, Addou, HK), 8 Oct 1976, DNSA; and Scranton, USUN 4283, 8 Oct 1976, FOIA.

75. See Habib, State 14991, 22 Jan 1977, FOIA, summarizing the assessment of CIA and INR.

76. Memcon (Giscard, HK), 10 Dec 1976, 5AG3-983, Archives de la Présidence, Paris; and CIA, "Perspectives for Planning and Programming," 3 Jan 1977, CREST.

77. *Newsweek*, 14 Feb 1977, 48.

78. INR, "Ethiopia: Radicals Stave off New Challenges," 26 Aug 1976, *FRUS 1969–1976, E-6*, doc 164; Tsongas and Bonker, "The Horn of Africa," [17 Dec 1977,] NSA/2, CL; and Hartman to Vance, 26 May 1977, NLC-23-20-4-5-5.

79. *NYT*, 9 Mar 1977, 12; and *WP*, 2 Mar 1977, 12. See CIA, Intelligence Memorandum: "Ethiopia: The Internal Political Balance," 10 Jan 1978, NLC-6-21-7-14-0.

80. INR, "Ethiopia: Radicals Stave off New Challenges," 26 Aug 1976, *FRUS 1969–1976, E-6*, doc 164. See Habib, State 14991, 22 Jan 1977, FOIA.

81. ZB to Carter, 21 Jan 1977, NLC 1-1-6-1-2, CL. Also, author's interview with Addou.

82. HK, State 8923, 14 Jan 1977, FOIA; and Habib, State 14991, 22 Jan 1977, FOIA.

83. CIA, "Intelligence Memorandum: World Trends and Developments," Feb 1977, 38–39, CIA-rr; and Hartman, State 35287, 16 Feb 1977, FOIA (emphasis added).

84. Hartman, State 35287, 16 Feb 1977, FOIA. For US focus on Djibouti (not Ogaden): ZB to Carter, 26 Jan 1977, NLC-1-1-6-27-4; and Jacobs, Mog 434, 14 Mar 1977, NA-AAD.

85. Bev Carter, Monrovia 873, 4 Feb 1977, FOIA. By late March, the Horn was the second item on the agenda. Christopher, State 70320, 30 Mar 1977, FOIA. For lack of reply: Henze to ZB, 18 Feb 1977, NSA-staff/5, CL.

86. DOS, "The Horn of Africa: US and Soviet Involvement," 27 Jan 1977, NLC-133-175-9-23-6; and DOS, Talking Points: "Somalia," n.d., NLC-133-176-1-49-5. See Vance, State 26383, 5 Feb 1977, NA-AAD.

87. Memcon (Siad Barre, Samsonov), 23 Feb 1977, "Journal of G. V. Samsonov" (Soviet ambassador to Somalia), 11 Mar 1977, CWIHP-va.

88. Young to Carter, Mondale, Vance, ZB, "Recommendations for Discussion Resulting from African Tour," 13 Feb 1977, NLC-128-12-5-23-6.

89. *Economist*, 19 Feb 1977, 61. These remarks were reported by the *CSM* and UPI, but not by the *NYT*, *WP*, or *LAT*. See *CSM*, 16 Feb 1977, 2; and UPI, *Ellensburg* [WA] *Daily Record*, 16 Feb 1977, 12. The State Department prepared a response to press queries about Young's comments, but none arose. See Hartman, State 36073, 17 Feb 1977, NA-AAD.

90. Young, USUN 726, 11 Mar 1977, NA-AAD.

91. Ibid.

92. Cohen, "Conditioning U.S. Security Assistance," 247. See DOS, "The Horn of Africa: US and Soviet Involvement," 27 Jan 1977, NLC-133-175-9-23-6; and US House, 1974, "Human Rights in the World Community," CD4. For the first country reports, US House, "Human Rights Practices," CD18. See Schoultz, *Human Rights*; Moyn, *Last Utopia*; Schmidli, "Human Rights"; Sellars, *The Rise*; and Kaufman, "The Bureau."

93. Vance in US House, "Foreign Assistance Appropriations for 1978, Part 1," CD10, 532.

94. US Senate, "Foreign Assistance, FY78," CD47, 151.

95. Ibid., 196.

96. Ibid., 196. See *NYT*, 25 Feb 1977, 1.

97. *NYT*, 27 Feb 1977, E16; and *WP*, 27 Feb 1977, edit C6. See State 40837, 23 Feb 1977, Ethiopia: Human Rights/1, NSA; charts in US House, "Foreign Assistance Appropriations for 1978, Part 1," CD10, 692–719; Ofcansky, "National Security"; and Lefebvre, *Arms for the Horn*, 153.

98. Official Government Communiqué of 1 Mar 1977, in *El País* (Montevideo), 2 Mar 1977, 1; and Communiqué of Argentine Foreign Ministry in *Nación* (Buenos Aires), 1 Mar 1977, 1. See also Schmidli, "Human Rights."

99. See *NYT*, 1 Mar 1977, 1; *NYT*, 2 Mar 1977, 10; and [n.d.] Mar 1977, SH Chron.

100. Ramos to Rodríguez, 8 Nov 1976, Gleijeses Papers.

101. Pérez Novoa to Fidel Castro, Addis Ababa 137, 10 Feb 1977, ibid. Also Memcon (Pérez Novoa, Ratanov [USSR Ambassador, Ethiopia]), 10 Feb 1977, "Diary of A. P. Ratanov," 30 Mar 1977, in Hershberg, "Anatomy," 53. The White House was aware of Mengistu's request: ZB to Carter, 11 Mar 1977, NLC-1-1-2-60-1.

102. "Visita de la delegación cubana a Etiopía," 20–27 Feb 1977, Gleijeses Papers.

103. "Report concerning a trip to the Democratic Republic of Somalia," in Ulianovskii to Ponomarev, 18 Feb 1977, in Hershberg, "Anatomy," 54–55; and Memcon (Samsonov [USSR Ambassador, Somalia], Siad Barre), 23 Feb 1977, ibid., 55–56.

See also Soviet Foreign Ministry, Third African Department, "Somalia's Territorial Disagreements with Ethiopia and the Position of the USSR," 2 Feb 1977, ibid., 52–53.

104. Tienken, Addis 1533, 15 Mar 1977, FOIA; Tienken, Addis 1568, 16 Mar 1977, FOIA; and Ticnken, Addis 1600, 17 Mar 1977, FOIA. See also Henze, ER, 16 Mar 1977, NSA-staff/5, CL.

105. See Tienken, Addis 1568, 16 Mar 1977, FOIA; Ramos to Rodríguez, 8 Nov 1976, Gleijeses Papers; "Visita de la delegación cubana a Etiopía," 20–27 Feb 1977, ibid.; Memcon (Honecker, Fidel Castro), 3 Apr 1977, DY30 JIV 2/201/1292, SAPMO; and Penfold to Johnson," 8 Mar 1977, FCO 31/ 2104, NA-UK.

106. CIA, "National Intelligence Analytical Memorandum: The Ethiopian Revolution and its Implications," 28 Mar 1977, CIA-rr. See Addis 1335, 5 Mar 1977, NSA.

107. Vance, State 63406, 22 Mar 1977, FOIA; ZB to Carter, 17 Mar 1977, NLC-1-1-3-8-8; and CIA, "National Intelligence Analytical Memorandum: The Ethiopian Revolution and its Implications," 18 Mar 1977, CIA-rr. See "The Ethiopian Revolution and its Implications," 28 May 1977, NLC-23-13-5-3-4.

108. Memcon (Casas, Ustinov, Akhromeyev), 27 Sep 1977, Gleijeses Papers.

109. See "Vermerk" (summary of conversation with Valdés Vivó), Berlin, 13 Mar 1978, DY30 IV 2/2.035/127, SAPMO, Berlin.

110. ZB to Carter, 11 Mar 1977, NLC-1-1-2-60-1.

111. [Dirección de inteligencia militar, EMG,] "Síntesis analítica sobre la revolución etíope," March 1977, Gleijeses Papers. All Cuban reports about the revolution were glowing. See, e.g., Ochoa to Raúl Castro, Addis Ababa 9, 19 Apr 1977, ibid.; and Maj. Calanas Rius to Viceministro Jefe Dirección Politica, 14 May 1977, ibid.

112. Jacobs, Mog 444, 15 Mar 1977, FOIA. For a more sober and accurate assessment, see "Cuban and Soviet Ventures in Africa," Jun 1977, Podgorny's 1977 Africa Tour/11, Program Files on Soviet Foreign Policy, RG 59, NA.

113. Memcon (Honecker, Fidel Castro), 3 Apr 1977, DY30 JIV 2/201/1292, SAPMO.

114. Ibid. See Malley, "20 heures."

115. "Current Foreign Assistance," in Tarnoff to ZB, n.d., in Shurtle to Steve, 4 May 1978, Christopher Papers/16, NA; and "The Case for Continued Assistance," ibid.

116. The *Prensa Latina* interview is reprinted as "An Interview with Ethiopia's Mengistu—The Man Carter Wanted Out," *Executive Intelligence Review* (8 Mar 1977): 2–4; and *Granma Internacional* (Havana), 27 Mar 1977, 3.

117. Memcon (Honecker, Fidel Castro), 3 Apr 1977, DY30 JIV 2/201/1292, SAPMO.

118. Ibid. Also Memcon (Bayeh, Sinitsin), 18 Mar 1977, "Diary of S. Y. Sinitsin," 30 Mar 1977, CWIHP-va.

119. Memcon (Honecker, Fidel Castro), 3 Apr 1977, DY30 JIV 2/201/1292, SAPMO.

120. *Newsweek*, 11 Apr 1977, 55.

121. Collins (INR), "USSR-Africa-Podgorny Trip; Clandestine Analysis," 1 Apr 1977, Podgorny's 1977 Africa Tour/11, Program Files on Soviet Foreign Policy, RG 59, NA; Vance, State 67010, 25 Mar 1977, ibid.; and Yevsyukov, "Reminiscences."

122. Vance to Carter, 5 Apr 1977, NLC-128-12-7-4-5. See DePree, Maputo 126, 8 Feb 1977, FOIA; Sikasula (Zambian ambassador, Maputo) to Mwale, 21 Apr 1977, 149 UNIP 7/23/61.

123. CPSU to SED CC, "Results of Podgorny's Visit to Africa," CWIHP-va; and Marturelos (Mogadicio) to Malmierca, Carlos Rafael, Valdés Vivó, Nogasshu, 11 Apr 1977, Gleijeses Papers.

124. See Vance to Carter, "Your Meeting with Crown Prince Fahd," May 1977, NLC-133-158-2-3-4.

125. Vance to Carter, 17 May 1977, NLC-128-6-15-1-6.

126. Ibid.; and Turki al-Faisal bin Abdel Aziz al-Saud, "Special Address at Georgetown University," 3 Feb 2002.

127. See Kennedy, "Persian Gulf," 25; Bronson, *Thicker Than Oil*, 131; *WP*, 21 Dec 1977, 1; and Bergsten, 16 Feb 1977, US House, "Foreign Assistance Appropriations for 1978, Part 1," CD10, 179.

128. Porter, Jidda 1010, 6 Feb 1977, NA-AAD. See also *NYT*, 23 Oct 1977, E2; CIA, "Trends in OPEC Economic Assistance, 1976," CREST; *NYT*, 30 Jan 1977, 1; and Wai, "The Sudan," 313.

129. *NYT*, 10 Mar 1977, 3. On the summit: "Afro-Arab Summit"; Gad, "Arab-African Economic Cooperation," 1 Mar 1977, 148 UNIP 7/23/59; and Kum Buo, "Illusion of Afro-Arab Solidarity," 46.

130. Toasts of the President and the Crown Prince, 24 May 1977, APP; and *WP*, 20 Dec 1977, 1. See: Remarks of the President and the Crown Prince at the Welcoming Ceremony, 24 May 1977, APP; *WP*, 21 Dec 1977, 1; and Bronson, *Thicker Than Oil*, 127. The US Treasury did not disclose Saudi holdings in US Treasuries and direct investments; $60 billion (in 1977 dollars) is the accepted estimate.

131. *NYT*, 21 Jun 1987, 1; and Mottram to Powell, 25 Sep 1985, published in *Guardian* (London), 28 Oct 2006, 9.

132. *NYT*, 21 Jun 1987, 1; and Kissinger, *Years of Upheaval*, 663.

133. CIA, "Intelligence Information Cable: Somalia/USSR," 29 Mar 1975, Hamrick Papers.

134. Loughran, Mog 1287, 3 Sep 1975, Hamrick Papers.

135. Jacobs, Mog 365, 6 Mar 1977, FOIA.

136. Loughran, Mog 365, 7 Mar 1977, NA-AAD. See Jacobs, Mog 582, 5 Apr 1977, NA-AAD.

137. PRM/NSC 21, 17 Mar 77, DNSA. Work on the PRM had begun at least two weeks earlier. See Henze's ERs on March 3, 4, and 14, 1977, Horn/5, CL.

138. Author's interviews with Addou, Moose, Hamrick, Petterson, and Easum.

139. Christopher, State 067050, 25 Mar 1977, FOIA.

140. Vance, ER, 24 Mar 1977, NLC-133-42-3-8-6. See Vance to Carter, "Official Working Visit by Egyptian President Anwar Sadat," n.d., NLC-133-157-3-3-4.

141. Mondale to Vance, 25 Mar 1977, NLC-133-42-3-8-6 (double underlining in original); and Clift to Mondale, 26 Mar 1977, NLC-133-106-6-54-1. Also author's interview with Mondale.

142. Hartman, State 38243, 18 Feb 1977, FOIA. Also Henze, ER, 17 Feb 1977, Horn/5, CL; and ZB to Mondale, "Somalia," [c. 29 Mar 1977,] in ZB to Henze, 24 Mar 1977, NSA-staff/1, CL.

143. Long quoted in Muir to Squire, 17 Jan 1978, FCO 31/2223, NA-UK.

144. Jacobs, Mog 538, 29 Mar 1977, forwarded in Vance, State 77651, 7 Apr 1977, FOIA. Ambassador Loughran was on sick leave.

145. DOS, Talking Points: "Somalia," n.d., NLC-133-176-1-49-5; Jacobs, Mog 538, 29 Mar 1977, forwarded in Vance, State 77651, 7 Apr 1977, FOIA; and *WP*, 28 Feb 1977, 20.

146. ZB to Mondale, "Somalia," attached to ZB to Henze, 24 Mar 1977, NSA-staff/1, CL; Vance to Mondale, 5 Apr 1977, NLC-133-42-3-8-6; and Henze to ZB, ER, 2 Mar 1977, Horn/5, CL.

147. Memcon (Vance, Owen), 1 Apr 1977, FOIA; and Gammon, Paris 09751, 3 Apr 1977, FOIA. Also Memcon (Owen, Vance), 1 Apr 1977, FCO 82/768, NA-UK; *Le Monde*, 5 Apr 1977, 1; and Colvin to Melhuish, "Vance's visit to Paris," 15 Apr 1977, FCO 36/2007, NA-UK.

148. *Le Monde*, 5 Apr 1977, 1 (interview with Sadat).

149. Memcon (Carter, Sadat, Mondale, Vance, ZB), 4 Apr 1977, NLC-25-109-8-2-3.

150. Memcon (Sadat, Vance, ZB), 4 Apr 1977, FOIA. See: Matthews, Cairo 873, 17 Jan 1977, FOIA; President's Diary, 4 Apr 1977, CL-online; ZB to Carter, 5 May 1977, NLC-1-2-2-29-9; and DOS, "The Military Supply Relationship," [1 Nov 1977,] NLC-5-3-9-2-2.

151. Porter, Jidda 2550, 4 Apr 1977, FOIA. Also: Henze, ER, 18 Mar 1977, NSA-staff/5, CL; and ZB to Carter, 26 Mar 1977, NLC-17-26-3-8-4.

152. Toast of the President at a Dinner Honoring the Egyptian President, 4 Apr 1977, APP.

153. Memcon (Carter, Sadat, Mondale, Vance, ZB), 5 Apr 1977, NLC-25-109-8-3-2.

154. *NYT*, 6 Apr 1977, 1.

155. Slonim, "New Scramble for Africa," 34.

156. *Time*, 18 Apr 1977, 18; and "Chronology of Events: Somali-US Relations 1976–77," [April 1978,] FOIA. See President's Daily Diary, 6 Apr 1977, CL online. This interview was the basis of "A Day in the Life of Jimmy Carter," an hour-long NBC special aired on April 14, 1977.

157. Vance to Carter, 6 Apr 1977, NLC-24-101-5-3-4.

158. Vance, State 78514, 7 Apr 1977, FOIA (emphasis in original); and Vance to Carter, 6 Apr 1977, NLC-128-12-7-5-4. See "Chronology of Events: Somali-US Relations 1976–77," [Apr 1978,] FOIA.

159. Henze, ER, 6 Apr 1977, NSA-staff/5, CL.

160. Henze, ER, 30 Mar 1977, NSA-staff/5, CL; and "PRM/NSC-21: The Horn of Africa," in Schaufele and Lake to Vance, 4 Apr 1977, Lake Papers/2, NA.

161. "PRM/NSC-21: The Horn of Africa," in Schaufele and Lake to Vance, 4 Apr 1977, Lake Papers/2, NA.

162. Vance, State 85332, 15 Apr 1977, FOIA; Schaufele and Lake to Vance, 8 Apr 1977, Lake Papers/2, NA; and "PRM/NSC-21: The Horn of Africa," in Schaufele and Lake to Vance, 4 Apr 1977, ibid.

163. PRC: Summary of Conclusions, 11 Apr 1977, NLC-7-67-9-4-8.

164. Schaufele and Lake to Vance, 8 Apr 1977, Lake Papers/2, NA.

165. Henze to ZB, 8 Apr 1977, Ethiopia/2, NSA. See Schaufele and Lake to Vance, 8 Apr 1977, Lake Papers/2, NA; and "Policy Review Committee Meeting," 11 Apr 1977, NLC-15-80-10-20-4.

166. PRC: Summary of Conclusions, 11 Apr 1977, NLC-7-67-9-4-8. See Vance, State 85332, 15 Apr 1977, NA-AAD.

167. Carter's comment on ZB to Carter, 11 Apr 1977, PRC Meetings/10, CL. See Carter's marginalia on Vance to Carter, 15 Apr 1977, NLC-24-101-5-2-5.

168. *NYT*, 20 May 1977, 2. The start date of the "Red Terror" varies from April to December 1977. In May 1978, the State Department estimated that the Terror had cost 1,500 to 2000 lives and 15,000 to 20,000 detentions. Amnesty International's figures were higher: 3,750 to 4,500 deaths from December 1977 to March 1978; 30,000 to 100,000 detainees in Addis alone and "barbaric torture of children as well as adults." "The Human Rights Question," in Tarnoff to ZB, in Shurtle to Oxman, 4 May 1978, Christopher Papers/16, NA.

169. See 19 Apr 1977, SH Chron; "Notes on Africa Group Meeting," 20 Apr 1977, NLC-133-15-3-17-6; and Henze, ER, 20 Apr 1977 and ER, 29 Apr 1977, NSA-staff/5, CL. Also Christopher, State 68802, 28 Mar 1977, FOIA; and Henze to ZB, 28 Mar 1977, NSA-staff/1, CL. Economic aid continued. See "Economic Assistance to Ethiopia," n.d., NSA-country/21, CL.

170. Henze to ZB, 21 and 22 Apr 1977, NSA-staff/1, CL.

171. Moose to Christopher, 29 Apr 1977, Christopher Papers/8, NA. See also Tienken, Addis 2472, 24 Apr 1977, Ethiopia/3, NSA; Vance, State 92313, 24 Apr 1977, FOIA; Vance, State 92315, 24 Apr 1977, NA-AAD; Wauchope, Asmara 336, 24 Apr 1977, FOIA; Ethiopia Working Group, Situation Report No. 9, 27 Apr 1977, NLC-6-21-8-27-5; and Ethiopia Working Group, Situation Report No. 10, 28 Apr 1977, NLC-6-21-8-29-3.

172. Vance, State 92359, 25 Apr 1977, FOIA; and Tienken, Addis 2705, 30 Apr 1977, NA-AAD.

173. Porter, Jidda 2863, 19 Apr 1977, NLC-1-1-5-54-5. See 15 Apr 1977, SH Chron.

174. 19 Apr 1977, SH Chron; and Henze, ER, 20 Apr 1977, NSA-staff/5, CL. See Miklos, Tehran 4896, 2 Jun 1977, NA-AAD.

175. Paul Henze wrote Brzezinski many memos questioning the pro-Somali tilt of Carter's policy, but Brzezinski did not include Henze's points in his memos to Carter. Henze's objections were not based on the perils of backing an aggressor; they were based on his conviction that Ethiopia was indelibly pro-Western and it was only a matter of time before it returned to a pro-American stance.

Chapter 5

1. *Time*, 25 Apr 1977, 49.

2. *NYT*, 15 Apr 1977, 38; and *NYT*, 18 Apr 1977, 30.

3. *NYT*, 19 Apr 1977, 24. See CIA Intelligence Memorandum, "The Impending Soviet Oil Crisis," Mar 1977, CIA-rr. Also Carter, *Keeping Faith*, 91–98.

4. The Energy Problem: Address to the Nation, 18 Apr 1977, APP. See "Jimmy Carter Energy Policy Speech," *NBC News*, 18 Apr 1977, VNA.

5. *NYT*, 18 Apr 1977, 30.

6. *NYT*, 21 Apr 1977, 35.

7. *WP*, Apr 17, 1977, 1. See Gallup Poll, 24 Apr 1977, *WP*, 1.

8. Lumet. *Network*; *NYT*, 19 Apr 1977, 1; West Virginia Remarks in a Panel Discussion on Energy, 17 Mar 1977, APP; and *NYT*, 20 Apr 1977, edit 20. For polls: *NYT*, 19 Apr 1977, 24; and *NYT*, 23 Apr 1977, 7, 25.

9. *WP*, 22 Apr 1977, B1.

10. Davidson to Darling, 23 Feb 1977, FCO 82/726, NA-UK.

11. See *CQ Weekly*, 19 Mar 1977, 488–90.

12. Drew, *American Journal*, 101; Tate to Carter, 18 Apr 1977, Handwriting/18, CL; and *CQ Weekly*, 26 Feb 1977, 361.

13. *WP*, 19 Apr 1977, edit 18.

14. *NYT*, 24 Apr 1977, E19; and *WP*, 20 Apr 1977, 15. See *Roll Call*, 5 May 1977, 1.

15. *CT*, 17 Apr 1977, 12. For the debates: *CR-House*, 23 May 1977, 15885–909; *CR-House*, 24 May 1977, 16171–265; and *CR-Senate*, 15 Jun 1977, 19266–98.

16. Bonker, "The Price of Peace in Rhodesia," in *CR-House*, 24 May 1977, 16181; and US Senate, "Foreign Assistance Authorization," CD49, 7. For increasingly detailed descriptions of the fund: US House, "United States Policy Toward Southern Africa," CD12, 32–33; and US Senate, "Security Assistance Authorization," CD50, 61–62. Also WOA, "Memo: Carter Requests Zimbabwe 'Carrot,'" 24 Mar 1977, WOA 58/210, Yale.

17. Pik Botha to Muller, 11 Feb 1977, CWIHP-va. See Vance to Carter, 4 Mar 1977, NLC-128-12-6-4-6.

18. Solarz in US House, "Foreign Assistance 1978, Part 3," CD16, 212, 215, 220, 230.

19. US Senate, "Security Assistance Authorization," CD50, 200 (Solarz), 102 (Javits).

20. US House, "Conference Report," CD21, 6, 5. See DOS, "Zimbabwe Development Fund," May 1977, NLC-133-13-26-22-7.

21. *CR-Senate*, 15 Jun 1977, 19286 (Helms); *CR-House*, 24 May 1977, 16175 (De La Garza), 16176 (Bauman), 16180 (Frenzel); *CR-House*, 21 Jul 1977, 24376 (Ashbrook); and *CR-House*, 24 May 1977, 16183 (Crane).

22. *CR-House*, 24 May 1977, 16176 (Bauman).

23. Ibid.

24. *CR-House*, 24 May 1977, 16186; and *CR-Senate*, 15 Jun 1977, 19286–87.

25. *CR-House*, 23 May 1977, 15907–8; and *CR-House*, 24 May 1977, 16172–77. See (no author), "Congressional Right Wing Attacks Black Africa," *Washington Notes on Africa* (Summer 1977), 7–8.

26. Author's interviews with Mondale and Young.

27. Lake and Petterson to Spiegel, 10 Mar 1977, Lake Papers/2, NA.

28. MemCon (Callaghan, Mondale), 22 May 1977, FCO 82/764, NA-UK; and Lake and Petterson to Spiegel, 10 Mar 1977, Lake Papers/2, NA. "Watershed" is in many documents briefing Mondale for the Vorster meeting.

29. MemCon (Owen, Vorster), 13 Apr 1977, NLC-133-17-1-11-2; MemCon (Owen, Smith), 13 Apr 1977, NLC-133-17-1-6-8; and Cabinet Minutes, 19 Apr 1977, Rhodesian Government: Cabinet Minutes, v. 5, Smith Papers. See Vance to Owen in State 79685, 8 Apr 1977, NLC-133-15-1-34-9; and Owen to Vance in Ramsbotham to Vance, 18 Apr 1977, NLC-133-15-1-28-6. All MemCons of Owen's April trip are British documents.

30. Author's interview with Kaunda; and MemCon (Owen, Nkomo), 10 Apr 1977, NLC-133-17-1-10-3.

31. MemCon (Owen, Nyerere), 11 Apr 1977, NLC-133-17-1-8-6; DePree, Maputo 683, 24 May 1977, NA-AAD; and MemCon (Owen, Mugabe), 11 Apr 1977, NLC-133-17-1-9-5. See MemCon (Owen, Machel), 12 Apr 1977, NLC-133-17-1-7-7; and MemCon (Owen, Muzorewa), 7 Apr 1977, NLC-133-17-1-12-1.

32. *Times* (Lusaka), 11 Apr 1977, edit 1; and MemCon (Owen, Nyerere), 11 Apr 1977, NLC-133-17-1-8-6.

33. Owen, *Time to Declare*, 306; *Daily Times* (Lagos), 15 Apr 1977, edit 3; *Daily News* (Dar), 12 Apr 1977, edit 1; *Times* (Lusaka), 11 Apr 1977, edit 1; *Daily Mail* (Lusaka), 15 Apr 1977, 1; Low, Lusaka 968, 12 Apr 1977, FOIA; *Daily Mail* (Lusaka), 12 Apr 1977, 4; and Low, Lusaka 994, 14 Apr 1977, FOIA.

34. Katzen to Mondale, 20 Apr 1977, NLC-133-15-3-15-8.

35. MemCon (Owen, Vance), in Vance, SecTo 4002, 2 May 1977, NLC-133-107-4-3-8; and Mondale to Carter, 15 Apr 1977, NLC-133-107-1-50-9.

36. Dodson to Mondale et al., 19 Jul 1977, Vertical/Cuba-defense, CL. For the initial plan: "Rhodesia: Aspects of a Settlement," c. April 1977, FCO 82/768, NA-UK. For its evolution: INR, "Southern African Developments," 1 Apr 1977, Brzezinski/14, CL; Owen to Vance, in Owen, 7 Apr 1977, FCO 948, FCO 35/2011, NA-UK; Vance to Owen, in Owen, FCO 949, 9 Apr 1977, FCO 36/2011, NA-UK; Vance to Carter, "Next Steps on Rhodesia," 2 May 1977, FOIA; Christopher, State 102357, 5 May 1977, FOIA; Christopher, State 24934, 8 May 1977, FOIA; and US House, "US Policy Toward Rhodesia," CD20, esp. 1–3.

37. See Vance, State 26132, for Young (forwarding Low, Lusaka 335), 4 Feb 1977, FOIA. On the war: Cilliers, *Counter-insurgency*, 27–44; Martin and Johnson, *Struggle*, 279–80; and Baxter, *Rhodesia*, 454–58.

38. MemCon (Owen, Vance), 10 Mar 1977, PREM 16/1486, NA-UK; MemCon (Waldheim, Rowlands), 17 May 1977, FCO 36/2037, NA-UK; and Honey, "Report on UN Conference," in Molotsi and Sogge, "Maputo Conference on Zimbabwe and Namibia," 10 Jun 1977, American Friends Service Committee, WOA 58/210, Yale. For Owen: Owen, Comments at 17th Cabinet Meeting, 28 Apr 1977, FCO 36/2012, NA-UK; Richard, MisNY, 28 Apr 1977, FCO 36/2035, NA-UK; and "Rhodesia: Recent History," in Wall to Renwick, 2 May 1979, FCO 36/2493, NA-UK. For ZANU's anxieties: "Robert Mugabe's Speech to UN Conference," 16 May 1977 in FBIS, "Materials on UN Conference in Support of the Peoples of Zimbabwe and Namibia," CREST; MemCon (Waldheim, Vance), 19 May 1977, FOIA; MemCon (Callaghan, Nkomo), 27 Jul 1977, FCO 73/287, NA-UK; and author's interview with Low.

39. "Report of the Interagency Group on Rhodesia," in Tarnoff to ZB, 16 Apr 1977, NSA-staff/119, CL. On mercenaries: Horne, *Barrel*, *passim*; and Voss, *Washingtons Söldner*, 197–246, 296–382.

40. Turner to Carter, 31 Mar 1977, enclosing CIA, "Effectiveness of Sanctions against Rhodesia," DDRS. For other sober reports on the difficulty of applying pressure on Smith: Schaufele to ZB, 17 May 1977, NLC-24-105-1-22-3 and "US Leverage in Southern Africa," [Apr 1977,] NLC-133-14-14-4-9. See also "DOS, "Some Additional Measures that can be Taken Regarding South Africa," [Apr 1977,] NLC-133-16-3-2-1.

41. Christopher, State 118021, 21 May 1977, NLC-133-123-4-23-8. For the anxieties: ZB to Interagency Group, in Thornton to ZB, 27 Apr 1977, NSA-staff/119, CL; Harrison to Laver and Duff, 1 Feb 1977, FCO 36/2034, NA-UK; and Crosland, FCO 58 to MisNY, 4 Feb 1977, FCO 36/2034, NA-UK. For the decision not to close: Derwinski to ZB, 6 Jun 1977, Subject/CO-50, CL; and Lanpher to Moose, 16 Dec 1977, NSA-staff/119-25, CL.

42. ZB to Carter, 6 Apr 1977, Vertical/classified, CL; and "A New Approach to Relations with South Africa," in ZB to Carter, 1 Apr 1977, Vertical/classified, CL.

43. ZB to Carter, 6 Apr 1977, Vertical/classified, CL; "A New Approach to Relations with South Africa," in ZB to Carter, 1 Apr 1977, Vertical/classified, CL; and Mondale to Vance, Young, ZB, 4 Apr 1977, NLC-7-6-10-1-6.

44. See Callaghan to Carter, 9 Apr 1977, Subject/CO-53, CL; Mondale to Vance, Young, ZB, 4 Apr 1977, NLC-7-6-10-1-6; Carter to Vorster in Carter to Bowdler (draft), [15 Apr 1977,] NLC-133-107-1-48-2; Bowdler, Cape Town 591, 19 Apr 1977, NLC -133-15-1-21-3; and York, Belgrade 3282, 21 May 1977, FOIA.

45. See Gillon, *Democrats' Dilemma*, 163–299; and Brock Brower, "The Remaking of the Vice President," *NYT Magazine*, 5 Jun 1977, 19ff. Also author's interview with Mondale.

46. See RAC files beginning NLC-133-, dated March and April 1977, at the Carter Library. Also author's interview with Mondale.

47. Mondale to Carter, 8 Apr 1977, NLC-133-14-14-16-6; Mondale to Carter, 26 Mar 1977, NLC-133-233-6-3-6; Mondale to Carter, 10 May 1977, NLC-133-12-6-1-3; and Aaron to Mondale, 31 Mar 1977, NLC-133-14-13-13-0.

48. "Scope Paper: Your Meeting with Prime Minister Vorster," n.d., NLC-133-123-5-2-0.

49. Carter to Callaghan in Clift to Aaron, 30 Apr 1977, NLC-133-15-2-38-4.

50. Mondale to Carter, 8 Apr 1977, NLC-133-14-14-16-6.

51. DOS, "Prime Minister Vorster's Objectives," May 1977, NLC-133-13-26-21-8 (emphasis in original). See ZB to Carter, 8 Apr 1977, NLC-133-14-14-16-6.

52. DOS, "An Approach to Prime Minister Vorster on South Africa," May 1977, NLC-133-13-26-14-6.

53. "Scope Paper: Your Meeting with Prime Minister Vorster," n.d., NLC-133-123-5-2-0.

54. Mondale to Carter, 10 May 1977, NLC-133-15-4-1-2 (emphasis added).

55. Clift, "Insert for VP's Lunch with the President," 25 Apr 1977, NLC-133-107-2-28-3.

56. Mondale to Carter, 10 May 1977, NLC-133-15-4-1-2.

57. DOS, "An Approach to Prime Minister Vorster on South Africa," May 1977, NLC-133-13-26-14-6.

58. Mondale to Carter, 8 Apr 1977, NLC-133-14-14-16-6.

59. See *NYT*, 17 Apr 1977, 3; *LAT*, 20 Apr 1977, B5; Range, "*Playboy*: Young," 66; and "Andrew Young," [26 May 1977,] FCO 82/773, NA-UK.

60. Aaron to Mondale, 24 Mar 1977, NLC-133-233-6-1-8.

61. Marginalia on Mondale to Carter, 10 May 1977, DDRS. Also author's interview with Mondale.

62. *Newsweek*, 28 Mar 1977, 25.

63. *WP*, 8 Mar 1977, 1 (armed forces); *LAT*, 15 Apr 1977, 1 (South Africa); *Newsweek*, 21 Mar 1977, 36 (Howard); *NYT*, 16 Apr 1977, 1 (British); *NYT*, 12 Apr 1977, 1 (communism); 12 Apr 1977, *LAT*, 2 (paranoia); *NYT*, 12 Apr 1977, 1 (Shaba); and *LAT*, 14 Apr 1977, B7 (intelligence).

64. *LAT*, 15 Apr 1977, 1; *WP*, 8 Mar 1977, 1; Richard, MisNY 438, 8 Apr 1977, FCO 82/735, NA-UK; and Q&A with Reporters, 8 Apr 1977, APP. For Foreign Office: Owen, FCO 217, 6 Apr 1977, FCO 82/735, NA-UK; Tait to Weir, 7 Apr 1977, FCO 36/2006, NA-UK; and Young to Richard, in Richard, MisNY 439, 8 Apr 1977, FCO 82/735, NA-UK.

65. *WP*, 10 Apr 1977, edit B6; *NYT*, 9 Apr 1977, edit 13; *Time*, 25 Apr 1977, 30; *NYT*, 27 Mar 1977, 3 (quoting Michel); and Michel, *CR-House*, 9 Mar 1977, 6809.

66. Robert Novak, *WS*, 13 Mar 1977, F3; *WP*, 11 Mar 1977, 25; Ashbrook, *CR-Extensions*, 19 May 1977, 15653; and *LAT*, 18 Apr 1977, 8.

67. William Safire, *NYT*, 14 Apr 1977, 25; and Stephen Rosenfeld, *WP*, 11 Mar 1977, 25.

68. Beard to Carter, 6 Jun 1977, WHCF/11-10, CL; *WSJ*, 22 Jun 1977, edit 24; Robert Novak, *WS*, 13 Mar 1977, in *CR-Extensions*, 22 Mar 1977, 8623; and Carl Rowan, *WS*, 13 Apr 1977, 19.

69. *NYT*, 27 Mar 1977, 3; and *Newsweek*, 28 Mar 1977, 30.

70. *NYT*, 14 Jul 1976, 19.

71. *Newsweek*, 28 Mar 1977, 30.

72. *The World* (Johannesburg), 23 May 1977, 1; and *NYT*, 19 Apr 1977, 2.

73. Author's interview with Young; *Time*, 21 Mar 1977, 31; and Maynes, FD, 14 Aug 1998.

74. US Senate, "Young's African Trip," CD53, 7.

75. Author's interview with Carter.

76. *WP*, 19 Mar 1977, B4; *NYT*, 13 Apr 1977, 11; *LAT*, 15 Apr 1977, 1; Dedication of Kennedy Center's African Room, 24 Apr 1977, APP; and MemCon (Callaghan, Mondale), 22 May 1977, FCO 82/764, NA-UK.

77. ADR [Air Vice-Marshall Harold Hawkins] to Gaylard, C151, 6 May 1977, ADR/8, box 4/006(m), Smith Papers. See *CT*, 20 May 1977, 2.

78. Mondale to Carter, 10 May 1977, DDRS. See MemCon (Mondale, Vorster), 19 May 1977, "First Meeting"; MemCon (Mondale, Vorster), 19 May 1977, "Second Meeting"; MemCon (Mondale, Vorster) 20 May 1977, "Third Meeting"; and all Mondale private papers.

79. "Scope Paper: Your Meeting with Prime Minister Vorster," n.d., NLC-133-123-5-2-0.

80. Spiers, London 6593 in Vance, State 91073, 22 Apr 1977, NLC-133-15-1-12-3 (continued in NLC-133-15-1-13-2). See MemCon (Owen, Vorster), 13 Apr 1977, NLC-133-17-1-11-2.

81. Mondale to Carter, 20 Apr 1977, NLC-133-15-1-22-1.

82. Mondale quoted in Aaron, Exit Interview, CL; and author's interview with Aaron.

83. ADR (Hawkins) to Gaylard, C151, 6 May 1977, ADR/8, box 4/006(m), Smith Papers; MemCon (Smith, Pik Botha), 15 Jun 1977, Meetings, box 4/002(m), ibid.; and Rhodesian Diplomatic Mission, "Notes of a Meeting held in Salisbury on Wednesday 15 Jun 1977," 22 Jun 1977, ibid. See Lake, *Tar Baby*, 198–285.

84. MemCon (Mondale, Vorster), 19 May 1977, "First Meeting," Mondale private papers.

85. See MemCon (Mondale, Vorster), 19 May 1977, "Second Meeting," Mondale private papers; Gleijeses, "Test of Wills"; and Gleijeses, *Visions*, 92–96, 146–58.

86. MemCon (Mondale, Vorster) 20 May 1977, "Third Meeting," Mondale private papers; MemCon (Vorster, Mondale), 19–20 May 1977, "Discussions between the South African and American delegations on matters concerning southern Africa," Aluka; MemCon (Mondale, Vorster), 19 May 1977, "Second Meeting," Mondale private papers; and MemCon (Mondale, Vorster), 20 May 1977, "Third Meeting," Mondale private papers.

87. MemCon (Mondale, Vorster), 20 May 1977, "Third Meeting," Mondale private papers.

88. Meehan, Vienna 4123, 20 May 1977, NLC-133-13-27-7-3.

89. MemCon (Tito, Mondale), 21 May 1977, NLC-133-105-8-10-8. See DOS, "Prime Minister Vorster's Objectives," May 1977, NLC-133-13-26-21-8.

90. MemCon (Mondale, Vorster), 20 May 1977, "Third Meeting," Mondale private papers; and York, Belgrade 3282, 21 May 1977, NA-AAD. See Comments appended to MemCon (Vorster, Mondale), 19–20 May, "Discussions between the South African and American delegations on matters concerning southern Africa," Aluka.

91. *NYT*, 21 May 1977, 1; and *CT*, 21 May 1977, 5.

92. Vance, State 121877, 26 May 1977, Subject/CO50-CO141, CL.

93. A cable from the US embassy in Belgrade (where Mondale traveled immediately after Vienna) provides a detailed summary of the talks, including the following comment by Vorster: "If you think we should scrap (homeland) governments and introduce one-man, one-vote in the central parliament, I say it can't be done." This does not appear in the official US and South African transcripts of the talks. York, Belgrade 3282, 21 May 1977, NLC-133-123-1-51-0.

94. Author's interviews with Mondale and Carter. Also, author's interview with Aaron.

95. Vance, State 121877, 26 May 1977, Subject/CO50-CO141, CL; *NYT*, 29 May 1977, 110; and "Southern Africa—Policy Review," [June 1977,] NLC-24-11-12-1-5.

96. Author's interview with Edmondson; Vance to Carter, 24 Jun 1977, NLC-15R-122-10-13-6; and Comments appended to MemCon (Vorster, Mondale), 19–20 May 1977, "Discussions between the South African and American delegations on matters concerning southern Africa," Aluka.

97. Author's interview with Mondale.

98. "Southern Africa—Policy Review," [June 1977,] NLC-24-11-12-1-5. See chapters 4 and 7 of Geldenhuys, *Diplomacy*.

99. "Southern Africa—Policy Review," [June 1977,] NLC-24-11-12-1-5.

100. Root, "Notes on Maputo Conference," n.d., WOA 58/210, Yale.

101. UN General Assembly, International Conference in Support of the Peoples of Zimbabwe and Namibia, 17 Dec 1976, A/RES/31/145; Tait to Alexander, 6 Apr 1977, FCO 36/2035, NA-UK; and marginalia on Simpson-Orlebar to Weir, 1 Apr 1977, FCO 36/2035, NA-UK. For the other Western countries: MemCon (Simpson-Orlebar, Pint), 21/22 Mar 1977, FCO 36/2035, NA-UK. West Germany and Canada began their UN Security Council terms on January 1, 1977.

102. MemCon (Hibbert, Laboulaye), 14 Apr 1977, FCO 31/2116, NA-UK.

103. MemCon (Owen, Aaron), 22 Apr 1977, FCO 36/2011, NA-UK. See: Simpson-Orlebar to Weir and Graham, 21 Apr 1977, FCO 36/2035, NA-UK; Richard, MisNY 486, 21 Apr 1977, FCO 36/2035, NA-UK; and author's interview with Moose (2002).

104. Simpson-Orlebar to Beattie, 25 Apr 1977, FCO 36/2035, NA-UK; Richard, MisNY 518, 28 Apr 1977, FCO 36/2035, NA-UK; Simpson-Orlebar to Mansfield, 28 Apr 1977, FCO 36/2036, NA-UK; and Wall to Rowlands, 29 Apr 1977, FCO 36/2036, NA-UK.

105. "Maputo Conference Brief no. 1: Rhodesia," in Reid to Rowlands, 13 May 1977, FCO 36/2037, NA-UK; and MemCon (Owen, de Guiringaud, Gencher [*sic*], Vance), 9 May 1977, NLC-23-19-2-2-2. See Rowlands to Owen, 28 Apr 1977, FCO 36/2036, NA-UK; and Owen, FCO 298, 7 May 1977, FCO 36/2036, NA-UK.

106. "Speech by President Machel," 16 May 1977, FCO 36/2037, NA-UK; and *NYT*, 19 May 1977, 5. On the Botswana raid: Christopher, State 112271, 16 May 1977, NA-AAD; Christopher, State 113169, 17 May 1977, NA-AAD; Christopher, State 112946, 17 May 1977, NA-AAD; and Smith to USG in Kirby, Johannesburg 1254, 20 May 1977, NA-AAD.

107. Kaunda to Carter, in Clingerman, Lusaka 1303, 14 May 1977, NLC-133-122-8-69-5; and Carter to Kaunda in Christopher, State 110995, 15 May 1977, FOIA. See Clingerman, Lusaka 1305, 15 May 1977, NLC-133-123-1-3-3; and Low, Lusaka 1318, 16 May 1977, FOIA. These threats caused Kaunda to postpone a planned state visit to Washington. See Mwale (Zambian minister of foreign affairs) to Vance in Clingerman, Lusaka 1251, 10 May 1977, NLC-133-107-4-14-6.

108. Remarks During a Televised Q&A, 17 May 1977, APP.

109. Root, "Notes on Maputo Conference," n.d., WOA 58/210, Yale.

110. De Chassiron, Maputo 187, 18 May 1977, FCO 36/2037, NA-UK.

111. No signature, "Text, as delivered, of Ambassador Young's Address," in Maputo 628, 19 May 1977, NA-AAD. Covers subsequent paragraphs. The State Department published only the prepared but undelivered speech: "United States Reiterates Support for the Independence of Namibia and Zimbabwe at Maputo Conference," 19 May 1977, *DOS Bulletin*, 11 Jul 1977, 55–58. USUN issued a press release with a draft of the delivered speech: "Statement by Ambassador Andrew Young," Maputo, 19 May 1977, *Press Release* USUN-27(77), 24 May 1977, WOA 58-210, Yale. The American Friends Service Committee, which sent an observer to the conference, issued a bulletin with excerpts from the delivered speech: "Andrew Young's Address to UN Conference (excerpts)," 10 Jun 1977, American Friends Service Committee, WOA 58/210, Yale. A *NYT* article contained excerpts not included in these versions: *NYT*, 20 May 1977, 5.

112. "Robert Mugabe Press Conference, May 19, 1977," 10 Jun 1977, American Friends Service Committee, WOA 58/210, Yale; and *WS*, 23 May 1977, 2.

113. DePree, Maputo 683, 24 May 1977, NA-AAD.

114. *LAT*, 17 May 1977, 2; and *WS*, 23 May 1977, 2.

115. Author's interview with McHenry.

116. *WS*, 23 May 1977, 2; *LAT*, 20 May 1977, B1; and *WP*, 20 May 1977, 1.

117. *WS*, 23 May 1977, 2; and *NYT*, 20 Apr 1977, 3.

118. No signature, "Text, as delivered, of Ambassador Young's Address," in Maputo 628, 19 May 1977, NA-AAD.

119. *Time*, 21 Mar 1977, 31; Root to Lockwood, 20/21 May 1977, WOA 58/210, Yale; and author's interview with Moose (2001). Also author's interview with Young. See *NYT*, 20 Apr 1977, 3.

120. MemCon (Owen, Mondale), 23 May 1977, FCO 36/2007, NA-UK; and Caradon, "Hope for Southern Africa," 22 May 1977, FCO 36/2037, NA-UK. See Miller, London 8531, 23 May 1977, NA-AAD.

121. Christopher, State 118004, 21 May 1977, NLC-133-14-10-4-3; and Owen, FCO 331, 23 May 1977, FCO 36/2037, NA-UK. See de Chassiron, Maputo 189, 19 May 1977, FCO 36/2037, NA-UK; and MemCon (Gaylard, Graham, Low), 25 May 1977, communications with South Africa, box 4/006(m), Smith Papers. For the draft declaration: "Preliminary Ideas for the Text of The Declaration and Programme of Action," 62–84, http://archives-trim.un.org/. For the final document: "Text of Final Declaration and Program of Action," *DOS Bulletin*, 11 Jul 1977, 59–65. For arm twisting: Vance to Owen in Christopher, State 117081, 20 May 1977, NLC-133-14-10-5-2.

122. "Maputo-Konferenz über Rhodesien und Namibia vom 16. bis 22.5.1977," 23 Mai 1977, doc. 129, *AAPD 1977*, 664-65; Owen (from Murray), FCO 331, 23 May 1977, FCO 36/2037, NA-UK; and "Owen's Meeting with Young, 26 May 1977: Line to Take," FCO 82/773, NA-UK.

123. Christopher to Carter, 21 May 1977, NLC-128-12-8-15-2; Young to Carter, 3 Jun 1977, Staff Secretary/30, CL; and US Senate, "Young's African Trip," CD53, 21.

124. See Kirby, Johannesburg 1283, 22 May 1977, NA-AAD.

125. MemCon (Christopher, Pik Botha) in Christopher, State 106075, 10 May 1977, NLC-133-107-4-14-6. For South African concerns: "Top Secret," 11 May 1977, NCL-1-2-3-9-6; South African *aide memoire* for Vance, 11 May 1977, NLC-133-16-5-4-7-1; and Bowdler, Pretoria 2560, 24 May 1977, NA-AAD. For example, the South African government discouraged Young from meeting with the banned Pan African Congress leader Robert Sobukwe, who was under house arrest 300 miles from Pretoria; Sobukwe's son and daughter had been living with the Youngs since 1974. (See Kirby, Johannesburg 1094, 9 May 1977, NA-AAD; and Hughes, Pretoria 2388, 14 May 1977, NA-AAD.) Mrs. Sobukwe, who was free to travel to Pretoria, was invited to Young's talk at the US embassy. Nelson, Cape Town 781, 13 May 1977, NA-AAD.

126. Author's interview with Moose (2001). This incident is briefly described in the Tanzanian press. See "Young Arrives in SA," *Daily News* (Dar), 22 May 1977, 2.

127. Bowdler, Cape Town 902, 4 Jun 1977, NA-AAD. See Nelson, Pretoria 2464, 18 May 1977, NA-AAD. Young did meet with representatives of the Soweto Students' Representative Council. See Bowdler, Pretoria 2560, 24 May 1977, NA-AAD; and "Southern Africa—Policy Review," [June 1977,] NLC-24-11-12-1-5.

128. Bowdler, Cape Town 902, 4 Jun 1977, NA-AAD; and *CSM*, 23 May 1977, 1. Young stayed at the home of Harry Oppenheimer, a South African businessman and critic of apartheid. See Bowdler, Cape Town 902, 4 Jun 1977, NA-AAD.

129. *Rand Daily Mail* (Johannesburg), 21 May 1977, 1; and ibid., 23 May 1977, 1.

130. *The World* (Johannesburg), 26 May 1977, 7 (transcript of Young's speech). See also Kirby, Johannesburg 1286, 22 May 1977, NA-AAD; and Young, "Statement . . . to South African Businessmen," Johannesburg, 21 May 1977, *Press Release USUN*-30 (77), 27 May 1977, Name/Young, CL.

131. *Rand Daily Mail*, 23 May 1977, 4; ibid., 24 May 1977, edit 14; and ibid., 23 May 1977, edit 10.

132. Bowdler, Pretoria, 24 May 1977, NA-AAD; and Bowdler, Cape Town 902, 4 Jun 1977, NA-AAD. See Hughes, Pretoria 2741, 3 Jun 1977, NA-AAD.

133. *CSM*, 29 Jun 1977, 23; and *The World*, 30 May 1977, edit 6. Also US Senate, "Young's African Trip," CD53, 24. For the speech: Kirby, Johannesburg 1307, 24 May 1977, NA-AAD.

134. *NYT*, 23 May 1977, 1; and *The World*, 30 May 1977, edit 6; Bowdler, Cape Town 902, 4 Jun 1977, NA-AAD.

135. *LAT*, 24 May 1977, edit D4; *NYT*, 17 May 1977, edit 30; *WP*, 8 May 1977, edit C6; and *WP*, 21 May 1977, edit 10. Also *CSM*, 16 May 1977, edit 28.

136. For Mondale's meetings: MemCon (Callaghan, Mondale), 22 May 1977, FCO 82/764, NA-UK; and MemCon (Owen, Mondale), 23 May 1977, FCO 36/2007, NA-UK.

137. For this and subsequent paragraphs: Address at Notre Dame, 22 May 1977, APP. On the writing of the speech, see Harvey Shapiro, "A Conversation with Jimmy Carter," *NYT Book Review*, 19 Jun 1977, 1.

138. AP, 23 May 1977, LexisNexis.

139. *LAT*, 28 Jan 1977, B3.

140. *NYT*, 6 Feb 1977, L14; and *LAT*, 16 Jan 1977, 9. Also *WP*, 16 Jan 1977, 3. See Gallup Poll #955, July 1976, question qn9b, *Gallup Brain*.

141. *WP*, 8 Feb 1977, 3. An exception was a speech to the fourth annual Conservative Political Action Conference in which Reagan criticized Carter's defense policies: *WP*, 6 Feb 1977, 20.

142. Ronald Reagan, "Human Rights and the Soviet Challenge," *LAT*, 23 Jun 1977, D7. This op-ed was adapted from the speech.

143. For the conversation with Kaunda and Nimiery: Bogosian, Khartoum 1764, 24 May 1977, NA-AAD; and Bogosian, Khartoum 1771, 25 May 1977, NA-AAD.

144. *CT*, 26 May 1977, 8; *WP*, 26 May 1977, 25; and Vance, State 122819, 27 May 1977, FOIA. Young lived in Queens from 1957 to 1961; for an analysis of racism there, see Logan, "Around City Hall."

145. Author's interviews with Graham and Renwick. On the London talks: Spiers, London 8800, 26 May 1977, NA-AAD.

146. Spiers, London 8719, 26 May 1977, NA-AAD. See *LAT*, 7 May 1977, 5. On Young's trip: "Top Secret," 23 May 1977, NLC-1-2-7-12-8; Henze, ER, 26 May 1977, Horn/5, CL; Young to Carter, 3 Jun 1977, Staff Secretary/30, CL; US Senate, "Young's African Trip," CD53, 1, 16, 25; and *NYT*, 7 Jun 1977, 12. On Cuban technicians: *WP*, 25 May 1977, 1.

147. *NYT*, 12 Jun 1977, 11. Also ABC, CBS, and NBC *Evening News*, 26 May 1977, VNA; *LAT*, 26 May 1977, 2; *NYT*, 27 May 1977, 1; and *WP*, 27 May 1977, 1.

148. Range, "*Playboy*: Young," 70.

149. Broomfield, *CR-House*, 7 Jun 1977, 17733; Martin, *CR-House*, 8 Jun 1977, 17910; Bauman, *CR-Extensions*, 7 Jun 1977, 17887; and Anderson, *CR-Extensions*, 9 Jun 1977, 18340. Also US Senate, "Young's African Trip," CD53, 13, 21–23, 27.

150. *NYT*, 8 Jun 1977, 6; News Conference, 13 Jun 1977, APP; and Q&A with Magazine Publishers Association, 10 Jun 1977, APP.

151. Vance to Owen, in Owen, FCO 949 to Washington, 9 Apr 1977, FCO 36/2011, NA-UK.

152. See VNA.

153. *WP*, 4 Jun 1977, 3.

154. Schaufele, FD, 19 Nov 1994; and Christopher, State 109473, 14 May 1977, enclosing Gammon, Paris 14331, from Schaufele to Vance, FOIA. On tensions between Young and Schaufele, see Greenstock to Ramsbotham, 14 Apr 1977, NA-UK. Also author's interviews with Moose (2002), Young, and DePree.

155. This portrait of Moose (this paragraph and next) is based on the documentary record, as well as author's interviews with Moose, Mondale, and Young. Also, *Economist*, 14 May 1977, 35; *WP*, 4 Jun 1977, 3; and *Afro-American* (Baltimore), 9 Aug 1977, 5.

156. Maynes, FD, 14 Aug. 1998.

157. William Safire, "The Suspicious 17," *NYT*, 9 Aug 1973, 35.

158. MemCon (Greenstock, Wisner, Tarnoff), 8 Jun 1977, FCO 82/735, NA-UK.

159. Author's interviews with Low and Moose (2001). On Moose's influence as a congressional staffer: Robert Sherrill, "Who Runs Congress? Well, there's Carl Marcy, Richard Moose . . ." *NYT Magazine*, 22 Nov 1970, 53ff.

160. Author's interview with McHenry; Low, FD, 5 Dec 1997; and author's interview with Graham. For the creation of the Low/Graham team: Vance to Christopher, 12 May 1977, FOIA; Christopher to Vance, 13 May 1977, FOIA; Seelye to Vance, 4 Jun 1977, FOIA; Dodson to Clift, 8 Jun 1977, Name/Low, CL; and Tarnoff to ZB, 18

Jun 1977, Subject/CO-50, CL. For a summary of the duo's travels: MemCon (Gaylard, Graham, Low), 25 May 1977, communications with South Africa, box 4/006(m), Smith Papers.

161. Low, FD, 5 Dec 1997.

162. Author's interview with Carter.

163. CIA, "Rhodesia: A Political Challenge to Prime Minister Smith," 13 Apr 1977, NLC-4-32-7-1-4. See Bowdler, Pretoria 1226, 15 Mar 1977, NA-AAD.

164. MemCon (Owen, Aaron), 22 Apr 1977, FCO 36/2011, NA-UK.

165. Author's interview with Edmondson; and Scott, Cape Town 99, 2 Mar 1977, FCO 36/2010, NA-UK. For Kissinger's refusal to allow ambassadors to circulate cables: Easum, Lagos 798, 21 Jan 1976, NSA-Country/5, GFL; and DePree, FD, 16 Feb 1994.

166. Author's interview with Moose (2001). Also author's interviews with Low, Easum, Edmondson, and DePree; and confirmed by author's interviews with Lake, McHenry, and Young (all of whom served in the United States). Also [no author] "Forging the Carter Policy," *Southern Africa* (Aug 1977): 28–30.

167. Author's interviews with Brzezinski and Thornton. Also SCC Meeting, 8 Feb 1977, Vertical/classified, CL; Vance, State 260172, 31 Oct 1977, DNSA; and MemCon (ZB, Fourie), 11 Nov 1977, NSA-subject/33, CL.

168. See Gleijeses, *Visions*, 159–63.

169. Author's interviews with Richardson, Renwick, and Moose (2001).

170. ZB, WR, 3 Jun 1977, NSA-subject/41, CL; and SCC Meeting, 8 Feb 1977, Vertical/classified, CL.

171. NSC Meeting (minutes), 3 Mar 1977, DDRS; and MemCon (Chona, ZB), 19 Jan 1977, NSA-staff/118, CL.

172. Author's interview with Carter; and Crocker, "Lost in Africa," 16.

173. Q&A with Publishers, Editors, and Broadcasters, 15 Apr 1977, APP; Maynes, FD, 14 Aug 1998; and Tarnoff to ZB, 27 Jul 1977, DDRS. Also King to Carter, 4 Jun 1977, Name/Moose, CL.

174. Author's interviews with Easum, Low, Thornton, Owen, and McHenry.

175. Author's interview with Carter.

176. Author's interview with McHenry; *Bilalian News*, 21 Oct 1977, 3; and Johnson, "Helping Blacks," 14.

177. Author's interviews with McHenry, Young, and Moose (2002).

Chapter 6

1. *Time*, 18 Apr 1977, 18. See chapter 4 above.

2. Vance, State 88966, 20 Apr 1977, NA-AAD.

3. Hartman to Vance, "The June 1 Quadripartite Ministerial Meeting," 26 May 1977, NLC-23-20-4-5-5. See "President's Briefing Book [for London Summit]" 4 May 1977, NLC-24-97-7-3-8; and Christopher (from Wisner), State 102503, 5 May 1977, NLC-133-16-4-19-2.

4. "The Ethiopian Revolution and its Implications," 28 May 1977, NLC-23-13-5-3-4; and CIA, Directorate of Intelligence, "Ethiopia: Assessment of Key Issues," 3 Jun 1977, NLC-SAFE-17B-3-10-2-8. See Eilts, Cairo 8238, 17 May 1977, NA-AAD. Based on interviews with Somali military officers, Gilkes asserts that a Somali army

captain commanded the first WSLF unit in the Ogaden in 1976. See Gilkes, "Revolution," 722.

5. ZB, WR, 13 May 1977, DDRS (dash in original). See "Human Rights Country Evaluation Plan: Somalia," attached to Derian and Harrop to Christopher, 8 Dec 1977, Christopher Papers/24, NA.

6. Thornton to ZB, 2 May 1977, NLC-24-97-7-2-9.

7. See "Policy Review Committee Meeting," 11 Apr 1977, NLC-15-80-10-20-4; 16 Apr 1977, SH Chron; and Henze, ER, 13 Apr 1977, NSA-staff/5, CL.

8. Vance to Carter, 14 Jun 1977, FOIA; and *Newsweek*, 27 Jun 1977, 45. See Henze, ER, 13 Jun 1977, Horn/5, CL. For attaché: ZB, WR, 26 May 1977, DDRS; and Vance to Carter, 14 Jun 1977, FOIA. For Moscow: CPSU CC to SED CC, "Visit to USSR of Somali Vice President Samantar," [1 Jun 1977,] in Hershberg, "Anatomy," 63–64.

9. *Newsweek*, 27 Jun 1977, 45 (the White House received an advance copy on June 13); and Henze to ZB, 14 May 1977, Horn/1, CL.

10. 3 May 1977, SH Chron; and Henze, ER, 9 May 1977, Horn/5, CL.

11. Katzen to Mondale, 5 May 1977, NLC-133-42-3-14-9.

12. Mondale to Carter, 13 May 1977, NLC-133-42-3-14-9. See Mondale to Carter, 12 May 1977, Horn/1, CL.

13. Presidential Daily Diary, CL-online.

14. Henze to ZB, 14 May 1977, Horn/1, CL; and Vance, State 118085, 23 May 1977, NA-AAD.

15. Vance to Carter, 17 May 1977, NLC-128-6-15-1-6. Also ZB to Carter, nd, NLC-128-6-15-1-6.

16. See North-South to Situation Room, 12 May 1977, NLC-24-105-1-89.

17. Wiley, Jidda 4432, 22 Jun 1977, NA-AAD.

18. West Diary, 24 May 1977, West Papers/22.

19. Memcon (Vance, Fahd), 24 May 1977, FOIA; and Eilts, Cairo 8402, 18 May 1977, NA-AAD.

20. Remarks to Reporters on the Crown Prince's Departure, 25 May 1977, APP.

21. *WP*, 25 May 1977, 1.

22. Vance, State 122819, 27 May 1977, FOIA; and *NYT*, 26 May 1977, 1. For Ethiopian denial: Raúl Castro to Fidel Castro, 2 Jun 1977, Gleijeses Papers.

23. *Newsweek*, 6 Jun 1977, 51. Also *NYT*, 26 May 1977, 1; and Walters, "Interview with Castro."

24. *WP*, 27 May 1977, 1; *NYT*, 26 May 1977, 1; and *Newsweek*, 6 Jun 1977, 51.

25. Exchange With Reporters at the Brunswick Airport, 30 May 1977, APP.

26. *NYT*, 4 Jun 1977, 1. Also Memcon (Vance, ZB, Garba), 21 Mar 1977, FOIA; Situation Room to ZB, 7 May 1977, NLC-4-3-2-11-0; *NYT*, 3 Jun 1977, 1; and Christopher, "Normalization of Relations," 11 Jun 1977, *DOS Bureau of Public Affairs*. See Gleijeses, *Visions*, 119–22; Schoultz, *Infernal*, 291–304, 323–24; and LeoGrande and Kornbluh, *Back Channel*, 159–68.

27. Vance, State 130125, 6 Jun 1977, FOIA (excerpts 3 Jun briefing); and *WP*, 7 Jun 1977, edit 16.

28. Memcon (Giscard, Carter), 9 May 1977, box 5AG3-984, Archives de la Présidence, Paris.

29. ZB, WR-15, 3 Jun 1977, NSA-subject/41, CL.

---

30. Vance to Carter, 17 May 1977, NLC-128-6-15-1-6.

31. "Chronology of Events: Somali-US Relations 1976–77," [April 1978], FOIA; *Time*, 18 Apr 1977, 18; and Carter's comment on ZB to Carter, 11 Apr 1977, PRC Meetings/10, CL. See Schaufele and Lake to Vance, 8 Apr 1977, Lake Papers/2, NA.

32. Address at Notre Dame, 22 May 1977, APP; and Q&A with Magazine Publishers Association, 19 Jun 1977, APP, (emphasis added).

33. Memcon (Mengistu, Ochoa, Pérez Novoa), 14 May 1977, Gleijeses Papers; and Raúl Castro to Fidel Castro, 13 May, 1977, ibid. For weapons: Raúl Castro to Fidel Castro, 19 May, 1977, ibid.

34. Ochoa to Raúl Castro, Havana, 7 Jun 1977, Gleijeses Papers; "Informe del G. D. Ochoa sobre entrevista con el Presidente Mengistu el día 6 junio 77," 10 Jun 1977, ibid.; and Fidel Castro to Mengistu, 9 Aug 1977, ibid.

35. *NYT*, 8 Jun 1977, 21. For CIA: Situation Room to ZB, 3 May 1977, NLC-1-2-2-12-3.

36. "The Ethiopian Revolution and its Implications," 28 May 1977, NLC-23-13-5-3-4.

37. Eilts, Cairo 7066, 27 Apr 1977, NLC 43-129-3-5-4. See Eilts, Cairo 8238, 17 May 1977, NA-AAD.

38. Memcon (Vance, Fahd), 24 May 1977, FOIA.

39. Lewis, TelAviv 6246, 22 Aug 1977, NA-AAD; and "Policy Review Committee Meeting," 11 Apr 1977, NLC-15-80-10-20-4. See Matthews, Cairo 873, 17 Jan 1977, FOIA; *NYT*, 10 Mar 1977, 3; Eilts, Cairo 12237, 22 Jul 1977, NA-AAD; Moshe Dayan, in *WP*, 7 Feb 1978, 1; and Hunter, "Israel and Ethiopia," 1.

40. See Memcon (Callaghan, Vance), 31 Mar 1977, FCO 82/768, NA-UK; East African Department, "Talks with the US Secretary of State," 2 May 1977, FCO 82/768, NA-UK; Siad to Callaghan, 25 May 1977, PREM 16/1870, NA-UK; and Memcon (Schaufele, Moose, Rowlands), 1 Jun 1977, FCO 36/2007, NA-UK.

41. See author's interview with Owen; "Quadripartite Talks," in Crowe to Private Secretary, 4 Mar 1977, FCO 82/756, NA-UK; Graham to Mansfield, 26 Apr 1977, FCO 36/2012, NA-UK; Carter, marginalia on ZB, WR, 3 Jun 1977, NSA-subject/41, CL; Vance to Carter, 14 Jun 1977, FOIA; Owen to Callaghan, 28 Jul 1977, PREM 16/1872, NA-UK; and *Le Figaro* (Paris) (interview with de Guiringaud), 18–19 Feb 1978, 10. Prior to the foreign ministers' quadripartite meetings, the four political directors held preparatory meetings. Assistant Secretary of State for European Affairs George Vest represented the United States at the political directors' meetings.

42. Memcon (Owen, de Guiringaud, Genscher, Vance), 9 May 1977, NLC-23-20-5-1-8; and Stoessel, Bonn 7380, 28 Apr 1977, NA-AAD. See Christopher, State 102503, 5 May 1977, NA-AAD; and Christopher, State 107685, 11 May 1977, NA-AAD.

43. Hartman to Vance, "The June 1 Quadripartite Ministerial Meeting," 26 May 1977, NLC-23-20-4-5-5. See the previous month's discussion of the Horn: Memcon (Owen, de Guiringaud, Genscher, Vance), 9 May 1977, NLC-23-19-2-2-2.

44. DOS Briefing Paper for June 1 Quadripartite Meeting, "The Horn of Africa," 25 May 1977, NLC-23-20-5-1-8.

45. Memcon (de Guiringaud, Vance), 30 May 1977, box 5AG3-984, Archives de la Présidence, Paris; and Memcon (Carter, Andreotti), 26 Jul 1977, NLC-23-21-6-4-3. Carter may have discussed this at the London Summit. See "President's Briefing Book [for London Summit]" 4 May 1977, NLC-24-97-7-3-8; and Eilts, Cairo 8401, 18 May 1977, NA-AA.

46. Memcon (quadripartite meeting), 23 Sep 1977, New York, B150/376, Berlin. See Vance to Carter, 14 Jun 1977, FOIA. British concern for Kenyan sensibilities is evident throughout their papers on the Horn: see esp. PREM 16/1870-72, NA-UK.

47. Henze to ZB, 2 Mar 1977, Horn/2, CL; and Henze, ER, 1 Apr 1977, Horn/5, CL. Kenyatta died on August 22, 1978.

48. Author's interview with Nimetz. Also author's interviews with Cahill, Moose (2001), Hamrick, and Henze. See *NYT*, 26 Jun 1977, 33; Kevin Cahill, "For a US Role in Somalia," *NYT*, 18 Jul 1977, L27; Vance, State 225871, 20 Sep 1977, FOIA; *Newsweek*, 26 Sep 1977, 42; Post and Holliday to Moose, 29 Sep 1977, FOIA; and *Newsweek*, 3 Oct 1977, 19.

49. Spiers, London 8776, 26 May 1977, FOIA; and *NYT*, 8 Jun 1977, 6. This hearing was not published.

50. Tarnoff to ZB, 2 Jun 1977, NLC-126-8-5-1-7.

51. ZB to Carter, [15 Jun 1977,] Horn/1, CL; and Jacobs, Mog 529, 28 Mar 1977, FOIA.

52. Vance, State 152186, 30 Jun 1977, FOIA. Also President's Daily Diary, CL-online; and author's interview with Addou.

53. The accounts of this meeting concur in all details. The most complete are Memcon (Carter, Addou), 16 Jun 1977, NSA-Brzezinski (7)/35, CL and Vance, State 152186, 30 Jun 1977, FOIA. Also Memcon (Carter, Addou), 16 Jun 1977, Horn/1, CL; 16 Jun 1977, SDC; and Vance, *Hard Choices*, 72–73.

54. Vance, State 152186, 30 Jun 1977, FOIA.

55. Memcon (Addou, Deptoff), 24 Jun 1977, SH Chron. See Henze, ER, 17 Jun 1977, Horn/5, CL. Also author's interview with Addou.

56. ZB to Carter, 15 Jun 1977, Horn/1, CL.

57. See *Crisis,* Dec 1976, edit 337; *Jet*, 3 Feb 1977, 6–7; *Freedomways*, 2nd quarter 1977, edit 69–70; Cobb (president, NAACP) to Mondale, 26 May 1977 and Carter to Cobb, 30 Jun 1977, Subject/CO-50-CO-141, CL; *Pittsburgh Press*, 3 Jul 1977, 26; and "Resolutions submitted . . . to the 68th annual convention," series V/2528, NAACP papers, LC. The best discussion of Carter and civil rights is Dumbrell, *Carter Presidency*, 86–109.

58. *NYT*, 2 Jul 1977, 7.

59. Vance, "The United States and Africa: Building Positive Relations," *DOS Bulletin*, 8 Aug 1977, 165–70. See *NYT*, 2 Jul 1977, 1; and *WP*, 2 Jul 1977, C1.

60. Vance, "The United States and Africa: Building Positive Relations," *DOS Bulletin*, 8 Aug 1977, 170–74.

61. "Jimmy Carter Answers Questions on Africa," [1976,] Persons: Carter/334, ANS. See *Afro American* (Washington), 5 Jul 1977, 7; *Afro-American* (Baltimore), 9 Jul 1977, 4; *Afro American* (Washington), Jul 19–23, 4; and *Bilalian News* (Detroit), 22 Jul 1977, 5. TransAfrica had been formed but was not yet an effective lobby. See chapter 10.

62. *NYT*, 1 Jul 1977, 5. See SRF, 13–21 Jun 1977, SH Chron; and Top Secret, 30 Jun 1977, NLC-1-2-5-62-5. For Zambian intelligence report: Makasa to Mwale, "Political Report No. 2 for May–June 1977," 149 UNIP 7/23/62. See Steigman, Libreville 1657, 1 Jul 1977, NA-AAD.

63. On the OAU conference: Zdenek Červenka, "OAU's Year of Disunity," *ACR 1977-1978*, A57–65; and "OAU Summit Conference," *Africa Research Bulletin*.

64. US Senate, "Young's African Trip," CD53, 15. See also DOS, "The Organization of African Unity," 24 Jan 1977, NLC-133-157-9-25-4.

65. Eteki Mboumoua quoted in 5 Jul 1977, Xinhua, LNA; and Červenka, *Quest for Unity*, xiv.

66. *Newsweek*, 18 Jul 1977, 18; Laitin, "War in the Ogaden," 102; *WP*, 5 Jul 1977, 15; and Hartman, Paris 22606, 4 Aug 1977, NA-AAD. See Memcon (Carter, Obasanjo), 11 Oct 1977, NSA (7)/35, CL.

67. *Time*, 18 Jul 1977, 36. On impact of resolution: Sellström, *Sweden*, 193–95. See also "On Interference in the Internal Affairs of African States," AHG/Res85 (XIV), in Legum, *ACR 1977–1978*, C4.

68. Brewster, London 10057, 17 Jun 1977, NA-AAD; "On Zimbabwe," AHG/Res84 (XIV), in Legum, *ACR 1977–1978*, C3; and "OAU Summit Conference," *Africa Research Bulletin*, 4487.

69. Clingerman, Lusaka 1918, 7 Jul 1977, FOIA; and *WP*, 16 Jul 1977, 3. Also DePree, Maputo 926, 28 Jul 1977, FOIA.

70. *WP*, 2 Jul 1977, 1. See also *Time*, 18 Jul 1977, 36.

71. Top Secret, 30 Jun 1977, NLC-1-2-5-60-7; and Eilts, Cairo 10389, 21 Jun 1977, NA-AAD. See Vance to Carter, 9 Jul 1977, NLC-7-18-5-3-7; Loughran, Mog 1263, 25 Jul 1977, FOIA; Chase, Alexandria 694, 28 Jul 1977, NA-AAD; and Chase, Alexandria 775, 2 Aug 1977, NA-AAD (includes an itemized list).

72. Author's interview with Addou; and Miklos, Tehran 4400, 18 May 1977, NA-AAD.

73. Vance, State 159686, 9 Jul 1977, NA-AAD; Moose, Draft report to President on Somali Arms request, 8 Jul 1977, SH Chron. See Eilts, Cairo 8401, 18 May 1977, NA-AAD; Sullivan, Tehran 5960, 6 Jul 1977, NA-AAD; Top Secret, 7 Jul 1977, NLC-1-2-4-30-1; Sullivan, Tehran 6018 & 6019, 7 Jul 1977, NA-AAD; and Sullivan, Tehran 6154, 12 Jul 1977, NA-AAD.

74. Top Secret, 30 June 1977, NLC-1-2-5-60-7. See footnote 162 below.

75. Christopher to Carter, 1 Jul 1977, NLC-128-12-10-1-4; "Vierer-Konsultationen über das Horn von Afrika," 15 Dec 1977, B150/382, Berlin; Hartman, Paris 20983, 20 Jul 1977, NA-AAD; Stoessel, Bonn 12293, 26 Jul 1977, NA-AAD; Brewster, London 12893, 4 Aug 1977, NA-AAD; and Vest to Vance, "June 23 [1977] Quadripartite Meeting: Africa," n.d, NLC-23-20-10-1-2. For quadripartite discussions: author's interview with Owen; Memcon (Owen, de Guiringaud, Genscher, Vance), 29 Sep 1977, FOIA; Vance, State 245649, 13 Oct 1977, FOIA; Vance to Carter, 7 Nov 1977, NLC-128-13-2-6-7; and Top Secret, 12 Nov 1977, NLC-1-4-4-25-5. For request to British: "Secretary's Visit to Iran and Saudi Arabia, 13–15 May 1977: Current African Issues," FCO 31/2117, NA-UK; Draft response to UK, 30 Jun 1977, SH Chron; Christopher to Carter, 1 Jul 1977, NLC-128-12-10-1-4; Top Secret, 4 Aug 1977, NLC-1-3-3-19-4; Brewster, London 13240, 10 Aug 1977, NA-AAD (the itemized Somalia request); and Wall to Meadway, "Arms Sales to Somalia," 25 Aug 1977, PREM 16/1870, NA-UK (another itemized list). For request to France: Global Issues Group to ZB, 15 Jul 1977, NLC-10-4-1-20-3; Loughran, Mog 1263, 25 Jul 1977, FOIA; Hartman, Paris 21427, 28 Jul 1977, NA-AAD; Memcon (Ratanov, Mengistu), 7 Aug 1977, in Hershberg, "Anatomy," 71–72; Noebel, London 1775, 18 Aug 1977, B150/374, Berlin; Hartman, Paris 26200, 9 Sep 1977, NA-AAD; and "Vierer-Konsultationen über das Horn von Afrika," 15 Dec 1977, London, B150/382, Berlin. For Germany: Stoessel, Bonn 12294, 26 Jul 1977, NA-AAD; Stoessel, Bonn 12787, 4 Aug 1977, NA-AAD.

76. Marginalia on Vance to Carter, 9 Jul 1977, NLC-7-18-5-3-7. For intelligence: SRF, 3 Jul 1977, SH Chron; and Top Secret, 13 Jul 1977, NLC-6-69-6-28-4.

77. CIA, "Interagency Assessment of the Ethiopian-Somali Situation," 10 Aug 1977, CREST. See Henze, ER, 6 Jun 1977, Horn/5, CL; and Henze to Aaron, 10 Nov 1977, Horn/1, CL.

78. "Versión del traductor Bernardo sobre informe del presidente [Mengistu] a Novoa el domingo 14 agosto/77," Gleijeses Papers; Memcon (Mengistu, Ochoa, Casas), 5 Sep 1977, ibid; and Memcon (Ustinov, Akhromeyev, Ochoa), 27 Sep 1977, ibid.

79. Memcon (Giscard, Vance), 2 Apr 1977, 5AG3/984, Archives de la Présidence, Paris. See Gammon, Paris 09751, 3 Apr 1977, FOIA.

80. For the list: Vance, State 161221, 12 Jul 1977, NA-AAD.

81. Tarnoff to ZB, 12 Jul 1977, Horn/1, CL; West, Jidda 5730, 19 Aug 1977, NLC-21-32-2-16-4; Loughran, Mog 1170, 12 Jul 1977, NA-AAD; and Vance to Carter, 9 Jul 1977, NLC-7-18-5-3-7, which includes the Somali arms request. Also author's interview with Moose (2001).

82. Moose to Vance, 8 Jul 1977, SH Chron.

83. Vance to Carter, 9 Jul 1977, NLC-7-18-5-3-7. Also Memcon (Moose, Addou), 8 Jul 1977, SH Chron.

84. Vance, State 161221, 12 Jul 1977, NA-AAD.

85. Memcon (Addou, Seeyle), 11 Jul 1977, SH Chron. Also author's interviews with Moose (2002), Hamrick, and Easum.

86. Vance to Carter, 13 Jul 1977, NLC-128-12-10-2-4; and Vance, State 170060, 21 Jul 1977, NA-AAD. Also, National Intelligence Daily, 15 Jul 1977, NLC-31-18-5-2-1.

87. Situation Room to ZB, 13 Jul 1977, NLC-1-3-2-14-0; Noebel, London 1775, 18 Aug 1977, B150/374, Berlin; and Makasa to Mwale, "Political Report No. 3 for July–August, 1977," 147 UNIP 7/23/55. See Memcon (Kenyatta, Owen), 5 Jan 1978, PREM 16/1872, NA-UK.

88. Carter, *White House Diary*, 56. See Quandt to ZB, 9 Jun 1977, DDRS; ZB to Carter, 18 Jul 1977, DDRS; and Quandt, *Camp David*, 63–78.

89. Memcon (Carter, Begin), 20 Jul 1977, NLC-25-110-7-14-9. See Moose to Habib, 20 Jul 1977, SH Chron; and *NYT*, 21 Aug 1983, 1.

90. Henze, ER, 20 Jul 1977, NLC-10-4-2-1-3; Loughran, Mog 1349, 8 Aug 1977, NA-AAD; and Henze, ER, 20 Jul 1977, NLC-10-4-2-1-3. Also Aaron to Henze, 11 Nov 1977, Horn/1, CL.

91. Top Secret, 2 Aug 1977, NLC-1-3-3-10-3; and Lewis, TelAviv 5669, 2 Aug 1977, NA-AAD. See Moose to Habib, 20 Jul 1977, SH Chron; Christopher, State 184546, 5 Aug 1977 NA-AAD; Top Secret, 5 Aug 1977, NLC-1-3-3-24-8; Top Secret, 6 Aug 1977, NLC-1-3-3-27-5; and Lewis, TelAviv 8529, 31 Oct 1977, NA-AAD.

92. Eilts, Cairo 12237, 22 Jul 1977, FOIA.

93. Ibid.

94. Post to Moose, Talking Points on Horn for meeting with Secretary, 14 Jul 1977, SH Chron.

95. Thornton and Richardson to Henze, 20 Jul 1977, Horn/1, CL.

96. Vance, State 161221, 12 Jul 1977, NA-AAD.

97. Vance, State 167604, 19 Jul 1977, FOIA.

98. Memcon (Habib, Addou), 15 Jul 1977, SH Chron; and Vance, State 167604, 19 Jul 1977, FOIA. On Siad's trip to Saudi Arabia: Sullivan, Tehran 6381, 19 Jul 1977, NA-AAD.

99. Vance, State 167604, 19 Jul 1977, FOIA. See "Discussion with Moose after his meeting with Addou," 15 Jul 1977, SH Chron.

100. Henze, ER, 22 Jul 1977, NLC-10-4-2-8-6.

101. Loughran, Mog 1249, 24 Jul 1977, FOIA.

102. Ibid. Also INR, Current Reports, 25 Jul 1977, NLC-SAFE17 B-3-14 1-5; and Loughran, Mog 1274, 26 Jul 1977, FOIA.

103. For the official Ethiopian declaration of the Somali attack: Stoessel, Bonn 12371, 27 Jul 1977, NA-AAD.

104. Hamrick, "The Horn of Africa: No Peace in Sight," [Sep 1977], Hamrick Papers. See Top Secret, 18 Jul 1977, NLC-1-3-2-32-0; West, Jidda 5117, 23 Jul 1977, NA-AAD; and *NYT*, 28 Jul 1977, 1. Estimates of the size of the "People's Army" vary; the Derg claimed it was 300,000; P. S. Gilkes estimates 100,000–120,000 (see Gilkes, "Revolution," 723); most estimates are lower.

105. Henze to ZB, 27 Mar 1978, Horn/2, CL.

106. Raúl Castro to Fidel Castro, 14 Jul 1977, Gleijeses Papers; Ochoa to Fidel Castro, 8 Jul 1977, ibid.; Vance, State 167604, 19 Jul 1977, FOIA; and Raúl Castro to Fidel Castro, 21 July, 1977, ibid. The date of the beginning of the war ranges from July 13 (Ethiopian documents cited in Tareke, *Ethiopian Revolution*, 191) to July 28 (*NYT*, 28 Jul 1977). US sources say July 23 (Top Secret, 25 Jul 1977, NLC-1-3-1-16-9), as did Mengistu in an address to the nation in January 1978 ("Imperialist Aggression from Vietnam to Ethiopia," Addis Ababa, 30 Jan 1978, PREM 16/1873, NA-UK). Cuban sources say July 24 ("Monografía de Etiopía," in Oramas to Malmierca, 14 Oct 1977, in Malmierca to Raúl Castro, 18 Oct 1977, Gleijeses Papers), while the Soviets say "by July 26" (Memcon [Ilichev, Kassim], 26 Jul 1977, CWIHP-va).

107. Russian Republic, *Rossiya*, 108. Nor is the US promise of arms to Somalia mentioned as a factor in the outbreak of the war in the well-informed report of the Zambian ambassador to Ethiopia. See Kalenga Kangwa to Siteke Mwale (Zambian minister of Foreign Affairs), "Regular Report No. 4/77 covering the period of June and July 1977," n.d., 149 UNIP 7/23/62.

108. Henze to ZB, 24 Aug 1977, Ethiopia-NSC/3, NSA-DC; Kangwa to Mwale, "Regular Report No. 4/77 covering the period of June and July 1977," n.d., 149 UNIP 7/23/62; and DOS, "The Horn of Africa," 12 Jul 1977, NLC-23-13-5-3-4. The most reliable sources on the Ogaden war are Tareke's *Ethiopian Revolution*, which is based on research in the Ethiopian archives, and the Cuban military reports from the front. US reports reveal Washington's perception of what was happening, but they are not based on good intelligence. This is true to an even greater extent of British, French, and West German reports. The declassified documents of the Italian Communist Party are even more disappointing.

109. See Henze to ZB, 24 Aug 1977, Ethiopia-NSC/3, NSA-DC; Vance, State 230604, 24 Sep 1977, NA-AAD; and Somali Ministry of Foreign Affairs, "Background to the Liberation Struggle of the Western Somalis," 1978, PREM 16/1873, NA-UK.

110. Dirección de inteligencia militar, EMG, "Parte especial sobre la situación in Etiopía para el 31.8 y el 1.9.77," [Sep 1977,] Gleijeses Papers.

111. CIA, "Interagency Assessment of Ethiopian-Somali Situation," 10 Aug 1977, CREST. See Memcon (Ratanov, Mengistu), 5 Sep 1977, CWIHP-va; INR, Current Reports, 6 Sep 1977, NLC-31-68-17-3-2; Henze, Khartoum [no number] to White House, 15 Sep 1977, NLC-7-6-10-4-3; and *NYT*, 29 Sep 1977, 56.

112. Tareke, *Ethiopian Revolution*, 199.

113. "Note sulla situazione etiopica," 15 Aug 1977, Note a Seg., 299-273, PCI, Istituto Gramsci, Rome. For Soviets: Memcon (Casas, Ustinov, Akhromeyev), 27 Sep 1977, Gleijeses Papers. For rumors re: Israel: W*P*, 1 Oct 1977, 12; Vance, State 244110, 12 Oct 1977, NA-AAD; Low, Lusaka 806, 13 Mar 1978, FOIA-DC; and Vance, State 65651, 15 Mar 1978, FOIA-DC.

114. There were only seven reports in all the major US press filed from near the front over the course of the war, and the reporters were always escorted by Ethiopian or Somali handlers: *NYT*, 1 Sep 1977, 3; *Newsweek*, 5 Sep 1977, 40; *WP*, 15 Sep 1977, 17; *Newsweek*, 26 Sep 1977, 43; *NYT*, 26 Sep 1977, 8; *NYT*, 29 Sep 1977, 1; and *Newsweek*, 17 Oct 1977, 54. For 15,000: Loughran, Mog 1434, 22 Aug 1977, Hamrick Papers. For rumors: Loughran, Mog 1288, 27 Jul 1977, FOIA; and Clarke, Djibouti 285, 8 Aug 1977, FOIA.

115. Henze, ER, 22 Aug 1977, NLC-10-4-6-12-7. See *NYT*, 15 Aug 1977, 57; and Tienken, Addis 05414, 9 Sep 1977, FOIA.

116. Carter to Vance, 18 Aug 1977, *FRUS 1977–1980, v. 13: China*, doc. 43. See Vance, *Hard Choices*, 75–83.

117. DOS, "Soviet, Chinese and Cuban Presence in Sub-Saharan Africa," July 1977, NLC-133-159-2-10-5; and DOS, "The Horn of Africa," [12 Jul 1977,] NLC-23-13-5-3-4.

118. Richard Holbrooke in Unger, Taipei 5269, 27 Aug 1977, *FRUS 1977–1980, v. 13: China*, doc. 54. See Young, USUN 1765, 3 Jun 1977, NLC-26-43-1-1-3.

119. Memcon (Vance, Teng Hsiao-ping [Deng Xiaoping]), 24 Aug 1977, DDRS. See Memcon (Vance, Hua Kuo-feng), 25 Aug 1977, DDRS.

120. Memcom (Vance, Huang Hua), 23 Aug 1977, DDRS. Also Henze to ZB, 26 Aug 1977, Horn/1, CL; and Henze to ZB, 31 Aug 1977, Horn/1, CL.

121. CIA, "China and the Horn of Africa," 12 May 1978, NLC-4-38-7-3-6. For the Somali vice president: Memcon (Vance, Huang Hua), 28 Sep 1977, *FRUS 1977–1980, v. 13: China*, doc. 62. For Chinese aid to Somalia: Toon, Moscow 16595, 15 Nov 1977, NA-AAD; Henze, ER, 15 Nov 1977, DDRS; Vance, State 278214/1, 20 Nov 1977, DDRS; Constable, Islamabad 12248, 15 Dec 1977, NA-AAD; Constable, Islamabad 12274, 16 Dec 1977, NA-AAD; and Toon, Moscow 18141, 16 Dec 1977, NA-AAD.

122. Memcom (Vance, Huang Hua), 23 Aug 1977, DDRS. See USDel Secretary Peking to White House, SecTo 9017, 23 Aug 1977, NA-AAD.

123. Christopher (Anderson/Wisner to Tarnoff), State 200949, 23 Aug 1977, NA-AAD; and Carter, "Being There," 164.

124. Tienken, Addis 4978, 17 Aug 1977, NA-AAD.

125. "Record of negotiations between Somali and Soviet officials in Moscow from 15–19 August 1977," 31 Aug 1977, Russian State Archive of Contemporary History (formerly the Center for Preservation of Contemporary Documentation), fond 5, opis 73, delo 1620, ll. 60–80 (hereafter "Record of negotiations"); INR, Current Reports, 18 Aug 1977, NLC-SAFE B-4-17-5-7; "Record of negotiations." The original Russian document includes Kasim's lengthy review of the history of the Horn and a heated discussion on 15 August, which are not included in the edited translation at CWIHP-va. See also Brewster, London 12893, 4 Aug 1977, NA-AAD.

126. Tienken, Addis 5744, 30 Sep 1977, NA-AAD; and Vance, SecTo 13075, 3 Jan 1978, NLC-16-42-4-13-0. For Siad's trip to Moscow: Memcon (Ratanov, Tienkin), 3 Sep 1977, in Hershberg, "Anatomy," 77; Memcon (Ratanov, Mengistu), 5 Sep 1977, in ibid., 77–78; and Loughran, Mog 1590, 20 Sep 77, Hamrick Papers. Also ZB to Carter, 6 Sep 1977, NLC-1-3-6-14-6.

127. Loughran, Mog 1333, 4 Aug 1977, FOIA; and Loughran, Mog 1627, 25 Sep 1977, Hamrick Papers.

128. Brewster, London 17304, 18 Oct 1977, NA-AAD.

129. Tienken, Addis 5744, 30 Sep 1977, NA-AAD; and Memcon (Casas, Ustinov, Akhromeyev), 27 Sep 1977, Gleijeses Papers.

130. Loughran, Mog 1590, 20 Sep 1977, Hamrick Papers; and Makasa to Mwale, "Political Report No. 3 for July–August, 1977," 147 UNIP 7/23/55. See Matthews, Cairo 16240, 29 Sep 1977, FOIA. On the deterioration of Somali-Soviet relations, see especially Westad, *Global*, 271–77.

131. For the speech: *Guardian* (London), 25 Jul 1977, 6. See *NYT*, 25 Jul 1977, 7; and *WP*, 25 Jul 1977, 14.

132. Thornton and Richardson to ZB and Aaron, 20 Jul 1977, NLC-24-97-7-16-4. They refer to a cable from Young that also questions the policy, but this cable is not available.

133. *NYT*, 27 Jul 1977, 3. See *WP*, 27 Jul 1977, 14; *CT*, 27 Jul 1977, 10; and *LAT*, 27 Jul 1977, 5. On British and French: Noebel, London 1775, 18 Aug 1977, B150/374, Berlin; and Wall to Meadway, 26 Aug 1977, PREM 16/1872, NA-UK.

134. Thornton to ZB and Aaron, 27 Jul 1977, NLC-21-32-2-12-8.

135. See ZB to Vance, 5 Aug 1977, NLC-21-32-2-15-5. More typical was Brzezinski's warning to Carter several days later not to do anything that "would be damaging to our efforts to detach Somalia from the Soviet Union." ZB to Carter, 18 Aug 1977, NLC-126-8-41-2-6.

136. Vance to ZB, 8 Aug 1977, NLC-21-34-2-14-6.

137. Henze to Hyland, 10 Aug 1977, Horn/1, CL.

138. Vance to Carter, 13 Sep 1977, NLC-21-19-15-1-1. See the September and October 1977 cables with this title in NA-AAD.

139. Vance, State 198297, 20 Aug 1977, NA-AAD; Loughran, Mog 1450, 23 Aug 1977, NA-AAD; and Tienken, Addis 5068, 23 Aug 1977, NA-AAD. For US efforts, see Loughran, Mog 1469, 28 Aug 1977, NA-AAD; Christopher, State 210166, 1 Sep 1977, NA-AAD. For Cubans, see DOS, "Cuban Objectives in Africa," 12 Jul 1977, NLC-23-13-5-3-4; Lane, Havana 535, 7 Nov 1977, NA-AAD; Streator, London 18457, 9 Nov 1977, NA-AAD; and Lane, Havana 583, 11 Nov 1977, NA-AAD.

140. Wyman, Lagos 10482, 12 Sep 1977, NA-AAD.

141. Vance, State 225871, 20 Sep 1977, NA-AAD.

142. Carter marginalia on Christopher to Carter, 3 Aug 1977, NLC-128-12-11-3-1; ZB to Vance, 5 Aug 1977, NLC-15-47-8-4-2; Henze to Hyland, 10 Aug 1977, Horn/1, CL; and *NYT*, 2 Sep 1977, 2. See ZB to Vance, 2 Aug 1977, NLC-6-69-6-29-3; Christopher to Carter, 9 Aug 1977, NLC-128-12-11-7-7; Wall to Meadway, "Arms Sales to Somalia," 25 Aug 1977, PREM 16/1870, NA-UK; and *WP*, 3 Sep 1977, 14. At the briefing on September 19, Hodding Carter declared that he had first announced the "go slow" in mid-August, but the record indicates the opposite: at the August 19 briefing, he vigorously denied a *NYT* story that the administration was pulling back. See *NYT*, 18 Aug 1977, 2; Vance, State 198215, 19 Aug 1977, NA-AAD; and Vance, State 225871, 20 Sep 1977, NA-AAD.

143. West, Jidda 6047, 31 Aug 1977, NA-AAD. See West, Jidda 5750, 19 Aug 1977, NA-AAD; West, Jidda 6507, 23 Sep 1977, NA-AAD; and Wiley, Jidda 7306, 25 Oct 1977, NA-AAD.

144. See Vance, State 218708, 13 Sep 1977, NA-AAD; and *Newsweek*, 26 Sep 1977, 42. See *WP*, 19 Sep 1977, 15; and *WP*, 20 Sep 1977, 12.

145. Vance, State 221656, 15 Sep 1977, NA-AAD.

146. Vance, State 225871, 20 Sep 1977, NA-AAD.

147. See Vance to ZB, 8 Aug 1977, NLC-21-34-2-14-6; and Tienken, Addis 5754, 1 Oct 1977, NA-AAD.

148. Christopher, State 237297, 1 Oct 1977, NA-AAD.

149. Ibid.

150. Memcon (Vance, Dobrynin), 17 Oct 1977, Carter-Brezhnev Project, NSA-online.

151. Hamrick, "The Horn of Africa: No Peace in Sight," [Sep 1977,] Hamrick Papers; Vest to Vance, "The September 29 Quadripartite Breakfast," [Sep 1977,] NLC-23-13-5-1-6; Memcon (Vance, Owen, de Guiringaud, Genscher), 29 Sep 1977, NLC-23-29-6-17-1; and Richard, MisNY 1602, 11 Oct 1977, PREM 16/1872, NA-UK. See Vance, State 237297, 1 Oct 1977, NA-AAD; Christopher, State 236037, 1 Oct 1977, NA-AAD; Brewster, London 16547, 4 Oct 1977, FOIA; and Brewster, London 18627, 11 Nov 1977, NA-AAD.

152. See Memcon (Carter, Waldheim), 4 Oct 1977, NSA (7)/35, CL; and Vance, SecTo, 7 Oct 1977, FOIA.

153. See Vance, State 278216, 19 Nov 1977, FOIA; and Memcon (Carter, Bongo), 17 Oct 1977, FOIA. See chapter 4.

154. See Vance to Carter, 13 Sep 1977, Ethiopia-NSC/3, NSA-DC; ZB to Carter, in Gates to ZB, 14 Sep 1977, Ethiopia-NSC/3, NSA-DC; and Henze to ZB, 18 Nov 1977, Horn/1, CL. Washington also extended increased aid to Chad.

155. *WP*, 28 Jul 1977, 1. See Eilts, Cairo 10389, 21 Jun 1977, NA-AAD; and Loughran, Mog 1577, 18 Sep 1977, NA-AAD.

156. AIPAC, "Memorandum: F-15s to Saudi Arabia–A Threat to Peace," n.d., West Papers/11; and *WP*, 30 Jul 1977, edit 14. See the shah to Carter, 27 Apr 1977, CL; Vance to Carter, 26 Jul 1977, CL; and Sullivan, Tehran 06611, 26 Jul 1977, DNSA.

157. *WP*, 28 July 1977, 1; and *WP*, 30 Jul 1977, 1. See Akins (US ambassador to Saudi Arabia) to Watson, 3 Oct 1976, West Papers/21. In April 1976, the Ford administration said it would sell six C-130 transport planes to Egypt; this was controversial, but it was not a weapons deal.

158. Christopher, State 188052, 9 Aug 1977, NA-AAD. Also Henze to ZB, 26 Aug 1977, Horn/1, CL; and Henze to ZB, 31 Aug 1977, Horn/1, CL.

159. Vance, State 252186, 20 Oct. 1977, FOIA.

160. In the hope of filling in some of the blanks, I consulted the journal of John West, the US ambassador in Jidda. In reams of pages about dinner parties and golf outings, Somalia was not mentioned. See West papers.

161. Eilts, Cairo 13245, 9 Aug 1977, FOIA; Christopher, State 188052, 9 Aug 1977, FOIA; Russian Republic, *Rossiya*, 109; and Eilts, Cairo 14756, 6 Sep 1977, NLC-21-16-14-20-4. For Egyptian aid to Somalia: Loughran, Mog 1343, 8 Aug 1977, NA-AAD; DOS, "Egypt's Concerns in Africa," Sep 1977, NLC-133-159-5-13-9; Loughran, Mog 1577, 18 Sep 1977, NLC-21-16-14-21-3; Christopher, State 295102, 10 Dec 1977, FOIA; Henze, ER, 19 Dec 1977, Horn/5, CL; Tsongas and Bonker, "The Horn of Africa," [17 Dec 1977], NSA/2, CL; Loughran, Mog 2236, 29 Dec 1977, NA-AAD; and DOS, "Developments in Africa,"[4 Jan 1978], NLC-133-161-1-8-6.

162. For Jordan: Moberly, Amman 27, 20 Jan 1978, PREM 16/1872, NA-UK; and Memcon (Callaghan, King Hussein), 22 Feb 1978, PREM 16/1873, NA-UK. For Sudan: Top Secret, 13 Dec 1977, NLC-1-4-7-20-7; and Wall, "Horn of Africa," 19 Jan 1978, PREM 16/1872, NA-UK. For Pakistan: Christopher, State 184981, 6 Aug 1977, NA-AAD; Hummel, Islamabad 8429, 18 Aug 1977, NA-AAD; Hummel, Islamabad 10908, 3 Nov 1977, NA-AAD; Hummel, Islamabad 11433, 21 Nov 1977, NA-AAD; Constable, Islamabad 12248, 15 Dec 1977, NA-AAD; and Cartledge to Wall, 17 Jan 1978, PREM 16/1872, NA-UK. For Iraq, UAE, and Kuwait: Raúl Castro to Fidel Castro, 5 May 1977, Gleijeses Papers; Top Secret, 12 Jul 1977, NLC-1-3-2-9-6; Eilts, Cairo 13245, 9 Aug 1977, FOIA; Mack, Baghdad 1403, 20 Aug 1977, NA-AAD; Loughran, Mog 1592, 20 Sep 1977, NA-AAD; Hamrick, "The Horn of Africa: No Peace in Sight," [Sep 1977], Hamrick Papers; and Memcon (Ali Nasser, Malmierca), 14 Mar 1978, Gleijeses Papers. For Morocco: Eilts, Cairo 10389, 21 Jun 1977, NA-AAD; and Henze to ZB, 26 Aug 1977, Horn/1, CL. For South Yemen: Scotes, Sana 3844, 1 Oct 1977, NA-AAD. For Singapore: Holdridge, Singapore 5383, 8 Dec 1977, NA-AAD.

163. Sullivan, Tehran 7124, 10 Oct 1977, NA-AAD. See Top Secret, 10 Aug. 1977, NLC-1-3-3-36-5; marginalia on Henze to Hyland, 10 Aug. 1977, Horn/1, CL; and Top Secret, 12 Aug. 1977, NLC-1-3-4-9-4.

164. Christopher, State 189617, 10 Oct 1977, NA-AAD.

165. Sullivan, Tehran 7143, 11 Oct 1977, NA-AAD.

166. Sullivan, Tehran 7186, 14 Oct 1977, NA-AAD.

167. "Vierer-Konsultationen über das Horn von Afrika," 15 Dec 1977, B150/382, Berlin; and Silverstein, "Licensed to Kill," 59. For US weapons, see Memcon (Mengistu, Aaron), 17 Feb 1978, in [unsigned, from Henze], Addis 534, 20 Feb 1978, NLC-7-6-10-19-7.

168. Memcon (Vierer-Konsultationen über das Horn von Afrika), 11 Nov 1977, doc. 322, *AAPD 1977*, 1546–48.

169. Mulley to Callaghan, 26 Sep 1977; Owen, FCO 846, 28 Sep 1977. See Kay, Jidda 701, 27 Sep 1977; marginalia on Mulley to Callaghan, 26 Sep 1977; Rowlands to Owen, [27 Sep 1977]; FCO to Moi, [27 Sep 1977]; Prendergast to Cartledge, 30 Sep 1977; and Cartledge to Prendergast, 6 Oct 1977. All PREM 16/1872, NA-UK.

170. Memcon (Carter, Barre), 16 Sep 1977, NLC-21-19-1-19-7; Vest to Vance, "The September 29 Quadripartite Breakfast," n.d., NLC-23-13-5-1-6; Memcon (Mueller, Harrop, Graham, Georgy), 4 Oct 1977 in Noebel, "Horn von Afrika," 19 Oct 1977, doc. 297, *AAPD 1977*, 1421–28; Vance to Carter, 7 Nov 1977, NLC-128-13-2-6-7; Hartman, Paris 32562, 17 Nov 1977, NA-AAD; "Quadripartite Discussions on the Horn of Africa," 10 Nov 1977, in Wall to Cartledge, 16 Nov 1977, PREM 16/1872, NA-UK; and Memcon (Owen, Vance, Habib), 8 Dec 1977, FCO 82/736, NA-UK. For French arms: Tienken, Addis 5491, 16 Sep 1977, FOIA; Memcon (Mueller, Harrop, Mansfield, Georgy), 10 Nov 1977, NLC-23-29-6-6-3; Brewster, London 18627, 11 Nov 1977, NA-AAD; LeMelle, Nairobi 14930, 17 Nov 1977, NA-AAD; Harrop to Vest, 17 Nov 1977, NLC-23-29-6-5-4; and Eilts, Cairo 20312, 6 Dec 1977, NA-AAD. For British denials: Memcon (Bolaños, Mansfield), 2 Dec 1977, FCO 99/22; and Memcon (Callaghan, Kenyan Vice President Moi), 6 Mar 1978, PREM 16/1873, NA-UK. For Italian arms: Memcon (Carter, Andreotti), 26 Jul 1977, NLC-23-21-6-4-3.

171. Telcon (Schmidt, Siad), 17 Oct 1977, in Memcon (Schmidt, Wischnewski), 17 Oct 1977, doc. 293, *AAPD 1977*, 1401, 1407; and *NYT*, 18 Oct 1977, 1. See Stoessel,

Bonn 16588, 5 Oct 1977, NA-AAD; Stoessel, Bonn 18040, 28 Oct 1977, NA-AAD; and Stoessel, Bonn 18545, 9 Nov 1977, NA-AAD.

172. Memcon (Schmidt, Afrah), 30 Nov 1977, doc. 341, *AAPD 1977*, 1635; and Memcon (Schlei, Haebser), 25 Nov 1977, B150/380, Berlin; Fergusson, "The Lufthansa Hijack," 24 Oct 1977, PREM 16/1872, NA-UK. There was dissent within the West German government about sending aid to Somalia, but Schmidt overruled it. See "Ausrüstungshilfe für Somalia," B136/17587, Koblenz.

173. Memcon (Schmidt, Bokah), 3 Nov 1977, doc. 315, *AAPD 1977*, 1513–17; and Memcon (Schmidt, Abdallah), 23 May 1978, B150/393, Berlin. For Sadat: Memcon (Schmidt, Afrah), 30 Nov 1977, doc. 341, *AAPD 1977*, 1635. For German aid: Henze, ER, 11 Nov 1977, Horn/5, CL; Harrop to Vest, 17 Nov 1977, NLC-23-29-6-5-4; Top Secret, 18 Nov 1977, NLC-1-4-5-3-8; Vance, State 276642, 18 Nov 1977, NA-AAD; and Stoessel, Bonn 19514, 23 Nov 1977, NA-AAD.

174. Memcon (Trudeau, Carter, Vance, ZB), 8 Sep 1977, NLC-24-62-8-5-3.

175. "Considerations on Regional Conflict," report following NSC Meeting, 10 May 1978, DDRS.

176. ZB, WR, 23 Sep 1977, DDRS; Memcon (Vance, Genscher), 30 Sep 1977, FOIA; and Situation Room to ZB, 4 Nov 1977, NLC-1-4-3-24-7. See INR, "Morning Summary," 20 Nov 1977, NLC SAFE 16 D-88-1-2-4.

177. Vance, State 252186, 20 Oct 1977, FOIA; Vance to Carter, 20 Oct 1977, NLC-128-13-1-13-0; and Vance, ER, 20 Oct 1977, NLC-15R-68-6-3-3.

178. *NYT*, 19 Oct 1977, edit 24.

179. Loughran, Mog 1385,14 Aug 1977, Hamrick Papers; Achille Occhetto, "Informazione del compagno Occhetto sulla situazione nel Corno d'Africa vista dalla Somalia," 5 Sep 1977, Note a Seg., 304-325, PCI, Istituto Gramsci, Rome; and Hamrick to Janka, [Sep 1977], "The Horn of Africa: No Peace in Sight." Also author's interviews with Hamrick and Addou.

180. Tienken, Addis 4978, 17 Aug 1977, NA-AAD. See ZB to Carter, 26 Aug 1977, NLC-1-3-5-18-3; and Kraft, "Letter from Addis Ababa," 61.

181. "Note sulla situazione etiopica," 15 Aug 1977, Note a Seg., 299-273, PCI, Istituto Gramsci, Rome. For Moscow's promises: Miklos, Tehran 10077, 14 Nov 1977, NA-AAD; and Westad, *Global*, 275.

182. Memcon (Vance, Huang Hua), 23 Aug 1977, DDRS; and Hamrick to Janka, [Sep 1977], "The Horn of Africa: No Peace in Sight." See Top Secret, 1 Aug 1977, NLC-1-3-3-4-0; Tienken, Addis 4753, 5 Aug 1977, FOIA; Tienken, Addis 4864, 11 Aug 1977, FOIA; "Draft cable to Addis," in Dodson to Mondale, 24 Aug 1977, Ethiopia-NSC/3, NSA-DC; and DOS, "The Horn of Africa," in Tarnoff to ZB, c. 25 Aug 1977, Ethiopia-NSC/3, NSA-DC. The Carter administration appointed a new ambassador to Addis on June 27, 1978; Ethiopia, which had withdrawn its ambassador to Washington in February 1975, announced in the summer of 1977 that it would appoint a new ambassador, and it did so in September.

183. DOS, "The Horn of Africa," in Tarnoff to ZB, [25 Aug 1977], Ethiopia-NSC/3, NSA-DC.

184. ZB, WR, 23 Sep 1977, DDRS; and Christopher, State 237297, 1 Oct 1977, FOIA. See Vest to Vance, "The September 29 Quadripartite Breakfast," n.d., NLC-23-13-5-1-6.

185. Memcon (Owen, de Guiringaud, Genscher, Vance), 29 Sep 1977, NLC-23-29-6-17-1.

Chapter 7

1. *NYT*, 1 Jun 1977, 1. See Moorcraft and McLaughlin, *Rhodesian War*, 164–66.

2. Richardson to ZB, 31 May 1977, NLC-24-105-1-18-8; and Memcon (Smith, Pik Botha), 15 Jun 1977, records of meetings, box 4/002(m), Smith Papers. See Christopher, State 124623, 30 May 1977, NA-AAD.

3. ADR (Hawkins) to Gaylard, C176, 26 May 1977, ADR/8, 4/006(m), Smith Papers.

4. Ibid.

5. Memcon (Smith, Pik Botha), 15 Jun 1977, records of meetings, box 4/002(m), Smith Papers.

6. Ibid.

7. "Inserts for VP's Lunch with President," 3 Jun 1977, NLC-133-107-5-1-9. See Clift to Mondale, 2 Jun 1977, NLC-133-107-5-2-8; and DePree, Maputo 734, 2 Jun 1977, NA-AAD. The UN Security Council discussed the raid on June 28 and 29; on June 30 it passed Resolution 411 "strongly condemning" Rhodesia, "condemning" South Africa "for its continued support of the illegal regime," and calling on all member states to extend aid to Mozambique. British and American pressure narrowly averted a vote on sanctions against South Africa. UN Security Council resolution 411, *Mozambique–Southern Rhodesia*, S/RES/411 (30 Jun 1977), http://undocs.org/S/RES/411(1977). See Mondale to Carter, 31 May 1977, NLC-133–14-13-12-1; and Vance to Carter in Christopher, State 125855, 1 Jun 1977, NA-AAD.

8. Rhodesian Diplomatic Mission, "Notes of a Meeting held in Salisbury on Wednesday 15 June 1977," 22 Jun 1977, records of meetings, box 4/002(m), Smith Papers; and Memcon (Smith, Pik Botha), 15 Jun 1977, ibid.

9. Memcon (Smith, Pik Botha), 15 Jun 1977, records of meetings, box 4/002(m), Smith Papers; and Rhodesian Diplomatic Mission, "Notes of a Meeting held in Salisbury on Wednesday 15 June 1977," 22 Jun 1977, ibid.

10. Memcon (Smith, Pik Botha), 15 Jun 1977, records of meetings, box 4/002(m), Smith Papers.

11. Rhodesian Diplomatic Mission, "Notes of a Meeting held in Salisbury on Wednesday 15 June 1977," 22 Jun 1977, records of meetings, box 4/002(m), Smith Papers; and Memcon (Smith, Pik Botha), 15 Jun 1977, ibid. On US-South African relations, see Zavelo, "In Transition."

12. US Senate, "Young's African Trip," CD53, 19; and Vance to Carter, 8 Jun 1977, NLC-7-18-4-1-0.

13. Richardson to ZB, 1 Dec 1977, NSA-staff/119, CL.

14. Gaylard to ADR, 7 Sep 1978, ADR/12, box 4/006(m), Smith Papers.

15. Brewster (from Ray Seitz), London 18559, 10 Nov 1977, NA-AAD.

16. See Martin and Johnson, *Struggle*, 279–80; Meredith, *Past Is Another Country*, 302–6; Jeremy Brickhill, "Daring to Storm the Heavens: The Military Strategy of ZAPU, 1976 to 1979," in Bhebe and Ranger, *Soldiers*, 48–72; and Moorcraft and McLaughlin, *Rhodesian War*, 129–35, 147–50. For a careful analysis of war deaths: Stedman, *Peacemaking*, 93. For a clear description of the armed forces: Moorcraft and McLaughlin, *Rhodesian War*, 47–68.

17. CIA, "World Trends and Developments," n.d., Feb 1977, CIA-rr; and CIA, "Rhodesia: Some Thoughts on a Partial Settlement," 10 Nov 1977, in Turner to ZB, 16 Nov 1977, NSA-staff/119, CL.

18. US Senate, "Young's African Trip," CD53, 20; and Renwick, BDOHP, 6 Aug 1998.

19. Hunter and Thornton to ZB, 20 Sep 1977, NSA-staff/119-25, CL; and author's interview with Low. On pensions: Memcon (Owen, Vance), 24 Jun 1977, FOIA.

20. Memcon (Owen, Vance), 24 Jun 1977, FOIA.

21. Author's interview with Graham.

22. Christopher to Carter, 29 Jun 1977, NLC-128-12-9-21-4.

23. Memcon (Genscher, Young), 19 Jul 1977, doc. 199, *AAPD 1977*, 1004; and [DOS,] "Southern Africa—Policy Review," in Dodson to Mondale, 19 Jul 1977, Vertical/Cuba-defense, CL (authorship is clear in: Richardson to ZB, 19 Jul 1977, Brzezinski/24, CL). See UK Cabinet, Conclusions, 28 Jul 1977, CAB/128/62/6, NA-UK).

24. Memcon (Carter, Owen), 23 Jul 1977, NSA-Brzezinski (7)/35, CL; "The Secretary of State's talks with Mr Vance," in Laver to Rowlands, 22 Jul 1977, FCO 36/2008, NA-UK; and Memcon (Carter, Owen), 23 Jul 1977, NSA-Brzezinski (7)/35, CL.

25. Presidential Campaign Debate, 22 Oct 1976, APP.

26. Memcon (Carter, Owen), 23 Jul 1977, NSA-Brzezinski (7)/35, CL; and Christopher, State 187016, 9 Aug 1977, DNSA.

27. Vance to Carter, [22 Jul 1977,] NLC-133-159-2-3-3.

28. Author's interview with Richardson; and ZB to Carter, 2 Aug 1977, NLC-5-13-4-14-3.

29. Callaghan to Carter, 4 Aug 1977, Brzezinski/14, CL.

30. Memcon (Carter, Nyerere), 4 Aug 1977, NLC-133-42-3-20-2 (emphasis in original).

31. Ibid.

32. ZB to Carter, "Points to Confirm with Nyerere," 4 Aug 1977, DDRS.

33. Memcon (Carter, Nyerere), 5 Aug 1977, NLC-133-42-3-20-2 (emphasis added). See ZB to Carter, "Points to Confirm with Nyerere," 4 Aug 1977, DDRS.

34. Owen, *Time*, 310.

35. Author's interview with Owen.

36. Vance, *Hard Choices*, 267.

37. Memcon (Carter, Trudeau), 21 Feb 1977, NLC-23-16-4-5-0.

38. Memcon (Genscher, Young), 19 Jul 1977, doc. 199, *AAPD 1977*, 1004.

39. Vance, *Hard Choices*, 269; author's interview with Owen; and Memcon (Owen, Vance), 12 Feb 1978, in Ferguson to PUS, 15 Feb 1978, FCO 73/316, NA-UK (emphasis added).

40. Callaghan to Carter, 4 Aug 1977, Brzezinski/14, CL.

41. Carter to Callaghan, in Meadway to Prendergast, 11 Aug 1977, FCO 36/2008, NA-UK.

42. Memcon (Owen, Nyerere), 13 Aug 1977, FCO 82/769, NA-UK. After his negotiations in the Middle East, Vance stopped in London, where he spoke with Nyerere on August 12.

43. Nyerere to Carter, in Spain, Dar 3316, 16 Aug 1977, NA-AAD.

44. See Memcon (Vance, Owen*)*, 11 Mar 1977, FOIA.

45. *Rhodesian Herald* (Salisbury), 19 Jul 1977, 4 (transcript of speech).

46. *Rhodesian Herald*, 20 Apr 1977, edit 10; *Rhodesian Herald*, 19 Apr 1977, edit 1; and *Rhodesian Herald*, 20 Apr 1977, 1. See Situation Room to ZB, 18 Jul 1977, NLC-1-3-2-31-1; and Graham to PS, 20 Jul 1977, FCO 36/2008, NA-UK.

47. See Muzorewa, *Rise Up*; and Mungazi, *In the Footsteps*, 109–28.

48. Author's interview with Graham. See Martin and Johnson, *Struggle*, 195–202; and Meredith, *Past Is Another Country*, 156–59, 201–2. For Sithole: N. Sithole, *African Nationalism*; N. Sithole, *Roots*; and M. Sithole, *Zimbabwe.*

49. ZB, WR, 22 Jul 1977, NSA-subject/41, CL. Also PRC Meeting: Summary of Conclusions, 22 Jul 1977, NLC-15-48-1-4-8; and Vance to Carter, 26 Jul 1977, NLC-133-159-2-8-8.

50. Author's interview with Graham. This is not a controversial point; it is laced throughout the British record. See, e.g., "The Role of Field Marshal Lord Carver . . . as Resident Commissioner Designate for Rhodesia," 20 Dec 1978, in Carver to Owen, 20 Dec 1978, FCO 73/319, NA-UK.

51. Memcon (Carter, Owen), 23 Jul 1977, NSA-Brzezinski (7)/35, CL.

52. Memcon (Callaghan, Kissinger), 25 Jun 1976, PREM 16/1092, NA-UK; and Laver to Aspin, 3 Jun 1976, FCO 36/1787, NA-UK.

53. Author's interviews with Graham and Low; and Martin and Johnson, *Struggle*, 287, quoting an unnamed journalist. See Memcon (Owen, Vorster), 13 Apr 1977, NLC-133-17-1-11-2. On Nkomo: J. Nkomo, *Story*; F. Nkomo, *Father Zimbabwe*.

54. [DOS,] "Southern Africa—Policy Review," in Dodson to Mondale, 19 Jul 1977, Vertical/Cuba-defense, CL (for authorship: Richardson to ZB, 19 Jul 1977, Brzezinski/24, CL); and PRC Meeting: Summary of Conclusions, 22 Jul 1977, NLC-15-48-1-4-8.

55. Memcon (Carter, Owen), 23 Jul 1977, NSA-Brzezinski (7)/35, CL; Carter marginalia on Mondale to Carter, 10 May 1977, DDRS; author's interview with Aaron; Low, Lusaka 1917, 7 Jul 1977, FOIA; Carter marginalia on Vance to Carter, 7 Jul 1977, NLC-128-12-10-4-1; and Memcon (Carter, Owen), 23 Jul 1977, NSA-Brzezinski (7)/35, CL. Also Vance to Carter, 14 Aug 1977, NLC-128-12-11-12-1.

56. Memcon (Callaghan, Nkomo), 27 Jul 2977, FCO 73/287, NA-UK.

57. "Brief for Meeting with Botha," 12 Aug 1977, FCO 82/769, NA-UK.

58. Transcript of Ian Smith's speech, in [unsigned], Pretoria 4568, 2 Sep 1977, FOIA; and DePree, Maputo 1067, 3 Sep 1977, FOIA.

59. Low, FD, 1 Feb 1994; Vance, State 162520, 13 Jul 1977, FOIA; and "Rhodesia: Proposals for a Settlement," Kissinger Proposals: Background, box 4/005, Smith Papers. See Great Britain, *Rhodesia: Proposals*. For the Smith regime's reaction: Settlement Coordinating Committee, 28 Sep 1977, v. 5, box 4/006(m), Smith Papers.

60. Moose and Lake to Vance, 19 Sep 1977, Lake/2, NA. See Top Secret, 19 Oct 1977, NLC-1-4-2-18-5.

61. Memcon (Owen, Brewster), 13 Sep 1977, FCO 36/2008, NA-UK; and Owen, FCO 2441, 9 Sep 1977, FCO 73/285, NA-UK.

62. Low, Lusaka 3390, 10 Nov 1977, NA-AAD.

63. Ibid. See Low, Lusaka 3583, 28 Nov 1977, NA-AAD.

64. Author's interview with Kaunda. See Vance to Carter, 17 Oct 1977, NLC-128-13-1-10-3, which makes it clear that Nkomo was at the meeting. Also Stephen Miles, BDOHP, 11 Nov. 1996. Owen implied to the British Cabinet that Whitehall had played no role in arranging the encounter. Cabinet Meeting, 15 Dec 1977, CAB/128/62/18, NA-UK. This is contradicted in all US accounts.

65. Low, Lusaka 3123, 15 Oct 1977, NLC-6-88-1-11-6.

66. Memcon (Carter, Obasanjo), 11 Oct 1977, NLC-20-7-7-2-3. Obasanjo told Carter that his sources heard this. There may have been follow-up meetings; and see Brewster, London 17950, 1 Nov 1977, NA-AAD.

67. "RE: Kaunda meets Smith," 13 Oct 1977, 150 UNIP 7/23/64; and "The Role of Field Marshal Lord Carver . . . as Resident Commissioner Designate for Rhodesia,"

20 Dec 1978, in Carver to Owen, 20 Dec 1978, FCO 73/319, NA-UK. Also "Rhodesia: Recent History," in Wall to Renwick, 2 May 1979, FCO 36/2493, NA-UK. For Mugabe's suspicions, see transcript of his press conference in Burns, Lusaka 3163, 19 Oct 1977, FOIA.

68. See Christopher to Carter, 26 Sep 1977, NLC-128-12-12-18-4; *NYT*, 2 Oct 1977, 7; Low, Lusaka 3123, 15 Oct 1977, NLC-6-88-1-11-6; and Vance to Carter, 17 Oct 1977, NLC-128-13-1-10-3.

69. Vance to Carter, 17 Oct 1977, NLC-128-13-1-10-3.

70. Vance to Owen, 17 Oct 1977, FOIA.

71. Vance to Carter, 20 Oct 1977, NLC-128-13-1-13-0. Also Top Secret, 20 Oct 1977, NLC-1-4-2-24-8.

72. Spain, Dar 4218, 20 Oct 1977, NA-AAD.

73. Vance, State 34233, 9 Feb 1978, FOIA.

74. Bowdler, Pretoria 3630, 25 Jul 1977, Easum Papers.

75. Mondale to Carter, 24 May 1977, NLC-133-16-1-8-7. See chapter 3 above.

76. In 1977, the UN Security Council included representatives of Benin, Libya, Mauritius, Pakistan, India, Panama, Venezuela, Canada, West Germany, and Romania, in addition to the five permanent members.

77. 31 Mar 1977, Tony Benn's diary, Thatcher Papers; and Owen, Cabinet Meeting, 29 Jun 1978, CAB/128/64/4, NA-UK. For UK exposure: Owen, "Africa," presented to Cabinet, 26 Jun 1978, CAB/129/201/16, ibid. For UK opposition: Memcon (Callaghan, Mondale), 22 May 1977, FCO 82/764, ibid.; and Memcon (Owen, Thorpe), 11 Jul 1977, FCO 36/2038, ibid.

78. DOS, "Southern Africa," May 1977, NLC-23-20-5-1-8; Reid to Mansfield, 7 Jul 1977, FCO 36/2008, NA-UK; and Ruete, London 1477, 5 Jul 1977, B150/371, Berlin.

79. [DOS,] "Southern Africa—Policy Review," in Dodson to Mondale, 19 Jul 1977, Vertical/Cuba-defense, CL (for authorship: Richardson to ZB, 19 Jul 1977, Brzezinski/24, CL); PRC Meeting: Summary of Conclusions, 22 Jul 1977, NLC-15-48-1-4-8 (emphasis in original); and Lake to Christopher, 8 Aug 1977, Christopher Papers/8, NA. For Iran: Moose to Vance, [31 Jul 1977,] NLC-6-88-5-5-9; Memcon (Carter, Barre), 15 Sep 1977, NLC-23-22-1-6-5; "Global Issues Paper: South Africa," in Richardson to Dodson, 26 Oct 1977, NLC-24-105-8-12-7; and Sullivan, Tehran 9554, 30 Oct 1977, NA-AAD.

80. Owen, "Rhodesia: UK-US Proposals," [12 Aug 1977,] B150/373, Berlin.

81. Brezhnev to Carter in Hyland to Carter, 6 Aug 1977, *FRUS 1977–1980, v. 6: Soviet Union*, doc. 41; and US Senate, "US Policy toward Africa," CD58, 20. See Carter to Brezhnev in Vance, State 1992990, 15 Aug 1977, *FRUS 1977–1980, v. 6: Soviet Union*, doc. 42. The best account of this incident is Hershberg, "Seventeen Days." For the South African nuclear program: Richelson, "U.S. Intelligence and the South African Bomb"; Liberman, "Israel and the South African Bomb"; Betts, "Diplomatic Time Bomb"; Van Wyk,"Ally"; and Rogers and Červenka, *Nuclear Axis*, 108–228.

82. INR, "New York Times article on South African Nuclear Development," in Jatzen to Mondale, 4 May 1977, NLC-133-107-3-17-4. See *NYT*, 30 Apr 1977, 1; and Rogers and Červenka, *Nuclear Axis*, 269–84.

83. Bowdler to Pik Botha, 18 Aug 1977, CWIHP-va (emphasis added); and British Foreign Office, "Soviet Allegations about South African Nuclear Weapons

Development," [Aug 1977,] CWIHP-va. See Vance to Pik Botha, 19 Aug 1977, CWIHP-va; and South African Embassy, Washington to Pik Botha, 31 Aug 1977, CWIHP-va.

84. Vance to Carter, 15 Sep 1977, NLC-128-12-12-10-2; Vorster to Carter, Oct 1977, CWIHP-va; and "Southern Africa," [Oct 1977,] NLC-23-22-4-13-4. Mondale's briefing papers for his May encounter with Vorster included a plea that Pretoria sign the NPT. See DOS, "South African Non-proliferation and Nuclear issues," [May 1977,] NLC-133-16-3-5-8.

85. News Conference, 23 Aug 1977, APP; and "Extract from Speech by Vorster at Congress of the National Party," 24 Aug 1977, CWIHP-va.

86. Aaron to ZB, 11 Nov 1977, NLC-133-215-1-8-6. See Brezhnev to Carter in Memcon (Vance, Dobrynin), 6 Mar 1978, doc. 87, *FRUS, 1977–1980, v. 6: Soviet Union*, 293–96; and Van Wyk, "Ally," 209.

87. Lawrence Livermore Laboratory, "South Africa: Motivations and Capabilities for Nuclear Proliferation," Sep 1977, CWIHP-va. See Mallaby to Reid, 21 Sep 1977, CWIHP-va.

88. See Červenka and Rogers, *Nuclear Axis*, 348.

89. See Young, USUN 3197, 22 Sep 1977, NLC-16-22-4-43-9.

90. Malan to Walls, 14 Sep 1977, Continued Logistical Support, Supplementary Files 17, Smith Papers. Also D. J. Rogers (Air Commodore), "Report of a Meeting held at Com Ops between Rhodesian and RSA Representatives on 10 September 1977," 12 Sep 1977, ibid.

91. Walls to Smith, 15 Sep 1977, ibid.

92. Intelligence Community, "Interagency Assessment, South Africa: Policy Considerations Regarding a Nuclear Test," 18 Aug 1977, NLC-6-70-1-14-2; Situation Room to ZB 15 Sep 1977, NLC-1-3-6-52-4; and Intelligence Community, "Interagency Assessment, South Africa: Policy Considerations Regarding a Nuclear Test," 18 Aug 1977, NLC-6-70-1-14-2.

93. Bowdler, Pretoria 4454, 29 Aug 1977, FOIA.

94. Vance to Carter, 12 Sep 1977, "Rhodesia: A Status Report," NSA-staff/119-25, CL.

95. Peter Gabriel, lyrics of "Biko," *Peter Gabriel*, 1980.

96. Vance to Carter, 13 Sep 1977, NLC-128-12-12-8-5.

97. Moose to Vance, 16 Sep 1977, FOIA. See Thornton to ZB, 14 Sep 1977, NSA-staff/119-25, CL; Moose and Lake to Vance, 16 Sep 1977, Lake/2, NA; and Thornton to ZB, 19 Sep 1977, DDRS.

98. PRC Meeting, 20 Sep 1977, PRC/41, CL. See ZB to Carter, 22 Sep 1977, PRC/41, CL; Aaron to Mondale, 26 Sep 1977, Vertical/Cuba, CL; and Tarnoff to ZB, [10 Oct 1977,] NLC-133-160-5-2-9.

99. Memcon (Carter, Obasanjo), 11 Oct 1977, NLC-20-7-7-2-3.

100. Memcon (Carter, Waldheim), 4 Oct 1977, Brzezinski (7)/35, CL. See UN Security Council resolution 415, *Southern Rhodesia*, S/RES/415 (29 Sep 1977), http://undocs.org/S/RES/415(1977); and Young, USUN 3643, 8 Oct 1977, FOIA.

101. DOS, "President Samora Moises Machel," [Jan 1977,] NLC-133-176-1-40-4.

102. Memcon (Carter, Machel), 4 Oct 1977, FOIA; DePree (who attended Carter's meeting with Machel), FD, 16 Feb 1994; and Memcon (Carter, Machel), 4 Oct 1977, FOIA.

103. Memcon (Carter, Machel), 4 Oct 1977, FOIA. Covers following two paragraphs.

104. Memcon (Carter, Waldheim), 5 Oct 1977, FOIA.

105. Vance, State 230604, 24 Sep 1977, NA-AAD.

106. Bowdler, Pretoria 5456, 13 Oct 1977, NLC-133-67-15-4-0.

107. Vorster to Carter, in Bowdler, Pretoria 5452, 13 Oct 1977, NA-AAD. See Clift to Mondale, 14 Oct 1977, NLC-133-67-15-4-0.

108. Bowdler, Pretoria 5486, 15 Oct 1977, NA-AAD.

109. Harrop and Lake to Vance, 20 Oct 1977, Lake/3, NA. See Young's interviews on VOA and ABC: Young, USUN 3920 and 3921, 20 Oct 1977, NA-AAD.

110. Young, USUN 4006, 22 Oct 1977, NA-AAD.

111. Ibid.

112. Ibid. Young's model was Resolution 221 (1966). See UN Security Council resolution 221, *Question concerning the situation in Southern Rhodesia*, S/RES/221 (9 Apr 1966), http://undocs.org/S/RES/221(1966)

113. "Response to South African Situation," [24 Oct 1977,] NLC-133-67-15-4-0; and PRC Meeting, 24 Oct 1977, Vertical/Cuba, CL.

114. See Harrop and Lake to Vance, 20 Oct 1977, Lake/3, NA; ZB to Vance, Brown, 25 Oct 1977, Lake/1, NA; and [South African UN Delegation,] SAUN 288, 12 Dec 1977, CWIHP-va. For a list of all options, "Other steps which could be taken," attached to Saunders (INR) to Christopher, 21 Oct 1977, Christopher Papers/19, NA.

115. For the resolutions and opening debate: Young, USUN 4028, 25 Oct 1977, NA-AAD.

116. Memcon (Vance, Tindemans), 20 Oct 1977, NLC-23-22-8-24-8.

117. Vance, State 255628, 26 Oct 1977, NA-AAD.

118. Vance, State 254729, 23 Oct 1977, NA-AAD.

119. Moose to Vance, [31 Jul 1977,] NLC-6-88-5-5-9. For Owen's change of direction: Briefing Paper for Quadripartite Discussions, 21 Jun 1977, NLC-23-20-10-1-2; Memcon (Genscher, de Guiringaud, Owen, Vance), 23 Jun 1977, NLC-23-13-5-3-4; and Memcon (Owen, Thorpe), 11 Jul 1977, FCO 36/2038, NA-UK.

120. News Conference, 27 Oct 1977, APP.

121. Vance, State 254803, 25 Oct 1977, NA-AAD. See Vance to de Guiringaud in Vance, State 258503, 28 Oct 1977, NA-AAD.

122. Author's interview with Owen; and Brewster, London 17909, 31 Oct 1977, NA-AAD.

123. Young, USUN 4217, 1 Nov 1977, NA-AAD; and Young, USUN 4230, 1 Nov 1977, DNSA. See Vance, State 259878, 31 Oct 1977, NA-AAD; and Vance, State 260818, 1 Nov 1977, DNSA.

124. See Young, USUN 4264, 2 Nov 1977, NA-AAD; Young, USUN 4295, 3 Nov 1977, NA-AAD; and Young, USUN 4363, 4 Nov 1977, NA-AAD. Also WOA, "Washington Notes on Africa," Spring 1977, 3. For Resolution 418, see UN Security Council resolution 418, *South Africa*, S/RES/411 (4 Nov 1977), http://undocs.org/S/RES/418(1977).

125. "An Interview with Vice President Mondale," *Meet the Press*, 6 Nov 1977, USIS: Official Text, FCO 82/727, NA-UK.

126. Young, USUN 4981, 24 Nov 1977, NA-AAD.

127. Ibid.

128. Ibid.

129. *NYT*, 27 Sep 1977, 30.

130. *NYT*, 3 Oct 1977, 1; and *NYT*, 30 Oct 1977, 1.

131. See, e.g., *NYT*, 4 Oct 1977, edit 36; and William Safire, *NYT*, 6 Oct 1977, 27.

132. *NYT*, 18 Oct 1977, 37; and Davidson to Willson, 21 Oct 1977, FCO 82/724, NA-UK. Gallup still gave him a 59 percent approval rating, but the percentage who "strongly approved" fell from 42 percent in March to 24 percent in October. NBC scored his approval at 46 percent and Harris (which the *NYT* used) at 48 percent.

133. News Conference, 27 Oct 1977, APP.

134. Ibid.

135. *WP*, 2 Nov 1977, 13.

Chapter 8

1. FBIS Trends, "Cuba-Africa," 9 Nov 1977, NLC-15-2-2-5-6.

2. Christopher, State 189266, 10 Aug 1977, FOIA-mf; and Henze to ZB, 31 Aug 1977, Horn/1, CL. For Siad's charge: Top Secret, 6 Aug 1977, NLC-1-3-3-27-5; and Christopher, State 188052, 9 Aug 1977, FOIA. For Cuban figures: MINFAR, "Misiones Internacionalistas Cumplidas por Cuba, 1963–1991," Havana, Jul 1998, Gleijeses Papers.

3. "Quadripartite Discussions on the Horn of Africa," 10 Nov 1977, in Wall to Cartledge, 16 Nov 1977, PREM 16/1872, NA-UK. See Memcon (Mueller, Harrop, Graham, Georgi), 4 Oct 1977 in Noebel, "Horn von Afrika," 19 Oct 1977, doc. 297, *AAPD 1977*, 1421–28; Memcon (Carter, Prince Saud), 25 Oct 1977, FOIA; and Memcon (Mueller, Harrop, Mansfield, Georgi), 10 Nov 1977, NLC-23-29-6-6-3.

4. Vance to Carter, 12 Nov 1977, NLC-7-19-3-4-7.

5. See Gleijeses, *Visions*, esp. 28–31, 43–53, and 119–26.

6. See Boss, Bruessel NATO 1455, "Horn von Afrika," 25 Nov 1977, B150/380, Berlin.

7. Mog Domestic Service, 13 Nov 1977, FBIS, NLC-6-69-6-40-0. For Cuban mission: Memcon (Ustinov, Akhromeyev, Ochoa), 27 Sep 1977, Gleijeses Papers. See Vought, Mog 1916, 13 Nov 1977, NA-AAD.

8. *NYT*, 14 Nov 1977, 1; and Toon, Moscow 16511, 14 Nov 1977, NA-AAD.

9. Vought, Mog 1926, 14 Nov 1977, FOIA.

10. Minutes of the Cabinet Meeting, 14 Nov 1977, Vertical, CL. Also Vance to Carter, 17 Nov 1977, NLC-128-13-2-14-8.

11. Minutes of the Cabinet Meeting, 14 Nov 1977, Vertical, CL. See Gleijeses, *Visions*, 37–45.

12. Meeting with Editors and News Directors, 11 Nov 1977, APP. Also *LAT*, 14 Nov 1977, 1. See Vance, State 277949, 19 Nov 1977, NA-AAD.

13. Richardson to ZB, 19 Nov 1977, NLC-24-11-4-5-3.

14. Vance, ER, 15 Nov 1977, NLC-128-13-2-12-0; and *NYT*, 17 Nov 1977, 1. See Drew, "Brzezinski," 115.

15. *NYT*, 5 Dec 1977, 11. For VOA: Reinhardt to ZB, 1 Dec 1977, Horn/1, CL; and ZB, WR, 16 Dec 1977, Brzezinski/41, CL. Brzezinski was on *Issues & Answers*, 11 Dec 1977.

16. ZB, WR, 18 Nov 1977, Brzezinski/41, CL (emphasis in original).

17. ZB, WR, 18 Nov 1977, Brzezinski/41, CL; Minutes of the Cabinet Meeting, 14 Nov 1977, Vertical, CL; and ZB, WR, 18 Nov 1977, Brzezinski/41, CL.

18. See "Quadripartite Discussions on the Horn of Africa," 10 Nov 1977, in Wall to Cartledge, 16 Nov 1977, PREM 16/1872, NA-UK; Habib, State 280070, 22 Nov 1977, NA-AAD; and Boss, Bruessel NATO 1455, "Horn von Afrika," 25 Nov 1977, B150/380, Berlin.

19. West, Jidda 7920, 17 Nov 1977, FOIA; and West, Jidda 8149, 1 Dec 1977, NLC-16-41-6-4-9. Also West Diary, 17 Nov 1977, West Papers/22; and Vance, State 276344, 18 Nov 1977, FOIA. For Siad's promises regarding Kenya: Wall to Cartledge, 16 Nov 1977, PREM 16/1872, NA-UK; Situation Room to ZB, 8 Dec 1977, NLC-1-4-6-37-0; Christopher, State 295102, 10 Dec 1977, FOIA; and Top Secret, 3 Jan 1978, NLC-4-7-2-6-2.

20. Vance, State 283211, 27 Nov 1977, NLC-16-109-7-18-8. See Vance, State 281934, 24 Nov 1977, NA-AAD.

21. Vance, State 281934, 24 Nov 1977, FOIA.

22. Vance, State 277991, 19 Nov 1977, FOIA; and Eilts, Cairo 19438, 26 Nov 1977, NLC-16-41-5-18-5. For refusal to Egypt: Top Secret, 5 Dec 1977, NLC-1-4-6-22-6; Situation Room to ZB, 8 Dec 1977, NLC-1-4-6-38-9; Bergus, Khartoum 4363, 13 Dec 1977, NA-AAD; and Top Secret, 14 Dec 1977, NLC-1-4-7-26-1.

23. Vance, State 283211 to Cairo, 27 Nov 1977, NLC-16-109-7-18-8.

24. Memcon (Schmidt, Sadat), 27/28 Dec 1977, B150/383, Berlin.

25. Lane, Havana 643, 19 Nov 1977, FOIA; and Canadian Embassy, Havana to FCO, 5 Jan 1978, FCO99/160, NA-UK.

26. Habib, State 278529, 21 Nov 1977, FOIA. See Memcon (Todman, Sanchez-Parodi), 21 Nov 1977, NLC-24-11-4-7-1.

27. Pérez Novoa to Raúl Castro, Addis Ababa 184, 12 Apr 1977, Gleijeses Papers; and Pérez Novoa to Raúl Castro, 12 Apr 1977, ibid. See Pérez Novoa to Raúl Castro, Addis Ababa 199, 15 Apr 1977, ibid.; Lane, Havana 807, 9 Dec 1977, FOIA; and Gleijeses, *Visions*, 45–47.

28. Memcon (Mengistu, Ochoa), Addis Ababa, 17 May 1977, Gleijeses Papers; and Memcon (Ochoa, Mengistu), Addis Ababa, 7 July 1977, ibid. See MINFAR, "La Misión Internacionalista en la República de Etiopía," n.d., ibid. For the Cuban medical mission: "Visita de la delegación cubana a Etiopía," 20–27 Feb 1977, ibid.; "Protocolo de las conversaciones sobre colaboración en la rama de la salud entre gobiernos de la República de Cuba y Etiopía," 23 May 1977, ibid.; and Ministerio de Salud Pública, "Informe sobre la visita realizada a Etiopía . . . del 17 al 23 de mayo de 1977," ibid. For the military mission: Ochoa to Raúl Castro, Addis 21, 23 Apr 1977, ibid.; and Raúl Castro to Fidel Castro, 25 Apr 1977, ibid.

29. Memcon (Mengistu, Ochoa, Casas), 5 Sep 1977, ibid. See Raúl Castro to Fidel Castro, 25 Apr; 5, 13, 19, and 26 May; 2, 10,16, 23, and 30 Jun; and 14 and 21 Jul 1977, ibid. For the Soviet mission: MINFAR, "Versión cable recibido de Etiopía, no. 886-135," 15 May 1977, ibid.; and Ochoa to Viceministro Primero, 27 May 1977, ibid.

30. Fidel Castro to Ochoa, 16 Aug 1977, in Gleijeses, *Visions*, 45.

31. MINFAR, "La Misión Internacionalista en la República de Etiopía," n.d., Gleijeses Papers; and Memcon (Mengistu, Ochoa, Casas), 5 Sep 1977, ibid. See Memcon (Mengistu, Soviet General Shapliguin, Ochoa), 16 Sep 1977, ibid.; and Ochoa to Raúl Castro, Addis 509, 17 Sep 1977, ibid.

32. Memcon (Fidel Castro, Mengistu), 28 Oct 1977, ibid.

33. Ibid.

34. "Monografía de Etiopía," in Oramas to Malmierca, 14 Oct 1977, in Malmierca to Raúl Castro, 18 Oct 1977, ibid.

35. Dirección Inteligencia Militar, "Resumen de la situación en Etiopía en el período del 1 al 7.11.77," 8 Nov 1977, ibid.; and MINFAR, "La Misión Internacionalista en la República de Etiopía," n.d., ibid.

36. "Quadripartite Discussions on the Horn of Africa," 10 Nov 1977, in Wall to Cartledge, 16 Nov 1977, PREM 16/1872, NA-UK. See Memcon (Mueller, Harrop, Mansfield, Georgi), 10 Nov 1977, NLC-23-29-6-6-3.

37. French study of Soviet objectives in the Horn, cited in Matlock, Moscow 18743, 30 Dec 1977, NA-AAD.

38. "Colloquio tra Berlinguer e Berkan Baye," Moscow, 3 Nov 1977, Note a Seg., 309-285, PCI, Istituto Gramsci, Rome.

39. Memcon (Ustinov, Akhromeyev, Ochoa), 27 Sep 1977, Gleijeses Papers; and INR, "Morning Summary, 20 Nov 1977, NLC SAFE 16 D-88-1-2-4. See Situation Room to ZB, 22 Nov 1977, NLC-1-4-5-17-3.

40. Brezhnev to Fidel Castro, 27 Nov 1977, Gleijeses Papers. For the decision: Fidel Castro to Ustinov, 25 Nov 1977, ibid.

41. Christopher, ToSec 120122, 11 Dec 1977, NA-AAD. For reports of airlift: Henze, ER, 9 Dec 1977, Horn/5, CL; and Matheron, Addis 6803, 10 Dec 1977, FOIA.

42. Marshall Shulman, quoted in Jay, Washington 566, 10 Feb 1978, PREM 16/1872, NA-UK; and Toon, Moscow 17909, 12 Dec 1977, Brzezinski/27, CL. The word *beznachitel'niy* (insignificant) is incorrectly transcribed as "*neznachitel'niy.*"

43. Christopher, State 297314, 13 Dec 1977, NA-AAD. See also Christopher, State 297297, 13 Dec 1977, NA-AAD.

44. Sullivan, Tehran 10878, 11 Dec 1977, NA-AAD. See Sullivan, Tehran 10877, 11 Dec 1977, ibid. For Pakistan: Vance, State 286616, 1 Dec 1977, ibid.; West, Jidda 8307, 7 Dec 1977, ibid.; Constable, Islamabad 12207, 14 Dec 1977, ibid.; and Cartledge to Wall, 17 Jan 1978, PREM 16/1872, NA-UK. For Turkey: Dillon, Ankara 9071, 14 Dec 1977, NA-AAD. The White House also asked Saudi Arabia to hamper Soviet access to Aden. Henze, ER, 19 Dec 1977, Horn/5, CL.

45. Ransom, Sana'a 4800, 6 Dec 1977, NA-AAD (both ellipses in original).

46. Christopher, State 295721 to Vance, 11 Dec 1977, NLC-16-110-2-14-5; Easum, Lagos 14354, 12 Dec 1977, FOIA; and Vance, ER, 16 Dec 1977, NLC-7-19-4-12-7. For Nigeria: Easum, Lagos 14541, 15 Dec 1977, NA-AAD. For Egypt: Christopher, ToSec 120031, 8 Dec 1977, ibid.; West, Jidda 8559, 17 Dec 1977, ibid.; and Eilts, Cairo 22250, 20 Dec 1977, ibid. For Ghana: Smith, Accra 9380, 15 Dec 1977, ibid.

47. Memcon (Heads of Gov't), Brussels, 5 Dec 1977, in Cartledge to Fergusson, 6 Dec 1977, PREM 16/1872, NA-UK.

48. Memcon (de Guiringaud, van Well, Owen, Vance), 7 Dec 1977, NLC-23-11-5-15-3.

49. Ibid.; and Vance, 8 Dec 1977, SecTo 12011, NLC-16-23-1-32-3. See Memcon (van Well, de Guiringaud, Owen, Vance), 7 Dec 1977, doc. 352, *AAPD 1977*, 1695.

50. Memcon (de Guiringaud, van Well, Owen, Vance), 7 Dec 1977, NLC-23-11-5-15-3; and DOS Briefing Book, "Secretary Vance's Visit to the NATO Ministerial, Brussels, December 7–9, 1977: Horn of Africa," Dec 1977, NLC-23-22-8-26-6.

51. "Vierer-Konsultationen über das Horn von Afrika," (Quadripartite Meeting), 15 Dec 1977, London, B150/382, Berlin.

52. Meeting with Editors and News Directors, 11 Nov 1977, APP; and Lane, Havana 807, 9 Dec 1977, FOIA.

53. Henze, ER, 14 Dec 1977, Horn/5, CL; CIA, "Increased Support for Ethiopia," 14 Dec 1977, ibid.; and Henze, ER, 14 Dec 1977, ibid. (emphasis in original). For Massawa: MINFAR, "Misiones Internacionalistas Cumplidas por Cuba, 1963–1991," Havana, Jul 1998, Gleijeses Papers. For US estimates of Cubans in Ethiopia: Situation Room to ZB, 8 Dec 1977, NLC-1-4-6-37-0; Henze, ER, 9 Dec 1977, Horn/5, CL; and ZB, WR, 9 Dec 1977, DDRS. For intelligence reports: CIA, "Increased Support for Ethiopia," 14 Dec 1977, Horn/5, CL; CIA, "Increased Soviet Military Advisor Role," 14 Dec 1977, CIA-rr; and CIA, "General Military Situation in Ethiopia," 14 Dec 1977, Horn/5, CL.

54. ZB, WR, 16 Dec 1977, Brzezinski/41, CL.

55. Christopher, State 297459, 13 Dec 1977, Brzezinski/27, CL. Also Vance, State 301330, 17 Dec 1977, FOIA.

56. Vance, State 306011, 23 Dec 1977, FOIA.

57. Thornton to ZB, "Annual Report," 8 Dec 1977, NLC-24-101-8-3-1. See Henze, ER, 28 Dec 1977, Horn/5, CL; and Memcon (Vance, Dobrynin), 14 Jan 1978, *FRUS, 1977–1980, v. 6: Soviet Union*, doc. 72.

58. Ian Smith, quoted in *NYT*, 25 Nov 1977, 1.

59. Meredith, *Past Is Another Country*, 292.

60. "Leading Personalities in Rhodesia, 1978," n.d., FCO 36/2718, NA-UK; and *NYT*, 25 Nov 1977, 1.

61. Vance, ER, 29 Nov 1977, NLC-7-19-3-10-0; Bowdler, Pretoria 6482, 30 Nov 1977, NA-AAD; *Rhodesian Herald* (Salisbury), 29 Nov 1977, 1; and *Rhodesian Herald* (Salisbury), 30 Nov 1977, edit 14. See Nesbit, Cowderoy, and Thomas, *Britain's Rebel*, 49–55; Petter-Bowyer, *Winds*, 430–47; and Moorcraft and McLaughlin, *Rhodesian War*, 150–51.

62. *NYT*, 29 Nov 1977, 9; *Guardian* (London), 28 Nov 1977, 1; and Robert Mugabe, "The Chimoio and Tembue Massacres," *Zimbabwe News* 9, no. 5/6 (Jul–Dec 1977): 34–36.

63. See *Daily News* (Dar), 5 Dec 1977, 1; Spain, Dar 4846, 5 Dec 1977, NA-AAD; and Bowdler, Pretoria 6698, 8 Dec 1977, NA-AAD. In fact, these photographs were of Grey's Scouts, a cavalry unit of the Rhodesian armed forces, torturing captives during operations in Rhodesia in November 1977; they were taken by AP photographer J. Ross Baughman, who was awarded the 1977 Pulitzer Prize for Feature Photography for them. See Rotkin, "A Puzzle." On Grey's Scouts: Moore-King, *White Man, Black War*.

64. *Noticias* (Maputo), 1 Dec 1977, 1; DePree, Maputo 1441, 1 Dec 1977, NA-AAD; and Petter-Bowyer, *Winds*, 441.

65. Bowdler, Pretoria 6482, 30 Nov 1977, NA-AAD; *Rhodesian Herald*, 30 Nov 1977, 1; and author's interview with Low.

66. *WP*, 1 Dec 1977, 1. See DOS, "South Africa," [Mar 1978,] NLC-23-23-7-1-3.

67. *NYT*, 3 Dec 1977, edit 22.

68. Vance, State 283188, 26 Nov 1977, NA-AAD. See [unsigned], London 19303, 25 Nov 1977, NA-AAD; and Vance, State 283151, 26 Nov 1977, NA-AAD.

69. Vance to Carter, 29 Nov 1977, NLC-133-215-1-23-9.

70. Carter's marginalia on Christopher, ER, 8 Dec 1977, NLC-7-19-4-7-3; Stevenson, Lilongwe 5, 3 Dec 1977, FOIA; and Carter's marginalia on Vance to Carter, 28

Dec 1977, NLC-7-19-4-2-8. For Carter and Muzorewa: Carter's marginalia on "Mandatory Elements of the UK-US Plan," in Vance to Carter, 1 Dec 1977, NLC-128-13-3-1-1; and Carter's marginalia on Christopher to Carter, 8 Dec 1977, NLC-128-13-3-6-6.

71. DOS, "Discussion Paper on Rhodesia," 30 Nov 1977, NLC-133-42-6-16-4.

72. Ibid.

73. Vance to Carter, 29 Nov 1977, NLC-133-215-1-23-9. See Vance to Carter, 1 Dec 1977, NLC-128-13-3-1-1; Vance, State 289252, 4 Dec 1977, NA-AAD; ZB, WR, 9 Dec 1977, DDRS; and Low, Lusaka 249, 27 Jan 1978, FOIA-mf.

74. DOS, "Discussion Paper on Rhodesia," 30 Nov 1977, NLC-133-42-6-16-4; and Vance to Owen in Vance, State 283233, 27 Nov 1977, NA-AAD.

75. Brewster, London 19422, 29 Nov 1977, NA-AAD. See Vance, ER, 29 Nov 1977, NLC-7-19-3-10-0.

76. The archival record on the Bingham Report in the British National Archives is voluminous. For a lively secondary account: Bailey, *Oilgate*. The Carter administration investigated rumors that US companies were shipping oil to Rhodesia: US House, "United States Policy Toward Rhodesia" CD20; Christopher, State 242781, 9 Oct 1977, NA-AAD; and Brewster, London 18754, 15 Nov 1977, NA-AAD.

77. Young, USUN 5498, 9 Dec 1977, NA-AAD. See Young, USUN 4030, 25 Oct 1977, ibid.; and Young, USUN 5126, 1 Dec 1977, ibid. On December 16, 1977, the General Assembly voted to ask the Security Council to impose an oil embargo on South Africa. (Resolution 32/116B, www.un.org) The tally was 113 to 0, with the United States, United Kingdom, France, Canada, and West Germany abstaining. See Young, USUN 5541, 9 Dec 1977, ibid.; Christopher, State 296540, 12 Dec 1977, ibid.; and Young, USUN 5593, 13 Dec 1977, ibid.

78. Brewster, London 20528, 16 Dec 1977, NA-AAD; and Young, USUN 5661, 15 Dec 1977, NA-AAD. For Owen's threat: Vance, SecTo 12011, 8 Dec 1977, NLC-16-23-1-32-3.

79. Memcon (de Guiringaud, van Well, Owen, Vance), 7 Dec 1977, NLC-23-11-5-15-3.

80. Eick, Cape Town 25, 3 Feb 1978, doc. 31, *AAPD 1978*, 188–91. For UK position: Owen to Washington, 10 Oct 1977, Lake/3, NA; Richardson to ZB, 1 Dec 1977, NSA-staff/119, CL; Young, USUN 5126, 1 Dec 1977, FOIA; and Brewster, London 20305, 14 Dec 1977, FOIA. For French veto: Vance, State 302458, 20 Dec 1977, NA-AAD.

81. Young, USUN 5184, 2 Dec 1977, NA-AAD.

82. Ibid.

83. Young, USUN 5720, 17 Dec 1977, NA-AAD.

84. Ibid. For the poll, see *NYT*, 15 Dec 1977, 31.

85. Richardson to ZB, 21 Dec 1977, NSA-staff/119, CL.

86. Vance to Carter, 1 Dec 1977, NLC-128-13-3-1-1; and Young, USUN 5498, 9 Dec 1977, NA-AAD.

87. See Vance, SecTo 12013, 8 Dec 1977, NA-AAD; and Young, USUN 5498, 9 Dec 1977, NA-AAD.

88. Christopher, State 296583, 13 Dec 1977, NA-AAD.

89. Young, USUN 5661, 15 Dec 1977, NA-AAD. See Brewster, London 20305, 14 Dec 1977, NA-AAD.

90. Carter to Nyerere in Vance, SecTo 13014, 30 Dec 1977, NA-AAD.

91. On the postponement: *WP*, 1 Feb 1978, 13. For the rising anxiety among the allies before the postponement: Memcon (Graham, Moose), 16 Jan 1978, PREM

16/1872, PRO; and Memcon (Genscher, Vance, Owen, de Guiringaud, Jamieson), 12 Feb 1978, doc. 44, *AAPD 1978*, 241–43.

92. Toast at a State Dinner, Tehran, 31 Dec 1977, APP.

93. Sullivan, Tehran 11321, 24 Dec 1977, NA-AAD. See Parsons, Tehran 2, 4 Jan 1978, FCO 82/898, PRO.

94. Vance, SecTo 13075, 3 Jan 1978, NLC-16-42-4-13-0. See Parsons, Tehran 2, 4 Jan 1978, FCO 82/898, NA-UK.

95. Henderson, Paris 16, 9 Jan 1978, FCO 82/898, NA-UK; Crowe to Mansfield, 13 Jan 1978, FCO 31/2223, NA-UK; and Memcon (Genscher, de Guiringaud), 6 Feb 1978, doc. 34, *AAPD 1978*, 201. Also Vance to Carter, "Your Visit to France, November 29–December 1," [the trip was subsequently delayed a month]," n.d., NLC-23-27-1-12-3; Matlock, Moscow 18743, 30 Dec 1977, NA-AAD; and "Weltreise Präsident Carters," 13 Jan 1978, doc. 9, *AAPD 1978*, 71–79.

96. News Conference, 12 Jan 1978, APP.

97. Ibid.

98. Ibid.

99. TASS, 13 Jan 1978, FBIS-SOV-78-009; and Addis Domestic Service, 17 Jan 1978, FBIS-SSA-78-011. Also TASS, 15 Jan 1978, FBIS-SOV-78-010.

100. Munro to Mansfield, 18 Jan 1978, FCO 31/2223, NA-UK; and Memcon (Graham, Moose), 16 Jan 1978, PREM 16/1872, NA-UK. Also Mansfield to Squire, "Anglo/US Relations," 9 Jan 1978, FCO 36/2205, NA-UK.

101. Henze to ZB, "Realities and Lessons of History in the Horn of Africa," 12 Jan 1978, Horn/1, CL.

102. Memcon (Schmidt, Siad Barre), 2 Jan 1978, B136/17587, Koblenz. See Eilts, Cairo 16750, 8 Oct 1977, NLC-16-41-1-15-2.

103. Abbot, Mog 13, 16 Jan 1977, PREM 16/1872, NA-UK; and Somali Embassy in London to Owen, 16 Jan 1978, FCO 31/2223, NA-UK.

104. Wall to Cartledge, 20 Jan 1978, PREM 16/1872, NA-UK; and Vance, State 18370, 24 Jan 1978, Horn 1, CL. For Italians: Memcon (Graham, Moose), 16 Jan 1978, PREM 16/1872, NA-UK; and Vance, ER, 24 Jan 1978, NLC-7-19-5-11-7. Also Munro to Mansfield, 19 Jan 1978, FCO 31/2223, NA-UK; and Henze to ZB, 24 Jan 1978, Horn 1, CL. Jackson writes that the participants agreed to "call for a Somali withdrawal from Ethiopia." (Jackson, *Carter and the Horn*, 76) They did no such thing; it would be three weeks before Carter called for Somalia to withdraw.

105. Maj. Girma Neway, quoted in *L'Unità* (Rome), 8 Feb 1978, 14. See Memcon (Kazankin, Stempel), 5 Feb 1978, DNSA. For analysis of the unreliability of sources: *Globe and Mail* (Toronto), 25 Jan 1978, 10; and *NYT*, 25 Feb 1978, 5. For Ethiopian denials: Memcon (Lamberz, Pepe), 3 Mar 1978, CWIHP-VA.

106. Hamrick to Janka, "The Somali-Ethiopian Situation: The UN Role," 6 Jan 1978, Hamrick Papers. Also Harrop, Vine, Lake to Vance, 17 Jan 1978, Lake/3, NA; Henze to ZB, 24 Jan 1978, Horn/1, CL; and Interagency Meeting, 26 Jan 1978, Horn/1, CL.

107. Puesto de Mando Especial to Raúl Castro, Havana, 12 Dec 1977, Gleijeses Papers. For fragging: Ochoa to Jefe Estado Mayor General, 20 Nov 1977, ibid. For mutilation: Ochoa to Jefe Estado Mayor General, 5 Dec 1977, ibid. For lack of training: Memcon (Raúl Castro, Mengistu), Addis Ababa, 10 Jan 1978, ibid.

108. Tareke, *Ethiopian Revolution*, 210; and Matheron, Addis 6646, 30 Nov 1977, NA-AAD.

109. Memcon (Raúl Castro, Mengistu), 6 Jan 1978, Gleijeses Papers; and Memcon (Raúl Castro, Mengistu), 10 Jan 1978, ibid. See MINFAR, "La Misión Internacionalista en la República de Etiopía," n.d., ibid.

110. Casas (from Raúl Castro) to Fidel Castro, 17 Jan 1978, ibid.; and Ustinov and Raúl Castro to Petrov and Ochoa, 19 Jan 1978, ibid. On the Cuban decision: Fidel Castro to Chief of the Soviet General Staff Ogarkov, 17 Dec 1977, ibid.

111. For the escalating estimates: Henze, ER, 27 Jan 1978, Horn/6, CL; Henze, ER, 9 Jan 1978, Horn/5, CL; Henze, ER, 17 Jan 1978, ibid.; "Talking Points for VP in Mexico," 19 Jan 1978, Horn/1, CL; [illegible] to Hunter, 23 Jan 1978, in Henze to ZB, 23 Jan 1978, ibid.; Annex 1, "The Cuban Role," in INR to Vance, 9 Feb 1978, NLC-6-21-7-8-7; Henze, ER, 6 Feb 1978, Horn/6, CL; DOS Briefing, in Vance, State 32544, 7 Feb 1978, FOIA; and The Secretary's News Conference, 10 Feb 1978, *DOS Bulletin*, Mar 1978, 14.

112. MINFAR, "Misiones Internacionalistas Cumplidas por Cuba, 1963–1991," Havana, Jul 1998, Gleijeses Papers. In a retrospective analysis, INR got the figures about right. INR, "Cuba's African Policy and its Effect on Relations with the US," 13 Mar 1978, FOIA.

113. Lane, Havana 906, 21 Dec 1977, NA-AAD; and Henze, ER, 10 Jan 1978, Horn/5, CL. See Henze, ER, 9 Jan 1978, Horn/5, CL; and Memcon (Rodriguez, Langer), 13 Feb 1978, Havana, US-USSR/117, NSA-DC.

114. Interagency Meeting, 26 Jan 1978, Horn/1, CL; Henze to ZB, 28 Jan 1978, ibid.; and "Summary of Conclusions, SCC Meeting on Horn of Africa," 26 Jan 1978, Brzezinski/28, CL.

115. [Parmenter,] "An Alternative View of the Situation in the Horn of Africa," [20 Jan 1978,] NLC-15-17-2-3-2 (for author and date: Henze to ZB, 1 Feb 1978, "Comments on CIA Paper," Horn/2, CL); and Walker, Dar 214, 18 Jan 1978, FOIA-mf.

116. Low, Lusaka 219, 25 Jan 1978, FOIA.

117. [redacted], State 19754, 25 Jan 1978, FOIA-mf. For Malta: "Draft Outline of Strategy/Contingency paper for Malta Talks," [14 Jan 1978,] FOIA; "Comparing the Anglo-American Proposals with the Salisbury talks," [14 Jan 1978,] FOIA; Brewster, London 1031, 19 Jan 1978, FOIA-mf; and Brewster, London 1317, 24 Jan 1978, FOIA.

118. Walker, Dar 402, 28 Jan 1978, FOIA-mf; and Vance, State 19583, 25 Jan 1978, FOIA. For Owen: *Times* (London), 3 Feb 1978, 6.

119. Vance, ER, 21 Feb 1978, NLC-7-19-6-9-9; and Brotherton, "Rhodesia," 25 Jan 1978, *Parliamentary Debates*, Commons, 5th ser., vol. 942, col. 1365.

120. Moose and Lake to Vance, 26 Jan 1978, Lake/3, NA.

121. 1 Feb 1978, AP (Gavshon), LNA. For death toll: *NYT*, 2 Feb 1978, 8.

122. Laingen, Valetta 116, 30 Jan 1978, FOIA-mf; Laingen, Valetta 131, 31 Jan 1978, ibid.; and BBC Domestic Television (interview with Owen), 1 Feb 1978, FBIS-WEU-78-023. Also Cabinet Meeting, 2 Feb 1978, CAB/128/63/3, NA-UK. For the Patriotic Front proposals: Laingen, Valetta 121, 31 Jan 1978, FOIA-mf.

123. *Afro-American* (Baltimore), 11 Feb 1978, 16; Owen, FCO 321, 8 Feb 1978, FCO 36/2232 (forwarding cable from Low); and Young, USUN 391, 4 Feb 1978, FOIA-mf.

124. *Malawi News* (Blantyre),12 Feb 1978, FCO 36/2130, NA-UK; Young, USUN 391, 4 Feb 1978, FOIA-mf; Young, USUN 2413, 6 Jun 1979, FOIA; Low, Lusaka 328,

4 Feb 1978, ibid.; *WP*, 4 Feb 1978, 12; and author's interview with Moose (2001). Also author's interviews with Young and Low.

125. *WP*, 4 Feb 1978, 12; Memcon (Owen, Vance), 12 Feb 1978, in Ferguson to PUS, 15 Feb 1978, FCO 73/316, NA-UK; and PRC: Summary of Conclusions, 17 Feb 1978, Vertical/Cuba, CL.

126. London Press Association, 2 Feb 1978, FBIS-WEU-78-024; and Churchill, "Rhodesia," 2 Feb 1978, *Parliamentary Debates*, Commons, 5th ser., vol. 943, col. 714.

127. Low, Lusaka 402, 9 Feb 1978, FOIA-mf. Also Vance, State 33928, 9 Feb 1978, FOIA; Spain, Dar 607, 10 Feb 1978, FOIA; Vance (from Moose), State 38164, 14 Feb 1978, FOIA; and Low, Lusaka 457, 14 Feb 1978, FOIA.

128. Annex 1, "The Cuban Role," in INR to Vance, 9 Feb 1978, NLC-6-21-7-8-7. See Tareke, *Ethiopian Revolution*, 203.

129. Ochoa to Fidel Castro, Daily Reports, 22–27 Jan 1978, Gleijeses Papers; Ochoa to Fidel Castro, Daily Reports, 27 Jan 1978, ibid.; Fidel Castro to Ochoa, 28 Jan 1978, ibid.; and MINFAR, "Misiones Internacionalistas Cumplidas por Cuba, 1963–1991," Havana, Jul 1998, ibid. Also Fidel Castro to Mengistu, 7 Mar 1978, ibid.; MINFAR, "La Misión Internacionalista en la República de Etiopía," n.d., ibid. (for the pilots and casualty estimate); and Tareke, *Ethiopian Revolution*, 205, gives the same casualty figure, based on Ethiopian sources. For Cuban losses: Ochoa to Fidel Castro, Daily Reports, 23 Jan 1978, Gleijeses Papers.

130. Henze, ER, 25 Jan 1978, Horn/6, CL; Henze, ER, 3 Feb 1978, ibid.; INR to Vance, 9 Feb 1978, NLC-6-21-7-8-7; and The Secretary: News Conference, 10 Feb 1978, *DOS Bulletin*, Mar 1978, 15.

131. "Core of presidential message to heads of state of Sudan, Saudi Arabia, Iran, and Egypt," 20 Jan 1978, Horn/1, CL. Also News Conference, 12 Jan 1978, APP; and Carter marginalia on Christopher to Carter, 16 Jan 1978, DDRS.

132. Easum, Lagos 2267, 22 Feb 1978, FOIA; National Intelligence Daily Cable, 19 Jan 1978, CREST; and Matthews, Cairo 4926, 14 Feb 1978, FOIA.

133. Memcon (Vance, Dobrynin), 14 Jan 1978, *FRUS, 1977–1980, v. 6: Soviet Union*, doc. 72; Toon, 12 Dec 1977, Moscow 17909, NLC-17-7-3-6-7; Memcon (Bushnell, Sanchez-Parodi), 10 Jan 1978, NLC-24-11-5-4-3; and Henze to ZB, 24 Jan 1978, Horn/1, CL.

134. Brind, Mog 60, 20 Feb 1978, PREM 16/1873, NA-UK; and Easum, Lagos 2110, 18 Feb 1978, FOIA.

135. Mengistu, "Imperialist Aggression From Vietnam to Ethiopia," (speech, 30 Jan 1978), PREM 16/1873, NA-UK.

136. Vance, ER, 27 Jan 1978, NLC-7-19-5-14-4.

137. Marshall Shulman, quoted in Jay, Washington 566, 10 Feb 1978, PREM 16/1872, NA-UK. See Christopher, State 295721, 11 Dec 1977, NLC-16-110-2-14-5; Christopher, ER, 12 Dec 1977, NLC-7-19-4-9-1; Carter to Brezhnev, in ZB to Toon, 21 Dec 1977, DDRS; Vance to Carter, 28 Dec 1977, NLC-7-19-4-2-8; "Oral Statement from US Leadership to the Soviet leadership," in Memcon (Vance, Dobrynin), 14 Jan 1978, *FRUS, 1977–1980, v. 6: Soviet Union*, doc. 72; "Non-Note From the Soviet Leadership to the US Leadership," 24 Jan 1978, ibid., doc. 73; Carter to Brezhnev, 25 Jan 1978, ibid., doc. 77; Marshall [Shulman] to Vance, 25 Jan 1978, FOIA; Carter to Brezhnev, 25 Jan 1978, DDRS; and Memcon (Vance, Ponomarev), 26 Jan 1978, Vertical (USSR-US)/117, NSA-DC.

138. Carter to Peréz/ Desai/ Tito, draft, Horn/1, CL; Carter to Obasanjo, draft, [17 Jan 1978,] Policy Documents—Ethiopia/3, NSA-DC; "Presidential Message to Heads of State of Sudan, Saudi Arabia, Iran, and Egypt," 20 Jan 1978, Horn/1, CL; Carter to Giscard, 27 Jan 1978, DDRS; "Giscard letter on the Horn," 6 Feb 1978, DDRS; "Oral Message to Giscard," 8 Feb 1978, Lake/1, NA; Carter to López Portillo, 13 Feb 1978, Subject/CO-25, CL; and Tito to Carter and Desai to Carter, in Gates to Aaron, 16 Feb 1978, NLC-6-21-6-10-5.

139. Vance, State 19760, 25 Jan 1978, FOIA. See Christopher, State 295721, 11 Dec 1977, NLC-16-110-2-14-5; and Presidential Directive/NSC-32, 24 Feb 1978, DNSA.

140. Easum, Lagos 2643, 2 Mar 1978, FOIA; and Eilts, Cairo 5845, 23 Feb 1978, FOIA. See "Soviet Non-Paper," in Vance, State 43255, 8 Feb 1978, *FRUS, 1977–1980, v. 6: Soviet Union*, doc. 82.

141. Lake, Vine and Harrop to Vance, 17 Jan 1978, "The Ogaden Conflict," Lake/3, NA; and Moose, Vest, Shulman, Lake to Vance, 25 Jan 1978, ibid.

142. [Parmenter,] "An Alternative View of the Situation in the Horn of Africa," [20 Jan 1978,] NLC-15-17-2-3-2.

143. Henze to ZB, 1 Feb 1978, "Comments on CIA Paper," Horn/2, CL; and Henze to ZB, "State's 5-Power Horn Meeting," 24 Jan 1978, Horn/1, CL. Also author's interviews with Brzezinski and Henze.

144. Henze to ZB, "Giscard letter on the Horn," 6 Feb 1978, DDRS; and Henze to ZB, "Presidential Emissary to Mengistu," 8 Feb 1978, Horn/2, CL.

145. Author's interview with Brzezinski. See Brzezinski marginalia on Henze, ER, 14 Feb 1978, NLC-27-6-1-3-2 and interview with Brzezinski, Albright, Denend, Odom, 18 Feb 1982, 19, CPP

146. *WP*, 27 Jan 1978, 30; and Mengistu to Carter, in Matheron, Addis 539, 3 Feb 1978, DDRS. Also: "Text of Oral Message from President Carter to Chairman Mengistu," 19 Jan 1978, Horn/1, CL; ZB to Carter, "Meeting with Ethiopian Ambassador," [19 Jan 1978,] ibid.; Henze, ER, 27 Jan 1978, Horn/6, CL; Christopher, State 23797, 28 Jan 1978, FOIA; Matheron, Addis 538, 3 Feb 1978, FOIA; Carter to Mengistu, in Tarnoff to ZB, 7 Feb 1978, Horn/2, CL; and Vance, State 39634, 15 Feb 1978, FOIA.

147. Emblematic is a long speech that Vance gave to the Los Angeles World Affairs Council on January 13, 1978. His survey of foreign policy issues the administration would confront in 1978 did not mention the Horn. "The Secretary: Foreign Policy Decisions for 1978," *DOS Bulletin*, Feb 1978, 23–26.

148. Matlock, Moscow 1734, 4 Feb 1978, Horn/2, CL. See Kornienko, *Kholodnaya voina*, 183.

149. Drew, "Brzezinski," 118.

150. See Brzezinski, *Power*, 178–82.

151. Cartledge to Wall, 17 Jan 1978, PREM 16/1872, NA-UK; and Henderson, Paris 106, 4 Feb 1978, ibid.

152. Top Secret, 9 Feb 1978, NLC-1-5-3-33-6. See INR to Vance, 9 Feb 1978, NLC-6-21-7-8-7; and Top Secret, 20 Feb 1978, NLC-1-5-4-18-2.

153. See: Memcon (Vance, Ponomarev), 26 Jan 1978, Vertical-USSR-US/117, NSA-DC; Henze, ER, 31 Jan 1978, Horn/6, CL; annex 3 of INR to Vance, 9 Feb 1978, NLC-6-21-7-8-7; and "US Military Hardware Transfers to Somalia," n.d., NLC-6-21-6-3-3.

154. INR, Current Reports, 10 Feb 1978, NLC-SAFE 17 B-8-39-8-6; and Thornton to ZB, 10 Feb 1978, Ethiopia/2, NSA-DC. This tentative thaw was halted by the Soviet invasion of Afghanistan. See Dawisha, "Soviet Policy," 34.

155. See Hamrick to Janka, 5 Jan 1978, Hamrick Papers; and "Recent Ethiopian Statements on Crossing the Somali Border," [13 Feb 1978,] NLC-6-21-7-13-1.

156. Brind, Mog 234, 30 Oct 1977, PREM 16/1872, PRO; and Moose and Saunders to Vance, 14 Feb 1978, NLC-6-21-6-4-2. See Memcon (Mengistu, Ochoa, Chapliguia), Addis, 10 Dec 1977, Gleijeses Papers; Somali Ministry of Foreign Affairs, "Background to the Liberation Struggle of the Western Somalis," 1978, PREM 16/1873, NA-UK; and Tareke, *Ethiopian Revolution*, 208, 212.

157. Giscard to Carter, 7 Feb 1978, NLC-133-215-4-10-0.

158. Anwar Sadat, at a 7 Feb 1978 meeting with senators, quoted by Senator Thomas Eagleton, *CR-Senate*, 8 Feb 1978, 2664; and DOS Noon Briefing, 7 Feb 1978, in Vance, State 32544, 7 Feb 1978, FOIA. Also: Statement issued after meetings with President Sadat, 5 Feb 1978, APP; and Parsons, Tehran 152, 21 Feb 1978, PREM 16/1873, NA-UK.

159. *WP*, 7 Feb 1978, 1; *Ha'aretz* (Tel Aviv), 7 Feb 1978, FBIS-MEA-78-027; and 4 Feb 1978, Riyadh Domestic Service, FBIS-MEA-78-025. See ABC, CBS, NBC, *Evening News*, 6 Feb 1978, VNA; "Sold Arms to Ethiopia," *Globe and Mail* (Toronto), 7 Feb 1978; Vance, State 32544, 8 Feb 1978, FOIA; and CBS *Evening News*, 10 Feb 1978, VNA.

160. Matthews, Cairo 4409, 8 Feb 1978, FOIA.

161. ZB, WR, 9 Feb 1978, DDRS.

162. See Oksenberg to ZB, [14 Jan 1978,] DDRS; Memcon (Carter, Huang Chen), 3 Nov 1977, *FRUS, 1977–1980, v. 13: China*, doc. 66; and Brzezinski, *Power*, 202–3.

163. Frank Press to Carter, 23 Jan 1978, DDRS; *WP*, 1 Feb 1978, 19; and Armacost and Oksenberg to ZB, 1 Feb 1978, DDRS. See Memcon (Carter, Vance, ZB, Mansfield), 7 Feb 1978, DDRS; ZB to Carter, [7 Feb 1978,] DDRS; ZB to Carter, 27 Jan 1978, DDRS; and ZB to Carter, 16 Feb 1978, DDRS.

164. ZB, WR, 9 Feb 1978, DDRS.

165. Thornton to ZB, 10 Feb 1978, NLC-24-109-3-1-0.

166. CIA, "USSR Weekly Review: The Soviet Union and the Horn," 2 Feb 1978, NLC-31-37-5-7-5; and CIA, "USSR: Motives and Dangers of Ethiopia Policy," [9 Feb 1978,] NLC-31-37-5-10-1. For Brzezinski's summary: ZB to Carter, 10 Feb 1978, NLC-1-5-3-34-5. See CIA, "Possible Repercussions of a Soviet Win in Ethiopia/Somalia," 6 Mar 1978, CIA-rr.

167. Hamrick, "Soviet Policy in Africa and the Horn," in Hamrick to Loughran, 15 Feb 1978, Hamrick Papers.

168. Ibid.

169. Author's interviews with Moose (2001) and Petterson. Also, author's interview with Hamrick.

170. William Griffith, "The Horn and US Policy," in Henze to ZB, 28 Jan 1978, *FRUS, 1977–1980, v. 6: Soviet Union*, doc. 78.

171. The Secretary: News Conference, 10 Feb 1978, *DOS Bulletin*, Mar 1978, 14 (emphasis added); Vance, State 19755, 25 Jan 1978, FOIA; Ayalew, quoted in ZB to Carter, "Meeting with Ethiopian Ambassador," [19 Jan 1978,] Horn/1, CL. See ABC, CBS *Nightly News*, 10 Feb 1978, VNA; and CBS *Evening News*, 14 Feb 1978, VNA.

172. Memcon (Vance, Jamieson, Genscher, de Guiringaud, Owen), 12 Feb 1978, PREM 16/1872, NA-UK. Also Murray, UKMis New York 392, 16 Feb 1978, PREM 16/1873, NA-UK. On the need for secrecy: Owen, FCO 291, 3 Feb 1978, PREM 16/1872, NA-UK.

173. Vance, State 40766, 16 Feb 1978, FOIA. See Interview with Representatives of Black Media Associations, 16 Feb 1978, APP. For Siad's evasive reply, Loughran, Mog 315, 18 Feb 1978, FOIA; Loughran, Mog 314, 18 Feb 1978, FOIA; and Loughran, Mog 318, 20 Feb 1978, FOIA. It is striking that in his memoirs, Brzezinski persists in calling the Somalis the "nominal aggressors" (Brzezinski, *Power*, 178).

174. Owen to Callaghan, 16 Feb 1978, PREM 16/1873, NA-UK.

175. [West,] Riyadh 125, 12 Feb 1978, NLC-16-43-1-31-2.

176. Author's interview with Aaron. Also Aaron, Exit Interview, CL; author's interview with Henze; and Harrop (who accompanied the mission), FD, 24 Aug 1993.

177. Memcon (Mengistu, Aaron), 17 Feb 1978, in [unsigned, from Henze], Addis 534, 20 Feb 1978, NLC-7-6-10-19-7; [unsigned, from Henze], Addis 536, 21 Feb 1978, NLC-7-6-10-20-5; Memcon (Mengistu, Aaron), 17 Feb 1978, in [unsigned, from Henze], Addis 534, 20 Feb 1978, NLC-7-6-10-19-7. Also: Aaron to Carter, 13 Feb 1978, NLC-133-215-4-15-5; Matheron, Addis 807, 17 Feb 1978, FOIA; Le Melle, Nairobi 2621, 18 Feb 1978, FOIA; Matheron, Addis 822, 18 Feb 1978, FOIA; Day, Addis 101, 20 Feb 1978, PREM 16/1873, NA-UK; and Matheron, Addis 851, 22 Feb 1978, Ethiopia/1, NSA-DC.

178. Author's interview with Aaron. See Memcon (Vest, Hibbert, Merillon, Blech), 3 Mar 1978, NLC-23-11-5-16-2.

179. Tareke, *Ethiopian Revolution*, 658; and DOS, "Soviet/Cuban Activities in Africa," backgrounder for NATO Summit, 30–31 May 1978, NLC-133-179-3-19-3. See MINFAR, "Misiones Internacionalistas Cumplidas por Cuba, 1963–1991," Havana, Jul 1998, Gleijeses Papers; MINFAR, "La Misión Internacionalista en la República de Etiopía," n.d., ibid.; and Tareke, *Ethiopian Revolution*, 207.

180. INR to Vance, 9 Feb 1978, NLC-6-21-7-8-7.

181. SCC: Minutes, 22 Feb 1978, Brzezinski/28, CL. Also: SCC: Summary of Conclusions, 21 [*sic*; should be 22] 1978, Ethiopia/2, NSA-DC. The White House announced Mengistu's noninvasion pledge. Digest of Other White House Announcements, 24 Feb 1978, APP.

182. Vance, ER, 2 Feb 1978, NLC-128-13-5-14-5 (emphasis in original).

183. SCC: Minutes, 22 Feb 1978, Brzezinski/28, CL.

184. Ibid. The task force had been recommended by William Griffith. See Griffith, "The Horn and US Policy," in Henze to ZB, 28 Jan 1978, *FRUS, 1977–1980, v. 6: Soviet Union*, doc. 78.

185. Brzezinski, *Power*, 182.

186. Unnamed official quoted in Drew, "Brzezinski," 104.

187. ZB, WR, 22 Sep 1978, Brzezinski/42, CL; and WGBH, "Interview with Zbigniew Brzezinski," 19 Nov 1986.

188. Brzezinski, *Power*, 182–83.

189. SCC: Minutes, 22 Feb 1978, Brzezinski/28, CL.

190. WGBH, "Interview with Zbigniew Brzezinski," 19 Nov 1986; and SCC: Minutes, 22 Feb 1978, Brzezinski/28, CL.

191. Jay, Washington 864, 3 Mar 1978, PREM 16/1873, NA-UK.

192. Meg Greenfield, *WP*, 8 Feb 1978, 19.

193. NSC: Minutes, 23 Feb 1978, Ethiopia/3, NSA-DC. For Turner's analysis: CIA Office of Regional and Political Analysis, "Soviet Attitudes on an Ethiopian Invasion of Somalia," 23 Feb 1978, NLC-31-37-5-13-8 (for pp. 5–6 of this document, which are misfiled, see NLC-31-76-4-11-8). See President's Daily Diary, 23 Feb 1978, CL-online.

194. NSC: Minutes, 23 Feb 1978, Ethiopia/3, NSA-DC.

195. Ibid.

196. Ibid.

197. Ibid.

198. Carter, *White House Diary*, 166.

199. NSC: Minutes, 23 Feb 1978, Ethiopia/3, NSA-DC; and Presidential Directive/NSC-32, 24 Feb 1978, DNSA. *New Yorker* correspondent Elizabeth Drew wrote an almost verbatim account of the disagreement at the February 22 SCC meeting. See Drew, "Brzezinski," 116.

200. James Reston, *NYT*, 24 Feb 1978, 27; and *WP*, 24 Feb 1978, 1. *LAT* and *Newsweek* also questioned Carter's leadership: *LAT*, 26 Feb 1978, edit D4; and "Dilemma on the Horn," *Newsweek*, 27 Feb 1978, 39.

201. See Gleijeses, *Visions*, 86–87.

202. *NYT*, 25 Feb 1978, 1. See ABC, CBS, NBC *Evening News*, 24 Feb 1978, VNA.

203. ZB, WR, 24 Feb 1978, Brzezinski/41, CL.

204. ZB to Mondale, Vance, Brown, "Presidential Directive/NSC 32," 24 Feb 1978, CL-online.

205. NSC: Minutes, 23 Feb 1978, Ethiopia/3, NSA-DC; and CNN, "Interview with Dr Zbigniew Brzezinski," 13 Jun 1997.

206. Armacost to ZB, 24 Feb 1978, FOIA-mf. Also Henze to ZB, "Possible Actions," 1 Mar 1978, DDRS.

207. Huntington to ZB, 7 Mar 1978, Horn/2, CL; Armacost to ZB, 24 Feb 1978, FOIA-mf; ZB to Carter, "Trip to the Far East," 27 Feb 1978, DDRS; and Carter, *White House Diary*, 174. For early planning of this trip: Oksenberg to ZB, 14 Jan 1978, FOIA-mf. Also Brzezinski, *Power*, 178–90.

208. *NYT*, 2 Mar 1978, 6.

209. Vance, State 52898, 1 Mar 1978, FOIA; and ABC *Evening News*, 1 Mar 1978, VNA.

210. *WP*, 2 Mar 1978, 1; and Vance in US Senate, "International Development Assistance Authorization," CD57, 218.

211. Vance in US Senate, "International Development Assistance Authorization," CD57, 218.

212. News Conference, 2 Mar 1978, APP.

213. "SCC Meeting on Horn of Africa," 2 Mar 1978, Ethiopia/3, NSA-DC. More heavily redacted versions in: DDRS and Ethiopia/2, NSA-DC. The summary of the meeting whitewashes the argument: SCC: Summary of Conclusions, 2 Mar 1978, DDRS.

214. "SCC Meeting on Horn of Africa," 2 Mar 1978, Ethiopia/3, NSA-DC.

215. ZB to Vance, "Instructions to Ambassador Loughran," [3 Mar 1978,] Horn/2, CL; and SCC: Summary of Conclusions, 2 Mar 1978, DDRS.

216. Brzezinski, *Power*, 183.

217. ZB to Carter, 3 Mar 1978, DDRS.

218. Ibid.

219. *NYT*, 3 Mar 1978, 3; *WP*, 6 Mar 1978, 1; and *WP*, 5 Mar 1978, 1.

220. *LAT*, 26 Feb 1978, edit D4; *CSM*, 7 Mar 1978, 1; and News Conference, 2 Mar 1978, APP. For Gallup poll: *WP*, 12 Feb 1978, 1.

221. *WP*, 26 Feb 1978, D8.

222. Art Buchwald, *LAT*, 23 Feb 1978, E2.

223. *NYT*, 25 Feb 1978, edit 20. An October 1977 Gallup poll found that only 7 percent of respondents considered foreign affairs "a major national problem."

224. *WSJ*, 23 Feb 1978, edit 26.

225. See MINFAR, "La Misión Internacionalista en la República de Etiopía," n.d., Gleijeses Papers. This source is most authoritative, but there is some disagreement about this date. See: 5 Mar 1978, Addis Ababa, FBIS-SSA-78-044.

226. MINFAR, "La Misión Internacionalista en la República de Etiopía," n.d., Gleijeses Papers; and *Newsweek*, 27 Feb 1978, 39. Also Ochoa to Fidel Castro, Daily Reports, 4–8 Mar 1978, Gleijeses Papers.

227. Vance, State 57913, 7 Mar 1978, FOIA. See Vance, ER, 7 Mar 1978, NLC-128-13-6-5-4.

228. Loughran, Mog 458, 8 Mar 1978, FOIA.

Chapter 9

1. *WP*, 17 Feb 1978, edit 16.

2. *NYT*, 16 Feb 1978, 1; and CIA National Foreign Assessment Center, "Rhodesia: Eight-Point Agreement," 16 Feb 1978, Incoming FOIA/6, NSA-DC.

3. Vance, State 41753, 16 Feb 1978, FOIA. Also *NYT*, 4 Mar 1978, 2; and Rowland Evans and Robert Novak, *WP*, 27 Feb 1978, 19.

4. *WSJ*, 17 Feb 1978, edit 16. Editorial comment on announcement of the Salisbury accords in the principal US newspapers spanned from the skeptical *NYT*, through the *WP*, which reserved judgment, to the guardedly optimistic *CSM*: *NYT*, 20 Feb 1978, edit 16; *WP*, 17 Feb 1978, edit 16; and *CSM*, 17 Feb 1978, edit 28.

5. Jay, Washington 15, 3 Jan 1978, FCO 36/2204, NA-UK.

6. PRC: Summary of Conclusions, 17 Feb 1978, Vertical/Cuba, CL; and Low, FD, 1 Feb. 1994. See DOS *Bulletin*, Mar 1978, 21. Young strongly disagreed with the PRC's conclusions. See Young, USUN 815, 8 Mar 1978, NLC-24-110-2-1-9.

7. For the full text of the settlement agreement: *Guardian* (London), 4 Mar 1978, 5. For a thorough critique: WOA, "The Rhodesia Settlement: Sell-out or Solution?" Mar 1979, US Foreign Relations: Rhodesia/253, WOA, Yale.

8. "What has been Accomplished," n.d., NSA-staff/119, CL. See Top Secret, 6 Mar 1978, NLC-1-5-5-24-4.

9. *WP*, 17 Feb 1978, edit 16.

10. *NYT*, 5 Mar 1978, edit E18. See *NYT*, 20 Feb 1978, edit 16; *WP*, 17 Feb 1978, edit 16; *CSM*, 17 Feb 1978, edit 28; and *WSJ*, 17 Feb 1978, edit 16.

11. *Guardian*, 4 Mar 1978, edit 16; and "Rhodesia," 16 Feb 1978, *Parliamentary Debates*, Commons, 5th ser., vol. 944: cols. 663–73.

12. ADR to Gaylard, 17 Feb, 1978, ADR/11, box 4/006(m), Smith Papers (transcript of interview with Owen on ITV's "News at Ten"); and CIA National Foreign Assessment Center, "United Kingdom: Pressures on Owen," 8 Mar 1978, incoming FOIA/6, NSA-DC.

13. Graham to PS, 22 Feb 1978, FCO 36/2232, NA-UK; and author's interview with Owen.

14. "Rhodesia: Talks with Mr Moose, 22 (and 23) February," in Laver to Graham, 21 Feb 1978, FCO 36/2232, NA-UK. Also Top Secret, 23 Feb 1978, NLC-1-5-4-37-1.

15. Low, Lusaka 569, 23 Feb 1978, FCO 36/2232, NA-UK.

16. Owen to Jay in FCO 458 to Washington, 24 Feb 1978, FCO 73/316, NA-UK.

17. Owen to Vance, 24 Feb 1978, ibid. Covers next two paragraphs.

18. Vance to Owen, in Brewster to Owen, 27 Feb 1978, FCO 36/2232, NA-UK; and author's interview with Owen. Also "Talking Points," in Owen, FCO 81 to Tel Aviv, 27 Feb 1978, FCO 36/2232, NA-UK.

19. Author's interview with Moose (2001).

20. Aaron to ZB, 4 Mar 1978, NLC-133-215-5-10-9; Aaron to ZB, 13 Mar 1978, NLC-133-215-5-22-6; and Brzezinski, *Power*, 140 (quoting from his diary).

21. Habib, Lake, Harrop to Vance, 28 Feb 1978, Lake/3, NA; administration official, quoted in Chester Crocker, "Lost in Africa," *New Republic*, 18 Feb 1978 16; and Habib, Lake, Harrop to Vance, 28 Feb 1978, Lake/3, NA.

22. Author's interview with Owen.

23. *Guardian & Observer* (London), 23 Apr 1978, 13. See *LAT*, 8 Mar 1978, 1.

24. Vance, State 60166, 9 Mar 1978, FOIA-mf.

25. Southern Rhodesia: Joint Statement, 8 Mar 1978, DOS *Bulletin*, Apr 1978, 30. Also Vance to Carter, 8 Mar 1978, NLC-128-13-6-6-3; and Vance, State 60429, 9 Mar 1978, FOIA.

26. *Daily Telegraph* (London), 29 Mar 1978, 5; and *Guardian & Observer*, 3 Apr 1978, 1.

27. *NYT*, 29 May 1978, 3.

28. Vance, State 63462, 12 Mar 1978, FOIA. See *NYT*, 6 Mar 1978, 2.

29. Vance, State 63495, 12 Mar 1978, FOIA; US intelligence report, "The Rhodesian Factor," [May 1977,] FCO 36/2007, NA-UK; and Vance, State 49199, 25 Feb 1978, FOIA. See Vance, ER, 18 Mar 1978, NLC-7-20-1-17-3.

30. Gates to ZB, 27 Feb 1978, NLC-6-79-5-21-1; and CIA National Foreign Assessment Center, "Rhodesia: Soviet Responses to a Settlement Without Nkomo," 24 Feb 1978, NSA-staff/119, CL. Also CIA National Foreign Assessment Center, "USSR Weekly Review," 9 Mar 1978, CREST. On Cuba's 1977 agreement, see chapter 7 above; and Gleijeses, *Visions*, 143–45.

31. Loughran, Mog 459, 9 Mar 1978, FOIA. See Vance, State 57913, 7 Mar 1978, FOIA.

32. Fidel Castro to Ochoa, 6 Mar 1978, Gleijeses Papers; and Fidel Castro to Ochoa (handwritten), 6 Mar 1978, ibid.

33. Fidel Castro to Mengistu, 7 Mar 1978, Gleijeses Papers.

34. Vance in US Senate, "Foreign Assistance, FY79," CD56, 467. Schweiker (R-PA) posed the question.

35. DOS Noon Press Briefing, in Vance, State 61170, 9 Mar 1978, FOIA; and Vance, State 61431, 10 Mar 1978, FOIA. Also draft cable to London et al., 9 Mar 1978, Lake/3, NA. After Siad's meeting with Loughran, the Somali government announced the decision to withdraw. Loughran, Mog 476, 9 Mar 1978, FOIA; and Loughran, Mog 477, 9 Mar 1978, FOIA.

36. TelCon (Schmidt, Carter), 9 Mar 1978, B150/388, Berlin; and News Conference, 9 Mar 1978, APP. Also Vance, State 60457, 9 Mar 1978, FOIA; and Vance, State 61122, 9 Mar 1978, FOIA.

37. *NYT*, 10 Mar 1978, edit 28; and *NYT*, 2 Mar 1978, 6.

38. Brzezinski, *Power*, 189, quoting his diary from 1980.

39. Westad, *Global*, 279.

40. For Brzezinski's explanation, see Drew, "Brzezinski," 118-21.

41. SCC: Minutes, 22 Feb 1978, Brzezinski/28, CL.

42. Tareke, *Ethiopian Revolution*, 214.

43. Based on a search of *NYT*, *WP*, *Sun* (Baltimore), *WSJ*, and *LAT*.

44. Owen Roberts, FD, 11 Feb 1991; and Memcon (Dobrynin, Harriman), 13 Apr 1978, 589/1, Harriman Papers. See State/NSC Paper #3, "Improving US Relations with African Countries," in Spiegel to Thornton, [16 Aug 1978,] Lake Papers box, NA.

45. *Sun*, 22 May 1978, 2; and Henze to ZB, 10 Mar 1978, Horn/2, CL.

46. See, e.g., Top Secret, 8 Feb 1978, NLC-1-5-3-27-3; Henze, ER, 8 Feb 1978, NLC-27-6-1-2-3; Christopher, State 37063, 11 Feb 1978, FOIA; Situation Room to ZB, 11 Feb 1978, NLC-1-5-3-38-1; Vance to Carter, 28 Feb 1978, Plains/38, CL; and Tarnoff to ZB, 7 Mar 1978, Horn/2, CL.

47. *Time*, 18 Apr 1977, 18; Henze, ER, 6 Mar 1978, Horn/6, CL; and *WP*, 18 Apr 1978, 19. For Saudi complaints about Somalis: SCC Meeting, "The Pro's and Con's of Encouraging Friendly Muslim Countries to Provide Increased Support for Somalia," 10 Feb 1978, Policy Documents-Ethiopia/3, NSA-DC. For Saudi policy at war's end: Lake and Moose to Vance, 1 Mar 1978, FOIA; and *NYT*, 10 Mar 1978, 1.

48. Brzezinski, *Power*, 189.

49. See Memcon (Vance, Gromyko), 25 May 1978, *FRUS, 1977–1980, v. 6: Soviet Union*, doc. 113; and Memcon (Carter, Gromyko), 27 May 1978, ibid., doc. 115.

50. See Pastor to Handeyside, 28 Jun 1978, NLC-24-77-2-2-7; Gleijeses, *Visions*, 43–45; LeoGrande and Kornbluh, *Back Channel*, 49–53, 168–72; and Schoultz, *That Infernal*, 325–28.

51. Young, USUN 1676, 27 Apr 1978, NLC-24-110-2-3-7; "SCC Meeting on Horn of Africa," 2 Mar 1978, Ethiopia/3, NSA-DC; and author's interview with Moose (2001). For US aid to Savimbi: ZB to Aaron and Bartholomew, 27 Apr 1978, NLC-7-32-2-13-3; Aaron to ZB, 27 Apr 1978, NLC-133-215-6-13-5; SCC, 15 May 1978, SCC/77, CL; marginalia on Vance to Carter, 19 May 1978, NLC-7-20-3-2-7; marginalia on Vance to Carter, 19 Jun 1978, NLC-7-20-4-11-6; and James Morton, FD, 18 Oct 1993. For French aid to Savimbi: Chambers, Brussels 11500, 12 Jun 1978, FOIA; Christopher, ER, 15 Jun 1978, NLC-7-20-4-9-9; and PRM 36, Response, Soviet/Cuban Presence in Africa, 18 Aug 1978, DDRS, X:6. See Gleijeses, *Visions*, 51–53.

52. Vance, *Hard Choices*, 114 (quoted), 114–19.

53. ZB to Carter, 27 Feb 1978, DDRS. See Henze to ZB, 1 Mar 1978, *FRUS, 1977–1980, v. 6: Soviet Union*, doc. 86; "SCC Meeting on Horn of Africa," 2 Mar 1978, Ethiopia/3, NSA-DC; NSC Staff, "A Proposal for Asian Policy Adjustments," in Oksenberg and Armacost to ZB, 13 Mar 1978, *FRUS 1977–1980, v. 13: China*, doc. 84; and Memcon (ZB, Dobrynin), 15 Mar 1978, *FRUS, 1977–1980, v. 6: Soviet Union*, doc. 91. See Warren Cohen and Nancy Bernkopf Tucker, "Beijing's Friend, Moscow's Foe," in Gati, *Zbig*, 85–103.

54. Brown to Carter, 11 Mar 1978, *FRUS 1977–1980, v. 13: China*, doc. 83. See Brzezinski, *Power*, 203–6.

55. Carter, "Being There," 164–65.

56. Carter's marginalia on Vance, ER, 14 Mar 1978, NLC-7-20-1-13-7. On sending Mondale, see Brzezinski, *Power*, 205.

57. Carter to Mondale and Vance, 16 Mar 1978, *FRUS 1977–1980, v. 13: China*, doc. 86.

58. Address at Wake Forest University, 17 Mar 1978, APP.

59. Béchir Ben Yahmed, "Ce que je crois: Démesure," *Jeune Afrique*, 22 Mar 1978, edit 15; and INR, "Cuba's African Policy and its Effect on Relations with the US," 13 Mar 1978, FOIA. Also CIA, "Soviet Involvement in Africa," [Mar 1978,] CREST.

60. INR, "Cuba's African Policy and its Effect on Relations with the US," 13 Mar 1978, FOIA; Young, Moose, Lake to Vance, 19 Dec 1977, Lake/3, NA; and Clingerman, Lusaka 4249, 4 Dec 1978, FOIA. See "President Machel of Mozambique," n.d., NLC-7-16-7-9-1. For US condemnation of raids: *NYT*, 30 Nov 1977, 9; and *NYT*, 4 Dec 1977, 46. For US aid: Vance to Carter, 16 Dec 1977, NLC-128-13-3-11-0; and ZB to Vance, 23 Dec 1977, Incoming FOIA-Rhodesia/6, NSA-DC.

61. CIA National Foreign Assessment Center, "Rhodesia," 10 Mar 1978, Incoming FOIA/6, NSA-DC; and Low, Lusaka 806, 13 Mar 1978, FOIA-mf. On fears about Zambia: CIA National Foreign Assessment Center, "Rhodesia: ZAPU Military Plans," 11 Mar 1978, Incoming FOIA/6, NSA-DC; Vance to Carter, 18 Mar 1978, NLC-128-13-6-13-5; Memcon (Vance, Mwale), 18 Mar 1978, in Vance, State 72802, 21 Mar 1978, FOIA; Low, Lusaka 1043, 28 Mar 1978, FOIA-mf; Brewster (from Low), London 7575, 12 May 1978, NLC-16-24-2-25-9; and ZB to Carter, [17 May 1978,], NLC-133-161-7-5-3.

62. ZB, WR, 24 Feb 1978, Brzezinski/41, CL; and Address at Wake Forest University, 17 Mar 1978, APP.

63. *NYT*, 18 Mar 1978, 9; and Memcon (Genscher, Stoessel), 22 March 1978, doc. 84, *AAPD 1978*, 407.

64. *WP*, 1 Apr 1978, 1; and *Daily Times* (Lagos), 1 Apr 1978, 1. Franklin D. Roosevelt passed through Liberia en route to the 1943 Cairo Conference, but it was not a state visit.

65. ZB to Carter, [25 Mar 1978,] NLC-24-107-3-4-9.

66. Harry Cahill, FD, 29 Jul 1993. The military aid request for Zaire was cut from $30 million to $17.5 million; Nigeria was slotted for a $2 million military training program. See *NYT*, 16 Jan 1978, 7; and Easum, Lagos 904, 21 Mar 1978, NLC-7-6-10-23-2.

67. See *Daily Times* (Lagos), 3 Apr 1978, 1; and *NYT*, 2 Apr 1978, 2. Author's interviews with Easum and Young.

68. Remarks at the National Arts Theatre, Lagos, 1 Apr 1978, APP.

69. Ibid.

70. Memcon (Carter, Obasanjo, ZB, Vance, Young, Brigadier Joe Garba), 1 Apr 1978, 10:40 am, NLC-24-107-5-3-8.

71. Kaunda to Carter in Low, Lusaka 1110, 1 Apr 1978, NLC-15R-50-2-6-3. See Nyerere to Carter, 3 Mar 1978, in Spain, Dar 940, 3 Mar 1978, NSA-staff/119, CL; Vance, State 62020, 10 Mar 1978, FOIA; Low, Lusaka 789, 12 Mar 1978, Carter-Brezhnev Project, NSA-DC; Vance to Carter, "Your Visit to Nigeria," 14 Mar 1978, DDRS; Vance, State 79045, 28 Mar 1978, FOIA; and Nyerere to Carter, in Spain, Dar 1326, 28 Mar 1978, NLC-15R-50-2-6-3.

72. Situation Room, "Africa Trends, No. 36," 1 Apr 1978, NLC-4-11-2-3-0; and Cooper, State 82605, 31 Mar 1978, FOIA. See Memcon (Owen, Vance), 12 Feb 1978, in Ferguson to PUS, 15 Feb 1978, FCO 73/316, NA-UK; and Owen's "Pilgrim's Speech," *Times* (London), 14 Mar 1978, 8.

73. Memcon (Carter, Obasanjo, ZB, Vance, Young, Brigadier Joe Garba), 1 Apr 1978, 10:40 am, NLC-24-107-5-3-8.

74. Easum, FD, 17 Jan 1990; and author's interview with Carter.

75. The Americans had hoped to arrange a summit meeting in Lagos with Carter, Callaghan, Obasanjo, and all the Frontline presidents, but the arrangements fell through. Young invited the foreign ministers instead. See Vance, ER, 14 Mar 1978, NLC-7-20-1-13-7; ZB to Carter, 16 Mar 1978, NLC-24-114-8-5-5; and Vance, ER, 17 Mar 1978, NLC-7-20-1-16-4.

76. Easum, FD, 17 Jan 1990. Also author's interviews with Easum, Young, and Moose (2001).

77. Easum, Lagos 4091, 2 Apr 1978, DNSA. The contrast with the draft communiqué, written before Carter's departure, is striking. See Vance, State 79086, 28 Mar 1978, FOIA-mf; and DOS, "Rhodesia," [Mar 1978,] NLC-23-23-7-1-3.

78. WP, 4 Apr 1978, edit 18; and Bowdler, Pretoria 2049, 11 Apr 1978, FOIA-mf.

79. NYT, 4 Apr 1978, edit 32; Time, 17 Apr 1978, 28; and Kaunda to Carter, 15 Apr 1978, in Clingerman, Lusaka 1324, 15 Apr 1978, FOIA.

80. NYT, 4 Apr 1978, 1.

81. NYT, 5 Apr 1978, 1.

82. Der Spiegel, 10 Apr 1978, 26–34, FBIS-WEU.

83. Amin Maalouf, "Le mal américain," Jeune Afrique, 26 Apr 1978, 14; and WP, 18 Apr 1978, 19.

84. Owen, Mansion House speech, quoted in Guardian, 6 Apr 1978, 1. Also Guardian, 7 Apr 1978, 13; and Memcon (Owen, Yacé), 8 May 1978, FCO31/2264, NA-UK. For US fears of Cubans in Eritrea: ZB to Carter, 7 Apr 1978, Brzezinski/28, CL; Matheron, Addis 1879, 24 Apr 1978, FOIA; and "Cuban/Ethiopian Relations," 20 Apr 1978, FCO31/2264, NA-UK. For Cuban policy in Eritrea: "Indicaciones del Comandante en Jefe para el Jefe de la misión militar cubana en Etiopía," n.d., Gleijeses Papers; Fidel Castro to Casas, 25 Nov 1977, ibid.; Casas to Raúl Castro, 8 Feb 1978, ibid.; Memcon (Soviet General Krivopliasov, Casas), 18 Mar 1978, ibid.; and Gleijeses, Visions, 325.

85. Carter to Vance, 14 Apr 1978, FRUS, 1977–1980, v. 6: Soviet Union, doc. 96. See Christopher, ToSec 40110, 17 Apr 1978, FOIA; "Remarks at a Town Meeting, Spokane, 5 May 1978, APP; and Lake to Vance, 23 May 1978, Lake/3, NA.

86. Memcon (Brezhnev, Vance), 22 Apr 1978, FRUS, 1977–1980, v. 6: Soviet Union, doc. 103. See Meeting of the CC CPSU Politburo, 27 Apr 1978, CWIHP-va.

87. Bowdler, Pretoria 2049, 11 Apr 1978, FOIA-mf. For the Patriotic Front's wariness: DePree, Maputo 428, 7 Apr 1978, FOIA-mf. For preparations for Malta 2: see especially the cables in FOIA-mf.

88. Conclusions: Cabinet Meeting, 6 Apr 1978, CAB/128/63/12, NA-UK.

89. Lake to Vance, 11 Apr 1978, Lake/3, NA.

90. Conclusions, Cabinet Meeting, 13 Apr 1978, CAB/128/63/14, NA-UK.

91. Ibid.

92. Vance to Carter, 11 Apr 1978, NLC-128-13-7-6-2. See Martin and Johnson, Struggle, 292.

93. Vance, SecTo 4074, 16 Apr 1978, Incoming FOIA/6, NSA-DC; author's interviews with Lake and Low; and Thornton to ZB, 15 Apr 1978, NLC-7-6-10-30-4. Also Vance, SecTo 4056, 15 Apr 1978, FOIA. Unfortunately, I could locate no detailed account of this meeting from the Patriotic Front's point of view.

94. Vance, Salisbury SecTo 4093, 17 Apr 1978, Incoming FOIA/6, NSA-DC. See Christopher, ER, 21 Apr 1978, NLC-7-20-2-16-3.

95. "The Role of Field Marshal Lord Carver . . . as Resident Commissioner Designate for Rhodesia," 20 Dec 1978, in Carver to Owen, 20 Dec 1978, FCO 73/319, NA-UK.

96. See Christopher to Carter, 21 Apr 1978, NLC-128-13-7-14-3; and Christopher, State 102659, 22 Apr 1978, FOIA-mf.

97. Memcon (Smith, Owen, Vance, et al.), 17 Apr 1978, SA v. 5, box 4/006(m), Smith Papers; and author's interview with Moose (2001). Also Executive Council to US and British Governments, in Gaylard to ADR, 25 Apr 1978, ADR/11, box 4/006(m), Smith Papers; and author's interview with Low.

98. For the first statement of this stance, see Low, Lusaka 1459, 25 Apr 1978, FOIA.

99. Mugabe quoted in *News of the World*, 9 Jul 1978 (in Rhodesian Ministry of Foreign Affairs, "Background Briefing: The Transitional Government and the American Conditions for the Lifting of Sanctions against Rhodesia," 18 Aug 1978, personal file, Smith 22, Smith Papers).

100. *WP*, 25 Feb 1978, B4. For Gallup: *WP*, 16 Mar 1978, 3; and *NYT*, 19 Mar 1978, 30.

101. Jay to Owen, 5 Jan 1978, PREM 16/1909, NA-UK. For the Panama treaties, see Pfeffer,"The Drill" and Clymer, *Drawing the Line.*

102. Reagan, "Cubans & Russians," handwritten, 13 Mar 1978, PP Ia/20, RL; and Reagan, "Desk-cleaning," 3 Apr 1978, PP Ia/21, RL (emphasis in original). For prior broadcasts about Cuba: "Cuba," 16 Nov 1976, PP Ia/4; "Update on Cuba," 2 Mar 1977, PP Ia/7; "Cuba II," 2 Mar 1977, PP Ia/7; "Cuba and Africa," 4 May 1977, PP Ia/9; "Cuba—Trouble in Paradise," 25 May 1977, PP Ia/10; "Cuba I," 6 Sep 1977, PP Ia/13; and " Cuba," 20 Feb 1978, PP Ia/19; all RL.

103. Ronald Reagan, "America's Purpose in the World," 17 Mar 1978, CPAC, www.conservative.org/cpac/archives/cpac-1978-ronald-reagan/ Also *CSM*, 22 Mar 1978, 3.

104. Ibid.

105. ZB, WR, 7 Apr 1978, Brzezinski/41, CL (emphasis in original); ZB, WR, 14 Apr 1978, ibid.; and ZB, WR, 21 Apr 1878, ibid. Also ZB, WR, 5 May 1978, ibid.; and ZB to Carter, 12 May 1978, NLC-1-6-3-6-5.

106. See chapter 6 above.

107. Oksenberg to ZB, 1 May 1978, NLC-6-1-1-4-9.

108. *NYT*, 30 Apr 1978, 1. See Christopher, ER, 1 May 1978, NLC-7-20-3-3-6.

109. Author's interview with Low.

110. US Senate, "US Policy toward Africa," CD58.

111. Donald to Owen, 9 Jun 1978, FCO99/162. See Situation Room to ZB, 23 May 1978, NLC-4-39-4-13-7; and Memcon (Vance, de Guiringaud, Genscher, Owen), 29 May 1978, NLC-23-11-5-12-6. On Shaba 2, see Gleijeses, "Truth"; Odom, *Shaba II*; Willame, "La seconde guerre"; and Gildea, "Case Study."

112. Vance to Carter, 16 May 1978, NLC-128-13-8-10-6; Vance to Carter, 17 May 1978, Subject/FO23, CL; ZB to Carter, 17 May 1978, Subject/FO23, CL; Carter to Giscard, 18 May 1978, Carter Brezhnev Project, NSA-DC; and Odom to Aaron, 19 May 1978, SCC/80, CL.

113. See *CT*, 28 May 1978, 4. The Red Cross concluded that there was no evidence of systematic killings by either side. See *WP*, 24 May 1978, 1; and *WP*, 11 Jul 1978, 9.

In the course of the crisis, 121 whites were killed. Approximately 300 black civilians and 419 black troops (Zairean and rebel) were killed, but these deaths did not get much coverage in the Western press.

114. Vance (from Moose), State 285045, 9 Nov 1978, FOIA; Vance to Carter, 17 May 1978, Subject/FO23, CL; and *NYT*, 22 May 1978, edit 20.

115. See CIA, Zaire Special Working Group, 21 May 1978, Action in Kolwezi, NLC-4-39-4-4-7. For a narrative of the operation: East African Department, Foreign Office, "Background: Kolwezi," 22 May 1978, FCO99/162, NA-UK.

116. Albright to ZB and Aaron, 27 May 1978, NSA-congress/1, CL. See interview with Brzezinski, Albright, Denend, Odom, 18 Feb 1982, 12-13, CPP; and Albright, *Madam Secretary*, 72–73.

117. *WP*, 21 May 1978, 1 (Byrd) and edit B6; and *CSM*, 23 May 1978, edit 28. For an opposing viewpoint: *CT*, 25 May 1978, edit B2.

118. French foreign minister quoted in Gleijeses, "Truth," 86; and *Guardian*, 18 May 1978, edit (quoting *Telegraph* and *Mail*), 14. For US editorials: *CSM*, 16 May 1978, 28; *WP*, 16 May 1978, 12; and *NYT*, 18 May 1978, 22.

119. *CSM*, 6 May 1978, 1; and *WP*, 4 Jun 1978, 1.

120. *WSJ*, 17 May 1978, edit 22 (Khaled); *WP*, 17 May 1978, 3; and *WP*, 17 May 1978, 3.

121. Lane, Havana 1320, 18 May 1978, FOIA-mf; [CIA,] "Shaba, Castro, and the Evidence," 6 Jun 1978, NLC-6-13-4-13-3 (for a version with different redactions: Vertical/Cuba Trip 2002, CL); and Situation Room, Morning Summary, 19 May 1978, NLC-4-39-3-5-7.

122. Remarks at the Welcoming Ceremony for President Kaunda, 17 May 1978, APP; and *Sun*, 18 May 1978, 2. For Kaunda's 1975 toast, see chapter 2 above.

123. *NYT*, 23 May 1978, 19.

124. Author's interview with McHenry; News Conference, 25 May 1978, APP; *CT*, 26 May 1978, 1; *WP*, 26 May 1978, 1; and *Time*, 5 Jun 1978, 26.

125. Author's interview with Clark. Also for Clark: *CQ Weekly*, 13 Jun 1978, 410; and *WP*, 25 Jun 1978, 1. For McGovern: *WP*, 21 May 1978, 1; *WP*, 24 May 1978, 1; and George McGovern, "Alarmism on Africa," *WP*, 1 Jul 1978, 15. On lifting Clark amendment: News Conference, 26 Jun 1978, APP; and Thornton to Aaron, Bartholomew, Pastor, 20 Jul 1978, NLC-24-110-3-37.

126. "Brzezinski on *Meet the Press*," 28 May 1978, DOS *Bulletin*, Jul 1978, 26–28.

127. *NYT*, 13 Jun 1978, 8; and Pastor to Aaron, 7 Aug 1978, NLC-6-13-4-12-4. See *Sun* (Baltimore), 18 Jun 1978, 2. For analyses of Castro's credibility: [CIA,] "Shaba, Castro, and the Evidence," 6 Jun 1978, NLC-6-13-4-13-3; CIA, "Cuba's Record of Deceit," [Jun 1978,] CREST; and Gleijeses, "Truth."

128. *NYT*, 10 Jun 1978, 1; and CIA, Zaire Special Working Group, 21 May 1978, Action in Kolwezi, NLC-4-39-4-4-7. See Cutler, Kinshasa 5120, 21 May 1978, FOIA-mf; Lake to Vance, 23 May 1978, Lake/3, NA; and Richard Rovere, "Affairs of State," *New Yorker*, 24 Jul 1978, 72–74.

129. Memcon (Gromyko, Vance), 31 May 1978, CWIHP-va. The redacted, American version is Memcon (Gromyko, Vance), 31 May 1978, *FRUS, 1977–1980, v. 6: Soviet Union*, doc. 120.

130. CIA, "Cuba's Record of Deceit," [Jun 1978,] CREST; and Gleijeses, "Truth." For the "proof" given to the congressional committees: Hetu (CIA), "Cuban and

Soviet Assistance to the Katangan Insurgents," 2 Jun 1978, NLC-26-64-6-1-6. Also Carter's handwritten notes, 2 Jun 1978, OSS/89, CL.

131. NATO Summit Remarks at the Opening Ceremonies, 30 May 1978, APP. See Lake and Gelb to Vance, 26 May 1978, Lake/3, NA.

132. *Guardian*, 1 Jun 1978, 5. Also Owen to Callaghan, n.d., FCO99/157, NA-UK; *Guardian*, 2 Jun 1978, 1; Owen, Conclusions of Cabinet Meeting, 8 Jun 1978, CAB/128/64/1, NA-UK; Owen, tel. 140 of 16 Jun 1978, FCO99/157, NA-UK; Shakespeare, "Anglo-Cuban Relations," 13 Jun 1978, FCO99/157, NA-UK; and Petersen, tel. 121 of 4 Aug 1978, FCO 31/2265, NA-UK.

133. Memcon (NATO Summit), 29 May 1978, doc. 167, *AAPD 1978*, 831; and "Zaire," in ZB to Carter, 2 Jun 1978, NLC-15-57-10-9-3. Also Brown to Carter, 2 Jun 1978, OSS/89, CL.

134. For an excellent analysis of the speech, see Strong, *Working*, 98–122. For Carter's handwritten draft: Handwriting/89, CL. For a typed copy with initial changes: "Annapolis Speech," NLC-126-13-2-1-4. Also Vance to Carter, (draft written by Lake), 25 May 1978, Lake/1, NA; and Vance to Carter (sent), 29 May 1978, FOIA. See *WP*, 8 Jun 1978, 18; and *WP*, 11 Jun 1978, 1. For "stapling," *WP*, 8 Jun 1978, 1; *Guardian*, 9 Jun 1978, 6; Rowland Evans and Robert Novak, *WP*, 14 Jun 1978, 27; and Fallows, "Passionless," 43.

135. Carter, *Why Not the Best?*, 44; and US Naval Academy Address at the Commencement Exercises, 7 Jun 1978, APP.

136. US Naval Academy Address at the Commencement Exercises, 7 Jun 1978, APP. The original used "state of affairs" instead of "future." Carter's handwritten draft: Handwriting/89, CL.

137. Joseph Kraft, *WP*, 8 Jun 1978, 23. Also *NYT*, 9 Jun 1978, 3; and Mary McGrory, *CT*, 14 Jun 1978, B4.

138. *NYT*, 8 Jun 1978, 1. Also *LAT*, 8 Jun 1978, 1; and *Times*, 8 Jun 1978, 17.

139. *WSJ*, 8 Jun 1978, 5; *CSM*, 9 Jun 1978, edit 28; and *LAT*, 9 Jun 1978, edit D6.

140. *WP*, 20 Jun 1978, edit 10. The *Post* published three more editorials about the speech: *WP*, 8 Jun 1978, edit 22; *WP*, 13 Jun 1978, edit 20; and *WP*, 22 Jun 1978, edit 26.

141. Vance to Carter, 29 May 1978, FOIA.

142. News Conference, 26 Jun 1978, APP.

143. Von Staden to Genscher, 5 Sep 1978, doc. 254, *AAPD 1978*, 1291. The word "loner" is written in English.

144. *WSJ*, 2 Jun 1978, edit 14.

145. *CSM*, 18 May 1978, 1.

146. *NYT*, 22 May 1978, edit 20; Memcon (Carter, Genscher et al.), 30 May 1978, doc. 170, *AAPD 1978*, 844–45; and Memcon (Schmidt, Carter, Callaghan, Giscard, Trudeau, Andreotti, Fukuda), 16 Jul 1978, B150/397, Berlin.

Chapter 10

1. Carter held twelve news conferences from January to June but only seven from July to December. See APP.

2. Memcon (Chikerema, Graham, Low), 10 Apr 1978, SA/5, box 4/006(m), Smith Papers. Also Memcon (Ndiweni, Graham, Low) and Memcon (Gaylard, Graham, Low), 14 Jun 1978, SA/5, box 4/006(m), Smith Papers.

3. Christopher, State 151837, 15 Jun 1978, FOIA.

4. See Tamarkin, *The Making*, 226–29; and Moorcraft and McLaughlin, *Rhodesian War*, 151–54. Martin and Johnson, who were well informed about guerrilla activity, estimate that there were 13,000 ZANU in Rhodesia in 1978. This is higher than most estimates. Martin and Johnson, *Struggle*, 292.

5. CIA, "The Soviet Role in Southern Africa: Key Judgments," 30 May 1977, CIA-rr. See Gleijeses, *Visions*, 59–63.

6. DCI, Interagency Intelligence Memorandum, "South Africa's Nuclear Options and Decisionmaking Structures," Jul 1978, CWIHP-va.

7. Richardson to ZB, 15 Feb 1978, enclosed in ZB to Carter, "Relations with Congress on Rhodesia," [16 Feb 1978,] NSA-staff /119-25, CL; and Albright to ZB and Aaron, 11 Mar 1978, NSA-congress/1, CL.

8. Memcon (Genscher, Vance, de Guiringaud, Owen), 29 May 1978, doc. 166, *AAPD 1978*, 825–26; and Owen, Cabinet Meeting, 29 Jun 1978, CAB/128/64/4, NA-UK.

9. Thatcher, "Business of the House," 29 Jun 1978, *Parliamentary Debates*, Commons, 5th ser., vol. 952, col. 1574.

10. Memcon (Owen, Chirau, Ndiweni), 4 Aug 1978, ZUPO visit to London, Smith Inventory 22, Smith Papers.

11. Moore to Carter, 3 Apr 1978, Handwriting/79, CL.

12. Ichord, *CR-House*, 6 Mar 1978, 5719–20; S. Con. Res. 69, *CR-Senate*, 7 Mar 1978, 5817; and *LAT*, 19 Mar 1978, F2. The resolution was referred to the Senate Foreign Relations Committee and did not emerge from it.

13. Moore to Carter, 3 Apr 1978, Handwriting/79, CL. In 1975, the Senate decreased the number required for a supermajority from two-thirds (67) to three-fifths (60).

14. US Senate, "Rhodesian Settlement?" CD59, 8.

15. *CR-Senate*, 28 Jun 1978, 19211, 19213, 19212.

16. Ibid., 19220.

17. Ibid., 19221 (Clark); and 19223 (McGovern).

18. Ibid., 19223.

19. *WP*, 11 Jul 1978, edit 10. For the vote, *CR-Senate*, 28 Jun 1978, 19224.

20. See *CR-Senate*, 28 Jun 1978, 19224. Lloyd Bentsen of Texas was the only southern Democrat to vote against the amendment.

21. Vance, *Hard Choices*, 287; International Organizations to ZB, 23 Jun 1978, NLC-24-53-7-9-1; ZB to Carter, 30 Jun 1978, NLC-1-6-7-26-9; [identifying marks removed; appears to be British High Commissioner in Zambia to FCO, 1 Jul 1978], Lake/1, NA; and Moose to Vance, 2 Jul 1978, Lake/1, NA. See Thornton to ZB, 30 Jun 1978, NLC-24-100-1-5-8.

22. ZB, WR, 7 Jul 1978, Brzezinski/41, CL.

23. "Bonn Summit: Heads of Government Dinner . . . on 16 July," 17 Jul 1978, Thatcher Papers.

24. Memcon (Smith, Fourie, Gaylard), 31 Jul 1978, records of meetings, box 4/002(m), Smith Papers.

25. Ibid.; "Rhodesia: Recent History," in Wall to Renwick, 2 May 1979, FCO 36/ 2493, NA-UK; author's interview with Owen; and Memcon (Owen, Sithole), 20–23 Feb 1978, Crane Collection, Hoover, quoted in Stedman, *Peacemaking*, 144.

26. Author's interview with Owen.

27. Memcon (Owen, Chirau, Ndiweni), 4 Aug 1978, ZUPO visit to London, Smith Inventory 22, Smith Papers. Also Memcon (Nkomo, Chirau, Ndiweni, Garba), 3 Aug 1978, ibid.

28. Garthoff, *Détente*, 674–77, 810.
29. Q & A with Western European and Japanese Reporters, 11 Jul 1978, APP. Shcharansky was sentenced on July 14, 1978, to thirteen years in prison and labor camp. After his release in 1986, he emigrated to Israel, where he became a politician, writer, and activist known as Natan Sharansky.
30. Vanden Heuvel, Geneva 10899, 15 Jul 1978, FOIA (a transcript of the unedited interview in English).
31. *NYT*, 13 Jul 1978, 1; *NYT*, 16 Jul 1978, 1; and *NYT*, 14 Jul 1978, 1. See *Le Matin* (Paris), 12 July 1978, 9. Also *WP*, 15 Aug 1979, 1; and Vance on *Issues and Answers*, 23 Jul 1978, DOS *Bulletin*, Sep 1978, 16.
32. Harry Byrd, *CR-Senate*, 13 Jul 1978, 20735.
33. Quoted in Link, *Righteous*, 102; and *NYT*, 21 Sep 1927, 27. Also Link, *Righteous*, 207; and Harrison, "Jimmy Carter."
34. Black and Black, *Rise*, 103–5, quotation 103.
35. *Roll Call*, 27 Apr 1978, 1.
36. Christopher, State 177401 (Harrop to Moose), 13 Jul 1978, FOIA; and Moore to Carter, 15 Jul 1978, NLC-128-6-12-2-8. See Lanpher to Bennet, 13 Jul 1978, Beckel/223, CL; Christopher, ER, 13 Jul 1978, NLC-133-7-1-9-6; and Moore to ZB, [17 Jul 1978,] NSA-congress/3, CL. The American Committee on Africa (ACOA) also lobbied members of Congress. See, e.g., Houser (Executive Director, ACOA) to Church, 28 Mar 1978, Senate Foreign Relations Committee: Africa, Church Papers/23.
37. DOS press briefing, 17 Jul 1978, in Talking Points: President's Wednesday Breakfast: Helms Amendment, 18 Jul 1978, Lake/4, NA.
38. Helms, *CR-Senate*, 19 Jul 1978, 21680; and Moore to ZB, [17 Jul 1978,] NSA-congress/3, CL.
39. Moore to ZB, [17 Jul 1978,] NSA-congress/3, CL. Also Lake to Christopher, 18 Jul 1978, Lake/4, NA.
40. Carter's April 1977 order to shutter the Information Office had been debated and delayed. See ZB to Interagency Group, in Thornton to ZB, 27 Apr 1977, NSA-staff/119, CL; ZB to Lipshutz (draft) in Richardson to ZB, 20 Dec 1977, NSA-staff/119, CL; and Memcon (Lake, Carbaugh, Lanpher), 13 Nov 1978, Lake Papers/4, NA. UNSC resolution 409 (1977) required the closing of the Office: UNSC resolution 409, *Southern Rhodesia*, S/RES/409 (27 May 1977), http://undocs.org/S/RES/409(1977).
41. Young, at the Australian National Press Club, Canberra, *Rhodesian Herald* (Salisbury), 9 May 1979, 3.
42. Kissinger quoted in *Economist*, 5 Aug 1978, 25; Muzorewa, Speech at Georgetown University, in *CR-Senate*, 19 Jul 1978, 21682–83; AP, *Lewiston Evening Journal* (Maine), 17 Jul 1978, 21; and *Sarasota Herald Tribune* (Florida), 20 Jul 1978, 6. For the meeting with Vance: Memcon (Vance, Garba), 26 Jul 1978, in Young, USUN 3027, 27 Jul 1978, FOIA; and Christopher to Carter, 26 Jul 1978, NLC-128-13-10-17-6.
43. Vance, ER, 21 Jul 1978, NLC-133-7-1-15-9; Vance and Owen, Press Conference, 20 Jul 1978, DOS *Bulletin*, Sep 1978, 17–18; and Vance on *Issues and Answers*, 23 Jul 1978, DOS *Bulletin*, Sep 1978, 13–16.
44. See Baker, 19 Jul 1978, Lake/4, NA; Christopher to Carter, 20 Jul 1978, NLC-128-13-10-12-1; Christopher, ER, 20 Jul 1978, NLC-7-20-5-16-0; Christopher, State 190604, 28 Jul 1978, FOIA; author's interview with Moose (2001); and Rowland Evans and Robert Novak, *Sarasota Herald Tribune*, 20 Jul 1978, 6.

45. Smith to Mondale, 24 Jul 1978, Beckel/223, CL; and Christopher to Carter, 20 Jul 1978, NLC-128-13-10-12-1.

46. Moore to Carter, 22 Jul 1978, NLC-128-6-12-3-7 (emphasis in original). See Christopher, ER, 14 Jul 1978, NLC-7-20-5-11-5.

47. *WSJ*, 17 Jul 1978, edit 10; *WP*, 11 Jul 1978, edit 10; and *NYT*, 24 Jul 1978, edit 16. Also *CT*, 20 Jul 1978, edit B2; and *CSM*, 24 Jul 1978, edit E3.

48. *CR-Senate*, 26 Jul 1978, 22745, 22747; and *CQ Weekly*, 29 Jul 1978, 1920. For full debate, *CR-Senate*, 26 Jul 1978, 22743–53.

49. Ibid., 22748.

50. Ibid., 22751 (Clark); and 22753 (Case). See ibid., 22745 (Javits).

51. Only thirty-nine senators voted to table the amendment; this group included eleven Democrats, all but one of whom was from the South.

52. Moore to Carter, 26 Jul 1978, Handwriting/96, CL.

53. *CR-Senate*, 26 Jul 1978, 22756.

54. DOS Statement, 26 Jul 1978, DOS *Bulletin*, Sep 1978, 18.

55. Christopher, State 190604, 28 Jul 1978, FOIA. See "Reclaiming Heritage: A Historical Profile of the NAACP and Africa," Mar 1977, NAACP VI/B4, LOC. Also "NAACP Task Force on Africa Report," *Crisis*, Apr 1978, 117–22; *CSM*, 10 Jul 1978, 5; "NAACP 70th Annual Convention Resolutions," NAACP V/2528, LOC; and "The 70th NAACP Annual Convention," *Crisis*, Oct 1979, 323–32.

56. See, e.g., Butler, Statement to House Subcommittee on Africa, 7 Sep 1978, NAACP V/2522, LOC; "Briefing on Zimbabwe-Rhodesian Sanctions," in Simmons to Hooks, 8 Jun 1979, ibid.; Margaret Wilson and Benjamin Hooks, "A Mockery of Rights in Rhodesia," *WP*, 22 Jun 1979, 19; and "NAACP Position on Rhodesian Sanctions," *Crisis* (October 1979): 352–54.

57. See Metz, "Anti-Apartheid Movement," esp. 337–45.

58. Author's interview with Richardson. For the group's early interest in Rhodesia, see: "First Press Statement," 10 Dec 1977, folder: "Birth of a Black Lobby," TransAfrica archive; "Statement to Senate," in Robinson to Church, 17 Jul 1978, Senate Foreign Relations Committee: Africa, Church Papers/23; *WP*, 23 Jul 1978, 1; *Economist*, 5 Aug 1978, 26; and *TransAfrica: News Report*, Fall 1978. Also Robinson, *Defending*, 96–98, 105–11; Pacific News Service, "New Black Lobby Pressures Carter on Africa," [rec'd Jul 3] 1978, WOA Yale, 45-29; and Christopher, State 245209, 27 Sep 1978, FOIA.

59. Price, "Real Democrats," 127; and CODEL (Diggs et al.), "The African-American Manifesto on Southern Africa," 25 Sep 1976, Diggs Papers/ 81. On the formation of the CBC: Adair, "Black Legislative Influence," 20–48. On the CBC and South Africa in 1977–1978: Metz, "Anti-Apartheid," 382, 405–59.

60. Author's interview with Richardson. In March 1978, Diggs was indicted and in October he was found guilty; he relinquished his committee chairmanships and his right to vote in the House for the remainder of the session; a month later, he won reelection overwhelmingly. On November 20, 1978, he was sentenced to three years in prison but in January 1979 he took his seat in the 96th Congress. He lost his bid to retain the chair of Africa subcommittee, and after a trial in the House (spearheaded by Newt Gingrich [R-GA]), he admitted guilt, apologized, was censured, resigned, and went to prison. See Robinson, *Defending*, 94–95; and Erhagbe, "Ideas," 369–72.

61. *CR-House*, 2 Aug 1978, 23938. For full debate: ibid., 23937–54.

62. Ibid., 23947.

63. Ibid., 23939.

64. Ibid., 23946.

65. *WP*, 3 Aug 1978, 1; and *WP*, 4 Aug 1978, edit 12. For the tally, *CR-House*, 2 Aug 1978, 23954.

66. Vance to Carter, 3 Aug 1978, Plains/39, CL; and Christopher to Carter, 8 Aug 1978 in Situation Room to Clough (for President), 9 Aug 1978, DDRS.

67. The senators on the committee were Howard Baker (R-TN), Joe Biden (D-DE), Clifford Case (R-NJ), Frank Church (D-ID), Dick Clark (D-IA), George McGovern (D-SD), John Sparkman (D-AL), and Charles Percy (R-IL). The representatives were Jonathan Bingham (D-NY), William Broomfield (R-MI), Dante Fascell (D-FL), Paul Findley (R-IL), Lee Hamilton (D-IN), Benjamin Rosenthal (D-NY), Steve Solarz (D-NY), Gerry Studds (D-MA), Larry Winn (R-KS), Lester Wolff (D-NY), and Clement Zablocki (D-WI).

68. US Senate, Committee on Foreign Relations and US House Committee on International Relations, "Conference: Senate 3075 and House Amendment Thereto," 10 Aug 1978, CD68, 39–52.

69. Ibid.; and Vance to Carter, 10 Aug 1978, DDRS.

70. See *CR-House*, 12 Sep 1978, 28997–29001.

71. ZB, WR, 4 Aug 1978, Brzezinski/41, CL; and *Economist*, 5 Aug 1978, 26.

72. On Carter's relations with Congress, see *CQ Weekly*, 26 Feb 1977, 360–63; *1977 CQ Almanac*, 21B–27B; *Roll Call*, 26 Jan 1978, 6; *1978 CQ Almanac*, 22C–28C; *1979 CQ Almanac*, 17C–23C; *1980 CQ Almanac*, 17C–23C; and Miller Center of Public Affairs, University of Virginia, "Jimmy Carter: Life in Brief," accessed July 21, 2015, http://millercenter.org/president/biography/carter-life-in-brief. Also author's interviews with Moose (2001), Lake, and McHenry.

73. Moore to Carter, 12 Aug 1978, NLC-128-6-12-6-4.

74. Information Section of Rhodesian Ministry of Foreign Affairs, "Background Briefing: The Transitional Government and the American Conditions for the Lifting of Sanctions against Rhodesia," 18 Aug 1978, personal file, Inventory 22, Smith Papers; and Brief by Flower to meeting of Executive Council, Ministerial Council, and Joint Operations Command, 3 Aug 1978 in Flower, *Serving Secretly*, 207–8.

75. Vance, *Hard Choices*, 291; and Thornton to ZB, 16 Aug 1978, NLC-24-100-2-3-9. See Memcon (Nkomo, Chirau, Ndiweni, Garba), 3 Aug 1978, ZUPO visit to London, Smith Inventory 22, Smith Papers.

76. Gaylard to ADR (Hawkins), C327, 18 Sep 1978, ADR/12, box 4/006(m), Smith Papers. I did not find a transcript of the meeting in the Smith papers or in the British, US, or South African archives.

77. Memcon (Schmidt, Nkomo), 29 Jun 1978, doc. 204, *AAPD 1978*, 204; and "The Role of Field Marshal Lord Carver . . . as Resident Commissioner Designate for Rhodesia," 20 Dec 1978, in Carver to Owen, 20 Dec 1978, FCO 73/319, NA-UK. See Memcon (Nkomo, Chirau, Ndiweni, Garba), 3 Aug 1978, ZUPO visit to London, Smith Inventory 22, Smith Papers.

78. Vance to Carter, 1 Sep 1978, Plains/39, CL. See "Rhodesia: Recent History," in Wall to Renwick, 2 May 1979, FCO 36/2493, NA-UK; and author's interview with DePree.

79. Author's interview with Owen. See [identifying marks removed; appears to be British High Commissioner in Zambia to FCO, 1 Jul 1978], Lake Papers/1, NA.

80. ADR (Hawkins) to Gaylard, 8 Sep 1978, C311, ADR/12, box 4/006(m), Smith Papers, quoting Low; Mugabe, "Report to the Catholic Commission on Peace and Justice," 1974, quoted in Stedman, *Peacemaking*, 53; and BBC "Focus on Africa," 21 Jan 1976, quoted in Martin and Johnson, *Struggle*, 210. See Sellström, *Sweden*, 182; Martin and Johnson, *Chitepo*; and White, *Assassination*.

81. Author's interview with DePree; and DePree, Maputo 1197 and 1198, 15 Sep 1978, FOIA.

82. Gaylard to ADR, 7 Sep 1978, ADR/12, box 4/006(m), Smith Papers; and Clingerman, Lusaka 3101, 5 Sep 1978, Incoming FOIA/6, NSA-DC.

83. Spain, Dar 3769, 4 Sep 1978, FOIA; Clingerman, Lusaka 3101, 5 Sep 1978, Incoming FOIA/6, NSA-DC; Moose and Bowdler (INR) to Vance, 6 Sep 1978, NLC-6-53-7-1-9; and Gaylard to ADR, 7 Sep 1978, ADR/12, box 4/006(m), Smith Papers.

84. Moose and Bowdler (INR) to Vance, 6 Sep 1978, NLC-6-53-7-1-9.

85. *CSM*, 7 Sep 1978, edit E1. See Moorcraft and McLaughlin, *Rhodesian War*, 154.

86. Smith to Vorster in Gaylard to ADR (Hawkins), 7 Sep 1978, ADR/12, box 4/006(m), Smith Papers.

87. See Vance, ER, 21 Mar 1979, NLC-7-21-5-9-7; Lulat, *United States Relations*, 236–37; O'Meara, *Forty Lost Years*, 229–49; Rhoodie, *Real Information Scandal*, esp. 156–203 for projects in the United States; Rhoodie, *PW Botha*, 48–78; and Rees and Day, *Muldergate*.

88. Geoffrey Hodgson, *Sun* (Baltimore), 30 Sep 1978, 15 (coining the term); *WP*, 8 Sep 1978, 15 quoting London *Times*; and Stewart, quoted in Conservative Research Department, "The Bingham Report," 28 Sep 1978, in Ridley to Leader's Consultative Committee, 29 Sep 1978, Thatcher Papers.

89. Christopher, State 235991, 16 Sep 1978, FOIA. See Smith to Vorster in Gaylard to ADR, 7 Sep 1978, ADR/12, box 4/006(m), Smith Papers; and Moose and Lake to Vance, Rhodesia Negotiations, in Lake and Moose to Newsom, 22 Sep 1978, Lake/4, NA.

90. Christopher to Carter, 27 Sep 1978, Plains/39, CL; Cabinet, 21 Sep 1978, CAB/128/64/12, NA-UK; and Marginalia on Christopher, ER, 19 Sep 1978, NLC-7-20-7-12-2. See Tarnoff to ZB, 27 Jul 1978, NSA-staff/118, CL; DOS, "Zambia: Economic and Military Needs and US Assistance," [Jul 1978,] NLC-6-88-1-14-3; and Vance, ER, 25 Oct 1978, NLC-133-7-2-14-9. On US aid to Kaunda: Low, Lusaka 3981 and 3982, 15 Nov 1978, NLC-24-98-2-14-0.

91. Christopher to Carter, 3 Aug 1978, Plains/39, CL; and "Zambia," 28 Sep 1978, CAB 128/64/13, NA-UK. See Callaghan to Cabinet, "Zambia," 26 Sep 1978, CAB 129/203/18, NA-UK. Also Brewster, London 17352, 24 Oct 1978, NLC-16-25-1-31-2. Kaunda also asked Sadat for arms, but Sadat was unable to help. See Eilts, Cairo 23480, 24 Oct 1978, NLC-16-55-1-26-5.

92. Jefe Dirección Inteligencia Militar EMG to Raúl Castro, 28 Sep 1978, Gleijeses Papers. See Gleijeses, *Visions*, 86–87.

93. "DR Item," 30 Oct 1978, NLC-133-216-4-26-2. See Gleijeses, *Visions*, 119–24; and LeoGrande and Kornbluh, *Back Channel*, 175–94.

94. DOS, "Soviet/Cuban Activities in Africa," backgrounder for NATO Summit, 30–31 May 1978, NLC-133-179-3-19-3. See CIA National Foreign Assessment Center, Africa Review, 27 Oct 1978, CREST. Also Situation Room to ZB, 2 Aug 1978, NLC-1-7-4-26-1; North/South to ZB, 11 Aug 1978, NLC-24-100-2-1-1; North/South

to ZB, 28 Jul 1978, NLC-24-100-1-13-9; Dirección Inteligencia Militar EMG to Colomé, 20 Oct 1978, Gleijeses Papers; and Unsigned, "Cuba's Activities in Latin America, the Caribbean, Africa, and the Middle East," [Apr 1979,] NLC-23-13-6-7-9.

95. INR Analysis, 18 Sep 1978, NLC-SAFE 17 B-13-71-10-1; and Jackson, 30 Nov 1978, Havana 468, FCO 36/2217, NA-UK. Also: Rhodesia Paper for NSC, attached to Moose and Lake to Vance, 5 Oct 1978, Lake/5, NA.

96. *NYT* wire, 23 Sep 1978. Also: *CSM*, 15 Sep 1978, 9.

97. CIA Office of Regional and Political Analysis, Africa, 20 Sep 1978, CREST. ZAPU had 12,000 trained men plus 10,000 in training, with an additional 14,000 available; ZANU had 10,000 trained, 3,000 in training, and 10,000 available. See Moorcraft and McLaughlin, *Rhodesian War*, 154–56; and Martin and Johnson, *Struggle*, 296–99.

98. Richardson to Thornton, 22 Sep 1978, NSA Staff/119-25; UNSC S/RES/253 (29 May 1968); and *Afro-American* (Baltimore), 14 Oct 1978, 1.

99. North/South to ZB, 21 Jul 1978, NLC-10-13-6-15-4 (emphasis in original); Hatch, *CR-Senate*, 3 Oct 1978, 33210; and DOS press briefing, 17 Jul 1978, Lake/4, NA. Also Harrop to Acting Secretary, 18 Jul 1978, Lake/4, NA.

100. Meg Greenfield, *WP*, 14 Dec 1977, 15; and Young, USUN 4335, 19 Oct 1978, FOIA. See Hatcher (Chair, TransAfrica) to Lake, 21 Sep 1978, Lake/9, NA; Hatcher and Robinson to Carter, 22 Sep 1978, Martin/92, CL; Goode (Director, National Conference of Black Lawyers) to Carter, 26 Sep 1978, ibid.; Robinson (for TransAfrica Board) to Carter, 3 Oct 1978, ibid.; Ron Brown (Urban League), *WP*, 11 Oct 1978, 24; and Benjamin Hooks, *Skanner* (Portland, OR), 26 Oct 1978, 3.

101. *WP*, 14 Dec 1977, 15; Meg Greenfield, *WP*, 14 Dec 1977, 15; and Cabinet Meeting minutes, 1 Aug 1977, Staff Secretary/41, CL. Also Mitchell to Watson, 25 Aug 1977, Name/Young, CL; "CBC Dinner," 24 Sep 1977, Name/CBC, CL; and *Bilalian News* (Detroit), 17 Oct 1977, 2.

102. Author's interview with Young.

103. Moore, Meeting with Rep. Parren Mitchell, 20 Sep 1978, Martin/22, CL. See Dumbrell, *Carter Presidency*, 100–2.

104. Moore, Meeting with CBC, 25 Sep 1978, Martin/22, CL; and ABC *Evening News*, 26 Sep 1978, VNA. Also NBC and CBS, *Evening News*, 26 Sep 1978, VNA; and *New York Amsterdam News*, 30 Sep 1978, 1.

105. Review of the Carter Administration by CBC, 29 Sep 1978, Martin/22, CL. See research.stlouisfed.org.

106. *WP*, 2 Oct 1978, B1. Also *CT*, 6 Oct 1978, 4:3.

107. Baker, *CR-Senate*, 2 Oct 1978, 33001; Hayakawa, *NYT* wire, 3 Oct 1978, 6; and *WS*, 3 Oct 1978, edit 10. Also Baker, *CR-Senate*, 4 Oct 1978, 33333; Dole, *CR-Senate*, 4 Oct 1978, 33430; and *WP*, 4 Oct 1978, edit 14.

108. Christopher, State 249886, 2 Oct 1978, FOIA. See Richardson to Thornton, 22 Sep 1978, NLC-24-108-3-4-8; Christopher to Carter, 27 Sep 1978, Plains/39, CL; and Carter and Callaghan to Nyerere, in Christopher, State 249884, 2 Oct 1978, FOIA.

109. Memcon (Vance, Moose, Mkapa), 3 Oct 1978, FOIA. For Machel: Memcon (Vance, Mwala), 4 Oct 1978, FOIA. See ADR to Gaylard, C371, 5 Oct. 1978, ADR v. 12, 4/006(m), Smith Papers.

110. Memcon (Vance, Mwala), 4 Oct 1978, FOIA. See *WP*, 9 Oct 1978, 23.

111. Announcement, 4 Oct 1978, DOS *Bulletin*, Nov 1978, 13.

112. *WP*, 8 Oct 1978, edit C6. Also *WSJ*, 6 Oct 1978, edit 20; and *CT*, 8 Oct 1978, edit B4. The black press was opposed: *Sun Reporter* (San Francisco), 5 Oct 1978, 7; and *Philadelphia Tribune*, 6 Oct 1978, 1.

113. *LAT*, 8 Oct 1978, 14; *WP*, 15 Oct 1978, 22; and *LAT*, 9 Oct 1978, 5. For a detailed exposition of Smith's argument, see Rhodesian Ministry of Foreign Affairs, "Background Briefing: The Transitional Government and the American Conditions for the Lifting of Sanctions against Rhodesia," 18 Aug 1978, personal file, Smith 22, Smith Papers. Smith was in the United States from October 7 to 20, 1978.

114. Memcon (Vance, Jay, Smith, Sithole), 9 Oct 1978, in Christopher, State 261346, 14 Oct 1978 in Mokoena, *Zimbabwe*; and Memcon (Smith, Vance), 10 [*sic*] Oct 1978, records of meetings, box 4/002(m), Smith Papers. Also "Ian Smith and the Kissinger Five Points," in Tarnoff to ZB, 9 Oct 1978, Lake/4, NA; and Vance, ER, 9 Oct 1978, NLC-7-20-8-7-7.

115. *CQ Weekly*, 14 Oct 1978, 2932; and *NYT* wire, 10 Oct 1978. Also Joint US-UK Statement, 9 Oct 1978, DOS *Bulletin*, Nov 1978, 13.

116. See *CSM*, 11 Oct 1978, edit 24; *WP*, 14 Oct 1978, edit 16; and Young, USUN 4335, 19 Oct 1978, FOIA.

117. *WP*, 15 Oct 1978, 22. See *NYT* wire, 20 Sep 1978; *WP*, 11 Oct 1978, B4; *NYT* wire, 15 Oct 1978; and ADR (Hawkins) to Gaylard, C406, 23 Oct 1978, ADR/12, box 4/006(m), Smith Papers.

118. See Thornton to ZB, 20 Oct 1978, NLC-24-100-2-12-9; Martin and Johnson, *Struggle*, 296–97; and Petter-Bowyer, *Winds*, 474–79.

119. See *NYT* wire, 21 Oct 1978; Hernández to Colomé, 26 Oct 1978, Gleijeses Papers; and Hernández to Colomé, 31 Dec 1978, ibid.

120. *NYT* wire, 22 Oct 1978 ("happy"); *Guardian*, 21 Oct 1978, 1 ("bigger"); and Smith to Jackson, 30 Oct 1978, personal file, Smith 22, Smith Papers. See Reid-Daly, *Selous Scouts*, 328–30.

121. Author's interview with Moose (2002).

122. "Notes of a Meeting held at the State Department, Washington, at 9:30 A.M. on Friday, 20th October 1978," records of meetings, box 4/002(m), Smith Papers ("disturbed"); Newsom to Carter, 20 Oct 1978, NSA-staff /119-25, CL ("objection"); and author's interview with Newsom. Also BZ to Carter, 25 Sep 1978, NLC-1-7-9-27-5; Moose and Lake to Newsom, 19 Oct 1978, Lake/4, NA; Memcon (Newsom, Smith), 20 Oct 1978, records of meetings, box 4/002(m), Smith Papers; and Joint US-UK Statement, 20 Oct 1978, DOS *Bulletin*, December 1978, 25.

123. *Guardian* (London), 20 Oct 1978, 1. See Low, Lusaka 3981, 15 Nov 1978, NLC-24-98-2-14-0.

124. Memcon (Vance, Mwala), 4 Oct 1978, FOIA.

Chapter 11

1. Thornton to ZB, 16 Aug 1978, NLC-24-100-2-3-9; and Jay to Owen, 4 Nov 1978, FCO 36/2206, NA-UK.

2. [DOS,] "Soviet/Cuban Activities in Africa," backgrounder for NATO Summit, 30–31 May 1978, NLC-133-179-3-19-3. For number of Cuban soldiers: Gleijeses, *Visions*, 45 (Ethiopia); 107 (Angola: the number of Cuban troops started to increase in May 1978 after Shaba 2; by January 1979, there were 23,000; therefore 20,000 in mid-1978 is a reasonable estimate); 535 n. 25 (Congo-Brazzaville).

3. PRM 36 Response: "Soviet/Cuban Presence in Africa," 18 Aug 1978, DDRS; and Experts' Committee, "Situation in Sub-Saharan Africa," in Christopher, State 230730, 12 Sep 1978, FOIA.

4. PRM 36 Response: "Soviet/Cuban Presence in Africa," 18 Aug 1978, DDRS. Also "The Cuban-Soviet Relationship," [Jun 1978,] NLC-12-19-1-9-8.

5. "Summary of Draft Responses to PRM-36," in Harrop and Lake to Vance, 12 Jun 1978, Lake/17, NA. Also Vance, State 149321, 13 Jun 1978, FOIA.

6. Dobrynin to Gromyko, 11 Jul 1978, Vertical: USSR-US/117, NSA-DC.

7. Tarnoff to ZB, 2 Aug 1978, DDRS; and "Summary of Draft Responses to PRM-36," in Harrop and Lake to Vance, 12 Jun 1978, Lake/17, NA. See Gleijeses, *Visions*, 119–26; Schoultz, *Infernal*, 304–28; and LeoGrande and Kornbluh, *Back Channel*, 168–96.

8. Moose and Walker to Vance, 21 Aug 1978, Lake/17, NA.

9. See Gleijeses, *Visions*, 92–103, 146–58; and Helman, Harrop and Katz to Vance, 5 Oct 1978, Lake/4, NA.

10. CIA, "Angola Cuba: Some Strains but No New Developments," 9 Apr 1978, CREST. See Thornton to ZB, 13 Apr 1977, DDRS; and Gleijeses, *Visions*, 92–103, 146–58.

11. See ZB, WR, 6 Oct 1978, Brzezinski/41, CL.

12. ZB marginalia on Thornton to ZB, 8 Nov 1978, NSA-country/3, CL. See Thornton to ZB, 18 Sep 1978, NLC-24-110-3-6-4.

13. Jay, Washington 5053, 22 Dec 1978, FCO 36/2206; and ZB, WR, 6 Oct 1978, Brzezinski/41, CL.

14. Moose and Lake to Vance, 5 Oct 1978, Lake/5, NA (emphasis added). See "National Security Planning Program: July 1, 1978–January 1, 1979," 11 Jun 1978, NLC-133-215-8-23-2.

15. NSC Meeting: Minutes, 6 Oct 1978, FOIA. See Agenda: NSC Meeting on Africa, 6 Oct 1978, NLC-133-216-4-12-7; and Brzezinski, *Power*, 139–42.

16. NSC Meeting: Minutes, 6 Oct 1978, FOIA.

17. Memcon (Carter, Gromyko), 30 Sep 1978, *FRUS, 1977–1980, v. 6: Soviet Union*, doc. 150.

18. Memcon (Carter, Obasanjo), 1 Apr 1978, NLC-24-107-5-3-8.

19. NSC Meeting: Minutes, 6 Oct 1978, FOIA.

20. Vance to Carter, 2 Sep 1978, Plains/39, CL.

21. Bowdler (INR) to Vance, 8 Sep 1978, Lake/16, NA; Edmondson, FD, 5 Apr 1988; and *CSM*, 23 Oct 1978, 1. On Owen: Moose and Lake to Vance, "Rhodesia Negotiations," in Lake and Moose to Newsom, 22 Sep 1978, Lake/4, NA. On PW Botha: O'Meara, *Forty Lost Years*, 223–28, 253–69; and Pottinger, *Imperial Presidency*, esp. 16–18, 121–24, 200–210.

22. See South African Military Intelligence,"Rhodesië: Militêre Bedreiging en Veiligheidsmagte," 23 Apr 1976, 1/156/1, v82, DFA, SA; Brief by Flower to meeting of Executive Council, Ministerial Council, and Joint Operations Command, 3 Aug 1978 in Flower, *Serving Secretly*, 208; Roger Riddell, "What Economic Road?" *Africa Report*, May/Jun 1978, 51–56; *CSM*, 26 Jul 1978, 4; "The Role of Field Marshal Lord Carver," 20 Dec 1978, in Carver to Owen, 20 Dec. 1978, FCO 73/319, NA-UK; INR (Mark), "Rhodesia: The Next Three Months," 1 Feb 1979, NLC-133-80-7-1-7; Anglin, "Zimbabwe," 671–72; Brownell, "Hole"; Wilkinson, "Impact," 115–18; and Moorcraft and McLaughlin, *Rhodesian War*, 151–56. For a chart of net immigration:

Stedman, *Peacemaking*, 94. For December flight: CIA Foreign Assessment Center, "Rhodesia: Looking Beyond the April Election," 2 Apr 1979, CREST. On the collapse of the economy: Callinicos, *After Zimbabwe*, 48–49.

23. *NYT*, 20 Jul 1978, 10; *CSM*, 30 Oct 1978, 8; and *NYT*, 17 Nov 1978, 8. See Funk to ZB, 26 Mar 1979, Funk/119, CL.

24. Parmenter (NIO for Africa) to DCI, "Warning Report: Sub-Saharan Africa," 20 Oct 1978, CREST.

25. *WP*, 5 Nov 1978, 1.

26. ZB, WR, 4 Aug 1978, Brzezinski/41, CL. In July 1978, 42 percent thought that the United States was "militarily weaker" than the Soviet Union. For an analysis of the conservative turn based on Americans for Democratic Action scores: *CQ Weekly*, 5 Feb 1977, 215–16; and *NYT*, 9 Nov 1978, 27. Also *Roll Call*, 21 Dec 1978, 4; *Roll Call*, 18 Jan 1979, 1; and Berman, *America's Right Turn*, 50–52.

27. ZB, WR, 9 Nov 1978, Brzezinski/41, CL.

28. See *Roll Call*, 9 Nov 1978, 1; Fenno, *Senators*, 110–23; and Smith, "Moving Right," 10–13.

29. *WP*, 27 Oct 1978, 1; Fenno, *Senators*, 112; and *WP*, 27 Oct 1978, 1.

30. *WSJ*, 8 Feb 1979, 18.

31. *WP*, 26 May 1978, 2; *WSJ*, 30 Oct 1978, 24; *CSM*, 13 Oct 1978, 23; *WP*, 9 Nov 1978, 3; and *WP*, 26 May 1978, 2. Also *Roll Call*, 23 Nov 1978, 1; and author's interview with Clark.

32. *NYT*, 9 Nov 1978, 27; and Memcon (Lake, Carbaugh, Lanpher), 13 Nov 1978, Lake/4, NA.

33. Moore to Carter, 3 Apr 1978, Handwriting/79, CL.

34. *WSJ*, 30 Oct 1978, 24.

35. Ibid.; Crowe to Barder, 10 Nov 1978, FCO 36/2206, NA-UK; Sanford Ungar, "South Africa's Lobbyists," *NYT Magazine*, 13 Oct 1985, 30; *NYT*, 22 Mar 1979, 12; and Rhoodie, *Real Information Scandal*, 173. See "Buying Some Friends," *Newsweek*, 2 Apr 1979, 41; and Rhoodie, *Real Information Scandal*, 173–74, 178.

36. Jay to Owen, 4 Nov 1978, FCO 36/2206, NA-UK.

37. Thornton to ZB, 1 Nov 1978, NSA-staff/119, CL.

38. See Brewster, London 19036, 17 Nov 1978, NLC-16-25-2-38-4.

39. CIA Foreign Assessment Center, *Africa Review*, 27 Oct 1978, CREST.

40. Low, Lusaka 3981, 15 Nov 1978, NLC-24-98-2-14-0; DePree, Maputo 1568, 5 Dec 1978, [US] FCO 36/2206, NA-UK; Australian Intelligence Service, "Rhodesia: Prospects for a Settlement," 19 Jul 1979, A1838 190-2-1/65, NA-AUS; and Edmondson (from Low), Pretoria 2498, 24 Mar 1979, [US], NA-UK. Also CIA Foreign Assessment Center, Africa Review, 23 Mar 1979, CREST.

41. CIA Foreign Assessment Center, *Africa Review*, 27 Oct 1978, CREST.

42. Ilichev, "Report on Soviet Delegation to Tanzania, Zambia, Mozambique and Angola," 6 Feb 1978, CWIHP-va. See Situation Room to ZB, 27 Jul 1979, NLC-1-11-6-19-2; CIA, "Soviet, Cuban and East German Interventionist Activities, 1977–1979," in Turner to ZB, 15 Aug 1979, NLC-24-13-7-1-3; and Martin and Johnson, *Struggle*, 316–17. On Chinese ties to ZANU: Taylor, *China and Africa*, 106–14. On US fears of Soviet aid to ZANU: Vance, 9 Feb 1979, State 34331, FOIA; and DCI, PRC Briefing: "Rhodesia," 4 Apr 1979, CREST. See Gleijeses, *Visions*, 139–45; and Kempton, *Soviet Strategy*, 100–104.

43. Gleijeses, *Visions*, 144 (quoting Castro). See Situation Room to ZB, 22 Nov 1978, NLC-1-8-6-27-7.

44. DOS suggestions for "Terms of Reference for Hughes-Low Mission" in Christopher, State 297991, 25 Nov 1978, FOIA. See Carter to Nyerere (draft) in ZB to Carter, 9 Jun 1978, NLC-133-215-8-18-8; and Memcon (Owen, McGovern), 14 Dec 1978, FCO 36/2233, NA-UK.

45. DePree, Maputo 1567, 5 Dec 1978, [US] FCO 36/2206, NA-UK; Lewen, Maputo 410, 5 Dec 1978, ibid.; and Allinson, Lusaka 960, 5 Dec 1978, [US], ibid.

46. Thornton to ZB, 1 Nov 1978, NSA-staff/119, CL; author's interview with Graham; and Wall to Owen, 10 Nov 1978, FCO 73/318, NA-UK.

47. Thornton to ZB, 24 Nov 1978, NLC-24-98-2-8-7; Thornton [quoting DOS] to ZB, 16 Nov 1978, NSA-staff/119, CL; and ZB, WR, 17 Nov 1978, Brzezinski/41, CL, with Carter's marginalia. See Brewster, London 19036, 17 Nov 1978, NLC-16-25-2-38-4.

48. Stowe to Wall, 20 Nov 1978, FCO 36/2233, NA-UK. See FCO to Jay, [27 Nov 1978,] FCO 36/2233, NA-UK; and Hutchinson to ZB, 21 Dec 1978, NSA-staff/119, CL.

49. Cabinet Conclusions, 19 Dec 1978, CAB 128/64/24, NA-UK. Also Vance to Carter, 19 Dec 1978, Plains/39, CL; and author's interview with Low. For the Hughes mission: DOS suggestions for "Terms of Reference for Hughes-Low Mission" in Christopher, State 297991, 25 Nov 1978, FOIA; Brewster, London 19476, 27 Nov 1978, FOIA; and Vance, State 300011, 27 Nov 1978, FOIA.

50. Author's interview with Owen.

51. Cabinet Conclusions, 19 Dec 1978, CAB 128/64/24, NA-UK. Also Owen, FCO 2932, 18 Dec 1978, FCO 36/2233, NA-UK; and Vance to Carter, 19 Dec 1978, Plains/39, CL.

52. CIA Foreign Assessment Center, "Military Weekly Review," 12 Jan 1979, NSA-DC.

53. See Taylor, *China and Africa*, 49, 93–100.

54. *NYT*, 17 Dec 1978, 1; Allinson, Lusaka 960, 5 Dec 1978, FCO 36/2206, NA-UK; and *NYT*, 17 Dec 1978, 1. See CIA Foreign Assessment Center, Africa Review, 6 Apr 1977, CREST.

55. Experts' Committee, "Situation in Sub-Saharan Africa," in Christopher, State 230730, 12 Sep 1978, FOIA. See Vance, ER, 30 Oct 1978, NLC-7-20-8-18-5; and Libby, *Politics*, 9, 243.

56. Norland, Gaborone 3832, 5 Dec 1978, FOIA. On Botswana and the Rhodesian war: Morapedi, "Dilemmas"; Polhemus, "Botswana's"; Mgadla, "Good"; Osei-Hwedie, "Botswana"; and Cilliers, *Counter-insurgency*, 193–95. UNHCR estimated in 1976 that 10,000 to 14,000 Rhodesian refugees fled to Botswana. Thompson, *Challenge*, 9–70. By 1978, that number had grown to 25,300. Osei-Hwedie, "Botswana," 430.

57. Memcon (Tarnoff, Pastor, Fidel Castro), "US/Cuban Relations," 3–4 Dec 1978, Havana, Vertical File, "Cuba: President Carter's Trip, May 12–17, 2002," CL. See Memcon (Tarnoff, Pastor, Rafael Rodríguez, Valdés Vivó, Padrón), "US/Cuban Relations," 2–3 Dec 1978, ibid. See Vaky and Pastor to Aaron and Newsom, 1 Aug 1978, NLC-24-12-2-1-8; LeoGrande and Kornbluh, *Back Channel*, 211–14; Gleijeses, *Visions*, 119–26; and Schoultz, *Infernal*, 330–31. Covers next three paragraphs.

58. Tarnoff and Pastor to Carter (through Vance and ZB), "Our Trip to Cuba, December 2–4, 1978," Vertical File, "Cuba: President Carter's Trip, May 12–17, 2002," CL; and Pastor to ZB and Aaron, 19 Dec 1978, ibid.

59. Author's interviews with DePree, Easum, Edmondson, Low, McHenry, Moose (2001 and 2002), Petterson, Richardson, and Thornton.

60. Author's interviews with Low, McHenry, and Moose (2001).

61. Author's interviews with Owen, Renwick, and Graham.

62. Author's interviews with Moose (2001), Thornton, Richardson, and Aaron.

63. "Memo for the file of a speech that was labeled as Off the Record and not for attribution by Ambassador Stephen Low at the Overseas Development Council, April 12th, 8 p.m. 1979," US Foreign Relations, Rhodesia/253, Africa News, Duke.

64. Author's interview with Newsom. Also, author's interview with Carter.

65. *LAT*, 5 Jan 1979, B20 (sunshine); and *Le Figaro* (Paris), 4 Jan 1979, 1. See Callaghan, *Time and Chance*, 541–53; Giscard, *Le pouvoir*, 363; and Brzezinski, *Power*, 295.

66. Carter to Mondale and Vance, 5 Jan 1979, NLC-128-4-12-3-9; and Callaghan, *Time and Chance*, 545. See Brewster, London 4703, 7 Mar 1979, NLC-16-26-1-20-3.

67. Callaghan, *Time and Chance*, 544; Giscard, *Le pouvoir*, 381; Schmidt, *Menschen und Mächte*, 232; and *Time*, 15 Jan 1979, 8.

68. *Le Monde* (Paris), 9 Jan 1979, 8; "Secretary of State's Meeting with Mr Vance," 21 May 1979, FCO 82/994, NA-UK; *Le Monde*, 16 Feb 1979, 9; Giscard, *Le pouvoir*, 377; Carter to Mondale and Vance, 5 Jan 1979, NLC-128-4-12-3-9; and Arthur (from Callaghan), Bridgetown 34, 8 Jan 1979, FCO 36/2504, NA-UK. For Schmidt's relationship with Carter, see Ham, "A Change."

69. Renwick to Duff, 15 Dec 1978, FCO 36/2233, NA-UK; Callaghan, *Time and Chance*, 544; and FCO to Callaghan [draft], "Five Power Talks on South Africa," [8 Jan 1979,] FCO 36/2504, NA-UK. Also Owen to Hughes in Moose to Lake and Harrop. 4 Dec 1978, Lake/1, NA; Carter to Mondale and Vance, 5 Jan 1979, NLC-128-4-12-3-9; and London 22746, 12 Jan 1979, A1838 190-2-1/55, NA-AUS. (Australian diplomatic cables are unsigned.)

70. Allinson, Lusaka 960, 5 Dec 1978, FCO 36/2206, NA-UK.

71. FCO to Callaghan [draft], [8 Jan 1979,] "Five Power Talks on South Africa," FCO; and Funk to ZB, 19 Jan 1979, Funk/119, CL.

72. Jay, Washington 4595, 17 Nov 1978, FCO 36/3322, NA-UK; and Muir to Spencer, 16 Apr 1979, FCO 36/2505, NA-UK.

73. Jay to Owen, 4 Nov 1978, FCO 36/2206, NA-UK; and Wall to Cartledge, 20 Dec 1978, FCO 36/2346, NA-UK.

74. Funk to ZB and Aaron, 27 Jan 1979, Funk/119, CL.

75. Jay, Washington 326, 25 Jan 1979, FCO 36/2521, NA-UK; Vance to Carter, 13 Jan 1979, Plains/39, CL; and Jay, Washington 326, 25 Jan 1979, FCO 36/2521, NA-UK. Also Fursland to Renwick, 31 Jan 1979, FCO 36/2538, NA-UK.

76. Memcon (Fidel Castro, Neto), 24 Jan 1979, Gleijeses Papers; and Vance to Carter, 13 Jan 1979, Plains/39, CL. Also CIA, "Fidel Castro's Message to President Carter," 11 Jan 1979, NLC-6-13-6-1-4; Funk to ZB and Aaron, 11 Jan, 1979, DDRS; and Christopher, ER, 21 Feb 1979, NLC-133-7-3-33-7.

77. Meredith, *Past Is Another Country*, 354.

78. Edmondson, Pretoria 298, 17 Jan 1979, FOIA. See Martin and Johnson, *Struggle*, 276.

79. Vance, State 34331, 9 Feb 1979, FOIA; and *CSM*, 15 Feb 1979, 24. For the liberated zones: Callinicos, *After Zimbabwe*, 34–39. For guerrilla strength: "Rhodesia: The Next Three Months" in INR (Mark) to Vance, 1 Feb 1979, NLC-133-80-7-1-7;

CIA, "Estimated Strength of the Rhodesian Security Forces During the April Election," 23 Mar 1979, CREST; and Josiah Tungamirai, "Recruitment to ZANLA," and Brickhill, "Daring to Storm the Heavens," in Bhebe and Ranger, *Soldiers*, 36–72.

80. *LAT*, 23 Feb 1979, 1.

81. Petter-Bowyer, *Winds*, 488–91, 489 quoted. See [MINFAR], "Resultado de la investigación realizada sobre la masacre del centro de entrenamiento de Boma por la Comisión del EMG," 7–12 Mar 1979, Gleijeses Papers; and *Guardian* (London), 27 Feb 1979, 1 and 28 Feb 1979, 8. On the training camp at Boma, see Gleijeses, *Visions*, 86–87; and chapter 8 above.

82. *NYT*, 27 Feb 1979, 3; *WP*, 27 Feb 1979, 1; and *Guardian*, 27 Feb 1979, 1. The London *Times* was on strike from November 30, 1978, to November 12, 1979.

83. Funk to ZB, 19 Jan 1979, Funk/119, CL.

84. Cabinet Conclusions, 19 Dec 1978, CAB 128/64/24, NA-UK; Vance to Carter, 29 Jan 1979, Plains/39, CL; and Owen to Callaghan, 26 Jan 1979, FCO 36/2538, NA-UK. Morocco was planning to fly the shah to exile in South Africa, Vance wrote Carter, "if another destination cannot be arranged." Vance ER, 26 Mar 1979, NLC-133-7-3-55-3.

85. Vance to Carter, 2 Feb 1979, NLC-128-14-4-2-8. Also Vance to Carter, 3 Feb 1979, NLC-128-14-4-3-7.

86. Memcon (Owen, Vance), 2 Feb 1979, FCO 36/2538, NA-UK; and Vance to Carter, 2 Feb 1979, NLC-128-14-4-2-8.

87. Memcon (Owen, McGovern), 14 Dec 1978, FCO 36/2233, NA-UK; and Edmondson, Cape Town 182, 2 Feb 1979, FOIA-mf. On Namibia: Gleijeses, *Visions*, 146–58. On South African bomb: Van Wyk, "Ally," 211–13.

88. Funk to ZB, 12 Feb 1979, Funk/119, CL; and Christopher to Carter, 21 Feb 1979, NLC-128-14-4-12-7.

89. Wall to Cartledge, 9 Nov 1979, FCO 36/2233, NA-UK; and "Press Release, 17 Mar 1979," DOS *Bulletin*, Jun 1979, 22. For British approaches to the US Congress: Memcon (Owen, seven members of US House), 21 Nov 1978, FCO 36/2233. NA-UK; Memcon (Owen, Javits), 11 Dec 1978, ibid.; Memcon (Owen, US Senate Foreign Relations Committee), 2 Feb 1979, FCO 36/2538, NA-UK; and Davidson to Thomas, 6 Feb 1979, FCO 36/2504, NA-UK.

90. Funk to ZB, 12 Feb 1979, Funk/119, CL.

Chapter 12

1. *NYT*, 15 Feb 1979, 1. See President's Daily Diary, 14 Feb 1979, CL.

2. Amstutz, Kabul 1060 (05:00Z), 14 Feb 1979, DNSA; Amstutz, Kabul 1061 (05:20Z), ibid.; Amstutz, Kabul 1063 (05:37Z), ibid.; Amstutz, Kabul 1068 (06:07Z), ibid.; Amstutz, Kabul 1070 (06:30Z), ibid.; Vance, State 38193, 14 Feb 1979, 07:04Z, DNSA; and Amstutz, Kabul 1072 (07:12Z), 14 Feb 1979, DNSA. See *LAT*, 14 Feb 1979, 1. The cables were sent in GMT (designated by "Z" for Zulu). Kabul was four-and-a-half hours later than GMT and nine-and-a-half hours later than EST. There was at least a fifteen-minute delay between events in Kabul and the arrival of cables in Washington. On the crisis, see Taylor (political officer, US embassy in Kabul), "Murder," 61–62; Cook, "Crisis in Kabul"; and Chapman and Flynn, "Assassination."

3. *CSM*, 15 Feb 1979, 1. See *WP*, 14 Feb 1979, 1.

4. The literature on US relations with Iran is vast. See esp. Bill, *Eagle*. During the February seizure of the embassy, a *WP* reporter and an *LAT* reporter were among the hostages. I have relied on their articles, supplemented by the following: *WP*, 15 Feb 1979, 15; *NYT*, 15 Feb 1979, 1; *CSM*, 15 Feb 1979, 1; *CT*, 15 Feb 1979, 1; Tomseth (political counselor, US embassy in Tehran), "Crisis"; and interviews with hostages in Wells, *444 Days*, 8–15. For a narrative with no footnotes, see Harris, *Crisis*, 158–60.

5. *NYT*, 15 Feb 1979, 1.

6. See Carter, *Diary*, 291.

7. *WP*, 15 Feb 1979, 15; and Wells, *444 Days*, 11–12. For the ham radio: *CT*, 16 Feb 1979, 4. For cook and marine: *WP*, 15 Feb 1979, 1; and *LAT*, 15 Feb 1979, 1. Six embassy contract employees, none of whom were US citizens, were killed in the crisis. Tomseth, "Crisis," 37.

8. Wells, *444 Days*, 13.

9. Amstutz, Kabul 1074 (08:20Z), 14 Feb 1979, DNSA.

10. Ibid.

11. Amstutz, Kabul 1075 (08:25Z), 14 Feb 1979, DNSA. See Chapman and Flynn, "Assassination."

12. Author's interview with Graham; *WP*, 15 Feb 1979, 1; and Wells, *444 Days*, 15.

13. Jack Perry, FD, 2 Jul 1992.

14. Mexico City, Toasts at the Luncheon Honoring President Carter, 14 Feb 1979, APP. This account is based on: *LAT*, 15 Feb 1979, 1; *CT*, 15 Feb 1979, 1, 5; President's Daily Diary, 14 Feb 1979, CL; and *CSM*, 16 Feb 1979, 1.

15. *CSM*, 16 Feb 1979, 1; *NYT*, 15 Feb 1979, 1; and Mexico City, Toasts at the Luncheon Honoring President Carter, 14 Feb 1979, APP.

16. *CT*, 15 Feb 1979, 1; *NYT*, 15 Feb 1979, 1; *CSM*, 16 Feb 1979, 1; and *LAT*, 15 Feb 1979, 2.

17. *CT*, 15 Feb 1979, 5; *LAT*, 15 Feb 1979, 1; *NYT*, 16 Feb 1979, 27; and *CSM*, 16 Feb 1979, 1.

18. *Le Monde* (Paris), 16 Feb 1979, 9; and *Le Figaro* (Paris), 16 Feb 1979, 2. For full transcript, see *Le Figaro* (Paris), 16 Feb 1979, 2–4; and *Le Monde*, 17 Feb 1979, 3–7.

19. *WP*, 16 Feb 1979, 30; *NYT*, 15 Feb 1979, D10; and *NYT*, 15 Feb 1979, 1.

20. *CSM*, 15 Feb 1979, edit 24; *NYT*, 15 Feb 1979, edit 26; *WSJ*, 15 Feb 1979, edit 20; and *LAT*, 15 Feb 1979, edit D10.

21. The State of the Union Annual Message to the Congress, 25 Jan 1979, APP.

22. CIA, "Cuban Involvement in Africa," 16 Apr 1979, CREST.

23. Christopher to Carter, 9 Dec 1978, Plains/39, CL.

24. *Rhodesian Herald* (Salisbury), 12 Jun 1979, edit 6; and *CR-Senate*, 29 Jan 1979, 1258, 1260.

25. *CQ Weekly*, 31 Mar 1979, 613. See Schweiker, *CR-Senate*, 9 Feb 1979, 2444. DeConcini and Schweiker to Colleague, 15 Feb 1979, DeConcini Papers/169; and Rhodesian Information Office, "Schweiker-DeConcini Resolution on Zimbabwe-Rhodesia: Background Notes," n.d., ibid. The resolution, S Con Res 24, had ten cosponsors.

26. See Vance to Carter, 1 Mar 1979, NSA-staff/119-25, CL; and Solarz to Vance, 2 Mar 1979, FOIA-mf. For the invitation: Edmondson, Cape Town 214, 7 Feb 1979, FOIA-mf.

27. "Report on the Security Council Meeting on the Question concerning the situation in Southern Rhodesia from March 2 to 8, 1979," 12 Apr 1979, enclosed in

Zambian UN ambassador to Chakula, 18 Apr 1979, 152 UNIP 7/23/70. See Young to Carter, [23 Feb 1979,] NLC-8-23-1-21-4.

28. See DePree, Maputo 318, 9 Mar 1979, FOIA-mf; Walker, Dar 1240, 19 Mar 1979, FOIA-mf; and Clingerman, Lusaka 1114, 3 Apr 1979, FOIA-mf.

29. See Robinson to Vance, 2 Feb 1979, Martin/92, CL; CBC to Vance, 6 Feb 1979, FOIA-mf; Brown to Vance, 23 Feb 1979, FOIA-mf; CBC press release, 7 Mar 1979, FCO 36/2504, NA-UK; and US Senate, "Rhodesia," CD61, 46.

30. Spain, Dar 836, 22 Feb 1979, FOIA-mf.

31. Memcon (Owen, McGovern), 14 Dec 1978, FCO 36/2233, NA-UK; and Jay, Washington 442, 31 Jan 1979, FCO 36/2504, NA-UK. See US House, "Executive-Legislative Consultation," CD34, 47; and McGovern's testimony in US House, "US Policy toward Rhodesia," CD26, 126.

32. See Vance to Carter, 28 Feb 1979, Plains/39, CL.

33. US Senate, "Impartial Observers," CD62, 4. A concurrent resolution is adopted by both houses and, since it is not presented to the president, is not legally binding.

34. Vance to Carter, 1 Mar 1979, NSA-staff/119-125, CL.

35. WS, 6 Feb 1979, 10; and Moose, Lake, Maynes to Vance, 1 Mar 1979, Lake/5, NA.

36. US Senate, "Rhodesia," CD61, 102, 122; and Davidson, "Congress and Rhodesia," 8 Mar 1979, FCO 36/2504, NA-UK. See Vance, ER, 15 Mar 1979, NLC-133-7-3-51-7.

37. CR-Senate, 28 Mar 1979, 6547–61 (full debate); 6557 (Helms); 6551–52 (Tsongas). On Tsongas, see Young to Carter, 30 Mar 1979, NLC-8-23-1-23-2.

38. See CR-House, 15 Mar 1979, 5368. For an excellent analysis of this vote: Weissman and Carson, "Economic Sanctions."

39. Author's interviews with Young, Easum, Low, and Moose (2001).

40. Solarz, FD, 18 Nov 1996.

41. Ibid.; and Vance, ER, 27 Apr 1979, NLC-133-7-4-12-9.

42. Solarz, FD, 18 Nov 1996. See Davidson to Thomas, 6 Feb 1979, FCO 36/2504, NA-UK; and Solarz, Journeys, 73–87.

43. Solarz, Journeys, 88. See US House, "US Policy Toward Rhodesia" CD26; and Weissman and Carson, "Economic Sanctions," 140.

44. Newsom, State 69720, 21 Mar 1979, FOIA-mf; CR-House, 9 Apr 1979, 7759; and US House, "US Policy Toward Rhodesia," CD26, 180–81 (emphasis added). Also Vance to Carter, 15 Mar 1979, Plains/39, CL and author's interview with Moose (2002).

45. Low, FD, 1988; Solarz, FD, 18 Nov 1996; and NYT, 3 Apr 1979, 4.

46. Renwick to Mansfield and Wall, 21 Feb 1979, FCO 36/2652, NA-UK.

47. CR-House, 9 Apr 1979, 7757. The resolution was HR 3715, H Con Res 110.

48. Ibid., 7758.

49. Ibid.

50. Ibid., 7763–67. Eleven Democrats who had supported Bauman's amendment switched their votes.

51. Vance to Carter, 9 Apr 1979, NLC-128-14-6-7-1. See Lanpher to Bennet, 16 Apr 1979, Beckel/228, CL.

52. Christopher to Carter, 21 Feb 1979, NLC-128-14-4-12-7; and Edmondson (from Low), Pretoria 2498, 24 Mar 1979, FOIA. See Flower, Serving Secretly, 198–99.

53. Albright to ZB, 10 Mar 1979, NSA-congress/1, CL; *Sunday Times* (London), 25 Mar 1979, 13; Edmondson, Cape Town 901, 15 Apr 1979, DNSA; and Situation Room to ZB, 19 Apr 1979, NLC-1-10-4-27-6. See NIO for Africa to Turner, "Talking Points for PRC meeting," 3 Apr 1979, CREST; and DCI, "South Africa: Domestic and Foreign Policy Implications of the Information Department Scandal," 4 Apr 1979, CREST. For the expulsions: CIA, "Current Foreign Relations, Issue No. 15," 18 Apr 1979, DNSA.

54. *WP*, 3 Dec 1978, C1; and Davidson to Jarrold, 20 Nov 1978, FCO 36/2351, NA-UK. In mid-1978 there was a vigorous debate in the Foreign Office about how to deal with "inevitable" economic sanctions on South Africa. Planning Staff, "Sanctions against South Africa," FCO 49/788, NA-UK.

55. Barder to Mansfield, 24 Jan 1979, FCO 36/2538, NA-UK; Carter to PW Botha, 6 Apr 1979, Lake/17, NA; and Carter's marginalia on Christopher to Carter, 31 May 1979, NLC-128-14-7-21-4. For the Namibia negotiations: Gleijeses, "Test of Wills."

56. *Sun* (Baltimore), 7 Feb 1979, 4.

57. See Minutes, Leader's Consultative Committee [LCC] Meeting, 15 Feb 1978, Thatcher Papers.

58. Minutes, LCC Meeting, 4 Oct 1978, ibid.

59. Ibid.; and Carrington, *Reflecting*, 290. See Carrington, *Reflecting*, 271–72.

60. Minutes, LCC Meeting, 4 Oct 1978, Thatcher Papers; and Summary, LCC, 4 Oct 1978, ibid.

61. *Guardian* (London), 12 Oct 1978, 15 (column by Peter Jenkins) and edit 14; *Sun* (Baltimore), 12 Oct 1978, 2; and *Guardian*, 12 Oct 1978, 6.

62. *Guardian*, 14 Oct 1978, 8.

63. *Guardian*, 4 Nov 1978, 3; and "Southern Rhodesia," 8 Nov 1978, *Parliamentary Debates*, Commons, 5th ser., vol. 957, col. 1122. The opponents included 114 Tories, plus Scottish and Welsh Nationalists and Ulster Unionists. There were 320 votes in favor of renewal.

64. *Guardian*, 9 Nov 1978, 6; and Thatcher to Churchill, 9 Nov 1979, Thatcher Papers.

65. See "Southern Rhodesia (United Nations Sanctions) Order 1968," 17–18 Jun 1968, *Parliamentary Debates*, Lords, 5th ser., vol. 293, cols. 350–425, 515–97.

66. "Southern Rhodesia Act 1965 (Continuation) Order 1978," 9 Nov 1978, *Parliamentary Debates*, Lords, 5th ser., vol. 396, cols. 435–46.

67. *Guardian*, 10 Apr 1979, 4; *WP*, 12 Apr 1979, 23; and *NYT*, 6 May 1979, 175. Also Vance, ER, 12 Sep 1977 [US], Thatcher Papers; *CSM*, 9 Mar 1979, 7; and Conservative General Election Manifesto, 11 Apr 1979, Thatcher Papers.

68. Vance, ER, 8 Feb 1979, NLC-133-7-3-29-2; Leahy to Parsons, 2 Mar 1979, FCO 82/984, NA-UK; and Brewster, London 4933, 9 Mar 1979, FOIA.

69. CIA Foreign Assessment Center, "Africa Review," 6 Apr 1977, CREST.

70. Brewster, London 7238, 10 Apr 1979, FOIA-mf.

71. Author's interviews with Moose (2001) and Lake.

72. Solarz, FD, 18 Nov 1996.

73. Carlucci, "Memorandum for the Record," 29 Mar 1979, CREST. Also Funk to ZB, 28 Mar 1979, Funk/119, CL.

74. Renwick to Mansfield and Wall, 21 Feb 1979, FCO 36/2652, NA-UK.

75. Lake to Vance, 4 Apr 1979, FOIA.

76. Ibid.; and author's interviews with Moose (2001) and Lake.

77. Author's interview with Lake; Lake to Vance, 4 Apr 1979, FOIA; and author's interview with Moose (2002).

78. Lake to Vance, 4 Apr 1979, FOIA.

79. Moose to Vance, 5 Apr 1979, FOIA-mf. Also Spiegel, "Problems with Memorandum on Rhodesia Strategy," [4 Apr 1979,] FOIA.

80. "Summary of Conclusions: PRC Meeting, 5 April 1979," in Dodson to Tarnoff, 10 Apr 1979, NLC-24-121-7-5-9.

81. Funk, *Life*, 204; Memcon (Squire, Funk), 11 Jan 1979, FCO 36/2504, NA-UK; and author's interview with Moose (2001).

82. Funk to ZB, 6 Apr 1979, Funk/119, CL. Also Squire to Varcoe, 6 Apr 1979, FCO 36/2505, NA-UK.

83. Funk to ZB, 11 Apr 1979, NLC-24-120-5-4-3; and Moose to Vance, 11 Apr 1979, FOIA. For the scenario: "Discussion Paper for PRC Meeting," in Moose and Lake to Newsom, [9 Apr 1979,] NLC-24-120-5-9-8.

84. Young, USUN 1555, 11 Apr 1979, FOIA-mf. Also Secret, NLC-1-10-4-5-0.

85. "President's Decision on Recommendations of PRC Meeting on Southern Africa, April 12, 1979," NLC-24-115-5-3-0; and Lanpher to Bennet, 16 Apr 1979, Beckel/228, CL. See "Discussion Paper for PRC Meeting," in Moose and Lake to Newsom, [9 Apr 1979,] NLC-24-120-5-9-8; and ZB to Carter, "Conclusions of PRC," [12 Apr 1979,] NLC-24-121-7-6-8.

Chapter 13

1. Funk to ZB, 23 Apr 1979, Funk/119, CL.

2. Situation Room to ZB, 13 Apr 1979, NLC-1-10-4-12-2; Low, Lusaka 1268, 16 Apr 1979, FOIA-mf; and Smith, *Betrayal*, 295. See Moorcraft and McLaughlin, *Rhodesian War*, 159; Petter-Bowyer, *Winds*, 495–501; and Stiff, *Silent War*, 282–83.

3. Edmondson, Pretoria 3766, 23 Apr 1979, FOIA.

4. Edmondson, Pretoria 3695 and 3696, 19 Apr 1979, FOIA-Rhodesia/20783, NSA-DC; Vance, State 103357, 24 Apr 1979, FOIA-mf; and DIA, "Rhodesia Election," 23 Apr 1979, FOIA-Rhodesia/6, NSA-DC.

5. *CR-Senate*, 23 Apr 1979, 8287. See Lord Boyd et al., "Report to the Prime Minister on the Election held in Zimbabwe-Rhodesia in April 1979," archive.org; American Conservative Union Observer Delegation, "Preliminary Report," 25 Apr 1979, FOIA-mf; Bauman (Chair, American Conservative Union) to Carter, 4 May 1979, FOIA-mf; Evans, "Eyewitness Report on the Rhodesian Elections," *CR-Senate*, 9 May 1979, 10394–97; Palley, "The Rhodesian Election Campaign," *CR-Senate*, 15 May 1979, 11218–24; Lord Chitnis, "Rhodesian Elections: A Confidence Trick," ibid., 11224–30; and "Report of American Observers of the Institute of American Relations on the Recent Elections in Zimbabwe-Rhodesia," ibid., 11257–262.

6. Funk to ZB, 23 Apr 1979, Funk/119, CL.

7. Edmondson, Pretoria 3696, 19 Apr 1979, FOIA-Rhodesia/20783, NSA-DC; CIA Foreign Assessment Center, "Rhodesia: Looking Beyond the April Election," 2 Apr 1979, CREST; and US House, "Rhodesia: Where Do We Go From Here?" CD28, 3. For a thorough analysis of intimidation: WOA, "The Rhodesian Election: Free and Fair?," 23 Apr 1979, AAA.

8. See Vance to Carter, 23 Apr 1979, NLC-128-14-6-17-0.

9. *NYT*, 22 Apr 1979, 1. There was irony in the fact that Helms later trumpeted Rustin's assessment of the Rhodesian elections. Sixteen years earlier, Helms had excoriated Rustin on his radio program as a communist and a "perverted" homosexual. This radio editorial—and the fact that Rustin was not given an opportunity to respond—formed the basis of an investigation that delayed the renewal of the station's license for eight months. See Link, *Righteous Warrior*, 80 and 106. See also *Daily Telegraph* (London), 24 Apr 1979, edit.

10. Brewster, London 9503, 15 May 1979, FOIA-Rhodesia/6, NSA-DC; and Low, Lusaka 1364, 25 Apr 1979, FOIA-Rhodesia/6, NSA-DC.

11. Helms, *CR-Senate*, 24 Apr 1979, 8437 and 30 Apr 1979, 8980; Helms, *CQ Weekly*, 28 Apr 1979, 808; and Ichord, *CR-House*, 2 May 1979, 9528. Also Schweiker, *CR-Senate*, 9 Feb 1979, 2444; Schweiker, *CR-Senate*, 23 Apr 1979, 8287; Bauman, *CR-House*, 25 Apr 1979, 8531–33; Rhodes, *CR-House*, 25 Apr 1979, 8509; Broomfield, *CR-House*, 25 Apr 1979, 8723; and Humphrey, Rhodes, *CR-House*, 30 Apr 1979, 8967.

12. Vance, State 103357, 24 Apr 1979, FOIA-mf; and *CQ Weekly*, 28 Apr 1979, 808.

13. ZB to Funk, 24 Apr 1979, NSA-country/3, CL.

14. Carter (handwritten notes), "Zimbabwe," 24 Apr 1979, Handwriting/127, CL.

15. ZB to Funk, 24 Apr 1979, NSA-country/3, CL.

16. Carter (handwritten notes), "Zimbabwe," 24 Apr 1979, Handwriting/127, CL.

17. Jay, Washington 915, 25 Apr 1979, FCO 36/2505, NA-UK.

18. Carter (handwritten notes), "Zimbabwe," 24 Apr 1979, Handwriting/127, CL (emphasis in original).

19. Squire to Renwick, 25 Apr 1979, FCO 36/2505, NA-UK; and Muir, "Rhodesia and Congress," 27 Apr 1979, ibid.

20. Squire to Renwick, 31 Jan 1979, FCO 36/2504, NA-UK; and Barlow to Renwick, 9 Feb 1979, ibid. Also Jay, 29 Mar 1979, Washington 843, ibid.; Gomersall to Spenser et al., 30 Mar 1979, ibid.; and Wall to Gomersall, 5 Apr 1979, ibid.

21. Memcon (Squire, Carbaugh), 26 Apr 1979 in Squire to Renwick, 27 Apr 1979, FCO 36/2505, NA-UK.

22. Helms to Carter (telegram), 5 May 1979, Beckel/228, CL; and Albright to ZB and Moore, 5 May 1979, NSA-congress/4, CL. The administration did not reply. See Helms, *CR-Senate*, 15 May 1979, 11238.

23. Squire to Renwick, 25 Apr 1979, FCO 36/2505, NA-UK.

24. Meeting with Members of UPI Advisory Board, 27 Apr 1979, APP; *Times* (Lusaka), 30 Apr 1979, edit; Press Conference, 30 Apr 1979, APP; and Albright to ZB, 2 May 1979, NSA-staff/119-25, CL.

25. See Brewster, London 8313, 26 Apr 1979, FOIA.

26. 1979 Conservative General Election Manifesto, Thatcher Papers; Smith, *Betrayal*, 298; and *Rhodesian Herald* (Salisbury), 5 May 1979, edit 4.

27. Telcon (Thatcher, Carter), 4 May 1979, FCO 82/976, NA-UK; and Carter to Thatcher, 11 May 1979, NLC-128-1-30-8-7. Also President's Daily Diary, 4 May 1979, CL-online; and Thatcher to Carter, 15 Jun 1979, Thatcher Papers.

28. *Guardian* (London), 7 May 1979, 10.

29. Theakston, *British Foreign Secretaries*, 122.

30. Quoted in Hudson, *Triumph or Tragedy?*, 150.

31. Moore, *Thatcher*, 450.

32. See Jay, Washington 915, 25 Apr 1979, FCO 36/2505, NA-UK.

33. See Helms, *CR-Senate*, 14 May 1979, 10858. For the debate, *CR-Senate*, 15 May 1979, 11214–66. This entire day is omitted from the LexisNexis Congressional database.

34. Helms, *CR-Senate*, 15 May 1979, 11238–40.

35. Ibid., 11239.

36. Harry Byrd, ibid., 11240.

37. Hatch, ibid., 11242; Schweiker, ibid., 11252; and Hayakawa, ibid., 11246 and 11256. Also Helms, ibid., 11238.

38. McGovern, ibid., 11241; Muskie, ibid., 11262; and Glenn, ibid., 11263.

39. See Shapiro, *Last Great Senate*, 30–35, 214–15.

40. H. Byrd, *CR-Senate*, 15 May 1979, 11240; and Jepsen, ibid., 11247. By calling the country "Zimbabwe-Rhodesia," the term the internal settlement leaders preferred, Byrd signaled that in his opinion the election had produced a legitimate government. The Carter administration avoided using this hyphenated name.

41. Garn, ibid., 11247.

42. Kennedy, ibid., 11245; and Hayakawa, ibid., 11246.

43. See McGovern, ibid., 11241.

44. Byrd to Theodore Bilbo, 10 Dec 1945, quoted in Smith, *Jim Crow*, 225; and *WP*, 21 Apr 1960, 2. See *CR-Senate*, 19 Jun 1964, 14480; *WP*, 2 Mar 2002, 23; and *WP*, 19 Jun 2005, 1. For Byrd's 2005 explanation of his membership in the Klan, see Byrd, *Byrd*, 54; for an apologia written by one of Byrd's staffers, see Corbin, *Last Great Senator*, ch. 1.

45. See President's Daily Diary, 3 May 1979, CL online; and Carter to Robert Byrd, 4 May 1979, Beckel/228, CL.

46. See Albright to ZB and Moore, 5 May 1979, NSA-congress/4, CL.

47. Vance, ER, 14 May 1979, NLC-128-14-7-9-8; and Vance to Carter, 7 May 1979, NLC-128-14-7-4-3. Also Jay, Washington 1015, 8 May 1979, FCO 36/2505, NA-UK.

48. Church, *CR-Senate*, 15 May 1979, 11245. See Vance, ER, 8 Jun 1979, FOIA.

49. Weissman and Carson, "Economic Sanctions," 144; and Helms, *CR-Senate*, 15 May 1979, 11249.

50. Author's interview with Moose (2001). Also Schweiker, *CR-Senate*, 9 Feb 1979, 2444; and ibid., 15 May 1979, 11251.

51. See *CR-Senate*, 15 May 1979, 11249–50; *CQ Weekly*, 19 May 1979, 958–59; Church in US Senate, "Trade Sanctions against Rhodesia," CD64, 12; and Weissman and Carson, "Economic Sanctions," 144–45.

52. Helms, *CR-Senate*, 15 May 1979, 11250, 11256, 11263. See *CQ Weekly*, 19 May 1979, 959. All nineteen in opposition were Democrats except Lincoln Chaffee (R-RI) and Charles Percy (R-IL). Twenty senators who had opposed lifting sanctions a year earlier voted for this resolution.

53. Helms, *CR-Senate*, 15 May 1979, 11255–56, 11264. Helms withdrew his revised amendment (lifting sanctions for one year), which superseded his original amendment (which did not have the one-year limit). Robert Byrd introduced a final amendment stating that it was "the sense of Congress" that sanctions should be lifted, but leaving the decision to the president; this amendment passed 83 to 11. *CR-Senate*, 15 May 1979, 11264–65.

54. *Rhodesian Herald*: 17 May 1979, 4; 18 May 1979, 4; and 17 May 1979, 4.

55. Smith, *Betrayal*, 301; *Sunday Mail* (Salisbury), 20 May 1979, 13 and 27 May 1979, 14; and Helms, *CR-Senate*, 15 May 1979, 11265.

56. *NYT*, 17 May 1979, 9; *Rhodesian Herald*, 22 May 1979, 3; *WS*, 17 May 1979, edit 10; Jay, Washington 1135, 16 May 1979, FCO 36/2505, NA-UK; and *NYT*, 17 May 1979, 9.

57. See Vance, ER, 27 Apr 1979, NLC-128-14-6-21-5; and Muir to Gomersall, 11 May 1979, FCO 36/2505, NA-UK.

58. Moose and Lake to Vance, 15 May 1979, Lake/6, NA.

59. Lord Boyd, "Report to the Prime Minister on the Election held in Zimbabwe-Rhodesia in April 1979," archive.org.

60. Jay, Washington 1145, 17 May 1979, FCO 82/992, NA-UK; and Jay, Washington 1122, 15 May 1979, FCO 36/2505, NA-UK.

61. ZB to Carter, [May 1979,] NLC-23-4-2-14-5; and "An Interview With Thatcher," *Time*, 14 May 1979, 33.

62. ZB to Carter, [May 1979,] NLC-23-4-2-14-5; and DOS, "The Foreign Affairs Posture of a Tory Government," [May 1979,] NLC-6-77-2-30-6.

63. Thatcher, "Debate on the Address," 15 May 1979, *Parliamentary Debates*, Commons, 5th ser., vol. 967, col. 86; Carrington, *Reflecting*, 288; and Funk to Aaron, 26 Apr 1979, Funk/119, CL.

64. Thatcher, "Debate on the Address," 15 May 1979, *Parliamentary Debates*, Commons, 5th ser., vol. 967, col. 86.

65. Carrington, *Reflecting*, 291; and *Guardian*, 6 May 1979, 12. For a scathing attack by the Conservatives' chief analyst on Rhodesian affairs, see Hudson, *Triumph or Tragedy?*, esp. 149–50.

66. Fraser, *Malcolm Fraser*, 493; and Bergbusch to FCC Ottawa, YNGR 2099, 14 Aug 1979, box 10667, pt. 4, Canada.

67. Fraser, *Malcolm Fraser*, 502.

68. Roberts (British HC, Canberra) to Yarnold, 15 May 1979, FCO 36/2505, NA-UK. See *Rhodesian Herald*, 5 May 1979, 3; and Evelyn Colbert, FD, 9 Sep 2004. Young was the guest of honor at Australian-American Week.

69. Vance to Carter, 19 May 1979, NLC-128-14-7-13-3; and *Guardian*, 19 May 1979, 1. Also Vance, *Hard Choices*, 296.

70. Peacock to Vance, 19 May 1979, in Freeth to Carrington, 21 May 1979, FCO 82/992, NA-UK.

71. Jay, Washington 1122, 15 May 1979, FCO 36/2505, NA-UK; and Day to Private Secretary, 18 May 1979, FCO 36/2539, NA-UK.

72. Carrington, *Reflecting*, 287. See Vance, *Hard Choices*, 295.

73. Memcon (Vance, Carrington), 21 May 1979, Funk/119, CL. See Memcon, (Carrington, Vance), 21 May 1979, FCO 82/992, NA-UK.

74. Memcon (Manasov, Valdés Vivó), 7 May 1979, CWIHP-va; and Diary of V. I. Vorotnikov, Memcon (Vorotnikov, Fidel Castro), 25 Jun 1979, CWIHP-va. See Martin and Johnson, *Struggle*, 305–8.

75. See Situation Room to ZB, 19 May 1979, NLC-1-10-7-26-4; "A New Cuban-Soviet Strategy on Rhodesia?" [19 May 1979,] NLC-SAFE 17-A-119-112-1-9; CIA, "Soviet Position in the Third World," [summer 1979,] NSA-DC; and CIA, "Cuba: Putting Africa on the Back Burner," 31 Aug 1979, NLC-24-371-8-6.

76. "Lord Carrington's Talks with Mr Vance," in Walden to Cartledge, 22 May 1979, Thatcher Papers. See ZB to Vance, 18 May 1979, [US,] Thatcher Papers; Day to Private Secretary, 18 May 1979, FCO 36/2539, NA-UK; Memcon, (Carrington, Vance), 21 May 1979, FCO 82/992, NA-UK; Memcon (Vance, Carrington), 21 May 1979, Funk/119, CL; Muir to Spencer, 23 May 1979, FCO 36/2506, NA-UK; MemCon (Carrington, Vance), 23 May 1979, FCO 36/2539, NA-UK; and MemCon (Thatcher, Vance), 23 May 1979, FCO 82/993, NA-UK. Also Vance, *Hard Choices*, 295–96.

77. Memcon (Vance, Carrington), 21 May 1979, Funk/119, CL.

78. Carrington's Meeting with Vance: Rhodesia, 21 May 1979, FCO 82/994, NA-UK; Carrington's Meeting with Vance: Steering Brief, 22 May 1979, ibid.; and Duff to Carrington, 23 May 1979, FCO 36/2539, NA-UK.

79. Carrington, "Address in Reply to Her Majesty's Most Gracious Speech," 22 May 1979, *Parliamentary Debates*, Lords, 5th ser., vol. 400, col. 240, FCO 82/992, NA-UK; and Renwick, *Unconventional Diplomacy*, 22.

80. Duff to Rhodesia Dept., 5 Jun 1979, FCO 36/2652, NA-UK.

81. See Funk to Aaron, 29 May 1979, Funk/119, CL.

82. See, e.g., Lake to ZB, 24 May 1979, Funk/119, CL; Christopher to Carter, 30 May 1979, ibid.; and ZB to Carter, [1 Jun 1979,] ibid.

83. *Rhodesian Herald*, 17 May 1979, edit 8.

84. Author's interview with Pastor.

85. Christopher to Carter, 30 May 1979, Funk/119, CL, with Carter's marginalia. Vance remained abroad, in Europe and the Middle East, after his London talks.

86. Funk to Aaron, 29 May 1979, ibid. (emphasis in original); and ZB to Carter, [1 Jun 1979,] ibid.

87. *WP*, 30 May 1979, 1; and *Atlanta Daily World*, 3 Jun 1979, edit 4.

88. ZB to Carter, 4 May 1979, NLC-1-10-6-12-0. Also *WP*, 20 May 1979, 1; and Renwick, *Unconventional Diplomacy*, 23.

89. "Report of the Commonwealth Committee on Southern Africa, June 1977–June 1979," June 1979, box 10667, pt. 2, Canada. See *Guardian*, 30 May 1979, 6; *Rhodesian Herald*, 30 May 1979, 3; Callinicos, *After Zimbabwe*, 49; Thompson, *Challenge to Imperialism*, 9–70; Astrow, *Zimbabwe*, 62; and White, "Civic Virtue," 105–6.

90. Muzorewa to Carter, 10 May 1979 in Edmondson, Cape Town 1116, 10 May 1979, Funk/119, CL. Also *Rhodesian Herald*, 12 May 1979, 1.

91. Edmondson, Pretoria 4036, 30 Apr 1979, FOIA-mf; *Rhodesia Herald*, 14 May 1979, 1; Edmondson, Pretoria 4994, 30 May 1979, FOIA; Edmondson, Pretoria 5085, 2 Jun 1979, FOIA; and Edmondson, Pretoria 5138, 4 Jun 1979, FOIA-mf.

92. *NYT*, 3 Jun 1979, 7; and Edmondson, Pretoria 5138, 4 Jun 1979, FOIA-mf.

93. *Guardian*, 14 May 1979, 6. Also DCI Briefing: "Rhodesia," 4 Apr 1979, CREST; *WP*, 21 May 1979, 1; and Smith, *Betrayal*, 311–13.

94. *NYT*, 5 Jun 1979, 2.

95. Smith, *Betrayal*, 293; *NYT*, 28 Apr 1979, 1; and Smith, *Betrayal*, 294, 307. See Jaster, "South Africa," 45–47.

96. *NYT*, 28 Apr 1979, 1. See *WP*, 22 May 1979, 1; and CIA, "Estimated Strength of the Rhodesian Security Forces During the April Election," 23 Mar 1979, CREST.

97. *Rhodesian Herald*, 30 May 1979, 1; Daily Report: Sub-Saharan Africa, 31 May 1979, *FBIS-SSA-79106*; and Funk to ZB, 23 Apr 1979, Funk/119, CL.

98. Muzorewa to Mondale, 24 May 1979, DDRS.

99. Statement by OAU, 22 May 1979, in US House, "Rhodesia: Where Do We Go From Here?," CD28, 18. See Tolbert (President of Liberia) to Solarz, 17 May 1979; Mogwe (Minister of Foreign Affairs, Botswana) to Solarz, 18 May 1979; Mbogua (Kenyan ambassador to United States) to Solarz, 23 May 1979; and Khartoum (Sudanese ambassador to United States) to Solarz, 28 May 1979; all in ibid., 13–17.

100. See CIA, National Intelligence Daily, 10 Feb 1979, CREST; and Obasanjo to Carter, 24 May 1979 in Wyman, Lagos 7308, 29 May 1979, FOIA.

101. Christopher, State 139103, 31 May 1979, FOIA. Also Christopher, State 139319, 31 May 1979, FOIA.

102. Easum, Lagos 4311, 29 Mar 1979, FOIA; Easum, Lagos 6565, 12 May 1979, FOIA; and *Guardian*, 17 May 1979, 1. Also CIA, National Intelligence Daily, 10 Feb 1979, CREST; *CSM*, 27 Apr 1979, 26; *WSJ*, 27 Apr 1979, 16; *Guardian*, 8 May 1979, 32; *CSM*, 17 May 1979, 6; *Guardian*, 17 May 1979, 1; Wyman, Lagos 6907, 18 May 1979, FOIA; and Brown, 24 Oct 1996, BDOHP.

103. *WP*, 31 May 1979, 1; and Easum, Lagos 6565, 12 May 1979, FOIA.

104. Wyman, Lagos 6907, 18 May 1979, FOIA; *WP*, 31 May 1979, 1; and *WP*, 29 May 1979, 16. Also CIA, National Intelligence Daily, 10 Feb 1979, CREST; Easum, Lagos 6565, 12 May 1979, FOIA; and Martin to Carter, 29 May 1979, Pinon/283, CL. Washington considered it unlikely that Lagos would jeopardize the pending multimillion dollar deal to export liquid national gas to the United States. See Obasanjo to Carter, 24 May 1979 in Wyman, Lagos 7308, 29 May 1979, FOIA; and ZB to Carter, WR, 1 Jun 1979, Brzezinski/41, CL.

105. Transcript of DOS press briefing, in Vance, State 139319, 31 May 1979, FOIA; and *Sun* (Baltimore), 1 Jun 1979, 2. Also *WP*, 31 May 1979, 1; *ABC Evening News*, 31 May 1979, VNA; *LAT*, 31 May 1979, 1; and *NYT*, 1 Jun 1979, 4.

106. *Globe and Mail* (Toronto), 29 May 1979, 18; *WP*, 31 May 1979, 1; and *WP*, 1 Jun 1979, edit 12. Nigerian officials warned Gulf Oil to expect retaliation if Carter lifted sanctions. Davidson to Renwick, 1 Jun 1979, FCO 36/2506, NA-UK; and Junior to Walker, 6 Jun 1979, FOIA-mf.

107. Andrew Young, "The Challenge of Leadership" (speech delivered in Atlanta), *The Black Scholar*, Jan/Feb 1979, 2–8.

108. Author's interview with Clark; and *NYT*, 15 Jun 1979, 3. See Muir, "Rhodesia: US Opinion," 26 Apr 1979, FCO 36/2505, NA-UK; and Martin to Carter, 29 May 1979, Pinon/283, CL.

109. Author's interview with Young.

110. Author's interview with Richardson. African Americans in the executive branch included Henry Richardson at the NSC; Anne Holloway, Ron Palmer, Clyde Ferguson, Goler Butcher, Bev Carter, and George Dally at the State Department; and Clifford Alexander, Percy Pierre, and Colin Powell at the Defense Department.

111. Vance to Carter, with Carter's marginalia, 25 Jan 1979, Plains/39, CL; and Hatcher (Chair, TransAfrica), Remarks at Meeting of Secretary of State and the Black Leadership, 25 Jan 1979, Martin/92, CL. Also Vance to Carter, 20 Jan 1979, ibid.; and Christopher to Carter, 31 Jan 1979, ibid.

112. See Moore, Meeting with the CBC, 27 Feb 1979, Martin/22, CL.

113. *Afro-American* (Baltimore), 9 Jun 1979, 5; Young to Carter and Vance, 27 Mar 1979, NLC-24-110-7-4-1; Funk to ZB, 6 Apr 1979, Funk/119, CL; CBC (Diggs, Collins, Gray) to Carter, 25 Apr 1979, Beckel/228, CL; and Jackson quoted in Fran

[Woode] to Carter, 23 May 1979, Staff Secretary/40, CL. Also Funk to ZB, 28 Mar 1979, Funk/119, CL; and Collins, *CR-House*, 21 May 1979, 12008.

114. Author's interviews with Thornton and Moose (2001). For Collins' testimony, see *CR-House*, 21 May 1979, 12008. Late in the process, the leaders of the CBC wrote Carter asking for a meeting to discuss Africa "in the immediate future"; they met with Carter a month later. Diggs, Collins, Gray to Carter, 2 May 1979, Beckel/228, CL. See Moore to Collins, 9 May 1979, Pinson/283, CL; and Collins, Gray, Diggs to Carter, 1 Jun 1979, ibid.

115. *Afro-American* (Baltimore), 9 Jun 1979, 5; and Thursday Lunch Group, *Newsletter*, Feb 1979, Martin/109, CL. Also *Rhodesian Herald*, 17 May 1979, 1.

116. Author's interviews with Young and Thornton.

117. See letters in: FOIA-mf; Beckel/228, CL; Martin/109, CL; and US Foreign Relations: Rhodesia/253, ANS. See also *Rhodesian Herald*, e.g., 17 May 1979, 1; and 29 May 1979, 4. For credit given to lobbies: *NYT*, 26 May 1979, 2; and *WP*, 30 May 1979, B1.

118. Memcon (Carrington, Vance), 21 May 1979, FCO 82/992, NA-UK; and author's interview with Renwick.

119. See US Senate, "Authorizing Appropriations," CD63, 10, 125, 151–52. Also *WP*, 7 Jun 1979, 1. Byrd's amendment lifting sanctions was passed by a 13-to-3 vote. Byrd, *CR-Senate*, 12 Jun 1979, 14328. The bill, S428, was then passed unanimously by the committee. US Senate, "Authorizing Appropriations," CD63, 137.

120. Funk to ZB, 25 May 1979, Funk/119, CL; and US House, "Rhodesia: Where Do We Go From Here?," CD28. Also, Vance to Carter, 27 Apr 1979, NLC-128-14-6-21-5; *NYT*, 13 May 1979, E5 (interview with Solarz); Squire to Renwick, 29 May 1979, FCO 36/2506, NA-UK; and Duncan, "Report." Duncan (D-OR) accompanied Solarz to Africa.

121. Solarz to Carter, 23 May 1979, Pinson/283, CL. See Vance, ER, 27 Apr 1979, NLC-133-7-4-12-9.

122. Davidson to Renwick, 1 Jun 1979, FCO 36/2506, NA-UK.

123. *Meet the Press* transcript, 3 Jun 1979, FCO 36/2506, NA-UK; and *CSM*, 7 Jun 1979, 1.

124. Ten Representatives to Carter, 31 May 1979, Beckel/228, CL. They were referring to the hearings organized by Solarz. See US House, "Economic Sanctions against Rhodesia," CD27.

125. Erlenborn and Pease to Colleagues, 4 Jun 1979, in *CR-Senate*, 11 Jun 1979, 14189; Bellmon, ibid., 14192; and Carrington, FCO 626, 7 Jun 1979, FCO 36/2652, NA-UK. See Erlenborn, *CR-House*, 9 Apr 1979, 7766–67; Spencer, 5 Jun 1979, FCO36/2652, NA-UK; and *CSM*, 7 Jun 1979, 1.

126. Lake to ZB, 24 May 1979, Funk/119, CL.

127. Author's interview with Carter.

128. "Statement to Congressional Leadership and members of foreign relations and foreign affairs committees," FOIA. Despite the title, this edited draft is basically the speech that Carter delivered in public. See Carter, "Trade Sanctions against Rhodesia," 7 Jun 1979, APP. Also Vance to Carter, [May 1979,] NLC-15-44-6-15-5; "Rhodesia Speech" 17 May 1979, NLC-133-232-5-2-9; "Negative Determination," 22 May 1979, NLC-6-89-2-4-2; Brewster, London 11087, 5 Jun 1979, NLC-16-26-6-73; and *NYT*, 10 Jun 1979, 10.

129. Carter, "Trade Sanctions against Rhodesia," 7 Jun 1979, APP. Covers following two paragraphs.

Chapter 14

1. Quoted in Zaremba, "Karol Wojtyła," 317.
2. Noskova et al., *Pol'ša*, 789; and Zaremba, "Karol Wojtyła."
3. See Trenor, "The Polish Desk."
4. Noskova, *Pol'ša*, 790. See CIA, "The Impact of a Polish Pope on the USSR," 19 Oct 1978, CIA-rr.
5. Vance, SecTo 4086, 30 May 1979, NLC-16-26-5-35-3.
6. This account is based on reports in *NYT, CSM, WP, LAT, CT, WSJ, Time*, and *Newsweek*. Also Kwitny, *Man*, 324–30; and Weigel, *Witness*, 304–23.
7. John Vinocur, *NYT*, 11 Jun 1979, 1.
8. The phrase is used by Andrew Young to describe marches during the US civil rights struggle in the 1950s and 1960s. Author's interview with Young. See Ponichtere, "One More Reason."
9. Noskova, *Pol'ša*, 790.
10. *NYT*, 1 Jun 1979, 1.
11. *NYT*, 5 Jun 1979, edit 20; *WP*, 4 Jun 1979, edit 26; and *WP*, 10 Jun 1979, edit D6.
12. *Time*, 18 June 1979, 26; *CSM*, 6 Jun 1979, edit 24; *NYT*, 5 Jun 1979, edit 20; and *WP*, 4 Jun 1979, edit 26.
13. *WP*, 4 Jun 1979, edit 26; *Time*, 18 June 1979, 26; *CSM*, 4 Jun 1979, edit 32; and *NYT*, 5 Jun 1979, edit 20.
14. Noskova, *Pol'ša*, 790.
15. *Afro-American* (Baltimore), 16 Jun 1979, 17; *WP*, 8 Jun 1979, B1; and *Time*, 25 Jun 1979, 21.
16. *WP*, 8 Jun 1979, B1.
17. *Philadelphia Tribune*, 1 Jun 1979, 3.
18. *Washington Informer*, 7 Jun 1979, 23. For unemployment: ibid., 14 Jun 1979, 20.
19. Author's interview with Moose (2001).
20. *Oakland Post*, 26 Jun 1979, 3. See: *The Skanner* (Portland, OR), 20 Jun 1979, 4 (NAACP); *Afro-American* (Baltimore), 16 Jun 1979, 16 (National Conference of Black Mayors); *Pittsburgh Courier*, 23 Jun 1979, 2 (SCLC); and *Washington Informer*, 21 Jun 1979, 3 (CBC). Also Jordan to Carter, 8 Jun 1979, Schneider/261, CL; and *Oakland Post*, 24 Jun 1979, 6.
21. *Amsterdam News* (New York), 16 Jun 1979, edit 18). See *Afro-American* (Baltimore), 26 Jun 1979, edit 4; *Washington Informer*, 7 Jun 1979, 23; *Washington Informer*, 14 Jun 1979, 20; *Sun-Reporter* (San Francisco), 21 Jun 1979, edit 7; and *Tri-State Defender* (Memphis), 23 Jun 1979, edit 5.
22. *Atlanta Daily World*: 12 Jun 1979, edit 6; 14 Jun 1979, edit 6; and 19 Jun 1979, edit 6. For Walls: Edmondson, Pretoria 5320, 11 Jun 1979, FOIA-mf. See Julian Bond to Editor, *NYT*, 6 Jul 1979, 20.
23. *LAT*, 8 Jun 1979, 1. See page 1 of the 8 Jun 1979 editions of *NYT, WP, WSJ, CT*, and *Sun* (Baltimore).
24. These editorials, written a fortnight later, strongly support maintaining sanctions: *Sun* (Baltimore), 20 Jun 1979, edit 18; *CSM*, 21 Jun 1979, edit 24; *CT*, 21 Jun 1979, edit B2; and *WP*, 22 Jun 1979, edit 18.
25. This and the following three paragraphs are based on these editorials: *WP*, 8 Jun 1979, 18; *LAT*, 10 Jun 1979, E4; *CSM*, 11 Jun 1979, 24; *NYT*, 11 Jun 1979, 18; *Sun* (Baltimore), 11 Jun 1979, 16; *WSJ*, 11 Jun 1979, 14; and *CT*, 11 Jun 1979, C2.

26. *NYT*, 10 Jun 1979, 10; and Trade Sanctions against Rhodesia, 7 Jun 1979, APP.

27. Renwick to Duff and Wall, 8 Jun 1979, FCO 36/2652, NA-UK; Memcon (Ridley, Christopher, 13 Jun 1979), 18 Jun 1979, FCO 36/2506, NA-UK; *NYT*, 10 Jun 1979, 10; and *Guardian* (London), 9 Jun 1979, 19.

28. Spencer to Renwick, 8 Jun 1979, FCO 36/2652, NA-UK; and Lake and Moose to Vance, 21 Jun 1979, Lake/5, NA.

29. Lake and Moose to Vance, 21 Jun 1979, Lake/5, NA.

30. Renwick to Duff and Wall, 8 Jun 1979, FCO 36/2652, NA-UK; O'Brien, Lusaka 1934, 9 Jun 1979, FOIA-mf; and Duff's minute on Renwick to Duff and Wall, 8 Jun 1979, FCO 36/2652, NA-UK.

31. Thatcher to Carter, 15 Jun 1979, FCO 82/977, NA-UK; Melhuish to Leahy and Parsons, 26 Jun 1979, FCO 82/979, NA-UK; and Lake and Moose to Vance, 21 Jun 1979, Lake/5, NA, with Vance's marginalia. Also FCO, "Meeting with President Carter, Tokyo, 28–29 Jun 1979," 21 Jun 1979, FCO 82/995, NA-UK.

32. Author's interview with Kaunda.

33. DePree, Maputo 718, 8 May [*sic*; it must be June] 1979, FOIA-mf; O'Brien, Lusaka 1934, 9 Jun 1979, FOIA-mf; McGuire, Maputo 721, 9 May [*sic*; it must be June] 1979, FOIA-mf; Easum, Lagos 7941, 12 Jun 1979, FOIA-mf; and author's interview with DePree. Also Wyman, Lagos 7863, 9 Jun 1979, FOIA; Brown, Lagos 295, 11 Jun 1979, FCO 36/2652, NA-UK; Allinson, Lusaka 390, 11 Jun 1979, FCO 36/2652, NA-UK; Obee, Dar 2696, 11 Jun 1979, FOIA-mf; and *Nation* (Nairobi), 12 Jun 1979 in Watts, Nairobi 321, 12 Jun 1979, FCO 36/2652, NA-UK.

34. Robinson, Washington 1414, 8 Jun 1979, FCO 36/2652, NA-UK.

35. Vance to Carter, 9 Jun 1979, NLC-128-14-8-7-9. See Robinson, Washington 1414, 8 Jun 1979, FCO 36/2652, NA-UK.

36. Scott, Cape Town 353, 11 Jun 1979, FCO 36/2652, NA-UK; *Rhodesian Herald* (Salisbury), 9 Jun 1979, edit 6; and *Sunday Mail* (Salisbury), 10 Jun 1979, edit 12.

37. Edmondson, Pretoria 5320, 11 Jun 1979, FOIA-mf; *NYT*, 9 Jun 1979, 1; and *Daily Mail* (Salisbury), 10 Jun 1979, 1.

38. *CQ Weekly*, 16 Jun 1979, 1185.

39. *CSM*, 12 Jun 1979, 4.

40. Vance, *Hard Choices*, 296; and US Senate, "Trade Sanctions against Rhodesia," CD64, 2–8. The House hearing was in closed session. For Vance's opening statement: *CR-House*, 12 Jun 1979, 14519; and *CR-House*, 22 Jun 1979, 16211–14.

41. US Senate, "Trade Sanctions against Rhodesia," CD64, 2–8.

42. See ibid., 30 and 22.

43. Robinson, Washington 1416, 8 Jun 1979, FCO 36/2652, NA-UK. Also US Senate, Committee on Foreign Relations, "Business Meeting," CD65; *CR-Senate*, 12 Jun 1979, 14324–25; *NYT*, 13 Jun 1979, 1; and *CQ Weekly*, 16 Jun 1979, 1185. Although there is no public record of the vote, the one senator who opposed the amendment must have been Helms.

44. *CR-Senate*, 12 Jun 1979, 14325.

45. *CR-Senate*, 12 Jun 1979, 14343, 14340, 14336. For the debate: ibid., 14320–46.

46. Ibid., 14321–22, 14325, 14338–39.

47. *CR-Senate*, 6 Jun 1979, 1372.

48. *CR-Senate*, 12 Jun 1979, 14340, 14337, 14370, 14336, 14395.

49. Atwood to Vance, 30 Jun 1979, NSA-staff/119-125, CL.

50. *CR-Senate*, 12 Jun 1979, 14343, 14329, 14339.

51. The 52–41 vote was on tabling the Tsongas (Javits) amendment. Twenty Democrats joined thirty-two Republicans in favor of tabling; eight Republicans joined thirty-three Democrats who opposed the motion. Seven did not vote. *CR-Senate*, 12 Jun 1979, 14346.

52. *WP*, 13 Jun 1979, 3; *NYT*, 10 Jun 1979, 1; *CSM*, 12 Jun 1979, 4; and *CSM*, 11 Jun 197, 5. Gallup gave Carter a 32 percent approval rating.

53. *Rhodesian Herald*, 14 Jun 1979, edit 6; *WP*, 13 Jun 1979, 1; *LAT*, 13 Jun 1979, 1; *WSJ*, 13 Jun 1979, 5; and *NBC Evening News*, 13 Jun 1979, VNA. Also *Sun* (Baltimore), 13 Jun 1979, 1; *CT*, 13 Jun 1979, 2; and *CBS* and *ABC Evening News*, 13 Jun 1979, VNA.

54. *NYT*, 13 Jun 1979, 1.

55. *NYT*, 14 Jun 1979, 4; and *Rhodesian Herald*, 14 Jun 1979, edit 6.

56. *NYT*, 8 Jun 1979, 1. For O'Neill: *WP*, 14 Jun 1979, 1.

57. Vance to Carter, 13 Jun 1979, NLC-128-14-8-10-5. For lobbying: Funk to Gates, 8 Jun 1979, Beckel/228, CL; Wexler and Martin to Carter, 13 Jun 1979, Pinson/283, CL; and Office of Media Liaison, "Zimbabwe-Rhodesia Economic Sanctions," 13 Jun 1979, Pinson/283, CL. Also Weissman and Carson, "Economic Sanctions," 150.

58. *CR-House*, 28 Jun 1979, 17199; and *NYT*, 17 Jun 1979, E2. Also *WP*, 22 Jun 1979, edit 18.

59. *Guardian*, 14 Jun 1979, edit 13; Wyman, Lagos 7833, 8 Jun 1979, FOIA; and Easum, Lagos 8242, 18 Jun 1979, FOIA. Also Easum, Lagos 7893, 11 Jun 1979, FOIA; Easum, Lagos 8192, 16 Jun 1979, FOIA; and author's interview with Easum.

60. Jay, Washington 1522, 14 Jun 1979, FCO 36/2506, NA-UK. See Wilkinson to Spencer and Renwick, 8 Jun 1979, FCO 36/2506, NA-UK.

61. HR 4439, "Relating to Sanctions against Zimbabwe-Rhodesia," 13 Jun 1979; and Atwood to Vance, 30 Jun 1979, NSA-staff/119-125, CL. See *CR-House*, 14 Jun 1979, 15023; and US House, "Zimbabwe-Rhodesia: The Issue of Sanctions," CD29, 4–5.

62. Vance to Carter, 13 Jun 1979, NLC-128-14-8-10-5. Also Newsom, State 147670, 8 Jun 1979, FOIA; "Supplemental Views of . . . Findley," in US House, "Zimbabwe-Rhodesia: The Issue of Sanctions," CD29, 11–12; and Weissman and Carson, "Economic Sanctions," 150.

63. *NYT*, 18 Jun 1979, 1; and *WSJ*, 19 Jun 1979, edit 22. See Memcons (Carter, Brezhnev), 16–18 Jun 1979, *FRUS, 1977–1980, v. 6: Soviet Union*, docs. 199–207.

64. *Newsweek*, 25 Jun 1979, 104.

65. US House, "Zimbabwe-Rhodesia: The Issue of Sanctions," CD29, 4–5; and *WP*, 16 Jun 1979, 1.

66. Bennet to Vance, 19 Jun 1979, FOIA-mf.

67. Vance to Carter, 20 Jun 1979, NLC-128-14-8-13-2. See Clift to Mondale, 20 Jun 1979, NLC-133-114-1-31-2.

68. 19–23 Jun 1979, President's Daily Diary, CL-online.

69. *CSM*, 22 Jun 1979, 6; *CR-Senate*, 21 Jun 1979, 15858; *NYT*, 29 Jun 1979, 2; Vance to Carter, 20 Jun 1979, NLC-128-14-8-13-2; and *NYT*, 28 Jun 1979, 19. Muzorewa's party held 43 seats; Smith's party, 28; two splinter black parties, 17; and Sithole—who was boycotting—12.

70. Edmondson, Pretoria 5549, 18 Jun 1979, FOIA-mf. See Moorcraft and McLaughlin, *Rhodesian War*, 162–63, 480–84; Baxter, *Rhodesia*; and Martin and Johnson, *Struggle*, 308–12.

71. *NYT*, 29 Jun 1979, 2; and *WP*, 21 Jun 1979, 22. See "Total National Strategy Guidelines for Zimbabwe-Rhodesia," 23 Mar 1979, SA DFAA, BTS 1/156/3 v.4 in Onslow, "Documents," 309–10; Australian Intelligence Service, "Rhodesia: Prospects for a Settlement," 19 Jul 1979, A1838 190-2-1/65, NA-AUS; Edmondson, Pretoria 5569, 19 Jun 1979, FOIA-mf; and Wilkinson, "Impact."

72. Low, Lusaka 2151, 26 Jun 1979, FOIA; Low, Lusaka 2234, 2 Jul 1979, FOIA; and *Guardian*, 27 Jun 1979, 1. Also Low, Lusaka 2153, 26 Jun 1979, FOIA; and Low, Lusaka 2155, 26 Jun 1979, FOIA-mf. See Petter-Bowyer, *Winds of Destruction*, 506–10.

73. *Rhodesian Herald*, 27 Jun 1979, 5; *WP*, 21 Jun 1979, 22; and *CSM*, 22 Jun 1979, 6. Also *WS*, 18 Jun 1979, 8; and *NYT*, 29 Jun 1979, 2.

74. See *CR-House*, 28 Jun 1979, 17195–225.

75. Solarz to Carter, 23 May 1979, Pinson/283, CL. See US House, "Zimbabwe-Rhodesia: The Issue of Sanctions," CD29.

76. *CR-House*, 28 Jun 1979, 17217 (Dellums); and *Washington Informer*, 21 Jun 1979, 3. See *CR-House*, 28 Jun 1979, 17202 (Collins).

77. *CR-House*, 28 Jun 1979, 17218 (Buchanan), 17204 (Fenwick).

78. Ibid., 17216 (Bingham), 17205 (Hyde), 218 (Rudd), 216 (Derwinski), 218 (Bauman).

79. See ibid., 17223–25. The Broomfield amendment was opposed by 216 Democrats and 26 Republicans; it was supported by 117 Republicans and 30 Democrats. The Solarz bill was supported by 236 Democrats and 114 Republicans; opposed by 27 Republicans and 10 Democrats.

80. *WSJ*, 9 Jul 1979, edit 16; and *Rhodesian Herald*, 30 Jun 1979, 1. See (all 29 Jun 1979): *NBC Evening News*, VNA; *NYT*, 2; *LAT*, 18; *Sun*, 10; and *CT*, 6.

81. Atwood to Acting Secretary, 2 Jul 1979, FOIA; and Atwood to Vance, 30 Jun 1979, NSA-staff/119-125, CL.

82. Albright to ZB, 30 Jun 1979, NSA-congress/2, CL; and Atwood to Vance, 30 Jun 1979, NSA-staff/119-125, CL.

83. Carter, *Diary*, 337, 335, 336.

84. *WP*, 7 July 1979, 1. The *WP* "obtained a copy" of the memo.

85. Address to the Nation on Energy and National Goals, 15 July 1979, APP.

86. *NYT*, 8 July 1979, E1. See Robinson, Washington 1831, 6 Jul 1979, Thatcher Papers.

87. See Mattson, "What the Heck."

88. ZB to Carter, 10 Jul 1979, Funk/119, CL (there is no hint of this advice in his memoirs: Brzezinski, *Power*, 142); *Rhodesian Herald*, 13 Jul 1979, 4; Robinson, quoted in *WP*, 10 Jul 1979, 2; and *WP*, 12 Jul 1979, 1. See Cartledge to Wall, Memcon (Thatcher, Helms), 4 Jul 1979, FCO36/2506, NA-UK.

89. *Rhodesian Herald*, 13 Jul 1979, 4; and *Sunday Mail* (Salisbury), 1 Jul 1979, edit 12.

90. *CSM*, 9 Jul 1979, edit 24. Also Robinson to Duff, 11 Sep 1979, FCO 36/2540, NA-UK.

91. Cartledge to Wall, Memcon (Thatcher, Helms), 4 Jul 1979, FCO36/2506, NA-UK. See Press Office Bulletin: Senator Helms, 4 Jul 1979, Thatcher Papers.

92. *WP*, 20 Jul 1979, 15. Carbaugh wrote to Thatcher asking her to give an interview to Evans and Novak. The prime minister minuted, "I can't give him an interview." Thatcher's marginalia on Cartledge to Thatcher, "Senator Helms and Mr. Carbaugh," 5 Jul 1979, Thatcher Papers.

93. Memcon (Thatcher, Waldheim, Carrington), 12 Jul 1979, FCO 36/2548, NA-UK; and Wall to Cartledge, 16 Jul 1979, Thatcher Papers.

94. Low, "Zimbabwe," 105. Also author's interview with Renwick.

95. Telcon (Carter, Thatcher), 4 Jul 1979, Thatcher Papers.

96. Thatcher to Carter (2), 7 Jul 1979, in FCO 814, 9 July 1979, FCO 36/2539, NA-UK; and *Rhodesian Herald*, 2 Jul 1979, edit 8. See Carrington, "Rhodesia," 10 July 1979, *Parliamentary Debates*, Lords, 5th ser., vol. 401, cols. 757–63.

97. Thatcher to Carter (1), 7 Jul 1979, in FCO 814, 9 Jul 1979, FCO 36/2539, NA-UK; and 12 Jul 1979, Washington 79449, A1838 190-2-1/65, NA-AUS.

98. 11 Jul 1979, London 35970, A1838 190-2-1/65, NA-AUS; and Atwood to Acting Secretary, 2 Jul 1979, FOIA. Also Atwood to Vance, 30 Jun 1979, NSA-staff/119-125, CL.

99. *CSM*, 13 Jul 1979, 3; US House, 25 Jul 1979, "Report to Congress on Rhodesia," CD30, 2, 21; and Carrington, "Rhodesia," 10 July 1979, *Parliamentary Debates*, Lords, 5th ser., vol. 401, col. 762.

100. Cook to Moose, 10 Jul 1979, NSA-staff/119, CL; Vance, State 178632, 11 Jul 1979, FOIA; and 12 Jul 1979, Washington 79449, A1838 190-2-1/65, NA-AUS. Also Moose to Vance, 11 Jul 1979, FOIA; Memcon (McCloskey, Muzorewa), 11 Jul 1979 in McCloskey to Moose, 13 Jul 1979, Lake/10, NA; and Memcon (Carrington, Mondale) in Wall to Renwick, 20 Jul 1979, FCO 36/2539, NA-UK.

101. Vance, *Hard Choices*, 298; Funk to ZB, 20 Jul 1979, NLC-10-22-3-12-0; and *Rhodesian Herald*, 12 Jul 1979, 4, 1. See *Rhodesian Herald*, 13 Jul 1979, 1.

102. *Rhodesian Herald:* 11 Jul 1979, edit 8; 14 Jul 1979, edit 6; 17 Jul 1979, edit 4; 19 Jul 1979, 5; and Smith, *Betrayal*, 310.

103. Address to the Nation on Energy and National Goals, 15 July 1979, APP.

104. Ibid.; *NYT*, 18 Jul 1979, 1; and *NYT*, 19 Jul 1979, 1. For rebuke: *WP*, 19 Jul 1979, 1.

105. *NYT*, 19 Jul 1979, 1.

106. *Rhodesian Herald*, 23 Jul 1979, edit 8. Carter immediately accepted the resignations of Joseph Califano (Health, Education and Welfare), Michael Blumenthal (Treasury), and Griffin Bell (Attorney General). Brock Adams (Transportation) and James Schlesinger (Energy) were forced out one day later.

107. US Congress, "Joint Conferees: HR 3363," CD2, 53.

108. Ibid., 53–54, 61, 63; *CR-Senate*, 2 Aug 1979, 22311; and *Rhodesian Herald*, 1 Aug 1979, edit 12. See *CR-House*, 2 Aug 1979, 22095–97 (discussion), 22105–106 (vote); *CR-Senate*, 2 Aug 1979, 22310–12; and US House, "Authorizing Appropriations," CD31, 12.

109. "Report of the Commonwealth Committee on Southern Africa, June 1977–June 1979," Jun 1979, box 10667, pt. 2, Block 23, RG 25, Canada.

110. *Observer* (London), 9 Dec 1979, 5.

111. Australian Department of Foreign Affairs, Department of the Prime Minister and Cabinet, "Southern Africa and CHOGM," 27 Apr 1979, A10756/ LC2512 Part 1, NA-AUS.

112. "Tanzania" (sheaf of handwritten notes), [1 Aug 1979,] Fraser Papers, M1356/11, NA-AUS.

113. For a summary of CHOGM debates about Rhodesia, 1966–1977: Rice, "Commonwealth Initiative," 30–37.

114. Beesley, Canberra YAGR 1916, "CHGM Lsaka [sic]: Australian Position," 29 Jun 1979, box 10667, pt. 2, block 23, RG 25, Canada.

115. Australian Department of Foreign Affairs, The Refugee Question at CHOGM, 2 Jul 1979, A10756/ LC2512 Part 1, NA-AUS; Prime Minister's Office and the Foreign Office, "Southern Africa and CHOGM," 27 Apr 1979, A12909/3135, NA-AUS; and Australian Department of Foreign Affairs and CHOGM Task Force to Cabinet, "CHOGM An Overview: Background," 29 Jun 1979, A1838 899/6/21/1 Part 6, NA-AUS.

116. Fraser to Thatcher, 19 May 1979, A1209, 1979/834, part 1, NA-AUS. Also Thatcher to Fraser, 5 Jun 1979, ibid.

117. Beesley, Canberra YAGR 1916, "CHGM Lsaka [sic]: Australian Position," 29 Jun 1979, box 10667, pt. 2, block 23, RG 25, Canada; Fraser to Clark, 17 Jul 1979, in (name illegible) High Commission, Canberra to FCC Ottawa, 19 Jul 1979, box 10667, pt. 4, ibid.; and Memcon (Fraser, Thatcher) 1 Jul 1979, A1209, 1979/834, part 2, NA-AUS. See Handwritten notes, Memcon (Fraser, Thatcher), 30 Jun 1979, ibid.; and Holdich to Fraser, "Trigger Points for Meeting with Mrs Thatcher," 30 June 1979, ibid.

118. PPS to Walden, "The Prime Minister's Visit to Canberra: Rhodesia," 3 Jul 1979, Thatcher Papers; and Transcript of Thatcher at National Press Club on 1 July, 1979 in Canberra 833542, 3 Jul 1979, A1209, 1979/834, part 2, NA-AUS. See Carrington, FCO 152, 1 Jul 1979, Thatcher Papers; 16 Jul 1979, London 36349, A1838 190-2-1/66, NA-AUS; and Fraser, *Malcolm Fraser*, 506. The Fraser administration struggled, and failed, to stop Thatcher from answering press questions. See Tebbit, Canberra 287, 6 Jun 1979, Thatcher Papers; "The Prime Minister's Visit to Australia," 15 Jun 1979, ibid.; and Tebbit, Canberra 339, 29 Jun 1979, ibid.

119. 12 Jul 1979, Washington 79449, A1838 190-2-1/65, NA-AUS. See Memcon (Thatcher, Waldheim), 12 Jul 1979, FCO 36/2548, NA-UK. Also 6 Jul 1979, Australian UN-NY14654, A1838 190-2-1/64, NA-AUS; and Memcon (Parsons, Maynes), 9/10 Jul 1979, FCO 82/980, NA-UK.

120. Nyerere to Thatcher, 10 Jul 1979, Thatcher Papers; and 20 Jul 1979, London 36789, A1838 190-2-1/66, NA-AUS. See 3 Jul 1979, Lagos 5729, ibid.; and 6 Jul 1979, Lagos 5758, ibid.

121. Walker, Monrovia 5433, 11 Jul 1979, FOIA; 21 Jul 1979, Lagos 5921, A1838 190-2-1/66, NA-AUS; and Walker, Monrovia 5691, 21 Jul 1979, FOIA. Also Memcon (Tolbert, Solarz) in Walker, Monrovia 6173, 8 Aug 1979, DDRS. On the banning of Muzorewa: *Rhodesian Herald*, 11 Jul 1979, edit 8; and *Rhodesian Herald*, 25 Jul 1979, edit 10.

122. *WP*, 23 Jul 1978, 1; "On Zimbabwe," AHG/Res84 (XIV), in Legum, *ACR 1977–1978*, C3; and Thatcher to Fraser in Carrington, FCO 439, 27 Jul 1979, Thatcher Papers. See 18 Jul 1979, London 36575, A1838 190-2-1/65, NA-AUS; and 23 Jul 1979, Canberra 836910, A1838 190-2-1/66, NA-AUS.

123. Peacock to Fraser, 26 Jul 1979, A1838 190-2-1/66, NA-AUS; 23 Jul 1979, Nairobi 8817, ibid.; and Walker, Monrovia 5691, 21 Jul 1979, FOIA.

124. Easum, Lagos 10280, 1 Aug 1979, FOIA. Also Easum, Lagos 10947, 13 Aug 1979, FOIA; Easum, Lagos 12093, 10 Sep 1979, FOIA; and Brown, 24 Oct 1996, BDOHP. The Nigerian government controlled 60 percent of the BP distribution network in Nigeria; this action gave it control of the remaining 40 percent.

125. *Nigerian Standard* (Lagos), 3 Aug 1979, 1; *Daily Times* (Lagos), 4 Aug 1979, back page; *Rhodesian Herald*, 2 Aug 1979, edit 8; and *Rhodesian Herald*, 14 May 1979, edit 6.

126. Situation Room to ZB, 31 Jul 1979, NLC-1-11-6-27-3. See Ingram, "Lusaka," 280.

127. *Rhodesian Herald*: 30 May 1979, edit 10; 16 Aug 1979, edit 12; and 30 Jul 1979, edit 10.

128. Speech for CHOGM Opening Session (draft), 23 Jul 1979, A10756, LC2512 part 1, NA-AUS. See McIntyre, *Significance*, 35.

129. See Peacock to Fraser, 29 Jul 1979, [Australian,] Thatcher Papers; Memcon (Peacock, Carrington), 31 Jul 1979, Thatcher Papers; and Hancock, "Australian policy." Jamaican prime minister Michael Manley spoke fulsomely about Fraser's role. See Kingston 3627, 10 Dec 1979, 1838 899/6/21/1 part 12, NA-AUS.

130. DOS, "Talking Points for Vice President Mondale's Office Meeting with Prime Minister Muldoon," [Sep 1978,] NLC-133-75-6-25-8; and Memcon (Thatcher, Muldoon), 1 Aug 1979, Thatcher Papers. See Gustafson, *His Way*, 95-97.

131. Fraser to Clark, in "Visit of Mr. Alan Griffith, June 5–6, 1979," box 10667, pt. 2, block 23, RG 25, Canada; and Clark to Fraser, attached to F.M. to Clark, "Letter from Prime Minister Fraser on Rhodesia," 25 Jul 1979, box 10667, pt. 4, block 23, RG 25, Canada. See Shenstone, "Discussion of Southern African Issues with Australians," 25 May 1979, box 10667, pt. 2, block 23, RG 25, Canada; Robertson, "CHGM—Visit of AT Griffith—Discussion on Africa," 6 Jun 1979, ibid.; [unsigned], Canberra YAGR 1655, "Ministerial Discussion on Southern Africa," 1 Jun 1979, ibid.; and Clark to Thatcher, in Richards, Yaounde 90, 30 Jul 1979, Thatcher Papers. For background, Kennair, *Forgotten Legacy*, 101–42.

132. Author's interview with Chona.

133. Vance to Carter, 4 Aug 1979, NLC-128-14-10-4-9; and *Sunday Mail* (Salisbury), 5 Aug 1979, edit 14. See "Prime Minister's Statement at Opening Session," 1 Aug 1979, Thatcher Papers; "Prime Minister's speech on Southern Africa" (draft), 3 Aug 1979, ibid.; and "Statement by the Prime Minister during the Opening Debate," 3 Aug 1979, annex A of Cabinet Meeting, 9 Aug 1979, CAB/129/207/3, NA-UK.

134. Vance to Carter, 4 Aug 1979, NLC-128-14-10-4-9. In an extended conversation with Canadian prime minister Joe Clark about British policy toward Rhodesia, neither leader mentioned new elections. See Memcon (Thatcher, Clark), 2 Aug 1979, Thatcher Papers.

135. Peacock to Fraser, "CHOGM Discussions in Dar es Salaam," 29 Jul 1979, A1838 190-2-1/67, NA-AUS; and Transcript of Nyerere's speech at Commonwealth Meeting, in 4 Aug 1979, Conference Post 140, ibid. Also Memcon (Peacock, Mkapa), 29 Jul 1979, Fraser Papers, M1356/11, NA-AUS; "Zimbabwe 'Sitrep,'" 30 Jul 1979, ibid.; and 4 Aug 1979, Conference Post 138, A1838 190-2-1/67, NA-AUS.

136. Memcon (Peacock, Carrington), 31 Jul 1979, Fraser Papers, M1356/11, NA-AUS.

137. Memcon (Fraser, Thatcher), 31 July 1979, A1838/899/6/21/7 part 1, NA-AUS; and Memcon (Thatcher, Fraser), 4 Aug 1979, Thatcher Papers.

138. F.M. to Clark, "CHOGM, Lusaka, August 1–8," 21 Jun 1979, box 10667, pt. 2, block 23, RG 25, Canada.

139. New Zealand's Muldoon suggested this small gathering. See Memcon (Thatcher, Muldoon), 1 Aug 1979, Thatcher Papers.

140. "Zimbabwe 'Sitrep,'" 30 Jul 1979, Fraser Papers, M1356/11, NA-AUS. For Clark: *Rhodesian Herald*, 29 May 1979, 4.

141. Memcon (Fraser, Thatcher, Carrington, Peacock), 4 Aug 1979, Fraser Papers, M1356/11, NA-AUS. Also Fraser, *Malcolm Fraser*, 509.

142. Memcon (Fraser, Thatcher, Carrington, Peacock), 4 Aug 1979, Fraser Papers, M1356/11, NA-AUS (emphasis added).

143. Renwick, *Unconventional Diplomacy*, 27. See ZB to Carter, [5 Aug 1979,] Funk/119, CL; and 6 Aug 1979, Conference Post 153, A1838 190-2-1/67, NA-AUS. For the communiqué: "Communiqué: Rhodesia," annex B of Cabinet Meeting, 9 Aug 1979, CAB/129/207/3, NA-UK. See Thatcher to Carter in Allinson, 5 Aug 1979, Lusaka 3, FCO 36/2539, NA-UK; and 5 Aug 1979, Conference Post 148, A1838 190-2-1/67, NA-AUS.

144. *Daily Times* (Lagos), 7 Aug 1979, 3; Situation Room to ZB, 8 Aug. 1979, NLC-1-11-7-25-4; and *Rhodesian Herald*, 6 Aug 1979, edit 6. Also ibid., 7 Aug 1979, edit 6; and ibid., 9 Aug 1979, edit 8.

145. Carter to Thatcher, 6 Aug 1979, FCO 36/2539, NA-UK.

Chapter 15

1. Carter, *White House Diary*, 349. See "Camp David Accords: The Framework for Peace in the Middle East," [17 Sep 1978,] CL-online.

2. For possible shift in PLO thinking: report of conversation between former West German chancellor Willy Brandt and Yasser Arafat, in Vance to Intelligence Summary Collective, IntSum 863, 30 Jul 1979, DNSA; interview with Arafat, *WS*, 12 Aug 1979, 1; "Autonomy and Possible Solutions," *Ha'aretz*, 19 Sep 1979, 4; and Hermann Eilts, FD, 12 Aug 1988. Also Quandt, *Peace Process*, 326–29; Spiegel, *Other Arab-Israeli Conflict*, 373–79; and Stein, *Heroic Diplomacy*, 253–60. For authorship of resolution: author's interview with Young. The PLO was granted observer status at the UN in 1974.

3. *WP*, 21 Aug 1979, 1.

4. Author's interview with Young. Also Young, *A Way Out of No Way*, 135–39; and Scheer, "Eyewitness." Kissinger gave this pledge to Israel as a Memorandum of Agreement on September 1, 1975, in connection with the second Sinai disengagement agreement.

5. See *Newsweek*, 27 Aug 1979, 14; and author's interview with Young.

6. *NYT*, 2 Aug 1979, 1; Vance to Intelligence Summary Collective, IntSum 863, 30 Jul 1979, DNSA; and *NYT*, 9 Aug 1979, 8.

7. "Remarks With Editors and News Directors," 10 Aug 1979, APP.

8. These allegations were widely reported: *Atlanta Constitution*, 16 Aug 1979, 1; ABC, CBS, *Evening News*, 16 Aug 1979, VNA; *Atlanta Constitution*, 23 Aug 1979, 1; CBS *Evening News*, 25 Aug 1979, VNA; *Time*, 27 Aug 1979, 10; *Newsweek*, 27 Aug 1979, 14; *Nation*, 8 Sep 1979, edit 162; *WP*, 29 Oct 1979, 22; and Jones, "National and International Consequences," 128. It is also very possible, as Wolf Blitzer alleges, that the National Security Agency bugged Young's conversation. See Blitzer, "Andy Young's Undoing."

9. *WP*, 16 Aug 1979, 1; and *NYT*, 19 Aug 1979, 1.

10. *LAT*, 14 Aug 1979, 1. See Reston (State Department spokesman), FD, 6 Jun 2005.

11. Author's interview with Young; *WS*, 17 Aug 1979, 4; and *NYT*, 6 Sep 1979, 18. See Blitzer, "Andy Young's Undoing."

12. *Atlanta Constitution*, 16 Aug 1979, 1. Also ABC *Evening News*, 16 Aug 1979, VNA. Young denied this report. See *NYT*, 19 Aug 1979, 1.

13. Author's interview with Young. See Friedman, "Intergroup Relations" 123–34; and *NYT*, 19 Aug 1979, 1.

14. See Rabinowitz, "Blacks, Jews, and New York"; and Friedman, "Race Relations," 78.

15. Maynes, FD, 14 Aug 1998.

16. Range, "*Playboy* Interview," 70.

17. Friedman, "Intergroup Relations," 139. Also *NYT*, 19 Aug 1979, 1; and author's interview with Young.

18. *NYT*, 15 Aug 1979, 1. Also *WP*, 15 Aug 1979, 1.

19. Finger, "Discussant," 141.

20. Author's interview with Carter.

21. Diary quoted in Carter, *Keeping Faith*, 491 (not included in *White House Diary*); and Fritchey, "Fall and Rise," 202.

22. *NBC Nightly News*, 14 Aug 1979, VNA. Also *ABC* and *CBS Nightly News*, 14 Aug 1979, VNA.

23. See *WP*, 16 Aug 1979, A1; and ABC *Nightly News*, 15 Aug 1979, VNA. Bush and Dole declared their candidacy in May 1979.

24. *NYT*, 15 Aug 1979, 1. Also the 15 Aug 1979 front pages of the *WP*, *LAT*, *CSM*, and *Sun* (Baltimore).

25. *NYT*, 16 Aug 1979, 1.

26. Diary quoted in Carter, *Keeping Faith*, 491.

27. Booker, "How Blacks Close to Carter," 7. See President's Daily Diary, CL-online; and *NYT*, 19 Aug 1979, 1.

28. See President's Daily Diary, CL-online.

29. Author's interview with Carter; and Young to Carter, 14 Aug 1979, Martin/109, CL. Also *NYT*, 19 Aug 1979, 1.

30. Author's interview with Young. Also "*Penthouse* Interview," 142. For Vance: Weisbord and Kazarian, *Israel in the Black American Perspective*, 130.

31. Scheer, "Eyewitness." See Young in US House, "US Interests in Africa," CD32, 17. Also author's interview with Young; *NYT*, 17 Oct 1979, 3; and Friedman, "Intergroup Relations."

32. Author's interview with Carter.

33. Carter, *Diary*, 352. Carter added this comment to his Diary when he edited it for publication in 2010.

34. For letters from African Americans decrying Young's firing, see Name/Hooks, CL; and "Young, Andrew, Departure from the White House," Martin/109, CL. Also Jesse Jackson, "Carter, Kennedy and the Black Vote," 24 Sep 1979, Name/Jackson, CL.

35. Carter to Young, 15 Aug 1979, Martin/109, CL. Also *WP*, 16 Aug 1979, 1; *Atlanta Constitution*, 16 Aug 1979, 17; *WS*, 16 Aug 1979, 1; *WSJ*, 16 Aug 1979, 2; and "The Fall of Andy Young," *Time*, 27 Aug 1979.

36. *Jet*, 30 Aug 1979, 5.

37. *WS*, 16 Aug 1979, 1; *Newsweek*, 27 Aug 1979, 14; and *WSJ*, 16 Aug 1979, 2.

38. Fritchey, "Fall and Rise," 202; and Dinnerstein, *Antisemitism*, 217.

39. Shattan, "Andy's Martyrdom," 9; and Baldwin, "Open Letter," 264.

40. Statement unanimously adopted by Black Leadership Meeting, "Blacks and US Foreign Policy," 22 Aug 1979, Name/NAACP, CL; Statement unanimously adopted by Black Leadership Meeting, "Ambassador Andrew Young, We are Proud of You," ibid.; Benjamin Hooks, "Victim of Double Standard," *WS*, 19 Aug 1979, C1; and Clark quoted in Logan, "Around City Hall," 137. Also CBS *Evening News*, 16 Aug 1979, VNA.

41. Fine, "Young Affair," 11, 13; and Brett Becker quoted in Logan, "Around City Hall," 138. Also, Alpert, "Our Black Friends," 4.

42. *WS*, 17 Aug 1979, 4.

43. Newhouse, "Sense of Duty," 71–72. The best sources on Lancaster House are Davidow, *Peace*; Low, "Zimbabwe"; Renwick, *Unconventional*; and Meredith, *Past Is Another Country*, 374–89. For the official report: Great Britain, *Southern Rhodesia*.

44. Young in US House, "US Interests in Africa," 18–19, CD32.

45. For the strategy: Duff to Renwick, 11 Oct 1979, FCO 36/2507, NA-UK; and Memcon (Soames, Kissinger), 19 Oct 1979, FCO 36/2507, NA-UK.

46. Smith, *Betrayal*, 319.

47. Carrington, *Reflecting*, 291. For the delegations: Great Britain, *Southern Rhodesia*, 1–2.

48. See Smith, *Betrayal*, 314–27; Renwick, *Unconventional*, 37; and Flower, *Serving Secretly*, 225–50.

49. Thatcher, "Rhodesia," 10 July 1979, *Parliamentary Debates*, Commons, 5th ser., vol. 967, col. 86. See Streator, London 17970, 12 Sep 1979, FOIA; and Great Britain, *Southern Rhodesia*, 3–8.

50. Robinson, Washington 2362, 20 Aug 1979, FCO 36/2507, NA-UK.

51. McHenry, USUN, 9 Nov 1979, in Mokoena and Gaymon, *Zimbabwe*.

52. *Economist*, 13 Oct 1979, 27. See, e.g., Vance, State 264744, 10 Oct 1979, FOIA; Wisner, Lusaka 3546, 9 Oct 1979, FOIA; Vance to Carrington, 21 Nov 1979, NSA-staff/118, CL; and Vance to Carter, 21 Nov 1979, NLC-128-14-13-16-3.

53. See Great Britain, *Southern Rhodesia*. On the land question in Zimbabwe, see esp., Riddell, "Land Problem"; Mlambo, "Land Grab"; and Onslow, "Land."

54. Fourie, *Brandpunte*, 146–47. See Smith, *Betrayal*, 320.

55. Vance, State 264744, 10 Oct 1979, FOIA. Also Wisner, Lusaka 3551, 10 Oct 1979, FOIA; and Christopher to Carter, 1 Nov 1979, NLC-128-14-13-1-9.

56. Author's interview with Chona.

57. Kaunda to Carter, 10 Oct. 1979, in Wisner, Lusaka 3570, 10 Oct. 1979, FOIA. Also Transcript of Nyerere's speech at Commonwealth Meeting, in 4 Aug 1979, Conference Post 140, A1838 190-2-1/67, NA-AUS. See: Mlambo, "Land Grab"; and Onslow, "Land."

58. Funk to ZB and Aaron, 12 Oct. 1979, NSA-staff/119, CL. Also Vance, *Hard Choices*, 299.

59. Davidow, *Peace*, 127, 65; Lanpher, FD, 25 Jun 2002; and *Time*, 29 Oct 1979, 52.

60. Brewster to Nkomo, 13 Nov 1979, [US], FCO 36/2507, NA-UK; and Carter's marginalia on Vance to Carter, 27 Oct 1979, NLC-128-14-12-18-2. Also Wisner, Lusaka 3569, 10 Oct 1979, FOIA; and Christopher to Carter, 26 Oct 1979, NLC-128-14-12-17-3.

61. Memcon (Carrington, Brewster) in Walden to Renwick, 15 Oct 1979, FCO 36/2540, NA-UK.

62. FCO, Rhodesia Department, "Rhodesia: Constitutional Conference: Essential Facts" in Walden to Alexander, 8 Oct 1979, FCO 36/2540, NA-UK; and Moose and Lake to Acting Secretary, 23 Aug 1979, Lake/5, NA. Also Vance to Carter, 21 Sep 1979, NLC-128-14-11-12-9; and Renwick to Walden, 21 Sep 1979, FCO 36/2507, NA-UK.

63. Moose to Vance, 6 Oct 1979, Lake/5, NA. Also Memcon (Carrington, Brewster, Lanpher), 7 Nov 1979, FCO 36/2507, NA-UK; and Vance to Carter, 10 Nov 1979, NLC-128-14-13-7-3.

64. Squire to Renwick, 13 Sep 1979, FCO 36/2549, NA-UK.

65. Ibid.

66. "Report by Lord Harlech on his visit to the U.S.A," 29 Oct 1979," FCO 36/2568, NA-UK.

67. Helms to Thatcher, 12 Sep 1979 in Alexander (Thatcher's private secretary) to Walden, 17 Sep 1979, FCO 36/2540, NA-UK (emphasis in original).

68. *Sunday Mail* (Salisbury), 23 Sep 1979, 6.

69. Moore, *Thatcher*, 501, based on interview with Carbaugh.

70. Nicholas to Duff, with marginalia, 17 Sep 1979, FCO 36/2507, NA-UK; Robinson to Duff, 11 Sep 1979, FCO 36/2540, NA-UK; and "Report by Lord Harlech on his visit to the U.S.A," 29 Oct 1979, FCO 36/2568, NA-UK. See Memcon (Alexander, Lucier, Carbaugh), 14 Sep 1979 in Alexander to Walden, 17 Sep 1979, FCO 36/2540, NA-UK; and Thatcher to Helms, 9 Oct 1979, ibid.

71. Lanpher, FD, 25 Jun 2002. See Layden to Renwick, 13 Sep 1979, FCO 36/2507, NA-UK.

72. Author's interview with Renwick; and Renwick to Walden, 21 Sep 1979, FCO 36/2507, NA-UK.

73. Lanpher, FD, 25 Jun 2002; and Carrington to Vance, in Carrington, FCO 1248, 21 Sep 1979, FCO 36/2540, NA-UK. See *NYT*, 20 Sep 1979, 3; and *Guardian*, 21 Sep 1979, 8. In his memoirs, Vance gives a sanitized account: Vance, *Hard Choices*, 300.

74. Christopher, State 254640, 27 Sep 1979, FOIA-mf. Also Vance, State 245916, 19 Sep 1979, FOIA-mf.

75. Soviet Combat Troops in Cuba: Remarks to Reporters, 7 Sept 1979, APP; and Peace and National Security Address to the Nation on Soviet Combat Troops in Cuba and SALT, 1 Oct 1979, APP. See Newsom, *Soviet*; Garthoff, *Détente*, 828–48; Schoultz, *Infernal*, 335–46; Gleijeses, *Visions*, 126–33; and LeoGrande and Kornbluh, *Back Channel*, 207–11.

76. Memcon (Vance, François-Poncet, Carrington, Genscher), 25 Sep 1979, FCO 36/2549, NA-UK.

77. See Vance to Carter, 17 Sep 1979, NLC-128-14-11-9-3; Vance to Carter, 19 Sep 1979, NLC-128-14-11-10-1; Vance, State 245916, 19 Sep 1979, FOIA-mf; "Dear [colleague]," 25 Sep 1979, NSA-staff/119-125, CL; Carter to Stennis, 25 Sep 1979, NSA-staff/119-125, CL; Christopher to Carter, 25 Sep 1979, NLC-128-14-11-15-6; and Christopher to Carter, 26 Sep 1979, NLC-128-14-11-16-5.

78. Christopher to Carter, 27 Sep 1979, NLC-128-14-11-17-4; and *NYT*, 2 Oct 1979, B13.

79. Houder to Moose, 25 Oct 1979, FOIA-mf. See US House, "DOD Authorization Act," CD33, 18. The Rhodesia provision of the bill was discussed briefly in the Senate and generated no debate in the House: *CR-Senate*, 24 Oct 1979, 29359–361; and *CR-House*, 26 Oct 1979, 29768.

80. Thirteen women and blacks were released quickly. One hostage was allowed to return home due to sickness.

81. Vance, State 289359, 5 Nov 1979, FOIA-mf.

82. Memcon (Carrington, Brewster, Lanpher), 7 Nov 1979, FCO 36/2507, NA-UK. Also Vance to Carter, 7 Nov 1979, NLC-128-14-13-5-5. For Carrington's statement: "Southern Rhodesia Bill," 13 Nov 1979, *Parliamentary Debates*, Lords, 5th ser., vol. 402, cols. 1096–1106.

83. Brewster, 27 Nov 1979, London 23515, FOIA-mf. See Memcon (Carrington, Brewster, Lanpher), 7 Nov 1979, FCO 36/2507, NA-UK.

84. Vance to Carter, 10 Nov 1979, NLC-128-14-13-7-3. On November 14, 1979, Carrington introduced an "enabling bill" to pave the way for the governor. For text: Brewster, London 22921, 19 Nov 1979, FOIA.

85. "Report by Lord Harlech on his visit to the U.S.A," 29 Oct 1979, FCO 36/2568, NA-UK.

86. Vance to Carter in Moose, Lake to Vance, 27 Oct 1979, Lake/5, NA; and Moose, Lake to Vance, 12 Nov 1979, ibid.

87. Vance to Carter, 13 Nov 1979, Funk/119, CL; and ZB to Carter, 13 Nov 1979, NSA-subject/50-68, CL.

88. "Sanctions Against Rhodesia," DOS *Bulletin* (Feb 1980): 11. Also marginalia on Moose, Lake to Vance, 12 Nov 1979, Lake/5, NA; and Carter to Vance, 14 Nov 1979, NSA-subject/50-68, CL.

89. See Great Britain, *Southern Rhodesia*.

90. Funk to ZB, 15 Nov 1979, Funk/119, CL. For the agreement: Great Britain, *Southern Rhodesia*, 34–39. See Henderson, 18 Nov 1979, Washington 3778, FCO 36/2507, NA-UK.

91. Vance to Carter, 16 Nov 1979, NLC-128-14-13-12-7. Also Wisner, Lusaka 4239, 23 Nov 1979, FOIA-mf.

92. DePree, Maputo 1457, 23 Nov 1979, FOIA-mf; and Edmondson, Pretoria 10367, 16 Nov 1979, ibid.

93. Vance to Carter, 15 Nov 1979, NLC-128-14-13-11-8. Also Funk to ZB, 15 Nov 1979, Funk/119, CL.

94. Vance to Carter, 15 Nov 1979, NLC-128-14-13-11-8. Also Atwood to Vance, 17 Nov 1979, FOIA-mf; and Henderson, Washington 3778, 18 Nov 1979, FCO 36/2507, NA-UK. See S. Con. Res. 52, *CR-Senate*, 15 Nov 1979, 32616; and H. Con. 213, *CR-House*, 15 Nov 1979, 32789.

95. US Senate, "Rhodesia," CD66, 5; Moose to Vance, 29 Nov 1979, FOIA-mf; and US Senate, "To Continue Discussion of Rhodesian Resolutions," CD67, 2. For Moose's testimonies: US Senate, "Rhodesia," CD66; and US Senate, "To Continue Discussion of Rhodesian Resolutions," CD67.

96. US Senate, "Rhodesia," CD66, 12.

97. US Senate, "To Continue Discussion of Rhodesian Resolutions," CD67, 3.

98. Ibid., 8, 5, 6.

99. Draft letter Vance to Church, 28 Nov 1979, Funk/119, CL. Also Vance to Church, 29 Nov 1979, FOIA.

100. Draft letter Vance to Church, with Carter's marginalia, 28 Nov 1979, Funk/119, CL. See Vance to Church, 29 Nov 1979, FOIA; and Vance to Helms, 3 Dec 1979 in Vance to Church, 3 Dec 1979, Lake/6, NA.

101. US Senate, "To Continue Discussion of Rhodesian Resolutions," CD67, 6; and Draft resolution attached to Vance to Church, 28 Nov 1979, Funk/119, CL. It was passed unanimously in the Senate. Vance, ER, 3 Dec 1979, NLC-15-74-7-47-6; and Vance to Carter, 6 Dec 1979, NLC-128-14-14-5-4.

102. A copy of the letter is in the Foreign Office files without any cover letter: Vance to Helms, 3 Dec 1979, [US] FCO 36/2507, NA-UK.

103. See Great Britain, *Southern Rhodesia.*

104. Lyne to Alexander, 4 Dec 1979, Thatcher Papers; and Memcon (Thatcher, Brewster), 5 Dec 1979, FCO 82/990, NA-UK. See Memcon (Thatcher, Vance), 10 Dec 1079, Thatcher Papers.

105. Author's interview with Renwick.

106. Henderson, Washington 4047, 5 Dec 1979, FCO 36/2507, NA-UK; and Vance, *Hard Choices*, 300.

107. Carrington, FCO 1834, 7 Dec 1979, FCO 36/2507, NA-UK.

108. Lake to Vance, 7 Dec 1979, Lake/6, NA.

109. Renwick to Duff, 8 Dec 1979, FCO 36/2507, NA-UK (emphasis in original). See Carrington, "Rhodesia," 11 Dec 1979, *Parliamentary Debates*, Lords, 5th ser., vol. 403, cols. 979–80.

110. Renwick to Duff, 10 Dec 1979, FCO 36/2507, NA-UK.

111. See ZB to Carter, 13 Dec 1979, NLC-1-13-5-7-4; Albright to ZB, 15 Dec 1979, NSA-congress/2, CL; and *WP*, 16 Dec 1979, 1.

112. Newhouse, "Sense of Duty," 78.

113. Gregory, "Zimbabwe Election," 22 (based on Gregory's 18 November 1979 interview with Mugabe); and 7 Sep 1979, London 40458, A1838 190-2-1/69, NA-AUS.

114. Author's interview with Renwick. See, e.g.: Smith, *Betrayal*, 288, 306; Thatcher, *Downing Street*, 73; and Renwick, *Unconventional*, 19.

115. Armstrong to Alexander, 28 Nov 1979, Thatcher Papers; Carrington in Memcon (Carter, Thatcher), part II, 17 Dec 1979, Thatcher Papers; and FCO, "Prime Minister's Visit to Washington: Rhodesia," 13 Dec 1979, FCO 36/2507, NA-UK.

116. Thatcher to Carter, 14 Dec 1979, FCO 36/2507, NA-UK.

117. On Brewster's threat: Davidow, *Peace*, 87–88.

118. Carter to Thatcher, 14 Dec 1979, Thatcher Papers.

119. DePree, FD, 16 Feb 1994; and Vance and McHenry to Carter, 3 Jan 1980, NLC-126-19-29-1-9. See Thatcher, *Downing Street*, 77–78; and DePree, "Mozambique."

120. Author's interview with Renwick; and *LAT*, 16 Dec 1979, 1. See Executive Order Revoking Rhodesian Sanctions, 16 Dec 1979, Speechwriters/26, CL; and Henderson, Washington 4219, 14 Dec 1979, FCO 36/2507, NA-UK.

121. Henderson diary, 23 Dec 1979, Thatcher Papers; and Visit of Prime Minister Margaret Thatcher, Remarks at the Welcoming Ceremony, 17 Dec 1979, APP. See Memcon (Thatcher, Carrington, Carter, Mondale, Vance, ZB), 17 Dec 1979, FCO 36/2507, NA-UK.

122. Memcon (Carter, Thatcher), part I, 17 Dec 1979, Thatcher Papers.

123. *NYT*, 18 Dec 1979, 1; and Renwick, *Unconventional*, 61.

124. Memcon (Thatcher, Carrington, members of US Congress), 17 Dec 1979, FCO 36/2507, NA-UK.

125. Visit of Prime Minister Thatcher, Toasts at the State Dinner, 17 Dec 1979, APP.

126. US Senate, "To Continue Discussion of Rhodesian Resolutions," CD67, 2, 29.

127. Squire to Renwick, 13 Sep 1979, FCO 36/2549, NA-UK.

128. Davidow, *Peace*, 22, 14; and Kennedy, *CR-Senate*, 19 Dec 1979, S19260–61.

129. Renwick, *Unconventional*, 19.

130. Author's interview with Renwick; and Renwick, *Unconventional*, 21. See Soames, "From Rhodesia"; and Carrington, *Reflecting*.

131. Thatcher, *Downing Street*, 73; Davidow, *Peace*, 22; and Davidow, *Dealing*, 15. Also Low, "Zimbabwe," 107–8.

132. Melhuish to Leahy and Parsons, 26 Jun 1979, FCO 82/979, NA-UK; and Vance, *Hard Choices*, 299.

133. DePree, FD, 16 Feb 1994; and Charlton, *Last Colony*, 80.

134. Low, "Zimbabwe," 103.

135. See Davidow, *Peace*, 45; and Jaster, *Regional Security*, 9.

136. Gregory, "Zimbabwe Election," 21.

137. *Daily Telegraph* (London), 12 Jan 1979, 5, edit 8. See Flower, *Serving Secretly*, 196–224.

138. "Nkomo in the Middle," *Newsweek*, 28 Jan 1980, 52. See Brownell, "Hole"; and Tamarkin, "White Political Elite."

139. Vance, State 34233, 9 Feb 1978, FOIA.

140. Carrington, *Reflecting*, 291; and Carrington in Kandiah and Onslow, "Britain and Rhodesia," 82.

141. Barlow and Day, minutes on Henderson to Carrington, "US Policy towards Rhodesia, May 1979 to April 1980," 13 May 1980, FCO 36/2751, NA-UK. See Davidow, *Peace*, 14.

142. Memcon (Fraser, Thatcher, Carrington, Peacock), 4 Aug 1979, Fraser Papers, M1356/11, NA-AUS.

143. See Rice, "Commonwealth Initiative," 64–208.

144. See Ginifer and Potgieter, *Managing Arms*; Onslow, "Freedom," 741; and Onslow, "Noises Off." Smith admitted that there were "in excess of 1000 South African troops" in Rhodesia during the elections. Smith, *Betrayal*, 323; see also Powell to Day, 23 Jan 1980, FCO 36/2751, NA-UK; and Powell to Morland, 23 Feb 1980, FCO 36/2751, NA-UK. For uniforms: Gerard Zilg, "Buying Time in Zimbabwe," *Nation*, 29 Mar 1980, 368. For helicopters: Ginifer and Potgieter. *Managing Arms*, 42–43.

145. On US diplomacy concerning the South African troops: North-South to ZB, 14 Jan 1980, NLC-10-26-5-1-8; North-South to ZB, 16 Jan 1980, NLC-10-26-5-15-1; Christopher, ER, 25 Jan 1980, NLC-128-15-1-14-7; Vance, ER, 30 Jan 1980, NLC-128-15-1-15-6; Vance, ER, 1 Feb 1980, NLC-128-15-2-1-0; and North American Department, "Recent Examples of American Failures to Consult, etc.," 20 Feb 1980, FCO 82/1030, NA-UK. Vance met with Carrington and discussed Rhodesia: Palliser, "Mr Vance's Visit," 20 Feb 1980, FCO 82/1030, NA-UK; and "Brief no. 10: Rhodesia," 21 Feb 1980, FCO 82/1030, NA-UK.

146. Author's interview with Carter.

147. Davidow, Salisbury 496, 27 Feb. 1980, NSA-country/89, CL. On elections: Vance, ER, 27 Feb 1980, NLC-128-15-2-20-9; and Vance, ER, 1 Mar 1980, NLC-128-15-3-1-0. On intimidation: *WP*, 24 Feb 1980, 1; *NYT*, 27 Feb 1980, 1; *NYT*, 1 Mar 1980, 1; *NYT*, 3 Mar 1980, 10; and Gerard Zilg, "Buying Time in Zimbabwe," *Nation*, 29 Mar 1980, 367–68.

148. Author's interview with DePree.

149. *Guardian*, 5 Mar 1980, 12.

150. North-South to ZB, 4 Mar 1980, NLC-10-27-5-8-8; and *Time*, 24 Mar 1980, 32.

151. *NYT*, 18 Apr 1980, 1; and *Newsweek*, 28 Apr 1980, 47–48.

152. Harriman to Carter, 22 Apr 1980, 600/2, Harriman Papers, LC. See Solodovnikov, "K istorii," 137–38; and "US/UK Talks on Africa," 28/30 Apr 1980, FCO 36/2751, NA-UK.

153. Brzezinski, *Power*, 143; and CIA, "Current Foreign Relations Report," 16 Apr 1980, in Mokoena, *Zimbabwe*.

154. Smiley, "Zimbabwe," 1083.

155. See *WP*, 17 Apr 1980, 27; and Solodovnikov, "K istorii," 137–38.

156. *NYT*, 17 Apr 1980, edit 26; *CSM*, 25 Apr 1980, edit 24; and *Atlanta Daily World*, 22 Apr 1980, edit 6.

Conclusion

1. Shrum, "No Private Smiles," 42.

2. Author's interviews with Newsom, Brzezinski, and Young. See interview with Brzezinski, Albright, Denend, Odom, 18 Feb 1982, 71–72, CPP.

3. See interview with Brzezinski, Albright, Denend, Odom, 18 Feb 1982, 48-53, CPP. Also author's interviews with Brzezinski and Young.

4. Author's interview with Brzezinski.

5. "Interview with Hamilton Jordan," 6 Nov 1981, CPP; Ramsbotham to Palliser, 16 Apr 197, PREM 16/1484, NA-UK; and author's interview with Carter.

6. Jay, "The United States: Annual Review for 1978," 9 Jan 1979, FCO 82/975, NA-UK.

7. Author's interview with Young.

8. Ramsbotham to Palliser, 18 Nov 1976, FCO 82/650, NA-UK.

9. McNally to Callaghan, 23 Nov 1976, PREM 16/1909, NA-UK.

10. Von Staden to Genscher, 5 Sep 1978, doc. 254, *AAPD 1978*, 1291; and *Guardian* (London), 19 Jun 1979, edit 10.

11. "Interview with Hamilton Jordan," 6 Nov 1981, CPP; and Fallows, "Passionless," 39.

12. Author's interview with Carter.

13. See Maynes, FD, 14 Aug 1998.

14. Mondale to Carter, 22 Jan 1979, Mondale/204, CL (emphasis in original).

15. See, e.g., Fallows, "Passionless," 42–43.

16. Commencement Address at Notre Dame University, 22 May 1977, APP.

17. Schlesinger, *Imperial Presidency*.

18. Memcon (Schmidt, Carter), 16 July 1978, B150/397, Berlin; Memcon (Carter, Genscher), 30 May 1978, doc. 170, *AAPD 1978*, 844–45; Giscard, *Le pouvoir*, 377; and *Daily Telegraph* (London), 31 Jul 1978, 1. See, e.g., Memcon (Giscard, Carter), 9 May 1977, box 5AG3-984, Archives de la Présidence, Paris; Memcon (Heads of Gov't), 5 Dec 1977, in Cartledge to Fergusson, 6 Dec 1977, PREM 16/1872, NA-UK; Memcon (Schmidt, Sadat), 27/28 Dec 1977, B150/383, Berlin; Memcon (Genscher, de Guiringaud), 6 Feb 1978, doc. 34, *AAPD 1978*, 201; Top Secret, 9 Feb 1978, NLC-1-5-3-33-6; and Memcon (Carter, Genscher), 30 May 1978, doc. 170, *AAPD 1978*, 844–45.

19. Jay to Owen, 5 Jan 1978, PREM 16/1909, NA-UK.

20. ZB, WR, 18 Nov 1977, Brzezinski/41, CL (emphasis in original).

21. Vanden Heuvel, Geneva 10899, 15 Jul 1978, FOIA (a transcript of the unedited interview in English, its original language).

22. *WP*, 1 Feb 1977, 17.

23. *NYT*, 12 Apr 1977, 1; and *NYT*, 22 May 1978, 1.

24. *US News & World Report*, 12 Jun 1978, 24.

25. Author's interview with Carter.

26. *NYT*, 8 Jun 1977, 6; News Conference, 13 Jun 1977, APP; and Q&A with Magazine Publishers Association, 10 Jun 1977, APP.

27. Author's interview with Young.

28. Ibid.

29. DeRoche, *Andrew Young*, 75, quoting DeRoche's interview with Young.

30. Remarks and Question-and-Answer, 21 Jul 1977, APP.

31. Author's interview with Carter.

32. *Newsweek*, 28 Mar 1977, 30.

33. *Time*, 23 Feb 1976, 29.

34. Kissinger, *Renewal*, 972.

35. Memcon (Tarnoff, Pastor, Fidel Castro), 3-4 Dec. 1978, Vertical/Cuba: President Carter's Trip, May 12-17, 2002, CL; and ZB to Carter, "Conversations in Havana," [20 Dec 1978,] ibid.

36. "Carter Speaks on South Africa," *Financial Mail* (Johannesburg), 5 Nov 1976, 500–10, Persons: Carter/334, Africa News, Duke.

37. "Memorandum for the record: 'Africa Trip Impressions,'" 27 Nov 1976, DNSA.

38. *WP*, 21 Dec 1978, 1.

39. "Statement by Ambassador Andrew Young, May 19, 1977," USUN *Press Release*, USUN-27 (77), 24 May 1977, WOA 58-210, Yale.

40. Author's interview with DePree.

41. Moose, "The Africa Bureau during the Administration of Jimmy Carter," in Anyaso, *Fifty Years*, 153.

42. Easum to Chester and Norma Easum, 23 Feb 1977, Easum Papers.

43. Author's interview with Carter.

44. Ibid.

45. Author's interview with Young.

46. Mary McGrory, "Winning the Hearts and Minds of Africa," *WS*, 10 Sep 1976, pp

47. Author's interview with Carter.

48. Author's interview with Owen.

49. *CR-Senate*, 28 Jun 1978, 19211–24.

50. Romano to DeConcini, 28 Feb 1979, DeConcini Papers/169; and Maynes, FD, 14 Aug 1998.

51. Young, 11 Apr 1979, USUN 1555, FOIA-mf.

52. *WP*, 3 Jul 1979, 17 (interview with Kissinger).

53. Trade Sanctions against Rhodesia, 7 Jun 1979, APP. See *CR-Senate*, 12 Jun 1979, 14395.

54. See Solodovnikov, "K istorii," 137–38.

55. Author's interview with Carter.

56. Author's interview with Kaunda and Chona.

57. See, e.g., Stedman, *Peacemaking*, 159; Davidow, *Peace*, 22; and Renwick, *Unconventional*, 19.

58. *Time*, 18 Apr 1977, 18.

59. Henze, ER, 17 Jun 1977, Horn/5, CL; and Memcon (Addou, Deptoff), 24 Jun 1977, SH Chron. See Memcon (Carter, Addou), 16 Jun 1977, NSA-Brzezinski (7)/35, CL and Vance, State 152186, 30 Jun 1977, FOIA. Also author's interview with Addou.

60. Mog Domestic Service, 13 Nov 1977, FBIS, NLC-6-69-6-40-0.

61. Author's interview with Carter.

62. Brzezinski, *Power*, 183.

63. Ibid., 189, quoting his diary from 1980.

64. McHenry, FD, 23 Mar 1993; and SCC: Minutes, 22 Feb 1978, Brzezinski/28, CL.

65. Author's interview with Carter.

66. Brzezinski, *Power*, 346–52.

67. "Interview with Jimmy Carter," 29 Nov 1982, 23, Miller Center of Public Affairs of the University of Virginia.

68. Commencement Address at Notre Dame University, 22 May 1977, APP.

69. Remarks at a Fundraising Dinner for Senator Strom Thurmond in Columbia, South Carolina, 20 Sep 1983, APP.

70. Remarks at the Annual Dinner of the Conservative Political Action Conference, 30 Jan 1986, APP.

71. "Kissinger's critique," *Economist*, 3 Feb 1979, 22; and "Kissinger's critique (continued)," *Economist*, 10 Feb 1979, 31.

72. Remarks at a National Republican Senatorial Committee Reception, 20 Oct 2006, APP.

73. Author's interview with Young.

74. Author's interview with Carter.

75. Author's interview with Mondale.

76. Author's interview with Carter.

77. Interview with Adam Michnik, in Vaughan, "Helsinki Final Act," 21–22. See Trenor, "Polish Desk."

78. Author's interview with Newsom. Newsom served in the State Department under every president from Truman through Carter, rising to ambassador to Libya, Indonesia, and the Philippines and undersecretary of state; he then became director of the Institute for the Study of Diplomacy at Georgetown University and a professor at the University of Virginia.

Bibliography

Archives

Australia
National Archives of Australia, http://www.naa.gov.au/

Canada
Library and Archives Canada/Bibliothèque et Archives Canada, Ottawa

Cuba
Piero Gleijeses shared documents with me that he gathered in the closed
    Cuban archives.

Federal Republic of Germany
Bundesarchiv, Koblenz
Politisches Archiv des Auswärtigen Amts, Berlin

France
Archives de la Présidence de la République sous Valéry Giscard d'Estaing,
    Archives Nationales de France, Paris

German Democratic Republic
Stiftung Archiv der Parteien und Massenorganisationen der DDR im
    Bundesarchiv, Berlin

Italy
Fondazione Istituto Gramsci, Archivio del Partito Comunista Italiano, Rome

South Africa and Rhodesia
Department of Foreign Affairs, Pretoria
Ian Smith Papers, Cory Library, Rhodes University, Grahamstown
South African History Archive, University of Witwatersrand, Johannesburg

United Kingdom

British Diplomatic Oral History Programme (BDOHP), Churchill Archives Centre, Cambridge University, http://www.chu.cam.ac.uk/archives/collections/BDOHP/

Margaret Thatcher Foundation Archive, http://www.margaretthatcher.org/

The National Archives, Kew

United States

African Activist Archive, Michigan State University, http://africanactivist.msu.edu/

Averell Harriman Papers, Library of Congress, Washington, DC

Charles Diggs Papers, Howard University, Washington, DC

Cyrus R. and Grace Sloan Vance Papers, Yale University, New Haven, CT

Dennis DeConcini Papers, University of Arizona, Tucson, AZ

Donald Easum personal papers (in author's possession)

Frank Church Papers, Boise State University, Boise, ID

Gerald R. Ford Library, Ann Arbor, MI

Jimmy Carter Library, Atlanta, GA

John Carl West Papers, University of South Carolina, Columbia, SC

Leroy T. Walker Africa News Service Archive, Duke University, Durham, NC

NAACP Papers, Library of Congress, Washington, DC

National Archives, College Park, MD

National Security Archive, Washington, DC

Records of the Washington Office on Africa, Yale University, New Haven, CT

Ronald Reagan Library, Simi Valley, CA

Sam Hamrick personal papers (in author's possession)

TransAfrica Archives, Washington, DC

Zambia

United National Independence Party Archive, Lusaka.

Interviews

I give only the position held by the interviewees that is relevant for this book.

Africans

Abdullahi Addou
> Somali Ambassador to the United States. March 17, 2007, Alexandria, VA; March 18, 2007, by telephone

Mark Chona
> Adviser to President Kaunda. March 5, 2009, Lusaka, Zambia.

Kenneth Kaunda
> President of Zambia. March 5, 2009, Lusaka, Zambia

Americans
David Aaron
> Deputy Assistant for National Security Affairs. March 18, 2007,
> Washington, DC
Zbigniew Brzezinski
> National Security Adviser. March 20, 2007, Washington, DC
Kevin Cahill
> Special envoy to President Siad Barre. May 7, 2007, by telephone
Jimmy Carter
> President. May 23, 2002, Atlanta, GA
Dick Clark
> Senator. June 12, 2001, Washington, DC
Willard DePree
> Ambassador to Somalia. June 11, 2001, Bethesda, MD
Donald Easum
> Ambassador to Nigeria. June 29, 1999, New York, NY
William Edmondson
> Ambassador to South Africa. October 17, 2002, Washington, DC
Sam Hamrick
> CIA expert on Horn of Africa. March 14, 2003, Culpeper, VA
Paul Henze
> NSC expert on Horn of Africa. March 18, 2007, Rappahannock, VA
Anthony Lake
> Director of Policy Planning, State Department. October 14, 2002,
> Washington, DC
Stephen Low
> Ambassador to Zambia. November 27, 2000, Washington, DC
Donald McHenry
> Ambassador to the United Nations. October 15, 2002, Washington, DC
Walter Mondale
> Vice President. March 29, 2007, Minneapolis, MN
Richard Moose
> Assistant Secretary of State for African Affairs. June 11, 2001 and
> October 13, 2002, Alexandria, VA
David Newsom
> Undersecretary of State for Political Affairs. June 14, 2001,
> Charlottesville, VA
Matthew Nimetz
> Counselor of the State Department. May 8, 2007, New York, NY
Robert Pastor
> NSC specialist on Latin America. June 5, 2013, by telephone

Donald Petterson
  Ambassador to Somalia. September 23, 2006, Brentwood, NH
Henry Richardson
  NSC specialist on sub-Saharan Africa. June 29, 2001, Philadelphia, PA
Thomas Thornton
  NSC expert on Africa. October 20, 2002, Baltimore, MD
Andrew Young
  Ambassador to the United Nations. July 16, 2002, Atlanta, GA

Britons
John Graham
  Ambassador and point man in Africa. November 20, 2002, Chipping
  Norton, UK
David Owen
  Secretary of State for Foreign and Commonwealth Affairs. November
  22, 2002, London, UK
Robin Renwick
  Head of Rhodesia Department, Foreign and Commonwealth Office.
  November 21, 2002, London, UK

Congressional Documents

1. US Congress. Senate Committee on Foreign Relations and House Committee on International Relations. "Joint Conferees: HR 6884." International Security Assistance Act of 1977, June 29, 1977. Washington, DC: GPO, 1977.

2. US Congress. Senate Committee on Foreign Relations and House Committee on Foreign Affairs. "Joint Conferees: HR 3363, Department of State Authorization Act, FY 1980–81." July 30, 1979. Washington, DC: GPO, 1979.

3. US House. "Aircraft Hijacking." Hearings before the Committee on Foreign Affairs, 91st cong., 2nd sess., September 17, 22, 23, 30, 1970. Washington, DC: GPO, 1970.

4. US House. "Human Rights in the World Community: A Call for US Leadership." A Report to the Subcommittee on International Organizations and Movements of the House Committee on Foreign Affairs, 93rd cong., 2nd sess., March 27, 1974. Washington, DC: GPO, 1974.

5. US House. "Review of State Department Trip through Southern and Central Africa." Hearings before the Subcommittee on Africa of the Committee on Foreign Affairs, 93rd cong., 2nd sess., December 12, 1974. Washington, DC: GPO, 1974.

6. US House. "US Policy and Request for Sale of Arms to Ethiopia." Hearings before the Committee on Foreign Affairs, 94th cong., 1st sess., March 5, 1975. Washington, DC: GPO, 1975.

7. US House. "Department of Defense Appropriations for 1977, Part 1." Hearings before the Subcommittee on Defense Appropriations of the Committee on Appropriations, 94th cong., 2nd sess., January 22, February 2–5, 1976. Washington, DC: GPO, 1976.

8. US House. "Report of Secretary of State Kissinger on his Visit to Latin America." Hearing before the Committee on International Relations, 94th cong., 2nd sess., March 4, 1976. Washington, DC: GPO, 1976.

9. US House. "Report of Secretary of State Kissinger on his Visits to Latin America, Western Europe, and Africa." Hearing before the Committee on International Relations, 94th cong., 2nd sess., June 17, 1976. Washington, DC: GPO, 1976.

10. US House. "Foreign Assistance and Related Agencies Appropriations for 1978, Part 1." Hearings before a Subcommittee of the Committee on Appropriations, 95th cong., 1st sess., February 16; March 2, 7, 8, 22, 24, 28, 29, 1977. Washington, DC: GPO, 1977.

11. US House. "Rhodesian Sanctions Bill." Hearings before the Subcommittees on Africa and International Organization of the Committee on International Relations, 95th cong., 1st sess., February 24, 1977. Washington, DC: GPO, 1977.

12. US House. "United States Policy Toward Southern Africa." Hearing before the Subcommittee on Africa of the Committee on International Relations, 95th Cong., 1st sess., March 3, 1977. Washington, DC: GPO, 1977.

13. US House. "Report 95-59: Amending the United Nations Participation Act of 1945 to Halt the Importation of Rhodesia Chrome." 95th cong., 1st sess., March 7, 1977. Washington, DC: GPO, 1977.

14. US House. "Foreign Assistance and Related Agencies Appropriations for 1978, Part 2." Hearings before a Subcommittee of the Committee on Appropriations, 95th cong., 1st sess., March 9, 10, 15, 17, 21, 22, 1977. Washington, DC: GPO, 1977.

15. US House. "Foreign Assistance Legislation for Fiscal Year 1978, Part 1." Hearings before the Committee on International Relations, 95th cong., 1st sess., March 16, 17, 22; April 18, 1977. Washington, DC: GPO, 1977.

16. US House. "Foreign Assistance Legislation for Fiscal Year 1978, Part 3." Hearings before the Subcommittee on Africa of the Committee on International Relations, 95th cong., 1st sess., March 17, 18, 23, 28, 29; April 28, 1977. Washington, DC: GPO, 1977.

17. US House. "Communication from the President of the United States." March 28, 1977. Washington, DC: GPO, 1977.

18. US House. "Human Rights Practices in Countries Receiving US Security Assistance." Report submitted to the Committee on International Relations by the Department of State, April 25, 1977. Washington, DC: GPO, 1977.

19. US House, Committee on International Relations (Zablocki). "International Security Assistance Act of 1977: Report." May 9, 1977. Washington, DC: GPO, 1977.

20. US House. "United States Policy Toward Rhodesia." Hearing before the Subcommittee on Africa of the Committee on International Relations, 95th Cong., 1st sess., June 8, 1977. Washington, DC: GPO, 1977.

21. US House (Zablocki). "International Security Assistance Act of 1977: Conference Report." July 15, 1977. Washington, DC: GPO, 1977.

22. US House. "Foreign Assistance and Related Agencies Appropriations for 1979, Part 2." Hearings before the Subcommittee on Foreign Operations Appropriations of the Committee on Appropriations, 95th cong., 2nd sess., January 25; February 22, 24; March 2, 9, 10, 14–17, 21-22; and April 4–5, 1978. Washington, DC: GPO, 1978.

23. US House. "Foreign Relations Authorization for FY 1979." Hearings before the Subcommittee on International Operations of the Committee on International Relations, 95th cong., 2nd sess., January 31; February 1, 7–8, 14, 16, 21, 23; March 14–15; April 5, 1978. Washington, DC: GPO, 1978.

24. US House. "Foreign Assistance Legislation for Fiscal Year 1979, Part 3." Hearings before the Subcommittee on Africa of the Committee on International Relations, 95th cong., 2nd sess., February 7–8, 14, 28; March 1–2, 1978. Washington, DC: GPO, 1978.

25. US House. "Foreign Assistance Legislation for Fiscal Year 1979, Part 1." Hearings before the Committee on International Relations, 95th cong., 2nd sess., February 21–24; March 2, 1978. Washington, DC: GPO, 1978.

26. US House. "United States Policy Toward Rhodesia." Hearings before the Subcommittee on Africa of the Committee on Foreign Affairs, 96th Cong., 1st sess., March 22, 27, 29; April 2, 1979. Washington, DC: GPO, 1979.

27. US House. "Economic Sanctions against Rhodesia." Hearings before the Subcommittee on Africa of the Committee on Foreign Affairs, 96th Cong., 1st sess., April 2; May 14, 16, 21, 1979, Washington, DC: GPO, 1979.

28. US House, Committee on Foreign Affairs (Solarz). "Rhodesia: Where Do We Go From Here?" 96th Cong., 1st sess., June 1, 1979. Washington, DC: GPO, 1979.

29. US House, Committee on Foreign Affairs (Solarz). "Zimbabwe-Rhodesia: The Issue of Sanctions," Report 96-283 to accompany HR 4439, 96th Cong., 1st sess., June 18, 1979. Washington, DC: GPO, 1979.

30. US House. "Review of President Carter's First Report to Congress on Rhodesia." Hearings before the Subcommittee on Africa of the Committee on Foreign Affairs, 96th Cong., 1st sess., July 25, 1979. Washington, DC: GPO, 1979.

31. US House. "Authorizing Appropriations for FY80–FY81 for the Department of State." Report 96-399, July 31, 1979. Washington, DC: GPO, 1979.

32. US House. "US Interests in Africa." Hearings before the Subcommittee on Africa of the Committee on Foreign Affairs, 96th Cong., 1st sess., October 18–19, 22, 24–25, 29; November 13–14, 1979. Washington, DC: GPO, 1979.

33. US House. "Department of Defense Authorization Act, FY 1980: Conference Report." Rpt. 96-546, October 23, 1979. Washington, DC: GPO, 1979.

34. US House. "Executive-Legislative Consultation on Foreign Policy: Sanctions Against Rhodesia" (by Raymond Copson). Foreign Affairs Committee Print: Congress and Foreign Policy, no. 6, September 1982. Washington, DC: GPO, 1982.

35. US Senate. "Nomination of Henry A. Kissinger." Hearings before the Committee on Foreign Relations, 93rd cong., 1st sess., September 7, 10–11, 14, 1973. Washington, DC: GPO, 1973.

36. US Senate. "Construction Projects on the Island of Diego Garcia." Hearing before the Committee on Armed Services, June 10, 1975. Washington, DC: GPO, 1975.

37. US Senate. "Soviet Military Capability in Berbera, Somalia." Report of Senator Bartlett to the Committee on Armed Services, July 1, 1975. Washington, DC: GPO, 1975.

38. US Senate. "Angola." Hearings before the Subcommittee on African Affairs of the Committee on Foreign Relations, 94th cong., 2nd sess., January 29; February 3–4, 6, 1976. Washington, DC: GPO, 1976.

39. US Senate. "US Policy toward Africa." Hearings before the Subcommittee on African Affairs and the Subcommittee on Arms Control, International Organizations and Security Agreements and the Committee on Foreign Relations, 94th cong., 2nd sess., March 5, 8, 15, 19; May 12–13, 21, 26–27, 1976. Washington, DC: GPO, 1976.

40. US Senate. "The Attempt to Steal the Bicentennial: The Peoples Bicentennial Commission." Hearings before the Subcommittee to Investigate the Administration of the Internal Security Act and Other Internal Security Laws of the Committee of the Judiciary, 94th cong., 2nd sess., March 17–18, 1976. Washington, DC: GPO, 1976.

41. US Senate. "International Security Assistance." Hearing before the Subcommittee on Foreign Assistance of the Committee on Foreign Relations, 94th cong., 2nd sess., March 26; April 5, 8, 1976. Washington, DC: GPO, 1976.

42. US Senate. "Threats to the Peaceful Observance of the Bicentennial." Hearings before the Subcommittee to Investigate the Administration of the Internal Security Act and Other Internal Security Laws of the Committee of the Judiciary, 94th cong., 2nd sess., June 18, 1976. Washington, DC: GPO, 1976.

43. US Senate. "Ethiopia and the Horn of Africa." Hearings before the Subcommittee on African Affairs, 94th cong., 2nd sess., August 4–6, 1976. Washington, DC: GPO, 1976.

44. US Senate. "Nomination of Theodore C. Sorensen." Hearing before the Select Committee on Intelligence. 95th cong., 1st sess., January 17, 1977. Washington, DC: GPO, 1977.

45. US Senate. "Nomination of Hon. Andrew Young as US Representative to UN." Hearing before the Committee on Foreign Relations, 95th cong., 1st sess., January 25, 1977. Washington, DC: GPO, 1977.

46. US Senate. "Rhodesian Sanctions." Hearings before the Subcommittee on African Affairs of the Foreign Relations Committee," 95th cong., 1st sess., February 9–10, 1977. Washington, DC: GPO, 1977.

47. US Senate. "Foreign Assistance and Related Programs Appropriations for Fiscal Year 1978." Hearings before a Subcommittee of the Committee on Appropriations, 95th cong., 1st sess., February 10, 21, 24; March 2, 8, 10, 16, 22, 24, 30; April 6, 27, 1977. Washington, DC: GPO, 1977.

48. US Senate. "Report 95-37: Rhodesian Sanctions." 95th cong., 1st sess., March 3, 1977. Washington, DC: GPO, 1977.

49. US Senate. "Foreign Assistance Authorization." Hearings before the Committee on Foreign Relations and the Subcommittee on Foreign Assistance on the International Development Act of 1977, 95th cong., 1st sess., March 23–25, 1977. Washington, DC: GPO, 1977.

50. US Senate. "Security Assistance Authorization." Hearings before the Subcommittee on Foreign Assistance, Subcommittee on Africa, and Subcommittee on Arms Control, Oceans, and International Environment of the Committee on Foreign Relations, 95th cong., 1st sess., April 21–22, 25; May 2, 1977. Washington, DC: GPO, 1977.

51. US Senate, "Markup: S. 1160, The FY 1978 Security Assistance Programs Authorization Bill." Subcommittee on Foreign Assistance of the Committee on Foreign Relations, May 3–4, 1977. Washington, DC: GPO, 1977.

52. US Senate, "The International Security Assistance and Arms Export Control Act of 1977: Report." Committee on Foreign Relations (Sparkman), May 16, 1977. Washington, DC: GPO, 1977.

53. US Senate. "Ambassador Young's African Trip." Hearing before the Subcommittee on African Affairs of the Committee on Foreign Relations, 95th cong., 1st sess., June 6, 1977. Washington, DC: GPO, 1977.

54. US Senate. "Arms Transfer Policy: A Presidential Report to the Committee on Foreign Relations." 95th cong., 1st sess., July 1, 1977. Washington, DC: GPO, 1977.

55. US Senate, Committee on Foreign Relations. "Perceptions: Relations between the United States and the Soviet Union." January 1, 1978. Washington, DC: GPO, 1978.

56. US Senate. "Act to Combat International Terrorism." Hearings before the Committee on Governmental Affairs, 95th cong., 2nd sess., January 23, 25, 27, 30; February 22; March 22–23, 1978. Washington, DC: GPO, 1978.

57. US Senate. "Foreign Assistance and Related Programs Appropriations for Fiscal Year 1979, Part 1." Hearings before the Subcommittee on Foreign Operations of the Committee on Appropriations, 95th cong., 2nd sess., February 22, 27; March 2, 7, 9, 14, 16, 21, 23; April 5, 1978. Washington, DC: GPO, 1978.

58. US Senate. "International Development Assistance Authorization." Hearings before the Subcommittee on Foreign Assistance of the Committee on Foreign Relations, 95th cong., 2nd sess., March 2–3; April 28, 1978. Washington, DC: GPO, 1978.

59. US Senate. "US Policy toward Africa." Hearings before the Subcommittee on African Affairs of the Committee on Foreign Relations, 95th cong., 2nd sess., May 12, 1978. Washington, DC: GPO, 1978.

60. US Senate. "A Rhodesian Settlement?" A Staff Report to the Committee on Foreign Relations, 95th cong., 2nd sess., June 1, 1978. Washington, DC: GPO, 1978.

61. US Senate. "Rhodesia." Hearings before the Committee on Foreign Relations, 96th cong., 1st sess., March 5, 7, 1979. Washington, DC: GPO, 1979.

62. US Senate. "Impartial Observers of the Forthcoming Election in Rhodesia." Report No. 96-41, 96th cong., 1st sess., March 21, 1979. Washington, DC: GPO, 1979.

63. US Senate. "Authorizing Appropriations for Fiscal Year 1980." Committee on Armed Services, Report 96-197, 96th cong. 1st sess., May 31, 1979. Washington, DC: GPO, 1979.

64. US Senate. "Trade Sanctions against Rhodesia." Hearing before the Committee on Foreign Relations, 96th cong., 1st sess., June 12, 1979. Washington, DC: GPO, 1979.

65. US Senate. "Business Meeting," June 12, 1979, unpublished, L-N.

66. US Senate. "Rhodesia," Hearings before the Committee on Foreign Relations, 96th cong., 1st sess., November 27, 29–30; December 3, 1979. Washington, DC: GPO, 1979.

67. US Senate. "To Continue Discussion of Rhodesian Resolutions." Hearing before the Committee on Foreign Relations, 96th cong., 1st sess., November 30; December 3, 1979, Washington, DC: GPO, 1979.

68. US Senate. "Conference: Senate 3075 and House Amendment Thereto." Committee on Foreign Relations and US House Committee on International Relations, August 10, 1978, unpublished, L-N.

Works Cited

Adair, Augustus Alven. "Black Legislative Influence in Federal Policy Decisions: The Congressional Black Caucus, 1971–1975." PhD diss., Johns Hopkins University, 1976.

Adams, Maurianne, and John Bracey, eds. *Strangers and Neighbors: Relations between Blacks and Jews in the United States.* Amherst: University of Massachusetts Press, 1999.

Adams, Russell. "An Analysis of the 'Roots' Phenomenon in the Context of American Racial Conservatism." *Présence Africaine* 116 (1980): 125–40.

"The Afro-Arab Summit: A New Blueprint for African Development?" *Bulletin of the Africa Institute* 3/4 (1977): 56–64.

Akten zur auswärtigen Politik der Bundesrepublik Deutschland: 1976 [Foreign policy documents of the Federal Republic of Germany: 1976]. Hrsg. vom Institut für Zeitgeschichte Munich-Berlin im Auftrag des Auswärtigen Amts (Ilse Pautsch, Matthias Peter, Michael Ploetz, Tim Geiger, eds.). Munich: R. Oldenbourg, 2007.

Akten zur auswärtigen Politik der Bundesrepublik Deutschland: 1977 [Foreign policy documents of the Federal Republic of Germany: 1977]. Hrsg. vom Institut für Zeitgeschichte Munich-Berlin im Auftrag des Auswärtigen Amts (Ilse Pautsch, Amit Das Gupta, Tim Geiger, Matthias Peter Fabian Hirlfich, Mechthild Lindemann, eds.). Munich: R. Oldenbourg, 2008.

Akten zur auswärtigen Politik der Bundesrepublik Deutschland: 1978 [Foreign policy documents of the Federal Republic of Germany: 1978]. Hrsg. vom Institut für Zeitgeschichte Munich-Berlin im Auftrag des Auswärtigen Amts (Ilse Pautsch, Daniela Taschler, Amit Das Gupta, Michael Mayer, eds.). Munich: R. Oldenbourg, 2009.

Albright, Madeleine. *Madam Secretary: A Memoir.* New York: Hyperion, 2003.

Alpert, Carl. "Our Black Friends and Colleagues," *The Jewish Press* 58, no. 49 (September 7, 1979): 4.

American Revolution Bicentennial Administration. *The Bicentennial of the United States of America: A Final Report to the People*. Washington, DC: GPO, 1977.

Anderson, Patrick. *Electing Jimmy Carter: The Campaign of 1976*. Baton Rouge: Louisiana State University Press, 1994.

Anglin, Douglas G. "Zimbabwe: Retrospect and Prospect." *International Journal* 35, no. 4 (1980): 663–700.

Anyaso, Claudia, ed., *Fifty Years of U.S. Africa Policy: Reflections of Assistant Secretaries for African Affairs and U.S. Embassy Officials*, Washington, DC: Association for Diplomatic Studies and Training, 2011.

Apter, Andrew. "The Pan-African Nation: Oil-Money and the Spectacle of Culture in Nigeria." *Public Culture* 8, no. 3 (1996): 441–66.

Astrow, André. *Zimbabwe: A Revolution That Lost Its Way?* London: Zed, 1983.

Auspitz, Lee et al., "America Now: A Failure of Nerve? A Symposium." *Commentary* 60, no.1 (July 1975): 16–87.

Bailey, Martin. *Oilgate: The Sanctions Scandal*. London: Hodder and Stoughton, 1979.

Baldwin, James. "Open Letter to the Born Again." *The Nation* (September 29, 1979): 263–64.

Baumhögger, Goswin, with Ulf Engel and Telse Diederichsen. *The Struggle for Independence: Documents on the Recent Development of Zimbabwe (1975–1980)*. Hamburg: Institut für Afrikakunde, 1984.

Baxter, Peter. *Rhodesia: Last Outpost of the British Empire, 1890–1980*. Alberton, South Africa: Galago, 2010.

Bennett, Gillian, and Keith Hamilton, eds. *Documents on British Policy Overseas*. Series 3, Vol. 3, *Détente in Europe, 1972–1976*. London: Frank Cass, 2000.

Berman, William. *America's Right Turn: From Nixon to Clinton*. Baltimore: Johns Hopkins University Press, 1994.

Bernstein, Richard. *The Founding Fathers Reconsidered*. Oxford: Oxford University Press, 2009.

Betts, Richard K. "A Diplomatic Time Bomb for South Africa?" *International Security* 4, no. 2 (Fall 1979): 91–115.

———. "The Tragicomedy of Arms Trade Control." *International Security* 5, no. 1 (Summer 1980): 80–110.

Bhebe, Ngwabi, and Terrence Ranger. *Soldiers in Zimbabwe's Liberation War*. Oxford: J. Currey, 1996.

Bill, James A. *The Eagle and the Lion: The Tragedy of American-Iranian Relations*. New Haven, CT: Yale University Press, 1988.

Bishara, Ghassan. "Interview of Zbigniew Brzezinski: 'Peace at an Impasse.'" *Journal of Palestine Studies* 14, no. 1 (Autumn 1984): 3–15.

Black, Earl, and Merle Black. *The Rise of Southern Republicans*. Cambridge, MA: Harvard University Press, 2002.

Blair, David. *Degrees in Violence: Robert Mugabe and the Struggle for Power in Zimbabwe*. London: Continuum, 2002.

Blight, James, and Peter Kornbluh. "Dialogue with Castro: A Hidden History." *New York Review of Books* 41, no. 16 (October 6, 1994): 45–49.

Blitzer, Wolf. "Andy Young's Undoing." *New Republic* (September 15, 1979): 11–15.

Bonafede, Dom. "Brzezinski—Stepping Out of His Backstage Role." *National Journal* 9, no. 42 (October 15, 1977): 1596–1601.

———. "Zbigniew Brzezinski." In *Fateful Decisions: Inside the National Security Council*, edited by Karl Inderfurth and Loch K. Johnson, 194–202. New York: Oxford University Press, 2004.

Booker, Simeon. "How Blacks Close to Carter Helped Him Get to the White House." *Jet* (February 10, 1977): 6–8.

Borstelmann, Thomas. *The Cold War and the Color Line: American Race Relations in the Global Arena*. Cambridge, MA: Harvard University Press, 2001.

Bourne, Peter G. *Jimmy Carter: A Comprehensive Biography from Plains to Post-Presidency*. New York: Scribner, 1997.

Bowden, Mark. *Guests of the Ayatollah: The First Battle in America's War with Militant Islam*. New York: Atlantic Monthly Press, 2006.

Brickhill, Jeremy. "Zimbabwe's Poisoned Legacy: Secret War in Southern Africa." *CovertAction Quarterly* 43 (Winter 1992–93): 4–59.

Brind, Harry. "Soviet Policy in the Horn of Africa." *International Affairs* 60, no. 1 (Winter 1983–84): 75–95.

Brinkley, Douglas. *Dean Acheson: The Cold War Years, 1953–71*. New Haven, CT: Yale University Press, 1992.

———. "The Rising Stock of Jimmy Carter: The 'Hands-on' Legacy of Our Thirty-ninth President." *Diplomatic History* 20, no. 4 (Fall 1996): 505–29.

Bronson, Rachel. *Thicker Than Oil: America's Uneasy Partnership with Saudi Arabia*. Oxford, UK: Oxford University Press, 2006.

Brownell, Josiah. *The Collapse of Rhodesia: Population Demographics and the Politics of Race*. New York: I. B. Tauris, 2011.

———. "The Hole in Rhodesia's Bucket: White Emigration and the End of Settler Rule." *Journal of Southern African Studies* 34, no. 3 (2008): 591–610.

Brzezinski, Matthew. *Casino Moscow: A Tale of Greed and Adventure on Capitalism's Wildest Frontier*. New York: Free Press, 2001.

Brzezinski, Zbigniew. *Africa and the Communist World*. Stanford, CA: Stanford University Press, 1963.

———. "America and Europe." *Foreign Affairs* 49, no. 1 (October 1970): 11–30.

————. *Between Two Ages: America's Role in the Technetronic Era*. New York: Viking, 1971.

————. "The Deceptive Structure of Peace." *Foreign Policy* 14 (Spring 1974): 35–55.

————. "Half Past Nixon." *Foreign Policy* 3 (Summer 1971): 3–21.

————. "How the Cold War Was Played." *Foreign Affairs* 51, no. 1 (October 1972): 181–209.

————. *Power and Principle: Memoirs of the National Security Adviser, 1977–1981*. New York: Farrar, Straus, Giroux, 1983.

————. "U.S. Foreign Policy: The Search for Focus." *Foreign Affairs* 51, no. 4 (July 1973): 708–72.

————. "U.S.-Soviet Relations." In *The Next Phase in Foreign Policy*, edited by Henry Owen and Morton H. Halperin, 130–32. Washington, DC: Brookings Institution Press, 1973.

Brzezinski, Zbigniew, and Samuel P. Huntington. *Political Power: USA/USSR*. New York: Viking, 1975.

Buckley, William F. Jr. "Young in Perspective." *The National Review* (September 14, 1979): 1134–35.

Byrd, Robert C. *Robert C. Byrd: Child of the Appalachian Coalfields*. Morgantown: West Virginia University Press, 2005.

Callaghan, James. *Time and Chance*. London: Collins, 1987.

Callinicos, Alex. *Southern Africa after Zimbabwe*. London: Pluto, 1981.

Cannon, James M. *Time and Chance: Gerald Ford's Appointment with History*. New York: HarperCollins, 1994.

Cannon, Lou. *Governor Reagan: His Rise to Power*. New York: PublicAffairs, 2003.

Capazzola, Christopher. "'It Makes You Want to Believe': Celebrating the Bicentennial in an Age of Limits." In *America in the Seventies*, edited by Beth Bailey and Dave Farber, 29–49. Lawrence: University Press of Kansas, 2004.

Carrington, Peter. *Reflecting on Things Past: The Memoirs of Peter Lord Carrington*. New York: Harper & Row, 1989.

Carter, Jimmy. *Always a Reckoning, and Other Poems*. New York: Times Books, 1995.

————. "Being There," a letter to the editor, *Foreign Affairs* 78, no. 6 (November–December 1999): 164–65.

————. *An Hour Before Daylight: Memories of a Rural Boyhood*. New York: Simon & Schuster, 2001.

————. "Jimmy Carter à *L'Express*: 'Voici ma politique étrangère.'" By Pierre Salinger. *L'Express* (August 23, 1976): 40–44.

————. *Keeping Faith: Memoirs of a President*. New York: Bantam, 1982.

———. *Palestine: Peace not Apartheid.* New York: Simon & Schuster, 2006.

———. *A Remarkable Mother.* New York: Simon & Schuster, 2008.

———. *White House Diary.* New York: Farrar, Straus and Giroux, 2010.

———. *Why Not the Best?* Nashville, TN: Broadman Press, 1975.

Carter, Jimmy, and Gerald R. Ford. *The Presidential Campaign 1976.* Washington, DC: Government Printing Office, 1978.

Casper, Clifford. "Tragic Pragmatism: Liberia and the United States, 1971–1985." MA thesis, North Carolina State University, 2012.

Caute, David. *Under the Skin: The Death of White Rhodesia.* Evanston, IL: Northwestern University Press, 1983.

Červenka, Zdenek. *The Unfinished Quest for Unity: Africa and the OAU.* New York: Africana, 1977.

Chapman, Robert, and Patrick Flynn. "Assassination by Fall Guy: Ambassador Adolph Dubs." *International Journal of Intelligence and Counter-Intelligence* 24, no. 3 (June 2011): 601–6.

Charlton, Michael. *The Last Colony in Africa: Diplomacy and the Independence of Rhodesia.* Oxford, UK: Blackwell, 1990.

Chomsky, Noam, and Carlos Peregrín Otero. *Radical Priorities*, 3rd edition. Oakland, CA: AK Press, 2003 [1981].

Cilliers, Jakkie. *Counter-insurgency in Rhodesia.* London: Croom Helm, 1985.

Clymer, Adam. *Drawing the Line at the Big Ditch: The Panama Canal Treaties and the Rise of the Right.* Lawrence: University Press of Kansas, 2008.

Clymer, Kenton. "Jimmy Carter, Human Rights, and Cambodia." *Diplomatic History* 27, no. 2 (April 2003): 245–78.

CNN. "Interview with Dr Zbigniew Brzezinski, June 13, 1997." *The Cold War.* "Episode 17: Good Guys, Bad Guys," first aired February 14, 1999. http://nsarchive.gwu.edu/coldwar/interviews/.

Cohen, Andrew. "Lonhro and Oil Sanctions against Rhodesia in the 1960s." *Journal of Southern African Studies* 37, no. 4 (December 2011): 715–30.

Cohen, Stephen B. "Conditioning U.S. Security Assistance on Human Rights Practices." *The American Journal of International Law* 76, no. 2 (April 1982): 246–79.

Congressional Quarterly (CQ). *Guide to 1976 Elections.* Washington, DC: Congressional Quarterly Press, 1977.

Congressional Research Service, Library of Congress. *Major U.S. Foreign and Defense Policy Issues* (February 1, 1977). Washington, DC: GPO, 1977.

Cook, Daniel. "Crisis in Kabul: The Kidnaping and Assassination of Ambassador Adolph Dubs, February 14, 1979." MA thesis, North Carolina State University, 2000.

Copson, Raymond. "East Africa and the Indian Ocean: A 'Zone of Peace'?" *African Affairs* 76, no. 304 (July 1977): 339–58.

Corbin, David. *The Last Great Senator: Robert C. Byrd's Encounters with Eleven U.S. Presidents*. Washington, DC: Potomac Books, 2012.

Critchlow, Donald. *The Conservative Ascendancy: How the GOP Right Made Political History*. Cambridge, MA: Harvard University Press, 2007.

Crocker, Chester. "Lost in Africa." *New Republic* (February 18, 1978): 15–17.

Cronkite, Walter. *A Reporter's Life*. New York: Knopf, 1996.

Crosland, Susan. *Tony Crosland*. London: Jonathan Cape, 1982.

David L. Wolper Productions. *Roots*. Burbank: Warner Home Video, [2007] 1977.

David, Steven. *Choosing Sides: Alignment and Realignment in the Third World*. Baltimore, MD: Johns Hopkins University Press, 1991.

———. "Realignment in the Horn: The Soviet Advantage." *International Security* 4, no 2 (Fall 1979): 69–90.

Davidow, Jeffrey. *Dealing with International Crises: Lessons from Zimbabwe*. Muscatine, IA: Stanley Foundation, 1983.

———. *A Peace in Southern Africa: The Lancaster House Conference on Rhodesia, 1979*. Boulder, CO: Westview, 1985.

Davis, Nathaniel. "The Angola Decision of 1975: A Personal Memoir." *Foreign Affairs* 57, no. 1 (Fall 1978): 109–24.

Dawisha, Karen. "Soviet Policy in the Arab World: Permanent Interests and Changing Influence." *Arab Studies Quarterly* 2, no. 1 (Winter 1980): 19–37.

Dean, John. "Rituals of the Herd." *Rolling Stone* (October 7, 1976): 38–58.

Democratic National Convention. *The Official Proceedings of the Democratic National Convention, New York City, July, 1976*. Washington, DC: Democratic National Committee, 1976.

DePree, Willard. "Mozambique: When Diplomacy Paid Off," *Foreign Service Journal* (March 2015), http://www.afsa.org/

DeRoche, Andrew. *Andrew Young: Civil Rights Ambassador*. Wilmington, DE: Scholarly Resources Press, 2003.

———. "Andrew Young and Africa: From the Civil Rights Movement to the Atlanta Olympics." Paper presented at "The South and Globalization," June 22, 2002, The University of Georgia, Athens, GA.

———. *Black, White, and Chrome: The United States and Zimbabwe, 1953 to 1998*. Trenton, NJ: Africa World Press, 2001.

Dinnerstein, Leonard. *Antisemitism in America*. New York: Oxford University Press, 1994.

Documenting the American South. "Oral History Interview with Andrew Young, January 31, 1974." Interview A-0080, Southern Oral History Program Collection #4007, http://docsouth.unc.edu/sohp/A-0080/menu.html.

Drew, Elizabeth. *American Journal: The Events of 1976*. New York: Random House, 1977.

———. *Portrait of an Election: The 1980 Presidential Campaign*. New York: Simon & Schuster, 1981.

———. "Reporter at Large: Brzezinski." *The New Yorker* (May 1, 1978): 90–130.

Dreyfuss, Joel. "Such Good Friends: Blacks and Jews in Conflict." *Village Voice* (August 27, 1979): 11–12.

Dudziak, Mary. *Exporting American Dreams: Thurgood Marshall's African Journey*. Oxford: Oxford University Press, 2008.

Dumbrell, John. *The Carter Presidency: A Re-Evaluation*. Manchester, UK: Manchester University Press, 1995.

Dunbar, Leslie W. "Thoughts on a Conflict." In *The State of Black America 1980*, edited by James D. Williams, 235–62. Washington, DC: National Urban League: January 22, 1980.

Duncan, Robert. "Report of a Study Mission to Africa." Washington, DC: GPO, 1979.

Du Preez, Sophia. *Avontuur in Angola. Die verhaal van Suid-Afrika se soldate in Angola 1975–1976* [Adventure in Angola: The story of South Africa's troops in Angola, 1975–1976]. Pretoria: J. L. von Schaink, 1989.

Easum, Donald. "Hard Times for the Africa Bureau, 1973–1975." In *Fifty Years of US Africa Policy: Reflections of Assistant Secretaries for African Affairs and US Embassy Officials*, edited by Claudia Anyaso, 104–39. Arlington, VA: Association for Diplomatic Studies and Training, 2011.

"Election '76: Jimmy Carter on Africa." *Africa Report* 21, no. 3 (May/June 1976): 18–20.

El-Khawas, Mohamed, and Barry Cohen. *The Kissinger Study of Southern Africa: National Security Study Memorandum 39*. Westport, CT: Lawrence Hill, 1976.

Ellerin, Milton. "Race and Ethnicity." In *American Jewish Year Book: A Record of Events and Trends in American and World Jewish Life, 1979*, edited by Morris Fine and Milton Himmelfarb, 107–11. Scranton, PA: American Jewish Committee (New York) and Jewish Publication Society of America (Philadelphia), 1978.

Engerman, David C. *Know Your Enemy: The Rise and Fall of America's Soviet Experts*. Oxford: Oxford University Press, 2009.

Erhagbe, Edward Oregbheme. "African-Americans' Ideas and Contributions to Africa, 1900–1985: From 'Idealistic Rhetoric' to 'Realistic Pragmatism'?" PhD diss., Boston University, 1992.

Evans, Alona. "Goldwater v. Carter." *The American Journal of International Law* 74, no. 2 (April 1980): 441–47.

Fallaci, Oriana. "Kissinger: An Interview." *The New Republic* (December 16, 1972): 17–22.

Fallows, James. "The Passionless Presidency." *Atlantic Monthly* 243, no. 5 (May 1979): 33–48 and 243, no. 6 (June 1979): 75–82.

Farer, Tom J. *War Clouds on the Horn of Africa: The Widening Storm.* New York: Carnegie Endowment for International Peace, 1979.

Farrell, John A. *Tip O'Neill and the Democratic Century: A Biography.* Boston, MA: Little, Brown, 2001.

Farsoun, Samih. "Andrew Young: The Two-Edged Sword." *Journal of Palestine Studies* 9, no. 2 (Winter 1980): 139–45.

Fenno, Richard F. *Senators on the Campaign Trail: The Politics of Representation.* Norman: University of Oklahoma Press, 1996.

Fine, Leonard. "The Andrew Young Affair . . . to be continued." *Moment* 4, no. 9 (October 1979): 9–13

Finger, Seymour Maxwell. "Discussant." In *Jimmy Carter: Foreign Policy and Post-Presidential Years*, edited by Herbert D. Rosenbaum and Alexej Ugrinsky, 141–43. Westport, CT: Greenwood Press, 1994.

Fishbein, Leslie. "*Roots*: Docudrama and the Interpretation of History." In *American History, American Television: Interpreting the Video Past*, edited by John O'Connor, 279–305. New York: Frederick Ungar, 1983.

Fitzgerald, Frances. "The Warrior Intellectuals." *Harper's* 252, no. 1512 (May 1976): 45–64.

Flower, Ken. *Serving Secretly: An Intelligence Chief on Record: Rhodesia into Zimbabwe, 1964 to 1981.* London: Murray, 1987.

Ford, Gerald R. *A Time to Heal: The Autobiography of Gerald R. Ford.* New York: Harper & Row, 1979.

Forman, Seth. *Blacks in the Jewish Mind: A Crisis of Liberalism.* New York: New York University Press, 1998.

Fourie, Brand. *Brandpunte: Agter die skerms met Suid-Afrika se bekendste diplomat* [Flashpoints: Behind the scenes with South Africa's most famous diplomat]. Cape Town: Tafelberg, 1991.

Francis, Samuel. "Conflict in the Horn of Africa." *The Heritage Foundation: Backgrounder 24*, July 13, 1977.

Fraser, Malcolm, and Margaret Simons. *Malcolm Fraser: The Political Memoirs.* Carlton, Australia: Melbourne University Publishing, 2009.

Friedman, Murray. "Black Anti-Semitism on the Rise." *Commentary* 68 (October 1979): 31–38.

———. "Intergroup Relations." In *American Jewish Year Book, 1981*, edited by Milton Himmelfarb and David Singer, 123–34. Scranton, PA: American Jewish Committee (New York) and Jewish Publication Society of America (Philadelphia), 1980.

———. "Race Relations." In *American Jewish Year Book, 1980*, edited by Milton Himmelfarb and David Singer, 77–86. Scranton, PA: American

Jewish Committee (New York) and Jewish Publication Society of America (Philadelphia), 1979.

———. *What Went Wrong: The Creation and Collapse of the Black-Jewish Alliance.* New York, Free Press, 1995.

Fritchey, Clayton. "The Fall and Rise of Andy Young." *The Nation* (September 15, 1979): 201–4.

Funk, Jerry. *Life Is an Excellent Adventure: An Irreverent Personal Odyssey. Or Trying to Decide What I Want to Be When I Grow Up.* Victoria, British Columbia, Canada: Trafford, 2003.

Galphin, Bruce. "Jimmy Who Goes to Washington." *Atlanta* (January 1977): 41–44; 82.

Gardner, Carl. *Andrew Young: A Biography.* New York: Drake, 1978.

Garthoff, Raymond L. *Détente and Confrontation: American-Soviet Relations from Nixon to Reagan.* Washington, DC, Brookings Institution Press, 1985.

Gati, Charles. *Zbig: The Strategy and Statecraft of Zbigniew Brzezinski.* Baltimore, MD: Johns Hopkins University Press, 2013.

Gelb, Joyce. *Beyond Conflict: Black-Jewish Relations: Accent on the Positive.* New York: Institute on Pluralism and Group Identity of the American Jewish Committee, 1980.

Geldenhuys, Deon. *The Diplomacy of Isolation: South African Foreign Policy Making.* New York: St. Martin's Press, 1984.

Gershman, Carl. "The World According to Andrew Young." *Commentary* (August 1978): 17–23.

Ghebhardt, Alexander. "Soviet and U.S. Interests in the Indian Ocean." *Asian Survey* 15, no. 8 (August 1975): 672–83.

Gildea, Tara. "A Case Study of Zaïre's Foreign Policy: Shaba I and II." Genève: Institut Universitaire de Hautes Études Internationales, 1990.

Giliomee, Hermann. *The Last Afrikaner Leaders: A Supreme Test of Power.* Charlottesville: University of Virginia Press, 2013.

Gilkes, P. S. "Revolution and Military Strategy: The Ethiopian Army in the Ogaden and in Eritrea, 1974–84." In *Proceedings of the Eleventh International Conference of Ethiopian Studies: Addis Ababa, April 1–6, 1991,* edited by Zewde Bahru, Richard Pankhurst, and Beyene Taddese, 721–36. Addis Ababa: Institute of Ethiopian Studies, Addis Ababa University, 1994.

Gillon, Steven. *The Democrats' Dilemma: Walter F. Mondale and the Liberal Legacy.* New York: Columbia University Press, 1994 [1992].

Ginifer, Jeremy, and Jakkie Potgieter. *Managing Arms in Peace Processes: Rhodesia – Zimbabwe: Disarmament and Conflict Resolution Project.* New York: United Nations, 1995.

Giscard d'Estaing, Valéry. *Le pouvoir et la vie.* Vol. 2: *L'affrontement* [The power and the life 2: The confrontation]. Paris: Compagnie 12, 1991.

Gleave, M. B. "The Dar es Salaam Transport Corridor: An Appraisal." *African Affairs* 91, no. 363 (1992): 249–67.

Gleijeses, Piero. *Conflicting Missions: Havana, Washington, and Africa, 1959–1976.* Chapel Hill: University of North Carolina Press, 2002.

———. *The Cuban Drumbeat: Castro's Worldview. Cuban Foreign Policy in a Hostile World.* London: Seagull Books, 2009.

———. "'Flee! The White Giants Are Coming!' The United States, the Mercenaries, and the Congo, 1964–65." *Diplomatic History* 18, no. 2 (Spring 1994): 207–37.

———. "Interview with Robert W. Hultslander, former CIA Station Chief in Angola, 1998." National Security Archive, http://www.gwu.edu/~nsarchiv/.

———. "A Test of Wills: Jimmy Carter, South Africa, and the Independence of Namibia." *Diplomatic History* 34, no. 5 (November 2010): 853–91.

———. "Truth or Credibility: Castro, Carter, and the Invasions of Shaba." *International History Review* 18, no. 1 (February 1996): 70–103.

———. *Visions of Freedom: Havana, Washington, Pretoria and the Struggle for Southern Africa, 1976–1991.* Chapel Hill: University of North Carolina Press, 2013.

Glickson, Roger. "The Shaba Crises: Stumbling to Victory." *Small Wars and Insurgencies* 5, no. 2 (Autumn 1994): 180–200.

Godwin, Peter, and Ian Hancock. *'Rhodesians Never Die': The Impact of War and Political Change on White Rhodesia, c. 1970–1980.* Oxford, UK: Oxford University Press, 1993.

Goldsborough, James Oliver. "Dateline Paris: Africa's Policemen." *Foreign Policy* 33 (Winter 1978–79): 174–90.

Good, Kenneth. "Zambia and the Liberation of South Africa." *Journal of Modern African Studies* 25, no. 3 (September 1987): 505–40.

Gordon, Tammy S. *The Spirit of 1976: Commerce, Community, and the Politics of Commemoration.* Amherst: University of Massachusetts Press, 2013.

Great Britain, Foreign & Commonwealth Office. *Rhodesia: Proposals for a Settlement, presented to Parliament by the Secretary of State for Foreign and Commonwealth Affairs by Command of Her Majesty, September 1977.* London: H.M.S.O., 1977.

———. *Southern Rhodesia: Report of the Constitutional Conference, Lancaster House, London, September–December 1979.* London: H.M.S.O, 1980.

Green, Reginald. "The East African Community: The End of the Road." In Legum, *Africa Contemporary Record, 1976–77,* pp. A59–A67.

Greene, John Robert. *The Presidency of Gerald R. Ford.* Lawrence: University Press of Kansas, 1995.

Greenfield, Richard. "Towards an Understanding of the Somali Factor." In *Conflict and Peace in the Horn of Africa: Federalism and Its Alternatives,* edited by Peter Woodward and Murray Forsyth, 103–13. Brookfield, VT: Dartmouth Publishing Co., 1994.

Gregory, Martyn. "The Zimbabwe Election: The Political and Military Implications." *Journal of Southern African Studies* 7, no. 1 (1980): 17–37.

Gustafson, Barry. *His Way: A Biography of Robert Muldoon.* Auckland: Auckland University Press, 2000.

Haile-Selassie, Teferra. *The Ethiopian Revolution, 1974–1991: From a Monarchical Autocracy to a Military Oligarchy.* London: Kegan Paul International, 1997.

Halliday, Fred. "A Curious and Close Liaison: Saudi Arabia's Relations with the United States." In *State, Society and Economy in Saudi Arabia*, edited by Tim Niblock, 125–47. London: Croom Helm, 1982.

Ham, Oliver. "A Change in German-American Relations: The German Nuclear Deal with Brazil, 1977." MA thesis, North Carolina State University, 2012.

Hamilton, Charles V. "On Politics." In *The State of Black America 1980*, edited by James D. Williams, 199–217. Washington, DC: National Urban League: January 22, 1980.

Hancock, Ian. "Australian policy towards Rhodesia/Zimbabwe." Paper delivered at the Australian Department of Foreign Affairs and Trade, 19 May 2011.

Hanhimäki, Jussi M. *The Flawed Architect: Henry Kissinger and American Foreign Policy.* New York: Oxford University Press, 2004.

Harris, David. *The Crisis: The President, the Prophet, and the Shah: 1979 and the Coming of Militant Islam.* New York: Little, Brown and Co., 2004.

Harrison, Stephen. "Jimmy Carter versus Congress: The Debate over Rhodesia and the Rise of Jesse Helms." MA thesis, North Carolina State University, 1999.

Haskins, James. *Andrew Young: Man with a Mission.* New York: Lothrop, Lee & Shepard, 1979.

Haykal, Muhammad H. *Illusions of Triumph: An Arab View of the Gulf War.* London: HarperCollins, 1992.

———. *Iran, the Untold Story: An Insider's Account of America's Iranian Adventure and Its Consequences for the Future.* New York: Pantheon Books, 1982.

Heard, Tony. *The Cape of Storms: A Personal History of the Crisis in South Africa.* Johannesburg: Ravan Press, 1990.

Henderson, Harold P., and Gary L. Roberts. *Georgia Governors in an Age of Change: From Ellis Arnall to George Busbee.* Athens: University of Georgia Press, 1988.

Henze, Paul. "Arming the Horn, 1960–1980." Wilson Center Working Paper 43, International Security Studies Program. Washington, DC: Woodrow Wilson International Center for Scholars, 1982.

———. *The Horn of Africa: From War to Peace*. New York: St. Martin's Press, 1991.

Hershberg, James, ed. "Anatomy of a Third World Cold War Crisis: New East-Bloc Evidence on the Horn of Africa." *Cold War International History Project Bulletin* 8/9 (Winter 1996): 38–102, 422.

———. "'Seventeen Days' (or Fifteen, Sixteen, or Eighteen, But Who's Counting?) The South African Nuclear Crisis (or Was It?) of August 1977." Paper delivered at "The Historical Dimensions of South Africa's Nuclear Program," December 10–12, 2012, Monash University, Pretoria, South Africa.

Hertzberg, Hendrik. "A Very Merry Malaise," *The New Yorker* (July 17, 2009). http://www.newyorker.com/news/hendrik-hertzberg/a-very-merry-malaise.

———. *Politics: Observations and Arguments, 1966-2004*. New York: Penguin Press, 2004.

Herzog, Chaim. "U.N. at Work: The Benin Affair." *Foreign Policy* 29 (1977): 140–59.

Hoffmann, Stanley. *Dead Ends: American Foreign Policy in the New Cold War*. Cambridge, MA: Ballinger, 1983.

Horne, Gerald. *From the Barrel of a Gun: The United States and the War against Zimbabwe, 1965–1980*. Chapel Hill: University of North Carolina Press, 2001.

———. "Race from Power: US Foreign Policy and the General Crisis of 'White Supremacy.'" *Diplomatic History* 23, no. 3 (Summer 1999): 437–61.

Hudson, Miles. *Triumph or Tragedy? Rhodesia to Zimbabwe*. London: H. Hamilton, 1981.

Hufbauer, Gary C. *Economic Sanctions Reconsidered,* 3rd Edition. Washington, DC: Peterson Institute for International Economics, 1985.

Hull, Galen. "Internationalizing the Shaba Conflict." *Africa Report* 22, no. 4 (July/August 1977): 4–9.

Hunter, Jane. "Israel and Ethiopia." *Israeli Foreign Affairs* 1, no. 6 (May 1985): 1, 8.

Inderfurth, Karl, and Loch K. Johnson. *Fateful Decisions: Inside the National Security Council*. New York: Oxford University Press, 2004.

Ingram, Derek. "Lusaka 1979: a Significant Commonwealth Meeting." *The Round Table* 69, no. 276 (1979): 275-83.

Isaacson, Walter. *Kissinger: A Biography*. New York: Simon & Schuster, 1992.

Jackson, Donna R. *Jimmy Carter and the Horn of Africa: Cold War Policy in Ethiopia and Somalia.* Jefferson, NC: McFarland & Co, 2007.

Jaster, Robert S. *A Regional Security Role for Africa's Front-Line States: Experience and Prospects.* London: International Institute for Strategic Studies, 1983.

———. "South Africa and Its Neighbours: The Dynamics of Regional Conflict." *Adelphi Papers* 209 (Summer 1986): 1–78.

Jefferys, Kevin. *Anthony Crosland.* London: Richard Cohen Books, 1999.

Johnson, Herschel. "A Close Encounter with Andrew Young." *Ebony* (April 1978): 110–112; 114, 116, 120, 122.

Johnson, Robert David. "The Unintended Consequences of Congressional Reform: The Clark and Tunney Amendments and U.S. Policy toward Angola." *Diplomatic History* 27, no. 2 (April 2003): 215–43.

———. *Congress and the Cold War.* New York: Cambridge University Press, 2006.

Johnson, Robert E. "Andy Young Talks About Things He Couldn't Talk About Before Now." *Jet* 56 (September 13, 1979): 14–16, 53–55.

———. "Helping Blacks by Helping Shape U.S. Foreign Policy: Young" (interview with Andrew Young). *Jet* 51 (February 10, 1977): 12–15.

Joint Center for Political Studies. *The Black Vote: Election '76.* Washington, DC: Joint Center for Political Studies, 1977.

Jones, Bartlett C. "National and International Consequences of Ambassador Andrew Young's Meeting with PLO Observer Terzi." In *Jimmy Carter: Foreign Policy and Post-Presidential Years*, edited by Herbert D. Rosenbaum and Alexej Ugrinsky, 123–39. Westport, CT: Greenwood Press, 1994.

Jordan, Vernon, Jr. "Introduction." In *The State of Black America 1980*, edited by James D. Williams, i–xii. Washington, DC: National Urban League: January 22, 1980.

Kabwit, Ghislain C. "Zaire: The Roots of the Continuing Crisis." *Journal of Modern African Studies* 17, no. 3 (September 1979): 381–407.

Kamarck, Elaine Ciulla. *Primary Politics: How Presidential Candidates Have Shaped the Modern Nominating System.* Washington, DC: Brookings Institution Press, 2009.

Kandiah, Michael, and Sue Onslow. "Britain and Rhodesia: The Route to Settlement," Institute of Contemporary British History (ICBH) Oral History Programme, July 5, 2005. London: ICBH, 2008.

Kane-Berman, John Stuart. *South Africa: The Method in the Madness.* London: Pluto Press, 1979.

Kaufman, Victor. "The Bureau of Human Rights during the Carter Administration." *Historian* 61, no. 1 (September 1998): 51–66.

Kaunda, Kenneth D., and Colin Morris. *A Humanist in Africa; Letters to Colin M. Morris from Kenneth D. Kaunda.* Nashville, TN: Abingdon Press, 1966.

———. *The Riddle of Violence.* San Francisco: Harper & Row, 1980.

Keller, Edmond J. *Revolutionary Ethiopia: From Empire to People's Republic.* Bloomington: Indiana University Press, 1988.

———. "Government and Politics." In *Ethiopia: A Country Study: Ethiopia,* edited by Thomas Ofcansky and LaVerle Berry. Washington, DC: Federal Research Division, Library of Congress, 1993.

Kempton, Daniel R. *Soviet Strategy toward Southern Africa: The National Liberation Movement Connection.* New York: Praeger, 1989.

Kennair, John. *A Forgotten Legacy: Canadian Leadership in the Commonwealth.* Bloomington, IN: Trafford, 2011.

Kennan, George, [X]. "The Sources of Soviet Conduct." *Foreign Affairs* 25, no. 4 (July 1947): 566–82.

———. "Hazardous Courses in Southern Africa." *Foreign Affairs* 49, no. 2 (January 1971): 218–36.

Kennedy, Edward. "The Persian Gulf: Arms Race or Arms Control?" *Foreign Affairs* 54, no. 1 (October 1975): 14–35.

King, Martin Luther, Jr. *Strength to Love.* Minneapolis, MN: Fortress Press, 1981 [1963].

Kissinger, Henry. *White House Years.* Boston, MA: Little, Brown, 1979.

———. *Years of Renewal.* New York: Simon & Schuster, 1999.

Korn, David. *Assassination in Khartoum.* Bloomington: Indiana University Press, 1993.

Kornbluh, Peter. "JFK & Castro: The Secret Quest for Accommodation." *Cigar Aficionado* (September/October 1999): 86–105.

Kornegay, Francis. "Africa and Presidential Politics." *Africa Report* 21, no. 4 (July/August 1976): 7–20.

Kornienko, Georgi. *Kholodnaya voina: svidetel'stvo ee uchastnika* [The Cold War: Testimony of a participant]. Moscow: Mezhdunarodnie Otnoshenia, 1994.

Kraft, Joseph. "Letter from Addis Ababa." *The New Yorker* (July 31, 1978): 46–63.

Kramer, Mark. "Anticipating the Grand Failure," in Gati, *Zbig,* 42–59.

Kreisler, Harry. "Reflections of a Diplomat: Conversation with Ambassador David D. Newsom." June 13, 2002, *Conversations with History,* Institute of International Studies, University of California, Berkeley, http://globe trotter.berkeley.edu.

————. "Reflections on Empire, Nationalism, and Globalization, with Kenneth D. Kaunda." November 3, 2006, 54:53, *Conversations with History*, Institute of International Studies, University of California, Berkeley, http://conversations.berkeley.edu/content/kenneth-d-kaunda.

Kum Buo, Sammy. "The Illusion of Afro-Arab Solidarity." *Africa Report* (September–October 1975): 45–48.

Kwitny, Jonathan. *Man of the Century: The Life and Times of Pope John Paul II.* New York: Henry Holt and Co., 1997.

Laitin, David. "The Political Economy of Military Rule in Somalia." *Journal of Modern African Studies* 14, no. 3 (September 1976): 449–68.

————. "The War in the Ogaden: Implications for Siyaad's Rôle in Somali History." *Journal of Modern African Studies* 17, no. 1 (March 1979): 95–115.

Laitin, David, and Said S. Samatar. *Somalia: Nation in Search of a State.* Boulder, CO: Westview Press, 1987.

Lake, Anthony. *The "Tar Baby" Option: American Policy toward Southern Rhodesia.* New York: Columbia University Press, 1976.

Lawson, Steven F. *Running for Freedom: Civil Rights and Black Politics in America since 1941.* Philadelphia, PA: Temple University Press, 1991.

Lefebvre, Jeffrey. *Arms for the Horn: U.S. Security Policy in Ethiopia and Somalia, 1953–1991.* Pittsburgh, PA: University of Pittsburgh Press, 1991.

Lefort, René. *Éthiopie: la révolution hérétique* [Ethiopia: The heretical revolution]. Paris: Maspero, 1981.

Legum, Colin. *Africa Contemporary Record: Annual Survey and Documents, 1975–76.* New York: Africana, 1976.

————. *Africa Contemporary Record: Annual Survey and Documents, 1976–77.* London: Collings, 1977.

————. *Africa Contemporary Record: Annual Survey and Documents, 1977–78.* London: Collings, 1978.

————. *Africa Contemporary Record: Annual Survey and Documents, 1978–79.* New York: Africana, 1979.

————. *Africa Contemporary Record: Annual Survey and Documents, 1979–1980.* New York: Africana, 1981.

Lellouche, Pierre, and Dominique Moisi. "French Policy in Africa: A Lonely Battle against Destabilization." *International Security* 3, no. 4 (Spring 1979): 108–33.

LeoGrande, William M., and Peter Kornbluh. *Back Channel to Cuba: The Hidden History of Negotiations between Washington and Havana.* Chapel Hill: University of North Carolina Press, 2014.

Lewis, I. M. *A Modern History of the Somali: Nation and State in the Horn of Africa.* Oxford: James Currey, 2002.

———. *Understanding Somalia and Somaliland: Culture, History, Society.* New York: Columbia University Press, 2008.

Libby, Ronald T. *The Politics of Economic Power in Southern Africa.* Princeton, NJ: Princeton University Press, 1987.

Liberman, Peter. "Israel and the South African Bomb." *The Nonproliferation Review* 11, no. 2 (Summer 2004): 1–35.

Link, William. *Righteous Warrior: Jesse Helms and the Rise of Modern Conservatism.* New York: St. Martin's, 2008.

Lockwood, Edgar. "The Future of the Carter Policy toward Southern Africa." *Issue: A Journal of Opinion* 7, no. 4 (Winter 1977): 11–15.

Logan, Andy. "Around City Hall." *The New Yorker* (June 27, 1977): 84–86.

———. "Around City Hall." *The New Yorker* (September 24, 1979): 134–45.

Low, Stephen. "The Zimbabwe Settlement, 1976–1979." In *International Mediation in Theory and Practice*, edited by Saadia Touval and I. William Zartman, 91–109. Boulder, CO: Westview Press, 1985.

Lowenthal, David. "The Bicentennial Landscape: A Mirror Held Up to the Past." *Geographical Review* 67, no. 3 (July 1977): 253–67.

Lubowski, Andrzej. *Zbig: The Man Who Cracked the Kremlin.* New York: OpenRoad, 2011.

Lulat, Y. G.-M. *United States Relations with South Africa: A Critical Overview from the Colonial Period to the Present.* New York: Peter Lang, 2008.

Lumet, Sidney, et al. *Network.* Burbank, CA: Warner Home Video, 2006.

MacLellan, David. *Cyrus Vance.* Totowa, NJ: Rowman & Allanheld, 1985.

Macmillan, Hugh. "The African National Congress of South Africa in Zambia: the Culture of Exile and the Changing Relationship with Home, 1964–1990." *Journal of Southern African Studies* 35, no. 2 (June 2009): 303–29.

Malley, Simon. "20 heures d'entretiens avec Fidel Castro" [20 hours of interviews with Fidel Castro]. *Afrique-Asie* (May 16, 1977): 8–21.

Mamdani, Mahmood. *Good Muslim, Bad Muslim: America, the Cold War, and the Roots of Terror.* New York: Pantheon Books, 2004.

Mangold, Tom, and Jeff Goldberg. *Plague Wars: A True Story of Biological Warfare.* New York: St. Martin's Press, 2000.

Marcus, Harold. *A History of Ethiopia.* Berkeley: University of California Press, 1994.

Marenches, Alexandre, with Christine Ockrent. *Dans le secret des princes* [In the princes' secret]. Paris: Stock, 1986.

Martin, David, and Phyllis Johnson. *The Chitepo Assassination.* Harare: Zimbabwe Publishing House, 1985.

———. *The Struggle for Zimbabwe: The Chimurenga War.* New York: Monthly Review Press, 1981.

Martinez, Ian. "The History of the Use of Bacteriological and Chemical Agents during Zimbabwe's Liberation War of 1965–80 by Rhodesian Forces." *Third World Quarterly* 23, no. 6 (December 2002): 1159–79.

Massie, Robert Kinloch. *Loosing the Bonds: The United States and South Africa in the Apartheid Years.* New York: Doubleday, 1997.

Mathews, K., and Samuel S. Mushi, eds. *Foreign Policy of Tanzania, 1961–1981: A Reader.* Dar es Salaam: Tanzania Publishing House, 1981.

Mattson, Kevin. *"What the Heck Are You Up To, Mr. President?" Jimmy Carter, America's "Malaise," and the Speech That Should Have Changed the Country.* New York: Bloomsbury, 2009.

Mayer, Jeremy D. *Running on Race: Racial Politics in Presidential Campaigns, 1960–2000.* New York: Random House, 2002.

Mazrui, Ali. "Black Africa and the Arabs." *Foreign Affairs* 53, no. 4 (July 1975): 725–42.

———. "The End of America's Amnesia?" *Africa Report* 22, no. 3 (May/June 1977): 6–11.

McAlister, Melani. "One Black Allah: The Middle East in the Cultural Politics of African American Liberation, 1955–1970." *American Quarterly* 51, no. 3 (1999): 622–65.

McIntyre, W. D. *The Significance of the Commonwealth, 1965–90.* Basingstoke, UK: Macmillan, 1991.

McWilliams, Carey. "Thoughts on the Bicentennial." *The Nation* 220, no. 14 (April 12, 1975): 420–23.

Mehmet, Ozay. "Effectiveness of Foreign Aid—The Case of Somalia." *Journal of Modern African Studies* 9, no. 1 (May 1971): 31–47.

Meredith, Martin. *Mugabe: Power, Plunder, and the Struggle for Zimbabwe.* New York: PublicAffairs, 2002.

———. *The Past Is Another Country: Rhodesia 1890–1979.* London: A. Deutsch, 1979.

Metz, Steven K. "The Anti-Apartheid Movement and the Formulation of American Policy Toward South Africa, 1969–1981." PhD diss., Johns Hopkins University, 1985.

Mgadla, Part T. "'A Good Measure of Sacrifice': Botswana and the Liberation Struggles of Southern Africa (1965–1985)." *Social Dynamics* 34, no. 1 (2008): 5–16.

Miller, Jake. "Black Viewpoints on the Mid-East Conflict." *Journal of Palestine Studies* 10, no. 2 (Winter 1981): 37–49.

Miller, Jamie. "Things Fall Apart: South Africa and the Collapse of the Portuguese Empire, 1973–74." *Cold War History* 12, no. 2 (2012): 183–204.

———. "Yes, Minister: Reassessing South Africa's Intervention in the Angolan Civil War, 1975–1976." *Journal of Cold War Studies* 15, no. 3 (2013): 4–33.

Minter, William. "Major Themes in Mozambican Foreign Relations, 1975–1977." *Issue: A Journal of Opinion* 8, no. 1 (Spring 1978): 43–49.

Mitchell, Diana. *African Nationalist Leaders in Zimbabwe: Who's Who 1980.* Salisbury, Zimbabwe: D. Mitchell, 1980.

Mlambo, Alois. "'Land Grab' or 'Taking Back Stolen Land': The Fast-Track Land Reform Process in Zimbabwe in Historical Perspective." *History Compass* 3, no. 1 (2005): 1–21.

———. *White Immigration into Rhodesia: From Occupation to Federation.* Harare, Zimbabwe: University of Zimbabwe Publications, 2002.

Mokoena, Kenneth, and Nicole Gaymon. *Zimbabwe, a Case Study in Diplomacy and Constitutional Negotiations.* National Security Documentation Research Series, no. 1. Washington, DC: National Security Archive, 1991.

Monson, Jamie. *Africa's Freedom Railway: How a Chinese Development Project Changed Lives and Livelihoods in Tanzania.* Bloomington: Indiana University Press, 2009.

Moorcraft, Paul L., and Peter McLaughlin. *The Rhodesian War: A Military History.* Barnsley, UK: Pen & Sword Military, 2008.

Moore, Charles. *Margaret Thatcher: The Authorized Biography: From Grantham to the Falklands.* New York: Knopf, 2013.

Moore-King, Bruce. *White Man, Black War.* Harare: Baobab Books, 1988.

Morapedi, Wazha. "The Dilemmas of Liberation in Southern Africa: The Case of Zimbabwean Liberation Movements and Botswana, 1960–1979." *Journal of Southern African Studies* 38, no. 1 (2012): 73–90.

Morgan, Kenneth O. *Callaghan: A Life.* Oxford, UK: Oxford University Press, 1997.

Morris, Kenneth E. *Jimmy Carter, American Moralist.* Athens: University of Georgia Press, 1996.

Moyn, Samuel. *The Last Utopia: Human Rights in History.* Cambridge, MA: Belknap Press of Harvard University Press, 2010.

Mtisi, Joseph, Munyaradzi Nyakudya, and Teresa Barnes. "Social and Economic Developments during the UDI Period." In *Becoming Zimbabwe: A History from the Pre-Colonial Period to 2008*, edited by Brian Raftopoulos and Alois Mlambo, 115–40. Harare, Zimbabwe: Weaver Press, 2009.

———. "War in Rhodesia, 1965–1980." In *Becoming Zimbabwe: A History from the Pre-Colonial Period to 2008*, edited by Brian Raftopoulos and Alois Mlambo, 141–66. Harare, Zimbabwe: Weaver Press, 2009.

Mungazi, Dickson. *In the Footsteps of the Masters: Desmond M. Tutu and Abel T. Muzorewa.* Westport, CT: Praeger, 2000.

Murphy, Philip. "'An intricate and distasteful subject': British Planning for the Use of Force Against the European Settlers of Central Africa, 1952–65." *English Historical Review* 121 (June 2006): 746–77.

Muzorewa, Abel. *Rise Up & Walk: The Autobiography of Bishop Abel Tendekai Muzorewa*. Nashville, TN: Abingdon, 1978.

Mwaipaya, Paul A. *African Humanism and National Development: A Critical Analysis of the Fundamental Theoretical Principle of Zambian Humanism*. Washington, DC: University Press of America, 1981.

Mwase, Ngila. "The Tanzania-Zambia Railway: The Chinese Loan and the Pre-Investment Analysis Revisited." *Journal of Modern African Studies* 21, no. 3 (1983): 535–43.

Nabudere, D. Wadada. "The Role of Tanzania in Regional Integration in East Africa." In Matthews and Mushi, *Foreign Policy of Tanzania*, 141–46.

National Council of Churches USA. "Andrew Young: NCC President, 2000–2001." November 1999. http://www.ncccusa.org/about/young.html.

Naughton, James. "Campaign without a Knockout Punch." *NYT Magazine* (June 6, 1976): 15, 60–65.

Ndlovu-Gatsheni, Sabelo J. *Reconstructing the Implications of Liberation Struggle History on SADC Mediation in Zimbabwe*. Johannesburg: South African Institute of International Affairs, 2011.

Nesbit, Roy C., Dudley Cowderoy, and Andrew Thomas. *Britain's Rebel Air Force: The War from the Air in Rhodesia, 1965–1980*. London: Grub Street, 1998.

Newhouse, John. "A Sense of Duty: Lord Carrington." *The New Yorker* (February 14, 1983): 47–83.

Newsom, David. *The Soviet Brigade in Cuba: A Study in Political Diplomacy*. Bloomington: Indiana University Press, 1987.

Njølstad, Olav. "Peacekeeper and Troublemaker: Jimmy Carter's Containment Policy, 1977-1978." PhD diss., Norwegian Institute for Defense Studies, 1995.

———. "Shifting Priorities: The Persian Gulf in US Strategic Planning in the Carter Years." *Cold War History* 4, no. 3 (April 2004): 21–55.

Nkomo, Fortune S. *Joshua Nkomo: Father Zimbabwe. The Life and Times of an African Legend*. Harare, Zimbabwe: Radiant Publishing, 2013.

Nkomo, Joshua. *The Story of My Life*. London: Methuen, 1984.

Noskova, Al'bina F., et al. *Pol'ša v XX veke. Očerki političeskoj istorii* [Poland in the twentieth century: Essays on political history]. Moscow: Indrik, 2012.

Nöthling, C. J. *Geskiedenis van die Suid-Afrikaanse Weermag, v.2: 1945–1994* [History of the South African Defence Force, vol. 2: 1945–1994]. Pretoria: SAMHIK, 1996.

"OAU Summit Conference," *Africa Research Bulletin* 14, no. 7 (July 1977): 4486–89.

Odom, Thomas P. *Shaba II: The French and Belgian Intervention in Zaire in 1978.* Fort Leavenworth, KS: US Army Command and General Staff College, Combat Studies Institute, 1993.

Ofcansky, Thomas. "National Security." In *Ethiopia: A Country Study*, edited by Thomas Ofcansky and LaVerle Berry. Washington, DC: Federal Research Division, Library of Congress, 1993, http://memory.loc.gov/frd/cs/ettoc.html

Ogunbadejo, Oye. "Conflict in Africa: A Case Study of the Shaba Crisis, 1977." *World Affairs* 141, no. 3 (1979): 219–34.

O'Meara, Dan. *Forty Lost Years: The Apartheid State and the Politics of the National Party, 1948–1994.* Randburg, South Africa: Ravan Press, 1996.

O'Neill, Tip, and William Novak. *Man of the House: The Life and Political Memoirs of Speaker Tip O'Neill.* New York: Random House, 1987.

Onslow, Sue. *Cold War in Southern Africa: White Power, Black Liberation.* London: Routledge, 2009.

———. "Documents: South Africa and Zimbabwe-Rhodesian Independence, 1979–1980." *Cold War History* 7, no. 2 (2007): 305–25.

———. "Freedom at Midnight: A Microcosm of Zimbabwe's Hopes and Dreams at Independence, April 1980." *The Round Table* (2008): 737–46.

———. "'Noises Off': South Africa and the Lancaster House Settlement 1979–1980." *Journal of Southern African Studies* 35, no. 2 (2009): 490–506.

———. "South Africa and the Owen/Vance Plan of 1977." *South African Historical Journal* 51, no. 1 (2004): 130–58.

———. "'We Must Gain Time': South Africa, Rhodesia and the Kissinger Initiative of 1976." *South African Historical Journal* 56, no. 1 (2006): 123–53.

———. "Zimbabwe: Land and the Lancaster House Settlement." *British Scholar* 2, no. 1 (2009): 40–74.

Onslow, Sue, and Anna-Mart van Wyk, eds. *Southern Africa in the Cold War, Post-1974.* Critical Oral History Conference Series, The Wilson Center, 2013.

Orwell, George, and Sonia Orwell. *In Front of Your Nose: 1945–1950.* Boston, MA: Godine, 2000.

Osei-Hwedie, B. "The Role of Botswana in the Liberation of Southern Africa." In *Botswana, Politics and Society*, edited by Wayne Edge and M. H. Lekorwe, 425–39. Pretoria: J.L. van Schaik, 1998.

Ottaway, Marina, and David Ottaway. *Ethiopia: Empire in Revolution.* New York: Africana, 1978.

Owen, David. *Time to Declare.* London: M. Joseph, 1991.

Paczkowski, Andrzej. *The Spring Will Be Ours: Poland and the Poles from Occupation to Freedom.* University Park: Pennsylvania State University Press, 2003.

Parker, Jim. *Assignment Selous Scouts: Inside Story of a Rhodesian Special Branch Officer.* Alberton, South Africa: Galago, 2006.

Parliamentary Debates (Hansard), Commons, 5th series (1909–80). http://hansard.millbanksystems.com/.

Parliamentary Debates (Hansard), Lords, 5th series (1909–). http://hansard.millbanksystems.com.

Patman, Robert G. *The Soviet Union in the Horn of Africa: The Diplomacy of Intervention and Disengagement.* Cambridge, UK: Cambridge University Press, 1990.

Peoples [*sic*] Bicentennial Commission. *America's Birthday: A Planning and Activity Guide for Citizens' Participation During the Bicentennial Years.* New York: Simon & Schuster, 1974.

Petter-Bowyer, Peter J. H. *Winds of Destruction: The Autobiography of a Rhodesia Combat Pilot.* Victoria, BC: Trafford, 2004.

Petterson, Donald. "Ethiopia Abandoned? An American Perspective." *International Affairs* 62, no. 4 (Autumn 1986): 627–45.

Pfeffer, Stephen. "'The Drill': The Emergence of the 'New Right' as a Force in U.S. Conservative Politics during the Panama Canal Debates, 1977–1978." MA thesis, North Carolina State University, 2006.

Pfister, Roger. *Apartheid South Africa and African States: From Pariah to Middle Power, 1961–1994.* London: Tauris Academic Studies, 2005.

Pipes, Richard. "Team B: The Reality Behind the Myth." *Commentary* 82, no. 4 (October 1986): 25–40.

Polhemus, James H. "Botswana's Role in the Liberation of Southern Africa." In *The Evolution of Modern Botswana*, edited by Louis A. Picard, 228–70. London: Rex Collings, 1985.

Ponichtera, Robert. "One More Reason for Communism's Collapse: Television in Poland, 1951–1989." Woodrow Wilson International Center for Scholars, November 12, 1997. http://www.wilsoncenter.org/publication/146-one-more-reason-for-communisms-collapse-television-poland-1951-1989.

Pottinger, Brian. *The Imperial Presidency: P.W. Botha, the First 10 Years.* Johannesburg: Southern Book Publishers, 1988.

Price, Tanya. "The Real Democrats: The Congressional Black Caucus and the Struggle for Power on Capitol Hill." PhD diss., Indiana University, 1993.

Quandt, William B. *Peace Process: American Diplomacy and the Arab-Israeli Conflict since 1967.* Washington, DC: Brookings Institution Press, 1993.

Rabinowitz, Dorothy. "Blacks, Jews, and New York Politics." *Commentary* 66, no. 5 (November 1978): 42–47.

Randel, William. "The Fife and Drum of Big Business." *The Nation* 216, no. 4 (January 22, 1973): 108–10.

Randolph, R. Sean. "The Byrd Amendment: A Postmortem." *World Affairs* 141, no. 1 (Summer 1978): 57–70.

Range, Peter Ross. "*Playboy* interview: Andrew Young." *Playboy* (July 1977): 61–83.

Rees, Mervyn, and Chris Day. *Muldergate: The Story of the Info Scandal.* Johannesburg: Macmillan South Africa, 1980.

Reeves, Richard. *Convention.* New York: Harcourt Brace Jovanovich, 1977.

Rehnquist, William. "A Tribute to Chief Justice Warren E. Burger." *Harvard Law Review* 100, no. 2 (1987): 969–1001.

Reid-Daly, Ron. *Pamwe Chete: The Legend of the Selous Scouts.* Weltervreden Park, South Africa: Covos-Day Books, 1999.

Reid-Daly, Ron, and Peter Stiff. *Selous Scouts: Top Secret War.* Alberton, South Africa: Galago, 1982.

Renwick, Robin. *Unconventional Diplomacy in Southern Africa.* New York: St. Martin's Press, 1997.

Republic of South Africa, Senate, *Debates.* Cape Town: Government Printer, 1974–1979.

Rhoodie, Eschel M. *PW Botha: The Last Betrayal.* Melville, South Africa: S.A. Politics, 1989.

———. *The Real Information Scandal.* Pretoria: Orbis, 1983.

Rice, Susan. "The Commonwealth Initiative in Zimbabwe, 1979–1980: Implications for International Peacekeeping." D.Phil thesis, New College, Oxford University, 1990.

Richelson, Jeffrey, ed. "U.S. Intelligence and the South African Bomb." Electronic Briefing Book 181, National Security Archive, http://www.gwu.edu/~nsarchiv.

———. "The Vela Incident: Nuclear Test or Meteoroid?" Electronic Briefing Book no. 190, National Security Archive, http://www.gwu.edu/~nsarchiv.

Riddell, Roger. "Zimbabwe's Land Problem: The Central Issue." In *From Rhodesia to Zimbabwe: Behind and Beyond Lancaster House*, edited by W. H. Morris-Jones, 1–13. London: F. Cass, 1980.

Rieff, David. "Realpolitik in Congo." *The Nation* (July 7, 1997):16–21.

Robbs, Peter. "Africa and the Indian Ocean." *Africa Report* 21, no. 3 (May/June 1976): 41–45.

Robinson, Randall. *Defending the Spirit: A Black Life in America.* New York: Plume, 1998.

Rodgers, Daniel T. *Age of Fracture*. Cambridge, MA: Belknap Press of Harvard University Press, 2011.

Rogers, Barbara, and Zdenek Červenka. *The Nuclear Axis: The Secret Collaboration between West Germany and South Africa.* London: Julian Friedmann, 1978.

Rose, Peter I. "Blacks and Jews: The Strained Alliance." *Annals of the American Academy of Political and Social Science* 454 (March 1981): 55–69.

Rothkopf, David. *Running the World: The Inside Story of the National Security Council and the Architects of American Power*. New York: Public Affairs, 2006.

Rotkin, Charles, "A Puzzle for the Press Club." *News Photographer* (June 1978): 51.

Rovere, Richard. "Letter from Washington." *The New Yorker* (March 8, 1976): 114–21.

Russian Republic, Ministry of Defense (Institute of Military History). *Rossiya (SSSR) v lokalnyh voinah i voennuh konfliktah vtoroi poloviny XX veka* [Russia (USSR) in local wars and military conflicts in the second half of the twentieth century]. Moscow: Kuchkovo Pole and Poligrafresursy, 2000.

Samatar, Ahmed. *Socialist Somalia: Rhetoric and Reality*. London: Zed Books, 1988.

Scheer, Robert. "Eyewitness: Andrew Young. Lessons From a Missed Opportunity." *Los Angeles Times* (September 12, 1993): 5.

———. "Jimmy, We Hardly Know Y'all." *Playboy* 23, no. 11 (November 1976): 98, 186–93.

———. "The Playboy Interview: Jimmy Carter." *Playboy* 23, no. 11 (November 1976): 63–86.

Schleicher, Hans-Georg. "Befreiungskampf Zimbabwe: Höhen und Tiefen der DDR-Afrikapolitik" [Zimbabwe liberation struggle: The ups and downs of the GDR's Africa policy]. In *Engagiert für Afrika: Die DDR und Afrika II* [Committed to Africa: The GDR and Africa II], edited by Ulrich van der Heyden, Ilona Schleicher, and Hans-Georg Schleicher, 49–72. Münster: Lit Verlag, 1994.

Schlesinger, Arthur. *The Imperial Presidency*. Boston, MA: Houghton Mifflin, 1973.

———. *A Thousand Days: John F. Kennedy in the White House*. Boston, MA: Houghton Mifflin, 1965.

Schmidli, W. M. "Human Rights and the Cold War: The Campaign to Halt the Argentine Dirty War." *Cold War History* 12, no. 2 (2012): 345–65.

Schmidt, Helmut. *Menschen und Mächte* [People and powers]. Berlin: Siedler, 1987.

Schneidman, Witney W. *Engaging Africa: Washington and the Fall of Portugal's Colonial Empire*. Lanham, MD: University Press of America, 2004.

Schoultz, Lars. *Human Rights and United States Policy toward Latin America*. Princeton, NJ: Princeton University Press, 1981.

———. *That Infernal Little Cuban Republic: The United States and the Cuban Revolution*. Chapel Hill: University of North Carolina Press, 2009.

Schraeder, Peter J., and Jerel A. Rosati. "Policy Dilemmas in the Horn of Africa: Contradictions in the US-Somalia Relationship." *Northeast African Studies* 9, no. 3 (1987): 19–42.

Schram, Martin. *Running for President, 1976: The Carter Campaign*. New York: Stein and Day, 1977.

Schwab, Peter. "Cold War on the Horn of Africa." *African Affairs* 77, no. 306 (January 1978): 6–20.

———. "Israel's Weakened Position on the Horn of Africa." *New Outlook* (Tel Aviv) (April 1978): 21–27.

Sellars, Kirsten. *The Rise and Rise of Human Rights*. Stroud, UK: Sutton, 2002.

Sellström, Tor. *Sweden and National Liberation in Southern Africa*. Vol. 2: *Solidarity and Assistance, 1970–1994*. Uppsala: Nordiska Afrikainstitutet, 1999.

Shapiro, Ira S. *The Last Great Senate: Courage and Statesmanship in Times of Crisis*. New York: PublicAffairs, 2012.

Sharter, Martin. "The Carter Promise." *Atlanta* (January 1977): 38–40.

Shattan, Joseph. "Andy's Martyrdom: The Sadness and the Junkets." *The American Spectator* 12, no. 12 (December 1979): 7–11.

Shirley, Craig. *Reagan's Revolution: The Untold Story of the Campaign That Started It All*. Nashville, TN: Nelson Current, 2005.

Shoup, Laurence. "Jimmy Carter and the Trilateralists: Presidential Roots." In *Trilateralism: The Trilateral Commission and Elite Planning for World Management*, edited by Holly Sklar, 199–212. Boston, MA: South End Press, 1980.

Shrum, Robert. "No Private Smiles: A Disquieting Look at the Carter Campaign." *New Times* (June 11, 1976): 23–25, 39–42.

Shubin, Vladimir G. *The Hot "Cold War": The USSR in Southern Africa*. London: Pluto Press, 2008.

Sibanda, Eliakim M. *The Zimbabwe African People's Union, 1961–87: A Political History of Insurgency in Southern Rhodesia*. Trenton, NJ: Africa World Press, 2005.

Silverstein, Ken. "Licensed to Kill: Shadowing Our Government's Favorite Arms Dealer." *Harper's* (May 2000): 52–66.

Sithole, Masipula. *Zimbabwe: Struggles within the Struggle.* Salisbury, Rhodesia: Rujeko Publishers, 1979.

Sithole, Ndabaningi. *African Nationalism.* Oxford: Oxford University Press, 1959.

———. *Roots of a Revolution: Scenes from Zimbabwe's Struggle.* Oxford: Oxford University Press, 1977.

Slonim, Shlomo. "Israel and the New Scramble for Africa." *Midstream: A Monthly Jewish Review* 23, no. 9 (November 1977): 30–35.

Smiley, Xan. "Zimbabwe, Southern Africa and the Rise of Robert Mugabe." *Foreign Affairs* 58, no. 5 (Summer 1980): 1060–83.

Smith, Graham. *When Jim Crow Met John Bull: Black American Soldiers in World War II Britain.* New York: St. Martin's Press, 1988.

Smith, Ian. *The Great Betrayal: The Memoirs of Ian Douglas Smith.* London: Blake, 1997.

Smith, Zack C. "Moving Right: Conservatives and the 1978 Election." *Georgia Political Science Association Conference Proceedings* (2006): 1–22.

Snow, Philip. "China and Africa." In *Chinese Foreign Policy: Theory and Practice,* edited by Thomas W. Robinson and David L. Shambaugh, 283–321. Oxford: Clarendon Press, 1994.

Soames, Lord. "From Rhodesia to Zimbabwe." *International Affairs* 56, no. 3 (Summer 1980): 405–419.

Soares, John A. "Strategy, Ideology, and Human Rights: Jimmy Carter Confronts the Left in Central America, 1979–1981." *Journal of Cold War Studies* 8, no. 4 (October 2006): 57–91.

Solarz, Stephen. *Journeys to War & Peace: A Congressional Memoir.* Waltham, MA: Brandeis University Press, 2011.

Solodovnikov, Vassily G. "K istorii ustanovleniia diplomaticheskikh otnoshenii mezhdu SSSR u Simbabwe" [On the history of the establishment of diplomatic relations between the USSR and Zimbabwe]. In *Afrika v vospominaniiakh veteranov diplomaticheskoi sluzhby* [Africa in the recollections of veterans of the diplomatic service], edited by the Institute of Africa, 134–74. Moscow: XXI Vek-Soglasie, 2000.

Somerville, Keith. "The Soviet Union and Zimbabwe: The Liberation Struggle and After." In *The Soviet Impact in Africa,* edited by R. Craig Nation and Mark V. Kauppi, 195–220. Lexington, MA: Lexington Books, 1984.

Southall, Tony. "Zambia: Class Formation and Détente – A Comment." *Review of African Political Economy* 12 (May–August 1978): 114–19.

Spiegel, Steven L. *The Other Arab-Israeli Conflict: Making America's Middle East Policy, from Truman to Reagan*. Chicago: University of Chicago Press, 1985.

Spies, F.J. du Toit. *Operasie Savannah. Angola 1975–1976* [Operation Savannah: Angola 1975–1976]. Pretoria: S.A. Weermag, 1989.

Staples, Robert, Clyde Taylor, Chinweizu, Chuck Stone, and Robert Chrisman. "*The Black Scholar* Forum: A Symposium on 'Roots.'" *The Black Scholar* 8, no. 7 (May 1977): 36–42.

Stedman, Stephen. *Peacemaking in Civil War: International Mediation in Zimbabwe, 1974–1980*. Boulder, CO: Lynne Rienner, 1991.

Stein, Kenneth W. *Heroic Diplomacy: Sadat, Kissinger, Carter, Begin, and the Quest for Arab-Israeli Peace*. New York: Routledge, 1999.

Stiff, Peter. *The Silent War: South African Recce Operations 1969–1994*. Alberton, South Africa: Galago, 1999.

Stockwell, John. *In Search of Enemies: A CIA Story*. New York: Norton, 1978.

Strack, Harry R. *Sanctions: The Case of Rhodesia*. Syracuse, NY: Syracuse University Press, 1978.

Strong, Robert A. *Working in the World: Jimmy Carter and the Making of American Foreign Policy*. Baton Rouge: Louisiana State University Press, 2000.

Stroud, Kandy. *How Jimmy Won: The Victory Campaign from Plains to the White House*. New York: Morrow, 1977.

Stuckey, Mary E. *Jimmy Carter, Human Rights, and the National Agenda*. College Station: Texas A&M University Press, 2008.

SURSIS (Saudi-US Relations Information Service). "Perspectives on Conflicts, Cooperation and Crises: A Conversation with Saudi Arabia's New Ambassador to the United States, Part 2." March 2, 2006, http://susris.com/2006/03/14/perspectives-on-conflicts-cooperation-and-crises-part-2/.

Tamarkin, Mordechai. *The Making of Zimbabwe: Decolonization in Regional and International Politics*. London: F. Cass, 1990.

———. "The White Political Elite in Rhodesia's Decolonization Crisis." *The Jerusalem Journal of International Relations* 12, no. 4 (1990): 81–106.

Tareke, Gebru. *The Ethiopian Revolution: War in the Horn of Africa*. New Haven, CT: Yale University Press, 2009.

Taylor, Ian. *China and Africa: Engagement and Compromise*. London: Routledge, 2006.

Taylor, James. "The Murder of Ambassador Dubs, Kabul 1979." In *Embassies Under Siege: Personal Accounts by Diplomats on the Front Line*, edited by Joseph Sullivan, 55–70. Washington, DC: Brassey's, 1995.

Thatcher, Margaret. *The Downing Street Years*. New York: HarperCollins, 1993.

Theakston, Kevin, ed. *British Foreign Secretaries since 1974*. London: Routledge, 2004.

Third World Round Up. "The Palestine Problem: Test Your Knowledge." *SNCC Newsletter* (June–July 1967): 4–5.

Thomas, Daniel C. *The Helsinki Effect: International Norms, Human Rights, and the Demise of Communism*. Princeton, NJ: Princeton University Press, 2001.

Thomas, William. "Black Leadership Question." *CQ Researcher* (January 18, 1980). http://library.cqpress.com/cqresearcher/cqresrre1980011800.

Thompson, Carol B. *Challenge to Imperialism: The Frontline States in the Liberation of Zimbabwe*. Boulder, CO: Westview Press, 1986.

Thompson, Hunter S. "Jimmy Carter and the Great Leap of Faith: An Endorsement with Fear and Loathing." *Rolling Stone* 214 (June 3, 1976): 54–64.

Tiruneh, Andargachew. *The Ethiopian Revolution, 1974–1987: A Transformation from an Aristocratic to a Totalitarian Autocracy*. New York: Cambridge University Press, 1993.

Tomseth, Victor. "Crisis after Crisis, Embassy Tehran, 1979." In *Embassies Under Siege: Personal Accounts by Diplomats on the Front Line*, edited by Joseph Sullivan, 34–53. Washington, DC: Brassey's, 1995.

Transnational Institute (Counter Information Services, London). *Black South Africa Explodes*. Washington, DC: Transnational Institute, 1977.

Trenor, Brian. "The Polish Desk: Radio Free Europe, Zbigniew Brzezinski, and Jimmy Carter's Polish Policy, 1976–1977." MA thesis, North Carolina State University, 2011.

Trento, Joseph. *Prelude to Terror: The Rogue CIA and the Legacy of America's Private Intelligence Network*. New York: Carroll & Graf, 2005.

Trofimov, Yaroslav. *The Siege of Mecca: The Forgotten Uprising in Islam's Holiest Shrine and the Birth of Al Qaeda*. New York: Doubleday, 2007.

Tubiana, Joseph, ed. *La révolution éthiopienne comme phénomène de société: témoignages et documents* [The Ethiopian revolution as social phenomenon: Testimonies and documents]. Paris: L'Harmattan, 1990.

Turki, Fawaz. "The Passions of Exile: The Palestine Congress of North America." *Journal of Palestine Studies* 9, no. 4 (Summer 1980): 17–43.

———. *Soul in Exile: Lives of a Palestinian Revolutionary*. New York: Monthly Review Press, 1988.

Turner, Stansfield. "The Naval Balance: Not Just a Numbers Game." *Foreign Affairs* 55, no. 2 (January 1977): 339–54.

UNA-USA National Policy Panel on Conventional Arms Control. *Controlling the Conventional Arms Race*. New York: UNA-USA, 1976.

Unger, Irwin. *Recent America: The United States since 1945*. Upper Saddle River, NJ: Prentice Hall, 2002.

United States, Department of State (Peter Samson, Laurie Van Hook, Edward C. Keefer, eds.). *Foreign Relations of the United States, 1969–1976, Vol. E–6, Documents on Africa, 1973–1976*. Washington, DC: GPO, 2006.

United States, Department of State (Myra Burton, Edward Keefer, eds.). *Foreign Relations of the United States, 1969–1976, Vol. 28, Southern Africa*. Washington, DC: GPO, 2011.

United States, Department of State (Melissa Taylor, Adam Howard, eds.). *Foreign Relations of the United States, 1977–1980, Vol. 6, Soviet Union*. Washington, DC: GPO, 2013.

United States, Department of State (David Nickles, Adam Howard, eds.). *Foreign Relations of the United States, 1977–1980, Vol. 13, China*. Washington, DC: GPO, 2013.

United States, Department of State (Kristin Ahlberg, Adam Howard, eds.). *Foreign Relations of the United States, 1977–1980, Vol. 2, Human Rights and Humanitarian Affairs*. Washington, DC: GPO, 2013.

Vance, Cyrus R. *Hard Choices: Critical Years in America's Foreign Policy*. New York: Simon & Schuster, 1983.

Van Wyk, Martha. "Ally or Critic? The United States' Response to South African Nuclear Development, 1949–1980." *Cold War History* 7, no. 2 (2007): 195–225.

Vaughan, Patrick. "Brzezinski and Afghanistan." In *The Policy Makers: Shaping American Foreign Policy from 1947 to the Present*, edited by Anna Kasten Nelson, 107–30. Lanham, MD: Rowman and Littlefield, 2009.

———. "Zbigniew Brzezinski and the Helsinki Final Act." In *The Crisis of Détente in Europe: From Helsinki to Gorbachev, 1975–1985*, edited by Leopoldo Nuti, 11–25. London: Routledge, 2009.

———. "Zbigniew Brzezinski: The Political and Academic Life of a Cold War Visionary." PhD diss., West Virginia University, 2003.

Verrier, Anthony. *The Road to Zimbabwe, 1890–1980*. London: Jonathan Cape, 1986.

Vorotnikov, Vitaly Ivanovich. *Gavana – Moskva: pamiatnye gody* [Havana – Moscow: Memorable years]. Moscow: Fond imeni I. D. Sytina, 2001.

Voß, Klaas. *Washingtons Söldner: Verdeckte US-Interventionen im Kalten Krieg und ihre Folgen* [Washington's mercenaries: Covert US intervention during the Cold War and its consequences]. Hamburg: Hamburger Edition, 2014.

Walker, Daniel Breck. "'Yesterday's Answers' or 'Tomorrow's Solutions'?: The Cold War Diplomacy of Cyrus Vance." PhD diss., Vanderbilt University, 2007.

Walters, Barbara. "An Interview with Fidel Castro." *Foreign Policy* 28 (Autumn 1977): 22–51.

Walters, Ronald. "The Black Initiatives in the Middle East." *Journal of Palestine Studies* 10, no. 2 (Winter 1981): 3–13.

Wander, Philip. "On the Meaning of 'Roots.'" *Journal of Communication* (Autumn 1977):64–69.

Watson, Denton. "The NAACP and Africa: An Historical Profile." *Crisis* (April 1977): 131–38.

Webb, Clive. *Fight against Fear: Southern Jews and Black Civil Rights.* Athens: University of Georgia Press, 2001.

Weigel, George. *Witness to Hope: The Biography of Pope John Paul II.* New York: Cliff Street Books, 1999.

Weisbord, Robert G., and Richard Kazarian Jr., eds. *Israel in the Black American Perspective.* Westport, CT: Greenwood, 1985.

Weissman, Stephen, and Johnnie Carson. "Economic Sanctions Against Rhodesia." In *Congress, the Presidency, and American Foreign Policy*, edited by John Spanier and Joseph Nogee, 132–60. New York: Pergamon, 1981.

Wells, Tim. *444 Days: The Hostages Remember.* San Diego, CA: Harcourt Brace Jovanovich, 1985.

Westad, Odd Arne. *The Fall of Détente: Soviet-American Relations During the Carter Years.* Oslo: Scandinavian University Press, 1997.

———. *The Global Cold War: Third World Interventions and the Making of Our Times.* Cambridge: Cambridge University Press, 2005.

WGBH. "Interview with Zbigniew Brzezinski, 1986." WGBH Media Library & Archives: Open Vault. November 19, 1986. http://openvault.wgbh.org/catalog/wpna-c1c1d6-interview-with-zbigniew-brzezinski-1986.

White, Luise. *The Assassination of Herbert Chitepo: Texts and Politics in Zimbabwe.* Bloomington: Indiana University Press, 2003.

———. "Civic Virtue, Young Men, and the Family: Conscription in Rhodesia, 1974–1980." *The International Journal of African Historical Studies* 37, no. 1 (2004): 103–21.

Wilentz, Sean. *The Age of Reagan: A History, 1974–2008.* New York: Harper, 2008.

Wilkinson, A. R. "The Impact of the War." *The Journal of Commonwealth & Comparative Politics* 18, no. 1 (1980): 110–23.

Willame, Jean-Claude. "La seconde guerre du Shaba" [The second Shaba war]. *Genève-Afrique* 16, no. 1 (1977–78): 9–26.

Willis, Ellen. "The Myth of the Powerful Jew, The Black-Jewish Conflict, Pt. 2." *Village Voice* 3 (September 3, 1979): 1–12.

Witcover, Jules. *Marathon: The Pursuit of the Presidency, 1972–1976.* New York: Viking, 1977.

Wolvaardt, Pieter, Tom Wheeler, and Werner Scholtz, eds. *From Verwoerd to Mandela: South African Diplomats Remember.* Johannesburg: Crink, 2010.

Woodroofe, Louise. *Buried in the Sands of the Ogaden: The United States, the Horn of Africa, and the Demise of Détente.* Kent, OH: Kent State University Press, 2013.

———. "Revolution in the Desert: The Ford Administration Responds to Upheaval in the Horn of Africa, 1974–1976." Seminar Paper for the Cold War Studies Centre at London School of Economics, October 25, 2005.

Woodward, C. Vann. "The Aging of America." *The American Historical Review* 82, no. 3 (June 1977): 583–94.

Woodward, Peter. *US Foreign Policy and the Horn of Africa.* Aldershot, UK: Ashgate Publishing, 2006.

Wooten, James T. *Dasher: The Roots and the Rising of Jimmy Carter.* New York: Summit Books, 1978.

Wrong, Michela. *I Didn't Do It for You: How the World Betrayed a Small African Nation.* New York: HarperCollins, 2005.

Yevsyukov, Petr H. "Reminiscences of the work in Mozambique" [in Russian]. In *Afrika v vospominaniiakh veteranov diplomaticheskoi sluzhby*, 134–74.

Young, Andrew. *An Easy Burden: The Civil Rights Movement and the Transformation of America.* New York: HarperCollins, 1996.

———. "Interview of Mayor Andrew Young." By David Hardin. *30 Good Minutes* (#2912), Chicago Sunday Evening Club, November 17, 1985. http://www.30goodminutes.org.

———. "*Penthouse* Interview: Andrew Young." By Allan Sonnenschein. *Penthouse* 14 (February 1983): 123–24, 126, 128, 134, 142, 144.

———. *A Way Out of No Way: The Spiritual Memoirs of Andrew Young.* Nashville, TN: Thomas Nelson, 1994.

———. "Why I Support Jimmy Carter." *The Nation* 222, no. 13 (April 3, 1976): 397–98.

Zaremba, Marcin. "Karol Wojtyła the Pope: Complications for Comrades of the Polish United Workers' Party." *Cold War History* 5, no. 3 (August 2005): 317–36.

Zavelo, Kelsey. "In Transition: The United States and South Africa, 1976–1977." MA thesis, North Carolina State University, 2015.

Ziołkowska, Aleksandra. *Dreams and Reality: Polish Canadian Identities.* Toronto: Adam Mickiewicz Foundation in Canada, 1984.

Ziołkowska-Boehm, Aleksandra. *The Roots Are Polish.* Toronto: Canadian-Polish Research Institute, 1998.

Index

Aaron, David: on Brzezinski, 128; and Ethiopia, 387–88; on foreign policy teamwork, 249; and Rhodesia, 218, 220, 226, 311, 327, 406–7, 500; and Shaba 2 crisis, 437; and southern Africa policy, 141; and Zambia, 474

Acheson, Dean, 38

Addou, Abdullahi: as ambassador, 195–97, 254–56; and arms sales to Somalia, 261–68, 272–76, 279–81; on Cuban troops in Ethiopia, 290; and Somalia's invasion of Ethiopia, 294, 680–81

Afghanistan: coup in, 432; Soviet influence in, 559; Soviet invasion of, 6, 650, 662, 667, 682, 685–87, 689; US ambassador's abduction and death, 510–11, 513, 516; US support to mujahideen in, 689

African-American Manifesto on Southern Africa (1976), 464

African Americans: and Carter, 12–13, 269–70; and Case-Javits Amendment, 579–81; in Congress, 162; and election campaign, 22, 34, 66, 69, 110, 116, 118, 133, 659, 670; lobbying by, 463–64; organizations, 119, 559, 671; and Palestinian issue, 618, 621; public opinion of, 640; and Rhodesia policy, 475–76, 521, 539, 568–70,

574, 596, 640, 644. *See also* Congressional Black Caucus

Afro-American (Baltimore), 372, 475, 579, 580

AIPAC (American Israel Public Affairs Committee), 293

Albright, Madeleine, 434, 448, 526, 543, 598

American Committee on Africa (ACOA), 785*n*36

American Israel Public Affairs Committee (AIPAC), 293

Amstutz, Bruce, 510

Anderson, John, 244

Angola: civil war in, 105; and Cold War politics, 3, 5–6, 10–11, 27–29, 114, 146–47, 167, 169–71, 208, 210, 323, 383–84, 684; Cuban troops in, 31–33, 37–38, 49, 133, 141–44, 188–89, 191, 259–60, 340–41, 343–45, 394, 409, 416, 482, 484–85, 487; and Rhodesia policy, 42–46, 52–53, 55–56, 58, 60, 90, 92, 105–8, 150–51, 506, 668; South Africa's invasion of, 421; and Zaire policy, 222, 436–37

Arab countries, 200, 272–73, 289, 292, 387. *See also specific countries*

Arafat, Yasser, 615

Argentina, 186–87

WOODROW WILSON CENTER PRESS
STANFORD UNIVERSITY PRESS